FORGERY AND COUNTERFORGERY

FORGERY

and

COUNTERFORGERY

The Use of Literary Deceit in Early Christian Polemics

BART D. EHRMAN

OXFORD
UNIVERSITY PRESS

Oxford University Press is a department of the University of Oxford.
It furthers the University's objective of excellence in research,
scholarship, and education by publishing worldwide.

Oxford New York
Auckland Cape Town Dar es Salaam Hong Kong Karachi
Kuala Lumpur Madrid Melbourne Mexico City Nairobi
New Delhi Shanghai Taipei Toronto
With offices in
Argentina Austria Brazil Chile Czech Republic France Greece
Guatemala Hungary Italy Japan Poland Portugal Singapore
South Korea Switzerland Thailand Turkey Ukraine Vietnam

Oxford is a registered trademark of Oxford University Press
in the UK and certain other countries.

Published in the United States of America by
Oxford University Press
198 Madison Avenue, New York, NY 10016

© Oxford University Press 2013

All rights reserved. No part of this publication may be reproduced, stored in a retrieval system, or transmitted, in any form or by any means, without the prior permission in writing of Oxford University Press, or as expressly permitted by law, by license, or under terms agreed with the appropriate reproduction rights organization. Inquiries concerning reproduction outside the scope of the above should be sent to the Rights Department, Oxford University Press, at the address above.

You must not circulate this work in any other form, and you must impose the same condition on any acquirer.

Library of Congress Cataloging-in-Publication Data
Ehrman, Bart D.
Forgery and counterforgery : the use of literary deceit
in early Christian polemics / Bart D. Ehrman.
p. cm.
Includes bibliographical references.
ISBN 978-0-19-992803-3
1. Christian literature, Early—History and criticism.
2. Literary forgeries and mystifications. I. Title.
BR67.E37 2014
270.1—dc23
2012009020

1 3 5 7 9 8 6 4 2
Printed in the United States of America
on acid-free paper

For J. Christiaan Beker and Bruce M. Metzger

In memoriam

CONTENTS

ACKNOWLEDGMENTS

I became seriously interested in questions of literary forgery just over twenty years ago in the course of doing research for my book *The Orthodox Corruption of Scripture*. It occurred to me at the time that the scribal falsification of texts is in many ways analogous to the forgery of texts. In both instances a writer (whether a scribe or an author) places his own words under the authority of someone else. Moreover, both practices were widely discussed and condemned in antiquity. To pursue the matter, I devoured Wolfgang Speyer's seminal treatment, *Die literarische Fälschung im heidnischen und christlichen Altertum,* a great book to which I have returned on a number of occasions in the two decades since. My debt to Speyer will be seen in the opening chapters of this book. It will be clear, however, that my study is altogether different, as I focus on the use of forgery in Christian polemics of the first four centuries.

Abbreviations are standard ones in the field; see, e.g., Patrick H. Alexander et al., *The SBL Handbook of Style* (Peabody, MA: Hendrickson, 1999), pp. 89–153.

There remains the happy occasion to thank those who have helped me in my work. As always, I am endlessly grateful to and for my wife, Sarah Beckwith, a remarkable human being, scholar, and dialogue partner, without whom my work, not to mention my life, would be immeasurably impoverished. My thanks to the National Humanities Center, which awarded me a fellowship in 2009–10, allowing me to pursue this academic passion without interruption, in the daily company of other scholars pursuing theirs. My thanks to my brother, Radd Ehrman, professor of Classics at Kent State University, for occasional help on matters of Greek and Latin literature and culture. My thanks to members of the UNC-Duke "Christianity in Antiquity" reading group (CIA), and members of the Duke-UNC "Late Ancient Studies Reading Group," for vigorously discussing sundry aspects of the work. My thanks to Elizabeth Clark, friend and colleague in the Duke Department of Religion, and to Zlatko Pleše, friend and colleague at UNC, for incisive comments and invaluable assistance on several of the chapters.

Early in my work I had the benefit of two bright and hard-working graduate students at UNC serving as my research assistants, Jared Anderson and Benjamin White. For the past three years, a massive amount of work has been undertaken with inordinate skill by Jason Combs, also a graduate student at UNC. Without his assistance, this book would have taken decades longer to write and contained thousands more errors. In the final stages, Maria Doerfler, graduate student at Duke, has joined forces and also done extensive and remarkable things, efficiently and with grace. To all of these research assistants I am deeply grateful.

I am especially indebted to three colleagues who read every word of the manuscript and made innumerable corrections and suggestions: Andrew Jacobs at Scribbs College, Joel Marcus at Duke Divinity School, and Dale Martin at Yale University. The world would be a happier place if every author had such friends, colleagues, and readers. All remaining mistakes are, alas, mine.

In the penultimate draft of the book I had determined to leave all foreign language materials cited in isolated and block quotations in their original languages, reasoning that this was, after all, meant to be a work of scholarship. My readers (all of them, actually) insisted that this was a very bad idea. I have yielded to their pleas (in this one instance) and asked the aforementioned Maria Doerfler, her of many languages, to translate the quotations (principally German, but also French and some of the Latin). She has complied in a remarkable way, and I cannot say how much I owe her. In places I have altered her translations, and the final responsibility for their accuracy (or inaccuracy) is all mine. I have resituated the original language quotations themselves to the footnotes. Unless otherwise noted, the translations of Greek texts are mine, including those of the New Testament.

Finally, thanks are due to my close friend and longtime editor Robert Miller at Oxford University Press, who has willingly and eagerly come forth from his normal world of college publishing to take on the task of editing the book.

I have dedicated the book to the memory of two of my former teachers at Princeton Theological Seminary: Bruce M. Metzger and J. Christiaan Beker. Among white, middle-class, New Testament scholars you could not find two more different human beings. But they both influenced me significantly, and they both shared my passion for learning the truth about early Christian literary deceit.

FORGERY AND COUNTERFORGERY

CHAPTER ONE

Introduction

Arguably the most distinctive feature of the early Christian literature is the degree to which it was forged.[1] Even though the early Christians were devoted to the truth–or so their writings consistently claimed—and even though "authoritative" literature played a virtually unparalleled role in their individual and communal lives, the orthonymous output of the early Christians was remarkably, even astonishingly, meager. From the period of the New Testament, from which some thirty writings survive intact or in part, only eight go under the name of their actual author, and seven of these derive from the pen of one man.[2] To express the matter differently, only two authors named themselves correctly in the surviving literature of the first Christian century. All other Christian writings are either anonymous, falsely ascribed (based on an original anonymity or homonymity), or forged.

Matters begin to change with the second Christian century, even though orthonymity continues to be the exception rather than the rule. It is worth considering, for example, what Pre-Enlightenment scholars accepted as the writings of apostolic and subapostolic times.[3] There were the *Homilies* and *Recognitions* of Clement, now known not to be works of the one who was reputedly the fourth bishop of Rome, but to be forged in his name. There were the writings of the early Pauline convert Dionysius the Areopagite, also forged. There were the letters of Paul himself to and from

1. I will be defining the term *forgery*, and related terms, soon, and justify the way I will be using them. See pp. 29–32. For now it is enough to state my general conception. A "forgery" is a literary work with a false authorial claim, that is, a writing whose author falsely claims to be a(nother) well-known person.

2. I am excluding for now the writings of Ignatius from this tally; were he to be considered—on the grounds that he probably wrote prior to the appearance of 2 Peter—then seven additional works and one additional author would be added to the totals.

3. See further, R. M. Grant, "The Appeal to the Early Fathers," *JTS* 11 (1960): 13–24.

Seneca, likewise forged. And there were the thirteen letters of Ignatius of Antioch, six of them forged and the others falsely and severely interpolated. When we move deeper into the second century and on into the third and fourth, we see a heightened interest in the production of "apostolic" works: Gospels by Peter, Thomas, Philip, all forged; Paul's letters to the Alexandrians and Laodiceans, forged; Jesus' correspondence with Abgar, forged; Apocalypses of Peter and Paul, forged. We can move backward into writings forged in the names of the greats from antiquity, Isaiah or the Sybil, or forward into the writings forged in the names of orthodox church fathers—Basil, Augustine, Jerome. The list goes a very long way.

Matching the abundant materials for the study of early Christian forgery is the remarkably sparse attention paid to it—as a broader phenomenon—in modern scholarship. Apart from studies of individual instances, which do indeed abound, and discussions of the relationship of pseudepigrapha to issues of canon, there is no full length study of the phenomenon in the English language, and only one reasonably comprehensive study in German.[4] There is none in any other language of scholarship.

The study of individual cases is, of course, crucial for the understanding of the broader phenomenon and so need continuously to be carried out with rigor and focus. But somewhat ironically, these examinations are often conducted precisely apart from a knowledge or appreciation of the wider phenomenon of early Christian forgery. Surely an individual instantiation of the practice cannot be studied in isolation, apart from its wider historical and cultural context.

The studies of forgery and canon are also vital in many ways, especially in assisting in the evaluation of the practices of and attitudes toward forgery in the early Christian tradition. Inevitably such studies draw on materials taken from the wider Jewish and pagan environments, often, though not always, with broad coverage and clarity of insight. But a focus on issues of canon can skew the discussion in certain ways, and there are other important questions that need to be addressed.

What are needed are fuller studies of the historical phenomenon, not only in relation to a set of theological concerns and not only with eyes focused on the early Christian forgeries that were eventually deemed to be Scripture. The canonical forgeries participated both in the broader stream of literary practices of antiquity and, more narrowly, in the literary practices of the early Christian communities. These broader practices should not be seen merely as background to the object of ultimate (theological) concern (the question of canon), but should be explored as a matter of intellectual inquiry in their own right. That is the intent and goal of the present study.

The focus of my concern will be the Christian literary forgeries of roughly the first four centuries CE. Later texts will be discussed only when they are in

4. Wolfgang Speyer's rightly famous *vade mecum*, *Die literarische Fälschung im heidnischen und christlichen Altertum: Ein Versuch ihrer Deutung* (München: Beck, 1971). It is now, obviously, over forty years old, but nothing has come along to replace or even to supplement it.

some way compelling, relevant, and especially noteworthy. In particular, for the purposes of this study, I am interested in forgeries that were engendered in the context of early Christian polemics. One could easily argue that these involve the majority of the relevant texts, but that statistical question is of no concern to me here. I am interested in polemics because they played such a major role in the history and development of the early Christian tradition and, as a consequence, in the production of early Christian forgeries. We know of numerous polemical contexts from the early Christian centuries, of course, and I am not restricting my vision to just one of them. Christians engaged in conflicts with non-Christian Jews and with antagonistic pagans; most of the polemical contexts, however, were intramural. There were internecine disputes over legitimate authority and authority figures. There were arguments over church structure and hierarchy, offices, ritual, and discipline. There were abundant and heated disagreements over specific theological teachings, from early eschatological disputes to later Christological and Trinitarian controversies. In all these contexts unknown authors produced forgeries, in large measure to help secure victory over their opponents through the authority provided by an assumed authorial name. Some of these forgers were remarkably successful in deceiving their reading audiences. Most of the forgeries produced have been lost or destroyed. But a striking number have survived, some through manuscript traditions down through the ages, others by chance discoveries made by professional archaeologists or rummaging fellahin.

We cannot understand these polemical forgeries if we fail to situate them in their context within the deceptive literary practices of the environment, the broader Greco-Roman world, including the part of that world that comprised Judaism. The study needs, then, to be carried out in relationship to that context, and so, in the following four chapters, it will begin by asking a set of questions about the wider phenomenon, seeking what can be known about the intent, function, motivations, and techniques of Greek and Roman forgeries. We will also examine the attitudes toward the practice, toward specific instantiations of it, and toward those who engaged in it: Were they seen to be lying? Were there culturally available justifications for their deceits? We will also evaluate the methods of detection that were employed by ancient critics intent on uncovering forgery.

The rest of the book deals with Christian forgeries of the first four centuries that appear to have been generated in polemical contexts. I discuss some fifty instances. In many cases I evaluate the scholarly debates that the texts have engendered—debates, in particular, over whether or not the text in question is authentic or forged. But there is much more to the matter of forgery than a mere Dass, as recent scholarship on forgery has so valuably stressed.[5] That is to say,

5. See especially the recent collection of essays edited by Jörg Frey, Jens Herzer, Martina Janssen, and Clare K. Rothschild, *Pseudepigraphie und Verfasserfiktion in frühchristlichen Briefen*. WUNT 246 (Tübingen: Mohr Siebeck, 2009).

knowing *that* a book is forged is crucial, but only as the beginning, not the end, of the investigation. Other—arguably even more important and interesting—questions involve such matters as the motivations and functions of the forgery. Why did an author choose to lie about his identity?[6] What was he trying to accomplish? How did the book he produced achieve his desired ends?

With respect to the first set of questions, whether or not a book is forged, I have taken three approaches in my analysis. Some books continue to be keenly debated among scholars (e.g., 2 Thessalonians, 1 Timothy, James); for these I provide a full discussion of the range of issues that suggest that the book is in fact forged. Other instances are less open to dispute (e.g., 2 Peter, the Pseudo-Ignatians), and in such cases I will simply state the most compelling reasons that have persuaded the majority of scholars. Yet other instances require no case to be made at all, as they are recognized as forgeries, for compelling reasons, by all hands (e.g., the Gospel of Peter; Jesus' correspondence with Abgar; the Apostolic Constitutions). The ultimate goal of the study is not to determine if this, that, or the other writing is forged, but to examine the motivation and function of forgery, especially in polemical contexts.

In the course of my discussions I will be especially interested in a kind of subcategory of forgery that I am calling "counterforgery" (Gegenfälschung). This term occasionally appears in the scholarship in two senses, which are not usually differentiated cleanly. On one hand, in a most general sense, a counterforgery involves a forged writing that opposes a specific idea, doctrine, point of view, or practice. But that, by the nature of the case, is true of virtually all polemically driven forgeries. And so I also propose a more specific kind of counterforgery, that is, one designed to counter the ideas, doctrines, views, or perspectives found precisely in another forgery (whether or not the author of the counterforgery realized that the book being opposed was forged). The value of this subcategory of polemical forgery will become evident in the discussions of individual cases.

In many instances readers may suspect that the forgeries I consider functioned in ways other than polemical. To anticipate that objection, I should here stress that it is important to recognize the multifunctionality of forgeries, which corresponds to the multifunctionality of all literary texts. Few writings are produced for a solitary reason. If one were to ask why Paul wrote the letter now known as 1 Thessalonians, a number of perfectly valid, but differing, responses could be given. He wrote it in order to resume relations with a community that he had founded and considered particularly dear; he wrote it to bring his apostolic presence into their midst while he was himself physically absent; he wrote it to remind his readers of the redemptive message they had earlier received; he wrote it to

6. That forgers were consciously lying about their identity in an effort to deceive their readers will be the burden of much of the following four chapters; in particular see pp. 128–32.

clarify the misunderstandings of some of the community concerning the nature of the eschatological gospel he had proclaimed; he wrote it to urge his readers to lead a life of high morality; and he probably wrote it for a handful of other reasons. It would be wrong to insist that he wrote the letter for just one reason, and it would be wrong to deny any one of these being the reason (or one of the reasons) he wrote it.

So too with forgeries in Paul's name, or the names of any of the famous figures from early Christianity. Rarely, if ever, do they fulfill just one purpose or serve just one function. They may serve several, possibly unrelated to one another. To take one obvious example, the Protevangelium Jacobi. The author calls himself James, and he almost certainly is claiming to be "that" James—the brother of Jesus, who, according to the account itself, would have been the son of Joseph from a previous marriage, that is, Jesus' older step brother. This, of course, would put him in a particularly strong position to tell the prehistory of Jesus' appearance in the world, which forms the subject for the bulk of the narrative. But why did the author write the account? In fact, the (forged) work may well have functioned on numerous levels. It may have been written to provide readers an entertaining account of the prehistory of Jesus' birth and of its immediate aftermath. It may have been produced to celebrate the greatness of the mother of God. More than that, it may have been created in order to answer pagan opponents of Christianity such as Celsus (and the fabricated claims of his "Jew"), by showing that the charges they leveled against Mary (a peasant girl who had to spin for a living), Joseph (a poor common laborer), and the child Jesus (born into poverty) were precisely wrong. But there is more. Against adoptionist Christians the account shows that Jesus was in fact the Son of God from his birth; and against Marcionites it shows that Jesus actually came into the world as a child—that he did not simply descend from heaven, fully grown, in the fifteenth year of Tiberius Caesar. The text, in other words, functions on a number of fronts in the proto-orthodox attempt to establish itself and its views in the face of opponents, Jewish, pagan, and heterodox Christian. Was it written to deal with just one set of problems? Possibly so. But it is virtually impossible to say, without having the author available to interview, since features of the account successfully counter the claims of this, that, or the other opponent of the proto-orthodox.

Finally, in view of my ultimate concerns in this study, I should emphasize what I will *not* be addressing here:

- I will not be discussing literary texts that have been taken by some scholars to be forgeries but that I consider to be authentic. Thus, for example, I will certainly be dealing with the fourth-century Pseudo-Ignatian letters, but I will not be discussing the seven letters of the Middle Recension, even though there is a history—some of it quite recent—of taking these letters also as forgeries. I do not find the recent arguments of Hübner and

Lechner to be any more persuasive than the older arguments by Weijenborg, Joly, and Rius Camps on the matter[7]; I think the seven letters are authentic, and so I will not be discussing them as polemical forgeries.
- I will not be examining pseudepigrapha that are not Christian in origin but came to be transmitted, cherished, and sometimes also altered by Christians as part of their literature (e.g., the Testaments of Twelve Patriarchs and the Greek Life of Adam and Eve).[8]
- I will not by and large be considering polemical forgeries from after the fourth century (e.g., Pseudo-Titus; the Narrative of Joseph of Arimathea).
- I will not be considering forgeries that are not polemical in some obvious way (e.g., the Prayer of the Apostle Paul or a number of other nonpolemical pseudepigrapha of the Nag Hammadi Library).
- Conversely, I will not be considering polemical works that are not forgeries (the Nag Hammadi Testimony of Truth, for example, makes no authorial claim).
- I will not be considering books that are no longer extant, in full or in part.
- I will not, for the most part, be considering falsely attributed books (since their authors made no false authorial claims: so, for example, the New Testament Gospels; the Epistle of Barnabas; Pseudo-Justin; Pseudo-Tertullian; etc.).
- I will not, with a few key exceptions in passing (such as the Sibylline Oracles and the Pseudo-Ignatians), be considering the closely related matter of false interpolations (e.g., in the writings of the New Testament).
- I will not be considering ancient instances of plagiarism, unless they have something to do with forgeries (e.g., possibly, 2 Peter).

I should stress that the preceding topics are all important and deserve full examination. But in this study, I will be restricting myself to books whose authors appear to make false authorial claims, for polemical purposes, within the Christian tradition of the first four Christian centuries.

---

7. Thomas Lechner, *Ignatius adversus Valentinianos? Chronologische und theologiegeschichtliche Studien zu den Briefen des Ignatius von Antiochen,* VCSup 47 (Leiden: Brill, 1999); R. M. Hübner, "Thesen zur Echtheit und Datierung der sieben Briefe des Ignatius Antiochien," *ZAC* 1 (1997): 44–72; Reinoud Weijenborg, *Les lettres d'Ignace d'Antioche* (Leiden: Brill, 1969); Robert Joly, *Le Dossier d'Ignace d'Antioche,* Université libre de Bruxelles, Faculté de Philosophie et Lettres 69 (Brussels: Éditions de l'université de Bruxelles, 1979); Josep Rius-Camps, *The Four Authentic Letters of Ignatius* (Rome: Pontificium Institutum Orientalium Studiorum, 1979). For responses, see Caroline Hammond Bammel, "Ignatian Problems," *JTS* n.s. 33 (1982): 66–97; Mark J. Edwards, "Ignatius and the Second Century: An Answer to R Hübner," *ZAC* 2 (1998): 214–26; and Andreas Lindemann, "Antwort auf die 'Thesen zur Echtheit und Datierung der sieben Briefe des Ignatius von Antiochien,'" *ZAC* 1 (1997): 185–95.

8. See, for example, M. de Jonge, *Pseudepigrapha of the Old Testament as Part of Christian Literature: The Case of the Testaments of the Twelve Patriarchs and the Greek Life of Adam and Eve* (Leiden: Brill, 2003). The only exceptions to my rule—e.g., the Sibylline Oracles—involve corpora that include originally Christian productions as well.

Finally, I want to take special care to circumvent a possible misreading of my study, which would think or claim that I am trying to advance some kind of positivist agenda in promoting one kind of Christian thought and its literature over another. When I call a text forged I am making a literary-historical claim about its author; I do not mean to imply any kind of value judgment concerning its content or its merit as a literary text (religious, theological, ethical, personal, or any other kind of merit). In particular, I am not claiming that it is somehow inferior in these ways to a work that is orthonymous. I am not, that is, contrasting later forged texts with texts that are somehow pristine, "original," and therefore better or more worthy of our attention.

Another way to express this caveat is this: my ultimate concerns do not lie (at least in this study) with theological or ontological questions of ultimate truth, but in historical questions about how Christianity developed as a religion. From a historical perspective—just to take an example—writings that were actually written by Paul were themselves products of their time, based on things Paul heard, experienced, and thought, just as were the writings produced by others in his name. As a historian I do not value the authentically Pauline writings any more or less than later "Pauline" writings that were forged.

PART I

Forgery in the Greco-Roman World

CHAPTER TWO

Forgers, Critics, and Deceived Deceivers

I begin with a series of anecdotes that establish some of the themes pursued throughout the course of my study. These historical narratives involve forgers who condemned forgery and deceivers who were deceived.

HERACLIDES AND DIONYSIUS

Heraclides Ponticus was one of the great literati of the classical age.[1] As a young man from aristocratic roots, he left his native Pontus to study philosophy in Athens under Plato, Speusippus, and eventually, while he was still in the Academy, Aristotle. During one of Plato's absences, Heraclides was temporarily put in charge of the school; after the death of Speusippus he was nearly appointed permanent head. His writings spanned a remarkable range, from ethics to dialectics to geometry to physics to astronomy to music to history to literary criticism. Diogenes Laertius lists more than sixty books in all. Ten more are known from other sources. Few texts remain, almost entirely in fragments.

Diogenes is our principal source of information outside the primary texts.[2] As is his occasional wont, he betrays much greater interest in regaling readers with amusing anecdotes than in describing Heraclides' contributions to the intellec-

1. For texts and fragments, see the standard edition of F. Wehrli, *Die Schule des Aristoteles*, Hefte VII, *Heracleides Pontikos* 2nd ed. (Basel: Schwabe 1969); and now Eckart Schütrumpf, *Heraclides of Pontus: Text and Translations* (New Brunswick, NJ: Transaction, 2009). For a full study, see H. B. Gottschalk, *Heraclides of Pontus* (Oxford: Clarendon Press, 1980). Contra Wehrli, who based his judgment on the comments of Diogenes Laertius, Heraclides is now seen as a member of the Platonic Academy, not a member of the school of Aristotle. So Gottschalk (pp. 2–6) and Schütrumpf (p. vii).

2. Texts and translation in R. D. Hicks, *Diogenes Laertius: Lives of Eminent Philosophers*, 2 vols. LCL (Cambridge: Harvard, 1972).

tual world of his day.[3] And so we are told that Heraclides' penchant for fine clothing and good food, which produced a noticeably corpulent figure, earning for him the epithet Heraclides Pompicus.

Of particular interest to Diogenes are instances in which Heraclides was involved in conscious deception. At one point, Heraclides had fallen desperately, even, he thought, mortally ill. Concerned for his postmortem reputation, he entrusted a family servant with the ploy. Feigning his death, he arranged for his pet snake to be placed, instead of his (not yet deceased) corpse, under the cover of the funeral bier; at the internment, those attending his funeral would take the appearance of the sacred snake as a sign that Heraclides had been bodily assumed into the realm of the gods. The plot failed, as it turns out; the snake prematurely slithered out from cover during the funeral procession, and it was immediately recognized that the entire proceeding had been a ruse. Heraclides was discovered, and, in the event, he was destined to live on, with more deceits in store.

This near-death experience is paired, by Diogenes, with an episode that did end Heraclides' life. When the region of Heraclea was suffering a famine, its citizens sent to the priestess at the oracle of Pythia to learn what they were to do in order to regain divine favor. Heraclides bribed the envoys and the oracular priestess herself to publish a fake prophecy: the Heracleans' plight would be resolved when they installed Heraclides as royalty with a golden crown, and vowed to bestow upon him honors worthy of a hero at his death. The citizens took the fabricated oracle to heart, but the falsity of the envoys and priestess was soon uncovered: when Heraclides was crowned as directed in the theater he was struck by a fit of apoplexy and died, thwarted in his desire for posthumous honors. The envoys were stoned to death, and the priestess was later dispatched by a poisonous snake at her shrine.

Even at the height of his career, the Diogenic Heraclides was involved in scandal. His literary treatise dealing with Homer and Hesiod was shown to be a bald plagiarism. And he committed forgery, according to the musician Aristoxenus, who claimed that Heraclides composed tragic plays in the name of Thespis. Richard Bentley was the first to argue that the few surviving fragments of Thespis are in fact Heraclidean inventions.[4]

What Heraclides is best known for, however, is an instance of deceit in which he was the victim rather than the culprit. This involves arguably the most famous instance of mischievous forgery in the history of the practice, Heraclides' deception at the hands of his former student Dionysius (Diogenes Laertius, *Lives*, 5.92–93).

Dionysius Spintharos ("the Spark") earned the epithet Metathemenos, the Renegade, in his old age, after a severe illness effectively disabused him of his

3. All anecdotes are taken from Diogenes Laertius, *Lives*, 5.6.

4. Richard Bentley, "Dissertation upon Phalaris," in *The Works of Richard Bentley*, ed. Alexander Dyce, vol. 1 (London: F. MacPherson, 1836; reprinted New York: Hildesheim, 1971), pp. 289–96.

lifelong Stoic view that pain, which is morally neutral, cannot therefore be considered evil.[5] According to Diogenes, earlier in life Dionysius played a trick on his former teacher, by forging a play called the *Parthenopaeus* in the name of Sophocles. In one of his works of literary criticism, Heraclides drew on the play, citing it as authentically Sophoclean. But Dionysius then informed him that in fact the play was a forgery, perpetrated by none other than himself. Heraclides refused to believe it, and so Dionysius brought forth evidence: at the opening of the play, the first letters in a group of lines formed an acrostic, "Pankalus," the name of Dionysius' own lover.

Heraclides insisted that the matter was a coincidence, until Dionysius brought forth two additional and yet more convincing proofs. The first was a subsequent acrostic that said, "An old monkey is not captured by a trap; yes, it is captured, but it is captured after some time." The final acrostic was irrefutable: Ἡρακλείδης γράμματα οὐκ ἐπίσταται οὐδ' ᾐσχύνθη (Heraclides does not know letters, and is not ashamed).[6]

Diogenes' passage has generated some scholarly discussion. In his edition of the fragments of the philosophers of the Aristotelian school, F. Wehrli gives reasons to think it was not the *Parthenopaeus* that was fabricated, but Diogenes' anecdote itself.[7] The story may be humorous and clever, but for the acrostics to have worked, Wehrli argues, Dionysius would have had to be relatively certain that Heraclides in particular would be deceived and make a public display of his ignorance.

Wehrli makes a strong point but perhaps is not completely suasive. Two of the three acrostics have no explicit connection to Heraclides; the other could just as easily have been placed in the text to satisfy Dionysius' rather scandalous sense of humor. If so, Heraclides just happened to step into a trap particularly suited for his corpulent frame.[8]

In any event, this is not the only instance of roguish forgery from the ancient world, designed to bamboozle an intellectual opponent. Galen indicates that Lucian decided to ridicule a much beloved, but unnamed, philosopher whom he considered a braggart and did so by penning an obscure and senseless philosophical treatise in the name of Heraclides. He had it presented to his enemy for an interpretation. When he complied, Lucian turned the tables, mocking him for being unable to see through the swindle.[9]

More to my purpose here, however, is the pure irony of Diogenes' own Heraclides. In a game of intellectual boomerang, the one who is guilty of swindles,

---

5. See H. von Arnim, *Stoicorum Veterum Fragmenta* (Leipzig: Teubner, 1903); vol. 1, pp. 93–96.

6. Some editors have proposed amending ουδ' to ου δε, so that the acrostic ends with ἐπίσταται, followed by Diogenes' comments, "but he was not ashamed." See Hicks, *Diogenes Laertius* ad loc.

7. Wehrli, *Schule*, pp. 62–63.

8. And one can think of other options. For example, it is possible that Dionysius knew that Heraclides was beginning a work on Sophocles; or, possibly—in a world of limited book distribution—he arranged for this work simply to fall into Heraclides' hands; and so on.

9. Galen, *In Hipp. Epid. II* comment II.

lies, plagiarism, and forgery—in a word, deceit—is himself a victim of deceit. The deceiver is deceived.

THE IRONIES OF THE APOSTOLIC CONSTITUTIONS

This ironic phenomenon has its rough parallels in the later Christian tradition. To begin with, we might look at a work universally recognized as pseudepigraphic, the late-fourth-century Apostolic Constitutions, a "church order" allegedly written by none other than the apostles of Jesus (hence its name) but in reality produced by someone simply claiming to be the apostolic band, living three hundred years after they had been laid to rest in their respective tombs.

We will be considering other aspects of this text in a later chapter.[10] For now it is enough to note that the book represents an edited composite of three earlier documents still extant independently, the third-century Didascalia Apostolorum, which makes up books 1–6 of the composite text; the Didache, which is found in book 7; and the Apostolic Tradition, wrongly attributed to Hippolytus, in book 8. Since this author has taken over earlier writings without acknowledgment, he could well be considered a plagiarist by ancient, as well as modern, standards. Consider, for example, the words of Vitruvius:

> While, then, these men deserve our gratitude, on the other hand we must censure those who plunder their works and appropriate them to themselves; writers who do not depend upon their own ideas, but in their envy boast of other men's goods whom they have robbed with violence, should not only receive censure but punishment for their impious way of life.[11]

In absolving our unknown compiler of the charge, it might be observed that plagiarism involves an author passing off someone else's work as his own, whereas in the case of the Apostolic Constitutions the author does not claim that *any* of the work is his own. He claims instead that it is the writing of the apostles. Ancient critics would certainly have considered the work a forgery, but it is not clear if they would have considered it a plagiarism.

As to the charge of forgery, it is worth observing that unlike the earliest of the borrowed documents, the Didache, the Apostolic Constitutions does not claim merely to stand in the apostolic tradition or to present a correct understanding of the teachings of the apostles. It claims to be written by the apostles. To this end, although the three earlier "church orders" are taken over more or less wholesale, some

10. See pp. 390–96 and the useful introduction in the first volume of Marcel Metzger's important edition of the text in the Sources Chrétienne, *Les constitutions apostoliques*, SC 320 (Paris: Cerf, 2008).

11. *Architecture*, book 7, preface 3. Translation of Frank Granger, *Vitruvius on Architecture, Books VI–X*, LCL (Cambridge, MA: Harvard University, 1934). For other discussions of plagiarism in antiquity, see, for example, Polybius *Histories* 9.2.1–2 and Pliny, *Natural History*, Preface 20–23, and my discussion on pp. 52–55.

important editing has taken place. The Apostolic Constitutions begins by naming its authors as "the apostles and elders."[12] As in the Didascalia, lying behind chapters 1–6, the apostles appear only rarely until toward the end; in 6.8, for example, the author reverts to a first-person plural "we went forth among the gentiles" and then to a first-person discourse in the name of Peter (6.9). The fourteen authors name themselves in 6.14 (the eleven disciples, Matthias the replacement of Judas, James the brother of Jesus, and the apostle Paul); in 6.12 they speak of themselves as the "twelve"—the original eleven and Matthias; elsewhere, on two occasions, Clement is added to the list. Moreover, the authorial fiction is inserted into the source documents at the very beginning of both book 7 ("We also, having followed our teacher Christ . . . are obliged to say that there are two ways") and book 8 ("Jesus Christ, our God and Savior, delivered to us the great mystery of piety. . . . These gifts were first given to us the apostles when we were about to proclaim the gospel").

More remarkably, starting in 8.16, certain directives for church offices are made in the first-person singular: "With respect to the ordination of deacons, I Philip make this constitution. . . . With respect to a deaconess, I Bartholomew make this constitution. . . . With respect to the sub-deacons, I Thomas make this constitution. . . ." And so on, in the names of other apostles. As Bruno Steimer has pointed out, only rarely does the author slip up and betray the pseudepigraphic character of his writing: James, one of the speakers (8.35.1), is said already to be dead (7.46.1–2); Peter both speaks in the first person and is spoken of in the third (7.11, but 2.24.4; 7.2.12); Paul is sometimes not included in the assembly (e.g., 2.55.1); and in one place, at least, Peter and Paul seem to differentiate themselves from the apostles (8.33.8).[13]

It is frequently stated that the Apostolic Constitutions claims as its ultimate author Clement of Rome, who allegedly is writing the words given him by the apostles.[14] This, however, is almost certainly wrong. Clement is not mentioned at the beginning of the book when the author addresses the readers in the names of the apostles, or in the beginning of any of the books' three main sections. He does appear twice in the first person (8.46.13; 8.47.85), and so he has been inserted as a co-author of sorts. But he is not the ultimate writer of the document. The passages that have been appealed to in support of a Clementine authorship are 6.18.11, where "the Catholic doctrine" is said to have been sent διὰ τοῦ συλλειτουργοῦ

---

12. Unless otherwise noted, English translations are my own. For a full translation, see James Donaldson, "Constitutions of the Holy Apostles," in Alexander Roberts and James Donaldson, eds., *Ante-Nicene Fathers*, vol. 7; reprint edition (Peabody, MA: Hendrickson, 2004; American edition original, 1886). Hereafter *ANF*.

13. Bruno Steimer, *Vertex Traditionis: Die Gattung der altchristlichen Kirchenordnungen* (Berlin: de Gruyter, 1992), p. 133.

14. Thus M. Metzger, "Les CA par contre ont été diffuses sous le nom de Clément, . . . Les CA sont donc un écrit pseudépigraphique," *Les Constitutions Apostoliques*, vol. 1, pp. 33–34; similarly Bruno Steimer, "Clemens agiert als Sekretär der versammelten Apostel; . . . also hat ihm der CA-Kompilator eine Vermittelrolle zugewiesen" *Vertex Traditionis*, p. 130.

Κλήμεντος; and again at the end the book at 8.47.85, where the writing is self-referentially said to have been addressed to the bishops δι᾽ ἐμοῦ Κλήμεντος. The book is clearly written "through Clement." But this does not mean that Clement is the one recording the words of the apostles. It means he is being imagined as the one who carried the book to the recipients and who could, then, vouch for both its authenticity, as having been written by the apostles, and its accuracy.[15]

The Apostolic Constitutions, then, tries to pass itself off as an authentically apostolic writing, even though it is not. This is a clear case of what I will later be defining as literary forgery: a writing that makes a false authorial claim, with the apparent intention of deceiving its readers.[16] A range of ironies emerge from this text as a result. One intriguing passage occurs in 8.3, where the author not only stresses his apostolic identity but also draws for his readers the ineluctable conclusion, in case they were too dense to catch it: "the one who hears us hears Christ, and the one who hears Christ hears his God and Father." What would it mean, then, to disobey the apostolic instructions of the book? The reader can draw her own conclusion.

At the same time, this authorial authority, rooted in a direct apostolic line heading straight to God, is rooted in a falsehood. The book is pseudepigraphic—literally, "inscribed with a lie." This makes the claim of apostolic succession all the more interesting, as the claim appears immediately after the author's reminder of how God "rebuked the way of those who . . . attempted to speak lies" (τῶν ψευδῆ ἐπιχειρούντων λέγειν . . . ἤλεγξε τὸν τρόπον; 8.3.1). Here a liar condemns the telling of lies.[17]

What is more, as with Heraclides Ponticus, here too the deceiver has been deceived. The alleged authors—the apostles of Christ, including Paul and James—claim that the books of the New Testament were theirs: ἡμέτερα δέ, τοῦτ᾽ ἔστι τῆς καινῆς διαθήκης (8.47.85). And so the author gives a list of which books those are, a

15. For discussions of διά in the context of letter writing and carrying, see the discussion on pp. 248–49 with reference to Silvanus' alleged role in the letter of 1 Peter.

16. This is a common view among the commentators on the Apostolic Constitutions, for example, Metzger, *Constitutions Apostoliques*, 1. 33–38; and Steimer, *Vertex Traditionis*, pp. 130–33. For an attempt to deny that the author intended to deceive his readers, see Joseph G. Mueller, *L'ancien testament dans l'ecclésiologie des Pères* (Turnhout: Brepols, 2004), pp. 77–84. Mueller's arguments fail to convince. He claims, for example, that since the Apostolic Constitutions condemns the use of forgery to authenticate a perspective, it would not use precisely the means that it condemns. This overlooks the fact that forgers commonly practiced what they condemned, as we will see; in fact, they condemned what they practiced precisely in order to convince their readers that they were not doing what they condemned. Mueller also argues that the author could not have used documents known in the community (the Didascalia, the Didache, and the Apostolic Traditions, along with the fourth-century canons that appear in 8.47), while seriously maintaining that these derived from the apostles, when the readers would have recognized them for what they were. This objection assumes that we know precisely what we do not: who was in the author's community and what texts they were familiar with, let alone whether he circulated his work in his own close-knit community.

17. On the question of whether pseudepigraphic writings were considered a form of lying, see below pp. 128–32. For now, it is enough simply to note the derivation of pseudepigrapha—writings inscribed with a ψεῦδος—a "lie."

list including all the books that eventually became the New Testament, with the exception of the book of Revelation. Strikingly, after listing the Gospels and the letters of Paul, James, John, Jude, and Peter, the author indicates that the New Testament is also to include the two letters of Clement and, to cap it all off, the Apostolic Constitutions themselves. The list ends with "our Acts of the Apostles" αἱ Πράξεις ἡμῶν τῶν ἀποστόλων (8.47.85)—in other words, not just the letters that the authors had earlier produced but also the account of their activities.

By naming 1 and 2 Clement as scriptural authorities—part of "our" New Testament—the alleged authors are establishing the authority of the bearer of their writing, Clement of Rome, companion of the apostles. Including their own writing, the Apostolic Constitutions, as Scripture is the natural corollary of the pseudepigraphic enterprise. If they wrote the other books of the New Testament, then surely their other writing—that is, the present one—is also sacred scripture. This is pseudepigraphy with chutzpah. The author is not just forging an apostolic writing; he is urging, in the name of the apostles, that the writing be deemed part of Scripture.[18] At the same time, to some extent this author is simply making explicit what other forgers clearly desired implicitly. Whoever wrote the extant letter of Laodiceans, the letter of 3 Corinthians, and the Gospel of Peter clearly expected their readers to accept their books as authentically apostolic and thus, surely, in some sense scriptural.

But, as intimated, the author of the Apostolic Constitutions is not only a deceiver; he is also deceived—in this case, about many of the books of the New Testament, which he did not in fact write but which were also, for that matter, not written by the apostolic authorities who are claimed as their authors. In making this mistake, our unknown author can certainly be excused. Virtually all Christians by the end of the fourth century assumed that the New Testament books were authentic; little did they know that the writings of Paul and the letters of Peter, James, and Jude would all come under criticism so many centuries later. All the same, here again we have a forger who has been fooled by other forgeries.[19]

What is yet more striking is that in two places this self-conscious pseudepigrapher explicitly condemns what he practices, insisting that his readers not read other forgeries. The first passage is in 6.16.1:

> We have sent all these things to you so that you might be able to know what our opinion is. And do not receive the books that have been patched together in our name by the ungodly. For you are not to pay heed to the names of the apostles, but to the nature of the things and to their undistorted opinions.

---

18. It is hard to imagine how someone could claim the author—the forger—was not trying to be taken seriously. Here is someone who insists that his own book be accepted as canonical.

19. I will justify the use of the term *forgery* for the canonical pseudepigrapha below, pp. 28–32. For now it is enough to note that the books falsely claiming to be written by Peter (for example) inside the New Testament are no different, in extending that false claim, from books that falsely claim to be written by Peter outside the New Testament.

The author goes on to mention books forged by the false teachers Simon and Cleobius[20] and their followers, who have "compiled poisonous books in the name of Christ and of his disciples," written in order to deceive others. He also speaks of "apocryphal books" written by the ancients, in the names of Moses, Enoch, Adam, Isaiah, David, and so on, that are "pernicious and alien to the truth," and he indicates that other "ill-named" persons have done so as well, writing books that malign the creation, marriage, providence, having children, the Law, and the prophets.

It is true, as J. Mueller has recently observed, that the author is not precisely condemning his own practice; he objects to heretical and apocryphal forgeries specifically because they teach false notions.[21] His own book, in his opinion, teaches the truth, something (for him) quite different. But it is also important to consider the issue in a wider perspective. His opponents—the ones who forged heretical books—would have seen the matter in just the opposite light and no doubt asserted that their views were apostolic whereas his were pernicious and poisonous. It is not up to the historian to adjudicate this theological dispute. Still, it is worth noting that the fact of the author even raising the issue of apostolic pseudepigrapha shows he is fully conscious of the circumstance of authors falsely writing in the name of apostles when he is doing so himself. And so the view of Steimer seems completely justified: "By adding a criterion for determining authenticity to his critique of forgery, the compiler of the Apostolic Constitutions avoids submitting his own work to the verdict that he himself has formulated. The criterion for authenticity provides him with a suitable means to polemicize as a forger against forgery."[22]

The second instance is 8.47.60, which condemns in no uncertain terms "anyone who publicly displays the pseudepigraphic books of the impious (τὰ ψευδεπίγραφα βιβλία τῶν ἀσεβῶν) in the church." Once more the author is principally concerned with forgeries that he judges to be heretical. And here again, the author opposes "pseudepigraphic books" of the heretics, without having any problem producing a pseudepigraphic book of his own. Among other things, as we will see, this kind of warning against forgeries proved to be a powerful tool in the hands of a forger, as it served, among other things, to throw the reader off the scent of his own deceit, as recognized, again, by Steimer.[23]

---

20. See 3 Corinthians, where the same two are mentioned.

21. *L'ancien testament*, pp. 79–80.

22. "Indem der CA-Kompilator seine Fälschungkritik durch ein Echtheitskriterium ergänzt, vermeidet er es, sein eigenes Werk dem selbst formulierten Verdikt zu unterwerfen; das Echtheitskriterium liefert ihm ein probates Mittel, als Fälschung gegen Fälschung zu polemisieren." *Vertex Traditionis*, p. 353.

23. "The warning against pseudepigraphal writings, which appears twice in the Apostolic Constitutions, must be considered the strongest argument in favor of its authenticity." ("Als stärkstes Argument der Authentizität ist die in der CA doppelt vorkommende Warnung vor pseudepigraphischen Schriften zu werten.") *Vertex Traditionis*, pp. 132–33.

What we have here in the Apostolic Constitutions, then, is not only a liar who condemns lying and a deceiver who is himself deceived; we also have a forger who condemns forgeries. His own forgery, in any event, was spectacularly successful. Later orthodox church leaders took him seriously when he claimed to be the apostolic band. From three centuries further on, for example, the so-called Trullan Council of 692 accepted as fully authoritative the eighty-five Apostolic Canons, which appear in 8.47 of the book. The rest of the Apostolic Constitutions was treated by the council as suspect, not because it was forged but because later heretics obviously intercepted the text and interpolated false passages into it. And so, as Canon 2 of the council reads:

> It has also seemed good to this holy Council, that the eighty-five canons, received and ratified by the holy and blessed Fathers before us, and also handed down to us in the name of the holy and glorious Apostles should from this time forth remain firm and unshaken for the cure of souls and the healing of disorders. And in these canons we are bidden to receive the Constitutions of the Holy Apostles [written] by Clement. But formerly through the agency of those who erred from the faith certain adulterous matter was introduced, clean contrary to piety, for the polluting of the Church, which obscures the elegance and beauty of the divine decrees in their present form. We therefore reject these Constitutions so as the better to make sure of the edification and security of the most Christian flock; by no means admitting the offspring of heretical error, and cleaving to the pure and perfect doctrine of the Apostles.[24]

THE FABRICATIONS OF EPIPHANIUS

As a further example of a forger who perpetrated a fraud, we might consider the work of a contemporary of the author of the Apostolic Constitutions, the doughty defender of the apostolic faith, Epiphanius of Salamis. Throughout his major work, the *Panarion*, an eighty-chapter refutation of all things heretical, Jewish and Christian, Epiphanius repeatedly demeans his opponents for using forged and apocryphal books. Nowhere is he more explicit in his condemnations than in his attack in book 26 on the Phibionites (known also as Gnostics and Borborites; he gives them numerous names). Among the false and forged books that this heretical sect used, Epiphanius explicitly condemns a book called Noriah, the Gospel of Perfection, the Gospel of Eve, the Lesser Questions of Mary, the Greater Questions of Mary, the Books of Seth, Apocalypses of Adam, the Birth of Mary, and the Gospel of Philip. Many of these books are now lost, although we do

---

24. Translation of Henry Percival from Philip Schaff and Henry Wace, eds., *Nicene and Post-Nicene Fathers*, Second Series, vol. 14. Reprint edition Peabody, MA: Hendrickson, 1994; American edition original, 1900), p. 361. Hereafter *NPNF*.

have still today an Apocalypse of Adam, the Gospel of Philip, the Birth of Mary (= Protevangelium Jacobi), and the Second Treatise of the Great Seth. Whether the extant versions are the books Epiphanius had in mind is anyone's guess.

Epiphanius is particularly well informed about the Phibionites and their literature, he tells us, because as a young man he was nearly seduced—literally—into their sect. According to his autobiographical, yet imaginative, account, as a young man he was approached by two attractive women who urged him to join with them in their sectarian worship, which, as we will see, was anything but sanctified (from Epiphanius' perspective). He nearly succumbed but in the end managed to escape their clutches, and he reported to the authorities what they were doing. The authorities went on a search and dispelled the band.

In the course of his near seduction, Epiphanius tells us, he managed to procure and read a number of the Phibionites' sacred books. One that particularly struck him was the Greater Questions of Mary, from which he quotes a passage in order to highlight its extraordinary, not to say completely scandalous, character. The passage concerns an encounter between Jesus and Mary Magdalene and replicates in Gospel form the interests and activities of the Phibionites who had allegedly forged it:

> For in the book called The Greater Questions of Mary (they have also forged one called the Lesser), they indicate that he [Jesus] gave a revelation to her [Mary]. Taking her to the mountain he prayed and then extracted a woman from his side and began having sexual intercourse with her; then he gathered his semen in his hand, explaining that "This is what we must do in order to live." When Mary became disturbed and fell to the ground, he again raised her and said to her, "Why do you doubt, you of little faith?"[25]

Epiphanius need only cite this passage to show how outrageous it was as a forgery and how implausible it was as an account from the life of Jesus. But one might wonder how plausible it is even as a Phibionite account of Jesus. Is it possible that the account was forged not by the Phibionites but by Epiphanius himself? There are in fact reasons for thinking that Epiphanius invented both the book and the episode.

The place to begin is with Epiphanius' detailed explanation of the scurrilous ritual activities of the Phibionites, which he narrates with scarcely shrouded voyeuristic pleasure. For their periodic Eucharistic celebrations, Epiphanius tells us, the Phibionite devotees came together to enjoy a sumptuous meal. When they arrived at the place of meeting, they greeted one another with a secret handshake, tickling the palm underneath, presumably to assure one another that they were legitimately part of the group, but perhaps also to set the stage for the intimacies

---

25. Translation mine. For the Greek text, see Bart D. Ehrman and Zlatko Pleše, *Apocryphal Gospels: Texts and Translations* (New York: Oxford University Press, 2011), p. 610.

to follow. After gorging themselves, the men and women matched up, each with someone other than their own spouse, in order to have indiscriminate sex together. But when the man reached climax, Epiphanius indicates, he would withdraw from the woman. They would then collect his semen in their hands and eat it, saying "This is the body of Christ." If the woman was in her period, they would also collect some of her menstrual blood and consume it, saying "This is the blood of Christ."

If, despite the ordained coitus interruptus, a woman by chance became pregnant, the group would perform a ceremonial abortion; they then cut up the fetus and ate it communally as a special Eucharistic meal.

Epiphanius also tells us that the Phibionite men who had advanced to roles of leadership no longer required women for their periodic celebrations. They are said to have engaged in sacred homosexual activities. Moreover, some members of the group practiced holy masturbation, consuming the body of Christ in the privacy of their own homes. This practice was justified by an appeal to Scripture: "Working with your own hands, that you may have something to give also to those in need."

According to Epiphanius, the Phibionites' ritual activities were closely tied to the theological views of the group. They are said to have believed that this world is separated from the divine realm by 365 heavens, each of them controlled by an archon who must be placated in order to allow the soul to rise through his realm. Since the soul first descended through all 365 heavens and then must reascend, it must pass by all the archons, twice. The journey occurred proleptically here on earth through a kind of empathy, as the man, during the course of the nocturnal sex liturgy, called out the secret name of one of the ruling archons, effecting a kind of identification with him that allowed safe passage through his realm. Since each archon must be passed by twice, as Epiphanius is quick to point out, each of the Phibionite men could expect to seduce female devotees on at least 730 festal occasions.

There was another link between the Phibionites' ritual activities and their theological system. Like other Gnostic groups, the Phibionites believed that human bodies were places of imprisonment for seeds of the divine, and the goal of the religion was to set the seed free. Since the seed comes to be implanted in the body through the sex act—literally in the exchange of bodily fluids—then the fluids were to be collected and consumed as an image of ultimate reunification. When, however, the seed was left inside the woman and a new body was formed, this allowed for the generation of another place of imprisonment. The fetus then was to be aborted in order to thwart the divinities keen on maintaining the system of entrapment. And so, whereas procreation defeated the true goal of existence and led to further entrapment and bondage, the ritualistic ingestion of semen, menses, and the occasional fetus provided liberation.

The Great Questions of Mary helped provide a textual basis—from the life of Jesus—for the ritual practices of the group. But did such a text actually exist?

The prior question is whether Epiphanius' description of the activities of the group is at all plausible. Historians have long treated Epiphanius in general with a healthy dose of skepticism.[26] No patristic source is filled with more invective and distortion; Epiphanius frequently makes connections between historical events that we otherwise know are unrelated, and he expressly claims to write horrific accounts precisely in order to repulse his readers from the heresies he describes (Pan. Proem. I. 2). His description of the Phibionites and their sex rituals, nonetheless, has been taken as historically grounded by a dismaying number of competent scholars. For Stephen Gero, the fact that other heresiological sources down into the Middle Ages mention the group (which he calls the Borborites) and level charges of immorality against them indicates that they did indeed exist and that they were indeed immoral.[27] But surely the perdurance of traditional slander is not the best gauge of historical veracity. So too Stephen Benko argues that the close ties between the ritual activities of the group and their theological views show that the account of Epiphanius is entirely plausible.[28] But this overlooks that it is Epiphanius himself who establishes the linkage, which may just as well show that he has invented a set of scandalous rituals imagined as appropriate to the nefarious theology of the group. How would we know?

One obvious place to start is with Epiphanius' sources of information. Because he had some contact with the group as a young man—was nearly seduced into it—it is sometimes claimed that he had special access to their liturgical practices. But this is scarcely plausible. Epiphanius indicates that he spurned the advances of the two attractive Phibionite women *before* being drawn into their orb. This must mean that he was never present for any of the ritual activities. And it defies belief that missionaries would inform outsiders about the scandalous and reprehensible activities of the group before they were admitted into the inner circle. Potential converts were not likely to be won over by accounts of ritualistic consumption of fetuses.

Epiphanius stands in a long line of Christian heresiologists who claimed that their opponents, especially Gnostics, subscribed to impenetrable and ridiculous mythological understandings of the world while engaging in outrageous and scurrilous behavior, all as part of their religion.[29] As far back as Irenaeus, two centuries earlier, we learn of Valentinians who allegedly taught that those who possess the divine seed should give their spirit to spiritual things and their flesh to fleshly things, so that indiscriminate copulation was not only permissible but

---

26. For an older, but still useful, if basic, study, see Gerard Vallée, *A Study in Anti-Gnostic Polemics: Irenaeus, Hippolytus, and Epiphanius*, Studies in Christianity and Judaism 1 (Waterloo, Ontario: Wilfred Laurier University, 1981). More generally, see Jon Dechow, *Dogma and Mysticism in Early Christianity: Epiphanius of Cyprus and the Legacy of Origen*, NAPSPMS 13 (Macon, GA: Mercer, 1988).

27. "With Walter Bauer on the Tigris: Encratite Orthodoxy and Libertine Heresy in Syro-Mesopotamian Christianity," in *Nag Hammadi, Gnosticism, and Early Christianity*, ed. Charles W. Hedrick and Robert Hodgson (Peabody MA: Hendrickson, 1986), pp. 287–307.

28. "The Libertine Gnostic Sect of the Phibionites according to Epiphanius," *VC* 21 (1967): 103–19.

29. For the link between charges of sexual deviance and heresy in ancient polemics, see the insightful analysis of Jennifer Knust, *Abandoned to Lust* (New York: Columbia University, 2005).

a *desideratum* for the pneumatichoi (*Adv. Haer.* I. 6.3–4); the Carpocratians are said to have practiced indiscriminate sex, and indeed their theology compelled them to violate every conceivable moral law and ethical norm so as to avoid being reincarnated ad infinitum (I.25.4); the heretic Marcus reportedly excited attractive women by inspiring them to speak in tongues, after which they became putty in his lascivious hands (I.13.3). Maligning the Other for sexual offenses was de rigueur among orthodox heresiologists.

And this is not the ammunition simply of Christian heresy hunters: throughout antiquity it was standard polemical fare to charge one's opponents with the most nefarious of crimes against nature and humanity, in particular indiscriminate sex, infanticide, and cannibalism. The Christians were charged with such activities by pagans such as Fronto, tutor to Marcus Aurelius, and by Jews such as the one introduced, or rather imagined, by Celsus. Jews had to fend off charges by pagan antagonists; pagans describe comparable activities in play among other pagans.[30]

That the polemic is standard should always give one pause in the face of any particular instantiation of it. But with groups of Gnostics we are on particularly thorny ground. The proto-orthodox heresiologists uniformly assumed that since various Gnostic groups demeaned the material world and bodily existence within it, they had no difficulty in demeaning the body. Moreover, since for Gnostics the body was irrelevant for ultimate salvation, reasoned the heresiologists, then the body could be used and abused at will. And so, for their opponents, the Gnostics engaged in all sorts of reprehensible bodily activities, precisely to demonstrate their antimaterialist theology.

This heresiological commonplace has been effectively refuted in modern times. The one thing the Nag Hammadi library has shown about Gnostic ethics is that the heresiologists from Irenaeus (and no doubt before) to Epiphanius (and certainly after) got the matter precisely wrong. Many Gnostic groups did devalue the body. But that did not lead them to flagrant acts of immorality. On the contrary, since the body was the enemy and was to be escaped, the body was to be treated harshly. One was not to indulge in the pleasures of the flesh precisely because the goal was to escape the trappings of the flesh. The Nag Hammadi treatises embody a decidedly ascetic ideal, just the opposite of what one would expect from reading the polemics of the proto-orthodox and orthodox heresiologists.[31]

Which takes us back to Epiphanius and his Greater Questions of Mary. Epiphanius, as we have seen, does claim to have read the Phibionites' literature, and this claim is sometimes taken to substantiate his account, even though he himself

30. On Fronto, see Minucius Felix, *Octavius*, 9.5; on Celsus, see Origen, *Contra Celsum*, 6.27; on Jewish apologia, see Josephus, *Contra Apionem*, 2.8; on pagan attacks on pagans, see the burlesque in *The Phoenician Miscellanies*. In general, see Stephen Benko, "The Charges of Immorality and Cannibalism," in *Pagan Rome and the Early Christians* (Bloomington: Indiana University, 1984), ch. 3.

31. See the now classic study of Frederik Wisse, "The Nag Hammadi Library and the Heresiologists," *VC* 25 (1971): 205–23.

both provides the account and makes the claim. Here as always Epiphanius must be taken with a pound of salt. The books of the Phibionites could not have been widely circulated outside the group—at least any books that documented their scandalous activities. So possibly Epiphanius read some of their theological or mythological treatises, and drew (or conjured up) his own conclusions. But did he read the Greater Questions of Mary and quote it accurately in his *Panarion*?

There is evidence that some such book did at one time exist: it is at least mentioned elsewhere, although there is no evidence that any other author of a surviving work actually had seen it.[32] But nowhere else, outside of Epiphanius, are we given any indication of its contents. The episode that Epiphanius cites of Jesus engaging in illicit sex, coitus interruptus, and consumption of his own semen coincides perfectly well with Epiphanius' description of the activities of the Phibionites themselves. Moreover, Epiphanius almost certainly fabricated the accounts of these activities: he had never seen them, no one from within the group would have told him about them, they could not have been described in their other literature, and they stand at odds with what we do know of the ethical impulses of all other Gnostic groups from antiquity. On these grounds I would propose that Epiphanius made up the account of the Greater Questions of Mary. The Phibionites may have had a long-lived reputation for scurrilous activities—thus Gero—but if they were like every other Gnostic group for which we have firsthand knowledge—and why would they not be?—then their antimaterialist theology did not lead to socially scandalous and illegal promiscuity, but to ascetic dismissal of the passions of the flesh. The conclusion seems inevitable: Epiphanius got the matter precisely wrong and then fabricated his accounts, and at least one document, in order to make his point.[33]

OTHER CHRISTIAN FORGERS WHO ATTACK FORGERY

Epiphanius would not be the first Christian author to condemn forgeries and then produce a forgery (or at least a fabrication) himself; nor would he be the last. Indeed, one of our earliest Christian writings of record may represent an analogous, if less outrageous, situation. As is well known, Paul's second letter to the Thessalonians warns its readers against an earlier letter "as if by us" to the effect that "the Day of the Lord is almost here" (2:2). In other words, the author is concerned about a forgery that has the potential of leading his readers astray about the true nature of eschatology. The irony—one to which we should be slowly growing accustomed by now—is that 2 Thessalonians is itself widely thought not

32. It appears, for example, as one of the thirty-five Gospel books in the Samaritan Chronicle II.

33. Technically speaking, the Greater Questions of Mary would not be a forgery in the sense that I will be defining it presently, but a fabrication—a made-up narrative.

to be by Paul, even though it claims to be written by Paul and goes out of its way to convince its readers that it really is by Paul (thus 3:17).[34] Among other things, the passage in 2:2 makes it relatively certain that forgeries in the name of Paul were being produced already in the New Testament period. If 2 Thessalonians is authentic, then Paul knows of a troubling forgery in his name already during his lifetime; if 2 Thessalonians is not authentic, then it is itself a forgery in Paul's name, in all probability not long after his death. Either way, there are Pauline forgeries in circulation. I will provide a fuller discussion of the matter later, but for now it is enough to state the widely held view that 2 Thessalonians is not Pauline. What this means, then, is that this is the first recorded instance in which a Christian forger—someone other than Paul claiming to be Paul—is warning his readers against a Christian forgery.

Here then is a ploy used at the beginning of the Christian era. And it was used for centuries to come, even after the invention of printing. In his lively and compelling book *Forgers and Critics*, Anthony Grafton points to no less a figure than Erasmus as another instance. Erasmus made a living off of exposing the forgeries, fabrications, and falsifications of his intellectual and religious tradition. Following in the path of the great Lorenzo Valla, for example, he showed compelling reasons for thinking that the famous correspondence between Paul and Seneca was forged: the letters are banal, Christ is hardly mentioned in them, Paul himself is portrayed as cowardly and timorous, and it is stupid to imagine that Seneca offered Paul a book "On the Abundance of Words" (De copia verborum) in order to help him write better Latin ("If Paul did not know Latin he could have written in Greek. Seneca did know Greek").[35]

But what goes around comes around. In 1530 Erasmus published an edition of the works of the third-century Cyprian, including a new treatise that Erasmus claimed to have found "in an ancient library," *De duplici martyrio* ("On the Two Forms of Martyrdom"). In this treatise the traditional martyrs are praised; but Cyprian also praises those who are martyrs in a different sense, who live a life of sacrifice (especially sexual) in the here and now. In Grafton's words, the treatise "takes a position highly sympathetic to Erasmus, who had always disliked the kind of Christianity that equated suffering with virtue, and had always preferred the human Christ hoping to avoid death in Gethsemane to the divine Christ ransoming man by dying at Calvary."[36] Grafton notes that the book is found in no manuscript that survives, it explicates passages of Scripture in ways paralleled in Erasmus's own commentaries, and the Latin writing style is very similar to Erasmus's own in such works as *The Praise of Folly*. Grafton's convincing conclusion:

---

34. For a fuller discussion, see pp. 156–71.

35. Cited in Grafton, *Forgers and Critics: Creativity and Duplicity in Western Scholarship* (Princeton: Princeton University Press, 1990), p. 43; quoting from P. S. Allen et al., eds., *Opus Epistolarum Des. Erasmi Roterodami* (Oxford: Clarendon, 1906–1958), 8:40.

36. Grafton, *Forgers and Critics*, p. 44.

> *De duplici martyrio* is not Erasmus' discovery but his composition; it marks an effort to find the support of the early Church for his theology at the cost—which he elsewhere insisted must never be paid—of falsifying the records of that Church. The greatest patristic scholar of the sixteenth century forged a major patristic work.[37]

From New Testament times to the early years of printing: forgers who condemn forgery. There are numerous examples between these two points. As Speyer has argued: "Frequently, however, the eras of incisive critique were also rich in forgeries. Hilduin of St. Denis, rather like Anastosius Sinaites, is critic and forger in one."[38] He later names as well the ninth-century archbishop of Rheims, Hincmar.[39]

Guilty parties leveling a charge are not found solely in the Christian tradition, of course, as we saw at the outset in the case of Heraclides Ponticus and Dionysius the Renegade. As a final example we might consider the charge leveled at the emperor Hadrian in the forged Historia Augusta, on the pen of (Pseudo-) Spartianus. Hadrian is faulted for instructing his freedmen to attach their own names to his autobiography, to provide it with something less than self-referential credentials: "So desirous of a wide-spread reputation was Hadrian that he even wrote his own biography; this he gave to his educated freedmen, with instructions to publish it under their own names. For indeed, Pflegon's writings, it is said, are Hadrian's in reality" (*Hadrian* 1.6).[40]

Yet again we have the exposure of a forged document (Pseudo-Hadrian) by a forger (Pseudo-Spartianus). The Historia Augusta is full of such irony, never found more elegantly than in the pseudonymously penned statement of *Aurelian* 1–2: "There is no writer, at least in the realm of history, who has not made some false statement." And this by an author who is writing, to use Ronald Syme's term, under a "bogus name."[41]

CONCLUSION: THE THEMES OF THE STUDY

These anecdotal accounts set the stage and express the themes for our detailed examination of the use of forgery in the context of early Christian polemics. Each

37. Ibid., p. 45.

38. "Oft aber waren Zeiten scharfsinniger Kritik auch reich an Fälschungen. Hilduin von St. Denis ist ähnlich wie Anastasios Sinaites Kritiker und Fälscher in einer Person," Speyer, *Literarische Fälschung*, p. 85.

39. Speyer, *Literarische Fälschung*, p. 200. See further H. Schrörs, *Hinkmar, Erzbischof von Reims* (Freiburg im Breisgau, 1884), pp. 398–400; Schrörs tries to exonerate Hincmar of the charge of forgery in pp. 507–12. But see B. Krusch, "Reimser Remigius Fälschungen," in *Neues Archiv Gesellschaft für ältere deutsche Geschichtskunde* 20 (1895): 531–37.

40. Translation of David Magie in *The Historia Augusta*, LCL (Cambridge, MA: Harvard University, 1921–32).

41. Ronald Syme, *Emperors and Biography: Studies in the Historia Augusta* (Oxford: Clarendon Press, 1971), ch. 1.

incident has involved the use of forgery in a polemical context, where the forgery, based on an authority claimed under the guise of an assumed name, provided ammunition for the assault on the views of another.[42] In each case, the forgery was meant to deceive its readers; that is to say, the authorial claims were meant to be believed. No one approved of someone else's forgery; the practice of forgery was condemned, in fact, even in works that were themselves forged. This is just one of the ironies that emerge from the ancient forged literature. One of its corollaries is that forgeries were sometimes used to counter the views of other forgeries. This is a phenomenon that I will be calling "counterforgery" in its narrow sense. We will see numerous instances of the phenomenon throughout the Christian tradition of the first four centuries.

Before looking specifically at the Christian materials, it will be important to have a more thorough grounding in the practice of forgery in the broader environment, defined here as the Greek and Roman worlds of antiquity and late antiquity. This will be the subject of Chapters Four and Five. First, however, I need to explain the terminology that I will be using throughout the study and justify my usage. That will be the subject of the next chapter.

---

42. This is true even of the Apostolic Constitutions, as we will see later in Chapter Twelve.

CHAPTER THREE

Terms and Taxonomies

Many scholars, especially Neutestamentlers, object to the use of the term *forgery* for the phenomenon I have so far described: a book written with a false authorial claim.[1] This is because of its negative connotations, sometimes asserted to be a modern and thus anachronistic imputation. I will deal with these objections in detail in Chapter Four. For now, it is enough to say that the terms used in antiquity were just as negative or even more so. What we call forgeries—books with false authorial claims—were typically called deceits, lies, and bastards.

THE TERMS OF FORGERY

Before discussing ancient terms, I need to clarify how I will be using modern ones. Those who object to the term *forgery* typically prefer to speak of pseudonymity or pseudepigraphy. Often these two terms are used synonymously, but that can lead to confusion, since other scholars, especially German and French, draw a clear distinction between them. Consider the differentiation of Eve-Marie Becker: "The terms pseudepigraphy and pseudonymity should not simply be used synonymously. In the case of pseudonymity, a fictitious author is chosen, in the case of pseudepigraphy, the work is ascribed to a real author."[2]

Rather than considering the two terms as categorically distinct, however, I prefer to see one as a subset of the other. For the purposes of this study, I will be using the term *pseudonymous* in a broad sense to refer to any writing that appears under

---

1. See, for example, the authors mentioned in note 32 on p. 78 and on pp. 128–32.

2. "Die Begriffe Pseudepigraphie und Pseudonymität sind nicht einfach synonym zu gebrauchen. Bei der Pseudonymität wird ein fiktiver Autor gewählt, bei der Pseudepigraphie wird das Werk einem realen Autor zugeschrieben." In "Von Paulus zu 'Paulus,'" in Jörg Frey et al., eds., *Pseudepigraphie und Verfasserfiktion*, p. 376.

a name other than that of the author. Roughly speaking, there are two kinds of pseudonymity. Some books, past and present, are written under a fictitious pen name. In modern times one naturally thinks of Mark Twain (Samuel Clemens) or George Eliot (Mary Anne Evans). The question of the "innocence" of the fiction is often open, even with the use of pen names. Evans chose a male name, in part, to facilitate the publication of her work. It was not a purely innocent act, but a closely reasoned one intended to effect a desired result. Even so, it was not "deceptive" in the way it would have been if she had written a novel claiming to be Jane Austen. In the ancient world there are examples of fictitious pseudonymity as well , as I will discuss later in this chapter: Xenophon wrote the *Anabasis* under the name of Themistogenes (a not altogether innocent choice, as we will see) and Iamblichus, in a different era, wrote his *Mysteries* as Abamon.

The other form of pseudonymity occurs when a book appears under the name of a well-known person who did not, in fact, write it. It is for this kind of pseudonymous writing that I will be using the more specific term *pseudepigraphy*. And so, all pseudepigrapha are pseudonymous, but not all pseudonymous writings are pseudepigraphic, as I am using the terms. Writings that appear under a false (known) name are again of two types. First, there are books that were originally published anonymously (or under a homonym) that were later ascribed by other writers, editors, scribes, or readers to well-known persons who did not actually write them. This kind of false ascription is not to be laid at the feet of the author, who produced the work without attaching any name to it (or simply his own name, which he happened to share with a well-known person). It is not an instance, then, of authorial deceit but of later misattribution.

The other kind of pseudepigraphon does involve an authorial claim. This is when an author indicates that he is a known (usually famous, at least locally) person, realizing full well that he is in fact someone else. As we will see in further detail, there are grounds for thinking that this kind of false authorial claim was typically meant to deceive the reader. Authors who wanted to commit such acts of deception had a variety of reasons. And they used a range of literary techniques to make the deception effective. All these matters we will consider at length in this chapter and the ones that follow. For now it is enough to establish the meaning of the term I will be using. This kind of pseudepigraphy is what I am calling "forgery," when an author claims to be someone else who is well known, at least to some readers. Forgeries involve false authorial claims.

The intention to deceive[3] is part and parcel of what it meant to produce a forgery; the claim to be a well-known person is not simply an innocent fiction.

---

3. I am quite aware of the problems posed by the notion of "intention." When Wimsatt and Beardslee first presented their claims about the "intentional fallacy," it was to explain and justify some of the hermeneutical principles of the "new criticism" (see W. K. Wimsatt, *The Verbal Icon: Studies in the Meaning of Poetry*, Lexington: University of Kentucky, 1954). Their concerns were principally literary, not historiographic. Philosophers as well have devoted considerable attention to the problem, and the issues obviously do have clear historiographic implications. In the second edition of my book *The Orthodox*

This distinction was critical to the greatest historian of ancient forgery, Wolfgang Speyer: "It is the intent to deceive that, beyond any particular literary purpose, makes a pseudepigraphon a forgery."[4] For Speyer, an authorial claim was deceptive and false when it functioned in some nonliterary way, that is, as something other than a fiction, in order to accomplish some desired end. This purposeful intention to deceive the reader is what made a falsely named writing a forgery. And if it was a forgery, it was a form of literary lying: "Only where intent to deceive—that is to say, dolus malus—exists, does [a work] attain to the status of forgery. Forgery thus belongs in the same category as the lie."[5]

As I have already indicated, the term *forgery* is no more derogatory than the ancient terms used to describe the same phenomenon. In the texts that I will be dealing with, the most common terms include the following (and their cognates, in various accidental formations; all have their translational equivalents in Latin):

a. *Ψεῦδος*, the common term for "lie." We have already seen the use of the term and some of its derivations—for example, ψευδεπίγραφα. As Armin Baum has argued in the most recent and useful analysis, in some contexts the term can, to be sure, mean an unintentional "falsehood." But Baum shows that this is not the normal meaning unless it is accompanied by some qualifying phrase, such as κατ' ἀγνοίαν.[6] Even beyond this, and more important still, the idea of an unintended falsehood (when one says something that is false, without knowing it or meaning to) is of no relevance to the term as it

---

Corruption of Scripture, I set forth in greater detail my views of the matter, specifically, of how historians who recognize the theoretical problems with reconstructing past intentions can nonetheless use the category of "intention" as a functional category (*Orthodox Corruption of Scripture: The Effect of Christological Controversies on the Text of the New Testament*, 2nd ed., New York: Oxford University, 2011, pp. 32–33 and 337–41). Here I am going a step further to claim that reasonable assumptions about (past) intention can be made. A good example of how historians can proceed is provided by Jason BeDuhn, "The Historical Assessment of Speech Acts: Clarifications of Austin and Skinner for the Study of Religions" in *MTSR* 12 (2000): 477–505. At the end of the day, persons both past and present have always had intentions, whether these are (completely) accessible or not. For BeDuhn, reconstructing intentions is a matter of establishing reasonable probabilities. The same can be said, of course, of all historical work: history as an act of "establishing the past" is itself nothing but plausible reconstruction.

4. ". . . macht die Täuschungsabsicht, die jenseits eines literarischen Zweckes liegt, ein Pseudepigraphon zur Fälschung." *Literarische Fälschung*, p. 94.

5. "Nur wo Täuschungsabsicht, also dolus malus, vorliegt, wird der Tatbestand der Fälschung erfüllt. Insofern gehört die Fälschung zur Lüge." Ibid., p. 13.

6. Armin Daniel Baum, *Pseudepigraphie und literarische Fälschung im frühen Christentum*, WUNT 138 (Tübingen: Mohr Siebeck, 2001), pp. 11–12. Someone familiar not with Baum's work but only with his title might wonder how his book differs from mine. Baum's overarching concerns involve the question of canon. Given the fact—which he establishes forcefully—that ancient persons, including Christians, considered forgery to be lying, is it possible that Scripture could contain any forgeries? This simply is not my concern. One of Baum's subsidiary concerns is to establish that a book that was not authored by the person named is not a forgery if its contents can be traced back directly to that person. That is a matter on which we disagree, for reasons that will be evident in the course of my study. See especially pp. 87–90.

occurs in the contexts we are concerned with here. The authors who wrote 1 Timothy, 3 Corinthians, and the Letter to the Laodiceans, claiming to be Paul, knew full well that they were not really Paul. Ancient people would call these literary productions ψευδεπίγραφα: writings that are inscribed with a lie. They were not inadvertent falsehoods.

b. *Νόθος*. This term refers to a child born out of wedlock, and carries with it all the negative connotations of our term *bastard*. A literary work is "illegitimate" if it does not actually belong to the person named as its author, just as a child is illegitimate if its real father is not known. For some authors, such as the much later Neoplatonist Olympiodorus, the term applies to books regardless of authorial intent: homonymous writings are, for him, νόθα.[7] My concern in this study is not with falsely ascribed (or purely homonymous) writings, but with writings with clear authorial claims. Ancients often referred to such a writing as a bastard (Latin: nothus or spurius).[8]

c. *Κίβδηλος*. This term, "counterfeit," is entirely negative in connotation as well, referring often to the adulteration of coinage, and denoting that which is false, deceitful, and fraudulent. Often it is used in contrast with ἀληθής.

Speyer lists twenty-six Greek terms, with Latin equivalents, sometimes used to describe the act of committing forgery, almost all of them with negative connotations, including διαφθείρειν, μεταχαράττειν, and ῥᾳδιουργεῖν; to his list could be added πλάσσειν and ἀναπλάσσειν, "to make up," "invent," "fabricate." Simply on the terminological level, this was not a respectable practice. When one considers what ancient authors actually said about the practice—a matter to which we will soon turn—there appears to be no reason to shy away from calling it what it is. *Forgery* is not an unnecessarily negative term, contrary to the claims of some New Testament scholars.[9] Books that made false authorial claims were thought of as lies, bastards, and counterfeits.

---

7. *Prolegomena*; CAG XII/1, 13, 4–14, 4. Greek text and German translation in Baum, *Pseudepigraphie*, pp. 239–41.

8. There may be some confusion over how the term is used in one of our key authors, Eusebius, since in his famous account of canonical writings in *H.E.* 3.25 he lists the Shepherd of Hermas as a νόθον, a seemingly inappropriate term for an orthonymous writing. But in fact the term may be entirely appropriate, since Eusebius seems to have followed his hero Origen in assuming that the Hermas claimed as the book's author was to be identified as the companion of Paul from Romans 16:14 (*H.E.* 3.3). Eusebius may have "known" that the author was not "that" Hermas, and therefore the book—along with the Acts of Paul, the Apocalypse of Peter, the Didache of the Apostles, and Barnabas—is not by the person named. Like these others, then, it is a νόθον, not fathered by the person named as its author. David Nienhuis (*Not By Paul Alone: The Formation of the Catholic Epistle Collection and the Christian Canon*, Waco: Baylor University, 2007, p. 65) is off the mark when he thinks that Eusebius means that the Shepherd is not a "legitimate offspring of the historic, apostolic church." This understanding stretches the meaning of the term in an idiosyncratic direction, failing to consider its typical usage both in Eusebius and in the broader Greco-Roman world. The term refers to authorship, not to standing within a religious tradition.

9. We will consider a host of examples later. For now it is enough to cite the suggestion (not meant in humor) of I. Howard Marshall, that instead of pseudonymity and pseudepigraphy—terms that employ

DESCRIPTIONS OF THE PHENOMENA

Normal and Special Cases: "Typical" Instances of Forgery

Practices of forgery are complex and not easily classified. In "normal" forgeries, if we may use the term, an author falsely claims to be a well-known person. But that claim can be made in a variety of ways and with different levels of insistence. Just considering examples from our earliest Christian writings, in a number of cases the author states his assumed name and does nothing further in his writing to assure his reader that he really is who he claims to be. That appears to be the case, for example, in such books as 1 Peter and James.

In other instances, the author uses validation techniques to assure his readers that he is the actual writer. We will see such techniques more fully in Chapter Five. For now it is enough to note several of the most obvious kinds. In some instances, the author inserts corresponding verisimilitudes into his account to make the reader think he really must be who he says he is. An outstanding set of examples occurs in 2 Timothy, where the author reminds his (fictitious) reader of their past interactions ("you have observed my teaching, my way of life, . . . my patience . . . my persecutions, my sufferings . . ." 3:10–11), but also gives to him personalized instructions: "Hurry and come to me quickly . . . and when you come bring the cloak that I left behind in Troas with Carpus, and also the books and especially the parchments" (4:9, 13). Such verisimilitudes assure the reader that this really is Paul writing to his young companion Timothy.

In other instances the author intensifies the claims through asseverations intended to demonstrate beyond doubt that he is who he claims to be. This happens, for example, in 2 Peter, whose author insists with some vehemence that he was actually there to see the majesty of Jesus on the Mount of Transfiguration (2 Pet. 1:16–18). He was among the "eyewitnesses" to the event and among those who "heard the voice that came from heaven." The argument that he makes depends on his telling the truth about the matter. So too the author of 1 Timothy, who swears an oath "I speak the truth, I am not lying," when he claims to be Paul, "preacher, apostle of the truth, and teacher of Gentiles" (2:7).

Sometimes the asseverations take the form of written guarantees of the author's identity, as happens, for example, in the famous conclusion of 2 Thessalonians: "This greeting is in my own hand, the hand of Paul, which is the sign in all my letters; this is how I write" (3:17).

---

the suggestion of falsehood—we use the more neutral terms allonymity and allopigraphy. His suggestion is rooted in his belief that if someone other than Paul wrote the Pastoral epistles, he did not mean to deceive anyone about it. I will have more to say about that—I think he is precisely wrong—in a later chapter. For now, I might simply ask which set of terms is true to the ancient discourse about the phenomenon and which one injects modern sensitivities into it. See I. Howard Marshall, *The Pastoral Epistles*, ICC (Edinburgh: T&T Clark, 1999), pp. 83–84.

There are other kinds of forgery that might be considered special cases, somewhat more complicated than the simple instance of an author claiming at the outset to be someone else. Here I will mention three such instances:

a. *Embedded forgeries.* Some writings do not make the explicit claim to be authored by a well-known person, but instead embed first-person narratives—or other self-identifying devices—in the course of their discussions, without differentiating the first person from the author. In these instances the reader naturally assumes that the person speaking in the first person is actually the writer of the account. A good example occurs in the Ascension of Isaiah, whose author does not self-identify at the outset but instead sets out an anonymous historical framework, written to sound very much like the prose narrative sections of the book of Isaiah itself. Partway through the narrative, however, and at key points throughout, the revelation given through Isaiah begins to be delivered in the first person. The (real) author of the account does not indicate that he is now quoting someone else, making the reader assume that the author has now begun speaking about what he himself experienced. This provides an unimpeachable authority for the account: it is revealed by none other than Isaiah. This kind of embedding strategy shows how blurry the lines of distinction can be between forgery and other kinds of writing. In many ways an embedded forgery is comparable to the use of speeches invented by historians and placed on the lips of their protagonists; but in those cases it is clear that the author has moved from narrative description to an (alleged) speech, even though the speech is invented. In an embedded forgery the narrator simply slips into another guise and becomes the authenticating figure. In another sense this kind of forgery is not so very different from fabrications of sayings reported to be from an authoritative figure, but that are actually the inventions of the author or of the unknown tradents who have passed them along in the oral tradition—such as many of the sayings of the Gospel of Thomas or later (or earlier) Gospel materials. But there again the sayings are attributed to another person and are presented by a narrator who is distinct from the one who is speaking, unlike what happens in the embedded forgery. For the latter, the narrator becomes the speaker (or participant in the action of the narrative). The Ascension of Isaiah, then, is a kind of forgery. The speaker who describes his experiences to the scribe recording the account is allegedly none other than Isaiah of Jerusalem himself.[10]
b. *Redactional forgeries.* There are a number of instances in which a book was originally circulated as an anonymous work, and was known in that

10. It should not be objected that since the Ascension of Isaiah is being recorded by Sebna the Scribe (1.5) Isaiah cannot be the author. Sebna is allegedly taking dictation in some form, as typically happened when authors "wrote" books. When the account turns to the first person, it is clear that Isaiah himself is doing the dictation. But this is simply an authorial ploy, a claim to be Isaiah by someone living 850 years later.

form for some time, before a later editor or scribe altered the text to make it present an authorial claim. The book is not then a forgery from its inception, but it becomes a forgery in the course of its transmission, not in the sense that the (original) author made a false authorial claim but in the sense that a later redactor reworded the text in such a way as to have the author (unwittingly) make such a claim. This is the case, for example, with the Infancy Gospel of Thomas. In the oldest parts of the textual tradition, this account of Jesus the mischievous wunderkind is simply narrated apart from any authorial claim. Only in later manuscripts is the name Thomas attached to it. Presumably this Thomas is to be taken as Jesus' twin brother Judas (Didymus), a particularly qualified authority to recount the miraculous childhood of the Son of God. But as Gero has argued, the attribution is late, probably from the Middle Ages.[11] The author himself made no authenticating claims.

c. *Non-pseudepigraphic forgeries.* There are other instances in which a book puts forth clear, but false, authorial claims without actually naming an author. This is true of one of the forgeries of the Hebrew Bible, the book of Ecclesiastes, which is allegedly authored by the "son of David," who is ruling as the king in Jerusalem, a man both inestimably rich and wise. Obviously the author means his readers to take him to be Solomon; but he never calls himself by name. This then creates an ironic situation: the author claims to be a famous person without actually naming himself. And so the book is a forgery (Solomon did not actually write it), but it is not, technically speaking, pseudepigraphic since it is not inscribed with the false name. A similar situation obtains much later in Christian circles in a book such as the "Martyrdom of Marian and James," whose author claims, falsely, to have been a personal companion of these two estimable martyrs, but never identifies himself by name.[12]

Some Not-So-Special Cases: When Forgery Is Allegedly Not Forgery

In Chapter Four we will see a number of scholars who, on general principle, are loath to label pseudepigraphic writings (especially canonical cases) forgeries, in part because they fail to see that false authorial claims involve deception. There are other scholars who posit special cases in which forgery is not really forgery. For these scholars, there are indeed instances of deception among the pseudonymous writings of antiquity, but other instances entailed special circumstances that make it inappropriate to label the pseudepigraphic writings in question forgeries.

---

11. Stephen Gero, "The Infancy Gospel of Thomas: A Study of the Textual and Literary Problems," *NovT* 13 (1971): 46–80, esp. p. 59.

12. See the discussion on pp. 505–6.

Wolfgang Speyer and "Genuine Religious Pseudepigraphy"

One commonly cited flaw in Speyer's rightly celebrated survey of pagan and Christian "Fälschungen" is his special category of "echte religiöse Pseudepigraphie" ("genuine religious pseudepigraphy"). Speyer notes that the category of forgery presupposes the concept of literary property: an author in some sense "owns" his work. Speyer traces this concept back to certain modes of Greek rational thought. When this kind of rationality is not in evidence in an ancient author, who instead writes under the inspiration of a divine being, Speyer maintains, the claim to authorship no longer consists of a deceit. In this case, it is the deity who is allegedly writing the book and the human inscriber is simply a tool in the hand of the divine. This kind of writing cannot be understood "scientifically," since it presupposes a different kind of thought and experience from that of the modern scholar:

> The final form of literary activity listed here, for which a deity is considered to be the originator of the written memorial, can be designated mythical or "religious pseudepigraphy." It is "genuine," as long as the belief in a divine revealer is vividly experienced as such . . . "genuine" religious pseudepigraphy could appear only in places not yet penetrated by rationalism, that is to say, primarily in regions at the margins of the Greco-Roman world.[13]

As examples Speyer has in mind certain kinds of oracular writing, or from Jewish circles, apocalypses truly based on revelatory experience. He thinks there are virtually no instances in the Christian literature.

This category is not unique to Speyer. In many ways it is similar to the view of J. Sint that "echte religiöser Ergriffenheit" (emotion) could lead to pseudepigraphic activity:

> It has become apparent, that a great number of writings can be explained only on the basis of religious motivations or motivations related to the psychology of religion. From the peculiarity of mythical thinking and genuine religious emotion the author obtains such persuasive power for his undertaking that we can no longer speak of conscious deception, that indeed ethical truth questions do not pose any problems for him and that he therefore could not fear being unmasked."[14]

---

13. "Die zuletzt genannte Form der Schriftstellerei, bei der ein Gott als der Urheber des schriftlichen Denkmals angesehen wird, kann als mythische oder 'religiöse Pseudepigraphie' bezeichnet werden. 'Echt' ist sie so lange, wie der Glaube an einen Gott als Offenbarer lebendig erlebt wird. . . . 'echte' religiöse Pseudepigraphie [konnte] nur noch dort auftreten, wohin die rationale Denkweise noch nicht gedrungen war, das heißt vornehmlich in den Randgebieten der griechisch-römischen Welt." *Literarische Fälschung*, p. 36.

14. "Daraus hat sich ergeben, daß eine große Anzahl psn Schriften nur aus religiösen und religionspsychologischen Entstehungsgründen zu erklären ist. Aus der Eigenart mythischen Denkens und echter

For Speyer, there are also instances in which the religious pseudepigraphy is "false" rather than "genuine." This is when a later author, cognizant of Greek rationalistic modes of thought and conversant with ideas of authorship, pretended to be under the inspiration of a divine being, and somewhat cynically then produced an imitation of a genuinely religious pseudepigraphon.

This further differentiation, however, reveals a principal problem with the category. It represents an attempt to render a historical judgment (what kind of pseudepigraphon is this work?) on the basis of a nonhistorical criterion (what is the state of mind of the author? Does he genuinely feel inspired by the divine?).[15] Inner psychological states are never accessible to the historian, and so surely they are not the best basis for forming historical conclusions. Hence the critique of E. J. Bickerman in his extended review of Speyer's work: "The hypothesis concerning 'genuine' religious pseudepigraphy is thus not only spurious, it is useless."[16]

Other objections are raised by H. Balz, who points out that the instances we have of Speyer's genuine religious pseudepigrapha are based on oral traditions that were later written down by an author. They are not, in other words, the product of immediate religious experience of divinely inspired prophets but are literary productions generated for the needs of communities.[17] More recently, and from another angle, P. Beatrice objects that Hesiod received his "information" about the genealogy of the gods from the Muses, yet signed the *Theogony* in his own name, just as the prophets of Israel who were conscious of being under the inspiration of God, and who spoke in his name, nonetheless produced orthonymous works.[18] When they did so, they were certainly not driven by the spirit of Greek rationalism. The other problem is that one might imagine how an author in a divinely inspired ecstatic trance might write in the name of the God who is using him as his vessel; but why would he be driven, then, to claim to be another

religiöser Ergriffenheit gewinnt der Verfasser für sein Vorgehen eine solche Überzeugungskraft, daß von bewusster Täuschung keine Rede sein kann, ja daß ihm die moralische Wahrheitsfrage gar nicht zum Problem wird und er darum seine Entlarvung nicht befürchten konnte." Josef A. Sint, *Pseudonymität im Altertum: Ihre Formen und ihre Gründe* (Innsbruck: Universitätverlag Wagner, 1960), p. 163.

15. Speyer claims that one can determine if a writing falls under the category based on "observations concerning language, style, composition and not least of all the psychology of such a writing" (Beobachtung von Sprache, Stil, Komposition und nicht zuletzt der Psychologie einer derartigen Schrift; p. 37). But he never explains the criteria that are to be used in making the judgment on these, or any other, grounds. As a result, the corpus of "genuine religious pseudepigrapha" appears to be a group of writings determined on the basis of a critic's "best guess."

16. "Donc, l'hypothèse de la pseudépigraphie religieuse qui est 'echt' est non seulement gratuite, elle est inutile." E. J. Bickerman, "Faux littéraires dans l'antiquité classique en marge d'un livre récent," in *Studies in Jewish and Christian History* (Leiden: E. J. Brill, 1986), p. 197.

17. Horst R. Balz, "Anonymität und Pseudepigraphie im Urchristentum: Überlegungen zum literarischen und theologischen Problem der urchristlichen und gemeinantiken Pseudepigraphie," *ZTK* 66 (1969): 412–13.

18. Pier Franco Beatrice, "Forgery, Propaganda and Power in Christian Antiquity," *JAC.E* 33 (2002): 45.

human? Why produce the writing in the name of someone else, rather than in the name of God?

In any event, since Speyer finds little evidence of any kind of genuine religious pseudepigraphy among Christian authors, his claims on this score are of little direct relevance for the current investigation.

Kurt Aland and the Authorial Spirit of God

By way of contrast, a much cited article by Kurt Aland declares that inspiration by the Spirit of God was precisely a Christian phenomenon and that it can explain the pseudepigraphic practices of the early church. The early Christian authors understood that the Holy Spirit was speaking through them when they wrote, much as he had spoken through them and their co-religionists when they orally delivered the Word of God to their hearers. When writing what the Spirit revealed, it would have been deceitful and false to claim their own names, as if the words were their own. As Aland puts it, "not only was the tool by which the message was given irrelevant, but . . . it would have amounted to a falsification even to name this tool, because . . . it was not the author of the writing who really spoke, but only the authentic witness, the Holy Spirit, the Lord, the apostles."[19] As a result:

> When pseudonymous writings of the New Testament claimed the authorship of the most prominent apostles only, this was not a skillful trick of the so-called fakers, in order to guarantee the highest possible reputation and the widest possible circulation for their work, but the logical conclusion of the presupposition that the Spirit himself was the author.[20]

According to Aland, it was only later in the life of the Christian community, once the age of prophecy had ceased, that works falsely written in the names of the apostles could be thought of as actual forgeries. This started happening in the midsecond century. By then "the possibility for the genesis of 'authentically pseudonymous' writings had passed."[21] Like Speyer, then, Aland maintains that there were authentic and inauthentic pseudepigrapha. Only the latter are to be deemed forgeries.

Despite the temporary popularity of Aland's view, there is little to commend it. For one thing, the claim that the earliest Christian authors would not write under their own names because they considered themselves inspired by the Spirit appears simply not to be true. Our earliest author is Paul, who names himself in no uncertain terms, and who certainly felt driven by the Spirit—at least as much

19. K. Aland, "The Problem of Anonymity and Pseudonymity in Christian Literature of the First Two Centuries," *JBL* 12 (1961): 44.

20. Ibid., pp. 44–45.

21. Ibid., pp. 48.

as, say, the forgers who produced books in his name in later periods (Ephesians, 1 Timothy, and so on). Moreover, as was the case with Speyer, Aland's view might well explain why an author refused to name himself—it was the Spirit talking, not him personally—but it cannot explain why an author *did* name himself, as some other (well-known) person. If it was the Spirit talking, why claim specifically to be Peter? Or James? Or Jude? Why not simply say "Thus says the Lord," or "Thus says the Spirit of God"? Or write anonymously altogether?

Moreover, it is worth noting that no ancient pseudepigrapher justifies his work on these grounds, and no ancient critic supplies this explanation for why works were forged. In the end, this is an attempt to justify a practice widely recognized in the ancient environment as deceitful. It is, in other words, theology, not history. And in the view of H. Balz it is not even good theology, as it means that these later "authentic pseudepigraphers" were more inspired by the Spirit than the Apostle Paul was.[22]

David Meade and the "Reactualization of the Tradition"

More influential in recent decades, at least in English-speaking circles, is the notion set forth in a revised Ph.D. dissertation at the University of Nottingham by David Meade, who argues that a good deal of the early Christian pseudepigrapha—at least those found in the canon—can be explained not as forgeries meant to deceive but as claims to stand within authoritative streams of tradition. Meade argues that the authors of the New Testament were appropriating modes of authorship with a venerable standing in the Jewish tradition (he pays no heed to the literary practices of the rest of the world). In Jewish writings, Meade avers, it was common to assume the name and the mantle of a fountainhead of a tradition, not in order to lie about one's own identity but in order (truthfully) to indicate one's traditional allegiances. This happened already in biblical sources.

So, for example, the book of Isaiah is not entirely the work of the eighth-century prophet of Jerusalem. The writings of two later authors, living in different contexts and addressing different situations, were added to those of their famous predecessor. This was not to deceive the reader but to inform her that the views and perspectives represented in this new account stood in the authoritative line of tradition begun by Isaiah himself. So too wisdom sayings produced centuries after the death of Solomon were attributed to the great king in order to apply his traditional wisdom to new situations. Similarly, later apocalyptic traditions were named after such figures as Enoch and Daniel.

In none of these instances was an author trying to deceive his readers. He was instead reactualizing the old tradition for a new context, showing how the old tradition was relevant and important for a new setting. This form of *Vergegenwärtigung*, then, does not represent the illicit borrowing of the name of another; it

---

22. "Anonymität und Pseudepigraphie," p. 419.

involves making a legitimate claim to stand in the other's line of tradition. And so, for example, with respect to the composite book of Isaiah, Meade can conclude:

> The anonymous/pseudonymous expansion of the Isaianic corpus is a recognition that Isaiah had become *part* of the tradition, and *the resultant literary attribution of that corpus must be regarded more as a claim to authoritative tradition by the participants in the process, and less a claim to actual authorship by Isaiah of Jerusalem.*[23] So too, the attribution of Ecclesiastes to Solomon, or of apocalyptic texts to Daniel and Enoch, "*is primarily an assertion of authoritative tradition, not a statement of literary origins.*[24]

And so, for Meade, the authors of New Testament pseudepigrapha, such as the Pastoral epistles, were not being deceptive when they claimed to be apostles. The author of 1 Timothy was informing his reader that he stood within the tradition established by the authentically Pauline epistles. He was genuinely attempting to apply Pauline views to the new situation that he was addressing. His claim to be Paul amounted to an assertion that his exhortations and perspectives were those of Paul himself—or would be, were Paul alive to address the new situation at hand. Vergegenwärtigung then is not forgery; it is a completely legitimate claim to stand closely within the Pauline tradition.

On one hand, this position is innately attractive: it acknowledges the historical fact that a number of the writings of the New Testament are pseudepigraphic, yet it absolves the authors of the charge of forgery. The view is nonetheless seriously flawed, on a number of grounds.

For one thing, Meade isolates the writings of the New Testament canon from the rest of the early Christian literature. Here again, this is theology, not history. Are there really *historical* grounds for claiming that 1 Timothy is pseudepigraphic Vergegenwärtigung but 3 Corinthians is a forgery? Was the author of 3 Corinthians not trying to make Paul speak for a new day? Does he not also stand—or at least try to stand—in line with Paul's teachings, for example, on the importance of the resurrection and life in the body?

In addition, Meade isolates these writings by situating them firmly, and only, in Jewish literary practices of the Bible, as if the New Testament authors were (1) Jews who (2) both knew and embraced the editorial practices that brought the various authors later named Isaiah altogether on the same scroll, or the various strands of the Danielic or Enochic traditions into a single work.

As to the first point, the vast majority of the early Christian authors, in particular the anonymous and pseudepigraphic writers after Paul (in other words, virtually all of them), were not Jews, did not originate in the Jewish tradition, and show

---

23. David G. Meade, *Pseudonymity and Canon: An Investigation into the Relationship of Authorship and Authority in Jewish and Earliest Christian Tradition* (Grand Rapids, MI: Eerdmans, 1985), p. 43; italics his.

24. Meade, *Pseudonymity and Canon*, p. 72; cf. p. 102 and passim. Italics his.

no signs of being intimately familiar with distinctively Jewish authorial practices, if any such thing ever existed. They were gentiles, who learned to write in gentile circles. They certainly did not have Jewish habits of Vergegenwärtigung hardwired into them. Even beyond that, it is very hard indeed to establish that Jewish modes of pseudepigraphy were distinctive. As Christopher Rowland has aptly observed, with respect to the most common form of Jewish pseudepigraphic writing from the time of the New Testament, the apocalypses: "a distinctively Jewish interpretation of Pseudonymity is difficult to uphold."[25] If that is true of Jewish apocalypses, how much more so of Christian writings, which were not written by Jews and were not tied, in terms of genre, to anything specifically Jewish.

It is striking, however, that Meade maintains that the writers of the New Testament pseudepigrapha not only stood within a thousand-year Jewish tradition of reactualization but were conscious of doing so. If this was a literary tradition in ancient Israel, why is it never mentioned in any source from antiquity? The reality is that ancient Jews, at least in the time that Meade is interested in, were in no way conscious of this literary "tradition." That is to say, first-century Jews, lacking access to nineteenth- and twentieth-century scholarship in higher criticism, did not know that Isaiah was the work of three authors put together onto one scroll. For them, and their Christian counterparts, there was one Isaiah and he wrote the entire book. And Daniel wrote Daniel and Solomon wrote Ecclesiastes. How could these later writers have stood in a tradition they did not know existed?

Moreover, many of the key (Jewish) examples that Meade cites simply do not relate to the (Christian) phenomenon he is trying to explain. Whoever wrote 2 Isaiah says nothing about being Isaiah, and we have no idea who put his anonymous writings on a scroll with those of his predecessor from 150 years earlier. How does that relate, then, to the author of 2 Peter, who goes out of his way to inform his readers that he really is Simon Peter and that he actually saw Jesus on the Mount of Transfiguration, so that he, as opposed to his enemies, knows whereof he speaks? Or to the author of 2 Timothy, who not only names himself as Paul but supplies extensive verisimilitudes to prove it? These are not commensurate cases.

On one point Meade is certainly correct. Whoever wrote 1 Timothy wanted his readers to think that he was standing within the Pauline tradition and that his views were those that Paul would have expressed had he been writing in the same situation. But of how many instances of pseudepigraphy can that *not* be said? One of the salient features of the ancient Christian literary tradition is precisely that authors taking contrary theological and practical positions appeal to the same authorities in support. Or rather, they claim to be the same authors, while advancing their own views, thinking that their views are, or would be, the views of the authors they are claiming to be. Whoever wrote the Coptic Apocalypse of Peter in order to denigrate the flesh and show its unimportance in the scheme of salvation

---

25. *The Open Heaven: A Study of Apocalyptic in Judaism and Early Christianity* (New York: Crossroad, 1982), p. 66.

appealed to Peter's authority in support of his view, and if pressed no doubt would have indicated that this really was Peter's view. But so too would the author of the Greek (Ethiopic) Apocalypse of Peter, who wrote to show that the fleshly existence ultimately matters and that salvation, and damnation, will be experienced precisely in the flesh. The first author would have considered the second a liar when he called himself Peter, and would have labeled his writing a forgery; the second would have responded in kind. Who is right? It may be possible for historians to adjudicate these claims, at least in theory. One of these writers may indeed be closer to the views of the historical man Peter. But given the fact that he has left us no writings, it is really very difficult to say. And even were we to give the palm to one writer or the other, the reality is that both of them fabricated narratives and then claimed to be Peter in order to deliver them. None of this material goes back to Peter. All of it is fabricated. Both works are forged.

In the end Meade's position that pseudonymous claims of the (canonical) writers is primarily about authoritative tradition rather than literary origins is based on a false and misleading dichotomy. In point of fact, the "authoritative" tradition that a forger lays claim to is made authoritative for the reader precisely because of the claim of literary origins. It is because the author is Peter, or Paul, or Thomas, or John, or Jesus, that the claims of his account are accepted as authoritative. In other words, in all these instances an author has lied about his identity in order to establish the veracity of his account. But so did other authors—sometimes claiming the same names—in order to authorize their discrepant accounts. Completely opposite views are advanced in the same name. All of them are acts of Vergegenwärtigung. But to excuse some of them and not others requires either a set of theological (not historical) norms or a pair of canonical blinders.

Harry Gamble sums the matter up as follows: "Others [outside of Meade] . . . find nothing distinctive in Jewish pseudepigraphy and regard both Jewish and early Christian pseudonymity merely as particular manifestations of a wider ancient practice of which Greco Roman literature offers many examples." Specifically with respect to Pauline materials, Gamble maintains: "Pseudonymous authorship is nothing else than it appears to be, namely the use of a revered apostolic name in order to assert the authority of teaching that was believed to be of value by its author, irrespective of its actual origins."[26]

Conclusion

Later we will discuss two other approaches to pseudepigrapha often taken by New Testament scholars in order to minimize the charges of deception: (1) the claim that nondeceptive pseudepigraphy was both widely practiced and sanctioned in the philosophical schools of antiquity, and (2) the assertion that the epistolary

---

26. Harry Y. Gamble, "Pseudonymity and the New Testament Canon," in Jörg Frey et al., eds., *Pseudepigraphy und Verfasserfiktion*, pp. 359, 361.

pseudepigrapha from early Christianity—at least the canonical cases—can be explained by appealing to the use of a secretary. Both claims, I will argue, are not supported by convincing evidence. These matters, however, need to wait until later chapters. At this stage it is more important to draw some preliminary conclusions. Forgery, based simply on the ancient terminology used to describe it, appears to have been a deceptive practice that was not widely sanctioned (more grounds will be given in Chapter Four). It cannot be explained away on the basis of alleged inspiration by the divine spirit(s); and it was not an innocent matter of reactualizing tradition. Forgery involved the conscious act of making a false authorial claim. Ancient writers considered it a form of lying. Before extending further evidence for this view, in the next chapter, we first need to continue our taxonomic efforts.

RELATED PHENOMENA

There are a number of literary phenomena that are closely related to forgery, and we do well to differentiate among them as clearly as possible.

Literary Fictions

It is widely recognized by scholars today, as it evidently was in antiquity, that some falsely named writings were not meant as deceptions but as literary fictions. This is particularly the case in certain letter collections and epistolary novels, written in the names of well-known figures but probably as rhetorical exercises rather than attempts to deceive a reading public. In many instances it is difficult to tell whether deception was part of the intent; in other instances the matter is clear. In either event this kind of pseudonymous writing has meager relevance for the present study, as there are no certain instances of pseudepigraphic fiction among the early Christian writings.[27]

The only full collection of epistolary fictions is in R. Hercher's 1873 volume *Epistolographi Graeci*, representing sixty letter writers and some sixteen hundred letters. Recent years have seen a burgeoning of interest in the matter, with a helpful bilingual collection of important specimens by C. D. N. Costa and several important studies, one of them book-length by P. Rosenmeyer.[28]

Costa usefully divides the fictional letters into two types. The first are "imaginary" (sometimes called "comic") letters. These are written under fictitious pen

27. See n. 35 below.

28. R. Hercher, *Epistolographi Graeci* (Paris: A. F. Didot, 1873; reprinted Amsterdam: A. M. Hakkert, 1965); C. D. N. Costa, *Greek Fictional Letters* (New York: Oxford, 2001); Patricia A. Rosenmeyer, *Ancient Epistolary Fictions* (Cambridge: Cambridge University Press, 2001). Other useful studies include Herwig Görgemanns, "Epistolography," *Brill's New Pauly* (Leiden: Brill, 2010); M. Hose, *Kleine griechische Literaturgeschichte* (Munich: C. H. Beck, 1999); M. Luther Stirewalt, *Studies in Ancient Greek Epistolography* (Atlanta: Scholars Press, 1993).

names, such as Aelian, Alciphron, and Philostratus, and appear to be produced by professional rhetoricians, or rhetoricians in training, on topics and themes to which they might devote declamations. They "aim to portray character and various levels of society, or to evoke a past age."[29] The other type comprises letters that are attributed to famous historical figures such as Phalaris or Themistocles, and especially to philosophers such as Anacharsis, Hippocrates, Diogenes, and Socrates. An earlier example would be Ovid's famous *Heroides*, which was clearly meant to be a fiction built on historically fictional characters. In this latter type, the figure in question is made to speak "in character," that is, these are written exercises in ethopoeia. Most of the philosophical letters have a didactic, moralizing aim, but they are also meant to reflect something of the character and personality of the supposed author.[30]

The thorough and enlightening discussion of Rosenmeyer shows, perhaps unwittingly, just how difficult it can be at times to differentiate between literary fictions and deceptions. She notes that R. Syme in particular has argued that these letters should not be termed forgeries, but are better understood as "impostures" (a term that does not seem hugely different in connotation), which "were doubtless created without any serious intent to deceive."[31] Rosenmeyer's principal concern is that these writings not be simply written off as of no importance—as they have been since Bentley's exposure of the letters of Phalaris—and so discarded as the chaff of history. They are important in their own right, when situated in their appropriate historical, cultural, and especially rhetorical contexts.

This is fair enough, but there are some questionable cases. Rosenmeyer herself points out that verisimilitudes were part of the exercise, as these letters speak about the mechanics of writing, sending, sealing, receiving, and so on, for one major reason: "The more realistic the epistolary moment appears, both in terms of the occasion and the specific letter, the more convincing it will be to its readers, who seek the literary thrill of reading someone else's private messages."[32] This sounds like a concession to the idea that the writers wanted to convince their readers, and it is difficult to draw a very clear line between that attempt and pure literary deception.

One might consider, for example, the two sets of Socratic epistles, one connected with Antisthenes, which urges a rigorous lifestyle, and the other with Aristippus, which supports hedonism. Both advocate their own perspective and inveigh against the other. And why is that? It is because, in Rosenmeyer's own words, "a treatise on the subject would be rejected as just another (mis)

---

29. Costa, *Greek Fictional Letters*, p. xiv.

30. There are debates over the genre of the "epistolary novel," that is, the use of fictional letters in order to create a coherent narrative. Rosenmeyer, for example, contends that there is only one set of letters that fits the description, the letters of Chion. (This obviously raises the question of how a genre with one literary representative is actually a genre.) Hose, *Kleine griechische Literaturgeschichte* finds seven.

31. Rosenmeyer, *Ancient Epistolary Fictions*, p. 195.

32. Ibid., p. 207.

interpretation of the philosopher; but a letter in the voice of the great man himself, or in that of his most highly regarded disciple, would be hard to refute."[33] That is exactly right; but it is also the reason that some of these fictions may be seen as going a step further in wanting their readers really to believe them to be actual letters written by the philosopher himself. It is at least possible, that is, that some of these works were produced not simply as rhetorical exercises but in order to perpetrate a literary deceit. However one judges that issue, fictions of this kind were difficult to keep in check. As Martina Janssen observes, there was no way to control their reception history, as later readers in another context may have taken an authorial fiction to be a bona fide authorial claim, so that an original rhetorical exercise came to function as a forgery, apart from any authorial intent.[34]

In any event, with only one or two possible exceptions—possibly the letters of Paul and Seneca?[35]—there are probably no literary fictions among the early Christian writings, produced simply as rhetorical exercises.

Pen Names

Pen names—or pseudonymity in the traditional, German, sense—were not common in antiquity, but were not unheard of either. This use of a pen name differs from a literary fiction of the first type described above in that the composition in question is not a rhetorical exercise in ethopoeia, but an actual writing with a purpose that extends beyond itself.

In some instances a pen name may have been relatively innocent, the opportunity to write a work anonymously under a name chosen at random. This appears to be the case with the work produced by the six purported authors of the Historia Augusta. Ronald Syme in particular has shown that the solitary author of this collection of imperial biographies was a learned but somewhat mischievous scholar from around 400 CE, who fabricated a good deal of information, much of it for his personal enjoyment.[36] He was remarkably successful in his endeavor to hide his identity: up to the end of the nineteenth century the work was held to be authentic and basically reliable. Though not everyone realized it at the time,

---

33. Ibid., p. 202.

34. Martina Janssen, "Antike (Selbst-)Aussagen über Beweggründe zur Pseudepigraphie," in Jörg Frey et al., eds., *Pseudepigraphie und Verfasserfiktion*, pp. 131–35.

35. This is the argument of the editor of the major critical edition, Claude W. Barlow, *Epistolae Senecae ad Paulum et Pauli ad Senecam* (Rome: American Academy, 1938): "Although the emphasis in a rhetor's school was upon oratory and the characteristic method of attaining oratorical perfection was by discussion and declamation, it seems nevertheless that writing as well as speaking must have formed a part of the training. The Correspondence between Seneca and St. Paul might then be considered as an exercise on a fictitious subject assigned by the teacher. . . . The possibility should also be mentioned that the Correspondence is the work of more than one hand, perhaps of two or three scholars in the same school, working in competition on a set problem" (p. 92). I owe this reference to Pablo Molina. See further discussion on pp. 520–27 below.

36. Syme, *Emperors and Biography*, pp. 1–16.

the death knell was struck in 1899 by Herman Dessau in a paper showing that the entire composition was the work of a single author writing centuries after the alleged authors. Dessau's argument: some of the characters mentioned in the work are fictitious and show signs of having been invented near the end of the fourth century.

In his chapter on "The Bogus Names," Syme categorizes all the cited names and authorities of the Historia Augusta, in ten categories, including the most significant: "fictitious characters who by their names reflect families eminent in the Roman aristocracy in the second half of the fourth century." He concludes that the author of the work was extremely erudite, but that he included a "profusion of details about food and drink and sex" which "were not meant to be taken seriously." Moreover, "he has his own silly or elaborate jokes." Syme's conclusion was that "this man is a kind of rogue scholar."[37]

In other cases we know full well the author of a book, but it is hard to discern a reason for the pen name. Thus Iamblichus wrote *On the Mysteries* as Abamon, but his reason is itself a mystery. T. Hopfner suggested that Iamblichus wanted to hide from his potentially Christian readers the fact that he and his fellow Neoplatonists were sometimes at odds with one another. The book, after all, is a response to Porphyry's attack on his former student for his attraction to the occult, in a letter ostensibly addressed to "Anebo," itself a name that has generated considerable discussion (is it too an invention?).[38] Hopfner's theory, however, seems rather unlikely, as Clarke, Dillon, and Hershbell point out, given Iamblichus' virtually complete disregard for Christians otherwise.[39] It may simply be that he recognized Porphyry's attack leveled at an alias for himself, and he responded in kind, pretending that the fictitious Anebo was his (the fictitious Abamon's) student as a "poke in the eye" to Porphyry, his own teacher.[40]

There are other instances where a pen name may have been chosen simply to protect the identity of the real author, in cases in which safety or other personal concerns were an issue: Janssen instances Nestorius' use of the name Heraclides in his *Liber Heraclidis*.[41] At other times the use of a pen name was not innocent at all. That is Plutarch's suspicion of Xenophon, when he wrote his *Anabasis* in the name of Themistogenes, an alleged general of Syracuse. This pseudonym is often taken to be a simple pen name, chosen for no particular reason. But as Plutarch points out (*Moralia* 345e), by discussing his own military activities in the third person, as a purported outsider, Xenophon was able to give himself greater credence and glory than if he had written the account in his own name.

---

37. See pp. 11, 13, 76, 95.

38. Theodor Hopfner, *Über die Geheimlehren von Jamblichus.* (Leipzig: Theosophisches Verlagshaus, 1922), p. x. For evaluation, see Emma C. Clarke, John M. Dillon, and Jackson B. Hershbell, trs. and eds. *Iamblichus On the Mysteries* (Atlanta: Society of Biblical Literature, 2003), p. xxviii.

39. *Iamblichus*, p. xxviii.

40. Ibid., p. xxx.

41. See her full discussion of pseudonyms, "Antike (Selbst-)Aussagen," pp. 137–47.

In yet other instances modern scholars have erred in thinking that a work was produced under a pen name. Aristophanes is sometimes said to have written his early plays pseudonymously, but D. McDowell has argued that in fact, given the mechanics of theatrical production, Aristophanes published them under the names of the persons who directed them, as those who were ultimately responsible for their contents.[42]

Homonymity

Ancient critics recognized full well the problems posed by homonymity, in a world where many names were common and few means were available to distinguish between authors of the same name. No one took the problem more seriously than the first-century BCE Demetrius of Magnesia, who wrote his book περὶ ὁμωνύμων ποιητῶν τε καὶ συγγραφέων not only to differentiate among homonymous writers, but also to tell anecdotes about them.[43] Diogenes Laertius, our principle source for the book, more commonly refers to it with the shortened title οἱ ὁμωνύμοι (e.g., 1.38.79; 7.31.169). It is cited by other authors as well, however, including Athenaeus (*Banqueters* 13.611B). An entire chapter is preserved by Dionysius of Halicarnassus.

Diogenes himself often deals with the problems of authorship posed by homonymity, reporting, for example, as just one instance, that the critics Panaetius and Sosicrates maintained that of all the writings commonly attributed to Ariston of Chios, the Stoic philosopher, only the letters were authentically his. Another thirteen titles, some in multiple volumes, went under his name, but were in fact written by Ariston the Peripatetic (*Lives* 7.163). With respect to the figure with whom we started, Heraclides of Pontus, Diogenes informs us that there were thirteen other literary figures who shared the name, one of them, confusingly enough, also known as Ponticus.

As one might expect, there are times when ancient critics have difficulty resolving issues of homonymity. And so, Quintilian wavers on the rhetorical writings assigned to Hermagoras:

> There are however books ascribed to Hermagoras which support the view under discussion; but either the attribution is wrong or the author was some other Hermagoras. For how can they possibly be by the Hermagoras who wrote so much so admirably about Rhetoric, since (as is clear also from the first book of Cicero's *Rhetoric*) he divided the subject matter of Rhetoric into Theses and Causes? (*Institutio Oratio* 3.5.14)[44]

---

42. *Aristophanes and Athens: An Introduction to the Plays* (New York: Oxford University Press, 1995), p. 34.

43. Diogenes Laertius, *Lives* 1.112.

44. Translation of Donald A. Russell in LCL (Cambridge, MA: Harvard University, 2002).

At other times there was less confusion, as in a case reported by Suetonius:

> For while some tell us that this same Ennius published a book "On Letters and Syllables" and another "On Metres," Lucius Cotta is right in maintaining that these were not the work of the poet but of a later Ennius, who is also the author of the volumes "On the Science of Augury." (*On Grammarians* 1.3)[45]

Numerous cases of homonymity have been uncovered only in modern times.[46]

What matters particularly for my purposes here, however, is the fact that some ancient critics posited homonymity as a chief reason that writings were transmitted under a false or wrong name, and were therefore to be termed νόθα. This is explicitly stated by the fifth-century Neoplatonist Olympiodorus, when he wants to explore διὰ πόσους τρόπους ἐνοθεύοντο τὰ βιβλία; the claim is repeated some years later by his student Elias.[47]

As is well known, the problems posed by homonymity were recognized by critics in the early Christian tradition as well. The best-known instance involved the third-century Dionysius of Alexandria, who argued that the book of Revelation was not written by the disciple John the son of Zebedee, but by some other John:

> That he was called John, and that this work is John's, I shall therefore not deny, for I agree that it is from the pen of a holy and inspired writer. But I am not prepared to admit that he was the apostle, the son of Zebedee and brother of James, who wrote the gospel entitled According to John and the general epistles. On the character of each, on the linguistic style, and on the general tone, as it is called, of Revelation, I base my opinion that the author was not the same. (Quoted in Eusebius, *H.E.* 7.25)[48]

Among other books in question were 2 and 3 John, which Jerome suggested may have been written by John the Presbyter rather than John the son of Zebedee (*Vir. ill.* 9); and the Shepherd, attributed to Hermas, but to which Hermas? Origen (*Romans Commentary* 10.31) and possibly Eusebius (*H.E.* 3.3) maintained that it was the Hermas mentioned by Paul in Romans 16:14, putting the composition

---

45. Translation of J. C. Rolfe in LCL (Cambridge, MA: Harvard University, 1914).

46. Thus Speyer (p. 38 n. 4), for example, notes the following: B. Capelle, "Un homiliaire de l'evêque arien Maximin," *RBén* 34 (1922): 81–108, and "Les homélies 'De lectionibus euangeliorum' de Maximin l'arien," *RBén* 40 (1928): 49–86: works of the Arian Maximus were transmitted as works of Maximus of Turin; and P. Courcelle, *Histoire littéraire des grandes invasions germaniques*, 3rd ed. (Paris, 1964), pp. 293–302: a poem attributed to Paulinus of Nola was actually written by Paulinus of Pella.

47. Olympiodorus *Prolegomena*; CAG XII/1, 13, 4–5; Elias *In Porphyrii Isagogen et Aristotelis Categorias Commentaria* (ed. A. Busse: Berlin, 1900), 128.1–22.

48. These and all translations of Eusebius are drawn from G. A. Williamson, *Eusebius: The History of the Church from Christ to Constantine*; rev. and ed. Andrew Louth (London: Penguin, 1965).

of the book back into apostolic times by a companion of the apostles, whereas the Muratorian Fragment insists that Hermas was the brother of the second-century bishop of Rome, Pius, and that it had been written "recently, in our own times." This was the view, of course, that eventually won out. Analogously, but somewhat later, the Adamantius who wrote De recta in deum fide was sometimes understood, wrongly, to be Origen; Rufinus reworked the dialogue by altering the places that showed it was written after Origen's day in order to use it to vindicate Origen's orthodoxy.[49]

Anonymity

There are far fewer anonymous writings from antiquity, and from Christian antiquity, than of other kinds of writing (orthonymous, falsely ascribed, forged). The reason is quite simple: anonymous works were almost always ascribed, usually incorrectly. This is due to what Wilamowitz famously described as a *horror vacui*. Speyer goes further in speculating that when libraries were collecting works, authors were assigned to them, with the most famous representatives of each genre then being ascribed works actually written by (anonymous) others: divine hymns were attributed to Homer, fables to Aesop, medical treatises to Hippocrates, and so on.[50]

Ancient critics sometimes discussed anonymity and its reasons, as when Clement of Alexandria claimed that the apostle Paul wrote the letter to the Hebrews anonymously because he realized that he was not much appreciated by the Jewish people to whom it was addressed: "In writing to Hebrews already prejudiced against him and suspicious of him, he was far too sensible to put them off at the start by naming himself" (Eusebius *H.E.* 6.14).

It is a genuine question as to why so many of the earliest Christian writings were produced anonymously (before being attributed). Michael Wolter argues that all these anonymata are principally concerned with differentiating their views, and the Christians who held them, from Jews and their religion. The use of anonymity, in his view, allowed the authors to claim implicitly that Jesus Christ himself was the authority behind their positions. Unfortunately, Wolter does not look at all the evidence, even within the New Testament, his area of principal concern. He leaves 2 and 3 John out of consideration, for some reason, and these are certainly not chiefly concerned with the relationship of the Christian gospel to Judaism. Moreover, for other anonymous books of the New Testament, Judaism is only one of a number of concerns at best (it is a matter of concern for Mark, but is it the *principal* reason the Gospel was written?), and for others it is not a concern at all (1 John). It might be

---

49. See V. Buchheit, "Rufinus von Aquileja als Fälscher des Adamantiosdialogs" in *ByzZ* 51 (1958): 314–28.

50. Speyer, *Literarische Fälschung*, p. 40; the reference from Wilamowitz occurs in note 4: *Göttingenische gelehrte Anzeigen* 158 (1896), p. 634 n. 1.

added that if one is seeking a historical explanation for the phenomenon, it will not do to restrict oneself to canonical writings: one also needs to deal with such works as the Didache, the Epistle of Barnabas, 2 Clement, and so on.

There may in fact have been a variety of reasons for Christian authors to remain anonymous. Wolter may be right that the choice was sometimes based on a desire to stress the authority of Christ himself, although that is not obvious from reading the texts. Possibly in some cases (2 and 3 John; the Didache) an author did not identify himself simply because he was already well known to the closely knit community to which he wrote. Or possibly, in the case of the Gospels, there was a generic consideration: like the histories of the people of God in the Jewish Scriptures (Joshua, Judges, Samuel, Kings), the stories of God's work among his people, Israel, are told anonymously. The Gospels, in this view, portray Jesus as a continuation of God's historical activities.

In any event, all of New Testament anonymata and almost all other anonymous writings of the early Christian centuries came to be attributed eventually (see below). An exception such as the Letter to Diognetus can be explained on the ground that it was so little known. This early apology, for example, is never quoted in any ancient source. Books that circulated for a long time anonymously almost always were attributed. This is true, for example, of the anonymous source that Eusebius quotes to malign the Roman adoptionists in his *Ecclesiastical History* 5.28. Theodoret later named the book the Little Labyrinth and attributed it, wrongly, to Origen. Modern scholars have proved no more successful, sometimes, since Lightfoot, wrongly assigning it to Hippolytus.[51] With an anonymous book like the Didache, it may be that the attribution of the teaching to the disciples was mistakenly taken to be a claim about authorship.

False Attributions

As we will see more fully in the next chapter, ancient Greek and Roman critics were deeply concerned over the attributions of writings. As far back as the fifth century BCE, Herodotus expressed his doubts concerning the attribution of the Cyprian poems and the Cyclic poem "The Heroes' Sons" to Homer, based on their material discrepancies with the Homeric epics themselves (2.117; 4.32). Centuries later, a fellow Halicarnassan, Dionysius, indicated that works attributed to Cadmus of Miletus, Aristaeus of Proconnesus, and other historians like them were not "universally accepted as genuine" (οὔτε . . . πιστεύονται; *On Thucydides*. 23). Quite often attributions were simply rejected off the cuff, showing that criticism was commonplace. Thus, for example, in talking about lewd songs to be publicly performed, Athenaeus quotes a passage from the work called the "Beggars," and admits that the common attribution of the work is probably wrong:

51. Theodoret, *Haer, Fab. Comp.* 2.5; J. B. Lightfoot, *The Apostolic Fathers: Clement, Ignatius, and Polycarp*, part 1, *Clement*, vol. 2 (London: Macmillan, 1889), pp. 377–80.

"Whoever wrote *Beggars*, generally attributed to Chionides, mentions a certain Gnesippus, playful writer of the lascivious muse . . ." (*Banqueters* 14:638d).[52]

As suggested earlier, attributions were sometimes simply made as a best guess or by simple mistake. This is probably the case for the attribution of the *Liber antiquitatum biblicarum* to Philo and the *Adversus omnes haereses* to Tertullian. The anonymous treatises *Cohortatio ad Graecos, De monarchia*, and *Oratio ad Graecos* sounded to some readers, as early as Eusebius (for at least the first two; he does not mention the *Oratio*) very much like Justin, and so they were attributed to him and were passed down in the manuscript tradition as his—wrongly, as is now known.[53] The same is true of later works that recorded the dialogues of Jerome and Augustine; they are sometimes attributed to these writers themselves, apparently on the ground that they were the principal speakers, even though they patently were not the authors.[54] Hundreds of sermons came to be attributed to Chrysostom, most of them wrongly.

In other instances attributions were not at all innocent. Whoever first thought of assigning the five books of the Torah to Moses did not do so out of purely antiquarian interests. On the Christian side, much the same can be said of the four books of the Gospels. Contrary to the extravagant claims of Martin Hengel, there is no reason to doubt that these books circulated for decades anonymously, before being attributed.[55] It is no accident that when these four books in particular—the ones in widest usage in the proto-orthodox communities—were assigned, it was to two of the disciples and two companions of the apostles. The attributions to Mark and Luke should cause no surprise. As early as Irenaeus and Tertullian we can see how the proto-orthodox logic worked: Mark gave Peter's version of the story (cf. Papias) and Luke gave Paul's. As Tertullian puts it: "that which Mark produced is stated to be Peter's, whose interpreter Mark was. Luke's narrative also they usually attribute to Paul. It is permissible for the works which disciples published to be regarded as belonging to their masters" (*Adv. Marc.* 4.5.3–4).[56] This

---

52. Translation of C. B. Gulick in LCL (Cambridge, MA: Harvard University, 1969).

53. Miroslav Marcovich. *Pseudo-Iustinus: Cohortatio ad Graecos, de Monarchia, Oratio ad Graecos* (Berlin: de Gruyter, 1990).

54. Thus the so-called thirty-seventh letter of Jerome, containing a dialogue of Jerome and Augustine, came to be assigned to Jerome himself, even though the author clearly differentiates himself from Jerome. So too the Dialogue *Contra Felicianum Arianum* came to be attributed to the main speaker Augustine, even though it was probably by Vivilius of Thapsus (see Ficker, *Studien zu Vigilius von Thapsus* 1897, pp. 77–79). In a similar way, the Dialogue *Adversus Fulgentium Donatistam* was also assigned to Augustine (see C. Lambot, "L'écrit attribute à S. Augustin *Adversus Fulgentium Donatistam*," in *RBén* 58 [1948], 177–222, esp. 183–84). On all these, see Speyer, *Literarische Fälschung*, pp. 32–33.

55. As expressed in various publications; see Hengel, *The Four Gospels and the One Gospel of Jesus Christ: An Investigation of the Collection and Origin of the Canonical Gospels* (London: SCM Press, 2000), pp. 34–56. Among refutations of Hengel's views, see, for example, F. Bovon, "The Synoptic Gospels and the Noncanonical Acts of the Apostles," *HTR* 81 (1988): 20–23.

56. Translation of Ernest Evans, *Tertullian, Adversus Marcionem: Books 4 and 5* (Oxford Early Christian Texts; Oxford: Oxford University Press, 1972), 271. All translations of this work will be from this edition.

is not to be misinterpreted—as it often is—to mean that Tertullian thought disciples could publish writings in the names of their teachers; Mark and Luke, in his opinion, published their works in their own names. But their views represent the views of their teachers. Thus the two greatest apostles of the church stand behind the Gospel traditions of these books.

And so the fourfold Gospel was based on the testimony of two personal disciples of Jesus and of his two principal apostles. Why were attributions made at all, after the books had originally circulated anonymously? The issues were complex, but can be boiled down to matters of differentiation (which Gospel is this?) and authority (is it based on a credible source?).

Other attributions as well may have been made for ulterior purposes. The anonymous letter that was early on assigned to Barnabas represents a view of Judaism and the Jewish Law that stands very much at odds with heterodox perspectives floated about by the likes of Marcion and various groups of Gnostics in the midsecond century. The book may be vitriolic in its opposition to Jews and Judaism, but it is not harsh toward the Old Testament. Quite the contrary, the Old Testament is presented as a distinctively Christian book, misunderstood, misinterpreted, and misappropriated by the Jews. It is, in fact, for the anonymous author, Christian Scripture. This became the proto-orthodox position in opposition to heterodox alternatives, which claimed that the Old Testament was not inspired by the one true, or ultimate, God. When Christians such as Clement of Alexandria falsely claimed that the anonymous letter was in fact written by Barnabas, they ascribed to it a significant authority. But not just any authority. Since Barnabas was otherwise so closely associated with Paul, the chief apostle of Marcion and much revered in some Gnostic circles, Paul himself was, by the indirection provided by the ascription, placed on the side of the proto-orthodox in the struggle to define the Christian understanding of the Old Testament.

Plagiarism

It is sometimes stated that plagiarism was either nonexistent or nonproblematic in Greek and Roman antiquity. As a prominent publication of the Jesus Seminar tells us: "The concept of plagiarism was unknown in the ancient world."[57] In point of fact, nothing could be further from the truth. Plagiarism was known, discussed, and condemned in ancient sources. As one of the best studies of the phenomenon, by Bernard Legras, summarizes: "In spite of the reticence of our sources and assuming that our texts are indeed admissible, we have been able to establish that plagiarism and forgery of literary works were considered offenses and punished."[58] Legras does go

---

57. Robert Funk, Roy W. Hoover, and the Jesus Seminar, eds., *The Five Gospels: The Search for the Authentic Words of Jesus* (New York: Macmillan, 1993), p. 22.

58. "Elle nous aura permis d'établir—malgré la modestie de nos sources et en admettant que nos textes soient bien recevables—que le plagiat et la forgerie d'oeuvres littéraires pouvaient être considérés comme des délits et sanctionnés." Bernard Legras, "La sanction du plagiat littéraire en droit grec et

on to qualify his statement: plagiarism and forgery were under legal sanction only in cases that appear to have affected the concerns of the state. There is no evidence of any proprietary laws, at any time or place, involving the concern to keep writings in general intact and safe from borrowing, or "stealing" as the ancients called it.

The phenomenon is in any event not unknown to our sources, as we have already seen in the case of Heraclides Ponticus, who, according to Diogenes Laertius, not only published extensively works of his own but also occasionally published works of others as if he had written them: "Chameleon complains that Heraclides's treatise on the works of Homer and Hesiod was plagiarized (κλέψαντα αὐτόν) from his own."[59] This was plagiarism by a man who, strikingly, wrote two separate treatises περὶ ἀρετῆς. Or consider his Athenian predecessor Aeschines, who stole dialogues of Socrates after the great man's death and was calumniated for it on more than one occasion, especially by Menedemus of Eretria, who claimed that "most of the dialogues which Aeschines passed off as his own were really dialogues of Socrates obtained by him from [Socrates's wife] Xanthippe. Moreover Aeschines made use (fraudulently: ἐσκευώρηται) of the *Little Cyrus*, the *Lesser Heracles*, and the *Alcibiades* of Antisthenes as well as dialogues by other authors" (Diogenes Laertius, *Lives*, 2.60).

At other times authors complained about writers who plagiarized their own work, none more memorably than Martial: "You mistake, you greedy thief of my works, who think you can become a poet at no more than the cost of a transcript and a cheap papyrus roll. Applause is not acquired for six or ten sesterces" (*Epigrams* 1, 66).[60]

When plagiarism was detected in antiquity, it often had actual social repercussions. Thus Vitruvius recounts an incident involving Aristophanes of Byzantium, one of the judges of a literary contest staged by the King of Pergamum to celebrate the dedication of his famed library. Aristophanes, we are told, had "read every book in the library," and when the authors who presented their work were judged, he ruled that only one was worthy of the prize, to the consternation of the other judges and the king. But Aristophanes demonstrated that except for the one, all the "others recited borrowed work whereas the judges had to deal with originals, not with plagiaries [ceteros aliena recitavisse; oportere autem iudicantes non furta sed scripta probare]."[61] The king was more than a little dubious about the claim, and so Aristophanes proceeded to quote passages from books in the library to prove his point. The result, Vitruvius tells us, was that the plagiarizers were forced "to confess they were thieves [coegit ipsos furatos de se confitieri]. The king then ordered them to be brought to trial for theft. They were condemned and

---

hellénistique," in E. Cantarella et G. Thür, éds., *Symposion* 1999 (Pazo de Mariñan, 6–9 septembre 1999; Cologne-Weimar-Vienne, Böhlau, 2003), 459.

59. *Lives*. 5.92. Unless otherwise indicated, this and the following quotations are taken from the translation of R. D. Hicks in LCL (Cambridge, MA: Harvard University, 1925).

60. Translation of Walter C. A. Ker, *LCL* (Cambridge, MA: Harvard University Press, 1979).

61. Translation of Granger; see p. 14 n. 11.

in disgrace, while Aristophanes was raised to high office and became librarian" (Book 7, Preface 7).

On occasion the condemnation for plagiarism led to even harsher reactions. Thus we learn of the expulsion of Empedocles from the school of Pythagoras, on the grounds of plagiarism: "Timaeus in the ninth book of his *Histories* says he [Empedocles] was a pupil of Pythagoras, adding that, having been convicted at that time of stealing his discourses (λέγων ὅτι καταγνωσθεὶς ἐπὶ λογοκλοπίᾳ τότε) he was, like Plato, excluded from taking part in the discussions of the school." (Diogenes Laertius, *Lives*, 8.54).

Elsewhere Vitruvius himself delivers a stringent judgment on those who engaged in the practice of plagiarism: "While, then, these men [viz. Those who left a written record of past events and philosophies] deserve our gratitude, on the other hand we must censure those who plunder their works and appropriate them to themselves" (Book 7, Preface 3). This attitude coincides with other ancient discourse about the practice, as in Polybius' off-the-cuff comment on authors who discuss "genealogies, myths, the planting of colonies, the foundations of cities and their ties of kinship"; Polybius laments the fact that since so much has already been written about such things, a modern writer who discusses them either rehashes what others have said or worse, "represents the work of others as being his own," a procedure that he calls "a most disgraceful proceeding" (ὃ πάντων ἐστὶν αἴσχιστον).[62]

Equally harsh is Pliny the Elder, who in his *Natural History* discusses his own practices of citation in contrast to those who are "of a perverted mind and a bad disposition" and steal the work of others to pass off as their own (*Natural History*, Preface 20–23):

> For I consider it to be courteous and to indicate an ingenuous modesty, to acknowledge the sources whence we have derived assistance, and not to act as most of those have done whom I have examined. For I must inform you, that in comparing various authors with each other, I have discovered, that some of the most grave and of the latest writers have transcribed, word for word, from former works, without making any acknowledgement; . . . For it is indeed the mark of a perverted mind and a bad disposition, to prefer being caught in a theft to returning what we have borrowed (obnoxii profecto animi et infelicis ingenii est deprehendi in furto malle quam mutuum redder).[63]

It is a genuine question concerning how relevant the ancient discourse on plagiarism is to the "unacknowledged borrowings" found throughout the early

62. *Histories*, 9.2.1; quotation from the translation of W. R. Paton from *Polybius: The Histories*, LCL (Cambridge, MA: Harvard University, 1922–1927).

63. Translation of H. Rackham, *Pliny: Natural History*, LCL (Cambridge, MA: Harvard University, 1938).

Christian literature. Assuming the two-source hypothesis, Matthew and Luke both acquired considerable amounts of their material, often verbatim, from Mark and Q, without acknowledgment. But if plagiarism is defined as taking over the work of another and claiming it as one's own, possibly the charge does not apply in these cases, as all the writings in question are anonymous. That is to say, the later Synoptic authors are not claiming anything as their own, as they do not even name themselves. The same would apply to the extensive and often verbatim reproduction of the Protevangelium Jacobi in such later texts as the Gospel of Pseudo-Matthew, in that the later author does not claim the earlier work as his own, since he is, in fact, writing pseudonymously.

A comparable situation obtains in the wholesale incorporation of the Didascalia Apostolorum, the Didache, and the Apostolic Traditions in the fourth-century Apostolic Constitutions. But here the situation is somewhat more complex. Two of these earlier works are anonymous, making it difficult to give credit where credit was due. The Didascalia, on the other hand, was inherited as a forgery—it falsely claims to be written by the apostles—and is itself embedded in another work that is also a forgery, also allegedly written by the apostles. Why would a forger need to credit an earlier work that he allegedly (but in fact did not) write himself?[64] Or consider the case of 2 Peter and Jude. There is little doubt that the former borrowed a good deal of the latter in its polemic against nefarious but unidentifiable opponents. But the source of the argument is a forgery, as is the text that uses the source. Can a forger commit plagiarism? In one sense he obviously has borrowed the work of another without acknowledgment, or as the ancient sources would put it, he has "stolen" his work. But in another sense he has not claimed that work as his own, since he does not give his own name so as to take credit for what his stolen material says. In all these instances we are dealing with complex literary relations that do not neatly line up in taxonomies of fraudulence, either ancient or modern.

Fabrications

It is widely thought that the invention of speeches and faux documents in historical narratives, and the creation of historical narratives themselves, are analogous to literary forgery. In all such instances an author fabricates materials and passes them off as historical when in fact they are products of his own imagination, much as a forger writes a work claiming to be someone else, possibly imagining, or purporting, that what he says is what the other person would have said had he had the opportunity. Sometimes it is inferred that since the fabrication of, say, speeches in historical narratives was seen as an acceptable practice, the forging of writings in the names of others must have been seen as acceptable as well. In the next chapter we will see that this leap of logic is an entirely modern one, as ancients are

64. See p. 14.

consistently negative in their appraisal of literary forgery. For now, it is enough to note that even with respect to fabrication there was not a consistent and universal opinion among ancient writers.

For the general approbation of historians who invented the speeches of their protagonists, appeal is normally made to the comments of Thucydides in his *History of the Peloponnesian War*:

> As to the speeches that were made by different men, either when they were about to begin the war or when they were already engaged therein, it has been difficult to recall with strict accuracy the words actually spoken, both for me as regards that which I myself heard, and for those who from various other sources have brought me reports. Therefore the speeches are given in the language in which, as it seemed to me, the several speakers would express, on the subjects under consideration, the sentiments most befitting the occasion, though at the same time I have adhered as closely as possible to the general sense of what was actually said.[65]

The practice of one historian, of course, does not necessarily reflect the practices of an era. But also to be considered is the sheer force of the ancient historians' dilemma: they needed, or at least wanted, to incorporate speeches in their accounts but usually had no means whatsoever of knowing what was actually spoken on the occasion. Moreover, there are other less frequently cited comments in our sources that reflect a similar attitude. And so, for example, Fronto mentions the practice of historians and annalists inventing letters thought to be appropriate to the occasion: "There are extant letters in both languages, partly written by actual leaders, partly composed by the writers of histories or annals, such as that most memorable letter in Thucydides of the general Nicias sent from Sicily."[66]

And as Cicero has his character Brutus state, when disagreeing with the first-person narrator's description of the death of Coriolanus: "At this he smiled and said: 'As you like, since the privilege is conceded to rhetoricians to distort history in order to give more point to their narrative' (concessum est rhetoribus ementiri in historias, ut aliquid dicere possint argutius)" (*Brutus*, 11. 42).[67]

Other authors, however, were willing to concede this privilege *only* to rhetoricians, not to historians, whose task it was to record what actually happened in the past—speeches and all—rather than to invent words and deeds that simply seemed appropriate. No one expressed this alternative view more forcefully than Polybius, whose comments are directed against the historian Phylarchus,

65. I, 22. Translation of Charles Foster Smith, *Thucydides: History of the Peloponnesian War: Books I and II*, LCL (Cambridge, MA: Harvard University, 1919).

66. *Ad Verum Imp.* 2, 1, 14. Translation of C. R. Haines, *Marcus Aurelius Fronto*, LCL, vol. 2 (Cambridge, MA: Harvard University, 1919), p. 43.

67. Translation of H. M. Hubbell, *Cicero V*, LCL (Cambridge, MA: Harvard University Press, 1962).

whose account of the Cleomenic War took very much a Thucydidian approach to speeches, much to Polybius' chagrin and even outrage:

> This sort of thing he keeps up throughout his history, always trying to bring horrors vividly before our eyes. Leaving aside the ignoble and womanish character of such a treatment of his subject, let us consider how far it is proper or serviceable to history (τὸ δὲ τῆς ἱστορίας οἰκεῖον ἅμα καὶ χρήσιμον ἐξεταζέσθω). A historical author should not try to thrill his readers by such exaggerated pictures, nor should he, like a tragic poet, try to imagine the probable utterances of his characters or reckon up all the consequences probably incidental to the occurrences with which he deals, but simply record what really happened and what really was said (ῥηθέντων κατ' ἀλήθειαν αὐτῶν), however commonplace. For the object of tragedy is not the same as that of history but quite the opposite. The tragic poet should thrill and charm his audience for the moment by the verisimilitude of the words he puts into his characters' mouths, but it is the task of the historian to instruct and convince for all time serious students by the truth of the facts and the speeches he narrates, since in the one case it is the probable that takes precedence, even if it be untrue, in the other it is the truth, the purpose being to confer benefit on learners.[68]

Later in his *Histories* Polybius similarly maligns the historian Timaeus for using rhetorical flourishes in the speeches he provides his characters, rather than indicating what was "really" said:

> As the proverb tells us that a single drop from the largest vessel suffices to tell us the nature of the whole contents, so we should regard the subject now under discussion. When we find one or two false statements in a book and they prove to be deliberate ones, it is evident that not a word written by such an author is any longer certain and reliable. But to convince those also who are disposed to champion him I must speak of the principle on which he composes public speeches, harangues to soldiers, the discourses of ambassadors, and, in a word, all utterances of the kind, which, as it were, sum up events and hold the whole history together. Can anyone who reads these help noticing that Timaeus had untruthfully reported them in his work, and has done so of set purpose? For he has not set down the words spoken nor the sense of what was really said, but having made up his mind as to what ought to have been said, he recounts all these speeches and all else that follows upon events like a man in a school of rhetoric attempting to speak on a given subject, and shows off his oratorical power, but gives no report of which was actually spoken. The peculiar function of history is to discover, in the first place, the words actually spoken, whatever they were, and

68. *Histories*, 2. 56.8–12; translation of W. R. Paton, *Polybius: The Histories*, LCL (Cambridge, MA: Harvard University, 1922).

> next to ascertain the reason why what was done or spoken led to failure or success. . . . But a writer who passes over in silence the speeches made and the causes of events and in their place introduces false rhetorical exercises and discursive speeches, destroys the peculiar virtue of history. And of this Timaeus especially is guilty, and we all know that his work is full of blemishes of the kind.[69]

At the very least, then, we can say that there was not a consistent view of the legitimacy of the practice of fabricating materials for historical accounts in antiquity. Whereas some writers—Thucydides, and the two objects of Polybius' scorn—accepted the practice, probably out of historiographic necessity, others strenuously objected. The vitriol of Polybius' protest may well suggest that he was in the minority on the matter. In neither side of the debate, in any event, do we find authors likening the practice to forgery. When Jewish authors such as Josephus, or Christian authors such as the anonymous and pseudonymous writers of various Christian Gospels, placed invented speeches on the lips of their protagonists, they were doing what was widely done throughout antiquity. Some writers approved the practice and others demurred.

Speeches and documents are not the only kinds of fabrications in historical writing. Often writers—historians, essayists, polemicists, or most anyone else—fabricated narratives of all sorts about real and fictitious characters: events, episodes, activities, controversies, practices, and on and on. We have seen a small sliver of this kind of fabricating narrative already with Epiphanius, who appears to have invented the ritual practices of the Phibionites, possibly based on his slight knowledge of their theological views, precisely in order to malign them. In generating such fabricated accounts, Epiphanius stood in a solid line of tradition that goes back as far as our earliest heresiologists. The harsh but undocumented invectives of the letter of Jude in the New Testament come to be fleshed out in its later ideological successors, such as Irenaeus, whose *Adversus Haereses* is the first proto-orthodox heresiological treatise to survive, and which is famous for its accusations against the shocking sexual practices of, for example, the Valentinians, Carpocratians, and Marcosians that I have already mentioned. As I suggested earlier, if one considers the rigorous ethic endorsed by the Gnostic sources themselves, it seems unlikely that any of the charges represent accurate representations; they are more likely fabricated.

Not all early Christian fabrications were malicious, of course. Long before we have any written texts of any kind, stories about Jesus were not only altered in the course of oral transmission, but also generated then: stories about his birth, his activities, his teachings, his controversies, his last days, his death and resurrection. And the fabrications continued long after the New Testament period, as so abundantly and irrefutably attested in the noncanonical accounts of his birth, life, death, and resurrection. And of his afterlife, as in Tertullian's claim that:

---

69. Ibid., 12, 25a1–25b4.

> So Tiberius, in whose reign the name of Christian entered the world, hearing from Palestine in Syria information which had revealed the truth of Christ's divinity, brought the matter before the Senate, with previous indication of his own approval. The Senators, on the ground that they had not verified the facts, rejected it. Caesar maintained his opinion and threatened dire measures against those who brought accusations against the Christians.[70]

This fabricated account was easily believed by later Christians; it is reiterated by Eusebius (*H.E.* 2.2.2). Further examples could be effortlessly multiplied many times over, for instance, from virtually every detail in the letters and narratives of the so-called Pilate cycle.[71]

So too the preliterary accounts of the apostles eventually embedded in the canonical Acts have their analogues in the later apocryphal Acts, whether stories of Peter raising a smoked tuna from the dead and depriving the magician Simon of his powers of flight in midair, or of John resuscitating Drusiana and castigating pestiferous bed bugs, or of Paul preaching a message of sexual abstinence that leads to the conversion of his most famous female follower, Thecla.

This final example is commonly cited in works dealing with forgery, by scholars who confuse Tertullian's comments in De baptismo 17 as referring to a presbyter of Asia Minor who allegedly forged the account in Paul's name. Thus, for example, the recent comment from an otherwise fine article by M. Frenschkowski : "This passage [in Tertullian] is significant not least of all because it once and for all disproves the myth of the unproblematic acceptance of pseudepigraphy in a Christian environment."[72] In fact, Tertullian's comments are not directly relevant to the question of whether or not forgery was widely seen as acceptable. The presbyter in question was charged not with forging an account but with fabricating it.

> But if the writings which wrongly go under Paul's name, claim Thecla's example as a licence for women's teaching and baptizing, let them know that, in Asia, the presbyter who composed that writing, as if he were augmenting Paul's fame from his own store, after being convicted, and confessing that he had done it from love of Paul, was removed from his office (sciant in asia presbyterum qui eam scripturam construxit quasi titulo pauli de suo cumulans conuictum atque confessum id se amore pauli fecisse loco decessisse).[73]

70. *Apology* 5; Rudolph Arbesmann, *Tertullian*, FC, 10 (Washington, DC: Catholic University Press, 1950), pp. 20–21. Subsequent quotations of this work will be from this edition.

71. For introductions, texts, and translations, see Ehrman and Pleše, *Apocryphal Gospels*, pp. 419–567.

72. "Diese Passage (in Tertullian) ist nicht zuletzt von Bedeutung, weil sie ein für alle mal die Legende von der problemlosen Akzeptanz von Pseudepigraphie in einem christlichen Umfeld widerlegen sollte." "Erkannte Pseudepigraphie?" in Jörg Frey et al., eds., *Pseudepigraphie und Verfasserfiktion*, p. 195.

73. Translation of S. Thelwall, *ANF*, vol. 3, p. 677.

The reconstruction of Tertullian's text is debated,[74] but the question of the presbyter's crime need not be. The "writings that wrongly go under Paul's name" were not accounts that Paul was alleged to have written. He was the subject of these writings, not the reputed author. At least as they have been handed down to us—assuming that what we have is what Tertullian is referring to[75]—the Acts are anonymous. The presbyter was being faulted, then, for making up stories about Paul that were not historically accurate.

In other instances the narrative fabrications of the early Christians served polemical purposes, although at times more subtly. As already pointed out, for example, stories of Jesus as a miracle-working wunderkind from the Infancy Gospel of Thomas functioned to discount an adoptionistic Christology that claimed that Jesus received his divine sonship—and so his divine power—only at his baptism. The story of Jesus emerging from his tomb as tall as a mountain from the Gospel of Peter functioned to show that his resurrection was decidedly bodily, in the face of claims that his afterlife was purely in the spirit, while his body experienced corruption. Stories of Peter besting Simon Magus in a series of miracle-working contests from the Acts of Peter illustrated the superiority of the proto-orthodox lineage of the Roman episcopacy over against various groups of Gnostic contenders. Stories of Pilate, Tiberius, and other Roman officials recognizing the clear divinity of Jesus from the Pilate Cycle functioned to counter the polemical charges of the cultured despisers of the new faith among the pagans, such as Celsus and Porphyry.

Christian fabrications served other purposes as well. Some satisfied early Christian curiosity about unknown aspects of the lives of Jesus and his followers (where was Jesus, exactly, during the time between his death and resurrection? Thus the Gospel of Nicodemus); others provided edificatory tales (God was on the side of the apostles in the face of horrible Roman opposition, as in the Apocryphal Acts); yet others were no doubt entertaining (Jesus' miraculous deeds as the mischievous five-year-old son of God in the Infancy Gospel of Thomas); some more directly supported one theological or ideological view or another (Paul's preaching of continence for eternal life, in the Acts of Thecla); and others performed apologetic service (the stories of the Protevangelium as answers to the charges against Mary, Joseph, and Jesus on the pen of Celsus).

Given their wide functionality, were such invented narratives generally seen as acceptable by the early Christians? On one hand, most Christians who heard such stories almost certainly did not consider them as anything but historical, and so were in no position to pass judgment on their character as fabrications. What would they have said if they were shown, beyond any reasonable doubt, that such

---

74. See Willy Rordorf, "Tertullien et les Actes de Paul (à propos de bapt 17, 5)," in *Lex Orandi Lex Credendi*, ed. Gerardo J. Békés e Giustino Farnedi (Rome: Editrice anselmiana 1980), pp. 475–84.

75. For a contrary opinion see Stevan L. Davies, "Women, Tertullian and the Acts of Paul," *Semeia* 38 (1986): 139–43, who argues that Tertullian is referring not to our extant Acts of Paul but to a lost pseudepigraphic letter of Paul. For an effective refutation, see Rordorf, "Tertullien et les Actes."

stories were made up? At the end of the day, it is impossible to say. But it does seem likely that Christians who approved of the stories and the lessons they conveyed would not have been particularly disturbed, taking, possibly, a Thucydidian attitude toward them. Christians with alternative perspectives, on the other hand, or non-Christians of all stripes would doubtless have considered such fabrications worthy of attack, more along the lines of a Polybius.

Falsifications

Even more closely related to the phenomenon of forgery is the practice of falsifying a text. When an author forges a writing, claiming to be someone other than who she is, she asserts that her words are those of another. So too a copyist who alters a text by adding a few words, or by interpolating entire passages, or by rewriting the text in other ways, is making the implicit claim that his own words—the ones he has interpolated or generated himself—are the words of the author of the (rest of the) text.

Textual alteration was widely discussed in antiquity, and just as widely condemned. Our earliest reference appears to be in Herodotus, who mentions a collector of oracles named Onomacritus, friend and counselor of the tyrant Pisistratus, who earlier in his life had been discovered to have inserted an oracle of his own into the verses of Musaeus, to the effect that the islands off Lemnos would disappear under water. Lasus of Hermione, a poet and musician who was Pindar's teacher, evidently suspected Onomacritus of making the interpolation and reported it to Hipparchus, who promptly banished Onomacritus from Athens.[76]

Onomacritus had a wide reputation for interpolating oracles into the alleged writings of Musaeus. Pausanias, for example, gives another instance: "I have read a poem in which Mousaios was able to fly, by the gift of the North-east wind; I think Onomakritos wrote it; nothing of Mousaios exists for certain except the *Hymn to Demeter*."[77] And Plutarch as well: "I forbear to mention how much blame men like Onomacritus, Prodicus, and Cinaethon have brought upon themselves from the oracles by foisting upon them a tragic diction and a grandiloquence of which they have had no need, nor have I any kindly feeling toward their changes."[78] Even the Christian Clement recounts the by then traditional view: "Onomacritus of Ath-

76. Oracles were important in Greek cities and were occasionally consulted, especially in times of crisis. The integrity of their text was, as a result, hugely important. It is not clear, however, why the sinking of the islands off Lemnos would have been such a politically charged issue. On the importance of Greek oracles, and thus of their integrity, see Hugh Bowden, "Oracles for Sale," in Peter Derow and Robert Parker, eds., *Herodotus and His World* (New York: Oxford University Press, 2003), pp. 256–74. My thanks to Prof. Bowden for the reference and for his communications on this topic. See also Michael A. Flower, *The Seer in Ancient Greece* (Berkeley: University of California Press, 2008).

77. Attica, 1, 22. 7. Translation of Peter Levi, *Pausanias Guide to Greece*, vol. 1 (London: Penguin, 1971).

78. Oracles at Delphi 407B-G. Translation of Frank C. Babbitt *Plutarch: Moralia*, vol. 5. LCL (Cambridge, MA: Harvard University Press, 1936).

ens, the reputed author of the poems attributed to Orpheus, is to be found in the reign of the Pisistratides *circa* the fiftieth Olympiad" (*Stromateis 1.21*).[79]

Strabo reports on an earlier Athenian textual alteration, this time in Homer's Iliad. In this case the falsification, made either by Pisistratus or Solon, had clear political implications, as it supported the Athenians' claim to the island of Salamis:

> At the present time the island is held by the Athenians, although in early times there was strife between them and the Megarians for its possession. Some say that it was Peisistratus, others Solon, who inserted in the *Catalogue of Ships* immediately after the verse, "and Aias brought twelve ships from Salamis," [Iliad 2, 557] the verse, "and, bringing them, halted them where the battalions of the Athenians were stationed," and then used the poet as a witness that the island had belonged to the Athenians from the beginning. But the critics do not accept this interpretation, because many of the verses bear witness to the contrary.[80]

Sometimes writings were falsified for philosophical rather than political reasons. Diogenes Laertius, for example, reports that the librarian of Pergamum, the Stoic Athenodorus, was condemned at trial for falsifying Stoic writings by deleting problematic passages from Zeno, founder of the sect:

> Isidorus likewise affirms that the passages disapproved by the [Stoic] school were expunged from his [Zeno's] works by Athenodorus the Stoic, who was in charge of the Pergameme library; and that afterwards, when Athenodorus was detected and compromised (φωραθέντος τοῦ Ἀθηνοδώρου καὶ κινδυνεύσαντος), they were replaced. So much concerning the passages in his writings which are regarded as spurious (περὶ τῶν ἀθετουμένων αὐτοῦ). (*Lives*, 7.34)

The falsification of texts of Homer, of course, generated early classical scholarship, especially as associated with the library in Alexandria.[81]

Falsification of texts was also a matter hotly contested within Christian circles of the first four centuries. Heretics were roundly and widely condemned for altering the texts of Scripture in light of their own doctrines.[82] Among the earliest and

---

79. Translation of John Ferguson, trans., *Clement of Alexandria, Stromateis: Books One to Three* (FC 85; Washington, DC: Catholic University of America Press, 1991), p. 119.

80. *Geography* 9.1.10. Translation of H. L. Jones in LCL (Cambridge, MA: Harvard University, 1927).

81. See esp. Rudolf Pfeiffer, *The History of Classical Scholarship from the Beginnings to the End of the Hellenistic Age* (Oxford: Clarendon, 1968).

82. The most extensive catalogue of these accusations is in A. Bludau, *Die Schriftfälschungen der Häretiker: Ein Beitrag zur Textkritik der Bibel.* (Münster: Aschendorf, 1925). Bludau claims—wrongly in my view—that these charges were more commonly directed against heretics for misinterpreting, not falsifying, Scripture. This view is largely based on Bludau's somewhat odd notion that since there were so many debates over Scripture in the early centuries, copyists (heretical or otherwise) would have been

most vitriolic accusers was Tertullian, who famously assaulted Marcion on these grounds:

> I say that mine is true: Marcion makes that claim for his. I say that Marcion's is falsified: Marcion says the same of mine. Who shall decide between us? Only such a reckoning of dates, as will assume that authority belongs to that which is found to be older, and will prejudge as corrupt that which is convicted of having come later. For in so far as the false is a corruption of the true, to that extent must the truth have preceded that which is false. An object must have been in existence before anything is done to it, as what it is in itself must be prior to any opposition to it. . . . Certainly that is why he has expunged all the things that oppose his view, that are in accord with the Creator, on the plea that they have been woven in by his partisans; but has retained those that accord with his opinion.[83]

As is clear, Marcion leveled the same charges against his own theological opponents, deemed as well to preserve false teachings.

False teachers were known to alter the texts not only of Scripture but also of any work that might prove harmful to their cause. And so the complaint of Dionysius of Corinth with respect to his own writings:

> When my fellow-Christians invited me to write letters to them I did so. These the devil's apostles have filled with tares, taking away some things and adding others. For them the woe is reserved. Small wonder then if some have dared to tamper even with the word of the Lord Himself, when they have conspired to mutilate my own humble efforts. (quoted in Eusebius *H.E.* 4, 23, 12)

Or the charges of Rufinus against heretical falsifiers who corrupted the writings of church authorities who opposed them:

> The heretics have followed this example of their father and this skill of their teacher. Whenever they have found treatises by renowned writers of old that have discussed things that pertain to the glory of God in detail and faithfully, so that every believer could make progress and receive instruction by reading them, they have not spared their writings, but have poured in the poisonous filth of their own doctrines, whether by interpolating what they had said, or by inserting things that they had not said. By this means, of course, the assertion of the man's own heresy was more easily advanced under the names of all the most learned and renowned among the ecclesiastical writers in view

---

reluctant to change the text. This is not a widely held view today; for an alternative, see my study *The Orthodox Corruption of Scripture.*

83. *Adv. Marc.* 4.4; translation of Ernst, *Tertullian*, pp. 267, 275.

> of the fact that some brilliant men among the Catholics appeared to have thought likewise.[84]

The normal way of falsifying a text was simply by altering it in the process of re-copying it. A particularly egregious example is cited by Origen with respect to the transcript of one of his debates:

> For a certain author of a heresy, when a discussion was held between us in the presence of many persons and was recorded, took the document from those who had written it down. He added what he wanted to it, removed what he wanted, and changed what seemed good to him. Then he carried it around as if it were from me, pouring scorn conspicuously on the things that he himself had composed. The brethren who are in Palestine were indignant over this. They sent a man to me at Athens who was to receive from me the authentic copy. Prior to this I had not even re-read or revised the work, but it was lying there in such a neglected state that it could hardly be found. But I sent it, and I say with God as my witness that, when I met the man who had falsified the work, [and asked him] why he had done this, he answered, as if he were giving me satisfaction: "Because I wanted to adorn and purify that discussion."[85]

Clearly, falsifiers of the text, like others who engaged in one kind of literary deception or another, felt both justified in what they did and offended by those who took umbrage. On other occasions falsifiers could be remarkably crafty, as in the case discussed by Rufinus about a manuscript containing the writings of Athanasius. It is a complicated story. Bishop Damasus was seeking to reconcile the Apollinarians to the rest of the church and had a theological treatise drawn up that could be agreed on by all sides. In this treatise, the term "Homo Dominicus" was applied to Christ, but the Apollinarists objected on the ground that it was a novelty, not part of the sanctioned terminology of their theological forebears. The author of the document attempted to defend himself by appealing to an earlier writing of Athanasius, which also used the term. But a representative of the Apollinarists found a way to undercut the precedent that this writing presented:

> When he had received the manuscript, he devised an unprecedented method of falsification. He erased the very passage in which the words were found, and then wrote in again the same words that he had erased. He returned the manuscript, and it was accepted as is.
>
> The debate about this very expression is stirred up once again; the manuscript is brought forward as evidence; the expression in question is found in it,

84. *De adult libr.* 7; translation of Thomas P. Scheck, *St. Pamphilus, Apology for Origen; with the Letter of Rufinus, On the Falsification of the Books of Origen* (FC 120; Washington, DC: Catholic University of America Press, 2010), p. 125.

85. Quoted in Rufinus, *De adult. libr.* 7; translation of Schenck, *St. Pamphilus*, p. 29.

> but in a position where there had been an erasure in the manuscript. The man who brought forward the manuscript is discredited, since the erasure seemed to be proof of corruption and falsification.[86]

No one was more famously connected with the alteration of inherited theological writings than Rufinus, who explicitly tells his readers that while translating the works of Origen he came upon passages that, in his opinion, could not have actually been written by him. His obvious solution to the problem was to return the texts to their pristine state by eliminating the offensive passages. As he states the matter in the Preface to his translation of *De principiis:*

> Wherever, therefore, I have found in his books anything contrary to the reverent statements made by him about the Trinity in other places, I have either omitted it as a corrupt and interpolated passage, or reproduced it in a form that agrees with the doctrine which I have often found him affirming elsewhere.[87]

Or as he says in his *Apology to Anastasius*:

> I used my own discretion in cutting out not a few passages; but only those as to which I had come to suspect that the thing had not been so stated by Origen himself; and the statement appeared to me in these cases to have been inserted by others, because in other places I had found the author state the matter in a catholic sense.[88]

And so we have the grounds for one of the vitriolic exchanges with Jerome, who responds to such editorial activity with characteristic zeal:

> I wish to know who gave you permission to cut out a number of passages from the work you were translating? You were asked to turn a Greek book into Latin, not to correct it; to draw out another man's words, not to write a book of your own. You confess, by the fact of pruning away so much, that you did not do what you were asked. You say that you have cut out many things from the Greek, but you say nothing of what you have put in. Were the parts cut out good or bad? Bad, I suppose. Was what you kept good or bad? Good, I presume; for you could not translate the bad. . . . It is a strange thing if you are to act like an unjust censor, who is himself guilty of the crime, and are allowed at your will to expel some from the Senate and keep others in it.[89]

---

86. *De adult libr.* 13; ibid., p. 135. See Mark Vessey, "The Forging of Orthodoxy in Latin Christian Literature: A Case Study," *JECS* 4 (1996): 495–513.

87. Preface of Rufinus; translation of G. W. Butterworth, *Origen on First Principles* (Gloucester, MA: Peter Smith, 1973), p. lxiii.

88. Translation of W. H. Fremantle in *NPNF*, 2nd series, vol. 3.

89. *Adv. Ruf.* 2.11. Translation of *NPNF*.

The widespread disapprobation of altering texts does not appear to have done much to stop copyists from engaging in such activities. One might nonetheless wonder what steps were taken to ensure the integrity of a text once put in circulation. The reality is that not much could be done. Occasionally there was legislation designed to protect against textual falsifications. The best known is the instance recounted in Pseudo-Plutarch's *Lycurgus*, the Athenian orator who urged passage of the law that the plays of Aeschylus, Sophocles, and Euripides were to be kept in a public archive, and that public officials were to use these official copies to check all performances in order to guarantee that there were no departures from the text. Any actor who did not stick closely to the "official" script was allegedly barred from further appearances on the stage.

This instance was the exception to the ancient rule. Without laws governing literary property, texts could be protected only by the relatively ineffective ploys of moral suasion and literary curses. Of curses, the best known is the conclusion to the Apocalypse of John:

> I testify to everyone who hears the words of the prophecy of this book: if anyone adds to them, God will add to them the plagues that are described in this book; and if anyone removes any of the words of the book of this prophecy, God will remove his share from the tree of life and from the holy city that is described in this book. (Rev. 22:19)[90]

Description of an analogous curse can be found in Jewish circles in the Letter of Aristeas. Once the translators of the Septuagint had miraculously produced their text, the leaders of the Jewish community are reported to have decided that its wording was never to be changed: "There was general approval of what they said, and they commanded that a curse should be laid, as was their custom, on anyone who should alter the version by any addition or change to any part of the written text, or any deletion either."[91]

Note the words: "as was their custom." Such curses were typical, not unusual. They recur in Christian writings of our period, for example in Irenaeus' now lost *Ogdoad*, as quoted by Eusebius:

---

90. For the formula "neither adding nor removing," see, among others, W. C. van Unnik, "De la règle ΜΗΤΕ ΠΡΟΣΘΕΙΝΑΙ ΜΗΤΕ ΑΦΕΛΕΙΝ dans l'histoire du canon," *VC* 3 (1949): 1–35. W. C. van Unnik, "'Die Formel nichts wegnehmen, nichts hinzufügen' bei Josephus," in idem, *Josephus als historischer Schriftsteller* (Heidelberg: Schneider, 1978), 26–49; C. Schäublin, "Μήτε προσθεῖναι μήτ' ἀφελεῖν," *MH* 31 (1974): 144–49; L. Feldman, *Josephus's Interpretation of the Bible* (Hellenistic Culture and Society 27; Berkeley: University of California Press, 1998), 37–46; M. Mülke, *Der Autor und sein Text: Die Verfälschung des Originals im Urteil antiker Untersuchungen* (Untersuchungen zur Antiken Literatur und Geschichte 93; Berlin: Walter de Gruyter, 2008), pp. 20–27, 266–68. I am obliged to Zlatko Pleše for these references.

91. Letter of Aristeas, 311. Translation of R. J. H. Shutt, in James H. Charlesworth, ed., *The Old Testament Pseudepigrapha*, vol. 2 (New York: Doubleday, 1985).

> If, dear reader, you should transcribe this little book, I adjure you by the Lord Jesus Christ and by His glorious advent, when He comes to judge the living and the dead, to compare your transcript and correct it carefully by this copy, from which you have made your transcript. This adjuration likewise you must transcribe and include in your copy. (*H.E.* 5.20)

Or in the lesser known but equally threatening comment near the conclusion of the Coptic *History of Joseph the Carpenter* : "Whoever takes away from these words or adds to them, and so considers me a liar, I will soon take vengeance on him" (30.7).[92]

It should be clear on a number of grounds that the alteration of texts was widely condemned in antiquity by authors who were pagan, Jewish, and Christian. Writers did not want copyists or editors to alter their words. They chastised and cursed anyone who did so. When falsifiers were detected in the act, they were censured, abused, and sometimes punished. An author's words were to be kept intact, because they were the author's own.

If authors objected to having words wrongly placed on their pens by falsifiers, it does not take much to imagine how they would react to words wrongly placed on their pens by forgers. In these instances a deceptive writer does not merely interpolate or alter the words of a text, implicitly claiming them to be the words of the author; he instead invents a text out of whole cloth, claiming that it presents the words of the author falsely named. In both cases the question is whether the written text derives from the person who is being claimed as its author.

92. Translation of Zlatko Pleše, in Ehrman and Pleše, *The Apocryphal Gospels*, p. 191.

CHAPTER FOUR

Forgery in Antiquity

Aspects of the Broader Phenomenon

Having looked at related phenomena from the Greco-Roman world, we can now redirect our focus to literary forgery itself, the practice of producing literary works with false authorial claims. The bulk of this study will consider the use of literary forgery and counterforgery in Christian polemical contexts of the first four centuries CE. To set the stage for that discussion, we need to look at the broader phenomenon in pagan, Jewish, and Christian antiquity, considering its extent and its widespread recognition and condemnation; the motives that drove authors to make their false claims; techniques they used to make these claims believable; the self-justifications that they made, or may have made, for engaging in the practice; and the means of detection used by ancient critics to expose forgery when they found it.

EXTENT OF THE PHENOMENON

It is impossible to quantify the extent of ancient forgery, although everyone who has worked seriously on the problem recognizes that it is a vast field.[1]

Pagan Literature

I will not attempt to provide here a comprehensive listing either of works identified as forgeries in pagan antiquity or pagan works now known or thought to be forgeries—two overlapping but not coterminous corpora. Numerous instances will be addressed throughout this chapter and the next. Instead, to give an idea of

1. None more so than Wolfgang Speyer and Norbert Brox, but including such recent scholars as Margaret Janssen and Armin Baum. See note 27 below.

the extent of the field here at the outset, I will summarize some of the incidental and direct comments about forgery in just one book of Diogenes Laertius' ten-volume work on the *Lives of Eminent Philosophers*.

In 2.39 Diogenes indicates that the (published) speech of Polycrates against Socrates is not authentic (μὴ εἶναι ἀληθῆ τὸν λόγον) since it mentions the rebuilding of the walls by Conon, which occurred ten years after Socrates' death. In 2.42 he indicates that the paean to Apollo and Artemis allegedly written by Socrates between the time of his condemnation and death (two lines of which Diogenes quotes) are debated: the critic Dionysodorus maintained that Socrates did not write it. So too Pisistratus of Ephesus denied that the works of Aeschines were actually written by him; the critic Persaeius attributed most of the seven books in question to Pasiphon, of the school of Eretria (2.61). With respect to Dialogues involving Socrates, we learn that Panaetius thought that those produced by Plato, Xenophon, Antisthenes, and Aeschines were authentic; but he doubted the authenticity of those ascribed to Phaedo and Euclides and he rejected all the others as inauthentic (2.64). The six books of essays attributed to Aristippus are said to have been accepted by some critics, whereas Sosicrates of Rhodes claimed that Aristippus had written none of them at all (2.84). As to the dialogues allegedly produced by Phaedo, Diogenes accepts as genuine (γνησίους) the "Zopyrus" and "Simon"; the "Nicias" is doubtful (δισταζόμενον), as is "The Elders"; the "Medius" is claimed "by some" critics to be the work of Aeschines or of Polyaenus; and some also attribute the "Cobblers' Tales" to Aeschines (2.105). Nine of the dialogues of Glaucon are thought to be authentic, but there are also extant thirty-two others that are considered spurious (οἳ νοθεύονται) (2.124). With respect to the "Medea" of Euripides, some claim that it is instead the work of Neophron of Sicyon (2.134).

All of this in just one volume of one ancient writing. In the same volume Diogenes also mentions two cases of plagiarism.[2] And Diogenes is not unique: as we have already seen, and will see yet more presently, there was a widespread practice of criticism among pagan literati of our period.

In Jewish Literature

The documented or suspected instances of forgery among Jewish writers of the time are not as extensive, in no small measure because there were far fewer Jewish writings of any kind.[3] In an earlier period, the so-called writing prophets of the Hebrew Bible (Isaiah, Jeremiah, Ezekiel, the Twelve), if they wrote at all, wrote in their own names (e.g., Isaiah, Amos) or anonymously (2 Isaiah; 3 Isaiah; editorial editions to Amos and others, for example). Only two books of the Hebrew

2. Xenophon appears to have published a book of Thucydides claiming it was his own (depending on how one reads the text; 2.57), and Aeschines, a follower of Socrates, published work he had received from Socrates' wife Xanthippe as if it were his own (2.60).

3. For a relatively succinct summary and discussion, see Speyer, *Literarische Fälschung*, pp. 150–68.

Bible can be considered forgeries in the sense that I am using it here. The visions of Daniel 7–12 claim to be written by the sage and prophet of the sixth century BCE but were almost certainly produced, in reality, four hundred years later by someone assuming the false name for reasons of his own. (I will be dealing with the question of apocalypses as pseudepigrapha shortly.) The book of Qoheleth is a textbook case of a non-pseudepigraphic forgery: its author clearly indicates that he is to be taken as Solomon (chs. 1–2), without naming himself, although he, once again, was writing many centuries after Solomon had passed from the scene.

Outside of the Hebrew Bible, orthonymous writings were, in the words of Annette Reed, "surprisingly rare among Second Temple Jews."[4] She names as exceptions ben Sira, Aristobulus, Eupolemus, Artapanus, and later Philo and Josephus. The authenticity of other works, such as the writings of Hecataeus and Manetho, are today hotly contested.[5] Even so, there are well-known forgeries, including the Wisdom of Solomon[6]; the Letter of Aristeas[7]; the Letter of Demetrius of Phaleron to Ptolemy II within the letter of Aristeas; the Decree of Artaxerses in the additions to the book of Esther; 3 Ezra 6.7–22, 6.24–27, 6.27–34, 8.9–24; the letters from and to the rulers of Sparta in 1 Macc. 12.2, 5–23, 14.20–23 (cf. Josephus *Antiquities* 12.225–28; 13.165–70); the letters between Solomon and Vaphres quoted in Eusebius (*Prep. Evang.* 9.31–32); between Solomon and Suron King of Tyre and Sidon (*Prep. Evang.* 9.33–34), the Decree of Alexander the Great in Sulpicius (*Severus Chron.* 2.17.2); and the Letter forged in the name of Herod's son Alexander mentioned by Josephus (*War* 1.26.3). Examples could be multiplied.[8]

---

4. Annette Yoshiko Reed, "Pseudepigraphy, Authorship, and the Reception of 'The Bible' in Late Antiquity," in *The Reception and Interpretation of the Bible in Late Antiquity,* ed. Lorenzo DiTommaso and Lucian Turcescu (Leiden: Brill, 2008), p. 478.

5. See Miriam Pucci Ben Zeev, "The Reliability of Josephus Flavius: The Case of Hecataeus' and Manetho's Accounts of Jews and Judaism: Fifteen Years of Contemporary Research (1974–1990)," *JSJ* 24 (1993): 215–34. For the famous but disputed letter of Judah Maccabee in 2 Maccabees, see Ben Zion Wacholder, "The Letter from Judah Maccabee to Aristobulus: Is 2 Maccabees 1:10b-2:18 Authentic?" *HUCA* 49 (1978): 89–133.

6. This is another case of non-pseudepigraphic forgery: the author does not say that his name is Solomon, but he claims to be a Jewish king who built a temple, and he describes events from Solomon's lifetime. The Muratorian fragment famously assigns the book to Solomon's friends—without denying that it implicitly claims instead to be by Solomon himself—but accepts it as canonical. Its authorship was doubted throughout the early church, for example by Origen in his *Commentary on John* 8, 37 (20.4.26); Jerome, *In libros Salom.* Praef; and Augustine (*Doctr. Christ.* 2, 8): "For two books, one called Wisdom and the other Ecclesiasticus, are ascribed to Solomon from a certain resemblance of style, but the most likely opinion is that they were written by Jesus the son of Sirach."

7. Among the extensive works of scholarship, see especially the full study of Sylvie Honigman, *The Septuagint and Homeric Scholarship in Alexandria: A Study in the Narrative of the Letter of Aristeas* (London: Routledge, 2003).

8. See especially Martin Hengel, "Anonimität, Pseudepigraphie und Literarische Fälschung in der Jüdisch-Hellenistischen Literatur," in *Pseudepigrapha I,* ed. Kurt von Fritz (Geneva: Vandoeuvres, 1972), pp. 231–308; Morton Smith, "Pseudepigraphy in the Israelite Tradition," also in *Pseudepigrapha I,* ed. von Fritz, pp. 189–215; and Eibert Tigchelaar, "Forms of Pseudepigraphy in the Dead Sea Scrolls," in Jörg Frey et al., eds., *Pseudepigraphie und Verfasserfiktion,* pp. 85–101.

A special question arises concerning the literary character of Jewish apocalypses, books certainly written in the name of someone other than the actual author. But is it appropriate in these cases to speak of "forgery," when pseudepigraphic authorship functioned as a standard element of the generic expectation of the works? In response, an obverse question might well be posed: Is there any reason that an entire (or almost entire) genre could not comprise, by its very nature, forgeries?

There has been extensive scholarship devoted to the question of the authorship of the Jewish apocalypses. None was more initially influential but subsequently renounced as D. H. Russell's work *The Method and Message of Jewish Apocalyptic 200 B.C.–A.D. 100.*[9] Russell contended that the pseudonymous authorship of Jewish apocalypses could be explained on the grounds of (1) corporate personality, in which ancient Jewish authors did not clearly separate the individual from his or her larger social group; (2) contemporaneity, in which Jews at the time did not neatly differentiate between the past and present; and (3) extension of personality, in which Jewish authors, such as those of the apocalypses, identified so closely with earlier figures that they could legitimately claim to write in their names. Each of these three points, as well as Russell's overall theory, has been effectively discounted by subsequent scholarship devoted both to the specific field of apocalyptic literature[10] and to pseudepigraphy more broadly.[11]

Apart from Russell, however, there is a broad, though not universal, sense among scholars of Jewish apocalypticism that the use of pseudonymity was so widespread as a practice that it must have been seen as conventional by the authors who produced the work and, correspondingly, "seen through" by their readers, who were not at all convinced that the resultant books were actually written by Abraham, Enoch, Ezra, Baruch, and so on. This broad sense is open to dispute, however, and has indeed been called into question by recent investigations. For one thing, one wonders where there is any actual evidence that the pseudepigraphic claims of the apocalypses were transparent fictions. It is striking that the one reader from antiquity who explicitly comments on the matter, Tertullian, insisted that Enoch's pre-diluvian composition (our 1 Enoch) is not invalidated by the fact of the flood: his direct descendant, Noah himself, no doubt could have reproduced the book verbatim after all surviving copies were destroyed by the deluge (*De cultu Fem.* 1, 3, 1).

Apart from the question of ancient "reader response," one needs to take seriously the functions and intentions of the genre itself, and of its pseudepigraphic character in particular. John Collins has repeatedly stressed that the authorial claim of the apocalypses functions precisely to make the *ex eventu* prophecies

9. London: SCM, 1964.

10. Thus Christopher Rowland, *The Open Heaven: A Study of Apocalyptic in Judaism and Early Christianity* (New York: Crossroad, 1982), who argues, among other things, that "a distinctively Jewish interpretation of pseudonymity is difficult to uphold," p. 66.

11. Meade, *Pseudonymity and Canon*, pp. 5–7.

believable. Readers who knew that Daniel was not really predicting the history of nations up to and following Antiochus Epiphanes would not have found much solace or assurance in his "prophecies." Only if his authorial claim is believed can his predictions about the imminent destruction of Antiochus have any effect. That is to say, since other prophecies (*ex eventu*, as we now know) came true, so too then, obviously, will the ones the reader is most interested in, namely those involving the current oppressor. Likewise for other apocalypses of Daniel's ilk, including those at Qumran.[12]

Karina Martin Hogan takes the matter a step further. While acknowledging that earlier scholars tried to get the ancient pseudonymous authors of the apocalypses off the moral hook (Speyer: "echte religiöse Pseudepigraphie"; Russell "corporate personality"; and so on), Hogan chooses to stress the historical consciousness of Jewish apocalypticists. In her view, pseudonyms were carefully and consciously chosen by the apocalyptic authors because these particular names provided links between the key historical periods with which the apocalypses were concerned. In particular, Noah, Moses, Daniel, Baruch, and Ezra were assigned apocalyptic visions because as traditional figures they bridged distinct historical periods and watershed events: Flood, Exodus, Babylonian Exile, and Restoration. As Hogan concludes about the real authors: "by casting Israel's history in the form of *ex eventu* prophecy, they bring a new perspective of determinism as well as an explicit claim to divine revelation, both of which set them apart from the biblical narratives and histories."[13] Once again, in any event, the authorial claim was conscious, even calculated.

A different angle taken by Michael Stone leads to a similar result.[14] Stone argues that the authority of the Jewish apocalypses did not come merely from the transmundane revelation they narrated, but also from the fact that they were written precisely to be taken as Scripture and were based, for that reason, on "ancient normative tradition." The claim to represent this tradition was secured by the name of the figure who conveyed the revelation. But that meant the name had to be explained and justified. This is what led to occasional self-conscious discussions of how the books were preserved from hoary antiquity to the present (cf. 1 Enoch 68.1; 81.1–5; 2 Enoch 10, 13, esp. 13.75–78; and so on): "That a need was felt to account for this is revealing. It betrays, by protesting overmuch, the awesome weight of the received scriptural tradition." These authors, in short, "were conscious in large measure of what they were doing, yet did it in dialectic with the received tradition," even if, as Rowland and others have insisted, "part of what they were doing was validated for them by their actual experiential practice." As

12. See, for example, John Collins, "Pseudepigraphy and Group Formation in Second Temple Judaism," in Esther G. Chazon and Michael Stone, eds., *Pseudepigraphic Perspectives: The Apocrypha and Pseudepigrapha in Light of the Dead Sea Scrolls* (Leiden: Brill, 1999), pp. 43–58.

13. "Pseudepigraphy and the Periodization of History in Jewish Apocalypses," in Jörg Frey et al., eds., *Pseudepigraphie und Verfasserfiktion*, pp. 61–83; quotation p. 82.

14. "Pseudepigraphy Reconsidered," *Review of Rabbinic Judaism* 9 (2006): 1–15.

a result, pseudepigraphic claims were done "partly ingenuously and partly very consciously."[15]

In light of these studies, there seems little reason to place pseudepigraphic apocalypses in a different category from pseudepigraphic prophecies, histories, epistles, and so on. For clear and distinct reasons, a writer claimed to be a figure from the distant past,[16] with the intent of convincing his readers that what he said about himself was true. Otherwise the apocalyptic visions would not "work" as visions.

With the testamentary literature we are dealing with a different phenomenon.[17] Even though the Testaments report the first-person narratives of their respective characters (the Twelve Patriarchs, Moses, Solomon, etc.), they do not claim to be written by these people. Instead, they function like embedded speeches or faux documents in, say, ancient histories, which purport to record the actual words of a key figure but which are, in reality, invented by the orthonymous (or, in the case of the Testaments, anonymous) authors themselves.[18]

In Christian Literature

There is little reason to cite every instance that has come down to us of forgery among the Christians of the first four centuries, as I will be discussing prominent cases throughout the bulk of my study. It is worth observing, however, that criticism was very much alive and well among Christian thinkers of the first four centuries. A bewildering number of writings, including many of those that eventually became part of the New Testament, were claimed by one Christian critic or another not to have been written by their alleged authors. As some examples: Augustine's Manichaean opponent Faustus argued that the Gospels were not actually written by apostles or companions of the apostles (*Contra Faust.* 32.2). Unnamed "heretics" rejected 1 and 2 Timothy, according to Clement of Alexandria, presumably meaning that they did not agree that Paul wrote them (*Strom.* 2.11). Eusebius indicates that the authorship of James was "disputed" (meaning some rejected it), because "few of the ancients quote it" (*H.E.* 2.23.25; 3.25); so too Jerome indicates that some writers considered the book pseudonymous (*Vir. ill.* 2.2). 2 Peter was doubted (Origen in Eusebius, *H.E.* 6.25.11) or rejected (Jerome, *Vir. ill.* 1); Didymus the Blind explicitly claims it was forged.[19] Jude too was "disputed" (meaning some rejected it) according to Eusebius (*H.E.* 2.23.25)

15. Ibid., pp. 12–13.

16. Except for such works as Revelation and the Shepherd, which were not forged.

17. See J. H. Charlesworth, ed., *The Old Testament Pseudepigrapha*, vol. 1, *Apocalyptic Literature and Testaments* (Garden City, NY: Doubleday, 1983), pp. 773–995.

18. As Anthea Portier-Young has pointed out to me, there is a possible exception with the Testament of Moses, in which Moses instructs Joshua to write down his words and deposit them in earthenware jars for safekeeping. Presumably the Testament itself is to be a replication of these words. See *TMoses*, 1.14–18.

19. "In epistolam S. Petri Secundam Enn.," *PG* 39 1774A.

and rejected because it quotes Enoch, according to Jerome (*Vir. ill.* 4). "Not all" considered 2 John and 3 John "genuine" according to Origen (Eusebius, *H.E.* 6.25). Revelation, as we have seen, was thought by some to be homonymous (thus Dionysius of Alexandria; Eusebius, *H.E.* 7.25); others ascribed it to a specific forger, Cerinthus (Gaius according to Eusebius, *H.E.* 3.28). Eusebius appears to reject Clement as the author of 2 Clement (*H.E.* 3.38) and labels Barnabas, the Apocalypse of Peter, and the Shepherd as νόθα (*H.E.* 3.25). The Gospel of Peter was eventually declared pseudepigraphic by Serapion (*H.E.* 3.25). So too Jerome labeled the Acts of Peter, the Preaching of Peter, the Apocalypse of Peter, and the Judgment of Peter nonauthentic (*Vir. ill.* 1). According to Eusebius, the Prophecies of Barcabbas and Barcoph were in fact invented by Basilides (*H.E.* 4.7.6–7). Paul's letters to the Laodiceans and the Alexandrians were labeled Marcionite forgeries by the Muratorian fragment. We have seen that Epiphanius names a number of Phibionite forgeries in book 26 of his Panarion; elsewhere he rejects Gospels written in the names of James, Matthew, and other disciples as Ebionite productions (book 30). Slightly later Jerome rejects the treatise "On Fate," allegedly by Minucius Felix, and Augustine exposes the letter of Jesus allegedly written to Peter and Paul (Augustine, *De cons. Evang.* 1. 10)

Early Christian authors similarly reject a long string of forged letters and documents: Athanasius was apparently the victim of an Arian letter forged in his name (*Apol. ad Const.* 19–21). There was also a forged summons to Augustine allegedly from Victorinus (Aug. *Epist.* 59, 2), a letter of Jerome suspected by Rufinus (*Adv. Rufin.* 3. 2), and another letter allegedly by Jerome about false translations of Scripture (*Adv. Rufin* 3.25; also 2.24). Jerome himself wonders if a letter of Augustine's is actually his (*Epist.* 102,1). Augustine doubts several books assigned to Pelagius (Aug. *De gest Pelag.* 1.19) and mentions a forgery in the name of Cyprian (*Epist.* 93.38). And a series of interpolations of false teachings amid the statements of Basil make it appear that he held these aberrant views (*Epist.* 129.1; 224.1).

And on and on. This list does not count all the books that scholars today widely accept as pseudepigraphic. Just in terms of the earliest Christian tradition, it is striking, as is often noted, that between Paul and Ignatius there is not a single Christian author who writes in his own name, with the possible exception of the "John" of the Apocalypse (which is homonymous).[20] Every other Gospel, epistle, treatise, or sermon is either forged or anonymous and then falsely attributed. No surprise, then, that K. M. Fischer can label the second half of the first century "the era of New Testament pseudepigraphy."[21]

---

20. 1 Clement may be seen as exceptional as well, in that it claims to be written by a group in Rome, and may well have been, by at least someone there. But since no authorial name is attached, it is perhaps best seen as anonymous.

21. "Die Zeit der neutestamentlichen Pseudepigraphie." "Anmerkungen zur Pseudepigraphie im Neuen Testament," *NTS* 23 (1967): 76.

From these sundry references it is also clear that ancients employed criticism during this early period. Jeremy Duff, in his otherwise helpful study "A Reconsideration of Pseudepigraphy in Early Christianity," is incorrect to claim that there are only six explicit discussions of pseudepigraphy in the first two Christian centuries. He names, as the six, 2 Thess. 2:1–3 (a letter "as if by us"); Dionysius of Corinth, who complains about false teachers interpolating his own writings; Serapion on the Gospel of Peter; Tertullian on the Acts of Paul; Tertullian on the Gospels of Mark and Luke (as actually Gospels of Peter and Paul); and the Muratorian Fragment with its comments on heretical forgeries.[22] Some of these, however, do not concern issues of authorship. Dionysius of Corinth is referring to the falsification of (his own) writings, not to forgery. And Tertullian, as we have seen, condemns the author of the Acts of Paul and Thecla not for forging the account but for fabricating it. Moreover, when Tertullian indicates that Mark and Luke are reasonably considered to represent the views of Peter and Paul (*Adv. Marc.* 4.5.3–4), he is not suggesting that Mark claimed to *be* Peter or that Luke claimed to *be* Paul. These authors (for Tertullian) wrote in their own names, not in the names of their authorizing figures.

On the other hand, there are other authors of the period who did indeed discuss pseudepigraphy, especially in Duff's wider usage of the term. Hegesippus, for example, maligned heretical forgeries in circulation, as Eusebius tells us: "And in discussing apocryphal books, as they are called, he states that some of them were fabricated by heretics in his own time" (καὶ περὶ τῶν λεγομένων δὲ ἀποκρύφων διαλαμβάνων, ἐπὶ τῶν αὐτοῦ χρόνων πρός τινων αἱρετικῶν ἀναπεπλάσθαι τινὰ τούτων ἱστορεῖ; *H.E.* 4, 22, 9). So too Gaius of Rome objected to those who "compose new scriptures" and contended that Paul's letters number thirteen, not accepting Hebrews as Pauline. As Eusebius indicates: "for then as now there were some at Rome who did not think that it was the Apostle's" (*H.E.* 6.20.3). Moreover, Gaius appears to have assigned the authorship of the book of Revelation to Cerinthus, who only falsely claimed to be John (Eusebius *H.E.* 3.28). So too, somewhat later, Dionysius of Alexandria indicates that his "predecessors" had charged that the book of Revelation was forged by Cerinthus in the name of John in order to get a hearing for his views (Eusebius, *H.E.* 7.25).

In addition, Irenaeus mentions numerous apocryphal and inauthentic writings by the heretics: "they adduce an untold multitude of apocryphal and spurious writings, which they have composed (πλῆθος ἀποκρύφων καὶ νόθων γραφῶν ἃς αὐτοὶ ἔπλασαν) to bewilder foolish men and such as do not understand the letters of the Truth" (*Adv. Haer.* 1.20.1).[23] Clement of Alexandria, as previously noted, mentions some who reject 1 and 2 Timothy because the former speaks of Gnosis falsely so-called (*Strom.* 2.11). Finally, as we have also seen, Origen was

22. Ph.D. thesis, University of Oxford, 1998, pp. 213–37.

23. *Against Heresies—Book I*, trans. John J. Dillon (ACW; New York: Newman Press, 1992).

even more forthright than Dionysius of Corinth in complaining about the falsification of his own work.[24]

As a net result, there is certainly no lack of materials from antiquity related to forgery—pagan, Jewish, and Christian. All the odder, as I indicated at the outset, that there are so few studies devoted to the topic. There are to be sure explorations of individual cases in droves,[25] as well as extensive studies of the relationship between pseudepigraphy and canon.[26] And there are articles written on this or that aspect of the broader problem,[27] many of them compiled into valuable collections.[28] But where are the monographs?[29]

---

24. See p. 64.

25. As will be abundantly clear in the chapters that follow.

26. Thus, e.g., Meade, *Pseudonymity and Canon*; Terry L. Wilder, *Pseudonymity, The New Testament, and Deception: An Inquiry into Intention and Reception* (Lanham, MD: University Press of America, 2004); and most helpfully Baum, *Pseudepigraphie und literarische Fälschung*.

27. See the bibliography. I would include under this rubric, as some of the most useful contributions: J. S. Candlish, "On the Moral Character of Pseudonymous Books," *Expositor* 4 (1891): 91–107; 262–79; Alfred Gudeman, "Literary Frauds Among the Greeks," in *Classical Studies in Honor of Henry Drisler* (New York: Macmillan, 1894), pp. 52–74; idem, "Literary Frauds Among the Romans," *Transactions and Proceedings of the American Philological Association* 25 (1894): 140–64; Arnold Meyer, "Religiöse Pseudepigraphie als ethisch-psychologisches Problem," *ZNW* 35 (1936): 262–79; earlier in *Archiv für die gesamte Psychologie* 86 (1932): 171–90; Frederik Torm, "Die Psychologie der Pseudonymität im Hinblick auf die Literatur des Urchristentums," *Studien der Luther Akademie*, Heft 2 (Gütersloh: Bertelsmann, 1932), pp. 7–55; Gustav Bardy, "Faux et fraudes littéraires dans l'antiquité chrétienne," *RHE* 32 (1936): 5–23; 275–302; Kurt Aland, "The Problem of Anonymity and Pseudonymity in Christian Literature of the First Two Centuries," *JTS* 12 (1961): 39–49; Wolfgang Speyer, "Religiöse Pseudepigraphie und literarische Fälschung im Altertum," *JAC* 8/9 (1965–66): 88–125; H. R. Balz, "Anonymität und Pseudepigraphie im Urchristentum," *ZTK* 66 (1969): 403–36; Martin Hengel, "Anonimität, Pseudepigraphie und 'Literarische Fälschung' in der Jüdisch-Hellenistischen Literatur," in *Pseudepigrapha I*, ed. Kurt von Fritz (Geneva: Vandoeuvres, 1971), pp. 231–308; Morton Smith, "Pseudepigraphy in the Israelite Tradition," *in Pseudepigrapha I*, ed. Kurt von Fritz, pp. 189–215; Bruce M. Metzger, "Literary Forgeries and Canonical Pseudepigrapha," *JBL* 91 (1972): 3–24; M. Rist, "Pseudepigraphy and the Early Christians," in *Studies in New Testament and Early Christian Literature: Essays in Honor of A. P. Wikgren; Novum Testamentum Supplement*, ed. David Edward Aune (Leiden: E. J. Brill, 1972), pp. 75–91; Franz Laub, "Falsche Verfasserangaben in neutestamentlichen Schriften: Aspekte der gegenwärtigen Diskussion um die neutestamentliche Pseudepigraphie," *TTZ* 89 (1980): 228–41; Pokorny, P. "Das theologische Problem der neutestamentlichen Pseudepigraphie," *EvT* 44 (1984): 486–96; E. J. Bickerman, "Faux littéraires dans l'antiquité classique en marge d'un livre récent," in *Studies in Jewish and Christian History* (Leiden: E. J. Brill, 1986); Jean-Daniel Kaestli, "Memoire et pseudepigraphie dans le christianisme," *RTP* 125 (1993): 41–63; Pier Franco Beatrice, "Forgery, Propaganda and Power in Christian Antiquity," *JAC.E* 33 (2002): 39–51; Michael E. Stone, "Pseudepigraphy Reconsidered," *Review of Rabbinic Judaism* 9 (2006): 1–15; Martina Janssen, "Antike (Selbst) Aussagen über Beweggründe zur Pseudepigraphie," in Jörg Frey et al., eds., *Pseudepigraphie und Verfasserfiktion*, pp. 125–79. See, in fact, all the essays, many of them lengthy, in the last-named volume.

28. E.g., Norbert Brox, ed., *Pseudepigraphie in der heidnischen und jüdisch-christlichen Antike* (Darmstadt: Wissenschaftliche Buchgesellschaft, 1977); and especially Martina Janssen, ed., *Unter falschem Namen: Eine kritische Forschungsbilanz frühchristlicher Pseudepigraphie* (Frankfurt: Peter Lang, 2003). See also Herzer, Janssen and Rothschild, eds., *Pseudepigraphie und Verfasserfiktion*.

29. E.g., on much broader issues: Archer Taylor and Fredric John Mosher, *The Bibliographical History of Anonyma and Pseudonyma* (Chicago: University of Chicago Press, 1951); and Edmund Kerchever

FALSE AUTHORIAL CLAIMS AND INTELLECTUAL PROPERTY

We have already seen substantial grounds for labeling literary works that make false authorial claims forgeries, for example in the clear instances of intended deceit considered in Chapter Two and in the ancient Greek and Latin terms used to describe the phenomenon, such as ψεῦδος, νόθος, and κίβδηλος. Scholars who object to the idea that deceit was involved in the practice typically claim that literary, or intellectual, property is a modern notion without an ancient analogue, so that authors who made false authorial claims were simply engaged in a widely accepted exercise that no one thought the worse of. And so, for example, in his commentary on the pseudepigraphic letter to the Ephesians, Andrew Lincoln declares:

> There is no reason to think of the device of pseudonymity in negative terms and to associate it necessarily with such notions as forgery and deception. . . . The idea of "Intellectual property," basic to modern discussion of legitimate claims to authorship, plagiarism, and copyright laws, played little or no role in ancient literary production.[30]

On these grounds, Lincoln indicates that literary pseudepigraphy (what I'm calling forgery) "was a widespread and accepted literary practice in both Jewish and Greco-Roman cultures."[31] Lincoln is not alone in expressing such opinions.[32]

The careful studies of Speyer, Brox, Grafton, Duff, and Baum, among others, however, have effectively destroyed this position. Ancients certainly did have a sense of intellectual property, and, as we have seen, critics thought and spoke badly of anyone who transgressed acceptable bounds by falsely claiming in writing to be a well-known person.[33] On the contrary, what is a modern invention is

---

Chambers, *The History and Motives of Literary Forgeries*, Burt Franklin Research & Source Works Series 508 (Oxford: B. H. Blackwell, 1891; Repr., New York: Burt Franklin, 1970). Those dealing with pagan and early Christian materials in particular, in addition to Speyer, *Literarische Fälschung*: Josef A. Sint, *Pseudonymität im Altertum: Ihre Formen und ihre Gründe* (Innsbruck: Universitätsverlag Wagner, 1960); Norbert Brox, *Falsche Verfasserangaben: zur Erklärung der frühchristlichen Pseudepigraphie* (Stuttgarter Bibelstudien, 79; Stuttgart: KBW, 1975); and Jeremy N. Duff, "A Reconsideration of Pseudepigraphy in Early Christianity" (Ph.D. thesis, University of Oxford, 1998).

30. *Ephesians*. WBC, 42 (Dallas: Word Books, 1990), p. lxxi.

31. Ibid., p. lxx.

32. See further the discussion on pp. 128–32 below. A harsh opponent of these views, Armin Baum (*Pseudepigraphie und literarische Fälschung*, p. 22) cites as examples of denying an ancient notion of literary property: F. Schmidt ("to some extent") in "'Traqué comme un loup.' A propos du débat actuel sur l'apocalyptique juive," *ASSR* 27 (1982): pp. 9–11; M. Casey, *Is John's Gospel True?* (London: Routledge, 1996), pp. 140–77, esp. p. 143, for the Jewish world; K.–H. Ohlig, *Die Theologische Begründung des neutestamentlichen Kanons in der alten Kirche*. KBANT (Düsseldorf: Patmos, 1972) p. 91, for the early Christians.

33. Speyer, *Literarische Fälschung*, pp. 112–28; Brox, *Falsche Verfasserangaben*, pp. 62–80; Grafton, *Forgers and Critics*, pp. 3–35; Duff, "Reconsideration," pp. 99–137; Baum, *Pseudepigraphie*, pp. 21–24 and passim.

the idea that ancient readers widely found false authorial claims acceptable.[34] This was recognized already by one of the pioneers of the modern study of forgery, Frederik Torm, some eighty years ago:

> The situation within Judaism and Christianity resembled that of the Greco-Roman world. *Either* one believed in the authenticity of a pseudonymous document and could then prize it highly, *or* one assumed its inauthenticity, in which case the writing in question became suspect already due to its pseudonymity. The notion that in this era pseudonymity was ever treated as a literary form in the religious realm and was indeed recognized as such is a modern invention. . . . [35]

Chief among the reasons for thinking that ancients were interested in knowing who actually wrote a literary work is what we have already begun to see repeatedly: ancient critics themselves addressing the issue with striking frequency. Speyer cogently speaks of an "extensive body of [ancient] writings, which does not serve any other purpose but to separate out inauthentic works from the literary remains of famous authors by means of philological and historical methods."[36] The ancient evidence is overwhelming. Just to give a fuller sense of the matter, I might mention some isolated instances.

Herodotus provides the first documented instances of Echtheitskritik, already in the fifth century BCE, when, among other things, he questions whether Homer authored the Cypria and the Epigoni epic (2, 116ff. and 4, 32). Ion of Chios, in his *Triagmi*, indicates that Pythagoras ascribed some of his own poems to Orpheus[37]; so too, Aristotle doubted that the Orphic poems were by Orpheus.[38] Extensive comments on authenticity—determining which works were γνήσια and which were νόθα—appear in the Neoplatonic commentaries on Aristotle, from Ammonius and Simplicius to Elias and David.[39]

---

34. As a side note: if intellectual property had been unknown, plagiarism would not have been an issue. As we have seen, it was a very serious issue indeed among ancient authors.

35. Es verhielt sich innerhalb des Judentums und des Christentums wie in der griechisch-römischen Welt. Entweder glaubte man an die Echtheit einer pseudonymen Schrift und konnte sie dann sehr hochschätzen, oder man nahm die Unechtheit an, und dann war die betreffende Schrift schon wegen ihrer Pseudonymität jedenfalls etwas anrüchig. Daß man in jener Zeit jemals auf religiösem Gebiet die Pseudonymität als eine literarische Form aufgefasst und ihre Berechtigung geradezu anerkannt hat, ist eine moderne Erfindung. . . . Torm, "Die Psychologie," reprinted in Brox, *Pseudepigraphie in . . . Antike*, p. 119. Emphasis his.

36. ". . . ein umfangreicheres Schrifttum . . . das keinen anderen Zweck verfolgte, als nach philologisch-historischer Methode die unechten Werke aus dem Nachlaß berühmter Schriftsteller auszusondern." *Literarische Fälschung*, p. 113.

37. According to Diogenes Laertius, *Lives* 8, 8.

38. Thus Johannes Philoponus, *Commentary on Aristotle's 'De Anima'* 1, 5.

39. See Carl Werner Müller, "Die neuplatonischen Aristoteleskommentatoren über die Ursachen der Pseudepigraphie," *Rheinisches Museum für Philologie*, NF 112 (1969): 120–26; reprinted in Brox, *Pseudepigraphie in der heidnischen und jüdisch-christlichen Antike*, pp. 264–71.

After the construction of the great libraries of Alexandria and Pergamum, Echtheitskritik became the task of the grammarians. Thus we learn, for example, from Quintilian:

> For not only is the art of writing combined with that of speaking, but correct reading also precedes illustration, and with all these is joined the exercise of judgment, which the old grammarians, indeed, used with such severity that they not only allowed themselves to distinguish certain verses with a particular mark of censure and to remove, as spurious, certain books which had been inscribed with false titles, from their sets, but even brought some authors within their canon and excluded others altogether from classification.[40]

And so, in the first half of the third century, Callimachus at the Alexandrian Museion categorized books in the library as genuine (γνήσια), inauthentic (i.e., forged: νόθα), or debated (ἀμφίβολα, ἀμφιδοξούμενα, ἀμφιβαλλόμενα).[41]

More specifically, in the later first century BCE, Dionysius of Halicarnassus expressed doubts ("Lysias" ch. 12 and "Dinarchus" chs. 2–3) about speeches of Lysias that were widely thought genuine, as we will see more fully later. Aulus Gellius indicates that Lucius Aelius maintained that only 25 of the 130 comedies circulating in the name of Plautus were authentic (*Noct. Attic.* 3.3.11–14). So too, numerous forgeries were in circulation in the name of Democritus: "Many fictions of this kind seem to have been attached to the name of Democritus by ignorant men, who sheltered themselves under his reputation and authority (nobilitatis auctoritatisque eius perfugio utentibus)" (10. 12.8).[42] Plutarch repeatedly speaks of his doubts concerning the genuineness of letters (*Brutus* 53, 7; *Lysand.* 14, 4). So too Pausanias on occasion, as when he expresses some mild doubt over the Hesiodic authorship of the *Theogony* (e.g., 9.27.2: "Hesiod, or the one who wrote the *Theogony* fathered on Hesiod"). Arguably the most famous critic of all was Galen, who took on the entire Hippocratic corpus, in part precisely to decide what was authentic and what not.[43]

---

40. Inst. Or. 1, 4, 3. Translation of John Selby Watson at http://honeyl.public.iastate.edu/quintilian/.

41. Thus Baum, *Pseudepigraphie*, p. 23, referencing Blum, *Kallimachos und die Literaturverzeichnung bei den Griechen* (Frankfurt: Buchhändler-Vereinigung, 1977), 27–244; Y. L. Too, *The Idea of Ancient Literary Criticism* (Oxford: Clarendon, 1998), 115–50, esp. 126–34; and R. M. Grant, *Heresy and Criticism: The Search for Authenticity in Early Christian Literature* (Louisville: Westminster, 1993), pp. 15–32. On the work of the Alexandrians' editing practices, see Franco Montanari, "Zenodotus, Aristarchus and the Ekdosis of Homer," in *Editing Texts,* ed. Glenn W. Most (Göttingen: Vandenhoeck & Ruprecht, 1998), pp. 1–21.

42. Translation of J. C. Rolfe in the 1927 LCL edition.

43. See L. O. Bröcker, "Die Methoden Galens in der literarischen Kritik," *Rheinisches Museum für Philologie* 40 (1885): 415–38. This is a learned classic, a careful exposition of the ways Galen engages in "criticism" in all its respects: lower criticism (textual); middle criticism (the detection of interpolations in authentic texts); negative higher criticism (establishing nonauthentic works, which Galen calls νόθα); and positive higher criticism (establishing authenticity of disputed works; Galen calls the authentic works γνήσια).

And we have already considered Diogenes Laertius and comments from the second book of his ten-volume work. Isolated other comments include his statement that the *Nautical Astronomy* attributed to Thales (εἰς αὐτὸν ἀναφερομένη) is said by others to be the work of Phocus of Samos (*Lives*, 1.23); that among the writings of Glaucon some thirty-two are to be considered spurious (οἳ νοθεύονται; 2.124); that the lecture notes of Strato "are doubted" (5.60); that some attribute Phlegon's play *Philosophers* to Poseidippus (7.27); and that a verse of Empedocles is perhaps to be assigned instead to Simonides (8.65). And on and on.

This listing of Greek and Roman sources intent on uncovering forgeries is not meant to be exhaustive. It is merely intended to illustrate a historical reality: ancient authors who mention pseudepigrapha do so because they are invested in knowing who really wrote the books produced in the name of known figures. Intellectuals were widely concerned to know whether a book's reputed author was its real author.

As we have already seen in part, there was an extensive discourse about authenticity in the early church as well, all of it implying a concern over what we might call literary property. To the discussions already cited, I might mention an expression of dismay over "heretical" forgeries from Ambrosiaster, who laments that just as the Devil sometimes assumes the guise of the redeemer in order to deceive believers, so too heretics write in the names of the sacred authors.[44] Ambrosiaster does not say here what he might think about forgers of his own theological persuasion; but there is no doubt what he thought of forgers with whom he disagreed. This naturally raises the broader question of the attitudes that ancient critics, especially Christians, had about the phenomenon of forgery.

COMPLAINTS ABOUT FORGERY

If there were no concept of intellectual property in antiquity, it would be virtually impossible to explain not only why plagiarists were condemned and sometimes punished, but also why authors complained about forgeries being produced in their own names. With his customary humor and bite, for example, Martial objects to forgers who produced poems, claiming to be him:

> My page has not wounded even those it justly hates, and fame won with another's blush is not dear to me! What does this avail me when certain folk would pass off as mine darts wet with the blood of Lycambes, and under my name a man vomits his viperous venom who owns he cannot bear the light of day? (*Epigrams*, 7.12)
>
> If some malignant fellow claim as mine poems that are steeped in black venom, do you lend me a patron's voice, and with all your strength and without stopping shout: "My Martial did not write that"? (7.72)[45]

44. *Ad Thess. Sec.* 2, 4, 1 (CSEL 81, 3, 239).

45. Translation of Walter C. A. Ker, *Martial: Epigrams* LCL (Cambridge, MA: Harvard University, 1968).

The best-known instance of complaint comes from Galen, a century later. In one of his many autobiographical accounts, he indicates that when passing by a bookseller in the Sandalarium he overheard an argument between a man who had just purchased a book with the title "Galen the Physician" and a trained amateur scholar, who read two lines and proclaimed "This is not Galen's language—the title is false."[46] Galen's own reaction was to write *De libris propriis*, the book about his books. Here he was straightforward about his goals: to allow those without the requisite grammatical and rhetoric training to know which books were actually his. And he certainly had a lot to be concerned about. By one modern account, some 13 percent of the surviving Galenic texts are forgeries.[47]

Among other things, these instances from Martial and Galen immediately give the lie to those New Testament scholars who claim that forgeries in the name of Paul, or Peter, or any other apostle, necessarily come from after their lifetimes, since no one would have dared forge a writing in the name of a person still living. Interestingly, this claim is often made by more conservative biblical scholars, who, ironically enough, tend to hold to the authenticity of 2 Thessalonians, a book in which "Paul" objects to a forgery circulating in his own name among the Thessalonians (2:2).

And "Paul" was not the only Christian who was both aware of and incensed by forgeries in his own name. We have already seen an analogous situation with Origen from a century and a half later.[48] A century still farther on we have the account of Athanasius, irate over a letter forged in his name by a theological opponent:

> I am sure you will be astonished at the presumption of my enemies. Montanus, the officer of the Palace, came and brought me a letter, which purported to be an answer to one from me. . . . But here again I am astonished at those who have spoken falsehood in your ears, that they were not afraid, seeing that lying belongs to the Devil, and that liars are alien from Him who says, "I am the Truth." For I never wrote to you, nor will my accuser be able to find any such letter.[49]

Forged letters became a real and widespread problem in the highly charged polemical environment of the Christian community at the end of the fourth Christian century and into the fifth. And so we have the complaint of Jerome:

> My brother Eusebius writes to me that, when he was at a meeting of African bishops which had been called for certain ecclesiastical affairs, he found there a letter purporting to be written by me, in which I professed penitence and

46. Translation of P. N. Singer, *Galen: Selected Works* (Oxford: University Press, 1997), p. 3.

47. See Ronald F. Kotrc and K. R. Walters, "A Bibliography of the Galenic Corpus," *Transactions and Studies of the College of Physicians of Philadelphia* Series 5. 1 (1979): 256–304.

48. See p. 64.

49. *Apol. Ad Const.* 19; translation of Archibald Robinson in *NPNF*, second series, vol. 4.

> confessed that it was through the influence of the press in my youth that I had been led to turn the Scriptures into Latin from the Hebrew; in all of which there is not a word of truth.

That he was not the author of the letter should have been obvious from the style; in any event, Jerome considers himself fortunate, tongue in cheek, for not being "self-accused" by the forger of truly criminal activity.

> It was impossible for him, accomplished as he was, to copy any style and manner of writing, whatever their value may be; amidst all his tricks and his fraudulent assumption of another man's personality, it was evident who he was. . . . I wonder that in this letter he did not make me out as guilty of homicide, or adultery or sacrilege or parricide or any of the vile things which the silent working of the mind can revolve within itself. Indeed I ought to be grateful to him for having imputed to me no more than one act of error or false dealing out of the whole forest of possible crimes. (*Adv. Ruf.* 2.24)[50]

In another place Jerome himself is falsely accused by Rufinus of forging a letter in the name of Pope Anastasius, a letter that, as it turns out, was genuine (*Adv. Ruf.* 3, 20). Elsewhere Rufinus feels that he has been unjustly accused of forging a letter in Jerome's name to a group of African bishops (Jerome, *Adv. Ruf.* 3, 25). Again, Jerome writes Augustine to ask if the letter he has received is actually by him (*Epist.* 102.1). As we have already seen, Augustine too exposed a forgery of a letter allegedly by Victorinus summoning him to a council meeting.[51]

It should not be objected that the forging of letters is generically different from the forging of literary works. Generic differences do matter. But many of the early Christian forgeries we will be examining—including those found in the New Testament—are precisely letters.

REACTIONS TO VIOLATORS CAUGHT IN THE ACT

There was no legislation in Greece and Rome to protect literary property rights, just as there was no legislation for all sorts of scandalous and socially unacceptable activities. Still, to that extent, forgery in antiquity is different from today, when forgers can be punished by law. At the same time, there is no doubt, as we have seen, that by the early Christian centuries there had long been a sense of intellectual property among ancient authors. Another indication is that ancient falsifiers of texts, fabricators of accounts, and forgers of literary works were regularly condemned, chastised, and sometimes even physically punished for their troubles.

---

50. Translation of W. H. Fremantle in *NPNF*, 2nd series, vol. 3.

51. Augustine, *Epist* 59, 1, 2.

In our first surviving account of Echtheitskritik, Herodotus tells us that Onomacritus was not only caught in the act of falsifying oracles but was severely punished for it by being banished from Athens.[52] This was not merely the peculiar whim of the local despot. Onomacritus and others like him who altered the oracular texts were open to widespread aspersion, as attested still many centuries later by Plutarch: "I forbear to mention how much blame men like Onomacritus, Prodicus, and Cinaethon have brought upon themselves from the oracles by foisting upon them a tragic diction and a grandiloquence of which they have had no need, nor have I any kindly feeling toward their changes" (*Oracles at Delphi* 407B).[53]

In a similar vein, the Stoic Athenodorus was relieved of his duties in the great library of Pergamum because he altered the texts of Zeno.[54] In Christian circles, as we have seen, Tertullian tells us of the presbyter of Asia Minor who resigned (by force?) his ecclesiastical office on being implicated in the fabrication of the Acts of Paul and Thecla (*De baptismo*, 17). In other instances, falsifiers and fabricators were simply maligned for their literary handiwork, as when Dionysius of Corinth leveled bitter complaints against those who heretically altered his writings,[55] or when Celsus castigated Christians for inventing Sibylline oracles that placed predictions of the coming of Christ on the lips of the ancient pagan prophetess.[56]

Much the same kinds of reaction are attested for those caught making false authorial claims. We have seen already the castigations of Martial on the pagan side and Origen on the Christian, leveled against brash authors who forged writings in their names.[57] Sometimes forgers were called to account, as when the fifth-century ecclesiastic Salvian was caught by his own bishop forging a writing in the name of Paul's companion Timothy. As we will see, Salvian wrote a self-serving justification in his own defense. For now it is enough to note that his bishop, Salonius, was not at all amused when he discovered that his former colleague and current underling had tried to promote his own views in the name of an authority who had been dead for four hundred years. That Salonius was upset and incensed is clear; how he reacted to Salvian's self-defense we will never know. We learn of the incident only from Salvian himself.[58]

In other instances we learn of real punishments for forgery. The philosopher Diotimus was caught having forged fifty obscene letters in the name of Epicurus. According to Athenaeus (*Banqueters* 13.611B), who names as his source Demetrius of Magnesia (the "Homonyms"), an Epicurean philosopher named Zeno tracked Diotimus down and murdered him. Forging could be serious

52. See p. 61.

53. Translation of Frank Cole Babbitt, *Plutarch's Moralia*, LCL (Cambridge, MA: Harvard University Press, 1927).

54. See p. 62.

55. See p. 63.

56. Origen, *Contra Celsum*, 7.56. See pp. 508–19.

57. See pp. 81 and 64.

58. See pp. 94–96.

business. This much we can learn from a Jewish source, Josephus, who indicates that a royal servant in the court of King Herod forged a letter in the name of Alexander that discussed his plan to murder his father Herod. The forger, a certain "Diophantus, a secretary of the king, an audacious fellow, who had the clever knack of imitating any handwriting [δεινὸς μιμήσασθαι πάσης χειρὸς γράμματα]; and who, after numerous forgeries, was eventually put to death for a crime of that nature."[59]

There are not many testimonials from antiquity about persons caught in the act of falsifying, fabricating, and forging documents. But every instance that we do have points in the same direction. These were not acceptable practices. On the contrary, they were condemned, maligned, castigated, and attacked. In the realm of polemical discourse and political realia, in particular, they were matters of real moment—sometimes, though rarely, of course, matters of life and death.

AUTHORS AS AUTHORITIES

We have seen that ancient attitudes toward the violation of intellectual property claims are relatively clear just from the vocabulary used to describe it. The terms used for plagiarism ("thievery," "robbery") and forgery ("lies," "adulterations," "bastards"), for example, were obviously harsh. Moreover, we have observed a keen interest in and serious intellectual energy devoted to establishing writings as authentic or spurious. Those who were found guilty of literary malfeasance were objects of derogation, if not worse.

In the rarified realm of literary criticism, deprecating comments were often simply off the cuff, as when Seneca the Elder, speaking of the works of the great rhetoricians, says, "In general there are no extant drafts from the pens of the greatest declaimers, or what is worse, there are forged ones (quod peius est, falsi)."[60] Still, critics wanted to know who said what, and they cast aspersions on the anonymous authors who claimed to be someone else. Thus, for example, Porphyry, in his *Life of Plotinus*, speaks of a book allegedly written by Zostrianus: "I myself have shown on many counts that the Zoroastrian volume is spurious and modern, concocted by the sectaries in order to pretend that the doctrines they had embraced were those of the ancient sage."[61]

For Seneca, Porphyry, and other ancient critics, one of the key reasons for wanting to know whether or not a writing was genuine (γνήσιον) was a widely

---

59. *Jewish War*, 1. 26. 3; translation of Thackeray as taken from Henry Leeming, *Josephus' Jewish War and Its Slavonic Version: A Synoptic Comparison of the English Translation by H. St. J. Thackeray with the Critical Edition by N.A. Meščerskij of the Slavonic Version in the Vilna Manuscript Translated into English by H. Leeming and L. Osinkina* (Leiden: Brill, 2003).

60. *Controv*. 1 Praef 11; Translation of Winterbottom from LCL (Cambridge, MA: Harvard University Press, 1974).

61. Translation of Stephen MacKenna, *Plotinus: The Enneads*, http://www.sacred-texts.com/cla/plotenn/enn001.htm.

shared cultural assumption that a symbiotic relationship existed between the author of a writing and its authority. That is to say, critics were not concerned about either the author or the contents of a writing in isolation from one another, but in tandem. The person of the author provided the authority for the account; at the same time, the contents of the account established the identity of the author. This symbiotic relationship was fully appreciated by early Christian critics and is a key to understanding their attitudes toward forged writings.

To some extent, the early Christian intellectuals, like their non-Christian counterparts, were interested on general grounds in knowing who the authors of various texts really were. And so, for example, Clement of Alexandria, one of the earliest of the trained Christian critics, both borrowed and mirrored the critical stances of his pagan contemporaries:

> It is said that the oracles attributed to Musaeus were composed by Onomacritus, Orpheus' *Mixing-Bowl* by Zopyrus of Heraclea, the *Descent to Hades* by Prodicus of Samos. Ion of Chios in his *Triads* records that Pythagoras attributed some of his work to Orpheus. Epigenes in his work *On Poetry Attributed to Orpheus* says that the *Descent to Hades* and the *Sacred Doctrine* are works of the Pythagorean Cercops and the *Robe* and the *Works of Nature*, writings of Brontinus.[62]

So too Tertullian, from the passage already mentioned: perplexed by the existence of the book of Enoch, Tertullian develops a lengthy argument to show that even if all the copies of the book had been destroyed by the flood in Noah's day, Noah himself, as Enoch's descendant, would have remembered his teachings handed down through the family line and so would have been able to reconstruct them, either of his own natural abilities or through the inspiration of the Holy Spirit. In either case, the book of Enoch extant today really is the book written by the antediluvian Enoch (*De cultu Fem.* 1.3.1).

Or there is Augustine dealing with the books of the Hippocratic corpus:

> But even in worldly writings there were well-known authors under whose names many works were produced later, and they were repudiated either because they did not agree with the writings that were certainly theirs or because, at the time when those authors wrote, these writings did not merit to be recognized and to be handed on and commended to posterity by them or their friends. Not to mention others, were not certain books that were produced under the name Hippocrates, the highly renowned physician, rejected as authoritative by physicians? Nor did a certain similarity of topics and language offer them any help. For, compared to the books that it was clear were really Hippocrates' books, they were judged inferior, and they were not

62. *Strom.* 1.21. Translation of Ferguson, *Clement*, 119–20.

known at the same time at which the rest of his writings were recognized as truly his.[63]

This widespread desire to find the actual, not just the reputed, author of a text puts a question mark beside the recent claim of Armin Baum that ancient critics did not consider a work forged so long as the contents could be thought to go back to the alleged author, whether or not he actually produced the book. In Baum's view, it did not matter so much whether the alleged author actually wrote the words; what mattered is whether the contents of the work could be traced back to the views of the alleged author. If so, ancient critics did not consider the book to be forged.[64]

Baum's detailed and learned study is useful in many ways, but this overarching thesis is problematic for a number of reasons.[65] It is true that the content of a book mattered to critics, and that it was one of the chief criteria used to establish claims of authorship. But there were other grounds as well, as we have already begun to see; moreover, these other grounds were employed precisely because ancient critics were genuinely interested in the historical question of who actually put pen to papyrus.

Before pursuing this particular issue further, it might be worthwhile pointing out a broader problem with Baum's line of argumentation, the inconvenient fact that numerous authors and groups of readers, holding wildly disparate philosophical or religious views, could claim that the contents of a particular text really were, or were not, those of the alleged author. In most instances there was no way then, and scarcely any way now, of adjudicating these claims. This will be an enormous issue once we come to the Christian materials in the following chapters. Various followers of Paul took contrary lines on such fundamental issues as the unity of the godhead, the nature of Christ, the viability of marriage and sexual relations, and so on. Some among these followers produced writings in Paul's name, all claiming that Paul himself authorized their views. The reality is that he authorized none of them. Baum's view may be theologically satisfying: apostolic pseudepigrapha can be accepted as apostolic, even if apostles did not write them, and no charge of forgery need be leveled against their pseudonymous authors. But the view is very hard to establish historically, given the nature of our evidence and our ability to trace multiple lines of thought back to apostles (e.g., that women can be active in the worship of the church or that they have to be passive and submissive instead—both views are "Pauline").

63. *Contra Faust.* 33.6; trans. by Roland Teske, *Answer to Faustus, a Manichean* (The Works of Saint Augustine: A Translation for the 21st Century, I/10) (Hyde Park, NY: New City Press, 2007). All subsequent quotations of the work will be from this translation.

64. Baum, *Pseudepigraphie*, passim.

65. One of the chief witnesses he appeals to for this view is Porphyry, in an obscure but oft-mentioned passage that discusses the writings of Pythagoras. As I will show in Chapter 5, however, Baum completely misconstrues Porphyry's comments.

That is to say, pseudonymous texts supporting divergent views, on Baum's assessment, would theoretically all have to be seen, historically, as nonproblematic in their authorial claims. But the ancients did not see it that way. If a book did not support the "correct" interpretation of Paul, then it could not be by Paul. And then it was labeled a lie, a deceit, and a bastard. The correct interpretation, however, was generally established not on historical-critical but on theological grounds. If a text agreed with the interpreter's own understanding of Paul, then it could be accepted as genuinely Pauline; if not, then it was forged.

Moreover, as I have begun to emphasize, in many instances in antiquity, critics both Christian and non-Christian were interested in the simple historical question of whether the alleged author of a work was its real author. This decision was not based purely on the question of the contents of a work, but on other grounds as well. Take the famous words of Origen on the authorship of Hebrews:

> If I were asked my personal opinion, I would say that the matter is the Apostle's but the phraseology and construction are those of someone who remembered the Apostle's teaching and wrote his own interpretation of what his master had said. So if any church regards this epistle as Paul's, it should be commended for so doing, for the primitive Church had every justification for handing it down as his. Who wrote the epistle is known to God alone: the accounts that have reached us suggest that it was either Clement, who became Bishop of Rome, or Luke, who wrote the gospel and the Acts. (Quoted in Eusebius, *H.E.* 6.25.11–14)

Origen's attitude may seem to justify Baum's view that only the contents mattered in establishing "genuine" authorship. But in fact it does not. Even though Origen agrees that the contents of the letter to the Hebrews are Pauline, he refuses to call it Pauline (even though he understands why others would want to do so). In other words, he refuses to do precisely what Baum's view suggests he should have done: accept the Pauline authorship of the book because of the Pauline contents. For Origen—at least in his one explicit discussion of the matter—the contents are not enough. He will not say a book is by Paul unless Paul actually wrote it.[66]

So too Origen's contemporary Dionysius of Alexandria, who was heavily invested in knowing who actually wrote the book Revelation. On the basis of a *stylistic* analysis, he shows that it could not have been John, the apostle and author of the Fourth Gospel and the book we now call 1 John. He concludes that it was

---

66. Elsewhere, Origen does indicate that Paul wrote Hebrews (*To Africanus*, 9; and possibly *De Principiis* 3.1.10, etc., although this is only in Rufinus' Latin, not the Greek; see also, though, *On Prayer*, 17; *Commentary on John* 2.6; 10.11). The easiest solution to these discrepancies is simply to suppose that he changed his mind on the question. It should be noted that elsewhere Origen shows an interest in knowing who actual authors were. With respect to the Petrine epistles, for example, he says that Peter "left us one acknowledged epistle, possibly two—though this is doubtful." With respect to the writings of John he says, "In addition, he left an epistle of very few lines, and possibly two more, though their authenticity is denied by some" (ἐπεὶ οὐ πάντες φασὶν γνησίους εἶναι ταύτας) (Eusebius, *H.E.* 6.25.8, 10).

instead produced by a holy and inspired man of the same name writing at the same time (Eusebius, *H.E.* 7.25.7).

Eusebius too was interested in knowing the actual authors of the early Christian writings. As one of his leading criteria he, the inveterate historian, looked to see how widely a book was used and attested by earlier authors. Writings that appear to have been unknown in earlier times were suspect, not just with respect to their canonicity but more specifically with respect to their authorship, two issues that were closely tied together (but by no means synonymous) in Eusebius' mind. Usage, though, was as important as content.

And so, for example, he has this to say about the epistles of James and Jude:

> Such is the story of James, to whom is attributed the first of the "general" epistles. Admittedly its authenticity is doubted, since few early writers refer to it (ἰστέον δὲ ὡς νοθεύεται μέν, οὐ πολλοὶ γοῦν τῶν παλαιῶν αὐτῆς ἐμνημόνευσαν), any more than to "Jude's," which is also one of the seven called general. (*H.E.* 2.23.25)

At stake here is not merely whether these books should be included in the canon, but also the fundamental issue that makes the canonical decision possible: Are these books genuinely by the ascribed authors? Or are they νόθα? On balance, Eusebius thinks the former. He engages in much the same line of argument with respect to the writings ascribed to Peter (*H.E.* 3.3.1–4). 1 Peter is genuine, because it is quoted widely; 2 Peter is not to be seen as canonical, even though some Christian leaders find it valuable. Other books such as the Acts of Peter, the Gospel of Peter, the Preaching of Peter, and the Apocalypse of Peter are to be rejected because they were not used in earlier times or in orthodox circles, to Eusebius' knowledge (*H.E.* 3.3.2). Again it may appear that Eusebius is concerned here only with issues of canon, but in fact the question of canon for him is closely tied to the more precise question of authenticity: a book not actually written by Peter and not widely accepted as being written by Peter is not to be included among the canonical writings of Peter. This is clear from the conclusion of his discussion: "These then are the works attributed to Peter, of which I have recognized only one epistle as authentic and accepted by the early fathers" (ἀλλὰ τὰ μὲν ὀνομαζόμενα Πέτρου, ὧν μόνην μίαν γνησίαν ἔγνων ἐπιστολὴν καὶ παρὰ τοῖς πάλαι πρεσβυτέροις ὡμολογημένην, τοσαῦτα. Note: γνησίαν [3.3.4]). That the issue for Eusebius was not merely canonicity but also authorship in se is seen by the circumstance that he applies the same kinds of criteria—especially lineage of usage (not contents)—in discussing works that he clearly did not consider canonical, such as 2 Clement (*H.E.* 3.38.4). If the book does not have an established lineage of usage from Clement's day, it is not to be attributed to Clement, independently of the question (Baum's) of whether the contents are Clementine.

Much the same could be said about Jerome, who determines that the letter to Jude is to be included among the Catholic epistles, but points out that it is rejected by other Christian critics because it quotes from the apocryphal book of Enoch (and surely no inspired author would quote as authoritative an apocryphal book!) (*Vir. ill.* 4). Here, as in Eusebius, the authority of the book resides in the actual author. In this instance the authenticity of the book is determined on the basis of its contents. This is not a case that supports Baum's perspective, however; for here the contents render a negative judgment (what is found in the book indicates that Jude could not have written it), not a positive one (the book is rightly attributed to Jude because the contents—apart from the wording and style—*do* go back to him). Moreover, Jerome, like Eusebius, is interested in the matter of authorship itself, that is, in who actually produced a book that goes under the name of a well-known person (and not simply on the grounds of contents).[67] Thus, for example, he argues that the work *De fato* ascribed to Minucius Felix is not actually by him, not because of its contents but because of its writing style: "although the work of a very learned man, [it] does not seem to me to correspond in style with the work mentioned above" (*Vir. ill.* 58). So too Theophilus, the sixth bishop of Antioch, composed many surviving genuine accounts, but the two books "On the Gospel" and "On the Proverbs of Solomon" are not authentic, because they "do not appear to me to correspond in style and language with the elegance and expressiveness of the above works" (*Vir. ill.* 25).[68]

And so there are two points that need to be stressed with respect to Christian approaches to forgery. On one hand, contrary to Baum, it was not simply the contents of a work that mattered; Christian critics were invested in knowing who actually wrote a work, on the basis of content, style, and established patterns of usage. On the other hand, this question of authorship did stand in a clear but ironically symbiotic relationship with the contents of a work. It was the contents that, in part (but only in part), helped determine whether an author actually wrote the book circulating under his name; but it was precisely the fact that he wrote the book that provided the authority for its contents.

Nowhere can this paradoxical situation be seen more clearly than in the famous incident of Serapion and the Gospel of Peter. Eusebius later narrates the event, from his first-hand knowledge of Serapion's autobiographical account, which is only partially quoted for us in the *Ecclesiastical History* (*H.E.* 6.12). Upon visiting the Christian community in the village of Rhossus, Serapion initially approved of their use of the Gospel of Peter, reasoning that if Peter had written a Gospel, it was obviously acceptable for liturgical use. Only after returning to Antioch did Serapion learn that the book had heretical tendencies. Procuring a copy for himself, he came to see that whereas most of it was perfectly acceptable, parts were definitely susceptible of a docetic reading. It was precisely on these grounds that he forbade the further use of the book and appears to have referred to it as the "so-called" Gospel of Peter (τοῦ λεγομένου κατὰ Πέτρον εὐαγγελίου).

67. See Vessey, "Forging," p. 507, n. 30.

68. Translations of Thomas Halton, *Saint Jerome: On Illustrious Men* (FC 100; Washington, DC: Catholic University of America Press, 1999), 84, 48. All subsequent translations of this work will be taken from this edition.

Here then is our symbiosis between literary author and authoritative literature: the Gospel would be authoritative had it been written by Peter; but the possibly heretical contents show that it could not have been written by Peter. And so the book is not authoritative. Eusebius himself adopts a similar line of thought, as when he attacks heretical forgeries in the names of the apostles Peter, Thomas, and Matthias, which "do not have the apostolic character" (ὁ τῆς φράσεως παρὰ τὸ ἦθος τὸ ἀποστολικὸν ἐναλλάττει χαρακτήρ; *H.E.* 3.25.6–7) "while the ideas and implication of their contents are so irreconcilable with true orthodoxy that they stand revealed as the forgeries of heretics." Both the style and contents are non-apostolic, and so they lack apostolic authority.

This understanding of the symbiotic relationship between authorial claims and authoritative contents did not originate with Eusebius, or with Serapion before him. It goes all the way back in the proto-orthodox heresiological tradition. Irenaeus, for example, attacks heretics for forging books in the names of others to lead their followers astray: "Besides those passages, they adduce an untold multitude of apocryphal and spurious writings [inenarrabilem multitudinem apocryphorum et perperum scripturarum, quas ipsi finxerunt], which they have composed to bewilder foolish men and such as do not understand the letters of the Truth" (*Adv. Haer.* 1.20.1).[69]

So too Tertullian: the fourfold Gospel of the orthodox is superior to the forgeries of Marcion—the heretic's creations are later in date than the apostolic writings and so must be seen as corruptions of an older truth (*Adv. Marc.* 4.5). And his contemporary, the author of the Muratorian Fragment, who rejects the letters to the Alexandrians and to the Laodiceans on the basis of their contents: they contain Marcionite teachings, were therefore not originally written by Paul, and so cannot be accepted as authoritative.[70]

The same view can be seen at the end of our period of concern, or just after, for example in the works of Augustine. Augustine uses a strictly historical argument in order to show that the theurgic letter allegedly written by Jesus to his disciples Peter and Paul could not be authentic: Paul was not one of Jesus' earthly followers. The forger of the letter must have been misled by seeing a Christian painting of the two apostles with Jesus and assumed then that the three were companions

---

69. Translation Dominic J. Unger and John J. Dillon, *St. Irenaeus of Lyons: Against the Heresies*, Vol. I (ACW 55; New York, Mahwah, NJ: Paulist Press, 1992), p. 76.

70. I do not find persuasive the attempt of A. Sundberg and M. Hahneman to redate the Muratorian Fragment from the late second to the fourth century (see A. C. Sundberg, "Canon Muratori: A Fourth Century List," *HTR* 66 [1973]: 1–41; and Geoffrey Mark Hahneman, *The Muratorian Fragment and the Development of the Canon*, Oxford: Clarendon, 1992). For incisive critiques, see Henne, "La datation du Canon de Muratori," *RB* 100 (1993): 54–75; C. E. Hill, "The Debate over the Muratorian Fragment and the Development of the Canon," *WTJ* 57 (1995): 437–52; J.-D. Kaestli, "La place du Fragment de Muratori dans l'histoire du canon. À propos de la these de Sundberg et Hahneman," *Cristianesimo nella storia* 15 (1994): 609–34; and especially Joseph Verheyden, "The Canon Muratori: A Matter of Dispute," in J.-M. Auwers and H. J. De Jonge, eds., *The Biblical Canon* (Leuven: Peeters, 2003), pp. 487–556.

during Jesus' earthly life. Since they were not, Jesus would not have written to the two of them:

> How, then, is it possible that Christ could have written those books which they wish to have it believed that He did write before His death, and which were addressed to Peter and Paul, as those among His disciples who had been most intimate with Him, seeing that up to that date Paul had not yet become a disciple of His at all? (*De cons. evang.* 1.10)[71]

As a result, the letter and the magical practices it supports were forged. In consequence, they have no authority. The authority of the writing resides in its authorship; and authorship is decided, at least in part, by the writing's contents. It is a two-way street.

As I pointed out earlier, however, this two-way street presented a problem to the early Christian critics, since it was a path accessible to just about anyone. No one saw that more clearly than Augustine himself, who protested against his Manichaean opponent Faustus: "Sinfulness has made you so deaf to the testimonies of the scriptures that you dare to say that whatever is brought forth from them against you was not said by the apostle but was written by some interpolator or other under his name" (*Contra Faust.* 33.6). Since authority resided in authorship, the easiest way to deny authority was to reject authorship. It is precisely this conundrum that made the literary and historical critical endeavors of the early Christian critics so vitally important. These faithful intelligentsia were not simply engaged in antiquarian endeavors when deciding which works were justifiably attributed to their alleged authors. This was theological discourse of the highest order, since authority resided in authorship. And so the contents of a work mattered insofar as they were genuinely penned by an authoritative figure. If the authorial claims were false, however, the text lost all claim to authority. Establishing the credibility of authorial claims was, as a result, central to the entire theological enterprise. It really did matter who wrote what.

71. Translation of S. D. F. Salmond in *NPNF*, series 1, vol. 6.

CHAPTER FIVE

Forgery in Antiquity

Motives, Techniques, Intentions, Justifications, and Criteria of Detection

The discussion of the previous chapter leads to an obvious question: If literary forgery was extensively condemned in the ancient Greek and Roman worlds, why was it, at the same time, so widely practiced? This question takes us directly to the matter of motivation: What drove so many authors to make false authorial claims? Wolfgang Speyer in particular has recognized motivation as a fundamental aspect of the broader phenomenon: "Failing to develop the intentions of forgers would be equivalent to failing to understand their forgeries. Motive alone explains the forgery."[1]

We are in the fortunate position of having vestiges of an ancient discourse on motivation. It is true that only rarely (and never in our period) do ancient forgers themselves explain why they did what they did.[2] And rarely (again, never in our period) is there systematic reflection on the matter by critics; only later writers attempted taxonomies of motivation. These are still worth examining. But from our period itself (prior to the fifth century CE) we do have numerous discussions of individual instances and clear ascriptions of motive by those who claim to have uncovered the deceitful practices of others. These discussions do not give unqualified indications of what individual forgers were actually thinking when they

1. "Der Verzicht auf ein Herausarbeiten der Absichten der Fälscher wäre gleichbedeutend mit dem Verzicht, die Fälschungen zu verstehen. Nur das Motiv erklärt die Fälschung." *Die literarische Fälschung*, p. 9.

2. We have only one writing from our period in which a forger admits to what he did, the letter of "Mithridates" that indicates why he produced pseudepigraphic responses by the addressees of the letters of Brutus (assuming, with Calhoun, that this letter is not itself pseudepigraphic). Unfortunately Mithridates does not explain his motivation. See Robert Matthew Calhoun, "The Letter of Mithridates: A Neglected Item of Ancient Epistolary Theory," in Jörg Frey et al., eds., *Pseudepigraphie und Verfasserfiktion*, pp. 295–330.

produced their work: a critic ascribing motivation to another is a different kind of "evidence" from forgers explaining their own motivations.[3] At the same time, the ancient discussions do give us a clear sense of what motivations were conceivable, sensible, and plausible in the ancient context. Before creating a kind of taxonomy of our own, we might consider the one instance, from a slightly later period, in which a forger attempted to justify his actions once they were detected.

A LATER DISCUSSION OF MOTIVATION

The author was a Christian presbyter of Marseille named Salvian, who around 440 CE published the book *Timothei ad Ecclesiam Libri IV*.[4] The name "Timothy," of course, had clear apostolic connections from Pauline times. In his letter to the church, "Timothy" inveighed against a community that had grown rich and soft, while advocating radical almsgiving to the church (in the divestment of property). In his concern for total commitment to the gospel and an ascetic style of life, Salvian was not far removed from the concerns of another author, from about the same time, a pseudonymous "Titus" (the other of Paul's Pastoral companions) who wrote a scathing attack on Christians who indulged in the joys of the flesh, condemning anyone, married or not, who engaged in sexual activities. The author of the forged letter of Titus was never discovered. But the author of the forged letter of Timothy was, by none other than his own bishop, Salonius of Geneva.

Long before the incident, Salonius and Salvian had been members of the monastic community at Lerins, where, for a time, Salvian was Salonius' teacher. But eventually the student surpassed the instructor in the ecclesiastical hierarchy, and when the letter of "Timothy" came to his attention, he immediately, for reasons never given, suspected that in fact it had been written by his former teacher and colleague. He evidently confronted Salvian on the matter, and Salvian wrote a letter in self-defense.

In this, his ninth letter, Salvian does not directly admit to having written *Timothei ad Ecclesiam*. But there is really no doubt about the matter, as he explains why the pseudonymous author (of whom he speaks in the third person) did what he did. That is to say, he explains his motivations.

On one hand, Salvian insists, the name of an author should not matter to a reader: "In the case of every book we ought to be more concerned about the intrinsic value of its contents than about the name of its author."[5] So too, "Since the

---

3. On the theoretical problem of establishing authorial intentions—which I am here differentiating from "motives," although obviously some of the hypothetical issues are the same—see p. 30, n. 32.

4. For the works of Salvian, see the edition in the *Sources Chrétienne*, 176, 220. The first English translation of *ad Ecclesiam*, with introduction, was published by A. Haefner, "A Unique Source for the Study of Ancient Pseudonymity," *ATh R* 16 (1934): 8–15.

5. I am using the translation of Haefner, "Unique Source"; see also Jeremiah F. O'Sullivan, tr., *The Writings of Salvian, The Presbyter* (Washington, DC: Catholic University Press of America, 1947).

name [of the author] is immaterial, there is no use in asking about the author's name so long as the reader profits from the book itself." These pleas ring hollow, however, in light of the rest of Salvian's self-defense: If he really thought that an author's name did not matter, why would he write pseudonymously? Why not write in his own name? Or even better, if names do not matter, why not write the book anonymously? The question is exacerbated by the fact that Salvian otherwise wrote extensively in his own name. His *De gubernatione dei* still survives, and other works were known in Christian antiquity.[6]

Still, Salvian's answer is straightforward. He recognizes his own insignificance and knows that readers do in fact think it matters who produced a writing. He therefore "wisely selected a pseudonym for his book for the obvious reason that he did not wish the obscurity of his own person to detract from the influence of his otherwise valuable book." If the authority of a book is rooted in the prestige of an author, then obviously a pseudonym is necessary: "For this reason the present writer chose to conceal his identity in every respect for fear that his true name would perhaps detract from the influence of his book, which really contains much that is exceedingly valuable."

Given this confession of motivation, what Salvian claims next may seem a bit surprising, if not downright duplicitous. Why did he choose the name Timothy in particular? Readers naturally took the name to refer to Paul's Pastoral companion, hence Salonius' distraught reaction. But in clear tension with his earlier assertion that an unknown person would not be accepted as an authoritative source, Salvian claims that he chose the name purely for its symbolic associations. Just as the evangelist Luke wrote to "Theophilus" because he wrote "for the love of God," so too the author of this treatise wrote as "Timothy," that is, "for the honor of God." In other words, he chose the pseudonym as a pen name.

Even though many critics today continue simply to take Salvian's word for it,[7] the explanation does not satisfy. If Salvian meant what he said, that the reason for choosing a pseudonymous name was to authorize the account—since a treatise written by an obscure or unknown person has no authority—then how can he also say that the specific pseudonymous name was not that of an authority figure (Paul's companion Timothy) but of an unknown, obscure, and anonymous person intent on honoring God?

Scholars determined to follow Salvian's lead in getting him off Salonius' hook have pursued various angles. Norbert Brox thinks it significant that Salvian claims in the letter to be humble ("we are urged to avoid every pretense of earthly vainglory. . . . The writer . . . is humble in his own sight, self-effacing, thinking only of his own utter insignificance"); for Brox, the choice of the pseudonym was

6. See the list of Gennadius, *Catalogus virorum illustrium*, 68, cited by O'Sullivan, *The Writings of Salvian*, pp. 5–6.

7. E.g., Norbert Brox, "Quis ille auctor? Pseudonymität und Anonymität bei Salvian," *VC* 40 (1986): 55–65.

consistent with ascetic practices of self-abnegation that Salvian, in part, endorsed in the treatise of "Timothy."[8] Brox notes that on two other occasions in his writings Salvian quotes himself, both times anonymously. He chose, in other words, to keep himself, and so his name, out of the limelight.

There is some merit to this view, but it does not really solve the problem.[9] Quoting oneself in the third person is not the same thing as writing in the name of someone else: if keeping out of the public eye was the key, then, as I have pointed out, Salvian could have written *Ad Ecclesiam* anonymously. Moreover, the other examples of the literary self-abnegation that Brox cites—starting with Paul's discussion of his ecstatic removal to the third heaven in 2 Corinthians—involve instances in which an author actually uses his own name (i.e., 2 Corinthians is orthonymous). Brox does not, that is, adduce anything analogous to Salvian's letter. What is completely analogous is the slew of forged writings from the early Christian tradition, numerous texts put in circulation by authors claiming to be apostles and companions of apostles, including letters allegedly written both to and by Timothy and Titus, canonical and noncanonical. Moreover, it should be reemphasized that Salvian did write other books using his own name.

Even less convincing is the more recent claim of David Lambert that Salvian's ninth letter was actually written as a preface to *Ad Ecclesiam*.[10] It is true that in the scant manuscript tradition it is located there; but one can easily imagine why a scribe might arrange Salvian's writings in that order, so as to explain the true nature of the authorship of the tractate. It can hardly make sense for Salvian to have put it there initially: the letter is a response to objections raised subsequent to the publication of the tractate, a self-defense for having circulated it under the name of someone else.

We do not know how Salonius reacted to Salvian's defensive ninth letter. But it is relatively clear how he reacted to the tractate *Ad Ecclesiam* itself. He considered it a forgery, he objected to the literary practice, and he called the author to account for it. Moreover, it is difficult to take Salvian at his word that he never meant anyone to think that he really was Timothy, the companion of Paul. Otherwise his explanation that no one would heed an unknown or obscure author makes no sense: Who is more unknown or obscure than a person who does not exist, or one whose name is not even given? But his explanation for why he could not write the book orthonymously is of considerable value: it shows that one of the motivations for producing pseudepigraphic works was to get a hearing for one's views, by claiming to be someone who deserved to be heard. That will be a fundamental point for the rest of our study.

Before stressing its importance for the polemical forgeries of early Christianity, we would do well to consider the range of motivations for forgery attested in our ancient sources.

---

8. Ibid.

9. For the following objections, see David Lambert, "*The Pseudonymity of Salvian's Timothy ad Ecclesiam*," *StPatr* 38, ed. Maurice Wiles et al. (Leuven: Peeters, 2001), pp. 422–28.

10. Ibid.

TAXONOMY OF MOTIVATIONS

It will be useful at the outset to differentiate between the concepts of motivation and intention. An intention indicates what a person plans to accomplish; a motivation indicates why she or he wants to accomplish it. A novelist may intend to write a best-selling book (that is what he would like to accomplish, his intention); but he may be motivated by a range of factors, including, for example, the desire to make a vast fortune and to become a household name. Later I will be furthering my argument that forgers in antiquity intended to deceive their reader into thinking they were someone other than who they really were.[11] But what drove them to do so? That is the question of motivation. I should stress that just as texts could perform a range of functions—rarely does an author write for just one reason—so too a forgery could be motivated by a number of reasons. The categories presented here, in other words, are not meant to be mutually exclusive.

To Make a Profit

It is sometimes, wrongly, claimed that the only reason for producing a forgery is to turn a profit. The New Testament scholar J. C. Fenton, for example, in an attempt to exculpate the authors of canonical pseudepigrapha from charges of deceit, argues that "A forger is one who writes in the name of another for his own profit: they [NT authors] did not do so. Forgery involves deceit for gain: pseudonymity did not."[12] Not only is this playing fast and loose with terminology (by fiat, a forger is out for personal profit), it overlooks an entire host of reasons that forgers had for doing what they did.

Still, it is true that on occasion—though not within the early Christian tradition—forgers were driven by a profit motive. The best-known evidence comes from Galen, who indicates that the construction of, and competition between, the libraries of Alexandria and Pergamum spawned an active forgery market, driven by the need of the respective librarians to boast holdings in Aeschylus, Sophocles, and Euripides, along with Plato, Hippocrates, Aristotle, and others.[13] As he puts the matter in one place: "For before the kings in both Alexandria and Pergamum eagerly endeavored to purchase ancient works, no one as yet produced pseudonymous writings (οὐδέπω ψευδῶς ἐπεγέγραπτο σύγγραμμα)." Once money could be made for such texts, however, all that changed: many pseudepigrapha were then written (πολλὰ ψευδῶς ἐπιγράφοντες).[14]

Galen is wrong about the first part, since there were ample numbers of forgeries before the construction of the Hellenistic libraries. But the idea that plays and

11. On intention, see p. 30, n. 3.

12. J. C. Fenton, "Pseudonymity in the New Testament," *Theology* 58 (1955): 55.

13. See, e.g., *In Hippocratis de natura hominis commentarium*, Book 2, Proem.

14. *In Hipp. De nat. hom. Comm.* 1. 44, the fuller passage is conveniently quoted in Baum, *Pseudepigraphie*, p. 224.

treatises in the names of the masters started to appear with alarming frequency once someone was willing to pay for them is completely plausible. Galen elsewhere gives a specific, related instance: one enterprising fellow took Hippocrates' *Nature of Man* and Polybius' *Regimen of Health*, both small-size volumes, and combined them in order to fetch a better price at one of the libraries.[15]

The evidence for this motive is not limited to Galen. In one of his humorous satires, *The Mistaken Critic*, Lucian charges:

> There is nothing invidious in fending off destitution by every means. . . . However you will permit me to praise one thing, anyhow, that very pretty performance of yours when you yourself—and you know it—composed the "Tisias' Handbook," that work of an ill-omened crow, thus robbing that stupid old man of thirty gold pieces; for because of Tisias' name he paid seven hundred and fifty drachmas for the book, gulled into it by you.[16]

After our period, Olympiodorus claims that since Juba, king of Libya, so loved Pythagorean writings, Ptolemy Philadelphius Aristotelian writings, and Pisistratus tyrant of Athens Homeric writings, they were willing to pay gold for them. As a result, many entrepreneurial types forged such works and sold them on demand.[17] John Philoponus confirms the report about both Juba and Ptolemy.[18] Furthermore, in one of the classic studies of forgery, A. Gudeman speculates that the hundreds of pseudonymous speeches and orations from antiquity are best accounted for by thinking that booksellers cobbled together as many school exercises on different orators as possible in order to have an exhaustive collection for sale, and so outdo their competition.[19]

For Political and Religious Authorization

More commonly, forgeries were produced for political and religious reasons (these are not always distinct, of course), to authorize or attack, under authority, political or religious figures and institutions. A number of instances are attested of forgers producing prophecies or oracular pronouncements for matters of state, such as when, at the beginning of the reign of Emperor Galba, a two-hundred-year-old set of verses was "discovered" in the temple of Jupiter Clunia indicating

15. *In Hipp. De nat. hom, Comm.* 2 pr. See Ann Ellis Hanson, "Galen: Author and Critic," in Glenn W. Most, ed., *Editing Texts, Texte edieren* (Göttingen: Vandenhoeck & Ruprecht, 1998), pp. 22–53, esp. p. 33.

16. *Mistaken Critic*, 30; translation of A. M. Harmon, *Lucian*, vol. 5; LCL (Cambridge, MA: Harvard University Press, 1972).

17. Olympiodorus, *Prolegomena*; for text, see Baum, *Pseudepigraphie*, pp. 238–41.

18. See Speyer, *Literarische Fälschung*, pp. 112, 333; C. W. Müller, "Die neuplatonischen Aristoteleskommentatoren über die Ursachen der Pseudepigraphie," *Rheinisches Museum für Philologie* 112 (1969): 120–26.

19. "Literary Frauds Among the Greeks," pp. 52–74.

that a ruler would come from Spain.[20] The verses may have been presented as an oracular pronouncement of Jupiter himself. If so, this is forgery with aplomb: the alleged author is not claiming to be a famous human authority but the king of the gods. In any event, there was a long tradition of such oracular forgeries; Alexander the Great was one beneficiary, as in the course of his conquests he was presented with a forged oracle on a copper plate near the city of Xanthus in Lycia, which indicated that the time would come when the Persian Empire should be destroyed by the Greeks.[21]

So too the supporters of Julius Caesar could find cold comfort in an oracle "discovered" in Capua, in the grave of its founder Capys, which predicted the murder of a "son of Ilium" by his own relatives, after which things would go badly in Italy. Speyer suspects that Octavian and Antony themselves were responsible for the forged oracle, as it provided them with divine sanction to ostracize the murderers. Suetonius, who reports the event, swears to its truthfulness: "And let no one think this tale a myth or a lie, for it is vouched for by Cornelius Balbus, an intimate friend of Caesar."[22] Somewhat later, Suetonius reports, Augustus was the victim rather than the culprit of a forgery. But in this case he had the last word, as he punished a certain Patavinus for having "circulated a most scathing letter about him (Augustus) under the name of the young Agrippa."[23] The forging of political letters was a salient issue in the earlier struggles for power at the end of the Republic, as Asconius informs us in no uncertain terms in his commentary on Cicero's *In toga candida*, faulting, once again, Antony, but this time Catilina as well (*In toga candida*, 94). Other forgeries involving political intrigues are reported by Josephus, including one I have already mentioned, a letter forged in the name of Herod's son Alexander that spoke of his plan to murder his father.[24]

At other times forgeries were used to authorize the establishment of religious institutions, such as the oracle at Abonoteichus established by Alexander, Lucian's infamous "False Prophet." To demonstrate the divine approval of the new oracle, according to Lucian, Alexander and a cohort forged a set of bronze tablets and buried them in the temple of Apollo in Chalcedon. When dug up, these divine writings indicated that Asclepius and his father Apollo were soon to move to Pontus and take up residence at Abonoteichus. Here is one instance in which a forgery was spectacularly successful (*Alexander the False Prophet*, 10).

---

20. Suetonius, *Galba*, 9.2

21. Plutarch, *Alexander*, 17.2 (who does not label it a forgery).

22. *Life of Julius*, 81; translation of J. C. Rolfe *Suetonius*, LCL (Cambridge, MA: Harvard University, 1951). See Wolfgang Speyer, *Bücherfunde in der Glaubenswerbung der Antike. Mit einem Ausblick auf Mittelalter und Neuzeit* (Göttingen: Vandenhoeck & Ruprecht, 1970), pp. 71–72.

23. *Life of Augustus* 51; translation of Rolfe in the Loeb.

24. *War* 1.26.3. For a further example involving Antipater, see *War* 1.32.6.

As Apologia

A closely related motivation, especially in Jewish and Christian circles, involves forgeries that functioned apologetically. Among Jewish instances, none is better known than the Letter of Aristeas, defending the divine origin of the Greek translation of the Hebrew Scriptures.[25] Also worth noting are the surviving Sibylline oracles.[26] The twelve books, numbered, somewhat confusingly, 1–9 and 11–14, have been heavily Christianized; but only book 6 (and possibly the fragmentary book 7) is completely Christian. All the others are Jewish in whole or part. We will be returning to a fuller discussion of the Sibyllines in a later chapter; here it is enough to note their apologetic function. The original Jewish oracles present an ancient, divinely inspired, pagan prophetess who discusses, sometimes cryptically, the institutions, practices, and views of Judaism. What better authority to shore up a religious tradition under periodic attack by its (non-Jewish) cultured despisers? When Christians took over the texts, they served a doubly apologetic purpose: a pagan prophetess favorable to Judaism and antagonistic to Rome predicts the incarnation of the Son of God. Now it is the Christian faith that is attested as divine by an inspired and unimpeachable source, pagan in origin and Jewish by inclination.[27]

Whether Jewish apologists made extensive use of the Sibyllina is difficult to say; but there is no ambiguity about the delight that Christians took in them, as they are explicitly mentioned as early as Justin and cited as early as Athenagoras.[28] They caused no little controversy by the end of the second century, as the pagan opponent of all things Christian, Celsus, accused Christians of inventing the prophecies themselves. Origen, in his inimitable style, challenged his long-dead opponent to prove it: "[Celsus asserts] that we have interpolated many blasphemous things in her verses, though he does not give any instance of our interpolation. He would have proved this point had he showed that the older copies were purer and had not the verses which he supposes to have been interpolated."[29]

Some Jewish apologetic forgeries served clear political purposes, including the letter mentioned by Josephus between Arius, King of Sparta (died 265 BCE), to the Jewish high priest Onias III, a letter that showed the Jews to be blood relatives of the Spartans—obviously of some apologetic moment for Jews in the

---

25. See the discussion on p. 66.

26. Among the significant studies, see esp. H. W. Parke, *Sibyls and Sibylline Prophecy in Classical Antiquity*, ed. by B. C. McGing (London: Routledge, 1988); and John J. Collins, "The Development of the Sibylline Tradition," *ANRW* II. 20 (1987): 421–59. Useful translations are available in Collins, "Sibylline Oracles," in James H. Charlesworth, ed., OTP (Garden City, NY: Doubleday, 1983), vol. 1, pp. 317–472.

27. See further pp. 508–19.

28. For a full study of the patristic attestations, see the now classic study of Bard Thompson, "Patristic Use of the Sibylline Oracles," *RR* 16 (1952): 115–36.

29. *Contra Celsum* 7.56; Translation of Henry Chadwick, *Origen: Contra Celsum* (Cambridge: University Press, 1953).

Hellenistic world.[30] The letter is cited as well in 1 Macc. 12.7–9. In other instances the apologia functioned more to justify Jewish religious practices (if, again, we can differentiate on any level between politics and religion). This is the case with the lesser-known Letter of Mordechai (adopted father of Esther) to Alexander the Great, a Jewish apologia for the worship of the one God instead of idols and for maintaining high ethical standards, including the refusal to assert power and to engage in sexual immorality. The letter, originally in Greek, occurs at the beginning of some manuscripts of the Alexander Romance, but dates from early imperial times.[31]

Christians too employed epistolary forgeries for apologetic ends. This continues to be the most plausible explanation for the correspondence of Paul and Seneca.[32] Christians of the late fourth century were perplexed by the fact that the great apostle of the early church, whose powerful and persuasive writings formed the basis not only of the New Testament but also of the church's entire theology, was completely unknown to other great thinkers of the day. The forged attempt to show that Paul was revered by none other than Seneca is widely seen today as rather feeble. Little of substance is said in the letters, and Seneca reproves the apostle for his rather pedestrian writing style. In Christian antiquity, on the other hand, the letters were a real boon, and were accepted as authentic—and as irrefragable evidence of the apostle's greatness—almost immediately. They are paraded to apologetic effect already by Jerome (*Vir. ill.* 12) and Augustine (*Epist.* 153,14).

One could well argue for a similar apologetic function lying behind the forged correspondence of Jesus and Abgar, cited by Eusebius and forming, then, the basis for the *Doctrina Addai*.[33] As we will see later, the letters serve an anti-Judaic purpose; but in no small measure they also elevate Jesus' importance. Far from being an obscure preacher from rural nowhere, he is recognized by one of the great kings of the region and his help is solicited in a time of need.[34] Royal acclamation comes to Jesus in yet other, nonepistolary, forgeries, including above all the Acts of Pilate and the other works of the Pilate cycle.[35] Here, rather than being guilty of crimes against the state, Jesus is portrayed as innocent, royal, and even divine—confessed to be divine, in fact, by the Roman governor Pontius Pilate, by

30. Actually the dates do not work; this must be Onias I (*Ant.* 12, 226f.). Josephus does not call the letter forged.

31. See esp. the discussion of Alfons Fürst et al., *Der apokryphe Briefwechsel zwischen Seneca und Paulus*, SAPERE XI (Tübingen: Mohr Siebeck, 2006).

32. For an alternative explanation, that the correspondence is merely a rhetorical exercise from a Christian school, see above, p. 45, n. 35. For fuller discussion see pp. 520–27.

33. For an English translation of the correspondence, see Ehrman and Pleše, *Apocryphal Gospels*, pp. 413–17.

34. Of even greater importance, as Maria Doerfler has reminded me: the letter serves to elevate the status of the Christian community in Edessa by connecting it directly to the earthly Jesus himself. See the study of the later *Doctrina* in Sidney Griffiths, "The *Doctrina Addai* as a Paradigm of Christian Thought in Edessa in the Fifth Century," *Hugoye* 6.2 (2003).

35. For translations see Ehrman and Pleše, *Apocryphal Gospels*, pp. 419–557.

King Herod, and by the Roman Emperor Tiberius himself. I will have more to say about the Pilate cycle in a later chapter.[36]

Defamation of Character

Polemics can be seen as the flip side of apologetics, attack rather than defense. Not surprisingly, assaults on others—for political, philosophical, or personal reasons—are among the most widely attested motivations for the production of forgeries in antiquity.

We have already seen instances of political attacks in Cicero's complaints as amplified by Asconius (*In toga candida*, 94); in the court of Augustus, as recorded by Suetonius (*Life of Augustus*, 51, 55); and in the household of Herod described by Josephus (*War* 1, 26, 3).

Philosophical attacks facilitated by forgery were at least as common, or even more so, judging at least from our surviving sources. One of the better-known instances is related by Pausanias in his story of Anaximenes, a rhetorician who, like all good rhetoricians, was skilled in imitating the style of others. Out of a personal vendetta against his fellow rhetorician Theopompus, Anaximenes wrote and widely circulated a treatise in his opponent's name, following closely his style; the treatise abused the citizens of Athens, Sparta, and Thebes. As Pausanias tells us, "Though Anaximenes was the author of the treatise, hatred of Theopompus grew throughout the length of Greece" (*Description of Greece*, 6.18.5).[37]

A comparable account is found in Diogenes Laertius, who indicates that Diotimus, a philosophical opponent of Epicurus, circulated fifty obscene letters in his name (*Lives* 10.3). This did nothing, as one might imagine, for Epicurus' reputation as a hedonist. Evidence that the story is not simply apocryphal is provided by Athenaeus, who indicates, as we have seen, that one of Epicurus' incensed followers, Zeno, tracked Diotimus down and murdered him for his spiteful act (*Banqueters* 13.611 B).

Other writings of Epicurus that were commonly accepted as authentic in antiquity spoke harshly of representatives of other philosophical schools. As Diogenes indicates:

> Epicurus used to call this Nausiphanes jelly-fish, an illiterate, a fraud, and a trollop; Plato's school he called "the toads of Dionysius," their master himself

---

36. Some have argued that the imperial rescripts designed to curtail and regulate the persecutions of Christians are best seen as apologetically driven forgeries by Christians (see Speyer, *Literarische Fälschung*, pp. 252–55). More recent scholars have found grounds for taking many of the rescripts as authentic. See Denis Minns, "The Rescript of Hadrian," in Sara Parvis and Paul Foster, eds., *Justin Martyr and His Worlds* (Minneapolis: Fortress, 2007), pp. 38–49; and Paul Keresztes, "The Emperor Antoninus Pius and the Christians," *JEH* 22 (1971): 1–18.

37. Translation of W. H. S. Jones, *Pausanias: Description of Greece*. LCL (Cambridge, MA: Harvard University, 1918).

> the "golden" Plato, and Aristotle a profligate. . . . Protagoras a pack carrier, the scribe of Democritus, and village school master; Heraclitus a muddler. . . . The Cynics foes of Greece; the Dialecticians despoilers; and Pyrrho an ignorant boor.[38]

Cicero says something similar.[39] W. Crönert, however, convincingly argues that these alleged writings of Epicurus in fact all derive from a single letter written by a single author, forged, again, in order to cast aspersions on Epicurus' reputation.[40] The letter is not one of those produced by Diotimus, since those, unlike this one, were obscene. In any event, slandering Epicurus through forgery appears to have been de rigueur.

Politicians and philosophers were not the only ones subject to forged assault, as we saw at the outset of the study in the case of the "Parthenopaeus" forged in the name of Sophocles by Dionysius the Renegade, in part to make his former teacher Heraclides look foolish. On several occasions Martial complains about poems forged in his name to sully his reputation.

> My page has not wounded even those it justly hates, and fame won from another's blush is not dear to me! What does this avail me when certain folk would pass off as mine darts wet with the blood of Lycambes, and under my name a man vomits his viperous venom who owns he cannot bear the light of day? (*Epigrams* 7.12)[41]
>
> The scurrilities of home-born slaves, low railing, and the foul insults of a hawker's tongue . . . [these] a certain skulking poet scatters abroad and would have them appear as mine. Do you believe this Priscus? That a parrot speaks with the voice of a quail. . . . Why should I toil to be known so evilly when stillness can cost me nothing? (*Epigrams* 10.3)[42]

With other public figures, the attacks were more direct, as comes out in the trial of Apuleius:

> And then there was that fabricated letter that was neither written by my hand nor plausibly forged. They intended it to show that I worked upon the woman by means of blandishments. But why use blandishments if I had put my trust in magic? Anyway, how did this letter come into their hands, for, naturally, it would have been sent to Pudentilla by way of a trusted person, as happens in such cases. And moreover, why would I write in such defective words, such barbarous

38. *Lives* 10, 8; translation of R. D. Hicks *Diogenes Laertius*.

39. *De natura deorum* 1.33; see also Sextus Empiricus, 599; Athenaeus, *Banq.* 8.354.

40. W. Crönert, *Kolotes und Menedemos* (Amsterdam: Adolf M. Hakkert, 1965), pp. 16–24.

41. Translations of Martial are from Walter C. A. Ker, *Martial: Epigrams* LCL, rev. ed. (Cambridge, MA: Harvard University, 1968).

42. See also 7.72, quoted on p. 81.

> language? . . . Yes, this is how things are, it is plain for everyone: the man who was not able to read a letter by Pudentilla in perfect Greek had less trouble in reading this one and put it across better, since it was his own. (*Apol.* 87)[43]

So too in Philostratus' defense of the rectitude of Apollonius in the face of published opposition: "And they have forged a certain letter (καὶ τινα ἐπιστολὴν ἀνέπλασαν) in the Ionic dialect, of tedious prolixity, in which they pretend that Apollonius went down on his knees to Domitian and besought him to release him of his bonds."[44]

Analogous instances occur in Christian sources, as when Augustine avers that the enemies of Christ have attempted to slur the Savior's reputation by associating him with magical practices, in a letter forged in his name addressed to Peter and Paul (*Cons. Evang.* 1.10). Jerome, as we have seen, on one occasion had to defend himself against slurs leveled against him in a forged correspondence: "he found there a letter purporting to be written by me . . . in all of which there is not a word of truth.[45]

The use of forgery in polemical contexts, in any event, was widespread, as seen clearly by Horst Balz: "Forgeries were considered literary means of war and were answered with counter-forgeries."[46] Further examples of this phenomenon from within the Christian literary tradition will occupy us for the bulk of this study.

To Supplement the Tradition

Some forgeries appear to have been produced in order to fill in a lacuna known to exist in a tradition. As an example, Plato indicates in the Phaedo (60 D) that while awaiting his death in prison, Socrates composed some "lyrics," based on Aesop's fables and the Prelude to Apollo. Later some such verses were in circulation, as attested by Diogenes Laertius, who indicates that some people claimed that Socrates composed a final paean to Apollo and Artemis between his condemnation and death, two lines of which are quoted: "All hail, Apollo, Delos' lord! Hail Artemis, ye noble pair!" The authenticity of the lines, however, were called into doubt, as noted by Diogenes himself: "But Dionysodorus denies that he wrote the paean."[47]

---

43. Translation of Vincent Hunink in Stephen Harris et al., *Apuleius: Rhetorical Works* (New York: Oxford University, 2001), p. 105.

44. *Life of Apollonius*, 7.35. Translation of F. C. Conybeare, LCL (Cambridge, MA: Harvard University, 1912).

45. *Adv. Rufin.* 2.24.

46. "Fälschungen galten als literarische Kampfmittel und wurden mit Gegenfälschungen beantwortet." "Anonymität und Pseudepigraphie im Urchristentum: Überlegungen zum literarischen und theologischen Problem der urchristlichen und gemeinantiken Pseudepigraphie," *ZTK* 66 (1969): 409.

47. *Lives* 2, 42.

The Christian tradition attests numerous forgeries intended to fill gaps in the dominical and apostolic traditions. In no small measure this accounts for the stories of Jesus' infancy in wide circulation, later to be written down in such works as the (redactionally) pseudepigraphic Infancy Gospel of Thomas and the Gospel of Pseudo-Matthew, and for the narratives of his activities between his death and resurrection, as in the Gospel of Nicodemus. From the apostolic side the most famous instance is "Paul's" extant letter to the Laodiceans, to which we will devote considerable attention later. If nothing else, the letter was occasioned in part by the mention of some such correspondence in the canonical, but also probably forged, letter to the Colossians (4:16). If a letter "from Laodicea" was said to have once existed, it is no surprise that someone—or more than one person, as we will see—invented a version of it. The surviving text may well have been meant also to provide an alternative to the Marcionite forgery already in circulation, much as somewhat later, the Christian Acts of Pilate, detailing episodes from Jesus' trial and death, were meant to replace the earlier, and extremely popular, but forged, pagan Acts of Pilate, which probably explained in narrative detail how Jesus fully deserved his fate.[48]

Philosophical Schools?

Judging from discussions of ancient practices of pseudepigraphy in New Testament scholarship, one might think that one of the most commonly attested contexts in antiquity for writing under an assumed name was in the philosophical schools, where, allegedly, students commonly wrote treatises of their own but signed them in the name of their teacher as an act of humility, since, after all, the thoughts of the student were simply those given him by one who was greater. In point of fact, this is one of the least attested motivations for pseudepigrapha in antiquity, and there are solid reasons for questioning whether it was ever a motivation at all. As this judgment stands at odds with what Neutestamentlers have been taught and have themselves taught for decades, it will be necessary to devote a considerable amount of attention to the issue and to the ancient evidence that lies at the heart of it.

Pseudepigraphy in the Philosophical Schools: The Widespread Scholarly View

The common view of New Testament scholars has been recently expressed in an otherwise helpful article on "Pseudonymity and the New Testament Canon" by Harry Gamble, who maintains that there were occasions in antiquity where "pseudonymous authorship appears to have been conventional and innocuous," giving as his key example the "followers of Pythagoras" who "composed

48. See the discussions on pp. 350–58 and 439–45.

philosophic and scientific works under his name, ascribing to him all that they knew."[49] So too, Margaret MacDonald, in her commentary on Colossians and Ephesians, can state: "Viewing Colossians (or Ephesians) as deutero-Pauline should not be mistakenly understood as meaning that these documents are simply examples of forgery. For example, to write in the name of a philosopher who was one's patron could be seen as a sign of honor bestowed upon that person."[50] So too in another standard commentary on Colossians, Markus Barth and Helmut Blank claim that: "Pseudonymous documents, especially letters with philosophical content, were set in circulation because disciples of a great man intended to express, by imitation, their adoration of their revered master and to secure or to promote his influence upon a later generation under changed circumstances."[51] And in a study of Ephesians Michael Gese maintains:

> Students to a greater or lesser extent put the thoughts of their teachers into writing, whereas great heads of schools frequently taught only orally. The authorial ascription therefore named the intellectual author to whom in the last instance the content of the work could be traced. People in antiquity did not perceive such an ascription as forgery.[52]

I cite these studies not because they are striking in their novelty, but because they express the *opinio communis*.[53]

This view, however, is not only expressed in commentaries on New Testament pseudepigrapha. It is a major contention among scholars of forgery as well, as a look at the recent study of Armin Baum and the older work of Norbert Brox makes particularly clear.[54]

---

49. "Pseudonymity and the New Testament Canon," in Jörg Frey et al., eds., *Pseudepigraphie und Verfasserfiktion*, p. 359.

50. Margaret MacDonald, *Colossians and Ephesians*, SP 17 (Collegeville, MN: Liturgical Press, 2000), p. 8.

51. *Colossians* AB 34B (New York: Doubleday, 1994), p. 123.

52. "Die Schüler brachten ja mehr oder weniger die Gedanken ihres Lehrers in schriftliche Form, während große Schulhäupter oftmals nur mündlich lehrten. Durch die Verfasserangabe wurde damit der geistige Autor benannt, auf den der Inhalt des Werkes letztlich zurückging. Eine solche Zuschreibung wurde vom antiken Menschen wohl nicht als Fälschung empfunden." *Das Vermächtnis des Apostels: Die Rezeption der paulinischen Theologie im Epheserbrief*, WUNT 2; 99 (Tübingen: Mohr Siebeck, 1997), p. 9. For another recent representative of the view, see Angela Standhartinger, *Studien zur Entstehungsgeschichte und Intention des Kolosserbriefs* (Leiden: Brill, 1999).

53. The most recent example of a scholar who presents the view nonproblematically is Richard Pervo, in his otherwise interesting *The Making of Paul: Constructions of the Apostle in Early Christianity* (Minneapolis: Fortress, 2010), pp. 6–10.

54. Baum, *Pseudepigraphie*, pp. 51–57; Brox, *Falsche Verfasserangaben*, pp. 71–75. It appears even in studies of Pythagoras himself. Thus David R. Fideler, "Introduction," in *The Pythagorean Sourcebook and Library: An Anthology of Ancient Writings Which Relate to Pythagoras and Pythagorean Philosophy*, compiled and translated by Kenneth Sylvan Guthrie (Grand Rapids, MI: Phanes Press, 1987):

One might ask what ancient evidence New Testament scholars provide in support of their assertions about the pseudepigraphic practices of the philosophical schools. In most cases—for example, in the vast majority of biblical commentaries —the answer is completely unambiguous: as a rule, they cite no evidence for the practice at all. The existence of the practice is simply asserted, stated as a fact, as if it must be so because so many scholars have assumed it is so. It is striking that those few (e.g., Baum) who do appeal to ancient evidence never cite any sources from the time of the New Testament or of the second century. In no small measure this is because no such evidence exists.

The sources that are sometimes discussed—at some length by Baum—come from later times. The two that have figured most prominently in the discussion are the Neoplatonists Porphyry and Iamblichus, who speak of the literary output of the school of Pythagoras, who lived eight hundred years earlier. As it turns out, however, one of these two sources, Porphyry, does not say what scholars have claimed he says, and the other, Iamblichus, is highly problematic for reconstructing what actually happened in the Pythagorean school. Neither source mentions anything about "common practices" of any of the other philosophical schools, let alone of philosophical schools in general, and neither says a word about practices of pseudepigraphy in the time period of our concern, the early Christian centuries.

OTHER ANCIENT SOURCES

Before turning our attention to the alleged evidence of Porphyry and Iamblichus, we might consider several other sources that could conceivably be used to support the idea that students of philosophers wrote with impunity in the names of their teachers. In his thirty-third epistle, Seneca indicates that whereas the sayings of the Stoic teachers all differ from one another, those of the Epicureans are unified: "With them, on the other hand, whatever Hermarchus says, or Metrodorus, is ascribed to one source. In that brotherhood, everything that any man utters is spoken under the leadership and commanding authority of one alone."[55] This statement could conceivably be construed as meaning that everything an Epicurean wrote he as-

---

> These writings are attributed to original members of the Pythagorean school which in fact is actually not the case [i.e., they did not actually write them]. This does not mean that these writings are "forgeries" in the modern sense of the word, for it was a fairly common practice in antiquity to publish writings as pseudepigrapha, attributing them to earlier, more renowned individuals. It was probably out of reverence for their master—and also perhaps because they were discussing authoritative school traditions—that certain Pythagoreans who published writings attributed them directly to Pythagoras himself.

It is worth noting that, as with most New Testament scholars, Fideler does not mention any ancient reflections on the phenomenon that have led him to his conclusion, and cites not a single piece of evidence for it.

55. *Epistle* 33, 4. Translation of R. M. Gummere in LCL, 3 vols. (Cambridge, MA: Harvard University, 1917–1925).

cribed to Epicurus. But in fact the comment says nothing about Epicurean authors writing books while claiming to be Epicurus. It is referring to oral communications and indicates that what others in the school say, they attribute to the authority (one might assume) of Epicurus himself. Even if Seneca is referring to writings of the school, the attribution of one's own views to Epicurus could, of course, be accomplished in orthonymous as easily as in forged writings (e.g., by quoting Epicurus).

Suetonius, in his treatise "On Grammarians," says of Antonius Gnipho:

> He wrote a great deal. Atieus Philologus, however, declares that he left but two volumes, "On the Latin Language," maintaining that the other works attributed to him were those of his pupils and not his own (nam cetera scripta discipulorum eius esse non ipsius). Yet his own name is sometimes found in them. (ch. 7)[56]

This comment does come closer to indicating that students of a philosopher might write a book claiming to be their teacher. On closer examination, however, it appears instead to indicate that anonymous books by students were sometimes falsely *attributed* to the teacher. It is not clear what it means that his own name was found in them; it is not obvious, in any event, that it must mean that his name was found in the authorial inscription (i.e., as placed there by the author himself, claiming to be Antonius Gnipho; it could just as well meant that his name is found in, say, an inscription added to the writing by a later editor). In any event, Suetonius does not indicate anything about this being a common practice, let alone an acceptable one. On the contrary, he seems to want to know who actually wrote the books.

Finally, Diogenes Laertius speaks of works written in Pythagoras' name by others. He claims that Pythagoras wrote three treatises, "On Education," "On Statesmanship," and "On Nature"; others were written in his name (*Lives* 8.6–8). Here again, however, there is no indication that Diogenes saw this as an acceptable practice—that is, as something other than forgery in the negative sense—and he says nothing about it being common. And he, like Suetonius, is interested in knowing who actually wrote the books.

THE PROBLEM OF PORPHYRY

In his extensive analysis of pseudepigraphy and canon, Armin Baum maintains that a key ancient witness to the common and accepted practice, in ancient philosophical schools, of writing treatises in the name of a teacher is the Neoplatonist Porphyry (234–304 CE).[57] In this he is followed by other scholars, including Martina Janssen in an otherwise full and insightful article.[58]

---

56. Translation Rolfe in LCL.

57. Baum, *Pseudepigraphie*, p. 53.

58. "Antike (Selbst-)Aussagen über Beweggründe zur Pseudepigraphie," in *Pseudepigraphie und Verfasserfiktion in frühchristlichen Briefen*, ed. Jörg Frey et al., p. 177.

Before evaluating what Porphyry actually says in the passage in question, it is worth pointing out that this alleged witness to the "common" practice in philosophical schools refers only to the school of Pythagoras and, yet more significant, dates 750–800 years after the fact.[59] How useful such a statement could be for understanding what was happening in early Christianity (say, two hundred years earlier) is very much open to question. But is Porphyry even referring to pseudepigraphic practices of Pythagoras' school, so many centuries earlier?

As Baum notes, the passage is not preserved in the Greek manuscript tradition of Porphyry, but only in an Arabic translation. The text is found in the lengthy book by Ibn Abi Usaybi'a, *Kitab 'uyun al-anba' fi tabaqat al-atibba,*[60] which, understandably, Baum did not actually read; he relied instead on the account of B. L. Van der Waerden.[61] I too do not read medieval Arabic. But the passage is important, and so I asked my colleague Carl Ernst, who specializes in Medieval Islam, to translate it for me. The passage does not say what Baum claims it does.

> But as for the books of Pythagoras the sage, which Archytas the Tarentine philosopher collected by himself, they are eighty books. But those that he made special effort, with all his strength, to compile, compose (*ta'līf*), and collect, from all the old men who were of the type of Pythagoras the philosopher, his school, and the inheritors of his sciences, man after man, these were two hundred books in number. And he who was unique in the essence of his intellect [i.e., Archytas] set aside from them the false books ascribed to the tongue of the sage and his name, which shameless people fabricated.

Ibn Abi Usaybi'a goes on to list twelve of the forged books.

Baum argues that in the passage Porphyry differentiates between eighty books that Pythagoras wrote, two hundred that his followers wrote (with impunity) in his name, and twelve that were later forgeries misrepresenting his views. But as can be seen, what the passage instead says is that Pythagoras wrote eighty books, that older men who belonged to the Pythagorean group wrote two hundred books, and that other books, of which Porphyry names twelve, were forgeries in the name of Pythagoras. The key point is this: Porphyry decidedly does not indicate that the two hundred books by Pythagoras' followers were written *in Pythagoras' name*. They were simply written by students of his school.

There is no problem with thinking that the followers of Pythagoras wrote books. We have these books more fully attested. They were written by the likes of Hippodamus, Okkelos, Philoaus, Periktyone, and Phyntis. They are orthonymous, and

59. Unless he is referring to the Hellenistic revitalization of the school, on which see p. 111.

60. Ed. 'Amir al-Najjar (4 vols., Cairo: al-Hay'a al-Misriyya al-'Amma lil-Kitab, 2001), vol. 1, pp. 244–45.

61. "Die Schriften und Fragmente des Pythagoras," *RESupp.* 10 (1965): 843–64; see also idem, *Die Pythagoreer. Religiöse Bruderschaft und Schule der Wissenschaft* (Zurich: Artemis, 1979), 272–73.

have been discussed in a number of important studies.[62] In other words, Baum has gotten the situation precisely wrong. The overarching claim of his study is that a book in antiquity was considered a "forgery" only if the *content* was judged not to derive from the named author, and Porphyry is appealed to as a witness—on the false assumption that Porphyry accepted the two hundred pseudepigraphic Pythagorean books since they taught the views of Pythagoras himself. But in fact, Porphyry is irrelevant to the question, because he does not mention two hundred books written by Pythagoras' followers in his name. He speaks only of two hundred books written by Pythagoras' followers.

Moreover, there can be no question about what Porphyry, at least according to this text, thought about books that were falsely produced in Pythagoras' name. Of these he says the following (again, from a private translation of Ernst):

> The criminal individuals who fabricated these lying books that we have mentioned, according to traditions that have reached us, are Aristotle the Younger, Nikos (Nuqūs) known as the essentially erroneous, one of the Cretans called Konios, Megalos, and Fūkhajawāqā (?), along with others even more reprehensible than they. And that was who proposed to them (others?) the fabrication of these lying books with the tongue of the philosopher Pythagoras and his name, so that [these writings] would be accepted among the moderns because of him, so they would honor, prefer, and share them.

Those who produced books in Pythagoras' name are called "criminal." Their books are "lying" "fabrications." They were written pseudepigraphically because by putting Pythagoras' name on them, the books were more likely to be accepted by their readers. For Porphyry this is a nefarious motivation.

In short, Porphyry cannot be used to establish the "common" practice in the philosophical schools—or even in the Pythagorean school—of publishing writings in the name of a revered teacher with impunity. Some followers of Pythagoras did produce such forged works, but the books were labeled lies and fabrications and the authors were called shameless criminals.

THE WITNESS OF IAMBLICHUS

The only other witness to the pseudepigraphic practices of the Pythagorean school writing within a full millennium of the death of its founder (apart from Diogenes Laertius) is another late antique neo-Platonist, Iamblichus (245–325 CE). Two passages from Iamblichus' writings are sometimes cited to establish the Pythagorean practices, but only one of them is germane to the question. The first

62. See Holger Thesleff, *An Introduction to the Pythagorean Writings of the Hellenistic Period* (Åbo: Åbo Academi, 1961). For collection of these texts see Kenneth Guthrie and Thomas Taylor, *The Pythagorean Writings: Hellenistic Texts from the 1st Cent. B.C.–3d Cent. A.D.*, ed. Robert Navon (Kew Gardens, NY: Selene Books, 1986).

occurs in Iamblichus' *Life of Pythagoras*: "Of the [Pythagoric] writings that are now circulating, some were written by Pythagoras himself, but others consist of what he was heard to say [τὰ δὲ ἀπὸ τῆς ἀκροάσεως αὐτοῦ συγγεγράφθαι]; for this reason the authors do not attach their own names to these books but attribute them to Pythagoras as being his (καὶ διὰ τοῦτο οὐδὲ ἑαυτῶν ἐπεφήμιζον αὐτά, ἀλλὰ εἰς Πυθαγόραν ἀνέφερον αὐτὰ ὡς ἐκείνου ὄντα)."[63] At first glance, this may indeed seem to indicate that Pythagoras' students published their own treatises in his name; but in fact, Iamblichus is referring to a very different phenomenon: the publication of Pythagoras' lecture notes by his students. These publications literally contain his own words, not those of the writers, and so it would not have been proper for them to claim the books for themselves. I will be dealing with the question of published lecture notes shortly.

The other reference in Iamblichus' *Life of Pythagoras*, on the other hand, does in fact deal with the publication of works by others in Pythagoras' name, and appears to say what scholars have said it says: "It was a fine custom of theirs also to ascribe and assign everything to Pythagoras, and only very seldom to claim personal fame for their discoveries, for there are very few of them indeed to whom works are ascribed personally."[64] Here Iamblichus indicates his own view about what happened among the followers of Pythagoras so many centuries earlier. But the relevance of this passage for understanding widespread views in antiquity is much open to dispute.

The first thing to note is that Iamblichus is referring only to the followers of Pythagoras. Nowhere does he say this was a widespread practice—or indeed, a practice at all—in any of the other philosophical schools. Moreover, it cannot be stressed enough that Iamblichus is writing eight hundred years after Pythagoras. Are there any grounds for thinking that he would actually know the practices of his school? If he does know, what are his sources of information? If they once existed, they do not exist any longer; this is the first we learn of such a practice.

It may be that Iamblichus is referring not to Pythagoras' immediate followers but to the later Pythagoreans of the Hellenistic period. But here too he would be speaking of literary practices from four hundred to five hundred years earlier. How would he know about these? And if he is right, why are these practices not mentioned by any authors—including biographers of Pythagoras—writing earlier? In fact, the questions keep on coming.

---

63. *Life of Pythagoras* 29. Translation mine.

64. Ch. 31; translation of John Dillon and Jackson Hershbell, *Iamblichus: On the Pythagorean Way of Life* (Atlanta: Scholars Press, 1991), p. 203. The translators themselves point out that whereas the claim may have made sense in the early years of the Pythagorean movement (although even here there are questions), "it hardly makes much sense subsequent to the publication of the pseudo-Pythagorean writings." One should press the question even harder: Does Iamblichus have any evidence (or rather is there any evidence) to support his claim? He certainly gives none. It looks instead to be his simple opinion of the matter.

LATER SUPPORTERS OF IAMBLICHUS' VIEW

It is true that two much-later Neoplatonists—Olympiodorus from the mid-sixth century CE and somewhat later his student Elias—also make this claim about the Pythagoreans. Elias is dependent on Olympiodorus and so cannot count as independent evidence. And Olympiodorus himself may simply be relying on the same neo-Platonic tradition as found in Iamblichus from more than two centuries earlier. In any event, Olympiodorus is the first writer to give us anything resembling a taxonomy of motives for the practices of pseudepigraphy. In his *Prolegomenon* Olympiodorus states his desire to establish the ways in which books are "forged" (or better, "bastardized," provided with false names; διὰ πόσους τρόπους ἐνοθεύοντο τὰ βιβλία) and the criteria one can use to "distinguish the genuine from the forged" (διαχωρίζειν τὰ γνήσια ἀπὸ τῶν νόθων). In Olympiodorus' judgment, books are forged/provided with false authorial names for three reasons: from the ambition/ambitious rivalry (φιλοτιμία) of kings; the affection/good will of students/disciples; and the homonymy of writers, writings, or notes/commentaries (ὑπομνήματα).[65]

His third category shows that he is concerned simply with the circulation of books under a wrong name (not forgery in the sense I am using it), since homonymy, as we have seen, does not involve a false authorial claim. He explicates his reference to the φιλοτιμία of kings by speaking specifically of Juba, king of Libya, who loved Pythagorean writings; Ptolemy Philadelphius, who loved Aristotelian writings; and Pisistratus tyrant of Athens, who loved Homeric writings. These kings, he indicates, were willing to pay gold for their beloved texts, leading enterprising scholars to invent them. His second category conforms with the statement of Iamblichus: students wrote books in the names of their teachers. He claims that this is true of "all" the books written in the name of Pythagoras. "For Pythagoras left no writings . . . and so his disciples out of affection/good will put the name Pythagoras on their writings (οἱ οὖν μαθηταὶ αὐτοῦ δι'εὔνοιαν ποιήσαντες συγγράμματα ἐπέγραψαν τὸ ὄνομα Πυθαγόρου)." As a result, for Olympiodorus, all of the writings in the name of Pythagoras are νόθα.

This statement is sometimes taken as an authoritative account of what happened in the philosophical schools.[66] Here again, however, it is not clear whether Olympiodorus is referring to forgeries in the name of Pythagoras by later writers or to publication of essays based on students' lecture notes (about which, below). And of course if Olympiodorus assumed that Pythagoras published nothing, then it only makes sense that he must draw the corollary: books that bear Pythagoras' name must have been written by students. And if they were written by students,

---

65. Olympiodorus, *Prolegomena*, 13; for Greek text and German translation, see Baum, *Pseudepigraphie*, pp. 238–43.

66. For example, by Mark Kiley, *Colossians as Pseudepigraphy* (Sheffield: JSOT Press, 1986), pp. 22–23.

they must have been produced with good will toward the master. And so it must have been an established and accepted practice.

As inexorable as the logic may have seemed to Olympiodorus, it cannot be seen as compelling today. Pythagoras was in fact widely thought to have written numerous books (although a number of ancients denied it). His followers did write books, but in their own names. There were, to be sure, books claiming to be written by Pythagoras that he did not himself write, just as there were books falsely written in the names of Socrates, Epicurus, Jesus, Peter, and Paul. To that extent, the practice was widespread. But this does not mean it was widely respected and approved. On the contrary, every indication is that even in antiquity the practice was widely condemned and censured. Whether forgers—Pythagorean or otherwise—themselves took the matter lightly is another question, one we will return to at the end of this chapter.

In any event, Olympiodorus lived a thousand years after Pythagoras himself. He shows no evidence of knowing what happened in the wake of Pythagoras, a millennium earlier. There is no reason to assume he is doing anything but repeating hearsay that had been in circulation in Neoplatonic circles since at least the time of Iamblichus, himself writing eight hundred years after the fact.

One is more or less left with an off-the-cuff comment by Iamblichus in support of this alleged practice in Pythagorean circles. It comes as no surprise that recent studies of the matter by scholars of Pythagoreanism draw a strongly negative conclusion, as summarized forcefully by Leonid Zhmud: "The only one (!), who reports such a practice is once again Iamblichus. Up to that point we do not hear of any concrete instance in which a Pythagorean ascribed his discoveries to Pythagoras, and we have furthermore no indication that such a tendency existed in his school."[67]

SOME COUNTER-INDICATIONS

I will draw some conclusions about the practices of forgery in the philosophical schools shortly, after raising several other issues. For now it is enough to provide some counterevidence to Iamblichus' assertion.

It is important to recognize that different Pythagoreans (even in the "school") had their own views and perspectives, and that they had no qualms about expressing them.[68] Most of these later authors wrote orthonymously, and we know of their writings. Others to be sure claimed to be Pythagoras. But this was not seen as an acceptable, let alone a widespread, practice. When these authors were

67. "Der einzige (!), der von einer solchen Praxis berichtet, ist wiederum Jamblichos. Bis dahin hören wir von keinem konkreten Fall, in dem ein Pythagoreer seine Entdeckungen dem Pythagoras zugeschrieben hätte, und wir haben auch keinerlei Hinweis darauf, daß es in seiner Schule solche Tendenzen gibt." *Wissenschaft, Philosophie und Religion im frühen Pythagoreismus* (Berlin: Akademie Verlag, 1997), p. 91; exclamation point his.

68. See esp. Thesleff, *Introduction*.

detected, their works were described as forgeries. We have already seen this to be the case with Porphyry and Diogenes Laertius.

Moreover, there were clear reasons for later Pythagoreans wanting to make their writings appear to derive from the great man himself. Among other things, H. Balz and others have argued that the practice provided a greater antiquity for certain Pythagorean views, a desideratum in the face of competing claims of other philosophical traditions.[69] In addition, we have other evidence of Pythagorean authors intentionally trying to deceive their readers about their authorial claims (what would have been the point if writing in the name of Pythagoras was widely accepted?). We have already seen that King Juba of Mauretania was willing to pay cash on the barrel head for writings of Pythagoras. Also, we have reports of forged Pythagorean manuscripts being artificially "enhanced" to make them look old and therefore authentic.[70] We also have several ancient accounts of faux "discoveries" of Pythagorean texts, meant to assure others of their great antiquity.[71]

There were numerous reasons for Pythagoreans to want to claim that their own writings were the productions of Pythagoras himself. But there is little indeed to suggest that they did so out of humility in a practice that was widely acknowledged in antiquity to be acceptable and sanctioned.

THE PUBLICATION OF LECTURE NOTES

As was already intimated, when it comes to the publication of students' lecture notes we are dealing with a different matter altogether. So far as we can tell, it was widely thought that the written dissemination of a teacher's "classroom" instruction should be under the teacher's name, since he was the one, after all, who had spoken the words. Not all teachers approved of the practice. But what was definitely derided was the alternative of publishing a teacher's words as one's own.

Quintilian gives an interesting instance of the practice, a case in which he was not thoroughly pleased that his words had been published by others:

> Two books on the art of rhetoric are at present circulating under my name, although never published by me or composed for such a purpose. One is a two days' lecture which was taken down by the boys who were my audience. The other consists of such notes as my good pupils succeeded in taking down from a course of lectures on a somewhat more extensive scale. I appreciate their kindness, but they showed an excess of enthusiasm and a certain lack of discretion in doing my utterances the honour of publication.[72]

---

69. "Anonymität und Pseudepigraphie," pp. 414–15; see also Speyer, *Literarische Fälschung*, pp. 139–42, and Duff, *Reconsideration*, p. 78.

70. See F. Jacoby, *FGrHist* 275 T 11.

71. See Livy 40.29; Pliny *Natural History* 13.84–87; and Philostratus, *Life of Apollonius*, 8.19–20.

72. *Quintilian Inst. Proem.* 7. Translation of H.E. Butler, *Quintilian I*, LCL (Cambridge, MA: Harvard University, 1920).

Quintilian explains the situation because he is now publishing a new treatise on the same topic, and wants it to be clearly understood that the new iteration will be superior to the two published by students in his name.

On the other hand, as we have seen already, students who published their teacher's words as their own were severely chastised for plagiarism. This is instanced in the case of Empedocles, mentioned by Diogenes Laertius: "Timaeus in the ninth book of his *Histories* says he was a pupil of Pythagoras, adding that, having been convicted at that time of stealing his discourses (λέγων ὅτι καταγνωσθεὶς ἐπὶ λογοκλοπίᾳ τότε) he was, like Plato, excluded from taking part in the discussions of the school" (*Lives*, 8.54).

The clearest instance, however, comes in one that is self-attested. Arrian, as is well known, did not attempt to write his own philosophical reflections based on the teachings of Epictetus, but instead recorded, to the best of his ability, what Epictetus himself said. Had he published the teachings under his own name, he would have been guilty, by ancient standards, of plagiarism (witness Empedocles: λογοκλοπία). And so he makes his intentions quite clear at the outset of the Discourses:

> Arrian to Lucius Gellius, greeting: I have not composed these Words of Epictetus as one might be said to "compose" books of this kind, nor have I of my own act published them to the world; indeed, I acknowledge that I have not "composed" them at all. But whatever I heard him say I used to write down, word for word, as best I could, endeavoring to preserve it as a memorial, for my own future use, of his way of thinking and the frankness of his speech.[73]

In short, it was perfectly acceptable to publish the notes of a teacher in his name; but to publish them in one's own name, as if they were one's own teachings, was seen as plagiarism. This is quite different, however, from writing one's own treatise and claiming that it was someone else's, even a beloved teacher's. If the words did not go back to the teacher himself, this would be forgery.[74]

---

73. Epictetus, *Discourses*. Translation of W. A. Oldfather in LCL (Cambridge, MA: Harvard University, 1926).

74. On the practice of publishing a philosopher's lecture notes, cf. Angela Standhartinger: "From antiquity too we know that much of what was published in the name of famous men had actually been written down by their students, whether in the form of notes taken at the actual event or as memories thereof after the fact. In the Pythagorean school and even more so in the Epicurean one, everything that was spoken or written by students counted as the intellectual property of the teacher and was frequently published under his name." ("Es war also in der Antike bekannt, daß vieles von dem, was man unter dem Namen berühmter Männer lesen konnte, eigentlich von ihren Schülern und Schülerinnen aufgeschrieben worden war, sei es als Mitschrift, sei es als nachträgliche Erinnerung. In der pythagoräischen Schule und mehr noch in der epikureischen galt alles, was von den Schülerinnen und Schülern gesagt und aufgeschrieben wurde, als geistiges Eigentum des Lehrers und wurde unter dessen Namen an die Öffentlichkeit gebracht"; *Studien zur Entstehungsgeschichte und Intention des Kolosserbriefs*, Leiden: Brill, 1999, p. 42). It is not clear where she derives her evidence that this was particularly common in Epicurean circles.

MEDICAL SCHOOLS

Much the same can be said about the ancient medical schools. Here again there are no indications that it was an accepted practice to publish one's own writing under the name of a beloved teacher as an act of humility or for the sake of giving credit where credit was due. Critics were, on the contrary, intent on knowing who actually produced the work. Nowhere is that clearer than in the one case we are best informed about, the Galenic evaluation of the Hippocratic corpus.[75]

We have in excess of one hundred Greek and more than thirty Latin writings in the name of Hippocrates. In such books as "Concerning the Genuine and Forged (νόθα) Writings of Hippocrates," Galen was particularly intent, as the title indicates, on determining which of the writings were genuinely those of the great physician himself and which were produced instead by his sons and students in his name. The latter writings he labeled as νόθα.

There were many possibilities. Some works, in his opinion, were authentically by Hippocrates. Others, such as *De victu acutorum*, were essentially authentic but were published posthumously by someone else, as shown by its disorderly train of thought and the occasional interpolation.[76] In some instances Galen ventured to indicate who the actual authors of the inauthentic works were, for example, Hippocrates' sons Dracon and Thessalus, his son-in-law Polybus, and others of his students. In other instances Galen had to resort to indicating that a work was not authentic, without suggesting the name of an author. Sometimes the more complicated works, such as *De natura hominis*, were said to have multiple authors, one of whom might have been Hippocrates.

As we have seen, Armin Baum has recently maintained that ancient authors considered books authentic so long as the contents could be attributed to the named author, whether or not he actually produced the book. To this end he sees as most significant Galen's views of the seven books on Epidemics. Books 1 and 3, Galen indicates, were actually by Hippocrates. Books 2 and 6, however, were composed by Thessalus after his father's death, on the basis of papers that he left behind. Galen does not suggest that these two books be deprived of Hippocratic authorship, but that they be entitled instead *"Books 1 and 2 of the Notes of Hippocrates" On Epidemics*. Since they are not to be attributed to their real author (Thessalus), in Baum's view, this shows that what matters is not the composer of the work, but the ideas in it. If these are Hippocratic, then the books are rightly attributed to him.[77]

---

75. The classic study, very much still worth reading, is L. O. Bröcker, "Die Methoden Galens in der literarischen Kritik," *Rheinisches Museum für Philologie* 40 (1885): 415–38. See as well A. Anastassiou and D. Irmer, eds., *Testimonien zum Corpus Hippocraticum*. pt. 2, *Galen; vol. 1 Hippokrateszitate in den Kommentaren und im Glossar* (Göttingen: Vandenhoeck, 1997). Scholars today, as both Dale Martin and Zlatko Pleše have reminded me, generally reject the authenticity of the entire Hippocratic corpus.

76. *In Hipp. Acut. Comment.* 2, 55; Anastassiou and Irmer, pp. 1–3.

77. Baum, *Pseudepigraphie*, pp. 58–59.

To an extent Baum is right about this, but not for the reason he thinks. It is not simply that the thoughts and ideas happen to be those of Hippocrates. What is important to note is that the books were written on the basis of papers that Hippocrates left behind. In other words, this is analogous to a student publishing the lecture notes of his teacher. The words really are the teacher's, and so should be attributed to him. To publish them under one's own name would be plagiarism. This is different altogether from publishing one's own views and claiming that they are someone else's. Galen labeled Hippocratic writings of that sort νόθα. For Galen it was extremely important to know which books were γνήσια. Books not giving the words of Hippocrates himself were inauthentic.

Galen was not the only one interested in such matters. From much later comes the clear statement of Augustine, who expresses well the general sentiment of antiquity:

> But even in worldly writings there were well-known authors under whose names many works were produced later, and they were repudiated either because they did not agree with the writings that were certainly theirs or because, at the time when those authors wrote, these writings did not merit to be recognized and to be handed on and commended to posterity by them or their friends. Not to mention others, were not certain books that were produced under the name Hippocrates, the highly renowned physician, rejected as authoritative by physicians? Nor did a certain similarity of topics and language offer them any help. For, compared to the books that it was clear were really Hippocrates' books, they were judged inferior, and they were not known at the same time at which the rest of his writings were recognized as truly his. (*Contra Faust.* 33.6)

Note carefully: determining the actual author mattered, not just to Augustine but to the critics that he references as writing before him. If a book is not authored by its alleged author, it lacks the authority that the imputed author bore. It is, on those grounds, "rejected."

CONCLUSION: THE USE OF FORGERY IN THE PHILOSOPHICAL SCHOOLS

One passage in Tertullian is sometimes cited to support the idea that it was an acceptable practice in antiquity for a disciple to publish a book in the name of his teacher.[78] This, however, is a complete misreading of Tertullian's point. What he says is this: "That which Mark produced is stated to be Peter's, whose interpreter Mark was. Luke's narrative also they usually attribute to Paul. It is permissible for the works which disciples published to be regarded as belonging to their masters."[79]

---

78. For example, Hindy Najman, *Seconding Sinai: The Development of Mosaic Discourse in Second Temple Judaism* (Leiden: Brill, 2003), p. 13.

79. *Adv. Marc.* 4.5.

Contrary to the common interpretation of this passage, Tertullian is not referring to pseudepigraphic practices, but to the authority that lay behind the canonical Gospels. That is to say, Tertullian is not indicating that Mark published his Gospel by calling it the Gospel of Peter, or that Luke published the Gospel of Paul. Each Evangelist wrote—in Tertullian's view—in his own name, but with the authority of another. The passage is thus of no relevance to the question of pseudepigraphy, let alone to the pseudepigraphic practices of the philosophical schools.

So too, Baum claims that since Justin Martyr refers to the Gospel of Mark as the Memoirs of Peter (Dial. 106.3), he considered it acceptable to publish under the name of one's teacher: the book's contents go back to Peter and are authoritative on those grounds.[80] This too is flawed reasoning. For one thing, P. Pilhofer has made a convincing case that Justin is not referring to canonical Mark at all, but to the Gospel of Peter (Justin never refers to the Gospel of Mark by name).[81] Beyond that, we have no evidence to suggest that the Second Gospel was ever circulated under Peter's name. If Justin is referring to it, he is describing it, not naming it. This is not at all the same as a writing claiming to be written by Socrates that was instead produced by a later follower. So too Origen's comment that Hebrews can be accepted as Pauline by those who want to do so, even though it was not written by Paul, because its views are consonant with Paul's. Here again we are not dealing with a book that *claims* to be written by Paul which can be accepted as Pauline, even though Paul did not write it. Hebrews is anonymous.

Forgery involves false authorial claims. Contrary to what is often said, the practice was not accepted, so far as we can tell, even within the philosophical schools—except, perhaps, by the people who practiced it, to whom we will return at the end of this chapter. Critics of the ancient world, however, found the practice objectionable. That is why they are so invested in knowing who actually wrote what. If it did not matter whether the book was written by a follower of Pythagoras or of Hippocrates or of Socrates, there would have been no reason for critics to invest so much effort in engaging in their critical investigations.

We know how falsifiers of philosophical texts were sometimes treated, as they tried to put their own words on the pens of their revered teachers: Athenodorus was removed from his duties in the Pergamum Library for "correcting" the writings of Zeno.[82] And we know how plagiarists were sometimes treated in the schools: Empedocles was forbidden access to the lectures of Pythagoras.[83] The reason for these attitudes is patent. Ancient readers of texts were widely concerned to know

80. Baum, *Pseudepigraphie*, p. 60.

81. Peter Pilhofer, "Justin und das Petrusevangelium," *ZNW* 81 (1990): 60–78; the attempted refutation by Thornton is far less persuasive; see Claus-Jürgen Thornton, "Justin und das Markusevangelium," *ZNW* 84 (1993): 93–110.

82. See p. 62.

83. See p. 54.

who the actual authors were. That, as Speyer repeatedly reminds us, was the entire reason for the extensive practice of Echtheitskritik.

It was, to be sure, acceptable to publish lecture notes in the name of the teacher who gave the lectures. This is what Arian did with the Discourses of Epictetus, and what some of the followers of both Hippocrates and Pythagoras did. But to write one's own work and to claim that it was the work of another—even a beloved teacher—was not acceptable. Such works were classified as νόθα.

To Establish the Validity of One's Views

There is one factor that ties together most of the motivations discussed so far, and I give it here as a final category even though in fact it appears to have broad application. Forgers typically produced writings in the name of others in order to establish the validity of their own views. As discussed earlier, the name of an author could carry authority. An author whose name carried no authority would sometimes claim a name that did.

This understanding of a forger's motivation comes to be clearly stated both within our period and afterward, never more so than in the sixth-century Christian Neoplatonist David in his comments on the writings of Porphyry: "When someone is unimportant and insignificant, and he wants his writing to be read, he writes in the name of an ancient and influential person, so that through that one's influence he can get his writing accepted."[84] Porphyry himself, as we have seen, indicated that this was what motivated the authors of the pseudo-Pythagorean writings. Aulus Gellius concurred with respect to a different instance: "Many fictions of this kind seem to have been attached to the name of Democritus by ignorant men, who sheltered themselves under his reputation and authority."[85]

Augustine cites this as the reason for the production of an anti-Christian letter embracing magical practices in the name of Christ himself:

> And it is quite possible that either the enemies of the name of Christ, or certain parties who thought that they might impart to this kind of execrable arts the weight of authority drawn from so glorious a name, may have written things of that nature under the name of Christ and the apostles.[86]

So too in the one instance we have from late antiquity of a Christian detected in the act of forgery, Salvian of Marseilles, who indicates that had he written the book *Ad Ecclesiam* in his own name, rather than in the name of Timothy, no one would have paid it any heed. And so he "wisely selected a pseudonym for his book

---

84. *In Porphyr Isage.* Pr. 1: Translation mine; Greek text in Baum, *Pseudepigraphie*, p. 214

85. *Attic Nights* 10.12.8. Translation of John C. Rolfe, *The Attic Nights of Aulus Gellius*. LCL (Cambridge, MA: Harvard University Press, 1978–1984).

86. *Cons Evang.* 1.10.

for the obvious reason that he did not wish the obscurity of his own person to detract from the influence of his otherwise valuable book." Or, as he then says, "For this reason the present writer chose to conceal his identity in every respect for fear that his true name would perhaps detract from the influence of his book, which really contains much that is exceedingly valuable."[87]

The same motivation is explicitly attested for the analogous case of textual falsification, in which one's own words are claimed to be the words of another; and so Rufinus indicates that heretics altered the writings of faithful Christian authorities: "By this means, of course, the assertion of the man's own heresy was more easily advanced under the names of all the most learned and renowned among the ecclesiastical writers in view of the fact that some brilliant men among the Catholics appeared to have thought likewise."[88] Similarly, some heretics tried to pass off a "false teaching" of Tertullian on the Holy Spirit by inserting his tractate on the Trinity, unnamed, into a collection of the writings of the impeccable Cyprian: "The result was that the heretics found a way of gaining credit for their perfidy by means of the authority of such a great man."[89]

Within Christian circles there seems to be no reason to doubt that the need for authority—in particular, apostolic authority—is what motivated most forgers to practice their craft.[90] That the apostles were unique authorities is evident from the earliest postapostolic times, for example in Ignatius, himself no mean authority, who could nonetheless tell his readers in Tralles: "But I have not thought that I, a condemned man, should give you orders like an apostle."[91] Later it was seen that apostolic books alone could carry Scriptural authority, as indicated by the Muratorian Fragment at the end of the second century, by Origen soon thereafter, and throughout our period, up to its end with Augustine.[92] The importance of apostolic writings for establishing Christian doctrine can be seen in a myriad of places throughout our literature; as just one example we might take the words of Jerome

---

87. See pp. 94–96.

88. *De adult libr. Orig.* 2. Scheck, *St. Pamphilus*, p. 125.

89. *De adult libr. Orig.*12. Scheck, *St. Pamphilus*, p. 133.

90. Among many others, see, for example, Petr Pokorný, "Das theologische Problem der neutestamentlichen Pseudepigraphie," *EvT* 44 (1984): 486–96.

91. My translation; see *The Apostolic Fathers*, LCL (Cambridge, MA: Harvard University, 2003).

92. The author of the Muratorian Fragment refuses to accept the Shepherd as canon in part because it was written by Hermes, the brother of the bishop of Rome, Pius; Origen (*Comm. In Matt* ser. 47, on Matt 24:23–28) indicates that the time of canonical writings was from the beginning of creation (Genesis) to the most recent writings of the Apostles "post quos nullis scripturis ita credendum est sicut illis" (see Baum *Pseudepigraphie*, pp. 154–55). Cf. Augustine: "But the books of later authors are distinct from the excellence of the canonical authority of the Old and New Testaments, which has been confirmed from the times of the apostles through the successions of bishops and through the spread of the churches. It has been set on high, as if on a kind of throne, and every believing and pious intellect should be obedient to it. . . . But in the works of later authors, which are found in countless books but are in no way equal to the most sacred excellence of the canonical scriptures, the same truth is also found in some of them, but their authority is far from equal" (*Contra Faust.* XI, 5).

about the virginity of Mary: "That God was born of a virgin we believe, because we read [that it was so]. That Mary was married after she gave birth we do not believe, because we do not read [that it was so]" (Natum deum esse de virgine credimus, quia legimus. Mariam nupsisse post partum non credimus, quia non legimus; *Adv. Helv.* 19).

Small wonder, then, that forgers wrote so many Gospels, epistles, apocalypses, and other works in the names of apostles. Among the names that carried authority, theirs carried the greatest authority of all. But they were not the only authority figures of the early church: Ignatius, Origen, Augustine, and Jerome themselves carried some weight, and so it is no surprise that forgers penned writings in their names as well—and in the names of others, whenever deemed appropriate. The issue was authority, and authority was indelibly linked to the names of authors.

TECHNIQUES

Forty years ago Wolfgang Speyer made a tantalizing claim that remains no less true today: "The history of literary gullibility has yet to be written."[93] Still, despite the astounding credulity of readers—modern as well as ancient—forgers have always made efforts to cover up the traces of their deceit. In many instances, it is simply enough for a forger to claim to be someone other than who he is. Anyone in antiquity who came across a letter of Paul addressed to a church (in Thessalonica, in Ephesus, in Colossae, etc.) naturally thought that Paul had written the letter, unless there was a glaring mistake that indicated otherwise. The forger's craft involved making sure there were no such mistakes: anachronisms, inconsistencies, or gaffes. But more than that, many, possibly most, forgers went out of their way to make their work believable. Some forgers, of course, were more skilled at deceit than others. The following are some of the ploys they typically used.

Imitation of Style

A good forger who wanted his readers to assume that he really was who he said he was tried to imitate the writing style of the author he was claiming to be. The ability to effect imitation was all part of a rhetorical education in ethopoeia, as Cribiore and many others have noted.[94] Not all forgers were good at it, and some apparently did not even make the effort. This was possibly the case with the famous incident recounted by Galen in *De propriis libris*, where an amateur scholar informed a dupe that the book in question was not by Galen, simply on the basis of the style of the first two lines. Caveat emptor. But most forgers almost certainly

93. "Die Geschichte der literarischen Leichtgläubigkeit ist noch nicht geschrieben." *Literarische Fälschung*, p. 85.

94. Raffaella Cribiore, *Gymnastics of the Mind: Greek Education in Hellenistic and Roman Egypt* (Princeton: Princeton University, 2001), pp. 228–30.

did their best, often with spectacular success. It took many centuries for anyone to realize that the writing style of Ephesians was not that of Paul.

We have only one instance from antiquity in which a forger actually acknowledges what he has done (not counting Salvian, who does not explicitly admit his guilt). This is the second century CE Mithridates, who forged a cover letter for a second edition of the letters of the general Brutus—from three centuries earlier—explaining why he himself had produced pseudepigraphic responses from the recipients of the various missives.[95] Among other things, Mithridates claims that in producing the letters he has tried to replicate the plausible contents of what they would have written and to have done so in an appropriately imitative style. But he admits it was not easy: "how difficult it turns out [to be] to contend with another person's skill when it is hard even to keep up one's own!"[96]

Verisimilitudes

In addition to using a familiar name and trying to imitate style, forgers would typically insert verisimilitudes in order to ground yet further the plausibility of their writings. As we will see when we turn to the Pastoral epistles, proponents of authenticity have long maintained that the personal touches that pervade 2 Timothy are the clearest indication that this book (and, often, by implication, its two companions) was actually written by Paul. Why would a forger bother to remind his recipient of their past relationship in such intimate detail? "I remember your tears, I long night and day to see you. . . . I remember your sincere faith, which first lived in your grandmother Lois and your mother Eunice and now, I am sure, lives on in you" (1:3–5). Why would a forger tell a feigned recipient to be sure to "bring the cloak I left at Troas with Carpus, and the books, and especially the parchments" (4:13)?

For scholars of forgery, the answer is obvious. A forger would invent such verisimilitudes precisely in order to convince the reader that he is who he says he is. This has been shown beyond any doubt in a now-famous article by Norbert Brox, "Zu den persönlichen Notizen der Pastoralbriefe,"[97] which demonstrates that "personal notes" are a standard ruse of the forger. Brox's position has been strengthened by further researchers, such as Lewis Donelson, who appeals to the forged letters of Plato, especially letters 12 and 13, in support:

---

95. See Robert Matthew Calhoun, "The Letter of Mithridates: A Neglected Item of Ancient Epistolary Theory," in Jörg Frey et al., eds., *Pseudepigraphie und Verfasserfiktion*, pp. 295–330. Calhoun summarizes the importance (yet neglect) of this letter in clear terms: "For scholars of the NT and early Christian literature the remarks of Mithridates on the production of pseudepigraphic letters should hold a comparable importance to what Thucydides has to say about the composition of speeches in historical narrative, since both directly address at a theoretical level phenomena that actually occur in Christian texts" (pp. 321–22). Among other things, Calhoun argues that the letter of Mithridates itself is not forged.

96. Translation of Calhoun, "The Letter," p. 303.

97. *BZ* 13 (1969): 76–94; reprinted in Brox, ed., *Pseudepigraphie in der heidnischen und jüdisch-christlichen Antike*, pp. 272–94.

> The particular genre of the pseudepigraphical letter displays in abundance the exact type of deception we find in the pastorals. The careless references to mundane affairs of daily life, the specific requests for ordinary and seemingly insignificant objects to be delivered, and even the attempt to display personal feelings are all fully documented in other letters.[98]

First-Person Narratives

One particular method of verisimilitude involves the use of first-person narrative, in which an author not only claims to be someone other than who he is, but also narrates events as a personal participant. We have already seen this ploy at work, for example in the canonical non-pseudepigraphic forgery, Ecclesiastes, where the author provides "autobiographical" discussions as King Solomon, and in the embedded forgery of the Ascension of Isaiah. It was also used in the earlier apocalypses, such as Daniel and Enoch, as well as in apocalypses of the Christian tradition such as those of Paul and Peter. It can be found in other narrative accounts too, such as the Coptic Apocalypse of Peter or the Gospel of Peter, or in narratives embedded in other sorts of texts, as in 2 Peter's first-person "recollection" of the transfiguration. The value of the first-person narrative is that it makes the writer an authority not only because of his name but also because of his firsthand experiences. This was clearly recognized, yet again, by Speyer:

> First person narrative and eye-witness report immediately inspire the belief in the hearer that the narrator has himself experienced that which he recounts. Such first-person narration and eyewitness report are practically characteristic of miracle stories and liars' tales. First-person narrative appears no less frequently in forgeries, frequently in conjunction with a false authorial claim.[99]

Discovery Narratives

An even bolder ploy was used by some forgers in order to explain why it is that a writing by an ancient author was not widely known by earlier readers. The reason: the book was hidden and discovered only in recent times.

Possibly the most famous instance among pagan writings is the account of the Trojan War allegedly written by a participant, Dictys of Crete, a companion of Idomeneus, widely read as authentic throughout the Middle Ages. The Preface of

---

98. Lewis R. Donelson, *Pseudepigraphy and Ethical Argument in the Pastoral Epistles* (Tübingen: Mohr/Siebeck, 1986), pp. 24–25.

99. Ich-Rede und Augenzeugenschaft veranlassen den Hörer unmittelbar zu dem Glauben, daß der Erzähler das, was er berichtet, selbst erlebt hat. . . . Die Ich-Rede und die Augenzeugenschaft sind für die Wundererzählung und die Lügenerzählung geradezu kennzeichnend. Nicht weniger oft begegnet die Ich-Rede in Fälschungen, und meist ist sie hier mit der Angabe eines vorgetäuschten Verfassernamens verbunden. *Literarische Fälschung*, p. 51.

the account, by Lucius Septimius, indicates how the book came to be uncovered, through pure serendipity.

> After many centuries the tomb of Dictys at Cnossos (formerly the seat of the Cretan king) collapsed with age. Then shepherds, wandering near the ruins, stumbled upon a little box skillfully enclosed in tin. Thinking it was treasure, they soon broke it open, but brought to light, instead of gold or some other kind of wealth, books written on linden tablets. Their hopes thus frustrated, they took their find to Praxis, the owner of that place. Praxis had the books transliterated into the Attic alphabet and presented them to the Roman Emperor Nero.[100]

The author of the account then indicates that he has translated the books into Latin, thus explaining both how they have mysteriously now appeared and why they are not circulating in a form of ancient Greek. The reality is that the entire set of books, preface and all, were forged.[101]

We have already seen a comparable account in the Pythagorean writings falsely claiming to be written by none other than the second (legendary) king of Rome, Numa, as reported by both Livy (*History of Rome*, 40, 29) and Pliny the Elder (*Natural History*, 13, 84–87). Livy indicates that the "discovery" was made in 181 BCE in a field under construction. Workers uncovered two large stone chests with lids fastened by lead. On them were inscriptions in Latin and Greek. One chest was said to be the sarcophagus of Numa Pompilius; the other was said to contain his books. There was no trace of the body in the one chest, but the other contained two bundles tied with waxed rope, each containing seven books, "not merely whole, but looking absolutely fresh" (non integros modo sed recentissima specie; *History of Rome* 40.29).[102]

Seven of these books dealt with pontifical law (of which, by tradition, Numa was the author); the seven in Greek dealt with "a system of philosophy which might have been current at that time" (septem Graeci de disciplina sapientiae quae illius aetatis esse potuit). Valerius Antias indicates that "they were Pythagorean, confirmation of the common belief, which says that Numa was a pupil of Pythagoras, being arranged by a plausible invention." As the books circulated, officials began to be worried about them; the praetor urbanus, Quintus Petilius, thought that a good portion of what was in them could be seen as subversive of religion: pleraque dissolvendarum religionum esse. After consultation he decided to have them publicly burned.

---

100. Translation of R. M. Frazer, *The Trojan War: The Chronicles of Dictys of Crete and Dares the Phrygian* (Bloomington: Indiana University Press, 1966).

101. See Stefan Merkle, "The Truth and Nothing But the Truth: Dictys and Dares," in G. Schmeling, *The Novel in the Ancient World* (Leiden: Brill, 1996), pp. 564–80.

102. For translation, see Evan Sage and Alfred Schlesinger, *Livy History of Rome Book XL–XLII*, LCL (Cambridge, MA: Harvard University, 1938).

Livy is not explicit about the authenticity of the books, but Pliny clearly suggests they were forged. The reason for thinking so: as an authority from the time of the alleged discovery pointed out, it was difficult to believe that books could have lasted so long without deteriorating.

These pagan examples have their clear counterparts in the best-known discovery narrative of Christian writings, the Apocalypse of Paul. The visions of Paul are introduced with this validation:

> In the consulship of Theodosius Augustus the younger and Cynegius, a certain nobleman was then living in Tarsus, in the house which was that of Saint Paul; an angel appeared in the night and revealed it to him, saying that he should open the foundations of the house and should publish what he found; but he thought that these things were dreams.
>
> But the angel coming for the third time beat him and forced him to open the foundation. And digging he found a marble box inscribed on the sides; there was the revelation of Saint Paul, and his shoes in which he walked teaching the word of God. But he feared to open that box and brought it to the judge; when he had received it, the judge, because it was sealed with lead, sent it to the emperor Theodosius, fearing lest it might be something else; when the emperor had received it he opened it, and found the revelation of Saint Paul, a copy of which he sent to Jerusalem and retained the original himself.[103]

As should be clear from these sundry examples, discovery narratives functioned not only to explain the long-absence of a book or set of books, but also to establish their authoritative credentials. In many instances the "discovery" is a result of divine intervention. This was the case as well, for example, with the "discovery" of bronze tablets by Alexander, Lucian's "False Prophet."[104] These tablets, which were planted by Alexander himself, indicated that Asclepeius and his father Apollo were planning to take up residence in Abonoteichus, the location of Alexander's soon-to-be-established faux oracle (*Alexander the False Prophet*, 10).

Lucian was not the only one who recognized how a discovery narrative could serve as a ploy. We also have Cicero's scathing comments on the "discovery" of lots as a means of divination. Cicero was quite forthright in his own opinion of the practice: "And pray what is the need, do you think, to talk about the casting of lots? It is much like playing at morra, dice, or knuckle-bones, in which recklessness and luck prevail rather than reflection and judgement."[105] But those who justified the use of lots claimed divine authorization, from a standard discovery narrative:

---

103. Translation of J. K. Elliott, *The Apocryphal New Testament: A Collection of Apocryphal Christian Literature in an English Translation* (Oxford: Clarendon Press, 1993).

104. See p. 99.

105. Translation of William A. Falconer, *Cicero: De Senectute, De Amicitia, De Divinatione*, LCL (Cambridge, MA: Harvard University, 1935).

> According to the annals of Praeneste Numerius Suffustius, who was a distinguished man of noble birth, was admonished by dreams, often repeated, and finally even by threats, to split open a flint rock which was lying in a designated place. Frightened by the visions and disregarding the jeers of his fellow-townsmen he set about doing as he had been directed. And so when he had broken open the stone, the lots sprang forth carved on oak, in ancient characters. The site where the stone was found is religiously guarded to this day. It is hard by the statue of the infant Jupiter, who is represented as sitting with Juno in the lap of Fortune and reaching for her breast, and it is held in the highest reverence by mothers.[106]

At other times discovery narratives were used to justify or explain political actions as foretold by a divine source (Suetonius, *Julius* 81 and *Galba* 9, 2). We are fortunate to have a full study of the phenomenon, covering these and a host of other related issues, in another important contribution by Wolfgang Speyer.[107]

Warnings Against Forged Writings

An equally clever, if less elaborate, ruse occurs in forgeries that warn their readers against reading forgeries. Who would suspect a forger of condemning his own practice? Such warnings occur occasionally in Christian writings; in these contexts, the warning is invariably directed against the forgeries of "false" teachers, as opposed to the writer who issues the warning, who sees himself, of course, as representing the truth. As already mentioned, we have a fairly elaborate example near the end of our period in the Apostolic Constitutions:

> We have sent all these things to you, that you may know our opinion, what it is; and that you may not receive those books which obtain in our name, but are written by the ungodly. For you are not to attend to the names of the apostles, but to the nature of the things, and their settled opinions. For we know that Simon and Cleobius and their followers, have compiled poisonous books under the name of Christ and of His disciples, and do carry them about in order to deceive you who love Christ, and us His servants. And among the ancients also some have written apocryphal books of Moses, and Enoch, and Adam, and Isaiah, and David, and Elijah, and of the three patriarchs, pernicious and repugnant to the truth. (6.16)[108]

Later in the text the forger issues a more severe warning: "If any one publicly reads in the Church the spurious books of the ungodly, as if they were holy, to the destruction of the people and of the clergy, let him be deprived" (8.47.60).

106. *On Divination*, 2.85.

107. *Bücherfunde in der Glaubenswerbung der Antike.*

108. Translation of James Donaldson in *ANF*, vol. 7.

Also as we have seen, a similar ploy appears already near the beginning of the period of our concern, in 2 Thess. 2:2. Here an author falsely claiming to be Paul warns against a letter "as if by us." An analogous concern is expressed by the forger of the Epistula Petri and the Contestio of the Pseudo-Clementine literature, whose false author warns his ostensible reader to protect his writings against falsifications.

Material and Literary Prophylaxes

Orthonymous writings sometimes employed forms of material and literary prophylaxis to assure their readers of their authenticity. Not surprisingly, forgers occasionally took the cue and inserted such forms of protection in their own works as a subterfuge. In the documentary realm we learn from Suetonius that Nero made provisions for the protection of wills: "It was in his [Nero's] reign that a protection against forgers (adversus falsarios) was first devised, by having no tablets signed that were not bored with holes through which a cord was thrice passed."[109] Sometimes authenticity was "guaranteed" by a sign or seal, as when Augustine indicates in Letter 59: "I have sent this letter sealed with a ring which has a head of a man looking to one side."[110] At other times the wording of a writing itself was to be taken as a sign of authenticity, as in the thirteenth letter of Plato, widely thought to be forged: "Plato to Dionysius, Tyrant of Syracuse, Wishes well-doing. Let this greeting not only commence my letter but serve at the same time as a token that it is from me" (σύμβολον ὅτι παρ' ἐμοῦ ἐστίν).[111] Something similar occurs in 2 Thessalonians, where some interpreters have thought that the author doth protest too much: "The greeting is in my own hand—the hand of Paul—which is a sign in my every epistle; this is how I write" (3:17).

Authors who wanted to implement a more sophisticated form of prophylaxis would sometimes resort to the use of embedded acrostics. Dionysius of Halicarnassus indicates that the acrostic was the mark of the pagan Sybilline oracles. After the collection of oracles was burned in the fire of 83 BCE, the Roman senate sent out envoys to collect copies from various places, especially Erythrea in Asia. But not all those collected were judged authentic. As Dionysius indicates: "Some of these are found to be interpolations among the genuine Sibylline oracles, being recognized as such by means of the so-called acrostics. In all this I am following the account given by Terentius Varro in his work on religion."[112]

---

109. *Nero*, 17; translation of J. C. Rolfe, *Suetonius: Lives of the Caesars*, LCL (Cambridge, MA: Harvard University, 1935).

110. Translation of Wilfrid Parsons, *Augustine, Letters 1–82*; FC, vol. 12 (Washington, DC: Catholic University Press of America, 1951), p. 300.

111. Translation of R. G. Bury, *Plato: Timaeus, Critias, Cleitophon, Menexenus, Epistles*, LCL (Cambridge, MA: Harvard University, 1929).

112. *Roman Antiquities*, 4.62.6. Translation of Earnest Cary, in LCL (Cambridge, MA: Harvard University, 1937–1950).

A later Christian forger accordingly followed suit and produced at least part of what is now book 8 of the Oracula Sibyllina with an elaborate acrostic that celebrated its own theme. The first letters of lines 217–50 produce the words ΙΗΣΟΥΣ ΧΡΙΣΤΟΣ ΘΕΟΥ ΥΙΟΣ ΣΩΤΗΡ. Acrostics could perform a variety of functions in forged works, as we saw at the outset with the mischievous Dionysius the Renegade and his pseudo-Sophoclean *Parthenopaeus*.

Confounding Through Intercalation

As a final technique of authentication, I might mention the practice of inserting forged material into writings judged to be authentic, in order to establish credentials through association. We have seen a comparable ploy with respect to the treatise of Tertullian on the Trinity, which according to Rufinus (*De adult. libr. Origen*) was inserted into a manuscript that otherwise contained the authentic letters of Cyprian, in an attempt to validate Tertullian's (discredited) views of the Holy Spirit. In this case, the Tertullian work was not forged; by leaving off the author's name, however, the culprit(s) managed to pass the work off as that of a respected and unquestioned authority.

Similar tricks were used by other pagan and Christian forgers. And so, for example, it is widely held that the epistles of Plato—most of them forged—acquired their standing by being placed in a corpus that contained, as well, writings that were authentic. And the six forged letters of the Long Recension of Ignatius were intermingled with the authentic seven, which were themselves interpolated by the forger of the six. In both these instances the perpetrators were remarkably successful; their handiwork was not uncovered until relatively modern times.

THE QUESTION OF INTENT

At the outset of this chapter I stressed the importance of differentiating between an author's intention and her motivation. Intention involves what an author wants to accomplish; motivation involves her reasons for wanting to accomplish it. There were numerous motivations that drove ancient authors to produce forgeries. In virtually every instance, however, their intention was the same. It was to convince their readers that they were the person they claimed to be. Their intention, in other words, was deceit.[113]

Many scholars have argued otherwise, maintaining that no deceit was involved in the production of literary pseudepigrapha. This view flies in the face of the convincing arguments of such older scholars as J. S. Candlish and Frederik Torm, the latter of whom could write already some eighty years ago that the idea that pseudonymous writings were widely seen in antiquity simply as a literary form

113. On the theoretical problem of intent, see p. 30, n. 3.

is a "modern invention."[114] The intervening years, regrettably, have seen no shortage of scholars who have subscribed to this "modern invention" of the notion of a literary forgery not meant to deceive its readers. Most of these scholars are experts in religion, and specifically in the New Testament. Their own intentions are in most instances clear: to absolve the authors of ancient forgeries of any guilt involved with lying and deception. All are heirs of the discredited scholars that Torm had in mind, such as the nineteenth-century J. Bernays: "Pagans, Jews and Christians have made use of the same [literary form]—one with greater, the other with lesser skill, but all without experiencing even the slightest scruple. This appeared to them to be a mere game of hide and seek, in which one deemed neither oneself nor another as a true forger."[115] In the English world some such views were expressed repeatedly, for example in the classic work on the Pastorals by P. N. Harrison: The author "was not conscious of misrepresenting the Apostle in any way; he was not consciously deceiving anybody; it is not, indeed, necessary to suppose that he did deceive anybody."[116]

Even though such views have long been discredited by scholars of ancient forgery, they continue to live on among Neutestamentlers, in part, no doubt, because those in the guild rely on the work of others in the guild, and do not as a rule read widely outside of it, for example in the work of scholars of ancient forgery. And so, for example, we find in a recent introduction to the New Testament by P. Achtemeier, J. Green, and M. Thompson a repetition of the old chestnut: "Pseudonymity appears to have been primarily a literary technique, and not one meant to deliberately deceive its readers."[117] Or writing in the wake of his student David Meade,[118] James Dunn can assert that an ancient pseudepigrapher standing in a(nother author's) tradition "could present his message as the message of the originator of that stream of tradition, because in his eyes that is what it was. . . . There was no intention to deceive, and almost certainly the final readers were not in fact deceived."[119]

Similar views are expressed by commentators who want to insist that New Testament pseudepigrapha are "transparent fictions"—meaning that the readers were meant to see through them and in fact did see through them, so that no deception was involved. This is R. Bauckham's claim with respect to 2 Peter: "Petrine

---

114. See p. 79.

115. "Heiden, Juden und Christen haben sich derselben [schriftstellerischen Form] bedient, der eine mit größerer, der andere mit geringerer Gewandtheit, alle aber ohne den leisesten Skrupel zu empfinden; es schien dies ein bloßes Versteckspiel, bei dem man weder sich selbst noch anderen als wirklicher Fälscher vorkam." J. Bernays, *Gesammelte Abhandlungen* 1 (1885) p. 250, as cited in Speyer, *Literarische Fälschung*, pp. 5–6.

116. *The Problem of the Pastoral Epistles*, 1921, p. 12.

117. Paul J. Achtemeier, Joel B. Green, and Marianne M. Thompson, *Introducing the New Testament, Its Literature and Theology* (Grand Rapids, MI: Eerdmans, 2001), p. 560.

118. See pp. 39–42.

119. "The Problem of Pseudonymity," in *The Living Word* (Philadelphia: Fortress, 1988), p. 84.

authorship was intended to be an entirely transparent fiction."[120] Even as good a scholar as Luke Timothy Johnson can write with approbation: "Later scholars [i.e., after Schleiermacher] became more sophisticated about pseudonymity, recognizing that it was both prevalent in antiquity and often a transparent fiction that did not seek to deceive."[121] Such views are virtually ubiquitous among New Testament commentators.[122]

Scholars who have considered the early Christian pseudepigrapha not in a cultural vacuum, however, but in relation to the broader phenomenon have, as a rule, taken an opposite stand. In his presidential address to the SBL, for example, Bruce Metzger asked the rhetorical question: "How can it be so confidently known that such productions 'would deceive no one'? Indeed if nobody was taken in by the device of pseudepigraphy, it is difficult to see why it was adopted at all."[123] The problematic notion of a "transparent fiction" was more carefully exposed, recently, by Annette Merz:

> The basic problem with this assumption of a transparent pseudepigraphy in ancient Christianity is that neither in the texts themselves are there any kinds of signals to the implied reader that allow us to discern a consciousness of this supposed genre, nor do we encounter pointers in other sources to such an attitude on the part of recipients.[124]

That deception was involved in the production of forgeries is the firm and emphatic conclusion of all the major studies of forgery, for example, those of Speyer, Brox, Grafton, and Baum. And for good reasons, as we will see. More representative of this less-apologetic perspective is the clear-headed recent statement of Harry Gamble: "It is undeniable, however, that irrespective of context, genre, or motive, pseudonymous writings are in their very nature deceptive, misleading the reader about the identity of the author."[125] Recall the words of the greatest modern scholar of forgery, Wolfgang Speyer: "Each forgery feigns a state of affairs that

---

120. *Jude, 2 Peter* WBC, 50 (Waco, TX: Word Books, 1983), p. 134.

121. *The First and Second Letters to Timothy*, AB 35A (New York: Doubleday, 2001), p. 57.

122. There is no need to provide an exhaustive list. Martina Janssen names the following as representative (from the late nineteenth to the late twentieth centuries): B. Hegermann, E. Reinmuth, Gerd Theissen, B. S. Easton, H. J. Holtzmann, H.-J. Klauck. A. Vögtle, and others. See Janssen, *Unter falschem Namen*, pp. 182–85.

123. Bruce M. Metzger, "Literary Forgeries and Canonical Pseudepigrapha," *JBL*, 91 (1972): 15–16.

124. "Das Grundproblem dieser Annahme einer offenen Pseudepigraphie im Urchristentum ist, dass weder in den Texten selbst irgendwelche Signale an die impliziten Leser zu finden sind, die ein Bewusstsein für diese postulierte Form der Rede erkennen lassen, noch in den sonstigen Quellen Hinweise für eine solche Einstellung auf Seiten der Rezipient Innen begegnen." *Die fiktive Selbstauslegung des Paulus: Intertextuelle Studien zur Intention und Rezeption der Pastoralbriefe* (Göttingen: Vandenhoeck & Ruprecht, 2004), p. 198.

125. "Pseudonymity and NT Canon," p. 356.

does not correspond to actual events. In this vein, forgery belongs to the realm of lie and deceit."[126]

Why then have scholars, especially New Testament commentators who have not looked at the broader phenomenon (and who, as a rule, do not cite any evidence), said otherwise? It is hard to escape the characteristically trenchant conclusion drawn by Anthony Grafton: "The only reason to assume that most earlier forgers were more innocent is our own desire to explain away a disquieting feature of the past."[127]

Reasons for acknowledging that the overriding intention of forgers was to deceive their readers should be quite obvious from everything that has been said over the past two chapters. How else can we make sense of the motivations that drove forgers to produce their works in the first place, the techniques they used to avoid detection, and the reactions they incurred when detected? How else can we explain the pains that orthonymous authors took to assure their readers that their writings were authentic and the widespread exercise of criticism by scholars wanting to detect and declare which works were orthonymous and which spurious?

With respect to motives: if forgers could make money for the production of "authentic" writings of Euripides or Plato, who would pay if the works were known to be forged? If a forgery was used to authorize an oracle or some other religious institution, who would be persuaded if the authority did not write the authorization? If a forgery was produced as an apologia—for example of the Jewish or Christian religion on the pen of an ancient pagan prophetess—who would be convinced if it was known to be the work of a later author simply claiming to be someone he was not? If a forgery was produced in the name of a famous person in order to defame his character, as in the case of the fifty obscene letters forged by Diotimus in the name of Epicurus, how could they obtain their desired result if no one thought they were orthonymous? And on and on. None of the motivations for producing forgeries makes sense if they were transparent fictions. And so L. Donelson can categorically state: "No one ever seems to have accepted a document as religiously and philosophically prescriptive which was known to be forged. I do not know of a single example."[128]

Moreover, if deceit were not involved, it is well nigh impossible to explain the techniques forgers used in order to pass their work off as someone else's. Not only would the competent forger claim to be another person; he would also try to imitate the style of the person's writing and introduce verisimilitudes into the writing. He sometimes might include a discovery narrative to explain why the writing was not widely known before. He might warn his readers against those who forge writings in his name. He might introduce various prophylaxes into his

---

126. "Jede Fälschung täuscht einen Sachverhalt vor, der den tatsächlichen Gegebenheiten nicht entspricht. Damit gehört die Fälschung in das Gebiet der Lüge und des Betruges." *Literarische Fälschung*, p. 3.

127. *Forgers and Critics*, p. 37.

128. P. 11.

account to assure his reader that it is genuine—seals, signs, acrostics, and the like. If he expected his reader to see through his ploy, why go to all the trouble? So too orthonymous writings tried to protect their integrity and to assure their readers by the same means. Why would this be necessary if forgeries were transparent? Why bother to protect what needs no protection?

And if no one was deceived, why are the reactions to forgers consistently negative and often harsh? Why do we have accounts of forgers being maligned, attacked, slurred, exiled, and murdered for their efforts—if no one was deceived and no one, frankly, cared? And why would ancient literary scholars need to go to all the bother of exposing forgeries and deciding for their readers which works circulating under an author's name were genuine and which were not, if no one was deceived?

All of the evidence points in the same direction. Forgers meant to deceive their readers. And they very often succeeded. So often did they succeed that in many instances—not just from early Christianity, but certainly at least from there—forgeries have not been detected until the modern period.

JUSTIFICATIONS FOR FORGERY: THE NOBLE LIE

Forgery therefore involved literary deception. For nearly as long as there have been forgers there have been critics trying to expose forgeries, as we will see in greater detail shortly. Forgery was not an acceptable practice in the ancient world, any more than other forms of lying and deception were acceptable practices. Why then did forgers engage in their craft? Here I am not asking the question of motivation, which I have already addressed, but the question of self-justification. Forgers engaged in a culturally despised activity. Some of these forgers—as we can assume, for example, within much of the Christian tradition—were proponents of traditional moral values. So how did they explain to themselves what they did? This is a topic to which we will return at greater length at the end of our study, when we query specifically why the Christian forgers did what they did, or at least how they justified their actions to themselves.

The psychological question can never, of course, be answered in any definitive way, as we have no access to the inner mental and emotional processes of our anonymous forgers. We know very little about these people. Among other things, we do not even know their names, let alone anything concrete about them. Nonetheless, it may be worth our while to try to situate the activities of forgers in some kind of plausible psychological or, at least, philosophical context, if we are to make sense of the practice in a broader way.

It is much to be regretted that we have such scant traces of forgers' self-reportage.[129] Sometimes appeal is made to Tertullian's discussion of the Acts of

129. See the informative discussion of Martina Janssen, "Antike (Selbst-)Aussagen über Beweggründe zur Pseudepigraphie," who, obviously, is more interested in the related question of self-described motivation.

Paul, produced by an unnamed presbyter of Asia Minor, who declared that he did it "for the love of Paul" (*De baptismo,* 17). Unfortunately, as we have seen, in this instance we are dealing not with a forgery but with the fabrication of a historical narrative (the author did not claim to be Paul). One author who did admit to producing pseudepigrapha—"Mithridates," who penned pseudonymous epistolary responses to Brutus from those to whom he had addressed letters—regrettably tells us nothing about how he understood what it was he was doing.

The one instance in which we have an ancient forger explain himself is the fifth-century Salvian of Marseille. As we have seen, Salvian refuses to admit guilt but states, as we have seen, that whereas readers should not assign authority to a mere name, he wrote in the name of Timothy because his own name carried no weight or authority. Salvian claims that he did nothing wrong: the "Timothy" named in the letter was not meant to be the apostolic companion of Paul but a pure pseudonym. He was writing "for the honor of God." This claim, as we have seen, stands in direct tension with Salvian's simultaneous insistence that for the book to be read it needed to be produced in the name of an authority. In any event, Salvian carefully avoids any admission of guilt, and if he refuses to acknowledge what he has done, then it is impossible for us to know how he justified it to himself. Possibly Salvian and most other forgers were so conflicted by what they were doing—deceiving others when they believed deceit was wrong—that they were unable even to explain to themselves why they did what they did.

There is no doubt, in any event, that the act of forgery was not just an act of deception but an active act of deception, involving a conscious literary lie. This is clearly recognized by Morton Smith, in his account of Jewish pseudepigrapha, where he states what should be—but regrettably is not always—obvious: even if a forger thought he had good reasons for doing what he did, "these considerations would not alter the fact that he knew he wrote the work, and he knew that the pretended author had not."[130]

In this connection it is important to stress again the difference between fiction and forgery. Antiquity had its own forms of writing that correspond roughly to our notion of fiction, and which were recognized as such, even if there continue to be debates among scholars about the nature of ancient fiction in relation to genres today.[131] But in a world of retold myths, epic poems, novels, and satires (cf. Lucian's "True Story") there was—even there—a tacit agreement between an author and a reader in which the requirement of factual reporting was suspended. As Michael Wood helpfully indicates, "Fiction is pure invention, any sort of fab-

---

130. "Pseudepigraphy in the Israelite Tradition," in *Pseudepigrapha I: Pseudopythagorica, Lettres de Platon, Littérature pseudépigraphique juive,* ed. Kurt von Fritz (Vandoeuvres-Génève: Fondation Hardt pour l'Étude de l'Antiquité Classique, 1972), pp. 206–7.

131. For an argument that nothing that corresponds to our sense of "fiction" existed in the ancient world, see Christopher Gill, "Plato on Falsehood–Not Fiction," in Christopher Gill and T. P. Wiseman, eds., *Lies and Fiction in the Ancient World* (Austin: University of Texas Press, 1993), pp. 38–87. For further discussion, see pp. 533–34.

rication. It is invention which knows it is invention; or which knows *and says* it is invention; or which, whatever it knows and says, *is known* to be invention."[132] The reports of forgery, on the other hand, consistently show that there was no agreement between author and reader for the assumption of a false name.[133]

There is no need for me at this stage to provide a lengthy evaluation of the ancient discourses on lying and deceit.[134] This is a matter to which I will return at the conclusion of our study. Suffice it to say, at this stage, that there was not one opinion about what lying was and under what circumstances it was acceptable. When Augustine wrote his two famous treatises on lying—the two most famous discussions from all of Christian antiquity—he staked out clear and precise positions both on what constituted a lie (a fissure between thought and utterance that is evident to the speaker in an act of speaking undertaken precisely with the intent of creating the fissure) and when telling a lie was admissible (never, under any circumstances whatsoever). But it is important to recall, with Paul Griffiths,

132. "Prologue," in Gill and Wiseman, eds., *Lies and Fiction in the Ancient World*, p. xvi. Italics his.

133. Even if Gill were right about ancient "fiction" (see note 131), my characterization would apply. There were some kinds of discourse that were adopted and accepted widely in antiquity—even if they involved narratives and discourses that were not factually true (e.g., epic poems, Platonic Dialogues, historians' speeches, and the like)—because they (1) fulfilled a kind of contract between the author and reader to be what they were and not something else and (2) attempted to convey what was true: philosophical "truth," a "true" representation of what a speaker would have said, a "true" conveyor of a culture's heritage/tradition, etc. Lacking that implicit contract, a "forgery" was widely thought to violate cultural standards, even if the author was trying to convey something that in his view was "true" (e.g., how Paul would have responded if he were faced with Gnostic teachings). Moreover, his views were often rejected as "false" even if they were, in fact, "true" (i.e., the writing is rejected independently of the question of whether Paul really would have responded this way or not).

134. There is, naturally, a sizeable literature. In addition to the essays in Gill and Wiseman, *Lies and Fiction*, the following are among the most useful for understanding key aspects of the Christian tradition: Franz Schindler, "Die Lüge in der patristischen Literatur," *Beiträge zur Geschichte des christlichen Altertums und der byzantinischen Literatur* (Amsterdam: Rodopi, 1969; originally published 1922); Gregor Müller, *Die Wahrhaftigkeitspflicht und die Problematik der Lüge: Ein Längsschnitt durch die Moraltheologie und Ethik unter besonderer Berücksichtigung der Tugendlehre des Thomas von Aquin und der modernen Lösungsversuche* (Freiburg: Herder, 1962; among other things, Müller acknowledges that "several fathers of this era consider permissible the 'lie from necessity'" ["einige Väter dieser Epoche die 'Notlüge' für erlaubt halten"] and numbers among them Origen, Didymus, Chrysostom, Jon Cassian, Theodoret, and others); R. P. C. Hanson, *Allegory and Event: A Study of the Sources and Significance of Origen's Interpretation of Scripture* (Richmond: John Knox, 1959; Hanson includes comments on divine deception, esp. in Origen's *Homilies* on Jeremiah; see XIX.15 and XX.3); Boniface Ramsey, "Two Traditions on Lying and Deception in the Ancient Church," *Thom.* 49 (1985): 504–33; David Satran, "Pedagogy and Deceit in the Alexandrian Theological Tradition," in *Origeniana Quinta*, ed. R. J. Daly (1992), pp. 119–24 (dealing with Philo, Clement of Alexandria, Origen); and the articles in *JECS* 9 (2009). There is an extensive literature on Augustine in particular, all referred to and surpassed by Paul J. Griffiths, *Lying: An Augustinian Theology of Duplicity* (Grand Rapids, MI: Brazos Press, 2004), a lucid, readable, intelligent, and helpful discussion, which embraces Augustine's view that consciously duplicitous speech acts are never acceptable, no matter what, as rooted in Augustine's understanding of the word in relationship to what it means to be human in relationship to God.

the most compelling commentator on Augustine's position, that especially with respect to the latter point, "Few Christians agreed with him when he wrote."[135]

On the contrary there was a widespread notion among thinkers from Socrates to Chrysostom—that is, throughout the entire period of our concern, and considerably prior—that lying was in some circumstances acceptable and not, necessarily, morally condemned. As Jane Zembaty has stated in a study of Plato's Republic, lying or deception was sometimes "justified by more important moral considerations."[136] Plato is known to have advocated the moral justification of lying to one's enemies, and more significant, to have proposed the "noble lie," reserved for the protectors of the state in his Republic, who needed to deceive their subjects in order to promote the greatest possible good. These notions did not originate with Plato, however; Socrates before him, for example, maintained that there were occasions in which lying was both necessary and useful, as when a field general needed to lie to his disheartened troops that reinforcements were near in order to spur them to more valiant efforts, or when a doctor needed to deceive a child in order to convince him to take medication that was good for him. Or so, at least, Xenophon reports in the *Memorabilia* (4, 2, 15–18).

Aristotle agreed with Plato, in Paul Griffiths' words, "damning some lies, excusing others, and recommending yet others (though they did not agree on which lies belong to which category)."[137] Sextus Empiricus showed that later Stoics accepted Plato's view (*Adv. Mathematicos)*, and by our period the idea had become a commonplace, as seen in its reappearance, in appropriately modified forms, in such widely disparate sources as Quintilian ("Is not this another case where the orator will not shrink even from lies, if so he may save one who is not merely innocent, but a praiseworthy citizen?")[138] and Heliodorus ("For lying is good whenever it benefits those who speak but does no harm to those who hear").[139]

Christian authors could and did appeal to numerous instances from Scripture itself in order to justify their own practices of lying and deception (as Augustine notes, disapprovingly): the midwives of Exodus 1:15–22, who protected the Hebrew babies from the unjust wrath of Pharaoh; Abraham and Isaac, who saved their own skins, and the posterity of Israel, by lying about their wives (e.g., Genesis 22); Rahab, who lied about the spies in Joshua 2; Michal, whose deception in 1 Samuel 19:11–18 saved David, the father of the future messiah; Jonathan, who lied to protect him a chapter later; and Jesus himself, who declared he was not going to Jerusalem in John 7, knowing full well that he was; and after his resurrection when he deceived his two followers on the road to Emmaus by assuming a false appearance in Luke 24. Even God is said to have employed deception in

---

135. *Lying*, p. 14.

136. Jane S. Zembaty, "Plato's Republic and Greek Morality on Lying," *JHP* 26 (1988): 531.

137. *Lying*, p. 13.

138. *Institutio Oratio*, 12.1.41. Translation of H.E. Butler in LCL (Cambridge, MA: Harvard University, 1929).

139. *Ethiopica*, 1.26.6. Translation mine.

Scripture, most famously in Jeremiah's lament, "O Lord, you have deceived me and I have been deceived" (Jer. 20:7).

We do not know, of course, what explanations or excuses forgers made to themselves when they engaged in their acts of conscious deception. But it has plausibly been argued by such scholars as Norbert Brox and Armin Baum that these authors—some of them? most of them?—subscribed to the secular and biblical idea of the "noble lie"—that it was better in some circumstances to practice deception so that a greater good might result. As Brox stresses:

> Notions that those kinds of deceptions, lies, and tricks carried out for the sake of truth and for the effective communication of truth, were expressly permitted were widespread, even if other contemporaries held different views. . . . Thus we cannot continue to say that all forgers (including Christian ones) must have forged with a troubled conscience.[140]

It is important not to miss the caveat, which cannot be worded strongly enough: "even if other contemporaries held different views." We do not have any evidence of any Christian forger being welcomed and supported for his attempt to achieve a greater good through an act of deception. Some Christians may indeed have approved such practices, just as other Christians may have approved of lying under oath, stealing, armed rebellion, and murder, if the circumstances required it.

In any event, it is not at all implausible that forgers themselves may have excused their activities to themselves on the ground that they were accomplishing more good than evil in lying about their identity in order to have their point of view heard. One can easily imagine a situation where later followers of Paul, Peter, James, Thomas, or any of the other apostles may have thought that by producing a writing in the name of their teachers—even if several generations or centuries removed—they could deal more effectively with a problem that had arisen or with a situation that had to be addressed. They may well have thought that their writing was very much what their teacher would have said, had he been alive at the time to say it.

But the reality is that other persons with alternative points of view—even precisely the opposite points of view—may well have thought the same things about their own lies and deceits. In either instance the forger may have felt that he

---

140. "Es gab verbreitete Vorstellungen, nach denen um der Wahrheit und um der wirksamen Vermittlung der Wahrheit willen Täuschung, List und Tricks ausdrücklich gestattet waren, auch wenn andere Zeitgenossen anderer Meinung waren. . . . Man kann also nicht weiterhin sagen, daß alle Fälscher (auch die christlichen) schlechten Gewissens gefälscht haben müssen." *Falsche Verfasserangaben*, pp. 91–92. A comparable notion involves the "antidote" given to heal a disease, as pointed out, based on passages in Plato, Clement of Alexandria, Origen, and Jerome, by Petr Pokorný, "Das theologische Problem der neutestamentlichen Pseudepigraphie": "The authors of the canonical Christian pseudepigrapha apparently felt justified in their actions primarily by virtue of the notion of fighting fire with fire" (Die Verfasser der kanonisierten christlichen Pseudepigraphen fühlten sich in ihrem Vorgehen offensichtlich vor allem durch die Thesen von dem Gegengift gerechtfertigt).

engaged in a noble lie and that he was justified in claiming to be someone other than he was. His opponents—conceivably, other forgers—would have felt quite differently, and would have called him a liar and would have labeled his work a νόθον. It is not just that the contents of the works were false; the author himself had tried to deceive his readers about his identity.

CRITERIA OF DETECTION

Throughout these opening chapters we have seen a steady stream of ancient witnesses to a consistent attitude toward forgery. Ancient critics were concerned to know the names and identities of the actual authors of texts; if a writing was suspected of being pseudepigraphic, there was an active interest in knowing who the real author was.[141] In no small measure, this was because of a widely unspoken assumption that the authority of a text resides in the person of the author. At the same time, the identity of the authorizing author was determined to some extent by the details of the text, so that a symbiotic relation existed between text and author: the author authorized the contents of the text, but the contents of the text established the identity of the author.

In an insightful study that effortlessly ranges from antiquity to early modernity, Anthony Grafton has shown that over the centuries the art of forgery grew and changed in relationship to the practice of criticism: the better critics became at determining forgery, the more skilled forgers became, by necessity, in hiding the traces of their deceit. As forgers improved their craft, critics further honed their skills, leading forgers to improve yet further.[142] This escalating scale of deceit and detection does not mean that the essential character of criticism changed over the centuries; as it turns out, the ancients used many of the same methods and appealed to many of the same criteria that critics use today.

Some form of Echtheitskritik goes back at least as far as Herodotus.[143] To be sure, as might be expected, in antiquity, as today, there was considerable gullibility on all sorts of matters, as sometimes lamented by the highly educated elite, such as Pliny the Elder: "It is astounding to what lengths Greek credulity (credulitas) will go; there is no lie (mendacium) so shameless as to lack a supporter."[144] And we have already seen what a modern critic has said about ancient credulity: "an uncritical approach to literature and gullibility of every kind were widespread. The history of literary gullibility has yet to be written."[145] Still, criticism

141. For a relatively full discussion of the use of critical methods to uncover forgery in antiquity, see Speyer, *Literarische Fälschung*, pp. 112–28.

142. *Forgers and Critics*, passim.

143. See the earlier discussion on pp. 61–62 and below p. 140.

144. *Natural History*, 8.82. Pliny, however, was not speaking of forgers but of werewolves!

145. ". . . waren literarische Kritiklosigkeit und Leichtgläubigkeit jedweder Art weit verbreitet. Die Geschichte der literarischen Leichtgläubigkeit ist noch nicht geschrieben." Speyer, *Literarische Fälschung*, p. 85.

was widely practiced, at least in the rarified atmosphere of the cultural elite. The following were among the criteria explicitly invoked in deciding whether a work was γνήσιος or ψεῦδος.

Style

First and foremost was the matter of literary style. We have already seen Galen's heartfelt approbation of the unnamed amateur critic who uncovered a forgery in Galen's own name simply by perusing the first two lines: οὐκ ἔστιν ἡ λέξις αὕτη Γαλήνου: "this is not the style of Galen." Galen himself was a master of style, and used stylistic considerations to great effect in his massive effort to establish the authentic Hippocratic corpus and to uncover the pseudepigraphic works within it. Just on the Hippocratic *On the Nature of Man*, for example, he is able to show that parts of the work, at least, could not have been forged at the time of the construction of the great Hellenistic libraries—invoking a different criterion—because they are quoted already by Plato, whereas other portions are of more recent vintage: "Those words must come from recent doctors who did not know the ancient style."[146]

The appeal to style was no Galenic invention. Two centuries earlier stylistic criteria were used to good effect by Dionysius of Halicarnassus. His essay on Dinarchus, the late-fourth-century Athenian orator, is nothing but a discussion of which speeches are genuinely his (γνήσιοι) and which are false, ψεῦδοι or ψευδεπίγραφοι. The grounds he appeals to time and again are stylistic: περὶ τοῦ χαρακτῆρος (ch. 5). Moreover, Dionysius claims that the same criterion can be applied to the works of Plato, Thucydides, Isocrates, or Demosthenes. Each author has a characteristic style, and Dionysius explains in rough form what it is. He then gives reasons for rejecting speeches that he considers "spurious" (ψεῦδοι). Elsewhere, in his evaluation of the writings of Lysias, he argues that the speech about the statue of Iphicrates is "devoid of charm and does not at all display the eloquence of Lysias."

So too Aulus Gellius, in the second century CE, weighed in on the question of the 130 comedies ascribed to Plautus. Noting that Varro had argued, largely on stylistic grounds, that only 21 of the plays were Plautan, Gellius himself considered that several more should be accepted, since they manifested "the characteristic features of his manner and diction" (*Noctes atticae* 3.3). So too Philostratus attacks those who ascribe *Araspes the Lover of Panthea* to Dionysius of Miletus, the great rhetor, indicating that they "are ignorant not only of his rhythms but of his whole style of eloquence, moreover they know nothing of the art of ratiocination."[147] The work instead was written by Celer, "the writer on rhetoric" who was in fact unfriendly with Dionysius from their youth onward, and "was not skilled in declamation" (*Lives of the Sophists* 1.22). So too in his *Life of Apollonius*,

146. See the discussion in Grafton, *Forgers and Critics*, p. 19.

147. Translation of Wilmer Wright, *Philostratus*, LCL (Cambridge, MA: Harvard University, 1952).

(7, 35) he indicates that the enemies of his protagonist had forged a letter (τινα ἐπιστολὴν ἀνέπλασαν) in his name, in which it was stated that Apollonius supplicated Domitian on his knees to be released from his bonds. Philostratus had no difficulty exposing the forgery: "Certainly Apollonius wrote his own will in Ionic; but a letter of his in that dialect I have never come across, though I have made a large collection of them, and I never observed verbosity in one of the Master's letters, since they are all brief and telegraphic."[148]

We have already seen that the educated elite among the early Christians were also adept at establishing authorship on the basis of considerations of style. Origen, for example, recognized that Hebrews could not have been written by Paul (Eusebius, *H.E.* 6.25); his contemporary Dionysius of Alexandria showed that the book of Revelation was not authored by the fourth Evangelist (Eusebius, *H.E.* 7.25); Jerome pointed out that his predecessors had called into question 2 Peter because of its stylistic differences from 1 Peter (*Vir. ill.* 1); so too he could argue that Theophilus of Antioch was not the author of certain biblical commentaries circulating in his name because they "ascribed to his authorship, which do not seem to me to match the elegance and style of the previous volumes" (*Vir. ill.* 25).

Anachronisms and Other Historical Problems

In addition to stylistic variations, ancient critics were keen to detect anachronisms and other historical problems that made it impossible for texts to have been written by their alleged authors. Returning to Dionysius of Halicarnassus, for example, and his criticism of the speech of Lysias about the statue of Iphicrates: not only does the speech differ stylistically from Lysias' other works, but the statue that it praises was not commissioned until seven years after the orator's death. Another speech in praise of Iphicrates defends its subject's actions during the War of the Allies, which occurred twenty years after Lysias had died. Dionysius argues on stylistic grounds that both speeches had been placed on the lips of Lysias by none other than Iphicrates himself (*Lysias* 12).

Somewhat later, Pliny the Elder speaks of a papyrus letter on display in a temple of Lycia which was allegedly written by Sarpedon during the Trojan war. Pliny objects on the grounds that the manufacture of papyrus in Egypt had not yet begun by the time of Homer (let alone Sarpedon), that in fact Egypt itself did not even exist yet. Since letters at the time were written on leaden tablets and linen cloths, the book cannot be authentic (*Natural History* 13, 88). So too Diogenes Laertius, citing Favorinus' *Memorabilia,* indicates that a speech of Polycrates against Socrates cannot be authentic (μὴ εἶναι ἀληθῆ τὸν λόγον) since it mentions the rebuilding of the walls by Conon, which did not take place until some years after the death of Socrates (*Lives* 2.39).

---

148. Translation of Christopher P. Jones, *The Life of Apollonius of Tyana,* LCL (Cambridge, MA: Harvard University, 2005).

At other times anachronisms took place on the level of historical linguistics. From Jerome's Prologue to his commentary on Daniel we learn that the enemy of the Christians, Porphyry, argued that the book of Daniel was a forgery that did not belong to the Hebrew Scriptures but was originally composed in Greek. This he deduced from the fact (which he had possibly picked up from Julius Africanus, who used it against Origen) that in the story of Susanna, Daniel uses the clever phrasing ἀπὸ τοῦ σχίνου σχίσαι . . . ἀπὸ τοῦ πρίνου πρίσαι "splitting the mastic tree . . . sawing the evergreen oak." This kind of alliterative pun obviously works in Greek but not in Hebrew. The book therefore does not go back to a Hebrew prophet of the sixth century BCE, but was composed in his name by a forger living in Hellenistic times.

Christian authors too were concerned with anachronisms and historical problems that called into question the authenticity of writings, both those they cherished and those written to oppose them. As mentioned, Tertullian was compelled to engage in a rather elaborate set of mental gymnastics to explain how Enoch could have written the popular apocalypse circulating in his name, given the circumstance that any such book must have perished in Noah's flood (*De cultu Fem.* 1, 3). Eusebius shows that the pagan Acts of Pilate in circulation during the reign of Maximin Daia could not be authentic, since it places the crucifixion of Jesus in the fourth consulship of Tiberius—that is, in his seventh year, whereas Pilate was not made governor of Judea, according to Josephus, until Tiberius' twelfth year (*H.E.* 1.9). So too, as we have seen, Augustine had no difficulty exposing a letter allegedly written by Jesus to his disciples Peter and Paul, on the ground that Paul was not a follower of Jesus during his earthly ministry (*De cons. evang.* 1, 10).

Internal Inconsistencies and Implausibilities

At other times pseudepigraphic writings were suspect because they contradicted the statements found in orthonymous works of the same author or contained other kinds of implausibilities. Herodotus, for example, doubted the Homeric authorship of the Cyprian poems because their account of the travels of Helen contradicted what was said in the Iliad and the Odyssey (2.117). At the end of our period Augustine cited inconsistencies between the claims of Pelagius made on trial with writings that allegedly were produced by him years earlier, arguing that the books were likely forgeries in his name produced by others (*De Gest. Pelag.* 1. 19). And as he states with reference to one of his other nemeses, Faustus:

> But even in worldly writings there were well-known authors under whose names many works were produced later, and they were repudiated either because they did not agree with the writings that were certainly theirs or because, at the time when those authors wrote, these writings did not merit to be recognized and to be handed on and commended to posterity by them or their friends. (*Contra faust.* 33.6)

Faustus himself claimed that it was completely implausible that the Gospel of Matthew was written by Matthew the tax collector, given the story of the call of Matthew in chapter 9, which is narrated in the third person:

> Hence, for the present we have allowed ourselves to do an injustice to Matthew until we prove that he did not write this but that someone else wrote it under his name. The indirect form of the same passage of Matthew teaches us this. After all, what does he say? "And when Jesus was passing by, he saw a man sitting at a tax collector's station by the name of Matthew, and he called him. But Matthew immediately got up and followed him." (Matt. 9:9) Who, then, when writing about himself, would say, "He saw a man sitting at a tax collector's station, and he called him, and he followed him," and would not rather say, "He saw me, and he called me, and I followed him." The only explanation is that Matthew did not write this but that someone else wrote it under his name. Even if Matthew wrote this, then, it would not be true, since he was not present when Jesus said this on the mountain. For how much better reason ought we not to believe this, given that Matthew did not write it but that someone else wrote it under the names of Jesus and Matthew? (17.1)

From the Roman world we have the *Apology* of Apuleius, which, as we have seen, mentions the work of his accusers who produced a "forged letter by which they attempted to prove that I beguiled Pudentilla with flattery. I never wrote it and the forgery is not even plausible" (*Apol.* 87). For one thing, his accusers charge him with using magic to entrance the rich widow: But if he used magic, why would he have needed to write a flattering letter? And how would they have obtained such a letter, which necessarily would have been private, not published?

In addition to these sundry criteria of detection used by a range of critics in antiquity, there were two that appear to be distinctively Christian, driven, at least in part, by theological views that characterized the orthodox understanding of the faith.[149]

Theological *Sachkritik*

In some early Christian discussions of authenticity there appears a critical logic that might appear peculiar to an outsider observer. The logic is founded on the idea that regnant orthodox views were rooted in the beliefs and preaching of the

149. Speyer overstates the case when he claims: "Christian criticism was dogmatically determined. Their 'Echtheitskritik' (assessments of authenticity) worked almost exclusively with the terms 'orthodox' and 'heretical'" ("Die Kritik der Christen war also dogmatisch bestimmt. Ihre Echtheitskritik arbeitete so fast ausschließlich mit den Begriffen <Rechtgläubig> und <Häretisch>"; *Literarische Fälschung*, p. 201). There were, as we have seen, other criteria used as well. But he does have a point: much of what passed as criticism in early Christian circles was theologically driven.

apostles of Jesus. Any writing that presents contrary positions could not, then, have been written by the apostles.

On one hand, this view is related to criteria mentioned earlier in which anachronisms and implausibilities can demonstrate a work's inauthenticity. Authorship was judged, in part, on contents. But this kind of *Sachkritik* is now given a theological edge. Writings out of line with orthodox Christian thinking cannot be associated with authors who stand at the foundation of the orthodox church. The circularity of the logic may seem all too patent to outsiders: orthodox Christians may have claimed the apostles as their theological forebears, but the historical figures of the apostles themselves were not so easily tamed. Multiple groups of Christians in, say, the second, third, and fourth centuries could all aver apostolic support for their views. In fact, all the groups of Christians that we know about did so, even when their views were diametrically opposed to one another. For one group to judge the authenticity of a writing based on its own set of theological perspectives is simply another way to contend that the apostles "are ours, not yours."

In any event, this kind of theological Sachkritik did occur on occasion, never more forthrightly than in the famous incident involving Serapion and the Gospel of Peter, already recounted.[150] Serapion forbade the future use of the book because of its occasional "docetic" affirmations. For him, the logic was inexorable. If parts of the book supported a theological perspective that he and his co-religionists found offensive or dangerous, then obviously they could not have originated from the pen of one of Jesus' earthly followers. Unlike the other criteria we have considered, this one is deeply rooted in heresiological concerns. It is theology, not history. Or at least it is theologically driven history.

Eusebius records a comparable debate over the book of Revelation. Some "orthodox" critics had charged that the book could not be by John, or even by a member of the true church, because it supported a sensualist vision of the future kingdom of God, involving "unlimited indulgence in gluttony and lechery at banquets, drinking bouts, and wedding feasts." Their conclusion: the book must have been forged in John's name by a heretic, most likely that nefarious opponent of orthodoxy, Cerinthus (*H.E.* 7.25). In less vitriolic terms Jerome indicates that some of his orthodox colleagues reject the book of Jude because it quotes the apocryphal book of Enoch, something no orthodox writer, obviously, would do (*Vir. ill.* 4).

A comparable logic drives Rufinus to explain how "orthodox" books could contain statements that do not toe the theological line:

> For it is shown in the case of saintly men of old and of those already judged to have been Catholics . . . that if anything is found in *their* works contrary to the faith of the Church, it should be thought to have been inserted by heretics rather than to have been written by the authors themselves. (*De adult. lib. Orig.*, 8)[151]

---

150. See pp. 90–92.

151. Scheck, *St. Pamphilus*, p. 130.

Established Patterns of Usage

The second distinctively Christian form of criticism also has analogues in the Greek and Roman worlds. We have seen that discovery narratives were adduced in large measure in order to explain why a work of such importance was not previously known. It had been hidden. Behind the ploy lies a concern of criticism: writings should have an established lineage to be accepted as authentic, rather than appearing just recently.[152]

Christians took this criterion to a new level, in no small measure because it related closely to another cherished notion, that the validity of a doctrine, practice, or policy was closely tied to its apostolic connections, and that lines of succession for all things orthodox could be traced directly back to the apostles of Jesus themselves. With few exceptions, orthodox Christians maintained that their beliefs represented the earliest forms of the tradition, and that false beliefs were later corruptions of the "original" teachings of the apostles. Clear lines of descent could be traced for both true and false positions.

This idea of succession morphed into an arbiter of literary authenticity, already by the time of Tertullian:

> These are the sort of summary arguments I use when skirmishing light-armed against heretics on behalf of the faith of the gospel, arguments which claim the support of that succession of times which pleads the previous question against the late emergence of falsifiers, as well as that authority of the churches which gives expert witness to the tradition of the apostles: because the truth must of necessity precede the false, and proceed from those from whom its tradition began. (*Adv. Marc.* 4, 5)

By the time of Eusebius the principle had solidified into a criterion. Christian—especially canonical—books are judged authentic largely on the basis of established usage among the orthodox Christian churches. Books that cannot trace a long lineage of use in such circles are suspect. And so, for example, in deciding which of Peter's writings were to be accepted as authoritative, Eusebius indicates that 1 Peter is genuine because it is quoted extensively in the writings of the early church fathers. 2 Peter was not widely known however, although some have found it worthy of a place in Scripture. But the Acts of Peter, the Gospel of Peter, the Preaching of Peter, and the Apocalypse of Peter—all attributed to him—are not to be accepted because they were not used by church writers of early days or in Eusebius's own day (*H.E.*3.3).

One might suspect that Eusebius here is concerned only with the question of canonicity, not of authenticity. But these two issues are indelibly linked for

152. Galen appealed to this criterion to establish that *De glandibus* was not actually a work of Hippocrates; none of the earlier physicians after the days of Hippocrates mentions it. See the discussion in Speyer, *Literarische Fälschung*, p. 126.

him, in no small measure because any writing by the apostle Peter would naturally need to be considered a scriptural authority. This connection is implied throughout his discussion, as when he summarizes his findings in terms of authorship: "These then are the works attributed to Peter, of which I have recognized only one epistle as authentic and accepted by the early fathers" (ἀλλὰ τὰ μὲν ὀνομαζόμενα Πέτρου, ὧν μόνην μίαν γνησίαν ἔγνων ἐπιστολὴν καὶ παρὰ τοῖς πάλαι πρεσβυτέροις ὡμολογημένην. Note again γνησίαν; 3.3.4). Elsewhere, on some such grounds, Eusebius can dispute the authenticity of James and Jude, considered νόθα precisely because they are not widely mentioned by "ancient" Christian writers (2.23). So too for patently noncanonical books. 2 Clement is not a work of Clement precisely because it is not widely attested in earlier sources; nor are the dialogues of Peter and Apion written in his name since "there is no mention whatever of them by early writers" (3.38).

Augustine in particular stresses both the secular and theological logic of this criterion, in a statement worth quoting at length:

> Were not certain books that were produced under the name Hippocrates, the highly renowned physician, rejected as authoritative by physicians? Nor did a certain similarity of topics and language offer them any help. For, compared to the books that it was clear were really Hippocrates' books, they were judged inferior, and they were not known at the same time at which the rest of his writings were recognized as truly his. But how is it proven that these books are really his when, compared to them, the books brought forth out of the blue are rejected? How is it proven so that, if anyone rejects this, he is not even refuted but laughed at, except because a series of physicians, from the time of Hippocrates down to the present time and thereafter, has commended them so that to have any doubt about them is the mark of a madman? How do people know that the books of Plato, Aristotle, Varro, Cicero, and other such authors are their works except by the same unbroken testimony of the ages following one upon another?
>
> Many authors have written extensively on the Church's writings, not, of course, with canonical authority but with some desire to be helpful or to learn. How is it determined who wrote what except by the fact that, in the times in which each author wrote them, he made them known and published them for those for whom he could, and from them they were passed on to future generations, one after another, with unbroken knowledge that was quite widely accepted, down to our times, so that, when asked whose book is whose, we do not hesitate what we ought to reply? . . . Since that is the case, who, then, is blinded by such great madness—unless he has been corrupted by agreeing with the wickedness and fallacies of lying demons—as to say that the Church of the apostles, so faithful and so numerous a harmony of brothers, could not have merited faithfully to transmit their writings to future generations, though the sees of the apostles have been preserved down to the present bishops in an utterly certain line of succession, especially since this is so much the case

> with any people's writings, whether outside the Church or even in the Church? (*Contra Faust.* 33.6)

The continuous attestation of books from the time of their author gives evidence of their authenticity, even in the case of secular writings. But that is even more the case with Christian writings, transmitted by faithful believers, unaltered over the years, in a way analogous to the famed apostolic succession, in which bishops can trace their lineage through their predecessors back to the apostles of Jesus themselves. With the Christian writings this is not just a matter of historical accident; it is an act of providence.

PART II

Forgery in Early Christian Polemics

CHAPTER SIX

Introduction to Forgery and Counterforgery in Early Christian Polemics

As we turn now to the central focus of this study, the use of literary forgery in early Christian polemics, several points already mentioned need to be returned to prominence. The first and most obvious involves the extent of the phenomenon being considered.

The literary landscape of the first several Christian centuries is littered with falsely attributed and forged writings. Among the twenty-seven books that were later deemed Scripture, only eight are orthonymous; one of these, the book of Revelation, was admitted into the canon only because of a quirk of homonymy. The other seven all stem from the pen of one man. The remaining books are either falsely attributed to early authority figures within the church (the Gospels, Johannine epistles) or forged. A fair critical consensus holds that six of the Pauline letters and the letters of Peter were written by someone other than the apostles claimed as their authors, and that James and Jude were falsely inscribed in the names of Jesus' brothers. A good case can be made that Hebrews is a non-pseudepigraphic forgery, with the hints in the closing meant to indicate that it was written by Paul, even though his name is not attached to it. In what follows I will argue that Acts and 1 John are also best seen as non-pseudepigraphic forgeries, as they too make false authorial claims without naming a specific author.

Outside the New Testament false attributions continue, in such works as 1 Clement and Barnabas, pseudo-Justin *Cohortatio ad Graecos, De monarchia,* and *Oratio ad Graecos,* and pseudo-Tertullian *Adversus omnes haereses.* Forgeries of apocryphal works continue apace throughout the second and third centuries, and indeed on into and through the Middle Ages, with Gospels assigned to such figures as James, Thomas, Matthew, Philip, and Nicodemus, epistles allegedly written, again, by Paul (Laodiceans, Alexandrians, correspondence with Seneca) and Peter (epistula Petri), and apocalypses as well in the names of Peter and Paul. Starting in the third century, "church orders" begin to appear, not merely claiming to convey the teachings of the apostles, as with the Didache, but actually produced, falsely, in their names, as in the Didascalia Apostolorum and the Apostolic Constitutions. Eventually writings appear in the names of subapostolic authorities, such as the pseudo-Ignatian letters and the pseudo-Clementine *Homilies* and *Recognitions*, as well as in the names of respected authorities from within the orthodox community, writings allegedly by Basil, Jerome, Augustine, Chrysostom, many of them produced within the alleged authors' own lifetimes.

We are dealing with a large and complex phenomenon. In the analyses that follow I will be considering some fifty instances of forgery from the first four Christian centuries. How many were actually produced at the time is anyone's guess.

It will be difficult to make sweeping generalities about these forged productions as an undifferentiated group. They were written at different times, in different places, by different authors, for different purposes. But as I will be limiting myself to forgeries that appear to have been generated out of polemical interests, one feature does appear to bind them together. Their authors assumed false names for one chief end: to provide for their views an authority that otherwise would have proved difficult to obtain had they written anonymously or in their own names. These were authors in the throes of controversy, eager to establish their views as both legitimate and authorized. To that end they employed means widely regarded throughout their environment as illegitimate and unauthorized.

Throughout our period orthodox writers regularly and roundly accused heretics of forging documents. We find the charge in our earliest surviving heresiologist, Irenaeus, who, for example, accuses the Cainites of making use of a forged Gospel of Judas Iscariot; at about the same time the Muratorian Fragment denigrates as Marcionite forgeries the "Pauline" letters to the Laodiceans and Alexandrians; and again, from roughly the same time, Serapion of Antioch pronounces the Gospel of Peter pseudepigraphic. At the end of our period Epiphanius maligns numerous forgeries of the heretics, including the seven books of Seth and the Gospel of Eve, not to mention that lascivious Greater Questions of Mary, a book that, as I argued in Chapter One, may have been his very own invention, possibly a case of casting a stone in a glass house.

In some instances one finds warnings not to be led astray by forged documents precisely in documents that are themselves forged. The charge is found at the very beginning of our period in the canonical work of 2 Thessalonians, which warns its readers not to be misled by a letter allegedly—but not actually—written by Paul. At the end of our period it is found in the Apostolic Constitutions, which warns its readers, in the names of the earthly apostles of Jesus, not to read writings falsely produced in the names of the earthly apostles of Jesus. All the Christian forgeries that warn readers to avoid forgeries are ultimately concerned with "false teachings," in an environment when knowing the "truth" was essential for salvation. This, of course, is one of the disturbing ironies of the early Christian tradition, that those invested in establishing and promoting the truth often did so by lying—in this case by lying about their true identities. They appear to have done so in order to deceive their readers into believing that they were authority figures who could, by their elevated status, establish the contours of the true faith. In short, they promulgated a falsehood in order to promote their understanding of the truth.

Sometimes the forged attacks on "false" teachings appear more subtly, in the phenomenon I am calling "counterforgery." To a certain extent every forgery that counters the views of another person, group, or writing is a counterforgery, and sometimes the term is used by scholars in this weaker sense. More poignantly, sometimes a forgery is used precisely to counter the views set forth in another work that is itself a forgery. It is in this stronger sense that I will predominantly be using the term here. It is not always the case that the forgery being opposed is recognized and named as a forgery—as does happen, however, in both 2 Thessalonians and the Apostolic Constitutions. More commonly it is impossible to know whether the forger realizes that the views under attack are in fact represented in a forged document; these, then, would be unwitting cases of fighting fire with fire.

Internecine conflicts were not the only polemical contexts within which the Christian writers of the first four centuries worked. Christians were embattled on several fronts at once; on the outside were the "unbelieving" Jews and the hostile pagans. Orthonymous writings of the so-called church Fathers attacked these Others and defended the true faith throughout the period; but so too did forged documents, believed by insiders to convey especial authority in view of their authorial claims. In many instances these forged attacks and apologiae served several purposes at once, intramural and extramural. And so it is important yet again to stress the potential multifunctionality of our surviving texts. Like many (most?) writings, Christian forgeries could and did serve a variety of purposes at one and the same time. The Coptic Gospel of Thomas polemicizes against apocalyptic expectations of other Christian teachers, against Judaism and Judaizing, and against theologies that stress the reality and importance of the flesh. It did not serve a solitary purpose. A writing such as the Protevangelium Jacobi serves nonpolemical ends of entertainment and of filling in lacunae from the stories of Mary and Jesus, but also apologetic aims in answering the charges against the savior and his mother by a pagan critic such as Celsus. It is not important to my study that the polemical functions of this or that forgery be seen as the one and only purpose of the work. On a practical level, the multifunctionality of several of these texts means that they will be discussed under more than one rubric.

The rubrics that I have devised are topical, guided to some extent by a loosely chronological logic. The earliest orthonymous Christian writings are concerned to no small extent with questions of eschatology. 1 Thessalonians, for example, is written, at least in part, to comfort those whose expectations of an imminent appearance of the Lord from heaven had been frustrated by the passage of time, and who were, as a result, concerned over the fate of those who had died in the interim. 1 Corinthians is written, again in part, to correct those within the community with an overly realized eschatology that claimed the benefits of the resurrected existence were already available and enjoyed in the present age, with little or nothing to expect in a cataclysmic break with the present in the future. Given this feature of early authentic writings, it is no surprise that our earliest surviving forgeries too deal with issues of eschatology—most obviously 2 Thessalonians but also, I will argue, Colossians and Ephesians (Chapter Seven). It is of some interest that the range of eschatological views that result through juxtaposition of the various perspectives found in these writings were all deemed worthy of hearing, in no small part because of the apostolic authority that lay behind them. And so, all of them were eventually accepted as canonical views, resulting in the paradoxical eschatology of "already and not yet." From early days, followers of Jesus were entrenched in theologies of paradox, later to come to fruition in complex Christological ("fully divine and fully human") and Trinitarian ("three persons but one God") views.

The eschatological questions did not cease with the passing of the first Christian generation, of course, and so later forged writings continued to take them on, both within the canon (2 Timothy; 2 Peter) and outside (Gospel of Thomas; Chapter Eight). Paul, the alleged author of most of these sundry works, was himself a debated topic from early days, as is evident from his own writings, such as the Corinthian correspondence and the letter to the Galatians. And so we find a number of early forgeries that are concerned either to promote or to attack Paul's authority, for example, 1 Peter, 2 Peter, and Acts (which I will argue, as I've mentioned, is a non-pseudepigraphic forgery) on one side of the issue (Chapter Nine), and James, Jude, the Epistula Petri, and the Pseudo-Clementine *Homilies* on the other (Chapter Ten). A closely related problem, best known precisely from the Pauline letters, has to do with the status of Jews and, relatedly, Jewish Christianity; these issues too were dealt with in polemical forgeries (including those discussed in Chapter Ten), such as the Gospel of Peter, the Epistula Clementis, the Didascalia, the Ascension of Isaiah, the Abgar Correspondence, the Gospel of Nicodemus, and other writings of the Pilate cycle (Chapter Eleven).

Also connected with Paul and his churches were problems of church hierarchy, structure, organization, and authority. Forgeries dealing with such issues abounded, from the Pastoral epistles of the New Testament through the "church order" literature (e.g., the Didascalia, Apostolic Church Order, Apostolic Canons, Apostolic Constitutions), but also in such writings as the Paraphrase of Shem from Nag Hammadi and the Ascension of Isaiah (Chapter Twelve).

Among the internecine theological conflicts that eventually emerged in the period, none proved so productive of forgery as those involving the nature, status, and relevance of "the flesh," especially because views of the flesh became intricately connected with so many other crucial and debated issues, such as the unity of the Godhead, the nature of creation, the person of Christ, the efficacy of his death, the reality of his physical resurrection, and the future fate of the believer. And so numerous forgeries written under apostolic authority emerged, arguing either against the flesh (the Coptic Apocalypse of Peter, the Book of Thomas the Contender, the Gospel of Thomas, the Paraphrase of Shem) or in favor of it (3 Corinthians, the Epistula Apostolorum, the Nag Hammadi tractate Melchizedek, the Apocalypse of Peter and the Apocalypse of Paul, and even, by misdirection, I will argue, the extant letter of Laodiceans; all in Chapter Thirteen).

Other theological debates engendered yet other forgeries from disputes with the Manichaeans (Abgar Correspondence) to the Arian controversies (the Pseudo Ignatians; Chapter Fourteen). And, as mentioned, a significant range of forgeries appeared as apologetic defenses of the faith, in quite diverse but manifest ways, including the Martyrdom of Polycarp (which I will argue is a non-pseudepigraphic forgery), the Protevangelium Jacobi, the Acts of Pilate, the correspondence of Paul and Seneca, and the Sibylline oracles (Chapter Fifteen). In the final chapter I return to the question of self-justification, asking how the forgers of early Christian documents may have explained to themselves the morality of their literary endeavors.

As should be clear from this overview, my concern in the study is less with establishing where forgery has occurred than in determining the function of the forgery, in particular as this relates to Christian polemics. But the function of a forgery, naturally, depends on the prior question, and so, where there are significant debates that need to be addressed, I take them on. Here I should reiterate my three-pronged approach. Works whose authorship continues to be a hotly debated topic—for example 2 Thessalonians or 1 Peter—I discuss at length, making a range of arguments in support of my view that they are in fact forged. Other works, about which there is less disagreement—for example 2 Peter—I devote much less argument to, appealing instead to widely accepted lines of reasoning. In yet other instances there is no scholarly disagreement of any moment—the Gospel of Peter or the Letters of Paul and Seneca, for example. In such instances I focus almost exclusively on the question of function.

It is my view that in every instance of forgery that I discuss, the intention of the forger was to deceive his readers into thinking he was someone other than who he was; his motivation was not only to receive a simple hearing of his views (although certainly that) but also to authorize his views through the authority provided by the status of his falsely assumed authorial name. His goal was to advance his own polemical agenda.

CHAPTER SEVEN

Early Pauline Forgeries Dealing with Eschatology

Eschatology was supremely important at the outset of the Christian movement. Jesus' apocalyptic proclamation of the coming kingdom, which was to appear before "this generation passes away" (Mark 13:30), found its mirror in the preaching of his earliest followers, who expected Jesus himself soon to return from heaven as the Son of Man. The message was continued in the missionary preaching of Paul and his followers, as evidenced in our earliest Christian writings, such as 1 Thessalonians and 1 Corinthians. Alternative eschatologies also appeared in the early stages of the Christian movement, as Paul's own writings attest. Some members of the Thessalonian congregation came to fear that those who had died already had lost out on their eschatological reward. Others in not-so-distant Corinth came to think that they had begun to reap the benefits of that reward in this life. Paul wrote in order to correct and comfort the despondent Thessalonians and to disabuse the enthusiastic Corinthians: there is a future reward, it will appear with the coming of Jesus, and it will involve a radical transformation not only of the world and its existing order, but also of the human body, as there will be resurrection of both the living and the dead into an immortal existence.

In view of the alternative perspectives more widely available, it comes as no surprise that some of the earliest Christian forgeries deal with just this issue of eschatology, produced by unknown authors claiming the authority of the apostle himself. At the end of the day it is impossible to provide relative datings of these pseudepigraphic efforts of Pauline Christians;[1] it is completely plausible to think,

---

1. Standhartinger and others have claimed that Colossians should be seen as our earliest Christian forgery, but there is really no way to date its appearance precisely, or even in relation to, say, 2 Thessalonians. See Angela Standhartinger, *Studien zur Entstehungsgeschichte und Intention des Kolosserbriefs* (Leiden: Brill, 1999), ch. 2.

however, that they emerged not long after the death of Paul himself, or even, conceivably, while he was still alive. There is no way to know.[2] In any event it may well be that just as 1 Thessalonians is the earliest surviving orthonymous Christian writing of any kind, its "sequel," 2 Thessalonians, is the earliest surviving Christian forgery.

SECOND THESSALONIANS

The History of the Question

Problems connected to the authenticity of 2 Thessalonians were first recognized by J. C. Chr. Schmidt in 1801.[3] Schmidt pointed out that 1 Thessalonians is a letter allegedly by Paul that maintains that the end is imminent, whereas 2 Thessalonians warns against a letter allegedly by Paul that maintained that the end is imminent (2:2). How could one explain this situation? If 1 Thessalonians were written first, would Paul not remember what he had written by the time he wrote 2 Thessalonians? If, conversely, 2 Thessalonians were written first, would Paul not remember that he warned his readers against precisely the views that he now embraced in the second letter? "In any case, it remains puzzling why he described in one letter the appearance of Christ as near, and in the other warned not to expect it as being near."[4]

Schmidt considers the obvious possibilities that Paul at some point changed his mind and rejected his earlier views, but he finds these possibilities wanting. In addition, he evaluates every part of 1 Thessalonians as being completely Pauline, including the words of the imminent coming of Christ. Is 2 Thessalonians then to be considered a forgery? No, for Schmidt, this letter too appears completely Pauline, with the exception of the offending passage, the warning of 2:1–2 and the fantasies about the Antichrist that follow. As he points out: "The accuser is frequently himself at fault and complains only in order to remove suspicion from his person."[5] In this case, though, it is not the whole letter that is forged; it is only the twelve verses in question. Once 2:1–12 are removed from the letter, 2:13 can be seen to follow the end of chapter 1 without obvious break. What we have, then, is not a forgery but a falsely interpolated pericope.

---

2. On whether forgeries in Paul's name could appear in his lifetime—an issue about which there really should be no debate—see p. 82.

3. J. E. Chr. Schmidt, "Vermutungen über die beiden Briefe an die Thessalonicher," in *Bibliothek für Kritik und Exegese des Neuen Testaments und älteste Christengeschichte*, vol. 2, fasc. 3 (Hadamar: In der neuen Gelehrten-Buchhandlung, 1801, pp. 383–84); the essay can be found in Wolfgang Trilling, *Untersuchungen zum 2.Thessalonicher* (Leipzig: St. Benno, 1972), pp. 159–61.

4. "In jedem Falle bleibt es rätselhaft, warum er in dem Briefe die Erscheinung Christi als nahe beschrieb, in dem andern aber davor warnte, sie nicht als nahe zu erwarten." As given in Trilling, *Untersuchungen*, p. 160.

5. "Der Ankläger ist oft selbst der Schuldige, und klagt nur, um den Verdacht von sich abzuwälzen."

As we will see, for later scholars it was precisely the peculiarly Pauline character of 2 Thessalonians—specifically its close resemblance to 1 Thessalonians itself—that, somewhat ironically, made it suspect. But Schmidt at least opened the debate with a plausible scenario, for directly at the point where 2 Thessalonians begins to diverge from its predecessor in theme it begins to contradict it in substance. It was many decades, however, before wider attention was drawn to the tensions between the two books, and between 2 Thessalonians and the other Pauline letters in general. In 1862 Hilgenfeld made the argument still favored by many scholars today, that 2 Thessalonians was forged precisely in order to replace its predecessor as Paul's (only) letter to the Thessalonians.[6] Thirty years later it had become yet more widely suspected that 2 Thessalonians could not be Pauline, as summed up in the arguments of Holtzmann: unlike the authentic Pauline letters, there was no anti-Jewish polemic in the book, in places it uses non-Pauline language, it contains a number of expansions of parallels from the first letter, and it contains no citations of the Hebrew Bible.[7]

These lines of argumentation can be easily picked apart and so were not widely convincing across the critical spectrum. A solid basis for seeing 2 Thessalonians as non-Pauline was not laid until Wrede's penetrating analysis of its relationship to 1 Thessalonians, about which I will have more to say presently. Trilling was the first to write a major commentary based on the assumption of non-Pauline authorship; important contributions by Marxsen, Krenz, and Bailey have furthered the discussion. There continue to be holdouts for Pauline authorship, most notably, among critical scholars, Robert Jewett and Abraham Malherbe. Malherbe can claim, in his Anchor Bible Commentary, that the "majority" of biblical scholars continues to hold to authenticity.[8] This may be true, but if so, it is simply because a sizeable plurality of biblical scholars (counting broadly) hold theological views that make the presence of literary forgeries in the canon of scripture untenable on principle. Among scholars with no such scruples, the balance swings in the other direction, and for compelling reasons.

2 Thessalonians as a Forgery

One reason the case for the inauthenticity of 2 Thessalonians has occasionally seemed wanting, even to some very fine scholars, is that critics have often resorted to a shotgun approach, citing every possible argument, good or bad, in support of their position. It is all too easy to dismiss bad arguments, leaving an appearance of evidence in balance, pro and con. And so, for example, the letter is often said to lack Paul's customary "warmth" (are all of Paul's writings necessarily warm? Even

---

6. A. Hilgenfeld, "Die beiden Briefe an die Thessalonicher," *ZWT* 5 (1862): 225–64.

7. H. J. Holtzmann, *Lehrbuch der historisch-kritischen Einleitung in das Neuen Testament*, 3rd ed. (Freiburg: J.C.B. Mohr [Paul Siebeck], 1892), pp. 213–16.

8. *The Letters to the Thessalonians: A New Translation with Introduction and Commentary* (New York: Doubleday, 2000), p. 364.

to the same congregation? Think of the different fragments of correspondence with the Corinthians—including 2 Cor. 10–13); the focus is on Christ as Kurios rather than on his cross (does Paul have to focus on the cross, in everything he says?); the letter does not employ the diatribe style (as if Paul was obliged to do so); the letter is lacking in justification language (do we need to read every Pauline letter with Lutheran blinders?). A scholar such as Malherbe can easily dismiss such claims, making the other arguments seem weak by association.

A better tack is to drive hard the compelling arguments. The two most striking involve (1) the impressive parallels to 1 Thessalonians, first pushed strenuously by Wrede, which, when examined closely, seem virtually inexplicable on grounds other than that a second author (not Paul) has used Paul's letter as a model for his own; and (2) the substantive differences *from* 1 Thessalonians in precisely the passage (recognized already by Schmidt) where the parallels evaporate. It is the combination of these two arguments that proves especially suasive. Where the author of 2 Thessalonians has borrowed words and phrases from 1 Thessalonians, of course he sounds like Paul (it is easy to take over the words of another writing, after all). And where he projects his own views onto the apostle, he in fact stands at odds with him. Add to these arguments some comments on differences in aspects of style in the author's free composition, and there are solid reasons for thinking that 2 Thessalonians was written by someone intent on authorizing a non-Pauline view in the name of the apostle himself.

The Relationship to 1 Thessalonians

Over a century ago Wrede showed that the parallels between 1 and 2 Thessalonians are massive and operate on various levels; his arguments have been confirmed and strengthened by Krenz and others.[9] As will be seen, these parallels do not indicate that Paul wrote both letters; on the contrary, a later author is imitating Paul.[10]

The easiest places to imitate the style and wording of a letter are its beginning and ending, and here the two Thessalonian letters are virtually identical. What is more, their concurrences make them stand alone among the Pauline writings: these are not the ways Paul begins and ends any of his other letters. With respect to the beginnings, we have the following:

---

9. W. Wrede, *Die Echtheit des zweiten Thessalonicherbriefs*. TU n.s. 9.2 (Leipzig: J. C. Hinrichs, 1903); Edgar Krentz, "A Stone That Will Not Fit: The Non-Pauline Authorship of Second Thessalonians," in J. Frey et al., eds., *Pseudepigraphie und Verfasserfiktion*, pp. 439–70. For a pithier statement, see Edgar Krentz, "Thessalonians, First and Second Epistles to the," *ABD* VI, 517–23 (on 2 Thess). For another, fuller overview, see John A. Bailey, "Who Wrote II Thessalonians?" *NTS* 25 (1979): 131–45.

10. Malherbe stresses that there are more differences than similarities between the two letters. That is certainly true—how could it not be?—but it is of no relevance to the question of whether a forgery (as opposed to Paul himself) made use of the first letter. He was under no obligation to replicate the letter in full. See Abraham J. Malherbe, *The Letters to the Thessalonians* AB 32B (New York: Doubleday, 2000), pp. 356–58.

> Παῦλος καὶ Σιλουανὸς καὶ Τιμόθεος τῇ ἐκκλησίᾳ Θεσσαλονικέων ἐν θεῷ πατρὶ καὶ κυρίῳ Ἰησοῦ Χριστῷ, χάρις ὑμῖν καὶ εἰρήνη. (1 Thess. 1:1)
>
> Παῦλος καὶ Σιλουανὸς καὶ Τιμόθεος τῇ ἐκκλησίᾳ Θεσσαλονικέων ἐν θεῷ πατρὶ ἡμῶν καὶ κυρίῳ Ἰησοῦ Χριστῷ, χάρις ὑμῖν καὶ εἰρήνη. . . . (2 Thess. 1:1)

They are virtually the same. The three named authors are identical in each place, and they are not further identified apart from their names. It is especially striking that in only these two letters of the entire Pauline corpus is Paul not described with an epithet such as "apostle" (as in most of his letters) or "slave" (Philippians) or "prisoner for Christ" (Philemon). Moreover, both letters refer to the church as comprising the people of a place—"of the Thessalonians"—as opposed to naming the city in which they dwell ("the church of God which is in Corinth"); this too is unlike any other Pauline letter.

So too the closing of the letters:

> ἡ χάρις τοῦ κυρίου ἡμῶν Ἰησοῦ Χριστοῦ μεθ᾽ ὑμῶν. (1 Thess. 5:28)
>
> ἡ χάρις τοῦ κυρίου ἡμῶν Ἰησοῦ Χριστοῦ μετὰ πάντων ὑμῶν. (2 Thess. 3:18)

Apart from the πάντων, this is a nine-word sequence of verbatim agreement. Other agreements occur throughout the letters, sometimes at the simple level of phrasing. In the following instances, the wording is found only in these two letters in the entire Pauline corpus. This should not be taken to mean that the second letter is "obviously Pauline," as some interpreters such as Robert Jewett would maintain: it is quite easy for a copyist to take over words from another letter.

- ἔργον πίστεως (found only, in the Pauline corpus, in 1 Thess. 1:3 and 2 Thess. 1:11)
- οἱ μὴ εἰδότες τὸν θεόν (as reference to pagans, only in 1 Thess. 4:5; 2 Thess. 1:8)
- πλεονάζειν used with ἀγάπη (only 1 Thess. 3:12; 2 Thess. 1:3)
- ἐρωτῶμεν δὲ ὑμᾶς, ἀδελφοί (only 1 Thess. 5:12; 2 Thess. 2:1; the verb occurs only two other times in the Pauline corpus, 1 Thess. 4:1 in the first person plural and Phil. 4:3, first singular)
- ἀδελφοὶ ἠγαπημένοι ὑπὸ θεοῦ/κυρίου (only 1 Thess. 1:4; 2 Thess. 2:13)
- κατευθύνειν (only 1 Thess. 3:11; 2 Thess. 3:5 and as an optative, both times)

In addition, στηρίξαι with ὑμῶν τὰς καρδίας is found in 1 Thess. 3:13 and 2 Thess. 2:17 (worded slightly differently, but both coming at the end of the body of the letter, in the internal benediction, before the paranesis), and only here in Paul's letters; only in 1 Thess. 4.7 and 2 Thess. 2:13–14 are "call and sanctification" joined together; and the root ατακ- is found in 1 Thess. 5:14 and 2 Thess. 3:6, 7, and 11, and nowhere else in the entire New Testament. Most striking, and most frequently noted is the close connection of 1 Thess. 2:9 and 2 Thess. 3:8: Νυκτὸς καὶ ἡμέρας ἐργαζόμενοι πρὸς τὸ μὴ ἐπιβαρῆσαί τινα ὑμῶν.

How are we to imagine such impressive and extensive verbal parallels? Is it likely that Paul remembered to the very word what he said at times in his earlier letter, creating verbatim agreements (found in none of his other writings from the same time) extending sometimes to sequences of nine, ten, or more words? Even if he wrote the second letter just, say, six weeks later, would he remember such phrases, which involve not only important ideas but also off-the-cuff comments and expressions? It is simple to see how a copyist may have taken over words and phrases here and there to make the letter sound so much like the first one. But why would Paul have done so, assuming, say, that he kept a copy on hand? Why would he delve into the heart of the first letter to pull out a word, a phrase, a sentence that he had earlier used to be sure to use it again? Is this how Paul ever writes?

We do have a way of knowing. There are other letters that deal with topics similar to one another: Galatians and Romans, for example. But such extensive "borrowings" are not found in them.[11] And we have yet other letters written—as allegedly were the Thessalonian epistles—to the same community within a relatively short period of time (1 and 2 Corinthians). Once again, there is nothing like this phenomenon to be found.

The agreements do not occur simply on the level of words, phrases, and sentences. The structure and layout of the two letters are strikingly parallel. Both, unlike any other Pauline letter, have two thanksgivings (instead of one), one at the outset and one in the body of the letter (1 Thess. 1:2–10; 2:13; 2 Thess. 1:3–12; 2:13).[12] They both contain an eschatological section, an admonition to be strong and to abide in the apostolic teaching, and a warning against idleness. Indeed, as Bailey has stressed, there is not a single major theme in 2 Thessalonians that is not also found in 1 Thessalonians.[13]

This is not how Paul wrote any of his other letters, by replicating the structure (to this degree) and taking over the vocabulary and even sentences of an earlier letter he wrote. But it is no stretch to imagine that this is how a forger would operate, to provide a Pauline feel to the letter. The evidence is clinched when seen in relation to the style and theology of the second letter, which differ from those of the first.

Issues of Style

It is altogether simple for a forger to take over the words and phrases of an author's other writing. It is a different matter to be able to imitate the author's style when engaging in free composition. Jewett sensibly objected to the stylistic arguments mounted by Trilling, because—as often happens in discussions of style in the Deutero-Paulines—Trilling offered no bases of comparison with the established

11. Not even in closely related passages such as Rom. 8:14–17 and Gal. 4:1–7.

12. For a basic overview of the parallel structures, see Bailey, "Who Wrote 2 Thessalonians?" p. 133.

13. Ibid., p. 134.

Pauline writings.[14] It is one thing to say that an author uses excessively long, complex sentences; it is another thing to show that this is somehow different from how Paul himself was known to write.

Two points should be kept in view at the outset of any discussion of Pauline style. The first is that the question is never whether Paul was capable of writing in one style or another. He was an educated author, and like all educated authors he could vary his style, to some degree at least, as he saw fit. But everyone does in fact typically write in a certain style, often without putting a great deal of thought into questions such as how to effect subordination, whether to prefer subordination to coordination, how to choose which conjunctions to prefer over others, how to construct participial clauses, how to employ the infinitive, and so on. Most authors, unless they are overwhelmingly conscious of being involved in a rhetorical exercise (for example, trained rhetoricians working on an oratorical production), simply write the way they write. No one can plausibly claim that Paul could not have written in the style of, say, Luke or the author of Hebrews, if he had really wanted to. At the same time, no one can plausibly claim that Paul did write that way.

The second point will require more extended discussion, and so I leave it to a short Interlude to come at the conclusion of the next chapter. It is often claimed by scholars of the New Testament that differences of writing style among, say, the Pauline or Petrine letters can be accounted for by the use of secretaries. This secretary hypothesis has become a panacea for all things authorially dubious, as even a quick survey of the commentaries makes abundantly clear. It nonetheless rests on an extremely thin, virtually nonexistent, evidentiary basis. All this I will try to show anon; I mention it here simply to forestall the anticipated objection that stylistic differences within the Pauline corpus derive from secretarial input.[15]

The most directed study of the style of 2 Thessalonians was undertaken by Darryl Schmidt, who showed on the basis of several unrelated but significant grounds that the letter differs, stylistically, from the undisputed Pauline letters.[16] Schmidt's essay does not engage in bland generalities about long sentences and strange style, but provides a detailed demonstration that 2 Thessalonians (and Colossians and Ephesians) are not written in Paul's typical style. Among his criteria, three are especially striking. First, he considers sentences as measured by the numbers of embedded clauses and levels of embedding. 2 Thess. 1:3–12 is often pointed to as a long and complex sentence. It is true, as Schmidt points out, that there are other sentences in the undisputed letters that are nearly as long (2 Cor. 6:3–10, 11:24–31). But these letters do not match the complexity of the sentences in 2 Thessalonians. Specifically, Schmidt takes the longest sentence in the opening thanksgiving section of each of the Pauline letters and measures

---

14. Jewett, *The Thessalonian Correspondence*, p. 11.

15. See pp. 218–22.

16. Darryl Schmidt, "The Syntactical Style of 2 Thessalonians: How Pauline Is It?" in *The Thessalonian Correspondence*, ed. Raymond F. Collins (Leuven: Peeters, 1990), pp. 383–93.

how many embedded clauses there are and how many layers of embeddedness. The results are quite telling: in Romans there are five embedded clauses at four layers of embeddedness; 1 Corinthians: six clauses at four layers; 2 Corinthians: five clauses at three levels; Philippians: six clauses at one level; 1 Thessalonians: ten clauses at five levels. Contrast these figures with the Deutero-Paulines: Colossians: twelve clauses at eight levels; Ephesians: eighteen clauses at thirteen levels; and most striking, 2 Thessalonians: a whopping twenty-two clauses at fifteen levels of embeddedness. The point, again, is not that this is an impossibly more complex style (it is not nearly as complex as that found in numerous other authors); the point is that it is an uncharacteristically Pauline style.

Schmidt then considers a different stylistic feature, the patterns of genitive constructions in nonphrase strings, of which there are three kinds: (1) article + noun + article + noun (genitive); (2) a genitive pronoun added to a string; (c) anarthrous nouns in the same kind of string. When calculated for every 1,000 words in the text, one finds the following frequencies of these kinds of strings (Appendix 2): Romans 12.8 strings per thousand words; 1 Corinthians 8.8 strings; 2 Corinthians 13.1 strings; Galatians 15.2 strings; Philippians 7.4 strings; 1 Thessalonians 10.8 strings; Philemon 11.9 strings. Again, the contrast with the Deutero-Paulines, and especially 2 Thessalonians is stark: Colossians 29.7 strings; Ephesians 31.7 strings; and 2 Thessalonians 26.7 strings.

Third, Schmidt considers the frequency with which a writing uses coordinating and subordinating constructions. Leaving out the ubiquitous καί, he finds the relative frequency of coordination versus subordination (per hundred words) to work out as follows: Romans 68:34; 1 Corinthians 77:47; 2 Corinthians 59:42; Galatians 65:44; 1 Thessalonians 49:38; Philippians 53:36; Philemon 50:38. Once again there is a contrast with the Deutero-Paulines, where subordination is far more relatively common: Colossians 18:25; Ephesians 27:26; 2 Thessalonians 41:37.

The ultimate payoff of these three measurements is that the general sense that scholars have had for many decades that 2 Thessalonians (and the other two Deutero-Paulines) contains a more complex style than the undisputed letters—including the author's model, 1 Thessalonians—is in fact borne out. It is indeed a more complex style. In isolation this kind of stylistic demonstration can carry little weight. Authors can and do vary their style, and statistical models are constantly challenged on grounds related both to the statistics and the models. But when taken in tandem with the earlier consideration, that the author of 2 Thessalonians has followed the structure and borrowed the words, phrases, and even sentences of 1 Thessalonians, the fact that the nonborrowed materials appear in a non-Pauline style appears far more formidable. Remaining doubts can be removed by the most complex of the three main arguments against Pauline authorship, the theology of the letter.

The Theology of 2 Thessalonians

As recognized already by J. E. Chr. Schmidt more than two centuries ago, the theological problem of 2 Thessalonians involves the divergent eschatological outlook of 2:1–12. There are two issues involved: Is the author addressing a problem of a realized or an imminent eschatology? And does his resolution of the problem contradict the views of 1 Thess. 4:13–5:11?

The first issue hinges to a great extent on the exegesis of 2 Thess. 2:2, and especially the key term ἐνέστηκεν. The readers are urged, with respect to the "parousia" of Christ and "our gathering together with him," not to be "quickly shaken or disturbed"—whether "by spirit, by a word, or by a letter as if from us" to the effect that ἐνέστηκεν ἡ ἡμέρα τοῦ κυρίου. In this context, does the perfect of ἐνίστημι mean that the day of the Lord "has already come and is now present," an eschatology analogous to what Paul disparages in 1 Corinthians, or that "it is virtually here and is soon to be realized," comparable, say, to the proclamation of Jesus in Mark 1:15, "the Kingdom of God is at hand" (ἤγγικεν ἡ βασιλεία τοῦ θεοῦ)?[17]

The use of the term ἐνίστημι in other Christian literature of the period is of only limited help. Twice in the writings of Paul and three times in the letter of Barnabas the word is clearly used to refer to "things present" as opposed to things "yet to come" (ἐνεστῶτα . . . μέλλοντα; Rom. 8:38; 1 Cor. 3:22; Barn. 1.7, 5.3, 17.2). On two other occasions it is used in this sense without the explicit contrast, in Barn. 4.1 and Heb. 9:9. At other times the usage—whether present reality or imminent occurrence—is ambiguous, as in Gal. 1:4 ("to deliver us from the present/from the impending evil age"). Somewhat less ambivalent is 1 Cor. 7:26, which like 2 Thess. 2:2 uses the perfect tense, but probably to imply a future event; it is because of the "impending distress" (probably) that one should not change one's marital status. In 2 Tim. 3:1 the term is used to denote something yet to come, but there it is an unambiguous future tense.

As is the case with all these other instances, it is the context that is decisive for the meaning in 2 Thess. 2:2. The passage appears to require the verb to refer to something that is yet to happen but is very much imminent. For one thing, it makes little sense to suppose that the audience would be deeply shaken or disturbed by thinking that they were already experiencing the glories of the eschatological day of the Lord. Others who held that view—the Corinthian enthusiasts, for example—seemed rather to have exulted in the idea. If, on the other hand, the destruction of all things was ready to occur at any moment, that could well frighten anyone, even those sure to be on the winning side.

But more than that, the eschatological view under attack can best be discerned in the argument used by the author to oppose it. What the author decidedly does not do is malign their aberrant eschatological notion by arguing that their present existence is anything *but* the glorious life of the kingdom. He does not, that is, correct their view by pointing out that they were still living in a world filled with evil, suffering, pain, and sin, or stress for them that they are living lives of hardship and suffering rather than glory, as, for instance, Paul does, using considerable sarcasm, in 1 Cor. 4:8, against opponents who thought very much this same thing.

---

17. The issue is debated, of course, throughout the commentaries.

Instead, this "Paul" shows the Thessalonians that they are wrong in their eschatological views, stated in 2:2, by giving them the correct apocalyptic scenario, in view of their incorrect one. The Day of the Lord is not come/almost here because first there must be "the rebellion" and then "the man of lawlessness" must arise, who will be slain by the Lord at his parousia. Why does the author explain that the "restraining power" needs to be released and that this anti-Christ figure has to arise before the end can come? It is because he is correcting a view that maintained that the end was almost here and that nothing yet need happen before it could come.

Thus the author is providing his readers with the true apocalyptic scenario in order to rectify the false one they held. That is to say, he does not correct a nonapocalyptic view by insisting on an apocalyptic one. He and his readers both agree that there is to be an apocalyptic sequence of events at the very end of the age, at the coming of the Day of the Lord. But they have come to imagine—on some grounds connected wrongly with him ("a letter as if by us")—a scenario that needs to be set straight. Their idea is not that there is to be no scenario at all; it is that it involves a scenario that can happen at any moment, imminently.

That is why the author opens his discussion of the issue by appealing to "the parousia of our Lord Jesus Christ and our assembling to meet him" (2:1). He is appealing here not to a new or different teaching that his readers do not accept. He is beginning his plea on a common ground of shared tradition: whatever their differences of eschatological outlook, they agree that the end will involve a return of Jesus and a gathering of the believers to join him. In arguing in this way, the author is indeed following an established Pauline approach, easily available to him from the other Pauline letters. When Paul wanted to argue against the enthusiasts in Corinth that the resurrection was a physical, future event, he did so by establishing common ground, that Jesus was bodily raised from the dead. 1 Corinthians 15 does not provide a demonstration that Jesus' resurrection was bodily; it is an argument based on the agreed belief that it was bodily. Since Jesus' resurrection was bodily, so too, by implication, will be the resurrection of those who follow him. But that necessarily means, for Paul, that it is a future event, not a past event already experienced.

So too in 2 Thessalonians. An author claiming to be Paul establishes the common ground he has with the readers, that the end involves the "parousia and gathering together with the Lord." If that is true, then the Day of the Lord has not yet appeared; it is yet to come. His readers have not worked through this implication carefully. The parousia and ingathering are to come as God's response to the evil in the world; it is then that he will overthrow all that is opposed to him to establish his kingdom. But the forces of evil have not yet been fully unleashed. Only when they are, with the appearance of the anti-Christ figure, will God respond by bringing Jesus back from heaven for judgment on the earth. The eschatology being opposed is not realized but absolutely imminent.

It should not be objected that Paul himself, in combating the enthusiasts of 1 Corinthians, also provided an apocalyptic scenario in order to show that they were wrong precisely in adopting a realized eschatology. That is not the function of 1 Cor. 15:50–57. Instead, the scenario there is given only after Paul has shown that his opponents' eschatological views are wrong, in order to lay out for them what is still to happen, once they are forced (in his opinion) to acknowledge that there is still an eschatology yet to happen. Moreover, the scenario in the Corinthian passage involves what will happen when Christ returns, not what needs to happen before he returns. To this extent, as well, it is incommensurate with the strategy of the author of 2 Thessalonians. And the reason is clear: one passage is opposing a realized and the other an imminent eschatology, as recognized by a range of recent scholars.[18]

There are several payoffs for this brief exegesis. For one thing, it means that the ἐνέστηκεν in 2:2 is indeed to be taken as an equivalent to the ἤγγικεν of Mark 1:15, so that the verse should be understood as meaning that the readers should not be disturbed by the notion that "the Day of the Lord is virtually here and soon to be realized." The Thessalonians can be assured, on the contrary, that the Day is not absolutely imminent.

As a result, the passage does indeed appear to contradict what Paul says in his undisputed letters, such as Rom. 13:12: ἡ νὺξ προέκοψεν, ἡ δὲ ἡμέρα ἤγγικεν or Phil. 4:5, ὁ κύριος ἐγγύς. Yet more important, the view stands at odds with 1 Thessalonians as well, where the end is to come suddenly and unexpectedly, "like a thief in the night" (5:2). It should not be objected that 1 Thessalonians does not claim that the day will come "like a thief" to the followers of Jesus, but only to the unwary on the outside. It is true that this is the rhetoric that Paul uses ("For you yourselves know full well"; 5:2). But his exhortations belie his rhetoric: if he really thought that his readers needed no reminder, he would scarcely have produced such a strenuous one. The exhortations that follow—to be alert and awake, lest they be caught off guard when the Lord arrives (1 Thess. 5:6–8)—make no sense unless the Thessalonians stood in need of warning. But that they do need to be warned about the imminence of the end stands at odds with what the author of 2 Thessalonians thinks: for this other author, the end will not come suddenly, without advance warning, like a thief in the night. There will in fact be plenty of warning, a whole sequence of events that must transpire. There is still some time to sleep and drink.

It may fairly be objected that the thief image of 1 Thessalonians speaks not of an absolutely imminent appearance of the Lord, but of a sudden appearance. However one stands on that issue, the reality is that the image is at odds with the view set forth by the author of 2 Thessalonians. For him the end is not coming right away, and it is not coming without advanced warning. Moreover, if it is true that this is what he actually taught the Thessalonians while he "was still with" them

---

18. Among important discussions arguing for an "imminent" eschatology for 2 Thess 2:2, see Andreas Lindemann, "Zum Abfassungszweck des Zweiten Thessalonicherbriefes," *ZNW* 68 (1977): 35–47; and especially A. M. G. Stephenson, "On the Meaning of ἐνέστηκεν ἡ ἡμέρα τοῦ κυρίου in 2 Thessalonians 2,2," in *SE* 4, ed. F. L. Cross (Berlin: Akademie-Verlag, 1968), pp. 442–51.

(2:5), then it is very difficult indeed to explain the problem of 1 Thessalonians, where members of the congregation are perplexed as to why the end has not happened right away and some have died in the interim (4:13–18). Paul's teaching would have been that it was *not* to come right away, and they would have known that. They thought otherwise—believing the end was imminent—because that is what Paul taught them. Conversely, if Paul is right in what he says in 1 Thess. 5:2, that they themselves "know well that the day of the Lord will come like a thief in the night," then it is well nigh impossible to understand how he can then tell them in 2 Thessalonians that the coming will not be sudden and unexpected, like a thief. It won't be like that at all, but will be anticipated by clear signs to all who can see. For 2 Thessalonians the coming of the Lord will not be like a burglar after dark; it will be like the much anticipated and broadcast arrival of a king.

It might be added that in view of the parallels to 1 Thessalonians advocates for the authenticity of 2 Thessalonians typically claim that it was written on the heels of the other letter. But how would Paul change his eschatological views so suddenly and decisively? Coupled with the problems posed by the parallels themselves, and the differences of style, the case for inauthenticity is very strong.

Nor does it resolve the tensions between the letters by following the suggestion occasionally made since Grotius in 1640, to reverse the chronological sequence of the two letters.[19] In that case the problems are simply compounded, as Krenz and others have noted. Under some such scenario, Paul first indicated that the Day of the Lord would not come except until some easily recognized signs had appeared (an anti-Christ entering into the Temple declaring himself divine), and then shortly after changed his mind and declared that the Thessalonians need to be constantly vigilant because the day would come like a thief, without advanced warning. Nor does it help to think, with Harnack, Dibelius, Goguel, and Schweizer—each of them with different scenarios—that the two letters are addressed by Paul to two different audiences in the Thessalonian church; there is in fact no indication of different audiences (quite the contrary), and the eschatological messages are in tension regardless of whom he addressed.[20]

Scholars who hold on to the authenticity of the letter occasionally mount arguments against the plausibility of it being a forgery, but in no instance can these parries carry conviction. Jewett, for example, claims that "there is scarcely enough time between Paul's death and C.E. 100 for a forgery to gain credence."[21] Here, however, unreflective "common sense" must give way to a wider knowledge of ancient practices of forgery. For as we have already seen, numerous ancient authors complained about forgeries—quite successful ones—circulating in their own names, even within their own lifetimes (not just forty years later). One naturally thinks of Martial, living in the same century as the Thessalonian correspondence

19. See the revival of the theory in T. W. Manson, "St Paul in Greece," *BJRL* 35 (1952–53): 428–47.
20. See the references and refutation of Bailey, "Who Wrote 2 Thessalonians?" pp. 136–37, 140–41.
21. See the discussion of Wrede in Jewett, *Thessalonian Correspondence*, p. 6.

(poems allegedly by him, circulating while he was still living and writing, and even in his home city); or of Galen some decades later (the whole point of *De libriis propriis*); or of Apuleius (a letter produced at his trial); or for later periods, thinking of written correspondence, letters in the names of such prominent figures as Jerome and Augustine, circulating in their own literary environs. The irony is that scholars who claim that 2 Thessalonians is authentic more or less have to admit that Paul himself envisaged the possibility of a Pauline forgery in his own lifetime, on the grounds of 2 Thessalonians itself (2:2).

It is sometimes claimed, similarly, that if the letter was sent to the Thessalonians, and if it contradicted what was said in 1 Thessalonians, they would have known and rejected it as inauthentic.[22] But this objection assumes that the letter would have been sent to Thessalonica. Why would it have been? It is a forgery! It could have been circulated absolutely anywhere in the Greek-speaking Christian world. Finally, it has sometimes been argued that there is no plausible historical context after Paul's day for such a letter, when apocalyptic fervor had died out from the Christian communities: "it appears in fact that the intense expectation of the parousia typical for Paul's lifetime tended to slacken after his death."[23] Even more than the other parries, this appears to be grasping at straws: imminent apocalyptic hopes have never yet died out, to our day, and never will within Christendom, world without end. Of greater moment, they certainly had not died out by the end of the first century. One needs only think of such texts as Didache 16 and (how can it not have occurred?) the book of Revelation.

2 Thessalonians as a Counterforgery

A good deal of exegetical ink has been spilled over the source of the Thessalonians' alleged disturbance that the Day of the Lord was imminent. The author tells them not to be upset μήτε διὰ πνεύματος μήτε διὰ λόγου μήτε δι' ἐπιστολῆς ὡς δι' ἡμῶν. Here again, there are two major issues. First, does the final phrase, ὡς δι' ἡμῶν apply to all three sources of information or only to the third? Has some kind of spiritual (ecstatic?) communication "as by us," some kind of oral teaching "as by us," and some kind of letter "as by us" been invoked? Or has the teaching come through a spiritual communication, an oral teaching, and a letter that by itself is allegedly "by us?"[24]

For the purposes of my discussion here, the decision does not much matter, as in both cases, the author is referring to a letter "as by us." Still, the exegetical

---

22. Jewett, *Thessalonian Correspondence*, p. 10.

23. Ibid., p. 6.

24. Among the better exegetical discussions, Eve-Marie Becker, "Ὡς δι' ἡμῶν in 2 Thess 2.2 als Hinweis auf einen verlorenen Brief," *NTS* 55 (2009): 55–72 opts for the first option—that the phrase applies to "spirit, word, and letter"—whereas Glenn S. Holland, "'A Letter Supposedly from Us': A Contribution to the Discussion about the Authorship of 2 Thessalonians," in *The Thessalonian Correspondence*, ed. Raymond F. Collins (Leuven: Peters, 1990), pp. 394–402, opts for the second.

decision is best made in reference to the broader context, and, as we will see, this context is significant for yet other reasons. For there is a second reference to "our letter" in 2:15, where the author urges his readers to stand fast and hold to the traditions ἅς ἐδιδάχθητε εἴτε διὰ λόγου εἴτε δι᾽ ἐπιστολῆς ἡμῶν. Since in this second case, there are only two items mentioned—a word and a letter—it does not appear to be an exact backward glance to the earlier list of three items. That in itself would suggest that the "spirit" was not included among the items connected with "us" in 2:2. And if all three items are not connected to "us," then it seems unlikely that two of the three were. It is the third item in the list that came "as by us."

Of greater moment for our reflections here is, second, the meaning and significance of ὡς in 2:2. Does the author refer to the earlier letter "as having (really) come from us" or "as if (but not really) having come from us"? Despite the widespread disagreement among exegetes, here too the wording of 2:15 must be decisive. If the author of 2:2 wanted to refer to a letter that "really did" come from us, he would scarcely have needed to provide the "ὡς" in the first place. He would simply have said "through our letter"—as he says in 2:15. The reference to a letter in 2:15, in fact, is given in contrast to the letter mentioned in 2:2. The earlier reference is to a letter "as if" by us, and is by implication denigrated by the author, who "corrects" the eschatology that this false letter conveyed. The later reference is to a letter that really is "ours," which is affirmed in what it taught its readers ("stand firm and hold fast to the traditions that you were taught" in that letter).

Hanna Roose has recently argued that by using the phrase ὡς δι᾽ ἡμων the author of 2:2 intentionally left the reference to the earlier letter ambiguous, because as a forger claiming to be Paul writing to the Thessalonians he wanted the earlier letter to look believably Pauline (really from us, i.e., 1 Thessalonians) while casting some doubt in the minds of his actual readers (it was not really from us).[25] This solution is probably too clever by half. Among other things it has to assume that there are no other references to Paul's "first" letter in 2 Thessalonians, since, if there are, then the ambiguity of 2:2 falls apart. But 2:15 does seem to be a reference to Paul's earlier letter (1 Thessalonians). How to resolve that problem? Roose, with a number of other scholars, including notably Lindemann, maintains that 2:15 refers not to an earlier letter but to the present one: the readers are to hold fast to the teachings found in it. This interpretation, however, overlooks the force of the aorist ἐδιδάχθητε in 2:15. The author is referring to a previous, past set of teaching that came by oral delivery (a word) and a written communication (a letter), not to the present letter.

This conclusion also shows the problem with the view widely taken otherwise, for example, by Lindemann and others, that 2:2 is to be understood to be a disparaging comment on 1 Thessalonians.[26] In this view, by a forger who wanted

25. Hanna Roose, "'A Letter as by Us': Intentional Ambiguity in 2 Thessalonians 2.2," *JSNT* 29 (2006): 107–24.

26. Andreas Lindemann, "Zum Abfassungszweck."

his readers to think that *this* letter (2 Thessalonians)—and its eschatological views—was the one from Paul, whereas the other, 1 Thessalonians, was the forgery. Were this view true, 2 Thessalonians would be a counterforgery with chutzpah. As Marxsen expresses the view, without reference to Lindemann's influential article, which was published five years earlier: "In truth, 2 Thessalonians must be regarded as Paul's first letter to the Thessalonians. It alone is the genuine Pauline letter. . . . The author of 2 Thess wants to edge out 1 Thess with his writing." Later: "The author of 2 Thess wants to replace 1 Thess with his writing."[27]

The problem overlooked by this view is, again, the positive reference to an earlier letter in 2:15. Whatever the author is castigating in 2:2, it is not the letter of 1 Thessalonians, as tempting as that view might be. The author in fact contrasts the δι᾽ ἐπιστολῆς ὡς δι᾽ ἡμῶν of 2:2 with δι᾽ ἐπιστολῆς ἡμῶν of 2:15. It is only the latter that is "actually" by the author; the other was not. This is an author who knows 1 Thessalonians, who realizes that it is accepted as authentically Pauline, who embraces it of necessity (and even copies it)—since he too wants to be thought of as Paul—and who speaks disparagingly of some other letter, allegedly but not really by Paul, which conveyed an aberrant understanding of eschatology. The irony is that this lost letter—whether it ever existed or not cannot be known—would have adopted an eschatology very much like that found in 1 Thessalonians, and the author does want to counter its views.

Eva-Maria Becker has recently played with the idea that this lost letter was an actual Pauline letter in circulation.[28] This is a possibility, but the reality is that whoever forged 2 Thessalonians, wanting to label this other letter (whether it existed or not) a forgery, would have had no way of knowing, at the end of the day, whether it was authentic or not, assuming it existed. And so for the interpretation of 2 Thessalonians the question is moot. What appears certain is that the letter of 2:2 is not 1 Thessalonians but a letter allegedly by Paul that the author wants to denigrate both in terms of authorship and, relatedly, authority. It conveys the false teaching of the eschaton. But since 2 Thessalonians affirms 1 Thessalonians, and yet proffers an alternative understanding of eschatology, one must conclude that its author wanted its readers to read the teaching of 1 Thessalonians in light of its own eschatological assertions. Or, to use the language that has recently come to be in vogue, 2 Thessalonians appears to be providing "reading instructions" for 1 Thessalonians.[29]

---

27. "Der 2. Thess. muss als der in Wahrheit erste Brief des Paulus an die Thessalonicher angesehen werden. Es ist der allein echte Paulus-Brief. . . . Der Verfasser des 2. Thess. will mit seinem Schreiben den 1 Thess. verdrängen." "Der Verfasser des 2. Thess. [will] mit seinem Schreiben den 1. Thess. ersetzen." Willi Marxsen, *Der zweite Thessalonicherbrief* (Zürich: Theologischer Verlag, 1982), pp. 35, 80.

28. Eve-Marie Becker, "Ὡς δι᾽ ἡμῶν."

29. The phrase is used explicitly of 2 Thessalonians recently by Hanna Roose, in reliance on Eckhart Reinmuth, "Die Briefe an die Thessalonicher," in N. Walter, E. Reinmuth, and P. Lampe, eds., *Die Briefe an die Philipper, Thessalonicher und an Philemon* (Göttingen: Vandenhoeck & Ruprecht, 1998), pp. 105–204. For the concept more broadly see, e.g., Annette Merz, "The Fictitious Self-Exposition of Paul: How

H. Roose, who sees the relation of the two letters in this light, has made a specific argument for how the "instructions" work, by describing the divergent understandings of the parousia in the two letters, arguing that when they are taken together as a unit the "Day of the Lord" and the "parousia" become coterminous, so that there is now a firm thematic unity between the events of 1 Thess. 4:13–18 on the one hand and 5:1–11 on the other. This view may be taking the matter a step too far, as surely Paul himself saw a firm thematic unity between these two passages that, off his pen, did not experience a chapter break between them. But it is true that when the letters are read together, the "imminent" and "sudden" eschatology of 1 Thessalonians is muted and altered.

It should not be objected that no one would place two such letters in a canon and assume they were complementary when they so clearly stand at odds with one another. Church leaders did place them in the same canon and Christian readers have always read them as complementary, as attested so elegantly by the advocates of the authenticity of 2 Thessalonians still today. But in fact their views were not seen as harmonious by the author of the second letter. He objected to an eschatology that insisted that Jesus was coming suddenly and unexpectedly, and in the imminent future, right away. 1 Thessalonians could certainly be read as conveying just such a message, but the author could scarcely denigrate that letter, as it was widely known to have come from the apostle himself. Another letter was (allegedly? actually?) available, however, that made the point even more strenuously and disturbingly, and this other letter too claimed to be written by Paul. Or so the forger averred. It was to counter this false letter that he produced a false letter of his own. He countered a forgery by producing a forgery. This is the first known instance of a Christian counterforgery, in the strong sense.[30]

In order to make his handiwork more effective, the author employed several of the known tools of the forger's trade. He replicated the distinctive vocabulary and adopted key instances of the phrasing of an authentic letter, structuring his along similar lines, and addressing most of the same major issues. He provided clear instances of verisimilitude, including a borrowed instance of "remembrance" of the time he had allegedly spent among the congregation, in words taken from the earlier letter (2 Thess. 3:8; 1 Thess. 2:9). He warned his readers against a forgery circulating in his name (2:2), a ploy to be repeated by later Christian forgers. And at the end he did perhaps "protest too much": "The greeting is in my own hand,

---

Might Intertextual Theory Suggest a Reformulation of the Hermeneutics of Pseudepigraphy?" in *The Intertextuality of the Epistles: Explorations of Theory and Practice*, ed. Thomas L. Brodie et al. (Sheffield: Sheffield Phoenix Press, 2006), pp. 113–32; and her earlier dissertation, *Die fiktive Selbstauslegung des Paulus: Intertextuelle Studien zur Intention und Rezeption der Pastoralbriefe* (Göttingen/Fribourg: Vandenhoeck & Ruprecht/Academic Press, 2004).

30. It will be seen that I am not here taking the position of Frank Hughes, who sees 2 Thessalonians as a counterforgery to the eschatological views of Colossians and Ephesians. Those views involve an immanent/realized eschatology, not an imminent (or sudden) eschatology. See Frank Witt Hughes, *Early Christian Rhetoric and 2 Thessalonians* (JSNTSSup 30, Sheffield: Sheffield Academic Press, 1989).

the hand of Paul, which is the sign in all my letters. This is how I write" (3:17). The first six words—ὁ ἀσπασμὸς τῇ ἐμῇ χειρὶ Παύλου—are precisely parallel to 1 Cor. 16:21, and are matched still more famously by Gal. 6:11. But in neither of these instances is Paul's final signing off—after his amanuensis had penned his dictation—said to be a mark of authenticity. It may have been that; but in both other instances it may as well have been a way of personalizing the letter for his readers. If this was the way Paul always finished his letters, it is more than a little strange that he does not end all his letters this way, and stranger still that he never refers to the practice as a prophylaxis against forgery.[31] At the same time, it is an odd claim to make in a (Christian) culture where letters circulated more commonly in copies rather than autographs. Did Paul himself expect only his handwritten copy to be read among his churches? If not, then it is hard to understand how he could have imagined 3:17 would be a bona fide demonstration of authenticity. On the other hand, it makes sense for a forger to make the claim. It did, after all, prove effective in throwing readers off the scent of the author's deceit, even though none of these readers saw a single iota of Paul's actual handwriting. Moreover, it was a ploy used by other forgers of antiquity.[32]

COLOSSIANS

The letter to the Colossians is sometimes taken to be the earliest surviving Pauline pseudepigraphon, and thus the earliest Christian forgery of any kind.[33] But there is obviously no way to say for certain: we do not know who wrote the letter, to whom, or where. As a result, it is virtually impossible to establish its relative chronology in relation, say, to 2 Thessalonians. It is also difficult—again, well nigh impossible—to identify with any level of certainty the adversaries who are being opposed, although I will argue below that they are probably to be taken as real, not imaginary. What is most clear is that the author of the book is using Paul's authority to attack them. Moreover, in doing so, the author has been more or less compelled, given the nature of the false teaching, to embrace eschatological views that stand at odds with Paul's. As we will see, eschatology is not a peripheral issue in the letter. It constitutes one of its central features.

---

31. Jewett maintains, on the contrary, that the statement of 3:17 would be a "risky method of supporting the acceptance of the forger" since it would call "into question the authenticity of every Pauline letter not bearing the 'mark' of Paul's signature at the end" (p. 6). There is no reason to think, however, that this author was overly concerned about the authenticity of Paul's other letters. Why would he care whether, say, Ephesians was accepted as authentic?

32. See Speyer, *Die literarische Fälschung*, pp. 57–58.

33. For example, Angela Standhartinger, *Studien zur Entstehungsgeschichte und Intention des Kolosserbriefs* (Leiden: Brill, 1999). The most recent representative of this view is Nicole Frank, "Der Kolosserbrief und die 'Philosophia': Pseudepigraphie als Spiegel frühchristlicher Auseinandersetzungen um die Auslegung des paulinischen Erbes," in Jörg Frey et al., eds., *Pseudepigraphie und Verfasserfiktion*, pp. 411–32.

Views of Authorship

In 1838, Ernst Mayerhoff was the first to question the Pauline authorship of Colossians. In his view, the language and style of the letter were not sufficiently Pauline, certain terms were used in non-Pauline ways, the author attacked a heresy not found until after Paul's day, and the book derived much of its teaching from Ephesians.[34] Many of these issues have remained important parts of the conversation still today. In 1857, Heinrich Ewald was the first to argue that the differences from the Pauline letters were because the letter was penned by a Pauline associate, Timothy, a view that continues to have representatives among those who see the letter as basically Pauline but distinctive in greater or lesser ways.[35]

Despite its popularity, this latter view is completely implausible. Not only is Paul named first as the author of the letter in 1:1, on two other occasions, the author—presumably not Timothy!—speaks of himself as "I, Paul" (1:23, 4:18), once indicating that he has written the greeting in his own hand. Moreover, as we will see, the problems presented by the letter involve not just the style—a serious matter in this instance—but also the very substance of its teaching. As Lindemann has pointed out, even if, to stretch the imagination, one of Paul's colleagues wrote the letter (claiming to be the apostle: "I, Paul"), Paul himself would surely have signed off on the contents. Yet it is precisely the contents that dissociate the letter from Paul. And so, quite apart from the issues of secretaries and coauthors—to be addressed in the next chapter—attributing the letter to a close co-worker appears to be a counsel of despair.[36]

The closely related view that Colossians, and others of the Deutero-Pauline letters, were the product of a "Pauline School" can also probably be put to rest. The idea of a Pauline school was first put forth by Hans Conzelmann in his important essay "Paulus und die Weisheit," and has been much bandied about over the past half-century since.[37] Even though no consensus ever emerged on the nature of such a school or the time of its inception, the benefits of the hypothesis for ques-

---

34. E. T. Mayerhoff, *Der Brief an die Colosser mit vornehmlicher Berücksichtigung der drei Pastoralbriefe*, ed. J. L. Mayerhoff (Berlin: Hermann Schültz, 1838).

35. Heinrich Ewald, *Die Sendschreiben des Apostel Paulus* (Göttingen: Dieterisch, 1857). In recent times, the position has been taken by James D. G. Dunn, *The Epistles to the Colossians and to Philemon*, NIGTC (Grand Rapids, MI: Eerdmans, 1996).

36. For a list of scholars holding the various views of authenticity, inauthenticity, and composition by a co-worker, see of Outi Leppä, *The Making of Colossians: A Study on the Formation and Purpose of a Deutero-Pauline Letter* (Göttingen: Vandenhoeck & Ruprecht, 2003), pp. 9–15.

37. *NTS* 12 (1965–66): pp. 231–44. The fullest recent assessment is Thomas Schmeller, *Schulen im Neuen Testament? Zur Stellung des Urchristentums in der Bildungswelt seiner Zeit* (Freiburg: Herder, 2001). For opposition to traditionally understood Pauline schools, see Peter Müller, *Anfänge der Paulusschule: Dargestellt am zweiten Thessalonicherbrief und am Kolosserbrief*, ATANT, 74 (Zurich: Theologische Verlag, 1988); and more recently Standhartinger, *Studien*, pp. 3ff. Still more recently Standhartinger appears to give back a good deal of ground: Angela Standhartinger, "Colossians and the Pauline School," *NTS* 50 (2004): 572–93, where she speaks of an *opinio communis* that the Deutero Paulines were "products of the School of Paul."

tions of pseudepigraphic authorship have always been obvious: without maligning authors for committing forgery, scholars could argue that close associates of Paul, who discussed and studied his teachings, produced writings in his name with impunity, much as the disciples of great teachers did in the cognate philosophical schools of their environment.

That this reconstruction is contextually untenable should be clear from our earlier discussions. There in fact is no evidence that students produced pseudonymous writings in the names of their teachers with impunity in the philosophical schools of the first century (or before or after).[38] This could scarcely, then, have been the context for the production of Pauline pseudepigrapha. Moreover, the references to Pauline authorship in these letters is not casual—a matter of an inscription, for example. The Deutero-Pauline letters insist with some emphasis that Paul himself was the author (thus the "I, Paul" references of Colossians, and the signature "with my own hand"). Whoever wrote these books wanted their readers to think they really were Paul.

Even beyond the contextual problem, one needs to ask seriously whether it makes sense to speak of a Pauline school. For one thing, we would not be talking about "a" Pauline school, but of many Pauline schools. Paul's communities, even in his own day, were wide-ranging in outlook and perspective, with followers of Paul claiming widely disparate views on a surprisingly broad range of topics. Eventually Paul's authority would be claimed for divergent understandings of such fundamental matters as the unity of the Godhead, the nature of Christ, the character of the created order, the means of salvation, the status of the flesh, the reality of the resurrection, the role of women in the church, and numerous other theological, liturgical, and practical issues. What could it possibly mean to speak of "a" Pauline school? Even in one of his earliest letters, 1 Corinthians, the one group of followers who claimed Paul as their leader ("I am of Paul") are presented as supporting views that Paul himself opposed. And this is not to speak of all the other Corinthians who looked up to him and yet advanced positions he found abhorrent.

One could argue that there were lots of Pauline schools, in lots of places, that took lots of positions, some of them in continuity with Paul and others of them not. But that in itself leads to the more fundamental question: Did Paul establish schools? We know that he started congregations. But schools? Did Paul establish places of learning, study, research, lecturing, and writing like the schools of antiquity? Where is the evidence of any such thing? Where does Paul ever mention, or even allude to, any such institution? It is fair enough to argue that the Deutero-Pauline letters evidence the oral transmission of Paul's teachings and discussions. But this kind of ongoing reflection does not require a "school." All it requires is a church. And that, of course, is what Paul does speak about, abundantly: churches, not schools. It is in the church context that proclamation, edification, and education took place.

Paul was no professional rhetorician, and nothing suggests that students were taking notes at his lectures. Moreover, Paul believed the end was near and

38. See pp. 105–19.

that the Gentile mission needed to be pursued. Why form a school? One might imagine—many have—that "the" Pauline school emerged with the delay of the end, as the Pauline churches became more firmly entrenched in the world. But here again we are faced with the pluriform nature of Pauline Christianities and the disappointing fact that nothing in the first century of Christianity's existence has any appearance of a philosophical school.

As a result, as helpful as the notion of a Pauline school may have once seemed to explain a product like the letter to the Colossians (or any of the other Deutero-Pauline epistles), the concept in the end is neither necessary nor even useful. To paraphrase Tertullian, "What has Athens to do with Colossae?"

This is not to deny that the letter to the Colossians bears strong resemblances to other literary products of the Pauline communities, especially Ephesians, and also to the writings of Paul himself. These similarities do not derive from comparable scholastic contexts, however. Instead, they suggest that here again we are dealing with an author who wanted his work to sound like Paul's.

The closest ties of the letter are to the orthonymous Philemon. The data are well known. Paul is said to be a prisoner in both letters (Col. 4:3; Phlm. 1, 9–14); in both Timothy is named as the cosender (Col. 1:1; Phlm. 1) and Onesimus is referred to as being sent to the recipient(s) (Col. 4:9; Phlm. 12). Five of the six persons who send greetings to the Colossians also send greetings to Philemon (Aristarchus, Mark, Epaphras, Luke, and Demas; Col. 4:10–14; Phlm. 23, 24); and special appeal is made in each letter to Archippus, one of three individuals addressed in Philemon (Col. 4:17; Phlm. 2). The conclusion reached by Victor Paul Furnish seems inescapable: these books were either written by the same author (notice: the similarities are not of the sort we found in 2 Thessalonians in relation to its model), or Colossians is written by someone wanting to imitate Paul with the letter of Philemon to hand.[39]

Evidence of Forgery

As with every instance of forgery, the case of Colossians is cumulative, involving multiple factors. None has proved more decisive over the past thirty years than the question of writing style. The case was made most effectively in 1973 by

39. "Colossians, Epistle to the," ABD, ed. David Noel Freedman (New York: Doubleday, 1992), 1.1090–96. E. P. Sanders ("Literary Dependence in Colossians," *JBL* 85, 1966, 28–45) went further and argued that Colossians 1–3 shows evidence of material that had possibly been collected from a range of Pauline letters: Romans, 1 and 2 Corinthians, Galatians and 1 Thessalonians. Leppä (*Making of Colossians*) has more recently argued that Sanders was right but that he did not go far enough; Colossians used all seven undisputed letters, and not just in the first three chapters. If he is correct, we would have a clear argument for the letter being forged by someone borrowing material from Paul's own work. Others, however, such as Standhartinger (*Studien*), are probably right that at the end of the day, there is simply not enough verbatim agreement to make the case. But as it turns out, this is not the strongest argument for forgery in any event.

Walter Bujard, in a study both exhaustive and exhausting, widely thought to be unanswerable.[40]

Bujard compares the writing style of Colossians to the other Pauline letters, focusing especially on those of comparable length (Galatians, Philippians, and 1 Thessalonians), and looking at an inordinately wide range of stylistic features: the use of conjunctions (of all kinds), infinitives, participles, relative clauses, repetitions of words and word groups, use of antithetical statements, parallel constructions, use of the preposition ἐν, the piling up of genitives, and on and on. In case after case, Colossians stands apart from Paul's letters.

Here I can mention a slim selection of his findings. How often does a book of Paul's use adversative conjunctions? Galatians 84 times; Philippians 52; 1 Thessalonians 29; but Colossians only 9. Causal conjunctions? Galatians 45 times; Philippians 20; 1 Thessalonians 31; but Colossians only 9. Consecutive conjunctions? Galatians 16 times; Philippians 10; 1 Thessalonians 12; but Colossians only 6. How often does the letter use a conjunction to introduce a statement (ὅτι, ὡς, πως etc.)? Galatians 20 times; Philippians 19; 1 Thessalonians 11; but Colossians only 3.

As a Fazit to part one, Bujard adds up conjunctions of all kind and indicates the percentage of their occurrence in relation to all words used: Galatians 239 (10.7 percent), Philippians 138 (8.5 percent), 1 Thessalonians 126 (8.5 percent), Philemon 28 (8.4 percent), but Colossians only 63 (4 percent). The average in all the undisputed letters is 10.4 percent; in Colossians it is 4 percent.

Bujard then uses another metric, adding up all the different conjunctions used in the Pauline letters: Galatians 33; Philippians 31; 1 Thessalonians 31; but Colossians only 21. But he goes further, subtracting from these totals the conjunctions that occur in all the letters in question (the shorter epistles: Galatians, Philippians, 1 Thessalonians, 2 Thessalonians, Philemon, Colossians, and Ephesians), since these are simply common words, not words necessarily distinctive of Paul. One is then left with the following numbers: Galatians 24; Philippians 22; 1 Thessalonians 22; but Colossians only 12. He then goes a step farther, subtracting those that occur in all but one of the letters in question (these are distinctive of Paul, not just common words). And the results remain consistent, if not more graphic: Galatians 20; Philippians 18; 1 Thessalonians 18; but Colossians only 8.

The findings involving conjunctions match those using other parts of speech. Bujard looks, for example, at the use of the infinitive. In Galatians the infinitive occurs 32 times (1.4 percent of all words), Philippians 39 (2.4 percent), 1 Thessalonians 48 (3.3 percent), but in Colossians only 11 (0.7 percent). The articular infinitive is used in Galatians 5 times, Philippians 16, 1 Thessalonians 13, but in Colossians never.

The same (or rather the inverse) results obtain with reference to the use of relative clauses. In Romans they make up 1.4 percent of all the words of the book,

40. Walter Bujard, *Stilanalytische Untersuchungen zum Kolosserbrief: als Beitrag zur Methodik von Sprachvergleichen* (Göttingen: Vandenhoeck & Ruprecht, 1973).

1 Corinthians 0.9 percent, 2 Corinthians 1.0 percent, Galatians 1.5 percent, Philippians 1.5 percent, 1 Thessalonians 0.3 percent, Philemon 1.4 percent, but Colossians 2.6 percent.

Bujard goes on like this for a very long time, page after page, statistic after statistic. What is striking is that all these features point the same way. When one adds to these the other commonly noted (though related) features of the style of Colossians—the long complex sentences, the piling up of genitives, the sequences of similar sounding words, and so on—the conclusion can scarcely be denied. This book is not written in Paul's style.[41]

Arguments based on style are strongly supported by considerations of content. In several striking and significant ways the teaching of Colossians differs from the undisputed letters. Most commonly noted is the eschatological view, to which we will return later in our discussion. In 1:13 the author insists that God (already) "has delivered us from the authority of darkness and transferred us into the kingdom of his beloved son." Already? An aorist tense? Is this Paul? More striking still is 2:12–13, and 3:1, which insist that believers have already experienced a kind of spiritual resurrection after having died with Christ: "you were also raised [aorist] in him through faith"; God "made you alive with him"; "if then you have been raised up with Christ"—statements in clear tension with Paul's emphatic statements elsewhere, such as Rom. 6:1–6, where it is quite clear that, whereas those who have been baptized "have died" with Christ, they decidedly have not been "raised up" with him yet. This is an important point in Paul's theology, not a subsidiary matter. The resurrection is something future, something that is yet to happen. So too Phil. 3:11—"if somehow I *might* obtain to the resurrection from the dead." And yet more emphatically in 1 Cor. 15—"in Christ all *shall be* made alive . . . we *shall* all be changed . . . the dead *will be* raised." It can easily be argued that this is a key—if not the single key—to understanding Paul's opposition to the Corinthian enthusiasts. They believed they were leading some kind of spiritual, resurrected existence, and Paul insisted that it had not yet happened. They may have died with Christ, but they had not yet been raised with him. That will come only at the end.

And what does the author of Colossians think? Believers have not only died with Christ but they have also been raised with him. They are already leading a kind of glorious existence in the present. This is the view Paul argues against in Corinth. Maybe he changed his mind. But given the stylistic differences—and the other matters of content to be discussed—it seems unlikely. Colossians is written

41. Markus Barth and Helmut Blanke make the remarkable argument that since Col. 1:1–2 and 4:18 differ so widely from Paul's epistolary style, they cannot be forged, as a forger would be sure to follow the style, whereas Paul was free to depart from it (*Colossians* AB 34B, New York: Doubleday, 1994, p. 121). Once again, Neutestamentlers would be well served to learn more about the practices of ancient forgery.

by someone who has provided a twist on a Pauline theme, moving it precisely in the direction Paul refused to go.[42]

There are other theological differences from Paul, frequently noted, all of them pointing in the same direction. A later author has taken up Pauline themes and shifted them in decidedly non Pauline ways. Unlike Paul, this author understands redemption as the "forgiveness of sins" (1:14; as does Eph. 1:7). The phrase occurs nowhere else in the Pauline corpus; indeed, the term ἀφίημι itself, in the sense of "forgive sins," is absent from Paul, except in the quotation of Ps. 32:1 in Rom. 4:7 ("Blessed are those whose lawless deeds are forgiven"). So too, analogously, with a different term, 2:13 speaks of trespasses being forgiven: χαρισάμενος ἡμῖν πάντα τὰ παραπτώματα. Χαρίζομαι is never used this way in the undisputed Paulines.[43] So too 3:13 speaks of "forgiving one another just as the Lord has forgiven you," using χαρίζομαι again.

This author speaks famously of "filling up what is lacking in Christ's afflictions" for the sake of the church (1:24), a shocking image for Paul; were Christ's sufferings in some way inadequate and needed to be completed? At the same time the author offers an exalted Christology (1:15–20), far beyond anything in the undisputed letters, even the Philippians hymn: Christ is the "image of the invisible God," the "first born of creation," "in him all things were created . . . and in him all things hold together," "in him all the fullness was well pleased to dwell." This is far closer to the Johannine prologue than Paul. As a result, in comparison with Paul, the author of Colossians seems to have a much higher view of Christ (1:15–20) and a much lower view of the efficacy of his death (1:24).

Other differences from Paul may not be as striking but bear noting as contributing to the overall sense of the letter. It seems very odd indeed to have "Paul" attack issues of Jewish legalism (sabbaths and festivals 2:16; "regulations" involving purity and kosher 2:20–21) without using Pauline vocabulary either to describe or attack it ("law," "commandment," "justification"). This is not a case of simply expecting Paul always to speak the language of δικαιόω and its equivalents in all of his letters; in this case the author is dealing precisely with the issues of relevance to the terminology, but he does not use it. When the "law" does make an appearance—without being named—it is said to be a "shadow of things to come" (2:17), a teaching that resonates with the views of Hebrews, but not with Paul.

Given Paul's ability to mix metaphor otherwise, possibly not too much weight should be placed on the fact that Christ here is described as the "head of the body"

---

42. It is true that there is still some eschatological reserve in Colossians, as often noted: 1:5 ("the hope laid up for you in heaven"), 1:27 (Christ is "the hope of glory"), 3:4 ("when Christ appears"), 3:6 ("the wrath of God is coming"). But these more traditional Pauline notions have been set in a broader context that is completely non-Pauline—indeed, anti-Pauline. This author maintains that believers have already been spiritually raised with Christ, a view that Paul takes care to argue against elsewhere.

43. The term otherwise occurs eleven times in Paul, never in reference to God forgiving sins: Rom. 8:32; 1 Cor. 2:12; 2 Cor. 2:7, 10 [tris]; 12:13; Gal. 3:18; Phil. 1:29; 2:9; Phlm. 22.

rather than the "body" itself (1:18), though the usage does give one pause.[44] When one considers, however, how Paul imagines the life "of the body" the differences are even more striking. The Haustafel of 3:18–4:1 has long been thought of as non-Pauline, and for reasons related to the realized eschatology already noted. In particular, this domestication of Paul in his embrace of family ideals stands at odds with Paul's firmly stated preference, for himself and others, for celibacy. Nowhere in Paul's letters do we find such a celebration of standard Greco-Roman ethics; on the contrary, Paul insisted on the superiority of the ascetic life free from marriage (1 Corinthians 7). This, indeed, was the appropriate response to a world that was in the process of "passing away." Here in Colossians, on the other hand, the world is not passing away (there is no imminent crisis); it is here for the long haul, and so are the Christians who make up Christ's body in it.[45] As a result, they need to adopt behavior appropriate for the long run. Relations to those living outside the community are especially important, not to inform them of the "impending crisis" but to maintain a proper upstanding relationship. In short, this is written by someone who knows the church has been here and will be here for the long run. There is no imminent expectation of the coming end.[46] On the basis of all these considerations,[47] it is clear that with Colossians we are not dealing with a letter of Paul, but a letter of someone wanting his readers to think he is Paul.[48]

---

44. Pervo has made the most recent argument that the shift of the image is significant for the authorship of the letter: *Making of Paul*, p. 67.

45. On the book's eschatological reserve, see note 42.

46. One other oddity of Colossians has sometimes been noted. In Paul's own letters he states unequivocally his unwillingness to "preach the Gospel" in a church founded by someone else (Rom. 15:20; see 2 Cor. 10:13–16; Gal. 2:9), because he does not want to build on someone else's foundation. Yet if Colossians is authentic, that appears to be exactly what he is doing here (unless Paul simply meant he was unwilling to visit someone else's church in the flesh). In any event, the Epaphras who is named here as one who established the community in Colossae (1:7) is said to be a fellow prisoner of Paul in Philemon (Phlm. 23). Has the author taken a known character and made him the founder of the church? Nothing in Philemon connects him either with the founding of the church in Onesimus' house or with Colossae.

47. It is sometimes pointed out that the earthquake that allegedly destroyed Colossae in 61 CE should have some bearing on the question of the authenticity of the letter—either that it must have been written before the earthquake (by Paul) or afterward by a forger, once the community had a chance to recover. Both views assume the letter was actually sent to Colossae. But if it is forged, there is absolutely no reason to think that it was. Moreover, recent scholars such as Standhartinger have given good reason for doubting that the town was ever destroyed by earthquake. Standhartinger, *Studien*, pp. 12–13.

48. The lengths to which some New Testament commentators will go to absolve the author of any intent to deceive can be seen in the recent comments of R. McL. Wilson, *Colossians and Philemon* (London: T&T Clark, 2005):

> The evidence from the ancient world makes it necessary to distinguish between dishonest forgery, undertaken for nefarious and malicious ends, and what might be described, paradoxical as it may appear, as "honest forgery" (p. 11). . . . It should be emphasized once again that the last option [that Colossians was not written by Paul] does not necessarily carry with it the stigma of fraud or forgery. That might apply in the case of a work written to propound some heretical doctrine, and as noted above many such works were later to be stigmatized as apocryphal

The Function of the Forgery: The Question of the Opponents

No issue in the interpretation of Colossians has so exercised interpreters as the identity of the opponents attacked in the heart of the letter, 2:8–23. Nearly forty years ago now, John Gunther could cite forty-four scholarly opinions about who the false teachers were.[49] Two decades later, in one five-year stretch, four major studies appeared on the issue, each arguing a different view.[50]

The inability to determine the precise nature of the opposing teaching has led to three extremes among scholars. The most common is to identify the opponents with some known, marginal group (the Essenes, Jewish Gnostics, devotees of the Mystery cults); another is to invent a group not otherwise known to exist by combining features of several that are known, creating an ahistorical amalgam that fits a theory of the opponents better than do the known facts of history (a Stocheia cult; Christians with Essene affinities); the third is to insist that since we do not know of any group that embodies the teachings intimated in the letter, no such group at all existed, and the author's opponents are imaginary.[51]

All these views appear to assume that if there were an actual group of false teachers under attack, we should have other evidence for its existence and thus should be able to name it. But why would that be so? The author is incensed by a group of Christians who deliver false teachings (2:8, 18, 20–21); we can know some of the things that they teach, but not everything. The author certainly would be under no obligation to spell out the nature of the "false teachings" for those of us interested two thousand years later. He sees them as a threat, but he clearly knows what he is referring to better than we ever can. That should give us no reason to despair and either wildly name them or claim that they must not have existed.

The latter claim was made most poignantly by Morna Hooker in a now-famous article.[52] In her view, if the opponents were a real problem, the author, on one

---

> or heretical, and therefore rejected. In the case of New Testament pseudepigrapha, however, the situation is somewhat different: these works came to be recognized by the Church as valid and authentic witnesses to the genuine Christian faith. . . . They witness to what the Church believed. (p. 31)

In this view, an "honest forgery" is one that supports the views that eventually became dominant within Christian orthodoxy. The dishonest forger, then, is one who had the misfortune of embracing alternative views.

49. John J. Gunther, *St. Paul's Opponents and Their Background* (Leiden: Brill, 1973).

50. Thomas Sappington, *Revelation and Redemption at Colossae* (Sheffield: JSOT Press, 1991); Richard DeMaris, *Colossian Controversy: Wisdom in Dispute at Colossae* (Sheffield: Sheffield University Press, 1994); Clinton Arnold, *Colossian Syncretism: The Interface between Christianity and Folk Belief at Colossae* (Tübingen: Mohr Siebeck, 1995); Troy Martin, *By Philosophy and Empty Deceit : Colossians as Response to a Cynic Critique* (Sheffield: Sheffield Academic Press, 1996).

51. For a nice listing of the traditional views, see Mark Kiley, *Colossians as Pseudepigraphy* (Sheffield: JSOT Press, 1986), pp. 61–65.

52. Morna Hooker, "Were There False Teachers in Colossae?" in *Christ and the Spirit in the New Testament*, ed. Barnabas Lindars and Stephen S. Smalley (Cambridge: Cambridge University Press, 1973), pp. 315–31; a more recent advocate of this view is Standhartinger, *Studien zur Entstehungsgeschichte.*

hand, would have provided more information about their views and, on the other, would have engaged in a more heated refutation, much as one finds in the letter to the Galatians. The second point is moot. The way Paul dealt with one set of problems in one set of circumstances has no bearing on how a different author—not Paul—would have dealt with another situation. As to the first point, one should always be loath to stipulate how polemicists should go about their business, and there is, as Alice reminds us, no accounting for tastes. This does not mean that we should be able to identify the opponents with an otherwise known group. Earliest Christianity was far more diversified than most of us have ever dared imagine, and local views could run the gamut of almost infinite variety.

In broad terms, the opponents appear to promote the worship of lower beings of the cosmic order–the famous but difficult-to-identify στοιχεῖα—either instead of, or more likely in addition to, Christ (2:8). The parallel in v. 18, which sums up the dual problematic of the opponents, suggests that these στοιχεῖα were conceived of as angelic beings, that is, lower divine entities on the celestial scale, far below the Christ celebrated in chapter 1 as he in whom the "fullness" of the divine completely dwells. The language of "disarming" in 2:15 may suggest that these lower beings were, in the author's view—though obviously not in the opponents'—insidious, not beneficent, beings. If so, the argument compares favorably to later forms of Christian polemic that maligned others for worshiping divine beings that were in fact demons.

This undue worship of inferior divine beings is accompanied by religious practices and scruples that may have been borrowed from Jewish cult: observance of special days such as Sabbath, festivals, new moons; purity concerns ("do not handle . . . do not touch"; 2:21); and dietary laws ("do not taste"). For the author, these ritual guidelines may give the "appearance of wisdom," in promoting sacred ascetic lifestyles in service of the divine, but in fact are of no use in the ultimate concerns of the believer, to check (real) fleshly indulgence (2:23).

The entire system proposed by those who threaten the readers with this false worship and pointless religious practices is summed up as "philosophy and empty deceit" (2:8). This deceit is obviously not the true worship that is available to believers in Christ. Contrary to what scholars sometimes assert, the threat posed by this alternative religiosity is internal, a threat to those who are already part of the body of Christ. It is not an invitation to deconvert and join some other religion (Jewish or pagan). That is to say, it is a challenge to become a different kind of Christian—although the author himself may have considered the "false teachers" as not Christian at all, as typically happened among polemicists standing in the proto-orthodox tradition. The opponents, though, appear to have seen their prescribed worship as important elements of their Christian tradition, not as non-Christian pagan or Jewish cult.

The author's response to these unnecessary add-ons to what he takes to be the "true" worship of Christ is, as widely recognized, already adumbrated in the celebrated Christ hymn of chapter 1, which is used to set up his direct refutation of chapter 2. It is precisely because Christ is the "image of the invisible God, the first born of the entire creation" that he alone is to be worshiped. The στοιχεῖα are among the things that were created in him: "all things were created through him and for him." Moreover, he is "before all things." He alone is "pre-eminent" and in him "all the fullness is pleased to dwell." The link between the hymn and the polemic is clearly made through the connections of 1:19 at the end of the first passage (ἐν αὐτῷ εὐδόκησεν πᾶν τὸ πλήρωμα κατοικῆσαι) and its loose reiteration in the second (ἐν αὐτῷ κατοικεῖ πᾶν τὸ πλήρωμα τῆς θεότητος σωματικῶς; 2:9). And so the issue in the controversy has to do with the adequacy of Christ. For this author, he is the embodiment of the fullness of divinity itself. He alone should be worshiped. There is no need for worship of lower beings of any sort, however powerful or important. And no need of secondary ascetic practices. Christ is all that one needs. Adding anything to the worship of Christ is empty deceit, merely human "philosophy," pointless and unnecessary religious exercise, and even, he suggests, the worship of malevolent beings.

In no small measure, the purpose of the letter, then, is to stress that believers who have been baptized into Christ already have complete access to him and the benefits that he conveys. They have no need of other divine beings or other religious activities. This is where the eschatology of the letter becomes crucial. For this author, those who have been baptized have not only died with Christ (as in Paul). They have already been delivered "from the authority of darkness and transferred . . . into the kingdom of his beloved son" (1:13). They have, that is, already experienced a spiritual resurrection. "You were also raised [aorist] in him through faith"; God "made you alive with him"; "you have been raised up with Christ."

In other words, precisely the theological feature of the letter that suggests it was not written by the Paul of the undisputed letters (the realized eschatology) is the feature that figures most prominently in its exposition of the superiority of the Christian faith, the central tenet of the letter. The non-Pauline eschatology is not a subsidiary matter tacked onto a letter dealing with other things; it is the centerpiece of the letter and the key to understanding its polemic. For this author, the believer's resurrection is a past, realized, spiritual event.[53]

---

53. In one of the most impressive studies of Colossians and its Sitz of recent years, Standhartinger (*Studien zur Entstehungsgeschichte*) recognizes that eschatology is the key, but she goes too far and in the wrong direction, coming up with a creative and imaginative thesis that is probably too imaginative by half: the author knows, as do his readers, that Paul is no longer living (thus she appeals to 4:3, 2:1, and 2:5 and cites Lohse, *Mitarbeiter*, p. 193; Charles Nielsen, *Status of Paul*; Margaret MacDonald, *Pauline Churches*, 127ff., and others; p. 3, n. 6). And so for her, he is writing a "letter from heaven" (Himmelsbrief), to encourage them in the face of his own death. What matters is not the polemic but the paranesis: be strong. As she puts it (p. 195): "the cause of the letter is not a specific theological position of a real group of opponents, but pessimism and discouragement in the face of the death of Paul." In her view, then, "Col intends to comfort the community/ies that have been discouraged and dispersed by the death of Paul through a 'heavenly letter' from Paul, and to counter the process of dispersal that the author fears will take place. . . . The theological concept of this part of the wisdom movement attempts to encounter eschatological doubts with an 'un-eschatological' concept of the presentist ascent of the

Colossians then may be considered a counterforgery in the weaker sense, in that it attacks a distinct—if hard to localize and identify—set of opponents representing an aberrant view. Here a later forger puts a non-Pauline (or anti-Pauline) eschatological view on Paul's pen in order to oppose "false teachers" who do not appreciate the full extent of the salvation Christ has brought. The letter did not need, of course, actually to have been sent to Colossae, whether or not the town still existed at the time.[54] As Standhartinger indicates, the specific address to Colossians in fact seems at odds with the universal tendency of the letter (1:6, 1:23, 1:28, 2:1, 4:16). As a result, she may be right that the letter was (pseudonymously) directed there for symbolic value. Colossae was a remote, little known place; this embrace of the fullness of the divinity in bodily form reaches into the very remote corners of the empire.[55]

EPHESIANS

I will deal with the letter to the Ephesians in somewhat less detail because it is less ostensibly polemical, in any traditional sense: it is not obviously directed against a group of enemies. But the letter does take non-Pauline eschatology even farther than Colossians, and at least one recent interpreter has seen it as an attempt to correct an important aspect of its predecessor. To that extent it can be seen, at least subtly, as polemical.

That the writing style of Ephesians stands out within the traditional Pauline corpus was seen already by Erasmus: "Certainly the style is so different from several of Paul's letters, that it might seem to be by another, were it not for the fact that the spirit and nature of the Pauline mind altogether vindicate it" (Certe stilus tantum dissonat a ceteris Pauli epistolis, ut alterius videri possit, nisi pectus atque indoles Paulinae mentis hanc prorsus illi vindicarent).[56] Evanson in 1792, and then Usteri in 1824, both maintained that its impersonal character and close proximity to Colossians made it suspect. But W. M. L. de Wette was the first to formulate the full

---

soul to God." ("nicht eine bestimmte theologische Position einer realen Gegnerinnen- und Gegnergruppe, sondern Pessimismus und Verunsicherung angesichts des Todes des Paulus Anlaß des Briefes ist. . . . Die Intention des Kol ist es, der/den durch den Tod des Paulus verunsicherten und auseinanderlaufenden Gemeinde(n) durch einen 'Himmelsbrief' des Paulus Trost zuzusprechen und dem von den Verf befürchteten Zerfallsprozeß entgegenzuwirken. . . . Das theologische Konzept dieses Teils der Weisheitsbewegung versucht, eschatologischen Zweifeln mit einem 'uneschatologischen' Konzept des präsentischen Aufstiegs der Seele zu Gott zu begegnen.") It is an intriguing position, but not probative, in my view, for two reasons. First, there is in fact nothing in the verses in question (4:3, 2:1, 2:5) to indicate that Paul is "dead." Quite the contrary, the language of the letter strives to assert just the opposite, especially the "I, Paul" passages already noted above. Second, and of key importance, the polemical language of the letter is not actually directed toward eschatological false teachings. That is to say, the eschatology is part and parcel of the author's discourse, but not as a response to alternative views. Instead, the author's eschatology is used to deal with a different kind of problem (worship of angels and so on, not the death of Paul).

54. See note 47.

55. Standhartinger, *Studien zur Entstehungsgeschichte*, pp. 15–16.

56. Erasmus, *Annotationes in Novum Testamentum* (Basel, 1519), p. 413.

argument against its genuineness in his *Einleitung* of 1826, an argument repeated in his commentary of 1843. In de Wette's view, the letter contains much that is "foreign to the apostle . . . or not worthy of him in its mode of writing and thought."[57]

A key contribution to the modern study was C. L. Mitton's 1951 analysis,[58] which laid out, in considerable detail, a wealth of arguments based on linguistics, style, literary dependence, historical circumstances, and doctrine. His demonstration against authenticity was not at all compromised by his adoption of the well-known but now discredited Goodspeed-Knox theory that the letter was originally designed as a "cover letter" for the *Corpus Paulinum*. Among the letters discussed so far, Ephesians is the most widely acknowledged to be pseudepigraphic among critical scholars, including such recent commentators as Sellin.[59]

As so often happens, the arguments against authenticity are at times far from compelling. It is widely pointed out, for example, that there is a lack of a concrete Sitz im Leben for the letter; no clear characterization of the recipients, who appear to be known only by hearsay; and no obvious situation to which the letter is addressed. But this scarcely speaks against Pauline authorship: there is no reason to think that Paul was constrained to write only one kind of occasional letter throughout his career. Was Paul for some reason not allowed to write a circular letter if he so chose? So too, it is often pointed out that the author himself is portrayed in rather colorless terms. But here as well, one might suspect that if Paul were to write another kind of letter from the seven about which we have detailed information, he may well have stood in relationship to it in a different way.

There are, nonetheless, compelling reasons for thinking that Paul did not in fact write the letter. The first and most obvious involves its relationship to Colossians, on which it appears to be patterned. If Colossians was forged—as it almost certainly was—there can be no thought of Paul himself imitating it in another piece of correspondence. Scholars evaluate the proximity of the two letters in various ways. Mitton's famous claim is that a third of the words in Colossians reappear in Ephesians. Lincoln gives more precise, though completely confirmatory, statistics: of 1,570 words in Colossians, 34 percent appear in Ephesians; of 2,411 words in Ephesians, 26.5 percent are in Colossians.[60] Hüneburg is somewhat more circumspect, recognizing that a good deal depends on how one counts the words found in parallel passages; by his tally somewhere between 26.5 percent and 50 percent of the words of Ephesians can be found in Colossians.[61]

---

57. Much that is "dem Apostel fremd . . . oder seiner nicht recht würdig scheint, in Schreib- . . . und Denkart." As quoted in Michael Gese, *Das Vermächtnis des Apostels: Die Rezeption der paulinischen Theologie im Epheserbrief*, WUNT 2, 99 (Tübingen: Mohr Siebeck, 1997), p. 1.

58. *The Epistle to the Ephesians: Its Authorship, Origin and Purpose* (Oxford: Oxford University Press, 1951).

59. Gerhard Sellin, *Der Brief an die Epheser*, KEK (Göttingen: Vandenhoeck & Ruprecht, 2008).

60. Andrew T. Lincoln, *Ephesians, WBC*, 42 (Dallas: Word Books, 1990), p. xlviii.

61. Martin Hüneburg, "Paulus versus Paulus: Der Epheserbrief als Korrektur des Kolosserbriefes," in J. Frey et al., eds., *Pseudepigraphie und Verfasserfiktion*, p. 390.

These kinds of bare statistics are scarcely probative; what matters are the individual instances. The passage that leaves no doubt is Eph. 6:21–22, which repeats an entire twenty-nine words from Col. 4:7–8 (leaving out just two words). Obviously this kind of parallel is impossible without one author copying another. Lincoln points out that there are three other passages that have seven words in common; these alone show that there must be a literary relationship between the letters (Eph. 1:1–2 and Col. 1:1–2; Eph. 3:2 and Col. 1:25; Eph. 3:9 and Col. 1:26); in two other passages five consecutive words are found (Eph. 1:7 and Col. 1:14; Eph. 4:16 and Col. 2:19).[62]

As might be expected, various solutions to the obvious literary ties of the two writings have been proposed throughout the history of the discussion. Mayerhoff in 1838 maintained that Ephesians is authentic and that Colossians was a secondary reworking of it by a later writer. De Wette in 1843 took the opposite side: Colossians is authentic and Ephesians was an imitation. Holtzmann in 1872 declared that both books, in their surviving form, are inauthentic: Colossians was based on an authentic Pauline letter, which had been used as the basis for a later author to create Ephesians, which in turn was used to create what is now Colossians. The majority of scholars today—despite the protests of E. Best—side with the priority of Colossians.[63] The most recent case has been made by Leppä: a number of the parallel passages in Ephesians appear to be elaborations of Colossians (Eph. 2:1–10 of Col. 2:12–13; Eph. 5:21–33 of Col. 3:18–19) and some passages of Ephesians appear to be conflations of disparate statements of Colossians (Eph. 1:7, cf. Col. 1:14, 20; Eph. 1:15–16, cf. Col. 1:4 and 1:9; Eph. 2:1–5, cf. Col. 2:13; 3:16; etc.).[64]

If this view is right, Ephesians was obviously forged, since Colossians, on which it was based, was forged. Confirmation comes in a range of arguments involving style, vocabulary, structure, and content. The stylistic considerations that led Schmidt to claim that 2 Thessalonians was non-Pauline speak with equal elegance for Ephesians—as well as for Colossians, in a case that is fully confirmed and ratified by Bujard's earlier but more extensive analysis. Unfortunately, nothing of Bujardian proportions exists for Ephesians, although it is frequently observed that the style is not Pauline, with its love of long and awkward sentences (1:3–14; 1:15–23; 2:1–7 with anacolouthon; 3:8–12; 3:14–19; 4:11–16; etc.), its strings of participles (1:13; 2:12; 2:14–16), strings of infinitives (3:16–18; 4:22–24); and repetitions of prepositions (1:3ff.; 4:12–13). Again, the question is not whether Paul was capable of writing in this way, but simply of whether he did. With respect to the long and complex sentences, one frequently cited statistic is that of Morton and McLeman, who pointed out that nine out of a hundred

62. Lincoln, *Ephesians*, p. xlviii.

63. Ernest Best, "Who Used Whom? The Relationship of Ephesians and Colossians," *NTS* 43 (1997): 72–96. For the older studies, see Victor Paul Furnish, "Ephesians, Epistle to the," in ABD, 2. 537.

64. Leppä, *Making of Colossians*, pp. 32–45.

sentences in the book comprise more than fifty words.[65] This stands in sharp contrast with passages of approximately equal length in Paul, for example, Romans 1–4, which has just three out of 581 sentences over fifty words; 1 Corinthians 1–4, which has one of 621 sentences; 2 Corinthians 1–3, with two of 334 sentences; Galatians, with one of 181 sentences; Philippians, with one of 102 sentences; 1 Thessalonians, with one of 81 sentences. Paul could obviously write long sentences. But it was not his characteristic style. One can only marvel at a supporter of authenticity like M. Barth, who suggests that "Paul himself is the man who could best afford to write in a non-Paulinistic way."[66] Whether here a secretary (or coauthor) hypothesis can best explain these stylistic data will be an issue addressed in an excursus in the next chapter.

Pointing in the same direction of style is the structure of the letter, which looks, at first glance, roughly Pauline, but is distinctive within the canonical corpus in containing both a blessing (1:3–14) and a thanksgiving (1:15–23). The word usage points in the same direction, in view of its occasional distinctiveness, although this is obviously not compelling in se. Still, as frequently noted, this author prefers the phrase "in the heavens" to Paul's "in heaven" (1:3, 20; 2:6; 3:10; 6:12), refers to the "Devil" instead of Paul's "Satan" (4:27, 6:11),[67] and uses the non-Pauline phrase "good works" (2:10). The final point—possibly the others as well—indicates a larger problem than mere linguistic preference. This author has a perspective that in many places may sound like Paul but in fact stands at odds with him, a matter to which we will turn momentarily.

Before doing so, it is important to stress more generally the strongest argument against the Pauline authorship of the letter, its non-Pauline contents. As different as Colossians is from Paul himself, Ephesians is more so, often in the same ways. There continues to be some element of eschatological reserve here, although not as much as Colossians. Thus, for example, the Spirit is the "down payment of our inheritance until we acquire it" (1:14) and it is in "the coming ages" (2:7) that believers will receive "the immeasurable riches of his grace"; moreover, the wrath of God is still "coming" (5:6). Nonetheless, the real significance of the resurrection of the dead is that it is a spiritual event that has happened (in the past) to believers, who are already enjoying the benefits of a raised existence. Even more than Colossians, this realized eschatology stands in sharp tension with Paul's carefully developed views in Romans 6, Philippians 3, and 1 Corinthians 15. Just as Christ himself has been "raised . . . from the dead and made to sit at his right hand in the heavenly places, far above every authority, power, and dominion" (1:20–21), so too the believers have also already been "made alive" (1:4), indeed, "made alive

65. A. Q. Morton and J. McLeman, *Paul: The Man and the Myth* (New York: Harper & Row, 1966), table 6.

66. Markus Barth, *Ephesians*, AB 34 (New York: Doubleday, 1974); vol. 1 (Eph. 1–3), p. 49.

67. Best tries to mute the force of this argument by pointing out that Paul too widely varies how he refers to Satan, referencing 2 Thess 3:3 "the evil one," and 2 Cor. 6:15 "Beliar." Does it need to be pointed out that one of these passages is forged and the other interpolated?

together with Christ . . . and raised . . . up with him and made . . . to sit with him in the heavenly places" (2:5–6). The exalted character of Christ who now rules over all the evil forces of this world is shared by the believers who have been raised with him and so likewise rule in the heavenly places. Believers are not even said, as in Paul, to have "died" to sin and the powers of the world; for this author, they *once* were dead, before coming to life in Christ; but now they are no longer subject to the powers and forces of the world.[68]

This is not the only material difference between Paul and the letter to the Ephesians. Like its model, Colossians, Ephesians too speaks of redemption in the un-Pauline way of ἄφεσιν τῶν παραπτωμάτων (1:7; cf. Col. 1:14); it too conceptualizes Christ as the head of the body, not the body (1:22–23 and especially 4:15–16, which sounds very much like Colossians—see Col. 1:18 and 2:19); it too, presents a Haustafel that appears to stand at odds with Paul's radical social ethic and endorsement of celibacy, and much more like the bourgeois ethic that the Christian church had begun to adopt once it recognized that it needed to "settle down" into life in the Roman world—a reconfirmation of the lack of eschatological urgency so characteristic of the authentic Paul.

Other statements of the letter are even more difficult to imagine as coming from the pen of Paul, including the claim—key to the teaching of the letter—that Christ had somehow "abolished the law of the commandments" by his death (2:15). Paul himself, with one of his characteristic emphatic declarations (μὴ γένοιτο!), insists that he does not believe the Law has been abolished; on the contrary, for him it is established in Christ (Rom. 3:31; cf., e.g., Gal. 6:2).

More than anywhere else, the key passage of Eph. 2:1–10 provides individual statements that seem, on the surface, to carry Pauline resonances, yet reveal themselves upon closer reflection to be strongly non-Pauline. The salvific pattern set forth here is often touted as vintage Paul: believers who were dead in their sins and alienated from God are made alive only by God's own gracious act in Christ, to be received by faith, not by "works," so that there is now no ground for boasting. Once the patina of Pauline phrases is scratched, however, the alien character of the passage is clearly shown. The historical Paul insisted in his own letters that before coming to Christ he was completely "blameless" with respect to the "righteousness that is in the Law" (Phil. 3:6). How could he now turn and say that he, like the pagans around him, followed "the passions of the flesh, the desires of body and mind?" Some such view may come from a misreading of Romans 7, but not from the pen of Paul talking about his own past. How could Paul, who insisted that believers "will be raised" with Christ, with an emphasis on the future state,

68. Given the occasional reserve of the author—there is still some kind of future for this world—Lindemann may press the matter too far by claiming that the author of Ephesians has sacrificed Paul's eschatology (*Die Aufhebung der Zeit: Geschichtsverständnis und Eschatologie im Epheserbrief* [Gütersloh: Gerd Mohn, 1975], p. 352). The Pauline eschatology has not been sacrificed; it has simply been muted and altered in a thoroughly non-Pauline direction. The view of Ephesians, again, appears to be precisely the one advocated by (Pauline?) enthusiasts in Corinth, whom Paul goes to some length to argue against.

declare that believers have already been raised and are in fact currently "seated in the heavenly places" with Christ, in a position of rule and authority removed from the evil forces of this world? How could Paul refer to the act of salvation as a completed event ("you have been saved") when for Paul salvation was an event to be eagerly expected, yet to come?[69]

Most important, in a letter dealing principally with the relation of Jew and Gentile in the body of Christ, how could the historical Paul speak of being saved by faith, and not by "good works"? Good works? Of course, Paul himself had no qualms about good deeds or the people who performed them; nor, obviously, did this author (2:8–10). But what has that to do with the Pauline view of justification? Paul's concern, especially in contexts of soteriology and the relationship of Jew and Gentile, was entirely with works "of the Law." Paul's own insistence that Gentiles do not need to keep the "works" of Jewish Law has somehow become transmuted into a claim that no one can be "good enough" to merit salvation. For Paul the issue was not moral probity; it was Jewish Law. This author has either very much misunderstood Paul's language or has rewritten it for a new situation, in which the words may sound similar but in fact mean something very different.

That the author was living after Paul is suggested by statements that may represent unintentional slips. And so, for example, in 2:20, the author speaks of the "apostles" as a founding group for the church, without any recognition that Paul himself was one of the constituent members of the group. Moreover, for Paul, Christ is not the "cornerstone" of the church: Christ himself (not the prophets and apostles") is the foundation (1 Cor. 3:11). Finally, and yet more striking, this author indicates that the central teaching of the gospel, that the Gentiles are to be joint heirs in the body of Christ with Jews, was "revealed to his holy apostles and prophets by the Spirit" (Eph. 3:5). But is he not missing something rather crucial? Paul thought that he himself was the one to whom this insight was supremely revealed. He was the apostle to the Gentiles, and he was the one who had to convince others.

There are, in short, numerous imponderable difficulties in thinking the letter to the Ephesians authentic. At the same time, one of the other striking features of the book is the lengths to which the author goes in order to make the letter sound like Paul's—in fact, to insist to his readers that he really is Paul. Obviously he names himself in 1:1 (no coauthor here), and uses a Pauline letter opening (1:1–2). The structure of the letter is, for the most part, Pauline (with the one key exception mentioned above) and it uses dozens of "Pauline sounding" words, phrases, and ideas. Apart from that, the author makes an inordinate number of self-references: "I Paul, a prisoner of Christ Jesus on behalf of you Gentiles" (3:1); "You have heard of the stewardship of the grace of God given me" (3:2); "how the mystery was made

---

69. See especially Rom. 5:9–10 and 1 Cor. 3:15, 5:5. The one possible exception of Paul using "salvation" language in a past sense is Rom. 8:24; but even there the entire point is that Christians have been saved "in hope," that is, in expectation of an ultimate event, yet to take place. This is precisely what is lacking in the Ephesians passage.

known to me by a revelation" (3:3); and "my understanding of the mystery" (3:4). He declares: "I was made a minister of this gospel . . . by the grace of God given to me" (3:7). He refers to himself as "the very least of all the saints" but claims that "grace was given [to me] to preach to the Gentiles" (3:8). He speaks of "my afflictions on your behalf" (3:13). He indicates that "I bow my knees before the Father" (3:14) and that "I [am] a prisoner of the Lord" (4:1). In the closing he asks his readers to "Pray . . . for me that a word might be given me" (6:19); he indicates that "I am an ambassador in chains . . . that I might declare it boldly" (6:20); he states that his readers may now "know how I am and what I am doing" (6:21); and he lets them know that "I have sent him [Tychicus] to you" (6:22).

How can a commentator like E. Best claim that this author was not trying to deceive his readers into thinking that he was actually Paul?[70] The author repeatedly goes out of his way to claim he was Paul. But he was not Paul. He was a follower of Paul, urging a non-Pauline set of theological views, writing later. Critics at the time would have labeled the book a νόθον or a ψεῦδος—creating an obvious irony, given the stress on the importance of "truth" found throughout the book (1:13; 4:15, 21; 5:9). Particularly piquant are 4:25 ("let everyone speak the truth with his neighbor") and 6:14 ("gird your loins with truth"), given the circumstances of the writing. Other critics have more sophisticated suggestions to absolve the author of his (from an ancient perspective) moral dilemma, but they too often appear to involve special pleading.[71]

---

70. Ernest Best, *Ephesians*, ICC (Edinburgh: T&T Clark, 1998), pp. 12–13. Among his arguments, Best claims that "had Tertullian been told that Ephesians had been written by a disciple of Paul he would have had no difficulty in accepting it, for he accepted the Gospels of Mark and Luke because they were written by the disciples, respectively, of Peter and Paul, saying that the works which disciples publish belong to their masters"; p. 13. This completely misconstrues ancient understandings of authorship, since, as pointed out earlier, Tertullian did not think that the author of Mark claimed to be Peter or the author of Luke, Paul.

71. For example, John Muddiman's recent solution to the puzzle of Ephesians (*The Epistle to the Ephesians*, BNTC, London: Continuum, 2001). For Muddiman, the letter embodies an authentic letter of Paul that has been thoroughly edited and revised, so that there are indubitable Pauline passages (3:1–4, 8; 4:20–21; 6:18–22) but also significant non-Pauline material, all together. This is an interesting attempt at a solution, but it is difficult to establish exegetically. There is no stylistic evidence in support, for example; and the problem is that the letter is thoroughly imbued with non-Pauline views. It is especially difficult to explain the parallels to the non-Pauline Colossians under this view. Muddiman claims that the differences from Colossians show that Ephesians was not modeled on it. But the question is not why they are different. They are different letters, so of course they are different. But why are they so similar? It is not convincing to argue that Ephesians cannot be a circular letter meant eventually to come back to Colossae, since then the Colossians would have been confused by the appearance of two such different letters coming from Paul. Why should we think the letter of Ephesians was meant to show up in Colossae? Or, as I have stressed, that Colossians was? But even more, the "solution" simply creates a problem of its own by pushing the problem back a stage, making the book a "redactional forgery." Whoever added the additional non-Pauline material and rephrased the Pauline material would, in this case, have published it as if it were Paul's letter itself. But it was not Paul's. It was this other person's letter, with his own ideas and thoughts (some of Paul's retained, others of his own added) published in the name of someone who in fact did not publish it.

The Polemics of the Letter

The Letter to the Ephesians may seem less germane to the focus of this study than other texts we will be examining. Its purposes are not ostensibly polemical and there is no clear-cut opponent described in its exposition. It is principally a celebration of Christian "unity": the unity of Jew and Gentile together in the body of Christ as the "mystery" that has been revealed (esp. 2:11–21) and the unity of both with God through the redemptive work of Christ (2:1–10). The paranetic section too stresses the importance of unity both in the Spirit (4:2–6) and in society (the Haustafel of 5:21–6:9, along with other exhortations). There are, course, many other themes and subthemes, a good deal of paranesis, and an attempt to "correct" views that the author finds inadequate (possibly, e.g., Gentile "boasting"). But polemic does not seem to be the dominant feature of the letter.

At the same time, even though "false teaching" is not the principal concern, it is—as with Colossians—an ongoing issue, as evidenced especially in the second half of the letter, as the readers are urged not to be carried away "with every wind of teaching by the cunning of others, by their craftiness in their wiles of deceit" (4:14); they are to "put away every lie" (4:25); they are to make sure that no one "deceive" them "with empty words"; and they are to gird their loins with truth (6:14). There is thus some concern about false teaching and wrong instruction, even if the content of the error is never brought to the level of expression. It is possible, obviously, that these exhortations are simply traditional language, in a letter that is more concerned with urging a unity in the body and to encourage its readers in their lives together.

There may be a case to be made, however, that the letter engages in a far subtler kind of polemic, as recently argued in an interesting article by Martin Hüneburg.[72] Hüneburg points out that despite the fact that Ephesians was modeled on Colossians and contains, as a result, many of its salient themes, it differs in a significant respect that may suggest the author was not simply writing a letter for purposes of his own, but was trying to correct a misdirection being taken by its model. In particular Hüneburg notes that unlike its model, Ephesians makes explicit appeal to the Jewish scriptures in the context of its exhortations. When one reads Colossians carefully, in fact, without the blinders provided by the rest of the Pauline corpus, there is nothing to suggest that the exalted status of believers and the full benefits of salvation that they now enjoy are closely tied to anything like a "history of salvation."

The historical Israel appears to be absent from Colossians, unlike Ephesians, where the historical people of Israel, and their Scriptures, figure prominently. In Ephesians, the body of Christ represents a reconciliation between "the commonwealth of Israel" with "you Gentiles in the flesh." A new circumcision has been provided; an alienation has been overcome; those who were "strangers to

72. "Paulus versus Paulus," pp. 387–409.

the promise" have now been brought into the fold through the blood of Christ, which has created "one new person in place of the two." The stress on the historical connections between the body of Christ and the people of Israel in the opening exposition of Ephesians, especially of chapter 2, is matched by an appeal (also absent from its model) to the Jewish Scriptures throughout the paranetic section (e.g., 4:8, 25; 5:31; 6:2–3).

It is completely plausible that among the concerns of the author of Ephesians was the ahistorical view of salvation presented by his model, where the act of salvation brought by Christ received through the new existence effected in baptism had lost its roots in the history of salvation to Israel as related in the Scriptures. Colossians is in danger of moving into the direction of salvation without a history of salvation. But not Ephesians. Here the Gentiles have joined the commonwealth of Israel and been made heirs of the promise, all as part of God's mysterious plan (not a new thing) for the salvation of the world.[73]

In short, Colossians was not merely a text to be imitated or a kind of Vorlage of Ephesians. It was a "Pauline" book that needed to be corrected and brought back into line. There is no "correction formula" here as one finds in 2 Thess. 2:2, possibly because the author of Ephesians saw Colossians as authentically, but dangerously, Pauline. He created a further close connection to his model through his reference to Tychicus in 6:21. But he extended its message by making the apostle now explain the economy of the salvation of Gentiles—the resurrected existence now already enjoyed by those who have been baptized into Christ—with reference to the larger salvation history of the people of God. If this view of the author's concerns is right, then Ephesians can be seen as a kind of counterforgery, intending to correct the views of its predecessor—or at least the implications of those views—in the name of an apostle who in fact did not write either work.[74]

73. Pervo makes a similar argument concerning the relationship of Colossians and Ephesians, in *Making of Paul*, p. 71.

74. A defense of the Pauline authorship of Ephesians can still be found in commentaries written, especially, by authors opposed to the notion of canonical forgery on principle. A good recent example is Harold W. Hoehner, *Ephesians: An Exegetical Commentary* (Grand Rapids, MI: Baker, 2002), who points out that it would be hard to see how those "who knew Paul would have accepted this as Paul's work so shortly after his death." This begs the question of audience. He goes on to state that "most pseudepigraphical works are apocalyptic and not epistolary in form" (p. 43), the force of which is hard indeed to penetrate. He also stresses the problematic of Eph. 6:21–22, asking the rather remarkable questions of how the historical Tychicus could have explained that he did not carry the letter, and why a pseudonymous author would ask for prayers if he was, in fact, already dead.

CHAPTER EIGHT

Later Forgeries Dealing with Eschatology

It should come as no surprise that apostolic forgeries involving variant eschatological views continued to appear after the earliest period of the Christian pseudepigraphic tradition. Once the overly sanguine expectations of an imminent end began not just to wane in some circles, but to disappear altogether, various Christian thinkers developed a variety of eschatological views, many of which stood at odds with one another. Some maintained that even though the early time table may have been wrong—the end was not to have come immediately in Jesus' generation—the basic scenario was right: the end was still to come right away, in their own time. Others contended that the apocalyptic scenario itself was flawed at the core: the Kingdom of God was not to be a future event to transpire literally on earth, but either a postmortem experience of the individual or a present reality in the resurrected existence enjoyed in the present, by both the individual and the collective body of the church. These alternative views found expression in the proclamation of various Christian leaders at the end of the first century and beginning of the second, and occasionally a writer would assume the guise of a prominent spokesperson, an apostle of Jesus, in order to authorize his position, as well as to polemicize against those advancing contrary positions.

One such forgery is the letter of 2 Timothy, written in part, allegedly, to oppose two teachers, Hymenaeus and Philetus, who insisted that "the resurrection is already past" (2:17–18). The authorship of 2 Timothy has become a matter of renewed interest over the past two decades, as some have argued that it, unlike its two Pastoral counterparts, should be credited as orthonymous;[1] others, including one major commentator, have mounted a spirited defense for the authenticity of all

1. See, e.g., Michael Prior, *Paul the Letter-Writer and the Second Letter to Timothy*, JSNTSup (Sheffield: University of Sheffield Press, 1989).

three of the Pastoral epistles.[2] In view of these ongoing discussions, it is important for the purposes of this study to explore at some length the question of authorship of the Pastoral corpus, before turning to the question of the eschatological polemic of 2 Timothy in particular. Later in the study we will return to the views of 1 Timothy and Titus, whose polemical concerns lie in a different direction.

THE PASTORAL EPISTLES

The question of the Pastoral epistles, as a group, is important historically, as these were the first writings of the New Testament whose authorship was seriously questioned in modern times. It is commonly stated that doubts were first expressed in 1807 by Friedrich Schleiermacher, in a public letter to J. C. Gass, *Über den sogenannten Ersten Brief des Paulus an den Timotheus: Ein Kritisches Sendschreiben.*[3] Jens Herzer has pointed out, however, that the authorship of 1 Timothy was questioned three years earlier by Johann Ernst Christian Schmidt, in his *Historisch-kritische Einleitung in das Neue Testament.*[4] The first to assert that all three Pastorals were to be considered as a group, to stand or fall together, was J. G. Eichhorn, in his own celebrated *Einleitung in das Neue Testament.* Eichhorn claimed that he had been questioning the authenticity of the books before Schleiermacher's letter appeared; his case against all three was based on historical, rather than stylistic questions.[5] These were largely the bases applied by F. C. Baur as well, who maintained that the opponents attacked in the letters were second-century Gnostics and so, obviously, not contemporary with Paul. The letters were therefore pseudepigraphic.[6] Baur's view moved toward a critical consensus with the 1880 commentary of Heinrich Holtzmann, *Die Pastoralbriefe, kritisch und exegetisch behandelt.*[7] Despite the outspoken minority of naysayers, the consensus by and large holds today, with the overwhelming preponderance of critical scholars maintaining that all three letters are clearly post-Pauline.

It should not be thought, however, that the question about the authenticity of the letters is simply a modern one. Hints and clear indications of doubt can be found among our earliest evidence. Our oldest extensive manuscript of the Pauline epistles, P^{46}, suffers a large lacuna in its missing final pages, but despite the intriguing claims of J. Duff, these have been shown by E. Epp not to have been

2. Luke Timothy Johnson, *The First and Second Letters to Timothy*, AB 35A (New York: Doubleday, 2001).

3. Berlin: Realschulbuchhandlung, 1807.

4. Jens Herzer, "Fiction oder Tauschung? Zur Diskussion über die Pseudepigraphie der Pastoralbriefe," in Jörg Frey et al., eds., *Pseudepigraphie und Verfasserfiktion*, pp. 489–536. For another recent brief history of scholarship, see Luke Timothy Johnson, "First Timothy 1, 1–20: The Shape of the Struggle," in *1 Timothy Reconsidered*, ed. Karl Paul Donfried (Leuven: Peeters, 2008), pp. 19–39.

5. 3.1 (Leipzig: Weidmannischen Buchhandlung, 1812).

6. *Die sogenannten Pastoralbriefe des Apostels Paulus* (Stuttgart: J. G. Cotta, 1835).

7. Leipzig: Englemann, 1880.

sufficient to have contained all three of the letters.[8] Whatever else they may have contained is anyone's guess. Marcion too did not have (or know about?) the three letters, as Tertullian stresses (*Adv. Marc.* 5.21). The same may have been true of Tatian (according to Jerome; *PL* 26.556). But that is not all: around 200 CE Clement of Alexandria reports that "some heretics" rejected 1 and 2 Timothy because of their contents (*Strom.* 2.52.6) and Origen notes that some orthodox Christians reject 2 Timothy because of its approbation of the magicians Jannes and Jambres in 3:8 (*Comm. on Matthew* ser. 117).

Supporters of the authenticity of the letters occasionally point to their use in other writers of the early church, most especially Polycarp. The matter of early usage is of historical interest, but it scarcely can be counted as evidence for Pauline authorship. Someone writing, say, twenty years after the books were placed in circulation may well have assumed that they were Paul's. After all, they claim to be Paul's. And certainly the fact that the authorship was more or less secure for centuries, down to the 1800s, is of no relevance at all.[9] The unconsidered opinion of thirteenth-century monks has no evidentiary value.

The Standard View of the Pastorals and Its Detractors

As already noted, the view adopted by Eichhorn in 1812, that the Pastorals are to be differentiated from the other Pauline letters, yet seen as a "zusammengehörende Gruppe," is still prevalent today, two centuries later. Norbert Brox states the case in these terms:

> Their unity and status as a closed group is documented further in the details, including their close relationship in terms of language (style, vocabulary), content, and presupposed church-historical situation. They speak the same high Greek, live in the same theological context, combat the same heresies, know on the whole the same organization and conception of the individual churches. . . .[10]

Aspects of this view are open to dispute, as we will see. In particular, there is no reason to think that the false teachings attacked by 1 Timothy and Titus are the same as those taken on by 2 Timothy, and the church structure and organization

---

8. Jeremy Duff, "P46 and the Pastorals: A Misleading Consensus," *NTS* 44 (1998): 578–90, answered in Eldon J. Epp, "Issues in the Interrelation of New Testament Textual Criticism and Canon," in *The Canon Debate: On the Origins and Formation of the Bible*; eds. Lee M. McDonald and James A. Sanders (Peabody, MA: Hendrickson, 2002), pp. 485–515; reprinted in E. Epp, *Perspectives on New Testament Textual Criticism: Collected Essays 1962–2004* (Leiden: Brill, 2005), pp. 596–639, here 613–19.

9. As intimated, for instance, by Luke Timothy Johnson, "First Timothy 1, 1–20," p. 19.

10. Ihre Einheitlichkeit und Geschlossenheit dokumentiert sich weiter im einzelnen bis in eine enge Verwandtschaft der Sprache (Stil, Wortschatz), des Inhalts und vorausgesetzt kirchengeschichtliche Situation hinein. Sie sprechen dasselbe gehobene Griechisch, leben in derselben theologischen Begriffswelt, bekämpfen dieselben Häresien, kennen im ganzen dieselbe Organisation und Verfaßtheit der Einzelkirchen." *Die Pastoralbriefe*, 4th ed. (Regensberg: Pustet, 1969), p. 12.

of the two letters is not evidenced in the third. But most scholars continue to see them as a group of three letters rather than individual, isolated productions. In its most extreme form this view is taken to mean that the three letters were produced—and are to be read—as a corpus, as stated by P. Trummer: "The pastoral epistles are not created merely as pseudepigraphal Pauline *epistles* per se, but are conceptualized also as a pseudepigraphal *pastoral corpus*."[11] And, more recently, G. Häfner.[12]

The consensus view of the letters was represented earlier by Brox: the three letters as a group differ in significant ways from the seven undisputed Paulines, or even from all ten other letters of the Pauline corpus. As pointed out, however, there have been lively objections raised from various quarters over the past two decades, in particular over the question of whether the three letters cohere sufficiently to be thought of as a corpus to be read as a unit rather than as individual productions. Among the detractors are, notably, Michael Prior, Jerome Murphy-O'Connor, Luke Timothy Johnson, William A. Richards, Rüdiger Fuchs, James Aageson, and Jens Herzer[13]—all of whom argue, on one set of grounds or another, that the letters differ sufficiently from one another as to warrant the view (at least in theory) that they may have been written by different authors. The most extreme position is taken by W. A. Richards, who claims that the Pastoral epistles represent the work of three authors, all writing for their own purposes, in different places, and in different times, possibly as much as sixty years apart.

I plan to map out a different view in the pages that follow, a modification of the broader consensus. In my judgment all three books were in fact written by the same author. But that does not mean they are to be read as an undifferentiated corpus. Each letter has its own concerns—those of 2 Timothy not necessarily coinciding, for example, with those of 1 Timothy—any more than the concerns of the orthonymous Galatians need be those of 1 Corinthians. In particular, the polemical purposes of the letters may differ. That does not mean, however, that they were written by different authors.

---

11. "Die Past sind nicht bloß als pseudepigraphe Paulus*briefe* geschaffen, sondern als pseudepigraphes *Corpus pastorale* konzipiert." Peter Trummer, "Corpus Paulinum—Corpus Pastorale: Zur Ortung der Paulustradition in den Pastoralbriefen," in *Paulus in den neutestamentlichen Spätschriften: zur Paulusrezeption im Neuen Testament*, ed. Karl Kertelge (Freiburg: Herder, 1981), p. 123.

12. Gerd Häfner, "Das Corpus Pastorale als literarisches Konstrukt," *ThQ* 187 (2007): 259: "If the letters are best read as a corpus, [that is to say] as a literary construct, this fact would speak against their composition by Paul." ("Sind die Briefe am besten als Corpus zu lesen, als literarisches Konstrukt, spräche dies gegen ihre Abfassung durch Paulus.")

13. Prior, *Paul the Letter Writer*; Murphy-O-Connor, "Paul the Letter Writer"; Luke Timothy Johnson, *The First and Second Letters to Timothy*; William A. Richards, *Difference and Distance in Post-Pauline Christianity: An Epistolary Analysis of the Pastorals* (New York: Peter Lang, 2002); Rüdiger Fuchs, *Unerwartete Unterschiede: Müssen wir unsere Ansichten über "die" Pastoralbriefe revidieren?* (Wuppertal: R. Brockhaus Verlag, 2003); James W. Aageson, *Paul, the Pastoral Epistles, and the Early Church* (Peabody, MA: Hendrickson, 2008); Jens Herzer, "Fiktion oder Täuschung?"

Those who want to stress that the three letters do not form a corpus make a methodological error when they stress, as they invariably do, that the three letters have so many differences among themselves. On one hand, many of those typically cited are simply differences of no moment: 1 Timothy deals with widows and deacons, but Titus does not; 1 Timothy deals with wealth as a problem, but Titus does not; Timothy is called an evangelist, but Titus is not; and so on. But why should two letters deal with all of the same topics and say exactly the same things?

When trying to establish common authorship, it is not the differences of two (or three) writings that matter, but the similarities. One should think of the analogous, though not identical, situation of the Synoptic Gospels. One could easily point to difference after difference between Luke and Matthew and conclude, then, that they derive from different sources. But it is the similarities they share—verbatim agreements in telling the same stories in the same sequence—that show their literary connections. So too, by analogy, with the authorship of the Pastorals. It is all too simple to point out difference after difference among them, but so what? One could just as easily point out the differences between 1 Thessalonians and Galatians, or between Ignatius's letters to the Smyrneans and the Romans. The question of relationship hinges on the similarities, which have to be explained, however one accounts for the differences.

It is true that taken in isolation, 2 Timothy does indeed look more like Paul than the other two letters, as I will be stressing momentarily. And for a time, I too was nearly persuaded that it might be orthonymous. But at the end of the day, the evidence is simply too overwhelming that the author of 2 Timothy must have been the author of the other two. This does not mean that we can amalgamate the three and pile up statistics based on the corpus to show how different they are, as a collection, from Paul. Each individual work has to be considered not just in relation to the other two, but also in relation to Paul. Nowhere is that more important than in considering the polemical thrusts of the letters. 1 Timothy and Titus appear to take on one set of opponents, and 2 Timothy another.

The One Author of the Pastorals

As a first step in laying out the modified consensus view it is especially important —in light of the demurrals of recent years—to establish the grounds for thinking that all three of the Pastoral epistles go back to the same author. The reason this matters for our discussions here should be patent: if 2 Timothy was written by the author of 1 Timothy, and 1 Timothy is forged, then 2 Timothy is necessarily forged. Not every egg should be set in this basket; as I will argue below, there are compelling reasons for thinking that each of the Pastorals individually, 2 Timothy included, does not go back to Paul. But the individual arguments are only strengthened by the circumstance that the same forger probably produced all three books.

1 Timothy and Titus

There has been far less disagreement over the joint authorship of 1 Timothy and Titus than over 2 Timothy in relationship to the other two.[14] There are in fact clear and compelling reasons for seeing 1 Timothy and Titus as products of the same pen, many of them being reasons for seeing all three as jointly authored (these latter reasons will be dealt with later). One of them reads very much like a kind of abridgment of the other; or the other reads like an expansion of the first. There are obvious parallels between them, for example in the instructions for the qualifications of leaders, the guidance given to "older men," to "younger men" and so on. In particular, there are numerous clear and specific parallels and overlaps that are virtually inexplicable apart from a literary relationship of some kind, either an abject borrowing of one author by another or, far more likely in this case, joint authorship. I mean the following data to be illustrative, not comprehensive; but they are more than enough to show some of the ties between the two books.

The connections start at the outset, where the phrase κατ᾽ ἐπιταγὴν θεοῦ σωτῆρος ἡμῶν of 1 Tim. 1:1 is matched by the κατ᾽ ἐπιταγὴν τοῦ σωτῆρος ἡμῶν θεοῦ of Tit. 1:3. It is virtually the same phrase, found in only these two places in the New Testament. The phrase τοῦ σωτῆρος ἡμῶν θεοῦ is itself found three times in each of these two letters, and nowhere else in the entire Pauline Corpus.

Moreover, the greeting to the addressee is far too close to be accidental, as nothing like it is found anywhere else in the New Testament, apart from 2 Timothy:

> Τιμοθέῳ γνησίῳ τέκνῳ ἐν πίστει, χάρις ἔλεος εἰρήνη ἀπὸ θεοῦ πατρὸς καὶ Χριστοῦ Ἰησοῦ τοῦ κυρίου ἡμῶν. (1 Tim. 1:2)
>
> Τίτῳ γνησίῳ τέκνῳ κατὰ κοινὴν πίστιν, χάρις καὶ εἰρήνη ἀπὸ θεοῦ πατρὸς καὶ Χριστοῦ Ἰησοῦ τοῦ σωτῆρος ἡμῶν. (Tit. 1:4)

This is the same writer, as shown by numerous words, phrases, and ideas, found in these two books but nowhere else in the Pauline corpus. Καιροῖς ἰδίοις is found in 1 Tim. 2:6 and Tit. 1:3, but never in Paul. Christ as an ἀντίλυτρον (1 Tim. 2:6) is matched by the verbal form λυτρώσηται in Tit. 2:14; the root never occurs in Paul. The phrase ἰδίους δεσπότας of 1 Tim. 6:1 is paralleled in Titus 2:9, but never in Paul. It should not be objected that this is because Paul does not have a Haustafel, since that is precisely the problem: Haustafeln are notably absent from the Pauline letters. In the same context, the warrant ἵνα μὴ τὸ ὄνομα τοῦ θεοῦ . . . βλασφημῆται of 1 Tim. 6:1 is found as ἵνα μὴ ὁ λόγος τοῦ θεοῦ βλασφημῆται in Titus 2:5. Elsewhere the instruction concerning the bishop, δεῖ οὖν τὸν ἐπίσκοπον

14. Schleiermacher maintained that 1 Timothy was the odd one out, and that view has been maintained on rare occasion over the years. See the most recent discussion of Jens Herzer, "Rearranging the 'House' of God: A New Perspective on the Pastoral Epistles," in *Empsychoi Logoi—Religious Innovations in Antiquity: Studies in Honour of Pieter Willem van der Horst*, ed. Alberdina Houtman et al. (Leiden: Brill, 2008), pp. 547–66. The striking similarities of 1 Timothy and Titus make this view implausible to most others.

ἀνεπίλημπτον εἶναι in 1 Tim. 3:2 is closely paralleled by the δεῖ γὰρ τὸν ἐπίσκοπον ἀνέκλητον εἶναι (Tit. 1:7), particularly striking in view of the fact that the term ἐπίσκοπος itself is so rare in the New Testament (only Phil. 1:1 in Paul).

The opponents of the author in both letters are teachers of the Law (1 Tim. 1:7; Tit. 1:10, 14; 3:9) who are interested in "genealogies" (1 Tim. 1:4; Tit. 3:9 the only two occurrences of the word in the New Testament), that involve ἔρις (1 Tim. 6:4; Tit. 3:9) and ζητήσεις (1 Tim. 6:4; Tit. 3:9; apart from 2 Tim. 2:23 the latter word never occurs in Paul).

The contents, polemics, instructions, and exhortations of the letters are simply too similar to think they come from a different pen, unless one author is copying another for purposes of his own. Even if that were the case, it should be noted that the copier (which would it be?) would necessarily be a forger, claiming to be Paul. But there are grounds for thinking that in fact neither book was written by Paul, as we will see.

1 Timothy and 2 Timothy

The question of the relationship of 1 and 2 Timothy is somewhat more pressing, given the forceful case made by critics such as M. Prior and J. Murphy-O'Connor that 2 Timothy is unlike the other two pastoral epistles and so, possibly, orthonymous. The arguments used to establish the point, however, are wanting, for the reason mentioned above. It is quite simple to point out the many ways that 2 Timothy differs from the other two Pastoral letters; but if one wants to establish joint authorship, it is to be done not on the basis of differences but similarities. The verbatim parallels have to be explained, and these cannot be tossed off as either accidental or, probably as we will see, the result of one author borrowing from the work of another. Here again I do not plan a comprehensive survey, but will simply restrict myself to some of the outstanding examples drawn from the first two chapters of 2 Timothy.

The greetings to the addressees in 1 and 2 Timothy are virtually identical and are unlike anything in Paul, except the address to Titus. Someone is either borrowing or the same author produced both:

> Τιμοθέῳ γνησίῳ τέκνῳ ἐν πίστει, χάρις ἔλεος εἰρήνη ἀπὸ θεοῦ πατρὸς καὶ Χριστοῦ Ἰησοῦ τοῦ κυρίου ἡμῶν. (1 Tim. 1:2)
>
> Τιμοθέῳ ἀγαπητῷ τέκνῳ, χάρις ἔλεος εἰρήνη ἀπὸ θεοῦ πατρὸς καὶ Χριστοῦ Ἰησοῦ τοῦ κυρίου ἡμῶν. (2 Tim. 1:2)

These two chapters share an abundance of unusual words and phrases. ἐπαγγελίαν ζωῆς occurs in 2 Tim. 1:1 and 1 Tim. 4:8; but never in Paul; χάριν ἔχω with the dative is found in 2 Tim. 1:3 and 1 Tim. 1:12 and nowhere else in the New Testament. The notion of laying on hands—ἐπιθέσεως τῶν χειρῶν—is found in the rest of the New Testament only in Acts 8:18 and Heb. 6:2, otherwise only in reference to Timothy in 1 Tim. 4:14 and 2 Tim. 1:6; in both of these latter instances it refers to the χάρισμα . . . ἐν σοί.

The non-Pauline phrase διὰ τῆς ἐπιφανείας τοῦ σωτῆρος ἡμῶν Χριστοῦ Ἰησοῦ of 2 Tim. 1:10 is matched by the μέχρι τῆς ἐπιφανείας τοῦ κυρίου ἡμῶν Ἰησοῦ Χριστοῦ of 1 Tim. 6:14. It should be noted that the term ἐπιφάνεια occurs only five times in the New Testament, once in 2 Thessalonians and all four other times in the Pastorals.[15] The striking self-description of Paul in 2 Tim. 1:11, εἰς ὃ ἐτέθην ἐγὼ κῆρυξ καὶ ἀπόστολος καὶ διδάσκαλος is paralleled in εἰς ὃ ἐτέθην ἐγὼ κῆρυξ καὶ ἀπόστολος, ἀλήθειαν λέγω οὐ ψεύδομαι, διδάσκαλος ἐθνῶν in 1 Tim. 2:7 with the odd exception of the oath that "Paul" for some reason would feel impelled to swear to his close companion. The term κῆρυξ occurs in the NT otherwise just in 2 Pet. 2:5.

The injunction τὴν παραθήκην μου φυλάξαι of 2 Tim. 1:12 has its counterpart in 1 Tim. 6:20 τὴν παραθήκην φύλαξον; the term παραθήκη occurs just one other time in the New Testament, also in 2 Tim: τὴν καλὴν παραθήκην φύλαξον (1:14). ὑποτύπωσις occurs only two times in the New Testament, 2 Tim. 1:13 and 1 Tim. 1:16. Somewhat more striking is ὑγιαίνω, which occurs three times in Luke, once in 3 John, and twice each in 1 and 2 Timothy (1 Tim. 1:10, 6:3; 2 Tim. 1:13, 4:3; along with four additional times in Titus). Particularly striking are the parallels between 2 Tim. 1:13 ὑγιαινόντων λόγων and 1 Tim. 6:3 ὑγιαίνουσιν λόγοις and 2 Tim. 4:3 ὑγιαινούσης διδασκαλίας and 2 Tim. 1:10 ὑγιαινούσῃ διδασκαλίᾳ. The latter phrase can also be found in Titus 1:9 and 2:1.

Δίωκε δὲ δικαιοσύνη is found identically in 2 Tim. 2:22 and 1 Tim. 6:11, and never in Paul–for obvious reasons, given Paul's teaching on justification (which is not "pursued" by believers!); so too ἐκ καθαρᾶς καρδίας in 2 Tim. 2:22 and 1 Tim. 1:5 is found nowhere else in Paul and only one other time in the New Testament (depending on the textual variant in 1 Pet. 1:22).

The term ζητήσεις occurs once in John and three times in Acts, but otherwise just in 2 Tim. 2:23 and 1 Tim. 6:4 (along with Titus 3:9; 1 Timothy also has a cognate hapax legomenon, ἐκζήτησις in 1:4). So too the phrase τὰς βεβήλους κενοφωνίας is found only in 2 Tim. 2:16 and 1 Tim. 6:20. Moreover, the otherwise unattested τῆς τοῦ διαβόλου παγίδος in 2 Tim. 2:26 is found as παγίδα τοῦ διαβόλου in 1 Tim. 3:7.

Many, many more verbatim agreements could easily be noted between the two letters, especially if we move beyond the first two chapters. But this is enough to make the point. Not only are there numerous words and phrases shared between the two books. That would be remarkable enough. But what makes the parallels particularly striking is that they are not Pauline words, found in other Pauline writings, orthonymous or forged; in fact, most of them are not words found (either at all or extensively) within the entire New Testament. There is clearly a literary relationship between these two books. And there is a good reason for thinking that it is not simply a relationship of one author borrowing the phrases of another—precisely *because* the words are distinctive to these two books (sometimes along with Titus). If one of the books served as the model for the other, the author of the second

15. In 1 Timothy it refers to the parousia, in 2 Timothy to the incarnation (or the resurrection?).

happened to pick out as the words to be replicated an inordinate number that are not found commonly elsewhere in the New Testament or Paul.[16]

And so, the different concerns expressed in 1 and 2 Timothy, problems they address, and responses they give to the problems do not require, or even suggest, that they were written by different authors, as is sometimes asserted. The linguistic parallels indicate they were written by the same author. He simply wrote the letters for different reasons.

2 Timothy and Titus

That all three letters were written by the same author should be clear from the foregoing: Titus and 1 Timothy are jointly authored, and so are 1 Timothy and 2 Timothy. This is a situation somewhat analogous to the Johannine epistles. There may be scant reason, in isolation, to think of 1 John as related to 3 John; but the reality is that whoever wrote 1 John also wrote 2 John; and the author of 2 John wrote 3 John; necessarily, then, 1 John and 3 John are jointly authored. The case of the Pastorals is even more certain because here there are so many striking similarities as well among the three, as we will see in a moment, and even between 2 Timothy and Titus, looked at by themselves.

And so, for example, 2 Tim. 3:17, πρὸς πᾶν ἔργον ἀγαθὸν ἐξηρτισμένος is closely tied to πρὸς πᾶν ἔργον ἀγαθὸν ἑτοίμους εἶναι of Titus 3:1; so too the virtual repetition of διὰ τῆς ἐπιφανείας τοῦ σωτῆρος ἡμῶν Χριστοῦ Ἰησοῦ in 2 Tim. 1:10 as ἐπιφάνειαν . . . σωτῆρος ἡμῶν Ἰησοῦ Χριστοῦ in Tit. 2:13. The concluding phrase "our Savior Jesus Christ" (2 Tim. 1:10; Tit. 1:4; 2:13) occurs nowhere else in the Pauline corpus (though cf. Phil. 3:20). The same can be said of the phrase εὐσεβῶς ζήσωμεν (Tit. 2:12) found in 2 Tim. as εὐσεβῶς ζῆν (3:12). The phrase μωράς . . . ζητήσεις in 2 Tim. 2:23 reappears precisely in Tit. 3:9, and nowhere else in the New Testament. Finally, the verb ἀποστρέφω is used only one time by Paul, in a quotation of Isa 59:20 in Rom. 11:26; but is used only twice in the New Testament with ἀλήθεια, 2 Tim. 4:4 and Tit. 1:14.

The Three Letters Together

The final coup de grace comes with the unmistakable and, otherwise inexplicable, verbal parallels of all three letters vis-à-vis Paul. Here the evidence cited individually above for the greetings of all three letters can be placed together. There is nothing like this in Paul, and it is impossible to imagine that the three could exist without a literary relationship:

> Τιμοθέῳ γνησίῳ τέκνῳ ἐν πίστει, χάρις ἔλεος εἰρήνη ἀπὸ θεοῦ πατρὸς καὶ Χριστοῦ Ἰησοῦ τοῦ κυρίου ἡμῶν. (1 Tim. 1:2)
>
> Τιμοθέῳ ἀγαπητῷ τέκνῳ, χάρις ἔλεος εἰρήνη ἀπὸ θεοῦ πατρὸς καὶ Χριστοῦ Ἰησοῦ τοῦ κυρίου ἡμῶν. (2 Tim. 1:2)

16. See further note 17.

> Τίτῳ γνησίῳ τέκνῳ κατὰ κοινὴν πίστιν, χάρις καὶ εἰρήνη ἀπὸ θεοῦ πατρὸς καὶ Χριστοῦ Ἰησοῦ τοῦ σωτῆρος ἡμῶν. (Tit. 1:4)

So too numerous other words and phrases. The phrase πιστὸς ὁ λόγος is never found in Paul, but is scattered throughout the three letters (1 Tim. 1:15, 3:1, 4:9; 2 Tim. 2:11; Tit. 3:8). So too ἐπίγνωσις τῆς ἀληθείας; it never is found in Paul but is in all three Pastorals (1 Tim. 2:4; 2 Tim. 2:25, 3:7; Tit. 1:1). The important term εὐσέβεια occurs never in Paul, but frequently in the pastorals (1 Tim. 2:2; 3:16; 4:7, 8; 6:3, 5, 6, 11; 2 Tim. 3:5; Tit. 1:1). The term μῦθος occurs never in Paul but does appear four times in the Pastorals (1 Tim. 1:4, 4:7; 2 Tim. 4:4; Tit. 1:14; one other time in the New Testament: 2 Pet. 1:16). As we have seen ζήτησις also never occurs in Paul but in all three Pastorals ([1 Tim. 1:4,] 6:4; 2 Tim. 2:23; Tit. 3:9); the same is true of the phrase ὑγιαινούῃ διδασκαλίᾳ (1 Tim. 1:10; 2 Tim. 4:3; Tit. 1:9; 2:1). The term ὠφέλιμος never occurs elsewhere in the New Testament, but four times in these books (1 Tim. 4:8 [bis], 2 Tim. 3:16; Tit. 3:8). The verb παραιτέομαι never occurs in Paul, and never as an imperative in the New Testament, except in all three of the pastorals (1 Tim. 4:7, 5:11; 2 Tim. 2:23; Tit. 3:10).

There is more to be said, but this is enough for our purposes. There is almost nothing in these particular words and phrases—except possibly the term "myths"—that makes them unsuitable for many of the other books elsewhere in the New Testament, or just for Paul. It is not that they are objectionable or puzzlingly unusual constructions. They are simply an author's preferred vocabulary. It is possible, of course, that one author wrote one of the books, and another author decided to copy many of its distinctive words and phrases to produce a book of his own. But given the facts that all three books have numerous similarities together while each of them has similarities with each of the others not shared by the third, the simplest solution is that one author produced all three books.[17] This is especially the case given the evidence, yet to be adduced, that each of the letters as well as the corpus as a whole was probably not written by Paul.

It seems odd to find—as one sometimes does—scholars who claim that each of the Pastorals was produced by a different author without even considering, for a moment, the linguistic arguments that show otherwise.[18] Those who do advance this view sometimes resort to linguistic arguments that appear to strain at gnats to swallow camels, as in an interesting and learned article of J. Herzer, which nonetheless maintains that the ecclesiologies of the 1 and 2 Timothy are at odds,

---

17. That is to say, if one were to posit that a Pauline imitator wrote 2 Timothy and an imitator of both Paul and 2 Timothy wrote 1 Timothy and Titus, then the hypothesis would require that the latter imitator chose as the specific linguistic features to replicate largely those not found otherwise in Paul. Moreover, this hypothesis requires three authors and three stages, whereas all of the data are more simply explained on the basis of two authors working at two stages: Paul and an imitator. As is true with the Synoptic Problem, the best solution should not unnecessarily multiply authors and stages for data that can be explained more economically.

18. So, for example, Jens Herzer, "Rearranging the 'House' of God."

in no small measure because the phrase οἶκος θεοῦ of 1 Tim. 3:15 is inconsistent with the οἰκία of 2 Tim. 2:20.[19] What of the dozens of distinctive and virtually impossible to explain verbal overlaps? It is even odder to find, on the far other side, a commentator like L. T. Johnson arguing against treating the three letters as a group produced by a single author, in the introduction to a commentary that treats 1 and 2 Timothy as two books by a single author (in his case, Paul, also, for him, author of Titus).[20]

Sometimes scholars, such as Gordon Fee, ask the rhetorical question of why a pseudepigrapher would have produced three such books instead of just one—overlooking the fact that Fee himself thinks that this is precisely what Paul did.[21] Apart from that, the rhetoric has no force. Why do we have fourteen letters between Paul and Seneca? Surely two or three would do. Why are their six pseudo-Ignatian letters instead of one? Why does any forger forge more than one work, even if he has similar things to say? With the Pastoral epistles one could imagine all sorts of reasons for an author wanting to write three letters. 2 Timothy, as I have been emphasizing, differs more from the other two than they do from each other, and so was obviously written for different reasons. As to the other two—just staying in the realm of pure speculation—one of them could have been a draft for the second; the second could have been an expansion of the first; they could have been written to different places, audiences, or times. They could have been merely two letters out of twenty that the person wrote. Maybe five or six others were reasonably similar; who knows? The answer, of course, is that no one knows. But one cannot object that a forger would not write three letters. Why would he not write three letters? Or thirty-nine? Even if the author wrote three and only three letters, one can imagine good reasons even for that; as Richard Pervo has recently pointed out, "Three is . . . a satisfactory and symbolic number, implying a true collection."[22]

In short, it appears that the same author produced the three Pastoral letters. Moreover, there are very good reasons for thinking this author was not Paul. Many of the strongest reasons have to do with the contents of the letters individually: what they actually say that stands at odds with views otherwise well documented for Paul himself. But the force of the argument for taking them as a collective should not be pushed aside. If one of these letters is forged, they are all forged, because they were all likely written by the same hand. In evaluating the question of authorship, Johnson is far less than generous, or at least being excessively rhetorical, when he claims that "the main argument against authenticity today is the sheer weight of scholarly consensus."[23] The reality is that the vast majority of the New Testament scholars who discuss the issue have read and mastered the

---

19. Herzer, "Rearranging."

20. *First and Second Letters to Timothy*, pp. 63–65.

21. *1 and 2 Timothy, Titus*. NIBCNT (Peabody, MA: Hendrickson, 1988), p. 6.

22. *Making of Paul*, p. 84. Pervo goes on to show that if one assumes that the three make up a corpus, they can be read as a kind of epistolary novel.

23. L. T. Johnson, "1 Tim. 1:1–20," p. 22.

scholarship and found that it is convincing, and have seen little reason then to reinvent the wheel.

Arguments from the Three Letters Together

It is true that bad arguments are often made to attack the Pauline authorship of the letters. It is commonly and roundly asserted that it is hard to locate the letters in Paul's ministry as laid out either in his own letters or Acts. But as Johnson points out, our hard information on Paul's ministry is extremely sparse: eight of the twelve years spanning 50 and 62 CE are summed up in the book of Acts in four lines.[24] But the arguments for considering the group as a whole pseudonymous are powerful, and we have already seen the opening gambit. Not only is a good deal of the vocabulary—terms, phrases, sentences—shared among the three letters, this shared vocabulary in particular is not Pauline.

Issues concerning the vocabulary and style of the Pastorals have been batted around for a very long time. The seemingly convincing case that P. N. Harrison made in 1921,[25] with its well-known lists and numbers of hapax legomena, was early on shown to be less than definitive by shorter studies, such as the pointed response by W. Michaelis.[26] But study after study continues to demonstrate the enormous linguistic problems.[27] The reality is that these letters are far less like Paul than anything in Paul.

This is recognized even by those who want to challenge the consensus opinion. The most recent attempt has been made by Armin Baum, who tries to explain one of the distinctive features of the letters: they violate the otherwise solid rule that shorter letters of Paul tend to use relatively fewer distinctive than common words. The pastorals have a vocabulary that is, by comparison with the other letters in the corpus, exceedingly rich; here there are approximately 20 percent more distinctive than common words.[28] This is a statistic that is obviously hard to explain on the assumption of Pauline authorship, especially when one looks at the hard data. As Baum shows, for example, 2 Timothy uses 451 different words, 161 (22 percent) of which are found only in 2 Timothy in the New Testament. In an average Pauline letter of this length we would expect only 42 distinctive words (12 percent). So how does one answer this incommensurability in favor of Pauline authorship? Baum does so with a theory: since it has been argued that written compositions tend to evidence richer word choice than oral communications, the

24. *First and Second Letters to Timothy*, p. 61.

25. P. N. Harrison, *The Problem of the Pastoral Epistles* (Oxford: Oxford University Press, 1921).

26. Wilhelm Michaelis, "Pastoralbriefe und Wortstatistik," *ZNW* 28 (1929): 69–76.

27. See, for example, Wolfgang Schenk, "Die Briefe an Timotheus I und II und an Titus (Pastoralbriefe) in der neueren Forschung (1945–1985)," *ANRW* II. 25, 4 (New York: Walter de Gruyter, 1987), pp. 3404–38.

28. Armin D. Baum, "Semantic Variation within the *Corpus Paulinum:* Linguistic Considerations Concerning the Richer Vocabulary of the Pastoral Epistles," *TynBul* 59 (2008): 271–92.

Pastoral epistles may have been planned as written works rather than dictated off the top of Paul's head.

It is hard to know where to begin with any such claim, but possibly it should be with the question of proof. One is hard pressed to know what evidence Baum might find persuasive for his view, since he presents it as a suggestion and so martials no argument. But what are we to think—that Paul's letter to the Romans, for example, was dashed off in a hasty mode of dictation, but 2 Timothy was carefully plotted and outlined as a literary text? Given the nature of the two letters, this seems, on the generous side, a shade unlikely. And the comparatively richer vocabulary itself cannot serve as the evidence that it happened this way, since that is the datum the theory is trying to explain.

Baum not only presents no evidence, he considers no obvious counterevidence, such as the observation of Quinn that the syntax of these letters sometimes breaks down, with "inordinately rough abrupt transitions (thus Titus 2:6–8; 1 Tim. 3:1a–b), inexplicable shifts in the inflection of verbs (1 Tim. 2:15), . . . sentence fragments that are without a verb or object to weld their endless phrases together (thus Titus 1:1–4; 1 Tim. 1:3–7)."[29] These do not give the appearance, at least, of being carefully plotted literary compositions.

There is more to the argument from vocabulary than a mere listing of unusual terms, even with an inordinately high level of frequency. More probative is the fact stressed so frequently, and for good reason, that some of the key terms actually shared with Paul take on other meanings—and this with words that matter a good deal to both Paul and the author of the Pastorals. And so, as commonly and rightly pointed out, δικαιοσύνη has lost its Pauline character involving justification by an act of God, and has become a virtue for the believer to pursue (thus 1 Tim. 6:11; 2 Tim. 2:22). So too "faith" is no longer a relational term, referring to a trusting relationship with God through Christ, or trust "in" the death of Christ for salvation. It is now the content of the religion (thus 1 Tim. 4:6; 5:8). In this linguistic world, the recurring phrase πιστὸς ὁ λόγος no longer sounds even vaguely odd.

As Harrison noted already in 1921, the vocabulary preferred by the author resonates more closely with the Christian language of the second century than with Paul. Yet more important, the historical situation of the church itself, embodied in the descriptions afforded by this vocabulary, appears to have moved far along from the days of Paul's charismatic communities. This is a factor that is completely underplayed and slighted by Johnson, who wants to see a solid continuity between the church of the Pastorals and the church of Paul.[30] What is far more salient to most readers is the radical discontinuity. We can get a good sense of "Pauline" churches from two corpora of letters, the Corinthian correspondence and the Pastorals. It is hard to see how these derive from contexts that are at all equivalent either temporally or ideologically. When Paul is deal-

29. Jerome D. Quinn, *The Letter to Titus* AB (New Haven, CT: Yale University, 1990), p. 5.

30. *1 and 2 Timothy*, p. 75: "one of the weakest arguments against authenticity."

ing with the manifest problems in the church of Corinth—disunity, immorality, disorganization, false teachings, and so on—why does he not write to the leader or leaders he has appointed in order to convince them to bring their people into line? Surely it is because there were no leaders, in that sense, who could do so. And the correspondence is completely unambiguous as to why. There were no "offices" in the Corinthian church that were conveyed by the laying on of hands (or by selection) to those who had set qualifications and the ability to lead. Each member of the community had a spiritual gift that was to be used for the upbuilding of the community; each person needed to use these gifts with ἀγάπη for the entire community, being concerned not for self-aggrandizement but for the good of the whole. If they followed the direction of the Spirit there would be harmony in the body of Christ as every part worked together for the greater good.

And what does the author of the Pastorals have to say about the spiritual gifts bestowed upon each member of the community given to benefit the body of Christ through their loving application? Nothing. His concerns are the leaders of the churches, "Paul's" personal representatives left behind to organize, structure, and direct the community, and the overseers and deacons who have responsibilities to fulfill. This is a different kind of community, and it does not take a degree in Weberian sociology to recognize what has happened in the historical movement from the chaos of Corinth to the structure of the Pastorals. The expectation of an imminent end of the age had waned (there would still be a future, to be sure), the sense of living in a short interim period had passed, and disorganization and local problems had led to sensible and logical solutions; there needed to be leaders in the church, these persons needed to be qualified, they needed to take charge and make decisions, and in particular they—not the Spirit through ecstatic utterance or the apostle (no longer living) through written communication—needed to pull in the reins on those proffering false and harmful teaching. The women who once exercised authority in the church through their teaching and prophesying needed to be brought to bay now that the church needed to be seen as a respectable institution. The leaders needed to be upright *men* admired even by those on the outside. Widows now had a special function in the life of the church (where does one find anything like *that* in the Pauline letters, Corinthians or otherwise?). Social relations needed to be normalized in the church and the serious asceticism that preferred the life of celibacy in light of the "impending disaster" had thus given way to a traditional set of social values that treasured marriage and family as solid Christian values.

It is true, as Johnson himself stresses, that the Pastoral epistles are not concerned to set up a church organization, as they are sometimes wrongly read. They are concerned with the qualifications of the leaders who man (literally) this organization—not with the duties that they are to perform. But this speaks even more for the pseudepigraphic character of 1 Timothy and Titus—the two letters I have been referring to—because these letters do not assume that a church hierarchy is starting to be established to replace the charismatic ordering of the churches of Paul's own day. They instead presuppose that a church hierarchy already is in place, to the extent that there are bishops, deacons, and widows who are to be enrolled. The author does not need to describe what each of these persons or groups does because this is already assumed. That is, it is common knowledge. These books were written well after the transition from a charismatic organization in which persons were authorized by the Spirit given at baptism. Now there are leaders with recognized skills and qualifications, who are ordained by the laying on of hands or selected from a pool of candidates.

It should not be objected that Philippians 1:1 presents us with the same situation already in Paul's lifetime. Overseers and deacons are mentioned there, but there is nothing either in that verse or the entire letter (or set of letters) of Philippians as a whole to indicate that these are persons selected for an office out of a pool of candidates, or that they were ordained by the laying on of hands. In fact, nothing is said about them at all, giving us no way of knowing whether they are comparable to the figures addressed in the Pastorals or not. If we assume they are it is not because of any evidence, since, in fact, there is no hint of evidence; it is simply a hopeful assumption. The fact that these Philippian overseers and deacons are never addressed in the letter(s) is itself far more telling: Paul does not tell them to correct the false teaching in the congregation, or to make sure Euodia and Syntyche fall in line, or to deal with any of the problems of the church. The differences from the Pastorals are apt.

The authorities for these Pastoral communities are not only the apostolic voice, delivered in writing; they also include written texts that have been elevated to a level of sacrality. This was true for Paul as well, who used the Jewish Scriptures to that end extensively (in at least some of his correspondence), and who could, as well, cite the oral traditions of the words of Jesus. The key difference with the Pastorals is found most clearly in 1 Tim. 5:18, where not just Jesus' teachings per se but a written text containing those teachings is deemed authoritative; in fact is labeled "Scripture." Whether the quotation comes from the (now-known) Gospel of Luke (10:7) or from some other written source, the dominical teachings are now known to be written and are on a par with the Scriptures cited so extensively by Paul. Here too we are in a period beyond Paul's time, at the end of the first century at the very earliest, when Gospel texts were assuming a position of authority in the local communities associated with Paul and others of the apostles.

It is important to stress that all of these various arguments are cumulative and all point in the same direction. The accumulation is not merely as strong as its weakest link. One argument after the other simply reinforces the one that precedes: the distinctive vocabulary, its non-Pauline character and force, the post-Pauline historical situation, the role of authorities in the church including written Gospel texts. At the same time, it cannot be stressed enough that specific comments of each of the individual books as well point in precisely the same direction, reinforcing the sense that if one of these books is forged, they all are forged.

Arguments from Each of the Books

The following passages represent statements that seem to stand at odds with the views of the historical Paul, as known from the undisputed letters. In no case can one say that Paul definitely would never have made any such statement. Large allowance must always be made for the flexibility of his thought, his ability to say seemingly contrary things, the possibility that his views developed over time, and the reality that he occasionally changed his mind, even about important matters. But it cannot help but strike the careful reader that so many of the comments in the Pastorals appear to run counter to Paul's views attested elsewhere. We are not dealing with one or two isolated statements. And so, these comments should not be treated in isolation from one another, but as a Gestalt that confirms the findings already set forth, that whoever wrote these letters, it appears not to have been Paul. Here again, my comments are meant not to be exhaustive but illustrative.

1 Timothy

As with the other two Pastorals, there is no point contending that 1 Timothy sounds completely unlike Paul. In many ways, or at least many places, it does sound like Paul, as one would expect from a letter forged by one of his later followers in his name. And there are numerous instances of verisimilitude—not nearly as many as in Titus or 2 Timothy, but numerous enough, as in the author's recollection of his former interaction with Timothy when he put him in charge of the congregation in Ephesus (1:3), his reflection on his past life as a blasphemer and persecutor of the church, acting out of unbelief (1:12–16), his indication that he is coming to pay a visit soon (3:14, 4:13); his personal attention to Timothy, urging him to take some wine for his stomach ailment (5:23); and so on.

At the same time, there are, scattered throughout the letter, comments that if nothing else create a real puzzle for those who think the apostle himself produced them. Right off the bat one must wonder about the author's view of the Jewish Law, which he declares is good "if someone uses it lawfully" (1:8). For Paul, is God's law good conditional on human obedience? On the contrary, in Romans at least, the Law is good unconditionally, regardless of how a person uses it, since it was given by God. The problem with the Law for Paul—a notoriously vexed issue in itself, of course—was intimately connected with the problem of sin, the cosmic power that compelled people to violate the dictates of God's (good) Law. There is nothing about the power of sin here in 1 Timothy. The author instead assumes that humans are able to keep the Law and thereby affirm its goodness. And would Paul say that "the Law is not set down for the one who is just/righteous" (1:9)? Quite the contrary, that in no small measure is whom the Law is for, those who have been given the Spirit of God so that they (and they alone) can do what the Law commands, for example by loving their neighbors as themselves, which is to be done precisely because the Law, which itself is good, demands that it be done (Gal. 5:13–14).

A related matter is Paul's relation to those who promote themselves as teachers of the Law (1:7). Paul himself was always intent on showing opponents who stressed their superior relation to the Law that he himself understood it better than they, through careful and often ingenious exposition of its teachings. Here, rather than fighting his opponents on their own ground—Paul's approach—this author simply ignores the Law and refuses to engage his opponents in their views. This "Paul" does not cite the Law, deal with the "false" interpretation of the Law, or explicate the status of the Law for those in Christ.

Just as the reference to the Law has the superficial sound of a Pauline teaching, so too does the problem of false teaching dealt with at the end of chapter 1: two false teachers are said to have been "handed over to Satan" in exchange for their misdeeds, an apparent reminiscence of the incident recounted in 1 Corinthians 5. But the differences are more striking than the similarities. Here—this never happens in Paul—the opponents are called by name. Moreover, the "handing over to Satan" is not a community affair; it is something the apostle himself has done. And the purpose of the act appears otherwise indeed; in Corinth it was for the "destruction of the flesh," which may well be taken as a death curse. In this instance it is for repentance: "that they may be trained not to blaspheme." The clear implication is that the miscreants will be welcomed back with open arms once they have learned their lesson.

The oath that the author swears in 2:7 has a Pauline feel to it, but it is delivered in a completely un-Pauline way. When Paul utters his oath in Gal. 1:20 ("the things I am writing you—see, before God, I am not lying!") it is to convince readers who may well have reasons of their own for not believing what he has to say; the oath, reasonably enough, is designed to convince them that he really is speaking the truth. So too the virtual oath of Rom. 9:1 "I am speaking the truth in Christ, I am not lying." For readers who might well suspect that Paul harbors an animosity toward the Jewish people, given everything he has said in the letter up to this point, Paul avers that nothing is farther from the truth; he insists that he is not lying about it. The author of 1 Tim. 2:7 also utters an oath: "I am telling the truth, I am not lying." This may sound like the other two instances, but it is strikingly different. Here "Paul" is writing to his close companion and erstwhile fellow-missionary Timothy, insisting that he really is a "herald, and apostle, and a teacher of the Gentiles." Why would the historical Paul have to swear to this? Why would Timothy suspect anything different? They were companions on the mission field together for years.

Not much need be said about the instructions to women in 2:11–15 to be silent and submissive and to exercise no authority over men. The women in Paul's churches were apostles and deacons; they were not silent in church or urged to be silent, but were told to speak their prayers and prophecies—congregational activities performed in the presence of men—with covered heads. The act of prophecy necessarily involves a woman in an authoritative position, as, of course, does serving as a deacon and, especially, an apostle. And to say that women's salvation is contingent on bearing children is completely removed from anything known from the apostle Paul. Among other things, it makes being "saved" a matter of life in this world rather than at the appearance of Christ at the end. And the idea that bearing children will somehow earn the right to be saved is not even in the right ballpark of a Pauline soteriology.

The views of marriage seem to stand at odds with Paul. It is true that he never did, in the surviving letters, actually "forbid marriage" (4:3); but he certainly discouraged it, in no uncertain terms, in view of the "impending disaster" (1 Cor. 7:27–27). Not this author. Bishops are actually required to be married men with households that they rule over (3:2, 4). So too the deacons (3:12). Young women, too, are to be married and have children (5:14). How does this coincide with Paul's wish that others—presumably leaders above all—be like him, celibate and single (1 Cor. 7:6–7)? How could he urge celibacy in one place and forbid it in another? Where, in fact, is the "impending disaster" that marks the urgency of Paul's mission and that drives his social ethics?

Is this author even Jewish? The idea that anyone would urge people "to abstain from foods" seems completely foreign to him (4:3), a sign of living in the latter days. For this author all foods are created by God and are good, and no food is to be rejected if received thankfully (4:4). Certainly Paul himself may have come to view laws governing kashrut as adiaphora, now that Christ has fulfilled the Law. But would it have seemed strange to him, and a sign of the end of time, that there were people out there actually forbidding the consumption of certain foods? Isn't that the religion he grew up in and espoused for most of his early life? Can he conceive of the kosher food laws as not having been given by God, as 4:4 implies, even if they have now been surpassed with the coming of Christ—if indeed they have been for the historical Paul, who certainly never tells Jews that they are to stop keeping kosher?

Moreover, the insistence that all foods be consumed stands at clear tension with the advice of the real Paul himself to the Corinthians and Romans, where he urges restraint and abstention from certain foods for the sake of others (1 Cor. 8:9, 13; Rom. 14:20). By contrast, here in 1 Timothy the scruples of others are mocked and maligned. Everything is to be eaten, regardless—or rather, precisely in the face of—the objections of others. The logic and the grounds of the ethics of eating differ here, but that is precisely the point. Following the "apostle's" teaching is far more important than being concerned over causing another to stumble.

There are numerous other points that stand in tension with the historical Paul, as already noted. Spiritual charisma is received by the laying on of hands rather than at baptism (4:14); God is the savior "especially" to those who have faith (especially? 4:10); widows are to be enrolled in the church, showing that the church is becoming a social institution (5:9); the presbyteroi—a word and concept found nowhere in Paul—are rulers of the church who deserve to be paid (5:17–18); the written words of Jesus are now Scripture (1 Tim. 5:18; cf. 1 Tim. 6:3); and on and on. Again, a few of these comments—and there are many more like them—may be explained away in isolation as a sensible development from Paul. But it is the collocation of odd comments, in combination with so many other factors, that shows that this is a book written after Paul's demise, by someone living in a later context when the church is established and settling in for the long run.

2 Timothy

Even though 2 Timothy was written by the same hand as 1 Timothy, there are reasons for thinking that it was not meant to be read with it, as the second letter directed to the same situation. Unlike the other letter, where Timothy is Paul's delegate left in Ephesus for the organization—or at least the instruction—of the church (1 Tim. 1:3), there is nothing here to indicate that he is to be thought of in this light. In fact, 4:12 may speak against the idea (Paul has sent Tychicus to Ephesus). Nothing indicates that Timothy is to be regarded as Paul's delegate in charge of a community. He is portrayed instead as a young man who needs to work to combat his youthful passions (2:22). He has been Paul's faithful companion until now, and he is urged to come meet Paul in Rome soon, and to bring some of Paul's prized possessions with him (4:9, 13, 21), as Paul awaits a second trial (4:16).

As with 1 Timothy, there are numerous passages that sound Pauline. It is no wonder that scholars since Harrison have "found" authentically Pauline fragments in the letter. But more than anything else it is the abundance of verisimilitude that continues to puzzle scholars who are otherwise not intimately acquainted with the ancient craft of forgery, persuading them that surely this must be the real Paul himself. This author remembers Timothy in his prayers (1:3), he recalls his tears (1:4), he longs to see him (1:4); he remembers his grandmother Lois and mother Eunice (1:5) and recalls how God's charisma was bestowed upon him by the laying on of hands (1:6); he refers to his enemies in Asia who have turned against him, citing two of them by name (1:15); but he indicates that Onesiphorus was faithful and came to find him in Rome after rendering him a service in Ephesus (1:16–18); he refers to other aspects of his past, including his persecutions at Antioch, Iconium, and Lystra (3:11); he himself is about to be sacrificed (4:6). And then comes the shower of verisimilitudes of 4:9–18, where the author cites names, places, and events from his life, thereby assuring the reader that he really is Paul, before the highly personalized greetings and benediction of 4:19–22.[31]

Given the comparative brevity of the letter, and the extent to which it is consumed with establishing the identity of the author through verisimilitude, it is no surprise that there are fewer passages that appear offensive to Pauline authorship here. But there are several that bear noting. Here again the spiritual gift is bestowed on Timothy by a leader of the community (in this case, Paul) laying on hands, rather than by the Spirit at baptism (1:6). The opponents of Paul are called by name, repeatedly (1:15: Phygelus and Hermogenes; 2:17: Hymenaeus and Philetus; 4:10: Demas; 4:14: Alexander). The love of money has become one of the issues in the community (3:2; cf. 1 Tim. 6:10), which seems to suppose a more established and occasionally prosperous constituency.

In particular it is hard to understand how this letter—if authentic—could be understood as a directive to the young Timothy. Here the problem is not

---

31. On the question of whether the verisimilitudes suggest authenticity, see the trenchant article of Brox, mentioned on p. 122.

the general one of how to fit the Pastoral epistles into a sensible chronology of Paul's life as established on the basis of his letters and Acts. The problem is that Timothy is being portrayed as a young companion of Paul (as seen already in 2:22), who needs to be warned against the passions that commonly afflict the young. At the same time, Paul is portrayed as in prison in Rome, having stood trial once, and awaiting a second trial (4:16). The letter is often read as a "last will and testament" of Paul, prior to his death. And although this characterization is sometimes challenged—especially by those who want to urge that the letter is authentic, since often these testaments are produced as fictions after the death of the protagonist—there is clearly something to it. Paul is expecting another trial, and he is fully expecting to be sacrificed: "The moment of my departure has arrived." He knows he is about to be condemned and executed, but looking back on his life, he knows he has "fought the good fight" (4:6–7).

But how does one reconcile these two data with anything like a sensible chronology of Paul's life? Timothy is still a young man but Paul is at the end of his life? In the book of Acts Timothy becomes associated with Paul rather early on, in Lystra (Acts 16:1). He is already an adult then, and already a disciple of Jesus. He then accompanies Paul on his missionary journeys. In Paul's own letters Timothy is a coauthor of what is probably the earliest surviving correspondence, 1 Thessalonians—so presumably they have been together for some years, prior to its having been written in, say, 49 CE. Even if Timothy was a young man then—there is nothing to indicate that he was—how could he still be young fifteen years later when Paul, on any reasonable chronology, is face-to-face with death at the end of a relatively long and productive ministry? On any reckoning Timothy must have been at least middle-aged by then. But not for the author of 2 Timothy. This author, not concerned with working out a viable chronology from Acts, which he probably did not know, or with Paul's other letters, with which, for the purpose, he probably did not bother, portrays Paul in his final days, and Timothy as a youthful companion. The chronology does not seem to work.

Titus

Like the other two Pastoral epistles, the book of Titus contains numerous passages that reflect the views of the historical Paul. This again is no surprise, as the letter comes from the pen of a later follower who saw himself as standing in the Pauline tradition. And here too there are a number of impressive verisimilitudes, especially in the closing, where the author urges his recipient to meet him at Nicopolis, where he has decided to spend the winter (3:12). Like the others, however, it also contains comments that are difficult to reconcile with the historical Paul.

We have already seen that the word *presbyteroi*—let alone the concept that it represents—is absent from Paul. Here, not only are there *presbyteroi*, but the recipient is urged to appoint *presbyteroi* in every town on Crete (1:5). This presupposes an amazingly successful mission on the island—were all the towns converted, with thriving Christian communities?—and also assumes that the churches were established and hierarchically organized. No Corinthian charismata here! And, as we have seen in other pseudo-Pauline writings, here too we find a Haustafel (2:2–10) for a community that is settled in for the long haul. The false teachers who have arisen within the communities are to be silenced, not argued with (1:9–11). The author himself offers no arguments against their deceptive "doctrine"; unlike Paul, he does not reason with them and show why they are wrong. He simply orders them to be rebuked for propounding "Jewish myths"—a strange injunction if from the real Paul, proud of his Jewish heritage.

But it is no stranger than the comment that follows, that "to the pure, all things are pure" (1:15). Is that why Jewish purity regulations and rules of kosher are no longer applicable, because they are rooted in foundationless Jewish mythology that now can be mocked, rather than revered for what it was, a set of good and true commandments given to God's chosen people to regulate their lives, at least before the coming of the messiah? Where in Paul are those who keep purity laws thought to be corrupt, unbelieving, detestable, and disobedient (1:15–16)? This does not appear to be Paul the Pharisee, "blameless with respect to the righteousness that is in the Law" (Phil. 3:6). On the contrary, this is an author who was once a slave to his passions and pleasures, who spent his days "filled with malice and envy, filled with hatred for others" (3:3). And now that he has been justified, this is one—contrast Paul—who simply refuses to engage in "stupid controversies" and "quarrels over the Law," deemed here as unprofitable and futile. Is this the author of Romans and Galatians?

There is some reason to suspect, on the other hand, that the author was intimately familiar with another Pauline letter, but this one too a forgery. The reminiscence of the author's former life in 3:3–8 sounds very much like an allusion to Ephesians 2:1–10, where "Paul" begins by outlining his former life as a pagan sinner (3:3; cf. Eph. 2:3), whom God has now "saved" (past tense! 3:5; cf. Eph. 2:5), not because of "good deeds" (no word of "works of the Law" here, 3:5; cf. Eph. 2:9), through Jesus Christ, by "grace" (3:7; cf. Eph. 2:5, 8), so as to be an heir of eternal life (3:7; cf. Eph. 2:7). The author indicates that this "word" that he is delivering is "faithful" (3:8). Does he mean that he has self-consciously derived his "word" from what he (wrongly) thinks is an actual description of the conversion of Paul, in the equally pseudonymous letter to the Ephesians?

Counter-Arguments for Authenticity

Taken collectively or as individual letters, the Pastoral epistles thus have appeared to a strong majority of critics to be pseudepigraphic productions of a post-Pauline age. Yet, as noted, there have been spirited defenses of their complete, or partial, authenticity over the years.[32] The idea of partial authenticity was most convincingly

---

32. I do not need to deal at any great length with scholars who continue to find the issue of forgery in the New Testament to be theologically or personally troubling, given all that I have shown so far. A

floated by P. N. Harrison, in his classic study of 1921 previously mentioned. There was a clear and certain attraction to his proposal, that even though in their final form the Pastoral letters did not come from Paul, they were ultimately based on bona fide fragments of Pauline correspondence. Objections were eventually raised, however, and the theory was finally demolished by Cook, who showed that the alleged differences between source and redaction required by the theory in fact do not exist. There is a unity of theme and style throughout the books.[33]

Some scholars still find it difficult to believe that a forger would employ such extensive verisimilitudes as found, in particular, in the opening and closing of 2 Timothy.[34] The most direct attack on such views occurs in a justly acclaimed article by Norbert Brox, in which he makes a completely compelling case that "Fake personal notes are well known as stylistic devices in ancient pseudepigraphy and do not come as a surprise in the Pastoral epistles either."[35]

Other scholars have wanted to insist that we take seriously the fact the most of Paul's other letters were coauthored, and that, as a result, we should expect large differences in content and, especially, vocabulary and style, in comparison with letters, such as the Pastorals, that he produced himself. On the surface of the matter, this seems like a sensible objection, and certainly worth considering. One obvious problem is that the letters in question differ not only in choice of words and stylistic preferences, but also, quite seriously, in substance. Are we to think that Paul signed off on the content of the earlier letters without agreeing on what they actually had to say?

There is, however, a larger problem with the assertion that coauthored letters will naturally differ from single-author letters. Where is the evidence? Luke Timothy Johnson has asserted that this solution can explain why the Pastorals

---

commentator such as I. Howard Marshall admits that the evidence is too strong against Pauline authorship, but he wants to insist that the Pauline follower who produced the letters did so "honestly"—not like the heretics who forged writings to promote their own "false" teachings (see p. 32, n. 9). This again is theology, not history. Such views lead then to his proposal, advanced with all seriousness, that in cases such as the Pastorals we speak not of pseudonymous but of allonymous writings, not of pseudepigraphy (let alone forgery) but allopigraphy.

33. David Cook, "The Pastoral Fragments Reconsidered," *JTS* 35 (1984): 120–31. The even more highly nuanced, hypothetical, and, one might say, overly fragmented theory of James D. Miller, *The Pastoral Epistles as Composite Documents* (Cambridge: Cambridge University Press, 1997) has also failed to persuade, for similar reasons.

34. As Lewis Donelson points out, this is simply not a problem for anyone who has read extensively in the forgeries of antiquity. He refers in particular, as an example, to the famous twelfth letter of "Plato," forged in order to validate yet other works of Plato that the author himself knows are forged (he may have forged them himself), including random irrelevancies to mask his motives by what appear to be off-the-cuff remarks. *Pseudepigraphy and Ethical Argument*, pp. 23–42.

35. Fingierte Personalnotizen sind als Stilmittel antiker Pseudepigraphie bekannt und stellen auch in den Pastoralbriefen nichts Erstaunliches dar; "Zu den persönlichen Notizen der Pastoralbriefe," *BZ* 13 (1969): 76–94, here 79–79; reprinted in Brox, ed., *Pseudepigraphie in der heidnischen und jüdisch-christlichen Antike*, pp. 275–76. Brox goes on to show that the verisimilitudes are not merely guises for authenticity, but they serve the rhetorical purposes—especially paranetic—of the letters as well.

may differ so much from the other Pauline letters.[36] But he offers not a shred of proof. This is odd for many reasons, not least of which is the fact that Johnson has made an outstanding career out of showing how parallels in the Greco-Roman environment can illuminate the writings of the New Testament in terms of genre, theme, vocabulary, rhetoric, and so on. The similarities of the New Testament literature with the literature of its surroundings provide lasting insights into its character and the force of its rhetoric. But when it comes to the Deutero-Pauline letters, Johnson wants to argue that the key to their interpretation is a phenomenon for which he cannot—or at least does not—cite a single parallel or analogy from antiquity: joint composition of letters (or in modern parlance, composition by committee). Why would this explanation for the distinctive character of the Deutero-Pauline letters be preferable to one for which there are abundant parallels and analogies scattered throughout all of antiquity, the use of literary forgery?

Something similar can be said of Michael Prior's use of the same argument in his study of 2 Timothy. Prior, at least, does try to find some evidence. After a diligent search, he locates some eighteen instances of coauthored letters from various ancient sources, mainly the papyri. After examining them, he then states "we have no way of knowing how the letters were composed, or what part each member of the coauthorship team played." That is precisely right: we literally have not a single clue. But then, in the very next sentence, Prior claims, "The indications are that the writers are on an equal footing."[37] But what indications would those be, if the examples do not give us any clues? Later, coming to the Pauline corpus, Prior asserts, "When seen against the background of ancient co-authored letters one would expect a real coauthorship for those letters."[38] Yet he provides no analysis of the "ancient co-authored letters" that would lead us to think that they should appear stylistically or materially different from single-authored letters.[39] This is a case made by assertion. If there is evidence to be adduced, then someone ought to adduce it. Until that happens, historians should be loath to accept as the "most probable" assertion one that has no demonstrable ancient analogy, in preference to what is abundantly attested in myriad places, that forgers produced works that differed stylistically and materially from those of the authors in whose name they wrote.

The Polemic of 2 Timothy

The polemical attack on false teachers is a prominent feature of all three Pastoral letters. By Johnson's count, 47 of the 242 verses of the books are involved with

36. "1 Timothy 1, 1–20," pp. 24–25.

37. Prior, *Paul the Letter Writer*, p. 39.

38. Ibid., p. 45.

39. Prior does explore the use of the first person singular and plural in Paul's letters, but when one examines the data he provides, it is to no effect. That Paul himself wrote these so-called co-authored letters by himself is suggested by Galatians 1:1, "all the brothers who are with me." Are we seriously to imagine that everyone pitched in?

polemic.[40] As Donelson states, "all three letters are peppered with warnings about false teachers . . . [who] appear to be the immediate occasion for writing the letters."[41] The polemic is especially evident in 1 Timothy and Titus, as it appears at the very outset of each letter (1 Tim. 1:3; Tit. 1:9–16); and at its conclusion (1 Tim. 6:20–21; Tit. 3:9–11), with scattered references, then, throughout. 2 Timothy is also littered with polemical statements and warnings. The opening section ends with the exhortation to "guard the good deposit that comes from the Holy Spirit that dwells in you" (1:14). The author is concerned that his teachings be "entrusted to faithful ones" who can teach others as well (2:2). The heart of the body of the letter involves the specific issue of greatest concern to the author, the false teachings of those who insist that the "resurrection has already happened" (2: 14–19) to which we will return momentarily. The false teachers are to be corrected, but not engaged (2:23–26), as they promote the work of "the devil" (2:26). These opponents appear closely connected with (identical with?) the moral reprobates about to appear in the last days (3:1–9). Other eschatological warnings involve false teaching in se, as members of the congregation will not endure "healthy teaching" but follow teachings that they prefer, turning from the "truth" in order to "stray after myths." Already the opposition is in full force, as evidenced by Alexander who "strongly opposed our words" and thus did the author "great harm" (4:14–15).

As stressed repeatedly above, the facts that the Pastorals were probably written by the same hand and that all engage in polemics should not be taken to mean that the polemical target is the same in all three letters, any more than the opponents of Galatians, 1 Corinthians, and Philippians are necessarily all the same. No one today would (or should) think of creating an amalgamation of Paul's polemical statements in these three letters to create some kind of hybrid opponent who embodied the negative characteristics intimated in each. Why scholars have been so eager to do so with the Pastorals is a mystery. The resulting amalgam is usually some kind of otherwise unknown group of "Jewish Gnostics," or occasionally some other interesting mixed bag, such as Spicq's converted Jews who use rabbinic and Hellenistic modes of interpretation of Scripture and privilege the Torah.[42] This passion for conflation is virtually ubiquitous in the literature, from authors as wide ranging as Robert Karris, Günter Haufe, Josef Zmijewski, I. Howard Marshall, and Lewis Donelson.[43] The real problem with this approach

40. Luke Timothy Johnson, "II Timothy and the Polemic against False Teachers: A Reexamination," *JRelS* 6 (1978): 1–26.

41. *Pseudepigraphy*, p. 117.

42. Ceslas Spicq, *Saint. Paul: les épîtres pastorales* (Paris: Gabalda, 1969), pp. 52–72.

43. Robert J. Karris, "The Background and Significance of the Polemic of the Pastoral Epistles," *JBL* 92 (1973): 549–63; Günter Haufe, "Gnostische Irrlehre und ihre Abwehr in den Pastoralbriefen," in *Gnosis und Neues Testament: Studien aus Religionswissenschaft und Theologie*, ed. Karl-Wolfgang Tröger (Güterslow: Gütersloher Verlagshaus Mohn, 1973), pp. 325–39; Josef Zmijewski, "Die Pastoralbriefe als pseudepigraphische Schriften—Beschreibung, Erklärung, Bewertung," *Studien zum Neuen Testament und seiner Umwelt* (1979): 97–118; I. Howard Marshall, *The Pastoral Epistles*; Lewis R. Donelson, *Pseudepigraphy and Ethical Argument*.

is not simply that the resultant composite picture does not resemble any known teacher or group; the same could be said even of unitary presentations of false teachers, such as that found in 3 Corinthians. The deeper problem is that there is in fact nothing in the letters themselves to make one think that the problems addressed in 2 Timothy are the same as those addressed in 1 Timothy and Titus, as scholars such as Johnson and Prior have recognized. As Murphy-O'Connor has stated the matter: "Nowhere has the assumption of the unity of the Pastorals been more pernicious than in treatments of the errors they oppose."[44]

Jerry Sumney has performed a particularly useful service of isolating the polemic of each of the letters and seeing from a minimalist view what each one has to say about the opponents.[45] Sumney can probably be faulted for being even too minimalist, in that he underreads some of the passages and does not see the close ties between 1 Timothy and Titus once the analysis is completed (every objection to the opponents of Titus can be found in 1 Timothy as well). I will later maintain that 1 Timothy and Titus are directed toward the same opponents. But nothing links them to the opponents addressed in 2 Timothy.

There are basic similarities in the unpleasant things said about the two groups. Like the opponents of the other Pastorals, those in 2 Timothy are full of vice (3:1–6); they dispute over words (2:14, 23); they are corrupted in mind and unproven in faith (3:8); and they turn aside to myths (4:4). There is nothing to indicate that these myths are Jewish teachings about the Law, as found in 1 Timothy and Titus. All of these polemical statements in fact are stock phrases that give us no real indication of what it is, exactly, these false teachers were teaching, a matter stressed years ago in an important article of Robert Karris.[46]

Other statements in the course of the polemic are more targeted and can provide us with some indication of who these false teachers were and what they proclaimed. For one thing, the author, in a clear departure from Pauline practice, actually names them. They are Hymenaeus and Philetus: persons, therefore, known, if only fictionally, to both the (fictional) audience and author. But since they are named, even if fictionally, it means that the author imagines the opposition to have arisen within the community among persons who are known. Moreover, some of the polemic directed against them is not simply undifferentiated slander. Since they are said to have swerved from the truth, they, again, are being conceived of as insiders, not external threats (2:18); so too the comment that they have been ensnared by the devil, which implies they had previously led an unensnared existence (2:26). What is more, they have misled others in the community (2:18), but they still have the chance to repent and come to know the truth (2:25). Most important is that their specific error is named directly:

---

44. "2 Timothy Contrasted with 1 Timothy and Titus," *RB* 98 (1991): 414.

45. Jerry L. Sumney, *"Servants of Satan," "False Brothers" and Other Opponents of Paul*, JSNTSup. 188 (Sheffield: Sheffield Academic Press, 1999).

46. Robert J. Karris, "The Background and Significance of the Polemic of the Pastoral Epistles," *JBL* 92 (1973): 549–63.

they maintain that "the resurrection has already happened" τὴν ἀνάστασιν ἤδη γεγονέναι (2:18).

Hints that this was to be the problem with the false teaching came earlier, though they were left unflagged, especially in the pithy summary of the "Pauline credo" in 2:11–13, with its neat repetition of future tenses at the appropriate moments: "if we died with him [aorist] we also will live with him [future]; if we endure we will also reign with him [future]; if we should deny him, even that one will deny us [future]." Paul himself could scarcely have said it better, and one is right to suspect the influence of a passage such as Rom. 6:5, 8.

As we saw earlier, this very Pauline insistence that the believer's death with Christ, in baptism, was past, but the future resurrection with Christ is yet future, formed the heart of the polemic against Paul's opponents in Corinth, who appear to have believed that they had already experienced the benefits of the resurrection in the present.[47] The irony, as we also saw, is that the later authors of Colossians and, especially, Ephesians appear to have developed their views precisely along the lines of these opponents of Paul in Corinth. As the author of Colossians expresses it, "You who were dead in the transgressions and uncircumcision of the flesh, God made you alive with him (aorist: συνεζωοποίησεν; 2:13; cf. the future συζήσομεν in 2 Tim. 2:11); or, as Ephesians states the matter yet more emphatically, "Even though we were dead in transgressions, he made us alive in Christ (same word in the aorist: συνεζωοποίησεν), and he raised us (aorist: συνήγειρεν) and seated us (aorist: συνεκάθισεν) in the heavenly places in Christ Jesus (Eph. 2:5–6).[48]

This is not a peripheral matter for any of these authors. Paul himself is quite emphatic that the death with Christ is a past event for those who have been baptized, but the resurrection with Christ is not to be thought of until Christ himself returns from heaven and the transformation of the mortal body takes place. That is clearly asserted in Romans 6 and stressed in 1 Corinthians 15. The reason for the emphasis in the latter passage is that it is directly related to Paul's opponents. Within his own community at Corinth the opposition was conceivably claiming his proclamation in support: nothing indicates that they saw themselves as standing in opposition to him or as outside of the tradition which he began. The writers of Colossians and Ephesians, like the opponents in Corinth, have also taken a Pauline datum—in Christ "all things are new" (see 2 Cor. 5:17)—and moved it in a non-Pauline direction, insisting that the resurrection had already occurred, even if there was more yet to come. But believers are already raised with Christ and are ruling with him in the heavenly places. They already are enjoying the benefits of the resurrected existence. The resurrection has occurred for those who are in Christ.

This in turn is just the position that the author of 2 Timothy opposes. The resurrection is not a past spiritual event. It is a future physical one. Those who think the eschatological moment is past have been ensnared by a false, non-Pauline

47. See p. 176.

48. See further pp. 176–77 and 185–86.

teaching. They may deliver an attractive perspective, but it will lead people astray. The polemic against people engaging in vice (3:1–6)—standard and stock as it is—may be germane here. Throughout proto-orthodox polemic against firmly realized eschatology one sees the logic, not that the opponents used, but that the polemic demands: the devaluing of the physical life in the flesh is connected with abuses of the flesh.

What is particularly intriguing is the circumstance that, as we have already seen, this author appears to be familiar with "Paul's" letter to the Ephesians. The evidence derives not only from the previously discussed restatement of Eph. 2:1–10 in Tit. 3:3–8, but also from 2 Timothy, as it is widely, and with good reason, thought that 4:12 (I have sent Tychicus to Ephesus) betrays knowledge of Eph. 6:21–22 ("Tychicus . . . will tell you everything; I have sent him to you"). If so, this is yet another indication, as if more is needed, that 2 Timothy is forged. Paul himself could scarcely have been expected to rely on a pseudepigraphon produced in his name.

But even if the author of 2 Timothy found Ephesians of some use for his own letter, he stood directly opposed to the eschatology that it presented. One might well suspect that what we have here is a correction of an earlier "aberrant" view in circulation in Paul's name, written, allegedly, by the apostle himself. It should be recalled that the author of 2 Timothy indicates that the eschatological error arose among Paulinists within the Pauline community, among people who, evidently, claimed Pauline support. At least this much can be said for the author of Ephesians. But the later Paulinist resisted this strain of Pauline thought by embracing another, one which, as it turns out, could find clear support in letters later judged by scholars to be orthonymous. The end has not come; the resurrection has not occurred. On the contrary (this is where the author differs from Paul himself), the church needs to settle in for the long haul, and establish itself as an efficiently working community characterized by "true" teaching.

The possibility that 2 Timothy presents us with a counterforgery was recognized already by Lindemann.[49] The author of the book does not provide us with a vague rejection of some kind of fantasized Gnostic teaching of the resurrection. He opposes a teaching that had arisen within the circles that the author himself is addressing, Pauline communities that had taken Paul's teaching of the "new creation" in Christ in the wrong direction and to a false extreme, in arguing that the resurrection is a spiritual event that had already occurred. For the author of 2 Timothy, this is non-Pauline, devilish, and wrong. The resurrection is a future event, yet to be experienced, notwithstanding "Pauline" letters, such as Ephesians, that indicate otherwise.

---

49. "One might therefore even consider whether the author here perhaps polemicizes directly against Col (as well as Eph)." ("Man könnte deshalb sogar erwägen, ob der Vf hier möglicherweise direkt gegen Kol (und auch Eph) polemisiert.") *Aufhebung*, p. 139.

EXCURSUS: THE SECRETARY HYPOTHESIS

Now that we have explored six of the Deutero-Pauline epistles, we are in a position to consider the hypothesis widely invoked by advocates of authenticity to explain how a letter allegedly by an author should differ so radically from other writings he produced. The notion that early Christian authors used secretaries who altered the writing style and contributed to the contents of a writing—thereby creating the anomalies that arouse the critics' suspicion—is so widespread as to be virtually ubiquitous. There is no need here to cite references; one need only consult the commentaries, not only on the Pauline corpus but on 1 and 2 Peter as well. At the same time, almost no one who invokes the secretary hypothesis sees any reason to adduce any evidence for it. Instead, it is simply widely assumed that since authors used secretaries—as Paul, at least, certainly did (Rom. 16:22; Cor. 16:21; Gal. 6:11)—these otherwise unknown persons contributed not only to the style of a writing but also to its contents. There is a good reason that commentators who propose the hypothesis so rarely cite any evidence to support it. The ancient evidence is very thin, to the point of being nonexistent.

The fullest study is by E. Randolph Richards, who is to be commended for combing all the literary sources and papyri remains in order to uncover everything that can reasonably be said about secretaries and their functions in the Roman world during our period.[50] He explores every reference and allusion in the key authors: Cicero, Pliny, Plutarch, Suetonius, and so on. He plows through all the relevant material remains from Oxyrhynchus and elsewhere. It is a full and useful study, valuable for its earnest attempt to provide the fullest accounting of evidence possible. Somewhat less commendable are the conclusions that Richards draws, at times independently of this evidence.

Richards maintains that secretaries in antiquity could function in four ways: as recorders of dictation; as copy editors who modified an author's style; as coauthors who contributed both style and content; and as composers who produced a letter from scratch, at the instruction of the "author."

The first category is both abundantly attested in the sources and completely nonproblematic. Secretaries often took dictation, either syllabatim or, if they had the requisite tachygraphic skills, viva voce. If Paul dictated a letter like Romans, his secretary Tertius simply wrote down what he was told, making himself known only in his somewhat temerarious insertion of 16:22. Otherwise he recorded the words as Paul spoke them. Whether Paul was composing orally or dictating from written drafts is another question, but of no relevance to the present issue. The words on the page are the words Paul spoke, in his style.

---

50. *The Secretary in the Letters of Paul*, WUNT 2.42 (Tübingen: Mohr Siebeck, 1991). His more recent discussion, *Paul and First-Century Letter Writing: Secretaries, Composition, and Collection* (Downer's Grove, IL: Intervarsity, 2004), adds little to the discussion; nor does the work of Jerome Murphy-O'Connor, *Paul the Letter-Writer: His World, His Options, His Skills* (Collegeville, MN: Liturgical Press, 1995).

It is with the second category that the significance and the evidence begin to move in opposite directions. If secretaries regularly edited the dictations they received, possibly taking down a draft by dictation and then reworking it into a style they preferred, then all sorts of options would open up for early Christian writings deemed pseudepigraphic on stylistic grounds. The differences between Colossians and the undisputed Paulines could be explained, as would the discrepancies between 1 and 2 Peter. What, then, is the evidence? And is it directly relevant?

Unlike the first category, the evidence that secretaries routinely reworked letters for style is very thin indeed. All of it derives from the very upper reaches of the Roman highest classes, among authors who used highly educated and skilled writers in helping them produce their correspondence. There is a serious question of how such data are relevant for a completely different social context, with the impoverished and lower-class authors of the Christian writings. Still, it is worth noting that Cicero, at least, appears to have allowed Tiro on occasion to assist him in stylistically shaping his letters. And Cicero suggests that the secretary of Atticus, Alexis, may have helped him similarly.[51] Moreover, Cicero speaks of one letter of Pompey that appears to have been written (or rewritten?) instead by Sestius, and intimates that Sestius wrote other writings in his name (mildly castigating Pompey for this proceeding).[52] Finally, there is an off-the-cuff comment in the handbook on style by Philostratus that the letters of Brutus may have been stylized by the secretary he used. This is not so much evidence for the historical Brutus (from three hundred years earlier) as evidence of what would have seemed culturally plausible in this later period.[53]

This evidence is notably sparse, but it does indicate that a secretary would occasionally edit an author's letter stylistically. Could this not explain, then, why Colossians differs so significantly (in style) from the other Pauline letters? Or why 1 and 2 Peter are so different from one another? Several points should be stressed. First, as already mentioned, the evidence all derives from fabulously wealthy, highly educated, upper-class elites with very highly trained secretaries. We have no evidence at all for the kinds of letters being dictated by a Paul, or, even more, by an illiterate Aramaic-speaking peasant such as Peter.[54] Second, the kinds of writings in question may be incommensurate. The vast majority of letters in Greco-Roman antiquity were very short and to the point. The letters of the papyri appear to average fewer than a hundred words; at the other end of the spectrum, letters of Cicero averaged around

51. Richards (*Secretary*, p. 46) cites Cicero, *Fam.* 16.10.2 and *Att.* 5.20, but he may be overreading the texts.

52. *Att.* 7.17, cited in Richards, *Secretary*, p. 96, note (in quo accusavi mecum ipse Pompeium).

53. Ibid., p. 52, n. 155. It should be noted that Richards uses this quotation in order to support his thesis that Brutus actually had a secretary compose his correspondence for him, but the text is explicitly addressing the issue of "epistolary style," not substance.

54. The term *peasant* has become a site of debate and even confusion in New Testament scholarship; I am using it in its most basic sense to refer to an uneducated person of low social status.

three hundred words, Seneca's around a thousand. The letters of Paul are much longer, on average about twenty-five hundred words.[55] What really matters, however, is not simply length, but complexity. The Christian letters we have examined so far in this study are not simply pieces of correspondence: they are complicated theological and paranetic treatises, with interwoven themes and subthemes, and intricate modes of argumentation, written in letter form. Apart from purely formal features (address, thanksgiving, body, closing, etc.) they are simply not like typical Greco-Roman letters, precisely because of what happens in the "body." What evidence is there that secretaries were ever given the freedom to rewrite this kind of letter—an extended treatise in letter form—in accordance with their preferred style? As far as I know, there is no evidence.

This latter point relates to the third. The kinds of "minor corrective editing" that Richards finds, for example, in the case of Tiro and Cicero[56] is far removed from the complete rewriting of the letters that would have been necessary to make an Ephesians or Colossians come in any sense from the hand of Paul. Here there are wholesale changes of style at every point. Where is the evidence that copy editing ever went to this extreme? If any exists, Richards fails to cite it.

Finally, it should be noted that in none of the instances we have considered so far, and in none of the ones we will consider throughout this study, are questions of style the only features of the letter that have led scholars to suspect forgery. The most definitive demonstration of a non-Pauline style comes with Colossians, and even there it was the content of the letter that confirmed that it was not written by Paul. Moreover, it should be stressed that the person actually writing the letter also repeatedly claims not to be a secretary but to be Paul himself ("I, Paul").

It is Richards's third and fourth categories that are particularly germane to the questions of early Christian forgery. What is the evidence that secretaries were widely used, or used at all, as coauthors of letters or as ersatz composers? If there is any evidence that secretaries sometimes joined an author in creating a letter, Richards has failed to find or produce it. The one example he considers involves the relationship of Cicero and Tiro, cited earlier by Gordon Bahr as evidence for co-authorship. In Bahr's words "Tiro took part in the composition of the letter."[57] But Richards points out that Bahr cites no evidence to support this claim, opting instead simply to assert the conclusion. Moreover, there is nothing stylistically in the Ciceronian correspondence to suggest a coauthorship. Richards concludes that at most Tiro sometimes engaged in "minor corrective editing." What is oddest in Richards' discussion, however, is the conclusion that he draws, once he discounts the evidence of Cicero, the one and only piece of evidence he considers: "Evidently then, . . . secretaries were used as co-authors."[58] It is not at all clear

55. See Richards, *Secretary*, p. 213, depending on Wikenhauser's *Einleitung*.

56. Richards, *Secretary*, p. 48.

57. "Paul and Letter Writing in the First Century," *CBQ* 28 (1966): 470.

58. Richards, *Secretary*, p. 48.

what makes this view "evident," given the circumstance that he has not cited a solitary piece of evidence for it.

There is better evidence that an author would sometimes commission someone else to write a letter in his name. This typically happened among the illiterate, who would hire a scribe for any necessary written communications. But this involved stock letters and documents, stereotyped and brief, of no relevance to the situation we are addressing with the early Christian pseudepigrapha. What about longer letters of some substance? Here there is at least some evidence, although all of it is connected with one author (out of how many?), Cicero. At one time Cicero asks Atticus "to write in my name to Basilius and to anyone else you like, even to Servilius, and say whatever you think fit." And in doing so he even urges Atticus to employ a deceit: "If they look for [my missing] signature or handwriting, say that I have avoided them because of the guards."[59] In addition to these passages, Richards places a good deal of weight on a letter of Rufus, a friend of Cicero who had promised to write him during his exile of 51 CE with news of Rome. Rufus indicates that he was too busy to fulfill his promise, and so "delegated the task to another."[60] This was a long and involved communication, and so is more like, in some respect, the lengthy letters of the early Christians we have been considering.

The problem is that the passage does not say what Richards says it says. Rufus never claims that he had someone else compose the account *in his own name*. He simply had someone else compose the account. That, of course, is a different matter altogether.[61]

And so, from all of antiquity, we are left with a few references to a secretary composing a letter in connection with Cicero. These references show that Cicero realized the practice was deceitful (he instructs Atticus to lie about the matter). Moreover, the correspondence involved short, stereotypical letters, not complex treatises in letter form. But is the evidence sufficient to establish a typical practice in antiquity of secretary-composed writings? Richards himself does not think so, as he repeatedly emphasizes: "Nowhere was there *any* indication that an ordinary secretary was asked, much less presumed, to compose a letter for the author. . . . [O]ne cannot assume that [Cicero's] use of such a questionable secretarial method is indicative of an acceptable custom of the day . . . [T]his secretarial method probably should not even be considered a valid option."[62]

What, on balance, is the evidence to support the secretary hypothesis to explain the early Christian pseudepigrapha? That secretaries took dictation in a variety of ways is clear and certain. This creates no problem for authorship: the author delivered an oral communication that was written down word-for-word by an amanuensis who simply performed the task of recording. In addition, on rare

59. *Att* 11.2,.4; 11.5. Cited by Richards, *Secretary*, p. 50, nn. 147, 148.

60. Cicero, *Fam*, 8.1.1; cited in Richards, *Secretary*, p. 51.

61. As Richards later admits, *Secretary*, p. 111.

62. Ibid., pp. 110–11, emphasis his.

occasions members of the upper-crust elite used their resources to hire highly literate secretaries to copyedit their letters in places. There is no evidence that this ever happened in other cultural settings, with, say, the poorer lower classes. Moreover, there is not a shred of evidence, at least none that Richards has been able to locate, to indicate that secretaries sometimes coauthored a letter. What is the evidence that secretaries actually composed letters in another person's name? Apart from a completely different phenomenon—the use of a scribe by illiterate persons to produce documents (wills, land deeds, sales contracts, etc.) or very brief stereotyped communications—the evidence appears to be limited to a few instances from the end of the life of Cicero, who admits that the practice involved a deceit, that is, that it was tantamount to forgery, willingly engaged in because of the impossible constraints placed upon his time.

In sum, what might we conclude about the evidence for the secretary hypothesis put forth by commentators wanting to affirm the authenticity of the Deutero-Pauline or Petrine letters of the New Testament? It is thin at best, almost nonexistent. Why then is the hypothesis so universally invoked? If it is not because of the evidence, it must be for other reasons, and one can only suspect that it involves wishful thinking. History, however, proceeds on the basis of evidence. What evidence exists, on the other hand, for the contrary position, that ancient authors forged writings in the names of other well known persons, not successfully replicating their style and producing anomalous content? That kind of evidence can be found all over the map. Scholars must constantly ask themselves whether evidence matters, that is, whether they prefer history or romance.

SECOND PETER

To this point we have considered only Deutero-Pauline letters in our query into forgeries produced to counter eschatological views that were deemed aberrant. "Aberrant" eschatology affected other writings as well, into the second century, including one that is distantly related to Paul, not because he is claimed as its author, but because its pseudonymous author, "Peter," appealed to Paul's support in opposition to the false eschatological teachings he addressed. The book of 2 Peter is a polemical treatise written to oppose Christians who maintained that there would be no future apocalyptic moment in which Jesus would return to right all that was wrong with the world. Unlike the "Pauline" letters we have considered so far, there is very little debate in this instance concerning authorship. More than any other New Testament writing, 2 Peter is widely recognized to be forged, even among scholars otherwise loath to admit the presence of pseudonymous works within the canon of Scripture.

2 Peter as Forgery

2 Peter is among the least well attested works of the New Testament from Christian antiquity, although it is found already in P^{72}, ca. 300 CE, along with 1 Peter

and Jude, the two canonical letters with which it is most closely associated. Still, during the first four centuries the book had an unsettled status among those interested in establishing the contours of the New Testament. Origen doubted its authenticity, in words quoted by Eusebius: "Peter . . . left us one acknowledged epistle, possibly two—though this is doubtful" (*H.E.* 6.25.8). Eusebius himself also considered 1 Peter genuine, but rejected 2 Peter, even though, as he notes, some readers have found it valuable: "Of Peter, one epistle, known as his first, is accepted, and this the early fathers quoted freely, as undoubtedly genuine. . . . But the second Petrine epistle we have been taught to regard as uncanonical" (*H.E.* 3.3.1). Somewhat later Jerome expressed the opinion of his day: "[Peter] wrote two epistles which are called Catholic, the second of which, on account of its difference from the first in style, is considered by many not to be his."[63] Most emphatic was Didymus the Blind, who indicated, "We must therefore not be ignorant of the fact that the epistle at hand is forged, which, even though published, is nevertheless not in the canon."[64]

Those modern scholars who do not share this concern with establishing the contours of the canon nonetheless agree with these ancient assessments of 2 Peter and often use the same faulty logic in support, that the book differs so significantly from 1 Peter that it could not have been written by the same author.[65] The flaw in the logic, as we will see, is that Peter probably did not write the first epistle either, so that variations from it say nothing, per se, about whether he wrote the second. Nonetheless, there are compelling reasons for thinking that 2 Peter came into existence long after the death of Jesus' disciple, and that it is simply one of a stack of a books that eventually appeared in his name. Still extant are the Gospel of Peter, the Epistula Petri of the Pseudo-Clementines, the Letter of Peter to Philip from Nag Hammadi, three apocalypses of Peter—all falsely claiming to be written by the great apostle. We will later see that Peter could not have written any of these books (no one, of course, claims that he did); but I will reserve that discussion for my assessment of 1 Peter, the one book scholars have been most inclined to consider authentic.

The grounds for considering 2 Peter a forgery are varied and numerous. The first has to do with the quality of the Greek. Even if we assume that Peter could write in Greek, an assumption I will challenge in the chapter that follows, it seems

---

63. *Vir. ill.* 1. Richard Bauckham is not right when he claims that Jerome argued that the differences between the two letters were due to the use of two different secretaries (*Jude, 2 Peter*, WBC 50, Waco: Word Books, 1983, p. 145). The passage in question is *Ad Hebidiam*, Epistula 120, 11 (c. 406/7): "Further, the two epistles, which circulate as Peter's, are also different in style among themselves and in character, and in word structure; from which we understand that he used different interpreters (or "translators": interpretibus—not secretaries) as necessary."

64. "Non est igitur ignorandum praesentem epistolam esse falsatam, quae licet publicetur, non tamen in canone est." *Enarr. In Epist.* Cathol. *PG* 39,1774.

65. Thus, for example, Peter H. Davids, *The Letters of 2 Peter and Jude* (Grand Rapids, MI: Eerdmans, 2006).

highly doubtful that he could have written Greek like this.[66] The style is widely assessed as overly elaborate, and the vocabulary is excessively rich. As Bauckham puts it, the author is "fond of literary and poetic, even obscure words."[67] This is not what one would expect of an Aramaic-speaking peasant.[68] By Elliott's count, there are proportionally more hapax legomena in 2 Peter than in any other writing of the New Testament: 58 of its 402 words (14.4 percent).[69]

In addition, there are the clear indications that the book was written in a later period, after the death of the apostles. Most obviously, it was written in order to deal with the massive delay of the parousia: there had been a long passage of time since Christians widely held to the expectation of an imminent end of all things, a problem dealt with in a variety of ways by other postapostolic writings, such as Luke-Acts and the Fourth Gospel. In particular we are told that "the fathers" have "fallen asleep" (i.e., died) since the original promises of the coming end (3:4). Moreover, when the author is speaking in character, he feigns a knowledge of his own approaching death, based in part on a prediction of Jesus himself (1:12–14; see, for example the post-Petrine John 21:18–19 as well), giving this book, as widely recognized, the character of a testamentary fiction.[70] He "knows" of his impending death and wants to give his readers his final instructions. As with all Testaments, this is a fiction put on the pen of someone already residing comfortably in his tomb.

Moreover, the author's knowledge of earlier Christian texts indicates that he was writing after the death of Peter. Most obviously, he makes extensive use of the letter of Jude. By Elliott's count, nineteen of Jude's twenty-five verses reappear in modified form in 2 Peter.[71] We will later see clear reasons for thinking that Jude was not produced by Jesus' brother, but is a forgery in his name written at a relatively late time, by someone looking back on the apostolic age. 2 Peter is, as a consequence, later still. Moreover, the author clearly knows of 1 Peter, as seen not only in what appears to be an explicit reference ("This, now, my beloved, is the second letter I have written to you", 3:1) but also in numerous similarities, to be mentioned later. I will be arguing in the next chapter that 1 Peter is forged; that would necessarily make 2 Peter a forgery as well. Equally striking, and widely noted, is the fact that this author already knows of a collection of Paul's letters (not just one or two in isolation), and that he is living at a time when Christians were already considering these letters to be Scripture (3:15–16). It is hard to imagine any such situation before the end of the first century, at best.

Finally, nothing that we know about the historical Peter as a Jewish missionary to Jews who continued to uphold the Law is true of this letter (e.g., Galatians 2).

---

66. Richard Bauckham, *Jude, 2 Peter*, WBC (Nashville, TN: Thomas Nelson, 1983), p. 137.

67. Ibid., p. 136.

68. See note 54.

69. "Peter, Second Epistle of," ABD, 5. 284.

70. Ibid., p. 283.

71. Ibid., p. 284.

There is, in fact, nothing Jewish about it. The reference to the false teachers who emerged from the community as those who had earlier escaped τὰ μιάσματα suggests they started out as pagans, not Jews (2:20). And the use of Scripture bears no relation to what we would suspect of a law-abiding believer like Peter. It is true that he speaks of the prophecy of Scripture (1:20); but even if he is referring to Jewish Scripture (as opposed to the writings of Christians that, like Paul's letters, are considered Scripture), there is nothing to suggest that the Law continues to be in force. On the contrary Scripture is read in a completely presentist way. The examples cited of disobedience in Scripture are merely illustrative of how God works. And there is no injunction to follow the dictates of Scripture. Quite the contrary, it is standard, high morals, not the works of the Law, that matter to this author.

It became common in Petrine forgeries to relate firsthand experiences with Jesus, a ploy that makes considerable sense: why else claim to be Jesus' right-hand man, if you cannot appeal to the authority that experience provides? And so the author of 1 Peter states that he was a "witness to the sufferings of Christ" (5:1). So too, the author of the Coptic Apocalypse of Peter claims to have observed the crucifixion of Jesus, somewhat oddly, while conversing with Christ on a hill nearby. And the author of the Greek Apocalypse of Peter, also on a hill, is taken by Jesus himself on a guided tour of the realms of the blessed and the damned.

The ironies in the case of 2 Peter in particular are nonetheless striking. This author insists that he was present at the transfiguration precisely in order to validate the status of his authority: his views, he avers, are not based on fictions (as opposed to the false teachers he opposes) but on facts and personal experiences (1:16–18). Yet this claim itself is a fiction written by a forger who has invented the tale of the personal experience, as recognized by J. Frey.[72] Moreover, this assertion of factual authority is used precisely in order to oppose the ψευδοπροφῆται and the ψευδοδιδάσκαλοι (2:1–3) who revile "the truth" and teach "false words"—all this in a ψευδεπίγραφον, a writing that is "inscribed with a lie" written by someone who deceives his readers about his own authoritative credentials. Rarely in early Christian texts do we find irony so exquisite.

The Polemical Function of the Forgery

In the next chapter I will argue that both the explicit reference to the letters of Paul as Scripture and the numerous resonances with Pauline thought in 2 Peter are not incidental to the polemical purposes of the letter but are, in fact, a fundamental component of them. For the purposes of the present chapter, it is enough

72. "This makes for a particularly daring argument if one keeps in mind that the author himself fictionally constructs the claim to eye-witness status" ("Darinliegt freilich ein besonders kühnes Argument, wenn man bedenkt, dass der Autor selbst den Anspruch der Augenzeugenschaft fiktional konstruiert"). Jörg Frey, "Autorfiktion und Gegnerbild im Judasbrief und im Zweiten Petrusbrief," in Jörg Frey et al., eds., *Pseudepigraphie und Verfasserfiktion*, p. 707.

to note the severity of the polemic and its centrality to the letter. The letter is, in fact, entirely polemical, directed against "false teachers" from within the community who adopt eschatological views counter to those received by the author from the early Christian apocalyptic tradition. The heart of the letter (virtually all of chapters 2 and 3) is directed to this polemic, and it is important to recognize that the charges of licentiousness that dominate chapter 2 are tied from the outset to the false teachings (2:1, "destructive heresies" that revile "the way of truth" and involve "false words"). In other words, the opponents are not simply unprincipled reprobates; they are false teachers whose errant views have, in the author's opinion, led to lascivious behavior. This connection between false teaching and immorality is reconfirmed in the author's antidote, which involves "holy and pious conduct" rooted in a correct understanding of eschatology (3:11–13). The idea that bad theology led to unconscionable behavior was to become standard fare among proto-orthodox heresiologists in the decades and centuries to follow.[73] And indeed, much of what the author says about his opponents involves stock polemic: they deny the Master; they secretly bring in heresies; they are licentious; they lead to the reviling of truth; they are greedy; they exploit with false words; they are sure to be destroyed; they despise authority; they are wild, dissipated, carousers.

With stereotypes such as these, we are handcuffed in trying to identify the opponents, if in fact there was some kind of actual, historical group lying behind the polemic. It may bear noting that the author's opposition to them resonates with later attacks on various Gnostic groups. His adversaries appeal to knowledge but are "without knowledge" (ἀγνοοῦσιν; 2:12); they urge freedom from bodily constraints (passim); they "revile the glorious ones" (comparable to Gnostic denigration of the world creators? 2:10); they base their views on myths rather than historical verities (1:16). But in the end, such charges cannot contribute significantly to any firm identification. Only two features of the opposition appear clear from the polemic leveled against them: the author insists that they are enemies who have emerged from within the Christian community, and they endorse false eschatological views.

As to the first point, 2:20 and 3:15–16 seem decisive. The opponents had formerly "escaped the pollutions of the world through the knowledge of our Lord and Savior Jesus Christ," but then they "became entangled in them again and were worse off than before." Obviously the opponents did not see themselves in this light, and may well have been amazed at the charges of immorality and licentious behavior leveled against them. But it appears that these enemies, at least as portrayed by the forger, have developed views at variance with the "original" teaching, and they have done so based on their interpretation of the letters of

73. See, for example, Frederik Wisse, "The Epistle of Jude in the History of Heresiology," in *Essays on the Nag Hammadi Texts in Honour of Alexander Böhlig*, ed. Martin Krause (Leiden: Brill, 1972), pp. 133–43.

Paul, which they, as "ignorant and unstable" persons, "twist as they do the rest of the Scriptures, to their own destruction." In other words, these are Christian Scripture scholars who have interpreted Paul in a way that this author finds offensive and scandalous.

This misuse of Paul coincides with a general approach to authority by the false teachers, as portrayed by their enemy, the forger of the letter. That the issue is authority is clear already in 1:20, where the author insists that the prophecies "of Scripture" are not a matter of private, personal exposition (ἰδίας ἐπιλύσεως). Prophecy came not from human θέλημα; it came from the Spirit of God. Presumably, then, human interpretations of prophecy—such as those practiced by the enemy—are strictly verboten. Here we seem to have an adumbration of modern hermeneutical debates, as this author simply wants the texts in question to "speak for themselves," since, after all, they are divinely inspired and can only be corrupted when humans apply their minds to them.

The teachings of prophetic scripture are consistent with the teachings of Jesus (3:2) and naturally of his apostles (3:2), especially "our brother Paul" (3:15). Since these are the writings explicitly invoked (though never quoted), is the author imagining that it was specifically the Christian prophets who were "moved by the holy spirit" and so "spoke from God" (1:21)? If so, the reference to "the rest of the Scriptures" (τὰς λοιπὰς γραφάς, 3:16) may be referring, as Lindemann has suggested, to Christian writings, rather than the "Old Testament."[74] Or, it may be, as in the standard interpretation, that the author is simply equating the two sets of writings in authority. In either event, the author positions two sets of indubitable authority against the fallacious reasonings of his opponents: (1) the clear meaning of authoritative texts when read without human sophistry, and (2) his own voice, as one who does not follow myths but knows the truth whereof he speaks since he, unlike they, was an actual companion of Jesus and beheld his glory on the holy mountain.

As pointed out, there are numerous connections between chapters 2 and 3, in which the "teaching" (the "destructive heresy") is tied to the "morality," attacked in notoriously vague but consistently nasty terms in chapter 2, terms that are largely drawn from the book of Jude. One would be hard-pressed indeed to reconstruct the teaching of the opponents from the invective directed against them in the earlier polemic : "irrational animals . . . blaspheming in things about which they have no knowledge . . . who consider it pleasure to revel during the day. . . . blots and blemishes who revel in their dissipated lives. . . . eyes full of adultery, incessantly in sin" and so on (2:12–14). To learn what the opponents actually say the reader needs to wait for chapter 3. The content of the false teaching is not that Christians need to be licentious. It is that the apocalyptic end proclaimed by Jesus, Paul, and the other apostles is not to be expected. It is this anti-apocalyptic

---

74. *Paulus im ältesten Christentum: Das Bild des Apostels und die Rezeption der paulinischen Theologie in der frühchristlichen Literatur bis Marcion* (Tübingen: Mohr Siebeck, 1979), pp. 93–94.

view that leads, in the author's opinion, to the immoral lifestyle of the enemies, possibly on the logic that if the end is not coming soon, there is plenty of time to enjoy the pleasures of the flesh, an argument that the opponents, if they actually existed, may have found astonishing.

The specific teaching of these "mockers" (3:3) is posed in terms of their blasphemous question and the implication they draw from it: "Where is the promise of his parousia? For since the fathers fell asleep, everything remains just as it was at the beginning of creation." The question has to do with the return of Jesus. There is no sign of it happening. The "fathers" must be the fathers of the church, the early Christian leaders who have all died, possibly in expectation that the end would occur within their own lifetimes. Rather than concede that these fathers were wrong, the opponents have interpreted their writings ("the letters of Paul . . . and the rest of the writings") in such a way as to show they were not, in fact, in error, because they did not predict a literal parousia of Jesus. It is not the fathers who have erred; it is the Christian group represented by the author of this rebuttal, 2 Peter, the group who has held on to the belief that an apocalyptic crisis was still imminent and who insisted that this had been the teaching of Jesus and his apostles all along (3:2). For the opponents this was not the proclamation of Jesus or the teaching of his apostles, and certainly not the teaching found in the letters of Paul. The end is not coming right away and it is not coming in the way sometimes proclaimed. These nonapocalyptic opponents claimed that their view had been the view of Jesus, his apostles, and Paul.

Such Christians could certainly find support for their view in earlier Christian writings, as amply attested in the few that still survive. The apocalyptic message proclaimed by the Jesus of Mark, some forty years after the founding of the new faith, came to be muted in Luke; by the time of John it came practically to disappear. As we will see shortly, it is polemicized against in the still later Gospel of Thomas. Not just Jesus but also Paul went through a radical de-apocalypticizing transformation at the hands of his later followers, as we have seen already, for example, in the letters of Colossians and, even more, Ephesians. This transformation continued in some Pauline circles of the second century, as among those Paulinists opposed in the Acts of Paul are those who declared that the resurrection is not a future, physical event: people are resurrected in their children, here, in this life.[75] We do not know if the opponents of 2 Timothy took this, or some similar line, but they too appear to have claimed Pauline support for their views that "the resurrection is past" (2 Tim. 2:18).

Pauline Christianity, much like Christianity at large, was enormously split on numerous issues, including this matter of eschatology. It was the nonapocalyptic view that eventually came to dominate within broader Christendom. It is no accident

75. Demas and Hermogenes teach that "the resurrection which [Paul] says is to come . . . has already taken place in the children, and that we rise again, after having come to the knowledge of the true God." *Acts of Paul* 14; translation of J. K. Elliott, *Apocryphal New Testament* (Oxford: Oxford University Press, 1993).

that the book of Revelation had such difficulty finding a place among the books of Scripture. Later chiliasts who believed in a literal millennium on earth, such as the early-second-century Papias, came to be mocked by writers such as Eusebius, who labeled his proto-orthodox forebear a man of "very little intelligence" (*H.E.* 3.39). The harsh words were directed against Papias not because he was, in fact, stupid, but because he was foolish enough to believe that there would be a utopian existence here on earth to be brought by an apocalyptic crisis at the end of the age. In other words, he was fool enough to agree with early Christian preaching.

So too did the author of 2 Peter. Was this one of the reasons this book too eventually had difficulty making it into the canon of Scripture? For this author, God created this world by his word and destroyed it with water (3:5–6). Next it will be destroyed by fire (3:7). The author adumbrates his view earlier in his short epistle, as when he refers to the (true) believers' "entrance into the eternal kingdom of our Lord and Savior Jesus Christ" (1:11) and in his abundant stress on the coming of real and palpable judgment on the false teachers throughout chapter 2. But it is in his reasoned response of 3:8:–15 that he sets forth views that contrast with the "destructive heresies" of his opponents. As proclaimed by Jesus and his apostles (3:2, 15–16) the end really is coming "soon." But temporal proximity is determined by a divine, not a human, calendar. And as Scripture teaches (Ps. 90:4), with the Lord a day is fully commensurate with a thousand years. There has been a (seeming) delay only because of God's forbearance, giving everyone a chance to repent. But the "Day of the Lord" is coming, like a thief, and it will involve a total, all encapsulating cosmic destruction (3:10, 12). In expectation of this apocalyptic moment, the true believers need to live in godly and pious ways (3:11).

In taking this stand, the author placed himself securely in the tradition that he understood to have stemmed from the apocalyptic proclamation of Jesus and his apostles, among whom he numbered himself. In order to provide particularly strong authorization for his views, he claimed to have seen firsthand the glory of Jesus, a glory that foreshadowed one yet to be revealed, on the "Day of the Lord," when destruction would come to this world. His views, in other words, were not simply those that stood within a noble tradition. They derived from the foundation of the church. The church is rooted in Scriptural prophecies, which anticipate a coming destruction, in the teachings of Jesus himself, and in the writings of Paul. This author was allegedly a companion of Jesus and a fellow apostle of Paul. As opposed to the "mockers" who have proclaimed a nonapocalyptic view of the faith, he writes to assure his readers that a clear and definite end is coming, and that it will be brutal, especially for those who think otherwise. These are "lying prophets" (ψευδοπροφῆται) and lying teachers (ψευδοδιδάσκαλοι). And the author has no scruples at all about telling a lie of his own, by writing a ψευδεπίγραφον, in order to attack the teachers of falsehood.[76]

76. Bauckham claims that since "Testaments" were by their nature fictional in character, it is "very implausible to suppose that most Jewish readers were so naïve as to read such speeches as accurate

THE GOSPEL OF THOMAS

As a final example of a forgery written, in part, to correct false eschatological notions, we can turn to the Gospel of Thomas. Unlike the other books we have considered, the Gospel of Thomas does not connect itself with the teachings of Paul; indeed, its eschatological views can be read as a rejection of Paul.

No one thinks the book was authentically produced by Didymus Judas Thomas. The name is known throughout Syriac traditions. "Judas Thomas" appears in the Syriac translation of John 14:22 (for "Judas not Iscariot"), in the Abgar legends that we will consider later, and especially in the fabricated Acts of Thomas. In that narrative of Thomas's missionary exploits there is no doubt concerning whose twin ("Didymus"/"Thomas") he is; the circumstance that he and his brother Jesus look just alike makes possible some of the most entertaining moments of the plot. Outside of the prologue of the Gospel, the author makes no use of the name (except saying 13, where it is not a self-designation and is probably a reference to a different Thomas). But the prologue is enough. The words that "the living Jesus" spoke are written by Didymus Judas Thomas. What greater authorization do these sayings need? They come from the pen of Jesus' own twin. Who better to know the secrets that can provide life eternal (saying 1)?

There are numerous themes developed throughout the collection, but as frequently noted, it is no accident that anti-apocalyptic sayings occur near the very beginning (saying 3) and the very end (saying 113), bracketing the whole. Five sayings altogether are particularly germane, and all five point in the same direction. This author, writing falsely in the name of Jesus' brother, insists, on his brother's authority, that there is to be no apocalyptic crisis at the end of the age to usher in God's good kingdom. The kingdom of God is here already, both within those who understand the secret teachings of Jesus and spread throughout the earth, for those who can see. Whether or not this view stands in direct tension with the apocalyptic teachings of the real, historical Jesus, as the majority of scholars continue to hold, they certainly stand at odds with the apocalyptic proclamation of his early apostles, such as Paul. The Gospel of Thomas was written, in some measure, to promote a nonapocalyptic eschatology and to polemicize against Christians who maintained that there was a future, physical kingdom yet

---

historical reports or that their authors were so naïve as to expect them to be so read." This, again, is history by assertion. What, exactly, makes either naïvety implausible? He goes on to claim that 2 Peter, itself a Testament, was meant as an "entirely transparent fiction" (*2 Peter and Jude*, p. 134), offering in support the point that the false teachers are spoken of in the present tense, rather than the conventional future tense—a sign to the readers of the book's fictional status. In response, it is hard to see how he can have it both ways (Testaments were read as fictions; this book differs from Testaments in a way to make readers take it as a fiction), making him appear to be grasping at straws. Moreover, if the author did not mean for his readers to take his identity seriously, it is difficult indeed to see why he roots his authority in a personal experience of Jesus on the Mount of Transfiguration, a real experience in contrast to the fantasies of the false teachers. Far more convincing is the counterposition of J. Frey, "Autorfiktion und Gegnerbild."

to come to earth. To that extent the eschatology of the collection appears to be much more in line with the views opposed by two of the forgeries we have already considered, 2 Timothy and 2 Peter, and closer to the views advocated by traditions now found in the falsely ascribed Gospel of John, where eternal life, for the most part, is portrayed as a present reality for those who believe in Jesus (thus 3:17–19, 36; 5:24; 11:25–27; etc.). In John, however, there continues to be some element of eschatological reserve in that it contains passages, possibly undigested fragments from earlier traditions, that still allow there will be a future apocalyptic event (5:25–29). Not so in the Gospel of Thomas. The kingdom is here and now; it is not a future, physical event to be anticipated.

Saying 3

The attack on an apocalyptic eschatology appears at the outset in saying 3. The saying presents a number of problems of text[77] and translation[78] that need not detain us here. T. F. Glasson has plausibly argued that it is to be understood as a midrash on Deut. 30:10–25 that establishes a connection between commandments, wisdom, and the reign of God within.[79] In any event, that the interpretation is advanced polemically is obvious: it is directed against "those who lead you," who maintain that the kingdom is a physical place that can be entered. This view is parodied: Is it in the sky? Is it in the sea? No, the kingdom is not a place that can be entered. "Rather, the kingdom of heaven is inside of you and outside" (ἐντὸς ὑμῶν ἐστι κἀκτός).[80]

The tie to Luke 17:20–21 is obvious: "the kingdom of God is among you" (again: ἐντὸς ὑμῶν ἐστιν). But the Thomasine saying differs significantly, at least from the way in which the logion appears in its broader Lukan context. There, Jesus is asked by the Pharisees—understood to be the enemy—when, not where, the kingdom is to come. Jesus replies that it will not come with observable signs, so that no one will be able to say "here it is or there." Instead, for Luke, the kingdom of God is in your midst. In this case ἐντός cannot mean "within" you, as it does in Thomas; Jesus is scarcely telling his opponents that they themselves have

77. We are fortunate to have a Greek fragment, POxyr 654, that is to be given primacy. There is, unfortunately, an important lacuna at l.15, normally filled with θεου, for "kingdom of God," but which DeConick argues should be filled with ουρανου, for "kingdom of heaven." If she is wrong, then the saying is even more closely tied to Luke 17:21. But she makes a good case: the lacuna has room for fourteen to seventeen letters; the standard reconstruction provides only twelve, whereas hers provides fifteen. April DeConick, *The Original Gospel of Thomas in Translation* (London: T&T Clark, 2006), 51.

78. The Coptic reads "those who draw you" (NETSOK). DeConick argues for a semitic original from NGD, meaning either to draw or to lead; the Greek, then, mistranslated the text, leading to the Coptic. *Original Gospel*, p. 52.

79. "The Gospel of Thomas, Saying, 3, and Deuteronomy XXX.11–14," *ExpTim* 78 (1976–77): 151–52.

80. Translations taken from Ehrman and Pleše, *Apocryphal Gospels*, pp. 303–35. Here, however, I have accepted DeConick's reconstruction of the text; see note 77 above.

the kingdom "in their hearts." No, for Luke the kingdom of God is present among them because it is manifest already in the ministry of Jesus. Thus, elsewhere Luke indicates that the kingdom of God has "come near" (10:9, 11) and in Jesus' ministry it is said already to have "arrived" (11:20). Moreover—and this is the key difference from Thomas—in Luke there is still a firm expectation that there is a decisive event to occur at the end of the age (21:7–32; see esp. v. 31). The experiences of the kingdom as present in the life and ministry of Jesus are therefore proleptic of the denouement that can still be expected. This is evident in the immediate context of 17:20–21 as well, where Jesus goes on to discuss the coming of the son of man (17:22–37).

That is not the case, however, for the Gospel of Thomas. Here the kingdom is already fully present, inside all those who know themselves, recognizing that they are "the sons of the living father."[81] This polemic is not only directed against chiliasts of the author's own day (early second century), proto-orthodox authors such as Papias, who still expected a future, physical, utopian kingdom to appear on earth. It is even more directed against the sacred texts that such proto-orthodox were beginning to cherish as authoritative, such as the Gospel of Mark (9:1; 13:30) and the letters of Paul (1 Thess. 4:14–17; 1 Corinthians 15, especially vv. 24–25, 51–57), which envisioned the kingdom as coming not only with the transformation of the creation (Rom. 8:18–25) but also with the resurrection of the body, which would be raised immortal. Thomas demurs. The kingdom will not be experienced as a place to be entered by a future, physically transformed body; it is to be experienced now, as an internal reality, enjoyed by those who know who they really are.

Saying 18

The polemic continues along a similar line in saying 18. Now, however, rather than being the unnamed "Christian leaders" who misunderstand Jesus' eschatological teaching, it is the earthly disciples, who, foolishly, for this Gospel, ask about "how our end will be." The saying clearly calls to mind the Synoptic tradition, where the disciples ask Jesus about the "end of the age" (Mark 13:3–4; Matthew 24:3; Luke 21:7), and where Jesus responds by delivering his apocalyptic discourse. One key difference is that in saying 18 the disciples ask their question in terms not of apocalyptic but of personal eschatology. They are interested in knowing their own fate, presumably after death. Such concerns are more in line with those of proto-orthodox texts like the Greek Apocalypse of Peter, also modeled on the Synoptic little apocalypse, but transformed from a description of the

81. Uwe-Karsten Plisch is wrong to say that lines 1–3 and 4–5 are unrelated. Knowing oneself means to recognize the fact that the kingdom is within; failing to know oneself is to lack the kingdom. *The Gospel of Thomas: Original Text with Commentary,* tr. Gesine Schenke Robinson (Stuttgart: Deutsche Bibelgesellschaft, 2008), pp. 43–44.

"end of the age" to an account of "life after death"—the fate of souls in the realms of the blessed and damned.

It is striking that in the Gospel of Thomas Jesus' response redirects the question, away from the issue of personal destiny and the temporality that it implies (the postmortem experience of the believer). To know the "end" one has to know the "beginning." The end, in fact, is not a new beginning, as the disciples mistakenly think. It is a return to the original beginning, which encapsulates the end. Those who recognize the beginning are already at the end; they have achieved the goal. That is to say, the end is not a cataclysmic break in history, as in apocalyptic eschatology, or the future fate of the soul, as in proto-orthodox transformations of that idea. It is instead a return to the beginning.

It is important to note that "the beginning" for this author is present. It "is." The one who understands this beginning—who knows the primordial condition—is still in the present, and yet experiences the return to Eden. Such a one "will not taste death." Since this final clause recalls saying 1, it should be clear that those who understand the secret sayings of Jesus are those who understand that the beginning is the end and so have achieved the Edenic existence of the kingdom. As saying 49 later expresses the matter: "You will find the kingdom; for you are from it and to it you will return."[82] DeConick has provided a clear exposition of saying 18: "It is implied by this dialogue that the community previously has misunderstood the End to refer to the eschatological renewal of creation through cosmic endings, rather than the mystical renewal of creation and the original Adam through encratic practice and personal transformation."[83]

It is true that even later proto-orthodox thinkers could stress the return to the beginning at the end, as seen, for example, in the comments of Origen:

> Seeing, then, that such is the end, when "all enemies shall have been subjected to Christ," when "the last enemy shall be destroyed, that is death," and when "the kingdom shall be delivered up to God and the Father by Christ to whom all things have been subjected," let us, I say, from such an end as this, contemplate the beginning of things. For the end is always like the beginning; as therefore there is one end of all things, so we must understand that there is one beginning of all things, and as there is one end of many things, so from one beginning arise many differences and varieties, which in their turn are restored . . . to one end, which is like the beginning." (*On First Principles*, 1.6.2)[84]

---

82. It may be worth noting that although the polemic is directed in part against an apocalyptic notion—even if modified in the direction of personal eschatology—the notion that Endzeit gleicht Urzeit—is central to Jewish apocalyptic thought, as recognized as early as Hermann Gunkel (*Schöpfung und Chaos in Urzeit und Endzeit: eine religionsgeschichtliche Untersuchung über Gen. 1 und Ap. Joh. 12*; Göttingen: Vandenhoeck and Ruprecht, 1895).

83. *Original Gospel of Thomas*, p. 102.

84. Trans. G. W. Butterworth, *Origen on First Principles* (Gloucester, MA: Peter Smith, 1973).

But even here "the end" is an apocalyptic event, not a present reality. The polemic of the saying in Thomas is especially stark in comparison with the apocalyptic sayings of Jesus found in the Synoptic tradition. In Mark 9:1, in particular, the disciples "will not taste death" until they see that the apocalyptic events of cosmic upheaval transform their world. How different that is from the disciples of Thomas, who "will not taste death"—period. For the kingdom is not a future physical event to come to earth. It is within those who come to understand the secret teachings of Jesus and, thereby, come to know themselves.

Saying 37

Jesus' anti-apocalyptic eschatology, and the disciples' failure to appreciate it, are continued in saying 37. Once again the disciples ask a future-oriented question, in this instance involving not their own fate so much as the return of Jesus: "When will you appear to us and when shall we see you?" And once again Jesus corrects the question by his response: the full revelation of divine truth does not come from something that Jesus will do, such as return in glory. It comes from something his disciples do: escape the material trappings of this world ("when you strip naked without being ashamed and take off your clothes . . . and stamp on them"). For this Gospel, Jesus is not one who "will be" seen; he is already here, in this world, for those who already see: "Split a piece of wood: I am there. Lift up the stone and you will find me there" (saying 77). The disciples will "see" Jesus ("the son of the Living One")[85] when they escape the material trappings of this world.

Valantasis argues that the "clothes" of this passage represent social encumbrances,[86] but they are better understood as the materiality of the body, as more widely interpreted. And even though the metaphor of "stripping" may call to mind baptismal language, as stressed by J. Z. Smith, others such as April DeConick and Jarl Fossum have noted that a range of Jewish and Christian texts use the image to refer to the removal of the body ("stripped").[87] Trampling on the body, then, refers to physical renunciation, for example in the kinds of ascetic lifestyle otherwise endorsed by the Gospel. Moreover, behaving like "little children" by stripping without shame may recall saying 18 and the need to return to "the

---

85. Richard Valantasis makes the interesting argument that by stripping off their clothes and trampling on them the disciples will see (i.e., come to know) not Jesus, but others of Jesus' followers. His reasoning is that since Jesus is described as "the living one" ("the living Jesus" of the prologue) then he could not also be the "son of the living one." His son must, then, be one like him: his followers. *The Gospel of Thomas* (London: Routledge, 1997), p. 113. It is probably better, though, to see the Son of the Living One as "the Son of God," since, after all, the Father too is described as a "living one," as in Saying 3 ("sons of the living father").

86. *Gospel of Thomas*, p. 113.

87. Jonathan Z. Smith, "The Garments of Shame," *HR* 5 (1966): 217–38; April DeConick and Jarl Fossum, "Stripped Before God: A New Interpretation of Logion 37 in the Gospel of Thomas," *VC* 45 (1991): 123–50.

beginning," that is, to human existence before the Fall. Returning to a prelapsarian state means enjoying the life of Eden; it is worth noting that Adam and Eve are described in Gen. 2:25 as naked and not ashamed. Only after eating the fruit do they cover themselves (3:7, because they were "afraid"). In other Christian texts, such as the *Liber Graduum* (341:2–5), Adam and Eve are described, prior to eating the fruit, as naked nursing babies who are not ashamed.[88]

In short, for saying 37, the disciples err in eagerly awaiting the physical return of Jesus. What matters is not an imminent parousia but a new way of life. Jesus' followers must escape their bodily constraints and the material trappings of this world in order to "see" Jesus as he really is, and thus return to an Edenic existence. The material world will not be destroyed by a decisive act of God in a future cataclysmic event; the world is to be escaped through renunciation of the body.

Saying 51

The disciples continue to demonstrate their lack of understanding in the opening question of saying 51: "When will the repose of the dead take place? And when will the new world come?" As Valantasis has pointed out, the question not only works against the tenor of the entire document—presupposing precisely the apocalyptic view that the author is at pains to polemicize against—it also fails to grasp the teaching of the immediately preceding saying 50, where "repose" is not for the dead but for the living. Once again Jesus corrects their misunderstanding: the "new world" is not a future event; it is already present for those who understand the teachings of Jesus and have achieved self-knowledge. The Kingdom is within those who know themselves.

Here, as in the preceding sayings, it is clear that we are witnessing developments within the Thomasine community as it shifts from an apocalyptic view inherited from other, earlier Christian traditions, and begins, then, to polemicize against them, stressing that the Kingdom is available in the here and now. DeConick has plausibly argued that the shift in the community's thinking occurred in stages, evident in the probable (though hypothetical) transmission history of this particular saying. Originally, in her view, the disciples asked "when will the resurrection [ΑΝΑΣΤΑΣΙΣ] of the dead occur?" This, then, was an apocalyptic view, that came to be displaced. But in a second stage the community's eschatology became personal, rather than apocalyptic, and as a result the question itself was changed: "When will the repose [ΑΝΑΠΑΥΣΙΣ—different in only three letters] of the dead occur?" Jesus' reply makes even better sense now: repose is present among those who know themselves (unlike the uncomprehending disciples) and so have recreated Eden in a prelapsarian state.[89]

---

88. See DeConick, *Original Gospel of Thomas*, 116.

89. Ibid., p. 183. Plisch argues that the text as we have it originally read ANASTASIS—resurrection—but was accidentally altered through scribal error. *Gospel of Thomas*, p. 132.

It is worth recalling in this connection that there are clear indications elsewhere that the question of when the resurrection will occur was hotly debated. Colossians and Ephesians both suggest that the resurrection of believers has, in some spiritual sense, already happened, a view evidenced as well, earlier, by Paul's opponents in Corinth. This is a view directly opposed by 2 Timothy (2:18). But it is adopted in modified form in the teachings of Paul's false followers, Demas and Hermogenes, in the Acts of Paul ("the resurrection which [Paul] says is to come . . . has already taken place in the children, and that we rise again, after having come to the knowledge of the true God," ch. 14), and in yet another form in the Gospel of Philip: "People who say they will first die and then arise are wrong. If they do not receive the resurrection first, while they are alive, they will receive nothing when they die" (Gospel of Philip 73).[90] This final perspective compares favorably with the view staked out in the Gospel of Thomas. The "repose" and the "new world" are not to be expected in the future: they have already come, "but for your part, you do not know it."

Saying 113

The disciples' eschatological misunderstanding comes to final expression in the climactic question of saying 113: "When will the kingdom come?" As already mentioned, the saying provides a closing bracket for the opening of saying 3, so that the Gospel begins and ends with the question of the kingdom, emphasizing in both places that it will not arrive in some undisclosed time in the future: "It will not come by waiting for it." Nor will it be a physical entity here on earth: "They will not say, 'Look, here it is,' or 'Look, it is there.'" Instead the kingdom is here and now, even though it is hidden from those who lack knowledge. For this Gospel, "knowledge" involves both an understanding of these secret teachings of Jesus and the self-knowledge that this understanding brings. And so, "the kingdom of the Father is spread out upon the earth, and people do not see it."

The polemic against the apocalyptic view here is extended through the use of familiar apocalyptic images. And so, for example, in the apocalyptic discourse of Mark 13:21–23 and Matt. 24:23–26 there are also false teachers who proclaim "Look, here is the Christ!" or "Look, there he is!" In this earlier conception the true followers are not to believe these false proclamations, for the end will not come with the physical appearance of Jesus as a human here on earth. It will come with cataclysmic signs in the heavens, when the sun grows dark, the moon fails to give its light, and the stars fall from the sky. That is when the "Son of Man" will come on the clouds of heaven and send out his angels to collect his chosen ones.

For the Gospel of Thomas nothing could be farther from the truth. Here, false teachers are not false simply because they wrongly think Jesus will physically

90. Translation of Marvin Meyer, *The Nag Hammadi Scriptures* (New York: HarperCollins, 2007).

return to earth before the catastrophic end; they are false because they think there will be a catastrophic end. They are not wrong in advancing a faulty apocalyptic scenario; they are wrong in advancing any kind of apocalyptic scenario. The kingdom is not coming as a future event. For this Gospel it is experienced here and now among those who interpret and implement Jesus' sayings correctly and so know who they really are. The kingdom is already spread out on the earth. It is not coming at a future time to a specific place. It is available to all who "find the meaning of these words." The kingdom of God is not imminent; it is immanent.

CHAPTER NINE

Forgeries in Support of Paul and His Authority

Most of the literary forgeries we have considered to this stage have involved the teachings of Paul. There were, of course, other Christian teachers, already in the first century, who claimed to represent the "true" understanding of the emerging Christian tradition more adequately than Paul. It may not be surprising, then, to find that a number of literary forgeries arose in the period, alternatively championing or challenging Paul's authority. In this chapter we will consider forgeries produced in support of the "Apostle to the Gentiles"; in the chapter that follows we will look at forgeries that call his authority, and his message, into question.

Two of the forgeries that we will be considering in this chapter are controversial among investigators today, one because many scholars question whether it has anything to do with Paul, his message, and his authority (1 Peter), the other because, in the judgment of most scholars, it makes no obvious authorial claim and so cannot be thought of as forged (the Acts of the Apostles). I will advance reasons for thinking that both scholarly opinions are wrong: these books are very much concerned with salvaging the image and authority of Paul, and both are best understood as forgeries.

FIRST PETER

Scholarship on 1 Peter has advanced dramatically since 1976, when J. H. Elliott declared it the "exegetical step-child" of the New Testament.[1] By 2004 Eugene Boring could note that during the preceding quarter-century more than sixty commen-

1. "The Rehabilitation of an Exegetical Step-Child: 1 Peter in Recent Research," *JBL* 95 (1976): 243–54.

taries on the epistle had appeared in English and the major languages of Europe.[2] One of the hotly debated issues in the period involved the question of authorship, an issue that goes far back in the history of its modern investigation. Already in 1788 Semler, who did not deny the letter to Peter, indicated that the letter closely paralleled the teachings of Paul and could be seen as a Pauline "imitation."[3] It was another twenty years before the Petrine authorship of the book was first challenged by H. H. Cludius, who maintained that the attribution of the letter to Peter was the result of a textual corruption in 1:1, where an original ὁ πρεσβύτερος was altered to read Πέτρος ἀπόστολος.[4] As we will see, since Cludius's day others too have proposed different textual changes of 1:1 to explain that the attribution is mistaken.

Arguments for 1 Peter as a Forgery

It is widely held today that the book was not written by Simon Peter. Boring claims that this is the general opinion among critical scholars, outside the ranks of those who disallow forgery in the New Testament on general principle.[5] A number of arguments are typically advanced for pseudepigraphy, some of them stronger than others. Among the more subsidiary are the following. First, there is almost nothing to suggest that Christianity had spread in Peter's day throughout the provinces of Asia Minor named in 1:1, making it highly unlikely that he, the historical Peter, would have written to churches there; moreover other traditions notably do not associate Peter with Christians in the general region. Next, if Peter himself had written the letter, it is very hard indeed to explain that in his references to "Christ" he gives no indication that he was his companion throughout his ministry; in fact, he gives no indication whatsoever that he had any personal knowledge of Jesus or his teachings (not even in 5:1, as we will see). Moreover, rather than identifying himself as a companion of Jesus, the author indicates that he is a "presbyter" (5:1), an office otherwise not associated with Peter, who appears rather to have been a missionary-apostle. Relatedly, the book shows that at the time of its composition "presbyters" were running the church as episkopoi (5:1–5; ἐπισκοποῦντες, v. 2). There is no evidence of this kind of structured leadership of the churches during the lifetime of Peter, although obviously it became the model of Pauline churches by the time of the Pastorals, some decades after Peter's death. Furthermore, the author uses the term *Christian* (4:16) as if it were in established usage, even though it is otherwise not attested, for example in the writings of Paul, until closer to the end of the first century, in the book of Acts.

2. M. Eugene Boring, "First Peter in Recent Study," *WW* 24 (2004): 358.

3. "One might call this an imitation of Paul, without begrudging it the name." (Imitationem Pauli liceret dicere, sine inuidia nominis.) *Paraphrasis in Epistolam I. Petri*, praef. Abs. 3; quoted in Ferdinand-Rupert Prostmeier, *Handlungsmodelle im ersten Petrusbrief* (Würzburg: Echer Verlag, 1990), p. 31 n. 66.

4. H. H. Cludius, *Uransichten des Christenthums nebst Untersuchungen über einige Bücher des neuen Testaments* (Altona: Hermann Heimart, 1808), pp. 296–302.

5. "First Peter in Recent Study," p. 359.

This final point relates to a much stronger argument against Petrine authorship. By the time this letter was written, it had become commonplace for followers of Jesus to suffer persecution "as a Christian," simply "for the name" (4:12–17). There is nothing to suggest that the mere name "Christian" was ground for persecution in apostolic times. Even in the later accounts of the book of Acts, there is no instance in which followers of Jesus suffered persecution "for the name." On the contrary, Christians are punished for what is recognized, correctly or incorrectly, as wrongdoing. The same can be said about the earliest instance we have of imperial opposition to the Christians under Nero, the persecution that, traditionally, is thought to have led to Peter's own martyrdom. As Tacitus makes abundantly clear, Nero rounded up the Christians of Rome and subjected them to brutal treatment and execution not because they were Christians per se, but because of arson (a false charge, according to Tacitus; *Annals* 15.44). It is not until we get to the famous correspondence of Pliny with Trajan around 112 CE that we find any instance of Christians persecuted simply for bearing the name Christian (Book 10). By Pliny's time it was known that calling oneself "Christian" meant something. Specifically it meant refusing to reverence and sacrifice to the gods of the state. That is why Pliny employed a simple device to decide whether persons who denied being Christian were telling the truth: all they had to do was repeat prayers he provided and offer incense to the image of the emperor. Those who refused to do so hung on to the name Christian; those who complied forsook the name. This does not mean that we can facilely locate 1 Peter to the time of Pliny. It simply means that the recognition that the name Christian was ground for persecution cannot be located anywhere near the lifetime of Peter himself. When the recognition arose afterward is uncertain, but it probably happened sometime between Nero and Trajan, and the book is accordingly best located to that period.

Supporting evidence comes in the argument advanced most convincingly by C. Hunzinger, that the veiled reference to Rome in the epithet "Babylon," named as the place from which the author writes (5:13), makes sense only after 70 CE, years after Peter's death.[6] That "Babylon" must refer to Rome is shown by the facts that (1) elsewhere in both Jewish and Christian texts (Rev. 14:8; 16:19; 17:5; 18:2, 10, 21) "Babylon" is a codeword for Rome, and (2) Peter is never associated in any of our traditions with either Mesopotamia or Egypt (where there was another Babylon), whereas he is frequently connected with Rome, indeed as its first bishop.

Other nicknames for Rome exist, however (Kittim, Edom). Why has the author chosen "Babylon"? As Hunzinger notes, the reasons for the identification become clear in light of Jewish apocalyptic texts. Passages such as 4 Ezra 3.1–2, 28, 31, and Syr. Baruch 11.1 probably show that Rome was thought of as (the new)

6. Claus-Hunno Hunzinger, "Babylon als Deckname für Rom. und die Datierung des 1 Petrusbriefes," in Henning Graf Reventlow, ed., *Gottes Wort und Gottes Land* (Göttingen: Vandenhoeck & Ruprecht, 1965), pp. 67–77.

Babylon because it too destroyed Jerusalem and, especially, the Temple. In other words, it is the catastrophe of 70 CE, in comparison with 586 BCE, that makes the identification both obvious and palpable. So too we find in the Sybilline oracles that Nero flees "from Babylon" (5.143), and later in the same oracle we find Babylon directly connected to the land of Italy, again because of the destruction of the Temple in 70 CE.[7] And so Hunzinger's conclusion: "The unanimity of the Jewish supporting data forces the conclusion that *the designation of Rome as Babylon came about under the impression of the renewed destruction of the Jerusalem temple*."[8] 1 Peter, therefore, could not have been written prior to 70 CE and, as a result, could not have been written by Peter, who apparently died years earlier.[9]

There is an even more compelling reason for thinking that Peter did not write this letter. In all likelihood, Peter could not write.

Peter as Illiterate

In his now-classic study of ancient literacy, William Harris gave compelling reasons for thinking that at the best of times in antiquity only 10 percent or so of the population was able to read.[10] By far the highest portion of readers was located in urban settings. Widespread literacy like that enjoyed throughout modern societies requires certain cultural and historical forces to enact policies of near universal, or at least extensive, education of the masses. Prior to the industrial revolution, such a thing was neither imagined nor desired. As Meir Bar Ilan notes: "Literacy does not emerge in a vacuum but rather from social and historical circumstances."[11]

Moreover, far fewer people in antiquity could compose a writing than could read, as shown by the investigations of Raffaella Cribiore, who stresses that reading and composition were taught as two distinct skills and at different points of the ancient curriculum. Learning even the basics of reading was a slow and arduous process, typically taking some three years and involving repeating "endless drills" over "long hours": "In sum, a student became accustomed to an incessant

---

7. See the discussion of the Sibyllina on pp. 508–19.

8. "Das einhellige jüdische Belegmaterial zwingt zu dem Schluß, daß *die Bezeichnung Roms als Babylon unter dem Eindruck der erneuten Zerstörung des Jerusalemer Tempels zustande gekommen ist.*" P. 76, italics his. Neugebauer and Thiede have called Hunzinger's view into question; Ferdinand-Rupert Prostmeier shows why their objections are not convincing (*Handlungsmodelle*, pp. 127–28, n. 327).

9. The argument is most recently embraced by Lutz Doering, "Apostle, Co-Elder, and Witness of Suffering: Author Construction and Peter Image in First Peter," in Jörg Frey et al., eds., *Pseudepigraphie und Verfasserfiktion*, pp. 645–81, who also points out that since the claim to authorship is false, there is no reason to think the book was actually written from Rome, any more than that it had to be written to the churches of Asia Minor. It was instead written by a later Christian who "knows" that Peter was closely associated with the Roman church.

10. William Harris, *Ancient Literacy* (Cambridge, MA: Harvard University Press, 1989).

11. Meir Bar-Ilan, "Illiteracy in the Land of Israel in the First Centuries CE," in *Essays in The Social Scientific Study of Judaism and Jewish Society*, ed. Simcha Fishbane et al. (Hoboken, NJ: Ktav, 1992), vol. 2, 47.

gymnastics of the mind."[12] These kinds of "gymnastics" obviously required extensive leisure and money, neither of which could be afforded by any but the wealthy classes. Most students did not progress beyond learning the basics of reading, to the second level of grammar. Training in composition came only after these early stages, and most students did not get to that point:[13] "the ability to articulate one's thoughts in writing was achieved only when much literature had been digested."[14] Especially difficult, and requiring additional training, was acquiring literacy in a second language. Indeed, as, Cribiore points out, "bilingualism did not correspond to biliteracy."[15]

All of these points bear closely on the question of whether an Aramaic-speaking fisherman from rural Galilee could produce a refined Greek composition such as 1 Peter. But before pressing that question, we should consider the issue of literacy specifically in Roman Palestine, a matter pursued most convincingly in studies by Bar-Ilan and Catherine Hezser.[16]

Bar-Ilan begins his analysis by referring to cross-cultural studies that have demonstrated that literacy rates are closely tied to broader social and cultural factors. Urban societies are always more literate than rural. Moreover, low birth rates, low population growth, and low life expectancy all relate to low literacy rates, and for good reason. With respect to life expectancy, for example: the use of the written word positively affects a society's hygiene, infant care, agricultural practices, and so on, all of which play a vital role in longevity. And so, for example, the more illiterate societies always suffer the highest rates of infant mortality.

Turning to hard historical evidence for ancient Israel, Bar-Ilan notes that the Talmud allows for towns where only one person could read in the synagogue (*Soferim* 11:2). Since all synagogues that have been discovered can accommodate more than fifty people, we are probably looking at literacy rates, in these places, at about 1 percent. When this figure is tied to the fact that the land of Israel was 70 percent rural, and only 10 percent was "highly" urban, one can take into account all the sundry factors and crunch the numbers: "it is no exaggeration to say that the total literacy rate in the Land of Israel . . . was probably less than 3%." Most of this 3 percent would have been wealthy Jews living in the major cities.

Hezser has devoted the only full-length study to this question in her monograph *Jewish Literacy in Roman Palestine*.[17] She agrees with Bar-Ilan on his statisti-

---

12. Cribiore, *Gymnastics of the Mind*, p. 250.

13. Ibid. See also her earlier study, Raffaella Cribiore, *Writing, Teachers, and Students in Graeco-Roman Egypt* (Atlanta: Scholars Press, 1996). Among the other significant studies of ancient education in reading and writing, see esp. Teresa Morgan, *Literate Education in the Hellenistic and Roman Worlds* (Cambridge: Cambridge University Press, 1998).

14. P. 177.

15. P. 175.

16. Meir Bar-Ilan, "Illiteracy," pp. 46–61; Catherine Hezser, *Jewish Literacy in Roman Palestine* (Tübingen: Mohr Siebeck, 2001).

17. See the preceding note.

cal claims: total literacy in Palestine was probably around 3 percent; those who were literate were largely located in urban areas; some villages and towns had a literacy rate of lower than 1 percent. In this connection Hezser makes the striking historical observation that "the only literary works which can with certainty be attributed to Palestinian Jews of the first century C.E. are the writings of Josephus and the no longer extant works of his opponent Justus of Tiberias" (both of whom "received a Greek education and were influenced by Graeco-Roman writing").[18] Moreover, Hezser argues that "writing seems to have mostly—and perhaps almost exclusively—been used by the political, economic, and religious-intellectual elites in late Roman Palestine." Was the fisherman Simon-Peter in this august group?

Before pursuing that question, we should look at the related issue of the use of Greek in first-century Palestine. Hezser evaluates the extent to which Palestinian Jews may have been able to converse in Greek more generously than other more recent studies devoted to the question, as we will see in a moment. But even she points out that Josephus is the only Jew of Roman Palestine to indicate that he learned Greek, and she notes that Josephus himself indicates that he could not write literary Greek without assistance from Greek speakers (*Contra Apionem* 1.9). Moreover, Hezser admits that we do not know whether Josephus studied Greek before coming to Rome.[19] She later acknowledges that most Jews in Palestine would have had only "a rudimentary knowledge of Greek," which involved knowing "a few phrases to lead to a simple conversation."[20] That is a long way from being able to write a high-level Greek composition, especially in light of the fact that simple conversational Greek took no special training, whereas learning to read (even in one's own language) took years of hard work, and composition took years more. Louis Feldman notes that "Josephus's admission (*Contra Apionem* 1.50 [= 1.9]) that he needed assistance in composing the version in Greek of the Jewish War illustrates that few attained the competence in the language necessary for reading and understanding Greek literature."[21]

The most persuasive studies of the use of Greek in Galilee in particular have been produced by Mark Chancey, who shows that scholars who maintain that Greek was widely spoken in the first century have based their views on very slim evidence, in which Palestinian data from over a number of centuries have been generalized into claims about the use of Greek in Galilee in the first half of the first century.[22] There is, in fact, scant evidence that Greek was widely used outside of the major urban areas. People living in rural areas spoke almost exclusively Aramaic.

---

18. P. 426.

19. P. 91.

20. P. 243.

21. *Jew and Gentile in the Ancient World: Attitudes and Interactions from Alexander to Justinian* (Princeton: Princeton University, 1993), p. 19.

22. Mark Chancey, *Greco-Roman Culture and the Galilee of Jesus* (Cambridge: Cambridge University Press, 2005).

These and other studies have made it clear that there were few educated people in Palestine in the days of Peter. Those who did have the benefits of education would have been taught Hebrew to enable them to read the Torah, unless they came from a fabulously wealthy aristocratic family in a major city. These fortunate few would have made up the bulk of the 3 percent of Palestine who could read. Moreover, most of the 3 percent who could read could not compose a sentence or a paragraph. Most of those who could compose a paragraph could not compose an entire book. Most of those who could compose a book could not do so in a foreign language, Greek. Most of those who could do so, could not compose it in elegant Greek. Was Peter, a lower-class fisherman from rural Galilee, among that minuscule fraction of the Palestinian population who could compose books in elegant Greek? He was not wealthy. He would have had no time or resources for an education. Let alone an education in reading a foreign language. Let alone education in Greek composition. Acts 4:13 is probably right: Peter was illiterate.[23]

In pursuing this line of inquiry, we might ask what we can know about Peter as a person, prior to his becoming a disciple of Jesus. The answer is that we do not know much at all. The Gospels are consistent only in portraying him as a fisherman from the village of Capernaum in rural Galilee. We can assume that since he was a common laborer, he was not from the landed aristocracy; and since he was from rural Galilee, he would have spoken Aramaic. What can we say about his home "town" of Capernaum?

The historical and social insignificance of the place can be seen by the fact that it is not mentioned in any source, including the Hebrew Bible, prior to the writings of the New Testament. In the Gospels it is portrayed as a fishing village on the "sea" of Galilee (Matt. 4:13; 8:5; 11:23; 17:24; Mark 1:21; 2:1; 9:33; Luke 4:23, 31; 7:1; 10:15; John 2:12; 4:46; 6:17, 24, 59). It is sometimes called a πόλις, although, as we will see, that designation is certainly wrong. Josephus mentions it only because he fell off his horse nearby and was taken there (*Life* 72); he calls it, more accurately, a "village" (κώμη). The rabbinic literature mentions it as a place of the minim (*Midr. Qoh.* 1.8.4; 7.26.3). There is no other literary evidence about the first-century town.

Most archaeologists associate it with Tel Hum, the ruins of which were discovered in 1838 by the American biblical archaeologist Edward Robbins, and identified as Capernaum in 1866 by the British engineer Charles Wilson. Based on the archaeological evidence, the best estimates place the population at around a thousand in the first century.[24] There is no suggestion from the material remains

---

23. Contrast the bizarre view set forth in the Louw/Nida, *Lexicon* *, 27.23, who reject the definition of "illiterate" for *agrammatos* in Acts 4:13: "this is highly unlikely in view of the almost universal literacy in NT times, and especially as the result of extensive synagogue schools." An understanding of ancient society and culture would go a long way in correcting this kind of mistake, even in such basic fields as lexicography.

24. James Strange in IDBSup., p. 140. Jonathan Reed estimates six hundred to fifteen hundred inhabitants in the time of Jesus (*Archaeology and the Galilean Jesus: A Re-examination of the Evidence,*

that it was a center of high intellectual activity. In fact, there is no evidence of intellectual life at all. As Jonathan Reed has pointed out, archaeologists have turned up no evidence of public buildings, such as shops or storage facilities. The local market must have been held in tents or booths in open unpaved public areas. The town was not built on any major international trade route; the Roman roads in the area are from the second century. There are no structures or materials associated with social elites (e.g., plaster surfaces, decorative frescoes, marble, mosaics, red ceramic roof tiles). The houses were constructed of rough stone basalt built without "the benefit of a skilled craftsman's techniques or tools," with insulation provided by mud or clay and smaller stones packed in the interstices, and thatched roofs.[25] There are no material remains of anything pagan; there are no inscriptions from the first century. Reed concludes that the population was "predominantly illiterate."

In short, Capernaum was a rather isolated and relatively unknown Jewish village in the backwaters of rural Galilee, with no evidence of any gentile presence. Its inhabitants were very poor. It was certainly not a polis, just an impoverished village.[26] If Bar-Ilan and Hezser are right that villages in rural Galilee could well have had literacy rates lower than 1 percent, maybe eight to ten persons in town would have been able to read in Peter's day. Or is this too generous? In any event, the handful of literate persons would have been the wealthiest and best-connected persons in the village. Simon Peter, on the other hand, was simply one of the local fishermen. Those in town who could read would be able to read Hebrew and would have spoken Aramaic. Could any of these handful compose a sentence? It is possible—but an entire book? It seems unlikely. Could they have composed a book in Greek? Almost certainly not. In highly literate Greek? It completely strains credibility.

What can we say, on the other hand, about the author of 1 Peter? It is widely noted that the language of the book is that of an educated Greek-speaking author. J. H. Elliott notes that the polished Greek style "[reveals] numerous traces

---

Harrisburg, PA: Trinity Press International, 2000, p. 152). The wildly inaccurate claims of Bellarmino Bagatti ("Caphernaum" *MB* [1983] 9) that Capernaum was a city of two thousand to fifteen thousand inhabitants, "as urbanized and urbane as anywhere else in the empire," were based, as Jonathan Reed has pointed out, on the erroneous estimates of Eric Meyers and James Strange, *Archaeology, the Rabbis and Early Christianity* (Nashville, TN: Abingdon, 1981), p. 58 (which Strange later modified as noted above), themselves based on the size of the town as described by Charles Wilson's report in 1871 [!] that the area of the ruins covered 30 hectares. In fact, the area is no more than 6 hectares, and is not as densely populated as Meyers and Strange originally thought (four hundred to five hundred persons per hectare).

25. Reed, *Archaeology*, p. 159.

26. The indication of Luke 7:1–10 that a centurion, with his century, was stationed in town is completely fictitious. Sometimes it is thought that since Zebedee had "hired servants" fishing must have been a relatively lucrative profession in Capernaum (Mark 1:16–20). But the reference is thoroughly literary. There is no reason to suspect that Mark ever visited the place on a tour of the holy land to note its affluence. Moreover, these "hired servants" may just as well have been very low-level peasants eking out a hand-to-mouth existence.

of literary refinement"[27] and "displays abundant affinities in vocabulary and style to classical writings, evidencing 'rhetorical competence' and 'literary refinement' of the author."[28] P. Achtemeier notes that, among other things, the author uses anaphora for parallel phrases; he employs antithetic as well as synthetic parallelism; he uses coordinate parallel expressions in which the first is negative, the second is positive, so as to stress a particular idea; in some places he produces a rhythmic structure and occasional long periods.[29] Twice the author uses εἰ with the optative, a refinement not found among most *koine* writers (3:14, 17). It seems scarcely possible that this is the writing of an Aramaic-speaking peasant from the hinterlands.

A related issue is the author's use of the Septuagint. Jews in rural Palestine familiar with Scripture would have heard it read in Hebrew. The vast majority of them would not have the opportunity or ability to study it on the page. The author of 1 Peter, on the other hand, is intimately familiar with the Jewish Scriptures. Apart from the quotation in 4:8, which is sometimes recognized as a direct translation of Proverbs 10:12 from the Hebrew,[30] the author invariably cites Scripture according to the Septuagint. This too is barely conceivable in a Galilean fisherman raised to speak Aramaic.

It is commonly argued that since Peter became a missionary to foreign lands after Jesus' death (Gal. 2:7; 1 Cor. 9:5), he must have picked up a knowledge of Greek in his travels. The reality, however, is that we simply have no way of knowing how Peter engaged in his missionary work. Did he use an interpreter? Did he learn enough Greek to communicate more easily? Even if he did so, that would scarcely qualify him to write a highly literary composition. Everyone in the Greek-speaking world could speak Greek. But only those with extensive training could learn to read. And only those who went past the first few years of training could learn how to compose a writing. Training in composition came only after everything else was mastered at the end of one's time with a grammatikos: alphabet, syllables, writing one's name, copying, reading scriptio continua, studying the poets, and so forth. It took years, plus a good deal of native talent, to become proficient. When exactly would Peter have found the time and resources to go back to school? And what evidence is there from the ancient world that *anyone* received a primary and secondary education precisely as an adult? To my knowledge there is no evidence at all.

In combination with all the other evidence indicated at the outset, there is really only one viable conclusion. The book of 1 Peter was not written by Peter, but by someone falsely claiming to be Peter. It is, in short, a forgery.[31]

---

27. John H. Elliott, "Peter, First Epistle of," *ABD* V, 269–78.

28. *1 Peter: A New Translation and Commentary* (New York: Doubleday, 2000), p. 64.

29. Paul Achtemeier, *1 Peter*, Hermeneia (Minneapolis: Fortress Press, 1996), p. 3.

30. Prostmeier, *Handlungsmodelle*, pp. 1–32.

31. I am completely unpersuaded by Karl Matthias Schmidt, *Mahnung und Erinnerung im Maskenspiel: Epistolographie, Rhetorik und Narrativik der pseudepigraphen Petrusbriefe* (Freiburg: Herder, 2003),

Attempts to Explain Away the Forgery

There have been numerous attempts to exonerate the author of 1 Peter of the charge that he wrote to mislead his reader into thinking he was Peter. As seen already, as far back as 1808 Cludius argued that 1:1 involved a textual corruption, where "the presbyter" was altered to read "the apostle Peter." A somewhat more interesting emendation was suggested by K. M. Fisher, who proposed that the book was originally written as a (Deutero-)Pauline epistle: rather than Πέτρος in 1:1 the author wrote Παῦλος.[32] This would make sense of the Pauline character of the letter otherwise, about which I will be speaking momentarily, although it would not get the author off the forger's hook, as in either case he would be claiming to be someone other than who he was.

Sometimes it is argued that Peter is the authority behind the letter, who commissioned someone else to write it for him. L. Goppelt and (many) others have suggested that it was written (ultimately) by Silvanus[33]; J. G. Eichhorn postulated that it was Mark[34]; Seufert put forward the author of Acts[35]; and Streeter, going yet further out on the precarious limb, proposed Ariston of Smyrna.[36] The one thing all of these guesses have in common is that they are based on virtually no evidence whatsoever. In addition, quite apart from the speculation involving specific names, we have already seen that there is nothing to suggest that it was an acceptable practice—or even a practice at all—for an "author" to have someone else write a work for him.[37] If he did commission such a work, this other person would be the author.

More commonly scholars have provided a toned-down version of the "commission" theory and suggested that the style, and possibly to some degree the substance, of the letter was provided by a secretary. More often than not, the secretary is named as Silvanus, in light of the conclusion of 5:12: διὰ Σιλουανοῦ ὑμῖν τοῦ πιστοῦ ἀδελφοῦ, ὡς λογίζομαι, δι' ὀλίγων ἔγραψα. Brox notes several of the problems with this identification of the Greek stylist behind the letter. For one

---

recapitulated in K. M. Schmidt, "Die Stimme des Apostels erheben: Pragmatische Leistungen der Autorenfiktion in den Petrusbriefen," in Jörg Frey et al., eds., *Pseudepigraphie und Verfasserfiktion*, pp. 625–44, that 1 Peter was meant to be a "fictional" letter. So far as we know it was never read that way, and there are no clear indications that the author meant for it to be taken that way—one of the major criteria for fictions over forgeries, in Schmidt's own reckoning. Decisive for Schmidt is 1 Peter 5:1, μάρτυς τῶν τοῦ Χριστοῦ παθημάτων, which he reads as meaning not that Peter saw the passion, but that he had been martyred. And if he was martyred, he must not be writing this letter! But throughout the book of Acts, as we will see, Peter is repeatedly referred to as a "μάρτυς" to Jesus, while still very much alive.

32. H.-M. Schenk and K. M. Fischer, *Einleitung in die Schriften des NT* (Berlin: Evangelische Verlagsanstalt, 1978), vol. 1. 199–203.

33. *A Commentary on 1 Peter* (Grand Rapids, MI: Eerdmans, 1993), pp. 14–15.

34. *Einleitung in das Neue Testament* (Leipzig: Weidmannischen, 1810), pp. 617–18.

35. "Das Verwandtschaftsverhältnis des ersten Petrusbriefs und Epheserbriefs," *ZWT* (1881): 379–80.

36. *The Primitive Church* (New York: Macmillan, 1929), pp. 136–39.

37. See pp. 218–22.

thing, transferring responsibility for the wording of the letter to Silvanus does not actually solve the problem of the Greek, since he too was an Aramaic-speaking Jew from Palestine (Acts 15:22). Moreover, if he did compose the letter, then, once again, it is he, rather than Peter, who was its real author. But even more, it is implausible to think that Silvanus wrote the letter, given his self-praise, then, in 5:12, and his reference, to himself, as having written the letter "through" himself. But even more important, as is now widely recognized, to write a letter διά someone is not to use that person as a secretary but as the letter carrier. 5:12 is not indicating that Silvanus composed the letter but that he took it to its destination.[38]

The ultimate problem with this view, however, is the one I dealt with at length in the preceding chapter. There is virtually nothing to support the so-called secretary hypothesis, which instead of ancient evidence rests on scholarly speculation. And one should always try to think through how, exactly, the hypothesis is supposed to have worked in a specific instance. In the case of 1 Peter, Peter himself could not have dictated this letter in Greek to a secretary any more than he could have written it in Greek. To do so would have required him to be perfectly fluent in Greek, to have mastered rhetorical techniques in Greek, and to have had an intimate familiarity with the Jewish Scriptures in Greek. None of that is plausible. Nor can one easily think that he dictated the letter in Aramaic and the secretary (Silvanus or anyone else) translated it into Greek. The letter does not read like a Greek translation of an Aramaic original, but as an original Greek composition with Greek rhetorical flourishes. Moreover the letter presupposes the knowledge of the Greek Old Testament, so the person who composed the letter (whether orally or in writing) must have known the Scriptures in Greek.

Given the lack of evidence for the use of secretaries in the ways needed for Peter to stand as the ultimate authority behind the letter, one is left having to make a choice. Which view is more probable, historically? A scenario that does not have any known analogy (Peter asking someone else to write the treatise in his name in a different language) or a scenario that has a very large number of analogies, since it happened all the time? Forgeries happened all the time. Surely that is the best explanation for the letter.

The Function of the Forgery

Apart from the name "Peter" at the outset of the letter and the reference to Rome ("Babylon") at the end, there is nothing in the book of 1 Peter to tie

38. Most recently see Lutz Doering, "Apostle, Co-Elder, and Witness of Suffering: Author Construction and Peter Image in First Peter," in Jörg Frey et al., eds., *Pseudepigraphie und Verfasserfiktion*, pp. 645–81. In other Christian writings from about the same time it is clear that writing "through" someone meant that the person carried the letter. Thus, decisively, Ign. Rom. 10. 1, Phil. 11.2, Smyr 12.1, Polyc-Phil. 14.1, and even Acts 15:22–23—where again Silas/Silvanus is designated as the letter carrier. Did the author of 1 Peter know this tradition of Silas and reemploy it here? Thus Harnack, *Die Chronologie der altchristlichen Literatur bis Eusebius* (Leipzig: J. C. Hinrichs, 1897–1904), 1. 459.

it specifically to the Petrine tradition. This makes the book decidedly different from all the other canonical books we have looked at so far, the Deutero-Pauline epistles that are clearly in trajectories that could trace themselves back to Paul, and 2 Peter, which goes out of its way to claim Petrine origins. In the case of 1 Peter, the authorial name is attached simply to provide apostolic credentials. There is nothing about the book itself that would make anyone think that it is Peter's in particular.

According to Galatians, Peter was the apostle-missionary to Jews (Gal. 2:8–9). But this book is not addressed to Jews, Peter's concern, but to gentiles. Thus 1:14 speaks of the "passions of your former ignorance" (a phrase hard to ascribe to Jews, but standard polemic against pagans); 1:18 refers to the readers as ransomed from the "futile manner of conduct passed down by their ancestors" (difficult to ascribe to Jews from a writer who sees Scripture as given by God); and most decisively, the author applies to his readers the words of Hosea 1:6, 9: "formerly you were not the people but now you are the people of God" (2:10). The author is speaking to converted pagans. [39] This is not the apostle to the Jews. And so, when he speaks of their "dispersion" in 1:1 he is not referring to the Jewish diaspora; these are Christians who are living away from their "true home" in heaven, temporarily.[40]

Moreover, there is nothing distinctive to Peter's views here, at least as these are known from the scant references to them in Paul, the only surviving author to mention Peter during his lifetime (e.g., Galatians 2). Nothing indicates that this author held to the ongoing importance and validity of the prescriptions of the Law: circumcision, kosher food regulations, Sabbath observance, Jewish festivals, for example. The significance of Scripture, for this author, is not that it provides guidelines for cultic activities in the community's life together. The "word of the Lord" is the gospel of Christ, not the Jewish Scriptures (1:25); the prophets looked forward to Christ and are fulfilled in him and in his new people the Christians (1:12; 2:6, 10); Scripture is important chiefly for its high ethical demands (3:8–12).

There are self-conscious epistolary conventions in the reference to the addressees in 1:1 and the closing greetings of 5:12–13. But both passages make the reader think of Paul, not Peter. The missionary sphere is Asia Minor, where Paul

---

39. The claim sometimes made (e.g., Elliott, "Peter, First Epistle of," *ABD* 5. 273) that since the author appeals to Jewish Scripture his readers must have been, or included, Jews overlooks the fact that gentiles in the church also used Scripture and that numerous writings, even in the New Testament, are directed to gentiles but use sophisticated modes of interpreting the "Old" Testament (cf. 1 Corinthians).

40. When Elliott argues in *Home for the Homeless: A Sociological Exegesis of 1 Peter, Its Situation and Strategy* (Philadelphia: Fortress, 1981) that the language of "resident alien" is to be taken literally as a description of the recipients, not figuratively in the sense of life in this world, apart from one's heavenly home, he makes some interesting sociohistorical points. But it is hard to believe that the author imagined all of his readers literally to be resident aliens wherever they happened to dwell. Would the letter not be read in churches with a variety of social groups present?

established churches but which is never associated in other traditions with Peter. The two persons mentioned at the end, Silvanus and Mark, are best known as Pauline associates (Silvanus: 2 Cor. 1:19; 1 Thess 1:1; 2 Thess 1:1; Acts 15:22–18:5; Mark: Col. 4:10; 2 Tim. 4:11: Phlm. 24).[41] The injunction to "greet one another with a kiss" is almost straight from Paul (Rom. 16:16; 1 Cor. 16:20; 2 Cor. 13:12; 1 Thess. 5:26) and occurs nowhere else.

The only possible bit of verisimilitude that might make a reader think of Peter is in 5:1, where the author claims to have been a witness of Christ's sufferings. As widely noted, however, this scarcely sounds like the Peter of the rest of the Christian tradition, at least as it has been handed down to us, who fled after Jesus' arrest, denied his Lord three times, and was notably absent from the crucifixion.[42] It may be germane that the book of Acts stresses Peter as a witness to Jesus, his death, and resurrection (1:8, 22; 2:32; 3:15; 5:32; 10:39, 41). Here too there is no sense that Peter actually observed Jesus suffer, so that there is no reason to suspect that is what the author of 1 Peter 5:1 had in mind either. But even more important, Peter in these other passages is not said to be uniquely qualified as a witness. In every instance he is simply one of the apostolic band who bear testimony to Jesus and the salvation he has brought. There is nothing about 1 Peter 5:1, then, that would make a reader think of Peter in particular from among the faithful band that bore witness to Christ. And this band includes not just the twelve apostles in Acts: Stephen too is called a μάρτυς (22:20) as, notably, is Paul himself (22:15; 26:16).

In view of all these considerations, the older claim of A. Jülicher and E. Fascher remains valid: "One can absolutely insist that if the first word 'Peter' were missing from our 'letter,' nobody would have guessed it might have been authored by Peter."[43] In fact, as already suggested above, everything in this letter instead sounds like Paul. This was recognized long ago by F. C. Baur and the "school" that he established. Far too often the view has been tarnished by the guilt of that association, as it was attached by Baur and his followers to his entire, complex, and now universally discounted theory of church history. But that attachment can itself be profitably abandoned without sacrificing all of the data that first brought

---

41. John Mark is connected with Peter in Acts 12–13; Silvanus could conceivably be thought of as loosely connected with Peter because of Acts 15. But this is very weak, since there he is connected with all the apostles, including Paul. Moreover, it is important to recall, as will be argued at greater length below, Acts too is invested in making links between Peter and Paul, and does so in no small measure by claiming that they had the same associates.

42. The one exception is the Coptic Apocalypse of Peter, which certainly postdates 1 Peter. See further the discussion on pp. 407–12.

43. "Man kann unbedingt behaupten, daß, wenn unserem 'Briefe' . . . das erste Wort *Petrus* fehlte, niemand auf die Vermutung, er sei von Petrus verfaßt, geraten sein würde." *Einleitung in das NT,* 7th ed. (Tübingen, 1931), pp. 192–93. I find Doering unpersuasive with regard to the point that the author is intent on painting a distinct portrayal of Peter ("Apostle, Co-Elder, and Witness of Suffering"). The allusions to Peter, if they exist at all outside of 1:1, are far too sparse and indeterminate.

it to mind. The Pauline character of 1 Peter stands out independently of the extravagant theories of the Tübingen school.[44]

It has nonetheless become virtually de rigueur to discount the Paulinisms of 1 Peter, as evidenced in such major commentaries as those of Goppelt, Achtemeier, and Elliott, and especially in such a full-length study as that of Jens Herzer.[45] Still, it should be pointed out that a book like Herzer's *Petrus oder Paulus* was perceived to be necessary precisely because 1 Peter does bear so many resemblances to a (deutero)Pauline letter, as we will see.

Herzer's lengthy analysis shows that the structure of the letter and the individual terms and phrases that it uses may sound like Paul, but they are not really like Paul. This is a fair enough observation, but it leads to a false conclusion, since the incongruity is precisely the point. If an author has his own point of view and wants to advance his own message, but at the same time wants to "sound" like someone else, he will use the characteristic words and phrases of the other, although obviously in his own sense. The result will be a book that on the surface sounds like that of the other author, but that underneath is quite different. That is why Ephesians and 2 Timothy seem both like and unlike Paul himself. On the surface there are numerous parallels to Paul's writings; dig deeper and they look odd by comparison. So too 1 Peter.

It is important in this connection to stress that no one is asking if Paul wrote 1 Peter. The question is whether the book sounds like Paul, and to pursue the question of why. The arguments that Herzer uses are precisely those that would be used to determine whether or not Paul was really the author of Colossians or 2 Thessalonians. But that is not the issue. Indeed, if 1 Timothy had Peter's name attached as the author, it would seem a lot less like one of Paul's writings than

---

44. Specifically, the views of Schwegler are not far off the mark: "[1 Peter is] the attempt of a Pauline author to mediate between the separate directions of Petrine and Pauline writers by putting into the mouth of Peter the witness to the orthodoxy of his fellow apostle Paul, a depiction, colored somewhat in a Petrine fashion, of the Pauline teaching. . . . We thus must recognize in the undeniably apologetic tendencies of this letter a historical situation, a historical motive, not from the apostolic, but from the post-apostolic era . . ." ("[1 Peter ist] der Versuch eines Pauliners, die getrennten Richtungen der Petriner und Pauliner dadurch zu vermitteln, dass dem Petrus ein Rechtgläubigkeitszeugnis für seinen Mitapostel Paulus, eine etwas petrinisch gefärbte Darstellung des paulinischen Lehrbegriffs in den Mund gelegt wird. . . . Wir haben also in der, nun einmal unleugbaren apologetischen Tendenz unseres Briefes eine historische Situation, ein historisches Motiv nicht der apostolischen, sondern der nachapostolischen Zeit zu erkennen") *Das nachapostolische Zeitalter* II, 24 (as quoted in Prostmeier, *Handlungsmodellen*, p. 27). The difference from the perspective I map out here will be clear. Unlike Baur, Schwegler, and others of their ilk, I do not propose a master plan that encompasses the entire sweep of early Christian history, including the sense that this entire history was divided between Paulinists and Petrines, the single greatest fault of the Tübingen Schule. On the contrary, I think the early Christian tradition was far more fragmented than the Baur thesis allows.

45. Goppelt, *Commentary*, 28–30; Achtemeier, *1 Peter* Hermeneia (Minneapolis: Fortress, 1996), 15–19; Elliott *1 Peter* Anchor Bible (New Haven, CT: Yale University Press, 2000), pp. 20–39. Jens Herzer, *Petrus oder Paulus? Studien über das Verhältnis des Ersten Petrusbriefes zur paulinischen Tradition* (Tübingen: Mohr Siebeck, 1998).

1 Peter does. As Eugene Boring has observed in his recent survey of "First Peter in Recent Study," the pendulum has swung too far in the wrong direction, away from recognizing the Pauline character of the book.[46]

The structure of the book itself, as William Schutter has observed, is Pauline, with names of the sender and receiver, a tripartite division of the letter, and the conclusion. It is not a slavish imitation of the Pauline letters, but the resemblances are palpable.[47] Yet more significant are the striking instances of important Pauline words and phrases and other features. The following list is meant to be suggestive rather than exhaustive.

- The mission field, in Asia Minor, as already noted, appears to be Paul's[48]
- ἀποκάλυψις 1:7, 13; 4:13 (the word appears thirteen times in the Pauline corpus, e.g., Rom. 2:5; 8:19; 1 Cor. 1:7; 2 Cor. 12:1, etc.)
- God judges all impartially according to their deeds 1:17 (cf. Rom. 2 and 2 Cor. 5:1)
- God raised Christ from the dead and "gave him glory" 1:21 (cf. Phil. 2:6–10)
- The gospel as the λόγος τοῦ θεοῦ 1:23 (cf. 1 Thess. 2:13)
- Christian teaching as "milk" 2:2 (cf. 1 Cor. 3:2)
- Giving oneself as a "sacrifice" 2:5 (cf. Rom. 12:1; Phil. 2:17)
- The quotation of Isa. 28:16 in 2:6 (I am laying in Zion a stone . . .) and of Isa. 8:14 in 2:8 ("a stone of stumbling"; for both see Rom. 9:33)
- The quotation of Hos. 2:25 in 2:10 (Rom. 9:25)
- Opposition to "desires" connected with sarx 2:11 (cf. Gal. 5:16, 24)
- "Be subject to every human institution" (2:13; cf. Rom. 13:1–7)
- The view of Christ's death as a substitutionary atonement, 2:24, 3:18 (this should not be thought of as a view shared by all early Christian writers with Paul; it is missing from the speeches of Acts—including Paul's—and from the Gospel of Luke[49])
- Dying to sin and living to righteousness 2:24 (Rom. 5:27–6:21)
- "Do not return evil for evil" 3:9 (Rom. 12:17; verbatim agreements)
- The "in Christ" formula 3:16; 5:10, 14 (in Paul, passim)
- Baptism as salvation 3:21 (cf. Rom. 6:1–6)
- Flesh and spirit applied to humans 4:6 (e.g., Rom. 8:5; Gal. 5:17)
- "The end of all things is at hand" 4:7 (cf. 1 Cor. 10:11)

---

46. Among older scholars who did not shy away from seeing the Pauline resonances of the book, see V. McNabb, "Date and Influence of the First Epistle of St. Peter," *Irish Ecclesiastical Record* 45 (1935): 596–613; F. W. Lewis, "Note on the Date of the First Epistle of Peter," *The Expositor* 5, 10 (1899): 319–20; W. Trilling, "Zum Petrusamt in NT," *ThQ* 151 (1971): 123–26; K. Kertelge, *Gemeinde und Amt im NT* (München: Kösel, 1972), p. 138.

47. William Schutter, *Hermeneutic and Composition in 1 Peter* (Tübingen: Mohr Siebeck, 1989).

48. For this point to stand, it scarcely matters that Paul is not recorded in Acts or the surviving letters as visiting all these provinces. He was known as the missionary to Asia Minor.

49. See Bart D. Ehrman, *The Orthodox Corruption of Scripture*, pp. 233–38.

- Preeminence of love 4:8 (1 Cor. 13; Gal. 5:14)
- Χάρισμα 4:10 (cf. 1 Cor. 12)
- Rejoicing in sufferings 4:13 (cf. 2 Cor. 6:10; 13:9 and generally 2 Corinthians, where Paul revels in his sufferings 2 Cor. 1:3–7; 4:7–12; 11:23–30)
- Suffering with Christ leads to glory 4:13 (cf. Rom. 8:17)
- And as noted, the conclusion in 5:12–14, including the references to Silvanus (cf. 2 Cor. 1:19; 1 Thess. 1:1; 2 Thess. 1:1); Mark (Phlm. 24; Col. 4:10; 2 Tim. 4:11); and the injunction to "Greet one another with a kiss" (Rom. 16:16; 1 Cor. 16:20; 2 Cor. 13:12; 1 Thess. 5:26)

Some of these words and phrases were, or became, "traditional stock." But some are distinctively Pauline ("in Christ" etc.). And there are so many of them. It is striking that other features of the letter resonate with the Pauline tradition known from the Deutero-Pauline letters:

- λυτρόω 1:18 (cf. Titus 2:14)
- The Haustafel of 2:18–3:7 (cf. Col. 3:18–4:6 and Eph. 5:22–6:9)
- Especially, within these instructions, the command for wives to be submissive 3:1, 5 (cf. 1 Tim. 2:11–15; Eph. 5:22; and the interpolation at 1 Cor. 14:34–35)
- The opposition to braided hair, gold, and costly clothes 3:3 (cf. 1 Tim. 2:9)
- Leaders are to oversee (ἐπισκοπέω) the flock 5:2 (cf. 1 Tim. 3:1, 2; Tit. 1:7);
- Διάβολος 5:8 (cf. Eph. 4:27; 6:11; 1 Tim. 3:6, 7, 11; 2 Tim. 2:26; 3:3; Tit. 2:3; but never in Paul)

There are simply too many Pauline parallels to be written off. They are scattered throughout the whole of this short letter. It is not a matter, as sometimes thought, of literary dependence on one or the other of the Pauline epistles (e.g., Romans and Ephesians).[50] This author is someone claiming to be Peter who is trying to sound like Paul. As Schenk and Fischer have stated the case, this author "actualizes for a new situation the Pauline heritage—and that in the name of Peter!"[51]

The counterarguments by those who refuse to see Pauline influences on the letter can be seen in their starkest form in the observation of Andreas Lindemann that the author of 1 Peter does not advance a view of justification by faith.[52] One could just as well argue, on the same ground, that 2 Corinthians is not Pauline.

---

50. See, e.g., Mitton, "The Relationship Between 1 Peter and Ephesians"; Kazuhioto Shimada, "Is 1 Peter Dependent on Ephesians? A Critique of C. L. Mitton," *AJBI* 17 (1991): 77–196; and K. Shimada; "Is 1 Peter Dependent on Romans?" *AJBI* 19 (1993): 87–137. These questions go all the way back to 1777 and J. D. Michaelis's claim that Peter had read Romans; so Herzer, *Petrus oder Paulus?* p. 5. For a negative judgment, see Achtemeier, *1 Peter*, pp. 15–19.

51. ". . . aktualisiert für eine neue Situation paulinisches Erbe—und das im Namen des Petrus!" Schenk and Fischer, p. 202.

52. Lindemann, *Paulus*, p. 258.

Paul Achtemeier too moves in the wrong direction, when he points out words and phrases of Paul not found in the letter ("flesh," "church," θλίψις, the old and new Adam, the body of Christ, righteousness by faith apart from the Law, the tension of Israel and the Church).[53] No one is claiming, or should claim, that the author of 1 Peter wanted to hit upon every Pauline theologoumenon in his brief letter. The author of the Pastoral epistles certainly did not do so, but one would be very hard pressed indeed to argue, on that ground, that he did not go out of his way to make his reader think that the letters were written by Paul. 1 Peter sounds much more like Paul than Titus does.

And it sounds much more like Paul than the Paul of Acts does. The Paul of Acts preaches to gentiles about the importance of Jesus without ever mentioning that his death was salvific. One could go a step farther. The Peter of 1 Peter sounds a lot more like Paul than the *Peter* of Acts does—even though Acts has as one of its overarching agendas to reconcile the two apostles theologically. The Peter of Acts does sound like the Paul of Acts (as opposed to the Paul of the undisputed letters); the Peter of 1 Peter sounds like the Paul of the letters (both undisputed and Deutero-). This is not necessarily because he happened to have access to the same letters of Paul that we have—although he may well have—but because however he inherited his Pauline traditions of Christology, soteriology, and ecclesiology, he used them, to good effect, to make the letter written by "Peter" sound like Paul.

This is not to say that the author lacked an agenda of his own. In fact there are distinctive features of the letter that make it clearly stand out from what now survive as the undisputed Pauline letters.[54] Although the many differences from the Pauline letters are interesting, it is important to stress again that this author was not trying to write a Deutero-Pauline letter, claiming to be Paul. He was writing a letter claiming to be Peter. But the letter, written in the name of Peter, sounds very much like a letter of Paul. So why did the author not simply claim to be Paul?

Reasons for the Forgery

The most widely proffered, but not fully convincing, explanation for why an author would claim to be Peter when writing like Paul is simply that he is trying to effect some kind of reconciliation between the two apostles, widely known to have quarreled publicly and widely thought to be at loggerheads about major theological and practical issues (as we will see at greater length in the next chapter). This

---

53. *1 Peter*, p. 18.

54. As some examples: somewhat oddly, the formulation that Christ "suffered" ὑπὲρ/περὶ ὑμῶν in 2:21; 3:18 never occurs in Paul (although Paul does indicate that Christ "died" for us Rom. 5:8; and for our sins in 1 Cor. 15:3.). In fact, Paul never uses πάσχω in reference to Christ. Christ as an "ἐπίσκοπος" or "ποίμην" 2:25 is never found in Paul; for this author, however, Christ is the chief Shepherd, and the leaders are to shepherd his flock (5:2–4). Possibly most striking, Christians are to continue living life "in the flesh" (4:1–2), a view Paul would have found either puzzling or downright offensive.

is the view expressed crisply, for example, by Wolfgang Trilling, who (without invoking Baur) stresses that the names used at the beginning and end of the letter are key. Peter himself was known to be a leading authority figure in the church; Mark and Silvanus were Paul's coworkers for the church of Asia Minor. And strikingly, all three were closely tied with the church in Jerusalem, whence their mission started. And so the letter is meant to effect a broad reconciliation of Paul with the other apostles and the Jerusalem church, and to show that these Jerusalem apostles embraced Paul's teachings, rather than rejected them.[55]

There is much to commend this view, as we will see. But the problem with it and with others of its ilk (going back to Baur) is that it refuses to consider the actual content of the letter of 1 Peter in order to explain its pseudepigraphic function. Surely this is not the best way to proceed. The subject matter of the letter must have some bearing on the reason it was written.

This was recognized by Norbert Brox in an important article that lamented the fact that so much effort had been placed in determining the authorship of 1 Peter and exploring its Paulinism without ever considering the main point of what the letter is actually about.[56] Oddly enough, whereas Brox provides a clear assessment of the content of the letter, he never circles back, in the article, to the question of why the letter should be written in the name of Peter in terms that sound like Paul. Earlier he had put forth a rather feeble argument that since the letter was written in Rome it was naturally attributed to the chief authority there, Peter. The association of Peter with Rome may indeed be significant, but there is no reason, if the ascription is false, to think that the alleged location of its origin is true: it may just as well be that since the letter was written by "Peter" it was said to be sent from Rome ("Babylon") because of Peter's close associations with the place. And we are still left with the question that Brox resolutely refuses to answer: Why Peter in particular? Why not Paul, also an authority on Roman soil? And is there really nothing in the substance of the letter, rather than the place of its origin, that makes sense of its Paulinisms?[57]

The letter is rich with themes and subthemes, but the one issue that ties together most of its sundry parts is the emphasis on suffering and endurance. The term πάσχω occurs more frequently in this short five-chapter epistle than in any other book of the New Testament—more than Luke-Acts combined, though

55. Wolfgang Trilling, "Zum Petrusamt im Neuen Testament: Traditionsgeschichtliche Überlegungen anhand von Matthäus, 1 Petrus und Johannes," *TQ* 151 (1971): pp. 123, 126.

56. "Situation und Sprache der Minderheit im ersten Petrusbrief," *Kairós* n.f. 19 (1977): 1–13.

57. Brox is precisely wrong when he argues, elsewhere, that it is anachronistic to imagine different forms of Christian faith belonging to one apostle or another (Peter, Paul, etc.) and correspondingly that an apostolic name would be used by ancient Christians to guarantee apostolic content ("Zur pseudepigraphischen Rahmung des ersten Petrusbriefes," *BZ* 19, 1975, 78–96). By no means is this view purely modern, as seen both from the New Testament (cf. "I am of Paul, I am of Apollos, I am of Cephas," 1 Cor. 1:12; or the conflict in Galatia) and from later writings such as the Pseudo-Clementines, as we will see in the next chapter.

suffering is a major concern there as well. For the author of 1 Peter, Christ suffered for the sake of others (2:21–24; 3:18), and his followers will follow in his steps and suffer as well (2:21; 4:1, 13). The believers' sufferings do not come from imperial authorities, so far as we can tell; these are to be obeyed as those who keep the public order (2:13–14). Instead, the opposition is unofficial and local, former friends and colleagues who are upset that, with their change of heart and lifestyle, the "Christians" no longer participate with them in their social and civic lives. These opponents of the Christians strike out at them in response (4:1–6). The Christians are to give no cause for persecution. They are to engage in no wrongdoing to warrant opposition (2:12; 3:16–17; 4:12–19). But they are always to be ready to explain why they live and believe as they do when called to account for it (3:15–16). Christians are constantly to recall that they are "exiles" in this world and will, as a result, be mistreated in this foreign land. But their real home is above, where they can expect an imperishable inheritance and great reward if they persevere to the end (1:1, 3–9, 11; 5:9–10).

The question of why this letter was forged must relate to the question of why it was written. It was written, presumably, to provide comfort and encouragement to Christians scattered in various places (the fictional designation: five provinces of Asia Minor) who were experiencing opposition and persecution at the hands of their former companions among the pagans. Why, as a subsidiary matter, was it written in the name of Peter in the style of Paul?

It may be worth observing, in this connection, that the book of Acts shares the dominant concern of 1 Peter with the problem of Christian persecution and suffering, and at the same time is completely committed to the question of the unity of the church, as manifest in the unity of the apostolic band. The presentation of the life, ministry, and proclamation of Paul in Acts is, in no small measure, affected by the author's concern to show that Paul aligned himself in toto with the Jerusalem church. And so, in contrast to Paul's own claims in Galatians, Acts indicates that immediately after his conversion he went to Jerusalem to meet with the apostles (Acts 9); in further contrast with Galatians, where it appears that Paul needed to use some rhetorical force to persuade the other apostles to agree with his law-free gospel, the author of Acts portrays Peter as the first to recognize that gentiles do not need to observe Jewish Law to be followers of Jesus (Acts 10–11). The Jerusalem conference itself is a virtual love fest in which James, Peter, Paul, and everyone else who matters is in complete agreement (Acts 15). Yet again in contrast to Galatians, where the fall out in Antioch appears severe and possibly permanent (Gal. 2:11–14), in Acts Peter and Paul are portrayed as in complete harmony. So aligned are they that it is virtually impossible to distinguish their public proclamations: Peter sounds like Paul and Paul sounds like Peter.

These ultimate concerns of Acts, involving both external circumstances of the church (persecution and suffering) and internal affairs (complete harmony of the apostles), are intimately related. The harmony of the church in the face of suffering demonstrates that God is at work in the community, despite the hardships that it faces; he is creating a harmonious body in the midst of attempts at disruption. In fact, hardships are overcome, in no small measure, through the unified efforts of the Christians in the face of it. Where there are splits and divisions in the community, the power of the group is threatened to dissipate (Ananias and Sapphira in ch. 5; Simon Magus in ch. 8; the "men from Judea" in ch. 15). It is only through the forceful and God-driven power of harmony that internal problems are resolved, allowing the church to stand as one in the face of external opposition. In short, suffering requires a unified front.

This lesson is not restricted to the account of Acts. To pick just one other example we might consider the book of 1 Clement, written at roughly the same time as Acts, near the end of the first century, and like 1 Peter, closely connected to Rome. Here the leading issue is harmony in the church, and the problems of schism among the leaders. The leadership in the church of Corinth has been usurped and the Roman church is writing in order to restore order, in this case by compelling the upstarts who have taken over places of leadership to give up their positions and return their predecessors to power. The book is about much more than that—as frequently noted, it is a very long letter indeed—but the overarching theme is unity, so much so that it can well be classified as a kind of literary "homonoia speech."[58]

At the outset of the letter, in order to show the terrible results of jealousy and envy (endemic to the Corinthian church and its leadership), the anonymous author points to examples from the Old Testament, before giving examples "in quite recent times." These latter are "athletic contenders . . . of our own generation" who suffered persecution from those who were envious of them, struggled, in fact, "even to death." He cites then just two "recent" examples among "the good apostles," Peter and Paul.

> Peter, who because of unjust jealousy bore up under hardships not just once or twice, but many times; and having thus borne his witness he went to the place of glory that he deserved. Because of jealousy and strife Paul pointed the way to the prize for endurance. Seven times he bore chains; he was sent into exile and stoned; he served as a herald in both the East and the West; and he received the noble reputation for his faith. . . . And so he was set free from this world and transported up to the holy place, having become the greatest example of endurance. (1 Clem. 5:4–7)

In this case the "envy and jealousy" come not from inside the community, but from outside. But it is striking that in a letter stressing the homonoia of the community, the author appeals to examples of suffering, and points to just these two apostles, Peter and Paul, and no others, unified with each other especially in their suffering.

---

58. See Bart D. Ehrman, *The Apostolic Fathers*, LCL (Cambridge, MA: Harvard University Press, 2003), 1. 18–20.

1 Peter shares with Acts and 1 Clement this concern of Christian endurance in the face of persecution. It is allegedly sent to the churches of Asia Minor, where the disharmony of the apostles was particularly well known, as evidenced in Paul's comments about his controversy with Peter in his letter to the Galatians, sent to one of the provinces named in 1 Peter 1:1. The letter of 1 Peter, directed to suffering, at the same time shows that the apostolic band is harmonized. Much as we find in the speeches of Acts, Peter is made to sound like Paul, embracing theological views very much in accord with his apostolic companion. By inverse logic, the words of Paul are now shown to sound like the voice of Peter. There is no split in the leadership of the church, at the highest levels. Peter and Paul, later shown to be unified in their sufferings in Rome, are shown to be at harmony in a letter allegedly written from Rome. It is Peter, writing as if he were Paul, who urges the Christians to stand firm in their trials, to suffer only for the name of Christ, not for any wrongdoing. Moreover, they are to be harmonized among themselves: hence the Haustafel, which functions in much the same way as it does in the Deutero-Pauline letters, to promote unity in the body among people in various social relations to one another.

In short, 1 Peter is a book that shows Peter and Paul standing face-to-face and agreeing point-by-point. If Christians are to face an antagonistic world with a unified front, then the unity of the ultimate leaders of the church—the apostles themselves—is particularly important. To show the deeply rooted harmony of the church in the face of ongoing opposition, an unknown author wrote a book of encouragement, claiming to be Peter, but sounding like Paul. This is a forgery that ostensibly deals with suffering of the Christians and that implicitly deals with the necessary corollary, the unity of the apostolic band.[59]

SECOND PETER

We have already considered 2 Peter in relation to its polemic against certain eschatological views. We can now look at the book more closely for its fervent

---

59. Another consideration–which is not exclusive to the one just discussed—involves the question of whether there was something specifically in the teaching of Paul on suffering that had created problems for the apostle that needed to be resolved by "Peter." We know that Paul's views of suffering did indeed create problems, for example, in the Thessalonian church, where he evidently taught that the miseries of this age were soon to end with the return of Jesus on the clouds of heaven. When that did not happen a good deal of anxiety arose in the community, as some of their members died in advance of Jesus' return. Had those who "were asleep" lost their reward? 1 Thessalonians is written, in part, to deal with that problem. As time dragged on, Paul's views may have continued to cause problems, as the imminent end to this world of hardship never appeared. 1 Peter may have been written, in part, to deal with that ongoing situation, to explain the reasons for suffering and to reassure readers that it is to be expected in this age, in part because Paul's views were being discredited. If so, then this could be Peter sounding like Paul precisely in order to provide Petrine support for a specific Pauline perspective. It is striking that Asia Minor is the region where Peter and Paul's conflict is best reported (Galatians) and where we first learn of Christians "suffering for the name" (Pliny's letter to Trajan).

support of the person and writings of Paul. As seen, 2 Peter has a completely different focus from 1 Peter. Here the problem addressed is not suffering caused by outsiders to the community, but false views promoted by insiders. These views concern the delay of the parousia, and the author is at great pains to emphasize that those who maintain a nonapocalyptic eschatology in the face of Jesus' non-appearance are not just misguided but are evil to the core, and profligate to boot. Several features of the second letter tie it to the first: it too is forged in the name of Peter, and precisely as his "second" letter (3:1). The salutations of the letters are close to each other in wording; the author who was a "witness to the sufferings of Christ" in the first letter (5:1) is one of the "eyewitnesses to his majesty" (1:16) in the second. Both letters warn against carousing either with former companions (in the first letter) or in the manner of the false teachers (in the second). Both stress the teachings of the prophets. And both are written, in part, to show Peter's support of Paul, indirectly in the first letter and far more directly and obviously in the second. Here Paul is invoked explicitly as an authority, indeed, his writings are deemed to be Scripture (3:15–16). Never did the two great apostles of the church appear more united.

The Pauline Character of the Opponents

The opponents attacked by the forger of the letter come from inside the Christian community.[60] They are those who had once come "to the knowledge of our Lord and Savior Jesus Christ," but who came to be "entangled" and "overpowered" by the "defilements of the world" so that their "last state has become worse for them than the first" (2:20). They once knew the "way of righteousness" but they turned back from it (2:21). The miscreants attacked in chapter 2 are the "scoffers" of chapter 3, who, "following their own passions," deny that there is yet to be an apocalyptic crisis with the reappearance of Jesus (3:3–4). Just as the secessionists from the Johannine community were labeled "anti-Christs" (1 John 2:18)—when they may well have viewed themselves as true adherents of the Christian gospel—so too these opponents are said to be "denying the Master who purchased them" (2:1).

More specifically, these opponents are Pauline Christians. They have Paul's writings, they interpret these writings, and they evidently treat them as authoritative texts, using them to establish their own perspectives, deemed by the author as highly aberrant (3:15–16). It is worth reflecting on the fact that the forger of this letter attacks these opponents for their licentious and loose living while admitting that their views derive from an apostolic authority, even if in corrupted form. This too seems reminiscent of polemics within the Johannine community, where some members have split off from the others (1 John 2: 18–19) because of certain Christological views (Christ did not come "in the flesh") that the author claims led to willfully sinful lifestyles (3:4–10; 4:7–12; they refuse even to love

60. See pp. 226–27.

one another). Theology and ethics were intimately linked in the minds of early Christian polemicists.

But what is there in the Pauline tradition that could possibly lead to the views attacked by the author of 2 Peter? We have already considered the "Pauline" eschatology. With respect to the ethics, is it possible that the persons attacked in 2 Peter derived these as well not from other sources, or from their naturally reprobate natures and desires, but from Pauline teaching, taken in a direction that the author of the letter opposes? More specifically, is it possible that they, like the authors of Ephesians and Titus, interpreted Paul's teaching of justification "apart from the works of the Law" to mean that what mattered was faith, not doing "good deeds" (see Eph. 2:8–9; Tit. 3:5)? We would be hard pressed to affirm that they actually took such a view to the extreme of supporting acts of moral degeneracy, but the view could be seen as leading in that direction by the author of 2 Peter. Some such view of moral living, as we will see, is attacked by James in a thinly disguised attack on Paul, or at least on a later interpretation of Paul, presumably among Pauline Christians. Specifically we learn that the opponents of 2 Peter "promise freedom" (2:19), again, a possible reminiscence of Paul's own teaching, of the believers' "freedom from the Law."

The opponents are also said to "despise authority" and to "revile the glorious ones" in 2:10. It is interesting, in this connection, to observe the opposite position evidently taken in Colossians, in its polemic against those who "worship angels" (Col. 2:18). As we will see later, the issue comes to a head with the letter of Jude, where a direct polemic against the view adopted by Colossians may be involved. In either event, as with the teachings of eschatology and ethics, the status of angelic beings may have been differently evaluated in various parts of the Pauline community.

The Forged Counter-Position

The author of 2 Peter is principally concerned to attack the Pauline corruptions of the faith by proffering the "correct" interpretation of Paul, in the name of his fellow apostle, Peter. In particular, Peter and Paul see eye-to-eye on the crucial issues of eschatology and ethics. It is interesting to note, as well, that by implication they see eye-to-eye on the interpretation of Scripture. This is an important issue because of what we know about the historical Paul and Peter, and their falling out in Antioch precisely over the understanding of the relevance of Scripture, specifically Scripture's kosher food laws and their implications (Gal. 2:11–14). We have no way of knowing how the historical Peter responded to Paul's charges of hypocrisy, and there are reasons for thinking that, in the general opinion of those present, Peter got the better of the argument.[61] And in particular, we have no way

61. As both Dale Martin and Joel Marcus have pointed out to me, in private communications. After the public confrontation Paul leaves Antioch and never mentions it as part of his mission field again. Moreover, had he won a resounding victory, he surely would have stressed the point with his readers.

of knowing whether the deep rift that so obviously troubled Paul, all those years later, was ever healed. But we can know that the issue involved the interpretation of Scripture and the question of its relevance to matters of real importance to the ongoing life of the Christian community, comprising both Jew and gentile.

Some later authors went out of their way to smooth over the differences between the two apostolic leaders, none more so than the book of Acts, as we shall see. But the efforts at palliation are at least as evident in the forged letter of Peter we are considering here. In this case Paul's views—on all topics—are compatible with Scripture; in fact they themselves are Scripture (3:15–16). Peter is the one who has the correct interpretation of Paul's writings, which he cherishes and regards as an ultimate authority for the life of the community. Peter and Paul are completely aligned on all matters of authority and interpretation. There is no rift here. By implication, then, even where Paul is not explicitly invoked—as in the attack on the licentious living of those who embrace "freedom" in chapter 2—he is implicitly on board with the polemic. This, then, is Paul fighting against Paul, the true Paul attacking the misinterpretations of Paul. And all in the name of Peter.

It would be interesting to know what the real, historical Paul—not to mention the real, historical Peter—would have to say about all this. With Peter we are handicapped, in having not a single word from his pen (since, indeed, he never used a pen). But we do have the writings of Paul, and it is worth noting that the views he stakes out in his letters are not those attacked in this one, advanced on his authority (3:15–16). There was not just a two-way split in the Pauline community, between those holding to an apocalyptic eschatology and those holding to a realized eschatology or between those living "lawlessly" and those insisting on a strict morality. As normally happens in history, things were far messier, with groups and individuals holding allegiance to Paul but advocating a variety of views, which covered the entire spectrum of options. How could that be? How could later Christians claiming Paul as an authority advocate differing—even opposing views—in his name? It should always be recalled that "authorities" may authorize certain views, but they do not necessarily dictate what those views will be.

And so, whereas Paul insisted that the end of all things was soon to happen with the reappearance of Jesus from heaven, and that he himself would be living to see it (e.g., 1 Thess. 4:13–18), other Paulinists—some in his own lifetime, but even more later—insisted that even though there was indeed to be an apocalyptic crisis with the coming of Jesus, there was a divinely ordained delay in the proceedings. That is roughly the view of 2 Thessalonians and 2 Peter, and the view of the Paulinist who produced Luke and Acts. Others of Paul's followers continued to think there would be *something* yet to come, in some undefined moment of the future, but that there was no urgency about the matter and that this was not a central component of the Pauline message. That is the view of such works as Colossians and, especially, Ephesians. And yet other Paulinists maintained that the end had already come in some sense in the death and resurrection of Jesus, and that believers were already enjoying the full benefits of salvation in the here and now. That is the view that Ephesians may be leaning toward, but it does not come to full expression in any of the Pauline writings that have survived from the early centuries—only in the views that are opposed as arising within Pauline communities, by Pauline believers who have left us no writings, such as the opponents of 2 Timothy and 2 Peter.

Paul himself was a lightning rod for all of these positions. Moreover, just as he was said to have advocated a "lawless" lifestyle, possibly in his own lifetime (Rom. 3:8), so too his authority was invoked by advocates of strict morality. In particular that happens here, in this letter of 2 Peter, which insists both that lawless living is contrary to Pauline teaching and that on this, and all other matters, the two great apostles stood in firm agreement.

THE ACTS OF THE APOSTLES

We have already seen two of the major thematic concerns of the book of Acts in our discussion of 1 Peter: the suffering of the Christians at the hands of antagonistic outsiders and the far-flung unity of the church, seen in particular in the harmony between Paul, the ultimate hero of the account, and the Jerusalem apostles, especially Peter, who dominate the action in the first third of the narrative. The latter theme begins to appear almost immediately after Paul's conversion in chapter 9. After leaving Damascus, he heads directly to Jerusalem to meet with the apostles and, with Barnabas's assistance, becomes their close associate (Acts 9:26–29). It is in the next chapter that the law-free Gospel for the gentiles is revealed in a vision—not to Paul, but to Peter, who acts on his new knowledge and converts gentiles in the Cornelius episode. It is Peter, then, who announces to the Jerusalem apostles that gentiles have received the spirit and been "given repentance unto life" (11:18). Paul's views are not controversial in this book. They are the views of the apostles before him, who act out their convictions of the law-free Gospel to the gentiles even before he is on the mission field, and who, most famously, endorse his own missionary activities at the climactic Jerusalem conference in chapter 15. Here Paul scarcely needs to defend himself, as Peter, Barnabas, and James all unite in affirming his mission to the gentiles in the most emphatic terms. The apostles of Jerusalem then send Paul back to his mission field with their blessing and enthusiastic support. Paul's mission in this account is both divinely sanctioned and wholeheartedly endorsed by the leaders of Jerusalem.

The apostolic unity is set out somewhat more subtly in the speeches of Acts, where, as I noted before, one is hard pressed to differentiate between the words of the Galilean fisherman and the Hellenistic intellectual. Paul's speeches sound little like the Paul we know from the surviving letters. It is likely that the earlier speeches in Acts are not those of the historical Peter either. Their unity of content results from the fact that they derive from the mind and pen of one man, the author of the narrative.

In order to effect this astounding harmony of Paul and his apostolic predecessors, especially Peter but also, notably, James, the author was compelled to smooth over their real, historical differences. The historical Peter had a serious falling out with the historical Paul, prompted by the appearance of people from James, when they both were in Antioch (Galatians 2). None of that can be found in Acts, where Paul's message and lifestyle conform closely with that of the Jerusalem apostles before him, including most emphatically the head of the Jerusalem church, James, and its leading spokesperson, Peter. This internal harmony is related to the broader concerns of Acts, in particular its celebration of the importance of Paul, his divine conversion and commission, his incredible miraculous powers, his persuasive preaching and teaching, his conversion of Jews and gentiles in moving the gospel through the world to the capital city of the empire, Rome itself. The book is, in no small measure, an encomium on Paul. But is it a forgery?

It is important to remember that a literary forgery, as I am using the term, refers to a text that makes a false authorial claim. In most Christian forgeries, an author claims to be someone other than who he really is in order to authorize his writing. In Chapter Three I explained a variety of ways authors make false authorial claims, one of which I termed an "embedded forgery." I repeat that discussion here: there are a number of writings from antiquity that do not explicitly claim to be authored by a well-known person, but instead use embedding devices, such as first-person narratives, without differentiating between the first person and the author. In these instances the reader naturally assumes that the person speaking in the first person is the writer of the account. A good example occurs in the Ascension of Isaiah, whose author does not self-identify at the outset, but instead provides an anonymous historical framework that involves Isaiah and that appears very much like the prose narrative sections of the book of Isaiah itself. Part way through the narrative, however, and at key points throughout, the revelation given through Isaiah begins to be delivered in the first person. The author of the account does not indicate that he is now quoting someone else. The reader assumes that the author has begun speaking about what he himself experienced. This provides an unimpeachable authority for the account: it is revealed by none other than Isaiah. The author is not Isaiah, however. This was a later writer making an implicit, but false, authorial claim. The book, then, is what I have been calling an embedded forgery.

The book of Acts, like the Ascension of Isaiah, is anonymous. But does it make a false authorial claim? The irony is that if it does so, the claim is made anonymously. That is to say, on no reckoning can Acts be termed pseudepigraphic (i.e., it is not a book inscribed with a false name). But it is also to be recalled that there are other instances of what I earlier termed non-pseudepigraphic forgeries, in which an author claims to be someone other than who he is, without actually naming himself. This is true, for example, of Ecclesiastes, whose author is allegedly the son of David ruling in Jerusalem, fantastically rich and wise. The author does not use the name Solomon, but that is clearly who he is claiming to be. He was not Solomon, however, but an unknown author living centuries later. Ecclesiastes is, then, a non-pseudepigraphic forgery. So too, I will be arguing, is the book of Acts, whose author wanted his readers to understand that he was for a time a traveling companion of Paul, even though he was not. This author used clear embedding devices in order to make his claim good. The claim functions to authorize his account, as an eyewitness to some of the events he narrates and as a bona fide authority even for those events that he did not personally observe. It was a remarkable strategy, and it proved to be extraordinarily effective, as readers to this day continue to attribute the book to Paul's traveling companion, Luke.

The "We-Passages"

The key to any discussion of the authorship of Acts is provided by the so-called "we-passages" that occur on four occasions (depending on how one accounts), narratives in which the author shifts from third- to first-person plural narrative. The scholarship on these passages may seem daunting in its scope, but it is even more disheartening in its execution, one suggestion even more implausible than the one preceding. Several full-length studies have been devoted to the question, the most recent by William S. Campbell, but including earlier important contributions by C. Thornton and J. Wehnert.[62]

The four passages in question are Acts 16:10–17, 20:5–15, 21:1–18, and 27:1–28:16. They include first-person-plural travel narratives (with Paul) from Troas to Philippi (16:10–11), from Philippi to Troas (20:5–6), from Troas to Miletus (20:13–15), from Miletus to Caesarea (21:1–9), from Caesarea to Jerusalem (21:15–17), from Caesarea to Fair Havens (27:1–8), and from Malta to Rome (28:11–16). It cannot be argued that first-person narrative is simply Luke's preferred technique for travelogues, given the third-person narratives of 14:20–28, 18:18–23, and elsewhere. But on the whole, the travel sections of these passages are narrated in the first person, and the scenes after travel in the third person.

In beginning to explore and explain these passages, it is important to note that they are not the only occurrence of the first person in the book. On the contrary, the author introduces his narrative in the first-person singular in the prefatory dedication to Theophilus. On any reckoning, the "we" of the later narratives must be seen as inclusive of the "I" of the preface. In other words, however one explains the we-passages from the perspectives of literary or source criticism, the author is making a back reference to an earlier passage, and thereby claiming not only to be the author of the narrative but also a participant in parts of it. This will be the gist of the argument that follows, that Acts is not simply a collection of narratives about the earliest Christian community. Its author wants to make an authorial claim to have been an eyewitness to some of the events that he narrates, so as to authenticate the narrative claims he makes, even though many of these claims can

62. William Sanger Campbell, *The "We" Passages in the Acts of the Apostles: The Narrator as Narrative Character* (Atlanta: Society of Biblical Literature, 2007); Claus-Jürgen Thornton, *Der Zeuge des Zeugen: Lukas als Historiker der Paulusreisen*, WUNT 56 (Tübingen: Mohr Siebeck, 1991); Jürgen Wehnert, *Die Wir-Passagen der Apostelgeschichte: Ein lukanisches Stilmittel aus jüdischer Tradition* (Göttingen: Vandenhoeck & Ruprecht, 1989).

be shown to be false, as can his assertion to have been an eyewitness to the life and preaching of Paul.

I begin the analysis with several observations about the passages in question. First, it should be observed that the we-sections are sometimes interrupted by short third-person narratives (20:9–12, 27:9–14, 27:21–26, 28:3–6), and that they contain a number of details that appear, at least, to be unnecessary to the narrative. These details, however, serve a useful function, as recognized by Samuel Byrskog: "Precisely, then, as seemingly ad hoc pieces of information within passages in first-person plural, they provide, whether historically accurate or not, the narrative with a realistic stamp."[63]

By far the most surprising aspect of the we-passages, however, apart from their existence at all, is their frequently noted abrupt beginnings and endings. It is their sudden and unexplained disappearance that is most unsettling. When did the author leave the company and for what reason? These and other related problems can be seen in the first of the passages, 16:10–17. How is it that "we" included Paul in 16:10 and 11, but then are differentiated from Paul in 16:17? That may make sense if an author had wanted to start easing out of the use of the first-person plural as a narrative ploy, but it is hard to understand if the narrative is a historically accurate description of a real life situation by an author who was there. Moreover, if "we" were with Paul when he rebuked the spirit of the possessed girl, how is it that only Paul and Silas were seized, not "we"? Did the eyewitness leave the company in 16:18 suddenly and for no expressed reason? If so, why is he still in Philippi much later in 20:6?

So too in the next passages in question, in chapters 20 and 21. Why is the narrative provided in the first person when traveling to Miletus (20:15) but then shifts to the third person once there? Was the author not present for the prayer in v. 36? Why did they not bring "us" to the ship in 20:38 if he sailed with Paul in the next verse? And in the next chapter, why does the author accompany Paul to Jerusalem in 21:18 and then disappear without an explanation or a trace in 21:19?

I will be arguing in what follows that the best explanation for these abrupt beginnings and endings is that the first-person pronoun was used selectively to place the author in the company of Paul, thereby authenticating his account. As Byrskog expresses the matter: "By presenting a narrator who speaks in first-person plural, the author himself appears, albeit vaguely, as present in the arena of history. Clearly, from a narrative point of view, the author is included among the 'we,' and that is sufficient. . . . The 'we' are, within the narrative of Acts, historical witnesses to the details and vividness of Paul's words and deeds."[64]

---

63. Samuel Byrskog , "History or Story in Acts—A Middle Way? The 'We' Passages, Historical Intertexture, and Oral History," in *Contextualizing Acts: Lukan Narrative and Greco-Roman Discourse*, ed. Todd Penner and Caroline Vander Stichele (Atlanta: Society of Biblical Literature, 2003), p. 263.

64. P. 264 Byrskog makes the mistake, however, of assuming that the "we" passages contain information that the author received "from people who had been involved"; p. 266. Unfortunately he provides no argument that the passages come from a source instead of from an authorial decision.

Various Solutions and Their Problems

The we-passages have generated a considerable amount of spilled ink. Nearly all the explanations can be summarized under four rubrics.

1. The Author of Acts Was a Companion of Paul on Some of His Travels

This explanation of the we-passages is the oldest and probably the most widespread. It was the dominant view before the modern critical study of the New Testament began. It is riddled with problems, however, and is rarely supported among scholars outside the ranks of the theologically conservative proponents of the complete historical accuracy of the narrative. For in fact, whatever one might say about "Luke," he does not appear to have been exceptionally knowledgeable about Paul, his life, and his message.[65] There are simply too many basic, fundamental, and detailed discrepancies between what Paul says about himself in the letters that he almost certainly wrote and the accounts of Acts. There is no need here to provide a detailed delineation. The discrepancies involve (1) his itinerary, with issues both large and small: after his conversion did Paul immediately go to speak with the apostles in Jerusalem, as Acts claims, or not, as Paul claims, emphatically, with an oath, in Gal. 1:18–20? When he traveled to Athens, was Timothy with him as in 1 Thessalonians 3, or not as in Acts 17? Was the Jerusalem conference Paul's third visit to Jerusalem or not? And on and on. (2) His missionary message. How could a companion of Paul think that Paul proclaimed idolatry as simply an honest mistake for which God was forgiving (as in Acts 17; contrast Romans 1)? Or how could an eyewitness and associate of Paul neglect to mention his theology of the cross? How could Paul preach to a crowd of gentiles and not even mention that it is Jesus' death that puts a person into a right standing before God (14:15–17; 17:22–31; cf. 24:10–21: and elsewhere, even to Jews)? (3) His life. The general portrayal of Paul as The Good Jew who never did anything in violation of the Jewish Law, rumors to the contrary notwithstanding, is hard indeed to reconcile with the Paul of the letters, who had no qualms at all with being a gentile to the gentiles, and who fell out with Peter on just these grounds.

2. The Author Used a Source for These Passages

More commonly it is thought that the author of Acts, not a participant in Paul's mission at any time, made use of a written document—usually thought of as a travel itinerary—that he incorporated more or less wholesale into his account without bothering to edit out the first-person-plural pronouns.[66] Sometimes the theory is

65. The classic study, which is still very much worth reading, is P. Vielhauer, "On the Paulinisms of Acts," in *Studies in Luke Acts*, ed. Leander Keck and J. Louis Martyn (Nashville, TN: Abingdon, 1966), pp. 33–50.

66. Among the many, many scholars who have taken some such line since the days of Dibelius, Barrett can be taken as representative: C. K. Barrett, *The Acts of the Apostles*, ICC, 2 vols. (Edinburgh: T&T Clark, 1998), p. xxix.

made a bit more complex, sophisticated, and, well, creative. In his detailed, full-length study, for example, Thornton maintains that the "itinerary" involved travel notes taken by Titus, provided to Luke (the real Luke, author of Acts) in scenes at which he, the author Luke, was actually present.[67] Oddly enough, Thornton argues that the "we" figure was not necessarily with Paul *only* for those events that are narrated in the first person, a concession that somewhat undercuts his case. Nor does the theory explain the abrupt beginnings and endings of the we-passages. Equally imaginative is the view of Wehnert that the passages come from an actual eyewitness—in this case, Silas—who was therefore reliable, and who passed along his account to the author orally; the first-person narrative was used, then, in order to signal to the reader that at this point the account was based on a source who was present at the event.[68] Similarly, in a more recent but much briefer analysis, Wedderburn maintains that the first person is used to signal a source who was actually present, as opposed to a written source. As it turns out, mirabile dictu, that source was none other than Luke.[69]

The highly speculative character of these particular views has not done much to win many converts, but they must be acknowledged as serious attempts to grapple with an intractable problem. Their real difficulty, however, has been widely recognized: there is nothing in the passages, other than the first-person pronoun, to raise any suspicion that we are dealing with material that has come from a source.[70] The passages are not distinct, stylistically or in any other significant way, from the surrounding narratives and they do not cohere, stylistically or in any other way, with each other in any unusual way. The stylistic unity of the passages with the rest of Acts was recognized as long ago as Harnack and emphasized in a classic study by Cadbury.[71] The most thorough study has been by Darryl Schmidt, who finds no "significant patterns that characterize all four sections" and notes that those syntactical constructions that seem noteworthy within them can be found elsewhere in Acts. Schmidt, in short, did not discover "any basis in the syntactic style of the text for isolating this material from the rest of Acts. It is neither uniform enough or distinctive enough to make that possible."[72]

---

67. Claus-Jürgen Thornton, *Der Zeuge des Zeugen*. Thornton firmly differentiates this view from the traditional "itinerary" hypothesis. On Thornton's case against forgery, see further note 107.

68. *Die Wir-Passagen der Apostelgeschichte.*

69. A. J. M. Wedderburn, "The 'We'-Passages in Acts: On the Horns of a Dilemma," *ZNW* 93 (2002): 78–98.

70. Thornton does claim that there are distinct features of the passages—more references to the "hosts" of the apostles and more precise designations of time, for example—but these could just as well be verisimilitudes required by the nature of the material. That is to say, they are standard fare among forged narratives. Stylistically the passages are not different from the rest of the narrative, showing authorial unity.

71. "'We' and 'I' Passages in Luke-Acts," *NTS* 3 (1957): 128–32.

72. Darryl Schmidt, "Syntactical Style in the 'We'-Sections of Acts: How Lukan is it?" *SBLSP* 28 (1989): 300–308.

And so, the stylistic unity of the work shows that whoever wrote the rest of the narrative of Acts also wrote the we-passages. Moreover, one cannot argue that the author edited out the stylistic oddities of the source otherwise to make it conform to his narrative, since the reason for thinking that the passages come from a different source in the first place is a stylistic oddity (the shift in person). If he edited everything else, why did the author of Acts not edit the pronouns? It is not convincing to argue that the first person pronouns were left in the source—or added to it—precisely in order to show that at this point of the narrative the author is using a source, even a particularly reliable source. When are first-person pronouns ever used in narratives to indicate the presence of a source?[73] What they are used for, with remarkable frequency, as will be seen shortly, is to verify that the author was an eyewitness to the accounts being narrated. First-person narratives authorize an account as having come from someone who would know the truth of what he relates, not in order to indicate that the author has used someone else's account.

3. The Use of First-Person Accounts in Narratives of Sea-Travel

First suggested by E. Plümacher and argued most influentially by Vernon Robbins, this is the view that the author of Acts was following standard narratological practice from antiquity, where travels on sea were typically narrated in the first person.[74] As Robbins puts it, after citing examples from the Odyssey, the Aeneid, Alcaeus, Heraclitus, Aeschylus, Varro, and others, "There is a natural propensity for portraying sea voyages through the medium of first-person narration."[75]

As attractive as the view appeared for a time, it has come under sustained attack by those who have looked yet deeper into the matter.[76] John Reumann, for example, rejects "the notion that 'we' for a sea voyage was a 'classical convention' in antiquity, let alone a necessary feature of style."[77] And after giving numerous counterexamples, Susan Praeder concludes: "There are first person and third person sea voyages in ancient literature, no passage is set in first person narration simply because it is a sea voyage, and there are no convincing parallels to the shifts

73. Ample refutations of Wehnert's claims along these lines (involving the first-person intrusions in Ezra and Daniel) can be found in the reviews of Chris Matthews, *JBL* 110 (1991): 355–57; and Gerard Mussies in *Filologia Neotestamentaria* 6 (1993): 70–76.

74. E. Plümacher, "Wirklichkeitserfährung und Geschichtsschreibung bei Lukas: Erwägungen zu den Wir-Stücken der Apostelgeschichte," *ZNW* 68 (1977): 2–22; Vernon K. Robbins, "By Land and by Sea: The We-Passages and Ancient Sea Voyages," *Perspectives on Luke-Acts*, ed. C. H. Talbert (Macon, GA: Mercer University, 1978), pp. 215–42.

75. "By Land and by Sea," p. 217.

76. See, for example, John Reumann, "The 'Itinerary' as a Form in Classical Literature and the Acts of the Apostles," in *To Touch the Text: Biblical and Related Studies in Honor of Joseph A. Fitzmyer, S.J*, ed. M. P. Horgan and P. J. Kobelski (New York: Crossroad, 1989), pp. 335–57; and Susan Marie Praeder, "The Problem of First Person Narration in Acts," *NovT* 29 (1987): 193–218.

77. Reumann, "The 'Itinerary,'" p. 357.

from third person narration to first person narration in Acts."[78] Instead, significantly for my purposes here, "first person and third person narration are signs of authorial participation and nonparticipation, respectively."[79]

In my view, that is exactly right. With the case of Acts, however, the claim to participation is false, since the author was not, in fact, a companion of Paul. And a book that makes a false authorial claim is a forgery.

4. The Author Is Making a False Claim to Have Been an Eyewitness

Historians were commonly maligned in antiquity for not knowing what they were talking about. Polybius, for example attacks the historical narratives of Timaeus because all of his knowledge was based on book learning, rather than personal experience. His fault: "he does not write from the evidence of his eyes."[80] As a nonparticipant in the kinds of stories he narrates "he is guilty of many errors and misstatements, and if he ever comes near the truth he resembles those painters who make their sketches from stuffed bags." He is like other historians "who approach the work in this bookish mood. We miss in them the vividness of facts, as this impression can only be produced by the personal experience of the author." Polybius goes on, then, to malign historical writers "who have not been through the events themselves."[81]

In his first preface, the author of Luke-Acts stresses his personal involvement in doing his research (book learning, of sorts) into the events he is to narrate (Luke 1:1–4). As we have seen, the first person "we" necessarily embodies the "I" of the two prefaces to the two works. It is best to understand the use of the plural pronoun in Acts as an authorizing technique. In using the pronoun in this way Luke is not—contrary to what is widely claimed—doing something highly unusual in Christian or other literature. Quite the contrary, the first-person pronoun (both singular and plural) was widely used in ancient texts, Christian and otherwise, precisely in order to provide authority for the account, as a rapid survey can show. This list provides a number of instances, and is meant to be illustrative rather than exhaustive:

- John 21:24—"And we know that his testimony is true." The author differentiates himself (as is not always recognized) from the "beloved disciple" to imply a personal acquaintance with him and his testimony and to provide a firsthand assurance of the accuracy of his testimony.

---

78. Praeder, "The Problem," p. 210.

79. Ibid., p. 212. It might be noted that whereas Praeder has shown the problem of the first-person narratives in Acts, and uncovered the weaknesses of the various solutions, she comes up with no compelling solution of her own.

80. *Histories of Polybius*, XII. 25g–h; translation of W. R. Paton, in LCL (Cambridge, MA: Harvard University Press, 1925), vol. 4.

81. It should be noted that Polybius is referring to the need for historians to have the *kinds* of experience necessary for the *kinds* of things they describe (military battles, political intrigues, etc.). But the same applies to the author of Acts: Does he have any personal experience of the missionary field that allows him to talk about it? Even more, does he have the experience of accompanying this particular missionary in his work?

- 1 Cor. 15:8—"As to one untimely born, he appeared also to me." Paul uses the first person to stress that he can attest to the reality of the physical resurrection of Jesus.
- 2 Cor. 12:2—"I know a person in Christ who, fourteen years ago, was snatched up to the third heaven." The "person" of course was probably Paul himself, and his account in the first person ("I know a person") provides authorization that in fact this is an event that really happened; in the context the narrative is used, in part, to establish Paul's credentials in the face of Corinthian opposition.
- 2 Peter 1:16–19—"We did not follow cleverly devised myths. . . . We heard this voice from heaven, for we were with him on the holy mountain. And we have the prophetic word made more sure." The author, falsely claiming to be Peter, uses a first-person-plural narrative to place himself with other apostles in the presence of Jesus at the crucial moment of the Transfiguration in order to validate his own message and to denigrate the message of his opponents (who were *not* eyewitnesses).
- 1 John 1:1–4—"What we have heard and seen with our eyes, what we beheld and our hands handled . . . and we have seen and bear witness and proclaim to you the eternal life . . . what we have seen and heard we proclaim also to you so that you might have fellowship with us; and our fellowship is with the father and with his son Jesus Christ; and we are writing these things to you so that our joy might be made complete." The prologue to 1 John is narrated in first-person plural, and it specifically stresses that the author and unnamed others (implied: the other apostles) had a real, tactile experience of the Word of Life.[82] The physicality of the manifestation of the word—stressed in the Prologue—plays an enormous role in the rest of the account, in opposition to the secessionists who have denied that "Jesus Christ came in the flesh." By narrating it in the first-person plural, the writer validates his alternative version, on the basis of personal experience.
- Gospel of Peter 26, 59–60—"But I and my companions were grieving and went into hiding, wounded in heart. For we were being sought out by them as if we were evildoers who wanted to burn the Temple. While these things were happening, we fasted and sat mourning and weeping, night and day, until the Sabbath. . . ." "But we, the twelve disciples of the Lord, wept and grieved; and each one returned to his home, grieving for what had happened. But I, Simon Peter, and my brother Andrew, took our nets and went off to the sea. And with us was Levi, the son of Alphaeus."[83] Unlike the canonical Gospels, this one is written in the first person by Peter, an unimpeachable authority for the accounts narrated.

---

82. See further pp. 421–25.
83. Translation of Ehrman and Pleše, *Apocryphal Gospels*, pp. 371–87.

- The (Greek) Apocalypse of Peter, passim—"When the Lord was seated on the Mount of Olives, his disciples came to him. And we besought him and entreated him. . . . 'Declare to us what are the signs of your coming and of the end of the world. . . . And our Lord said to us. . . . And I, Peter, answered and said to him. . . . And he showed me in his right hand the souls of all men." And so on. In the Akhmim fragment the realms are seen by Peter himself: "And I saw also another place opposite that one, very squalid; and it was a place of punishment. . . . And I saw the murders and those who were accomplices. . . ."[84] The first-person narrative authorizes the account: Peter himself was given the tour of heaven and hell by Jesus.
- The Coptic Apocalypse of Peter, passim—"The Savior . . . said to me, Peter, blessed are those who belong to the Father. . . ." "When he said this, I saw him apparently being arrested by them. I said, "What do I see Lord?" The entire account is narrated in the first person to verify the accuracy of what is reported to be the teachings of Jesus and the true account of his crucifixion.[85]
- The Apocryphon of John:—"One day when John the brother of James . . . went up to the temple, . . . a Pharisee named Arimanios came up to him and said to him, "Where is your teacher, whom you followed?": I said to him. . . . The Pharisee said to me. . . . When I John heard this . . . I was distressed within. . . . At the moment I was thinking about this, look the heavens opened, all creation under heaven lit up, and the world shook." The first-person narrative authorizes the vision that follows, and the mystical revelation that it entails of the origins of the pleroma and the world of humans.[86]
- The Apocryphon of James, passim—"You have asked me to send you a secret book revealed to me and Peter by the master, and I could not turn you down. . . . Be careful not to communicate to many people this book, that the Savior did not want to communicate even to all of us, his twelve disciples."[87] The author can assure the reader of the truth claims of the book, available only to the chosen few.
- Many others of the Nag Hammadi writings, for the same reasons.
- Irenaeus, *To Florinus*, quoted by Eusebius in *H.E.* 5. 20—"When I was still a boy I saw you in Lower Asia in Polycarp's company. . . . I have a clearer recollection of events at that time than of recent happenings . . . so that I can describe the place where the blessed Polycarp sat and talked, his goings out and comings in, the character of his life, his personal appearance, his addresses to crowded congregations. I remember how he spoke of his intercourse with John and with the others who had seen the Lord; how he

84. Translation of J. K. Elliott, *Apocryphal New Testament*, pp. 593–612.
85. Translation of Marvin Meyer, *The Nag Hammadi Scriptures*, pp. 487–97.
86. Ibid., pp. 107–32.
87. Ibid., pp. 23–30.

repeated their words from memory; and how the things that he had heard them say about the Lord, his miracles and his teaching, things that he had heard direct from the eye-witnesses of the Word of Life, were proclaimed by Polycarp. . . ." Irenaeus can vouch for his firsthand knowledge of Polycarp, who had firsthand knowledge of the apostle John. Since Eusebius quotes this correspondence, he stands within a direct line of eyewitnesses back to the apostles of Jesus.

- Protevangelium Jacobi, ch. 18—"But I, Joseph, was walking, and I was not walking. I looked up to the vault of the sky, and I saw it standing still, and into the air, and I saw that it was greatly disturbed, and the birds of the sky were at rest. I looked down to the earth and saw a bowl laid out for some workers who were reclining to eat."[88] The chapter was not found in the oldest version of the Protevangelium but was added by a later redactor; its move from the third-person narrative about Joseph to a firsthand account of how time stood still when the Son of God appeared serves to authenticate the miraculous event of the incarnation by an eyewitness.
- Infancy Gospel of Thomas 1—"I, Thomas the Israelite, make this report to all of you, my brothers among the Gentiles, that you may know the magnificent childhood activities of our Lord Jesus Christ—all that he did after being born in our country."[89] In the epilogue found in the Latin version, an editor adds the claim, "I have written the things that I have seen . . . and behold, the entire house of Israel has seen . . . how many signs and miracles Jesus did. . . ." Both are editorial additions to the text, making them redactional forgeries. Both function to verify the accuracy of the reporting.
- Pseudo-Matthew, prologue—"I, James, son of Joseph the carpenter, who have lived in the fear of God, have carefully recorded everything I have seen with my own eyes that occurred at the time of the birth of the holy Mary and of the Savior."[90] The claim to be Jesus' half-brother allows the author to set forth his narrative as deriving from an eyewitness.
- The Apostolic Constitutions 1.1 and passim—"The apostle and elders to all those who from among the gentiles have believed in the Lord Jesus Christ. . . ." "When we went forth among the Gentiles to preach the word of life. . . ." "We the twelve assembled together at Jerusalem . . ." "I Philip make this constitution. . . . I Bartholomew make this constitution . . . I Thomas make this constitution. . . . I Matthew . . . make a constitution. . . ." "I James, the son of Alphaeus, make a constitution. . . ." These directions for church leaders and polity come straight from the apostles themselves.
- The Martyrdom of Polycarp 9.15—"As he entered the stadium a voice came to Polycarp from heaven. . . . No one saw who had spoken, but those

88. Translation Ehrman and Pleše, *Apocryphal Gospels*, pp. 31–71.

89. Ibid., pp. 3–23.

90. Ehrman and Pleše, *Apocryphal Gospels*, pp. 73–113.

among our people who were there heard the voice." "And as the fire blazoned forth we beheld a marvel—we to whom it was granted to see, who have also been preserved to report the events to the others." At precisely the moments at which the reader may doubt the account—when, that is, a supernatural element is introduced—the author introduces a first-person voice to assure the reader of the accuracy of what is related.[91]

- The Martyrdom of Ignatius, 7—"Now these things took place on the thirteenth day before the Kalends of January, that is, on the twentieth of December, Sun and Senecio being then the consuls of the Romans for the second time. Having ourselves been eye-witnesses of these things. . . . When, therefore, we had with great joy witnessed these things, and had compared our several visions together, we sang praise to God, the giver of all good things, and expressed our sense of the happiness of the holy [martyr]; and now we have made known to you both the day and the time [when these things happened]."[92] The accuracy of the report is guaranteed by having come from eyewitnesses.
- The Martyrdom of Marian and James, 1—"I refer to Marian and James. . . . Both of these . . . were bound to me not only by our common sharing in the mystery of our faith but also by the fact that we lived together in a family spirit. . . . And it was not without reason that in their close intimacy they laid upon me the task which I am about to fulfill."[93] A close companion of the martyrs presents himself as a particularly reliable witness to their deaths. The first person recurs throughout the narration, although the narrator, for some reason, is, unlike his companions, not in danger.

In some of these scattered examples, the first-person narrative is in the singular, in others, the plural. In some instances it dominates from beginning to end (Coptic Apocalypse of Peter); in others the first person appears after an initial third-person narration (Protevangelium; Apocryphon of John); in yet others the first person disappears into a third-person narration (Infancy Thomas). In a number of cases the first person is not identified, but is anonymous (John 1; 21; 1 John 1; Martyrdom of Polycarp; Martyrdom of Marian and James). Whether these first-person narratives represent accurate claims (Irenaeus?) or not (Apocalypse of Peter) they all are unified in having one thing in common. They all function to authenticate the reports in which they are embedded.

We have already seen from Polybius the importance of eyewitness testimony in antiquity in general. This can be seen, as well, in the writings of Thucydides on the pagan side and Josephus on the Jewish, as Campbell has recently stressed. For Thucydides, for example, the movement to the first person "emphasizes the

91. See further pp. 493–502.

92. Translation of *ANF*, 1.129–31.

93. Translation of Herbert Musurillo, *Acts of the Christian Martyrs* (Oxford: Clarendon Press, 1972), 194–213.

author/narrator's knowledge and authority."[94] Indeed, for all these authors, "The author/narrator frequently attempts to establish his trustworthiness by lifting up his personal involvement in or thorough research and critical assessment of the subject matter."[95]

Eyewitness testimony was certainly important for the early Christians as well. Consider the words of Theophilus of Antioch:

> Seeing that writers are fond of composing a multitude of books for vainglory,—some concerning gods, and wars and chronology, and some, too, concerning useless legends and other such labor in vain—on their account I also will not grudge the labour of compendiously setting forth to you, God helping me, the antiquity of our books . . . that you may not grudge the labor of reading it, but may recognise the folly of other authors. For it was fit that they who wrote should themselves have been eye-witnesses of those things concerning which they made assertions, or should accurately have ascertained them from those who had seen them; for they who write of things unascertained beat the air. (*ad Autolycum* 3, 1–2)[96]

It is interesting in this connection that Augustine's nemesis Faustus denied that the Gospel of Matthew was valid precisely because it did not contain an eyewitness report of Jesus' life and ministry (August., *Contra Faust.* 17,1).

The relevance of these parallels for understanding the we-passages of Acts should be obvious. Here too is an anonymous first-person narrator. Does this first-person narration function like the other examples we have cited, six of them from the New Testament, or not? Without accepting Wehnert's somewhat extravagant theory of these passages, it is easy to agree with his general assessment of the function of the first-person narratives:

> The narrated subject of a text . . . periodically becomes the narrating subject, takes the place of the author and in doing so vouches for the unconditional reliability of the depiction for the reader. . . . Who could narrate one's own story better and more precisely than the person directly affected by it?[97]

---

94. Campbell, *The 'We Passages,'* p. 30.

95. Ibid., p. 43. Where I disagree with Campbell is in his claim that the author of Acts—or of any of these other books he deals with—is interested purely in literary, narratological matters, and not with establishing precisely the historicity of his account. The prologue of Luke is clear evidence, in my judgment, that the author's interests are not purely literary.

96. Translation of Marcus Dods in *ANF*, vol. 2.

97. "Das erzählte Subjekt eines Textes . . . wird phasenweise zum erzählenden Subjekt, nimmt den Platz des Autors ein und verbürgt dadurch dem Leser die unbedingte Zuverlässigkeit der Darstellung. . . . Wer könnte die eigene Geschichte besser und genauer erzählen als der Betroffene selbst?" Wehnert, *Die Wir-Passagen*, pp. 182–83.

A similar view was earlier expressed by van Unnik, "He who could claim to have been present at a certain event, was a generally accepted source of true information . . . autopsia was a safeguard against fallacies and opened the way of the truth."[98] Or consider the concession of Wedderburn: "It is hard to avoid the conclusion that the author wishes to suggest that he was present on the journeys described and that the first person plural signals this participation."[99]

Except that the author of Luke was *not* a personal companion of Paul who participated in his journeys. His claim to have been a companion is false. This, then, is a book making a false authorial claim. It is, in other words, a forgery.

The History of "Our" Reception

To take the matter a step further, it is important to notice how the we-passages function in Acts. They put the writer in connection with Paul on his journeys, making him an eyewitness and thus self-authorizer of the account. In light of the genre considerations discussed by Plümacher and Robbins, it makes considerable sense that the author has inserted these references into passages in which sea travel was involved. That was not a requirement of sea-travel narratives, as Praeder and others have shown; but it was a common enough characteristic of them, and so the sea passages made a sensible location for the occasional insertion of a self-verifying but false self-reference. He could just as well have chosen other places, had he wanted.

In support of the thesis that the author created these first-person narratives in order to establish himself as a participant in the ministry of Paul, it is well worth observing how these passages—and the larger narrative of Acts within which they were embedded—were read in antiquity. Here there is no ambiguity about the evidence at all. The we-passages were everywhere taken to be clear and certain indications that the author was an eyewitness to the ministry of Paul and that his account, as a result, was well-informed and accurate. This "history of reception" as we will see, gives the lie to those scholars today who maintain that if an author wanted to portray himself as an eyewitness, he would have had to do a much better and thorough job of it. The job this author did was thorough enough as it was and his editorial work was fully effective. Because of these we-passages, from the earliest (known) readers of Acts down to our own day, it has simply been assumed that the account was produced by a companion of Paul and is, therefore, to be trusted.

Our earliest extensive references to the text[100] come in the writings of Irenaeus, who indicates that the author, "Luke was inseparable from Paul, and his fellow-labourer in the Gospel, he himself clearly evinces." Irenaeus goes on to mention

98. "Once More St. Luke's Prologue," in *Essays on the Gospel of Luke and Acts," Neot* 7 (1973): 14.

99. Wedderburn, "The We Passages," p. 85.

100. All possible allusions to Acts from early Christian writings (including those in the NT) up to Irenaeus can be found in C. K. Barrett, *The Acts of the Apostles*, ICC (Edinburgh: T&T Clark, 1998), 1.30–48.

the we-passages, and then explicates the significance of having an eyewitness produce the accounts: "As Luke was present at all these occurrences, he carefully noted them down in writing, so that he cannot be convicted of falsehood or boastfulness, because all these [particulars] proved both that he was senior to all those who now teach otherwise, and that he was not ignorant of the truth" (*Adv. Haer.* 3.14.1).[101]

At about the same time—assuming a late second century date for the text[102]—we have the words of the Muratorian Fragment: "The third book of the Gospel is that according to Luke. Luke, the well-known physician, after the ascension of Christ, when Paul had taken him with him as one zealous for the law, composed it in his own name, according to [the general] belief" (2–6). Later it indicates:

> The Acts of all the apostles were written in one book. For "most excellent Theophilus" Luke compiled the individual events that took place in his presence—as he plainly shows by omitting the martyrdom of Peter as well as the departure of Paul from the city [of Rome] when he journeyed to Spain. (34–39).[103]

It is worth noting that already by this time—the time of our earliest recorded "readers response" (180 CE or so?)—it is a "general belief" that Luke was the author of the book and that he was an eyewitness to the life of Paul.

Soon thereafter Clement of Alexandria dubs Luke the author of Acts (*Strom.* 5.12). Some few years later, Tertullian's views are interesting and worth noting: he downplays the importance of Luke as a person only because he needs to do so when attacking Marcion's use of Luke's Gospel, and only that Gospel:

> Now Luke was not an apostle but an apostolic man, not a master but a disciple, in any case less than his master, and assuredly even more of lesser account as being the follower of a later apostle, Paul, to be sure: so that even if Marcion had introduced his gospel under the name of Paul in person, that one single document would not be adequate for our faith, if destitute of the support of his predecessors. (*Adv. Marc.* 4.2.2)[104]

And so Tertullian grudgingly concedes that the author of Luke followed Paul—obviously because he cannot deny it, since that was the established tradition already.

So too in the so-called anti-Marcionite Prologue to Luke (which has nothing obviously anti-Marcionite about it): "Luke was a Syrian of Antioch, by profession

---

101. Translation in Roberts and Donaldson, eds., *ANF*.

102. On the date of the Muratorian Fragment, see p. 91, n. 70.

103. Translation of Bruce M. Metzger, *The Canon of the New Testament*, pp. 305–6.

104. Translation of Peter Holmes, *ANF*, 3.

a physician, the disciple of the apostles, and later a follower of Paul until his martyrdom. . . . Later the same Luke wrote the Acts of the Apostles."[105] Eusebius too accepted the standard tradition (*H.E.* 3.4.1). Jerome expresses it even more strongly: Luke was Paul's companion "in all his journeying" (*Vir. ill.* 7).

The tradition—unthinkable without the clues provided by the we-passages—continues down to the present day, not just among lay readers of the Bible but among noted scholars of the New Testament, from across a wide spectrum, including the likes of D. Bock, J. Fitzmyer, J. Jervell, C. K. Barrett, and C.-J. Thornton, just to pick several very different scholars from a host of possibilities. And so Barrett can declare about the we-passages: "The *prima facie* inference to be drawn from them is that the person who wrote them was present at the events he describes."[106] And as C.-J. Thornton states, somewhat rhetorically, "The We-passages of Acts do not contain anything that ancient readers would not have considered completely realistic. They could glimpse in them only a report concerning the actual experiences of the author. Had the author not participated in the journeys that are narrated in this we-format, his stories about these would be—from an ancient point of view as well—lies."[107]

It is possible now to draw some simple but far-reaching conclusions. By the end of the second century, everyone who ventures an opinion concerning the authorship of Acts indicates that it was written by Luke, a companion of Paul, who wrote about things that he himself observed. The "fact" that the author was a companion was shown by the we-passages. Since the author was an eyewitness, he was a reliable source for the accounts he narrated.

Since that is the case, there is absolutely nothing peculiar at all in thinking that the author edited his account precisely in order to achieve that end, that is, that this is the effect that he had in mind. Nothing more was needed—no additional first-person narratives, no further self-identification. All the author had to do in order to authorize his account as based on eyewitness testimony and therefore to

105. For discussion (and this translation) see Fitzmyer, *Luke*, pp. 38–39. Metzger dates this prologue to the end of the fourth century, not to the second.

106. *Acts of the Apostles*, 2.xxvii.

107. "Die Wir-Erzählung der Apostelgeschichte enthalten nichts, was antike Leser nicht für völlig realistisch gehalten hätten. Sie konnten darin nur einen Bericht über die wirklichen Erlebnisse des Autors erblicken. Hätte der Autor die in Wir-Form geschilderten Reisen gar nicht mitgemacht, so wären seine Erzählungen darüber—auch nach antiken Verständnis—Lügen." Thornton, p. 141. Thornton places a lot of stock in the testimony of Irenaeus and argues that his testimony must reflect tradition from the early second century. Moreover, if the book of Acts was itself written in the reign of Titus or Domitian, then historical Luke and others like Timothy would have been alive, making it implausible, in his judgment, that someone would have ascribed it to Luke, unless he really wrote it. There is nothing persuasive in this argument. False ascriptions could indeed occur during an author's lifetime (it is not even an *in*scription). We have ample evidence of actual forgeries in the alleged author's lifetime: witness Galen, Martial, and 2 Thessalonians. Moreover, there is no reason to think that the historical Luke would have been physically present in the sundry places where this narrative was circulated, to make certain that no one said it was his. And what evidence, actually, do we have about the historical Luke—for example, the date of his death? None at all.

make it trustworthy as historically accurate was to provide a few passages written in the first person, passages that are stylistically like all his other passages, and so do not appear to have come to him from a different source.

Objections to the View

It is sometimes argued that if "Luke" had really wanted to convince his readers that he was a companion of Paul and an eyewitness, he would have done much more to make it obvious: name himself in the preface, introduce more first-person narratives, stress that he really was present to see these things happen, and so on.[108] I have already shown why this argument strikes me as unpersuasive. Starting with the first author to comment on the matter, Irenaeus in about 180 CE, and for the next eighteen hundred years, virtually every reader of the narrative of Acts was persuaded that it was written by an eyewitness, a companion of Paul. How could a ploy have been any *more* successful?

Others have argued that we have no analogy for what Luke allegedly did: introduce a first-person narrative without warning to authenticate the account.[109] That view is completely wrong, as we have already begun to see, but it is also important to recognize that Luke had no analogy for a number of his most important literary decisions. So far as we know, he had no predecessor in writing an account of the early church from a historical perspective, or in providing it with a first-person preface without hinting at his own identity, or in making it part of a two-volume work in which the two volumes are actually different genres of literature. To put it otherwise, Luke wrote a Gospel , which was a kind of religious biography, *and* a general history of the early church, and made them two volumes of the same work. Where is the analogy for that? So why does Luke need analogies for anything that he chose to do? In addition, it needs to be stressed that there are abundant analogies for the insertion of the first person into accounts in order to authorize their accuracy, as we saw above; in many instances, these eyewitness authorities are left anonymous, as they are in Acts, and yet they function to demonstrate the validity of the account.

Finally, it is sometimes argued that Luke was too obscure a figure in the early church for anyone to think of as the potential author of the account, if he were not really the author; anyone wanting fully to authorize the account would have chosen someone more prominent, like Timothy or Silas.[110] Unfortunately, this argument claims far more than we could possibly know. For one thing, when someone insists that Luke is too obscure a figure, we might ask, too obscure for whom? Our data from the first century of the church are frustratingly sparse. We have no way of knowing who was obscure or who was well known in most times and places.

---

108. Thus, among many others, Praeder, "The Problem of First-Person Narrative."

109. Thus Thornton, *Der Zeuge des Zeugen*.

110. The argument is forcefully advanced in ibid.

How can we possibly know who the local favorites among the early Christian missionaries were? In any event, this objection really has little to do with what the author was trying to achieve, since he never claims to be Luke but simply asserts that he was an occasional companion of Paul on his travels.[111]

The Purposes of the Forgery

We are left with the question of the purpose and function of the book of Acts—and indeed of Luke-Acts as a whole—an issue that luckily I do not need either to address or to resolve here in its broadest terms. There were undoubtedly multiple purposes for a work of this length and scope, and scholars have long debated the issues. More germane to my concerns here are the purpose and function specifically of Acts as a forgery. Here there is less room for dispute. The we-passages show that the author was (allegedly) a companion of Paul and therefore an eyewitness to his ministry. They provide assurance to the reader that the account is true and accurate.

Among other things, this is a "history" that celebrates Paul's miraculous conversion by a vision of Jesus himself, as recounted on three occasions in the narrative so as to highlight its importance. The book stresses Paul's divine commission to preach the gospel; it emphasizes his supernatural miracle-working power, his compelling preaching, the divine interventions that allow him to overcome all opposition and personal antagonism. Paul is portrayed as the one figure most responsible for the spread of the gospel "to the ends of the earth" (1:8), eventually in the capital city of Rome itself. Paul is the leading spokesperson in the church, God's chosen one to fulfill his mission on earth. The book in short, is both an encomium on Paul and an apology for his life, ministry, and message, allegedly written by someone who was there to see these things happen. But why would an apology be necessary?

We have already seen, and will see in greater length in the next chapter, that Paul was a controversial figure in the early church. So far as we can tell, he had at least as many enemies as friends. In most of his undisputed letters (Romans, 1 Corinthians, 2 Corinthians, Galatians, Philippians) he counters the views of his enemies and attacks their persons. These are enemies from *within* the Christian

---

111. Thornton's argument that the author really was a companion of Paul fails to convince, in part because his objections to the notion that the author tried to mislead his readers about his identity fall flat. Among other things, he claims that (1) a pseudonymous book would not be written in the lifetime of the alleged author. Yet we know of flat-out forgeries contemporary with their alleged authors. (2) The author would have claimed to be an eyewitness in the preface of the work. But how do we know what an author would have done? And why should we tell him what he should have done? (3) First-person narratives were not used to establish the credibility of historical accounts. This is just wrong. (4) If he were a fictional author, he would have dedicated it to a better-known person, such as Seneca. Again, we have no reason for thinking that we know what an anonymous author would have done, and he clearly had other compelling reasons for dedicating the book to Theophilus.

church, inimical teachers who take opposing points of view, and argue, in the context of their opposition, precisely against Paul, his message, and his authority for preaching it. And these are simply the enemies that we know about (though only allusively), from within his own churches. It is impossible for us to gauge how widely Paul was maligned by those in the churches founded by others, or for what reasons.

Acts answers many of the objections raised against Paul and his gospel message. It is not that the author of the book had access to the Pauline letters and writes a direct response to them; he never mentions Paul even writing letters to his churches, and if he did know Paul's writings, he did not know them well. Otherwise it is hard to explain why, in so many places, he appears to contradict them. The situation instead appears to be this: there were widely known charges leveled against Paul, some of them evidenced in his letters, and the author of Acts writes, in part, to set the record straight.

The Judaizers of Galatians claimed that Paul had no authority for his message and that he had corrupted the teachings of the apostles of Jerusalem, especially the pillars of the church, Peter, James, and John. Acts shows that in fact the authority for Paul's message came directly from the resurrected Jesus himself, and that his views were in complete harmony with the apostles before him, with whom he consulted immediately upon being converted and with whom he agreed on every major (and minor) point about both the gospel message and his mission to proclaim it.

The super-apostles of Corinth attacked Paul for being weak in speech and paltry in person. Acts shows that in fact he was a powerful and effective rhetorician, a great worker of miracles, and empowered by God in all his work. No human force could bring him down and his divinely appointed mission could not fail. If he is stoned in one place, he simply gets up and goes on to evangelize the next.

The opponents who maligned Paul to the Romans maintained that his gospel message discounted the role of Israel in the plan of God, severed God's relationship with the Jews, and led to a lawless and godless lifestyle. Acts shows on the contrary that Paul himself was a good, pious, faithful Jew from beginning to end, never doing anything opposed to the laws of his people, never urging lawless lifestyles, even among the gentiles; and Paul's mission was always "to the Jew first." It was unfaithful Jews who have rejected Paul; Paul never rejected Jews or the Jewish faith. His gospel was the fulfillment of all that is true in Judaism.

As we will see in the next chapter, eventually it was Paul's "lawless" gospel—which for him meant a gospel message that all people are restored to a right relationship with God apart from keeping the Jewish Law—that created the biggest rift between his followers and their Christian opponents, as there were other Christians for centuries to come who insisted that faith in Jesus was necessarily a Jewish faith, and that Paul had corrupted the truth of the message of Jesus. For them, Paul was not a divinely commissioned spokesperson of God; he was, instead, the personal enemy of Peter, James, and other apostles of the church. Acts is an early attempt to rescue Paul from such charges, an account allegedly by a personal companion of Paul meant to set the record straight. Paul was converted directly by Jesus, he was empowered by the Spirit just as was Jesus himself and his disciples after him, he proclaimed the true gospel, and he was God's tool in fulfilling the divine plan—which is why he was both powerful and unstoppable. Most important for the purposes of internecine Christian polemic, Paul never did anything to violate the laws God had given to his people the Jews. Moreover, in all his views—about Jesus, the salvation he brought, the role of the Jewish Law, the standing of the gentiles among the people of God—he saw eye-to-eye with the other apostles, and in particular the leaders of the church in Jerusalem. He and they proclaimed the same message.

Even so, the message that they all proclaim in Acts is not, historically, the message of either the historical Paul or of the historical Peter and James. It is the message of "Luke," a later, anonymous author falsely claiming to have been a one-time companion of Paul.

CHAPTER TEN

Forgeries in Opposition to Paul and His Message

In the previous chapter I noted that the apostle Paul appears to have had as many enemies as friends. We have seen a good deal of what those who revered Paul had to say about him, both by producing forgeries in his name (as in the Deutero-Pauline epistles) and by pseudonymously supporting him and his message, however it was understood, either subtly (as in 1 Peter) or not so subtly (as in 2 Peter and Acts). In this chapter we turn to Paul's literary opponents, who attacked Paul's person and message in the guise of authorized, usually apostolic, writings. Here again, some of the writings, such as the Epistula Petri, which introduces the Pseudo-Clementine *Homilies*, are transparent in their attack on the unnamed Paul; others are far subtler in their polemic, such as the New Testament book of Jude. And a number fall somewhere along the spectrum between these two.

In all cases it must be remembered that the polemic against Paul may not be opposition to the Paul as he has been reconstructed by modern scholars from the seven undisputed letters (the so-called real Paul). Ancient readers knew nothing about this modern consensus of an authentic Pauline corpus or the views that could result from applying historical-critical methods to it. They interpreted and attacked the Paul that had come down to them in writings (some of them forged) and in the oral tradition—skewed as he and his message may have been in these media.

We begin with the most discussed canonical instance of anti-Paulinism, the New Testament letter of James, asking whether it is in fact directed against Paul (real or imagined) and, of particular relevance to our present concerns, whether it can be considered a forgery.

THE EPISTLE OF JAMES

The letter of James begins simply enough: "James, a slave of God and of the Lord Jesus Christ, to the twelve tribes in the dispersion, greetings" (1:1). A number of persons are named James in the New Testament, including the father of Joseph (Jesus' "father," Matt. 1:16), the son of Zebedee (Matt. 4:21 etc.), the son of Alphaeus (Matt. 10:3 etc.), the father of Jude (Luke 6:16), and, most famously, the brother of Jesus (Mark 6:3 etc.). There is a compelling two-pronged argument that the author of this short letter intends his readers to understand that he is the best known James, Jesus' brother, the head of the church in Jerusalem. On one hand, the author does not further identify himself, to indicate which James he is, in a world where the name was exceedingly common. This must mean that he can assume—at least he thinks he can assume—that his readers will know "which" James he is. That would work if this were a letter written to his own close-knit community, for whom further identification would be unnecessary. But the letter is addressed instead—this is the second prong—to the twelve tribes of the dispersion. That is, it is going everywhere.

There have been protracted debates about the ostensible recipients of the letter. Obviously it is not being sent to the twelve Jewish tribes, since these no longer existed; and there is nothing to suggest that it was being sent to non-Christian Jews around the world, as its interests are Christian (even though Christ himself is mentioned only twice). More plausibly, then, the letter is being addressed to Jewish Christians scattered throughout the empire or, possibly, to Christians in general. Since there is nothing uniquely Jewish about the letter (nothing non-Jewish either), perhaps the final option is the best.

With respect to authorship, in any event, the point is that this is a letter intended to be read far and wide by someone who simply calls himself "James" without indicating which James he was; the recipients would have no way of knowing his identity unless they assume he is "that" James: the most famous one of all, the brother of Jesus in charge of the mother church in Jerusalem. It is worth noting in this connection that this particular James is often named in the New Testament without further qualifier (Acts 12:17; 15:13; 21:18; 1 Cor. 15:7; Gal. 2:12).

There are other forgeries produced in the name of James from the early Christian centuries, including the Protevangelium Jacobi, which I will discuss in a later chapter, and three works discovered at Nag Hammadi: the Apocryphon of James and two separate Apocalypses of James. Later times saw the production of yet other forgeries in his name as well.[1] No one thinks James wrote any of these other works. Why should we think he wrote the one that came to be included in the

1. E.g., a fifth-century anti-Jewish account of the Jewish mistreatment of Jesus and the early Christians, preserved in one Syriac and one Armenian manuscript; the James Liturgy of the sixth century, preserved in eighth- and ninth-century Greek and Syriac manuscripts, instrumental in the separation of the Syrian "Miaphysites" from the catholics; and the report of John Chrysostom, preserved in one Sahidic manuscript of the tenth century, to have discovered an ancient book by James that described Jesus' ascent to the seventh heaven; on this last see E. A. W. Budge, "An Encomium on Saint John the Baptist," in *Coptic Apocrypha in the Dialect of Upper Egypt* (Oxford: Oxford University Press, 1913), pp. 128–45, 335–51.

New Testament? My view is that it, like the others, is forged in his name. One leading reason for thinking so is that like his compatriot Peter, as discussed in the previous chapter, James could almost certainly not write.

The History of the Suspicions

Questions about the authorship of the letter are ancient. As is often noted, the book is not included among the writings of Scripture listed in the Muratorian Fragment. In this case it is impossible to know, however, whether the author actually rejected the book or simply was not familiar with it. Eusebius, on the other hand, deals with the matter directly, indicating that the letter, which was "the first of the epistles that are called catholic" was (sometimes? often?) regarded as forged (ὡς νοθεύεται) since "many of the ancients do not mention it." He, however, accepts the book as canonical since it was used "in most of the churches."

> Such is the story of James, to whom is attributed the first of the "general" epistles. Admittedly its authenticity is doubted [ἰστέον δὲ ὡς νοθεύεται μέν], since few early writers refer to it, any more than to Jude's. . . . But the fact remains that these two, like the others, have been regularly used in very many churches. (*H.E.* 2.23.25)

Jerome says something similar: "[James] wrote a single epistle, which is reckoned among the seven Catholic Epistles, and even this is claimed by some to have been published by someone else under his name, and gradually as time went on to have gained authority" (*Vir. ill.* 2).

Generally, of course, the book was accepted as canonical and attributed to James, the brother of Jesus. Even Luther, who denied that the book was "apostolic" because it "did not preach Christ," did not deny that James had written it. The first to question authorship seriously was Wilhelm de Wette in his widely used *Einleitung* of 1826; but it was F. H. Kern who first pushed hard for pseudepigraphic authorship, in 1835.[2]

Arguments for Forgery

There are solid reasons for thinking that whoever wrote this letter, it was not James, the brother of Jesus. The first, as already mentioned, is that James of Nazareth could almost certainly not write.

Whoever produced this letter was a highly literate native speaker of Greek, grounded in Hellenistic modes of discourse and able to use abundant rhetorical devices and flourishes. It is often noted that the book employs sophisticated use

2. F. H. Kern, *Der Charakter und Ursprung des Briefs Jakobi* (Tübingen: Fues, 1835).

of participles, infinitives, and subordinate clauses. Even Luke T. Johnson, a supporter of authenticity, points out that the language consists of "a form of clear and correct *koine* with some ambitions toward rhetorical flourish . . . comparable in quality if less complex in texture, to that of Hebrews."[3] Johnson also notes that the author makes vigorous use of rhetorical devices found in many Greco-Roman moral discourses, but associated especially with the diatribe.[4] Matt Jackson-McCabe concurs: not only does the author evidence a "relatively high proficiency in Greek grammar, vocabulary, and style"; he is "more generally at home in literate, Hellenistic culture," using commonplaces of Greco-Roman moralistic literature (horses with bits, ships and rudders, controlling the tongue in order to control the body, etc.).[5]

It seems unlikely that an Aramaic-speaking peasant from rural Galilee wrote this. Here I can simply refer the reader back to the discussion of literacy in antiquity, and in Palestine in particular, in the preceding chapter.[6] What applied to the fisherman Peter applies to the common laborer James as well (an apprentice carpenter? We don't know how he earned a living), or even more so. As far into the backwoods as Capernaum was, the little hamlet of Nazareth was more so; excavations have turned up no public buildings, let alone signs of literacy. Even if James's well-known brother could read—and so was considered highly exceptional by his townsfolk (Luke 4:16; cf. Mark 6:2)—it would have been Hebrew; nothing suggests that Jesus could write; if he could do so it would have been in Hebrew or Aramaic, not Greek. And by all counts he was the star of the family.

This was a part of the world where literacy was likely 1–2 percent or even less. Where would James have learned to write Hebrew? Or to read Greek? To write Greek? To write literary Greek? Greek that shows knowledge of the diatribe? And that uses rhetorical flourishes known from Greco-Roman moralists? All of that would have taken many years of intensive education, and there is precisely zero indication that James, the son of a local τέκτων, would have had the leisure or money for an education as a youth. Moreover, there were no adult education classes to make up the deficit after his brother's death years later. One should not reason that James could have picked up Greek after Jesus' death on some of his travels. If he did learn any Greek, it would have been of a fumbling kind for simple conversation; writing literacy was not (and is not) acquired by sporadic conversations in a second language—especially writing literacy at this level. And James certainly would not have mastered the Scriptures in Greek, as the author of this letter has done (see 2:8–11, 23; 4:6). And so, despite the remarkably sanguine claims of some scholars about the Greek-writing skills of uneducated rural peasants of Nazareth, it is virtually impossible to imagine this book coming from the

3. *The Letter of James*, AB 37A (New York: Doubleday, 1995), p. 7.

4. Ibid., p. 9.

5. Matt Jackson-McCabe, "The Politics of Pseudepigraphy and the Letter of James," in Jörg Frey et al., eds., *Pseudepigraphie und Verfasserfiktion*, p. 621.

6. See pp. 242–47.

pen of James.[7] The conclusion of Matthias Konradt is understated at best: "it remains questionable . . . whether one might expect the rhetorical and linguistic niveau of James from a Galilean craftsman's son."[8] More apt is the statement of Wilhelm Pratscher: "Even if one assumes a widespread dissemination of Greek in first century C.E. Palestine, one will nevertheless scarcely consider possible the composition of James by the brother of the Lord, especially when one compares it to the markedly simpler Greek of the Diaspora-Jew Paul."[9]

Other arguments support the claim that James the brother of Jesus almost certainly did not write the letter.[10] Of key importance is the fact that precisely what we know about James of Jerusalem otherwise is what we do not find in this letter. The earliest accounts of James—one of them from a contemporary—indicate that he was especially known as an advocate for the view that Jewish followers of Jesus should maintain their Jewish identity by following the Jewish Law. This seems to be the clear indication of Gal. 2:12 in the famous Antioch incident: "Certain men from James" influenced Cephas no longer to eat with the gentiles, out of "fear of those from the circumcision." The most sensible construction of the incident is that these "men" were representatives of James's perspective, that he was a leader of the so-called circumcision party, and that this group of Christians, with him at the head, insisted on the ongoing importance of Jews maintaining their Jewish identity, which meant, in light of concerns stemming from rules of kashrut, not eating with gentiles.

---

7. Contra J. N. Sevenster, *Do You Know Greek? How Much Greek Could the First Jewish Christians Have Known?* (Leiden: Brill, 1968), who argues that James would have known Greek. Sevenster's study has been superseded, indeed, demolished by the more recent investigations of M. Chancey, M. Bar Ilan, and C. Herzer mentioned in the previous chapter. And so, Lindemann, *Paulus*, is precisely wrong to maintain "The Greek of James is indeed the weakest argument against its authenticity" ("In der Tat ist die griechische Sprache des Jak das schwächste Argument gegen seine Echtheit," p. 241, n. 57). And when John Painter (*Just James: The Brother of Jesus in History and Tradition*, Edinburgh: T&T Clark, 1997) maintains that James *could* have been the author, since as a Galilean he would have been fluent in Greek, he is simply arguing on the basis of assertion, flying in the face of the evidence; his further claim that we need to take into account "the educative effect of the Jesus tradition" fails to address the hard issues (p. 238). Training in Greek composition was not part of first-century catechism.

8. "Es [bleibt] gleichwohl fraglich . . . dass einem galiläischen Handwerkersohn das rhetorische und sprachliche Niveau des Jak zuzutrauen sei." "'Jakobus, der Gerechte': Erwägungen zur Verfasserfiktion des Jakobusbriefes," in Jörg Frey et al., eds., *Pseudepigraphie und Verfasserfiktion*, p. 578.

9. "Selbst wenn man eine weite Verbreitung des Griechischen im Palästina des 1. Jh.s n. Chr. annimmt, wird man eine Abfassung des Jak durch den Herrenbruder selbst kaum für möglich halten, insbesondere, wenn man daneben das merklich einfachere Griechisch des Diasporajuden Paulus stellt." *Der Herrenbruder Jakobus und die Jakobustradition* (Göttingen: Vandenhoeck & Ruprecht, 1987), p. 211.

10. Sometimes in discussions of authenticity, the letter's allusions to dominical traditions are brought into play, by advocates of both positions. But it should not be thought that the author's failure to quote his brother explicitly demonstrates that James did not write the book; one can imagine all sorts of reasons for the absence of direct quotations. At the same time, the many parallels with the sayings of Jesus do not demonstrate that the author was his brother. Most early Christians would have known the teachings of Jesus, and many of them would have been interested in replicating these sayings in their reflections on the ethical lives of Christians.

So too, the book of Acts. Despite its concern for the gentile mission and its insistence that gentiles not convert to Judaism to be followers of Jesus, Acts portrays James as a Jew deeply concerned that Jewish followers of Jesus maintain their Jewishness. Nowhere is this more evident than in the incident in Acts 21:18–24, where James, after agreeing with Paul about gentiles, nonetheless wants Paul, as a Jew, to demonstrate to other Jews that he has not at all abandoned his own commitment to keeping the Law. The incident is obviously to be suspected historically, as an invention of "Luke." But even as such, it confirms the traditional view that James, a Jewish follower of Jesus, was known to be intent not to violate anything in the rituals prescribed in the Jewish Law.

So too in the fragmentary report of book 5 of Hegesippus' now lost *Memoirs*, quoted by Eusebius (*H.E.* 2.23), possibly dating to the early second century. Here James is said to have remained a Nazirite his entire life, to have had special access to the Jewish Temple, and to have prayed there so regularly that his knees became as calloused as a camel's. Moreover, according to this account, James's concern was entirely for the Jewish people, many of whom he converted to the consternation of the Jewish leaders in Jerusalem, leading to his martyrdom by the sanctuary. Hegesippus indicates that this happened immediately before the siege of Jerusalem; Eusebius claims that it is what led (theologically) to the destruction of Jerusalem.

What all of these early accounts suggest about James of Jerusalem is that he was known to be particularly invested in seeing that Jewish followers of Jesus maintained their distinctiveness, vis-à-vis the rest of the world, by holding fast to their Jewish identity culturally and cultically.

The book of James hints at a James-like audience, as it is addressed to "the twelve tribes." What is striking is that none of the cultural or cultic concerns of James of Jerusalem is in evidence in the book. Just the opposite. The book is thoroughly concerned about the "Law," but not about the aspects of the Law that James himself is reported to have been invested in. Here, in the book of James, the Law more or less involves the love commandment (2:8) and the Decalogue (2:10–12). There is nothing about ritual. Or cult. Or kosher food laws. Or Sabbath or feast days. Or circumcision. Or anything at all involving Jewish ethnic identity. The Law is a moral code given by God, applicable to all people. In other words, just those aspects of Law otherwise attested as of supreme interest to James of Jerusalem are absent here. It cannot be replied that this is to be expected in a letter written principally to gentiles; the address indicates that the intended audience is Jewish (-Christian).

One can go farther and argue that what is emphasized in this letter runs precisely counter to what we would expect from the pen of James, leader of the "circumcision party." As we will explore more fully in a moment, this author is concerned not with the "works of the Law" in the sense used by Paul in opposition to "those of the circumcision"—that is, the aspects of the Law that established Jewish identity in a pagan world. The concern is with "good works," that is, doing good deeds to benefit other people. There is no reason to think that the historical James would have objected to the notion that good deeds were an important aspect of the life of one following Jesus. But it is not the area of Law that he is otherwise identified with. His own interests were the same as Paul's, even if he took a position contrary to the apostle of the gentiles on those issues. He was interested in "works of the Law," not "good deeds."

In this connection it is interesting to notice which sins and failures occupy the author of the letter. They are by and large not explicit violations of the Torah but moral shortcomings such as showing favoritism, not controlling one's speech, and failing to help those in need. So too, what is "true religion" for this author? It has little to do with specific requirements of the Torah per se. It involves "bridling" the tongue and "visiting orphans and widows in their affliction" (1:26–27). It also involves "keeping unstained from the world," which would seem to open up the door for a discussion of cultural separatism. But instead of detailing the importance of maintaining Jewish identity in light of "the world's" staining influence, the author speaks only of upright moral behavior. Again, this is not an "un-Jewish" concern; it simply is not the concern attested otherwise for James of Jerusalem. This author speaks of "fulfilling the entire Law" but says not a word about Sabbath, circumcision, purification laws, kashrut, or festivals.[11]

Further indications that the letter is not written by James are given by the intimations that it was written at a relatively late date within the development of early Christianity, after James had died, presumably sometime in the 60s. For one thing, the debate over whether it was important for Christians to engage in "good works" is itself evidenced in the post-Pauline period. In Paul's day, and James's, the pressing issues had to do with the relationship of believers in Jesus to the "works of the Law." Only later, as we will see more fully below, did that concern migrate into a conflict over the importance, or irrelevance, of doing good deeds for salvation.

Another indication of a late date is the concern over ostentatious wealth in the community. Wealthy people have come into the congregations and caused problems, both by their very presence (the problem of favoritism, 2:1–5) and by their actions (dragging the poor into court, 2:6). That rich members of the community formed a sizable minority is evident from the charge of 5:1–6. And how early in the history of the Christian communities could this have been a problem? Surely not in the first decades. So too we learn that even though the "coming of the Lord is at hand" (5:8–9), people need to exercise the patience of Job in waiting for it. This seems to indicate that a good deal of time has passed in the expectation of the parousia, so much so that people have grown highly impatient and need proverbial patience in order to quell their anxieties. Consonant with these considerations is the fact that "elders" appear to be in charge of the community (5:14), a development that appears closer to what we find, say, in the Pastoral epistles than in the letters of Paul written during James's lifetime.[12]

---

11. Cf. Matt 22:34–50; Rom 13:9; Gal 5:14, where "love," not "works of the Law," fulfills the Law.

12. It is important to note that the use of the term *synagogue* to refer to the Christians' gathering does not indicate that the letter is either early or "Jewish," as shown, for example, by such texts as Ignatius *Polycarp* 4:2 ("let there be more frequent synagogues"), *Shepherd,* Commandments 11:9 ("the synagogue of upright men"), and Dionysius of Alexandria, according to Eusebius, *H.E.* 9.9.2, 7.11.11.

These indications of late date (and the Hellenized language) not only show that the letter was not written by James, but also that it was not commissioned by him in his lifetime—a view that is rendered highly improbable on other grounds as well, as discussed earlier when I considered the widespread but faulty view among scholars that early Christian authors employed others to write their works for them.[13] This book, in short, claims to be written by someone who did not write it. It is our earliest extant work produced in the name of James, brother of Jesus, and head of the church in Jerusalem. But like its later counterparts, it too is forged in his name. Why then was it forged?

James as a Counterforgery

Luke Johnson has made a strong case that there is no hard evidence of real animosity between the historical James and the historical Paul, basing his argument in large measure on Paul's neutral references to James in 1 Cor. 15:7; Gal. 1:19, 2:9, 2.12; and possibly 1 Cor. 9:5.[14] This reading may falter on the Antioch incident of Gal. 2:11–14, as already mentioned. If "James" is not to be blamed for the highly controversial stance of Cephas—who acted "out of fear for the circumcision party"—why would Paul bother to specify that it was the representatives of James who created the problem in the first place? Paul's stance, in any event, is clear: these "men from James" represented a completely intolerable view that threatened the essence of his gospel message. Would James have agreed? We have no way, ultimately, of knowing. What we do know is that later traditions portrayed James and Paul at loggerheads. This can be seen, for example, in the graphic account of the Pseudo-Clementine *Recognitions*, where Paul is said to have tried to murder James for his missionary success among Jews in Jerusalem (a passage we will consider at greater length later in this chapter[15]) and by implication in the Epistula Petri, where James is the recipient (eager and willing, one might infer) of the letter of Peter in which Paul, though not named, is clearly described as "the man who is my enemy." The tradition appears to have lived on in some Christian groups who swore allegiance to Jerusalem and the church started there, ruled by James, such as the Ebionites, who understood Paul as Christian enemy number one.

Despite occasional disclaimers, there should be no doubt that Paul, or at least the tradition associated with Paul, is under attack in the letter attributed to James in the New Testament. Johnson is absolutely right to object that there is more to the book than 2:14–26; but it is also the case that this passage is where the principal polemic lies. Moreover, the themes of these thirteen verses resound throughout the short letter. The book is about nothing if not "doing good works" and so being a "doer of the word" instead of simply a hearer. It is overwhelmingly

---

13. See pp. 218–22.

14. *Letter of James*, pp. 94–96.

15. See pp. 305–8.

concerned with followers of Jesus living out their faith. All the paranesis is directed to that end, and the book is almost completely paranesis.

Moreover, Johnson is wrong to argue that "there is absolutely no reason to read this section [i.e., 2:14–26] as particularly responsive to Paul."[16] Much to be preferred, for clear and compelling reasons I will enumerate, is Kari Syreeni: "Not only does [James] heavily draw on Paul, it goes very decidedly into a debate with well-known Pauline statements. The reluctance of many scholars to see a literary dependence here is stunning."[17] Stunning indeed, but understandable. Who wants two of the leading authorities of early Christianity to stand at loggerheads? But at loggerheads they stand—at least in the opinion of the author of this letter, who put words on the pen of James in order to attack what he understood to be the views of Paul. What I will be arguing—here I stand at some variance with Syreeni—is that even though the author based his argument against Paul on "authentic" Pauline traditions, he read these traditions through the lens provided by later Pauline interpreters, so that what he attacked was not (the "real") Paul but a kind of Deutero-Paul, one evidenced, in fact, in surviving Pauline forgeries. The book of James, in other words, is a counterforgery.

James as Dependent on Paul

The evidence that James depends on Pauline formulations for its polemic is clear and compelling; it hinges on verbatim agreements, conceptual formulations, and polemical constructions that are simply too closely aligned to be discounted.

James 2:21 and Rom. 4:2 (and Gal. 3:7)

> James 2:21: Ἀβραὰμ ὁ πατὴρ ἡμῶν οὐκ ἐξ ἔργων ἐδικαιώθη.
> Rom. 4:2: εἰ γὰρ Ἀβραὰμ ἐξ ἔργων ἐδικαιώθη.

---

16. Johnson, *Letter of James*, p. 249. Johnson bases his argument on two claims, that for James ἔργα are never connected to the law, and that the common elements in the two authors is just as easily explained as resulting from the fact that they were both first-generation of a messianic movement that had faith in Jesus as the messiah. This view is effectively refuted by Matt Jackson-McCabe, *Logos and Law in the Letter of James: The Law of Nature, the Law of Moses, and the Law of Freedom* (Leiden: Brill, 2001). Among other things, Jackson-McCabe points out that there are simply too many verbal connections with Paul to be accidental (as I will show). Moreover, it is not true that ἔργα are not connected with the law in James—as seen most clearly in 1:25 and also in 2:1–13. (Below I argue that what Paul and James *mean* by ἔργα is different; but that is another matter.) Moreover, although it is true that typical discussions in ancient first-generation members of the Jesus messianic movement do tie "attitude and action" (faith and works), it is equally important to note that the terms used to *express* this important tie, outside of James and Paul, are never πίστις and ἔργα—let alone in connection to whether one can be considered "righteous" (using δικαιοῦσθαι) by faith apart from ἔργα.

17. Kari Syreeni, "James and the Pauline Legacy," in *Fair Play: Diversity and Conflicts in Early Christianity*, ed. Ismo Dunderberg et al. (Brill: Leiden, 2002), p. 401.

The precise verbal overlap alone would be significant, but it is important as well to recognize that for James, both the concept of justification and the example of Abraham appear completely out of the blue in 2:21. "Being justified" has not been part of the discourse of faith and works until this point: δικαιόω occurs here for the first time in the letter. This shows that James is responding to someone who made justification—and more specifically, Abraham's justification—the key point in a discussion of faith and works. This point is made nowhere in early Christian literature, outside of Paul and James.

Moreover, both James 2:23 and Rom. 4:3 quote Gen. 15:6 in order to establish their (contrary) views about Abraham in relationship to his justification. Again, nowhere else in early Christian (or Jewish) literature is Gen. 15:6 brought to bear on the question of justification, let alone justification by works or by faith.

In addition, it is worth noting that the author of James 2:21 understands that Christian believers are the children of Abraham ("Abraham our father"), the one who was justified "by works." This stands in stark contrast with Gal. 3:7: "those who are from faith, these are the children of Abraham."

James 2:24 and Gal. 2:16 and Rom. 3:28

> James 2:24: ὁρᾶτε ὅτι ἐξ ἔργων δικαιοῦται ἄνθρωπος καὶ οὐκ ἐκ πίστεως μόνον.
>
> Gal. 2:16: εἰδότες ὅτι οὐ δικαιοῦται ἄνθρωπος ἐξ ἔργων νόμου ἐὰν μὴ διὰ πίστεως Ἰησοῦ Χριστοῦ.
>
> Rom. 3:28: λογιζόμεθα γὰρ δικαιοῦσθαι πίστει ἄνθρωπον χωρὶς ἔργων νόμου.

The parallels among the passages, much noted for centuries, are striking still today: all of them contain a verb of knowing, an indefinite "person," the verb "justified" in the passive voice, and the antithetical contrast of works and faith. Nowhere else in all of early Christian literature are these elements combined. Yet the two authors take what appear to be—at least on the surface—opposite sides of the argument, one insisting that a person is justified not by "works" of the Law but by faith, the other that a person is not justified by faith alone but by "works." The passages are far too close to have been accidentally created in such similar yet contrary fashion. And so, as Lindemann, in the company of many others, has noted: "The section James 2:21–24 in any case touches so closely upon Romans 3–4 that it raises suspicions of a literary relationship."[18]

The difficulty with Lindemann's claim, which echoes the views widely held at least since Luther, is that it imagines only two possible alternatives: literary independence (of James and Paul) or literary dependence. As I will argue below, this

18. "Der Abschnitt Jak 2, 21–24 berührt sich jedenfalls so eng mit Röm 3.4, daß eine literarische Beziehung doch zu vermuten ist." Andreas Lindemann, *Paulus*, p. 247. See also, among a large host, Wiard Popkes, "James and Scripture: An Exercise in Intertextuality," *NTS* 45 (1999): 213–29.

overlooks other options, especially "secondary orality," where Paul's writings influenced how people, even illiterate followers, may have discussed (and here and there altered) his views. This would be a kind of literary dependence mediated not through manuscripts but through an oral tradition, and would make sense of the fact, noted by many, that technically speaking James does not contradict Paul, since his construal of the key terms of the debate—"faith" and "works"—differs from Paul's. That does not mean there is not dependence. Given all the linguistic and conceptual parallels, some kind of dependence is necessary. But it may mean that James is not simply "misreading" Paul. He may have inherited these Pauline formulations in some way other than a direct literary connection with copies of Romans and Galatians in hand.

Other Indications of Dependence

Before developing that idea, it is important to note several other indications that James is reacting to or otherwise influenced by Pauline formulations, whether he learned of these in writing or by other means. Thus for example, James' reference to νόμον τέλειον τὸν τῆς ἐλευθερίας (1:25; cf. 2:12) seems to stand in sharp contrast to Paul, for whom the Law is a matter of slavery (Gal. 4:24; 5:1) and brings a curse (Gal. 3:10). In addition, as Popkes has pointed out, the only places in early Christian writings where the love command of Lev. 19:18 is portrayed as the crown of the Law, but not used as part of the "two greatest commandments," are James 2:8–11, Rom. 13:8–10, and Gal. 5:14. Popkes convincingly argues for other connections with Paul,[19] leading him to conclude: "James does not treat an isolated theological motive (in 2:14–16) but writes from the background of the development of (Pauline) missionary churches. It is even possible that he may have gained access to several Pauline key texts, albeit probably not directly but mediated through oral or written communication."[20] Note the final phrase.

Understanding the polemic of James requires one to place him in relation to the tradition he is opposing. That is the problem with the position taken by scholars such as N. W. Niebuhr, who argues that one should read James on "its own

---

19. Thus James 3:13–18 is close to 1 Corinthians 2–3, down to the wording (genuine wisdom over against earthly psychic eagerness for quarrels). Among other phrases and ideas that appear Pauline are "Lord of glory" 2:1 (cf. 1 Cor. 2:8), the contrast of "desire and death" 1:13–15 (cf. Rom. 6:11–13, 23; 7:7ff), and God's preference for the poor (2:5; cf. 1 Cor. 1:26–28). Moreover, the climactic chain of conclusions in 1:2–3 is like Rom. 5:3–5 (and 1 Peter 1:6–7). On the other hand, Martin Hengel, "Der Jakobusbrief als antipaulinische Polemik," in *Tradition and Interpretation in the NT: Essays in Honor of E. Earle Ellis,* ed. G. Hawthorne and Otto Betz (Grand Rapids, MI: Eerdmans, 1987), pp. 248–78, is overly fanciful when he sees everything in the letter (esp. 3:1–12; 4:13–16; 5:13–16) as anti-Pauline.

20. "Jak behandelt nicht ein isoliertes theologisches Thema (in 2, 14–16), sondern schreibt auf dem Hintergrund der Entwicklung der (paulinischen) Missionskirchen. Möglicherweise gewann er sogar Zugang zu einigen paulinischen Kerntexten, evtl. freilich nicht auf direktem Weg, sondern durch mündliche oder schriftliche Vermittlung." *Der Brief des Jakobus* (Leipzig: Evangelische Verlagsanstalt, 2001), p. 39.

terms" without importing a knowledge of Paul. Margaret Mitchell's response is apt: in order to read James on its own terms, one *must* read it in light of Paul, "if Paul was one of those terms!"[21]

James as Independent of Paul

Even though James has picked up phrasing, concepts, contrasts, and Scriptural proofs from Paul, his actual position, as often noted, may not be contradictory to Paul's. True, he certainly sounds contrary to Paul. For James a person is justified by works, not by faith alone; for Paul a person is justified by faith, not by doing the works of the Law. The problem is that Paul and James appear to mean different things by both "faith" and "works."

I do not need to provide a lengthy disquisition on Paul's use of the two words. Faith, for Paul, refers to a trusting relationship with God through Christ, or a trust in Christ's death for justification. It is a relational term. But not for James. When James speaks of "faith" he refers to an intellectual acknowledgment of theological claims: "You believe that God is one? You do well. Even the demons believe, and they shudder" (2:19). For James, the intellectual assent to what we might call propositional truths cannot put a person into a right standing before God. One needs to do "works."

But what he means by "works" also differs from Paul. Paul's "works of the Law" are the demands that the Law makes on Jews qua Jews. In Paul's view, justification does not come by keeping these demands. If it did, then there would have been no reason for Christ to die. This does not mean, of course, that Paul thought that "doing good deeds" was unrelated to a right standing before God. Much of his surviving correspondence, after all, involves urgent paranesis. Believers are still to "work out their salvation with fear and trembling" (Phil. 2:12). But there is nonetheless an important terminological difference from James. For James, "works" are not the demands of the Law placed on Jews. They are good deeds. One needs to do good deeds in order to be justified. And so, the terse summary of Pratscher: "Indeed, Paul in no way represents the understanding of faith that James attacks."[22] For Paul, too, there is no such thing as ("true") faith without obedience (Rom. 1:5) or active love (Gal. 5:6).

---

21. Margaret Mitchell, "The Letter of James as a Document of Paulinism?" in *Reading James with New Eyes: Methodological Reassessments of the Letter of James*, ed. Robert L. Webb and John S. Kloppenborg (London: T&T Clark, 2007), p. 75. I am not, however, persuaded by Mitchell's rather eccentric attempt to show that the author of James was actually a later Paulinist trying to reconcile Paul (of Galatians) with Paul (of 1 Corinthians). In support she points to other later Paulinists such as 1 Clement and Polycarp, who make similar rhetorical moves to the same end. The difference, however, is stark. James states a Pauline theologoumenon and then argues against it so as directly to oppose a "Pauline" teaching. None of her other authorities does this.

22. "Paulus vertritt ja keineswegs den von Jak attackierten Glaubensbegriff." Wilhelm Pratscher, *Der Herrenbruder Jakobus und die Jakobustradition* (Göttingen: Vandenhoeck & Ruprecht, 1987), p. 214.

One can well argue—and for centuries, competent scholars have done so, with some vehemence—whether the real, historical Paul would have disagreed with the views set forth by the author of James. My guess is that the answer is yes, since for Paul justification does not come by doing good deeds (either instead of or in addition to faith) but by faith in Christ. But the question is of no moment for my present discussion. One might also ask whether the author of James would have disagreed with the conception of justification put forth by the real, historical Paul. My guess here is that the answer is no, once the terms of the debate were clearly laid out. But again, it is beside the point for the present discussion. The point here is that the author of James is clearly dependent on Pauline formulations for his contrasting views, whether he understood Paul rightly or not, and yet he attacks these formulations in terms that are not actually commensurate with Paul's conception of them. Why is that?

One obvious solution, and the one most frequently suggested, is that James simply misread Paul. This is always a possibility, but another one presents itself as well. What is most interesting is that the Pauline notion that "works of the Law" cannot justify was eventually transformed precisely in the Pauline tradition itself into a teaching about "good deeds." We have seen this already in both Eph. 2:1–10 and Tit. 3:5–8. In these instances, later Paulinists took Paul's teaching about the Jewish Law, and either unwittingly or knowingly altered it—or at least extended it—into a teaching about engaging in meritorious action. For the forger of Ephesians, for example; it is not doing good deeds that brings salvation; it is grace alone (2:1–10).

James is not attacking the position of Paul himself, as scholars have reconstructed him today on the basis of the undisputed letters.[23] But he does seem to be attacking a position that could be read out of the Deutero-Pauline epistles. Or to put it differently, the author of James is reading Paul—either the Pauline letters themselves (Gal. 2:16; Rom. 3:28, 4:2), or Pauline traditions circulating orally, based on those letters—through the lens provided by later Paulinists, as evidenced in the Deutero-Pauline letters. If he actually had access to literary forms of the later Pauline tradition, for example, the letter of Ephesians itself, then his writing is not just a forgery. It is a counterforgery.

---

23. And so, I am obviously arguing against those who continue to read James through Lutheran eyes as standing in conflict with Paul himself, as for example, Lindemann, *Paulus in ältesten Christentum*: "James 2:14–26 in this regard must be understood as an explicit disagreement with Paul. James does not reject a 'degenerate' Paulinism . . . he simply rejects the assertion that humanity is justified by faith alone" ("Jak 2, 14–26 ist insofern zu verstehen als expliziter Widerspruch gegen Paulus. Jak wendet sich nicht gegen einen 'entarteten' Paulinismus . . . er wendet sich einfach gegen die Behauptung, daß der Mensch aus Glauben allein gerechtgesprochen werde," p. 248). Lindemann does acknowledge that James's "misreading" of Paul corresponds to what is found in post-Pauline authors who favored his teaching (Eph. 2:8–9; 2 Tim. 1:9; Tit. 3:5–7; 1 Clem. 32:4; Pol. Phil. 1:3). But that is just the point. James is attacking a later understanding of Paul embodied in forged Pauline traditions by later Paulinists.

Why James?

Why then did this counterforger choose the name James for his attack on a later Pauline position on faith and works? Dibelius saw the choice of the pseudonym as ideologically innocent.[24] Unlike the Deutero-Pauline letters, which invest considerable effort in convincing their readers that it is indeed Paul who is writing, this author simply states his name in 1:1 and provides no attempt at verisimilitude. Since James of Jerusalem was known for his "righteous" living, and since this book wants to stress the importance of living out one's faith, the connection was obvious. This view, however, overlooks the early traditions of conflicts between the historical James and the historical Paul. It can scarcely be an accident that this anti-Pauline letter is put on the pen of one of his best known early opponents.

Other more recent authors have gone too far in other directions. Most recently David Nienhuis, for example, advances the creative argument that the author of the book of James was the same person who compiled the seven-letter corpus of the Catholic epistles in order to complement the seven-letter canon of Pauline writings then in circulation, these others produced by the "pillars" of the Jerusalem church.[25] This happened, according to Nienhuis, at the end of the second century, as there is no knowledge of the book of James before Origen. The author in particular was interested in countering the growing influence of Marcionism on the church, and its rabid Paulinism. There are enormous problems with this reconstruction. Irenaeus already shows evidence of knowing the book of James, for example,[26] and little in the writing could be seen as directed against distinctively Marcionite teachings. [27] On the contrary, the views the book counters are easily situated in the post-Pauline situation of the church at the end of the first century. Of more importance for the present discussion, Jude was not one of the "pillars" of the Jerusalem church. The collection could scarcely have been made in order to have writings of the "pillars" set in opposition to Paul. As a corollary, the author of the present epistle did not choose the name James for that reason.

At the end of the day, the simplest explanation of the authorial claim is probably the best. James was considered an impeccable authority in the early church as the "brother of the Lord" and the leader of the church in Jerusalem. Moreover,

---

24. *James: A Commentary on the Epistle of James*, tr. Michael W. Williams (Philadelphia: Fortress, 1976).

25. David R. Nienhuis, *Not by Paul Alone: The Formation of the Catholic Epistle Collection and the Christian Canon* (Waco, TX: Baylor University, 2007).

26. Irenaeus does not directly quote James, but he does, like James, follow a quotation of Gen 15:6 with the comment that Abraham "was called a friend of God" (*Adv. Haer.* 4.16.2). Nienhuis discounts this evidence on the simple grounds that Abraham is called the "friend of God" in Jewish literature as well (p. 36). But the point is the quotation and the epithet are combined in precisely the same way in both James and Irenaeus. That is hard to imagine as a historical accident.

27. It is too easy for Nienhuis to claim that the author hid his anti-Marcionite agenda so as not to be guilty of anachronism; one could just as well argue that the author was anti-Valentinian, anti-Thomasine, or anti-Sethian.

he was known to be an opponent of Paul, whether or not the tradition is rooted in a historical conflict. And so, an author who wanted to attack a "Pauline" position —possibly not knowing that it was not Paul's own, but a position that had later developed within some Pauline communities—chose his pseudonym wisely. In the letter of James we have a forger attacking a Deutero-Paul for views that Paul himself, so far as we know, never held. In doing so it stands in sharp contrast with pro-Pauline works that we have already considered. These include such works as the book of Acts, which shows Paul and James completely on the same page—theologically, practically, and every other way—and, interestingly, the book of 1 Peter, with which, as M. Konradt in particular has shown, the book of James has a number of striking similarities, even though their stand on Paul was precisely at odds.[28]

THE EPISTLE OF JUDE

Jude is the shortest forgery of the New Testament, and like many of the others, it is filled with invective against its opponents, even if scholars have found it difficult to discern what, exactly, these enemies of truth were thought to have proclaimed.

Jude the Brother of James

An initial question to be addressed concerns the book's authorial claim. There are a number of persons named Jude/Judas in the New Testament : Judas Iscariot (Mark 3:19 and parallels; twenty-two occurrences altogether), Judas the son of James (the apostle, Luke 6:16), who may also be Judas "not Iscariot" of John 14:22, Judas the Galilean in Acts 5:37, Judas who owns a house in Acts 9:11, Judas who is called Barsabbas in Acts 15:22. There are solid reasons for thinking that the author of this letter is claiming to be one specific and arguably the best-known Jude of the early church, the brother of Jesus mentioned in Mark 6:3 (along with James, Joses, and Simon). The author identifies himself as the "brother of James" in v. 1, and Mark 6:3 provides us with the only James-Jude brother relationship in the New Testament. Moreover, one would normally identify oneself in relationship to one's father, not one's brother. The brother in this case must be an unusually well-known person to serve as an identity marker for the author—in this case, a well-known Christian. By far the best known James of

28. Matthias Konradt, "Der Jakobusbrief als Brief des Jakobus," in Petra V. Gemünden et al., eds., *Der Jakobusbrief: Beiträge zur Rehabilitierung der 'strohernen Epistel'"* (Münster: Lit Verlag, 2003), pp. 16–53. Thus the parallels of James 1:2–3 with 1 Pet. 1:6–7 in particular show that the relationship was probably on the literary level Πειρασμοὶ ποικίλοι. . . . τὸ δοκίμιον ὑμῶν τῆς πίστεως: "[begegnet man] in der gesamten antiken Literatur nur an den genannten beiden Stellen." Konradt, "Jakobus, der Gerechte: Erwägung zur Verfasserfiktion des Jakobusbriefes," in Jörg Frey et al., eds., *Pseudepigraphie und Verfasserfiktion*, p. 579. Cf. also James 4:6–10 with 1 Pet. 5c–9 (both replace LXX κύριος with θεός) and James 1:18, 21 with 1 Pet. 1:22–2:2 (conversion as rebirth).

the early church, of course, was James the brother of Jesus, head of the church in Jerusalem. The author of this short text, therefore, is almost certainly claiming to be a brother of both James and Jesus (cf. Mark 6:3; Matt. 13:55).

In a moment we will see why the author may have wanted to identify himself in relation to James rather than Jesus. Some scholars have objected that Jude was too obscure a name for an author to choose as a pseudonym.[29] The objection has more rhetorical than substantive force, however. On one hand, how many "nonobscure" figures were there to choose from in the early church? The objection seems to assume that everyone writing pseudepigraphically would choose the names Peter or Paul. On the other hand, and more pressing still, how could Jude be thought of as obscure (leaving Hardy out of the equation)? He was widely known as extraordinarily well connected: his one brother was "the" leader of the earliest Christian community; his other brother was the Savior of the World. Not bad credentials for an early Christian author.

More than that, as J. Frey and others have shown, the author is claiming not just to be a brother of James (and thus a brother of Jesus) but also to be closely connected to the letter written by this brother, the New Testament book of James. The connection to this earlier letter is suggested already by the author's use of the same identifying formula, Ἰησοῦ Χριστοῦ δοῦλος. Moreover, J. Daryl Charles has noted the inordinately large number of verbal parallels between the two books: 93 cases of verbal agreement out of 227 different words used, 27 of these terms occurring two or more times in both letters: "Astonishingly, *each* of the twenty-five verses of Jude averages approximately four words found in the epistle of James—an extraordinary rate of verbal correspondence." His conclusion: "Aside from Jude–2 Peter and Colossians-Ephesians comparisons, the verbal correspondence in James and Jude, considering the brevity of the latter, is unmatched anywhere else in the New Testament."[30] The writer of the letter of Jude, then, is claiming a derived authority; as Vögtle has put it, Jude's reference to his literary predecessor gives him a status as "einen zweiten Jakobus."[31]

Jude as a Forgery

Jude was rejected by some proto-orthodox and orthodox writers. Eusebius indicates that like the book of James, it was thought by some to be forged (ἰστέον

---

29. An issue raised, for example, in Jörg Frey, "Autorfiktion und Gegnerbild im Judasbrief und im Zweiten Petrusbrief," in Frey et al. eds., *Pseudepigraphie und Verfasserfiktion*, pp. 683–732.

30. J. Daryl Charles, *Literary Strategy in the Epistle of Jude* (Scranton, PA: University of Scranton Press, 1993), p. 77. Charles goes astray only in trying to explain these similarities as deriving from the circumstance that the two authors were writing in the same Jewish Galilean milieu, as if both would have had similar training in Greek composition. Given what we have seen about literacy rates in rural Galilee, Frey "Autorfiktion und Gegnerbild" is much more convincing in seeing in these linguistic parallels evidence for literary dependence.

31. Anton Vögtle, *Der Judasbrief. Der 2 Petrusbrief* (Düsseldorf: Benzinger Verlag, 1994), p. 17.

δὲ ὡς νοθεύεται μέν), although it was publically read in many churches and thus, possibly, canonical:

> Such is the story of James, to whom is attributed the first of the "general" epistles. Admittedly its authenticity is doubted [ἰστέον δὲ ὡς νοθεύεται μέν], since few early writers refer to it, any more than to Jude's, which is also one of the seven called general (λεγομένων καθολικῶν). But the fact remains that these two, like the others, have been regularly used in very many churches. (*H.E.* 2.23.25)

Jerome voiced a more specific doubt about the book: since it quotes from 1 Enoch, it was regarded by many as non-Scriptural and rejected:

> Jude the brother of James, left a short epistle which is reckoned among the seven catholic epistles, and because in it he quotes from the apocryphal book of Enoch it is rejected by many (a plerisque reicitur). Nevertheless by age and use it has gained authority and is reckoned among the Holy Scriptures. (*Vir. ill.* 4)

Modern times have seen a healthy split among scholars who see the book as authentically written by the brother of Jesus and of James, and those who consider it forged.[32] Numerous factors give the palm to the latter group. For one thing, the book gives every indication of being produced relatively late in the first century, after the "age of the apostles." The apostles themselves are referred to as living in the past, and as predicting the "last time" when the author is now living—differentiated from the time of the apostles themselves (vv. 17–18). The author speaks of "the faith" as the content of the body of knowledge that makes up the Christian religion, a usage found in the Pastorals but not in earlier Christian writings such as those of Paul, despite occasional scholarly claims to the contrary.[33] That this "faith" was "delivered once and for all to the saints" assumes an event that transpired in the now distant past.

More important for our purpose here, there are highly convincing reasons for thinking that whoever wrote this letter, it was not Jude, the Aramaic-speaking peasant from Nazareth.[34] Here again, as with the book of James, we need to deal with the problem of language. This author too is not just writing-literate; he

32. For a list of scholars on both sides since 1880, see Richard Bauckham, *Jude and the Relatives of Jesus in the Early Church* (London: T&T Clark, 1990), p. 174 n. 261. Bauckham himself makes a spirited defense for authenticity.

33. See, for example, Peter H. Davids, *The Letters of 2 Peter and Jude*, who instances Paul's usage in 2 Cor. 13:5 ("your faith"), and Gal 1:23 ("preaching the faith he once tried to destroy"). But neither reference means what Jude means by "the faith." The first is a reference to "your faith"—which is not a body of knowledge or truths to be confessed; the latter reference uses the term to refer to a group of believers who put their trust in Christ. Again, that is different from "the body of knowledge that we call the faith." Even Davids admits that the use of the term in Jude compares most favorably with the Pastorals.

34. On Jude as a "peasant," see p. 219, n. 54.

writes very good Greek, not the sort of skill one can acquire simply by spending time on the mission field without years of serious literary training.[35] As R. Bauckham points out, the book employs "wide and effectively used vocabulary"; some of its terminology is "rather specialized" (σπιλάς, φθινοπωρινός, πλανήτης); other words are relatively rare (ἀποδιορίζέιν, ἐπαφρίζέιν). The author has "command of good Greek idiom," his "sentence construction is handled with considerable rhetorical effect." Bauckham goes on to speak of the author's "almost poetic economy of words, scriptural allusions, catchword connections, and the use of climax."[36] In the fullest study of Jude's style, J. Daryl Charles speaks of the author's "elevated use . . . of rhetorical invention, composition, and style," and mentions, in particular, his use of "parallelism, antithesis, figures of speech, repetition, ornamentation, vivid symbolism, word- and sound-play."[37]

In addition, it should be pointed out that the author is not only flawlessly fluent in Greek composition, but he also knows the Hebrew Bible, evidently in Hebrew.[38] Moreover, he knows the book of 1 Enoch, arguably in Aramaic.[39] As a result, we have here an author who is not merely literate—able to read, apparently effortlessly—in three languages, but fully writing-literate in one of them (a second language for him, if he were a native of rural Palestine). How could this be true of Jesus' brother, an Aramaic-speaking peasant from a small hamlet of Galilee, who no doubt like his father was a common laborer?[40]

As a side note, I might mention that we have some record about Jude's family from later times, which gives us no indication that it came from the upper

35. The unreflective claims of R. Bauckham notwithstanding (see Richard J. Bauckham, *Jude, 2 Peter*, WBC, 50, Waco, TX: Word, 1983, pp. 6–16, esp. pp. 15–16). Writing literacy did not come from hearing others speak the language and picking up conversational Greek for oneself. It took substantial training in a school setting, requiring years of hard work. See pp. 242–47.

36. Bauckham, *Jude, 2 Peter*, p. 6.

37. *Literary Strategy in the Epistle of Jude*, pp. 62–63.

38. So Bauckham, who argues that in two quotations (vv. 12, 13) the author bases his argument on wording found in Hebrew, not Greek, text; in three references to the OT (vv. 11, 12, 23) his vocabulary does not correspond to that of the LXX; p. 7. This assumes, of course, that the LXX text available to us today was a stable entity then as well.

39. So Bauckham, p. 7.

40. As I have repeatedly stated, becoming reading-literate in just one language took years and considerable resources; becoming writing-literate—at the level required to compose a book—took still more years. And that was in one's native tongue. To become writing-literate in a second language required intensive training. Where would Jude have found the time or resources to manage this training? It is true that his brother, Jesus, may have been extraordinary among his townspeople for learning to read (Hebrew), but that is a far cry from being able to compose a book in Hebrew, let alone in Greek. And everything suggests that Jesus was the outstanding exception in the family. Anyone who suggests that a person like the historical Jude could have learned Greek composition simply by traveling the world as a missionary has not taken seriously the scholarship on ancient literacy and on the educational systems of antiquity. Contrast Bauckham: "if his [Jude's] missionary travels took him among strongly Hellenized Jews there is no reason why he should not have deliberately improved his command of Greek to increase his effectiveness as a preacher"; p. 15.

classes that could afford the time and money for education. Hegesippus tells the story of Jude's grandsons brought before the emperor Domitian, when he learned they were from the line of David and so, possibly, instigators of a kind of messianic uprising against the state. These men convinced Domitian that they were poor farmers who could barely eke out an existence working full time on the land, showing him their calloused hands as proof. And so he set them free (Eusebius *H.E.* 3.19–20). There can be little doubt that the report is apocryphal. It defies belief that the Roman emperor himself would cross-examine Jewish peasants from Palestine, let alone that he would do so out of fear that their insurgency might cripple his empire. But the story does show how Jude's family was remembered in the early church: not as aristocratic elites with wealth and leisure to receive the refined benefits of higher education. Just the contrary, they continued to be known as lower-class peasants who engaged in full-time manual labor simply to survive. Nothing suggests that their progenitor, Jude, was any different.

In short, the book of Jude appears to have been written relatively late in the first century, after the age of the apostles, by a highly educated Greek-speaking (and -writing) Christian who was able to negotiate the complexities of both the Hebrew Bible and surviving Aramaic literature. Whoever this elite, well-trained figure was, he was not the Aramaic-speaking peasant of Nazareth, the brother of Jesus and James.

The Nature of the Polemic

The epistle of Jude presents an outpouring of invective against a group of persons who have allegedly infiltrated the Christian community, wreaking havoc in their wake. In the influential view of Frederik Wisse, the "heresy" promoted by these persons has no real content.[41] These persons are accused of being wildly licentious (v. 4) and of denying "our only Master and Lord Jesus Christ" (v. 4). This shows that the predictions of the apostles have come to pass, that the readers are indeed living "in the last time" (v. 17). Wisse appears to be absolutely right that the author of this short piece of polemic must grossly exaggerate the character of his opponents: "It is beyond belief that persons of this description could have been accepted and tolerated in a Christian congregation, much less have slipped in unnoticed."[42] But he probably goes too far in claiming that the author would have not written pseudonymously to an unspecified group of readers if he had wanted to address a specific problem. Pseudepigraphic polemics regularly attack specific problems and deal with concrete issues. Moreover, we can indeed say some things more concretely about the views of these enemies to the true "faith once delivered to the saints" (v. 3).

For one thing, the opponents are portrayed as having come from the outside and having infiltrated the community (v. 4). It is not at all clear that we should

41. Frederik Wisse, "The Epistle of Jude."

42. Ibid., p. 136.

accept their outsider status: this part of the polemic could easily have arisen from the concern not to concede that "the truth" was perverted from the inside. But that the opponents were *eventually* inside the community should at least be clear. Otherwise it is impossible to explain the author's vexation.

Modern interpreters have taken the portrayal of the enemies as licentious reprobates to two equally unlikely extremes. Some, such as Gerhard Sellin, have discounted all of the language of moral iniquity and claimed that modern interpreters have read licentiousness into the book instead of out of it.[43] Even though other parts of Sellin's understanding of the book are attractive, it is difficult to concede to him this particular point. Whatever else the author wanted to say about his opponents, charges of antinomian behavior figure prominently (thus: ἀσέλγεια v. 4, ἐκπορνεύσασαι v. 7 [spoken about Sodom and Gomorrah, but the opponents behave "in a similar way"]; σάρκα . . . μιαίνουσιν, v. 8; συνευωχούμενοι, v. 12; αἰσχύνας, v. 13; κατὰ τὰς ἐπιθυμίας ἑαυτῶν πορευόμενοι, v. 16; κατὰ τὰς ἑαυτῶν ἐπιθυμίας πορευόμενοι τῶν ἀσεβειῶν, v. 18). The other extreme is represented by Bauckham, who claims that the author is concerned with antinomianism and nothing but antinomianism.[44] This view overlooks other charges leveled against the opponents, or at least it has to force them into an uncomfortable antinomian mold, as they are said to "deny . . . Christ" (v. 4); to "revile glorious ones" (v. 8); to follow the error of Balaam and the rebellion of Korah (v. 11); and to be grumblers, boasters, and flatterers (v. 16)—none of which necessarily involves licentious lifestyles.

Something more specific about the enemies' alleged antinomian behavior is suggested by v. 4: they "alter the grace of our God into licentiousness" (τὴν τοῦ θεοῦ ἡμῶν χάριτα μετατιθέντες εἰς ἀσέλγειαν). In other words, they take the teaching of χάρις too far, thinking that the Christian religion is all about grace, not about how one lives. For them—in the judgment of their opponent, the author—antinomian living is a consequence of the teaching of grace. In an earlier period, Paul himself, an advocate of χάρις, was accused of holding some such view: "Just as some claim that we say, ' let us do evil so that good might come'" (Rom. 3:8). Paul naturally denies the charge, but one can see how it might be taken, by others, to be the logical conclusion of his teaching of divine grace and the justifying effect of faith apart from "works of the Law." But the charge makes even better sense against later forms of Paulinism, such as that represented in the book of Ephesians, a forgery that states quite explicitly that one is saved not by doing good deeds but solely by the grace (χάρις) of God: "For you have been saved by grace, through faith—and this is not from yourselves, it is the gift of God, not from works, so that no one may boast" (Eph. 2:8–9).

The author of Ephesians takes Paul's teaching on faith and grace a step beyond Paul, in indicating that good behavior can have no bearing on "being saved." The opponents of Jude allegedly take the matter a step further still: antinomian

43. Gerhard Sellin, "Die Häretiker des Judasbriefes," *ZNW* 77 (1986): 206–25.

44. *Jude, 2 Peter*, pp. 11–13.

activity demonstrates the full grace of God, which alone brings salvation. Or at least the author of Jude *portrays* his opponents as making that argument. Whether they did so or not is anyone's guess; but it does give one pause that Paul himself was falsely accused of something similar already decades earlier.[45] In any event, this charge against what appears to be a (post-)Pauline position can help explain why the author claims to be Jude, the brother of James. As Sellin recognized, this author is uniting with the epistle of James in opposing a view of grace that renders the moral life of the Christian immaterial.[46]

But there is even more in the polemic of Jude to suggest that the opponents are being constructed as representing a form of Pauline Christianity. One of the specific charges leveled against them is that they denigrate and revile angels. Bauckham, who sees the problem with the opponents purely in antinomian terms, has difficulty explaining this charge. In his view, these angels are possibly the ones who delivered the Law; they are reviled by those who violate it—an implausible view, since nothing is said about the "glorious ones" being those who delivered the commandments to Moses. A better alternative has been proposed by Sellin and, to some extent dependent on him, Frey.[47] The denigration of angelic beings was part of the Pauline tradition.

Before turning to Paul, consider the comments of Jude. According to v. 8, the opponents not only "defile the flesh," they also "reject authority" and "revile glorious ones." In v. 10 again they are said to "revile what they do not understand." They are unlike the archangel Michael, who did not dare to revile the Devil (v. 9). Moreover, the one explicit quotation of the short epistle is of 1 Enoch in vv. 14–15, a passage that also relates to angels, as does the allusion to the Book of the Watchers (presumably) in v. 6.[48] As Frey notes, the "decisive point for the author lies in his angelology."[49]

---

45. Sellin, "Die Häretiker," goes too far in thinking that the τοῦτο of Jude 4 ("this condemnation") is inexplicable as a reference to the judgment described in v. 15, since there it is κρίσις rather than κρίμα. In his view it is a cross-reference back to Rom. 3:8. But it is hardly conceivable that a reader would make that link rather than the other, especially since the two words can be used synonymously, and in 15 it is found in a quotation (it obviously is not referring to the judgment of v. 6, as that refers to the angels, or of v. 9, which is about Michael and the Devil; only vv. 4 and 15 refer to the judgment of humans).

46. Sellin, "Die Häretiker," p. 211, n. 17.

47. Ibid.; Jörg Frey, "Autorfiktion und Gegnerbild im Judasbrief und im Zweiten Petrusbrief," in Jörg Frey et al., eds., *Pseudepigraphie und Verfasserfiktion*, pp. 683–732.

48. Sellin "Die Häretiker," argues that vv. 6–7 are part of the polemic against the opponents, but this is taking the case a step too far. These two verses indicate past instances of judgment against the disobedient, not charges against the false teachers.

49. "Autorfiktion und Gegnerbild," p. 698. Sellin is too extreme in insisting that the entire polemic of the book involves the relationship to angels, as when he argues that "defiling the flesh" in v. 8 refers to humans and angels inappropriately entering into one another's spheres. That would be an odd meaning for "defiling the flesh," given the other language invoking licentiousness. Rather, these opponents revile angels *and* carry the teaching of "grace" to an inappropriate extreme. One can imagine numerous possible connections between the two prongs of this attack. Are the opponents, for example, thought to despise all authority—angelic beings and moral codes?

Where in the Christian tradition are angels devalued? As Frey points out, we already see a movement in this direction, possibly, in the undisputed Paul, where the phenomenon of glossolalia already places believers on the same level as angels (1 Cor. 13:1). Moreover, for Paul, rulers, powers, and authorities are considered inferior forces, subject to Christ in the end (1 Cor. 15:24). And believers are said to be the future judges of angels (1 Cor. 6:3). In Galatians Paul devalues the Law precisely because it was given through angels (Gal. 3:19).

This depotentizing of angels is carried out yet further in the Deutero-Pauline epistles. Angelic powers are part of the creation overcome by Christ (Col. 1:16; 2:10; Eph. 1:21); they are stripped through Christ's triumph over the powers (Col. 2:15), and for that reason they are decidedly not to be worshiped (Col. 2:18). This final verse is especially key for Sellin and Frey. As Frey states: "It is thus certainly imaginable that an attitude like the one mentioned by the author of Colossians appeared to the author of Jude as a denial of the cosmological and eschatological significance of the angels and the order represented by them."[50] Or as Sellin earlier put it:

> Connections . . . may well exist between the author of Colossians, who polemicizes against angel-worshippers, and the heretics of the Epistle of Jude. After all, it becomes apparent in Col 2:18 that the tenets of the Law and the service of angels, on one hand, and antinomianism and the despising of angels, on the other hand, belong together. The heretics of the Epistle of Jude thus appear to me to be standing in a Pauline tradition whose oldest witness is Colossians.[51]

Despite the attractiveness of this position, it should be pointed out that the polemic of Jude appears to be directed at Pauline Christians who have taken their views (whether actually or simply in the author's fertile imagination) yet a step farther than that evidenced in the Deutero-Pauline epistles of Ephesians and Colossians. Just as the opponents do not merely insist that χάρις apart from good works brings salvation (as in Ephesians), but go much farther (allegedly) in promoting an actual antinomian lifestyle, so too the opponents do not merely discourage the worship of angels (as in the Deutero-Paulines), but they (allegedly) actively denigrate them. Thus even though the opponents do not take a position attested in any of the canonical Pauline writings, they stand in a clear Pauline trajectory.

---

50. "Es ist daher durchaus denkbar, dass eine Haltung, wie sie der Autor des Kol zur Sprache bringt, dem Verfasser des Jud als Leugnung der kosmologischen und eschatologischen Bedeutung der Engel und der durch sie repräsentierten Ordnung erscheinen." "Autorfiktion und Gegnerbild," p. 700.

51. "Wohl . . . könnte es Verbindungslinien geben zwischen dem Verfasser des Kolosserbriefes, der gegen die Engel-Verehrer polemisiert, und den Häretikern des Judasbriefes. Aus Kol. 2,18 geht ja hervor, daß Gesetzesvorschriften und Engeldienst einerseits, Antinomismus und Verachtung der Engel andererseits zusammengehören. So scheinen mir die Häretiker des Judasbriefes in einer paulinischen Tradition zu stehen, deren ältestes Zeugnis der Kolosserbrief darstellt." "Die Häretiker," p. 222.

It is impossible to say whether any such opponents really existed. But they certainly existed in the imagination of the author, whose attacks appear to be directed against Pauline Christians.[52] It is this opposition to Paul—at least as conceived in the mind of the author—that explains, then, the choice of the pseudonym "Jude." P. Davids is off-base to argue that an author wanting to choose a false name would not have chosen an "obscure" figure such as Jude, as we saw out the outset. Indeed, this author chose to polemicize against the Pauline tradition in a way that makes patent sense. By choosing the name Jude he has established his credentials as one closely related to James of Jerusalem, and he, in fact, stands in clear lines of continuity with the letter allegedly written by his more famous brother. His grounds of attack are different, but the target is the same: Paulinists whose radical views had led to the rejection of all authority, angelic and moral.[53]

THE EPISTULA PETRI

Although the Epistula Petri is one of the "introductory writings" of the Pseudo-Clementine *Homilies*, it is not altogether clear that it was composed to serve that function. The "Preachings" of Peter at issue in the letter are not the *Homilies* of Clement themselves. Indeed, they appear to be a collection of writings that were earlier sent by Peter to "James, the lord and bishop of the holy church" (1:1),[54] whether this was an actual collection, or more likely, a fiction alluded to simply to provide the occasion of the letter. Moreover, Clement is not mentioned in the letter. For these reasons, despite common scholarly opinion, the letter may have been composed independently and was only added to the *Homilies* secondarily.[55]

The purpose of the letter is to instruct James to follow the example set by Moses among "those who belong to his people" for the transmission of sacred literature. Just as Moses passed his books only to specially selected individuals who could

---

52. As I have stressed, such an author would have had no way of knowing that the views of these Paulinists differed from the views of Paul, lacking, as he did, access to modern critical analyses of the Pauline corpus and the modern scholarly reconstruction of the "real" Paul.

53. And so Frey's conclusion is apt: "The choice of pseudonym in this regard does not serve to legitimatize the text and its content, or serves only in a very limited way; it serves primarily the assignation [of the text] to a particular line of tradition that is characterized by the figure of James and is represented by the Epistle of James, and that takes a critical stance against various developments in the Pauline-Deutero-Pauline tradition." ("Die Wahl dieses Pseudonyms dient insofern nicht oder nur sehr wenig der Legitimation des Schreibens und seines Inhalts, sondern primär der Zuordnung zu einer Traditionslinie, die durch die Gestalt des Jakobus markiert und durch den Jakobusbrief repräsentiert ist und verschiedenartigen Entwicklungen in der paulinisch-deuteropaulinischen Tradition kritisch gegenübertritt.") "Autorfiktion und Gegnerbild," p. 702.

54. All translations are from Johannes Irmscher and Georg Strecker, "The Pseudo-Clementines," trans. R. McL. Wilson, in *New Testament Apocrypha*, ed. Wilhelm Schneemelcher (Louisville, KY: Westminster/John Knox, 1992).

55. For a recent statement of other opinions, see Graham Stanton, "Jewish Christian Elements in the Pseudo-Clementine Writings," in *Jewish Believers in Jesus*, ed. Oskar Skarsaune and Reidar Hvalvik (Peabody, MA: Hendrickson, 2007), pp. 305–24.

be trusted, so too the books of Peter's preaching are not to be given to "any one of the gentiles," nor to any "of our own tribe" before they have gone through a period of trial to demonstrate that they are trustworthy. The reason for Peter's concern is clear: there have been some gentiles "who have rejected my lawful preaching [that is preaching about and in accordance with the Law], and have preferred a lawless and absurd doctrine of the man who is my enemy" (2.3). These gentile enemies have tried to "distort my words by interpretations of many sorts as if I taught the dissolution of the Law" (2.4). But for Peter this is a heinous charge, for he would never oppose "the Law of God which was made known by Moses" and which was borne witness to by Jesus, who indicated that none of the Law will ever pass away while there is a heaven and earth (quoting Matt. 5:18). Peter, in other words, is in full support of the Mosaic Law, which continues in full force; to think otherwise is to oppose God, Moses, and Jesus (2.5). It is only "the man who is my enemy," and the gentiles he has influenced, who have twisted Peter's words to make him appear to say otherwise.

No one thinks that the actual author of this short letter was Peter himself. But it was certainly someone who wanted his readers to think he was Peter. And the identity of his opponent is no mystery: it is Paul ("the man who is my enemy") and his followers ("the gentiles").

The idea that care was needed in passing along important texts was a commonplace in the ancient world, where books copied by hand were open not only to misinterpretation but also to physical alteration. Comparable concerns can be found, for example, in Galen's *De libris propriis* 11: "I ordered that these notes should be shared only with those who would read the books with a teacher." So too in the Apocryphon of James from Nag Hammadi, a writing also connected with Peter:

> You have asked me to send you a secret book revealed to me and Peter by the master, and I could not turn you down, nor could I speak to you, so [I have written] it in Hebrew and have sent it to you , and to you alone. But since you are a minister of the salvation of the saints, do your best to be careful not to communicate to many people this book that the Savior did not want to communicate even to all of us, his twelve disciples. (1.8ff.)[56]

That Paul is the unnamed "man who is my enemy" is not open to much doubt.[57] This is someone who has an enormous effect on "the gentiles" and who preaches a "lawless gospel." This latter phrase is shorthand for a gospel message that pro-

---

56. Translation of Marvin Meyer, *The Nag Hammadi Scriptures*, p. 23.

57. See Pierluigi Piovanelli, "'L'Ennemi est parmi Nous': Présences rhétoriques et narratives de Paul dans les Pseudo-Clémentines et autres écrits apparentés," in *Nouvelles intrigues pseudo-clémentines—Plots in the Pseudo-Clementine Romance: Actes du deuxième colloque international sur la littérature apocryphe chrétienne, Lausanne—Genève, 30 août—2 septembre 2006*, Frédéric Amsler et al., eds. (Prahins, Switzerland: Éditions du Zèbre, 2008). I am obliged to Maria Doefler for this reference.

claims a person can be made right with God without keeping the Jewish Law, an apt description of Paul's message in a book such as Galatians, sent to gentiles and insisting on justification apart from "works of the Law." It is striking that the author of the Epistula Petri is particularly concerned that this "enemy" proclaims that Peter himself supports his "lawless gospel." That is precisely Paul's claim in Galatians, as he indicates that the pillars of the Jerusalem church, James, Cephas, and John, "added nothing to me" and in fact "gave me and Barnabas the right hand of fellowship" (Gal. 2:6, 9). According to Paul, Peter agreed with his law-free gospel. However one construes the precise nuances of the matter—a much-disputed topic—the Antioch incident of Gal. 2:11–14, in Paul's eyes, was a matter of Peter's hypocrisy. Whereas Peter had formerly, in Jerusalem, agreed with Paul's gentile gospel, and acted out this agreement in having table fellowship with gentiles (who obviously were not keeping kosher), he changed his mind and his behavior so as not to give offense, once members of "the circumcision" came to town as representatives of James. In Paul's eyes, Peter's offense was that he began to act as if he did not agree with the law-free gospel after he had already, overtly, agreed.

The Epistula Petri may well be referring to the account of the Antioch incident in Galatians when it charges its enemies with maintaining that Peter agreed with "the dissolution of the Law" but that he "did not express it openly"—in other words, that he held to a Pauline view, but did not publicly say so. This is the charge that Paul levels against Peter in the passage of Galatians, before stating baldly: "knowing that a person is not justified by works of the Law, but through faith in Jesus Christ, even we have believed in Christ Jesus, so that we might be justified by faith in Christ and not by works of the Law, because from the works of the Law will no one be justified" (2:16). This, then, is the "lawless" gospel that Peter opposes in the Epistula Petri, and that his enemies falsely accuse him of affirming.

It is striking that other forgeries of early Christianity do indeed claim that Peter agreed with Paul in his law-free gospel message. As we have seen, that is one of the overarching themes of the book of Acts, a non-pseudepigraphic forgery allegedly by one of Paul's own companions. In Acts it is not Paul who first learns that the gospel is to come to gentiles apart from the Law, but Peter (Acts 10). And it is not Paul who first converts gentiles to the law-free faith, but, again, Peter (Acts 10–11). Moreover Peter and James—even more than in Paul's account of Galatians 2—are completely aligned with Paul's law-free gospel in Acts; at the Jerusalem Conference of Acts 15 everyone sees eye-to-eye: the gentiles are not to keep the Law in order to receive salvation through Jesus. This, for Acts, is the explicit message of Peter, the alleged sender of the Epistula Petri (Acts 15:7–11); James, the alleged recipient of the Epistula (Acts 15:13–21); and Paul, the enemy described in the letter (Acts 15:12).[58]

---

58. See Annette Yoshiko Reed, "'Jewish Christianity' as Counter-history? The Apostolic Past in Eusebius' Ecclesiastical History and the Pseudo-Clementine *Homilies*," in *Antiquity in Antiquity: Jewish and Christian Pasts in the Greco-Roman World*, eds. Gregg Gardner and Kevin L. Osterloh (Tübingen: Mohr Siebeck, 2008), p. 177, n. 17.

A similar message is presented in the forged 1 Peter, which advocates a Pauline gospel in the name of Peter, and yet more obviously in the forged 2 Peter, where the author not only doth protest too much that he really is Peter, but also claims to be on the same theological page as Paul, whose writings he classifies among "the Scriptures" (2 Pet. 3:16). There are in fact interesting and ironic similarities between 2 Peter and the Epistula Petri. In the latter "Peter" expresses his chagrin over those who have twisted his teachings by false interpretation, making him sound as if he supports the lawless gospel message of his enemy (Paul). 2 Peter, on the other hand, complains of alleged followers of Paul who twist Paul's words away from a Petrine view. And so, in one book it is the writings of Peter that are twisted, in the other it is the writings of Paul. In both instances the twisting involves false and, one might say, unauthorized interpretations. But in the case of 2 Peter, the false interpretations portray Peter and Paul as standing at odds with one another; in the case of the Epistula Petri they portray them as standing in unity.

It is not difficult to imagine that the Epistula Petri arose because of other forgeries, some of them in the name of Peter, that maintained that Peter and Paul agreed on the Pauline understanding of a so-called law-free gospel. If so, then it would be another instance of counterforgery. Its subsequent attachment to the Pseudo-Clementine *Homilies* makes sense, not only because it celebrates the importance of Peter, but also because it does so at the expense of Paul, a theme that recurs at other places in the *Homilies,* as we will see below.

It is interesting, then, to trace the history of Peter and Paul through these various writings. The historical Peter himself may well have held to the ongoing importance of the Law, at least for Jews. That would explain his actions in Antioch, as maligned by Paul in Gal. 2:11–14. Again, on the historical level, this may indeed have led to a falling out between the apostle to the circumcised and the apostle to the uncircumcised. Later, forgeries were produced taking a stand on this conflict. In the not-so-subtle account of the non-pseudepigraphic forgery allegedly produced by one of Paul's own companions, the book of Acts, the two apostles are portrayed as being in complete and perfect harmony. With greater subtlety the same lesson is conveyed in the forged 1 Peter. Later still all subtlety is once again abandoned, when yet a third Paulinist forged the letter of 2 Peter. On the other side of the equation an anti-Paulinist forged the Epistula Petri in order to counter this (false) opinion that the two apostles saw eye-to-eye, since, for this author, the harmony of the two would necessarily mean that Peter ultimately agreed with Paul. But for the Epistula Petri, the two did not agree, because Paul was the enemy. Moreover, in their dispute, Peter was right and Paul was wrong. And what is more, James of Jerusalem agreed with Peter.

THE EPISTULA CLEMENTIS

Another forgery that survives as one of the introductory writings to the Pseudo-Clementine *Homilies* is the Epistula Clementis. Although not usually recognized as such, the Epistula is a kind of "church order," comprising instructions about different church offices given to Clement, ordained to be the bishop of Rome by the apostle Peter. The key emphasis at the beginning and end of these orders concerns this ordination, as Peter passes along to his unwilling successor the power to bind and to loose. The overarching concern of the book, then, is to show that Clement is the one who carries Peter's authority in the governance of the church. As W. Ullmann puts it, "What we are here confronted with is the perfectly clear and unambiguous institution of an heir by St. Peter. . . . Clement was elevated onto the throne, the cathedra, of Peter by the apostle himself."[59]

The letter falsely claims to be written by Clement to "James, the lord and bishop of bishops, who governs the holy church of the Hebrews at Jerusalem" (1.1).[60] This address functions to establish the authority of James and, by implication, the importance of a Jewish understanding of the faith: James is both the leader of the "church of the Hebrews" and the "bishop of bishops." More particularly the address stresses the connection of Rome and Jerusalem, the two ultimate seats of power in the early church, whose two leaders are in complete agreement. Of special interest, Clement, bishop of Rome who has all the power of Peter to bind and loose, and so is superior to every convert to the faith, is subordinate not only to Peter but also to James, "who rules . . . the churches everywhere." This then is a Jewish-Christian forgery meant to promote a kind of Jewish Christianity. Correspondingly, the letter is written in no small measure to oppose Paul and the kind of Christianity he represents.

It is interesting to note, in this connection, the emphasis placed on Peter, often in implicit contrast to Paul. Peter is the "first fruit of our Lord, the first of the apostles to whom the Father first revealed the Son" (1.3). Here there seems to be a clear contrast with the Paul of the undisputed letters, who gloried in the fact that at his conversion "[God] was pleased to reveal his Son to me" (Gal. 1:16). It was Peter, the Epistula Clementis avers, who was a "table-companion and fellow traveller" with Jesus (1.3). Later in the *Homilies* this long acquaintance with Jesus will be used to set Peter over against Paul, who knew Jesus only from a brief vision (Hom. 17.13–19). Peter was appointed, "as the most capable of all" to "enlighten the darkest part of the world, the West, and was enabled to achieve it" (1.3). For those familiar with other early Christian literature, the contrasting claims of Paul are stark: he himself expressed a wish to preach in Rome (Rom. 1:15) and planned a mission to the far West (Rom. 15:22–29). Moreover, according to the Roman 1 Clem. 5:7, it was precisely Paul who took the gospel to the West.

For the Epistula Clementis it was Peter who proclaimed Christ "to all the world . . . saving men by his God-willed teaching" (1.5). Later Clement is called "the better first-fruits among the gentiles who are saved through me [Peter]"

---

59. W. Ullmann, "Some Remarks on the Significance of the *Epistola Clementis* in the Pseudo-Clementines," *StPatr* 4 (1961): 332.

60. All translations are from Johannes Irmscher and Georg Strecker, "The Pseudo-Clementines," in Schneemelcher, ed. *New Testament Apocrypha*.

(3.4). It is not Paul who was the God-appointed missionary to the gentiles. The letter also speaks of "the evil one [who] has begun a war against His bride" (4.2). This may well be a reference to the devil as "the evil one." But it is also important to note that the way the evil one works is principally from inside the community, as Peter explicitly states at the end of the letter:

> If anyone remains a friend to those with whom he (the bishop) is at enmity, and speaks with those with whom he does not consort, he is himself one of those who wish to destroy the Church. For he who is with you in the body, but in his mind is not with you, he is against you, far more dangerous than the enemies who are visible outside, since with seeming friendship he scatters those within. (18.3–4)

Given the celebration of both Peter and James, and the obvious contrast being made between Peter and Paul—not to mention the context of the letter, coming in its transmitted state after the Epistula Petri and before the *Homilies*—it may well be that Paul is the enemy within.

In an even subtler way, this letter may evidence long-standing tensions between Peter and Paul, specifically with regard to the legitimate leadership of the church of Rome. Here it is Peter—emphatically not Paul—who is the chief apostle of the Roman church; he ordains his successor directly by a public ceremony of laying on of hands. Clement is presented as Peter's most important gentile convert to the faith and follower, who assumes the mantle of leadership only unwillingly.[61]

This view stands in contrast with the position taken by Irenaeus, who indicates that prior to Clement there were two other bishops, Linus and Anecletus, and that Peter and Paul *together* were responsible for the bishopric of Clement.[62] Irenaeus explicitly states that the church in Rome, which was "very great, very ancient, and universally known" was "founded and organized . . . by the two most glorious apostles Peter and Paul" (*Adv. Haer*. 3.3.2) Both apostles committed the church into the care of Linus, who was succeeded by Anecletus, and then Clement. Clement himself knew both apostles and had "the preaching of the apostles still echoing in his ears and their tradition before his eyes" (*Adv. Haer*. 3.3.3). Irenaeus' concern to stress the unity of Peter and Paul in the subsequent Roman leadership is especially clear in the following claim:

---

61. The tradition that Peter personally ordained Clement as bishop of the Roman church, directly after himself, without intermediating bishops, is also found in Tertullian, *Prescription*, 32.

62. Ullmann's view ("Significance," pp. 296–98) that the view of Clement's ordination derived from a careful reading of Irenaeus is flawed. On one hand, the tradition is also in Tertullian (see n. 61). Moreover, Ullmann's exegesis of *Adv. Haer.* 3.3.2–3 involves overreading: both Peter and Paul "hand over" the bishopric of Rome to Linus. Is that really categorically different from Clement, who was "called" to the position? It appears, instead, that Irenaeus is working to show the transitions of Roman leadership in such a way as to smooth over the stormy differences between Peter and Paul, which otherwise affected various factions within the Roman community.

> This succession, the ecclesiastical tradition from the apostles, and the preaching of the truth, have come down to us. And this is most abundant proof that there is one and the same vivifying faith, which has been preserved in the church from the apostles until now, and handed down in truth. (*Adv. Haer.* 3.3.3)

It is worth noting in this connection that Linus and Clement, mentioned by Irenaeus, are both associated in the New Testament with Paul (2 Tim. 4:21; Phil. 4:3), but never with Peter.

How different is the view of the Pseudo-Clementines themselves, and of the writings that now introduce them, including the Epistula Clementis, which presses for the superiority of Peter at the expense of Paul, and stresses that it was he alone who chose his successor to sit on his cathedra.

The orthodox concern for a unified Pauline-Petrine front in the leadership of Rome is found in a different way, later, in Eusebius, who indicates (contra Irenaeus) that Linus was called to be the bishop of the church only after Paul and Peter had been martyred (*H.E.* 3.2). Moreover, for Eusebius, Linus was the first bishop after Peter, and Clement the third (no reference to Anecletus; *H.E.* 3.4). Eusebius does not indicate who ordained Linus or Clement, but he does note that Clement was Paul's companion and co-worker, with reference, again, to Phil. 4:3.

Yet more interesting, from about the time of the Pseudo-Clementine *Homilies*, the Apostolic Constitutions indicates that the first bishop of Rome was Linus, who was ordained by Paul, and that the second was Clement, ordained by Peter (7.46). Does this reflect an early conflict found among factions in Rome, where some claimed that Paul was the one responsible for establishing the line of bishops and others claiming that it was Peter? Were there divisions in Rome comparable to what are earlier attested for Corinth ("I am of Paul, I am of Apollos, I am of Cephas"; 1 Cor. 1:12)? If so, it is no mystery which side of the debate eventually won out, as the less-than-conciliatory view represented in the forged Epistula Clementis became dominant: Peter founded the church and appointed his own successor, thus beginning the Roman apostolic line traced back to the chief disciple himself.

At every point, there were conciliatory voices, which cannot, however, agree among themselves about how to effect the conciliation. For some, both apostles appointed Linus; for others, Peter appointed Clement, Paul's companion; for others Paul appointed the first successor and Peter the second. Conciliation between the two apostles is found in other literature as well, including the forged pro-Pauline documents we have considered so far and the even more famous letter of 1 Clement, falsely attributed, not by accident, to Clement of Rome, but in fact written by the Roman church precisely to the church of Corinth, earlier divided along apostolic lines (1 Cor. 1:12), in which Peter and Paul are jointly portrayed as the two great apostles of the earlier generation (1 Clement 5).

It would be a mistake, however, to see the Epistula Clementis as being principally concerned with establishing a polemical position against Paul. The vast bulk of the letter is an early church order, with instructions and exhortations to the bishops, presbyters, deacons, and catechists of the church, and an extended analogy of the church as a ship with different crew members sailing over the rough seas of life. Moreover, the letter is set up to be an introduction to the Clementine *Homilies*. But in another sense the "set up" is precisely the point, as the *Homilies* too imagine a real threat from within, associated to some extent, at least with Paul. Here too is a forgery that, in part, attacks Paul's views with the authority of Peter and, by implication, James, as mediated through Clement, bishop of the church of Rome and the one who was ordained to his position through Peter, the one who had been given the power to bind and to loose.

PSEUDO-CLEMENTINE RECOGNITIONS AND HOMILIES

The Pseudo-Clementine *Recognitions* and *Homilies* represent two reworkings of an earlier Christian novel that described, principally, the conversion of the Roman Clement to the Christian faith through the ministration of the apostle Peter, and the proclamations and missionary adventures of the two afterward. The novel itself—the so-called Grundschrift—was probably composed in the early third century; its two surviving, heavily modified, iterations appear to stem from fourth-century Syria.[63] Both the *Recognitions* and *Homilies* are forged in the name of Clement himself; the former begins with the claim "I Clement, who was born in the city of Rome was from my earliest age a lover of chastity" (1.1), and goes from there. The *Homilies* begin similarly.[64]

Until recent years, the overwhelming concern of scholarship on the Pseudo-Clementines involved the vexed question of sources and of sources behind the sources: their extent, literary character, theological views, polemical targets, and dates. Few problems in early Christian studies have proved more intractable and convoluted. Since my interests in the present study are not with hypothetical sources that may have been forged, but with surviving texts, I will not delve into the source questions and the detailed arguments that have generated the *opinio*

63. The *Homilies* are usually dated to 300–320, and survive in their original Greek; the *Recognitions* are dated to 360–380 but survive only in the Latin translation of Rufinus. For the texts see Bernhard Rehm, *Die Pseudoklementinen: I Homilien*, ed. J. Irmischer (Berlin: Akademie-Verlag, 1953; 2nd ed., ed. F. Paschke, 1965; 3rd ed., ed. G. Strecker, 1994); Rehm, *Die Pseudoklementinen II Rekognitionen in Rufins Übersetzung*, ed. F. Paschke (Berlin: Akademie Verlag, 1965; 2nd ed., ed. G. Strecker, 1994).

64. For histories of research, see F. Stanley Jones, "The Pseudo-Clementines: A History of Research," *Second Century* 2 (1982): 1–33, 63–96; and F. Amsler, "État de la recherché récente sur le roman pseudo-clémentin," in F. Amsler et al., eds., *Nouvelles intrigues pseudo-clémentines—Plots in the Pseudo-Clementine Romances* (Lausanne: Éditions de Zèbre, 2008), pp. 25–45. A useful general overview can be found in Graham Stanton, "Jewish Christian Elements in the Pseudo-Clementine Writings," in Skarsaune and Hvalvik, eds., *Jewish Believers in Jesus*, pp. 305–24. A fuller introduction is F. Stanley Jones, "Introduction to the *Pseudo-Clementines*," in Jones, ed., *Pseudoclementina Elchasaiticaque inter Judaeochristiana: Collected Studies* (Orientalia Lovaniensia Analecta 203, Leuven: Peeters, in press).

communis that has more or less emerged here in the twenty-first century, except to say that the Grundschrift is widely thought to have been a Jewish-Christian production that, in part at least, represented a polemic against Marcionite understandings of the faith,[65] and that the source behind *Recognitions* 1.27–71 is widely taken to have been an attempt to rewrite, in some sense, the Christian history presented in the book of Acts, about which I will have more to say later.[66]

More recent scholarship, particularly in the insightful work of Nicole Kelley and Annette Yoshiko Reed, has bypassed the question of sources and approached the Pseudo-Clementines in their final form, asking what they can tell us about the social and theological conflicts within Christianity at the time and place of their production, fourth-century Syria.[67] These sophisticated analyses are relevant to such matters as the production and promotion of (some kind of) "Jewish Christianity" and the subtle polemics against unnamed opponents. For the present, however, I am principally interested in the several passages—incorporated, it appears, from earlier sources—that reflect opposition to Paul. In two of these passages the ostensible target is Simon Magus, Peter's nemesis on the missionary trail throughout the narratives. Scholars have long recognized that in some instances Simon is a cipher for Paul himself. This does not mean that in every episode involving Simon one should think of Paul. Quite the contrary, scholars such as Mark Edwards and, especially, Dominique Côté have shown that Simon is not a simple, coded figure, standing necessarily for Paul, his later follower Marcion, or even Simon Magus himself. He is a composite

---

65. So Han J. W. Drijvers, "Adam and the True Prophet in the Pseudo-Clementines," in Drijvers, "Adam and the True Prophet in the Pseudo-Clementines," in *Loyalitätskonflikte in der Religionsgeschichte*, FS Carsten Colpe, ed. Christoph Elsas and Hans Kippenberg (Würzburg: Königshausen und Neumann, 1990), pp. 314–23. More recently, with a different spin, see F. Stanley Jones, "Marcionism in the Pseudo-Clementines," *Poussières de christianisme et de judaïsme antiques*, ed. A. Frey and R. Gounelle (Prahins: Editions du Zèbre, 2007), pp. 225–44. It is a mistake to conclude, however, that since the work was anti-Marcionite, it could not also be Jewish-Christian, as Drijvers avers. See F. Stanley Jones, "Jewish Christianity of the *Pseudo-Clementines*," in *Companion to Second-Century Christian 'Heretics,'* ed. Antti Marjanen (Leiden: Brill, 2005), pp. 315–34.

66. See especially F. Stanley Jones, "An Ancient Jewish Christian Rejoinder to Luke's Acts of the Apostles: Pseudo-Clementine *Recognitions* 1.27–71," *Semeia* 80 (1997): 223–45; and his fuller study, *An Ancient Jewish Christian Source on the History of Christianity Pseudo-Clementine "Recognitions" 1.27–71*, SBLTT 37, Christian Apocrypha Series 2 (Atlanta, GA: Scholars Press, 1995).

67. Nicole Kelley, *Knowledge and Religious Authority in the Pseudo-Clementines: Situating the Recognitions in Fourth Century Syria* (Tübingen: Mohr Siebeck, 2006); and Kelley, "Problems of Knowledge and Authority in the Pseudo-Clementine Romance of *Recognitions*" *JECS* 13 (2005): 315–48; Annette Yoshiko Reed, "'Jewish Christianity' after the 'Parting of the Ways': Approaches to Historiography and Self-Definition in the Pseudo-Clementines," in *The Ways That Never Parted: Jews and Christians in Late Antiquity and the Early Middle Ages*, ed. Adam H. Becker and Annette Yoshiko Reed (Tübingen: Mohr Siebeck, 2003), pp. 189–231; Reed, "'Jewish Christianity' as Counter-history?" pp. 173–216; and Reed, "Heresiology and the (Jewish-)Christian Novel: Narrativized Polemics in the Pseudo-Clementine *Homilies*," in *Heresy and Identity in Late Antiquity*, eds. Eduard Iricinschi and Holger M. Zellentin (Tübingen: Mohr Siebeck, 2008), pp. 273–98.

figure encompassing the bad features of all these persons, and more.[68] It is nonetheless equally clear that in some of the polemic against Simon we are seeing polemic against Paul.

Recognitions 1.66–71

The one place where Paul is clearly in view and under attack, but not under the cipher of Simon, is in *Recognitions* 1.66–71. This is the concluding episode of the first instruction given to Clement by Peter, and as just noted, is widely taken to have been drawn from an earlier source that comprises 1.27–71, to be discussed as a whole later.[69] The instruction traces the history of God's interaction with humans from the creation of the world down to Clement's own day. In his speech Peter predicts that the Jerusalem Temple would be destroyed because the "time of sacrifices" has "passed away" with the coming of Jesus.[70] The Jewish sacrificial system, established by Moses as a compromising and temporary measure, has now been surpassed. This declaration causes an uproar among the Jewish priests, who are calmed by Gamaliel, called "a chief of the people," even though in fact he is portrayed as a secret Christian. Gamaliel promises that a public debate will be held on the next day to "oppose and clearly confute every error." His Jewish listeners assume that he means to confute the Christians, though in fact, as a secret follower of Jesus himself, he evidently plans to vindicate the Christian cause.

Gamaliel comes the next day to the scene of the debate with James, "the chief of the bishops," who enters into a public discussion with the chief priest Caiaphas. On the basis of arguments taken from the Jewish Scriptures, James shows that two advents of the Christ were foretold, one in humility and one in glory, and argues that no one could receive the remission of sins or enter the kingdom of heaven without being baptized in water "in the name of the threefold blessedness, as the true Prophet taught." James, as it turns out, is remarkably successful in his proclamation, such that over the course of seven days "he persuaded all the people and the high priest that they should hasten straightway to receive baptism." In other words, the entire Jewish nation, including its priestly leaders, are on the verge of converting to become followers of Jesus.

And then Paul arrives on the scene (ch. 70). He is not named, but it is quite clearly him: he is described as "one of our enemies" and in the next chapter he receives letters from the high priest to persecute the believers in Jesus in Damascus, an obvious reference to Acts 9. Just as the Jewish nation is about to turn to faith in

68. M. J. Edwards, "The *Clementina*: A Christian Response to the Pagan Novel," *CQ* 42 (1992), p. 462; Dominique Côté, "La fonction littéraire de Simon le magician dans les Pseudo-Clémentines," *LTP* 57 (2001): 513–23.

69. See pp. 318–20.

70. All quotations of the Pseudo-Clementine *Recognitions* and *Homilies* are taken from Thomas Smith, "Pseudo-Clementine Literature," *ANF*, vol. 8.

Jesus, Paul intervenes and creates a ruckus, argues publicly with James, and begins "to excite the people and to raise a tumult" and "to drive all into confusion with shouting and to undo what had been arranged with much labor." He then turns to violence, starts a riot so that "much blood was shed," and himself "attacked James and threw him headlong from the top of the steps" of the Temple, thinking that he had killed him (1.70).

This is obviously not a positive portrayal of Paul. He is the enemy; he is violently opposed to James—tries, in fact, to kill him. He prevents the wild success of the Christian mission, which was on the verge of converting the entire Jewish nation, even the high priest, to faith in Christ. This, to be sure, is the "pre-Christian" Paul. But there is no word anywhere in the book of his repenting of what he did or converting. For the *Recognitions*, penned in the name of Clement, the eventual leader of the church in Rome and Peter's right-hand man, Paul remains the enemy.

Homilies 2.15–18

Anti-Pauline polemic may also lie behind the famous discussion of the divinely ordained "pairs" (syzygies) in Hom. 2.15–18. In this address to Clement Peter provides a kind of schematized *Heilsgeschichte*, according to which God sends forth all things, including human beings, in pairs, with the inferior and the wicked preceding the superior and the good. And so, the temporary world precedes eternity; ignorance precedes knowledge. So too with "the leaders of prophecy": the wicked Cain came before the righteous Abel, Ishmael preceded Isaac. Peter then applies the logic to his own situation:

> It were possible, following this order, to perceive to what series Simon (Magus) belongs, who came before me (Simon Peter) to the Gentiles, and to which I belong who have come after him, and have come in upon him as light upon darkness, as knowledge upon ignorance, as healing upon disease. (ch. 17)

Later Peter points out that the Anti-Christ comes before Christ returns. And so on.

As earlier noted, Simon Magus is not simply a cipher for Paul throughout Peter's discourses. But one cannot help but draw the inferences in this case, as it is Paul in the Christian tradition who first goes out in the gentile mission field as the apostle to the gentiles.[71] In this understanding of things, Peter must follow in Paul's footsteps to correct those he has led astray.[72]

---

71. Even in Acts, although Peter is the first to convert a gentile (Acts 8), it is Paul who first engages in a sustained gentile mission.

72. Although even here Simon cannot be seen as "Paul without remainder." Peter goes on to describe Simon in the following chapter, and to discuss his history; clearly he is not thinking directly of Paul here.

Homilies 17.13–19

A much clearer polemic against Paul occurs in *Homilies* 17.13–19, an attack by Peter on "Simon's" authorization to preach his version of the gospel based on an alleged vision of Christ. As Graham Stanton has recognized, in this case "there can be no doubt at all that behind the mask of Simon Magus stands Paul."[73] Among other things, as Stanton notes, whereas the authenticating visionary experience is widely associated with Paul (cf. Galatians 1–2; Acts 9), in the Pseudo-Clementines Simon Magus never (elsewhere) appeals to a vision of Jesus.

The scene begins with Simon objecting to Peter's claims about Jesus. He, Simon, has had a vision, and since visions come from God, one need not question their reliability. Peter, however, gets the upper hand in his reply. The one "who trusts to apparition or vision and dream is insecure. For he does not know to whom he is trusting. For it is possible either that he may be an evil demon or a deceptive spirit, pretending in his speeches to be what he is not" (ch. 14). Moreover, no one can question or converse with a vision, only with a living person. Indeed, it is evil demons who appear to the impious enemies of God. What is more: "Statements of wrath are made through visions and dreams, but the statements to a friend are made face to face . . . not through riddles and visions and dreams, as to an enemy" (ch. 18). Peter then draws his conclusion: "If, then, our Jesus appeared to you in a vision, made Himself known to you, and spoke to you, it was as one who is enraged with an adversary."

Simon's alleged vision contrasts with Peter's own interaction with Jesus: "But can anyone be rendered fit for instruction through apparitions? And if you say, 'It is possible,' then I ask, 'why did our teacher abide and discourse a whole year to those who were awake?'" (ch. 19). Peter then issues a challenge:

> But if you were seen and taught by Him, and became His apostle for a single hour, proclaim His utterances, interpret His sayings, love His apostles, contend not with me who accompanied Him. For in direct opposition to me, who am a firm rock, the foundation of the Church, you now stand. If you were not opposed to me, you would not accuse me, and revile the truth proclaimed by me. (ch. 19)

Here we see the real issue: it is a conflict between Peter, the firm rock, and the apostle Paul, the unstable visionary, who uttered a contrary proclamation on the basis of an alleged revelation, and in so doing stood opposed to the one who spent an entire year in the presence of Jesus and was chosen by him to serve as the foundation of the church. As Stanton points out, that the author has the conflict of Peter and Paul clearly in mind is shown above all by the verbal links between the passage and the account of the Antioch incident in Gal. 2:11–14. In the *Homilies* Peter claims that Paul stands opposed to Peter (ἐναντίος ἀνθέστηκας μοι) just as

73. "Jewish Christian Elements," p. 315.

in Gal. 2:11 Paul claims that he stood opposed to Peter (κατὰ πρόσωπον αὐτῷ ἀντέστην; same verb). And in both cases the opposition is said to be because Peter stood κατεγνωσμένος.[74]

Paul, Peter, Barnabas, and Clement

By no stretch of the imagination can the Pseudo-Clementine *Recognitions* and *Homilies* be seen as principally polemical confrontations with Paul and Pauline Christianity. These are long, complex, and involved books with an array of other agendas.[75] At the same time, there are clear anti-Pauline elements scattered throughout their narratives and speeches. These anti-Pauline elements stand in stark contrast with the views we saw earlier in forgeries that championed Paul and his message, most notably the New Testament book of Acts. In these fourth-century forgeries, Paul's vision of the resurrected Jesus is not affirmed as an experience that authorizes his gospel message; on the contrary it is maligned and mocked. Here Paul is not shown standing shoulder-to-shoulder with Peter in his missionary activities; instead he is portrayed as one of Peter's enemies, attacked with some vehemence by the one chosen by Christ to be the foundation for the church. So too with James, whom Paul tries to murder and whose success in converting the entire Jewish nation is disrupted by none other than Paul. Here Paul's law-free gospel is portrayed as being at odds with the gospel of Christ, as we will see further in the chapter that follows.

In this connection it is interesting to see how two of the "co-workers" of Paul known from the New Testament writings are portrayed here. Barnabas figures importantly in the Pseudo-Clementine narrative (see *Recognitions* 1.7–13). He is the one who, at the beginning of the account, first comes to Rome, makes contact with the pagan Clement, preaches the true gospel in his presence, urges him to sail to Palestine to learn the truth of the gospel, and then meets him in Judea and introduces him to Peter, the hero of the account. There is nothing that ties Barnabas to Paul here; on the contrary, he is Peter's man and follows Peter's gospel. In fact, the reason he does not personally accompany Clement to Judea, but must precede him, is because he has to hurry back to celebrate a Jewish festival: "he hastened his departure, saying that he must by all means celebrate at Judea a festal day of his religion that was approaching" (1.10). Barnabas, companion of Peter, and responsible for the fate of the future leader of the Roman church, Clement, is Jewish to the core, continuing to observe Jewish festivals still as a Christian. Is this a poke at the Pauline law-free gospel? In any event, not just Peter but also Barnabas stands over against Paul in this account, even though in the book of Acts Barnabas is closely connected precisely with Paul.

---

74. Ibid., p. 316.

75. For a sense of the range of issues, see the most recent collection of essays, *The Pseudo-Clementines*, ed. Jan N. Bremmer (Leuven: Peeters, 2010).

Then there is Clement. In the New Testament he has no connection with Peter but only with Paul, his "co-worker" who "contended together with me in the gospel" (Phil. 4:3). But not in these books forged in his name. He is converted by Peter, he follows Peter, he accepts Peter's gospel, he accepts Peter's castigation of Paul. And so not only Barnabas but also Clement has been taken from Paul and given to Peter, the foundation of the church who stands against Paul, his authority, and his message.

The Counterforgery of Recognitions 1.27–71

It has generally been conceded by scholars of the Pseudo-Clementines that the anti-Pauline polemic of *Recognitions* 1.66–71 is part of a larger unit (chapters 27–71), which was taken over by the author, but not from the Grundschrift.[76] The grounds are solid: it is a coherent unit, it has no parallel in the *Homilies,* and its views in some ways contrast with those of the *Recognitions* otherwise, for example, in the elevated role it gives to Jesus in relationship to Moses.[77] Gerd Lüdemann argued that the passage was intended to present an alternative view of the development of church history to that found in the New Testament book of Acts, in fact that it "sets out to correct a section of Luke's Acts with its own version of the story."[78]

No one has developed this line of thought more fully than F. Stanley Jones, and although the argument is generally made with reference to the source itself, the same can be said of its incorporation in the fuller account of the *Recognitions.*[79] Jones lists a number of parallels between the account and the book of Acts, including as the most secure: Rec. 1.65.2–3 parallels Acts 5:34–39 (Gamaliel calming the crowd); Rec. 1.71.3–4 parallels Acts 9:1–2, 22:4–5, 26:10–12 (Paul arranges with the high priest to persecute the Christians); and Rec. 1.36.2 parallels Acts 3:22–23 (quotations of Deut. 18:15 and Lev. 23:29). Several other overlaps Jones considers "probable": Rec. 1.34.2 parallels Acts 7:8 (summary of the genealogy of Isaac, Jacob, and the twelve patriarchs); Rec. 1.41.1–2 parallels Acts 2:22–24 (Jesus is crucified even though he performed signs and wonders); and Rec. 1.71.2 parallels Acts 4:4 (five thousand flee Jerusalem to Jericho). Jones finds twenty-two other instances of parallels that he considers "possible." What he finds particularly striking is that in many of these instances the overlaps include aspects of Lukan redaction, showing that the author of this portion of the *Recognitions* is actually using Acts.

---

76. See especially Jones, *An Ancient-Jewish Christian Source;* and Jones, "An Ancient Jewish-Christian Rejoinder."

77. See Reed, "'Jewish Christianity' after the 'Parting of the Ways.'"

78. "Anti-Paulinism in the Pseudo-Clementines," in *Opposition to Paul in Jewish Christianity,* ed. G. Lüdemann and Eugene Boring (Minneapolis: Fortress, 1989), pp. 169–94; see esp. p. 183.

79. See note 66.

More than that, the author behind *Recognitions* 1.27–71 has changed the story of Acts in significant ways. Here Paul, as we have seen, is the villain rather than the hero of the story; he hinders instead of promotes the Christian mission; and he is never said to convert. In Jones's opinion, the author of this source behind the *Recognitions* wanted to outstrip Acts by writing a better history; in fact, his account was intended to "replace Acts."[80]

There are clear problems with this view as a wholesale explanation for Rec. 1.27–71. Most obviously, the majority of the passage does not cover the same scope or material as the book of Acts: it is a description of the history of the world from its very beginning up to the seventh year after Christ's death. Most of it, in other words, has nothing to do with Acts, as recognized by Stanton: "so many of its traditions are unrelated to Luke's Acts that rivalry as a primary purpose should not be pressed too far."[81] Moreover, the way the passage treats Acts is not noticeably different from the way it treats its other sources, principally the Hebrew Bible, in radically shortening the narrative and emphasizing certain key points. Surely one would not argue that its author was trying to replace the Hebrew Bible as well.[82]

Even so, Lüdemann and Jones have made a good point, that the retelling of the incidents from Acts is, in Stanton's words, "tendentious and imaginative."[83] To that extent, its narrative appears intent on countering the views of Luke, clearly from a Jewish-Christian (as opposed to Pauline) perspective. This portion of the Pseudo-Clementines can thus be considered a kind of counterforgery.

There may be a trace of Christian supercessionism in this passage as well, particularly in its polemic against Jewish animal sacrifice. The key text is the indication of why Moses allowed animal sacrifice in the first place—as a concession to the faulty religious leanings of his fellow Israelites who were not ready to abandon their pagan practices altogether:

> When meantime Moses, that faithful and wise steward, perceived that the vice of sacrificing to idols had been deeply ingrained into the people from their association with the Egyptians, and that the root of this evil could not be extracted from them, he allowed them indeed to sacrifice, but permitted it to be done only to God, that by any means he might cut off one half of the deeply ingrained evil, leaving the other half to be corrected by another, and at a future time. (Rec. 1.36)

80. "Jewish-Christian Rejoinder," p. 243.

81. Stanton, "Jewish Christian Elements," p. 318.

82. Jones's claims that the source attempts to write a "better history" than Acts is convincing only to the extent that any alternative account tries to do better than the one that it is opposing. But the specific arguments that he uses are for the most part unpersuasive. For example, the claim that the source focuses on only one encounter between the apostles and the Jewish leaders shows that it "has definitely provided a better arranged and more vivid account" (*Ancient Jewish Christian Source*, p. 241) rests on subjective evaluations of plot and structure. One need always ask: Better for whom? And on what grounds?

83. "Jewish Christian Elements," p. 322.

When Christ came as the prophet predicted by Moses in Deuteronomy 18, he fulfilled what Moses anticipated, by substituting baptism for sacrifice. As Annette Reed has argued, this attack on the practice of Jewish sacrifice would have been completely moot at the time of the writing, since the Temple had already been destroyed and no sacrifices were being performed in any event; moreover, the author is not maligning the religion of Moses but, as it were, affirming it. There is nothing "anti-Jewish" in the passage, to the extent that Jesus stands with Moses, not against him; Jews who have not accepted Christ are not condemned but are simply urged to change their minds: "the author's Christian supercessionism looks a lot like Jewish messianism."[84] In any event, this understanding that Jesus has superseded Moses at all stands at some tension with the rest of the *Recognitions* and the *Homilies*, as Reed has shown. But since the Christology, and the relationship of "Jews" and "Christians," is largely effected in nonpolemical terms through these two works, they are of less relevance to my present concerns.[85] In a broader sense, however, one could see the whole of the Pseudo-Clementine *Recognitions* and *Homilies* as having a subtle but comparable polemical agenda:

> H(omilies) and R(ecognitions) appeal to the authority of this apostle [Peter] to promote an account of early church history that counters the epistles of Paul and the Book of Acts. Most notably, they exalt James and Peter as the true guardians of Jesus' message and the authentic leaders of the apostolic community, while condemning Paul and the law-free mission associated with him.[86]

Broader Polemic in the Pseudo-Clementines

Whereas *Recognitions* 1.27–71 has sometimes been seen as a counterforgery to the book of Acts, Annette Reed has argued that the *Homilies* taken as a whole can be seen as standing in direct tension with that other great historian of Christianity's first four centuries, Eusebius.[87] A broad comparison of Eusebius's ten-volume work with the twenty-book *Homilies* shows numerous parallels. They are practically contemporaneous, Eusebius from 290–312 CE, the *Homilies* from a few decades later. Eusebius wrote from Caesarea, the *Homilies* come from Syria. Many of their concerns are the same: tracing apostolic succession, establishing ecclesiastical authority, responding to pagan critiques, defending orthodoxy against heresy, and explaining the relationship of the Christian church to Judaism. In addition, both extensively use earlier source materials.

---

84. "'Jewish Christianity' after the 'Parting of the Ways,'" pp. 212–13.

85. For exposition of key passages, see Reed, "'Jewish Christianity' after the Parting of the Ways.'" For the Jewish Christian elements of the Pseudo-Clementines more broadly, see most recently F. Stanley Jones, "The Jewish Christianity of the *Pseudo-Clementines*," in *A Companion to Second-Century Christian 'Heretics,'* ed. Antti Marjanen and Petri Luomanen (Leiden: Brill, 2008), pp. 315–34.

86. Reed, "Jewish Christianity after the 'Parting of the Ways,'" p. 198.

87. Annette Yoshiko Reed, "'Jewish Christianity' as Counter-history?" pp. 173–216.

Reed compares the views of the two under a number of enlightening rubrics. Eusebius maintains that apostolic succession occurs in all of the main churches of the orthodox tradition through "the successions of the holy apostles" (*H.E.* 1.1); the *Homilies* are concerned only about the succession through the Jerusalem church, and specifically Peter (Hom. 2.6–12; 3.15, 19; 11.35), who passes along the teaching of the "true prophet." Eusebius claims that Christianity, though continuous with the religion of Abraham and those before him, is discontinuous with Judaism, basing his argument on Gen. 49:10, that a scepter would fall away from Judah, opening up the way for the "new" thing to arrive in Jesus (e.g. *H.E.* 1. 6. 1–8); the *Homilies* claim that Moses and Jesus are both to be identified with the true prophet (Hom. 2.16–17; 3.17–21) and that they represent a single teaching (Hom. 8.6–7). The incarnation was not needed because of the failure of the Jews, but in order to allow the message to go to the gentiles (Hom. 3.18.3–19.1). Eusebius asserts that the mission to Jews was destined to fail, leading to the mission to gentiles (e.g., 2.1.8); the *Homilies* insist that the mission to the Jews was unnecessary, since Jews can be saved by the teachings of Moses (Hom. 8.5–7). The mission is for the pagans alone. Eusebius maintains that orthodoxy precedes heresy, which is by nature derivative and impotent; the *Homilies*—in the teaching of the syzygies (Hom. 2.15–18)—claims that the false comes prior to the true, and that falsehood is far from impotent (as seen in the successes of "Simon"). For Eusebius, Christianity is a new "ethnos"; this obviously poses a problem, then, for Jewish converts (what are they, exactly?); the *Homilies* use the term *Jew* even for gentile followers of Jesus (Hom. 11.16).

In light of these contrasts, Reed postulates that Eusebius provides a "parade example" of what Amos Funkenstein has called "counter history": "the process by which another group's history and sources are appropriated and reworked in the service of contrasting aims."[88] As she notes, Eusebius draws extensively on Josephus and Philo to describe the failings of Judaism; moreover, he relies on Hegesippus, himself possibly a "Jewish Christian" to narrate the history of "Jewish Christianity." If this view of Eusebius is right, then the possibility further presents itself that "the *Homilies* was compiled, at least in part, to counter this counter-history." That is to say, with many of the same concerns as Eusebius, the *Homilies* spin the tale in precisely a contrary way. This involves not merely alluding to Paul "in order to exclude him," but also telling the entire story of the Christian mission and message in a way that stands at odds with the "orthodox" historian. It is, then, a counterforgery in what I am calling the weak sense, a forgery designed to counter views found in another writing, in this case a writing that was destined to attain the status of orthodoxy and to determine how historians understood the development of the Christian church for many centuries to follow.

---

88. Reed, "'Jewish Christianity' as Counter History," pp. 212–13, with reference to Amos Funkelstein, *Perceptions of Jewish History* (Los Angeles: University of California Press, 1993), pp. 36–49.

CHAPTER ELEVEN

Anti-Jewish Forgeries

Many of the writings that we considered in the previous chapter attacked Paul while advancing a contrary understanding of the Christian gospel that can be called, despite all the term's well-known problems, "Jewish-Christian." The predominant tendency among our surviving sources, however, both forged and orthonymous, lies in the opposite direction. Indeed, attacks on Jews as people and on Judaism as a religion quickly became de rigueur in most of the Christian circles we have close familiarity with from the literary record. The history of Christian anti-Judaism is complex, but inordinately well documented, and I do not need to trace even its broad lines here.[1] The rise of anti-Jewish sentiment within a range of Christian communities—proto-orthodox and heterodox—led, as one might expect, to the production of forgeries that, under the name of authoritative figures, castigated Jews and the religion they practiced.[2] In

1. Among the standard works, see especially Marcel Simon, *Verus Israel: A Study of the Relations Between Christians and Jews in the Roman Empire 135–425 AD* (New York: Oxford, 1946, French original 1948); Rosemary Ruether, *Faith and Fratricide: The Theological Roots of Anti-Semitism* (New York: Seabury, 1974); and John Gager, *The Origins of Anti-Semitism: Attitudes Toward Judaism in Pagan and Christian Antiquity* (New York: Oxford University, 1983). Among the more valuable of the spate of recent literature, see Daniel Boyarin, *Border Lines: The Partition of Judaeo-Christianity* (Philadelphia: University of Pennsylvania, 2004); Adam H. Becker and Annette Yoshiko Reed, *The Ways That Never Parted: Jews and Christians in Late Antiquity and the Early Middle Ages* (Minneapolis: Fortress, 2007).

2. It is tempting to include the book of Hebrews as an instance of a forged polemic against Jews. But even though it does indeed appear to be a forgery, at the end of the day it is difficult to establish its function as primarily, or even covertly, polemical. It is the postscript of 13:22–25 that seems to carry the implicit claim that the author was Paul (even though he certainly was not Paul). Especially striking is v. 23: "You should know that our brother Timothy has been released; I will see you with him if he comes quickly." That the passage was originally part of the letter, see Harry Attridge, *The Epistle to the Hebrews* Heremenia (Philadelphia: Fortress, 1989), p. 13 and ad loc. Claire Rothschild in particular has made a

this chapter we will consider a number of these works, starting with one of the great archaeological discoveries of texts in modern times, the Gospel of Peter.

THE GOSPEL OF PETER

For centuries the best-known account of a Gospel of Peter came in Eusebius' description of its encounter and exposure by Serapion, bishop of Antioch at the very end of the second century. Eusebius includes in his report a lengthy but frustratingly partial citation of Serapion's own pamphlet dealing with the matter. Serapion first heard of the Gospel of Peter while making his episcopal rounds in the village of Rhossus. Learning that the church there used Peter's Gospel, but not perusing it for himself, he deemed it acceptable for use. Only later was he informed that the book had been propagated by a group of Docetists. After examining it, Serapion decided that it was for the most part orthodox; but it contained certain "additions" to the Gospel story that he considered spurious and dangerous. On these grounds he forbade future use of the book, appending to his account a list of the offensive passages. It is much to be regretted that Eusebius chose not to cite this appendix, as we are, as a result, unable to determine for certain if the fragmentary Gospel of Peter discovered in 1886–87 is in fact the one Serapion considered objectionable. But there are good reasons for assuming that it is, as we will see.

First, however, it is important to note that Justin Martyr, some fifty years before Serapion, also gives evidence of knowing the Gospel of Peter, in a much-controverted passage in his Dialogue with Trypho. On fifteen occasions throughout

---

lively and impassioned case that the book is meant to be taken as a Pauline letter, by an author living well after Paul's day: "The author of Hebrews composed the postscript in imitation of Paul in order to pass off the text as one of his prison letters. . . . The author did so, not as an afterthought, but as a way of carrying out the book's original intention. That is, the postscript is a deliberate forgery by an otherwise unknown early Christian author, claiming Paul's authorship for a work he composed to be published as part of an existing *corpus Paulinum*" (*Hebrews as Pseudepigraphon: The History and Significance of the Pauline Attribution of Hebrews*, Tübingen: Mohr Siebeck, 2009, p. 4). Rothschild's argument is that the entire letter—not just the postscript—contains numerous allusions to Paul's own writings, and that it cites an inordinate number of passages of Scripture also cited by Paul. In her judgment the Pauline materials throughout the book do not come to the author from some kind of "common stock" of early Christian traditions. They are intentional allusions to Pauline teachings, given to verify to the readers that the author is Paul.

I am inclined to agree that the letter—especially because of its ending—is written by someone who wants his readers to think he is Paul. At the same time, I do not see the letter as polemical (Rothschild does not contend that it is either). It is true that one of the major concerns of Hebrews is that its readers not (re?)turn to Judaism. And so most of the book is designed to show that Jesus is superior to anything Judaism has to offer (he is greater than the angels, than Moses, than Joshua, than the high priests, than the sacrifices, and so on). As a result, one might see in this a polemic against Judaism. But in fact the author does not attack Jews or the Judaism of his day; the form of Judaism he discusses is biblical Judaism. Even when he indicates that God "finds fault with them" (8:8), the author is referring to Israelites in the days of Jeremiah, not to Jews in his own time. The Judaism discussed in the book, therefore, is not a contemporary religion subject to polemical attack. And yet more important, it is not an evil to be abrogated. The Jewish religion of biblical times was a good religion, given by God, that has now been transcended.

his writings, Justin refers to the Gospels by calling them the ἀπομνημονεύματα, the "Memoirs." In most instances he explains that these are specifically the "memoirs of the apostles," and in one case he makes it quite clear that he is referring to literary productions, Gospels, produced by apostles: οἱ γὰρ ἀπόστολοι ἐν τοῖς γενομένοις ὑπ' αὐτῶν ἀπομνημονεύμασιν, ἃ καλεῖται εὐαγγέλια (I *Apol.* 66.3). On the one occasion we are most interested in, however, he refers one set of Memoirs to a specific apostle:

> Καὶ τὸ εἰπεῖν μετωνομακέναι αὐτὸν Πέτρον ἕνα τῶν ἀποστόλων, καὶ γεγράφθαι ἐν τοῖς ἀπομνημονεύμασιν αὐτοῦ γεγενημένον καὶ τοῦτο, μετὰ τοῦ καὶ ἄλλους δύο ἀδελφούς, υἱοῦς Ζεβεδαίου ὄντας, ἐπωνομακέναι ὀνόματι τοῦ Βοανεργές, ὅ ἐστιν υἱοὶ βροντῆς. . . . (*Dial.* 106.3)
>
> And when it says that he changed the name of one of the apostles to Peter, and when also this is written in his Memoirs, that he changed the name of . . . the sons of Zebedee to Boanerges, which is "sons of thunder. . . ."

Scholars such as Hilgenfeld and Harnack maintained that the reference should be read in the most straightforward sense, so that the possessive pronoun "his" refers to its nearest antecedent, "Peter," making this the earliest reference to the existence of the Gospel of Peter.[3] Naysayers have taken a variety of positions, some arguing that "his" refers to Jesus, so that the αὐτοῦ is some kind of objective genitive, or that it refers specifically to the Gospel thought by Papias to be Peter's version of the Gospel, that is, the Gospel of Mark—thus, most emphatically, Claus-Jürgen Thornton, in an article that is more learned than compelling.[4]

Against the passage referring to the Gospel of (= about) Jesus is, to begin with, a simple question of grammar, overlooked by such advocates of the view as Paul Foster, in his recent full-length commentary.[5] Objective genitives occur with nouns of action (love, hate, vision, and so on). A "memoir" (like a "book") does not seem to qualify; Foster, at least, provides nothing analogous. But what is more, how can a personal pronoun in the genitive be an objective genitive? "His book" or "his writing" or "his anything" surely indicates possession (the one who owns it) or derivation (the one who created it). Yet more significant, we have the other uses throughout Justin's writings, where "Memoirs of the Apostles," clearly refers to the books that the apostles wrote, as explicated in the reference cited above of 1 *Apol.* 66.3. That is to say, the genitive following ἀπομνημονεύματα is consistently a genitive of source or origin. Is there any compelling reason, apart

3. A. Hilgenfeld, "Das Petrus-Evangelium über Leiden und Auferstehung Jesu," *ZWT* 36 (1893): 447; A. Harnack, *Bruchstücke des Evangeliums und der Apocalypse des Petrus* (Leipzig: J. C. Hinrichs, 1893), 37–38.

4. "Justin und das Markusevangelium," *ZNW* 84 (1993): 93–110.

5. *The Gospel of Peter: Introduction, Critical Edition, and Commentary* (Leiden: Brill, 2010), pp. 97–99.

from a general unwillingness to see this as a reference to the Gospel of Peter, not to take it this way here?[6]

On the contrary, a compelling case for reading it this way has been made by P. Pilhofer. In particular Pilhofer is opposed to the idea that Peter's "Memoirs" could be a reference to the Gospel of Mark. Taking it this way presupposes knowledge of Papias, whom Justin never mentions, even though he may be front-and-center in the minds of modern scholars thinking about the Gospel of Mark in relation to Peter. But there are positive reasons for thinking that Justin has the Gospel of Peter in mind, that Justin has, in fact, been influenced elsewhere by the accounts distinctive to it. As Pilhofer points out, where Justin's comments on the life of Jesus overlap with the surviving narrative in the Akhmim fragment of the Gospel of Peter, he appears to rely on it in substance. For example, the guilt of the Jews in the death of Jesus–they are the ones who actually kill him—is the same in both (e.g., *Dial.* 85.2 "who suffered and was crucified by your people under Pontius Pilate"; cf. *GPet.* 5–10); and in both accounts the disciples are said to have fled after Jesus' crucifixion (*Dial.* 53.5; cf. *GPet.* 26, 59), unlike in the New Testament Gospels.

Two specific passages especially merit attention. According to 1 Apol. 35.6, it is the Jews, not the Roman soldiers, who mock Jesus (thus also *GPet.* 5–10, but not the Gospels of the New Testament);[7] and in *Dial.* 97.3, when Jesus' clothes are divided, the phrase used is λαχμὸν βάλλοντες, a phrase that never occurs in Greek literature before Justin, with one exception: *Gospel of Peter* 12, καὶ λαχμὸν ἔβαλον. Confronted with these similarities, Foster asks which direction the dependence was more likely to go, from the Gospel of Peter to Justin or the other way around. He opts for the latter option, but how can that be the better alternative? Which would be more likely, that a Gospel writer would comb through the lengthy, discursive writings of an apologist in order to ferret out isolated and scattered dominical traditions to include in his Gospel account, or that an apologist would rely on a Gospel text for his occasional references to the life of Jesus? Surely it is the latter. And we need constantly to recall that after referring to Peter in *Dial.* 106.3, Justin does refer to "his Memoirs."[8] This point has been recently

6. Foster argues that since the infinitive used before the αὐτοῦ and the infinitive used after the αὐτοῦ both have as the subject Jesus, then the αὐτοῦ must not be changing the person being discussed. There's a certain force to the argument, but it ultimately fails because it overlooks both the closest antecedent for the pronoun and the established usage of Justin in his other references to the Memoirs, not to mention the problems involving the use of an objective genitive with "Memoirs." *Gospel of Peter*, pp. 97–99.

7. Among the similarities between the accounts that Foster writes off ("The Writings of Justin Martyr and the So-Called Gospel of Peter," in *Justin Martyr and His Worlds*, ed. Sara Parvis and Paul Foster, Minneapolis: Fortress, 2007, 108–9): the use of διασύρω in Justin and σύρω in Gospel of Peter; the use of ἐκάθισαν in both to associate Jesus with a judicial function; and the request for Jesus to judge. These are indeed strong points of contact and cannot be dismissed, as Harnack earlier recognized (*Bruchstücke*, pp. 38–40).

8. Thornton's attempt to refute Pilhofer fails to convince. Rather than dealing with Pilhofer's arguments, for the most part, Thornton makes an argument of his own, that the reference in *Dial.* 106.3

reemphasized by Katharina Greschat, an advocate for Pilhofer's view, who provides additional supporting evidence.[9]

The reason Justin's witness matters is, in part, that it provides a *terminus ante quem* for the Gospel of Peter as the first half of the second century, when it was already in circulation and known in Rome, and in fact accepted by a prominent proto-orthodox teacher there as a scriptural authority. This conclusion also shows, as a sidelight, that whether or not Justin used a Gospel harmony, as Bellinzoni and others have argued, he also used separate Gospels.[10]

The discovery of the Akhmim fragment of the Gospel of Peter by a French archaeological team in the 1886–87 season caused a wide stir, and raised a number of immediate questions. The first was whether this fragment was part of the Gospel known to Serapion. Generally scholars thought the answer was yes. But this raised the question of the alleged docetism of the text, with some scholars finding traces of a docetic Christology in the comment that when crucified, Jesus "was silent as if he felt no pain" (v. 10), in his cry from the cross "My power, O power, you have left me" (v. 19), in the note that he was then "taken up" (while his body was still obviously on the cross; v. 19), and in the very un-humanlike appearance of his body, tall as a mountain, after the resurrection (v. 40). In the resurgence of interest in the Gospel in more recent decades, however, some scholars have argued that a docetic view was more often being read into the text rather than out of it, and that as a consequence there is no compelling reason to see this book as the one known to Serapion.[11] In response it might be pointed out that Serapion indicated that parts of the Gospel were perfectly orthodox and others could be read heretically, and that is certainly true of the fragment that we have. Finally, scholars were obsessed with the relation of this Gospel to the canonical four: Did it use them? Was it independent of them? Or, as in the famous but rather uninfluential

---

speaks of Jesus "changing" the name of Simon to Peter (not giving him a nickname), and of calling James and John Boanerges. Among our Gospels, these naming events happen only in Mark, so that Justin is referring to Mark as Peter's Memoir. A good deal rests on Thornton's claim that in the other Gospels Simon's name is not actually changed to Peter; for them, Peter is a nickname. But for the Gospel of Peter and Justin, Jesus made a name change. On one hand, the argument fails to take seriously enough the fact that Simon's name was decidedly *not* permanently changed in Mark, since Jesus calls him "Simon" in 14:37. Moreover, this cannot be an argument that the Gospel of Peter is not being invoked, when the episode is not found in the Akhmim fragment, which provides only portions of the Passion narrative. Thornton's case is driven in fact by a completely different agenda: he wants to establish that by the time of Justin there was already a fourfold Gospel canon in Rome in the midsecond century, decades before its (otherwise) earliest attestation in Irenaeus. By making Peter's Memoir Mark, Thornton can show that all four Gospels are quoted in Justin's work.

9. "Justins 'Denkwürdigkeiten der Apostel' und das Petrusevangelium," in Thomas J. Kraus and Tobias Nicklas, eds., *Das Evangelium nach Petrus: Text, Kontexte, Intertexte,* TU 158 (Berlin: de Gruyter, 2007), pp. 197–214. Although Greschat shows that "his memoirs" is not the Gospel of Mark, but the Gospel of Peter, she does not see the need to posit *direct* literary dependence of Justin.

10. *The Sayings of Jesus in the Writings of Justin Martyr* (Leiden: Brill, 1967).

11. E.g., Jerry McCant, "The Gospel of Peter: Docetism Reconsidered," *NTS* 30 (1984): 258–73. See the most recent discussion of Paul Foster, *Gospel of Peter*, pp. 157–65.

proposal of J. D. Crossan, was the Gospel based on an earlier account, the Cross Gospel, a now-lost source of the canonical versions that is better represented in Peter than in any of them?[12]

All of these concerns are fueled more by an interest in seeing how the Gospel relates to external factors (Serapion, docetism, the canonical Gospels) than by a concern with what we find within the Gospel itself. Two features of the Gospel are significant for my present purposes: it makes a clear, but false, authorial claim; and its narrative is driven, in no small measure, by a polemical agenda of showing that the Jews were responsible for the death of Jesus.

The Pseudepigraphic Claim

No one doubts that the account is forged. Whereas most of the narrative is given in the third person, things change in vv. 26–27:

> But I and my companions were grieving and went into hiding, wounded in heart. For we were being sought out by them as if we were evildoers who wanted to burn the Temple. While these things were happening, we fasted and sat mourning and weeping, night and day, until the Sabbath.[13]

The author, then, was allegedly one of the disciples. It is at the very end that we learn which one he is: "But I, Simon Peter, and my brother Andrew, took our nets and went off to the sea. And with us was Levi, the son of Alphaeus, whom the Lord . . ." (v. 60). And that is where the text breaks off, in the middle of a sentence. We are fortunate that it did not break off a verse earlier: we would never have known which of the Twelve this author was claiming to be.

With very few exceptions most scholars date the account to sometime in the (early) second century.[14] Most important for our purposes, unlike the anonymous earlier Gospels that came to be included in the canon, this one is written by an author making a false self-identification. It is a forgery in the name of Simon Peter.

The Anti-Jewish Agenda

One of the Gospel of Peter's distinctive emphases is evident at the outset of the surviving fragment: ". . . but none of the Jews washed his hands, nor did Herod or any of his judges.[15] Since they did not wish to wash, Pilate stood up. Then King

---

12. *The Cross That Spoke: The Origins of the Passion Narrative* (San Francisco: Harper & Row, 1988).

13. Translations are from Ehrman and Pleše, *The Apocryphal Gospels*, pp. 371–87.

14. See Foster, *Gospel of Peter*, 169–72. Crossan's early dating of the alleged Cross Gospel has not received much support, although he found one convert in Paul Mirecki, author of the ABD article "Gospel of Peter," vol. 5, pp. 278–81.

15. Cf. Matt. 27:24.

Herod ordered the Lord to be taken away and said to them, 'Do everything that I ordered you to do to him.'"

The fragment begins in the middle of the scene of the hand-washing at Jesus' trial. Pilate is not explicitly said to have washed his hands, but that is clearly what has happened in the preceding lines that are now lost. Unlike the Matthean parallel, however, here the emphasis is on what "the Jews"—Herod, the Jewish king, and his Jewish judges—specifically refuse to do. They are the ones, not Pilate, responsible for Jesus' death. Indeed, in the next line we learn that it is the Jewish king Herod, not the Roman governor, who orders Jesus' execution.

It is not just the Jewish leaders (King Herod and his judges) who are maligned for their role in the crucifixion: "none of the Jews" washed his hands. The emphasis continues throughout the account. Herod delivers Jesus "over to the people" (τῷ λαῷ) for punishment (v. 5), and they, the Jewish people, are the ones who mock and then crucify him:

> Those who took the Lord began pushing him about, running up to him and saying, "Let us drag around the Son of God, since we have authority over him." They clothed him in purple and sat him on the judgment seat, saying, "Give a righteous judgment, O King of Israel!" One of them brought a crown made of thorns and placed it on the Lord's head. Others standing there were spitting in his face; some slapped his cheeks; others were beating him with a reed; and some began to flog him, saying, "This is how we should honor the Son of God." They brought forward two evildoers and crucified the Lord between them. (vv. 6–10)

The author is not hesitant to lambaste the Jews for what they have done: "Thus they brought all things to fulfillment and completed all their sins on their heads" (v. 17). Later they realize just how evilly they have behaved and foresee the divinely ordained punishment. Jerusalem will now be destroyed by God as a result: "Then the Jews, the elders, and the priests realized how much evil they had done to themselves and began beating their breasts, saying 'Woe to us because of our sins. The judgment and the end of Jerusalem are near'" (v. 25).

But this does not stop them from doing yet more mischief. The disciples of Jesus are forced to go into hiding because the Jews are trying to track them down "as if we were evildoers who wanted to burn the Temple" (v. 26). Too late do the Jewish people realize that they have put an innocent man to death: after the clear signs given at his death, they bemoan what they have done, although they are not said to repent: "If such great signs happened when he died, you can see how righteous he was!" (v. 28). Then the Jewish leaders accompany the Roman guards to watch the tomb, and with them observe Jesus raised from the dead, and go in to tell Pilate:

> Greatly agitated, they said, "He actually was the Son of God." Pilate replied, "I am clean of the blood of the Son of God; you decided to do this." Then everyone approached him to ask and urge him to order the centurion and the

> soldiers to say nothing about what they had seen. "For it is better," they said, "for us to incur a great sin before God than to fall into the hands of the Jewish people and be stoned." And so Pilate ordered the centurion and the soldiers not to say a word. (vv. 45–49)

Rather than convert, they arrange a cover-up. And at the end they are still to be feared, as the women going to the tomb realize: "Now Mary Magdalene, a disciple of the Lord, had been afraid of the Jews, since they were inflamed with anger" (v. 50).

One feature of the text worth noting is that even though the Jewish leaders and the Jewish people are so obviously painted as the culprits in the death of Jesus and its aftermath, the disciples of Jesus are themselves concerned to keep the Jewish Law, rigorously. And so they appear to observe the Sabbath day (v. 27) and to have kept the feast of unleavened bread (v. 58). Why, in an anti-Jewish text, are Jesus' followers portrayed as pious Jews?

One might suspect that this is a case of historical verisimilitude. But it is also possible that Jesus' followers are to be understood to be the "true" Jews, the ones who really do perform God's will, as opposed to those who call themselves Jews but are opposed to it. This possibility relates to some of the ironies embedded in the narrative, which call to mind those highlighted in another anti-Jewish account, the Gospel of John. The most obvious irony in the Gospel of Peter's crucifixion scene is the fear, expressed twice, that Jesus' body needs to be removed from the cross before the Sabbath, so as not to violate the Jewish Law. For this account, Jews who have just killed the messiah of God are concerned not to break the Law. This is reminiscent of the irony of the Fourth Gospel, where at Jesus' trial the Jewish leaders refuse to enter the Praetorium because they want to be ritually pure in order to eat the Passover meal that evening (John 18:28), not realizing that it is precisely the Passover Lamb they are about to slay in their execution of Jesus.

Other ironies abound in the Gospel of Peter's brief narrative. The Jewish people who revile Jesus think they have authority over him, not realizing that he is the Lord (v. 6); they mockingly call him the King of Israel and demand a judgment, when in fact they will be judged for what they have done to him (vv. 7, 25); they crown him, slap him, beat him, and flog him, since that is their way of honoring the Son of God, who will return the favor when it comes time to destroy Jerusalem (v. 25). All these ironies heighten the heinous behavior not just of the Jewish leaders but also of the Jewish λαός.

What then is the function of the anti-Judaism in the text? Some scholars have argued that the attacks are directed against the Jewish leaders but not the Jewish people. And so J. D. Crossan can argue that "The Gospel of Peter is . . . more 'anti-Jewish' with regard to the authorities than any of the canonical gospels but also more 'pro-Jewish' with regard to the *people* than any of them."[16] But it is extremely

16. "The Gospel of Peter and the Canonical Gospels: Independence, Dependence of Both?" *Forum* 1 (1998): 28. Italics his.

difficult to see how this can be read out of a text that accuses the Jewish people of crucifying Jesus. Denker similarly sees the account as pinning the blame for the cover-up of the resurrection on the Jewish leaders (that part is true) in order to win Jews over to the Christian message,[17] a view similar to A. Kirk's that the blame on the Jewish leaders would lead Jewish people to reject them in favor of the church.[18] Neither of these views can explain why the Jews as a people are so harshly treated in the text. T . Nicklas argues that the author wanted to stress that Jews were fulfilling Scripture in their rejection of Jesus, but that once they realize what their leaders have done in hiding the message of the resurrection, they would be more inclined to convert.[19]

J. Verheyden critiques all these views, and argues that the Gospel of Peter is not promoting any particular agenda when it portrays the Jews as guilty in the death of Jesus. The author instead is simply recounting, unreflectively, the traditions about Jesus' death as they have come down to him. Had he wanted to pin significant blame on the Jews, he would have been more explicit in his denunciation, rather than stating Jewish involvement in a rather banal and matter-of-fact manner. In Verheyden's view, the author of the Gospel of Peter

> has no great design or theologically profound message to offer. His agenda is far more modest. He tells a story that was known to all, and he does this in a way that appeals to an audience that was probably as little concerned with doctrine as it was eager for being confirmed in its opinions and prejudices about those who it was convinced had murdered Jesus.[20]

In my view this is taking the matter too far. As seen above, the account is permeated with anti-Jewish comments from beginning to end. The Roman governor Pilate is exculpated for the death of Jesus; it is the Jews who are responsible. And not just the Jewish leaders, but the Jewish people. Even if this is simply how the author "knows" the story—Verheyden's view—he has learned it as it has been passed through a virulently anti-Jewish matrix, far more virulent than even what we find in the New Testament. The Jews killed Jesus, and God will now destroy Jerusalem in punishment. And even though Jews realize with horror what they have done and the fate that now is to befall them, not one of them repents.

To return to our question, how are we to account for such vitriol against the Jews? Why need we look any farther than the rising tension with and hatred of Jews among (some) Christians of the second century? This was a century that saw the appearance of the epistle of Barnabas with its audacious claim that Jews

---

17. *Doketismus*, pp. 78–92.

18. A. Kirk, "The Johannine Jesus in the Gospel of Peter: A Social Memory Approach," in *Jesus in Johannine Tradition*, ed. R. T. Fortna and T. Thatcher (Louisville: Westminster John Knox, 2001), pp. 319–21.

19. T. Nicklas, "Die 'Juden' im Petrusevangelium (PCair. 10759). Ein Testfall," *NTS* 47 (2001): 221.

20. Joseph Verheyden, "Some Reflections on Determining the Purpose of the 'Gospel of Peter,'" in Kraus and Nicklas, eds., *Das Evangelium nach Petrus*, p. 299.

have always misunderstood their own religion and that the Old Testament is a Christian, not a Jewish, book; a century that saw the rise of the Christian *adversus Ioudaeos* literature with such authors as Justin and, soon thereafter, Tertullian; a century that saw the most heinous charges of deicide leveled against the Jews in the Paschal Homily of Melito. And we will see similar charges to those leveled against Jews in the Gospel of Peter in yet other passion narratives of still later times, when we come to the Pilate literature.

For now, we might conclude by returning to the issue of forgery. Given the anti-Jewish element of the book, why did its author decide to call himself Peter? The question is easier to ask than answer; in no small measure we are handicapped by the size of the small fragment of the text that survives. Any assessment of its authorial claim would necessarily depend on what could be found in the rest of the now-lost materials. But even with what little we have, one can think of reasons for an unknown author of such a second-century account to claim to be Peter. On one hand, the mere claim lends credibility to this version of the story and thereby assures a wider readership. But even beyond this, is it an accident that this, the most anti-Jewish of our early Gospels, is placed on the pen of an apostle who was thought to insist most strongly on the Jewish character of the gospel, and to have been a missionary specifically to Jews?

Peter became a battleground over which the Jewishness of Christianity was fought. In the Pseudo-Clementine literature he is portrayed as a proponent of a form of Christianity that adhered to the Law of Moses (see, e.g., the *Epistula Petri*). In the Pseudo-Clementine *Homilies,* he avers that Jews who follow Moses are on a soteriological par with gentiles who follow Jesus. In these lengthy romances, Judaism is affirmed and Jews are praised, by Peter, the head disciple and foundation of the Christian church. But not in the Gospel of Peter. Here Jews are enemies of God who crucify their own messiah; their leaders hide the truth of Jesus' resurrection and persecute Jesus' disciples. At the end of the day, both sets of writings—the Pseudo-Clementines and the Gospel of Peter—use Peter, the Jewish follower of Jesus and well-known evangelist among the Jews, to set forth their visions of the message of Jesus in relationship to Judaism. In the Gospel the portrayal is hateful: Jews are responsible for executing Jesus and God will exact on them a penalty.

THE ASCENSION OF ISAIAH

The Ascension of Isaiah is unusual in being a Christian apocalyptic text written about, and partially in the name of, a great prophet of the Old Testament. The book is clearly divided into two parts. The first five chapters describe the Martyrdom of Isaiah under the wicked Israelite king Manasseh at the instigation of the false prophet Belchira, who is empowered by Beliar. These chapters include a description of Isaiah's prophecy of the coming and reception of Christ on earth, and the apostasy that will follow his ascension. The latter is the one major event between the departure of the "Beloved," the book's favored epithet for Christ, and the apocalyptic end. This opening section of the book ends with Isaiah's death, as he is sawn in half with a "treesaw."

Chapters 6 through 11 recount an earlier vision of Isaiah, in which he ascends through the seven heavens, observing the angelic hosts at each level, until he reaches the highest heaven, the realm of God himself, whence he observes the descent and reascent of the Beloved through the realms below, assuming a different angelic form on his descent so as not to be recognized en route, and providing, as required, the proper passwords to be allowed passage. There follows a description of the incarnation and crucifixion, and then the Beloved's reascent in glory.

Scholarship on this apocalypse has long been obsessed with theories of sources.[21] As Richard Bauckham notes in his concise history of research, since W. Gesenius in 1821, most scholars have agreed that the Ascension of Isaiah is not the unified work of a single author.[22] For much of the second half of the twentieth century the theory of R. H. Charles held sway, that the book comprises three earlier sources, a Jewish Martyrdom of Isaiah, edited by a Christian (much of chs. 1–5), a Testament of Hezekiah (3:13b–4:18), and the Vision of the book's final six chapters. In 1973 A. Caquot tried to isolate the Jewish source behind the Martyrdom, but all such attempts—along with the idea of any such independent source at all—were destroyed by the work of Mauro Pesce, who showed that the Martyrdom is not a Christianized version of a Jewish source, but a Christian text through and through, based in part on Jewish haggadic traditions.[23] Pesce's view is now widely held. The Martyrdom is so obviously and thoroughly Christianized that it is difficult to remove Christian elements to obtain a Jewish core. It is filled with references to the Beloved, for example, and there are traces of an incipient trinitarianism, as in 1.7: "the Beloved of my Lord and the Spirit that speaks in me."

E. Norelli has argued at length that chapters 1–5 are a coherent and unified work by a single author, with a central theme involving the conflict between true and false prophecy. In addition, he maintains that the Vision of chapters 6–11 is an earlier composition that had circulated independently, which was later joined to the Martyrdom by the author of the latter, who composed 11.41–43 to bind the two parts together. The two major portions of the work, then, reflect different phases of the history of the community of prophets from which they emerged.[24]

---

21. For an overview, see Jonathan Knight, *Disciples of the Beloved One: The Christology, Social Setting and Theological Context of the Ascension of Isaiah,* JSPSUp 18 (Sheffield: Sheffield Academic Press, 1996), pp. 28–32.

22. Richard Bauckham, "The Ascension of Isaiah: Genre, Unity and Date," in *The Fate of the Dead: Studies on the Jewish and Christian Apocalypses,* NovTSup 93 (Leiden: Brill, 1998), pp. 363–90.

23. *Il "Martirio di Isaia" non esiste: L'Ascensione di Isaia e le tradizione giudaiche sull'uccisione del profeta* (Bologna: Centro Stampa Baiesi, 1984).

24. E. Norelli, *L'Ascensione di Isaia: Studi su un apocrifo al crocevia dei cristianesimi* (Bologne: Centro editorial dehoniano, 1994).

Bauckham wants to take the matter a step further still. In his judgment the entire Ascension is the single composition of a solitary first-century Christian author who used the book of Daniel as his generic model, with its opening narrative only loosely connected with the visions in the second half of the book. This view, however, may propose an implausibly early date for the final product of the Ascension. There is nothing in Christian literature of the first century analogous to the descent and reascent of the Beloved through the seven heavens, using passwords as necessary to pass through the realms controlled by others.

Jonathan Knight places the final text after the apostolic age, given comments made in 3.21–31, but before "full-blown Gnosticism," since the Vision evinces parallels with Gnostic thought yet lacks Gnostic cosmology such as is known from the writings of the Nag Hammadi library that date from the midsecond century. Here too, however, one should be wary of placing too much emphasis on a unilinear ideological development among texts, as if Gnostic writings written after 150 CE necessarily evidence developed cosmogonic myths. As we will see, the early to middle second century provides a plausible date for the Ascension. Certainly no detailed account of a divine being's ascent and descent through the layers of the heavens—replete with passwords—can be found earlier.

The Pseudepigraphic Character of the Book

As mentioned in an earlier chapter, the Ascension of Isaiah is a textbook example of "embedded pseudepigraphy." The book as a whole does not claim to be written by Isaiah, but periodically through the course of its narrative "Isaiah" inserts himself to describe his own history and vision. And so the narrative begins in the third person and continues that way up to 3.30 ("for each will say what seems pleasing in his own eyes"[25]) and then suddenly, without explanation, moves into the first person in 3.31 ("And they will set aside the prophecies of the prophets which were before me and also pay no attention to these my visions . . ."). The narrative continues in the first person (see 4.1, 13, 20) before returning to the third person in 5.1. So too in the Vision, chapter 6 describes Isaiah entering into a trance in the third person, but Isaiah himself begins to narrate his vision in the first person starting in 7.2 ("In that moment when I was prophesying according to things heard by you, I saw a sublime angel . . ."). So too at the end, there is an abrupt shift from first to third person, at 11.35–36 ("'This have I seen.' And Isaiah told it to all who stood before him . . ."). Thus the author of the book often removes himself from consideration and feigns the identity of Isaiah himself. It should not be argued that this is simply the generic device of apocalypses and so should not be taken seriously as an authorial claim. As I showed in an earlier chapter, pseudepigraphy is indeed a regular feature of both Jewish and Christian apocalypses, but the authorial claims were meant to be believed and trusted.

25. Translations of C. Detlef G. Müller, in Schneemelcher, *New Testament Apocrypha*, vol. 2.

Whoever wrote the book of Daniel in the second century BCE meant his readers to take seriously his claim to be the wise man and prophet of four hundred years earlier; otherwise his "predictions" would have carried no probative force. These books were not written under innocent pseudonyms, but were forged.[26]

We should also guard against thinking that the goal of forgers of apocalypses was the same in every case. Each apocalypse pursues its own agenda and the authorial question needs always to be pursued in that light. In some apocalypses the function of the authorial claim makes particular sense, when, for example, the seer foretells what will happen in the future even though he is, in fact, relating what had already happened in the past, thereby verifying his "vision" for his reader. But that is not the case with the Ascension of Isaiah, which is not concerned to relate the course of human history through a variety of maleficent kingdoms aligned against God (contrast Daniel). And so how might we explain the authorial function here?

Knight provides one explanation worth considering.[27] In his judgment, the book is principally about the defeat of Beliar by Christ, and is written to provide hope for Christians who are undergoing persecution in the early second century. For this author the end is near and the persecuting powers will soon be overthrown. In other words, this apocalypse and its authorial claim function in a way similar to the canonical apocalypses of Daniel and Revelation. Knight's view, however, may rely too much on his understanding of how apocalypses work in general; there is less to commend it from the specifics provided by this text in particular. Persecution may be part of the picture, in that the deaths of both Jesus and Isaiah figure prominently. But it is certainly not the entire picture. The bigger picture involves the revelation of heavenly secrets that make sense of earthly realities, and not just the realities of suffering. Also at stake are the reality of the incarnation, the hidden identity of Jesus, his rejection on earth, and the apostasy that arose in the wake of his departure. At its heart, this apocalypse is deeply concerned with theology.

The Theological Dimensions of the Text

The theological views of the text have long puzzled interpreters. Its view of Christ is often described as "naïvely docetic," in that Christ is said to have come to earth in the "likeness" of a human, after transforming his appearance at will through the heavenly realms (3.13). He was born after Mary was pregnant for just two months (11.13); and he nursed not because he needed nourishment but simply to avoid being recognized for who he really was (11.17). Darrell Hannah has shown, however, that the account is not thoroughly docetic. Christ really suffers torment, is crucified, and dies, before being raised from the dead.[28]

---

26. See my discussion on pp. 72–74.

27. Knight, *Disciples*.

28. Darrell D. Hannah, "The Ascension of Isaiah and Docetic Christology," *VC* 53 (1999): 165–96.

So too the account is clearly Trinitarian but not especially nuanced: "And there they all named the primal Father and his Beloved, Christ, and the Holy Spirit, all with one voice" (8.18). Moreover, both the Beloved and the Holy Spirit are worshiped (9.40). At the same time they flank the throne of God, presumably as subordinates, and only the Holy Spirit, not the Beloved, is described as an angel (9.40). Instead, the Beloved assumes the appearance of an angel only as it suits his purposes during his descent. In Hannah's convincing explication, the account is not theologically rigorous, written to promote a refined theological perspective. Nor is it naïvely docetic. It is simply theologically naïve.[29]

One aspect of the theology of the book that merits particular attention is its relationship to Johannine theology known from the writings of the New Testament, with which it shares many features—both with the Gospel of John, where Isaiah is said to have seen the glories of heaven (John 12:41), and with the book of Revelation, where another seer is granted a vision of the divine realm. At the same time the author of the Ascension stands at clear odds with some of the views of the Fourth Gospel. John maintains that no one has ascended to heaven except the one who has previously descended, that is Christ, the Son of Man (John 3:13). Not so for the Ascension, where the prophet of old ascended to the highest realm. Moreover, according to John, Isaiah had a vision of the pre-incarnate Christ in the realm of glory (12:41), since indeed, no human has ever seen God the Father, except Christ himself (John 6:46; see also 1:18, 5:37; 1 John 4:12, 20). The Ascension stresses, on the other hand, that Isaiah saw not just Christ on his throne, but God the Father himself (9.39).[30] It is possible, as Robert Hall has argued, that there is some competition among the communities behind these two literary productions, although it may be going too far to suggest that we can know the inner workings of these groups.[31]

The commonalities and differences between the Johannine community and the author of the Ascension of Isaiah may suggest that they were in direct contact with one another at points of their history. Their different perspectives do not require completely separate historical developments. It should always be remembered that the secessionists shared a history with but rejected the theology of the community behind the Johannine epistles. Something similar can be said of the book of Revelation, with its many ties to the fourth Gospel but its radically

---

29. Darrell D. Hannah, "Ascension," and Hannah, "Isaiah's Vision in the Ascension of Isaiah and the Early Church," *JTS* 50 (1999): 80–101.

30. He appears to be able to see God, but not the "glory" that surrounds him; 9.29, 10.2, 11.24.

31. Robert G. Hall, "The *Ascension of Isaiah*: Community Situation, Date, and Place in Early Christianity," *JBL* 109 (1990): 289–306. Hall goes beyond what the evidence suggests in reconstructing a number of competing prophet groups in early Christianity; moreover, this set of competitions is probably not the best primary setting for the book. Among other things, Hall appears to overread AscIsa. 3.21–31, seeing it as directed against other groups within Christianity that specifically reject the doctrine of the descent and ascent of the Beloved. As I will argue later, broader issues in the apostasy appear to be involved. The ascent-descent motif does not figure in the passage.

divergent eschatology. The traditions behind Ascension of Isaiah as well may have been forged in connection with the views behind the Gospel of John, but developed in different directions.

The Anti-Jewish Emphasis of the Text

On one point, however, the two books appear in close proximity: their views of Jews and Judaism. For both, Judaism is the God-given, true religion; but the Jews are maligned as the enemies of God. I do not need to make that case for the Fourth Gospel in this context, with its affirmation of Jewish Scripture and, say, festivals, and its simultaneous assault on "the Jews," children of the Devil (ch. 8). But it is important to consider how these views play out in the Ascension of Isaiah. Here, even though polemic is not the driving force of either the Martyrdom or the Vision, there is ample opposition to Jews throughout, with the implicit claim that Jews have forsaken their own religion. That appears to be the reason the great Hebrew prophet Isaiah is chosen as the subject and, indeed, pseudepigraphic presence, in the book; he testifies to the truth, and his views are rejected (much like John 1:11; "He came to his own, and his own did not receive him").

Thus we are told that Beliar caused "many in Jerusalem and in Judah" to "depart from the true faith" (1.9) and there is reference to the great "apostasy of Israel" under Manasseh (2.1–6). In 3.1 "Belchira . . . appeared as a false prophet in Jerusalem, and many in Jerusalem joined with him." The prophet Isaiah is martyred because of his vision of Christ (3.13, 5.15) and the Jewish leaders and people look on in approbation (5.12). Christ too is opposed by the people of Israel: "The adversary envied him and roused the children of Israel against him. . . . They delivered him to the king and crucified him" (11.19; note that here, as in the Gospel of Peter, it is the Jews who kill Jesus). There are parallels between the deaths of Isaiah and Christ: the former is executed because of his vision of the latter; both suffer at the hands of the people of Jerusalem inspired by Beliar; the death of both involve tree imagery (crucified on a tree; sawed in half by a treesaw). It should be emphasized that all these things were predicted in advance, not only by the prophet Isaiah but also in all the Psalms and prophets (4.21). The Jews, in other words, should have known.

In addition to these individual passages, it is important to consider the overall thrust of the book, as Greg Carey has done in an important article.[32] Carey's thesis is that the book as a whole embodies a kind of anti-Jewish polemic: "Its narrative rhetoric argues that a prominent Hebrew prophet such as Isaiah knew the pattern of Christian proclamation centuries in advance, that his knowledge was rejected in Jerusalem, and that Isaiah's martyrdom resulted from his proclamation of the Beloved."[33] As Carey observes, Christian authors of the second and third century

---

32. "*The Ascension of Isaiah*: An Example of Early Christian Narrative Polemic," *JSP* 17 (1998): 65–78.

33. Ibid., p. 65. Emphasis his.

commonly used the book of Isaiah in order to promote their anti-Jewish agenda. The Epistle of Barnabas uses Isaiah to advance his view of Christian supersessionism (14:5–8, quoting Isa. 42:6–7, 49:6–7). Justin uses Isaiah to show how Jews have falsely rejected the virgin birth and shown their own hardheadedness (Dialogue 43; 66–67, 77–78, 84). Origen uses Isaiah to very similar ends in the *Contra Celsum* (1.28–29, 32–38), stressing Isaiah's message that the proclamation will be taken, then, to the gentiles (2:78, citing Isa. 65:1; 1:53 citing Isa. 42:4).

And so, at the time of the writing of the Ascension, Christians in other contexts were engaged in anti-Jewish polemic and using the prophecies of Isaiah to accomplish these ends. As we will see in Chapter Twelve, an attack on Jews is not the only emphasis of the Ascension—or even its only polemical thrust—but it is certainly one of them. As Carey summarizes: "Despite its Christological and visionary emphases, the apocalypse's entire narrative structure communicates an apologetic against non-Christian Jews."[34]

THE GOSPEL OF THOMAS

We have already considered the Coptic Gospel of Thomas with respect to its rejection of an apocalyptic eschatology, and there is no need here to repeat my introductory comments on the book as a whole.[35] One other area of obvious polemic in the book involves the sayings that discuss Jews and the Jewish religion. Here there is a fairly specific orientation: the relevant logia may vary in their harshness, but they uniformly demean both Jewish cultic practices and the Jewish people.

Saying 6

This is the first saying in the collection that broaches the issue of Jewish acts of piety, as the disciples ask Jesus about how they are to be practiced: "Do you want us to fast? And how should we pray? Should we give alms? And what kind of diet should we observe?"[36] One immediately thinks of the Sermon on the Mount, where Jesus deals with some of these issues; but as DeConick has pointed out the order is reversed in Matt. 6:1–8 (alms, prayer, fasting), so there is probably not any literary dependence.[37] What is most striking is that the Jesus of Thomas does not seem to answer the disciples' questions—or at least the answer is delayed until saying 14. So close are the two logia that some scholars have argued that they were originally a unity separated in the course of transmission, either because a page came to be displaced (the question appeared on the bottom of the page and the answer at the top of the next, but another page came to be interca-

34. Ibid., p. 74.

35. See pp. 230–31.

36. All translations of the Gospel of Thomas are drawn from Ehrman and Pleše, *Apocryphal Gospels*, pp. 303–35.

37. *Original Gospel of Thomas*, p. 62, with other reasons also adduced.

lated between the two),[38] or because of a fluke at the oral stage of the tradition in a recitation of the sayings of Jesus.[39]

Even taken as an integrated saying, as it stands, logion 6 appears to disdain these acts of piety—which are to be understood as Jewish, not simply human (see saying 14 and its appeal to kashrut).[40] Jesus' reply vitiates the need to fast, pray, and give alms, that is, to engage in external acts of Jewish piety. Instead, one is to be truthful and to observe the negative golden rule. It is personal behavior that matters before God, not Jewish religious customs and laws: "For there is nothing hidden that will not be revealed, and nothing that is covered will remain undisclosed." Acts of Jewish piety are therefore irrelevant at best.

Saying 14

If, as it seems, the response of saying 14 is to be taken with the questions of saying 6, then acts of Jewish piety are not merely irrelevant; they are harmful: "Jesus said to them, 'If you fast, you will bring sin upon yourselves; and if you pray, you will be condemned; and if you give alms, you will do harm to your spirits.'" The next part of Jesus' response may seem, at first, irrelevant to these conditional clauses and their condemnations, but in fact it may be the key to understanding them. Jesus moves into the question of food, specifically whether those engaged in the Christian mission should try to observe kosher food laws. He answers with a resounding no:

> And when you go into any land and walk in the countryside, if they receive you, eat whatever they place before you and heal the sick among them. For whatever goes into your mouth will not defile you; rather, it is what comes out of your mouth that will defile you.

The concerns of missionaries are not food regulations. They are instead the welfare of other people ("heal the sick") and proper speech. What one eats is not what defiles a person, but the speech that comes from the mouth. The Christian missionary proclamation is to have precedence over kosher concerns. Is this the original context for the denigration of the other pious activities at the opening of the logion? Acts of Jewish piety are far less important than the mission. A similar concern, with a similar perspective, is found elsewhere in the Jesus tradition, especially Luke 10:8–9. There, however, Jesus speaks of entering a different "town" whereas here he speaks of entering a different "land." The mission has expanded since the logion preserved in Luke, and naturally it is harder to find kosher food in foreign lands than in the various towns of Israel.

---

38. Allowed as a possibility by Valantasis, *Gospel of Thomas*, p. 63.

39. DeConick, *Original Gospel of Thomas*, p. 87.

40. Contra Valantasis, *Gospel of Thomas*, p. 63.

The stress on "what comes out of your mouth" may have a deeper meaning in the context of the Gospel of Thomas. This is a Gospel that is all about discourse. It consists exclusively of sayings of Jesus, sometimes set in dialogic context; and it is the "interpretation of these sayings" that provides eternal life (saying 1). Teachings are of ultimate importance for this author, and presumably for his community. As Valantasis puts it, "The search for the interpretation of the sayings takes precedence over the traditional pious practices."[41] But the matter can be expressed even more firmly. Traditional practices are not only bypassed by the need to read, interpret, and teach; engaging in these earlier practices is seriously detrimental, leading to sin, condemnation, and spiritual damage. This is a new religion that displaces the old and declares it harmful.[42]

Saying 27

It is clear that saying 27 must relate to the preceding two in its condemnation of cultic practices. But how does it do so? On the surface it seems to embrace what they spurn, by claiming that one will not "find the kingdom" if one does not "fast from the world," and will not "see the Father" if one does not "make the Sabbath a Sabbath." Does this not require Jesus' followers to practice acts of Jewish piety: fasting and Sabbath observance?

It is worth noting that fasting here is not said to involve abstention from food (the normal meaning of the word, not just in Jewish piety), but from the world. As such, the saying appears to embrace a broader ethic than a periodic religious fast: it means abstaining from the pleasures and activities of life in order to obtain the kingdom of God. Rather than pushing for a Jewish ritual practice it is urging a more rigorously ascetic lifestyle, a disengagement from life.

A variety of interpretations have been proffered for the enigmatic injunction to "make the Sabbath a Sabbath." It could mean, for example, that one should truly observe the Sabbath (make it a *real* Sabbath); alternatively, it could be playing on the term *rest*, and be saying that one should rest from taking a day of rest—that is, precisely, *not* observe the Sabbath.[43] The latter interpretation would coincide well with both the first part of the saying and with sayings 6 and 14, and so is probably to be preferred.

Another option has been proposed by Peter Nagel, who points out that the words used for "Sabbath" are given variant spellings in the surviving Coptic text (SAMBATON and SABBATON). This leads him to suggest two meanings for them: in one instance Sabbath refers to the day of the Sabbath, and in the other it

41. *Gospel of Thomas*, p. 80.

42. For further interpretation, see A. Marjanen, "Thomas and Jewish Religious Practices," in R. Uro, ed., *Thomas at the Crossroads: Essays on the Gospel of Thomas* (Edinburgh: T&T Clark, 1998), pp. 163–82.

43. Both possibilities are suggested by Zlatko Pleše in Ehrman and Pleše, *Apocryphal Gospels*, p. 317, n. 37.

means "week" (as in Luke 18:12; Mark 16:9).[44] This leads to a possible reconceptualization of the saying, as spelled out in the expansive translation/interpretation of Plisch:

> If you do not refrain from the world
> (and not only from a part of it, as certain food, etc.)
> You will not find the kingdom;
> If you do not observe the (entire) week as Sabbath
> (instead of only some "holy days")
> You will not see the father.[45]

In this rendering, it is important for the Christian to enter into repose permanently, not just temporarily. In that sense, once again, Jewish practices are superseded and no longer in force. They are, in fact, harmful. Jewish language, then, is being used to oppose Jewish religious practice.

Saying 39

This saying presents a direct polemic against Jewish Pharisees and scribes. They know how to enter into God's Kingdom and can provide this knowledge for others, but they have refused to do so. They "have taken the keys of knowledge and hidden them. They have neither entered nor let those wishing to enter do so." And so the Jewish leaders have not only condemned themselves before God, they have brought about the condemnation of other people.

The polemic is comparable to what one finds in the New Testament, especially in the famous set of "woes" found in Matthew 23. The saying itself appears to be a conflation of tradition otherwise known from Matt. 23:13 and Luke 11:52. The obvious contrast in the Gospel of Thomas is with Jesus himself, who not only has the keys of knowledge but reveals the divine secrets, the correct interpretation of which can bring eternal life (saying 1).

Saying 40

This brief saying may not be directed against Jews and Judaism per se, but against anyone who is not rooted in God: "A grapevine has been planted outside of the Father. And since it is not strong, it will be pulled up by its root and perish." Plisch takes it as a reference to people in general who do not find the source of their sustenance in the Father.[46] So too Valantasis understands the saying as

44. "Wenn ihr nicht den Sabbat zum Sabbat macht?" in *Sprachen Mythen, Mythizismen. Festschrift Walter Beltz*, in *Hallesche Beiträge zur Orientwissenschaft* 32 (2001): 507–17.

45. Uwe-Karsten Plisch, *The Gospel of Thomas: Original Text with Commentary* (Stuttgart: Deutsche Bibelgesellschaft, 2008), pp. 93–94.

46. *Gospel of Thomas*, p. 113.

polemical, but simply directed against "another religious community."[47] But it should not be overlooked in this connection that the Hebrew Bible sometimes portrays Israel as a grapevine or vineyard, occasionally with negative implications about its viability (Ps. 80:9–10; Isa. 5:1–7; Jer. 2:21). Read in light of these passages, the saying does not provide an aphoristic truth claim about "any" grapevine that happens to be "planted outside of the Father." Instead it makes a statement of fact, that a grapevine "has been planted outside the father." This specific grapevine is weak, and will be destroyed. It is hard not to take the saying as directed against historical Israel, to be destroyed because it is not located within the sphere of the true God.

Saying 43

This saying is surprising in several ways. For one thing, it begins with a challenge from the disciples to Jesus, which stands at odds with the normal Thomasine portrayal of the disciples as obedient, if sometimes slow, students of the master: "Who are you to say these things to us?" Jesus' frank reply is damning especially in the broader context of the Gospel of Thomas: his disciples do not understand who he is, despite his teachings. Since it is only through understanding Jesus' teachings that one can have eternal life, the consequences of their ignorance—and the challenge of his authority—are rather stark.

But Jesus castigates them even further, likening them to "Jews": "Rather, you have become like the Jews; for they love the tree but hate its fruit; and they love the fruit but hate the tree." This is surely a negative characterization in which the disciples are damned by association. But is there a specific meaning to "fruit" and "tree" in this context? Valantasis thinks there is, but gives a rather palliative interpretation. The tree represents Judaism and the fruit represents Christian faith: "The saying suggests that it is futile to differentiate such tree and fruit, loving one and hating the other. Even with animosity between the sibling religions, the mutuality and correlativity of the two traditions coexist inseparably."[48] Surely the negative characterization of Jews and Judaism elsewhere in the text, however, does not favor an interpretation endorsing mutual love and respect. DeConick's view is better. The disciples are like the Jews who are unable to decide whether to love the tree or the fruit: "This is the voice of a community which is in the process of separating itself from its Jewish roots."[49]

At the same time, the saying is more than that. The Jews are portrayed negatively here, as those who cannot decide what to love and what to hate. The supposed followers of Jesus who cannot understand him are like that: without knowledge—the correct understanding of his teachings—they do not know

---

47. Valantasis, *Gospel of Thomas*, p. 116.

48. Ibid., p. 140.

49. *Original Gospel of Thomas*, p. 165.

what to think; and if they do not know what to think, they will never inherit eternal life. Like the Jews.

Saying 52

In this saying the disciples exclaim that Jesus is the fulfillment of the Jewish prophets, only to earn his rebuke for listening to dead voices rather than the voice of the living: "His disciples said to him, 'Twenty-four prophets spoke in Israel, and they all spoke about you.' He said to them, 'You have abandoned the one who lives in your presence and have spoken of the dead.'"

There has been considerable speculation concerning who the twenty-four prophets of Israel were. They are probably best understood as the books of the entire Hebrew Bible, as in 2 Esdras 14:45, where Ezra is instructed to publish all the Scriptures he has inscribed: "The Most High spoke to me, saying, 'Make public the twenty-four books that you wrote first, and let the worthy and the unworthy read them.'" For many early Christians, Jesus came in fulfillment of Scripture, and Scripture provided testimony to who he is; Judaism is thus the forerunner of Christianity that prepared the way for Christ. For the Jesus of the Gospel of Thomas, on the other hand, the Hebrew Bible is dead and defunct, and the religion it supports is of no value. It is not the Old Testament that is to be studied, but the sayings of the living Jesus.[50]

Saying 53

Following the rejection of ancient Israel and its scriptures in saying 52, saying 53 makes a direct attack on the Jewish practice of circumcision, comparable to the attack on other aspects of Jewish cultic life in saying 14. When the disciples ask whether circumcision is beneficial, Jesus delivers a stark reply: "If it were beneficial, their father would beget them already circumcised from their mother. But true circumcision in the spirit has become entirely profitable." It is important to note that Jesus does not simply express the superiority of spiritual over physical circumcision, as the saying could easily be misread. The final clause does indeed indicate that spiritual circumcision is beneficial, as found in texts of the Hebrew Bible (Jer. 4:4) and other early Christian writings, including those associated with Paul (Rom. 2:25–29, 3:1–2; Phil. 3:3). But in this case the superiority of spiritual circumcision is coupled with a complete rejection of physical circumcision, which is of no value at all. This is a vivid contrast with Paul's own view (Rom. 3:1–2), that circumcision is valuable "much and in every way." For this author, circumcision is of no value whatsoever; otherwise, boys would be born circumcised. Since they are not, circumcision does not come from God.

---

50. This stands in precise contrast, for example, with the Pseudo-Clementine *Recognitions* 1.59, which instead *affirm* the Scriptural prophets precisely because Christ bears witness to them.

This denigration of circumcision is at the same time a denigration of what it means to be Jewish. Rather than representing the sign of the covenant made between God and his people, circumcision is to be rejected as of no religious value. To this extent the Jesus of Thomas embraces a view found in other anti-Jewish writings, such as Justin's *Dialogue with Trypho* 19.3: "As I already explained . . . it is because circumcision is not essential for all men, but only for you Jews, to mark you off for the suffering you now so deservedly endure."[51]

THE DIDASCALIA APOSTOLORUM

The so-called church orders include such books as the Epistula Clementis (although as earlier noted, it is not usually included in the group), the Didache, the Apostolic Tradition, the Apostolic Church Order, the Didascalia Apostolorum, and the Apostolic Constitutions. There is some question over whether it is appropriate to consider these books, and others like them, as a coherent genre, but in any case they do tend to discuss a range of topics related to the administration of the church (not all topics are found in each book): church organization, ethical and to some extent doctrinal instruction; the appointment of church officers; the duties of each office; church discipline; and instructions for liturgical acts such as baptism, eucharist, and ordination. The Didascalia Apostolorum is notable within the group for its strong anti-Jewish slant. It was allegedly written by the twelve apostles after the death of Jesus, but like the Epistula Clementis and the Apostolic Constitutions (which takes it over virtually wholesale), it too is forged. For those who wanted an authoritative account of the church—its offices, organization, beliefs, ethics, and so on—no better option existed than a book of instructions from the apostolic band itself.

The Didascalia was originally written in Greek, but is now preserved completely in Syriac, with extensive portions in Latin. Traditionally it is dated to the early third century, although the most recent study of Alistair Stewart-Sykes places its final composition in the early fourth century.[52] It was first published in 1856 by Lagarde from a single Syriac manuscript. One of the great scholars and translators of the work, R. H. Connolly, considered it to be a unified text,[53] a view that held sway for most of the twentieth century, up to the more recent

51. Translation of Thomas Falls, *The Writings of Justin Martyr* (Washington, DC: Catholic University of America Press, 1948). I do not include a discussion of saying 104, where Jesus again appears to denigrate the Jewish practices of prayer and fasting, because I am convinced by the interpretation of DeConick (*Gospel of Thomas*, p. 282), that since fasting was connected in Jewish texts with atonement and demonic battles, Jesus' response is simply a claim not to have needed atonement and not to have needed help in spiritual warfare. In her opinion, this saying arose in the Thomasine community before they developed anti-Jewish attitudes and lifestyles.

52. Alistair Stewart-Sykes, *The Didascalia Apostolorum* (Turnhout: Brepols, 2009), p. 54.

53. *Didascalia apostolorum: The Syriac Version translated and accompanied by the Verona Latin fragments, with an introduction and notes* (Oxford: Clarendon, 1929). See e.g., p. xxxvi.

investigations of Paul Bradshaw and now, most notably, Stewart-Sykes.[54] Whatever one makes of the integrity of the text, the author(s) were clearly dependent on earlier traditions that have been incorporated into the work. In its final form, the book presents the "teaching" of the twelve disciples. Unlike some of the other church orders, there is no detailed instruction on liturgical practices; and, as we will see, large portions of the book are neither (directly) polemical nor written in the first person. Among the topics it addresses are sin and its consequences, penance, bishops and how they should judge and forgive, the need to support bishops and honor all the clergy, the settlement of disputes, the role of widows and deaconesses, the Christian relation to the Jewish Law (this is where the book becomes polemical, and where the author most frequently reverts to first-person discourse), and the related theme of heresy.

The most recent, detailed, and somewhat convoluted source-redaction analysis of the work comes in the new translation and introduction of Stewart-Sykes. In addition to two major sources underlying the bulk of the instruction, Stewart-Sykes claims that there were two later redactors. He labels one the "deuterotic," because he opposed the "secondary legislation," that is, the Jewish Law given by Moses as a punishment to the Jews for their idolatry, after he delivered the true Law of God, the Decalogue. The other redactor is called the "apostolic" because it was he who inserted the first-person authorial claims in the names of the apostles. If this view is right, then the final product that circulated in the manuscript tradition is what I have called a "redactional forgery." The older sources and their combination into the bulk of the text were written anonymously; but by redacting the piece in the names of the apostles, sometimes narrated in the first person, the apostolic redactor has made not only his occasional additions but also the redacted whole a forgery.

The jury is still out on Stewart-Sykes's complicated redactional analysis of the work. But it is clear that some redaction, at least, has taken place, in many instances awkwardly, as there are serious editorial seams in the work that become evident upon a close reading. [55] In particular Stewart-Sykes makes a good point about the apostolic redactor: the topics addressed in the first person tend, as a whole, not to be those of the rest of the book, and in these passages the tone turns polemical, just when authorization for certain views becomes especially important. As we will see more fully, the apostolic first-person narrator inserts himself only rarely in the early chapters of the book (e.g., Matthew in 2.39.1)[56]; by the end

54. Paul Bradshaw, *The Search for the Origins of Christian Worship*, 2nd ed. (New York: Oxford University, 2002), p. 93; and Stewart-Sykes, *Didascalia*, passim.

55. As just one example, in the account of the Jerusalem conference discussed in 6.12.3 the author indicates that he is the "apostles" and differentiates himself from "James." But then the author has "I James" speak as if he is one of the twelve and includes himself among the apostolic band: "we, the apostles" (6.12.12, 14).

56. NB: I will not be following the twenty-four chapter divisions of the manuscripts, as these do not allow for easy cross-referencing and checking, but the more refined book-chapter-verse divisions provided by F. X. Funk and retained by Stewart-Sykes.

of the book, however, the device becomes common. And it is not difficult to identify the first-person narrator's overarching concerns. It is in the context of heresies and schisms that the first person becomes prominent, especially in discussions of the secondary legislation. The fundamental aim of this part of the text is "to dissuade Christians from keeping the Jewish Law."[57]

One may well wonder why the redactor did not edit his work more exhaustively by setting up a pseudepigraphic frame at the outset. G. Schöllgen—writing well before Stewart-Sykes's complex source-redaction analysis but anticipating it in at least one key point—gives a compelling explanation:

> A possible, indeed perhaps the most plausible, explanation for the limited presence of the frame in the first third appears to me to be the assumption that the Didascalia was originally not conceptualized as an apostolic writing and sought to proceed only by means of extensive argumentation from Scripture against problems in communal practice.[58]

The Authorial Claims of the Text

The issue of authority—a matter of concern for all the church orders—is clear at the outset of the book, even without the first-person narrator. The Didascalia is written "from the command of the Savior" (1). The later pseudepigraphic references, then, when they do start to appear, make that "command" all the more plausible. This teaching comes from Christ through the apostles. Still, the most peculiar feature of the authorial claims of the Didascalia is precisely their uneven spread.[59] The unidentified narrator at the beginning of the book continues until 2.14.9, where suddenly the author speaks in the first-person plural in reference to Judas Iscariot praying with "us" but doing "us" no harm.[60] Obviously one is to take the first person to be the other eleven disciples, but nothing more is said about the matter at this point.

As one moves through the book, first-person references begin to appear, more or less out of the blue, without any self-identification and without pushing any obvious ideological or theological agenda (2.6.16, 2.7.1, 2.8.1, 2.52.3, 3.9.2, 4.9.2). At other times it is clear that the apostles are the "we,"—as in the recollection

57. Stewart-Sykes, *Didascalia*, p. 24.

58. "Eine mögliche, vielleicht die plausibelste, Erklärung für die Rahmenabstinenz des ersten Drittels scheint mir die Annahme zu sein, daß die Didaskalie ursprünglich gar nicht als Apostelschrift konzipiert war und lediglich mit Hilfe extensiver Schriftargumentation gegen die Mißstände in der Gemeindepraxis vorgehen wollte." Georg Schöllgen, "Pseudapostolizität und Schriftgebrauch in den ersten Kirchenordnungen. Anmerkungen zur Begründung des frühen Kirchenrechts," in *Stimuli: Exegese und ihre Hermeneutik in Antike und Christentum. Festschrift Für Ernst Dassmann*, ed. George Schöllgen and Clemens Scholten (Münster: Aschendorffsche Verlagsbuchhandlung, 1996), p. 115.

59. So also B. Steimer, *Vertex Traditionis*, p. 55.

60. The author does use a first-person pronoun occasionally before this, e.g., in 1.1.3 ("our" Lord), 1.2.4 ("Let us"), and especially 1.7.17 ("we . . . you"). But he gives no indication at these points that he is presenting himself as the apostolic band.

of Jesus' washing the disciples' feet in 3.13.4–5. The first occurrence of a first-person singular narrative is 2.39.1, "I Matthew." In this instance the reference is occasioned by the mention of "tax collectors" in the previous paragraph; but it is probably significant that this is also the first context in which "false brothers" are discussed.

It is not until the final third of the book that the first-person narration becomes prominent. When looked at as a whole, the alternations between first and third persons are awkward. For example, even though, in the final product, this is the apostles talking, they sometimes talk about themselves in the third person, as in 2.20.1, "for to the bishop it was said through the apostles."[61] Or in 2.26.7, "the presbyters are also to be reckoned to you as a type of the apostles." It seems especially odd for Matthew to speak in the first person in 2.39.1 ("I, Matthew") but then to have the Gospel of Matthew referred to impersonally, "Now in the Gospel of Matthew it is written thus" (5.14.11).

On the other hand, it is perhaps not surprising that once the text moves to discuss doctrinal matters, the basis for correct teaching is not made merely by natural arguments and appeals to Scripture, but by the personal authority of the apostles who were with Jesus, spoke with him, ate with him, and were witnesses to him (5.7.25–26). Doctrine in particular needs special apostolic authorization. So too when the author tries to settle a major controversy over the celebration of Passover, he speaks in the first person in the voice of the apostles who personally participated in the Last Supper (5.14.1–5, 5.17.1). And again, when the matter of heresies and schisms appears, the first-person narrator can appeal to having heard the Lord himself (6.5.1–4). In particular, he stresses that God has departed from "the people" (i.e., the Jews) and moved into "the church" (i.e., the Christian community), and this has happened "by means of ourselves the apostles" (6.5.4). Satan too has come to the church, for example in the person of "Simon the sorcerer," whose encounters with the true representatives of God are narrated in the first person by the apostles, and in particular "I, Peter" (6.9). Most especially, "because the entire church was in danger of falling into heresy, we twelve apostles gathered together as one in Jerusalem to determine what should be done" (6.12.1). They decided that they would write up this "didascalia," so that the entire book, in this final redaction, is understood to be the document that emerged from the Jerusalem conference, convened to attack false teaching (6.13.1).

This claim to apostolic authorization for its teaching had its effect. Epiphanius, for example, held the document to be apostolic (*Panarion*, 70, 10ff.).

Nature of the False Teaching

Stewart-Sykes has a clear vision of the function of the deuterotic redactor: "The fundamental aim of the redactor is to deal with the challenges posed by Jewish

61. Throughout I will be using the translation of Stewart-Sykes, *Didascalia*.

Christians."[62] Unlike the earlier works we have studied in this chapter, the opponents here, in other words, are not Jews from outside the church but Christians who insist on still following aspects of the Jewish Law. For the most part, the attack on Judaism is, therefore, indirect; but as we will see, there is also direct polemic against Judaism itself as a false religion. That is why, ultimately, followers of Jesus are not to practice it.

Most of the Didascalia is not polemical in nature. When the polemic does begin to appear, however, it is in relation to the Jewish Law. In an important passage early on (1.4.7–10), the author indicates that the true Law is the "Decalogue and the judgments." What he calls the "deuterosis"—the "secondary legislation"—is the Law given after the incident of the Golden Calf, when Moses returned up the mountain and received all of the Law other than the ten commandments. Christians are to avoid this secondary legislation: "Keep away from all its instructions and commands, so that you do not lead yourself astray and bind yourself and weigh yourself down with ancient bonds which cannot be undone" (1.4.7). Christ came, for this author, in order to fulfill the Law (i.e., the true Law, the Decalogue) and to weaken the bonds of the secondary legislation, making them null and void for his followers.

This early passage is an adumbration of the fuller exposition near the end of the book, 6.15–23. Christians are not to follow the Law that was given in order to punish Jews for their sins: "You who have been converted from the people [i.e., from among the Jews] who believe in God and in our Saviour Jesus Christ should not now be continuing to keep to your former conduct, keeping pointless obligations and purifications, and separations and baptismal lustrations and distinction between foods" (6.15.1).

The temptation to follow the secondary legislation is not limited to converts from Judaism, however, as the author earlier addresses "especially you who are of the gentiles" (5.14.22). And so the problem involves both ethnically Jewish Christians who continue to follow the prescriptions of Torah and gentile Christians who have been convinced, presumably by them, to do so as well. For this author, the true Law of God, which certainly is to be followed, is "simple . . . pure, and holy." It is the Decalogue, as shown by a curious kind of gematria. Since it is specifically a "Deca"-logue, it can be represented by the letter iota (the numeral ten); and it is iota that begins the name ΙΗΣΟΥΣ (6.15.2). And so the Decalogue is for the followers of Jesus, and only the Decalogue: "Thus the law is indissoluble, whereas the secondary legislation is transitory. For the law is the Decalogue" (6.15.3–4).

The secondary legislation was given by God out of anger, when the children of Israel committed idolatry in the incident of the Golden Calf: "Then was the Lord angry, and in the heat of his anger, yet in his merciful goodness, he bound them to the secondary legislation as to a heavy load and the hardness of a yoke" (6.16.6).

62. *Didascalia Apostolorum*, p. 3.

This deuterosis required them to make frequent burnt offerings, to observe strict food laws, purifications, "and much else that is astounding" (6.16.9). Followers of Jesus, however, have been "released from the worship of idols through baptism, as from the secondary legislation. For in the Gospel he renewed and fulfilled and confirmed the Law, and abolished and abrogated the secondary legislation" (6.17.1). That, in fact, is why Christ died: "to redeem us from the bonds of the secondary [legislation]" (5.5.3).

Anyone who continues to try to keep the secondary legislation, therefore, is "guilty of the worship of the calf" (6.18.9); what is more, "if you uphold the secondary legislation you are also asserting the curse against our Saviour. You are ensnared in the bonds and so are guilty of the woe as an enemy of the Lord God" (6.18.10).

It should be clear from the foregoing that the main target of the pseudepigraphic polemic is a form of Jewish Christianity, defined, in this instance, as a Christianity that insists on the ongoing validity of Jewish ritual observances. The author appears to have other opponents in view as well, and indeed he may not have neatly differentiated among them. For one thing, Jews who are not followers of Jesus also come under attack, on grounds that can easily be imagined. They are no better than "pagans [who] go in the morning to worship and serve their idols when they rise from sleep" (2.60.2). They are, in fact, "vainly called Jews" (2.60.3), by resting on the Sabbath they show that they are "idle." They do not have any faith. Most severely, "they do not confess the murder of Christ, which they brought about through transgressing the law, and so repent and be saved." They are, then, without "excuse before the Lord God" (2.60.4). Indeed, they "made the Lord angry by not believing in him," (5.16.1) and they hate the Christians (5.14.23).

The other target of attack is a group of "heretics" whose crimes of unbelief are spoken of in such general terms that it is impossible to know exactly who they were or what they believed. The names Simon and Cleobius (6.8) may be traditional, picked up, perhaps from 3 Corinthians, which I will discuss in a later chapter. The charges against these heretics may also have been derived from this Pauline forgery, as they are accused of refusing to use the laws and the prophets, of blaspheming God the Almighty, and of not believing in the resurrection (6.10.1)—all charges dealt with not only in 3 Corinthians but throughout the writings of proto-orthodox heresiologists attacking "Gnostics." At the same time the opponents are said to forbid marriage and the eating of meat, charges commonly associated with overly rigorous encratites (also Gnostics?); yet others insist simply on not eating pork and on getting circumcised—charges involving, now, the secondary legislation (6.10.3–4). It may be that in this instance the author is simply attacking heresy in general, rather than having specific targets in mind. In any event, he claims that the rise of these opponents is what prompted the Jerusalem conference and the writing of this very didascalia (6.12.1), even though, as I have noted, the vast bulk of the instruction has nothing to do with such false teachings.

The author shows a particular awareness of, and irritation toward, other Christian leaders who "come falsely under the name of apostles" (6.13.2), who are evidently having an influence on the churches. One hardly need note the thick irony, in this book that falsely claims to be written by the apostles, actually produced some two centuries after their demise. Who the author has in mind as apostolic impostors is anyone's guess. If he knew of actual writings celebrating the importance of the Jewish Law for Christians—such as the forged Epistula Petri or the forged Grundschrift lying behind the Pseudo-Clementine *Recognitions* and *Homilies*—then we would be altogether justified in labeling his work a counterforgery in the strong sense. C. Fonrobert, on the other hand, has argued that the immediate occasion for the book was not Christian literary activity but non-Christian Jewish—specifically that the book and its instructions for Christians is a response to rabbis in the process of codifying what became the Mishnah:

> The Didascalia spends so much time arguing about the "second legislation," and the correct way of reading Scripture, because it recognizes that there are other ways of reading, potentially legitimate or persuasive ways of reading at that, that challenge the sense of Christian identity that the Didascalia itself wants to convey.[63]

At the end of the day it may be impossible to decide this issue. But it bears repeating that the explicit target of the author's polemics in almost every instance is false teachers within the Christian community. Only rarely, as we have seen, does he attack non-Christian Jews; instead, his concern is with followers of Jesus who keep the Jewish Law. This may tilt the scale in favor of seeing the context as less a confrontation with local rabbinic activities and more a concern over Judaizing practices within the Christian communities themselves.[64] And as we will see in a later chapter, there are other polemical issues touched upon by the author, again involving internal church dynamics.

THE ACTS OF PILATE

Unlike the other books we have considered in this chapter, the Acts of Pilate was massively popular throughout the Middle Ages. More than five hundred manuscripts still survive in Latin, Greek, Coptic, Syriac, Aramaic, Armenian, and

---

63. Charlotte Elisheva Fonrobert, "The Didascalia Apostolorum: A Mishnah for the Disciples of Jesus," *JECS* 9 (2001): 501–2.

64. At the same time, it is important to affirm Fonrobert's overarching point about Jews and Christians in antiquity, that neither Rabbinic Judaism nor Christianity was a fixed point along a spectrum, and that a document such as the Didascalia cannot neatly be located somewhere along the line between them. There were obviously massive interchanges and nuanced relationships among people who self-identified as Jews and/or Christians, as is becoming increasingly clear among scholars who refuse to think simplistically about the so-called parting of the ways.

Georgian. The manuscripts in the vernaculars of Europe are even harder to tally. They can be found in Castilian, Catalan, French, Italian, Occitan, Portuguese, German, English, Danish, Dutch, Old Norse, Swedish, Gallic, Irish, Bulgarian, Polish, Old Slavonic, and Czech.[65]

Patristic References to an Acts of Pilate

We appear to have references to an Acts of Pilate before any such book existed. The first occurs in Justin's First Apology, where he indicates, about the passion of Jesus, "That these things really happened, you can ascertain from the Acts of Pontius Pilate" (35.9).[66] Later he states "That Christ did perform such deeds you can learn from the Acts of Pontius Pilate" (48.3). The second reference shows that these "Acts" are not thought of as some kind of official *acta* recording the events of Jesus' trial, but a fuller account of some kind. Historians have always treated both references gingerly. Directly before the first of them, Justin also suggests that his reader can learn about the town of Bethlehem "by consulting the census taken by Quirinius, your first procurator in Judea." Apart from the fact the Quirinius was never a procurator in Judea, there is the problem that the census itself, referred to in Luke 2, was almost certainly Luke's invention (or that of Luke's community or oral source), designed with the express purpose of locating Jesus' actual birth in Bethlehem despite the fact that everyone knew that he came from Nazareth. Justin, in other words, is making things up. There was no census record to consult, and no Acts of Pilate. He may well have simply assumed that they must have existed.

Some decades later Tertullian refers, not to acta, but to correspondence allegedly sent from Pilate to the emperor Tiberius. Tertullian's first reference does not actually mention Pilate, but indicates that "So Tiberius . . . hearing from Palestine in Syria information which had revealed the truth of Christ's divinity, brought the matter before the Senate, with previous indication of his own approval" (*Apol.* 5.2). Here again we are dealing with an obvious fiction, both with respect to Tiberius' attempt to obtain the senate's approbation of Jesus' divine status and to his receipt "from Palestine" of correspondence to that effect. The second reference clarifies that the alleged correspondence came from Pilate: "All these facts about Christ were reported to Tiberius, the reigning emperor, by Pilate who was by now a Christian himself, as far as his conscience was concerned" (*Apol.* 21.24). That Pilate eventually became a Christian was later narrativized in some of the writings of the Pilate cycle. The presence of the tradition in Tertullian's reference to a correspondence does not inspire confidence in the report, which is fully implausible even on its own merits.

---

65. See Rémi Gounelle and Zbigniew Izydorczyk, *L'Évangile de Nicodème ou Les Actes fait sous Ponce Pilate* (Belgium: Brepols, 1997); and especially Z. Izydorczyk, *The Medieval Gospel of Nicodemus: Texts, Intertexts, and Contexts in Western Europe*, Medieval and Renaissance Texts and Studies, 158 (Tempe: Arizona State University, 1997).

66. Translation from T. Falls, *Writings of Saint Justin Martyr.*

A further reference occurs in the "Passion of Tarachus, Probus, and Andronicus," three martyrs during the Great Persecution of 304 CE. Here it is not a Christian but a pagan governor, Maximus, who confronts the accused with the existence of an Acts of Pilate: "Nonsense! Don't you know that he whom you invoke is an evil man who was hanged on a cross under the authority of a governor named Pilate, whose Acts are still preserved?"[67] In this case there is reason to think that the governor—whether a fictional character speaking for the author/narrator or a real person—was referring to an actual, existing document. For we have solid evidence that there did indeed at one time exist a pagan version of the Acts of Pilate, propagated in the context of Christian persecution at the beginning of the fourth century.

The evidence comes from Eusebius, who both mentions the document and exposes it as a nonhistorical fabrication. In speaking of the activities of pagan priests under the persecuting zeal of the emperor Maximin Daia, he indicates that they forged an Acts of Pilate as part of their strategy in attacking the Christians: (*H.E.* 9.5) "They actually forged *Memoranda* of Pilate and our Savior (πλασάμενοι δῆτα Πιλάτου καὶ τοῦ σωτῆρος ἡμῶν ὑπομνήματα), full of every kind of blasphemy against Christ."[68] He goes on to speak of the distribution of the book:

> These, with the approval of their superior, they sent to every district under his command, announcing in edicts that they were to be publicly displayed in every place, whether hamlet or city, for all to see, and that they should be given to children by their teachers instead of lessons, to study and learn by heart.

Stephen Mitchell has pointed out the strategic significance of the emperor's decision to make the text available not simply in the major urban areas of the empire, but also in more remote rural places: "Official persecution hitherto . . . had made little impression on the countryside of much of the empire. Retreat to the chora was a natural and effective response of threatened Christians, if they had the means and opportunity to do so."[69] By spreading propaganda against the Christians into the countryside, Maximin was able to compromise the traditional safe havens of the Christian elite who could escape the cities for areas with other overriding concerns.

Eusebius had access to this fabricated account and had no difficulty exposing it as historically worthless. Its narrative—if that's what it was—was set in the fourth consulship of Tiberius, that is, in the seventh year of his reign. But Josephus, as Eusebius points out, indicates that Pilate was not made governor of Judea until

67. My translation of the French from Gounelle and Izydorczyk, *L'Évangile de Nicodème*, p. 106.

68. Translation of G. A. Williamson, *Eusebius*.

69. Stephen Mitchell, "Maximinus and the Christians in A.D. 312: A New Latin Inscription," *JRS* 78 (1988): 121. For general background on Maximin Daia and his persecution of Christians, see Robert Grant, "The Religion of Maximin Daia," in *Christianity, Judaism, and Other Greco-Roman Cults*, ed. J. Neusner (Leiden: Brill, 1975), pp. 143–66.

the twelfth year of Tiberius' rule: "This clearly proves the forged character of the *Memoranda* so recently published, blackening our Saviour; at the very start the note of time proves the dishonesty of the forgers" (*H.E.* 1.9).

We no longer have this fabricated pagan Acts of Pilate and can only guess at what it contained. Z. Izydorczyk suggests that since the audience included the general populace and school children learning how to read, the account may have been very basic indeed: "possibly a list of charges against Jesus and some account of the trial."[70]

The Christian Acts of Pilate

Our first certain reference to a Christian "Acts of Pilate" comes over a half century after Eusebius, in the writings of Epiphanius (377 CE). While attacking the Quartodecimans in chapter 50 of his *Panarion*, Epiphanius indicates that they based their celebration of Easter on the eighth day before the calends of April (March 25) on the dating provided in the "Acts accomplished under Pontius Pilate." Epiphanius challenges this dating because he has seen multiple manuscripts of the work with textual variation at just this point; the date is therefore not secure. Among other things this reference shows that the Christian Acts of Pilate was in wide circulation by the 370s; it was in use among Quartodecimans; and Epiphanius had seen it in numerous manuscript copies, which he was able to collate at a key point. Ten years later, from 387 CE, we have an Easter Homily actually written by a Quartodeciman, who does just what Epiphanius claimed the group did, arguing for the date of Easter based on the "Acts Done Under Pilate."[71]

There are reasons for thinking that the Christian version cannot have been written *before* the fourth century, despite the rather quirky claim of F. Scheidweiler that it was available already in the second Christian century.[72] For one thing, if such a document were in circulation, surely Eusebius would have known about it, and would have delighted in exposing the pagan version as a fabrication based on the "true" account of Pilate's role in and attitude toward Jesus' crucifixion. Moreover, Gounelle and Izydorczyk give material reasons for thinking that the Christian version as it has come down to us is most plausibly placed in the fourth century. In their judgment, the superior royalty of Christ makes best sense once Christianity had become a legitimate religion.[73] Moreover, the oath that Pilate

---

70. *Medieval Gospel of Nicodemus*, p. 24.

71. Gounelle and Izydorczyk draw the obvious conclusion that the Acts of Pilate was in circulation in Asia Minor by no later than the second half of the fourth century. *L'Évangile de Nicodème*, p. 108.

72. In Schneemelcher, *New Testament Apocryphya*, 1.501–4. Scheidweiler's argument is demolished by Jean-Pierre Lémonon, *Pilate et le gouvernement de la Judée: textes et monuments* (Paris: J. Gabalda, 1981).

73. *L'Évangile de Nicodème*, p. 110.

takes before the sun (3.1; see also 12.1) reflects a practice otherwise not known before the fourth century.[74]

Given what can be established about the dates of the two respective Acts of Pilate, it has been widely argued that the Christian version was written to counter the claims of the pagan, which appeared some years earlier. Representative of this view are G. W. H. Lampe ("If this was the purpose of Maximin's publication, it is tempting to think that the Christian *Acts of Pilate* may have been composed as a counter-blast to it"[75]) and Z. Izydorczyk ("One suspects, admittedly on circumstantial evidence, that the AP known to us remain in some relation to those circulated under Maximin. Possibly, they were a Christian response to the polemics against Christianity evoked by Eusebius"[76]). If this view is correct, then in the surviving Acts of Pilate we have another instance of a counterforgery.

Given its extensive attestation, in many languages over many centuries, the text of this work is highly unstable, even to the extent that it has been known under a variety of names. Eventually it was most widely called the Gospel of Nicodemus, since, as we will see in a moment, it claims actually to have been written by Nicodemus himself (which is why it is a forgery). But the thorough investigations of Gounelle and Izydorczyk have shown that some variation on the title "Acts of What Happened to Our Savior Jesus Christ Under Pontius Pilate, Governor of Judea" lay at the base of all the early versions of the text in Latin and the oriental languages, apart from the Slavonic, and is used in fifteen of our oldest manuscripts in the Greek tradition (starting in the twelfth century). In their view, the earliest form of the book was probably entitled "The Acts Accomplished Under Pontius Pilate." The famous account of the Descent to Hell, found in Tischendorf's B text of the Gospel, was probably not added until the sixth century. According to Gounelle, the title "Gospel of Nicodemus" became popular only in the twelfth century.[77]

The Acts of Pilate as a Forgery

Despite the earlier form of its title, the Acts of Pilate claims not to be written by Pilate but by the Rabbi Nicodemus, as stated at the outset of the narrative: "Nicodemus related all the things that happened after the crucifixion and suffering of our Lord and delivered them over to the high priests and the other Jews. The same

74. Attested otherwise in the Apostolic Constitutions 21.52.1 and the fourth-century *Lives of the Caesars* 39.13 (*L'Évangile de Nicodème*, p. 110).

75. "The Trial of Jesus in the Acta Pilati," in *Jesus and the Politics of His Day*, ed. E. Bammel and C. F. D. Moule (Cambridge: Cambridge University Press, 1984), p. 176.

76. *Medieval Gospel of Nicodemus*, p. 24.

77. Rémi Grounelle, "Évangile de Nicodème ou Actes de Pilate," in Pierre Geoltrain and Jean-Daniel Kaestli, *Écrits apocryphes chrétiens* (Paris: Éditions Gallimard, 2005), pp. 251–59. For a fresh English translation of the A text (chs. 1–16) and parts of the B text (including the Descent to Hell), see Ehrman and Pleše, *Apocryphal Gospels*, pp. 419–89.

Nicodemus compiled these writings in the Hebrew tongue."[78] The account begins then with a kind of discovery narrative:

> I, Ananias, a member of the procurator's bodyguard, well versed in the law, came to know our Lord Jesus Christ from the divine Scriptures, coming to him by faith and being deemed worthy of holy baptism. I searched out the public records composed at that time, in the days of our master Jesus Christ, which the Jews set down under Pontius Pilate. These public records I found written in Hebrew, and with God's good pleasure I have translated them into Greek, so that all who call upon the name of our Lord Jesus Christ might know them. This I did in the seventeenth year of our master, the emperor Flavius Theodotius, the sixth year of Flavius Valentinianus, in the ninth indiction. (424–25 CE)

Despite the claims of the prologue, the book could hardly have been composed, originally, in Hebrew. In one of its early, amusing scenes, Pilate's courier indicates that when in Jerusalem he heard the "children of the Hebrews" crying out their acclamations to Jesus at the triumphal entry. A dispute then arises with the Jewish leaders in Pilate's court over the Greek translation of the Hebrew words the courier heard spoken on the occasion. The Greek explanations given in the text would have made no sense if in fact the scene was not originally composed in Greek (the Hebrew phrasing is itself transliterated and then translated into Greek). The claim to have been written in Hebrew, then, is simply a clumsy verisimilitude.

Even though the document is widely thought to have been a response to the pagan fabrication of an Acts of Pilate, rarely has anyone considered why a narrative of this sort would be appropriate as a counterforgery.[79] Part of the answer may lie in one of the commonly accepted features of the account, its harsh treatment of Jews, especially the Jewish leaders who force Pilate to have Jesus crucified out of jealousy. The centrality of the Jewish leaders is established at the outset of the narrative: "The chief priests and scribes called a meeting of the council—Annas, Caiaphas, Semes, Dathaes, Gamaliel, Judas, Levi, Nephthalim, Alexander, Jairus, and the other Jews—and they came to Pilate, accusing Jesus of many deeds" (1.1). The willful blindness of these Jewish leaders to Jesus' unique identity not only as the king, a point stressed throughout the account, but also as the son of God, is hammered home time and again, chapter after chapter. It begins with the famous scene of the bowing standards in 1.5–6. When Jesus enters into Pilate's praetorium, the standards—topped with an image of Caesar—held by pagan slaves, bow down in obeisance before him. The Jewish leaders are incensed and accuse the slaves of bowing. Jesus is dismissed, the Jewish leaders get twelve of their own burly men to take the standards, six

78. Prologue. Translations taken from Ehrman and Pleše, *Apocryphal Gospels*.

79. For further reflections on its value as a counterforgery, in the context of early Christian apologetics, see pp. 484–85.

to each one. Jesus is brought back into the room, and once again the standards bow before him.

For the reader this is clear and certain proof both of Jesus' unique standing before God (even the image of the emperor worships him) and of the Jewish leaders' hardheaded and hardhearted refusal to accept it. They proceed to bring false charges against him, especially that he was "born of fornication" (alluding to the Virgin Birth tradition), and they refuse to heed when reliable witnesses testify to the contrary. Pilate in his confusion asks the witnesses about Jesus' accusers:

> "Why do these people want to kill him?"
>
> They replied to Pilate, "They are filled with religious zeal, because he heals on the Sabbath."
>
> Pilate said, "They want to kill him for doing a good deed?"
>
> They replied, "Yes." (2.6)

The entire trial scene pits Pilate, who wants Jesus released, against the recalcitrant Jewish leaders, who want him crucified. At one point Pilate curses the whole lot of them, not just the leaders: "Your nation is always causing riots, and you oppose those who are your own benefactors." He goes on to narrate how the children of Israel were in constant rebellion against Moses, and even against God himself, despite the miracles done on their behalf. Miracles figure prominently in this account as well, as witnesses whom Jesus has healed come forward, testifying to what he has done. The Jewish leaders remain unmoved and eventually force Pilate's hand.

But Pilate is even more reluctant here than in the (briefer) canonical accounts, repeatedly trying to release Jesus and urging the Jewish leaders to try him themselves. When he finally yields to their insistence, it is not the leaders alone who have accepted responsibility. As in Matthew it is the Jewish people as a whole who speak the hateful words accepting the responsibility for Jesus' blood. "Pilate said to them, 'I am innocent of the blood of this righteous man. You see to it yourselves.' The Jews replied, 'His blood be upon us and our children'" (4.1). Unlike in Matthew, the scene is repeated for good measure, so that "the Jews" make their fateful declaration twice: "Then Pilate took water and washed his hands before the sun and said, 'I am innocent of the blood of this righteous one. See to it yourselves.' Again the Jews cried out, 'His blood be upon us and our children'" (9.4). As if that were not enough, after Jesus' death the Jewish authorities decide to punish Joseph of Arimathea for providing Jesus a proper burial, and he rebukes them, recalling the earlier scene:

> "Now the one who is uncircumcised in the flesh but circumcised in heart has taken water to wash his hands before the sun, saying, 'I am innocent of the blood of this righteous one; see to it yourselves!' And you replied to Pilate, 'His blood be upon us and our children.' Now I am afraid that the wrath of the Lord may come upon you and your children, just as you have said." The Jews

> were deeply embittered when they heard these words and they attacked Joseph, seized him, and locked him in a house with no window, setting guards at the door. (12.1)

Once again, it is not just the leaders who are at fault: it is "the Jews." And yet there are at least a few "Jews" who come off well in the narrative, most notably Joseph of Arimathea himself, who is later awarded a special postresurrection audience with the risen Jesus, and Nicodemus, the stalwart member of the Sanhedrin who desperately tries to have Jesus released rather than executed (ch. 5), and who, then, later, allegedly writes up the entire account. For this author "the Jews" may be a recalcitrant group—especially their leaders—but their problem is less that they were Jewish than that they were not Christian.

How then would this forgery serve to counter the pagan Acts of Pilate in circulation on imperial order some years earlier, in the days of Christian persecution? As we will explore more fully in a later context,[80] from the earliest days of Christian apologetics, followers of Jesus were confronted with an enormous problem in the face of Roman opposition. Their lord had been crucified by the governing authorities. By following a convicted insurrectionist, they were themselves, obviously, antagonistic to the state. It was this known antagonism that led to persecution—not belief in one God, or in Christ's divinity, or anything else. Christians were a political problem and this was obvious on the most basic level: they followed Jesus, crucified under Pontius Pilate for crimes against the state.

The obvious apologetic solution suggested itself early on to Christians who realized that it was a much better thing to be on the side of the authorities than in opposition to them. If Jesus' death was a miscarriage of justice, yet not because of an incompetent decision by the Roman governor—if Jesus did nothing to deserve his fate and if the governor was, in fact, drawn to him—then his followers too were not interested in opposing the state. In fact, they could support the state and its authorities. But how could one sell that story? The easiest way was to produce a counternarrative that stood opposed not only to history as it was known to have happened but also to the formulations of it that were highly inimical to the Christian cause. The counternarrative is found already in our earliest Gospel, Mark, where it is the Jewish leaders who hand Jesus over to Pilate and insist on his death; it is strengthened in Luke, where Pilate declares Jesus innocent three times; it is strengthened further in Matthew, where Pilate washes his hands of Jesus' blood and hears the crowd respond that they will assume full responsibility themselves (passing it on to their children). Matters go to an even more unlikely extreme in the Gospel of John, where it is the Jewish leaders who actually crucify Jesus, a view attested in still later works such as the Gospel of Peter.

The exoneration of Pilate serves not only an obvious apologetic purpose; it also makes it possible to denigrate the Jews, hated on other grounds, principally

80. See ch. 15.

for refusing to admit that Jesus really is the messiah. This double purpose is nowhere more evident than in the Christian Acts of Pilate, allegedly written by a good Jewish rabbi who saw Jesus as the true king and Son of God, as opposed to most of the other Jews, who were hardheaded, hardhearted, hateful villains who opposed both the Roman authority embodied in Pontius Pilate and the divine authority embodied in Jesus Christ.

OTHER WORKS IN THE PILATE CYCLE

Among the other works traditionally located in the Pilate cycle are several written in the names of well-known figures connected with the Passion of Jesus: Pontius Pilate, Herod Antipas, and Joseph of Arimathea (others are anonymous narratives). A number of these may well have been produced toward the end of the period of our concern: the first four Christian centuries. No one thinks that any of them is authentic. They were written by later Christians intent on applying their imaginations to the question of what those connected with Christ might have said about their role in his death and resurrection. In some instances these authors may have been motivated by rumors that some such writings once existed, as found in the references of Justin and Tertullian previously mentioned, or possibly the later report of Eusebius (based on Tertullian):

> Our Saviour's marvellous resurrection and ascension into heaven were by now everywhere famous, and it had long been customary for provincial governors to report to the holder of the imperial office any change in the local situation, so that he might be aware of all that was going on. The story of the resurrection from the dead of our Saviour Jesus, already the subject of general discussion all over Palestine, was accordingly communicated by Pilate to the Emperor Tiberius. For Pilate knew all about Christ's supernatural deeds, and especially how after death he had risen from the dead and was now generally believed to be a god. It is said that Tiberius referred the report to the senate, which rejected it. The apparent reason was that they had not gone into the matter before, for the old law still held good that no one could be regarded by the Romans as a god unless by vote and decree of the senate; the real reason was that no human decision or commendation was required for the saving teaching of the divine message. (*H.E.* 2.2.1–2)

The Anaphora Pilati

The "Report" of Pontius Pilate to the Emperor Tiberius relates the events of Jesus' trial, death, and resurrection from the perspective of the Roman governor, but in much briefer compass than the Acts of Pilate. Like that other account, the Anaphora celebrates Jesus' miraculous character, exculpates Pilate for his death, and inculpates the Jews. It is doubtful that the surviving Report is the one referred to by Tertullian, if in fact he really knew of an actual document (which seems unlikely). As it survives in the manuscript tradition, the Anaphora does not appear to date from a period earlier than the late fourth century.[81]

The first half of the brief account is largely devoted to testimony of Pilate himself to the wondrous deeds Jesus performed during his public ministry, recorded in no small measure to show the blindness of the Jews in rejecting him. And so we are told, the "whole multitude of the Jews" is hardened to these signs, and thus turn Jesus over to Pilate without being able to "convict him of a single crime" (v. 1).[82] His one fault, in their eyes, is "that Jesus accomplished these deeds on the Sabbath." Pilate, on the other hand, sees the truth: "For my part, I know that the gods we worship have never performed such astounding feats as his" (v. 5).

The Jewish leaders and people are unmoved, however, and to prevent a general rebellion, Pilate orders Jesus crucified. The astounding deeds Jesus had performed while living are surpassed by those that transpire at his death and resurrection, which take up most of the second half of the narrative:

> The light did not cease that entire night, O King, my master. And many of the Jews died, being engulfed and swallowed up in the chasms in that night, so that their bodies could no longer be found. I mean to say that those Jews who spoke against Jesus suffered. But one synagogue was left in Jerusalem, since all the synagogues that opposed Jesus were engulfed. (v. 10)

Presumably it was the synagogue of Jesus' followers that survived destruction. For this account, the nonbelievers received what they deserved for refusing to recognize Jesus as the one sent from God.[83]

The Letter of Pilate to Claudius

The letter allegedly written by Pontius Pilate to the emperor Claudius (!) has survived in several textual forms.[84] A Latin version accompanies the accounts of the Descent to Hades from the B text of the Acts of Pilate. In Greek it is quoted in Pseudo-Marcellus, *The Passion of Peter and Paul*. Yet different forms occur in

---

81. See Ehrman and Pleše, *Apocryphal Gospels*, pp. 491–99; and Rémi Gounelle, "Rapport de Pilate, réponse de Tibère à Pilate, comparution de Pilate," in *Écrits apocryphes chrétiens*, vol. 2, ed. Pierre Geoltrain and Jean-Daniel Kaestli (Paris: Gallimard, 2005), pp. 303–4, 306–7.

82. Quotations of all works from the Pilate cycle are taken from Ehrman and Pleše, *Apocryphal Gospels*.

83. Another work of the Pilate cycle, the *Paradosis Pilati*, is sometimes, wrongly, taken as a direct response of Tiberius to the Anaphora; it may indeed have been conceived in that way, but it is stylistically different and is almost certainly written by another hand. As it does not claim to be written by Tiberius, but is an anonymous narrative about his reaction to Jesus' crucifixion, it need not concern us further here. See Ehrman and Pleše, *Apocryphal Gospels*, pp. 501–9; and Gounelle, "Rapport de Pilate," pp. 301–9.

84. Jean-Daniel Dubois and Rémi Gounelle, "Lettre de Pilate à l'empereur Claude," in *Écrits apocryphes chrétiens*, vol. 2, ed. Geoltrain and Jean- Kaestli, pp. 357–63.

Armenian and Syriac, and as incorporated in the fifth century *Acts of Peter and Paul* (chs. 40–41), whose anonymous author has probably taken the letter over from an earlier source. This final iteration may represent the apocryphon in its earliest surviving form.

In these Acts the letter is cited in the following context. Years after Jesus' death, we are told, the apostle Simon Peter and the heretic Simon Magus appear before the emperor Nero. When the emperor hears about Christ, he asks Peter how he can learn more about him. Peter tells him to retrieve the letter sent by Pilate years earlier to his predecessor, the emperor Claudius, and to have it read aloud. He does so, and the text of the letter is then reproduced.

It is not clear what to make of the anachronistic reference to Claudius as the emperor at the time of Jesus' death. The forger of the letter, living so long after the fact, may simply not have known the facts of Roman imperial history. It is also possible that the surviving letter was originally said to have been sent to Tiberius (as in Tertullian and as mentioned in the Anaphora), and that a later editor—conceivably the author of the fifth-century *Acts* that presents the letter—altered the name of the addressee (e.g., to make it refer to Nero's immediate predecessor).[85] In any event, the letter could have been composed any time between Tertullian and the fifth-century *Acts of Peter and Paul.* Scheidweiler and Elliott have suggested that it may have served as the basis for the Anaphora Pilati, in which case it would likely have arisen somewhat earlier in that period.[86]

The themes of the letter resonate with other works in the Pilate cycle. The Jews are totally oblivious to what God has done in sending Christ into the world:

> Pontius Pilate, to Claudius. Greetings. I myself have uncovered what has just now happened. For the Jews, out of envy, have brought vengeance both on themselves and on those who come after them by their terrible acts of judgment. They have been oblivious to the promises given to their ancestors, that God would send them his holy one from heaven, who would naturally enough be called their king; he promised to send this one to earth through a virgin. And now this one has come to Judea, during my governorship.

Despite his many miracles—or to be more accurate, precisely because of his many miracles—the Jewish leaders sought to have Jesus executed:

> They saw that he brought light to the eyes of the blind, that he cleansed lepers, healed paralytics, drove demons out from people, raised the dead, rebuked the winds, walked on the waves of the sea, and did many other miracles; and that all

85. Dubois and Gounelle ("Lettre de Pilate") maintain that the letter was originally composed as part of the Latin "Passion of Peter and Paul," thus explaining its supposed origin from the time of Nero's immediate predecessor.

86. Felix Scheidweiler, "The Gospel of Nicodemus / Acts of Pilate and Christ's Descent into Hell," in *New Testament Apocrypha*, ed. Schneemelcher, p. 205.

> the people of the Jews called him the son of God. For this reason the chief priests were moved by envy to seize him and deliver him over to me; and they told lie upon lie, saying that he was a magician and that he acted contrary to their law.

As a result, Pilate himself is not responsible for Jesus' death; the stiff-necked and godless Jews are. In fact, it is not Pilate who has Jesus crucified in order to placate the Jewish leaders; they do the foul deed themselves: "Since I believed their accusations, I delivered him over to their will, after having him flogged. And they crucified him."

Moreover, after they commit the foul deed, they bribe the guards at the tomb to say that he was not raised from the dead. And that, indicates Pilate, is the reason for his letter: "In case someone else might lie about it and you be led to believe the false reports told by the Jews."

A reply of the emperor (Tiberius) to Pilate survives from manuscripts of the later Middle Ages, but as it appears to have been written no earlier than the eleventh century,[87] it is of no concern to us in this context.

The Letter of Herod to Pilate

The letter allegedly written by Herod Antipas to Pilate, found in a fifteenth-century Greek manuscript, is first attested in a Syriac version of about the sixth century. The document may have been forged in the late fourth century.[88] In it, Herod affirms the divine principle that "each will receive his due" for the evil deeds he has done. In his case, Herod's beheading of John the Baptist has been divinely reciprocated in the grisly death of his stepdaughter, Herodia, who literally loses her head when she is swept away by a flood: her torso is borne downstream but her severed head is left in the grasp of the hands of her mother, who was trying to save her. Herod too is facing God's judgment: as he writes, "already worms are coming up from my mouth." Here the author of the letter appears to confuse Herod the tetrarch of Galilee, connected with Jesus' death, with Herod Agrippa, who according to the book of Acts was eaten by worms and died (Acts 12:23). So too, the soldier Longinus, who stuck a spear in Jesus' side on the cross, meets a gruesome fate, condemned to be torn apart by a lion every night, only to have his body restored during the day in preparation for another night's agony, much as Prometheus of Greek myth.

There are clear connections between this text and the Acts of Pilate and the Anaphora Pilati. The Roman governor Pilate is portrayed in a positive light, representing the gentiles who will receive the future kingdom, as opposed to the Jews, represented by Herod, who have been rejected by God. Among its anti-Jewish sentiments is Herod's condemnation of the Jewish leadership, and with them the entire Jewish people, the one-time "children of light":

---

87. Thus Gounelle. "Rapport de Pilate."

88. See Montague R. James, *Apocrypha Anecdota*, second series (Cambridge: University Press, 1897), pp. xlv–xlviii, 66–70; Ehrman and Pleše, *Apocryphal Gospels*, pp. 523–27.

> There is no peace for the priests, says the Lord. Death will soon overtake the priests and the ruling council of the children of Israel, because they unjustly laid hands on the righteous Jesus. These things will be fulfilled in the culmination of the age, so that the Gentiles will become heirs of the kingdom of God, but the children of light will be cast out, because we did not keep the commandments of the Lord nor those of his Son.

The Letter of Pilate to Herod

As a final forgery to be considered from the Pilate cycle, the Letter of Pilate to Herod is principally concerned with showing how Pilate, along with his wife Procla and Longinus, the soldier at the cross, all converted to become followers of Christ after the resurrection.[89] One might expect the letter to have close connections with the one preceding, but apart from the titles and the appearance of some of the same names (Herod, Pilate, Longinus), the letters have almost nothing to do with one another, and in fact stand at odds in their views. Nowhere is this clearer than in their respective accounts of Longinus. In the Letter of Herod, the solder is subject to cruel and eternal torment as an unbeliever; in the Letter of Pilate he converts to become a blessed devotee of Jesus after being confronted by him, personally, after the resurrection. It may be that the two letters were combined in the textual tradition (this one is found in the same Syriac and Greek manuscripts) simply because of their comparable titles.

This letter is also much less ostensibly polemical against the Jews, although an implicit polemic may be found in its historically remarkable claim that Pilate became a Christian convert after the resurrection. This claim may stand at odds with everything that we can know about Pilate, sparse as that is; but it stands very much in line with what some Christians wanted to say about him, in no small measure because it demonstrates yet further his basic sympathy with the cause of Christ. And if Pilate was sympathetic with Christ, who was antipathetic? It was obviously the Jews, culpable for his murder and responsible for the suffering that they have, as a result, brought upon themselves.[90]

THE ABGAR CORRESPONDENCE

The two letters of the Abgar correspondence form part of the larger Abgar legend, recounted by Eusebius (*H.E.* 1.13) and, in a later version, by a fifth-century

---

89. See Ehrman and Pleše, *Apocryphal Gospels*, pp. 517–21.

90. One other interesting document of the Pilate cycle, the Narrative of Joseph of Arimathea, is also forged, but probably after our period; two others, the Mors Pilati and the Vindicta Salvatoris, are anonymous narratives rather than forgeries. Texts and introductions for all three can be found in ibid., pp. 537–85.

Syriac work, the *Doctrina Addai*.[91] It may well be, as will be argued below, that the legend was built around the correspondence, which existed independently of it. The legend itself tells of the conversion of Edessa to Christianity after the resurrection through the preaching of Jesus' apostle Thaddeus (Eusebius) or Addai (*Doctrina*). Eusebius claims to have uncovered the story in the archives of Edessa, and to have translated it literally from the Syriac. Sebastian Brock, among others, has argued that both claims are improbable.[92] Where Eusebius actually found the tradition cannot be known. Eventually it came into wide circulation: it is preserved in Greek, Latin, Syriac, Coptic, Armenian, Arabic, Persian, and Slavonic witnesses.

There have been long and hard debates over the legend as a whole in both of its basic iterations, especially over when it came into existence and what its overarching purpose is. The classic views of F. C. Burkitt and of W. Bauer have been superseded in modern times by the intriguing thesis of H. J. W. Drijvers that the legend was generated at the end of the third century among the proto-orthodox minority of Christians in eastern Syria in order to counter the religious claims that the Manichaeans made for Mani, the founder of their religion.[93] In a later chapter I will consider whether the letters themselves may have derived from the context of anti-Manichaean polemic. For now I need say only a few words about the anti-Jewish slant of the correspondence. We can leave the larger legend to one side, as it is not itself a forgery but an anonymous narrative.

The correspondence comprises two letters. The first is a short missive from the king of Edessa, Abgar Uchama ("the Black") to Jesus, acknowledging Jesus' miracle-working powers: "I have heard about you and your healings, which you perform without medications or herbs. As the report indicates, you make the blind see again and the lame walk, you cleanse lepers, you cast out unclean spirits and demons, you heal the chronically sick, and you raise the dead."[94]

Abgar has drawn the appropriate conclusions from the tales he has heard: "Having heard all these things about you, I have concluded one of two things: either you are God and do these things having descended from heaven, or you do them as the Son of God." His principal concern, however, is for his own, unspecified illness. He would like Jesus to come to Edessa to heal him, and at the same time to escape the animosity of the Jews in his homeland: "For I have also heard

---

91. For Syriac text and English translation, see George Howard, *The Teaching of Addai* (Ann Arbor, MI: Society of Biblical Literature, 1981).

92. Sebastian Brock, "Eusebius and Syriac Christianity," in *Eusebius, Christianity, and Judaism*, ed. Harry Attridge and Gohei Hatta (Detroit: Wayne State University, 1992), pp. 212–34.

93. See pp. 455–58. F. C. Burkitt, *Early Christianity outside the Roman Empire* (Cambridge: Cambridge University Press, 1899); Walter Bauer, *Rechtgläubigkeit und Ketzerei im ältesten Christentum* (Tübingen: Mohr/Siebeck, 1934), ch. 1; H. J. W. Drijvers, "Addai und Mani: Christentum und Manichäismus im Dritten Jahrhundert in Syrien," *Or. Chr. A.* 221 (1983): 171–85. For a recent discussion of how the legend functioned in its later context, see Alexander Mirkovic, *Prelude to Constantine: The Abgar Tradition in Early Christianity* (Frankfurt: Peter Lang, 2004).

94. Translations from Ehrman and Pleše, *Apocryphal Gospels*, pp. 413–17.

that the Jews are murmuring against you and wish to harm you." Here then is another piece of anti-Jewish rhetoric that highlights the Jewish animosity toward Jesus (and, presumably, all things Christian).

In his brief reply, Jesus blesses Abgar for "believing without seeing" (an allusion to John 20:29) but informs the king that he cannot come because he needs to fulfill his mission, that is, by being crucified. After his ascension, however, he will send an apostle to heal the king and "provide life both to you and to those who are with you" (that is, to lead them to salvation).

There are various indications that this short correspondence originated independently of the legend of the conversion of Edessa. It can at least be affirmed that it circulated separately[95]: copies of the letter in Greek can be found in two inscriptions at Euchaita in northern Anatolia, on a stone at Philippi in Macedonia, and on a stone at Kirk Magara near Edessa, all dating from the fifth century. Later it can be found in an inscription at Ephesus on a stone over the door of a house and on a papyrus that was possibly used as an amulet. In addition, according to Judah Segal, "texts of the Abgar-Jesus correspondence are frequent in Coptic, and in many forms—on stone, on parchment, on ostraca, and as amulets on papyrus."[96]

In addition to the surviving remains themselves, we have the evidence from the pilgrim Egeria that citizens of Edessa in later times considered the correspondence significant for its magical powers, as containing a letter from the Son of God himself (*Peregrinatio Egeriae* 19). It was brought forward in times of war, miraculously scattering the armies laying siege to the city. Eventually a copy of the correspondence was affixed to the city gates to ward off enemies. This miraculous character of the correspondence was based in no small measure on the last line of Jesus' letter, which is not found in Eusebius's account, but is present both in the surviving Greek fragments of the letter and in the account found in the *Doctrina Addai*, where Jesus assures Abgar that "Your city will be blessed, and the enemy will no longer prevail over it." This line itself can still be found in inscriptions, ostraca, and amulets.[97]

It is possible that these various sources for the correspondence extracted it from the fuller legend. It is worth noting, however, that Egeria herself gives no evidence of knowing the fuller legend, but speaks only of the correspondence.[98] Moreover, the letter indicates that Jesus himself will send an apostle to Abgar after his ascension, but the legend indicates that it is Thomas who does so, with no indication of or even allusion to dominical inspiration. It may well be, then, that the legend sprang up around the correspondence in a second stage of the

95. For the following epigraphic and manuscript notes, see Judah Segal, *Edessa, the "Blessed City"* (Oxford: Clarendon Press, 1970), p. 75.

96. Ibid., p. 75. For discussion of papyrus fragments later discovered in Egypt, see Rolf Peppermüller, "Griechische Papyrusfragmente der *Doctrina Addai*," *VC* 25 (1971): 289–301.

97. Thus Drijvers.

98. The only factum that she mentions not in the letters themselves is that the letter of Jesus was brought to Edessa by Ananias; but this is also found in the superscript to the letter.

tradition. The tradition itself is internally uneven: the *Doctrina Addai* does not speak of a letter from Jesus, possibly under the influence of the notion that Jesus never wrote anything. Instead, according to the *Doctrina,* he sent an oral reply through a messenger.

Both Augustine and Jerome indicate that Jesus never produced any writings.[99] Other traditions exist, however, indicating that he both was able to write and did write. The best known is the apocryphal Pericope Adulterae that later found its way into manuscripts of the Fourth Gospel, where Jesus is literally said to "write" (καταγράφειν) on the ground (not draw or doodle), a passage that Chris Keith has recently argued was originally designed precisely to show that Jesus was writing-literate.[100] Two other writings allegedly by Jesus survive, the letter that Jesus writes from the cross, addressed to the Cherubim of heaven, in the Narrative of Joseph of Arimathea (although in that case one might suppose the letter was dictated . . .) and the Second Treatise of the Great Seth from Nag Hammadi, which, however, is allegedly written by the heavenly, not the earthly Jesus. As a result, the correspondence with Abgar is the only piece of writing allegedly produced by Jesus himself that survives. And appropriately enough, it is in response to a letter forged by the same writer, in the name of the king of Edessa, who is concerned about Jesus' fate at the hands of the recalcitrant Jews, who obviously do not recognize his supernatural character, despite the miraculous signs he performed.

As it turns out, a similar set of themes is played out in a second pair of letters preserved in the Abgar legend, at least in its later iteration in the *Doctrina Addai.* This is a correspondence between Abgar and the emperor Tiberius, allegedly written after Jesus' death. The themes of the correspondence sound very much like what one finds throughout the Pilate cycle. Abgar informs the emperor that the Jews have wrongfully crucified their own messiah: "I write and make known to your powerful and great rulership, that the Jews under your authority who live in Palestine have gathered together and crucified the Messiah who was unworthy of death."[101] They did this despite the fact that Jesus "performed signs and wonders and had showed to them mighty powers and signs." In response, Abgar has wanted to take his armies into Palestine and wipe out the Jews, but he restrains himself out of respect for the emperor.

In his reply, Tiberius indicates that he was already informed about the malevolent actions of the Jews in a letter from Pilate, and that he is now prepared to take legal actions against the culprits: "I am ready whenever I have quiet to make a legal charge against the Jews who have acted unlawfully." Pilate himself has been punished by being "dismissed in disgrace" for his part in the affair, "because he deserted the law and did the will of the Jews, and for their appeasement crucified the Messiah who . . . should have been honored instead. . . . It is right that he

99. Augustine, *Faust.* 28.4; *Cons.* 1.7.11; Jerome, *Comm. Ezech.* 44.29 (PL 25.443).

100. *The Pericope Adulterae, the Gospel of John, and the Literacy of Jesus* (Leiden: E. J. Brill, 2009).

101. Translation of Howard, *Teaching of Addai.*

should have been worshiped by them, particularly since they saw with their own eyes everything which he did."

This forged correspondence presupposes the existence of an exchange between Pilate and Tiberius, as referred to earlier in this chapter. Eusebius himself knows about such an earlier exchange, but shows no knowledge of these letters between Abgar and the emperor. It appears that their forger produced his account sometime in the late fourth, or even the early fifth, century and, like the sundry authors of the writings found in the Pilate cycle, was intent not only on imagining the unimaginable—a Tiberius agonized over the death of the Jewish messiah—but also on imagining it in the harsh anti-Jewish terms of his own day.

CHAPTER TWELVE

Forgeries Involving Church Organization and Leadership

From the earliest of times, Christian churches of every description encountered difficulties of organization and leadership. From the early years of the movement we are best informed about the churches connected with Paul, where problems arose that could make even the most stalwart apostle tremble. Nowhere is that clearer than in the Corinthian correspondence, directed to a community organized (if one can use the term) according to a charismatic principle that enabled considerable chaos to reign not only in the worship services but also in the life of the community in general, especially in competing factions and their outspoken representatives. Within such communities factionalism often played itself out in the realm of theological discourse, as subcommunities and individuals advocated views of the faith in opposition to the rest. Small wonder that the church as a whole could not continue to structure itself along such lines, that hierarchical organization and established leadership soon took hold in order to provide both clarity and direction for a church settling in for the long haul.

But even more conventionally organized communities experienced serious internal problems and conflicts over how the church should be structured and who should be granted roles of leadership. Concerns for church order are evidenced throughout our literature, whether orthonymous (Paul's letters), anonymous (e.g., the Didache), or forged. At the early stage of our literary record, nowhere are the concerns more evident than in two of the Pastoral epistles, 1 Timothy and Titus, forged in Paul's name by the same author who produced 2 Timothy, which we have already considered for another reason and in a different context.

1 TIMOTHY AND TITUS

In that earlier discussion I provided a preliminary sketch of all the background issues of relevance to the question of the pseudonymous character of these two books, and I do not need to repeat that discussion in detail here. My argument can be summed up quickly: all three of the Pastoral epistles were written by the same author; that author was not Paul; strong arguments for this conclusion obtain from considering the three letters as group; but the strongest arguments derive from each letter individually. The arguments involving 1 Timothy and Titus were already advanced in that earlier context. Moreover, it is important to reiterate that these books were not produced within some kind of "Pauline school" (a modern scholarly invention),[1] nor can their differences be explained (in support of their authenticity) on the grounds that others of Paul's letters were produced by committee, whereas these come from the man himself.[2]

To restate one other fundamental point: even though the three letters were written by the same author, that does not justify the scholarly attempt to conflate their contents into one mega-Pastoral letter, interpreting the three as a unified and uni-functional canon, as done over the past several decades, for example, by such scholars as G. Haufe and P. Trummer, in a different way by Richard Pervo, and most recently by G. Häfner.[3] The character, concerns, and presupposed historical situation of 2 Timothy, in particular, are not those of the other two, and leveling out their differences—particularly when trying to ferret out the teachings of the opponents—creates an amalgam that is both unrecognizable and unhelpful.

For this reason, a number of scholars have argued that the three need to be considered as individual productions, just as one today is more inclined to study Galatians or Philippians as its own literary production, not simply in relation, say,

---

1. See the discussion on pp. 172–74.

2. See the discussion on pp. 218–22.

3. Günter Haufe, "Gnostische Irrlehre und ihre Abwehr in den Pastoralbriefen," in *Gnosis und Neues Testament: Studien aus Religionswissenschaft und Theologie*, ed., Karl-Wolfgang Tröger (Güterslow: Gütersloher Verlagshaus Mohn, 1973), pp. 325–39, argued that all three were combating the same opponents, and they were Gnostic (p. 325). The most influential twentieth-century spokesperson in support of this view of the corpus Pastorale is Peter Trummer, "Corpus Paulinum—Corpus Pastorale"; for him, the Pastorals were by a single author and were meant as a conclusion for the Pauline corpus. Even more extreme is Gerd Häfner, "Das Corpus Pastorale," who argued, contrary to recent claims of such scholars as L. T. Johnson and W. Richards, that the Pastorals were generated and were meant to be read as a corpus of writings; the corpus is not an epistolary novel, but it has some of the characteristics of the genre, and the books are to be read in the order 1 Timothy–Titus–2 Timothy. Moreover, the claim that no single opponent emerges when the three are taken together as a unit, Häfner avers, is not necessarily true. Everything said about opponents can be subsumed under some such category as "Jewish-Christian Gnosis." The idea that the letters could be read as an epistolary novel was most influentially advanced by Richard Pervo, "Romancing an Oft-Neglected Stone: The Pastoral Epistles and the Epistolary Novel," *Journal of Higher Criticism*, 1 (1994): 25–47. Among the very basic problems of the thesis was the fact that Pervo was forced to argue that the entire "genre" of epistolary novel contains but one work, the letters of Chion of Heraclea. How can there be a genre of *one* writing? (He did allow that the Socratic letters were related, but not closely.) Moreover, the differences, as Pervo pointed out, between the Pastorals and the letters of Chion are stark: the Pastorals are a good deal longer, two of the three do not carry much of the narrative, and their coherence is not progressive, sequential, and narratological. As a conclusion, Pervo states that if the author of the Pastorals wanted to write a work of the genre, he "was not very successful" (p. 40).

to Romans. It is easy to take this move toward individuation too far, however, as William Richards does in positing three different authors for the three Pastorals, living decades apart.[4] The books should be treated individually, but they still share a number of important features. In particular 1 Timothy and Titus have a good deal in common, in language, concept, theme, and presupposed (i.e., alleged) historical situation. Nowhere is that more evident than in the two overarching concerns of the letters: the attack on false teaching and the concern to establish appropriate church leaders.

The Alleged Historical Situation of the Letters

The concerns to silence false teachers and to appoint appropriate church leaders make particular sense in the historical contexts that the letters presuppose. These situations are roughly similar to one another, and are unlike the ostensible situation of the third of the Pastoral epistles. In 2 Timothy, Paul was in prison awaiting trial and anticipating his imminent death. Not so for 1 Timothy and Titus. As a result, if one does read the letters as a corpus, it would be natural to assume that these two were written somewhat earlier in Paul's life. It is in the allusions to Paul's situation that the great bulk of the letters' verisimilitudes occur. These may not overwhelm the reader, as those in 2 Timothy threaten to do, but they are abundant enough to show that the author was quite intent on making these letters appear actually to be by the apostle himself.

In 1 Timothy Paul is hoping to come visit his young colleague (4:12) soon (3:14). He had earlier left Timothy in the city of Ephesus to lead the church, to control the false teaching that had erupted there (1:3–7, 18–20), and to be sure that the "right" people were appointed to positions of leadership (3:1–15). It is probably not technically correct to call Timothy the "bishop" of the church, although he certainly does exercise the key leadership role as the one in charge, as seen especially in 4:11–16. But unlike the resident bishop and the deacons, he is passing through. There is some question of whether Paul's designation of him as a "deacon"(4:6) is meant in a technical or general sense; and it is not clear what "gift" was bestowed upon him through "prophetic utterance" when he was ordained by the presbyterial "laying on of hands" (4:14). But however one understands this complicated passage, it does appear that a leadership role has been passed on to Timothy by leaders before him, including the apostle Paul himself.

A very similar situation is assumed for Titus. Here again there is no word about Paul being in prison; on the contrary, he is hoping to meet up with Titus in Nicopolis, where he has decided to spend the winter (3:12). In the meantime, Paul has left Titus behind on the island of Crete in order to appoint presbyters in all the cities there (1:5). These presbyters are evidently meant to serve as bishops of the churches (1:7). Titus is also to bring under control false teachers who are

4. *Difference and Distance.*

troubling the congregations (1:13) and to work for the social unity and appropriate behavior of the individuals, of different sorts and walks of life, who make up the churches (2:1–10). Here too Titus is envisaged as the ultimate leader of the church on Crete, so long as he is resident among them (2:15).

The Direct Polemic of the Letters

The direct polemic of both letters involves false teachers and "Paul's" insistence that his appointed delegates bring them under control. This is the first and most urgent message to issue from the apostle's pen in 1 Timothy, immediately after the letter opening: "charge certain persons not to teach anything heterodox" (ἵνα παραγγείλῃς τισὶν μὴ ἑτεροδιδασκαλεῖν). And it is also the last note sounded at the end of the letter before the final farewell, "avoid the worthless empty talk and the contradictions of falsely-named gnosis" (ἐκτρεπόμενος τὰς βεβήλους κενοφωνίας καὶ ἀντιθέσεις τῆς ψευδωνύμου γνώσεως). The topic of false teaching dominates both the opening and final chapters. If that is how an author begins and ends a letter, we can be reasonably sure that it is his principle concern.

So also with Titus. Here, too, the letter begins with an attack on false teachers. Titus is to "correct what is defective," (1:5) and appoint leaders who "hold firm to the true word that is taught" (ἀντεχόμενον τοῦ κατὰ τὴν διδαχὴν πιστοῦ λόγου), who can deliver "sound teaching" (ἐν τῇ διδασκαλίᾳ τῇ ὑγιαινούσῃ) and refute anyone who contradicts it (1:9). The false teachers must "be silenced" (1:11). The letter, again, ends on a similar note. Titus is to avoid foolish controversies (μωράς . . . ζητήσεις), genealogies, and dissentions, and arguments over the law, "for they are not of profit and futile" (3:9–11). Moreover, any "heretical person" (αἱρετικὸν ἄνθρωπον) is to be admonished once or twice, and then shunned for good (3:10), since anyone like that is "perverted, sinful, and self-condemned" (3:11).

It is much harder to know what exactly it is that the false teachers were (allegedly) saying, whether or not they actually existed.[5] For our purposes here, it does not much matter if the opponents were real or imagined: all we have in any event is the letters themselves, and the author has presented us with a set of false teachers that he portrays as dangerous. Although he provides more information about them in 1 Timothy, the polemical thrust of Titus is very similar. None of the characterizations in the latter is missing from the former, so that even though these are not the same false teachers attacked in 2 Timothy, they do seem to represent a single set of adversaries in these two letters.

It is clear from 1 Timothy that the opponents are imagined as coming from inside the congregation. They have "swerved away" and wandered off into "vain reasoning" (1:6), suggesting that once they had walked the straight and narrow. This is confirmed in the two cases the author mentions, "Hymenaeus" and "Alexander,"

---

5. The most careful analysis, methodologically, is Jerry Sumney, *"Servants of Satan."* See my comments on p. 215.

who have made a "shipwreck of their faith" by rejecting their conscience; these were obviously members of the believing ship's crew before disaster struck, and "Paul" had to "deliver them over to Satan" to teach them no longer to commit their blasphemies (1:20). Later "Paul" indicates that the false teachers—not just the two he has named—are those predicted to come in the end of time, when "some will depart from the faith by holding fast to deceitful spirits and teachings of demons" (πνεύμασιν πλάνοις καὶ διδασκαλίαις δαιμονίων). He returns to the topic at the end of the letter, where he speaks of teachers from within the congregations (6:3) who do not "agree with the sound words of our Lord Jesus Christ" and the "teaching that accords with piety" (6:3). There is some hint, at least, that these teachers have gone astray from "the faith" out of love of money (6:9–10).

As so often happens in this kind of polemic, many of the accusations leveled against the false teachers reveal more about the author's prowess in generating vituperation than about the specific teachings that he finds objectionable.[6] In addition to being fond of deceitful spirits and demonic doctrines (4:1), these teachers are "puffed up with conceit," ignorant, and morbidly passionate for controversy and verbal arguments; they are "depraved" in their minds, they lack the truth, and they are pious for the sake of material reward (6:3–7). All this may or may not be true, but it can get us nowhere if we want to know what it is, exactly, these people teach.

In several places, however, the polemic becomes more specific. We may not, at the end of the day, have a coherent picture, and certainly not a complete one, but there are a few features of the false teachings that emerge over the course of the letter. For one thing, the opponents imagine themselves to be "teachers of the Law" (νομοδιδάσκαλοι; 1:7), even though they do not know what they are talking about. Presumably, from the pen of "Paul," this means that the opponents base their views on the Jewish Scriptures, or possibly the Torah exclusively. One might think that since they are characterized as ignorant, that they would be gentile Judaizers rather than Jews, but that would be pressing the polemic too hard, as it is quite easy to accuse even a qualified expert of being an ignorant dilettante.

It is also hard to know how their passion for νόμος relates to their obsession with "myths and endless genealogies" (1:4). Are these Jewish myths and Old Testament genealogies? Or are they cosmogonies such as known from later Gnostic texts? (The latter would not rule out the possibility that the proponents were ethnically and culturally Jewish.) The author returns to the opponents' "empty and ridiculous" myths in 4:7. If this were actually Paul speaking, it would be hard to assume that he would use such disparaging terms about the Jewish Scriptures; on the other hand, if it were Paul, it would also be hard to imagine Gnostic theogonies and cosmogonies sufficiently advanced, at such an early period, to have

6. On the problem of the polemical stereotypes, see the now-classic article of Robert J. Karris, "The Background and Significance of the Polemic of the Pastoral Epistles," *JBL* 92 (1973): 549–63; and Luke Timothy Johnson, "II Timothy and the Polemic against False Teachers: A Reexamination," *JRS* 6 (1978): 1–26.

caused real and present danger to Christians in Ephesus. The "falsely called gnosis" of 6:20 sounds warning bells for anyone attuned to later second-century heresiology. But that may well be an incautious knee-jerk reaction created by deep and intimate association with Irenaeus. At the end of the day, it is hard to know what the author is referring to.

What is somewhat clearer is that the author attacks his opponents for a kind of rigorous asceticism. They "forbid marriage" and "urge abstinence from foods" (4:3). The author objects that God created these foods to be received with thanks. Unfortunately, since the author does not specify which foods he has in mind, it is not clear whether he is attacking kosher food laws or general ascetic discipline involving abstention from luxuriant or otherwise all-too-desirable edibles. The comparisons and contrasts with Paul himself are intriguing at just this point. Even though Paul did not forbid marriage, he certainly discouraged it (1 Corinthians 7); and even though he allowed all foods—even those offered to idols—he did urge his Corinthian inquiring minds to abstain for the sake of the conscience of others, and, at least in one place, because of the demons (1 Corinthians 8, 10). The false teachers of 1 Timothy, in any event, whether seeing themselves as Paulinists or not (assuming the teachers' existence, whether they are fictional or real), actually forbid marriage and the consumption of certain foods.

What then, in summary, can we say about the teachings of the opposition? Since F. C. Baur, there have been scholars all too ready to speak of them as Gnostics. Myths, genealogies, speculations, pointless asceticism, and "falsely-called" gnosis—it all adds up. On the other hand, there is obviously no full-blown Gnostic speculation here. We don't know what the myths and genealogies are. In Titus, as we will see in a moment, the myths are specified as "Jewish." And the genealogies could as easily be connected with Scripture as with theogonies and cosmogonies known from second-century sources, Gnostic and heresiological. It may be safest to say, then, that we know some of the characteristics of these false teachers but do not have a complete picture. They stress the Jewish Law; they focus on myths and genealogies; they urge asceticism; and they rely on gnosis. It may well be that these are forerunners of groups that eventually became Gnostic, as such are some of the characteristics that could be found among groups that were to emerge later. Possibly they are proto-Gnostics. Considered within their own time, such a designation would be anachronistic: they were who they were and are not necessarily best understood in light of what later teachers would build on the foundations they laid.

The one tie of these teachers to the opponents of 2 Timothy comes in the person of Hymenaeus (1:20; cf. 2 Tim. 2:17–18). As earlier noted, by specifying an enemy, the author distances himself from Paul, who steadfastly refused, at least in his surviving literary remains, to name names. It is also odd that what the author says here—that "Paul" has turned Hymenaeus over to Satan—stands at some tension with what he says in 2 Timothy, where Hymenaeus continues to cause a disturbance in the church. One might suppose that 1 Timothy is being imagined as having been written at a later time, when Paul finally became sufficiently vexed with the fellow to give him the apostolic boot; but that solution does not accord well with the clear indications that the author envisages 2 Timothy as a kind of "last testament," written near Paul's death, making 1 Timothy, therefore, necessarily earlier. Possibly the author wanted to create another tie between the two letters and simply did not realize that he had created a certain snafu; or, if one wants to play the game of reconciliation a bit, possibly he imagined that Hymenaeus learned his lesson after spending time with Satan, returned to the fold, but then began to misbehave again later. In any event, the reference to this Pauline headache in 1 Timothy seems to suggest that Hymenaeus' behavior is ethically problematic, and that the bad actions are connected to bad theology, since Paul needs to teach him not to "blaspheme." In 2 Timothy the problem involves belief that the resurrection is past. Possibly the author sees the opponent as problematic on numerous fronts, all in one way or another tied together, as was the situation in a remarkably similar case many years earlier with Paul and the enthusiasts at Corinth. One stark difference, on the other hand, as already noted, involves what it means to deliver a person "over to Satan."[7]

As might be expected with a briefer letter, when we move to the explicit polemic of Titus we have even less to go on. Here again there are numerous empty and stereotyped charges that are of little value for determining what the imagined or real opponents actually stood for. They allegedly stand *against* "healthy teaching" (1:9); they are "insubordinate, speakers of vain things, and deceivers" (1:10); they disrupt entire families by teaching for financial profit (1:11); as Cretans they are "liars, wicked beasts, and lazy gluttons" (as one of their own, a fellow Cretan, says; or was he, as all Cretans were, also a liar, so that in fact these charges against them are not true? 1:12); they are not "sound in the faith" (1:13); they are "loathsome, disobedient, and not fit for any good deed" (1:16); moreover, they are "heretical" (αἱρετικὸν ἄνθρωπον), perverted, sinful, and self-condemned (3:10–11), to echo some of the polemic of 1 Timothy.

Here again, though, there are some specific identifying features of the enemy, and in many ways what is said dovetails well with 1 Timothy (though not 2 Timothy). It is striking, however, that the enemies who are particularly "insubordinate . . . deceivers" are especially those who "are from the circumcision" (1:10). In other words, the worst enemies, though evidently not all of them, are ethnically Jewish. This then makes sense of 1:14–15, that they pay close attention to "Jewish myths," and "human commandments" that have to do with purity regulations.[8] This is another passage, as noted earlier, that is difficult indeed to assign to Paul, who may have seen that the Law was a problem, but not that it was filled with myths and human (as opposed to divine) injunctions.[9] As in 1 Timothy, the false teachers are involved with "foolish controversies, genealogies, dissensions, and arguments over

7. See p. 207.

8. There is an obvious connection (although it is not as obvious what to do with it) between 1:15, πάντα καθαρὰ τοῖς καθαροῖς and Mark 7:19, also written by a non-Jew, καθαρίζων πάντα τὰ βρώματα. See also Acts 10:14–15 and Rom. 14:20.

9. See pp. 206, 211.

the Law" (3:9). With the emphasis on the "members of the circumcision," Jewish myths, purity requirements, and legal disputes, these opponents are more obviously Jewish than those of 1 Timothy; but there is nothing in the description here that runs at odds with the other book. As indicated earlier, J. Sumney may be taking the matter too far when he imagines that the two groups are presented as unrelated. There is a lot of overlap, and not just in the stereotyped polemic.

In any event, Titus is not to argue with the opponents (3:9), but to admonish them in order to return them to the truth (3:11). That is the function of the bishop as well (1:7, 9).

The Indirect Polemic of the Letters

In addition to the direct, if frustratingly ambiguous, attack on false teaching in 1 Timothy and Titus, there are elements of indirect polemic as well, one of which—the appointment of suitable leaders—is probably connected with the explicit polemic, as we will see momentarily. The other is presented just in 1 Timothy, and involves the much debated issue of the role of women in the church.

Women in the Church

It is not clear that all of the injunctions to and about women in 1 Timothy are to be seen as arising out of specific polemical contexts. In some instances, such as the instructions to widows in 5:3–10, the directives may simply involve situations that have arisen as the church has grown and developed. In other words, there is no need, and probably scant reason, to envision a controversy with other Christian leaders insisting that widows should be younger or not enrolled. Even here, however, the author cannot restrain his all-too-obvious opinion of women in the church, as is most evident in his comments on the "younger widows" of 3:11–15, who have, many of them, already "strayed after Satan," who have learned to be "idle" as they make the rounds from house to house as "gossips" and "busybodies," and who are inclined to "grow wanton" against Christ and get remarried. Such language is polemical not because it is directed against another set of teachings, but because it is directed against a group of people vilified as if it were in their very nature to gad about as idle busybodies.

The point comes to a head in the infamous 2:11–15, about which enough has been said over the past fifty years to require, in this context, only a few brief words. That women are instructed to be "silent and submissive" and not to "exercise authority over a man" simply cannot be reconciled with the Pauline policy, as restrictive as it was, that required women to prophesy and pray in church only while wearing head coverings (1 Cor. 11: 2–16). Either women can speak in church or they cannot; and prophecy by its very nature asserts authority.[10] Moreover, the

10. One convenient way around the problem is to think of the γύναι and ἄνδρες of the passage as husbands and wives, in view of 3:2. Still, apart from the fact that it does not let the author off the hook—even

idea that women would be saved not by faith in Christ, for example, but by having babies is, to put the most generous spin on it, un-Pauline at best.

As in the discussion of the "young widows," this restriction, or rather curtailment, of the participation of women in the church is polemical in the sense that it is opposing an activity that almost certainly was thought to have been common: women teaching and exercising authority in the church. But can we say anything more specifically about the background to the attack? In one of the most important and interesting studies of the Pastoral epistles in recent years, Annette Merz has argued that the author is not merely on the attack against an established practice, but that he understands the practice to be rooted in a misreading, or at least an inadequate reading, of the Pauline letters themselves. In this view, the author writes the Pastorals, in part, in order to redirect the reading of a passage that Merz takes to be authentically Pauline, 1 Cor. 14:34–35.[11]

This argument is part of Merz's larger project of suggesting a theoretically sophisticated intertextual approach to the Pastoral epistles. The standard approach to intertextuality appeals to the texts that a passage refers to in order to help clarify how the passage is to be interpreted: "The openness of texts to a variety of interpretations is largely due to the dialogue between those texts which are evoked in their reception."[12] As Merz points out, however, the process of interpretation can work both ways. When the concern of the interpreter involves how to interpret a passage, and its various intertexts are invoked to that end, then it is a "text-oriented" approach. But it is also significant that once the passage is interpreted, its meaning, newly established, is often applied back to the intertexts themselves in order to deepen their meaning as well. As an example that Merz draws from the Pastorals, when 1 Tim. 5:18 invokes Deut. 25:4 ("Do not muzzle an ox that is treading") in order to support its view that church leaders deserve to be paid, Christians familiar with this interpretation who then read the passage in Deuteronomy are more inclined to take it in the sense that it is used in 1 Timothy, so that it is understood even in its original Old Testament context to refer to paying one's minister. This inversion of the interpretative process, in which the intertext is subject to a new interpretation, is a "reference-oriented" approach to intertextuality.

Merz contends that the Pastorals are meant to provide reference-oriented strategies of interpretation for their intertexts. Or to use the terminology that has come to be in vogue, the Pastorals provide "reading instructions" for the Pauline letters to which they allude. Anyone who reads the Pastoral epistles as having

---

here, wives must be silent and submissive, and exercise no authority—the immediately preceding context of 3:8–9 (men and women, not husbands and wives) makes the interpretation implausible.

11. *Die fiktive Selbstauslegung des Paulus: Intertextuelle Studien zur Intention und Rezeption der Pastoralbriefe* (Göttingen/Fribourg: Vandenhoeck & Ruprecht/Academic Press, 2004); see also her shorter study, "The Fictitious Self-Exposition of Paul: How Might Intertextual Theory Suggest a Reformulation of the Hermeneutics of Pseudepigraphy?" in *The Intertextuality of the Epistles: Explorations of Theory and Practice*, ed. Thomas L. Brodie et al. (Sheffield: Sheffield Phoenix Press, 2006), pp. 113–32.

12. Merz, "Fictitious Self-Exposition," p. 117.

come from Paul as part of his corpus of writings interprets the various passages in the Pauline letters in light of one another. The other letters can and are, then, read through the lens of the Pastorals, just as, historically speaking, they were, and are, read by readers who naturally assume that they are orthonymous.

Normally this process of reference-oriented intertextual reading implies both an alternative way of reading a text and one or more readers who read it that way. That is to say, the process is innately polemical. And so the idea that office holders in the church should be paid may seem to stand at odds with what Paul says in 1 Corinthians 9. But in fact if 1 Corinthians 9 is read in light of 1 Timothy 5, then those who oppose paying their preachers are put in a compromising position by "Paul" himself. So too the requirement that young widows remarry (1 Tim. 5:14) seems to stand at odds with what Paul, and many of his readers, thought, based on 1 Corinthians 7. Merz in particular argues that "Paul's" instructions in 1 Tim. 6:1–5 about Christian slaves and slaveholders has close parallels (verbal and conceptual) to Philemon 16, which could be read as suggesting that slaves were to be manumitted by their Christian owners; but not for the author of the Pastorals, who insists, as a way of countering this reading of Philemon, that slaves are to remain in their subjection to their Christian masters.

With respect to the issue of women in the church, Merz argues that 1 Tim. 2:11–15 is to be understood as a guide for reading the less forthright injunctions of 1 Cor. 14:33–36. In this connection she stresses the well-known verbal parallels between the two passages, and suggests they are no accident: ἡσυχίᾳ / σιγάτωσαν; μανθανέτω / μάθειν; ὑποταγῇ / ὑποτασσέσθωσαν; ἐπιτρέπω / ἐπιτρέπεται. Moreover, the author has shifted from the more vague λαλεῖν to the more precise διδασκεῖν, and has filled out the rather ambiguous "as the Law says" to the specific Torah interpretation of Adam and Eve (Genesis 3). Most striking, the author has moved from a passive οὐ γὰρ ἐπιτρέπεται αὐταῖς λαλεῖν to the more explicit prohibition, διδάσκειν δὲ γυναικὶ οὐκ ἐπιτρέπω.

As a result, as Margaret Mitchell approvingly notes, the possible ambiguities of 1 Corinthians, which in one place appear to allow women to exercise authority (11:2–16), are overcome with an explicit directive that shows how Paul is to be read.[13] Contrary to the practice, possibly built on the writings of Paul (Gal. 3:28, etc.), women are not to be allowed to be actively involved in the church's liturgy.

As insightful and potentially enlightening this interpretive move is, its difficulties reside in the obvious questions of the status of 1 Cor. 14:34–35 itself. The reference-oriented reading works only if there was a referent text in place, and there continue to be compelling reasons for thinking that the Corinthian passage is an interpolation.[14] If the Pastorals are referring to the altered form of the text

13. Margaret M. Mitchell, "Corrective Composition, Corrective Exegesis: The Teaching on Prayer in 1 Tim 2, 1–15," in Karl Paul Donfried, ed., *1 Timothy Reconsidered* (Leuven: Peeters, 2008), pp. 41–62.

14. The strongest arguments are that the views expressed in the verses stand at odds with Paul's overall view that women could be active in the church—as seen in his comments from Romans 16, as an obvious example—and more specifically with his exhortation earlier in chapter 11, which is reconciled

of 1 Corinthians 14, the interpolation would have had to have been made at an extremely early date. Moreover, one could just as easily maintain that the verbal and conceptual parallels exist precisely because a later copyist, familiar with the words of 1 Tim. 2:11–15, decided to reinscribe their teaching by inserting a comparable passage into the text of 1 Corinthians. If so, the author of the Pastorals is not obsessed with guiding the reading of another Pauline epistle but is simply concerned with a practice that he deems inappropriate and even dangerous, as women speak out and exercise authority over men. As we will see, this is a common anxiety for the forged church orders, which show a constant concern that the activities of women needed to be regulated in the names of the apostles.

The Church Offices

One of the overarching concerns of both 1 Timothy and Titus is obviously the leadership of the church. As I have already observed, it is important to note that the author does not take steps toward establishing the sundry church offices. By the time of his writing, there were already bishops and deacons in the churches with which he was familiar. In other words, this writer is not advancing beyond the charismatic communities known, say, from the Corinthian correspondence to propose a more hierarchically structured organization. He was living in an age in which the hierarchy was already in place and in which church leaders were ordained to office; communities were no longer run by Spirit-filled members who received gifts at baptism. The question the author is concerned to address involves the qualifications of these leaders. The emphatic insistence that only the "right people" be allowed to occupy leadership roles may well relate to the other polemical concerns of the letters. Here only a few words need to be said about these roles.

It is clear from 1 Timothy that the ἐπίσκοπος is ultimately in charge of the church, after the apostle himself and his appointed delegate, Timothy. This much is evident from 3:5: just as the bishop manages or runs his own household, so too he is to manage or run the church. Since one can "aspire to be bishop," the leaders appear to be chosen from candidates who wish to be considered; they are not chosen completely by lot or some other divinely ordained procedure. Presumably the same applies to the deacons as well.[15] It is not clear how the πρεσβύτεροι (plural) of 5:17 who "rule" relate to the bishop (singular) of 3:1–7, or to the διάκονοι

with the injunctions of 14:34–35 only with severe difficulty. The fact that the passage in chapter 14 flows even better without the verses in question exacerbates the problem. But the debates rage on. For a rather weak argument that there is textual support for the omission, see Gordon D. Fee, *The First Epistle to the Corinthians* (Grand Rapids, MI: Eerdmans, 1987), ad loc. A recent study that supports the view that the passage is interpolated is Pervo, *Making of Paul*, pp. 46–48, with a nice chart giving the parallels of the two passages.

15. As often noted, it is difficult to understand 3:11 as referring to anything other than women deacons, given the context of 3:8–10 on the one hand and 3:12 on the other. But why then are qualifications for the women deacons not mentioned?

of 3:8–13, whether the "elders" are a separate group of men or instead are the men who inhabit the other two categories. If they are a separate group, it seems odd that the author does not spell out their qualifications, as he does for the others. In Titus they are to be "appointed" (1:5). In any event, it is somewhat unclear whether there are three offices involved here (bishop, presbyters, deacons) or just two (bishop, deacons), both of which constitute "elders."

Titus is instructed to "appoint presbyteroi in every city" (1:5). Obviously, since they are to be appointed, the presbyteroi are not simply older men, but (older?) men who have a leadership role in the churches. Since the author goes on to describe the qualifications of the episkopos two verses later, without indicating that he is talking about someone else now, a reasonable assumption is that the appointed elders in fact are appointed to be overseers. The qualifications of 1:7–9 are similar to those found in 1 Timothy, although there is a greater emphasis here on the need for the bishop to silence false teachers (1:9–11). There is no reference to the διάκονοι in this briefer letter.

For our purposes one of the most interesting questions has to do with the polemical function of these concerns over church leadership. As I have noted, both of these books begin and end with injunctions about false teaching and contain similar doctrinal concerns scattered throughout. Is this concern for "healthy teaching" unrelated to the need to allow only the right people in leadership roles? Or, rather, are the overarching polemical concerns of these books directly connected with their interest in leadership? As just indicated, Titus itself makes the connection directly, especially in 1:7, 9–11. Just as Paul's personal delegates are instructed to get the false teachers under control, so too are the bishops.

One of the salient purposes of these forgeries, then, is to give apostolic authorization for a church hierarchy that was needed in no small measure because of the variegated and dangerous teachings that had emerged in the Pauline communities near the end of the first century (assuming that this is when the letters were written, if not later). In the broader picture, how could "false" teachings most effectively be countered? By setting forth the true, apostolic teachings. When there were no longer apostles around to provide these teachings, one solution was to employ a form of literary deceit more widely used in the surrounding world at large. Claiming to be an apostle, an author could write treatises promoting the proper understanding of the faith, lying about his identity in order to advance the cause of truth. Moreover, true teaching could best be enforced from the top down, by leaders of the churches who saw the truth and were willing to silence anyone who violated it. And how was one to authorize the "right kind" of church leadership? Forgery again proved to be a useful tool. Writing in the name of Paul, a later forgery could presuppose the proper church hierarchy, insist on certain ecclesiastical arrangements, such as keeping women silent, and promote the cause of having the right leaders in charge.

Eventually within the proto-orthodox tradition this insistence on apostolic doctrines (even if found in forgeries) and on apostolic church structures (again, supported pseudepigraphically) created the need for other forms of authorization. This need is what drove the development of the various arguments over "succession" in which both the teachings of the orthodox churches and the bishops of those churches could be established as standing in continuity with predecessors who were appointed by those who stood directly in the line of the apostles. And since the apostles learned at the feet of Christ, and Christ came from God, the church hierarchy and the doctrine it proclaimed was divinely sanctioned. Those who proposed different structures or different theological views could be cast out as schismatics and heretics who had alienated themselves from the Almighty.

The Pastorals and the Acts of Paul

In pursuing the motivating factors behind the forgery of the Pastoral epistles, we need to consider a once-popular opinion that these three books were written, at least in part, in order to counter the views embodied in the second-century Acts of Paul. I will not be dealing with the Acts of Paul as a possible forgery or counterforgery per se, since so far as we can tell from both patristic references and the scant manuscript tradition, the book, or set of books, did not claim Paul as the author but only as the leading subject of its narrative. The author, in other words, did not make a false authorial claim.

There is a debate over whether Tertullian has in mind the same Acts of Paul that has come down to us in our scattered manuscripts, when he makes his famous deprecatory comment that "it was a presbyter in Asia who put together that book compiling the work from his own materials in the name of Paul. Having been convicted, he confessed that he had done it out of love for Paul" (*De baptismo* 17).[16] Stevan Davies has mounted a multipronged argument that Tertullian has in mind an actual forgery that no longer survives, rather than the extant Acts; but W. Rordorf and A. Hilhorst have provided convincing refutations and defenses of the traditional view,[17] and in the end, the matter does not affect the questions I want to pursue here, which involve instead the relation of the surviving Acts, especially the Thecla story, to the Pastoral epistles. It does bear emphasizing, in any event, that Tertullian does not accuse the author of the Acts of Paul of forging the document but of fabricating it—a major difference (that is, it was "written in Paul's name" because the "Acts of Paul" names Paul in its title). This

16. Translation of Stephen J. Davis, "A 'Pauline' Defense of Women's Right to Baptize? Intertextuality and Apostolic Authority in the Acts of Paul," *JECS* 8 (2000): 453–59.

17. Stevan L. Davies, "Women, Tertullian and the Acts of Paul," *Semeia* 38 (1986): 139–43. His argument is that unlike what Tertullian indicates about the work produced by the Asia Minor presbyter, the surviving Acts of Paul was not written in Paul's name, does not give Thecla the right to baptize, was not written to augment Paul's fame, and did not come to be held in disgrace among the proto-orthodox circles to which Tertullian belonged. See then the responses of A. Hilhorst, "Tertullian on the Acts of Paul," in Jan Bremmer, ed., *The Apocryphal Acts of Paul and Thecla* (Kampen: Pharos, 1996), pp. 150–63; and Willy Rordorf, "Tertullien et les Actes de Paul."

too is the claim of Jerome, who stresses that the book is apocryphal precisely because it is historically inaccurate (*Vir. Ill.*, 7). Jerome's proof: if such a story as Paul and the baptized lion had actually occurred, surely Luke would have known of it and included it in his canonical account of Paul's ministry! Moreover, it should be stressed that according to Tertullian, the offending presbyter was not expelled from office, as often claimed. After admitting to what he had done, he left office himself.[18] The Acts of Paul was judged—at least by these two authors—as an unacceptable fabrication.

But can the Pastoral epistles be understood as forgeries meant to counter the claims of these apocryphal tales? If so, how does one explain their relative dating? Already a century ago Hans Helmut Mayer argued that the Pastorals were directed, in part, against some of the views found in the Acts of Paul, a view influentially popularized by Dennis MacDonald in the early 1980s.[19] To evaluate the view, we need to consider some of the important data.[20]

There are six proper names that occur in the Thecla story connected with Paul. Five of them occur, as well, often in related connections, in the Pastoral epistles: (1) Demas (AP, 3.1; 2 Tim. 4:10; also Col. 4:14 and Phlm. 24) in both places deserting Paul, both times for greed; (2) Hermogenes (AP, 3.1; 2 Tim. 1:15), whose name occurs only in these two places in early Christian literature, and in both places he is twinned with a companion and deserts Paul in Asia Minor; (3) Onesiphorus (AP 3.2; 2 Tim. 1:16; 4:19), mentioned in early Christian literature only in these two places, and in both instances he is connected with Asia Minor, he befriends Paul when Paul is in prison, and he appears with his family; (4) Titus (AP 3.2; 2 Tim. 4:10; Tit. 1:4; ten times in 2 Corinthians and Galatians); and (5) Alexander (AP 3.26; 1 Tim. 1:20; 2 Tim. 4:14), who is said to oppose Paul, in both places, and only there. The one exception is Castellius (AP 3.14), who appears in the Acts only as a governor at the trial, not in Paul's ministry per se.

It is also worth noting that in both corpora there are two people connected with Paul who indicate that the resurrection has already taken place (Demas and Hermogenes in AP; Hymenaeus and Phileus in 2 Timothy). Moreover, both corpora connect a "coppersmith" with Paul, either Alexander (2 Timothy) or Hermogenes (AP).

In addition, there are four place names mentioned in the Acts of Paul, three of which also recur in the Pastorals: Iconium (3.1; 2 Tim. 3:11; five times in Acts); Antioch (3.1; 2 Tim. 3:11; sixteen times in Acts, once in Galatians); and Lystra

---

18. Hilhorst, "Tertullian on the Acts of Paul."

19. H. H. Mayer, *Über die Pastoralbriefe* (Göttingen: Vandenhoeck & Ruprecht, 1913). Dennis Ronald MacDonald, *The Legend and the Apostle: The Battle for Paul in Story and Canon* (Philadelphia: Westminster, 1983).

20. In addition to MacDonald, *Legend and the Apostle*, see Richard Bauckham, "The Acts of Paul as a Sequel to Acts," *The Book of Acts in Its Ancient Literary Setting*, ed. Bruce Winter and Arthur Clark (Grand Rapids, MI: Eerdmans, 1993); pp. 105–52; and Carston Looks, *Das Anvertraute bewahren. Die Rezeption der Pastoralbriefe im 2 Jahrhundert* (Munich: Hebert Utz, 1999), pp. 435–52.

(1.3; 2 Tim. 3:11; five times in Acts). The one exception is Myra (AP 3.40; twice in Acts).

Some of the material parallels between the works are similarly impressive. For example, from outside the Thecla story, in AP 11.1, we learn that Luke from Gaul and Titus from Dalmatian were awaiting Paul at Rome. Compare this with 2 Tim. 4:10–11, where Paul is writing from prison, presumably from Rome, and he indicates that Titus has gone "to Dalmatia" and that "Luke alone is with me." More striking still is the famous account of Paul and the baptized lion in the Acts of Paul. At this point of the narrative, Paul has been staying with Priscilla and Aquila in Ephesus, and everyone else has turned against him. With no support, he makes a bold witness before the governor and the crowd. The governor condemns him to be eaten by a ferocious lion, but the lion—Paul's previous acquaintance and convert—refuses to eat him and they both flee the scene unharmed. Compare this with 2 Tim. 4:16–19, where "Paul" indicates that no one took part at his defense and that everyone deserted him; but "the Lord stood by me and strengthened me so that the message could be fully proclaimed through me and all the Gentiles could hear." Moreover, at that time, "Paul" indicates that he "was saved from the mouth of the lion." He continues on, then, to send his greetings to Prisca and Acquila.

Despite these verbal and material overlaps, there are antithetical emphases in these two corpora that make their relationship of particular interest. And so, for example, 2 Tim. 3:6–7 attacks those who enter into households and capture weak women. This is precisely what the apostle himself appears to do in the Acts of Paul, certainly in the case of Thecla and later with Artemilla and Eubula. Similarly, Titus 1:10–11 speaks of opponents who upset entire households. Evidently these Christian teachers urge some form of asceticism, since Titus responds by asserting that with the pure all things are pure (i.e., nothing is forbidden). Thecla's household in the Acts of Paul was certainly turned topsy-turvy by Paul's proclamation in the home of Onesiphorus next door, a proclamation that has a rigorously ascetic bent. 1 Tim. 4:3 opposes those who are driven by deceitful spirits and the doctrines of demons to forbid marriage. So too, the Pastor requires leaders of the churches to be married, and urges young widows to remarry and have babies. In the Acts of Paul, Paul may not condemn marriage, but he certainly discourages it, as in the lead case of Thecla; moreover, it is his enemies Hermogenes and Demas who offer the teaching, contrary to Paul, that the resurrection happens precisely in one's progeny. In 1 Tim. 2:15 women are said to be "saved" by having children; whereas in the Acts of Paul women learn, through Paul's beatitudes, that it is the celibate who abstain from sex who will be blessed. So too, whereas the Pastor's women are not allowed to teach, but must be silent and submissive, in the legends Paul commissions a woman to go forth and teach (AP 3.39, 41, 43). Finally, whereas 1 Tim. 4:3 opposes those who abstain from certain foods, Paul in the Acts appears to maintain a vegetarian diet (AP 3.23–25).

And so, without yet drawing a specific conclusion concerning the direction in which the influence went, it is difficult to withstand the conclusion of J. Rohde that the Acts of Paul accepts as "legitimate teaching" what the Pastorals reject as "false."[21] Indeed, it would be a mistake to claim that the two corpora are unrelated, on the ground, for example, that so much material present in each—the legends of the Acts and the teaching of the Pastorals—is neither found nor maligned in the other. No one need think that the single purpose of either body of writings was to attack the other; but some such polemic could well have been at least one of its purposes. At all times we need to recall that texts, as a rule, are generated for multiple reasons and serve multiple purposes. And so we are justified in considering the reason and purpose of the Acts of Paul in relation to the Pastoral epistles.

The most provocative view of the relation of the two corpora was the aforementioned monograph of Dennis MacDonald, *The Legend and the Apostle: The Battle for Paul in Story and Canon.*[22] In his study, MacDonald explored three episodes of the Acts of Paul: the Thecla story, the account of the baptized lion, and the martyrdom of Paul. He argued that these stories were based on oral traditions that had been in circulation principally among Christian women in Asia Minor, so that Tertullian's presbyter was simply writing down accounts he had heard. The Pastoral epistles, on the other hand, were written in opposition to these oral traditions. There is not, in other words, a direct literary dependence between the two works, one way or the other; nor is the Acts of Paul responding to views eventually embodied in the Pastoral epistles. The relationship is the reverse: the Pastorals are responding to oral traditions that were later put in writing in the Acts of Paul.

Despite the attractiveness of the theory, it suffers from a weak set of arguments used to undermine a more obvious solution, that whoever wrote the Acts of Paul was reacting to the (earlier) Pastoral epistles. MacDonald argues that the influence did not go in this direction because, first of all, any author, such as the composer of the Acts of Paul, who "wanted to alter the traditional memory of a historical figure" (the author of the Pastorals), "would be more likely to use forged letters than a collection of stories."[23] But surely this is not self-evident; if the Pastorals themselves can be read as a kind of narrative—as Richard Pervo and others have tried to do[24]—there is no reason they could not be responded to by a narrative. And there is certainly nothing to preclude an author writing a narrative that had, as a subsidiary purpose, the opposition to a view of his protagonist set forth in some other influential writing, regardless of genre. MacDonald goes on to argue that if the author of the Acts was opposing the Pastorals, "we would

---

21. "Pastoralbriefe und Acta Pauli," *SE* 5 (1968): 309. Rohde goes on to argue that the AP is not necessarily polemicizing against the message of Paul in the Pastorals, since there is so little direct polemic in AP, as opposed to Pastorals. Rather than being principally polemical—even if there are anti-Gnostic traces—the legends are by and large edificatory and entertaining. Rhodes's view may be true, but there is little reason to deny that the views of the Acts are antithetical to those set forth in the Pastorals, and vice versa.

22. See note 19.

23. *Legend and the Apostle*, p. 63.

24. See note 3.

expect to find him authenticating the narrative in order to secure credulity over against the epistolary opposition." Here again, there is no reason that we should tell authors what they ought to do, or expect them to take what in the modern critical mind seems to be a more effective approach.

Most important for MacDonald is his claim that a theory of literary dependence is able to explain the similarities between the two texts, but not the differences in the details. For example, in the Acts of Paul Hermogenes is associated with Demas; but in the Pastorals he is associated with Phygelus. If one is dependent on the other—as arguably shown by the similarities—it is hard to account, in MacDonald's view, for such differences.

The major problem with this position is that it requires far too narrow an understanding of how literary dependence can work and overlooks an entire range of possibilities involving secondary orality. It is not necessary to suppose that an author who is responding to a text will have the writing on his knee, comparing every line as he proceeds to write his narrative (or epistle). He may just as well—especially in an ancient context—have heard the earlier text read aloud, possibly multiple times, and decided then to respond to its themes. Many of the names and places may well be recalled, but it is altogether possible that the specifics get lost. I myself have read the Pastoral epistles literally hundreds of times in both Greek and English, and I could not tell you, without looking it up, with whom Hermogenes is associated in the text, or even if Phygelus is mentioned in it. One should not respond by insisting that matters were different in past oral cultures; if studies of oral cultures have taught us anything, it is that stories were not remembered or repeated precisely the same way in every iteration.

There is a broad consensus that the Acts of Paul as we have it are the product of the late second century. If these are the works referred to by Tertullian in *De baptismo* 17—which continues to be a strong consensus—and if he is correct that they were first put together near the end of the second century, then on virtually any reckoning they came into existence some time after the Pastorals. If, as appears evident, there is some kind of relation between the two corpora, the most sensible solution is to think that the author of the Acts is responding in narrative form to the image of Paul, and of his views, found in the earlier texts. He worked to rewrite Paul in significant ways. Paul's message is now one of rigorous ascetic celibacy (whereas in the Pastorals he condemned asceticism and urged women to have babies); women are now empowered and allowed to teach and preach; and the unity of the home is not to be protected.

At the same time, it should be stressed that even if the Pastorals were not written as responses to the Acts of Paul, the traditions and views embodied in these later accounts were not invented out of whole cloth sometime late in the second century. Ascetic impulses can be found early in the Christian movement, as evidenced not only in the Pastorals. Paul himself urged celibacy in view of the "impending crisis" and insisted that "it is good for a man not to touch a woman." Women were afforded active roles in the churches, as seen, most strikingly and emphatically, by Paul himself, as attested in Gal. 3:28; Rom.

16:1, 7; and 1 Corinthians 11. Other Paulinists objected to such views, urging the value of the extended family and the Haustafeln that kept everyone in their place, arguing for the "freedom" of the whole person in Christ, propounding the virtues of marriage and sexual activities. The apocalyptic urgency that created an unworldly and, seen from a Roman point of view, antisocial attitude among Christians eventually lost out to (what cannot help but appear to observers today to be) a bourgeois ethic.

In that environment the Pastoral epistles were written, in part to oppose views advocated by other Paulinists, opponents who could well appeal to Paul himself for their views. These views did not die out with the writing of opposing forgeries in Paul's name. They lived on in some circles that passed along the oral traditions they inherited about the apostle, which stressed the importance of the ascetic, celibate life and celebrated the important roles that women could play in the church. Eventually these traditions came to be written down in such works as the Acts of Thecla. The Pastoral epistles may not be counterforgeries in the strong sense of being produced in order to oppose the view found in another identifiable forgery, or even an existing legendary fabrication; but they are counterforgeries in the weaker sense of opposing views associated otherwise with Paul by using the best set of ammunition available to the unknown author: the name of the apostle himself. The real, but unknown, author lied about his own identity in order to bring the apostolic voice to bear on a set of issues that were very much a matter of intense debate in his own day.

THE FORGED CHURCH ORDERS

We have already seen that several of the "church orders" produced in our period were forged. This would include the Epistula Clementis, the Didascalia, and the Apostolic Constitutions, the last of which could also be considered a case of plagiarism, depending on how far one stretches the meaning of the term.[25] The earliest examples of the genre were not always forged: witness the anonymous Didache, which avers to propound the teaching of the twelve apostles, but whose author does not claim to be the apostolic band or even one of its members. So too the Apostolic Tradition, later attributed, wrongly, to Hippolytus of Rome.[26] Other church orders fall outside of our time period.[27]

There have been long debates over the character of these documents and their instructions for church organization and administration. Do they represent descriptive and reasonably full accounts of the protocols that governed the life of the Christian community? Or do they deal only with issues and problems that

25. Depending, that is, on whether a forger can commit plagiarism, given the circumstance that he is not actually claiming someone else's work to be his own, as he is writing it in the name of another. See p. 14.

26. See Joseph Mueller, "The Ancient Church Order Literature: Genre or Tradition?" *JECS* 15 (2007): 337–80.

27. See the full study of twelve texts in B. Steimer, *Vertex Traditionis*.

have arisen within an author's purview, and do not therefore provide a full representation of the organizational and administrative issues that a community had to address, the bulk of which would have been nonproblematic and therefore in no need of discussion? That is to say, are these church orders reasonably exhaustive and descriptive accounts? Or are they selective, polemical, and prescriptive?

The decision between these two options obviously matters. If the church orders are principally descriptive, then in them we gain an extensive insight into the lives of the pre-Constantinian churches, at least in the regions from which they derive, and by subtraction we can see what these churches were not doing as well. If they are principally polemical and prescriptive, they are not protocols for the most important activities of the community, but *Tendenzschriften* that deal only with what the author perceives as the problems and (possibly deplorable) state of affairs in his community. This too would be helpful historically, as it would show us what internal organizational issues were being debated in the Christians communities of the first three hundred years.

Bruno Steimer, in his study *Vertex Traditionis,* a 1991 dissertation at Regensburg, takes the first position. The book deals with twelve church orders, starting with the Didache and moving up through the fifth-century Clementine Octateuch. Steimer is chiefly concerned with establishing the generic features of these works, but he deals extensively with issues related to pseudepigraphy throughout, especially in a closing section exclusively devoted to the question. In this final section he argues that although pseudonymity is not a generic requirement, it is one of the ways that the author of a church order could most successfully perform his task, in that the apostolic pseudonym naturally provided legitimation for the positions he asserts. That is to say, the apostles are typically presented as "formal authorities" to back up the views that are advanced and work to show that these orders were normative for the church from the outset, all the way back to the apostles of Jesus themselves.[28] The pseudepigraphic claims, therefore, function to gain the works acceptance and universal validity.

Steimer summarizes the important matters dealt with in this literature, most of them involving the church as an institution: the qualification and selection of leaders, their duties, church discipline, ethical and doctrinal instruction, observance of rituals such as baptism and eucharist, and so on. In Steimer's view, these books represent the church's actual practice, and to that extent they are descriptive accounts. For that reason, it is possible to recreate extensively the activities of the early churches, since the most important church concerns are addressed "mit Umfassendheit."[29]

A trenchant review of Steimer's work by Georg Schöllgen provides compelling counterarguments to this view.[30] Schöllgen focuses on the Didache, the Apos-

---

28. Ibid., p. 344.

29. Ibid., p. 270.

30. Georg Schöllgen, "Der Abfassungszweck der frühchristlichen Kirchenordnungen: Anmerkungen zu den Thesen Bruno Steimers," *JAC* 40 (1997): 55–77.

tolic Tradition, and the Didascalia, arguing that for these three, "nowhere is it clear that they intend to order life in their communities comprehensively. There is no 'pretended universalization of order' to speak of."[31] For Schöllgen, the church orders do not represent a codification of the typical praxis of the community; rather, they deal with problems that had arisen—such as those, quite obviously, involving itinerant prophets and apostles in the Didache. This is shown especially by the fact that the authors have had to cement their views in writing, accompanied with paranesis, under the authority of the apostles. The authors are trying to argue a case in light of abuses in the community, involving such matters as the roles of women, alternative forms of governance, and care of the poor. They do not simply indicate something about the status quo. Among other things, church orders represent an attempt to make the monepiscopate more central to the life of the community.[32]

In particular, the forged character of these books shows that they were not written simply to state the current state of affairs: "Pseudepigraphy is thus a clear argument against the 'reflection theory': Why should a church order, which does not intend anything but 'to put into writing' the community's practice, do so not in the name of its actual authors or its community, but instead takes the risk of being unmasked as an act of deception?" The use of pseudepigraphy served then to justify practices where there were controversies about them: "The borrowed authority of the apostles was intended to make the text binding in a way that the author could not have achieved by publishing it under his own name."[33]

It is especially significant for Schöllgen that these documents are scripturally based. The authority of the apostles, as found in Scripture, was important for establishing the veracity of the claims made in them. And so the apostolic character of the church orders is in a sense an extension of the authority of Scripture, so that these too function as Scripture in dealing with community problems that had arisen.[34] What is more, when a book like the Didascalia lik-

---

31. "An keiner Stelle deutlich, daß sie die Absicht haben, das Leben in ihren Gemeinden umfassend zu regeln. Von einer 'prätendierten Universalität der Ordnung' kann keine Rede sein," "Der Abfassungszweck," p. 64.

32. P. 69.

33. "Die Pseudepigraphie ist zudem ein deutliches Argument gegen die Widerspiegelungstheorie: warum sollte eine Kirchenordnung, die nichts anderes im Sinn hat, als die Gemeindepraxis zu 'verschriftlichen,' dies nicht unter dem Namen ihres tatsächlichen Verfassers bzw. seiner Gemeinde tun, statt sich in die Gefahr zu begeben als Betrugsmanöver entlarvt zu werden?" . . . "Die geliehene Autorität der Apostel soll der Schrift die Verbindlichkeit verleihen, die der Verfasser bei einer orthonymen Veröffentlichung nicht hätte erreichen können." Both quotations p. 76.

34. As Schöllgen argues elsewhere concerning the relationship of scripture citation and pseudepigraphic authorship in the Didascalia: "The apostolic frame obviously serves the purpose of making the Didascalia's interpretation of Scripture binding vis-à-vis competing interpretations." ("Der apostolische Rahmen dient ganz offensichtlich dem Zweck, die Schriftinterpretation der Didaskalie gegen konkurrierende Interpretationen verbindlich zu machen.") "Pseudapostolizität und Schriftgebrauch in den

ens the office of the bishop to the office of the apostle, with similar functions ascribed to both (νουθετεῖν, διδασκεῖν), the bishop is presented as having the same role in his congregations that the apostles have for the entire church. They are the mouth of God and the witness to the divine will, through the proper interpretation of Scripture.

In short, when considering the church orders, we are dealing with inherently polemical literature, even when the polemics are below the surface. Sometimes, of course, the polemics are front and center, as we have already observed with the Didascalia. At other times, however, they are far more subtle, as we can see by looking at other aspects of these works.

The Didascalia

We have already considered the Didascalia at some length with respect to the anti-Jewish character of its teaching on the "secondary legislation," which was put into the document, according to the theory of Stewart-Sykes, by the deuterotic redactor, who worked before an editor inserted the apostolic claims that make the text pseudepigraphic.[35] There is no need at this stage to review all of the relevant background information on the document itself and its (possible) redactional states. Rather we can turn to consider several of its other polemical interests, also advanced in the names of the apostles after the death of Jesus.

The Role of the Bishop

Some readers have suspected that the heightened emphasis on the role of the bishop in the life of the community is not simply descriptive of situations that widely obtained at the time of the author's writing, but represent a plea to grant the bishop greater authority. It is striking that eight of the twenty-seven chapters of the book deal with the office, responsibilities, and behavior of the bishop. Charlotte Methuen contends that "the Didascalia must be seen as part of an ongoing struggle to establish a more hierarchical Church centered on the bishop, which led to the discrediting of other forms of authority and the groups which supported them."[36] In particular she has in mind church groups that stressed the possibility of women exercising authoritative roles in the work of teaching and baptizing, a matter to which we will turn momentarily. But it is also possible that the stress on the bishop was driven by broader concerns of localizing the power of the local congregation in the hands of one authority figure who was able thereby to marginalize and overturn schismatic and heretical factions advocating alternative forms of polity or the age-old bugbear, "false teaching."

---

ersten Kirchenordnungen," in G. Schöllgen and G. Scholten, eds., *Stimuli: Exegese und ihre Hermeneutik in Antike und Christentum*. (Münster: Aschendorff, 1996), p. 117.

35. See pp. 344–50.

36. Charlotte Methuen, "Widows, Bishops and the Struggle for Authority in the *Didascalia Apostolorum*," *JEH* 46 (1995): 213.

The Celebration of Easter

In an analysis that only an inveterate source critic could love, Alistair Stewart-Sykes provides a long and complicated discussion of the multiple redactions of what comes down to us as chapter 21 of the Didascalia, a chapter that discusses passion week and the sequence of days leading up to the celebration of Easter. It is by all accounts a complicated and confusing part of the text, with instructions concerning what to perform on which days in relation to Jesus' last week and, as well, in relation to the Jewish feast of Pascha:

> Thus it is required, brothers, that you investigate carefully in the days of the Pascha and perform your fasting with all diligence, making a beginning when your brothers from the people [i.e., the Jews] are keeping the Pascha. (5.17.1) . . . Therefore from the tenth, which is the second day of the week, you shall fast in the days of the Pascha. You shall sustain yourselves with bread and salt and water only, at the ninth hour, until the fifth day of the week. However on the Friday and Saturday you shall fast entirely. (5.18.1) . . . For this reason you likewise are to mourn on their behalf on the sabbath day of the Pascha, until the third hour of the night following. And then, at the resurrection of Christ, rejoice and be glad on their behalf, and break your fast. (5.20.9) You shall observe it in this way whenever the fourteenth of the Pascha should occur, for neither the month nor the day falls at the same time each year, but is changeable. Thus you should be fasting when that people performs the Pascha; yet be careful to conclude your vigil within their (week of) unleavened bread. (5.20.10)

In an attempt to make sense of the various comments of the text, Stewart-Sykes argues that the book originated as a document that embraced a Quartodeciman perspective, but that it was later edited to oppose this perspective.[37] The result was a view that supported the observance of Easter on Sunday, but within the Quartodeciman milieu—that is, during the celebration of the Pascha, but always on a Sunday—a compromise position hammered out in the midst of some rather fierce controversy over the celebration of this most important festival in the life of the church.

The Role of Women

Several scholars have argued that a particular concern of the Didascalia is to control the activities of women in the church. G. Schöllgen, for example, maintains that the directions given to widows not to engage in pastoral duties, but to do good deeds only in the sphere of the home, represent a polemic against other practices that were being followed, a view supported by Carolyn Osiek and, strongly, Charlotte Methuen.[38]

---

37. *Didascalia*, p. 43.

38. Schöllgen, "Der Abfassungszweck," p. 68; on Osiek and Methuen, see pp. 389–90 below.

The instructions given to and about widows occur in book 3. A widow must be over fifty years of age (3.1.1)[39]; she is not allowed to remarry more than once: "After this she is a harlot" (3.2.2). The author is especially concerned about widows who are "talkative or loud, or garrulous, or fond of strife" (3.5.1). Widows are not to instruct in doctrine, since "when a woman speaks of the incarnation and suffering of Christ, [the gentiles] shall sneer and scoff, rather than glorifying the word of the old woman, and she shall be subject to a harsh judgement for her sin" (3.6.1). Women, then, are not to teach, but "solely to pray and beseech the Lord God" (3.6.2). The author's apostolic logic: when the Lord "sent us, the twelve" to proclaim the gospel, he "did not send with us the women disciples who were with us . . . to instruct or save the world." Impeccable logic, of its sort. The author instructs widows not to "wander or go from house to house" (3.6.4), and is especially concerned for widows who go about begging for alms, "caring only for mammon" (3.7.3–4).

In particular he stresses that women are not allowed to baptize, even other women (3.9.1–2). But they may serve as deaconesses who can speak to other women in the houses of pagans and to anoint with oil other women at their baptism, although it must be the man who pronounces the invocation of the divine names at the ceremony (3.12.1–3). Moreover, women are allowed to educate other women who come out of baptism, "so that the mark of baptism may be kept intact in chastity and holiness" (3.12.3).

In short, as summarized by Carolyn Osiek, women are not considered empowered subjects in this text; they are "reduced to cloistered ignoramuses who can be trusted with nothing"; they cannot speak to pagans or else they will make Christianity an object of ridicule (3.5); they must stay at home to pray and spin, or they will be spiritually bankrupt (3.6, 7); they can engage in no ministry unless ordered by the bishop or deacon, whom they must obey (3.8); for them to baptize would be dangerous both to themselves and to the ones they baptize (3.9); just as the altar does not move about, so too they must stay at home (3.6.3).[40]

As indicated, several scholars have suggested that the vehemence with which these injunctions are set forth suggests that the author is trying to prescribe a form of church authority in the face of opposition from another model. Thus Methuen: "The tone and content of these instructions make it likely that they are a polemic against women who do indeed baptize and teach and who in so doing assume a function and authority which the author regards as the exclusive province of the bishop."[41] And Osiek: "The length of texts devoted to the subject and the vehemence expressed are exceptional, however, and seem to indicate a reaction to some real or imagined threatening situation."[42]

39. A "not" has inadvertently dropped out of Stewart-Sykes's translation of 3.1.1 ("Widows who are to be appointed: should be less than fifty years of age"!).

40. Carolyn Osiek, "The Widow as Altar: The Rise and Fall of a Symbol," *SecCent* 3 (1983): 168.

41. Methuen, "Widows, Bishops, and the Struggle for Authority," p. 200.

42. "The Widow as Altar," p. 168.

According to Methuen's reconstruction of the historical *Sitz*, a group of widows who are accustomed to teaching and baptizing have come into the Didascalia's community from another group: "The strength of his reaction against the widows suggests that they might come from outside the Didascalia congregation, representing a group which subscribes to a different pattern of ministry and authority, and, moreover, to one which grants freedom and authority to women."[43]

In response, it might be pointed out that there is nothing in the polemic to suggest any outside influence. More likely the author's polemic is directed against what has traditionally happened in the community and what continues to happen in his own day. He is writing to prevent women from engaging in activities they were already involved with.

Osiek puts the matter in a sensible broader context:

> The more hierarchically structured Christian churches of the second and third centuries often felt themselves to be in a state of siege because of the threat posed by the more "charismatic" or loosely structured communities that more often than not seem to have allowed a great deal of freedom and responsibility to women, especially in the area of religious leadership.

As a result,

> the attempt to restrict severely the activities of widows is, no doubt, part of the well-known reaction against the freedom exercised by women in rival Christian groups. Or, more specifically, it could be a reaction against the very important role played by members of the order of widows in neighboring churches.[44]

To this extent, the Didascalia would be a kind of counterforgery, in the broad sense, produced, in its final redaction, in the names of the apostles in order to rein in a dominant practice in which women, and especially widows, were exercising considerable authority in their roles in the church.

The Apostolic Constitutions

At the outset of our investigation we saw a number of key aspects of the Apostolic Constitutions.[45] The book is a heavily redacted text that combines three otherwise extant documents in order to make a more all-encompassing church order: the Didascalia (in what are now chs. 1–7); the Didache (ch. 8), and the Apostolic

43. "Widows, Bishops, and the Struggle for Authority," p. 203. Methuen argues as well that the Didascalia is specifically directing its polemic against a group of women as known from the Acts of Thomas.

44. Osiek, "The Widow as Altar," pp. 168–69. See also Bonnie Bowman Thurston, "The Widows as the 'Altar of God,'" SBLSP 24 (1985): 279–89.

45. See pp. 14–19.

Tradition (ch. 8). To the end is added the eighty-five "Apostolic Canons," which may have had a separate transmission history at some stage, but are now known only in their connection with this larger work.[46]

Thomas Kopecek has noted that the Greek text of the Apostolic Constitutions was first edited in the sixteenth century by a Spanish Jesuit, Franciscus Turrianus, whose interest in the work, as a Roman Catholic, was to appeal to its apostolic authority in order to refute the Protestant understanding of the church. In the centuries that followed, Anglican divines cited the final book of the work in order to advance their views of the liturgy, as sanctioned by the apostles. As Kopecek points out, "This interpretation died hard."[47]

Possibly this late use of the document can provide a clue as to the purpose of its original concoction. For it does indeed appear to have been generated in order to justify certain ecclesiastical structures through the sanctioning power of the pens of the apostles. It was only when the sources of the work were discovered and evaluated that scholars abandoned any claims to its apostolic provenance.

Pseudepigraphic Character and Date

Of the three sources that were used to construct the Apostolic Constitutions, only the Didascalia came to the editor/author (in its final redacted form) as pseudepigraphic; the other two works were anonymous. But when edited into a larger whole, all three works have become pseudonymous, and in fact the compiler of the Apostolic Constitutions has gone well beyond the Didascalia itself in emphasizing his book's apostolic origins. As noted earlier, the apostolic claim is made, now, at the beginning of each of the major divisions (beginnings of books 1, 7, and 8). On occasion throughout the work the author speaks in the first-person plural as eyewitnesses and disciples of the earthly Jesus, as in 2.55.2:

> After His passion [we] the twelve apostles, and Paul the chosen vessel. . . . We therefore, who have been vouchsafed the favour of being the witnesses of His appearance, together with James the brother of our Lord, and the other seventy-two disciples, and his seven deacons, have heard from the mouth of our Lord Jesus Christ, and by exact knowledge declare "what is the will of God, that good, and acceptable, and perfect will."[48]

Or in book 6, when speaking of the Jerusalem Conference of Acts 15:

> But because this heresy did seem the more powerful to seduce men, and the whole Church was in danger, we the twelve assembled together at Jerusalem. . . .

---

46. For that reason I will not be giving them a separate treatment, even though they too are falsely written in the names of the apostles.

47. Thomas A. Kopecek, review of Marcel Metzger, *Les Constitutions Apostoliques*, vol. 1 in *JTS* 38 (1987): 209.

48. Translation of James Donaldson in *ANF*.

> We deliberated, together with James the Lord's brother, what was to be done.... And when one said one thing, and some another, I Peter stood up and said to them [etc.] ... (6.12)

In Book 8, "we, the twelve apostles of the Lord," (8.4) along with Paul and James (the brother of Jesus), give instructions, individually by name: "I, Peter, say that a bishop to be ordained is to be ... chosen by the whole people ..." (8.12); "And I James, the brother of John, the son of Zebedee say, that the deacon shall immediately say ..." (8.12); "Concerning the ordination of deacons, I Philip make this constitution" (8.17). And so on. The apostolic band contained in the first-person plural is not always the same throughout that text. Thus, for example, 6.12 mentions the Eleven, Matthias, and James, but does not include Paul among the "we" who are speaking. Yet, in addition to the twelve, Paul, James, and Clement all elsewhere speak in the first person.

Sometimes the author alludes to the lives of individual members of the twelve in the first person, as they occasionally speak out to say something to identify themselves, for instance, Matthew, who calls himself the tax collector (2.24.4); Thomas, the one who was lacking in faith (5.19.1); and especially Peter, who recalls his conflicts with Simon Magus (4.7.2, 6.7.4). At other times the author quotes the writings of the New Testament as if the apostles themselves were simply speaking the words (as opposed to him, the author, quoting texts); or he speaks of personal episodes rather than quotations of Scripture, as in 2.46: "It is also a duty to forgive each other's trespasses, ... as the Lord determined when I Peter asked Him, 'How oft shall my brother sin against me and I forgive him'"; or 5:7: "He ... sent a piece of money out of a fish's mouth by me Peter...."

The point of all this heightened first-person narrative is occasionally hammered home, in case readers are too dull to figure it out for themselves: "We who have eaten and drunk with Him, and have been spectators of His wonderful works, and of His life, and of His conduct, and of His words, and of His sufferings.... We teach you all these things which he appointed us by His Constitutions" (5. 7).

Scholars have long questioned whether the final document was compiled over time by a number of editors, or instead was the product of a single redactor's work. An early proponent of multiple redactors was Johann Sebastian von Drey in 1829;[49] the consensus today, however, leans toward a single redactor, for compelling reasons that are, however, of little moment for our present concerns.[50] There is also a strong consensus that the final product was made in Syria, probably Antioch, at the end of the fourth century. That date would accommodate the discussion of the minor church offices (subdeacon, reader, singer, deaconess, etc.) in 8.12 and, in particular, the list of festivals that includes Christmas in 5.13, since

49. "Über die apostolischen Constitutionen, oder neue Untersuchungen über die Bestandtheile, Entstehung und Zusammensetzung, und den kirchlichen Werth dieser alten Schrift," *ThQ* 11 (1829): 397–477, esp. p. 410.

50. Compiled by Steimer, *Vertex Traditionis*, pp. 119–20.

Chrysostom indicates in a homily of 386 CE that the Christmas festival in Antioch began to be celebrated ten years earlier.[51]

The Tendencies of the Author

There have been long, hard, protracted, and occasionally pointless arguments over the inclination of the author/final editor of the Apostolic Constitutions, especially of his theological proclivities.[52] The concern is not merely a modern one, as shown by Canon 2 of the Trullanum (692–93 CE), which was quoted at the outset of this study, but which is of sufficient relevance to warrant quoting again:

> It has also seemed good to this holy Council, that the eighty-five canons, received and ratified by the holy and blessed Fathers before us, and also handed down to us in the name of the holy and glorious Apostles should from this time forth remain firm and unshaken for the cure of souls and the healing of disorders. And in these canons we are bidden to receive the Constitutions of the Holy Apostles [written] by Clement. But formerly through the agency of those who erred from the faith certain adulterous matter was introduced, clean contrary to piety, for the polluting of the Church, which obscures the elegance and beauty of the divine decrees in their present form. We therefore reject these Constitutions so as the better to make sure of the edification and security of the most Christian flock; by no means admitting the offspring of heretical error, and cleaving to the pure and perfect doctrine of the Apostles.[53]

From the outset of the critical investigation, it was believed that the passages in question ("certain adulterous matter") were Arian, a view that dominated until the pivotal investigations of F. Funk, who argued that the author was in fact orthodox, with Apollinarian tendencies.[54] One upshot was that the text in its final form would likely date later than normally understood, sometime in the fifth century. Funk's view was in turn attacked by C. H. Turner, who pushed for the traditional view that the author/editor was Arian,[55] a view supported in the next generation with additional argumentation by Bernard Capelle.[56] Later still, in 1972, Georg

51. "*Hom. in diem natalem Domini nostri Jesu Christi,*" in Migne *PG* 49, 351, cited in Steimer, *Vertex Traditionis,* p. 121 n. 61.

52. See Metzger, *Les constitutions apostoliques,* vol. 2, pp. 10–110; Metzger, "La théologie des Constitutions apostoliques par Clément," *RevScRel* 57 (1983): 33–36; and especially Steimer, *Vertex Traditionis,* pp. 122–29, to whom I am especially indebted in my survey here.

53. Translation of Henry Percival from Philip Schaff and Henry Wace, eds., *NPNF,* second series, vol. 14 (reprint edition Peabody, MA: Hendrickson, 1994; American edition original, 1900), p. 361.

54. Franz X. Funk, *Die Apostolischen Konstitutionen. Eine literar-historische Untersuchung* (Rottenburg: W. Bader, 1891), pp. 105–7, 367.

55. "Notes on the Apostolic Constitutions," *JTS* 16 (1915): 54–61 and 523–38.

56. "Le texte du 'Gloria in excelsis,' *RHE* 44 (1949): 439–505.

Wagner claimed specifically that the author was a neo-Arian of the Eunomian type, that in fact Eunomius was the possible author.[57]

A different approach to studying the theological comments of the author/redactor involved making a more precise identification by associating him with other writings from the same period. In particular it had been argued as far back as James Ussher in 1644 that the author of the Apostolic Constitutions also forged the Pseudo-Ignatian letters.[58] Objections were raised to the identification over the years, but the view was put on firmer ground by the great Harnack.[59]

The conclusion was made even more certain by Dieter Hagedorn, who, in a 1973 edition of a late-fourth-century Arian commentary on the book of Job, explored thirty-five points of contact that it shared with the Apostolic Constitutions.[60] On some occasions, in dealing with the same topics, the two works use precisely the same somewhat unusual phrases. Hagedorn pointed to three explanations that could be adduced for these parallels: the two (different) authors used the same source; or one of them edited the work of the other; or they were the same person. He went on to argue that the final option was most plausible.[61]

One significant result of this conclusion is that the author of the Job commentary actually identifies himself. He was named Julian. Whoever Julian was, he also compiled the Apostolic Constitutions and forged the Pseudo-Ignatian letters. And from the Job commentary there can be little doubt about his theological views. He was, in Hagedorn's view, strongly "Arian."[62]

At the same time, it should be stressed that the inability of scholars to mount a compelling and definitive demonstration of the theological tendencies of the Apostolic Constitutions themselves, based simply on the surviving text, shows that the author—probably Julian—did not have a distinctively theological agenda to promote in this particular writing, even though his theological views may have crept into the text at points. That is to say, he forged this writing—it is a redactional forgery—for reasons other than theology. This too is the conclusion of Marcel Metzger, editor of the three-volume edition for the Sources Chrétienne.[63]

---

57. "Zur Herkunft der Apostolischen Konstitutionen," in *Mélanges liturgiques offerts au R. P. dom Bernard Botte à l'occasion du cinquantième anniversaire de son ordination sacerdotale (4 juin 1972)* (Louvain, Abbaye du Mont César, 1972). For the views of S. Schwartz and J. Lebreton, see Steimer, *Vertex Traditionis*, p. 125.

58. *Polycarpi et Ignatii epistolae* (Oxford: Leonard Lichfield, 1644), LXIII–LXIV.

59. *Die Lehre der zwölf Apostel nebst Untersuchungen zur Geschichte der Kirchenverfassung und des Kirchenrechts* (Leipzig: J. C. Hinrichs, 1884), 244–65.

60. Dieter Hagedorn, *Der Hiobkommentar des Arianers Julian* (Berlin: Walter de Gruyter, 1973).

61. P. lii.

62. See further the discussion of the Pseudo-Ignatian letters on pp. 460–80.

63. "The view that the compiler and his school took recourse to pseudepigraphy for the purpose of surreptitiously imposing Arian doctrines and formulae is untenable in light of a complete examination of the Apostolic Constitutions and the local historical context." ("Que la compilateur et son atelier aient recouru à la pseudépigraphie pour imposer subrepticement les thèses et les formules ariennes, cette opinion ne peut tenir devant un examen complet des CA et du contexte historique local.") *Les constitutions apostoliques*, vol. 2, p. 11.

Metzger's reasoning is compelling. The compiler of the work prefers to use biblical rather than philosophical terminology: terms such as ὀυσία, πρόσωπον, ὑπόστασις, and their adjectives are missing from the account, as are the terms typically used in the Trinitarian controversies, such as ὁμοούσιος, ὁμοιούσιος, ἀνόμοιος, etc. Moreover, the author leaves out all incontestably "Arian" theological terms and phrases, and does not provide any trace of a polemic against Nicene orthodoxy. These linguistic facts are hard to explain if the writing was, in fact, meant to serve as a piece of Arian propaganda. Instead, the polemical emphasis, in Metzger's opinion, resides in what we earlier considered, an attack on Judaism and Jewish Christianity, or more specifically against views such as those found in the Pseudo-Clementines. In Metzger's opinion, the theology of the book, when examined in se, is simply some form of late Origenism.[64]

This view did not go down well with reviewers who had difficulty believing that an Arian might well be interested in discussing something other than Christology—such as church liturgy, church offices, and church discipline. And so, T. Kopecek complains that Metzger devotes only thirty pages of his introduction to a discussion of the theology of the Apostolic Constitutions, but twice as many to an account of its institutional and liturgical descriptions.[65] In response it might be pointed out that this is, after all, what the book is: a church order, not a theological treatise.

If Julian did not forge the Apostolic Constitutions as an "Arian" apologia, why did he stress his alleged apostolic credentials—far more than his most extensive source, the forged Didascalia, let alone the anonymous Didache and the Apostolic Tradition? The obvious response is that he wants to stress that his views about church structure and administration come with direct apostolic authority: "When ye have learned this constitution from us, ye who are ordained bishops by us at the command of Christ, may perform all things according to the commands delivered you, knowing that he that heareth us heareth Christ, and he that heareth Christ heareth His God and Father" (8.3.2). It is hard to appeal to greater authority than that.

In a sense Julian takes the matter further than his predecessors. As seen, a book like the Didascalia uses Scripture to support its own apostolic claims, showing that the apostles who produced the sacred texts are now speaking with an equally authoritative voice in this text. Julian, on the other hand, has the apostles declare that his own book is Scripture. As seen at the climax, in canon 85 (8.47), the Apostolic Constitutions itself is one of the books of the New Testament, as are the two books produced by its carrier and authenticator, Clement of Rome. Moreover, by warning its readers against the "spurious books of the ungodly" on two occasions (6.16.1, 8.47.60), the author assures his readers that even though there may be forged books in the names of the apostles out

64. *Les constitutions apostoliques*, vol. 2, p. 18.

65. See note 47.

there, this is not one of them. This one, indeed, comes from the apostles themselves. "The warning against pseudepigraphal writings that appears twice in the Apostolic Constitution should be considered the strongest argument in favor of its authenticity."[66]

The Apostolic Church Orders

Date and Character

The Apostolic Church Orders was first published in 1692 by J. Leutholf, from the Ethiopic, with a Latin translation, in *Iobi Ludolfi (alias Leutholf dicti) ad suam Historiam Aethiopicam antehac editam Commentarius.*[67] J. W. Bickell published the Greek text, with German translation, 150 years later.[68] The most recent edition is by Alistair Stewart-Sykes.[69]

Although, as Steimer indicates, there is a broad consensus that locates the Apostolic Church Orders to the first part of the fourth century,[70] the consensus has been challenged by Stewart-Sykes, who argues that the nature of the polemic suggests a date (of the final redaction) a century earlier: "200–235 would be a reasonable suggestion."[71]

The work is a composite text consisting of a two-ways teaching similar to that found in the Didache, but placed on the pens of the twelve apostles (chs. 1–15),[72] followed by a brief church order that deals with the appointment, qualifications, and duties of church officers (bishop, presbyters, readers, deacons, widows), as well as of laity and women (chs. 16–30), also given in first-person narrative by the apostles.[73] Stewart-Sykes, as is his wont, provides a complex source and redactional analysis. An earlier influential assessment of sources was made by Adolf Harnack.[74]

---

66. "Als stärkstes Argument der Authentizität ist die in der CA doppelt vorkommende Warnung vor pseudepigraphischen Schriften zu werten." Steimer, *Vertex Traditionis*, pp. 132–33.

67. Frankfurt am Main, 1691, pp. 304–14.

68. In *Geschichte des Kirchenrechts* 1 (Giessen, 1843), pp. 107–32.

69. *The Apostolic Church Order: The Greek Text with Introduction, Translation and Annotations* (Strathfield, Australia: St Pauls, 2006).

70. *Vertex Traditionis*, p. 65.

71. *Apostolic Church Order*, p. 78.

72. There is nothing to require Speyer's judgment that the document was produced in order to replace the Didache. Instead, it simply gives the Two Ways teaching a different iteration, and combines it with a church order. See Speyer, *Literarische Fälschung* p. 223.

73. Faivre attempts to find clever connections between what each apostle says and what is known about that apostle from other sources ("Apostolicité et pseudo-apostolicité dans la 'Constitution ecclésiastique des apôtres': L'art de faire parler les origines," *RevScRel* 66, 1992, 19–67). Thus, for example, Cephas speaks about the role of women in part because in 1 Cor. 9:5 he is connected with a wife; and Andrew talks about the symbolic theological connection of the deaconate between men (ANΔPAEI) and women. In most instances, including these two, the connections appear to be a considerable stretch and fail to convince.

74. *Die Lehre der zwölf Apostel*, pp. 210–16.

The Pseudepigraphic Character and Polemic

The forger opens his account by making an apostolic claim: "In accordance with the command of our Lord Jesus Christ the Savior we gathered ourselves together as he laid down for us" (ch. 1).[75] The first-person narrative recurs throughout the text until the end: "Peter said: 'Brothers, we do not command these things as those who have the power to compel, but as having a command from the Lord'" (ch. 30). Several oddities have frequently been noted in the list of apostolic names given in the Preface: both Cephas and Peter appear, as do both Nathaniel and Bartholomew. Moreover, even though twelve names are listed, only eleven apostles are given speaking roles in what follows. The exception is Jude the son of James. Stewart-Sykes follows T. Schermann in thinking Jude was a late addition to the text by a final redactor.[76]

The only real polemic of the text appears in the strong emphasis placed on the minimal role to be filled by women in the church. Apart from the laity in general, they are the only group discussed that is not to be involved with church offices, and the restrictions placed on them are made quite plain. The discussion begins in chapter 24 with Andrew urging the apostles "to establish ministry for the women." Peter suggests they consider the eucharist (ch. 25) and John points out that at the Last Supper, Jesus "did not permit the women to stand alongside of us." Martha had said it was because Jesus had seen Mary smiling, but Mary indicates that she did not, in fact, laugh. Instead, Jesus had previously said "that the weak would be saved through the strong" (ch. 26). Cephas states that women are to pray sitting on the ground, instead of standing—possibly in order to differentiate them from the men (ch. 27).[77] James concludes that the only ministry women can have is "the ministry of supporting women in need" (ch. 28).[78]

Although the discussion is not extensive—the treatise itself is quite short—it does appear that the work, like the Didascalia, is concerned to restrict carefully what women can do in liturgical service. Unlike the Didascalia, there is no office of widow or deaconess here. Possibly this text is earlier. It is certainly less detailed. Stewart-Sykes argues that the injunctions concerning women in chapters 24–28 were added by a final redactor to a previously existing church order, with one purpose: "The whole point of the discussion is to subordinate women's ministry, and in particular to legislate against women's participation in the celebration of the eucharist."[79]

---

75. Translations are taken from Stewart-Sykes, *Apostolic Church Order*.

76. T. Schermann, *Eine Elfapostelmoral oder die x-Rezension der "beiden Wege"* (Munich: Lentner 1903); Stewart-Sykes, *Apostolic Church Order*, p. 34.

77. Stewart-Sykes conjectures that the text originally involved an injunction for the women not to prophesy standing, lest they become physically out of control; *Apostolic Church Order*, pp. 113–14, n. 46.

78. Stewart-Sykes proposes an alternative translation, "supporting women in chains," and suggests that if followed the passage may refer to some kind of exorcistic ministry, a view he then rejects.

79. *Apostolic Church Order*, p. 49. It should be noted that the polemic is not an assertion of too much authority exercised specifically by deaconesses, as Jean Daniélou suggested (*The Ministry of Women*

It is interesting to see Mary and Martha mentioned in the context of a discussion of women's role at the eucharist. As Francois Bovon has pointed out, both women appear at the eucharist in the Acts of Philip 8.2, where Mary prepares the bread and salt for the meal and Martha ministers to the crowds.[80] Stewart-Sykes concludes that the passage "seems directly to speak to the situation envisaged by K [=Apostolic Church Orders], to the extent that we may suggest that K is a direct response to the liturgical role of women presupposed by Acts of Philip."[81] He goes on to suggest that the author knew of Montanist groups, with women officers, and such Gnostic groups as produced the writings connected with Mary Magdalene, and he ponders whether the final redactor "is alarmed by the situation that obtains and, rather than recognizing that this is ancient tradition, believes this to be a Gnostic innovation, so using Gnostic tools (the dialogue) and anti-Gnostic tools (apostolicity) to oppose it."[82]

Faivre agrees, concluding that in view of the role mapped out for women in the treatise, the pseudepigraphic authorship plays a decisive role in the theological claims of the text. The attribution of the church order to the apostles establishes the antiquity of the contents of the books, provides literary unity for the material, and "above all . . . gives to more recent materials an authority equal to that of authentic materials."[83]

FORGED REVELATORY TEXTS

Several forged texts that can be grouped together as "revelatory" also reflect internal Christian debates over church organization and leadership. These documents all appear to have been forged, in part, to oppose aspects of proto-orthodox forms of Christianity. Two of these texts come to us from the Nag Hammadi Library; the other is one we have already considered in the context of anti-Jewish polemic in Chapter Eleven, the Ascension of Isaiah.

The Ascension of Isaiah

As we have seen, the Ascension of Isaiah contains certain motifs otherwise widely associated with Gnostics, in particular, the ascent and descent of the Beloved, who changes into a new shape in each realm of the heavens and delivers the passwords

---

in the Early Church, London: Faith Press, 1961, p. 20). As Roger Gryson pointed out (*The Ministry of Women in the Early Church*, Collegeville, MN: Liturgical Press, 1976, p. 48), deaconesses are not mentioned here. The office of deaconess instead may have emerged from just the roles to which women were restricted in documents such as this.

80. "Mary Magdalene in the Acts of Philip," in *Which Mary? The Marys of Early Christian Tradition*, ed. F. Stanley Jones (Leiden: Brill, 2003), pp. 82–83.

81. *Apostolic Church Order*, p. 53.

82. Ibid., p. 54.

83. "Surtout, elle donne aux matériaux plus récents une autorité égale à celle des matériaux authentiques," "Apostolicité et pseudo-apostolicité," pp. 64, 66.

necessary to be granted passage. On the whole, however, the book appears to be most closely aligned with proto-orthodox theological views, even if Darrell Hannah is right that these views are somewhat "naïve."[84] Included in a vision narrated in the opening section of the book (the Martyrdom of Isaiah) is a polemical passage that appears to be directed against the leaders of the author's community, who are maligned for downplaying the importance of prophecy for the life of the church, presumably in favor of more worldly oriented hierarchy such as eventually came to dominate the orthodox tradition (3:21–31).

Robert Hall has argued that in this polemic the Ascension reflects competition among various prophetic groups in its community. For him, the text "issues from an early Christian prophetic school in conflict with other similar early Christian groups."[85] In fact, however, there is little in the text to suggest that the controversy was between prophetic groups; on the contrary, the polemic appears to be directed against a (majority) group that spurns the prophetic activities of the author and his smaller community.

The passage in question is preceded by a summary of an Isaianic vision of the Beloved's descent, crucifixion, resurrection, and ascension, followed by the coming of the Holy Spirit (3.13–20). We are then told that "afterwards, when he is at hand, his disciples will forsake the teachings of the twelve apostles" (3.21).[86] The main problem in the life of the community will be its leaders: "many who will love office though they are devoid of wisdom" (3.23). Indeed, "many elders will be lawless and violent shepherds to their sheep. . . . They will have no holy shepherds" (3.24). The leaders will be covetous; and there will be "much slandering and boasting" (3.26). More important, "there will not be many prophets nor such as speak reliable words, except a few here and there" (3.27). As a result, "great discord will arise among them" (3.29). And possibly most significant of all, they "will set aside the prophecies of the prophets which were before me and also pay no attention to these my visions" (3.31).

The first-person narrator here, of course, is Isaiah, and it is passages such as these that make the work an embedded forgery, as discussed earlier. The polemic of the passage is directed against church leaders who reject the authority of prophecy, both the visions of this Isaiah and of the other prophets of the church that arose before him.[87]

---

84. See pp. 335–37.

85. Robert G. Hall, "The *Ascension of Isaiah*: Community Situation, Date, and Place in Early Christianity," *JBL* 109 (1990): 289. Hall provides an interesting assessment of the text, but much of it comes through a rather flat mirror reading, in which any description of Isaiah and his school is taken to refer to the prophetic author and his real-life school. This is taking the approach developed by J. Louis Martyn for his reading of the Fourth Gospel to an extreme (see Martyn, *History and Theology in the Fourth Gospel*, New York: Harper and Row, 1968). For critique, see Greg Carey, "The Ascension of Isaiah: An Example of Early Christian Narrative Polemic," *JSP* 17 (1998): 65–78.

86. Translation of C. Detlef G. Müller, in Schneemelcher, *New Testament Apocrypha*.

87. It appears less likely that the author is objecting to the leaders rejecting the writings of the Old Testament prophets, since the focus is on "these my visions"—that is, the visions recorded in this very book, and hence specifically "Christian" prophecy made in the names of the prophets of old.

It is interesting to observe, in this connection, the movement away from charismatic authority in some proto-orthodox writings that discuss church leadership and organization. The Pastoral epistles, obviously reflect a very different ecclesial situation from, say, the Corinthian correspondence. In Corinth, the church was organized and run by those endowed with spiritual gifts given at baptism, including such revelatory powers as prophecy and speaking in tongues. Not so for the Pastorals, where the right to direct the church comes through the laying on of hands by the elders, given to those who meet certain standards and qualifications. Even the "prophetic utterances" that "pointed to" Timothy are ratified and brought under control of the "council of elders" through some kind of ritual of ordination (1 Tim. 4:14). Direction for this community comes from "scripture . . . preaching . . . teaching" (1 Tim. 4:13), not through relatively uncontrolled and uncontrollable prophetic utterance. Presupposed here is a hierarchical structure, which saw the apostle as the one ultimately in charge, then his appointed delegate, and then the ordained bishop and deacons. Such a community has scant space for ecstatic utterance or visions to guide the life of the community, and it is not a stretch to imagine that the hierarchy was put in place precisely to provide controls for the kind of organizational chaos that could erupt under a more charismatic system, as indeed did erupt in the community at Corinth in Paul's time. The Ascension of Isaiah appears to be reacting to this kind of relatively new "system," so that we are well served seeing in it a counterforgery, in the strong sense, to the forged apostolic authorizations of church structure such as seen in the Pastoral epistles.

We can see the same movement toward hierarchical structure play itself out, more or less before our eyes, in the Didache. For this community there continue to be charismatic prophets who visit the churches from outside and give it instructions. But they are to be treated gingerly, and at this stage of the community's history, somewhat skeptically (Didache 11–13). This is a different community from both those of the Pastorals and of the Ascension of Isaiah. But the same mechanics are involved in the development away from charisma and toward hierarchy. It is particularly striking in this connection that although the Didachist entertains healthy doubts about the viability of charismatic directives for the church, it also issues instructions for the community to appoint bishops and deacons (ch. 15), who presumably would be permanent and grounded fixtures, as opposed to the wandering charismatics who were clearly being seen already as a problem.

The Ascension of Isaiah then presents a kind of counterattack against this move toward orthodox hierarchy. The settled, antiprophetic leadership of the church is peopled by covetous, boastful, and envious leaders who are "devoid of wisdom" and who move the community in the wrong direction. God speaks through the prophets—not merely the prophets of old, such as Isaiah, but through the prophets of the present day, who have visions of God and learn the truths necessary for the proper guidance of the community.

The Coptic Apocalypse of Peter

The Coptic Apocalypse of Peter appears as tractate 3 in codex 7 of the Nag Hammadi Library. It can probably be dated to the early third century.[88] We will be looking at the work in greater length in the next chapter, since the principle thrust of its polemic involves its negative views of the flesh, over against the proto-orthodox insistence on the fleshly existence of both Christ and his followers. But there are also clear polemical charges leveled against the church hierarchy that this author, and his community, rejected, a hierarchy that has every appearance of being a majority, proto-orthodox church structure.

The Anti-Institutional Polemic

The author identifies himself as Jesus' own disciple at the outset of the treatise: "He said to me, Peter . . ." (7.70.20).[89] It is interesting to note the clear parallels between this Petrine forgery and others that are still preserved. The concluding portion of the treatise is its most famous feature, an eyewitness account of the crucifixion of Jesus, with a decidedly Gnostic twist. One cannot help but recall the words of the earlier forger of 1 Peter, who declared that he was "a witness to Christ's sufferings" (1 Pet. 5:1). The parallels with 2 Peter are particularly numerous, as I will note in a moment.

The author of the account admits that only a few of his readers will acknowledge his revelation and so come to saving knowledge. As the Savior tells him, "From you I have established a base for the remnant whom I have summoned to knowledge" (71.19–20). Those without this knowledge are "blind ones who have no guide" (72.12–13). It is, in other words, the revelatory vision of Peter, not the church leaders, that is to lead the people. And so we learn that those who teach the community, the priests and scribes who praise the Savior, are "blind and deaf" (73.13–14). They think they are praising the Savior but they are instead blaspheming.

And they welcome as their followers those who "praise the men of the propagation of falsehood, those who will come after you" (74.10–12). These would be Peter's supposed successors, who were presumably the leaders of the churches in his wake. But the members of the community "will become greatly defiled and they will fall into a name of error and into the hand of an evil cunning man and a manifold dogma, and they will be ruled heretically" (74.16–23). Moreover, "some of them will blaspheme the truth and proclaim evil teaching" (74.22–25).

These church leaders proclaim what they think is truth, but they misunderstand what it is they preach; at the same time, they arrogantly think they have a corner on the truth: "some who do not understand mystery speak of things which

---

88. Thus Henriette W. Havelaar, ed., *The Coptic Apocalypse of Peter (Nag-Hammadi Codex VII, 3)* (Berlin: Akademie Verlag, 1999).

89. Translations are those of James Brashler and Roger A. Bullard in Robinson, *NHL*.

they do not understand, but they will boast that the mystery of the truth is theirs alone" (76.27–34). What is more, "many others who oppose the truth and are the messengers of error, will set up their error and their law against these pure thoughts of mine. . . . They do business in my word" (77.22–78.1). The author then moves to specifics, making it perfectly clear that he has been referring to the appointed leaders of the (proto-orthodox) churches: "And there shall be others of those who are outside our number who name themselves bishop and also deacons, as if they have received their authority from God. They bend themselves under the judgment of the leaders. Those people are dry canals" (79.22–31).

These appointed officers of the church will be hugely successful. Peter fears that "there are multitudes that will mislead other multitudes of living ones, and destroy them among themselves. And when they speak your name they will be believed" (80.3–7). To this the Savior responds: "for a time determined for them in proportion to their error they will rule over the little ones" (80.8–11). But these leaders "say evil things against each other" (74.26–27) and they "are divided among themselves" (82.33).

The Targets of the Polemic

There is strong disagreement among scholars whether the Coptic Apocalypse of Peter, in its entirety, is directed against only one set of enemies or is, instead, fighting battles on numerous fronts, with three or even as many as seven opposing groups in view.[90] What can be said, clearly, is that the main enemy of its polemic in the portions just cited is the proto-orthodox church structure with its bishops and deacons (and, as we will see in Chapter Thirteen, with its doctrine of crucifixion rooted in an understanding of the need for Christ actually to have died in the flesh for salvation). How does one explain this anti-ecclesiastical rhetoric precisely on the pen of Peter, chief of Jesus' disciples, allegedly first bishop of Rome and hero of the proto-orthodox community?

The foundational study of the polemic of the Coptic Apocalypse of Peter, still very much worth reading more than thirty years on, is Klaus Koschorke, *Die Polemik der Gnostiker gegen das kirchliche Christentum.*[91] Koschorke argued that there are seven groups attacked in various portions of the text, but that they all can be subsumed under one major group, which consists of the leaders of the proto-orthodox churches. At stake ultimately is the struggle between the two groups, the Petrine Gnostics on one hand and the leaders of the proto-orthodox churches on the other. This is a battle over winning support from the masses of Christians.

Henriette Havelaar goes a step farther, arguing that the community behind the Coptic Apocalypse of Peter was a splinter group from the proto-orthodox

90. See Havelaar, *The Coptic Apocalypse of Peter,* ch. 6. For an argument that seven heretical groups are under attack, and that the polemic against the bishop and deacons is specifically directed against a Manichaean group, see Michel Tardieu, "Hérésiographie de l'Apocalypse de Pierre," in *Histoire et conscience historique dans les civilisations du Proche-Orient ancient* (Leuven: Peeters, 1989), pp. 33–39.

91. Leiden: Brill, 1978.

majority, a group that started out within the community, developed "aberrant" views, was excluded from the community, developed these views further, and then entered into a polemical exchange with the larger group. Although Havelaar does not draw attention to the similarities, the model is highly reminiscent of the views of the Johannine community and its secessionists mapped out by J. Louis Martyn and Raymond Brown.[92] The model, in this case, would explain why both communities make use of similar traditions. The Coptic Apocalypse of Peter, like proto-orthodox writings, uses a good number of the books that later became part of the New Testament; it focuses on the passion narrative and stresses the relationship between Peter and Jesus. At the same time, there are striking differences, precisely at the places of overlap, for example in the value of church offices and in the reality of the flesh and fleshly suffering of Jesus.

An even more specific proposal has been developed by Birger Pearson, who takes up the argument of Terrence Smith that there is a direct literary relationship between the Coptic Apocalypse of Peter and the pseudepigraphic 2 Peter.[93] Pearson maintains that Smith is wrong to think that the Apocalypse is a direct polemic against 2 Peter (if it were, it would be a counterforgery in the strong sense); instead he thinks the Apocalypse is reading the book of 2 Peter in a Gnostic way, appropriating its message, sympathetically, in a different context.[94]

In particular, Pearson is impressed by the fact that the Apocalypse portrays Peter as "the founder of the Gnostic community and the chief protagonist in a struggle against orthodox ecclesiastical Christianity." This is Peter, the founder of the Roman church, of all people.[95] It is also striking that the work makes extensive use of materials drawn, evidently, from the Gospel of Matthew, which was otherwise used to establish Peter as the "rock" of the Catholic church.[96] But there are especially striking verbal parallels with 2 Peter, which Pearson lists at length. Most intriguing is the polemic against church leaders as "dry canals" (79.30–31), strikingly close to 2 Peter's polemic against those who "are waterless springs" (2:17). In Pearson's view, the author of the Coptic Apocalypse has slightly modified the image in light of "an Egyptian geographical environment."[97]

One is also struck by the "strong eschatological expectation" of the Coptic Apocalypse, which may not be expected in a Gnostic work. But judgment is said to come on the false teachers at the parousia; and nowhere is the parousia more

---

92. On Martyn, *History and Theology*; Brown, *Community of the Beloved Disciple* (New York: Paulist, 1979).

93. Birger A. Pearson, "The Apocalypse of Peter and the Canonical 2 Peter," in *Gnosticism and the Early Christian World*, ed. James Goehring et al. (Sonoma, CA: Polebridge Press, 1990), pp. 67–74; in reference to Terrence V. Smith, *Petrine Controversies in Early Christianity: Attitudes towards Peter in Christian Writings of the First Two Centuries* (Tübingen: Mohr/Siebeck, 1985), pp. 43–54, 137–41.

94. Havelaar is not convinced that there is any relationship between the two works at all. *Coptic Apocalypse*, ch. 5.

95. Pearson, "Apocalypse of Peter," p. 68.

96. For use of NT materials in the Apocalypse of Peter, see Havelaar, *Coptic Apocalypse*, ch. 5.

97. P. 71.

in evidence than in 2 Peter. "Now we have a Gnostic text that not only contains a vigorous eschatological expectation but even uses 2 Peter itself in giving expression to it." Pearson cites a number of other parallels between the two texts as well, and concludes that the author of the Coptic Apocalypse has found 2 Peter "a very congenial piece of Petrine teaching, one that can freely be used in his own presentation of Petrine *gnosis*."[98]

The Coptic Apocalypse does not engage with polemic against the views of 2 Peter, however; instead, it uses the language and images of 2 Peter in order to attack the proto-orthodox ecclesiastical establishment. Here we have two Petrine forgeries, one building on the other and interpreting it in its own context in order to attack Christians who also use Peter for precisely the opposite purpose, to justify the church hierarchy that was destined to prevail within the early Christian movement. The Coptic Apocalypse of Peter, then, is a minority voice in the struggle to establish dominance within the broader community. Its protests went virtually unheard, as the church refused to move away from a hierarchical organization, but in just the opposite direction, as Peter came to be thought of as the head of the church or Rome, the leader of all the churches of Christendom. It was the "dry canals" that won the day, and the Peter of orthodoxy who triumphed over the Peter of the Gnostics.[99]

The Paraphrase of Shem

The Paraphrase of Shem, the first tractate in Nag Hammadi codex 7, is another Gnostic apocalypse, although there are debates over its particular Gnostic allegiances. Given our limited knowledge of the followers of Basilides, it is difficult to conclude with M. Tardieu that the text is best understood as a Basilidean production.[100] The view of Michel Roberge appears more credible, that even though the

---

98. P. 71.

99. Some scholars have argued that the Apocryphon of James from codex 1 of the Nag Hammadi Library has a polemical bent similar to the Coptic Apocalypse of Peter. Madeleine Scopello in particular has urged that the figure of Peter in the text is portrayed as a somewhat dull and unreceptive recipient of Jesus' revelation, in contrast to the hero of the text, James. In this view, the ultimate point of the text is that Gnostics require no intermediaries for salvation, unlike the members of the proto-orthodox church, who require the ecclesiastical structure to be saved. This may, however, be an overreading of the book in a polemical direction not warranted by the text itself. (Madeleine Scopello, "The Secret Book of James," Introduction in Marvin Meyer, ed., *The Nag Hammadi Scriptures*, pp. 19–22.) By contrast, see also Donald Rouleau, *L'Épître apocryphe de Jacques (NH I, 2)*, Bibliothèque copte de Nag Hammadi, Section "Textes" 18 (Quebec: Les Presses de l'Université Laval; Louvain: Peeters, 1987), pp. 25–27, who stresses that in the account, Peter as well as James is set apart by Jesus to receive his revelation, and they both receive it equally; the other disciples ask both of them what the revelation was at the end, and they both reply and give the right answer. It is true that Peter betrays a misunderstanding of Jesus, but James too is represented as not comprehending Jesus and his message (chs. 5–6).

100. "Commemoration gnostique de Sem." In *La commemoration*, ed. Ph. Gignoux (Louvain: Peeters, 1988), pp. 219–23. Tardieu dates the text to the end of the fourth century, as an attack on the post-Constantinian church.

author "follows his own way," he appears to have been heavily influenced by both Sethian and Valentinian systems, the latter, in particular, because he embraces a tripartite anthropology comprising psychics, noetics, and pneumatics.[101]

The revelation in the text is delivered by the son of infinite Light, Derdekeas, to Shem, the son of Noah. For our purposes, it is important that the account is written in the first person, allegedly by Shem himself, "The paraphrase about the unbegotten Spirit—what Derdekeas revealed to me, Shem. . . . My thought in my body snatched me away from my race and carried me up to the summit of creation. . . . I heard a voice speaking to me, Shem, since you are from pure power. . . ." (1.1–19).[102] Like other apocalypses, in other words, this is pseudepigraphic. The revelation involves both a Gnostic cosmogony and anthropogony, but then moves to a historical description of key salvific events: the flood, the overthrow of Sodom, the baptism of the Savior, and his ascent at the crucifixion, ending in two eschatological discourses and a description of Shem's ascent to the planetary spheres.

Of particular interest is the polemic of the work, which begins in 30.4–31.14 with the appearance of the "demon" who comes "to baptize with an imperfect baptism and to disturb the world with bondage of water." This is none other than John the Baptist, whose water baptism is a baptism "in error" and is described as "the baptism of the demon." This denigration of John's baptism sets up the discourse directed against the church's practices of baptism.

The polemical character of the account is evident in a revelation of Derdekeas to Shem in 34.16–36.24: "Many in the generation of Nature will seek the security of power, but they will not find it, nor will they be able to fulfill the will of Faith. For they are the seed of universal Darkness" (35.7–13). In contrast are "the perceptive." As Derdekeas reveals "I disclosed to them all the concepts and teaching of the righteous" (36.9–11). The others—those who are not perceptive and are tied to "the flesh"—will be led astray, thinking that baptism in water will save them. This becomes clear in the disparagement of Christian baptism by Derdekeas:

> Then many who wear flesh that leads them astray will descend into the harmful waters by means of the winds and the demons, and they are bound with the water. But water will provide an ineffective treatment. It will mislead and bind the world. . . . O Shem, people are deceived by the many forms of demons, and they think that through the baptism of unclean water this substance that is dark, feeble, ineffective, and disturbing will take away sins. They do not know that coming from the water and going to the water are bondage, error, defilement, envy, murder, adultery, false witness, heresies, robberies, lusts, babbling, wrath, bitterness. (36.25–38.28)

101. "The Paraphrase of Shem," in Marvin Meyer, ed., *Nag Hammadi Scriptures*, pp. 437–47.

102. Translations are taken from Roberge, "Paraphrase of Shem."

The upshot of this revelation then becomes clear: "I proclaim to those who have a mind that they must abandon defiled baptism . . . for where water has been invoked, there is Nature with a ritual formula, a lie, and injury."

There follows a peculiar description of the beheading of a female figure "Rebouel." The gruesome act, however, is presented as a good thing. Rebouel has "the perception you will reveal upon the earth," and so Shem can proclaim, "Blessed is Rebouel among all generations of people, for you alone have seen and will listen" (40.12–15). What is the meaning of her beheading? Roberge argues, "Just as Rebouel is declared blessed in her beheading, so the noetics should not hesitate to separate from the great church (early orthodoxy) which practices baptism, and enter the community of those who possess gnosis."[103]

This, in short, is another case of Gnostic polemic against proto-orthodoxy, one that in particular rejects the practice of baptism: "the writing is best explained as the product of a group living on the fringe of Christianity and urging the members of the great church to separate and join the community of those who possess gnosis."[104] It is impossible to identify the target of the attack with any greater specificity; but it is worth noting, with J.-D. Dubois, that the polemic accords well with the two treatises that follow the Paraphrase of Shem in codex 7, the anonymous Second Treatise of the Great Seth and the forged Apocalypse of Peter, which we have already considered. In Dubois's opinion, it is probably no accident that these three polemical attacks on proto-orthodoxy are grouped together in the codex.[105]

---

103. Ibid., p. 445.

104. P. 445. Roberge goes on to make the less plausible suggestion that the polemic may instead have focused on Elchasaites, with their practice of multiple baptisms and therapeutic baths.

105. J.-D. Dubois, "Contribution à l'interprétation de la Paraphrase de Sem," *Deuxième journée d'études coptes* (Louvain: Peeters, 1986), pp. 150–60.

CHAPTER THIRTEEN

Forgeries Involving Debates over the Flesh

None of the theological controversies of the second and third Christian centuries was as heated or prolonged as the debate over the status of the flesh, both the real flesh of Jesus before and after his resurrection and the flesh of his followers, alternately spurned and embraced by Christians of varying persuasion. The debates over the flesh were carried out not only in the realm of the heresiological literature—with famous stands taken by such stalwart advocates of orthodoxy as Irenaeus and Tertullian—but also within a surprising number of forged texts from the period. We have, as a result, apostolic pseudepigrapha that take positions on both ends of the spectrum, some arguing against the "grotesque" notion that Christ was a man of real flesh and that his resurrection—and that of his followers—involved a reanimation of the flesh, and others arguing with equal vehemence the opposite view, that Christ's incarnation was fully in the flesh, as was his resurrection, in anticipation of the fleshly resurrection of his followers, yet to be. As might be expected, we have fewer surviving representatives of the former position, in no small measure because its supporters succumbed and their literary advocacies were, as a result, relegated to the trash heaps of perverse theological curiosities. We begin with these few apostolic denigrations of the flesh.

FORGERIES THAT OPPOSE THE FLESH

The Coptic Apocalypse of Peter

I have already discussed one important aspect of the Coptic Apocalypse of Peter in the preceding chapter, as this striking revelation to Peter of the true nature of the crucifixion of Jesus was written, in no small measure, to oppose the hierarchical developments within the proto-orthodox community. The treatise attacks not only church leaders, however, but also anyone who maintains that Christ was really a man of the flesh, whose bodily torment and death had any role to play in human salvation. It is no accident that the separationist Christology of the text—in which a clear demarcation is made between the fleshly shell of the Savior and his true inner essence—is placed on the pen of Peter, otherwise celebrated as the leader of the proto-orthodox community that this author opposes.

Peter and True Insight

The Petrine authorship of the book is established in its opening sentence, "As the Savior was sitting in the temple . . . he said to me, 'Peter, blessed are those above belonging to the Father. . . . '"[1] One is immediately drawn to parallels in the canonical traditions, especially the apocalyptic discourse of Mark 13, given at the explicit request of Peter and other disciples while overlooking the Temple. The connections to 1 Peter (whose author was "a witness to Christ's sufferings") and yet more extensively 2 Peter, have already been discussed.

Early on in the treatise the polemical tone is set. It is the ones who "belong to the Father" who are blessed; and Peter is reminded that the Savior intended that those "who are from the life . . . may hear my word and distinguish words of unrighteousness and transgression of law from righteousness" (70.24–32). And so there is a clear difference between the true teaching of the Savior and teachings that derive from elsewhere. So too these sundry teachings differentiate groups of alleged followers from one another. Only a few (the "remnant") hear the true revelation of Christ and so come to saving knowledge: "From you I have established a base for the remnant whom I have summoned to knowledge" (71.19–21). Those without this knowledge are "blind ones who have no guide" (72.12–13). These "others" are polemicized against throughout: they "say evil things against each other" (74.26–27) and "are divided among themselves" (82.33). The object of attack, as we have seen, is the proto-orthodox community headed by the deceived "bishops and deacons" (79.25–26).

The group is misguided not only because they follow blind leaders who are "dry canals" (79.31) but even more because they subscribe to false views, insisting on the importance of the fleshly body of Christ and on the salvific significance of his death. Looking only to the externals, they do not see the true, inner, hidden meaning of both Christ and his crucifixion. To illustrate this problem at the outset, the author presents the strange scene in which the Savior instructs Peter to see precisely by putting his hands over his eyes, and to hear by placing his hands over his ears (72.10–73.22). After an initial confusion, Peter comes to understand the point. What seems to be happening in the physical world of sensation in fact masks what is really happening, as can be detected not through the physical senses, which need to be obliterated, but through spiritual insight, which comes only when one turns from the outward and physical. Only some people

1. Quotations taken from James Brashler and Roger Bullard, "Apocalypse of Peter," in *NHL*.

can see: those who abandon the importance of flesh and the physical nature of existence. It is those who look with their physical eyes who are blind ("If you want to know their blindness, put your hands upon your eyes . . . and say what you see"; 72.13–17).

The Christological Polemic

The primary target of the author's polemic is the false teaching about the importance of Christ's (real) death. The blind leaders of the opposition, and their followers, called the "men of the propagation of falsehood" err because they "cleave to the name of a dead man, thinking that they will become pure" (74.11–15). That is to say, they think that it is the crucifixion that brings salvation (the dead Jesus instead of the living one). On the contrary, those who hold such views "will become greatly defiled and they will fall into a name of error and into the hand of an evil cunning man and a manifold dogma and they will be ruled heretically" (74.16–22).

The alternative Christology proposed by the author is not, strictly speaking, docetic (i.e. phantasmal), but separationist, in which the outer shell of the man Jesus, which gets crucified, is of no ultimate significance for salvation; it is the real Jesus, the inner spiritual being, that matters.[2] That the suffering of the shell has no connection with the real savior is a view found in other Nag Hammadi treatises as well, including the First Apocalypse of James (5.3, 5.31.17–18), the Second Apocalypse of James (5.4), and the Letter of Peter to Philip (8.2).[3] The view is portrayed with particular poignancy here, in the famous culminating scene of the tractate, where Peter observes the crucifixion of Jesus from afar, while speaking to the Savior:

> When he had said those things, I saw him seemingly being seized by them. And I said, "What do I see, O Lord, that it is you yourself whom they take, and that you are grasping me? Or who is this one glad and laughing [above] the tree. And is it another one whose feet and hands they are striking?"
>
> The Savior said to me, "He whom you saw [above] the tree, glad and laughing, this is the living Jesus. But this one into whose hands and feet they drive the nails is his fleshly part, which is the substitute, being put to shame, the one who came into being in his likeness." (81.3–23)

To his increased amazement, Peter then sees "someone about to approach us resembling him, even him who was laughing." This one was filled "with a Holy Spirit" and is also said to be the Savior. "And there was a great ineffable light

2. On the difference between a docetic and a separationist Christology, see Ehrman, *Orthodox Corruption of Scripture*, pp. 140–45, 212–19.

3. Cf. Havelaar, *Coptic Apocalypse of Peter*, p. 190: "the idea of a division between the real Savior who cannot suffer and the material Jesus who is crucified is a common theme in the Nag Hammadi corpus."

around them and the multitude of ineffable and invisible angels blessing them." This one—seemingly yet another image of Christ—explains:

> He whom they crucified is the first-born, and the home of demons, and the stony vessel in which they dwell, of Elohim, of the cross, which is under the Law. But he who stands near him is the living Savior, the first in him, whom they seized and released, who stands joyfully looking at those who did him violence, while they are divided among themselves. Therefore he laughs at their lack of perception, knowing that they are born blind. So then the one susceptible to suffering shall come, since the body is the substitute. But what they released was my incorporeal body. But I am the intellectual Spirit filled with radiant light. He whom you saw coming to me is our intellectual Pleroma. (82.4–83.13)

There are numerous well-known ambiguities about this passage. Among other things, although interpreters are broadly agreed that there is a clear and fundamental distinction made between the material body of Christ and his real spiritual self, there are strong disagreements about the nature and unity of the latter, with some scholars such as Luttikhuizen thinking that it (the nonmaterial part) consists of two essences, corresponding more or less to soul and spirit, and others such as Havelaar who speak of a "tripartite Savior," comprising the "intellectual Pleroma," the "intellectual or Holy Spirit" and the "incorporeal body or living Savior" that is connected to the material body.[4] This disagreement is not of vital significance for my purposes here. What matters instead is the differentiation drawn between the material part of Christ, which is crucified, and the spiritual part(s), which cannot and do not suffer. The fleshly part of Christ is "the home of demons" and belongs to "Elohim" the creator God of this world. It is of no real importance to the living Jesus. Those who think they can harm the living Jesus are "blind" and do not "know what they are saying" (81.30–32). That is why the Savior "laughs at their lack of perception, knowing that they are blind" (83.1–3). The opponents of Christ think they have destroyed the Savior, but in fact they have only put themselves to shame. It is not the fleshly body of Jesus—and thus his physical death—that ultimately matters. That was a charade. What matters is the inner Jesus, the spiritual Savior who escapes torment and cannot be killed.

So too with the followers of the Savior. Their material flesh is not what matters. What matters is the spirit within. And so, as Havelaar notes, the crucifixion of Jesus is "an example of the repudiation of the material world."[5]

---

4. Gerard P. Luttikhuizen, "The Suffering Jesus and the Invulnerable Christ in the Gnostic *Apocalypse of Peter*," in Jan Bremmer, ed., *The Apocalypse of Peter* (Leuven: Peeters, 2003), pp. 187–99; Havelaar, *The Coptic Apocalypse of Peter*, p. 179.

5. Havelaar, *Coptic Apocalypse of Peter*, p. 186.

One of the striking features of the passage is the Savior who laughs at his own crucifixion. We meet this image elsewhere, most notably in the Gospel of Basilides, unfortunately no longer extant, but mentioned by Irenaeus (*Adv. Haer.* 1.24.4), and in the Second Treatise of the Great Seth (7.62.27–64.20). The idea that the Savior could be killed was, for many Gnostics, completely risible. Jesus laughs for other, but related, reasons four times in the Gospel of Judas. A comparable motif occurs in the "Gnostic" chapters of the Acts of John, where John is portrayed as laughing at the wooden cross. A similar view, without such humor, occurs in the Letter of Peter to Philip, which insists that Jesus was "a stranger to these sufferings" (8.139.21–11). As with this final instance, the authority of such views was significantly heightened when expressed not simply as a trustworthy revelation of secret knowledge, but pseudepigraphically in the name of one who would know. In the Coptic Apocalypse it is to Simon Peter, Jesus' closest disciple, the foundation on which, allegedly, the (proto-orthodox) church was built, that Jesus reveals his true spiritual nature and the complete insignificance of his material, fleshly existence.

False Teachers and False Teachings

It is central to the understanding of the Coptic Apocalypse of Peter that its two parts—the revelation of Jesus concerning the false teachers of the church and the vision of Peter revealing the false understandings of Christ's material nature—are linked thematically by ideas of knowledge and ignorance. The church leaders who are misled and who mislead others are like those who crucify Jesus, thinking that they know the truth when in fact they are misled by appearances. The ultimate reality is not material but spiritual. The church leaders are blind and ignorant, people of the flesh instead of the spirit, devoted to the creator Elohim and so enslaved to the Law, rather than perceiving the true divine being who is the radiant savior.

These church leaders not only fail to understand the true God, thinking that he is Elohim, and Christ, thinking that he is a dead man: they also misunderstand Peter, who is the foundation for the "remnant" that has knowledge. Peter sees that Christ is not the "dead man" who was crucified, but the living, laughing savior who is an incorporeal body (83.7) and who was "released" from his flesh (82.30). Just as God and Christ are falsely proclaimed by the proto-orthodox community, so too Peter is falsely claimed in support of the community's errant theological and Christological views. The forgery of the book functions, then, not only to correct the proto-orthodox community in its doctrinal assertions but also to rob it of its apostolic foundation. The person claimed by the proto-orthodox as the guarantor of the truth of its message shows that this message is rooted in ignorance, blindness, and error.

Part of this error is the claim that truth was anticipated in the Scriptures given by the God of the Old Testament. In fact, prior to the coming of Christ "they did not find him, nor was he mentioned among any generation of the prophet. He has now appeared among these, in him who appeared, who is the Son of Man" (71.6–12). It is not the scriptures of Elohim that reveal Christ, as the proto-orthodox insist. Only Christ himself reveals the truth of God. And it has nothing to do with the material world of the creator.

This pseudonymous attack on materiality, on the significance of Jesus' real bodily death, and on the world of the flesh comes to us as a minority voice among the extant Christian writings of antiquity. As we will see, the proto-orthodox position is, as one would expect, far better represented in our surviving remains. The one-time vitality of this Gnostic view should not be underplayed, however. The orthodox response was so virulent and extensive precisely because of the attractiveness and widespread effect that the opposition to the flesh had in the early Christian movement. Some of the proto-orthodox response came likewise in forgeries, some of them penned in the name of Peter, including at least one other apocalypse that he allegedly wrote.

The Book of Thomas the Contender

The Book of Thomas the Contender comes to us as tractate 7 of codex 2 from Nag Hammadi. It is generally recognized as a late-second- or early-third-century work, whose major theme, in the words of John Turner, is "unbending asceticism that condemns anything to do with the flesh, supplemented by the Platonic-Hermetic-Gnostic theme of salvation by self-knowledge."[6] The book allegedly records the words of Thomas as written by "Matthias," who could be either Matthew the disciple and Gospel writer or Matthias the apostle elected to replace Judas Iscariot after the resurrection. In either case, the work is pseudepigraphic, or, rather, doubly pseudepigraphic, as it purports not only to be written by an apostle but also to record faithfully the words delivered to another (Thomas). Thomas and Matthew are linked in other Thomasine writings (cf. Gospel of Thomas, 13) and other Gnostic works, such as the Pistis Sophia, where Mariam exclaims that Jesus secretly taught his revelation to Philip, Thomas, and Matthew (1.43).

The book comprises two parts, a lengthy dialogue between Jesus and his twin brother Judas Thomas, and a monologue delivered by Jesus (the final two-fifths of the text).[7] The discussion is placed just before Jesus' ascension (138.23). In a way reminiscent of the Gospel of Thomas, it begins with "the secret words that the savior spoke to Judas Thomas" (138.1–2).[8] In this case, however, it is clear that Thomas is to be understood specifically as the brother of Jesus, as Jesus addresses

6. John D. Turner, "The Book of Thomas and the Platonic Jesus," in Louis Painchaud and Paul-Hubert Poirier, eds., *L'évangile selon Thomas et les textes de Nag Hammadi* (Québec: Presses de l'Université Laval / Louvain: Peeters, 2007), p. 601.

7. Turner suggests that the book may represent a secondary combination of two originally distinct treatises: (1) an older dialogue that had been created by dissecting an earlier epitome of Plato's teaching on the soul and making it into a series of expositions on this teaching by Jesus in response to questions; and (2) a collection of dominical sayings reminiscent of Q, with woes and blessings. When the two works were combined, the whole was then attributed to Thomas. See Turner, "The Book of Thomas."

8. Quotations are taken from John D. Turner, "The Book of Thomas the Contender," in *NHL*.

"brother Thomas" (138.4) and indicates that "it has been said that you are my twin and true companion" (138.7–8). There is obviously no one better to receive the Savior's ultimate teachings about this world and the humans in it.[9]

The revelation is almost entirely about gnosis, self-knowledge:

> I will reveal to you the things you have pondered in your mind . . . examine yourself and learn who you are, in what way you exist, and how you will come to be. . . . It is not fitting that you be ignorant of yourself. . . . For he who has not known himself has known nothing, but he who has known himself has at the same time already achieved knowledge about the depth of the all. (138.6–18)

Whether or not one ultimately considers the book "Gnostic," there are certainly Gnostic terms and concepts in it: "depth of the All" (138.18), the Pleroma (138.34), the doctrine for the perfect (139.10), "you will find rest" (145.11); the Archon in charge of this world who will punish those attached to it (142.26–143.7). But ultimately there is no Gnostic mythology either explicated or underlying the views of the text. Instead, it presents a view of rigorous asceticism grounded in Platonic understandings of image versus reality, and a concordant denigration of the flesh. The book may well have been amenable to a Gnostic construal, and could conceivably have been produced, in its current state, by a Gnostic author, but its concerns are not distinctively Gnostic.

Of greater importance for my purposes here is the centrality of the "flesh" to the text. This can be seen at the outset, when Thomas asks to be told about the things that are invisible, leading Jesus to deliberate on the physical, visible (human) body that will decay, controlled by the blaze of lust and destined to perish and be lost (138.10–139.12, 33–37). This then is the point of the entire treatise; it is an attack on the flesh and on those who cave in to its fiery desires. And so human bodies are said to be "bestial" (139.6). Jesus teaches that the body survives by eating other creatures and so changes; but anything that changes "will decay and perish, and has no hope of life from then on" (139.4–6). Moreover, bodies come into being through intercourse, just as happens with "beasts"; as a result humans cannot beget anything that is nonbestial (139.8–11). The goal of existence is for the "elect" to "abandon bestiality," that is, escape their fleshly

9. It is not important to my purposes here to determine where the book fits more broadly within the Thomasine tradition of early Christianity. Turner argues that the book occupies a "median position" between the Gospel of Thomas and the Acts of Thomas, in terms of date, dominance of the figure of Thomas, and development of genre (it lies between a list of sayings and a full narrative). Moreover, in this sequence the notion of sexual renunciation becomes increasingly dominant from one book to the next. Paul-Hubert Poirer, however, does not think the three books can be linked together ("The Writings Ascribed to Thomas and the Thomas Tradition," in *The Nag Hammadi Library after Fifty Years*, Leiden: Brill, 1997, pp. 295–307). Schenke goes even farther to argue that the Book of Thomas stands outside the Thomasine tradition (H.-M. Schenke, *Das Thomas Buch [Nag Hammadi-Codexes II, 7]*, Berlin: Akademie-Verlag, 1989, 65).

bodies (139.28–31). For in fact, "the vessel of their flesh will dissolve." And so Jesus pronounces a "woe" on those "who hope in the flesh and in the prison that will perish" (143.10–11).

One problem with those who live in and for the flesh is that they "suppose that the imperishable will perish too" (143.12–13); that is, they think that this life in the flesh is all there is, and that nothing survives the death of the body. And so Jesus pronounces a series of twelve woes on those who give themselves up to the desires of the flesh, who hope in the flesh, who are in the grip of the burning of lust of their flesh, who engage in sexual intercourse and do not receive the true doctrine (143.9–145.1). These woes are followed by three blessings for those who have "prior knowledge of the stumbling blocks," who are persecuted for their message, but who "will be released from every bondage" (145.1–8). Jesus' final exhortation sums up his urgent message:

> Watch and pray that you not come to be in the flesh, but rather that you come forth from the bondage of the bitterness of this life. . . . For when you come forth from the sufferings and passions of the body, you will receive rest from the good one, and you will reign with the king. (145.8–14)

As intimated in some of the preceding quotations, a controlling metaphor of the work is the image of "fire." The illuminating power of the "light" of the sun is set in contrast with the "fire" that burns within human bodies and makes them drunk in mind and deranged in soul (139.33–37). This fire is the bodily passions, "The lust that scorches the spirits of men" (140.3–4). Ironically, this fire will "blind them with insatiable lust and burn their souls" (140.25–26). It is an imitative fire, which gives people an "illusion of truth" but in fact leads them to be imprisoned "in a dark sweetness" (140.21–24).

This passage is nothing so much as an exposition of Plato's Allegory of the Cave: the sun, the fire, the people bound by chains who do not recognize the true light because of the effects of the fire, the ultimate contrast of images versus reality, and so on (*Republic*, 514–20). The heavy Platonism of the Book of Thomas is, in fact, evident throughout, as elucidated in particular by Turner: "In the Book of Thomas, the teaching of Jesus has become Platonized, while Plato's teaching on the soul has become Christianized." The "metaphysical axis" of the book is the Platonic opposition between appearance and reality; its hortatory force is the insistence that the soul must be set free from the bodily appetites that constrain it.[10]

In addition, there is a good deal of eschatological incentive in the piece, which Turner argues is also platonically inspired, but which may as well have come from the early Christian tradition. "Only a little while longer" and that which is visible "will dissolve" (141:14–15). When it does, "shapeless shades . . . will forever

10. Turner, "Book of Thomas and the Platonic Jesus," pp. 606–7. Turner's article enumerates numerous parallels with the *Phaedo, Phaedrus, Republic,* and *Timaeus*.

dwell upon the corpses in pain and corruption of soul" (141.16–18). Moreover, people "will be thrown down to the abyss and be afflicted by the torment of the bitterness of their evil nature" because they "fulfill the lust of their fathers" (141.32–34). Those who do not come to the truth will find that the fire they follow (the lust of their flesh) will be "the fire that will burn them" (142.2). Those who reject the message of Jesus will be turned over to "the ruler above who rules over all the powers as their king" and he will cast them into the abyss and imprison them in "a narrow dark place" (142.28–35). These souls will be scourged with fire and find fire wherever they turn (142.42–143.7). The flesh may be destined for extinction, but the fire of its passions will burn forever.

It is clear that the forger of this text was involved in some kind of community conflict. The "woes" that are leveled against others are directed toward members of the larger community, those who refuse to engage in the ascetic life that Christ demands and instead value the flesh and so indulge in its passions. This polemical context is seen as well in 141.19–143.7, where Thomas wonders what to say to the "blind" people who do not agree with the teaching. The Savior replies that scoffers will devour each other and suffer horribly in the afterlife. And in fact there is little reason to try to convert the outsiders. This document is meant for those inside the ascetic subgroup of the community; those outside are "ignorant fools" and "blind," and so beyond the pale. They place their hope in the flesh, and for that reason they will be punished forever, not raised to eternal glory. It is those who escape the flesh, and the demands of its desires, who will be liberated to enjoy a blessed afterlife.

The authority for these views is ensured by the identity of its authors. These are the words delivered directly by Jesus himself to his twin brother Thomas, faithfully recorded by the apostle Matthias.

The Gospel of Thomas

We have already examined sayings of the Coptic Gospel of Thomas in chapters dealing with eschatology and anti-Judaism. A third and final set of polemics evident in the text involves sayings that denigrate the flesh and the material world it inhabits. Six of the 114 sayings merit investigation.

Saying 29

When Jesus claims that "If the flesh came into being because of the spirit, it is a marvel"[11] he is almost certainly not referring to the "Holy Spirit" but to the spirit that resides within humans, set here in contrast to the human flesh.[12] It is difficult to imagine that flesh arose because of spirit, for example as a place of housing or imprisonment. But the option, that the "spirit came into existence be-

11. Translations taken from Ehrman and Pleše, *Apocryphal Gospels*, pp. 303–35.

12. Contra DeConick, *The Original Gospel of Thomas*, p. 135.

cause of the body," is beyond imagining. That would be a "marvel of marvels." Already Johannes Leipoldt recognized that this alternative does not mean that hearers should be struck with awe that such a thing has happened; on the contrary, "marvel of marvels" indicates that this is a hypothetical possibility that the saying rejects.[13] Read in this way, the three parts of the saying cohere and form an original unity, contra Plisch, who contends that part three of the saying—"I marvel at this, how this great wealth has come to dwell in this poverty"—as incongruous must not originally have belonged with the other two.[14] The parts do in fact belong together, and they function to show the denigration of the flesh as inferior to the spirit. "This great wealth" is the spirit; "this poverty" is the flesh—a completely impoverished existence. It is a marvel to the author that the greatness of spirit has made its home in such a pathetic vessel.

And so Valantasis is probably wrong when he claims that the saying's "problematizing of the world does not denigrate it, but makes it a place of wonder."[15] The world is, to be sure, a place where wonder takes place. But this material existence is itself impoverished and the saying maligns it. That is why, in saying 27, Thomas indicates that one must "fast from the world"; and it is why, as we will see, saying 56 insists that in fact this world is a dead "corpse."

Saying 37

We have already considered the meaning of this verse and some of the scholarship devoted to it in Chapter Eight.[16] In part the verse rejects the expectation of the disciples that there is to be a future apocalyptic salvific moment. But in championing an alternative perspective the saying undermines a basic assumption of futuristic eschatology: this material word and the physical bodies that people inhabit are to be transformed in a cataclysmic act of God. For the Gospel of Thomas, salvation does not come *in* the body through an act of future redemption; it comes *from* the body as people learn that this fleshly existence is to be superseded, and so escaped, in order to experience the joys of salvation. It is "when you strip naked without being ashamed and take your clothes, place them under your feet like little children, and stamp on them" that salvation occurs. Here clothes are emblematic of the physical, material body inhabited by the spirit. It is only by discarding it and trampling on the physical shell of one's existence that the spirit can be set free, and so "will see the Son of the Living One, and . . . not be afraid."

Saying 56

The terse saying 56 arguably summarizes better than any other the Gospel of Thomas's understanding of the material world: "The one who has come to know

---

13. Johannes Leipoldt, *Das Evangelium nach Thomas* TU 101 (Berlin: Akademie Verlag, 1967), p. 62.

14. *The Gospel of Thomas*, p. 96.

15. *The Gospel of Thomas*, p. 104.

16. See pp. 234–35.

the world has found a corpse; and the one who has found the corpse, the world is not worthy of that person." The world, when truly known, is recognized as a dead entity; those who come to this recognition are superior to the world because they are the ones who have life, as suggested, for example, in saying one.

It is only because DeConick insists on a thoroughly encratitic interpretation of the Gospel that she decides the verse must be textually corrupt, proffering as an emendation "Whoever has come to know the world has mastered the body. The world does not deserve the person who has mastered the body."[17] This, though, is a textual emendation driven by an interpretive principle. If the text is not forced into a procrustean bed of encratic thought, the logion makes perfectly good sense as transmitted. The material world is dead, not alive; those who know this will live and thus are superior to that which is dead. And so as Plisch can summarize, "Whoever comprehends what this world, the material world . . . , in its essence really entails, recognizes that it is dead," and so "this world recognized as a corpse is worthless for the one who has this comprehension."[18]

The saying thus has a good deal in common with the Gospel of Philip 73.19–23: "This world is a corpse-eater. All the things eaten in it themselves die also. Truth is a life-eater. Therefore no one nourished by [truth] will die."[19] It is also very close to the virtual doublet in Gospel of Thomas 80, which prefers the term σῶμα to πτῶμα for "body"/"corpse." The term σῶμα occurs only three times in the Gospel (sayings 29, 80, 87) and carries negative connotations each time. For that reason Plisch suggests translating it as "dead body" (i.e., corpse). Valantasis argues that in fact saying 80 and 56 represent two different Coptic renditions of the same Greek saying; but that would mean that the saying was literally repeated twice in the Gospel, which seems somewhat unlikely.[20]

Saying 110

Saying 110 is comparable. In this case a person is said to "find" the world, which surely means, in the context of this Gospel, "finds the true meaning of the world." That person will "become wealthy" and then should "renounce the world." This does not mean that the person who acquires true knowledge of this world will thereby amass worldly wealth, although this apparently is not obvious to Plisch, who suggests that literal riches are in view here.[21] On the contrary, a person who discovers what the world really is—a corpse, as we have seen—has acquired great spiritual wealth far in excess to anything the world has to offer. That is why the person is to renounce the world: it cannot provide anything of value, especially in

17. *Original Gospel of Thomas*, p. 192.

18. *Gospel of Thomas*, p. 140.

19. Translation of Wesley Isenberg, *NHL*.

20. Moreover, Valantasis assumes that the "body" refers to the body of believers. But in fact the saying denigrates the body, rather than affirming it. DeConick proposes the same textual emendation for saying 80 as for saying 56.

21. *Gospel of Thomas*, p. 110.

comparison with the great wealth that inheres in the true knowledge that brings life. Knowing the world must lead one to reject it.

Saying 87

Saying 87 provides a forceful statement that any dependence on the physical body leads to a wretched existence—whether it is another body that depends on the body or the soul that does. DeConick proposes an interesting alternative understanding of the verse, arguing that EISHE here does not mean "depend on" but "hang," in the sense of "hang by crucifixion," as the word is used of Jesus' crucifixion in the Coptic version of Matt. 20:19, Mark 15:14, Gal. 5:24, Heb. 6:6, Acts 2:23, and Luke 23:39. If so, then possibly the verse should be translated as "Miserable is the body crucified by a body. Miserable is the soul crucified by these together." As such, the saying means something like "the body suffers because of its own nature, while the soul suffers because it is united with the body." And so, "the point of the logia [87 and 112], in fact, is that *embodiment is a dire situation with suffering resulting for both body and soul.*"[22] Parallels, as DeConick points out, can be found in Clement of Alexandria, who speaks of bodily pleasure and pain as "nailing" the soul to the body (*Strom.* 2.2; cf. the *Book of Thomas the Contender*) and talks of the soul that is constantly undergoing torture through its bodily sensations (*Strom.* 5.14).[23]

Saying 112

A doublet of saying 87 appears in the terser construction of saying 112: "Woe to the flesh that depends on the soul. Woe to the soul that depends on the flesh." The problem here is specifically the "flesh," denigrated as bringing woe, both to itself and to the soul. A comparable woe is pronounced in the *Book of Thomas the Contender* discussed earlier, "Woe to you who hope in the flesh and in the prison that will perish" (143.10–11). For both authors, flesh and soul cannot be dependent on each other, and neither can be redeemed by the other. The flesh will perish but the soul can live on. Thus a person needs to strive to become, as the Gospel of Thomas puts it, "a solitary one," renouncing the flesh and living as a soul, not dependent in any way on the material trappings of the body (see sayings 16, 49, 75).

FORGERIES THAT CELEBRATE THE FLESH

It should not be surprising to find that forgeries celebrating the flesh—both of Christ and of the believers—far exceed those that denigrate it. The side that wins preserves the texts. It is only through the lucky happenstance of the Nag

22. DeConick, *Original Gospel of Thomas*, p. 254; italics hers.

23. See also R. Uro, *Thomas: Seeking the Historical Context of the Gospel of Thomas* (London: T&T Clark, 2003), pp. 58–62, who discusses the Platonic context for the problem of souls being united with bodies.

Hammadi discoveries that we have been graced with the few forgeries discussed above. The winners, on the other hand, preserved one forgery favoring the flesh as part of the canon of the New Testament, two others that were considered canonical by some of the proto-orthodox at certain times and places, and several others that were widely popular in various parts of the proto-orthodox community.

First John

Like the book of Acts, the letter of First John is not normally treated as a forgery. And like Acts, the book is not pseudepigraphic. Its author does not falsely claim to be a (specific) famous person. But he does make a false authorial claim of another sort to validate and legitimize his account. By my definition that makes the book a forgery.

The Polemic of the Letter

To make sense of the authorial claim, we should first consider the polemical situation that the author addresses.[24] Judging from the author's derogatory comments, it is clear that a group of one-time insiders have split off from the author's (larger?) community, in part because of a harsh difference over Christology. The "secessionists," as Raymond Brown has dubbed them,[25] appear to have embraced a docetic Christology, in many ways comparable to what was known perhaps a decade or so later to Ignatius of Antioch, and later still found among the followers of Marcion and some groups of Gnostics.[26]

The key passage is 2:18–19, which describes a group of "antichrists" who "went out from us." Clearly, these "opponents of Christ" were once members of the community, who have now left. The author wants to insist that even though these persons were once part of the larger group, "they were not of us, for if they had been of us, they would have remained with us." The author calls them "antichrists"—the first recorded use of the term—because in his opinion they have

---

24. There are, of course, a large number of theories about the relationship of the letter to the Fourth Gospel, with nearly every possible view represented by reasonable scholars, including a range of views of the relationship of the two prologues. On all this, one can simply consult the commentaries. Since the epistle does not deal with problems involving the Jewish synagogue, but is instead concerned with a secessionist movement that almost certainly occurred later in the community's history, the simplest and now probably most widespread solution to the relationship of the books is that they derive from two authors living at different times and addressing situations out of a very similar tradition rooted in the same community. With respect to the similar prologues, the author of 1 John appears to try to imitate that of his more famous predecessor, and is not altogether successful in the attempt.

25. See *The Community of the Beloved Disciple* (New York: Paulist, 1979) and his valuable commentary *The Epistles of John* (Garden City, NY: Doubleday, 1982).

26. This is not the view of Brown himself, who thinks the secessionists simply undervalue the salvific importance of Jesus' humanity. This view, however, cannot explain all the polemical emphases of the letter, including the prologue. See my assessment in *Orthodox Corruption of Scripture*, pp. 153–57, esp. n. 66.

adopted views that oppose Christ, a remarkable claim for a group of persons evidently committed to Christ. One hint concerning their aberrant view comes then in 2:22. These persons deny that "the Christ is Jesus." It is not widely enough recognized among commentators that this denial involves an identification formula that answers the question "who is the Christ"?[27] For this author, but not his opponents, it is the man Jesus. But what does that mean?

It cannot mean that the opponents are Jews who do not confess the messiahship of Jesus, since the subgroup started out as part of the Christian community. They must, then, be believers in Jesus who have developed Christological views that the author considers tantamount to a denial of the community's confession that the Christ is actually the man Jesus (cf. John 20:30–31). What those views might have been becomes clearer in a subsequent reference to the "antichrist" in 4:1–3. The true Christological confession for this author is that "Jesus Christ has come in the flesh." In contrast, "every spirit that does not confess Jesus" (i.e., "that Jesus Christ has come in the flesh") is not from God. This is "the spirit of the antichrist."

What matters for this author is that believers acknowledge that Christ really came "in the flesh." Anyone who denies that view is an antichrist. The secessionists do not subscribe to a separationist view, such as that occasionally associated with Cerinthus, but a pure docetic view, in which Christ was assumed to be a phantasm, not actual flesh and blood.[28] That can explain why the author stresses the physical nature of the Christ even in the prologue, as we will see in a moment, and why he emphasizes, throughout his short letter, that it is precisely Jesus' "blood" that brings expiation for sin (1:7, 2:2, 4:10, 5:6). The real blood of Jesus is needed for real expiation; there was nothing phantasmal about it.

In many respects the secessionists appear to embrace a Christology that comes to prominence some time later among the docetists attacked by Ignatius in his letters to Smyrna and Tralles.[29] These opponents reject the idea that Jesus Christ "truly" came "in the flesh" and was killed and raised ἐν σαρκί; instead, they teach that he only "seemed" (δοκεῖν) to be what he was and to do what he did (thus Ign. Smyrn. 1.1–2, 2.1, 3.1–3, 4.2, 5.2, 7.1; Ign. Tral. 9.1–2). For them Jesus was a spirit without a real body of flesh, who assumed the form of a human for a short while. It is significant that Ignatius stresses, on the contrary, that Jesus' body could be perceived and handled (ψηλαφάω; Ign. Smyrn. 3.2), much as the prologue of 1 John emphasizes that the Word of Life could be heard and handled (ψηλαφάω). An especially striking parallel occurs in Ignatius' condemnation of his opponents for "not confessing that he bore flesh" (Ign. Smyrn. 5.2, μὴ ὁμολογῶν αὐτὸν σαρκοφόρον), which is closely parallel to 1 John 4:2 "every spirit that confesses

27. See ibid., p. 200, n. 63.

28. See ibid., pp. 153–55, and its discussion of 1 John 5:6.

29. I have borrowed much of the following two paragraphs from my discussion in ibid., pp. 155–56.

Jesus Christ having come in the flesh" (πᾶν πνεῦμα ὃ ὁμολογεῖ Ἰησοῦν Χριστὸν ἐν σαρκὶ ἐληλυθότα).

Moreover, just as in 1 John, Ignatius stresses the reality and importance of Jesus' real death in which he shed real blood. The opponents in Smyrna and Tralles are explicitly said to believe that Christ, who was not real flesh, only "appeared to suffer" (λέγουσιν τὸ δοκεῖν αὐτὸν πεπονθέναι, Ign. Smyrn. 2.2; Ign. Trall. 10.1), whereas Ignatius emphasizes that Christ truly (ἀληθῶς) suffered, died, and was raised, and that anyone who fails to believe in Jesus' blood is subject to judgment (Ign. Smyrn. 6.1) because Christ's real suffering is what effects salvation (Ign. Smyrn. 1.2, 2.1; cf. 1 John 1:7, 2:2, 5:6).

Thus the polemical emphases of 1 John seem to parallel those found soon thereafter in Ignatius' opposition to the docetic Christians of Smyrna and Tralles. There is no reason to insist that the targets of attack are one and the same, but the two sets of opponents do appear to embrace highly comparable views. Both of them claim that the Christ is not the "man" Jesus, that in fact Christ was not really a flesh-and-blood human. For both the author of 1 John and Ignatius, if Christ was not really in the flesh, he could not really shed blood. And if Christ did not shed his blood, there is no expiation for sin.

The Claims of the Prologue

It is this understanding of the opponents of 1 John that makes best sense of the prologue and its emphasis on the real, tangible appearance of Christ: "That which was from the beginning, that which we have heard, that which we have seen with our eyes, that which we have beheld and our hands handled." The author wants to stress, at the very outset of his letter, the Christological theme that will play such a vital role in his harsh polemics. Christ was a physical being who could actually be heard, seen, and handled. He was no phantasm. But who, exactly, is the "we" who have heard, seen, and handled him?

To answer the question, we should first consider how the author uses first-person pronouns throughout the letter. On a number of occasions the first-person plural indicates the entire Christian community, of which the author is one: for example, "we should be called the children of God. . . . The world does not know us" (3:1–2); "we know that we have passed out of death unto life" (3:14); "they are of the world, we are of God" (4:5–6). In other places the author uses the first-person singular, in all but one instance to indicate that he is the one writing to the larger community: "My little children, I am writing this to you" (2:1); "Beloved I am writing you no new commandment" (2:7); "I am writing to you, little children" (2:12); and so on. In these instances the author differentiates himself ("I") from his readers ("you"). This differentiation also occurs in several instances of the use of the first-person-plural pronoun. In some such instances the author differentiates between his readers and himself, even though they are all part of the larger Christian community: "you have heard that anti-Christ is coming . . . therefore we know that it is the last hour" (2:18). More important, in other instances the author differentiates between his readers and a group of persons that the author includes himself among;

this latter group is decidedly not the entire Christian community: "This is the message we have heard from him and proclaim to you" (1:5). "We" in this instance cannot be "all Christians" because "you" includes Christians as well. The "we" then is a subgroup among the Christian community.

It is this latter kind of differentiation that is the key to understanding the first-person pronoun of the prologue. It is true, as noted everywhere in the commentaries, that the grammar of 1:1–3 is both confused and confusing.[30] What matters for my purposes here, however, is simply the first-person pronoun itself. In this case the author is not claiming simply to be a member of the entire Christian community who has "heard . . . seen . . . and handled" the incarnate word of life. He is a part of a smaller community that has had these tangible experiences involving Christ, and he is relating them to his readers. To begin with, that is evident from the graphic nature of the language—the community may have "seen . . . and heard" Christ in a metaphorical sense; but they certainly did not "handle" him. As Brown has observed: "clearly the author is claiming participation in a physical contact with Jesus."[31] Moreover, and yet more compelling, the author makes a clear differentiation here between himself and his readers, between "we" and "you": whereas "we have heard . . . have seen . . . have looked upon . . . and handled with our hands"(v. 1), it is to "you" that the author has proclaimed these things (v. 2). Thus only some believers have been in real, physical contact with Christ, and can attest to his physical existence as one who could be observed, heard, and handled. And the author includes himself among this select group. In other words, the author is claiming to have been among the inner group of Jesus' followers who can bear witness to his real, physical nature.[32]

---

30. Among the sundry options, the one proposed by Strecker has considerable merit, that the neuter relative used four times in 1—despite the fact that it is neuter (which, of course, is the problem)—in conjunction with the περί clause of 1b, "refers to nothing other than the Christ event to which the author testifies" (Georg Strecker, *The Johannine Letters*. Hermeneia. Trans. Linda Maloney [Minneapolis: Fortress, 1996; German original 1989], p. 10). But even more persuasive is Raymond Brown, that the pronoun refers to "that entity that became human" (so that the pre-existent Logos in some sense is depersonalized). *Epistles of John*, pp. 151–54.

31. P. 163. Brown goes on to claim that the author is not *really* indicating that he had real contact with Jesus, since he was writing much later and could not have been an eyewitness to Jesus' ministry. R. Schnackenburg too refuses to believe that the author could really be claiming to be an eyewitness, since he was not one (*The Johannine Epistles*, New York: Crossroads, 1992, ET of 7th German edition of 1984, original 1953, p. 55). Both of these exegetical opinions overlook the pseudepigraphic character of the author's claims. This oversight creates a contradiction in the interpretation. On one hand, Schneemelcher indicates that in the prologue the author is "expressing a prophetic self-consciousness in which he appropriates to himself the experience of a witness who actually saw and heard," but he then indicates that "1 John does not otherwise betray a 'prophetic self-consciousness'" (p. 55).

32. Without compelling reason, Judith Lieu asserts the contrary: that "the assertion that 'we have heard . . . we have seen' is not a claim to an eyewitness experience of the historical ministry of Jesus made by a group of the original disciples." Her logic is the same as Brown's and Schnackenburg's (see the preceding note): that since this author was not an eyewitness, he could not be claiming to be one. She too, then, fails to consider the possibility that the author wants to portray himself as an eyewitness,

Except that he cannot be. He is an author living and writing long after the fact.[33] In asserting that he was an eyewitness to the life of Jesus, he is advancing a false authorial claim. This then is a forgery, a book whose author claims to be someone other than who he is.

It is important to note that this way of reading the prologue is "normal." Historically, the author—because of this passage—was taken to be an eyewitness to the ministry of Jesus. The first explicit quotation of the Johannine epistles comes from Irenaeus, who cites 2 John on two occasions and 1 John once, evidently thinking they are the same writing, and attributing them to John, the Lord's disciple (*Adv. Haer.* 1.16.3; 3.16.5, 8).[34] About the same time, the Muratorian Canon indicates that John wrote the Gospel and his epistles in which he indicates that he saw, heard, and touched Christ (quoting 1 John 1:1). Tertullian cites 1 John more than forty times and refers to it as the work of John. So firmly entrenched was the idea that John had written the anonymous three epistles that later writers who doubted they were by John the son of Zebedee were constrained to identify the author as a *different* John. As Judith Lieu observes, "there was never any alternative tradition of authorship."[35] The view had lasting power, down to the present, as seen in some of the less critical commentaries, such as that of Plummer, who speaks of the author as "the last survivor of those who had heard and seen the Lord."[36]

When more critical commentators—Brown, Lieu, Schnackenburg, and others—reject the idea that the author is claiming to be an eyewitness to the fleshly reality of Jesus in his public ministry,[37] it is almost always because they are convinced that in fact he was not an eyewitness. The fault of the interpretation derives from a failure to understand the world of ancient forgery. What we have in 1 John is an author who very much wanted his readers to think he was an eyewitness, even though he was not. In this he was following established patterns of forged writing from antiquity, seen already, for example, in the author of 2 Peter who was

---

precisely in order to validate his claims about the real fleshly existence of Christ. As a result, she proposes a rather obscure and romantic understanding of the first-person pronoun in the prologue: "its chief effort is to invite its readers to be attuned to the echoes and associations of the unequivocal authority of sensory experience, to attest it, and to determine whether they will affirm it and, by affirming it, whether they will shape their own lives by the pattern of consequences that the rest of the letter will trace." In response I would say that this is precisely not the "chief effort" of the author. He instead wants his readers to know that he is an authority who has actually experienced the incarnate word of life as a physical, tangible entity, so that they can rest assured that Christ really did come in the flesh. See Judith Lieu, *I, II, and III John: A Commentary*, NTL (Louisville: Westminster John Knox, 2008), pp. 35–43, quotation pp. 40–41.

33. See note 24.

34. See the discussion in Brown, *Epistles of John*, pp. 9–10.

35. *I, II, and III John*, p. 3.

36. A. Plummer, *The Epistles of S. John* (Cambridge: Cambridge University, 1886), p. 14.

37. See notes 31 and 32 above; John Painter, *1, 2, and 3 John*. SP (Collegeville, MN: Liturgical Press, 2002), pp. 129–30.

bound and determined to have his readers know that he really was present at the transfiguration of Jesus, or the author of 2 Timothy, who loaded his letter with verisimilitudes to make himself appear to be Paul, or, in fact, the authors of virtually all the pseudonymous documents we have considered. This author is simply applying the craft of the forger.

First John as a Forgery

The reason behind the false authorial claim of 1 John was keenly recognized by Strecker. Since the author is opposing "the false teachers who . . . represent a docetic Christology . . . it is important to assert the 'empirical' reality of the Christ event." And so he begins the letter "with a testimony that the Christ lived on earth as visible, audible, and tangible." It is true, Strecker concedes, that the author does not use a pseudonym. But "he is still writing this document under fictitious circumstances. He pretends to be an eye- and ear-witness, even though that does not correspond to historical reality." And his motive is clear: "such a fiction is appropriate to underscore the claims of this document and hence the author's intention to put the docetic teaching of the opponents in its place."[38]

It cannot be objected that the author would be known to his readers, on the basis of the evidence of 2 and 3 John, sent by the same author to a community of people who knew his identity. There is nothing to suggest that the letter of 1 John was sent to the same community,[39] or, more precisely, the self-same house church, as the other two letters. Indeed, there is good evidence that it circulated as a separate composition. Otherwise it is hard to explain why 2 and 3 John did not have a wider acceptance as authoritative texts early on. Origen, for example, knows of these two smaller letters but never quotes them, questions whether they are canonical, and observes that they are not everywhere accepted as coming even from the same author.[40] Brown concludes that the three letters were not transmitted as a corpus and that whereas 2 and 3 John were assumed to have been written by the somewhat shadowy "presbyter" John, 1 John was understood to have been writ-

---

38. Strecker, *Johannine Letters*, p. 14. It should be noted that the author's claim is quite different from that of the author of the Fourth Gospel, who does indeed say "we beheld his glory" (1:14), but does not claim to be an actual eyewitness. On the contrary, he appears to be claiming to speak of the glory revealed to all believers; he is one who has believed "without seeing" (20:29). Evidence for this interpretation comes at the end of the Gospel, where the author clearly indicates that he was not one of the disciples (20:30–31), and at the scene of the crucifixion where the author indicates that he himself is not the one who observed the event but that he derived his information from one who had (19:35).

39. Indeed, Strecker can maintain that a different author produced 1 John, on the basis of the facts that he does not call himself a πρεσβεύτερος, that the letter is of a different form (critically), and that there are different views of theology and church discipline ("what one finds here is an independent author in the Johannine school tradition"; *Johannine Letters*, p. xl). I do not find this view persuasive, in part because I think 2 John 7 is difficult to explain if not from the same author as 1 John 4:2–3. But it is not at all implausible that the author sent a general letter into broader circulation, claiming to be an eyewitness to what he attests, rather than simply to a single house church.

40. Eusebius, *H.E.* 6.25.10.

ten by the apostle himself. They may have originally circulated, then, in different communities.

In many respects, then, 1 John is a forgery comparable to the book of Acts. Both writings are, strictly speaking, anonymous. But both authors make false authorial claims through the use of first-person discourse, used in order to establish themselves as eyewitnesses to that which they testify. Both books, in other words, are what I have already termed "non-pseudepigraphic forgeries." In the case of Acts the author claims to be an eyewitness to the life and teachings of Paul; in the case of 1 John the author claims to be an eyewitness to the incarnation of Christ. The latter claim is made for purely polemical reasons.[41] It is directed against one-time members of the community who have created a schism and gone off to form their own community (assuming that it is they, and not the author's own group, who have left), due in large part to a variant understanding of Christology. The author buttresses the beliefs of his own (sub)community, that Christ was a real flesh-and-blood human, by writing an anonymous tractate, choosing anonymity not because his readers know full well who he is but precisely so that he can claim to be someone other than who he is. By assuming the guise of an eyewitness to the life of Jesus, he can provide the necessary authorization for the Christological views that he feels compelled to advance. Against those who claimed that Jesus did not "come in the flesh," this author attests that he himself heard, saw, and handled Jesus, the "Word of Life" who "was made manifest" (1:1–2). As was the case with so many others, the author's false claims about himself were readily believed, and the book was eventually accepted as a part of sacred Scripture, written by Jesus' own disciple, John the son of Zebedee.

Third Corinthians

Within the short compass of the two letters known, together, as 3 Corinthians we find an entire range of vital issues related to early Christian debates over the status of the flesh: Is the flesh important in the divine scheme? Did Jesus have real flesh? Was he raised in the flesh? Will believers too be raised in the flesh? This final question is related to the issue addressed in 2 Timothy; here, however, the question is not simply about the fact of the future resurrection but also about its character.

The Textual Tradition of the Letters

The scholarly discussion of 3 Corinthians began with J. Ussher's mention of a lacunose Armenian manuscript in 1644.[42] The correspondence was not published

---

41. A case could be made that the anonymous author of 1 John wanted to be known not only as a disciple who was in Jesus' physical presence, but also as the author of the Fourth Gospel; hence his attempt to imitate the Prologue of his predecessor.

42. *In Polycarpionam epistolarum Ignationarum syllogen annotationes* (Oxford), p. 29. For a full sketch of the manuscript tradition, see Vahan Hovhanessian, *Third Corinthians: Reclaiming Paul for Christian Orthodoxy* (New York: Peter Lang, 2000), 3–10.

however, for another seventy years, making its first appearance in a work by F. Masson.[43] The first critical editions were of the Armenian.[44] The book came into English through a translation by William Whiston,[45] later superseded by a rendition of none other than Lord Byron.[46] It came into German through a translation of W. F. Rink.[47] In most of the surviving Armenian manuscripts, the correspondence occurs as part of the New Testament between 2 Corinthians and Galatians.

The Syriac tradition is known through Ephrem's four-volume biblical commentary (which survives in Armenian translation), which D. Bundy argues is itself pseudepigraphic (falsely ascribed rather than forged).[48] Latin manuscripts began to appear at the end of the nineteenth century; we now have six.[49] The Coptic version, found in the Heidelberg Papyrus, was discovered by Carl Schmidt in 1904 and published in 1905.[50] Finally, and most important, the sole Greek witness, which, dating from the third century, is by far the earliest manuscript evidence, was found among the Bodmer papyri and published as Bodmer Papyrus X by Michel Testuz in 1959.[51]

Whereas earlier scholars such as Harnack believed that 3 Corinthians was originally part of the Acts of Paul,[52] today it is generally ascribed an independent origin and circulation. For one thing, only the Heidelberg papyrus presents it as part of the Acts; the other manuscripts present it as part of the New Testament. Moreover, among the manuscripts of the Acts of Paul only the Heidelberg manuscript contains the correspondence. Still more important, there are clear anomalies between the narrative of the Acts and the letters. According to the cor-

---

43. *Histoire critique de la république des lettres* Tome X (Amsterdam/Utrecht, 1714), pp. 148–71.

44. J . Zohrab, *Astuatsashunch' Matean Hin Ew Nor Ktakarants'* (= Scriptures of the Old and New Testaments; Venice: Srboyn Ghazaru, 1805; reprinted Delmar: Caravan Books, 1984), pp. 25–27.

45. In part II of *Collection of Authentic Records Belonging to the Old and New Testament* (London: William Whiston, 1727).

46. See Rowland E. Prothero, *The Works of Lord Byron: Letters and Journals*, IV (New York: Scribner's, 1900), pp. 429–33.

47. *Das Sendschreiben der Korinther an den Apostel Paulus und das dritte Sendschreiben Pauli an die Korinther* (Heidelberg: C. F. Winter, 1823). For further information on manuscript discoveries, summarized here, see Steve Johnston, "La Correspondance apocryphe entre Paul et les Corinthiens: un pseudépigraphe paulinien au service de la polémique anti-gnostique de la fin du II siècle" (M.A. thesis, University of Laval, 2004), 1–30; and Hovhanessian, *Third Corinthians*, pp. 3–10.

48. "The Pseudo-Ephremian *Commentary on Third Corinthians:* A Study in Exegesis and Anti-Bardaisanite Polemic, " in *After Bardaisan: Studies on Continuity and Change in Syriac Christianity in Honour of Professor Han J. W. Drijvers*, ed. Gerrit J. Reinink and Alexander Cornelis Klugkist (Louvain: Peeters, 1999), pp. 51–63.

49. See the discussion in Hovhanessian, *Third Corinthians*, pp. 6–9.

50. *Acta Pauli: Aus der Heidelberger Koptischen Papyrushandschrift Nr. 1* (Leipzig: J. C. Hinrichs, 1905), pp. 125–45.

51. *Papyrus Bodmer X–XII* (Geneva: Bibliotheque Bodmer, 1959). See as well his "La Correspondance apocryphe de saint Paul et des Corinthiens," in *Littérature et théologie pauliniennes* (Louvain: Desclée de Brouwer, 1960), pp. 217–23.

52. Adolf Harnack, "Die apokryphen Briefe des Paulus an die Laodicener und Korinther," in *Apocrypha IV*, 2nd ed. (Berlin: de Gruyter, 1931), pp. 6–23.

respondence, heresies present a grave threat to the Christians in Corinth; but in the narrative, once Paul arrives in the city there is no word about heresy. On the contrary, Paul is pleased with the progress of the Corinthian believers. Relatedly, during Paul's visit he makes no mention of an earlier correspondence and mentions none of the problems addressed in it. What is more, whereas Cleobius is presented as an arch-heretic in the Corinthians' letter to Paul, in the narrative he is portrayed as a spirit-filled Christian. And so, it appears that the correspondence originated independently of the Acts of Paul, as recognized not long after the publication of the Bodmer papyrus, for example, by Klijn.[53]

Technically speaking the correspondence consists of four parts: a narrative introduction to the Corinthians' letter to Paul, the letter itself, a narrative introducing Paul's reply, and that letter itself. As S. Johnston has conveniently summarized, different surviving witnesses attest each of these four parts. Our oldest and only Greek witness, the third-century Bodmer Papyrus, attests only the two letters themselves, without narrative introduction. On these grounds it is generally thought today that the sequence of composition and redaction was as follows: the letters themselves were first composed and circulated, narrative introductions to each were later added, and the whole was subsequently inserted into the Acts of Paul.[54] Luttikhuizen, in opposition to Testuz, has made a strong case that the Armenian and Syriac versions drew the correspondence from the Acts of Paul—rather than from an independent manuscript transmission—since they contain the second introductory narrative.[55]

The Themes of the Correspondence

As they stand now, the letters place a particular stress on the importance of the flesh: the fleshly existence of Christ, the fleshly nature of his resurrection, and the fleshly character of the resurrection of believers yet to come. In the first letter, allegedly written to Paul by Stephanus, Daphnus, Eubulus, Theophilus, and Zeno, we learn that two false teachers, Simon and Cleobius, have arrived in Corinth

---

53. "There are reasons to suppose that the correspondence was not written by the same author as the Acts of Paul." A. F. J. Klijn, "The Apocryphal Correspondence between Paul and the Corinthians," *VC* 17 (1963): 13.

54. One might be tempted to postulate, further, that the two letters were composed independently of one another. The second letter, from Paul to the Corinthians, can easily stand on its own, apart from the earlier set of inquiries of the first letter; moreover, in this letter Paul mentions neither the first letter nor the heretics who are its principal concern. In addition, whereas the first letter assumes that Paul has already been delivered from his legal troubles ("the Lord has delivered you from the godless," v. 8), in the second he is in prison (v. 1) and in chains (v. 34). The differences between the letters, however, are as difficult to explain on the hypothesis of the first being written later as an introduction to the second as on the standard view that both were written together, as a unit. Moreover, the opening statement of the second letter does appear to preserve an allusion to the first: "I marvel not that the teachings of the evil one had such rapid success" (in possible reference to "they overthrow the faith of some").

55. Gerard Luttikhuizen, "The Apocryphal Correspondence with the Corinthians and the Acts of Paul," in Jan Bremmer, ed., *The Apocryphal Acts of Paul and Thecla* (Kampen: Pharos, 1996), pp. 75–92.

and proclaimed "pernicious words" that have destroyed "the faith of some."[56] In particular they have declared that

> one must not appeal to the prophets and that God is not almighty, there is no resurrection of the body, man has not been made by God, Christ has neither come in the flesh, nor was he born of Mary, and the world is not the work of God but of angels. (vv. 10–15)

Paul's response is more or less a point-by-point refutation, given at much greater length than the succinct summary of the false teachings themselves. As Paul has learned "from the apostles before me who were always with Jesus Christ," Christ was certainly "born of Mary . . . that he might come into this world and save all flesh by his own flesh and that he might raise us in the flesh" (vv. 5–6).[57] God is called both the "almighty" and the "maker of heaven and earth," and is said to have "sent the prophets first to the Jews" (v. 9). Salvation "of the flesh" comes through the (real) body of Christ (v. 16). Those who "assert that heaven and earth and all that is in them are not a work of God" are "not children of righteousness but of wrath" (v. 19). Moreover, "those who say that there is no resurrection of the flesh shall have no resurrection" (v. 24). Paul concludes his polemic by giving three arguments for the real, physical resurrection of the flesh: the sowing of seeds, the story of Jonah, and an apocryphal account of a corpse that was revived when thrown on the bones of Elisha (vv. 26–32). Those who accept this message, as "received by the blessed prophets and the holy gospel," will be rewarded; those who have rejected it will be punished with fire, "since they are Godless men, a generation of vipers" (vv. 34–37).

Third Corinthians as a Forgery

No one thinks that either letter is authentic.[58] There are, however, a substantial number of Pauline themes and verisimilitudes. Connections with 1 and 2 Corinthians in particular abound: Paul's tribulations (v. 2; cf. 2 Cor. 1:3–10, 11:23–28); the imminent appearance of Christ (v. 3; cf. 1 Cor. 15:51); Paul's claim that he delivered to the Corinthians what he also "received" (v. 4; cf. 1 Cor. 15:3); the body as a temple of righteousness (v. 17; cf. 1 Cor. 6:19); an attack on those who say that "there is no resurrection" (v. 24; cf. 1 Cor. 15:12); the resurrection compared to

56. Translations are taken from J. K. Elliott, *Apocryphal New Testament.*

57. The letter presents an interesting notion of the incarnation, unlike anything in Paul's New Testament letters. Here God is said to have sent the Holy Spirit into Mary so that Christ could be born of her (vv. 5, 13–14). God also sent a "portion of the Spirit" into the Jewish prophets, as a kind of preliminary to the sending of the Spirit into Mary. This appears to be a kind of Spirit Christology comparable to the Logos Christology of contemporary thinkers such as Justin (where the Logos is in the Greek philosophers, but becomes fully manifest in Christ).

58. At least, no scholar of the Western world. For anyone with residual doubts, S. Johnston devotes fifty-five pages to a demonstration ("La Correspondance apocryphe," pp. 78–133).

sown seeds (vv. 26–27; cf. 1 Cor. 15:36–37); the coming judgment (v. 37; cf. 2 Cor. 5:10). A large number of other Pauline words and phrases are scattered throughout: "prisoner of Jesus Christ" (v. 1; cf. Phil. 1:7, Phlm. 1); "seed of David" (v. 5; cf. Rom. 1:3); believers' "adoption" (v. 8; cf. Rom. 8:15–17); "children . . . of wrath" (v. 19; cf. Eph. 2:3); the "marks" that Paul bears (v. 33; cf. Gal. 6:17); "that I may win Christ" (v. 34; cf. Phil. 3:8–9); "that I may attain to the resurrection of the dead" (v. 33; cf. Phil. 3:11); and many others. Clearly the author knows Paul's letters and imitates their phrasing. In this case we are not dealing with a forger who is simply claiming to be an apostle and providing little "evidence" to support his claim (as, say, with the letters of 1 Peter or Jude). This author wants to sound like Paul.[59] Even so, as we will see in a moment, he fails miserably on several fronts.

The function of the forgery is to use the apostolic name to oppose heretical groups who denigrate the flesh and the fleshly resurrection. Over the years scholars have failed to resist the vain temptation to nail down the identity of the opponents with greater precision. And so, for example, Rist argued that the opponents were Marcionites of an Apelles sort: "the best organized and the most aggressive 'heresy' during the latter part of the second century."[60] W. Rordorf proposed that the opponent was Saturninus;[61] M. Muretow held that it was Simon Magus;[62] Hovhanessian suggested the Ophites.[63] Most commonly, however, it is recognized that there is not a specific group of "heretics" in view, but a kind of teaching, found in various guises among the Marcionites and sundry Gnostics. This is the conclusion of Klijn: "we are not able to say that the correspondence was written against one particular kind of heresy. The correspondence probably describes a tendency in the early church."[64] And Luttikhuizen: "we may be dealing with a *general* warning against the invasion of Gnostic ways of thinking into Christianity rather than with the refutation of a specific group of Gnostics."[65] Or Johnston: the letter is an attack on "all the gnostic ideas that circulated during his era."[66]

---

59. In my judgment M. Rist is precisely wrong to claim that the author's "indistinct echoes of Paul's words" were not "designed to give his composition an appearance of authenticity." See M. Rist, "III Corinthians as a Pseudepigraphic Refutation of Marcionism," *Iliff Review* 26 (1969): 55.

60. Rist, "III Corinthians," p. 58. Rist gives six very good points of comparison with what is known of Marcion and one with Apelles. Klijn ("Apocryphal Correspondence"), however, makes a valid objection to this view: Apelles maintained that one angel, not a plural number of angels, was the creator. Rist sees this as a trivial difference.

61. Hérésie et orthodoxie selon la correspondance apocryphe entre les Corinthiens et l'Apôtre Paul," in *Orthodoxie et Hérésie dans l'Eglise ancienne*, ed. H. D. Altendorf. *Cahiers de la Revue de Théologie et de Philosophie* 17 (1993): 21–63.

62. "Über den apokryphen Briefwechsel des Apostels Paulus mit den Korinthern," *Theologische Boten* (1896).

63. Rist, "III Corinthians," pp. 130–31.

64. "Apocryphal Correspondence," p. 22.

65. Ibid., p. 91. Italics his.

66. "L'ensemble des conceptions gnostiques qui circulaient à son époque." *La correspondance apocryphe*," p. 222. A different approach to establishing the opposition is proposed in a recent study by Benjamin White, who suggests that rather than trying to identify the false teachers by what is said about

At the same time, given the popularity of Paul among both Marcionites and sundry Gnostic teachers, it is worth entertaining the idea that the author believed himself to be countering teachings that claimed support in Paul's own proclamation. We have seen such a contest over Paul in 2 Peter, whose pseudonymous author objected to the "ignorant and unstable" false teachers who "twist" Paul's letters "to their own destruction" (2 Pet. 3:16). Already in Paul's own day we know of groups of his own devotees who, in his opinion, seriously misconstrued his message. This at least is true of one of the groups in Corinth who claimed to be "of Paul," in opposition to others who claimed to be "of Cephas," "of Apollo," or "of Christ." Possibly the most striking feature of the historical Paul's intervention in this Corinthian dispute is that he does not side with his own party, but attacks them along with all the others for misunderstanding the true meaning of the gospel, even though this was a group that specifically appealed to his authority for their views.

Many of the themes of 1 Corinthians—especially, but not exclusively, those involving splits in the community—are replicated a generation later in the letter of 1 Clement, also written to Corinth, the church, remarkably, said to be the recipient of the apocryphal correspondence we are now considering. Like 3 Corinthians, 1 Clement is deeply concerned about the teaching of the future resurrection, and is invested in arguing for its reality in the face of those who denied it (esp. 1 Clem. 24–26). Both letters appeal to nature in support of their views: the claim, "if one will not take the parable of seeds . . ." (3 Cor. 26), is not formally far removed from "he shows us the magnificence of his promise even through a bird" (1 Clem. 26.1). In fact, there is good reason for thinking that 3 Cor. 26 ("For they do not know, O Corinthians, about the sowing of wheat") is an allusion to 1 Clement 24:4–5 ("We should consider the crops: how, and in what way, does the sowing occur?"). Both passages are based on Mark 4:26–27; and there are several striking verbal parallels: βάλλω, τῶν σπερμάτων (Mark has σπόρον instead), εἰς τὴν γήν (Mark has ἐπὶ τῆς γῆς), and γυμνή (not in Mark).[67] Still, even though there is a literary connection between these two writings, it would be difficult to show, historically, that Clement's opponents were the same as 3 Corinthians docetists.[68]

What is clear is that Paul could be, and was, appealed to by various sides in debates over both the resurrection and the related issue of the status of the flesh. It

---

them, it may be better to see how "Paul" is being constructed as their opponent; as it turns out, this Paul is very much like the Paul of the Pastoral epistles and of Irenaeus. The opponents, then, take contrary views. Benjamin L. White, "Reclaiming Paul? Reconfiguration as Reclamation in 3 Corinthians," *JECS* 17 (2009): 497–523.

67. Johnston gives a nice synoptic comparison of the two passages, but points out a key difference: whereas 1 Clement is simply interested in demonstrating that there will be a resurrection, 3 Corinthians stresses that it will specifically be a resurrection "of the flesh."

68. In support, for example, of Walter Bauer's claim that the problem addressed by 1 Clement is a group of Gnostics in Corinth. See *Orthodoxy and Heresy in Earliest Christianity*, pp. 105–6.

is no accident that the Marcionites—harsh opponents of the flesh—appealed to forged letters of Paul to the Alexandrians and Laodiceans (according to the Muratorian Canon). 3 Corinthians can well be seen, then, as a kind of counterforgery to the views of certain Paulinists (Marcion and some Gnostics), and possibly to actual forgeries that they produced. It also counters the views found in certain docetic fabrications, such as the Acts of John and its remarkable portrayal of a phantasmal Christ (e.g., Acts of John 93),[69] as well as (possibly) Gnostic works not connected with Paul, such as the *Book of Thomas the Contender* considered earlier. And when "Paul" claims in the letter that "I delivered to you first of all what I received from the apostles before me who were always with Jesus Christ" (v. 4; cf. 1 Cor. 15:3), the forger provides an even more precise counterforgery to claims such as those found in the forged Epistula Petri and the book it introduces, the Pseudo-Clementine *Homilies*, where Paul stands precisely at odds with the views of Peter, the one who was with Christ for his public ministry and knew Christ far better than did Paul, who acquired his "knowledge" from a brief and unreliable vision. Here then, in 3 Corinthians, we have a "Paul" who appears to be fighting against other "Pauls."

What is most striking of all is that this particular "Paul" stands at odds with what we know about the real, historical Paul, at least as he is represented in the undisputed Pauline epistles. This has been shown above all by Benjamin White in his recent analysis of 3 Corinthians.[70] For one thing, the forged letter—in dealing with the question of Christ's nature—places almost no importance on the death of Jesus, and overlooks questions about the Jewish Law, focusing instead on the role of the Spirit in the teachings of the prophets. Of greater importance, the pseudonymous author embraces views found nowhere in Paul, such as the incarnation of Christ through Mary and the remarkable "proofs" of the resurrection through the stories of Jonah and the bones of Elisha. Most significant, however, is that the author presents views that stand precisely at odds with Paul. In particular, the author has taken Paul's teaching of the resurrection of the "body" (σῶμα) and transformed it into a doctrine of the resurrection of the "flesh" (σάρξ). As White has shown, the stress on "flesh" is not simply different from Paul, it is counter to Paul, who insisted that "flesh and blood cannot inherit the kingdom of God" (1 Cor. 15:50). For Paul, the flesh is the fallen part of humans that cannot and will not be redeemed. It is the body that is to be raised, not the σάρξ. As a result, 3 Corinthians represents a forged attempt to salvage Paul that does so only by altering a critical aspect of his actual message.

At the same time, the author was standing in a clearly demarcated line of Pauline tradition, as White has further shown. In particular, his views coalesce strikingly with the views of Paul found in the Pastoral epistles and in the somewhat later writings of Irenaeus. Here then we find the irony we have run across before.

69. See p. 433 below.

70. See note 66.

Paul is used to combat Paul; but it is a "twisted" Paul—to use the language of 2 Peter—that has been created in order to counter an otherwise "twisted" Paul.

Melchizedek

It may seem highly irregular to include a Gnostic treatise among early Christian texts that champion the flesh and oppose a docetic understanding of Christ, but that is precisely what we have in "Melchizedek," the first treatise of codex 9 discovered at Nag Hammadi. The surviving copy is a highly lacunose revelation to Melchizedek by the angel Gabriel that includes a liturgical rite spoken by Melchizedek. The original text comprised 750 lines. Only 19 of these survive complete, 467 are fragmentary, many of them largely so. The remaining 264 lines, over a third of the entire treatise, are lost altogether.

The pseudepigraphic character of the piece is nonetheless intact. The author claims to be the famous but mysterious royal/priestly figure known from Genesis 14, Psalm 110, and Hebrews 5–7: "And [I immediately] arose—I, Mel[chizedek]—and I began to [glorify] God" (14.15–18); [71] "For I have a name: I am [Melch]izedek, the priest of [God] Most High" (15.7–10); "and they said to me, '[Greetings, Mel]chiz[ed]ek, [Priest] of God [Most High]'" (19.12–14). Whether in this tractate Melchizedek is to be identified as Christ himself, or as distinct from him, has been a matter of dispute.[72]

The book shows strong ties to the Sethian tradition, as seen, for example, in 5.17–19, "I [am Gamal]iel. It is to [snatch away] the assembly of the [children] of Seth that I have come."[73] Among its Gnostic features are a myth of descent through the realms of the aeons (but cf. *Ascension of Isaiah*) in 1.1–5: "Jesus Christ, the Son of God . . . from . . . the aeons, that he might pass through all of the aeons and see in each one of the aeons the nature of the aeon, as to what kind it is, and that he might put on as a garment sonship and goodness. . . ." Moreover, a host of Gnostic divinities are invoked by the piece: Autogenes, Barbelo, Aithops, Doxomedon, Domedon, Harmozel, Oraoiael, Daveithe, Eleleth (5.23ff.); and later Barbelo Doxomedon Harmozel, Oriael, and others (16.17ff.).

In view of the tractate's Gnostic character, what is most peculiar is precisely its anti-docetic Christology, which luckily survives in one of the few intact passages, in a series of polemically contrasting statements:

> Furthermore, they will say of him
> "He was not born," though he was born;
> "he does not eat," though he does eat;

---

71. Quotations taken from the translation of Birger Pearson in Marvin Meyer, ed., *Nag Hammadi Scriptures*.

72. See Birger Pearson, "Melchizedek," in Marvin Meyer, ed., *Nag Hammadi Scriptures*, pp. 597–98.

73. The fragmentary reference to the name Gamaliel is secure, in light of the rest of the text. The verb is unfortunately missing; "snatch away" is Pearson's hypothesis. In any event, the Sethian focus is clear.

"he does not drink," though he does drink;
"he is not circumcised," though he was circumcised;
"he is without real flesh," though he came in the flesh;
"he did not suffer death," <though> he did endure suffering;
"he did not rise from the dead," <though> he did rise from the dead. (5.1–11)

As Birger Pearson has noted, the balanced set of contrasts compare favorably to other Christological statements found throughout the early Christian literature, of varying persuasion. One thinks most immediately of the famous contrasting claims of the Acts of John, which function to emphasize precisely the opposite Christological point (in favor of a docetic interpretation):

> So then I have suffered none of those things which they will say of me. . . . You hear that I suffered, yet I suffered not; and that I suffered not, yet I did suffer; and that I was pierced, yet I was not lashed; that I was hanged, yet I was not hanged; that blood flowed from me, yet it did not flow; and, in a word, that what they say of me I did not endure, but what they do not say, those things I did suffer. (Acts of John 101)[74]

More stark still are the disaffirmations of the Manichaean Psalms of Heracleides:

Amen, I was seized; Amen again, I was not seized.
Amen, I was judged; Amen again, I was not judged.
Amen, I was crucified; Amen again, I was not crucified.
Amen, I was pierced; Amen again, I was not pierced.
Amen, I suffered; Amen again, I did not suffer. . . . (Ps. Heracl.)[75]

These docetic statements are what one might more naturally expect to find in a Gnostic treatise such as Melchizedek. But instead, the tractate's material similarities are much closer to the paradoxical affirmations of the proto-orthodox Ignatius: "For there is one physician, both fleshly and spiritual, born and unborn, God come in the flesh, true life in death, from both Mary and God, first subject to suffering and then beyond suffering, Jesus Christ our Lord."[76] At the same time, as Pearson points out, whereas the Ignatian statements are presented as paradoxes, those in Melchizedek are polemical contradictions, in which false Christological views are directly countered.

How does one explain such strong anti-docetic polemic in a Gnostic treatise? Pearson considers the possibility that the tractate is connected to the eponymous

74. Here and in the pages that follow I will use the translation of Knut Schäferdiek, in Schneemelcher, *New Testament Apocrypha*, vol. 2.

75. Translation of Charles Allberry, *A Manichaean Psalm-Book Part II* (Stuttgart: W. Kohlhammer, 1938), 191.

76. Ign. Eph. 7.2; my own translation, *Apostolic Fathers*, vol. 1 in LCL.

group of Melchizedekians referred to by several heresiologists. In particular Epiphanius maintained that the Gnostic Melchizedekians subordinated Christ to Melchizedek and affirmed that Christ originated from Mary, that is, that he was born as a man (*Pan.* 55). Interestingly, a low Christology is also attested for the group in both Hippolytus (*Refut.* 7.24) and Pseudo-Tertullian (*Haer.* 8). For them, Christ was purely human, a "mere man," in contrast to the heavenly power of Melchizedek, of which he was the image. The conclusion to hand is that this group stressed the real, fleshly humanity of Christ and his actual suffering in order to contrast these with their more exalted views of Melchizedek.

On the other hand, given the overwhelming unreliabilities of the heresiological reports—Epiphanius being the most obvious and extreme case—there may be a better explanation for the presence of an anti-docetic Christology in a Gnostic work. Schenke proposes a somewhat more economical solution. The Gnostic tractate of Melchizedek that we now have was at one point edited and revised along proto-orthodox lines, creating the odd amalgam that we now have:

> The simplest solution[:] the assumption that in Melch the degree of secondary Christianization of Sethian gnosis has reached such force that it exceeded its categorical boundaries and that the Sethianism here lost its gnostic character. That is to say: Melch would represent a Christianized Sethianism that is no longer gnostic at all.[77]

However one evaluates the genesis of this odd tradition, it is clear that here in Melchizedek we have one Nag Hammadi document that simultaneously evinces clear Gnostic tendencies and celebrates the importance of the real fleshly character of Christ and his real tangible suffering.

The Epistula Apostolorum

The Epistula Apostolorum presents us with another emphatic declaration of the importance of the flesh of Christ and the future fleshly resurrection of his followers, in the face of false teachers who proclaim a docetic gospel. The document was unknown until Carl Schmidt discovered a Coptic fragment at the Institut de la mission archéologique française in Cairo in 1895.[78] The complete Ethiopic text, extant in five manuscripts, was published by Louis Guerrier and Sylvain Grébaut

---

77. ". . . die einfachste Lösung [scheint] die Annahme zu sein, daß in Melch der Grad der sekundären Verchristlichung der sethianischen Gnosis eine solche Stärke erreicht hat, daß es zu einer kategorialen Grenzüberschreitung gekommen ist und der Sethianismus hier seinen gnostischen Charakter verloren hat. Das heißt, Melch würde einen verchristlichten Sethianismus repräsentieren, der überhaupt nicht mehr gnostisch ist." "Melchisedek (NHC IX,1), in Hans-Martin Schenke, Hans-Gebhard Bethge, and Ursula Ulrike Kaiser, eds., *Nag Hammadi Deutsch*, 2nd ed. (Berlin: De Gruyter, 2010), p. 475.

78. See Carl Schmidt, *Gespräche Jesu mit seinen Jüngern nach der Auferstehung. Ein katholisch-apostolisches Sendschreiben des 2. Jh.* (Leipzig: J. C. Hinrichs, 1919).

in 1912.[79] It is generally thought that the Coptic presents the better form of the text, which was originally composed in Greek, even though it is more fragmentary than the Ethiopic.

A range of dates has been plausibly argued for the work, from around 120 CE to the late second century. In addition to the general tone and theological character of the text, a good deal hinges on how one evaluates the striking claim of chapter 17, presented in variant forms in the Coptic and Ethiopic, concerning the time of the second coming of Christ. According to the Coptic this will occur when the "hundredth part and the twentieth part is completed"—that is, 120 years after Christ. According to the Ethiopic it will be "when the hundred and fiftieth year is completed." The obvious interpretive issues involve the thirty-year difference between the two accounts and the question of when one is to begin the timetable: at Jesus' birth, for example, or at his death? The temporal discrepancy is most easily explained by the passage of time, with the Ethiopic translation having been created some years after the 120th year had already been completed. As to when the counting should begin, it seems unlikely that the highly anticipated end of all things would be dated from Jesus' birth, as that was not celebrated in the second century, but from his death and resurrection, which was commemorated not only every year at Easter but every single week of the year. If, as seems most plausible, the Coptic preserves the earlier form of the text, then it was in all likelihood produced sometime before 150 CE or so, possibly close to that time.[80]

Manfred Hornschuh provided the pivotal study of the text in 1965.[81] Notwithstanding his many stunning insights, some of Hornschuh's overarching claims appear today rather quaint, if not quite bizarre, especially his contention that the Epistula "cannot be understood either as a document of ancient Christian origins nor as the gnosis of early Catholicism." For Hornschuh, the document is not "early Christian" because it has a divergent understanding of the person and work of Christ (in his view, the Christology is ultimately docetic, even though the

79. *Le testament en Galilée de notre-Seigneur Jésus Christ* (Paris: Firmin-Didot, 1912).

80. See further Charles E. Hill, "The *Epistula Apostolorum*: An Asian Tract from the Time of Polycarp," *JECS* 7 (1999): 1–53. J. de Zwaan bypasses the dating provided by chapter 17 in favor of the issues raised and resolved concerning the Quartodeciman controversy, but as a result dates the work almost certainly too late to 195 CE; "Date and Origin of the Epistle of the Eleven Apostles," in *Amicitiae Corolla: A Volume of Essays Presented to James Rendel Harris, D.Litt., on the Occasion of His Eightieth Birthday*, ed. H. G. Wood (London: University of London Press, 1933), 344–55. So too J. K. Elliott's claim that the "consensus" places the text in the third quarter of the second century does not take chapter 17 with sufficient seriousness (*The Apocryphal New Testament*, p. 556). Options for the location of the composition are almost literally all over the map, Asia, Syria, and Alexandria being the leading suspects. In addition to the articles of Hill and de Zwaan, see A. Stewart-Sykes, "The Asian Context of the New Prophecy and of *the Epistula Apostolorum*" *VC* 51 (1997): 416–38.

81. *Studien zur Epistula Apostolorum* (Berlin: De Gruyter, 1965). The more recent full-length study of Julian Hills, *Tradition and Composition in the Epistula Apostolorum* (Minneapolis: Fortress, 1990), is less concerned with the theological and polemical investments of the text than with its structure, composition, and the relation of tradition and redaction.

polemic is anti-docetic)[82]; it is not "early Catholic" because it assigns no significance to the church and church offices. The book instead reflects a situation in which the author belongs to a minority anti-Gnostic group that has been forced out of the larger (Gnostic) community.

Hornschuh is certainly right in his stress that the book is anti-Gnostic. But there is no reason to see the book as a secessionist document or to deny its essentially proto-orthodox orientation. Apart from the now obsolete construction of "Frühkatholizismus," Hornschuh's view does not consider the wide range of possibilities open to a proto-orthodox author. Not everyone had to obsess over church hierarchy and offices. Moreover, the book goes out of its way to stress important aspects of the emerging regula fidei, as we will see.

The book is presented as a revelatory letter that "Jesus Christ revealed to his disciples" (ch. 1).[83] It does not assume the form of an epistle, however, but of a postresurrection dialogue, known now so well from precisely the kinds of Gnostic texts to which the book sets itself in opposition. Its pseudepigraphic character, in any event, is clear from the outset. It is a letter describing the experiences of the eleven disciples with the risen Christ after his death and resurrection, written in the first-person plural. The eleven are named and, as has happened before, both Peter and Cephas are said to belong to the apostolic band, as are both Nathaniel and Bartholomew.[84]

The occasion of the letter is the teachings of "the false apostles Simon and Cerinthus." The writer stresses that "in them is deceit with which they kill men." The alternative views of the forger are stated at the outset, as he assures his readers in the names of the true apostles that "we have heard and felt him after he has risen from the dead" and that he "has revealed to us things great, astonishing, real" (ch. 2). The author then launches into a proto-orthodox regula: "Christ is God and Son of God, who was sent from God, the ruler of the entire world, the maker and creator of what is named with every name. . . ." The bulk of the book provides an account of Jesus' teaching to the eleven after appearing to them in his resurrected body, prior to departing from them in the final chapter. That the teaching

82. "Läßt sich weder als ein Dokument des Urchristentums noch der Gnosis noch des Frühkatholizismus begreifen." On docetism: "The fact that Jesus is risen in the flesh has therefore meaning only as a fact that is supposed to demonstrate the reliability of Jesus's teaching" ("Das Faktum, daß Jesus im Fleische auferstanden ist, hat mithin nur die Bedeutung eines Tatbeweises, der die Gläubigkeit der von Jesus verkündigten Lehre demonstrieren soll"). Further, "The determination of the Risen One's bodiliness serves only as proof and for the confirmation of the teaching concerning the resurrection of the flesh. The Epistula Apostolorum is thus quite distinct from the views of Ignatius and Irenaeus" ("Die Feststellung der Leiblichkeit des Auferstandenen dient nur zum Beweis und zur Bestätigung der Lehre von der allgemeinen Auferstehung im Fleische. Von den Anschauungen des Ignatius und des Irenäus ist die Epistula Apostolorum weit geschieden"; p. 60). I could not disagree more. Throughout his *Studien* Hornschuh uses an essentialized understanding of what it means to be "Christian" and shows that the Epistula Apostolorum does not stack up well against it.

83. Translations of C. Detlef G. Muller in Schneemelcher, *New Testament Apocrypha*.

84. See p. 397.

is needed because of dangerous heresy is reiterated in Jesus' final words to his disciples: "There will come another teaching and a conflict; and in that they seek their own glory and produce worthless teaching an offence of death will come thereby, and they will teach and turn away from my commandment even those who believe in me and bring them out of eternal life." Both the teachers and those who heed them "will be eternally punished."

That the form of this revelation is closely related to what can be found in Gnostic "secret revelation" resurrection dialogues was recognized early on, by Schmidt himself.[85] Schmidt, however, maintained that the book was not meant to attack Gnostics, but to confirm the "catholics" in their faith.[86] Hornschuh, on the other hand, rightly saw that this is a false dichotomy. The Epistula Apostolorum confirms "catholic" views precisely by contradicting the views of their opponents: "One can scarcely deny that the important parts of the letter are to be understood in no other way than as a refutation of the Gnostics."[87]

Hornschuh notes comparable motifs in such Gnostic works as the Gospel of Mary, the Apocryphon of John, the Sophia of Jesus Christ, and the Pistis Sophia. More could easily be named.[88] The conclusion is near to hand: the author took up the weapon of his enemies in order to fight against them.[89] One major difference, as Hornschuh notes, is that whereas for Gnostics the revelations made by the resurrected Jesus entailed esoteric knowledge for insiders, for the author of the Epistula Apostolorum they are for broad publication. Here they are given in a letter for universal distribution: "As we have heard it, kept it, and have written it for the whole world" (ch. 1).

Of yet greater moment is the substance of the teaching. And in this book, it is all about substance: the flesh of Christ, the fleshly nature of his resurrection, and the fleshly character of the believers' resurrection yet to come. Even though the incarnation is described in a Gnostic-like account (though see Melchizedek and the Ascension of Isaiah) of the descent of Christ through "the heavens" (ch.

---

85. "In the most worrisome fashion, the author thus touches upon the pseudepigraphal activity of the Gnostics who in addition to the general instruction during their public teaching had chosen in particular the post-resurrection period for their special revelations" ("Damit streift der Verfasser auf das bedenklichste der pseudepigraphische Schriftstellerei der Gnostiker, die neben der allgemeinen Unterweisung während der öffentlichen Lehrtätigkeit besonders die Zeit nach der Auferstehung für ihre Spezialoffenbarungen sich ausgesucht hatten"). Schmidt, *Gespräche*, p. 202.

86. *Gespräche*, p. 198.

87. "Man [wird] schwerlich bestreiten können, daß wichtige Partien des Briefes nicht anders zu verstehen sind denn als Widerlegung der Gnostiker," Hornschuh, *Studien*, p. 7. Hornschuh tried to be more precise in naming the opponents, and settled on a group of Basilideans (p. 94). Most scholars today are, rightly, more reserved in thinking that we can pinpoint one Gnostic sect over another. Among other things, if the Basilideans were in view, why are they set under the guise specifically of Simon and Cerinthus? It is better to think here in terms of a general polemic against Gnostic teachings found among a number of groups.

88. See, e.g., Pheme Perkins, *The Gnostic Dialogue: The Early Church and the Crisis of Gnosticism* (New York: Paulist Press, 1980).

89. Hornschuh, *Studien*, p. 7.

13), in which he passed by "the angels and archangels in their form and as one of them," becoming "like an angel to the angels," when he went "into Mary" he "became flesh" (ch. 14). And this was not an appearance. He was flesh and he remained flesh, as emphasized throughout the account. After his resurrection his disciples "thought it was a ghost" but he demonstrated to them that "I am he who spoke to you concerning my flesh, my death, and my resurrection" (ch. 11). At his insistence the disciples feel him and his wounds; and he tells Andrew "look at my feet and see if they do not touch the ground (Ethiopic: leave a footprint). For it is written in the prophet, 'The foot of a ghost or demon does not join to the ground' (Eth.: "leaves no print on the ground").

This passage provides a stark contrast to the docetic Acts of John, and its famous passage in which the apostle realizes that Jesus did not have a real body and notices to his amazement that the resurrected Jesus leaves no footprint:

> I will tell you another glory, brethren; sometimes when I meant to touch him I encountered a material, solid body; but at other times again when I felt him, his substance was immaterial and incorporeal, and as if it did not exist at all. . . . And I often wished, as I walked with him, to see if his footprint appeared on the ground—for I saw him raising himself from the earth—and I never saw it. (Acts of John, 93)

Not so with the *Epistula Apostolorum*. After Jesus' resurrection, "we felt him, that he had truly risen in the flesh" (ch. 12). As Jesus later stresses, "I have put on your flesh, in which I was born and died and was buried and rose again" (ch. 19). Moreover, just as Christ rose "in the flesh" so too "you also will arise" (ch. 21). For indeed: "The flesh of every one will rise with his soul alive, and his spirit" (ch. 24; repeated in chs. 25 and 26). Moreover, those who teach "another teaching" will experience real punishment involving physical pain in the afterlife (ch. 29); those who suffer physical persecution in this world, on the other hand, will receive a heavenly reward (ch. 38).

Clearly in the Epistula Apostolorum we are dealing with a counterforgery on numerous levels. In the weak sense, it is a book that counters widespread and popular views that claimed that Christ did not really and permanently come in the flesh. More specifically, it is countering such notions as found in the book's generic parallels in the Gnostic revelation dialogues. This would include such a writing as the Nag Hammadi letter of Peter to Philip, which also records a (non-pseudepigraphic)[90] postresurrection revelation of Christ. Here, though, Christ is not a fleshly being after his resurrection; he comes to the disciples as a light and a voice. Moreover, even though he appeared to experience his Passion, it was all an appearance: "My brothers, Jesus is a stranger to this suffering" (138.21–22).

---

90. Only the opening letter of the account, not the revelation dialogue, is forged.

But in the strongest sense, the Epistula Apostolorum is countering views found precisely in other forgeries. Numerous striking parallels can be found, for example, with the *Book of Thomas the Contender*, discussed earlier, which contained "secret words" as opposed to those here that are to be published throughout the whole world (138:1); which insisted that salvation comes only when spirits remove themselves from the world of flesh (139.28–30); which taught that the "vessel of the flesh will dissolve and . . . [be] brought to naught" (141.5–8); which pronounces a woe on "you who hope in the flesh and in the prison that will perish" (143.10–11); and which ends with the exhortation "Watch and pray that you not come to be in the flesh, but rather that you come forth from the bondage of the bitterness of this life" (145.8–10).

Not so for the Epistula Apostolorum, a proto-orthodox forgery that stresses in the names of the apostles that Christ took on real flesh, remained in the flesh, rose in the flesh, and informed his followers that they too would rise, in the flesh.

The Letter to the Laodiceans

The Letter of "Paul" to the Laodiceans survives in a large number of manuscripts of the Latin Bible from the sixth to the fifteenth centuries.[91] The letter is a pastiche of Pauline phrases with no obvious theme or purpose. Apart from the opening line, drawn from Gal. 1:1, the borrowings are almost entirely from Philippians. About a tenth of the letter represents "filler" provided by the author, which is also without character or color.[92]

Scholars have long vied with one another to see who could express the greatest contempt for the letter's sheer banality. Thus Leon Vouaux in 1913: "It is indeed as trivial as possible;[93] Karl Pink in 1925: "The letter is a pitiful concoction without any kind of personal note on behalf of the author, without a trace of heresy, without bias or purpose";[94] Adolf Harnack in 1931: "It is with regard to content and form the most worthless document that has come down to us from Christian antiquity";[95] and most recently Régis Burnet, who moves the lament to the title of an article: "Pourquoi avoir écrit l'insipide épître aux Laodicéens?"[96] The letter

91. The first critical edition was produced by Brooke Foss Westcott, *A General Survey of the History of the Canon of the New Testament*, 4th ed. (London: Macmillan, 1875), pp. 561–76.

92. Pervo is unusual in seeing the letter as something other than a pastiche; he wants to stress the epistolary character of the piece, as constructed, and to read it, then, with a generous spirit. See *Making of Paul*, pp. 106–9.

93. "Elle est en effet aussi anodine que possible." *Les actes de Paul et ses lettres apocryphes . . .* (Paris: Letouzey et Ané, 1913), p. 321.

94. "Der Brief [ist] ein armseliges Elaborat ohne jede persönliche Note des Verfassers ohne Spur von Häresie, ohne Tendenz und Zweck"; "Die pseudo-Paulinischen Briefe," *Bib* 6 (1925): 190.

95. "Es ist übrigens nach Inhalt und Form die wertloseste Urkunde, die aus dem kirchlichen Altertum auf uns gekommen ist"; *Apocrypha IV: Die apokryphen Briefe des Paulus an die Laodicener und Korinther*, 2nd ed. (Berlin: de Gruyter, 1931), p. 3.

96. Viz., "Why Was the Insipid Letter to the Laodiceans Written?" *NTS* 48 (2002): 132–41.

nonetheless serves an interesting historical function, as I will argue below: it appears to be a forgery meant to provide an indirect counter to those who would deny the value of the flesh.

The early references to the letter are confused and confusing. The Muratorian Fragment speaks of Marcionite forgeries of "Pauline" letters to the Alexandrians and the Laodiceans. The former no longer survives in any form; with respect to the latter, it is impossible to determine if the unknown author of the canon has our extant letter in view. If so, it is difficult to know why he would have considered it Marcionite, had he actually managed to read it.[97] Tertullian, soon thereafter, also indicates that the Marcionites had a letter to the Laodiceans, but claims that this was none other than an edited and renamed version of Ephesians (i.e., not a separate production; *Adv. Marc.* 5. 11, 17). Epiphanius complicates matters when he argues that Laodiceans was a separate, fifteenth Pauline letter; but when he quotes from it, he cites Eph. 4:5 (*Panarion*, 42.9.12).

With just these earliest references to a Laodicean letter, then, we are left with a host of puzzles. In the early centuries was there just one letter to the Laodiceans (the one we now have) which was sometimes mistakenly identified as an edition of Ephesians by people who had not actually seen it? Or were there two (e.g., ours and one forged by Marcionites)? Or three (ours, the Marcionites', and an edited form of Ephesians)? And just with respect to our earliest reference: Did the author of the Muratorian Fragment have our letter in mind but not realize that it was not, in fact, Marcionite? Did he have another letter in mind, and not know about our letter? Or did he have our letter and think (as later Harnack would argue) that it was a Marcionite production?

After Epiphanius, references to the letter proliferate.[98] It is only with the Pseudo-Augustinian *Speculum* of the fifth-sixth centuries, however, that we have an actual quotation of our Laodiceans. Moreover, the author of this falsely attributed work sees the letter as canonical. This is also about the time of our earliest manuscript evidence for its existence, in the codex Fuldensis, produced by Victor of Capua in 546 CE. The letter is now found in the better manuscripts of the Vulgate[99]; it came to be widely respected in the West despite the condemnation of Jerome (*Vir. ill.* 5) and others. It was reproduced in German Bibles prior to Luther, for example, and in Czech Bibles until the seventeenth century, where it was placed between Colossians and 1 Thessalonians.[100] But it was rejected unanimously in the Greek-speaking East, most notably at the Second Council of Nicea in 787 CE.[101]

97. Pink ("Die pseudo-Paulinischen Briefe") argued that the author of the Muratorian Fragment did not realize that the Marcionites had renamed Ephesians Laodiceans (as Tertullian indicates) and so supposed that a separate letter must have existed, not being familiar with the letter that we now have.

98. For a full listing, see Pink, "Die pseudo-Paulinischen Briefe."

99. See Burnet, "Pourquoi," p. 132.

100. Thus ibid., p. 133.

101. See Vouaux, *Les actes*, p. 320.

There have been long debates over the original language of the letter, with Westcott arguing that it was written in Latin and his colleague J. B. Lightfoot, who provided the first full collations, arguing for Greek.[102] Harnack opted for a totalizing view, suggesting that it was originally produced in both a Latin form (known to the Muratorian Fragment) and in Greek. That, however, is more a council of despair than a conclusion, and in any event, even with a bilingual edition, one of the two would necessarily have to have been written first.[103] As to when the letter was produced, in theory it could have been any time before our first hard evidence for its existence—the *Speculum*—though most scholars date it much earlier, to the end of the second century, a date that makes good sense in view of its possible occasion and purpose, as will be seen.

This matter of occasion and purpose has long vexed scholars. The most common explanation is also the most obvious one, that the letter was produced by someone intent on filling the lacuna occasioned by the reference in Col. 4:16: "When this letter is read by you, see also that it is read in Laodicea and that you as well read the one from Laodicea."[104] If Paul mentions a letter sent to the Laodiceans, there must once have been one, and some unknown forger set out to create it. Burnet objects that the letter could not have been generated on these grounds, since Colossians speaks of a letter ἐκ Λαοδικαίας rather than a letter πρὸς Λαοδικαίαν. And it is true that as early as Chrysostom it was sometimes thought that the reference in Col. 4:16 was not to a letter Paul had written but a letter Paul had received.[105] But there is no reason to push the language so hard. The Colossians passage is frequently read even today as referring to a letter sent by Paul to the Laodiceans, which the Colossian church would get, therefore "from" them, and there is no reason that a forger might not have construed the passage in this way as well. It scarcely need be stressed that since Colossians itself is forged, there is no way of knowing whether the reference to a Laodicean letter indicates real knowledge of some such writing or represents, instead, a simple verisimilitude of the earlier forger.

Even without pressing the logic of the preposition used in Col. 4:16, one might still question if its reference to a now-lost letter can explain the banal concatenation of Pauline phrases that have come down to us as the letter to the Laodiceans. Why would anyone feel compelled to produce such a letter, simply because one was once "known" to exist? Surely something drove the forgery outside of idle curiosity or

102. For Westcott see note 91; J. B. Lightfoot, *Epistle to the Colossians and to Philemon* (London: Macmillan, 1904), pp. 291–92. Lightfoot provided a retroversion to the "original" Greek.

103. See Harnack *Apocrypha IV*. Pink had argued that the Graecisms, cited by Lightfoot, do not require a Greek original, since so much of the letter is drawn from Pauline works originally penned in Greek. He goes on to argue that the letter draws on vocabulary invented by Tertullian (thus "dilectio" and "retractus") and so was written in Latin no earlier than the mid-third century. But the first occurrence of the terms in Tertullian does not prove that he invented them. Their appearance in the letter therefore indicates nothing about its original language or date.

104. Thus, for example, Vouaux, *Les actes* and Pink, "Die pseudo-Paulinischen Briefe."

105. Chrysostom, *Homily 12* on Col. 4:16.

the desire to supply what was lost. Was it, really, just a random writing exercise? Why then would it have been put into such wide circulation? And how might the author's motivation relate to the character of the letter he produced, which, had he signed his real name to it, would have opened him up to the charge of plagiarism?

The most radical view came in the later writings of Adolf Harnack, who changed his tune toward the end of his career and decided that in fact our surviving letter is the Marcionite forgery denounced by the Muratorian Fragment.[106] The letter, in Harnack's judgment, was forged not by Marcion, but by one of his followers. The forger kept his work, with its Marcionite tendencies, very subtle so as to escape detection and enable broad distribution. And his ploy obviously worked. No one except the anonymous author of the Muratorian Fragment recognized the writing for what it was. Until Harnack.

Harnack argues that, despite all previous scholarship, the Marcionite character of the writing can be shown irrefutably (unwiderleglich). His most important points are the following:

- Marcion's "Apostolos" began with the letter to the Galatians, which provided the foundation for all that follows, starting with Gal. 1:1. And that is the verse with which the letter to the Laodiceans begins.
- Philippians begins with the words "I give thanks to my God." Laodiceans echoes the thanksgiving with a key change that reveals the author's modalistic (i.e., Marcionite) Christology: "I give thanks to Christ" (v. 3).
- On two occasions in vv. 4–5 the author warns against the vapid preaching of false teachers, which stands over against the "veritas evangelii." This phrase, "the truth of the Gospel" is a Marcionite terminus technicus. Moreover, by stressing that this true gospel is "preached by me," the author sets his (Paul's) proclamation over that of other evangelists or apostles—a key Marcionite emphasis.
- Marcion denied the promise of knowledge of "eternal life" to those who adhered to the Old Testament and, especially, to the catholic Christians. "Eternal life" became a catchword of his proclamation and for his church. And strikingly the phrase "eternal life" shows up twice, unexpectedly, in this letter in vv. 5 and 10 (cf. v. 7).

Harnack concludes: "These observations are decisive: our letter is a Marcionite forgery."[107] As indicated, however, for him the letter did not derive from Marcion

106. The fullest statement of the view is found in *Marcion: Das Evangelium vom fremden Gott; eine Monographie zur Geschichte der Grundlegung der Katholischen Kirche*, "Beilage III: Das Apostolikon Marcion," part D: "Der Laodicener- und der Alexandrinerbrief" (Leipzig: J. C. Hinrichs, 1924), pp. 134*–49*, which is based on an article published the previous year in *Sitzungsberichte der Preuß. Akademie*, Nov. 1, 1923.

107. "Diese Beobachtungen entscheiden: unser Brief ist eine Marcionitische Fälschung." *Marcion*, p. 143*.

himself. For one thing, Marcion renamed Ephesians Laodiceans, and so had no reason to create a separate letter to the Laodiceans. What is more, the letter was not produced as Marcion produced his other "biblical" writings, which was through editing, not creating/compiling. And so one of Marcion's followers produced it after his lifetime but before the Muratorian Canon, 160–190 CE. This unknown author wanted to fill the gap left by Col. 4:16 and did so by bringing the clandestine Marcionite teachings (die heimlich Marcionitischen Lehren) to expression in a way that catholic Christians would not be able to detect. And so he worked with Pauline phrases, principally from Philippians, because it was relatively easy, using this epistle, to make the composition appear harmless. Fearing to show his hand, he did not include any explicitly Marcionite teachings in the letter.

If anyone could make a case for the banal letter of the Laodiceans being a Marcionite forgery, it would have been the mighty Harnack. But he won virtually no converts to his view. Each of his points individually appears weak: (1) if the author wanted to stress Galatians at the outset, why would he not quote it more extensively throughout, and use at least one phrase that actually mattered for the Marcionite cause? (2) the exchange of God and Christ was exceedingly common in early scribal and homiletical contexts, and never required a Marcionite modalism for explanatory force; (3) false teachers are a problem for every Christian group, not just the Marcionites; (4) so too eternal life was a ubiquitous concern. More than that, there simply is no Marcionite theology in the letter. To claim that the author worked subtly would be an understatement: even heresiologists known for their ability to sniff out heresy where none existed did not detect a whiff of Marcionism in the letter. The letter would certainly not have been accepted in the West had there been the least thing to suspect in it; moreover, there would be no reason for the author of the Muratorian Canon to oppose the Marcionite "Laodiceans" if in fact this pastiche of Pauline phrases were it. There must, then, be a different explanation.

The most recent attempt at solving the problem is by R. Burnet, who tries to use the set of commonplaces that constitute the letter to advantage, in arguing that the letter has no point except to exist precisely as a letter of Paul.[108] Unlike Paul himself, who used his letters as a substitute for his oral message when personally present, this letter has no message: it simply is "Paul" making himself present. Moreover, since the letter talks of eternal life—and thus eternity—this letter is not from the historical Paul but from the Paul living in eternity. It is Paul writing from heaven. The purpose of the letter is not to convey a message but to convey an apostolic presence from the world beyond.

Burnet's hypothesis, which, he admits with a bit of understatement, is "sans avoir de preuve" (p. 140), is that the Christians in Laodicea were jealous of the fact that Paul had written a letter to the Colossians, and so created a letter of their

---

108. "Pourquoi."

own, so that they too could claim to have an apostolic presence in their midst. The letter was important for them for its status as an object; not for the message it conveys (since it conveys none).

Unlike Harnack, Burnet does not attempt to offer any argument for his hypothesis, which must, as a result, remain as unprovable as any baseless hypothesis. It should be noted, however, that there is no evidence that the letter was actually produced in, read in, cherished in, or preserved in Laodicea. Nothing connects it with Laodicea other than its address. Any real association with the Christians there—about whom we know next to nothing—is necessarily imaginary.

A more compelling option was suggested by Wolfgang Speyer, although he did not explicate it in any detail. This is a view that turns Harnack's suggestion precisely on its head: our letter to the Laodiceans is not the Marcionite forgery mentioned by the Muratorian Fragment, but a proto-orthodox counterforgery, produced precisely to oppose the (now-lost, if it ever existed) Marcionite version.[109]

If hard-pressed one could dig as deep into the well as did Harnack to find characteristics of the letter that could be taken in anti-Marcionite ways. The author, claiming to be Paul, tells his reasons to avoid false teaching that leads "away from the truth of the gospel" (v. 4). And why? Because of what will happen on the "day of judgment" (v. 3). That day will be survived by those who do the appropriate "good works" (v. 5). The author stresses his own suffering, which will lead to salvation (vv. 6–7). The author is happy to die for the sake of the gospel (v. 8). These are all tactile phenomena. The author stresses the importance of the physical response to the gospel: to do good, to act for God, to suffer, to die—all for God. Salvation does not come from an empty belief in a docetic Christ, but a hard-fought life of love and service.

But not too much can be made of the tactility expressed in the letter. The reason for thinking it is an anti-Marcionite forgery is that it exists. This is comparable to the supposition of Burnet, but in this case there is both an argument and a logic. What we know historically is this. In proto-orthodox circles, as evidenced in the Muratorian Fragment and Epiphanius, for example, it was known—or at least believed—that a Marcionite forgery existed, a letter of Paul to the Laodiceans. This forgery, whether real or imagined, was almost certainly conceived of on the basis of Col. 4:16, and was with equal certainty a forgery that actually (or imaginarily) pressed a Marcionite agenda (which, among other things, opposed the material world, Christ's flesh, and the importance of human flesh). Proto-orthodox writers not only knew of the existence of this forgery; they also, naturally, opposed it. But what would be the best way to show that the Marcionite forgery was not the letter Paul was referring to in Col. 4:16? What better way than to produce the *real* letter of Paul to the Laodiceans? If the real item existed, the Marcionite version would be exposed as a forgery.

---

109. Speyer, *Die literarische Fälschung*, p. 229.

And so a proto-orthodox author produced the "real" thing. That is why the letter is both completely banal and totally dependent on other Pauline letters. There was no point to the forgery other than its existence, to show that the Marcionite forgery was a fraud. But it had to sound very much like Paul to be convincing. And who sounds more like Paul than Paul? The forger then simply borrowed a large number of phrases from Galatians and, especially, Philippians, strung them together, gave them a Pauline epistolary frame and format, and thereby accomplished his aim. The letter he produced was "the" Letter to the Laodiceans. To counter the Marcionite forgery it did not have to replicate anti-Marcionite polemic. All it had to do was sound like Paul. The author succeeded spectacularly. The letter circulated as part of the New Testament throughout a large chunk of the Latin Middle Ages.

The Apocalypse of Peter

The Apocalypse of Peter, to be differentiated from the Coptic Apocalypse of the same name, was discovered during the winter excavation season of 1886–87 by a French archeological team, digging in Cemetery A at al-Hawawis in the desert necropolis of Akhmim. It is one of four texts included in the sixty-six page book that included, as well, the Gospel of Peter.[110] Debates over the date of the manuscript have been most satisfactorily resolved by Cavallo and Maehler, who place the hand in the late sixth century.[111] Since the discovery, two small Greek fragments have appeared, shown by M. R. James to derive from a single manuscript. One of these is now in the Bodlean; the other is in the Erzherzog Rainer collection in Vienna.[112]

The Ethiopic version of the apocalypse was uncovered from the manuscript tradition of the Pseudo-Clementines, and published in 1907 and 1910 by E. Grébaut, though not recognized as belonging to the same account as the Greek text until 1911, again by M. R. James.[113] Today it is generally recognized that the Ethiopic version, which was probably derived from Arabic, is the older of the two, and that the surviving Greek text has been seriously edited, possibly in order to make it more closely aligned with the Gospel of Peter in the same codex.[114] The

110. The fullest and best account of the discovery and of the codicological issues involved is in Peter van Minnen, "The Greek *Apocalypse of Peter*," in Jan Bremmer and István Czachesz, eds., *The Apocalypse of Peter* (Leuven: Peeters, 2003), pp. 15–39.

111. G. Cavallo and H. Maehler, *Greek Bookhands of the Early Byzantine Period, A.D. 300–800* (London: University of London, Institute of Classical Studies, 1987), no. 41.

112. The first full study of the text of the Akhmim text was Dieterich's *Nekyia; Beiträge zur Erklärung der neuentdeckten Petrusapokalypse* (Leipzig: Teubner, 1893), conducted, obviously, prior to the discovery of the more accurate Ethiopic version.

113. Grébaut, "Littérature éthiopienne ps. Clémentine. La second venue du Christ et la resurrection des morts," *ROC* (1907): 139–51; (1910): 198–214, 307–23, 425–39; M. R. James, "A New Text of the Apocalypse of Peter," *JTS* 12 (1910/11): 36–54, 362–83, 573–83.

114. Thus Müller: "That the Ethiopic version is authentic and offers the original text of the Apocalypse of Peter, albeit in parts somewhat distorted, can scarcely be contested any longer today." C. Detlef G. Müller in Schneemelcher, *New Testament Apocrypha*, 2.625.

differences between the two versions matter a good deal for interpretation. As van Minnen points out, the Akhmim fragment edits away all positive "references to things Jewish."[115] Of yet greater significance for our purposes in this chapter, the future punishments of the damned in the Ethiopic account are transformed in the Greek into punishments in the present for those dwelling in heaven and hell.

Date

There have been numerous debates over the date of the writing. As it is cited by Clement of Alexandria (Eusebius, *H.E.* 6.14.1; *Ecl. Proph.* 41.2, 48–49) and named by the Muratorian Fragment, it can clearly date no later than the mid second century.[116] Some scholars have urged greater precision in the dating, notably D. Buchholz and especially R. Bauckham, who base their arguments on the interpretation of the parable of the fig tree in chapter 2.[117] Here Peter asks for an explanation of the parable, and Christ launches into a detailed exposition. The fig tree "is the house of Israel."[118] Once its branches sprout, then "shall deceiving Christs come, and awaken hope (with the words): 'I am the Christ.'" One in particular will arise who "is not the Christ." And when the followers of Jesus reject this one, "he will kill with the sword (dagger) and there shall be many martyrs." These "shall be reckoned among the good and righteous martyrs who have pleased God in their life."

Bauckham argues that this passage refers to the false messiah Bar Kochba and to his slaying of Christians who refused to participate in the second revolt, as mentioned by Justin (see 1 *Apol.* 31). The Apocalypse, then, can be dated to the time of the second revolt, 132–35 CE. Other scholars, however, such as van Minnen, have made convincing counterarguments. Even if ch. 2 refers to the events under Bar Kochba—which is not clear, as the references are far from precise—that would simply mean that the text would date to some period later than 135; Bar Kochba, in that case, may be used by the text as an example of the *kind* of antichrist that will arise.[119] E. Tigchelaar goes even farther: the text at issue is corrupt, most of the terms used of the messianic figure are stock, there is no evidence that Bar Kochba killed "many" Christians, and many of the historical references of the text work as well for the events of 115–17 CE. One payoff is that we cannot use the

115. "The Greek *Apocalypse*," p. 28.

116. See Dennis D. Buchholz, *Your Eyes Will Be Opened: A Study of the Greek (Ethiopic) Apocalypse of Peter* (Atlanta: Scholars Press, 1988), p. 17. Buchholz counts twelve direct references to the account and eighteen indirect references (pp. 20–81). A more conservative presentation can now be found in Thomas J. Kraus and Tobias Nicklas, eds., *Das Petrusevangelium und die Petrusapokalypse: Die griechischen Fragment mit deutscher und englischer Übersetzung* (Berlin: de Gruyter, 2004), pp. 87–99.

117. Richard Bauckham, "The *Apocalypse of Peter*: A Jewish Christian Apocalypse from the Time of Bar Kokhba," *Apocrypha* 5 (1994): 7–111; reprinted in Bauckham, *The Fate of the Dead: Studies on the Jewish and Christian Apocalypses* (Leiden: Brill, 1998), pp. 160–258. Original pages are indicated here. Buchholz, *Your Eyes Will Be Opened.*

118. Translations taken from C. Detlef G. Müller in Schneemelcher, *New Testament Apocrypha.*

119. Van Minnen, "The Greek *Apocalypse.*"

second revolt as the hermeneutical lens for reading the account.[120] At most we can say that the document was produced at least by the middle of the second century.

Whenever it was produced, the Apocalypse of Peter proved to be a historically significant book. It was considered to be part of Scripture by Clement of Alexandria[121] and the scribe of codex Claramontanus. It is listed as a disputed book in the Muratorian Fragment and the Stichometry of Nicephorus. Eusebius saw it as spurious (*H.E.* 3.3.2, 3.25.4, 6.14.1), but Sozomen reported that it was used in public worship on Good Friday (*H.E.* 7.19). It is not, however found in the Gelasian Decree.

Narrative

The Apocalypse of Peter is noteworthy as the first surviving account of a guided tour of the realms of the damned (chs. 3–12, Ethiopic) and the blessed (chs. 13–16; the Greek reverses the sequence). The beginning of the narrative sounds very much like the opening of the famous apocalyptic discourse of Mark 13 and its Synoptic parallels: "And when he was seated on the Mount of Olives, his own came unto him, and we entreated and implored him severally and besought him saying unto him, 'Make known unto us what are the signs of thy parousia and of the end of the world.'"

The bulk of the narrative, then, recounts in graphic detail and some voyeuristic glee the fates awaiting souls in the age to come. The account concludes with an alternative version of the transfiguration, in which Peter volunteers to build "three tabernacles," one for Jesus, one for Moses, and one for Elijah; a voice comes from heaven affirming that Christ is the beloved Son, and then a great cloud comes to take away all three of them.

Bauckham in particular has argued that the narrative is not to be seen as a variation on the apocalyptic discourse of the Synoptics but as a postresurrection narrative.[122] If he were right, the work would present the final words of the resurrected Jesus to his followers and could be seen as a kind of counterforgery to the Gnostic revelation dialogues. In this it would be much like the Epistula Apostolorum, as here—contrary to the Gnostic counterparts—the real physical experiences of the afterlife are quite emphatically in the flesh. But the account, as we will see, is anti-Gnostic wherever one places it in the story of Jesus, and it is very hard indeed to deny that the opening sets the stage for an alternative description of the small apocalypse of Mark 13 and its parallels. Moreover, the conclusion is not an ascension narrative, as Bauckham is forced to argue, but contains all the elements

---

120. Eibert Tigchelaar, "Is the Liar Bar Kokhba? Considering the Date and the Provenance of the Greek (Ethiopic) *Apocalypse of Peter*," in Bremmer and Czachesz, eds., *The Apocalypse of* Peter, pp. 63–77.

121. James A. Brooks, "Clement of Alexandria as a Witness to the Development of the New Testament Canon," *SecCent* 9 (1992): 41–55.

122. *Apocalypse of Peter*, pp. 19–20.

of the transfiguration scene (Peter's presence; Moses and Elijah; the voice from heaven; the cloud).

In any event, the "tour" (real or imagined) that Christ gives Peter of the respective realms of the dead focuses on the tactile experiences of the afterlife. Most attention has been paid to the horrific punishments meted out to sinners. Five times in the account the author stresses that each one will be treated "according to his deeds" performed while living. Nowhere is the point more emphatic than at the outset, where Christ proclaims:

> Recompense shall be given to each according to his work. As for the elect who have done good, they will come to me and will not see death by devouring fire. But the evil creatures, the sinners and the hypocrites will stand in the depths of the darkness that passes not away, and their punishment is the fire, and angels bring forward their sins and prepare for them a place wherein they shall be punished for ever, each according to his offence. (ch. 6)

What has struck scholars most is that many of the punishments of hell work on the principle of the lex talionis. This is not simply a Jewish notion, as István Czachesz points out by recalling the clever line in Aelius Theon's *Progymnasmata*: "Didymon the flute player, on being convicted of adultery, was hanged by his namesake."[123] But as also widely noted, not all of the punishments described in the book are "kind for kind." In the helpful taxonomy of Bauckham, four of the twenty-one torments are specifically body part for body part; and six others could be construed this way. Others, however, replicate common human punishments made eternal (whips, burnings); others reflect what happens typically to exposed human corpses (being eaten by birds); and yet others have traditional associations with the Jewish place of punishment, Gehenna (darkness, fire).[124] In any event, the punishments are individualized for different kinds of sin; they are as a whole meant to vindicate God's justice; they are retributive, not reformatory (too late for all that!); and they are eternal—a fact stressed eleven times in the older form of the Ethiopic, though edited out in the Greek, possibly because the editor had an alternative understanding of eschatological realities. This final point is worth stressing. In the Ethiopic version the punishments describe what will be; in the Greek they are what is occurring in the present. One cannot help but suspect that the de-apocalypticized version represents a transformation generated by the failure of the end to materialize, or at least the heightened sense that it probably never would materialize in the way formerly anticipated.

---

123. István Czachesz, "The Grotesque Body in the *Apocalypse of Peter*," in Bremmer and Czachesz, eds., *The Apocalypse of Peter*, p. 108.

124. See Callie Callon, "Sorcery, Wheels, and Mirror Punishment in the *Apocalypse of Peter*," *JECS* 18 (2010): 29–49.

The Polemical Nature of the Text

Even though the Apocalypse of Peter engages in rather obvious attacks on certain immoral activities and the people who engage in them, it does not level its assault on any groups of heretics or false teachers (in contrast, as we will see, to the Apocalypse of Paul)—or of nonbelievers (e.g., Jews, apart from the possible reference to Bar Kochba). The explicit polemic involves sins, primarily of the flesh. Still, that in itself may be significant in view of the theological debates of the early and middle second century. It is striking and well worth noting that what is emphasized here, in the name of Peter, is the physical fate of humans, in the flesh. They experience either brutal torment or eternal ecstasy. The book in other words, may well function polemically in emphasizing precisely a doctrine that, at the time of its composition, was in wide dispute among various Christian groups, not in the manner of, say, 3 Corinthians, which addresses the issue of the flesh head on as a polemical issue, but by emphasizing the importance of flesh through the words of Christ himself, delivered to his disciples, especially Peter. A number of discussions of the book miss this forest for the trees, not realizing that the flesh is one of the book's ultimate concerns.

The stress on the flesh is clear in the opening eschatological discourse, where Christ emphasizes that on the "day of God" there will be "the decision of the judgment of God" when all people will be gathered before the Father, who will command hell to open up and give up everyone in it. Then, most notably "the beasts and the fowls shall he command to give back all flesh that they have devoured, since he desires that men should appear (again); for nothing perishes for God" (ch. 4). This, then, is "the resurrection of the dead on the day of judgment"—a raising of all flesh to face judgment in the flesh.

The fleshly character of suffering is particularly evident in what Czachesz has called the "grotesque body," the all-too physical "combination of the ludicrous and fearful" in the detailed torments of the damned.[125] So too with the godly ecstasies narrated in chapter 16, experienced in a beautiful garden with sweet fragrances, to satisfy the bodily senses. It might also be noted that, at the end, it is precisely "men in the flesh" who come to welcome Christ into heaven (ch. 17).

The Pseudepigraphical Character

The forger establishes his false identity at the outset, first as one of Jesus' disciples ("we entreated and implored him severally," ch. 1) and then more concretely as the head disciple himself ("I, Peter, answered and said unto him," ch. 2). The authorial pretense is maintained throughout the narrative, although to some extent it is more pronounced in the later Greek version, where the visions of the damned are narrated in the first person rather than the third (e.g., "I saw another place . . ." Greek ch. 21, and so on). At the end as well, we have, in both versions, first-person

125. "The Grotesque Body."

narrative, spoken by Peter: "I approached God Jesus Christ and said to him . . ." (ch. 16).

A key question that is rarely asked and even more rarely answered in scholarship on the text involves precisely the pseudepigraphic claim. Why does the author feign to be Peter, in particular? In his discussion of *Petrine Controversies* Terence Smith raises the question and never answers it.[126] Bauckham suggests that it is because Peter is the principal disciple and important in Matthew, the author's favorite Gospel. But that too does not get us very far.

It may be more useful to consider the stress the author places on the physicality of the afterlife, where rewards and punishments will be in the flesh. Peter, as we have seen, was sometimes associated with an alternative eschatology, in which the flesh was belittled. Docetic understandings of Christ, and thus denigrations of the importance of the flesh generally, can be found in the Coptic Apocalypse of Peter, the letter of Peter to Philip, and—as read, at least, by Serapion and his associates, whether or not this was the authorial "intention"—in the Gospel of Peter. This author responds by stressing the opposite perspective and authorizing his view by appeal, again, to Peter himself. The flesh matters, and will continue to matter into the afterlife.

It is interesting to consider the connections between the two Apocalypses of Peter in this regard, one of them devaluing the flesh and the other emphasizing it. It may be pushing the matter too far to claim that one of them was written in response to the other. They are, after all, dealing with different subject matters. But if nothing else their similarities and differences do highlight the varying interpretations of the flesh attributed to the chief apostle by forgers antagonistic to one another's views. Both the docetic Coptic Apocalypse of Peter and this proto-orthodox version involve revelations of Christ directly to Peter, that is, visionary experiences that Christ mediates; both take place near the end of Jesus' life; both reveal what cannot be perceived by the normal processes of human observation; both are concerned with spiritual blindness; both see the need to differentiate between truth and error; both have ultimate, eschatological implications to their views of the flesh.

The distinctions between the two accounts are yet more revealing.

- In the Coptic apocalypse Peter does not understand what he sees and is told that what is perceived by physical sight is not the ultimate reality. In the proto-orthodox apocalypse Peter understands perfectly well what he sees and his vision represents itself as the ultimate reality.
- In the Coptic apocalypse ultimate reality transcends the flesh and resides in the realm of the spirit. In the proto-orthodox version ultimate reality is precisely in the flesh.

---

126. Terence V. Smith, *Petrine Controversies*: "It is therefore difficult to determine the precise reason for the writer's appeal to the Peter-figure." Smith goes on to suggest that the references to Peter's martyrdom in Rome (Eth 14, Rainer fragment) may provide a clue, but then decides not: "though the martyrdom is referred to, the writer does not attempt to use it as a buttress for any Petrine/Roman primacy." So too he thinks that a concern for persecution related to Peter cannot explain it (p. 48).

- In the Coptic apocalypse the ultimate goal of salvation is to be removed from the body and its sensations; the end comes when the physical body is transcended. In the proto-orthodox version salvation comes in the body and its sensations, and the end comes when the physical body is rewarded or tormented.
- In the Coptic apocalypse the literal teachings of Peter lead to blindness and error. In the proto-orthodox Apocalypse it is the literal teachings of Peter about the literal events of the future that constitute ultimate truth.
- In the Coptic apocalypse the orthodox Christians are condemned for clinging to the name of a dead man. In the proto-orthodox version Jesus is a crucified man whose example should be followed and whose martyrs are counted as pleasing to God.
- In the Coptic apocalypse Jesus tells Peter to be strong; since Jesus will be with him, none of his enemies will prevail against him. In the proto-orthodox apocalypse Jesus sends Peter to his martyrdom: "Leave and go to the city of the west and drink the wine about which I have told you."[127]

And so, even though the two "revelations" are about two different matters—Christ's crucifixion and the fate of the dead—the books are very much at odds with one another at a number of key points. The Coptic version is explicitly countering a set of views that is endorsed by the proto-orthodox version, whose own polemic is much more subtle but recognizable nonetheless. The flesh matters. In Buchholz's summary, the author "was involved in the debate over the believers' resurrection bodies. He insists on a very physical, future resurrection for believers."[128] This view is presented specifically in a forgery in the name of Peter, chief of the disciples, and counters writings—including some forgeries—that take, or were believed to take, precisely the opposite perspective, also in the name of Peter, including not only the Coptic Apocalypse of Peter but also the Gospel of Peter and the Letter of Peter to Philip.

The Apocalypse of Paul

Far more influential on the history of Christian thought than the Apocalypse of Peter, though clearly dependent on it for many of its traditions, was the Apocalypse of Paul, which was originally composed in Greek but came to be translated into a number of languages: Latin, Syriac, Coptic, Armenian, Slavonic, and Ethiopic.[129] The work as we have it is dated at the outset: "In the consulate of Theodosius Augustus the Younger and of Cynegius, a certain respected man was

127. Ch. 14, translation of Buchholz.

128. *Your Eyes Will Be Opened*, p. 396.

129. The most important recent edition is T. Silverstein and A. Hilhorst, *Apocalypse of Paul: A New Critical Edition of Three Long Latin Versions* (Geneva: P. Cramer 1997).

living in Tarsus. . . ."[130] Commonly this is taken to indicate that the book was composed, in its final form, around 388 CE.[131] But this in fact is merely the terminus ad quem. And so Silverstein has influentially argued for a later date of around 420 CE and Piovanelli for a slightly earlier one of 395–416 CE.[132] Most recently Hilhorst agrees with an early-fifth-century date for the existing text, but, along with others, stresses that an earlier iteration of the account, lacking the prologue, appears to be attested at least 150 years earlier, as some form of the account was probably known to Origen. Origen quotes the text in a fragment preserved by the thirteenth-century Syrian author Bar Hebraeus (*Nomocanon* VII, 9); moreover Origen's Homily 5 on Psalm 36 describes the fate of souls that appears to parallel the Apocalypse of Paul 13ff. Hilhorst's conclusion is that "some version of the *Apocalypse of Paul* must have existed in the first half of the early third century."[133]

Despite its widespread popularity—down at least to Dante—the work was roundly condemned in orthodox circles, including in the Gelasian Decree. Augustine had nothing good to say about it:

> And from this circumstance, with a most foolish presumption, certain vain persons have devised an *Apocalypse of Paul,* which the sound Church does not accept, full of some fables or other, asserting that this it is about which he had said that he had been caught up to the third heaven and there had heard "unspeakable words, which it is not granted to man to utter." In any event, their audacity would be intolerable if they had said that he had heard [words] which it is not *yet* granted to man to utter; but since he said "which it is not granted to man to utter," who are those people who dare to utter these [words] impudently and unsuccessfully?[134]

Nor did Sozomen:

> So the work entitled The Apocalypse of the Apostle Paul, though unrecognized by the ancients, is still esteemed by most of the monks. Some persons affirm that the book was found during this reign, by Divine revelation, in a marble

130. Translation of H. Duensing and Aurelio de Santos Otero, in Schneemelcher, *New Testament Apocrypha.*

131. Thus, for example, Elliott, *Apocryphal New Testament,* 616.

132. T. Silverstein "The Date of the 'Apocalypse of Paul,' " *MS* 24 (1962): 335–48; P. Piovanelli, "Les origines de l'Apocalypse de Paul reconsidérées," *Apocrypha* 4 (1993): 25–64, esp. 45–59.

133. Anthony Hilhorst, "The *Apocalypse of Paul*: Previous History and Afterlife," in Jan Bremmer and István Czachesz, eds., *The Visio Pauli and the Gnostic Apocalypse of Paul* (Leuven: Peeters, 2007), pp. 1–22. Piovanelli disputes these data, claiming that neither of the passages of Origen need necessarily refer to the Apocalypse and noting that all of our surviving witnesses derived from the fifth-century edition of the text (so that there are no physical remains of the earlier version). Duensing and de Santos Otero concur, marshaling the odd argument that since Sozomen indicates that "none of the ancients" knew the document, Origen could not have quoted it.

134. Augustine *Tract. Ioh.* 98, 8. Translation of John Rettig, *Augustine: Tractates on the Gospel of John* FC, 90 (Washington, DC: Catholic University Press of America, 1994).

box, buried beneath the soil in the house of Paul at Tarsus in Cilicia. I have been informed that this report is false by Cilix, a presbyter of the church in Tarsus, a man of very advanced age, as is indicated by his gray hairs, who says that no such occurrence is known among them, and wonders if the heretics did not invent the story.[135]

Arguably the most famous feature of the book is the opening discovery narrative that Sozomen refers to, and which I have already discussed.[136] The account itself begins with a lamentation on the sinfulness of humans by the sun, moon, stars, and sea (chs. 3–10). Paul is then taken up to the third heaven where he is shown the fate of souls from on high, in particular that of one righteous and one unrighteous man (chs. 11–16). There follows a tour of the realms of the blessed and the damned, based in part on the visions of the Apocalypse of Peter. Throughout the account it is assumed that the rewards of the blessed are given temporarily until the soul returns to the body for the final judgment day: "And they roused the soul saying: Soul take knowledge of your body which you have left, for in the day of resurrection you must return to that same body to receive what is promised to all the righteous" (ch. 14). One can assume that the torments described in such graphic detail are, likewise, preliminary to those yet to come at the resurrection.[137]

The torments of the damned have a good deal in common with those earlier assigned to Peter's vision: here too there is a stress on the physicality of both ecstasy and torment, the former, in this case, being described in graphic terms reminiscent of the famous superlatives of Papias.[138] But there are also key differences from the author's model.[139] Whereas the patriarchs, prophets, and righteous of the Old Testament are praised, there appears a strain of anti-Jewish sentiment in the statement of chapter 48: "See, Moses, what those of your people have done

---

135. *Ecclesiastical History* 7.19. Translation of Chester D. Hartranft, *NPNF*, second series, vol. 2.

136. See p. 125. A comparable account is found, most famously, in Dictys. For other discovery narratives, see V. Saxer, *Morts, Martyrs, reliques, en Afrique Chrétienne aux premiers siècle* (Paris: Éditions Beauchesne, 1980, 245–46); F. Bovon, "The Dossier on Stephen, the First Martyr, *HTR* 96 (2003): 279–315; Pierluigi Piovanelli, "The Miraculous Discovery of the Hidden Manuscript, or the Paratextual Function of the Prologue to the Apocalypse of Paul," in Bremmer and Czachesz, *The Visio Pauli*, pp. 23–49; and esp. W. Speyer, *Bücherfunde*.

137. Piovanelli has argued that by the time of the writing—after the triumph of Christianity starting in 313 CE—the idea of an apocalyptic renewal of the heavens and earth had given way to an individualized judgment in the afterlife. That may be true enough, but it almost certainly was not a shift created by the conversion of the emperor and the massive shifts of religious allegiance that occurred in its wake, since we have earlier evidence of this eschatological transformation, most notably in the Apocalypse of Peter of the mid-second century.

138. Duensing and de Santos Otero (p. 715) oddly enough take this as an indication of the *late* date of the account.

139. Czachesz finds it significant that there is nothing said about the torment of Christian persecutors, and argues on these grounds that the final recension must have occurred some time after Constantine. Thus "Torture in Hell and Reality. The *Visio Pauli*," in Bremmer and Czachesz, eds., *The Visio Pauli*, pp. 130–43.

to the Son of God." Of far greater significance is the heightened attention given to Christians. On one hand, the wilderness ascetics are praised early in the account, whereas those who do not fulfill their ascetic practices are roundly condemned (chs. 9–10; again, e.g., ch. 23). Among the blessed are the married souls who nonetheless remain chaste (ch. 22). On the other hand, those who fast but who are proud and who praise themselves cannot enter the city of Christ (ch. 24). Moreover, church people who are not totally committed to a Christian lifestyle are punished in boiling fire; these include those who spent some of their days in prayer, but others in sin, and who were involved in idle disputes; and those who took the eucharist but then committed fornication (ch. 31).

Yet more striking is the punishment suffered specifically by Christian leaders. There are gory eternal torments lying in wait for a presbyter who is punished severely for not fasting and for offering communion while in a state of fornication (ch. 34); for a bishop who was not just and did not pity widows and orphans (ch. 35); for a deacon who used the oblations for himself and committed fornication (ch. 36); for a reader who did not keep the precepts of God (ch. 36); for those who disparaged the Word of God and did not obey it (ch. 37); for those who stopped fasting too soon (ch. 39); and for would-be monks who did not live the life of a monk (ch. 40).

But above all there are the heretics, who falsely hold to a docetic Christology and deny the importance of the flesh. It is here that the real polemic can be found. The worst punishment of all—"seven times greater than these" (ch. 40)—is the "well" filled with an unbearable stench, and peopled by "those who have not confessed that Christ came in the flesh and that the Virgin Mary bore him, and who say that the bread of the eucharist and the cup of blessing are not the body and blood of Christ" (ch. 41). Others are tormented by cold and gnashing of teeth and cubit-long worms with two heads: "They are those who say that Christ has not risen from the dead and that this flesh does not rise" (ch. 42).

Here then we have the implicit polemic of the earlier Apocalypse of Peter taken to an extreme and made explicit. Not only does the physicality of the afterlife emphasize the importance of the flesh in the face of those who deny it; the most horrendous torments are reserved precisely for such heretical naysayers. For this orthodox author there can be no crime more heinous or deserving of eternal and excruciating torment than the sin of denying that Christ himself came in the flesh and that the resurrection would be in the flesh. Eternity would indeed be a fleshly existence, as those who refused to acknowledge it would discover to their eternal horror.

CHAPTER FOURTEEN

Forgeries Arising from Later Theological Controversies

If the various theological controversies from the end of the third century and into the fourth generated a large number of literary forgeries, most of them have since been lost. The ones that survive are not modern discoveries but old standards, known throughout the ages because, in no small measure, these authors were unusually successful in their deceitful endeavors. One of the most historically significant of these works was the forged Ignatian letters, to which I will devote the greatest attention in this chapter. But we would do well to return to two other forgeries that we have examined in previous contexts, as, in part, their production was spurred by the theological controversies of their day.

THE ABGAR CORRESPONDENCE

We have already discussed the forged correspondence between Jesus and King Abgar Uchama in the context of anti-Jewish polemic.[1] These letters do not only malign Jews for their role in the death of Jesus, however; they also function in a more patently theological way. As Han J. W. Drijvers has shown, the letters appear to have been forged as an anti-Manichaean polemic.

As we have seen, the letters appear in the context of the larger Abgar legend, known from both Eusebius and the *Doctrina Addai*. My primary concern here is not with the legend per se. Even though it is certainly a fabrication of later times, it is not a forgery. The correspondence at the beginning of the legend, however, is forged, or rather doubly forged, one letter allegedly written by the king of Edessa and the other by Jesus himself. Taken as a Gestalt, the letters and the legend have been subject to considerable dispute. Burkitt argued that the complex grew out

1. See pp. 362–66.

of a historical kernel, in which the Christian conversion of Abgar VIII the Great (177–212 CE) was retrojected back onto Abgar V Uchama (ruler: 4 BCE–7 CE and 13–50 CE) in order to provide a greater antiquity for the church of Edessa.[2] W. Bauer argued, in contrast, that the entire legend, including the letters, was an invention ex nihilo, meant to support the claims of the orthodox party in Edessa to have an apostolic origin.[3] J. Segal argued that the complex originated as a Christian parallel and counterpart to the story of the conversion to Judaism of the royal dynasty of Adiabene, as preserved in Josephus.[4] And there have been other theories.[5]

In a series of publications Drijvers has shown the problems with these various views, before reaching his own conclusion[6]: "The Abgar legend likely arose at the end of the third century in Edessa as a propaganda text for the orthodoxy of that era."[7] Specifically, the propaganda is directed against a dominant form of Syrian Manichaeanism.

As I argued earlier, however, in contrast to Drijvers, the letters appear to have originated independently of the legend.[8] Even so, they too, as well as the legend, may have arisen during an anti-Manichaean campaign by orthodox Christians in Edessa. The grounds for seeing the correspondence in this light are given by Drijvers, who notes not only that letters were important to the Manichaean tradition in general, but also that, as known from Augustine, the Manichees claimed to have letters of Christ in particular (*Contra Faust.* 28.4). There are convincing reasons for seeing the Abgar correspondence as a counterforgery designed to undercut the claims (and possibly even the letters) of the Manichees.

Especially significant, in this regard, is Jesus' promise to Abgar in the second letter: "After I have ascended I will send you one of my disciples to heal your illness and to provide life both to you and to those who are with you."[9] This appears

2. F. C. Burkitt, *Early Eastern Christianity* (London: John Murray, 1904), ch. 1.

3. Walter Bauer, *Orthodoxy and Heresy in Earliest Christianity*, ch. 1.

4. Judah Segal, *Edessa, the "Blessed City,"* pp. 68–69.

5. See e.g., J. J. Gunther, "The Meaning and Origin of the Name, 'Judas Thomas,'" *Mus* 93 (1980): 113–48. On the whole question, see Sebastian Brock, "Eusebius and Syriac Christianity," in Attridge and Hata, eds., *Eusebius, Christianity, and Judaism*, pp. 212–34; and Alexander Mirkovic, *Prelude to Constantine*. Mirkovic's concern, however, is not with the origin of the legend but with its function in the early centuries of circulation.

6. Most thoroughly in H. J. W. Drijvers, "Addai und Mani: Christentum und Manichäismus im dritten Jahrhundert in Syrien," *OrChrAn* 221 (1983): 171–85; recapitulated in "The Abgar Legend," in Schneemelcher, *New Testament Apocrypha*, 1.492–99. See also "Facts and Problems in Early Syriac Speaking Christianity," *SecCent* 2 (1982): 157–75.

7. "Die Abgar-Sage ist wahrscheinlich am Ende des dritten Jahrhunderts in Edessa entstanden als eine Propagandaschrift der damaligen Orthodoxie"; "Addai und Mani," p. 172.

8. See pp. 364–66.

9. Translation from Ehrman and Pleše, *Apocryphal Gospels*. In the later *Doctrina Addai*, Jesus' reply is delivered orally rather than in writing. It is usually thought that this is a change from the older version of the story, influenced by the view that Jesus was known not to have written anything (so Augustine, *Contra Faust.* 28.4; Jerome, *In Ezek.* 44. 29; Gelasian Decree 5.8.1.2).

to be an allusion to John 16:7–8 and its promise of the sending of the Spirit: "It is better for you that I depart; for if I do not depart, the Comforter will not come to you; and if I go, I will send him to you. When he comes, he will convince the world. . . ." As Drijvers notes, Mani understood himself to have been sent in fulfillment of this Johannine promise. The letter of Jesus, then, provides a counterclaim. Moreover, Mani understood himself to be sent from God as a healer: "I am a physician [doctor] from Babylon," he says to the Sassanic king Shapur, whom he then heals—a close parallel to what is said to be about to happen to Abgar, not through the coming of Mani but through his counter, the apostle to be sent from Jesus.[10] Drijvers concludes: "It becomes clear that the reply Jesus sends to Abgar is a trenchant version of the saying concerning the Paraclete, which is perhaps intended to counter Manichaean claims and the Manichaean mission."[11] For this correspondence, Christianity will establish itself with the appearance of Jesus' apostle, not with the coming of missionaries from Mani.[12]

Drijvers notes that there is an internal discrepancy between the letter of Jesus and the legend of Addai. The letter claims that Jesus will send an apostle to Abgar, but in the legend, it is Judas Thomas who does so. This is "an anomaly" in the sequence of the narrative."[13] But neither Drijvers nor anyone else who sees the letters as, originally, a piece, has an adequate explanation for the discrepancy. In fact, as seen earlier, the disjuncture is easiest accounted for by assuming that the letters and legend both sprang from the same polemical impulse, but were only secondarily added together. This would explain, as well, why they had separate histories of transmission (Egeria, for example, knows the letters but betrays no knowledge of the legend).[14]

At the same time, the impulse behind the legend appears to have been very much like that behind the earlier letters. As Drijvers repeatedly emphasizes, one of Mani's first apostles, sent in 240 CE into the Roman empire where he healed and converted the queen of Palmyra, Zenobia, was named Addai. This cannot be a coincidence. Now the one (a Christian apostle) who comes to Edessa to heal and convert the King is Addai. Or, one might think, the *real* Addai: "This

---

10. Quotation from M. 556, I, ed. F. W. K. Muller, *APAW* (1904): 87, as cited by Drijvers, "Facts and Problems," p. 163, n. 24.

11. "Es stellt sich also heraus, dass der Antwortbrief Jesu an Abgar eine pointierte Version des Parakletspruches ist, die vielleicht gegen den manichäischen Ansprüchen und der manichäischen Mission gemeint ist"; "Addai und Mani," p. 180.

12. Drijvers also suggests that the allusion to John 20:29 at the outset may have been picked up from the Manichaean literature, as the Manichaeans may have used it to explain why the eyewitnesses got it wrong and only the later Mani got it right; "Addai und Mani," p. 181.

13. Ibid., p. 181.

14. Drijvers' view that it was the last line of the letter ("your city will be blessed and the enemy will no longer prevail over it") that led to a separate transmission history of the letters, apart from the stories, fails to convince. Why would the line not, then, be found in Eusebius, if he knew both the letters and the legend? It is easier to believe that the correspondence originally had a transmission history of its own and that the final line was added in some witnesses but not others.

is an ingenious piece of propaganda: A *Christian* apostle in rivalry with Mani, whose best-known apostle was actually called Addai."[15] "The Christian Addai is a borrowing from Manichaeism."[16] Drijvers points out other, probably noncoincidental, similarities between Manichean legends and the Abgar tradition.[17] The conclusion to be drawn from these parallels is clear: "The Abgar legend is a document of Christian propaganda which originated in a historical situation in Edessa at the end of the third century, in which the Manichean version of the Christian faith and the Manichean mission were sharply threatening orthodoxy, which formed only a minority."[18]

This propaganda campaign, however, took place in stages. It started with a set of forged letters between Jesus and the King of Edessa, which had their own history of transmission; it continued with a similarly oriented set of stories; it came to fruition in the combining of the two sets of documents. The combination yielded a notable inconsistency that was overlooked in antiquity, and is still ignored by scholars today. But the final product ultimately proved valuable for the orthodox community of Edessa.

THE PSEUDO-CLEMENTINE HOMILIES AND RECOGNITIONS

We have already considered the Pseudo-Clementines in relation to their "Jewish" orientation and their resultant anti-Pauline (or possibly anti-Marcionite) polemic. Here I can say just a few words about other theological issues involved in their production.

The final editions of both the *Homilies* and *Recognitions* bear the marks of the time of their redaction, as both appear to have been edited sometime in the fourth century by Christians with "Arian" tendencies.[19] There is little to indicate that this redactor was intent on advancing his Arian views with polemical intent, however, and so I need say but little about the matter.

The common view of the *Homilies* was expressed well over a century ago in an influential study by Charles Bigg. From his analysis of *Hom.* 20:7, Bigg concluded: "If we suppose that we have in the present *Homilies* the product of an

15. "Abgar Legend," p. 495. Emphasis his.

16. "Facts and Problems," p. 161.

17. Interestingly, in the Manichaean legend, Mani's "heavenly twin clothes him with miraculous healing power and charges him to proclaim the message of the truth." This is, in the Addai Legend, "exactly the same task for which Judas Thomas sends Addai to Edessa." It is, then, a later feature of the legend, as the letters originally indicated that it would be Jesus who sent an apostle, not his twin. Moreover, in the *Doctrina Addai*, the portrait of Jesus painted by Hanan appears to stand in the place of the venerated portrait of Mani. "Facts and Problems," p. 165–66.

18. "The Abgar Legend," p. 496.

19. On the problem presented now by the term *Arian*, see below, pp. 474–75.

Arian Christian of Syriac nationality who fancied that he found in Ebionitism a solution of the great problem—a historical and quasi-philosophical doctrine of the Arian savior—we should not perhaps go far wrong."[20]

This general perspective is widely shared today, for example, in the most recent full-length study of Nicole Kelley.[21] So too *Rec.* 3.2–11 has long been recognized as containing an Arian perspective. The theology of the passage was so problematic—confused, confusing, or dangerous—that Rufinus tells us that he refused to include it in his translation:

> There are also in both collections some dissertations concerning the Unbegotten God and the Begotten, and on some other such subjects, which, to say nothing more, are beyond our comprehension. These, therefore, as being beyond our powers, I have chosen to reserve for others, rather than to produce in an imperfect state.[22]

This is not to say that there are not theological polemics in the Pseudo-Clementines. Indeed, Kelley has made a compelling case that the books do have polemical intent. Eschewing questions of sources, she examines the final form of the text of the *Recognitions* for what it can tell us about the concerns of the editor, living in fourth-century Syria. In her view, the prominent motif that "true knowledge" can come only from the prophets of Scripture, and in particular from the True Prophet (Christ), is meant to function polemically, in order to counter other popular avenues of knowledge widely used in the author's environment. In particular, the author/editor is intent on combating those who insist on the epistemological importance of both astrology and philosophy. That is why the heroes of the tale are shown to be experts in both disciplines, and yet converts away from them. They personally know what astrology and philosophy can provide, and they have realized their ultimate shortcomings: "Despite its insistence on its heroes' expertise in the different paths to knowledge, the text also suggests that philosophy and astrology cannot really provide the access to true knowledge which they claim. . . . True knowledge comes only from prophets."[23]

The author was confronted with a maelstrom of religious opinion, belief, and doctrine in his fourth-century Syrian environment. Rather than attack any one set of false teachings, he takes them on all at once, setting forth the true understanding of religion in opposition to any who stand in a different tradition or take another theological view. As Kelley summarizes:

---

20. Charles Bigg, "The Clementine Homilies," in *Studia Biblica et Ecclesiastica: Essays Chiefly in Biblical and Patristic Criticism*, vol. 2 (Oxford: Clarendon Press, 1890), p. 192.

21. *Knowledge and Religious Authority in the Pseudo-Clementines* (Tübingen: Mohr/Siebeck, 2006), p. 15.

22. Prologue to the *Recognitions*; translation of Thomas Smith in *ANF*, vol. 8.

23. *Knowledge and Religious Authority*, p. 28.

> In an environment characterized by a multitude of competing truth claims, the *Recognitions* functions as a multi-pronged attack not just against *one* group such as the Marcionites or Pauline Christians, but against several different varieties of belief. In this way the text redescribes the field of competition, so that it ceases to be a bewildering array of rival religious claimants and becomes something more manageable: a choice between prophetic and false knowledge, and ultimately a choice between salvation or damnation.[24]

THE PSEUDO-IGNATIAN LETTERS

Arguably the most historically influential set of forgeries of the late fourth century are the Pseudo-Ignatian letters. As has long been recognized, these were produced in the context of the Christological controversies racking the church at the time. Over the centuries they came to be used in a wide variety of other contexts, most notably in the wake of the English Reformation, in the numerous vitriolic exchanges over the validity of church hierarchy between the likes of Anglican Archbishop and scholar extraordinaire James Ussher and the young but outspoken Puritan John Milton.[25]

In addition to the seven Ignatian letters widely regarded as authentic today, ten other letters were circulated at various times and places in the medieval and early modern period. These ten come in two corpora. One corpus appears to have been a late medieval addition to the collection, and so will not concern us here. This comprises four letters, two from Ignatius to John, the disciple of Jesus, one addressed to Mary, the mother of Jesus, and the last a reply from Mary to Ignatius. The forger of these short missives appears to have had access to the so-called Long Recension of Ignatius, about which I will speak in a moment, in particular the forged letter of Ignatius to Mary of Cassabola, which is addressed to χριστόφορος θυγάτηρ Μαρία, christifera filia Maria. The letter to the Blessed Virgin uses the same epithet, "christiferae mariae suus Ignatius" and indicates that the author has written to her before. These four letters are only in Latin, probably their original language. Lightfoot plausibly suggested that they date no earlier than the eleventh century. Nonetheless, the forger was inordinately successful with his deceit: there are far more manuscripts of this correspondence than of the Long Recension itself, and far more quotations from it. As Lightfoot indicates, "in some quarters indeed S. Ignatius was only known through them."[26]

The remaining six forgeries circulated with heavily interpolated versions of the seven authentic Ignatian letters. For reasons we will see, it is almost universally thought that the interpolator and the forger were one and the same; taken

---

24. Ibid., pp. 206–7.

25. See the fascinating historical survey of J. B. Lightfoot, *The Apostolic Fathers: Clement, Ignatius, and Polycarp* (London: Macmillan, 1889–90, reprinted Peabody MA: Hendrickson, 1989); part 2, vol. 1, *Ignatius and Polycarp*; pp. 237–46.

26. *Apostolic Fathers*, p. 235.

together, it is these interpolated and forged letters that are usually referred to as the Long Recension.

The forgeries involve letters of Ignatius to the churches of Tarsus, Antioch, and Philippi; a personal letter to Hero, his successor to the bishopric of Antioch; a letter from Mary of Cassobola to Ignatius; and his reply. These six letters, along with the interpolated versions of the seven authentic letters, were known to be "Ignatius" until the mid-seventeenth century, when critical examinations of Ussher and others, and important manuscript discoveries, changed the picture. Problems were initially detected through comparisons of the texts of the letters with quotations of Ignatius in the writings of Eusebius and Theodoret. The differences were so stark that it was difficult, as Ussher indicated, to imagine "that one was reading the same Ignatius who was read in antiquity" (eundem legere se Ignatium qui veterum aetate legebatur).[27] In addition, it was noted that the Long Recension (the only one known at the time) contained serious anachronisms and revealing blunders, such as its references to Basilides and Theodotus among the false teachers Ignatius opposed (Trall. 11), when in fact they lived long after his day, and when he named Ebion a heresiarch (Philad. 6), as Tertullian and those after him had done. Moreover, it was noted that Eusebius knew of only seven letters—casting immediate doubts on the other six (*H.E.* 3.36).

Ussher was particularly taken by the fact that several late medieval writers,[28] including the thirteenth-century Robert Grossteste of Lincoln, cited the letters of Ignatius in a textual form that was different and shorter than that otherwise known. Ussher reasoned that an alternative textual tradition must have once existed, at least in England. He embarked on a mission to find remnants of this other tradition, and was rewarded in uncovering two Latin manuscripts that contained the seven Eusebian letters in a shorter form, which coincided with the medieval citations of the text, lacking the passages so obviously tied to the theological and ecclesiastical concerns of the fourth century (although these manuscripts included the additional, forged letters as well). On the basis of his discovery, in 1644 Ussher published a new Latin edition of the Ignatian corpus: just the Eusebian letters in the noninterpolated form (although Ussher considered the letter to Polycarp spurious).[29]

Two years later, Ussher's views were confirmed by Isaac Voss's publication of a Greek manuscript from Florence that preserved six of the Eusebian letters in their shortened form—all but the letter to the Romans, which had a separate history of transmission.[30] Finally, in 1689 the French scholar T. Ruinart published the Greek text of Romans as uncovered in a tenth-century manuscript from Paris, making then the original form of the authentic corpus completely available.[31]

27. Quoted in ibid., p. 237.

28. For the following two paragraphs I depend on my discussion in *The Apostolic Fathers*, 1. 210–11.

29. *Polycarpi et Ignatii epistolae* (Oxford: Lichfield, 1644).

30. *Epistolae genuinae S. Ignatii martyris* (Amsterdam: Blaev, 1646).

31. *Acta primorum martyrum sincere et selecta* (Paris: Muget, 1689).

Debates over the full extent of the authentic Ignatian corpus continued to rage after the seventeenth century. In the mid-nineteenth century the flames of controversy were stoked by William Cureton, who claimed to have discovered manuscript evidence of an "original" corpus containing only condensed versions of the letters to Polycarp, Ephesians, and Romans.[32] But with the massively documented studies of Theodore Zahn and J. B. Lightfoot, the seven-letter corpus in the uninterpolated form posited and then discovered by Ussher and his successors was put on solid ground.[33] The twentieth century saw renewed questions, as authors such as R. Weijenborg, R. Joly, and J. Rius Camps, and most recently R. M. Hübner and T. Lechner, argued that some, or all, of the letters of the Middle Recension (= the uninterpolated seven letters known to Eusebius) were forged.[34] The majority of scholars remains unconvinced, however, and I take the common view here: the seven "Eusebian" letters go back to Ignatius (Ephesians, Magnesians, Trallians, Romans, Philadelphians, Smyrneans, and Polycarp). These were interpolated and six additional letters were forged (Tarsians, Antiochians, Hero, Philippians, Mary Cassobola, and from Mary Cassobola), creating the Long Recension.[35]

The Author

It is widely and almost certainly correctly thought that the same person who interpolated the authentic Ignatian letters forged the remaining six. As Zahn and Lightfoot exhaustively demonstrated, the interpolations and the forgeries share many of the same verbal and stylistic features, ecclesiastical views, practical concerns, polemical targets, theological positions, and uses of Scripture; sometimes they even replicate the same passages and similar paraphrases. With respect to theological investments, for example, Lightfoot has argued that the "same doctrines are maintained, the same heresies assailed, and the same theological terms employed."[36] Amelungk has provided charts of the remarkable parallels between the forgeries and the interpolations, claiming that four-fifths of the material of the former is paralleled in the latter. Of the letter to Hero he claims that it is "actually plagiarized from the [letter] to Polycarp."[37]

The only serious challenge to the unity of authorship has come from Jack Hannah, who claimed that Lightfoot was right that the forger of the additional letters produced his work in the fourth century, but argued that the textual affinities of

32. William Cureton, *The Ancient Syriac Version of Saint Ignatius* (London: Rivington, 1845).

33. Lightfoot, *Apostolic Fathers*. Theodore Zahn, *Ignatius von Antiochien* (Gotha: Perthes, 1873).

34. Weijenborg, *Les lettres d'Ignace*; Joly, *Dossier*; Rius-Camps, *The Four Authentic Letters*; Hübner, "Thesen zur Echtheit und Datierung"; Thomas Lechner, *Ignatius adversus Valentinianos*.

35. See further p. 6, n. 7.

36. Lightfoot, p. 248; much of Zahn's argument is recapitulated in Arnold Amelungk, "Untersuchung über Pseudo-Ignatius," *ZWT* 42 (1899): 508–81.

37. "eigentlich ein Plagiat von dem [Brief] an Polycarp." Amelungk, "Untersuchung," p. 553.

the Scripture citations in the interpolations indicate that they were made by a different person two centuries earlier, about 140 CE in Ephesus, "probably within twenty-five years of the originals."[38] The interpolations were then used by the forger for his subsequent creations. This is an interesting view, but it was demolished in the one article devoted to its refutation, by Milton Brown, who effectively reasserted the traditional view.[39]

This traditional view maintains that the author was writing in the second part of the fourth century. Numerous features of the forged materials (including here, for the sake of convenience, the interpolations under the rubric of "forged") show that they were written long after Ignatius' day, not least the extensive citation of the writings that eventually became the Scriptures of the New Testament, not cited as canonical authorities by Ignatius himself. We will be considering this use of Scripture anon. There are also several telling anachronisms in the text, including not just the post-Ignatian heresiarchs of Tralles 11, already mentioned, but also a striking list of later church offices in Antiochians 12: "the sub-deacons, the readers, the singers, the doorkeepers, the laborers, the exorcist, the confessors . . . the keepers of the holy gates."[40] As Lightfoot notes, the first mention of the office of laborers is in the rescript of Constantius of 357 CE; the offices of doorkeepers and singers are first mentioned in in the canons of the Council of Laodicea of 363 CE. Moreover, "the fact that the writer can put such language into the mouth of S. Ignatius without any consciousness of a flagrant anachronism would seem to show that these offices were not very new when he wrote."[41]

Somewhat less obvious, but equally compelling and of particular interest to our concerns here, the forger, as we will see, uses a good deal of coded theological language that, despite its frequent subtlety, betrays a concern for the Christological debates of the mid to late fourth century.

What is yet more striking, we appear to have two other works from the hand of this same author, in one of which he names himself. As we have already seen, the forger of the Pseudo-Ignatians appears also to have forged the Apostolic Constitutions, another work with polemical intent, not written in the name of a one-time companion of the apostles, but of the apostles themselves, and allegedly delivered by Ignatius's near contemporary Clement of Rome.[42] It is now also widely recognized, based on the investigative work of D. Hagedorn, that the forger also produced a Commentary on Job, and that his name was Julian.[43]

In the manuscript tradition, this commentary is attributed to Origen, but that cannot be right, as Hagedorn shows. Not only does the theology differ from

---

38. Jack W. Hannah, "The Setting of the Ignatian Long Recension," *JBL* 79 (1960): 222.

39. Milton P. Brown, "Notes on the Language and Style of Pseudo-Ignatius," *JBL* 83 (1964): 146–52.

40. Translations are taken from A. Cleveland Coxe in *ANF*.

41. Lightfoot, *Apostolic Fathers*, p. 258.

42. See, for example, A. Harnack, *Die Lehre der zwölf Apostel*, pp. 241–68; and C. H. Turner, "Notes on the Apostolic Constitutions I-III," *JTS* 16 (1914–15): 54–61, 523–38; 31 (1930): 128–41.

43. Dieter Hagedorn, *Der Hiobkommentar*.

Origen's in significant ways, but the book also mentions Lucian of Antioch as a person of the past; Lucian, however, died some fifty years after Origen. The catenae sometimes ascribe the work to an unspecified Julian, which has often been taken to be Julian of Halicarnassus. But R. Draguet long ago showed that this cannot be right either: the commentary represents an arianizing theology of the second half of the fourth century.[44] One manuscript of the catenae attributes it instead to Julian, a deacon of Antioch; and in fact Julian is named in the prologue of the commentary itself. This then is probably the author; he cannot, however, be identified with anyone else who bears the name from the period. All that we can learn about him comes from the works—one orthonymous and two forged—that he left behind.

The benefit of identifying the author of the Pseudo-Ignatians as Julian is that it helps solidify our knowledge of his views and perspectives, which are less guarded in the Job Commentary than elsewhere. The reasons are transparent: in his other two works he is claiming to be other people and so he was compelled to present his views under the guise of others. As a result, his theological views are often more opaque, most obviously in the Pseudo-Ignatians themselves, where a number of scholars, basing their judgments only on what was available to them, the texts themselves, have argued incessantly concerning the doctrinal investments of the forger, most maintaining that the author was one kind of Arian or another (e.g., Zahn, Harnack, Amelungk, Perler) or, instead, Apollinarian (Funk, Diekamp). A number of scholars have proposed specific authors—Eusebius of Emesa, Evagrius Ponticus, Euzoius—or persons closely connected with them.[45] Surveying the discussions up to his time, Hagedorn concludes that there is simply no *opinio communis*.[46]

In the commentary, on the other hand, the author was not hampered by the demands of his pseudepigraphic art from presenting in more straightforward fashion his own theological perspective. And here it is quite clear that he is an "Arian" of what was once called a "strong" sort, someone who would have been comfortable in many ways with the positions of, say, an Aetius or Eunomius.[47]

Hagedorn makes a compelling case that Julian authored all three works, on the basis of striking commonalities among them in theological views, dogmatic terminologies, topoi, and style. He provides a list of thirty-five points of contact between the Job Commentary and the Apostolic Constitutions. Both works often

---

44. "Un commentaire grec arien sur Job," *RHE* 20 (1924): 38–65.

45. For early views, and an explicit discussion and refutation of Funk's claim that the author was Apollinarian, see Amelungk, "Untersuchungen." For Eusebius of Emesa: Othmar Perler, "Pseudo-Ignatius und Eusebius von Emesa," *Historisches Jahrbuch* 77 (1958), 73–82; Evagrius Ponticus (completely unconvincingly): Reinoud Weijenborg, " Is Evagrius Ponticus the Author of the Longer Recension of the Ignatian Letters?" *Anton* 44 (1969): 339–47; Euzoius or associate: James D. Smith, III, "Reflections on Euzoius in Alexandria and Antioch," *StPatr* 36 (2001): 514–20.

46. *Hiobkommentar*, xli.

47. On the problems involved with using the term *Arian*, see esp. Lewis Ayres, *Nicaea and Its Legacy: An Approach to Fourth-Century Trinitarian Thinking* (Oxford: Oxford University Press, 2004), pp. 2–4, 13–14. See further pp. 474–75 below.

deal with precisely the same topics, using precisely the same somewhat unusual expressions.[48] It is virtually impossible to imagine, as he notes, that two authors could independently attest such verbatim agreements in so many instances. Either two authors used the same source, or one author heavily edited or used the work of the other, or they are the same person. A careful analysis leads to the final result: Julian is the compiler of the Apostolic Constitutions.[49]

Verbal parallels between the Job Commentary and Pseudo-Ignatius are also significant. Hagedorn cites numerous instances, most of them impressive. As just three examples:

1. ὦ πάντων δαιμόνων πονηρότερον ἐκ κακονοίας δαιμόνιον (Job Comm. 24.14)
   ὦ πάντων πονηρῶν πνευμάτων πονηρότερον ἐκ κακονοίας πνεῦμα (Philipp. 11)
2. σοφὸς τοῦ κακοποιῆσαι. Τὸ δὲ καλὸν ὅτι ποτέ ἐστιν ἀγνοεῖ (Job Comm. 292.3)
   σοφὸς γάρ ἐστι τοῦ κακοποιῆσαι. Τὸ δὲ καλὸν ὅτι ποτέ ἐστιν ἀγνοεῖ (Philipp. 4)
3. καὶ τῆς ἐντολῆς ἐκστήσας τοὺς οὐδὲν αὐτὸν ἀδικήσαντας (Job Comm. 299.2)
   καὶ τῆς ἐντολῆς ἐκστήσας τοὺς οὐδὲν ἀδικήσαντάς σε (Philipp. 11)

On the basis of such verbatim similarities, Hagedorn concludes strongly: "The only possible explanation for the topical and linguistic/stylistic parallels between the three works is the identity of their author."[50]

Moreover, this author, Julian, shows his theological cards in the Commentary on Job. A key passage is the loaded comment on Job 37:22–23:[51]

> There is no one who is similar (οὐκ ἔχων τὸν ὁμοιούμενον) to him [ὁ παντοκράτωρ] with respect to his being or his power. In being because he is ἀγένητος; in power because he is the father of the son. Nor is anyone else the cause of all things or the παντοκράτωρ; nor is there another mediator of the genesis of these things except the μονογενὴς Θεός. (There follows a citation of John 1:1–3). He is not the Word as a "voice" nor is he God, in the sense of having no beginning (ἄναρχος); but he is "Word" in the sense of being born directly from the will and power, not by the suffering of nature (οὐ πάθει τῆς φύσεως), not through a division of his being (οὐ διαιρέσει τῆς οὐσίας). . . . Great is the glory of the All powerful; great is the honor due to him . . . ; he is incomparable both in nature and in power (ἀσυγκρίτου καὶ φύσει καὶ δυνάμει). There is nothing equal to him [of the same substance] or like him (οὔτε οὖν ὁμοούσιόν τι ἐξ αὐτοῦ . . . οὔτε ὁμοιούσιον). For he is incomparable, and we will find no other that is like him and his power (ἀσύγκριτος γάρ ἐστι καὶ οὐχ εὑρήσομεν ἄλλον ὅμοιον αὐτῷ καὶ τῇ ἰσχύι αὐτοῦ).

48. *Hiobkommentar*, xlii–xlviii.

49. Ibid., xlix.

50. "Die einzige mögliche Erklärung für die sachlichen und sprachlich-stilistischen Parallelen zwischen allen drei Werken ist die Identität ihres Autors." Ibid., lii.

51. Translation mine, based on the Greek text in Hagedorn, *Hiobkommentar*, pp. 245–46.

This strong rejection of both ὁμοούσιος and ὁμοιούσιος shows Julian's allegiances. For Hagedorn he was a "true-blood Arian"—specifically a disciple of Aetius or Eunomius. Since arguments over the term ὁμοούσιος did not appear until some thirty years after Nicea, starting with the Synod of Sirmium in 357 CE, this work must date sometime after that. And since, in his view, the neo-Arians did not survive the purge of Theodosius and the Council of Constantinople (381 CE), the work probably dates somewhat earlier. Hagedorn suggests a date between 357–365 and argues that the work was produced in Syria.[52]

This date works well for the forgery of letters in the name of Ignatius of Antioch as well. But several caveats are in order. For one thing, it is—as already intimated—inordinately difficult to get a handle on the theological views presented in the Pseudo-Ignatian letters themselves, in no small measure because so many nuances are involved with their language. Moreover, if we accept the identity of authorship among the three works of Julian, this does not mean he has expressed exactly the same views in all three. In no small measure that is because authors' views often shift over a period of time, especially in a period where theological niceties were being thrashed about and refined, and borders were constantly shifting between what was acceptable and what was execrable. At no time was that more true than in the period between the second quarter and the end of the fourth century. As two extreme cases from opposing ends of the spectrum, there is Arius, who at the end of his life claimed to support the decisions of Nicea, and Marcellus of Ancyra, who retracted many of his most distinctive views once they could not stand up either to criticism or the test of time.[53] We should not, in short, simply assume that if Julian wrote both the Commentary to Job and the Pseudo-Ignatian forgeries, the theology between the works will be identical. In fact, there are many similarities, as the forged works embrace some kind of "Arian" perspective and attack views endorsed by Marcellus and his followers who supported a miahypostatic (to use Lienhard's phrase) view. But there are differences as well, and it is important not to suppose that the author was strictly neo-Arian at the time he produced his works.[54] On the contrary, as we will see, the Pseudo-Ignatians appear to take several stances that run counter to traditional neo-Arian views.

Purpose of the Forgeries

Possibly the most important aspect of the Pseudo-Ignatians has been almost entirely overlooked by previous scholars interested in learning the motivation

52. His argument: Julian uses the Lucianic revision of the Septuagint, he cites the exegesis of Lucian of Antioch, he discusses alternative interpretations of "the Syrians," and Antioch was a stronghold of Arianism.

53. See, e.g., Joseph Lienhard, *Contra Marcellum: Marcellus of Ancyra and Fourth-Century Theology* (Washington, DC: Catholic University of America, 1999), ch. 4.

54. This is why it is important to look at a range of issues, not simply theological content, when evaluating the authorial claims of such works as the Pastoral epistles or Colossians and Ephesians.

behind the forgeries (and interpolations). This investigation has always proceeded by looking carefully at the nuances of the author's theological affirmations, to see whether he can best be described as a Nicene, Apollinarian, "semi-Arian," neo-Arian,[55] and so on. These affirmations are then set down in categories provided by systematic theology. This approach, however, has almost always missed the forest for the trees. In particular, scholars have worked hard to identify the author's theological alignments without asking why he may have wanted to create the forged materials in the first place. Thus, for example, the justly great Lightfoot, who argues that Pseudo-Ignatius cannot be located precisely: the author has some Arian leanings but is not exactly Arian, he is somewhat Apollinarian, but not really. Yet Lightfoot, in the end, never asks why the letters were forged. This is a question, in fact, that has scarcely ever been raised.

It is important to recognize that these letters were not meant to be a set of theological treatises, produced in the way modern systematic theologians produce theirs. As we will see, the letters are largely polemical, ostensibly, though not really, addressed to certain people and in almost every instance dealing with situations of conflict. This is widely known. But what has not been sufficiently appreciated is that the letters do not explicitly attack positions of the author's own day. They instead appear, on the surface, to be directed to theological aberrations of the second century, aberrations that the forger—incorrectly, as it turns out—seems to have thought were already a problem in the early years of that century, in the days of Ignatius. The targets of all the explicit polemic are such Christological heresies as psilanthropism (where Christ is not divine but a "mere man"); Gnosticism and Marcionism (with the claim that the unknown God did not create this world and that Christ is not the son of the creator); the related, but not coterminous, problem of docetism (where Christ is not a human at all, but is fully God); and Sabellianism (where Christ and God the Father are not separate beings but one being in two modes of existence).

It is true that the proto-orthodox attacks against these various second-century heresies, in the works, say, of Irenaeus, Hippolytus, and Tertullian, were replicated in the fourth century, as enemies of various theological persuasions accused their adherents of following tenets long denounced as heretical. Marcellus, for example, was regularly and roundly charged with being a kind of Sabellius redivivus, and accusations of psilanthropism were mutually leveled by heresiologists against one another.[56] But the striking feature of Pseudo-Ignatius' denunciations of heresies in nearly all of his explicit polemic is that, at least on the surface, they are phrased not in the sophisticated language of fourth-century Arian controversies, but in language that was, for the most part (though not entirely) appropriate two hundred years earlier. No wonder Hannah could think that the interpolations, at least, were roughly contemporaneous with Ignatius's own generation; on the surface they sound as if they are.

---

55. On the problems of using terms connected with "Arian," see pp. 474–75.

56. See, e.g., Lienhard, *Contra Marcellum*, pp. 210–40.

At the same time, there are places where the author used coded language that was sufficiently nuanced to express some of his key theological views. He evidently did so because he wanted to provide support for his own perspective and to show the genealogical lines of the tradition that could be traced back to a known postapostolic person—one known to the apostles—whom Eusebius indicates was the second bishop of Antioch after Euodius. The author forged these letters to show what Ignatius would have said as a leading heresiologist of his time, but more than this, as a reputed authority, both as the bishop of a major see, and above all as one of the first known Christian martyrs. As a concerned church leader, "Ignatius" naturally opposes false teaching, and this forger thinks, wrongly, that he knows what those teachings would have been in Ignatius's day. In some cases, he is off by several decades. Of equal importance, however, is that in the course of constructing this picture of Ignatius the martyr-heresiologist, the author slips in, here and there, theological views that are his real and ultimate point. These are subtle and hard for us to track, but they are in there, embracing some kind of "Arian," or at least dyohypostatic (again, Lienhard's phrase) understanding of the godhead. The other heresies that are explicitly attacked, in other words, serve as "covers" for the real issues that the forger wants this authority to address.

And so, the solution to the dilemma of the Pseudo-Ignatian forgeries (including the interpolations) is to see the ostensible polemic as a smoke screen, used by a highly trained and intelligent author who sought to establish, explicate, and support his own theological position by putting it on the lips of a great proto-orthodox leader of the faith, the famed martyr bishop Ignatius. By having Ignatius attack heresies thought to be from his own day, the author afforded himself the opportunity, in other places, to express his real theological agenda, by having Ignatius proclaim a theology that was, in fact, the forger's own.

Several subsidiary points need to be made before proceeding to a more detailed analysis. First, the author is clearly engaged, consciously, in the act of forgery, as is made clear both by all of his attempts at verisimilitude, some of which we will examine shortly, and by the fact that he altered in highly significant ways the authentic letters of Ignatius, in effect putting his own words on the pen of an author living more than a century and a half earlier. Moreover, the forger is not only concerned with theology and with conveying his particular Christological views under the authority of Ignatius. As is true of most authors, he has multiple interests.[57] These other interests include emphasizing the preeminence of the bishop, the ability of young men to serve as bishops, the importance of the church structure, the social relations of Christians, the relationship of church and state, and a large range of ethical issues, including opposition to rigorous asceticism.

---

57. See, for example, Norbert Brox, "Pseudo-Paulus und Pseudo-Ignatius: einige Topoi altchristlicher Pseudepigraphie," *VC* 30 (1976): 181–88, who deals with a very limited aspect of the problem posed by the Pseudo-Ignatians, arguing that the author modeled his work on Pastorals, especially (though somewhat obviously) in his correspondence with Mary.

Important Features of the Forgeries and Interpolations

I will not be able to provide an exhaustive examination of all the important features of the forger's work. A full analysis, however, is long overdue, and a full critical commentary on the Pseudo-Ignatians (including the interpolations) is a major desideratum in the field.

It is clear, in any event, that the author has gone out of his way to make his work believably Ignatian through the myriad verisimilitudes he provides. Thus, for example, we have the opening statement of the letter to the Tarsians: "From Syria even unto Rome I fight with beasts, not that I am devoured by brute beasts . . . but by beasts in the shape of men . . . I therefore the prisoner of Christ, who am driven along by land and sea, exhort you" (ch. 1).[58] Or the opening statement of the letter to the Antiochians, "The Lord has rendered my bonds light and easy since I learnt that you are at peace"; or its postscript "I write this letter to you from Philippi"; or from a passage in medias res, "What I spoke to you while present I now write to you" (ch. 7). The letter to Hero, as might be expected, given its subject matter, is especially full of examples: "I hand over to thee the Church of Antioch. . . . The bishops Onesimus, Bitus, Damas, Polybius, and all they of Philippi (whence also I have written to thee), salute thee in Christ . . ." (chs. 7–8). "Salute Cassian, my host, and his most serious minded partner in life, and their very dear children. . . . Salute by name all the faithful in Christ that are at Laodicea. Do not neglect those at Tarsus. . . . I salute in the Lord Maris, the bishop of Neopolis. . . . Salute thou also Mary my daughter . . ." (ch. 9). Especially profligate in this respect is the letter to Mary, where "Ignatius" waxes eloquent on the competing merits of writing as opposed to speaking face-to-face, and in a later section where he pretends to be under military guard (ch. 4), although here, evidently, he is imagined as being under house arrest in Antioch (whence he can fulfill her request) rather than en route to Rome. Verisimilitudes are not lacking to the additional comments of the interpolation, as seen, for example, in Ephesians 12, "I am the very insignificant Ignatius, who have thrown my lot with those exposed to danger."

All the verisimilitudes in the world cannot compensate for the author's occasional slips, however, as noted earlier, both in his delineation of false teachers who came after Ignatius' day in Tarsians 11 and in the list of minor church offices, some of which are otherwise unattested until the second half of the fourth century (subdeacons, readers, singers, doorkeepers, laborers, exorcists, confessors; Antiochenes 12).

In the interpolations there is a steady effort to expand upon what is already found in the authentic letters, not always in theologically, or at least christologically, interested ways. And so, for example, in Magnesians 5, instead of the Ignatian comment "there are two kinds of coins, the one of God, the other of the world, and each of these has its special character stamped upon it" we have

58. All quotations of the long recension of Ignatius are taken from Roberts and Donaldson, eds., *ANF*, vol. 1.

> Two different characters are found among men—the one true coin, the other spurious. The truly devout man is the right kind of coin, stamped by God Himself. The ungodly man, again, is false coin, unlawful, spurious, counterfeit, wrought not by God but by the devil. If anyone is truly religious, he is a man of God; but if he is irreligious, he is a man of the devil, made such, not by nature, but by his own choice. The unbelieving bear the image of the prince of wickedness. The believing possess the image of their Prince. . . .

Such expansions dominate the interpolations. The author is especially extravagant in his use of Scripture, in particular the writings that by his time had constituted the New Testament. And so, for example, in Ephesians 9, where Ignatius himself may indeed allude to both 1 Peter and John 12, the forger provides nine explicit citations to provide scriptural backing for his views, drawing from John 14, 16, 17; Psalm 119; 1 Peter 2, and Ephesians 1. Similar abundance can be found in Ephesians 10; Magnesians 8, 10, 12; Trallians 11; and Romans 8, 9.

In a number of instances the author tries to clear up difficult passages, often using more theologically loaded but still nuanced language. And so, in Magnesians 6, the Ignatian reference to deacons who are "entrusted with the ministry of Jesus Christ, who was with the Father before the ages and has been manifest at the end" gets modified to language more acceptable to an author embroiled in later debates: "are entrusted with the ministry of Jesus Christ. He, being begotten by the Father before the beginning of time, was God the Word, the only begotten son, and remains the same forever; for 'of his kingdom there shall be no end.'" Here, as we will see, is not just theology, but theological polemic, directed against those (of the fourth century) who denied that Christ was the Son before he became incarnate and those (same ones) who maintained that in fact the kingdom of Christ would indeed come to an end.

At other times the author's interests coincide roughly with those of Ignatius, who was thought to have not, perhaps, stressed a point with sufficient emphasis. Thus, on the question of the relationship of Christ and "Judaizers," Ignatius said in Magnesians 10: "It is outlandish to proclaim Jesus Christ and practice Judaism. For Christianity did not believe in Judaism, but Judaism in Christianity." This gets changed to "it is absurd to speak of Jesus Christ with the tongue, and to cherish in the mind a Judaism which has now come to an end. For where there is Christianity there cannot be Judaism. For Christ is one. . . ."

The Theological Investments

The most obvious and striking feature of the Pseudo-Ignatians is their theological investments. Theology is prominent in the author's mind; the letters written to the churches (Tarsians, Antiochians, Philippians) all begin, immediately after the letter openings, with strong theological polemic. And so, for example, in the letter to the Tarsians, after extending an epistolary greeting, the author launches into his attack: "I have learned that certain of the ministers of Satan have wished to disturb you, some of them asserting that Jesus was born [only] in appearance. . . . Others, again, hold that He is a mere man, and others that this flesh is not to rise again . . ." (ch. 2). So too the letter to the Antiochenes, "[Guard] against those heresies of the wicked one which have broken in upon us, to the deceiving and destruction of those that accept them . . ." (ch. 1).

Many of the interpolations as well involve true and false belief, and it becomes quite clear, especially here, that the author sees doctrine as a matter of life and death—or rather of eternal life and eternal damnation: the one who "sets at nought His doctrine shall go into hell" (Eph. 16); "If any man does not stand aloof from the preacher of falsehood, he shall be condemned to hell" (Philad. 3). It is hard to imagine anything more important, then, than true teaching.

This teaching, for the author, involves a clear affirmation of the Trinity, a doctrine that is inserted throughout the authentic letters of Ignatius. And so, for example, in Trallians 1, the phrase "By the will of God and Jesus Christ" becomes "by the will of God the Father, and the Lord Jesus Christ, His Son, with the co-operation of the Spirit"; in the preface to Romans the statement "is named from Christ, and from the Father" becomes "is named from Christ, and from the Father, and is possessed of the Spirit"; and in Philadelphians 4, the phrase "according to [the will of] God" becomes "there is but one unbegotten Being, God, even the Father; and one only begotten Son, God, the Word and man; and one Comforter, the Spirit of Truth."

In many other instances, the theological affirmations are presented in ostensibly polemical fashion. As noted, the polemics appear, on the surface, to be directed against older heresies presumably imagined as obtaining in the days of Ignatius. Despite the anachronisms, the polemical objects can all be assigned the second century, rather than the late fourth century. And so we find the warning of Tarsians 2:

> Certain ministers of Satan have wished to disturb you, some of them asserting that Jesus was born only in appearance, was crucified in appearance, and died in appearance; others that He is not the son of the Creator, and others that He is Himself God over all. Others, again, hold that He is a mere man, and others that this flesh is not to rise again.

Here then are attacks on docetism ("in appearance"), Gnosticism (or Marcionism; "not the son of the Creator"), Sabellianism ("God over all"), psilanthropism ("mere man"), and a condemnation of the flesh, such as found in the Gnostic works discussed in Chapter Thirteen.

A similar list applies to Antiochians 5, where some false teachers are said to declare "that there is but one God, only so as to take away the divinity of Christ." Others confess Christ, "yet not as the Son of the Maker of the world, but of some other unknown being, different from Him whom the Law and prophets have proclaimed." Others "[reject] the incarnation," and others declare "Christ to be a mere man." Here then one might think of Jewish Christianity (the unity of God without the divinity of Christ), Gnosticism, docetism, and adoptionism (or psilanthropism). A similar set of opponents is found in Hero 2, all of them second-century "deviations," but some of them post-Ignatian.

Such opposition is also found outside the congregational letters, especially in the exchange with Mary Cassobola, the predominant purpose of which is to support the possibility of young men serving as bishops, but in which theological affirmations nonetheless appear, in clear opposition to such groups as the adoptionists on the one hand and the Marcionites on the other (Christ preexisted but became human through the Virgin Mary, in fulfillment of the prophets, ch. 1). It occurs in the interpolations as well, as in Trallians 6:

> They alienate Christ from the Father, and the law from Christ. They also calumniate His being born of the Virgin; they are ashamed of His cross; they deny His passion; and they do not believe His resurrection. They introduce God as a Being unknown; they suppose Christ to be unbegotten; and as to the Spirit, they do not admit that He exists. Some of them say that the Son is a mere man, and that the Father, Son, and Holy Spirit are but the same person, and that the creation is the work of God, not by Christ, but by some other strange power.

Even though, as we will see, some of this is coded language for theological conflicts of the author's own day, a good deal of it could be directed against second-century Marcionites, adoptionists, docetists, Gnostics, and Sabellians. So too with an interpolation in Philadelphians 6, which explicitly attacks Simonians and Ebionites, and without naming them takes on the Marcionites, the Gnostics, the psilanthropists, and the docetists for good measure, not to mention those who are either excessively ascetic (calling "lawful wedlock, and the procreation of children, destruction and pollution" and deeming "certain kinds of food abominable") or heedlessly licentious (affirming that "unlawful unions are a good thing" and placing "the highest happiness in pleasure").

If we examine what the author affirms, and not merely what he rejects, a clearer picture of his place in the theological and christological debates of the fourth century begins to emerge. To start with, the forger stresses that there is one God, who alone is unbegotten, ὁ μόνος ἀγέννητος θεός (Hero 6; Eph. 7; cf. Antioch. 7; Magn. 7). It is only the heretics that teach that Christ too is ἀγέννητος (Philip. 7; Trall. 6). The one God is above all things (τοῦ θεοῦ τῶν ὅλων; Hero 7; Philip. 1), and he alone is almighty (εἷς θεός ἐστιν ὁ παντοκράτωρ; Magn. 8). This, as we will see, sets God the Father in contrast to his μονογενὴς υἱός, who is mentioned alongside him, but is begotten, not unbegotten, and is not God over all things, and does the will of the Father (e.g., Philip. 1; Philad. 4; Eph. 3). Throughout his work, the forger tries to walk the tightrope that led to the fall of many a fourth-century theologian, by avoiding clearly heretical teachings from different ends of the spectrum. And so, from Philippians 2, we learn that for him there is "one God and Father, and not two or three," just as there are not "three Sons or three Paracletes." There is, instead, "one Father, and one Son, and one Paraclete." But also, and equally important, there is not "one [person] having three names, nor . . . three [persons] who became incarnate." And so the author is determined to avoid a Sabellian view on the one hand, but some kind of tritheism on the other. For him, there may be one God, but there are "three" (what? beings?) who are "possessed of equal honour" (ἀλλ' εἰς τρεῖς ὁμοτίμους). The latter phrase, as we will see, has wreaked no little havoc among interpreters trying to make sense of the author's views (is ὁμοτίμους the same, or equivalent, to ὁμοούσιους? Or not?).

Some of the author's most emphatic teachings concern his views, specifically, of Christ. He has no difficulty calling Christ "God," although in most instances the term is anarthrous, and is, in the editing of the authentic Ignatians, made anarthrous. Thus Christ can be called θεὸς και ἄνθρωπος (Philip. 5); he is the "flesh-bearing God" σαρκοφόρον θεόν (Smyrn. 5); or, with the rare use of the article, the God Word τὸν θεὸν λόγον (Smyrn. 1). It is only the false teachers who preach God but disaffirm/deny/destroy Christ's divinity (καταγγέλλει θεὸν ἐπ' ἀναιρέσει τῆς τοῦ Χριστοῦ θεότητος; Antioch. 5).

Christ is emphatically not God the Father or fully equal to him. Hero 6 is typical in making the differentiation: ὁ μόνος ἀγέννητος θεὸς καὶ ὁ κύριος Ἰησοῦς Χριστός. With some rhetorical flair, the author attacks Satan for claiming that Christ is "God over all, and the Almighty" (Philip. 7). In Antiochenes 14 he differentiates between the one who is unbegotten and the one who is begotten "before the ages" (ὁ ὢν μόνος ἀγέννητος διὰ τοῦ πρὸ αἰώνων γεγεννημένου). The distinction between Father and Son is carefully kept, even where the Son is called "God." This can be seen, for example in the changes that the interpolator made to the famous hymnlike confession of Ephesians 7. No longer is Christ himself called, as in the authentic Ignatius, the "one physician." Now it is God "the Father and the Begetter of the only-begotten Son" who is "our physician"; at the same time "we have also as a physician τὸν κύριον ἡμῶν θεὸν Ἰησοῦν τὸν Χριστόν." As seen, Christ is still divine, but now, in this new version of the passage, Christ is no longer called ἀγέννητος; quite the contrary, only God is called ὁ μόνος ἀληθινὸς θεός, ὁ ἀγέννητος καὶ ἀπρόσιτος, the Lord of all, the father and begetter of the μονογενής. Christ, significantly, is indeed the "only-begotten Son and Word before time began"; he later became a human through the virgin Mary.

The distinction between Christ and God is seen as well in the interpolator's elimination from Ignatius's letters of the so-called exchange of predicates, so that, for example, the "blood of God" becomes the "blood of Christ" (Eph. Pref.). Similarly, the author typically changes phrases such as "Jesus Christ our God": καὶ Ἰησοῦ Χριστοῦ, τοῦ θεοῦ ἡμῶν, in Eph. 1, becomes κυρίου ἡμῶν Ἰησοῦ Χριστοῦ τοῦ σωτῆρος ἡμῶν. So too in the preface to Romans he shifts from ἐν Ἰησοῦ Χριστῷ, τῷ θεῷ ἡμῶν, to ἐν θεῷ διὰ Ἰησοῦ Χριστοῦ. There are a few occasions, however, where the editor appears to be inconsistent, using the article in describing Christ's divine status, as in the Preface to Romans: κατὰ πίστιν καὶ ἀγάπην Ἰησοῦ Χριστοῦ, τοῦ θεοῦ καὶ σωτῆρος ἡμῶν; and later in chapter 6: ἐπιτρέψατέ μοι μιμητὴν εἶναι πάθους Χριστοῦ τοῦ θεοῦ μου. One cannot immediately rule out the possibility that the editor was occasionally inconsistent or less than rigorous.

What can be said with greater certainty, in any event, is that he goes out of his way to emphasize that even though the divine Christ may be worthy of equal honor to God (whatever that is taken to mean) he is decidedly subordinate to him as the Son of the Father. Christ's subordinate status is evident throughout the forged and interpolated letters. As examples, Christ is said to do all things "according to the will of the Father" (Eph. 3); he established all things "according to the will of the Father" (Eph. 18); Christ becomes "subject to" God (ὃς καὶ μετὰ πάντων ὑποτάσσεται; Tars. 5); just as the church "depends on" Christ, Christ "depends on" God the Father (μακαρίζω τοὺς ἀνακεκραμένους αὐτῷ, ὡς ἡ ἐκκλησία τῷ κυρίῳ Ἰησοῦ καὶ ὁ κύριος τῷ θεῷ καὶ πατρὶ αὐτοῦ; Eph. 5); so too all in the church are to be obedient to the bishop as the bishop is to Christ and Christ is to the Father (Philad. 4). In Smyrneans 7 we are explicitly told that Jesus Christ "rejoiced in the superiority of the Father" (χαίρων τῇ τοῦ πατρὸς ὑπεροχῇ); in Smyrneans 9 Christ is subject to the Father just as those in the church are subject to their leaders and those lower in the church hierarchy are to those higher (οἱ λαϊκοὶ τοῖς διακόνοις ὑποτασσέσθωσαν, οἱ διάκονοι τοῖς πρεσβυτέροις, οἱ πρεσβύτεροι τῷ ἐπισκόπῳ, ὁ ἐπίσκοπος τῷ Χριστῷ, ὡς αὐτὸς τῷ πατρί).

Along with his concern to clarify—as best he could, we might assume—the relationship between Christ and God the Father, the forger was determined to understand the humanity of Christ, who, as we have seen, is described as an ἄνθρωπος. The most striking feature of the author's view is that even though the Incarnate had a human body, he did not have a human soul. In its place was the Logos: "God the Word did dwell in a human body, being within it as the Word, even as the soul also is in the body, because it was God that inhabited it, and not a human soul" (Philad. 6).[59] Probably it was because of that that Christ, as a human, "could not be tempted" by the Devil in the wilderness (the author asks the Devil: πῶς πειράζεις τὸν ἀπείραστον; Philip. 11); and why he "lived a life of holiness without sin" (Smyrn. 1). After his life ended, it was the Word, which had previously indwelled him, that "raised up again His own temple on the third day" (Smyrn. 2).

The Author's Polemical Target

As repeatedly noted, it has proved remarkably difficult over the years for scholars to nail down the object of the author's polemic. On one hand, it is clear that he is opposed to all sorts of heterodoxy stemming from the second century—docetism, psilanthropism, Marcionism, Gnosticism, Sabellianism, and Ebionitism. It would be also fair to say, in general terms, that based on the parallels to the Job commentary, the author is almost certainly an "Arian" of some kind. But that term itself has fallen on hard times, for good reasons. Rowan Williams notes that it became more or less a term of disapprobation applied indiscriminately to anyone

---

59. This was obviously a key passage for Funk's identification of the author as an Apollinarian; see, though, note 65 below.

who did not subscribe to Nicene orthodoxy: "The anti-Nicene coalition did not see themselves as constituting a single 'Arian' body: it is the aim of works like Athanasius' *De synodis* to persuade them that this is effectively what they are, all tarred with the same brush."[60] Even such a die-hard dyohypostatic as Eusebius of Caesarea could in effect deny that he was Arian.[61] It is striking that in his theological writings *Contra marcellum* and *De ecclesiastica theologia,* Eusebius never uses either the term *Arian* or the name *Arius;* so too other harsh opponents of miahypostatics such as Eusebius of Emesa and Cyril of Jerusalem.[62]

Moreover—the point I stressed earlier—even though the author's Job Commentary comes out strongly for a neo-Arian position that appears close to those taken by an Aetius or Eunomius, this does not mean that this set of writings will as well. We know nothing about the life story of Julian of Antioch, whether he remained consistent in his Trinitarian views with the shifting of the doctrinal tides over the years, or whether he wrote these two works in close proximity to one another. It is hard to believe that a theologian such as Julian, who insisted on the absolute supremacy of God the Father, and the subordination of the Son, would be willing to say that the two were ὁμοτίμους. At the same time, that is the claim of Pseudo-Ignatius himself, even though he too stresses the superiority of the only unbegotten God and the subordination of his only begotten Son.

In any event, the counter arguments of Lightfoot that the author could as well be seen as a Nicene Christian fail to convince.[63] However one might decide to label the author positively, a number of his comments indeed appear to be coded statements of polemic, directed against a specific target. This target does not need to be identified with any person that we otherwise have knowledge of, any more than the author Julian need be someone mentioned in our other surviving records. What is reasonably clear is that a number of the author's nuanced statements show that he is combating a hyper-monotheistic, virulently anti-Arian, strict miahypostatic view such as that embraced by, and often accorded

60. *Arius: Heresy and Tradition,* rev. ed. (Grand Rapids, MI: Eerdmans, 2001), p. 166. See also note 47 above.

61. See especially Lienhard, *Marcellus,* p. 108.

62. Ibid., p. 194. It is interesting to consider the First Creed of the Dedication at the Council of Antioch, whose "Arian" bishops rejected the label Arian: "We have not been followers of Arius. For how could we, as bishops, follow a presbyter? Nor did we receive any other faith except the one handed down from the beginning. We ourselves were the examiners and testers of his [Arius's] faith. We admitted him; we did not follow him." Quoted in ibid., p. 168.

63. For example, Lightfoot argues that the author speaks of the Son as "begotten before the Ages." But he admits that most Arians would have no trouble saying that as well. He indicates that the author condemns those who see Christ as a mere man as well as those who deny that he is God; that too could be and was part of Arian polemic. And he points out that the author calls Christ "God"—but so too do Arians. Lightfoot also maintains that Arians would not consider Christ "unchangeable" by nature (on the basis of a passage in the Thalia); but Perler has argued that whereas extreme Arians may not have made the claim, those like Eusebius of Caesarea easily could have done so (Othmar Perler, "Die Briefe des Ignatius von Antiochian: Frage der Echtheit—neue, arabische Übersetzung," *FZPhTh* 18, 1971, 381–96). At the end of the day, the author simply uses too much "Arian" language to be dismissed.

to, Marcellus of Ancyra (whether Marcellus himself was the actual target or not). This view was commonly labeled Sabellian by its enemies, because of its insistence that there was only one hypostasis, God the Father, and that only the Word (not the Son) was preexistent with the Father.

According to Marcellus, the Word emerged from the Father for the purpose of creation and later, then, became flesh at the incarnation. It was when it took on flesh that the Word became the Son; indeed none of the traditional Christological titles, apart from Word, apply to the Preincarnate. At the end of all things, when the time is fulfilled, the Word will return into the Father, at which point the kingdom of the Christ will come to an end.[64]

The opponent of these views—Julian of Antioch, forger of the Pseudo-Ignatian letters—was some kind of "Arian,"[65] who is most clearly seen in what he attacks, either explicitly or with subtlety. It is hard to know why he does not take the hard neo-Arian views expressed in the Job Commentary. Is it because he is pretending to be Ignatius? Because his views are slightly different at this point of his life and authorship? Because he is more intent on opposing an aberrant view than setting forth the niceties of his own? In any event, his "Eusebian"-type opposition to a Marcellian miahypostatic view is relatively pronounced throughout this forged response in the name of Ignatius.[66]

And so, for example, Antiochenes 1 attacks those who "deny Christ under pretense of maintaining the unity of God"—the latter being one of the ultimate concerns of miahypostatic views. Philippians 4 insists that not only is there one God the Father, there is also one Son, God the Word. Repeatedly, throughout Julian, the forger's, writings, Christ is portrayed as a separate being from God. Christ, moreover, is the "Son" (not just the Word) "before the ages" (Antioch. 14); Christ (not just the Word) is begotten by the Father before the ages (Magn. 11); Christ is the Son of God before time (Polyc. 3). Magnesians 6 strongly asserts an anti-Marcellian position: Jesus Christ was begotten before the ages and was not only God the Word but the only begotten Son, and he "remains the same forever" and "of his kingdom there will be no end"—the most strident and frequent position taken by opponents against Marcellus.

---

64. For the fullest and best synthesis of Marcellus's life and theology, see Lienhard, *Contra Marcellum*; in addition see Ayres, *Niceae*, pp. 62–69.

65. That he was not a Nicene of Apollinarian leanings was shown long ago, especially in Amelungk's refutation of Funk, "Untersuchung"; his conclusion stands close to the position staked out here; pp. 521–22. What he does not realize is that the subtle views are set up by the smokescreen. See also Lightfoot, *Apostolic Fathers*, part 2, vol. 1, pp. 254–61.

66. Others who have seen the author as an Arian of a more-or-less-Eusebian mode include Perler, "Die Briefe des Ignatius von Antiochian," pp. 381–96, with Perler earlier making a more specific proposal, in "Pseudo-Ignatius"; and K. J. Woollcombe, "The Doctrinal Connexions of the Pseudo-Ignatian Letters," *StPatr* 6 (1962): 269–73. Amelungk has helpfully deduced a large number of parallels between the Pseudo-Ignatians and the Ekthesis makrostichos in particular, possibly a source for Julian's work; see the tabular results in Amelungk, "Untersuchungen," pp. 573–81.

An even more direct assault on Marcellus is found in the edited version of Magnesians 8, as long ago recognized by Lightfoot. The authentic letter spoke of "Jesus Christ His Son, who is his word proceeding from silence."[67] The interpolator significantly altered the passage with important theological result, so that now it reads, διὰ Ἰησοῦ Χριστοῦ τοῦ υἱοῦ αὐτοῦ, ὅς ἐστιν αὐτοῦ λόγος, οὐ ῥητός, ἀλλ' οὐσιώδης· οὐ γάρ ἐστιν λαλιᾶς ἐνάρθρου φώνημα, ἀλλ' ἐνεργείας θεϊκῆς οὐσία γεννητή:

> through Jesus Christ his Son, who is his Word, not a literal utterance but having a real existence; for he is not a speaking of an articulate utterance [meaning that he is not just words that can be aurally sensed] but is a being begotten of divine power [that is, he has a real existence as an ousia, but is begotten as such by God].[68]

Lightfoot argues that this statement opposed the Marcellian view that Christ did not have a separate ousia from the Father but was an energy emitted by the Father for the purposes of creation and redemption, who then was absorbed back into the Father when these tasks were completed.[69] Moreover, it stresses, contrary to Marcellus, that the Preincarnate was not Word in name only, a Word that was inside the Father until spoken and not the Son (until the incarnation).[70]

For this author not only is the divine Christ a distinctive being, begotten before the ages, he is subordinate to God, contrary to the views of Marcellus and others more or less in the Athanasian camp or to the left of it. Hence the stress we have seen already: Christ does the will of the Father, he does nothing apart from the Father (Magn. 7); he is subject to the Father, dependent on the Father, obedient to the Father (Eph. 5; Philad. 4; Smyrn. 7, 9). This is a subordinationist Christology. It makes sense, then, that the author portrays his opponent(s) in contrary, Sabellian terms. Thus, as we have seen Satan (the author of the heresy held by the opponent) is attacked in Philippians 7 for maintaining that Christ himself is God over all. So too Marcellus and his followers were often accused of being Sabellian, since they were so miahypostatic that they (seemed to have) denied the Son a separate existence. It bears noting that in his *De ecclesiastica theologia* Eusebius accused Marcellus of being Sabellian on forty occasions; moreover, a number of later anti-miahypostatic tractates—including Pseudo-Athanasius' *Fourth Oration against the Arians* and Basil of Caesarea's *Contra Sabellianos et Arium et Anomoeos*—attacked Marcellus and his followers under the thinly disguised figure of

67. On the famous textual problem, where scribes nervous about the claim being taken in a Gnostic way added a negative, so that now the Word does *not* come forth from "Sige," see Lightfoot, *Apostolic Fathers*, part 2, vol. 2, pp. 126–28.

68. Translation mine.

69. *Apostolic Fathers*, part 2, vol. 1, p. 268.

70. On Marcellus's views, see Lienhard *Marcellus*, p. 218.

Sabellius.[71] Finally, it should be noted that Eusebius explicitly maligned Marcellus for his view that Christ had a specifically human soul (*De eccl. theol.* 1.20.43, 45); the author of the Pseudo-Ignatians is emphatic that the incarnate Christ had a human body and the divine Logos in the place of a human soul, a view that has been wrongly read as Apollinarian, but is in any event clearly anti-Marcellian.[72]

Some Remaining Ambiguities

It would not be prudent to claim to have ascertained the precise theological position of the author of the Pseudo-Ignatian corpus, when so many stalwarts in the field have failed. What is relatively clear is that the author Julian has here used the proto-orthodox martyr-bishop Ignatius to oppose an Über-Nicene view such as found in Marcellus and those like him, who stressed the complete unity of God at the expense (it was thought) of the separate existence of the Son. This miahypostatic position is roundly attacked in the polemics of the corpus through its emphasis on the preexistence of the Son (not just the Word), his separate existence from God, and especially his subordination to God. All of this could simply be called Origenist, but that does not get us very far, as so many theological views of the fourth century could trace their lineage—had they wanted to do so—to the great Alexandrian.

Even though Julian himself appears to have been neo-Arian in his Commentary on Job, the views in the Ignatian forgeries (and interpolations) are more muted, and ambiguities remain. When the author stresses that there is only one God, not two or three (Philip. 2), that may simply be a defense against the charge of ditheism or tritheism, but it could also be an attack on those who, like Origen, had no qualms about calling Christ a "second God"—a view acceptable as well to a range of Arians. The "Eusebian" dyohypostatic view stressed that although there were two hypostases, they were not equal; Eusebius, in fact, makes the emphatic declaration that δύο ὑποστάσεις τιθέντα. οὐδὲ γὰρ ἰσοτίμους αὐτὰς ὁριζόμεθα (*De eccl. theol.* 2.7.3). That seems difficult to reconcile with the claim of Pseudo-Ignatius that the Father, Son, and Holy Spirit are, precisely, εἰς τρεῖς ὁμοτίμους (Philip. 2). Are the three ὁμοτίμους but not ἰσοτίμους? Moreover, when the author claims that the opponents "alienate Christ from the Father" (Trall. 6) is that an attack on neo-Arians? And does the claim that Christ is "unchangeable in nature" (Philip. 5) stand counter to a neo-Arian view, as Perler maintains?[73]

In sum, while a good deal remains ambiguous, several points seem clear. In view of linguistic considerations, the author of the Pseudo-Ignatians appears

71. See ibid., pp. 210–40.

72. Apollinarius saw the Logos as taking the place of the νοῦς or πνεῦμα, not the ψύχη, though the matter came to be complicated in later Apollinarians. Other aspects of the author's teaching, however, seem to distance him from Apollinarius. See further Lightfoot, *Apostolic Fathers,* part 2, vol. 1, pp. 271–73, and note 65 above.

73. "Pseudo-Ignatius und Eusebius von Emesa," pp. 80–81.

to be Julian of Antioch, who also produced the Apostolic Constitutions and the Commentary on Job. In the latter he takes a strong neo-Arian stand. In the Pseudo-Ignatians, for one reason or another (written for a different purpose? At a different time in his life, when his views were somewhat altered?) the line he takes is somewhat more moderate, comparable to a traditional Eusebian dyohypostatic perspective. But there is little doubt about his principal theological opponent—whether a real figure or a person or group imagined for the occasion. He attacks in particular an extreme Nicene perspective that emphasized the unity of God, the one hypostasis, at the expense, in the author's opinion, of the individual existence of Christ and his subordination to the Father.

Other Emphases of the Author

Throughout this study I have stressed that forgeries—like other literary works—need to be seen as multifunctional, and this is certainly the case with the Pseudo-Ignatians. The author was not concerned simply to attack false theological teachings. He had a wide range of interests, as is evident from even a casual perusal of his work. Among other things he devoted a considerable amount of effort to expanding the paranetic sections of the authentic Ignatian letters (see e.g., Philad. 4) and in providing paranesis of his own (e.g., Antioch. 9–10). In that regard he was interested in the social arrangements of the Christians in their family lives (the Haustafeln in the chapters just mentioned); in ethical instructions against crimes such as magic, pederasty, and murder (Antioch. 11); and against fanatically rigorous asceticism (Hero 1). He was particularly concerned to develop Ignatius' own stress on the church hierarchy (e.g., Eph. 5). The bishop is to be followed as the head of the church (Hero 3, Tars. 8, Trall. 7, Smyrn. 9, and lots of other places). The author was especially keen to stress—in an elaboration on a theme of the Pastoral epistles, as N. Brox has recognized[74]—the validity of young bishops (Magn. 3 and both letters in the correspondence with Mary).

In addition, he had other polemical targets, not just the dubious theologians he saw as the primary threat. In particular, he was concerned with Jews and/or Judaizers who, in this case, were not necessarily ciphers for his overly emphatic miahypostatic opponents.[75] And so, he explicitly attacks the "Christ killing Jews" (Magn. 11; Philad. 6) and indicates that Jews both do battle with God and "killed the Lord" (Trall. 11). Christ stands over against "the Jews," his enemies: "The Word raised up again His own temple on the third day, when it had been destroyed by the Jews fighting against Christ." For him, Judaism no longer served a useful (or any) function, and had legitimately passed away: "It is absurd to speak

74. N. Brox, "Pseudo-Paulus."

75. On the use of "the Jew" as a convenient label against fellow Christians in fourth-century controversies, see, e.g., Christine Shepardson, *Anti-Judaism and Christian Orthodoxy: Ephrem's Hymns in Fourth Century Syria* (Washington, DC: Catholic University of America Press, 2008).

of Jesus Christ with the tongue, and to cherish in the mind a Judaism which has now come to an end" (Magn. 10). For that reason, Jewish festivals were no longer to be kept: "Let us therefore no longer keep the Sabbath after the Jewish manner, and rejoice in days of idleness" (Magn. 9). In fact, anyone who keeps Sabbath "is a Christ killer" (Philip. 13); so too is anyone who celebrates the Passover with the Jews. This final attack may be directed against Quartodecimans; but given the propensity of some Christians in some places to celebrate Jewish holidays with Jews—famously acknowledged and attacked by other stalwart fourth-century proponents of Christian orthodoxy such as John Chrysostom[76]—the author may indeed have in mind otherwise orthodox Christians celebrating real festivals with real Jewish friends and neighbors.

76. See for example Robert Wilken, *John Chrysostom and the Jews: Rhetoric and Reality in the Fourth Century* (Berkeley: University of California, 1983).

CHAPTER FIFTEEN

Apologetic Forgeries

In the preceding chapters I have focused on Christian forgeries that attack views thought to be problematic or dangerous—the standard province of polemics. The obverse of the battle coin is apologia, the defense put up against the attacks of others.[1] Early Christian forgeries were used in the intellectual defense of the faith against non-Christian opponents, and it is that apologetic function of forged writings that I will consider in this chapter.[2]

Several of the forgeries I have already discussed may well have functioned, in one sense or another, apologetically.

THE ACTS OF THE APOSTLES

The Acts of the Apostles, a non-pseudepigraphic forgery that strives, among other things, to champion Paul, his message, and his mission, has often been read as an apology of sorts, not just for Paul (and Jesus) but for the Christian movement as

1. For recent works on the early Christian apologists, see Bernard Pouderon, *Les apologistes grecs du IIe siècle* (Paris: de Cerf, 2005); and Mark Edwards, Martin Goodman, and Simon Price, eds., *Apologetics in the Roman Empire: Pagans, Jews, and Christians* (Oxford: Oxford University Press, 1999). Still worth reading as backdrop to the apologetic movement is the classic of Pierre de Labriolle, *La réaction païenne: étude sur la polémique antichrétienne du Ier au VIe siècle* (Paris: L'artisan du Livre, 1934). For a recent, interesting attempt to limit the genre of the "apology" strictly, as a form introduced by Justin and perfected but brought to an end by Tertullian, see Sara Parvis, "Justin Martyr and the Apologetic Tradition," in Sara Parvis and Paul Foster, eds., *Justin Martyr and His Worlds* (Minneapolis: Fortress, 2007), pp. 115–27. For my purposes here, "apologetic forgeries" refers not to forgeries necessarily in the literary form, or genre, of "apologia," but to forgeries that function apologetically.

2. Here I leave to the side the question of whether Christian apologiae were meant to convince outsiders, or to provide insiders with ammunition for their debates with others. I subscribe to the latter view, but the issue does not affect the questions I will be addressing throughout the chapter.

a whole.[3] To some extent, though not completely, this apologetic thrust hinges on the identification of Theophilus. If he is thought of as a Roman official of some kind—whether an actual figure or one dreamt up for the occasion—it would make sense that the history of the Christian church that follows would be oriented toward convincing him that the movement comes from God, that there is nothing illegal or immoral about it, that its success is evidence of its truth claims, and that any social conflict that has erupted with its appearance is due not to rabble-rousers among the Christians but to the recalcitrant Jews who have rejected not only God but also his messiah and the people who follow him. This bilateral approach that sets its apologetic sights on both pagans, to whom apology is made, and Jews, who are faulted and condemned in the process, became a regular feature of the early Christian apologetic literature, for reasons that are not hard to fathom. For Christian thinkers intent on establishing the legitimacy of the religion as ancient only one real option was available: to present the Christian faith as the "true" form of Judaism, a religion that could be traced as far back as Moses—who lived four centuries before the pagan Homer—and beyond him all the way to Abraham. In a world that respected antiquity and suspected novelty, Judaism was a religion with venerable roots, and Christians needed to claim them as their own. It was a claim hard to sustain, given the thriving communities of non-Christian Jews, far outnumbering the followers of Jesus, legitimately able to claim themselves to be "true" Jews. They, unlike most Christians, actually followed Jewish laws and traditions. And if they were the Jews, what were the Christians but a set of interlopers who tried to usurp Israel's rightful place as the people of the one Creator God? As a matter of survival, then, Christian apologists had to attack contemporary Judaism as an aberrant form of the faith that descended from Abraham and Moses.

This is one of the factors that led to the early animosities between Jews and Christians, and it played itself out narratively not just in the minds of Christians but also on the written page, in a book such as Acts which portrays the Jews in a negative light, blaming them for the Christians' woes and portraying them as troublemakers who have refused to accept the true prophet and messiah sent from their own God. The persecution of Christians in this book does not usually originate with Roman mobs or officials incensed at the claims made for Jesus. It almost always originates with Jews, who have rejected their own messiah.[4] Thus the apologetic function of the book depends in part on its castigation of Jews and the true religion that they belligerently refuse to embrace.

And so the book absolves Christians—especially the apostles, and in particular Paul—of any wrongdoing. The apologetic *Tendenz* is seen especially in the speeches delivered to pagan officials in the book, speeches that dominate the final quarter of the narrative in the episodes of Paul on trial. These speeches are not

---

3. For earlier discussion of Acts, see pp. 263–82.

4. For an exception, see Acts 19.

historical recollections; they are apologetic models for Christian readers who also needed to defend themselves against charges that the author considered unfair and unjustified. The Christians have done nothing to rouse the ire of the state; they are simply following the true understanding of the Jewish faith made available now with the coming of the messiah. Any social unrest that accompanies the movement originates with the wicked machinations of unbelieving Jews.

We will see this correlation of antagonism to Jews and apology to gentiles in such works as the Acts of Pilate, the Martyrdom of Polycarp, and the Sibylline Oracles. In the case of the Acts of the Apostles, the intertwined themes are connected to the identity of the pseudonymous author. He is not simply someone who is basing his work on hearsay. He has done substantial research into the matter (Luke 1:1–4), and more than that, he was personally there to see how the principal figure in his narrative—the apostle Paul himself—engendered unwarranted hatred by the Jews, leading to his arrest and trials, where he delivered his apologetic addresses. The alleged author, then, is well situated to show that the followers of Jesus are no threat to the social order.

FIRST PETER

Another forgery that is both closely connected with Paul and related to issues of apologia is the letter of 1 Peter.[5] Unlike Acts, 1 Peter is not principally framed to convey an apologetic message; it instead gives instructions for Christians confronted with animosity and opposition, urging them to behave in ways that reveal their innocence in the face of charges—unofficial, in this case—brought against them: "Be prepared at all times to provide an apologia to everyone who asks you for a word concerning the hope that is in you" (3:15). As noted earlier, the book is especially obsessed with the issue of Christian persecution and suffering. The author is particularly concerned that Christians suffer only for doing what is right, not what is wrong (3:17). Suffering "as a Christian" is to be expected, since Christ himself had to suffer (3:18). But his followers should suffer for their faith, not because they have done anything to incur legitimate animosity: "For what credit is there if you sin and suffer for it, but endure it? But if you do what is good and suffer, and endure it, this is acceptable to God" (2:20). Christians are to lead moral and upright lives, in no small measure because doing so may pay the ultimate apologetic reward of leading others to join the faith: "Abstain from the fleshly passions which do battle against your soul; keep your conduct good among the gentiles, so that when they malign you as evil doers they may see your good works and give glory to God on the day of visitation" (2:11–12).

The Christians' behavior should not merely be acceptable to outsiders, it should be exemplary. They should "no longer live according to human passions

5. See discussion on pp. 239–59.

but according to the will of God" (4:2). In this they display a newness of life that should attract the right kind of attention:

> The time that is already past is sufficient to fulfill the will of the gentiles, participating in licentiousness, passions, drunkenness, revels, drinking parties, and lawless idolatries. They are surprised when you do not run around with them in the same wild profligacy, and they blaspheme—but they will render an account to the one who is ready to judge the living and the dead. (4:3–4).

In addition, Christians are to subject themselves to every civil authority (2:13–14), "for it is the will of God that by doing good you might silence the ignorance of the foolish" (2:15). On the home front, Christians are to follow established lines of authority. Slaves are to obey masters (2:18) and women are to be submissive to husbands, "so that if some are disobedient to the word, they might be gained through the behavior of their wives without them saying a word" (3:1). In short, believers are to be model citizens, slaves, and spouses; they should not break the law or acceptable moral codes (4:15); but if they suffer "as a Christian" that is all to the good, as in the long run it may have a positive effect, for both sufferer and oppressor (3:16–17).

This exhortation to speak and live apologetically is given by one of early Christianity's ultimate authorities, the apostle Peter, "witness to Christ's sufferings," who himself, of course, was reputed to have suffered the ultimate penalty, in having been martyred under Nero in Rome. The letter, though, was not actually written by Peter from beyond the grave, but by a forger who was intent on using Peter's name to provide authorization for the message he needed to deliver.

THE ACTS OF PILATE

As a final example of a previously examined forgery that functioned apologetically, we should consider anew the fourth-century Acts of Pilate.[6] As already indicated, the genesis of the book has generated considerable interest among scholars, in no small measure because of the intriguing circumstance mentioned by Eusebius, that earlier in the fourth century, during the reign of Maximin Daia, a pagan version of an "Acts of Pilate" appeared and made an enormous splash among readers throughout the Empire.

Although this pagan Acts of Pilate does not survive, the Christian version does. In this imaginative account, as we have seen, rather than condemning Jesus justly for warrantable crimes, Pilate finds Jesus completely innocent of all charges. It is only the recalcitrant Jews who force his hand. Pilate himself is convinced that Jesus is the true King. So too is everyone else in the narrative, apart from the Jewish antagonists. Even the standards bearing the image of Caesar bow down,

6. See the discussion on pp. 350–58.

of their own accord, before him. Caesar himself, then, recognizes not just Jesus' complete innocence but his divine royalty.

This in itself is an apologetic motif, but in many ways it is the very existence of this Christian version of an Acts of Pilate that functions as an apology. This appears to be a case of counterforgery, a forged Christian Acts countering an earlier forged pagan Acts. To that extent, the book is the apologetic equivalent to the polemical letter of the Laodiceans, whose very existence shows that the Marcionite forgery could not really be by Paul. With the Acts of Pilate, the Christian edition discredits and refutes the pagan account simply by giving the "true" version of the story. To do so it had no need to refer explicitly to the earlier work. Its appearance and dissemination themselves corrected the errant portrayal of the older forgery.

In addition to these forgeries that we have already considered under other rubrics, there are several whose primary function may well be considered apologetic, including one that was, in many ways, more historically and culturally significant than many of the books that eventually became Scripture, the Protevangelium Jacobi.

THE PROTEVANGELIUM JACOBI

The title, Protevangelium Jacobi, is not original or even ancient. It comes from the first publication of the book by G. Postel in 1552, *Protevangelion sive de natalibus Jesu Christi et ipsius Matris virginis Mariae, sermo historicus divi Jacobi minoris.*[7] The title is appropriate to the book's contents, as the narrative relates events leading up to and immediately following the birth of Jesus, especially those involving Mary: her own miraculous birth, upbringing, young life, and engagement to Joseph. In addition, the account narrates, as a kind of Christian midrash on the infancy narratives of Matthew and Luke,[8] the circumstances of Jesus' birth, Mary's continued virginity (demonstrated famously by a midwife's postpartum inspection), and the opposition to the Christ child by King Herod, leading to the miraculous protection of John the Baptist and his mother, while his father, Zacharias, the high priest of the Jews, is murdered in the Temple. The book is allegedly written by "James," by whom is certainly meant the brother of Jesus, or for this account, his stepbrother, the son of Joseph from a previous marriage.

---

7. The bewildering array of long and explanatory titles found in the manuscripts include such niceties as "Narrative and History Concerning How the Very Holy Mother of God was Born for Our Salvation" (Tischendorf ms C); or "Narrative of the Holy Apostle James, the Archbishop of Jerusalem and Brother of God, Concerning the Birth of the All Holy Mother of God and Eternal Virgin Mary" (ms A). Our earliest manuscript, Bodmer V of the third or fourth century, simply calls it "The Birth of Mary, the Revelation of James."

8. See Edouard Cothenet, "Le Protévangile de Jacques: origen, genre et signification d'un premier midrash chrétien sur la Nativité de Marie," *ANRW* 2.25.6 (1988): 4252–69.

The account is usually dated to the second century, for reasons we will see below, and became particularly popular in eastern Christendom.[9] It was not unknown in the West: there are still fragments of a Latin version and, more important, it was taken over by the widely read Gospel of Pseudo-Matthew, which popularized many of its stories. But for the most part the Protevangelium was not transmitted in the West because its portrayal of Jesus' brothers as sons of Joseph from a previous marriage was roundly condemned by no less an authority than Jerome, in whose forcefully stated view Jesus' alleged brothers were in fact his cousins.[10] This interpretation was closely tied to Jerome's ascetic agenda; for him, not only was Mary a perpetual virgin, but so too was Joseph, the earthly father of the Lord. The Protevangelium was explicitly condemned in 405 CE by Pope Innocent I[11] and eventually in the sixth-century Gelasian Decree.

The earliest reference that is virtually certain comes in Origen's *Commentary on Matthew* 10.17 (on Matt. 13:55), where he claims that the view that James was the son of Joseph from a previous marriage is taught either in the Gospel of Peter or the Book of James, the latter of which, he says, stresses the ongoing virginity of Mary. As this is a key theme of the Protevangelium, there is little doubt that Origen is referring to our text. More questionable are possible references in Clement of Alexandria, who knows the story of Mary's postpartum inspection by a midwife, but does not indicate the source of his knowledge (*Strom.* 7. 16. 93), and earlier in Justin, who knows the tradition that Jesus was born in a cave outside Bethlehem, but does not refer to the Protevangelium itself (*Dial.* 78).

Whenever the Protevangelium achieved its final form (if one can speak of a "final" form for a textual tradition as malleable as this one),[12] the text as it has come down to us gives clear signs of being based on yet earlier sources available to the pseudonymous author. Not only is chapter 18 narrated in the first person (Joseph describing how "time stood still" when the son of God came into the world), so too is the postscript: "I James, the one who has written this account" (ch. 25). Obviously, the first person of chapter 25 is different from the first person of chapter 18; the two accounts almost certainly come from different sources, or at least from one later redaction of another source. Harnack made the influential argument that there are three major sources that have been incorporated into the longer account: (1) a kind of biography of Mary in chapters 1–17, beginning with the circumstances of her miraculous birth to the wealthy Jerusalemite Joachim and his hitherto barren wife, Anna, and through her holy

9. The book survives in some 150 Greek manuscripts and a range of eastern versions: Coptic, Syriac, Ethiopic, Armenian, Georgian, and Slavonic.

10. *De perpetua virginitate beatae Mariae adversus Helvidium.*

11. Letter 6 to Exuperius of Toulous 7.30.

12. See the extensive collations of manuscripts in two unpublished Duke University dissertations: B. Daniels, "The Greek Manuscript Tradition of the Protevangelium Jacobi" (1956); and George Zervos, "Prolegomena to a Critical Edition of the Genesis Marias (Protevangelium Jacobi): The Greek Manuscripts" (1986).

and protected infancy, to her upbringing in the Jerusalem Temple, where she is daily fed by an angel, through her engagement to the elderly Joseph, and then her virginal conception; (2) an account of Joseph and the birth of Jesus in chapters 18–20, including the trip to Bethlehem, the firsthand account of Joseph's vision of time standing still, and the narrative of the postpartum inspection of Mary, which showed her to be a virgin even after giving birth; and (3) an account of the death of Zacharaias, the father of John the Baptist, in the wake of Herod's wrath, in chapters 22–24.[13]

Other scholars, such as de Strycker, have argued for an original unity of the text, largely on the grounds of literary style and vocabulary.[14] What is clear, in any event, is that the subject matter does shift in the final chapters of the book, where Mary, the key figure of the narrative as a whole, disappears from sight, and the family of John the Baptist assumes center stage. Even if this latter account was "original" to the text, it probably comes from a different oral or written source, as did the vision of Joseph in chapter 18.

Whatever his sources, it is not difficult to reconstruct some of the driving forces that led the pseudonymous author to generate his account. The canonical Gospels are notoriously silent about key issues and events involving the time up to and including Jesus' appearance into the world. This Gospel tries to fill in some of the gaps. It would be a mistake, however, to see the Protevangelium driven by biographical concerns pure and simple, or even by the impulse to provide an encomium on Mary, as such scholars as Hock have maintained.[15] The narrative does indeed function in both of these ways. But it also functions apologetically, to answer charges leveled against Jesus by non-Christian authors who were opposed both to him and to the religion founded in his name. It answers these charges pseudonymously, in a forgery allegedly written by Jesus' own (step)brother, James, who would obviously be well positioned to know the family secrets about events leading up to Jesus' appearance in the world.

The Pseudepigraphic Framework

There can be little doubt that by using the pseudonym "James" the author meant for his readers to identify him as Jesus' brother, the leader of the church in the Jewish capital, James of Jerusalem. Not only does he not identify himself further, so that readers naturally assume it must be "that" James, but at the end he associates himself with the holy city (cf. Gal. 2:9):

---

13. Adolf von Harnack, *Geschichte der altchristlichen Literatur bis Eusebius* (Leipzig: J. C. Hinrichs, 1958 [original 1897]), 2: 598–603.

14. Emile de Strycker, *La Forme la plus ancienne du Protévangile de Jacques* (Brussels: Société des Bollandistes, 1961).

15. Ronald Hock, *The Infancy Gospels of James and Thomas* (Santa Rosa, CA: Polebridge, 1995). pp. 14–20.

> But I James, the one who has written this account in Jerusalem, hid myself away in the wilderness when there was a disturbance at the death of Herod, until the disturbance in Jerusalem came to an end. There I glorified God, the Master, who gave me the wisdom to write this account. (ch. 25)[16]

This Herod, then, is "Herod the Great," known to be violently opposed to the family of Joseph (Matthew 2). But it is also possible that the author is making an implausible intertextual connection, or that he is himself somewhat confused about the facts of biblical history, by referring to the association of "James" and "Herod" from Acts 12:1–2. In the latter episode, it is another James (the son of Zebedee) who is persecuted, and by one of the other Herods (Antipas), who had him executed. According to the Protevangelium, James escaped the persecution, which in any event happened after Herod's death; but possibly the author meant the passage to provide a foreshadowing of persecution yet to come (another James, another Herod). History knows of no connection between James of Jerusalem and Herod Antipas, but one should not object that this text, of all texts, could be expected to get the historical record straight.

In any event, in the Protevangelium, Joseph is said to have grown sons already when he is chosen to be Mary's husband (9.2); of these one is named Samuel (17.2). The James writing the book is obviously another son, and so an impeccable authority for events involving his "brother."[17] As H. Smid points out, the fact that he claims to be writing after the persecution of Herod had died down is meant to indicate that the book was produced very soon after the events described, while Jesus was still a child.

The Apologetic Character of the Text

The Protevangelium is widely thought to have as one of its purposes the "defense" of Mary against the attacks of pagan critics such as Celsus.[18] Mary Foskett claims that this view is held by the "majority of interpreters," although she herself prefers Hock's position that the book is meant as an encomium, not an apologia.[19] It is not clear, however, that these generic options are to be imagined as mutually ex-

16. Translations taken from Ehrman and Pleše, *Apocryphal Gospels*, pp. 31–71.

17. Thus, in his commentary on the book, H. Smid states the obvious conclusion: "The author of PJ poses as James, the step(brother) of Jesus. The object of this identification is to make his story that of an eyewitness, able to complete the account in all 'necessary' points, on the basis of Matt 1 and 2 and Luke 1 and 2." Harm R. Smid, *Protevangelium Jacobi: A Commentary* (Assen: van Gorcum, 1965), p. 168.

18. See, for example, Albert Frey, "Protévangile de Jacques," in *Écrits apocryphes chrétiens*, vol. 1, ed. François Bovon and Pierre Geoltrain (Paris: Gallimard, 1997), pp. 73–80; P. A. Van Stempvoort, "The Protevangelium Jacobi, the Sources of its Theme and Style and their Bearing on its Date," in SE, pp. 413–15; Cothenet, "Le Protévangelium," p. 4257; and Smid, *Protevangelium*, pp. 15–17: "It is probable that P.J. is a direct reply to the accusation of Celsus, at any rate to a similar indictment" (p. 16).

19. *A Virgin Conceived: Mary and Classical Representations of Virginity* (Bloomington: Indiana University Press, 2002), p. 20.

clusive. Encomia, among other things, can perform apologetic functions, and no one thinks that the narrative is in the *form* of an apologia.

The narrative may not be a direct response to Celsus' Ἀληθὴς Λόγος, but if not, it is a response to an attack on Mary and Jesus that was remarkably close to it in tenor and content. Celsus' attempt to disprove that Jesus could be a true son of God is worth quoting at length. The charges are placed on the lips of an antagonistic Jew:

> After this he represents the Jew as having a conversation with Jesus himself and refuting him on many charges as he thinks: first because he fabricated the story of his birth from a virgin; and he reproaches him because he came from a Jewish village and from a poor country woman who earned her living by spinning. He says that she was driven out by her husband, who was a carpenter by trade, as she was convicted of adultery. Then he says that after she had been driven out by her husband and while she was wandering about in a disgraceful way she secretly gave birth to Jesus. And he says that because he was poor he hired himself out as a workman in Egypt, and there tried his hand at certain magical powers on which the Egyptians pride themselves. (1.28)
>
> . . . The mother of Jesus is described as having been turned out by the carpenter who was betrothed to her, as she had been convicted of adultery and had a child by a certain soldier named Panthera. (1.32)[20]

Then, in an attempt to attack the idea that Jesus was conceived by the Spirit of God:

> Then was the mother of Jesus beautiful? And because she was beautiful did God have sexual intercourse with her, although by nature He cannot love a corruptible body? It is not likely that God would have fallen in love with her since she was neither wealthy nor of royal birth; for nobody knew her, not even her neighbours. It is just ridicule also when he says: When she was hated by the carpenter and turned out, neither divine power nor the gift of persuasion saved her. (1.39)

Obviously a good deal of these attacks on Mary and Jesus could actually have been spoken by Jewish as well as pagan opponents; the story of Panthera is well known from Jewish sources.[21] What is striking for our purposes here is that virtually every objection raised by Celsus' Jew is answered by the narrative account of the Protevangelium, a correspondence too impressive to be written off as coincidental:

- Did Jesus invent the story of his virgin birth? The narrative shows that Mary really was a virgin. In fact, Joseph was given a test that revealed he

20. Translations taken from Chadwick, *Contra Celsum*.

21. See the discussion in ibid. (p. 31, n. 3), in reference for example to Tosephta Hullin, 11.22–23. For a fuller listing of passages, see Raymond Brown, *The Birth of the Messiah: A Commentary on the Infancy Narratives in Matthew and Luke* (New York: Doubleday, 1977), pp. 534–37.

did not father Jesus, and Mary was given a virginity test to show that she conceived without ever having sex. They passed with flying colors, to the amazement of all who looked on. Moreover, the special nature of the birth was shown by the fact that time stood still when the savior appeared into the world, by the vision of glory at the cave that both Joseph and the midwife witnessed, and above all by the postpartum inspection of Mary by the doubting Salome. She was intact, even after giving birth.

- Was Jesus born in a remote Jewish village? On the contrary, he was born near Bethlehem, famous as the home of King David; moreover, his birth occurred there because Joseph and Mary had traveled on order of the Roman emperor Augustus (17.1). Furthermore, the birth of Jesus in Bethlehem is specifically said to be a fulfillment of prophecy (21.2).
- Was Jesus' mother a simple country woman? In fact, her father Joachim was extremely wealthy (1.1); he appears to have lived in Jerusalem, the capital city, in close proximity to the Temple of God (7.2); and he was customarily allowed to offer his gifts to God first, before all other Israelites, showing his extraordinarily high status. Moreover, Mary would be highly revered "among all generations" 6.2); and the "entire house of Israel loved her" (7.3). In fact, "all the generations of earth" would bless her (12.1).
- Did she earn her living by spinning? No, she did not need to earn a living. Early in life her needs were supplied by her fabulously wealthy father; then she was fed by an angel of God in the Temple (8.1); and then she was supported by a wealthy businessman, her espoused Joseph. When she did spin it was not to make money but in order to fulfill a sacred duty, as she was given the honor of spinning part of the curtain for the holy Temple of God (10.1–2).
- Did she live a life of poverty? Quite the contrary, her father was extremely rich and her husband, Joseph, was a well-to-do man of business.
- Was she a commoner (not of royal blood)? In fact, she came from a family that was inordinately wealthy and among the upper-tier aristocrats of the land. More than that, she enjoyed divine favor from the time of her birth through her upbringing in the Temple, where she was fed by an angel of God.
- Was she completely unknown, even to her neighbors? No, actually, "all Israel" knew her, even when she was still a child. As she grew, she became a favorite of the aristocratic priests who were at the center of the religion.
- Was her husband a lowly carpenter? On the contrary, he was a major building contractor (9.2).
- Was she expelled from her house and divorced by her husband when he discovered that she was pregnant? In fact, he was dissuaded by an angel of the Lord from abandoning her, and he "watched over her," (14.2) taking her into his home.
- Was she (legally) convicted of committing adultery? No, she was tried on the charges of adultery and legally exonerated by a sacred test that showed she had never had sexual relations (chs. 15–16).

- Was the real father of the child a soldier named Panthera? On the contrary, she conceived by the Word of God, the living God, and the power of God (11.2–3).
- Was Jesus then an illegitimate child? In fact, he was the literal son of God, destined to be "a great king to Israel" (20.3) and who was himself worthy of worship.
- Did no one believe her story? On the contrary, everyone believed her, in no small measure because God revealed the truth in dreams and sacred tests to the satisfaction of all: Joseph, the Jewish priests, and the Jewish people.

It is true that there are other charges that Celsus levels against the infant Jesus—especially involving his "escape" to Egypt—that do not appear to be answered by the narrative of the Protevangelium. That may either be because of oversight, because the author simply chose not to respond to everything, because the ending of the narrative at some point became muddled or lost (when it shifts to the preservation of John from the wrath of Herod, rather than Jesus), or because it was not written directly to counter Celsus per se, but to counter the kinds of attacks that are now known from Celsus. In any event, it is quite clear from the point-by-point refutation that what we are dealing with here is a narrative that serves not only to entertain its readers with stories about Mary's life and the coming into the world of the infant Jesus, and not only to provide an encomium on the mother of the Son of God. It also is an account that serves to stave off the attacks on both Mary and Jesus by opponents of the faith, both pagan and Jewish.

Other Polemical Targets?

In view of the emphases of the Protevangelium, it can well be imagined that the author's apologetic agenda, directed to outsiders, found its complement in certain polemical motives related to intramural conflicts. For example, in addition to defending the character of Jesus' divine birth from attacks by opponents such as Celsus, the narrative could just as well function to debunk the views of adoptionists, such as the Ebionites from the Jewish side or the Theodotians from the gentile one, both of whom held that Jesus was naturally born of the union of Joseph and Mary and only acquired his divine sonship at his baptism.[22] In the Protevangelium, on the contrary, Jesus was miraculously conceived and miraculously born the Son of God—God's son from birth—born to one who was herself miraculously conceived, born, and raised to be a fit vessel for the Son of God.

One might imagine as well that the views of the Protevangelium may have been prompted by views expressed by Christian thinkers on the opposite end of the theological spectrum from the adoptionists, that is, docetists such as Marcion,

---

22. This is an option suggested, for example, by Cothenet (cf. Justin *Dialogue* 48), "Le Protévangile," p. 4257.

who denied that Jesus appeared as a human being into the world as an infant at all , but that he descended in the appearance of a grown man during the reign of Tiberius (Tertullian *Adv. Marc.* 4.7). Proto-orthodox writers accused Marcion of altering the Gospel of Luke to promote this view.[23] The forger of the Protevangelium takes the opposite side and approaches the matter from the opposite tack. Rather than truncating Luke (as Marcion is alleged to have done), this author expands it, precisely back into the period where Marcion refused to go, accepting as authoritative very "Jewish" traditions about Jesus' prehistory that Marcion, who opposed all things Jewish, would have found repugnant.[24]

It should not seem odd that a writing such as the Protevangelium could fulfill these various apologetic and polemical functions at one and the same time. Already Tertullian recognized that Marcion's understanding of Christ coming into the world coincided with the non-Christian Jewish view, that he was not the Christ predicted by Scripture:

> So, then, since heretical madness was claiming that that Christ had come who had never been previously mentioned, it followed that it had to contend that that Christ was not yet come who had from all time been foretold: and so it was compelled to form an alliance with Jewish error, and from it to build up an argument for itself. (*Adv. Marc.* 3.6)

Or as he says more pithily (he restates the argument repeatedly):

> It is now possible for the heretic to learn, and the Jew as well, what he ought to know already, the reason for the Jew's errors: for from the Jew the heretic has accepted guidance in this discussion, the blind borrowing from the blind, and has fallen into the same ditch. (3.7)

At the same time, an anti-docetic function of the text may appear less plausible since the physical nature of the boy Jesus is not emphasized at all, except to the extent that Mary was obviously physically pregnant before giving birth; hence the horror of Joseph and the Jewish priests.[25] But when Jesus comes into the world he scarcely seems to be a real child who has experienced a real birth: he does not

---

23. It is not altogether clear that Tertullian and the later heresiologists who deal with the matter are right to think that Marcion truncated Luke by eliminating the offensive opening two chapters. It is equally plausible that the text of Luke inherited by Marcion in the early second century lacked the chapters, and that they were added only later. But it was widely *thought* among the proto-orthodox that Marcion took his penknife to these chapters, and this is all that matters for the present argument.

24. For a supporter of this view, see John L. Allen, "The Protevangelium of James as an Historia: The Insufficiency of the Infancy Gospel Category." SBLSP 30 (1991): 508–17.

25. Although one could still imagine a specifically anti-Marcionite polemic, as the account makes plain that Jesus came into the world as a child born (in some sense) of Mary, not as an adult descended straight from heaven.

appear to have come through the birth canal (hence the postpartum "proof") and he is able already to walk (as he toddles over to his mother) and to perform miracles (curing Salome's burning hand). If this was a forger who wanted to stress the reality of the fleshly appearance of Jesus, who appeared in the world as a real human being, born like other humans, he did a rather bad job of it.

It is more likely, then, that if polemics are involved at all, they are directed against an adoptionistic view of Christ. What seems relatively certain is that whether or not internecine conflicts affected the account, the apologetic need was foremost. This is a forgery that defends Jesus and his mother against the charges leveled against them by antagonistic opponents of the faith, allegedly written by someone uniquely qualified to know the truth of the matter.

THE MARTYRDOM OF POLYCARP

In a very different apologetic vein are the martyrologies that begin to appear in the Christian literary tradition beginning in the early third century. I give that date in full cognizance of its problems. Normally the first instantiation of the genre is taken to be the Martrydom of Polycarp, usually dated to within a year of Polycarp's execution, which is variously located—based on a number of complex factors—to the middle of the second century or a bit later (156 CE? 177 CE?).[26] But the date of the narrative correlates to the time of Polycarp's death only if we take at face value the author's claim to have been eyewitness at the event. That, however, is precisely the point that must be decided. Whether it is a contemporary account, or one written much later, the Martyrdom of Polycarp has clear apologetic features. In this it is like the other martyrologies that sprang up in its wake, which strive to show both that the Christians were innocent of any wrongdoing that might have warranted their harsh treatment and that in the midst of their suffering they received such divine succor as to reveal the ultimate truth of the religion for which they were willing to die.

The description of the arrest, trial, and martyrdom of Polycarp comes to us in the form of a letter allegedly written by a member of Polycarp's home church of Smyrna who had, along with the others, observed the execution. It is addressed to the church of Philomelium: "The church of God that temporarily resides in Smyrna to the church of God that temporarily resides in Philomelium, and to all congregations of temporary residents everywhere, who belong to the holy and universal church (Pref.)."[27]

The account was not, of course, actually written by the entire church, but by someone belonging to it. We learn at the end of the letter that this was a person named Evaristus (20.2: "the one who is writing the letter"; this would make him either the actual author or the scribe taking dictation). Marcion (unrelated to the

---

26. See Bart D. Ehrman, *The Apostolic Fathers*, vol. 1, p. 362.

27. Translation from ibid.

heretic of the same name; 20.1) was the one who allegedly carried the letter and authenticated its contents (διὰ τοῦ ἀδελφοῦ ἡμῶν Μαρκίωνος).[28] The letter has not come down to us in a straight line of transmission, however. According to the concluding colophon, it was copied several times within solidly proto-orthodox avenues of production, but came to be lost until a preternatural vision revealed its existence to Pionius, himself a later martyr, whose own death is described (in a different text) in ways highly reminiscent of Polycarp's, as we will see. Pionius' copy of the letter, then, brought the account out of hibernation and made it more widely available:

> Gaius transcribed these things from the papers of Irenaeus, a disciple of Polycarp; he also lived in the same city as Irenaeus. And I, Socrates, have written these things in Corinth from the copies made by Gaius. May Grace be with everyone. And I, Pionius, then sought these things and produced a copy from the one mentioned above, in accordance with a revelation of the blessed Polycarp, who showed it to me, as I will explain in what follows. And I gathered these papers together when they were nearly worn out by age. . . . (22.2–3)

It is clear even from a superficial reading of the "Martyrdom" that it was never meant to be a disinterested account of the death of Polycarp, but had from the outset literary pretensions and apologetic motives. The author engages in polemics against other groups, including the Jews who are especially eager to participate in the killing of the Christian witness, and, from a completely other sphere, the voluntary martyrs (Montanists?) who, contrary to the Gospel (and contrary to Polycarp), needlessly offer themselves up as sacrifices to the cause. Yet more germane for our purposes, the account goes out of its way to show that Polycarp's death was "in conformity with the Gospel"; on page after page the events mirror episodes known from the canonical accounts of Jesus' passion. In addition, the author stresses not only that true martyrs were doing the will of God, but that as a reward God gave them strength to endure their inhumane torments with a fortitude that could only be ascribed to divine intervention (e.g., 2.2–4). One result was the amazement of the crowds who looked on, who realized that the Christians were not normal humans (2.2–4, 3.2, 16.1). In other words, this work is driven by an apologetic impulse to defend the divine character of this persecuted religion.

Older Questions About Historicity

It has long been recognized that there are problems with taking the Martyrdom of Polycarp at face value as a straightforward historical record of what actually happened to the bishop of Smyrna. The numerous parallels to the Gospel records of Jesus' death appear contrived in places, the account is chock full of miraculous

28. On the use of διά to designate the letter carrier, see above, pp. 248–49.

elements, some of which—one immediately thinks of the dove that emerges from Polycarp's side when the executioner slices him open—are too dubious even for the most credulous of critical readers, and the events in the aftermath of his death, when the Christians gather his remains to store in a sacred place to be revered on the "birthday" of his death, are difficult to assign to a generously early date. Or so it has seemed, at least, to some scholars since Lipsius first raised questions about the authenticity of the account in 1874.[29] It was four years later that a thorough assault was made by Theodor Keim,[30] who argued that the Martyrdom was dependent on the Letter of Lyons and Vienne and on the Acts of Thecla (Polycarp's blood dowsing his fire was drawn from the miraculous thunderstorm that dowsed Thecla's). The account, then, could not date from before the end of the second century. Moreover, the phrase "the catholic church in Smyrna" (16.2) indicates, for Keim, that it was written at a time when local churches were differentiating themselves from one another, and that Smyrna had a number of churches in its midst, only one of which was claiming to be the "catholic" church. This, for Keim, must indicate a date no earlier than Cyprian. Moreover, the lull in the persecution at the time the letter was written would fit the period immediately following the persecution of Decius. Some such mid-third-century date makes sense, as well, of a number of other themes in the book: the sacrificial deaths of martyrs in relation to the death of Christ (a theme first found in Tertullian); the reverence of a martyr's death day; the valuation of the martyr's bones as "precious stones" (not attested otherwise till the third century); and so on. Keim's conclusion: the account achieved its shape only some time in the third century.[31]

Scholarship in this field, however, is resilient, and most historians continued to take the account at face value as an eyewitness report, with, perhaps, a few excesses at key points. A major shift occurred with the work of Hans von Campenhausen, who provided a critically respectable way of isolating a historical kernel in the account, while recognizing that it is also filled with literary and theological excesses that occasionally compromise its historical veracity.[32] Von Campenhausen's famous and influential claim was that an original bare-bones account of the death of Polycarp had been redacted several times over the years, into the form we now have. The grounds for evaluating the various redactions were not only the anachronisms and supernatural elements, but also the fact that when Eusebius cites the account, he intimates the existence of a different, much shorter version of the events.

Von Campenhausen argued that the original eyewitness account of Polycarp's death underwent four redactions, most of them after Eusebius' day. An anti-Montanist redactor added to the account the condemnation of Quintus and of

29. R. A. Lipsius, "Der Märtyrertod Polykarps," *ZWT* 17 (1874): 188–214.

30. Theodor Keim, *Aus dem Urchristenthum: geschichtliche Untersuchungen* (Zurich: Orell Fsli, 1878), pp. 126–32.

31. Ibid., p. 132.

32. Hans Freiherr von Campenhausen, "Bearbeitungen und Interpolationen des Polykarpmartyriums," *SHAW. PH* (1957): 5–48.

voluntary martyrdom in chapter 4, as well as the reverence for the martyrs in 17.2–3 and 18.2. A "Gospel Redactor," working after Eusebius, added the well-known parallels that showed Polycarp's death was very much like that of Jesus. A later redactor added several miraculous elements to the account (5.2, 15.2). Finally both the epilogue dating the event (ch. 21) and the colophon indicating the transmission history of the text (ch. 22) were added at a later stage. Once one removes these *Interpolationen,* one is left with an authentic account of Polycarp's death recorded by an eyewitness.

Von Campenhausen's view was controversial and found considerable resistance among some reviewers, who found the proliferation of redactors excessive.[33] It nonetheless had its attractions, as indicated by the most recent study—critical of the authenticity of the account—by Candida Moss: "Contesting the integrity of the account itself has formed a kind of via media for scholars wishing both to account for anachronisms and to preserve the historical quality of the account."[34] As Dehandschutter noted, "This theory became a 'commonplace' for much research within German scholarship."[35] Since the 1980s, however, it has fallen on hard times, as seen in the works of Dehandschutter, Saxer, and Buschmann.[36] As Schoedel was able to state: "Although serious doubts have been entertained about the integrity of MPol, critical opinion is now moving in the opposite direction. . . . Here, then, is the final rejection of the notion that originally MPol would naturally have contained a more or less factual account uncontaminated by miracles and explicit theological reflection." [37]

And yet, one is still left with enormous problems. If the questions raised concerning the integrity of the account cannot be sustained, one still has a report that both claims to be by an eyewitness and that presents numerous nonhistorical and anachronistic features. In light of the latter, can the book really be accepted as coming from an eyewitness?

A renewed attack on the authenticity of the account was launched by Silvia Ronchey in 1990.[38] Ronchey argued that the Martyrdom derives from the late third century (260–80 CE), about a century after Polycarp's death (which she dates to 167 CE), and was written largely for polemical reasons. The account

33. E.g., H. I. Marrou in *TLZ* 84 (1959): 361–63.

34. "On the Dating of Polycarp: Rethinking the Place of the *Martyrdom of Polycarp* in the History of Christianity," *Early Christianity* 1 (2010): 543.

35. B. Dehandschutter, "The Martyrium Polycarpi: A Century of Research," *ANRW* 2.27. 1 (Berlin: New York: de Gruyter, 1993), p. 494.

36. See, e.g., ibid. Victor Saxer, "L'authenticité du 'Martyre de Polycarpe': Bilan de 25 ans de critique," *Mélanges de l'école française de Rome. Antiquité* 94 (1982): 979–1001; Gerd Buschmann, *Martyrium Polycarpi—eine formkritische Studie. Ein Beitrag zur Frage nach der Entstehung der Gattung Märtyrerakte,* BZNW 70 (Berlin/New York: de Gruyter, 1994), pp. 15–70.

37. "Polycarp of Smyrna and Ignatius of Antioch," *ANRW* 2.27.1 (Berlin/New York: De Gruyter, 1993), pp. 353–54.

38. *Indagine sul martirio di San Policarpo: Critica storica e fortuna agiografica di un caso giudiziario in Asia Minore* (Nuovi Studi Storici, 6; Rome: Istituto Italiano per il Medio Evo, 1990).

comes from a single author and is not heavily redacted. In her view, Lipsius and Keim were right to recognize that the anachronisms of the text need to be taken seriously as markers of a late date; moreover, the denunciation of voluntary martyrdom in the Quintus episode of chapter 4 is aimed at Montanists, specifically in the church of Philomelium, and thus could be possible only in the third century when Montanism was strong in Phrygia. Other non-historical features involve the downplaying of the role of the imperial governor in Polycarp's death, the elevated role of the mob, and of the Jews in particular. All these features are to be explained as an attempt to exculpate the Roman governor. The text is, in other words, a pro-Roman polemic—or rather apologia—dated best in the late third century.

Renewed Questions of Authenticity

It must be said that reviewers were not kind to Ronchey's monograph, and few found it convincing.[39] But as Moss has vigorously argued more recently, one does not need to follow Ronchey in all of her positions in order to recognize the enormous problems with the text. In fact, given these problems it is very hard indeed to see how the account can be accepted as anything like trustworthy—that is, an authentic, eyewitness account.

To begin with—a factor rarely noted—it is precisely the claims of the author to be an eyewitness that show we are not dealing with an eyewitness account. One should notice where the author's asseverations occur. They occur at the very points of the narrative that are the most incredible and least susceptible of critical acceptance. Whenever a miracle happens, the author vouches for its occurrence by claiming to have observed it. The first time this happens is already in the summarizing account of the unbelievable noble endurance of torments by the Christian martyrs:

> For who would not be astounded by their nobility, endurance, and love of the Master? For they endured even when their skin was ripped to shreds by whips, revealing the very anatomy of their flesh, down to the inner veins and arteries, while bystanders felt pity and wailed. But they displayed such nobility that none of them either grumbled or moaned, clearly showing us all that in that hour, while under torture, the martyrs of Christ had journeyed far away from the flesh, or rather, that the Lord was standing by, speaking to them. (2.2)

39. See, for example, Dennis Trout in *Spec* 68 (1993): 251–53; T. D. Barnes, *JTS* 43 (1992): 237–38; and esp. Jan den Boeft and Jan Bremmer, "Notiunculae Martyrologicae V" *VC* 49 (1995): 146–64. Den Boeft and Bremmer in particular stress that the late date does not account for details in the text that make better sense with a second-century dating. They do not consider the possibility that such indicators of an early date could just as easily have been passed down orally in the accounts of Polycarp's death, before the account was written many years later.

Not only did the Christians face brutal and excruciating torture, but they—all of them—refrained even from uttering a moan. That showed "to us" that they were receiving divine succor.

Credulity is strained even more in the next two eyewitness reports. The first is when Polycarp enters the place of his final trial: "But as he entered the stadium a voice came to Polycarp from heaven: 'Be strong Polycarp, and be a man.' No one saw who had spoken, but those among our people who were there heard the voice" (9.1). This voice from heaven, then, was not heard by anyone else; it was a miraculous exhortation available only to the Christians with privileged access to the heavenly realm.

The final eyewitness guarantee of a miracle is the most striking. It occurs at the first attempt of the enemies of God to destroy his cherished saint:

> When [Polycarp] sent up the "Amen" and finished the prayer, the men in charge of the fire touched it off. And as a great flame blazoned forth we beheld a marvel—we to whom it was granted to see, who have also been preserved to report the events to the others. For the fire, taking on the appearance of a vaulted room, like a boat's sail filled with the wind, formed a wall around the martyrs' body. And he was in the center, not like burning flesh but like baking bread or like gold and silver being refined in a furnace. And we perceived a particularly sweet aroma, like wafting incense or some other precious perfume. (15.1–2)

The fire does not touch the martyr's body, but forms a wall around him; his body was not burned; and what wafted from the pyre was not the smell of reeking flesh but of perfume. Not everyone noticed this, though, but only the eyewitness who can guarantee the truth of the report since he and the other Christians were there, were really there.

The problem with this alleged eyewitness report should be clear. It is precisely at the most disputable and incredible parts of the narrative that the author inserts himself as someone who can testify to what he heard, saw, and smelled. He does not insert himself at nonproblematic points. His self-assertion is meant, then, to provide much-needed assurance for anyone inclined to think that those tortured ever might have moaned, or who doubt that voices come down from the heavens, or who might reasonably think that the flesh of martyrs could burn or stink.[40]

Apart from the miraculous elements of the text—which include the martyr's blood gushing forth in such profusion as to douse the flames of his pyre, and a dove emerging from his side and flying to the heavens—there are other clearly nonhistorical features of the text, which should at least give one pause before too readily insisting that this really is a firsthand report. For one thing, it defies belief that the animal games and execution of criminals described in the text could have happened in a "stadium" (8.3, 9.1). Animal hunts happened in amphitheaters,

40. The first person recurs later in the account as well, in the adoration of the martyr's relics, which I will address later.

where the high walls would protect the crowds from hungry beasts who might want the choice morsels on offer by spectators, as Gary Bisbee notes:

> Τὸ στάδιον would most properly denote a race track and not a place of butchery such as was the amphitheater. The stadium was normally a long and open-ended construction, often amounting to little more than a race track between two hills upon which spectators sat. A stadium would not have had the high inner walls that an amphitheater possessed to keep wild animals and gladiators from killing spectators.[41]

This was not written by someone who was there, or possibly by someone who was *ever* present at animal hunts, gladiatorial contests, or Christian executions. This conclusion is borne out by the fact that there is no official trial of the condemned, but only a summary mock trial that does not follow any known legal precedent (even though allegedly "observed" by an eyewitness). Even Bisbee, who very much wants to find something historical lying behind the traditions of the narrative, acknowledges that the account as we have it is not a real trial, based on a surviving commentarius. If a real trial did take place, it would have happened sometime before the scene in the stadium.[42] But it is difficult to imagine when that might have been, given the flow of the narrative. It is better, with Moss, to see this account as modeled not on something that actually happened but on the Gospel accounts.[43]

The other pretensions to historicity in the account also fail. In chapter 21 the author gives us a precise indication of when the martyrdom took place: the eighth hour "on the second day of the new month of Xanthikos, February 23," when "Philip of Tralles was high priest" and "Statius Quadratus was proconsul." In this attempt to locate the narrative in time and place, however, the author has blundered. Timothy Barnes has shown that the dates simply do not work. Philip the Asiarch was high priest in 149–50, but "no conceivable argument will put the pro-consulate of Statius Quadratus before 153/4."[44] There was, in other words, a three year gap—and no one writing at either time could fail to know that the two terms did not overlap. This is written by someone living later.

And what he is writing is a kind of historical legend. The legendary character of the account is seen in numerous details, including the remarkable "coincidences" that make Polycarp's trial and death so much like that of Jesus: Polycarp does not turn himself in but waits to be betrayed (1.2); he knows about his coming execution in advance and predicts it to his followers (5.2); he prays intensely before his arrest (7.1–3); he asks that God's will be done (7.1); the official in charge of

41. *Pre-Decian Acts of Martyrs and Commentarii*, HDR, 22 (Philadelphia: Fortress, 1988), p. 121.

42. Bisbee, *Pre-Decian Acts*.

43. Moss, "Dating," pp. 549–50.

44. T. D. Barnes, "A Note on Polycarp," *JTS* n.s. 18 (1967): 436.

his arrest is named Herod (6.2); Polycarp rides into town on a donkey (8.1); and so on. These are literary touches, not historical recollections. So too other parts of the story, including the remarkable account of Germanicus in chapter 3, who evidently has a wild beast standing meekly by, waiting for his suicidal impulse. To leave this life, he drags the beast-in-waiting onto himself, forcing it to kill him. It is hard indeed to know how we are supposed to imagine this actually worked.

And then there is Quintus, the voluntary martyr turned coward. As Moss has argued, the Quintus episode creates enormous problems for the traditional dating of the text, seen simply from a traditio-historical perspective. If the account dates, say, from 155–167 (as we have seen, scholars differ), then we have the unparalleled situation that this text is the earliest to recognize the category of "martyr" at all; at the same time it is also the first to refer to voluntary martyrs; and yet further, it is the first to condemn the practice of voluntary martyrdom. As Moss notes: "it is remarkable to suppose that the first text to construct an ideology of martyrdom accurately anticipates later 'enthusiasm' for an as-yet-undefined practice."[45]

Problematic for entirely other reasons is the account of what happens in the aftermath of Polycarp's death. The Jews, moved by the devil, are intent not to allow the Christians to collect Polycarp's body "even though many were desiring to do so and to have a share in his holy flesh" (ch. 17). And so, the centurion ordered the body to be burned. That did not hinder the Christians' enthusiasm for Polycarp's material remains, however: "And so, afterwards, we removed his bones, which were more valuable than expensive gems and more precious than gold, and put them in a suitable place." It is there that the author anticipates celebrating, with his fellow believers, the "birthday of his martyrdom."

One might be able to imagine some kind of "cult of the martyr" already at the time of Polycarp's death, as Saxer and others have argued.[46] But where do we observe anything like this adoration of the martyr's relics? Outside of this text, we do not find such a thing, as Moss has noted, until the third-century Acts of Thomas (dated ca. 230 CE).[47] Polycarp's body is not simply treated here with respect and given a decent burial. His bones are considered more precious than gems and gold and are stored where worship takes place. Yet "the practice of collecting and venerating the bodies of the martyrs is unparalleled in second-century Christian literature."[48] The author, in fact, has to defend the practice by claiming that the adoration of the remains of the martyr would never replace the worship of Christ (17.2). This defense shows that the practice was far enough advanced

45. "Dating," p. 562.

46. "L'autenticité du Martyre de Polycarpe."

47. Moss, "Dating," p. 567.

48. Ibid., p. 566. Moss also argues that the text provides an "apologia for the absence of relics." Strictly speaking, however, this is not true, since the bones in fact are the relics, even if the other parts of the body no longer survived.

as to be open to attack. In other words, it came at a time when adoration of relics was a known and criticized phenomenon.

Equally telling is one other portion of the text meant to ensure its authenticity, but which, when examined critically, has precisely the opposite effect. The colophon, as cited already above, provides a kind of history of transmission of the text, in which Irenaeus had a copy of the book among his papers, which was then copied by Gaius, whose work was copied by Socrates; then, many years later, when the copy of Socrates was old and falling to ruin, it was revitalized by Pionius, who received a revelation from the martyred Polycarp himself, presumably telling him where to find the manuscript. The general implausibilities of the case—involving visions of a long-dead Polycarp and the miraculous recovery of his story—speak against anything like historicity. The narrative functions, in fact, like the eyewitness reports generally in this account, to make believable that which, on the surface, defies belief. If this closing account were historical, it would be passing strange that Irenaeus himself, the ultimate authority cited, never mentions either the letter of Polycarp or the martyrdom. It cannot be objected that the colophon was added only later after the original text had long been in circulation; we have no manuscripts that lack it, but only an extended form in the Moscow manuscript that heightens its original emphases. The idea of a story of discovery is by now familiar to us. It functions here as it does in other places, such as the Apocalypse of Paul, to explain why the account has now surfaced in the middle to late third century (after the days of Pionius) when it was previously unknown to interested Christian readers.

From all these historical problems, it should be clear that the Martyrdom of Polycarp does not go back to an eyewitness account written within a year of the event, say 157 or 166 CE. It was written at least some fifty years later. It was not really produced by Evaristus, carried and authenticated by Marcion, on behalf of the Christians of Smyrna who, along with the two named figures, actually saw these things take place. It is a legendary account written simply as if by eyewitnesses. And so it is a forgery. The events it narrates had been in oral circulation down to the time of the author, which is no doubt why there are remnants of historical reminiscences that do indeed make sense in a second-century setting.[49] The story was not made up whole cloth. But it was also not a firsthand account. Its attempts to validate its miraculous claims are simply part of the forgery; by claiming to have been there, the author can establish the truth claims of his message.

It should be reemphasized that the author is interested in other forms of polemic as well. He is most emphatically opposed to voluntary martyrdom that the orthodox later came to associate—rightly or wrongly is beside the point, for our purposes—with the Montanist movement (ch. 4). Moreover, it is the Jews who are said to be the most eager (and accustomed) to gather the firewood to burn the Christians (13.1); and they are key in the refusal to provide access to the corpse

49. See den Boeft and Bremmer in note 39.

once the deed is done (17.2). They are the enemy, more than the governor who is driven by the mobs to condemn Polycarp. Here again, then, the apologetic impulses of the text accompany its opposition to the Jews. Its major contention, however, is that God was on the side of Polycarp as he was on the side of the other martyrs who preceded him in dying a death "in conformity with the Gospel." At the end of the day, this is apologia in martyrological guise, produced as an eyewitness testimony by a forger who wanted his readers to know that they could rest assured in the factual accuracy of his legendary report.

OTHER MARTYROLOGIES

The Martyrdom of Polycarp is not the only martyrology to come down to us from the early church that is written as a first-person narrative in order to authenticate the accuracy of its tales. There are, of course, a large number of martyr texts. Those with the greatest (though often slight) claims to "reliability" have been collected in the handy edition by Mursurillo.[50] More than anyone else, Gary Bisbee has tried to show how one can establish what is historical in them.[51] There are no grounds, however, for seeing any of them as thoroughly accurate representatives of what actually happened. Most of the accounts are simply third-person narratives; some of them, though, do contain first-person passages that function to "guarantee" the accuracy of the report. With the exception of the well-known first example that we will consider, the first-person narrators are not named, however, and so in these instances we are dealing with non-pseudepigraphic forgeries.[52]

The Passion of Perpetua

Augustine was the first to express doubts about the authorship of the "diary" kept by Perpetua prior to her martyrdom in 203 CE. When speaking of Perpetua's

---

50. Musurillo, *Acts of the Christian Martyrs*. He includes twenty-eight of the accounts that he considers "the most reliable" or at least "extremely important and instructive"; p. xii.

51. *Pre-Decian Acts*. Bisbee's approach involves ascertaining whether some kind of (actual) historical commentarius lies behind each of the respective Acts.

52. There have occasionally been scholars who have wanted to claim that the famous persecution in Lyons and Vienne in the days of Marcus Aurelius was made up by an imaginative Christian author out of whole cloth. See, for example, James Westfall Thompson, "The Alleged Persecution of the Christians at Lyons in 177," *AJT* 16 (1912): 359–84. The article was savaged by Harnack, *TLZ* 3 (1913): 74–77; and M. Paul Allard, *Revue des questions historiques* (1913): 53–67. Thompson attempted a lengthy and rather defensive response in *AJT* 17 (1913), 249–58. I will not provide an analysis here because, even though the account contains first-person narrative, it is not clear to me that this is an authorial ploy. Winrich Löhr, "Der Brief der Gemeinden von Lyon und Vienne (Eusebius, h.e. V, 1–2(4))," *Oecumenica et patristica*, 1989, pp. 135–149, argues that the letter was not forged, but that it does contain literary elements to combine fact with fiction, in particular in an attempt to theologize the conflict as one between God and Satan, to stress the opposition to Montanism, and to create literary tension and drama and to highlight the character of those martyred, over against those who caved in.

brother Dinocrates, Augustine says in passing " . . . nor does the saint herself, or whoever it was who wrote the account. . . ."[53] Whereas many scholars continue to think the diary an authentic production of Perpetua herself,[54] others have harbored considerable doubt. A particularly interesting case has been made by Thomas Heffernan, who focuses on how the verb tenses and sequences work in the piece.[55] Although Heffernan acknowledges that the genres of "diary" and "autobiography" were not set in stone in antiquity, they do evidence a difference in reference to time. Autobiography "provides attempts to a coherent interpretation of the past from a future perspective."[56] A diary, on the other hand, gives accounts of the past as fragments of experience as perceived from the present. Diaries, then, do not provide unified coherence between past events; they tend to be episodic and to lack any kind of teleology. An autobiography, in contrast, reconstitutes the self as an agent in an attempt to impose meaning on events.

For Heffernan, the Passio Perpetua is a kind of "hybrid of these two types." But what is most striking is that the verb tenses fit an autobiographical mode, in which the past connections are used to provide temporal coherence. Terms such as "after a few days," or "many days," or "a few hours later" indicate the passage of time and so provide a kind of narrative sequence. The reason this matters: "Such periodicity is not typical of a narrative written diurnally, in snatches when the hideous oppression of the prison abated; rather it suggests a composition written sometime after the events have transpired."[57]

If Heffernan is right, then what we have in the Diary of Perpetua is not a diary, but a later author—claiming to be Perpetua—writing in autobiographical mode, pretending to write a diary. In other words, the "diary" would be a forgery, a conclusion reached by other scholars on yet other grounds.[58] Like the other martyrological texts, it functions apologetically in showing that, contrary to appearances, God is at work in the lives and sufferings of the martyrs, empowering them in the

---

53. "On the Origin of the Soul," 1.12. Translation of Peter Holmes and Robert E. Wallis, *NPNF*, first series, vol. 5.

54. See, recently, J. N. Bremmer, "Perpetua and Her Diary: Authenticity, Family, and Visions," in W. Ameling, ed., *Märtyrer und Märtyrerakten* (Stuttgart: Franz Steiner Verlag, 2002), pp. 77–120.

55. Thomas J. Heffernan, "Philology and Authorship in the *Passio Sanctorum Perpetuae et Felicitatis*," *Traditio* 50 (1995): 315–25.

56. Ibid., p. 320.

57. Ibid., p. 322.

58. See, for example, Ross Kraemer and Shira L. Lander, "Perpetua and Felicitas," in Philip Esler, ed., *The Early Christian World*, vol. 2, Routledge Worlds Series (London: Taylor & Francis, 2000), pp. 1048–65, who assert that there are "myriad" problems in the account, although they mention only a few. In particular, they note that the only contemporaneous evidence for Perpetua outside the Passio is Tertullian, who mentions her in passing and without referring to either a text or a commemoration; it is not, in fact, until the fourth century that text and commemoration are secured, starting with the liturgical Calendar of Rome in 354 and the comments of Augustine. Most striking are the parallels evidenced between the specifics of the Passio and the "prophecy" of Joel 2:28–29 (cf. Acts 2:17–18), where sons and daughters are said to prophesy, the spirit is poured out, the young see visions, and the old dream dreams.

face of horrible opposition and torment, and using them as a witness to the truth of the gospel.

The Martyrdom of Pionius

Probably written sometime around 300 CE, the Martyrdom of Pionius "is the only substantial martyrdom that we possess which pretends to date from the period of the Decian persecution."[59] The opening of the account is a bit odd, in that it indicates that the bulk of the writing—which is narrated almost entirely in the third person—is a book by Pionius about himself (even though for the most part it does not employ the first person):

> More fitting is it that we should remember the martyr Pionius seeing that this apostolic man, being one of us, kept many from straying while he dwelt in the world, and when he was finally called to the Lord and bore witness, he left us this writing for our instruction that we might have it even to this day as a memorial of his teaching. (1.2)[60]

The account does not move into the first person until near the end, and then it is clearly not Pionius speaking, as the author claims to have witnessed the miracles that transpired at the martyr's death. The entire account, however, bears the marks of literary license, if not wholesale invention, since, as widely recognized, it is modeled on the Martyrdom of Polycarp. As we have seen, Pionius, not coincidentally, is named in the earlier martyrdom as the one who received a revelation from the long-dead Polycarp concerning the whereabouts of the lost account of his martyrdom. The account of Pionius' own martyrdom, perhaps not remarkably, is dated to the anniversary of Polycarp's (a century later); it too occurs on a Great Sabbath. Here, as in the earlier account, the Christian martyr is wounded, but acts as if he is not. Here too the execution occurs, remarkably, in a stadium. A figure named Marcion appears in both texts—here in connection with a follower of the heretic who is martyred along with the orthodox man of God. The Jewish antipathy is as strong here as in the earlier account. The author speaks of Jews as the "enemies" (4.8), and asks rhetorically "Who forced the Jews to sacrifice to Beelphegor? Or partake of the sacrifices offered to the dead? Or to fornicate with the daughters of foreigners ? Or to sacrifice their sons and daughters to idols? To murmur against God? To slander Moses?" (4.11) With biting contrast the author indicates that "*we* did not slay our prophets nor did we betray Christ and crucify him" (13.2).

---

59. Musurillo, *Christian Martyrs*, p. xxix. For a recent study, which deals with some of the problems of the eyewitness claims and the possibility that the account preserves some historical information, see E. Leigh Gibson, "Jewish Antagonism or Christian Polemic: The Case of the Martyrdom of Pionius," *JECS* 9 (2001) 339–58.

60. Translation taken from Musurillo, *Christian Martyrs*.

It is not until the end of the account that the author introduces a first-person narrative:

> For after the fire had been extinguished, those of us who were present saw his body like that of an athlete in full array at the height of his powers. His ears were not distorted; his hair lay in order on the surface of his head; and his beard was full as though with the first blossom of hair. His face shone once again—wondrous grace!—so that the Christians were all the more confirmed in the faith, and those who had lost the faith returned dismayed and with fearful consciences. (22.2–4)

Here too, then, we have an author who wants to be both an eyewitness and a faithful testifier to the miraculous events surrounding the martyrdom of one beloved of God. But the account, as widely recognized, is an invention; the author was merely claiming to have seen it take place. Here again we have an instance of non-pseudepigraphic forgery.

The Martyrdom of Marian and James

There is no better way to show the unusual authorial problems of the early-fourth-century Martyrdom of Marian and James than to provide a lengthy citation of its narrative, in which the author is the closest companion of the martyrs who accompanies them at the time of their arrest:

> To me have these noble witnesses of God left the task of proclaiming their glory, I refer to Marian and James, among the dearest of our brethren. Both of these as you are aware, were bound to me not only by our common sharing in the mystery of our faith, but also by the fact that we lived together in a family spirit. . . . It was their wish that their battle . . . should be communicated to their fellow Christians through me. . . . And it was not without reason that in their close intimacy they laid upon me the task which I am about to fulfill. For who can question the common life we shared in times of peace when the same period of persecution discovered us living in unbroken affection? (1.2–4)
>
> We were on our way together to Numidia. . . . But an entire band of violent and unscrupulous centurions swooped on the country-house which sheltered us as though it was a notorious centre of the faith. . . . And while the ripe hour of the divine choice made more stringent demands on them, it also bound me to them with a tiny share in my brothers' glory; for I too was dragged from Muguae to Cirta. . . . For in exhorting me with special intensity they betrayed by their effusive joy the fact that they too were Christians. They were then questioned and were led off to prison. . . . (2.1; 4.3, 6, 9–10)

It is difficult indeed to understand how the author himself was not arrested and sent to prison, if he really was such a close companion and eyewitness of all these things. Musurillo can simply assume that "the author had presumably been freed as not falling under the Valerian edicts" (p. xxxiv) although the account says nothing of the matter. Moreover, Musurillo admits that "some scholars have had serious doubts about the authenticity" of the account (p. xxxiii). A serious option worth entertaining is that here again we have a martyrology written in the first person not because the author was really there to see these things happen, but in order to stimulate interest in his account and assure the reader of its accuracy.

The Martyrdom of Montanus and Lucius

Often thought to have been based on work produced by a disciple of Cyprian,[61] the Martyrdom of Montanus and Lucius is another account of the execution of Christian clergy under the persecution of Valerian. It is allegedly written by one of the Christians who was arrested, as a kind of memoir that cannot help but call to mind the Passion of Perpetua, as here too a number of visions of those who are jail-bound are presented, reliably, by a first-person narrator:

> Love and a sense of obligation have urged us to write this account, that we might leave to all future brethren a loyal witness to the grandeur of God and a historical record of our labours and our sufferings for the Lord (1.1). . . . All of us were arrested (2.1). . . . We got the news of our sentence from the soldiers: the governor had threatened us the day before with fire. . . . (3.1)[62]

At chapter 12 the narrative shifts to a different "first person," reminiscent, again, of the Passio Perpetua: "This was the joint letter written to us from prison. . . . Flavian privately enjoined on me the task of adding to their account whatever might be missing. Hence I have added the rest as was necessary." This new author continues on, then, with a third-person narrative (with occasional references to himself as an observer) to the end. The first-person narrators are here again interspersed with third-person narrations, both to add immediacy to the account and to verify the accuracy of its reports. Not everyone has been fooled, however; in their 1890 edition of *The Passion of Sts. Perpetua and Felicitas*, J. Rendell Harris and S. K. Gifford called it "a deliberate forgery."[63]

The Acts of Ignatius (Antiochene Version)

The legendary account of Ignatius' death by wild beasts in the arena in Rome comes to us in several forms, the most important of which, historically, is the so-called Antiochene version, which provides us, as well, with the authentic letter

61. Ibid., xxxv.

62. Translations taken from ibid.

63. Thus ibid., p. xxxv.

of Ignatius to the Romans, otherwise lacking from the epistles' textual tradition. Since Lightfoot's withering criticism, the Acts themselves have rarely been taken seriously as historical.[64] The surviving account is normally thought to derive from the fifth century, although Bisbee argues, somewhat implausibly, that it is ultimately based on a near contemporaneous second-century commentarius. In any event, the work that we have is late.[65]

The widely recognized problems with the account, as recounted by Lightfoot and Bisbee, include the following[66]:

- The trial before the emperor Trajan in Antioch is dated to 106–07 CE, the ninth year of his reign; but Trajan did not come to Antioch until some seven years later.
- The route taken by Ignatius in the Acts does not coincide with that presupposed in the authentic letters.
- Whereas there is no persecution of the churches of Asia Minor in evidence in the authentic Ignatian letters, it is presupposed here.
- Ignatius' own letter to Polycarp intimates that the two first met while Ignatius was en route to his martyrdom; in the Acts they have been companions from long before, as they both sat at the feet of the disciple John.
- There is no reference to the Acts in either Eusebius or Jerome; and no manuscript attests the Acts until the sixth century.

Even though the trial of Ignatius is here narrated in the third person, the author moves to a first-person account, strikingly, as in the Acts of the Apostles, during a sea voyage leading to martyrdom: "Therefore continuing to enjoy fair winds, we were reluctantly hurried on in one day and a night" (ch. 5).[67] The account describes Ignatius' martyrdom by the wild beasts (ch. 6), and we are told that "only the harder portions of his holy remains were left, which were conveyed to Antioch and wrapped in linen, as an inestimable treasure left to the holy church by the grace which was in the martyr" (ch. 6). The account itself is then ensured through a first-person declaration:

> Having ourselves been eye-witnesses of these things, and having spent the whole night in tears within the house . . . it happened, when we fell deeply asleep, that some of us saw the blessed Ignatius suddenly standing among us and embracing us, while others saw him again praying for us, and still others saw him dripping with sweat, as if he had just come from his great labor, and standing by the Lord. When, therefore, we had with great joy witnessed

64. *Apostolic Fathers*, 2.2, 383–90.
65. As admitted by Bisbee, *Pre-Decian Acts*, pp. 146–49.
66. For these arguments, see Lightfoot and Bisbee, as cited in notes 64 and 41.
67. Translation taken from Bisbee, *Pre-Decian Acts*.

> these things and had compared our several visions together, we sang praise to God. . . . (ch. 7)

Here, then, as with the much-earlier Martyrdom of Polycarp, the first-person narrative serves to validate the claim to have observed a divine miracle.

All these martyrologies appear to have served multiple functions among their Christian readership. On one level they were entertaining, if in a rather grisly way. They also provided models of behavior for those who themselves might be threatened with persecution, torture, and death. And, importantly for our purposes, they were apologiae for the truthfulness of the Christian message in the face of opposition to it. Justin suggested that his observation of Christian martyrs played a role in his conversion (2 *Apol.* 12), and Tertullian famously argued against his belligerent pagan opponents that "We become more numerous every time we are hewn down by you: the blood of Christians is seed" (*Apol.* 50). The texts describing martyrdoms functioned in a similar way at the literary level, apologetically. They revealed the truth of the Christian gospel in the face of violent opposition to it, with the valiant deaths of the martyrs testifying to the power of God in the midst of a world that brought all its power to bear against him and his servants.

THE SYBILLINE ORACLES

Markedly different, but also fulfilling an apologetic function, the Sybilline oracles consist of twelve books of Jewish and Christian origin that present the "predictions" of the ancient pagan Sibyl. An anonymous Byzantine scholar of the sixth century CE compiled the surviving collection, which spans a seven-hundred-year period. He claims that he brought these writings together because he wanted to provide in one place oracles otherwise widely dispersed, which together, he avers,

> expound very clearly about Father, Son, and Holy Spirit, the divine Trinity, source of life; about the incarnate career of our Lord and God and Savior Jesus Christ, the birth, I mean, from an unchanging virgin, and the healings performed by him; similarly his life-giving passion and resurrection from the dead on the third day and the judgment which will take place. (Prologue)[68]

In fact, the majority of the oracles are not about the Trinity or Christ at all, but are of non-Christian Jewish origin. Two of them are indeed Christian (one, certainly), and several others represent Christian redactions of Jewish originals (through heavy interpolation).

Because of a fluke of transmission, the twelve books are numbered 1–8 and 11–14. The background to the collection involves the famous but no longer

---

68. Translation of John J. Collins, "Sybilline Oracles," in James H. Charlesworth, ed., *OTP*, vol. 1 (New York: Doubleday, 1983).

surviving pagan Sibylline oracles of Roman and, predominantly, Greek extraction. The full story of these "original" oracles is found elsewhere and need not deter us at great length; the story from Republican through early Imperial times, though, can be summarized briefly.[69]

From an early age there were known to be prophecies of the great Sibyl, an ancient Greek prophetess of astounding longevity attuned to communications of the gods, which she delivered in hexameter verse, often with the use of acrostics. As these prophecies proliferated over time, and came to be associated with numerous locations, stories arose of Sibyls living in different places. Varro made the canonical claim that there were ten Sibyls altogether.

In Roman times the best-known collection of the oracles came to be stored in the temple of Jupiter Optimus Maximus on the capitol in Rome; these were consulted by the quindecimviri, on direction of the Senate, when divine instruction was sought in times of plague, famine, and prodigy. Evidently the collected books indicated the necessary ritual for dealing with dire situations. There is record of the books having been consulted some fifty times between 496 and 100 BCE. In 83 BCE, while Sulla was fighting his way up through Italy, the temple was destroyed, and with it the deposit of Sibylline books. That oracles had been widely in circulation before the event is shown by what happened in the wake of their disappearance from the capitol. In 76 BCE the consul Caius Curio proposed a commission to go to Erythrea in search of replacement oracles. The results were disappointing: only about a thousand verses were gathered from private sources (about a third of what had been lost). Further expeditions yielded other oracles in other localities. The quindecimviri were given the task of editing what had been collected. We do not know the criteria they used, but they evidently detected and expunged certain verses as interpolations.

In 28 BCE Augustus transferred the books to his new marble temple of Apollo on the Palatine. In 12 BCE, when he became pontifex maximus, Augustus ordered the retrieval of all circulating prophetic books in Greek and Latin. Those that were anonymous or of unsuitable authorship were burned, some two thousand of them. Others were added to the official collection. Evidently these actions were undertaken to ensure that no unauthorized oracles would be in circulation; individuals were no longer allowed to possess any.

In 19 CE Tiberius had to deal with a popular rumor of a sibylline prophecy that Rome would perish "when thrice three hundred years have passed over" (a prophecy taken to refer to contemporary times). Tiberius intervened, declared the verses spurious, inspected all books of oracles in circulation, and burned the ones he disapproved of.

Eventually all the books were lost or destroyed. What we have now are Jewish and Christian versions, in which forgers, claiming to be the great Sibyl herself,

69. See John J. Collins, "The Development of the Sibylline Tradition," *ANRW* II.20.1 (1987): 421–59 and esp. H. W. Parke, *Sibyls and Sibylline Prophecy*, on which the following précis depends.

place Jewish and Christian ideas, views, and predictions on the lips of the ancient prophetess.[70] Many of the Jewish creations are associated with Alexandria and evidence several obvious polemical and apologetic functions: to condemn idolatry; to propagate the Jewish faith, especially monotheism and ethics; and to stress the coming of eschatological judgment, particularly as this relates to the ultimate doom and downfall of Rome. As noted, the surviving Christian Sibyllina correlate to the Pseudo-Ignatian writings in that they constitute both original compositions and extensive redactions. In my discussion here I will deal with the interpolations first and then consider the original, forged, creations. In each instance we are probably dealing with different authors, who had, however, similar purposes. Among other things, they shared the common goal of apologia: the great and trustworthy pagan prophetess, the Sibyl, attests to the truth of the Christian message, and, especially, the truth of the Christian Savior.

The Christian Interpolations

As samples of how Christian authors placed their views both in the context of Jewish oracles and, as a consequence, on the lips of the ancient Sibyl, we can consider the striking examples from books 1, 2, and 8. Books 1 and 2 were originally a unity, composed together, by a Jewish author, but redacted at some time in the midsecond century, according to the dating of Collins.[71] Together these two books recount (or rather "predict") the appearance of ten generations of humans on earth, leading up to the time of the end. For some unknown reason—possibly in the course of the Christian redaction—generations eight and nine have dropped out of the work. The tenor of the book is established at the outset:

> Beginning from the first generation of articulate men
> Down to the last, I will prophesy all in turn,
> Such things as were before, as are, and as will come upon
> The world through the impiety of men. (1.1–4)

There follows a discussion of the creation and "fall," and then the history of the human race in ten generations. A major Christian interpolation occurs in ll. 324–400, in the midst of a discussion of the seventh generation of humans (the Titans). The interpolation is about Christ, his incarnation, life, death, resurrection, and ascension, and its effect on the Jews:

> Then indeed the son of the great God will come,
> Incarnate, likened to mortal men on earth,

---

70. The textual tradition is complex. For this and all other "introduction" issues involving dating, redaction, and structure, see Collins, "Development."

71. "Sibylline Oracles," p. 332.

Bearing four vowels, and the consonants in him are two.
I will state explicitly the entire number for you.
For eight units, and equal number of tens in addition to these,
And eight hundreds will reveal the name
To men who are sated with faithlessness. But you, consider in your heart
Christ, the son of the most high, immortal God. (ll. 324–31)

The clever gematria is of the name ΙΗΣΟΥΣ, whose letters add up, remarkably, to 888. Not only, however, does the interpolation provide a pagan prediction of the coming of Christ. Closely tied to it is a vitriolic attack on the Jewish people, pronounced here by a pagan oracle in support of a Christian agenda. And so the oracle says that "Israel, with abominable lips and poisonous spittings will give this man blows" (ll. 365–66); it also speaks of a "new sprout" that will emerge among the nations, who will "follow the law of the Great one" (by implied contrast with the old stump, ll. 383–84). The rhetoric becomes especially strong in ll. 387–400: the "Hebrews" will "reap a bad harvest"—meaning that they will reap their awful reward for killing Christ. Specifically "a Roman king will ravage much gold and silver"; there will "be a great fall for those men when they launch on unjust haughtiness"; "the Hebrews will be driven from their land, wandering, being slaughtered, they will mix much darnel in their wheat . . . receiving the wrath of the great God in their bosom, since they committed an evil deed."

The interpolation is thus both apologetic, predicting reliably the coming of Christ, and polemical, against the Jews. This is a combination we have seen before and will see yet again. The Christian redaction of book 2 moves along similar lines, describing the final judgment from a Christian perspective, with Christ as judge, and providing graphic descriptions of the torments of the damned, all accompanied with more anti-Jewish invective.

Book 8 of the Oracles is particularly intriguing. There has been considerable scholarly dispute over how to divide the oracle, with Johannes Geffcken proposing a complex solution that derives three passages from a pagan source, intermingled with Christian redactions,[72] and Collins suggesting a simpler division of the book roughly in half, in which lines 1–216 are Jewish (except for ll. 131–38, and a Christian interpolation involving eschatology in ll. 194–216) and 217–500 are Christian.[73] This Christian section begins in ll. 217–50 with one of the best-known and intriguing features of the surviving Sibyllina, an acrostic poem, the first letters of each line spelling out the words ΙΗΣΟΥΣ ΧΡΙΣΤΟΣ ΘΕΟΥ ΥΙΟΣ ΣΩΤΗΡ ΣΤΑΥΡΟΣ. Throughout the poem there is a strong emphasis on the flesh: Christ will "judge all flesh" (ll. 218–19); the flesh of the dead will arise (l. 227); "fire will torment the lawless forever" (l. 228). The conclusion then is

72. *Komposition und Entstehungszeit der Oracula Sibyllina* (Leipzig, J. C. Hinrichs, 190), pp. 38–46.
73. Collins, pp. 315–16.

striking: “This is our God, now proclaimed in acrostics, the king, the immortal savior, who suffered for us” (ll. 249–50).

The rest of the Christian interpolation involves a poetic celebration of Christ, a condemnation of idolatry, the need for ethical rigor in the face of the coming judgment, a paean to God, and a recounting of the incarnation event. Here too there appear to be some (implicit, at least) anti-Jewish materials: “They will stab his sides with a reed on account of their law” (l. 296). Even though one might take the referent to be the Romans, the following statement makes it appear to be to the Jews: “every law will be dissolved . . . on account of a disobedient people” (ll. 300–01). This interpretation is confirmed later, in ll. 305–8, when the Temple curtain is rent, “for no longer with secret law and temple must one serve the phantoms of the world.” Later still the author appeals to “daughter Sion,” and speaks of the “yoke of slavery, hard to bear, which lies on our neck . . . the godless ordinances and constraining bonds” (ll. 324–28). And so, once more, we find a mixture of apologetics and polemics, the latter possibly against those who minimize the importance of the flesh, and certainly against the Jews.

The Christian Creations

Book VI of the Sibyllina is completely and incontrovertibly a Christian creation. The poem is quoted by Lactantius thirteen times in *De ira dei,* and so must date some time before 300 CE. A more precise date is not possible. The book presents a short twenty-eight-line hymn to Christ. There is no evidence of a pagan or Jewish substratum, and nothing, in fact, that connects it to the Sibyl, apart from its appearance in the collection. The high Christology of the piece is evident at the outset:

> I speak from my heart of the great famous son of the Immortal,
> To whom the Most High, his begetter, gave a throne to possess before he was born. . . .

Here, as in the interpolations, there is a good deal of anti-Jewish polemic. Christ is said to come to “a disobedient people” (l. 11); the people of the “land of Sodom” have “evil afflictions . . . in store” (l. 21),[74] for the people of this land “did not perceive your God when he came before mortal eyes” (ll. 22–23). The author goes on to say that these people were the ones who crowned Christ with thorns and gave him gall to drink (ll. 23–25). As a result, the Jewish people will suffer: “That will cause great afflictions for you” (l. 25). The poem ends with a paean to the cross, the “blessed” wood that will ascend from earth and “see heaven as home when your fiery eye, O God, flashes like lightning” (ll. 26–28).

74. Sodom represents Jerusalem in Rev. 11:8.

John Collins considers book VII also to be a Christian composition, but in this case there is at least a modicum of doubt.[75] There are certainly Christian elements in the oracle, but there are scant grounds for deciding whether these came in by way of interpolation or were part of the original wording. In any event, Collins is certainly right that the book consists of a loose collocation of oracles, some of them judgments against the nations, bracketed, significantly, with descriptions of the past destruction by flood and the future destruction by fire. The Christian elements are for the most part found in ll. 64–90. Here Christ is referred to as "your God" and is the one who was not recognized by the inhabitants of Coele-Syria (ll. 64–66). A high Christology is evident here in the reference to "the sovereign Word, with the Father and Holy Spirit"; moreover, the incarnation is explicit: Christ "put on flesh but quickly flew to his Father's home" (ll. 69–70).

One key passage is found in the ritualistic prescriptions of ll. 76–84. Sacrifice to God is to be made, but not by burning incense or slaughtering animals (ll. 77–78). Instead the worshiper is to take a wild dove and set it off while gazing to heaven. Then she is to pour a libation of water on pure fire, while crying out the following prayer: "As the father begot you, the Word, so I have dispatched a bird, a word which is swift reporter of words, sprinkling with holy waters your baptism, through which you were revealed out of fire" (ll. 82–84). Whereas Geffcken and Kurfess consider this to be a Gnostic ritual, and see other traces of Gnostic thought in the use of such terms as "the first ogdoad" (l. 140), John Gager has made an impassioned plea for restraint, arguing that ambiguous ritualistic formulations and isolated Gnostic-like terms a Gnostic text doth not make; far better simply to see the book as in some sense "syncretistic."[76] Much of the rest of the book deals with judgments on the nations and individuals, especially at the end when fire will devour the earth and all those who live on it, a fire that will torment them not briefly but for the years of ages forever (ll. 127–28).

The Sibyllina as Apologetic Forgeries

It is fair to ask whether it is right to see the Christian Sibylline materials as forgeries, in any ordinary sense of the term. On one level they may not seem "forged" in that they represent claims to inspired divine prophecy. On the other hand, the Sibyl was indeed considered to be a human author (although a highly unusual one), who was often thought of as being a historical person from hoary antiquity, and these sundry Christian writers—both the interpolators and literary creators ex nihilo—were claiming to be her. At the least we can say that these books are redactional forgeries, in the sense laid out earlier in the study.[77] Even if book 6 was not originally attributed to the Sibyl (the matter is difficult to judge), in its

75. Collins, "Sibylline Oracles," pp. 408–9.

76. John G. Gager, "Some Attempts to Label the Oracula Sibyllina Book 7," *HTR* 65 (1972): 91–97.

77. See pp. 34–35.

surviving context it conveys her words. So too with the redacted books: in their present state they represent Christian reflections that are now given not by unknown poets and theologians, but by the great prophetess of Greek antiquity. The authors and redactors do not claim to be conveying the words of a divine being (Apollo, for example), but the words of a seer.

There is another form of Sibylline materials that survives from Christian antiquity, outside of the collection of Oracula Sibyllina that have come down to us. This involves references to and quotations of the Sibyl in Christian writers of the early centuries. Some of the quotations do not correspond with what can now be found in the surviving fourteen books, and so they require a different treatment. In many of these Patristic references the apologetic function of the Christian Sibyl is particularly evident.

Apart from the reference to the Sibyl in the Shepherd of Hermas (a case of false identification, when Hermas thinks the elderly lady representing the church is the ancient prophetess; Vision 2.4), the first clear references occur in Justin: "Indeed Sibyl and Hystaspes foretold that all corruptible things are to be destroyed by fire" (*Apol.* 1. 20). This is an apt summary of what is found in the surviving books; but it is so general as to make closer identification impossible. More telling are the quotations in Pseudo-Justin *Cohortio* (a misattributed, not forged, work). This anonymous apologist refers to the Sibyl on numerous occasions, especially in chapters 16 and 37–38. In chapter 16 we are told that the "ancient and very old Sibyl" was called by Plato and others a "prophetess"; she is said to have taught through her oracular verses that there is "only one God." The author then provides three quotations of the Sibyl, one indicating that there is "only one unbegotten God" (cf. O. S. 3.11–12), another that the people who worship idols have "strayed from the Immortal's ways" since the idols are the "workmanship of our own hands, and images and figures of dead men" (cf. O.S. 3.721–73); and the other that people should worship the one great God and abjure all shrines, altars, idols, and sacrifices (cf. O.S. 4.24–30). It is striking that all three of the quotations are drawn from, or at least are very similar to, the Jewish, not the Christian, Sibyllina.

The discussion intensifies in chapters 37–38. Chapter 37 discusses the Sibyl but provides no oracular pronouncements. The Sibyl is said to have been of Babylonian extraction, the daughter of Berosus, author of the "Chaldean History." She is said to have gone to the hot springs at Cumae; the author himself has actually seen, he says, the basilica where she bathed and prophesied. She was proclaimed a prophetess by Plato in the Phaedrus, and is one of those he refers to in the Meno who are clearly shown to be inspired by God when they speak in plain and manifest terms the truth about which they are personally unaware. Her prophecies were recorded by ignorant amanuenses, which is why the meter sometimes does not work. She herself, coming out of a trance, did not know what she had said.

This entire discussion is intended to establish the Sibyl as a completely trustworthy source. And what is it that she allegedly said? According to chapter 38, she predicted "in a clear and patent manner, the advent of our Savior Jesus Christ.

She also taught that the gods of the idols have no real existence; and she uttered prophecies about the advent of Christ and the things he would do."[78]

Here, then, the author is reliant on early Christian forms of the Oracula Sibyllina, thought to be utterances of a pagan priestess who prophesied the truth when in a state of ecstasy, inspired by the one true God.

An even more extensive use of the oracles of the Sibyl is found in the writings of Lactantius, especially the *Diviniae Institutiones*. Lactantius uses the Sibyl more than any other ecclesiastical writer, and in fact quotes Sibylline material 50 percent more often than he quotes the Old Testament. Unlike Pseudo-Justin, he does not provide long quotations, but only sentences here and there. Still, he cites hundreds of lines altogether. Lactantius shows that he is acquainted in particular with what became books 3–8. He quotes the text in order to discuss monotheism, everlasting life, the "fall," the coming of the Son of God, his life and miracles, passion, resurrection and second coming, the last judgment, and the general resurrection. In particular, for Lactantius, the Sibyl is a prophetess who foretold Christianity: "Since these events are true and certain of fulfillment, being in agreement with prophecies uttered by the seers, and since Trismegistus and Hystaspes and the Sibyls have foretold the same destinies, it is indisputable that all hope of life and salvation rests on the religion of God alone" (*Epitome Institutionum*, epilogue).[79] The apologetic function of the material could hardly be more patent.

A similar function can be found in the citation of the Sibyl in the forged Apostolic Constitutions: "But if the Gentiles laugh at us, and disbelieve our Scriptures, let at least their own prophetess Sibylla oblige them to believe, who says thus to them in express words:

> But when all things shall be reduced to dust and ashes
> And the immortal God who kindled the fire shall have quenched it
> God shall form those bones and that ashes into a man again,
> And shall place mortal men again as they were before.
> And then shall be the judgment, wherein God will do justice,
> And judge the world again. But as many mortals as have sinned through impiety
> Shall again be covered under the earth;
> But so many as have been pious shall live again in the world
> When God puts His Spirit into them, and gives those at once that are godly both life and favour
> Then shall all see themselves. (5.1.7)[80]

78. Translation of M. Dods, *ANF*, vol. 2.

79. Translation of E. H. Blakeney, *Firmiani Lactantii Epitome Institutionum Divinarum/Lactantius' Epitome of the Divine Institutes* (London: SPCK, 1950), 123.

80. Translation of Collins, "Sybilline Oracles," p. 322.

In a similar way Augustine declared in *The City of God* that the acrostic of book 8 was a genuine prophecy of Christ:

> It was at this same time, according to some accounts, that the Erythraean Sibyl made her predictions. Varro, we note, informs us that there were a number of Sibyls, not only one. This Sibyl of Erythraea certainly recorded some utterances which are obviously concerned with Christ. . . . This I discerned in conversations with that eminent man Flaccianus, who was, amongst other things, proconsul, a man of most ready eloquence and profound learning. We were talking about Christ, and he produced a Greek manuscript, saying that it was the poems of the Erythraean Sibyl. He showed me that in the manuscript the order of initial letters in one passage was so arranged as to form these words: IESOUS CHREISTOS THEOU UIOS SOTER, the translation of which is "Jesus Christ, the Son of God, the Saviour. (City of God, 18.23)[81]

He then quotes the acrostic poem.

Altogether, according to the statistics compiled by B. Thompson in a short but extremely useful article on the subject,[82] twenty-two Patristic sources preserve some eight hundred lines of the oracles. Clement of Alexandria, for example, quotes them eleven times, amounting to forty-six lines; Theophilus quotes a large portion of book 3, etc.

That Christians were particularly interested in the Sibyl and in the forged prophecies that supported the claims and theological views of their faith is especially evident in the charges occasionally leveled against them by pagans, that they had interpolated their own words into her writings. The first time we find the charge is in the *Ἀληθὴς Λόγος* of Celsus. After telling the well-known story of the Stoic Epictetus, who removed himself so far from his own suffering that he calmly explained to his master that he should not have broken his leg, Celsus asks why Jesus, if he were so great, did not react similarly:

> What comparable saying did your God utter while he was being punished? If you had put forward the Sibyl, whom some of you use, as a child of God you would have had more to be said in your favour. However, you have had the presumption to interpolate many blasphemous things in her verses, and assert that a man who lived a most infamous life and died a most miserable death was a god. (7.53)[83]

Origen's reply may have satisfied his Christian readers, but knowing what we do today about the composition of the Sibyllina Oracula, it seems, in fact, a bit wanting:

---

81. Translation of Henry Bettenson, *St Augustine, Concerning the City of God Against the Pagans* (Penguin Books, 1972), 788–89. All subsequent quotations of this work will come from this edition.

82. Bard Thompson, "Patristic Use of the Sibylline Oracles," *RR* 16 (1952): 115–36.

83. Translation of H. Chadwick, *Contra Celsum*, p. 440.

> Then for some unknown reason he wanted us to call the Sibyl a child of God rather than Jesus, asserting that we have interpolated many blasphemous things in her verses, though he does not give an instance of our interpolations. He would have proved this point had he showed that the older copies were purer and had not the verses which he supposes to have been interpolated. (7.56)

Although the charge of forgery is not found in (surviving) pagan attacks against Christians, it is referred in several other Christian sources that counter these attacks. A half century after Origen, Lactantius could claim, "Some, refuted by these testimonies, are accustomed to have recourse to the assertion that these poems were not by the Sibyls, but made up and composed by our own writers" (*Institutions*, 4.15.26).[84] Even more striking is the extensive discussion by none other than the Christian Constantine, in his "Oration to the Assembly of the Saints," preserved for us by Eusebius (assuming for the moment that the speech actually goes back to Constantine, an issue that does not much matter for my point).[85] The passage, though lengthy, deserves to be quoted in full, as it shows both the apologetic value of the Sibyl for the Christian cause and the pagan charge that the "predictions" in fact represented Christian forgeries:

> My desire, however, is to derive even from foreign sources a testimony to the Divine nature of Christ. For on such testimony it is evident that even those who blaspheme his name must acknowledge that he is God, and the Son of God if indeed they will accredit the words of those whose sentiments coincided with their own. The Erythraean Sibyl, then, who herself assures us that she lived in the sixth generation after the flood, was a priestess of Apollo, who wore the sacred fillet in imitation of the God she served, who guarded also the tripod encompassed with the serpent's folds, and returned prophetic answers to those who approached her shrine; having been devoted by the folly of her parents to this service, a service productive of nothing good or noble, but only of indecent fury, such as we find recorded in the case of Daphne. On one occasion, however, having rushed into the sanctuary of her

84. Translation of William Fletcher in *ANF*, vol. 7.

85. On the authenticity of the speech, see Hal Drake, *Constantine and the Bishops: The Politics of Intolerance* (Baltimore: Johns Hopkins University Press, 2002), p. 293:

> Its authenticity questioned during an earlier period of hypercriticism (during which scholars freely dismissed whole passages for not conforming to what their science told them the emperor should have said), it then became cautiously admitted as a representative piece of fourth-century propaganda, though still held unlikely to be Constantine's own. Recent scholars have been more willing to concede authenticity, although the enthusiastic identification of parallels in other writers such as Lactantius was beginning to sound like yet another search for alternative authors until T. D. Barnes came to the sensible conclusion that words delivered by the emperor, no matter who wrote them, could safely be considered to be the emperor's own.

I owe this reference to Maria Doerfler.

> vain superstition, she became really filled with inspiration from above, and declared in prophetic verses the future purposes of God; plainly indicating the advent of Jesus by the initial letters of these verses, forming an acrostic in these words: Jesus Christ, Son of God, Saviour, Cross. The verses themselves are as follows. (chs. 18–19)[86]

Constantine then provides a full quotation of the acrostic poem, and continues by refuting the charge of forgery:

> Many, however, who admit that the Erythraean Sibyl was really a prophetess, yet refuse to credit this prediction, and imagine that someone professing our faith, and not unacquainted with the poetic art, was the composer of these verses. They hold, in short, that they are a forgery, and alleged to be the prophecies of the Sibyl on the ground of their containing useful moral sentiments, tending to restrain licentiousness, and to lead man to a life of sobriety and decorum. Truth, however, in this case is evident, since the diligence of our countrymen has made a careful computation of the times; so that there is no room to suspect that this poem was composed after the advent and condemnation of Christ, or that the general report is false, that the verses were a prediction of the Sibyl in an early age. For it is allowed that Cicero was acquainted with this poem, which he translated into the Latin tongue, and incorporated with his own works.

Constantine, needless to say, was wrong about this.

Sibyllina Oracula as Counter-Forgeries

It is possible to see the Christian Sibylline Oracles—both those that survive (as interpolations of forgeries) and those quoted in patristic writers—not only as forgeries created for apologetic purposes, but specifically as counterforgeries. Among the weapons pagans used to oppose Christians were (forged) oracular pronouncements of their own, delivered with all the power of divine authority in the names, of course, of the pagan gods. And so, for example, Eusebius recounts an incident during the persecution of Maximin Daia, when a sheriff of Antioch named Theoctecnus forged an oracle to justify persecution of the Christians; he "displayed his magic arts by spurious oracular utterances. . . . This man aroused the demon against the Christians: the god, he said, had commanded 'the emperor's enemies,' to be cleared right out of the city and its neighborhood" (*H.E.* 9.2–3).

Years later Augustine could claim that pagan opponents of Christianity "thought up some sort of Greek verses, supposedly the effusions of a divine oracle, given to someone consulting it," which indicated that Jesus' disciple Peter

86. Translation of Ernest C. Richardson, *NPNF*, Second Series, vol. 1.

"used sorcery to ensure that the name of Christ should be worshipped for 365 years, and that on the completion of that number of years it should come to an immediate end." Augustine readily exposes the false claim of the oracle: the allotted amount of time had passed already, and the church was thriving more than ever (*City of God* 18.53). Later, in the same source, Augustine discusses Porphyry's *ΕΚ ΛΟΓΙΩΝ ΦΙΛΟΣΟΦΙΑΣ*, which mentioned an oracle of Apollo against the Christians. Augustine proffers the expected objection: "Is anyone so dense as to fail to realize that these oracles were either the inventions of a cunning man, a bitter enemy of the Christians, or the responses of demons devised with a like intent?" (19.23; see also 20.24 and 22.25).

If pagans were using forged oracles to oppose the Christians, is it any surprise that Christians responded in kind, by forging oracles of their own to defend themselves and their faith?[87] They could not forge oracles as having come from the gods of Greece and Rome, known to be either nonexistent or demonic. But an outlet existed in the person of the Sibyl, an actual human who went into a trance and under the power of inspiration delivered the truth of God. There is, in fact, a possible suggestion within the surviving Oracula Sibyllina themselves that Christians may have been inventing these texts as counterforgeries, in this case not against pagans but against Jews, who were known to have a good number of Sibylline oracles, as most of the surviving books derive ultimately from Jewish circles. The passage in question comes from Book 7:

> But they will endure extreme toil who, for gain
> Will prophesy base things, augmenting an evil time;
> Who putting on the shaggy hides of sheep
> Will falsely claim to be Hebrews, which is not their race.
> But speaking with words, making profit by woes,
> They will not change their life and will not persuade the righteous
> And those who propitiate God through the heart, most faithfully.
> (7.132–138)

Normally, the false "Hebrews" here are taken to be non-Jewish Christians of some kind. But might they, even more radically, be taken to be actual Jews, who, for Christians, were not in fact "true Jews," because by rejecting Christ they had rejected their own God? As this book itself says, in further attacking Jews: "Ah, Coele-Syria, . . . wretched one, you did not recognize your God, whom once Jordan washed in its streams" (7.64–67). And so, it should be at least considered possible that the forger of this part of book 7 produced his Christian interpolation precisely as a counter to the Jewish Sibylline prophecies that he saw here before him, which needed to be "corrected" in line with true religion.

87. For other examples, including Diocletian's appeal to the oracle of Didyma (Eusebius, *de vita Const.* 2.50–51; Lactantius, *De mort. pers.*, 11.7), see Speyer, *Literarische Fälschung*, pp. 250–51.

THE LETTERS OF PAUL AND SENECA

As a final example of apologetic forgeries, we might consider the letters allegedly exchanged by Paul and the Roman philosopher Seneca. There are fourteen letters in this famous correspondence, eight of them from Seneca to Paul and six from Paul to Seneca. The first reference to the correspondence comes in Jerome's *De viris illustribus* (393 CE):

> Lucius Annaeus Seneca of Cordova, a disciple of the Stoic Sotion, and paternal uncle of the poet Lucan, was a man of very temperate life whom I would not place in a catalogue of saints, were it not that I was prompted to do so by those *Letters from Paul to Seneca* and *from Seneca to Paul* which are very widely read. In these, when Seneca was Nero's teacher and the most influential person of the period, he said that he wished to have the same position among his own [i.e., the pagans] which Paul had among the Christians. Two years before Peter and Paul were crowned with martyrdom, he was put to death by Nero. (*Vir. ill.* 12)[88]

Soon afterward Augustine mentions them: "Rightly did Seneca say, who lived at the time of the apostles, some of whose letters to the apostle Paul are still read" (*Epist.* 153. 14).[89] As A. Fürst notes, it is significant that the correspondence is not mentioned by Lactantius in the early fourth century.[90] This absence cannot simply be written off as an argument from silence; Lactantius frequently cites Seneca otherwise and highly evaluates him, and had he known of the letters, and thought them authentic, he scarcely could have failed to cite them. In any event, the terminus ante quem for their appearance is 392 CE, and plausibly they date from some decades before that, so, say, middle of the fourth century.[91] They were certainly composed in Latin, given, among other things, Seneca's castigation of Paul for his feeble Latinity.

That Paul and Seneca would have exchanged letters may have seemed altogether plausible to the fourth-century forger who created the correspondence and to the reading audience that eagerly accepted his work as authentic. The two

---

88. Translation of Thomas Halton, *Saint Jerome: On Illustrious Men* (FC 100; Washington, DC: Catholic University Press, 1999), pp. 20–22.

89. Translation mine.

90. Alfons Fürst et al., *Der apokryphe Briefwechsel zwischen Seneca und Paulus* (Tübingen: Mohr Siebeck, 2006), pp. 6–7.

91. A more precise date was unsuccessfully attempted by Édmond Liénard, who notes that there are many parallels between the correspondence and the letters of the Roman senator Quintus Aurelius Symmachus (345–402 CE). Liénard argues, then, that the letters were written just a few years before Jerome attests to their existence. "Sur la Correspondance Apocryphe de Sénèque et de Saint-Paul," *RBPH* 11 (1932): 5–23. Fürst has demonstrated the problem with this line of argumentation: the letters, in fact, have numerous points of contact and parallels with a good number of other fourth-century letter writers as well, and simply conform in many ways to the rhetorical conventions of the time (*Der apocryphe Briefwechsel*, pp. 7–8).

great figures were contemporaries; both of them died in Rome. Paul appeared before Seneca's own brother, Gallio, the proconsul of Achaia, in one of his trial scenes in Acts (18:12–17). Moreover, when the historical Paul sent forth greetings from prison (in Rome?) to the Philippians, he includes a salutation from "those of Caesar's household" (4:22), which could include any number of people, including Nero's then advisor, Lucius Annaeus Seneca. Moreover, it has long been noted, classically by J. B. Lightfoot, that there are many clear parallels between the authentic writings of the two authors, especially in their teachings on ethics.[92] That the two would have corresponded with one another may have seemed likely to ancient Christian readers, even if it appears completely out of the question for modern scholars.

The Character and Emphases of the Letters

The letters are filled with various verisimilitudes, as can be seen simply from the way the correspondence begins in letter 1:

> Seneca to Paul, greeting. I believe that you have been informed, Paul, of the discussion which my friend Lucilius and I held yesterday concerning the apocrypha and other matters: for some of the followers of your teachings were with me. We had retired to the gardens of Sallust, and it was our good fortune that these disciples whom I have mentioned saw us there and joined us, although they were on their way elsewhere. You may be sure that we wished that you, too, had been present. . . .[93]

Many of the letters from Seneca are filled with praise of Paul. This undoubtedly relates to the reason they were written in the first place. And so, for example, from letter 1: "when we had read your book . . . we were completely refreshed. These thoughts, I believe, were expressed not by you, but through you. . . . For they are so lofty and so brilliant with noble sentiments that in my opinion generations of men could hardly be enough to become established and perfected in them." Or from letter 7: "For the holy spirit that is in you and high above you expresses with lofty speech thoughts worthy of reverence . . . I confess that Augustus was affected by your sentiments. . . . He was amazed that one whose education had not been normal could have such ideas."

In turn, Paul, somewhat less than humbly, accepts Seneca's praise and intimates that it is fully deserved: "I count myself fortunate in the approval of a man who is so great. For you, a critic, a philosopher, the teacher of so great a ruler, nay even of everyone, would not say this unless you spoke the truth" (letter 2).

---

92. See Lightfoot, *Saint Paul's Epistle to the Philippians* 2nd ed. (London: Macmillan, 1869), pp. 268–331.

93. Translations taken from Elliott, *Apocryphal New Testament.*

At the same time, although Seneca is awed by the content of Paul's writings, he is more than a little underwhelmed by his lack of rhetorical style: "I do wish you would obey me and comply with the pure Latin style, giving a good appearance to your noble utterances, in order that the granting of this excellent gift may be worthily performed by you" (letter 13). In letter 9 he indicates that he has sent his correspondent a "book on elegance of expression," presumably a Latin equivalent of Strunk and White, to help Paul along in his writing.[94]

The most frequently commented aspect of this correspondence is its almost complete lack of substance, otherwise. There is very little content to the letters. The one exception is letter 11, where there is, finally, a good bit of meaty material and hints at courtly gossip, of a very serious nature. The letter discusses the fire in Rome and Nero's role in it. At the same time, because it is so different in conception, content, and style from the other letters, because it is dated out of sequence with the rest (occurring between letters dated 58 and 59 CE, even though it is given the date 64 CE), and because it has a completely different (negative) view of Nero from elsewhere in the correspondence, it is generally conceded to have come from another forger.[95] In any event, it provides the most "substance" of any of the letters. Seneca writes as follows:

> Do you think I am not saddened and grieved because you innocent people are repeatedly punished? Or because the whole populace believes you so implacable and so liable to guilt, thinking that every misfortune in the city is due to you? . . . The source of the frequent fires which the city of Rome suffers is plain . . . Christians and Jews, charged with responsibility for the fire—alas!—are being put to death, as is usually the case. The ruffian, whoever he is, whose pleasure is murdering and whose refuge is lying, is destined for his time of reckoning, and just as the best is sacrificed as one life for many, so he shall be sacrificed for all and burned by fire. One hundred thirty-two private houses and four thousand apartment-houses burned in six days; the seventh day gave respite.

The insipid character of the rest of the letters is the subject of frequent comment, as early as Erasmus: "I do not see how he could have made up these letters in a more feeble or inept fashion."[96] A nineteenth-century study by G. Boissier states: "Never has a clumsy forger made such great spirits speak more foolishly."[97] And the most recent lengthy analysis sums up the common view: "The notice-

---

94. There exists some evidence that highly trained pagan authors generally considered Paul's letters a bit barbaric. See Zahn, *Geschichte* 2, 2, 620–21; Harnack *Geschichte*, 1, 763–65; E. Bickel, *Lehrbuch der Geschichte der römischen Literatur* 2nd ed. (Heidelberg: C. Winter, 1961), 15.226–27.

95. Thus, most recently, Pervo, *The Making of Paul*, p. 112.

96. "His epistolis non video quid fingi possit frigidius aut ineptius," *Epistola* 2092.

97. "Jamais plus maladroit faussaire n'a fait plus sottement parler d'aussi grands esprits." G. Boissier, "Le Christianisme de Sénèque," *Revue des deux mondes* 92 (1871): 43. I owe this reference to my student Pablo Molina.

able peculiarity of the epistolary exchange between Seneca and Paul is the fact that content apparently does not matter; what matters are only the names of the correspondents."[98]

The Correspondence as Forgery

The Senecan correspondence was popular throughout the Middle ages; from the thirteenth century up to the sixteenth it was regularly included in the manuscripts of Seneca's writings. It has nonetheless been recognized as forged since the advent of historical criticism. Already Valla, in 1440, demonstrated its inauthenticity on stylistic grounds.[99] Erasmus, after commenting on the insipid character of the writings, cited above, went on to say "nonetheless, whoever was the author, he wrote so as to persuade us that Seneca had been a Christian."[100] Lightfoot expressed the matter with characteristic clarity: "The poverty of thought and style, the errors in chronology and history, and the whole conception of the relative positions of the Stoic philosopher and the Christian Apostle, betray clearly the hand of a forger."[101] Only very few scholars, most of them Italian, have thought it possible that parts of the correspondence are authentic.[102]

But why would someone forge a set of letters with virtually no substance? We have seen another instance of the phenomenon in the Greek letter to the Laodiceans, and we would not be far afield to suspect that the reason for that cipher may apply to these as well: it was the fact of their existence that mattered, not the character of their contents. But that has not always been the explanation for the forged Senecan correspondence. For some time, the *opinio communis* was far more specific, as Harnack argued that the letters were produced for a concrete purpose, in order to commend Paul and his writings, or even the entire Bible, to recently converted fourth-century Christians of the educated classes, by showing an enthusiastic approbation by Seneca.[103] Fürst, however, shows the flaw in the reasoning: Seneca did not enjoy a high reputation among educated pagans of the fourth century, and his philosophy played virtually no role in the Neoplatonic thought world of late antiquity.[104]

---

98. "Die auffällige Eigenheit des Briefwechsels zwischen Seneca und Paulus ist die, dass es in ihm offenbar gar nicht um Inhalte geht, sondern um die Namen der Korrespondenten und nur um diese"; Fürst, *Der apokryphe Briefwechsel*, p. 11.

99. L. D. Reynolds and H. G. Wilson, *Scribes and Scholars* (Oxford: Clarendon, 1991), 142.

100. "et tamen quisquis fuit auctor, hoc egit ut nobis persuaderet Senecam fuisse Christianum."

101. *Philippians*, p. 271.

102. See Ilaria Ramelli, "L'epistolario apocrifo Seneca-san Paolo: alcune osservazioni," *VetChr* 34 (1997): 299–310.

103. Adolf von Harnack, *Geschichte der altchristlichen Literatur bis Eusebius*, vol. 1 (Lepizig: J. C. Hinrichs, 1893), p. 765; see also Theodore Zahn, *Geschichte des neutestamentlichen Kanons* II/2 (Leipzig: A. Deichert, 1892), p. 621.

104. Fürst, *Der apokryphe Briefwechsel*, p. 17.

An alternative was proposed by the editor of the first critical edition of the letters in 1938, Claude Barlow, who suggested that the simple, unadorned style of the letters indicates they may have originated as a rhetorical school exercise.[105] If they were that, however, one would have to judge that the student did not receive high marks, as the faux Senecan letters are striking precisely for their failure to approximate Seneca's elegant style. But the fatal blow to the view, attractive as it is on first sight, is that school exercises in rhetoric were by their nature designed to say something, to invent an imaginary substance as the topic of correspondence. That is precisely what is lacking here.

A more promising, but ultimately failed, proposal was floated by Bernhard Bischoff, who produced the editio princeps of a Latin letter recently discovered, in which a certain Annas (allegedly) wrote to Seneca condemning idolatry and pagan religion generally. This is a letter, in other words, that advances a kind of Jewish apologia. In fact, according to Bischoff, the Annas named in its title is to be seen as none other than Annas II, Jewish high priest for a short time in 62 CE, and so a contemporary of Seneca. Bischoff maintained that the letter was actually written in the fourth century, and he ascribed it specifically to a Jewish author because there are (1) numerous parallels to the Wisdom of Solomon and (2) no specific Christian content.[106]

According to Bischoff, the existence of this Jewish letter cannot be thought of as unrelated to the Christian correspondence, also involving Seneca. One of the works may well have served as a motivating factor for the production of the other. In his provocative summary, Bischoff states:

> Since the possibility cannot be excluded that either the Christian author of the Seneca/Paul letters knew the Annas epistle, or that the Jewish author was aware of that fictional correspondence, one of the two fictional writings might be a counter-move against the other side's attempt to let the philosopher appear in conjunction with a representative of its own faith. If one considers content, the Annas letter may be able to lay claim to priority, which would suggest a fourth century date for its origin.[107]

---

105. Claude Barlow, *Epistolae Senecae ad Paulum et Pauli ad Senecam (quae vocantur)* (Horn, Austria: F. Berger, 1938).

106. "Der Brief des Hohenpriesters Annas an den Philosophen Seneca—eine jüdisch-apologetische Missionsschrift (Viertes Jahrhundert?)," in *Anecdota Novissima: Texte des vierten bis sechzehnten Jahrhunderts.* (Stuttgart: Anton Hiersemann, 1984), pp. 1–9.

107. "Da nicht auszuschließen ist, daß entweder dem christlichen Verfasser der Seneca-Paulus-Briefe die Annas-Epistel oder dem jüdischen Autor jene fiktive Korrespondenz bekannt war, kann eine der beiden Fiktionen ein Gegenzug gegen den Versuch der anderen Seite sein, den Philosophen in Verbindung mit einem Repräsentanten ihrers Glaubens erscheinen zu lassen. Wägt man den Inhalt ab, so dürfte die Priorität bei dem Annas-Brief liegen, was für seine Entstehung im IV. Jahrhundert sprechen würde"; P. 5.

This view found wide acceptance soon after its publication, for example by Wolfgang Wischmeyer and even, with some minor revisions, the great Arnaldo Momigliano.[108] Eventually, however, A. Hilhorst showed that it was completely implausible. Hilhorst provided a new critical edition of the letter of Annas with text-critical and interpretive notes, and a brief discussion of its character and origin. On one hand, Hilhorst expressed skepticism over whether the letter was to be thought of as addressed, originally, to Seneca. The incipit that mentions Seneca is not followed by an epistolary opening. A forger creating a letter to Seneca would surely place his name in the text. Instead the letter is addressed to "the brothers." The title of the work is therefore a later addition to the text and tells us nothing about the original design of its author.

Even more than that, Hilhorst insisted that the letter appears to be Christian rather than Jewish. "Fratres" in the address indicates co-religionists, not potential converts. And the term is quite common in specifically Christian writings. In addition, one has to deal with a specific set of historical probabilities. The reality is that we do not have a single prose writing from antiquity, in Latin, written by a Jewish author .[109] What then is the likelihood that this one letter would be the exception, when nothing in the letter would prevent it from being seen as Christian? As Hilhorst states his case: "If I am right that there is no intrinsic evidence that the *Epistola* was written by a Jew any more than by a Christian, then it is reasonable to attribute this text to an environment in which all other a Latin writings of this kind originate, that is, Christianity."[110]

Hilhorst's view has been forcefully supported, with additional arguments by Rainer Jakobi,[111] who among other things points out that Christian authors such as Justin, Clement of Alexandria, and Lactantius made abundant use of the Wisdom of Solomon, that a number of the arguments of the letter can be found in the works of Christian writers, and that there do indeed appear to be Christian allusions in the text. In particular, the author appears to know Lactantius, the Vulgate,

---

108. Wolfgang Wischmeyer, "Die Epistula Anne ad Senecam: Eine jüdische Missionsschrift des lateinischen Bereichs," in *Juden und Christen in der Antike*, ed. J. Van Amersfoort and J. van Oort (Kampen: Kok, 1990), pp. 72–93; Arnaldo Momigliano, "The New Letter by 'Anna' to 'Seneca'" *Athenaeum* n.s. 63.1–2 (1985): 217–19. For Momigliano, the author of the letter was indeed a Jew. But, he points out, even though the incipit mentions Seneca, the letter itself is addressed to fratres. The name Seneca is therefore a "secondary interpolation" possibly made by a Jewish editor; the edited form of the letter then became the incentive for a somewhat later Christian writer to forge the correspondence of Paul and Seneca.

109. A. Hilhorst notes that there are some Jewish inscriptions in Latin that survive, but they almost never demonstrate any literary pretensions. "The *Epistola Anne ad Senecam*: Jewish or Christian?" in G. J. M. Bartelink et al., ed., *Eulogia*. Festschrift A. A. R. Bastiansen (Steenbrugge: Abbatia S. Petri, 1991), pp. 147–61.

110. P. 161. It should be noted that this argument could be circumvented if it were shown that the letter is a Latin translation of a Greek original; but there appears to be no evidence that this is the case.

111. *Die sogenannte 'Epistula Anne ad Senecam'* (Torun: Wydawn, Uniwersytetu Mikołaja Kopernika, 2001).

and the commentary on Isaiah by Jerome. All this provides us with the religious identity of the author and his date: the author is a Christian and he is writing after Jerome's commentary, that is, sometime soon after 410 CE.

More than that, the Annas of the incipit is not meant to be a reference to the high priest. The letter is allegedly by Annaei Senecae, created by someone already familiar with the Paul-Seneca correspondence. The letter is written to show that the great stoic philosopher had a highly enlightened view of religion and that he anticipated the attacks on pagan idolatry to be popularized by Christian apologists a century after his day.

If then the letters of Paul and Seneca can be explained adequately by none of the options cited above, we might return to the suggestion made earlier, which in fact is the most common view of the matter. The letters function—by the very fact that they exist—as a kind of Christian apologia. The background to their construction can plausibly be reconstructed as follows. It was widely "known" in the fourth century that there had been no connections between Paul and the great minds of his day ("knowledge" based on the available sources on Paul, such as the book of Acts and the various legends incorporated in the Acts of Paul). Moreover, his style of writing, and even the extent of his learning, were open to suspicion.[112] Naturally questions arose: Was the great apostle to the gentiles really so great? Why was he not more significant historically? Why was he not connected with other major thinkers of the time? Why are his writings not more weighty intellectually and polished stylistically? A forger produced the correspondence with Seneca to answer these questions, and very little substance was required to achieve that end. Paul was known and adored by the greatest philosopher of his day, who considered his ideas divinely inspired, all the more so since his inferior writing style showed that he did not learn his message through rigorous academic training. It must have come, then, straight from God. Even the Roman emperor was amazed at Paul's learning.

And so, as Stefan Krauter has recently observed, the letters of Paul and Seneca may seem insipid and disappointing to modern readers who hope to find some substance in them—for example, of the relationship of Stoic and Christian thought—or at least some good imperial gossip. But the letters should not be criticized on these grounds. The various anachronisms and fissures of the correspondence are there simply because the author had little vested interest in doing anything other than showing that Paul and Seneca exchanged letters in which Paul was praised.[113] A similar view is taken by the most exhaustive recent analysis of Fürst:

> The text is crafted from conventions and phrases that are commonplace in late ancient epistolography. With these simple means, garnished with several

---

112. On his style, see note 94 above.

113. Stefan Krauter, "Was ist 'schlechte' Pseudepigraphie? Mittel, Wirkung und Intention von Pseudepigraphie in den Epistolae Senecae ad Paulum et Pauli ad Senecam," in Jörg Frey et al., eds., *Pseudepigraphie und Verfasserfiktion*, pp. 765–85

> splendid ideas, the author generates the one impression that was apparently his aim, namely that Seneca and Paul were supposedly friends. . . . The letters desire nothing further but to show by means of the chosen genre that Seneca and Paul had contact with one another.[114]

The driving force behind the association of Paul with Seneca in particular is that even though Seneca was not an important figure in pagan literary circles at the time,[115] he was indeed important to a range of Latin theologians, starting with Tertullian, who approvingly speaks of "Seneca saepe noster" (*De anima* 20.1), and moving through Lactantius up to Jerome, who numbered Seneca among the saints. His philosophy may have played little role in the development of Christian thought, but his person was considered important. So too with these letters: it is their existence as encomia on Paul, more than their contents, that matter.

The long-range effect was significant, for both Paul and Seneca. Paul hereafter was seen as closely connected with the greatest mind of his day, who praised him for his divinely inspired thought, and Seneca's status among Christians was elevated by his association with Paul. The letters came to be included as standard fare among the manuscripts of the writings of Seneca down to the invention of printing.

---

114. Der Text ist gebastelt aus Konventionen und Phrasen, wie sie in der spätantiken Epistolographie gang und gäbe sind. Mit diesen schlichten Mitteln, garniert mit einigen famosen Einfällen, erzeugt der Autor den einzigen Eindruck, der offenbar vermittelt werden soll, dass nämlich Seneca und Paulus Freunde gewesen sein sollen. . . . Die Briefe wollen nichts weiter, als mittels der gewählten Gattung demonstrieren, dass Seneca und Paulus miteinander Kontakt hatten"; *Der apocryphe Briefwechsel*, pp. 3, 12.

115. See p. 523 above.

CHAPTER SIXTEEN

Lies and Deception in the Cause of Truth

I have come to the end of my study and can now summarize my findings in a few words. I will then conclude by examining the one major issue I have not yet addressed at any length. Throughout the study we have seen that forgery was widely considered a form of literary deceit. But we have not considered the ethics of the practice. In the early Christian tradition, were there circumstances in which literary deceit may have been considered acceptable? That is to say, how would forgery have been evaluated in early Christianity as a moral, or immoral, practice?

SUMMARY AND EXPLANATION OF OUR FINDINGS

Arguably the most striking finding of my study is the most basic. In the early centuries of the church Christians produced a large number of literary forgeries. We have considered some fifty examples from the first four Christian centuries. Many of these are highly significant historically and culturally. Among the earliest surviving writings of the Christians—those that make up the New Testament—nearly half (13/27) are forged.[1]

I have restricted my study, with only a couple of minor exceptions, to the forgeries that have survived in manuscript tradition and that are tied closely to the polemical agendas of the early Christians in their various internecine and extramural struggles. We know, of course, of other forgeries that do not survive but that were, at one time, known and discussed.[2] Moreover, toward the

1. For my tally I am including Acts, Ephesians, Colossians, 2 Thessalonians, 1 Timothy, 2 Timothy, Titus, Hebrews, James, 1 Peter, 2 Peter, 1 John, and Jude.

2. See, e.g., pp. 19–20, if one chooses to trust Epiphanius.

end of our period forgeries continued apace, especially with the sea-change that came with the conversion of Constantine and the proliferation of writings of all sorts among Christian intellectuals. Sometimes these later forgeries involved shenanigans connected with important figures in the theological and ecclesiastical life of the church of the fourth century. Such is the case with a no-longer surviving letter forged for unfriendly purposes in the name of Athanasius, as he himself tells us in a letter he wrote to Constantius in opposition to Arian opponents:

> I am sure you will be astonished at the presumption of my enemies. Montanus, the officer of the Palace, came and brought me a letter, which purported to be an answer to one from me, requesting that I might go into Italy, for the purpose of obtaining a supply of the deficiencies which I thought existed in the condition of our Churches. Now I desire to thank your Piety, which condescended to assent to my request, on the supposition that I had written to you, and has made provision for me to undertake the journey, and to accomplish it without trouble. But here again I am astonished at those who have spoken falsehood in your ears. . . . For I never wrote to you, nor will my accuser be able to find any such letter. (*Apol. ad const.* 19)[3]

Years later, Jerome describes a malicious letter, no longer extant, written to castigate his intentions in performing his translation work:

> My brother Eusebius writes to me that, when he was at a meeting of African bishops which had been called for certain ecclesiastical affairs, he found there a letter purporting to be written by me, in which I professed penitence and confessed that it was through the influence of the press in my youth that I had been led to turn the Scriptures into Latin from the Hebrew; in all of which there is not a word of truth. When I heard this, I was stupefied. . . . Letters were soon brought me from many brethren in Rome asking about this very matter, whether the facts were as was stated: and they pointed in a way to make me weep to the person by whom the letter had been circulated among the people. He who dared to do this, what will he not dare to do? It is well that ill will has not a strength equal to its intentions. Innocence would be dead long ago if wickedness were always allied to power, and calumny could prevail in all that it seeks to accomplish. It was impossible for him, accomplished as he was, to copy any style and manner of writing, whatever their value may be; amidst all his tricks and his fraudulent assumption of another man's personality, it was evident who he was. It is this same man, then, who wrote this fictitious letter of retractation in my name, making out that my translation of the Hebrew books was bad, who, we now hear, accuses me of having translated the Holy Scriptures with a view to disparage the Septuagint. . . . I

3. Translation of M. Atkinson and A. Robinson, *NPNF*, second series, vol. 4.

> wonder that in this letter he did not make me out as guilty of homicide, or adultery or sacrilege or parricide or any of the vile things which the silent working of the mind can revolve within itself.[4] (*Adv. Rufin.* 2, 24)

Examples could be multiplied.[5]

In addition to restricting myself to works that survive, I have focused on just one kind of early Christian forgery, those written in the context of early Christian polemics—whether internal struggles among various Christian groups trying to establish, in the face of opposing views, what Christians should believe or how they should live, attacks on Jews and Judaism, or apologia in the face of pagan assault. I have not considered non-polemical forgeries, and so have left out of our examination, for example, a number of Nag Hammadi treatises such as the Apocryphon of John, The Gospel of Philip, or the two Apocalypses of James. These do indeed use a pseudonym to advance a particular understanding of the religion (and to that extent are obviously arguing against alternative perspectives), but they are not especially polemical in their content or rhetoric.

As it turns out, however, the majority of our early Christian forgeries do in fact appear to have been generated out of a polemical context. The reason has to do with much larger issues in the development of the Christian religion, which I will mention here in only very brief compass. As is widely recognized, Christianity—by which I mean all the various groups of devotees who paid allegiance to Christ in one way or another, and considered themselves to be his followers—was distinctive in the Roman world in a number of ways. As opposed to followers of other religions, most Christian groups were exclusivistic in their views, maintaining that they had the "true" understanding of the faith (whether they were Sethian, Valentinian, Thomasine, Marcionite, Ebionite, Proto-orthodox, or something else), and that knowing the truth was in fact the key to practicing true religion. Christians ("true" Christians of whatever variety) were right, and everyone else was in error. Conversion was required, and conversion meant abandoning one's old religion, whether that was some form of Judaism, one of the many hundreds (thousands) of "pagan" cults, an "aberrant" Christian sect, etc. A person had to believe the "right" things to be on the right side of God, from the very beginning of the Christian movement.

If being right mattered, then accepting the right teachings mattered. But how was one to know the right teachings when there were so many alternative views available, not just within the Christian movement, but competing with it from the outside? Authorities were needed. Authorities who could speak the truth from God. And so there developed the notion of apostolic succession. God sent Christ, who chose his apostles, who spoke the truth and passed it along to their hand-selected successors. But what happens when Christianity spread, and there

4. Translation of W. H. Fremantle in *NPNF*, second series, vol. 3.

5. E.g., Basil, *Epist.* 224,1; Augustine *Epist.* 59.1–2.

were very few people left who actually knew the successors of the apostles? In one strain of thought, apostolic succession was carried down to and through the bishops of the main churches, who could be trusted to convey the apostolic teachings learned from Jesus who was sent from God. Another way to get back to the apostles was by reading the writings they had produced. Apostolic writings then became the order of the day. Even apostles of Jesus who, in real life, could not have written a paragraph in Greek had their souls depended upon it—Simon Peter, James the brother of Jesus, and John the Son of Zebedee, for example—had writings attributed to them. Many of these writings were produced by later authors who could not possibly have had any real connection with the apostles. They wrote forgeries, but they did so no doubt—at least in their own views—for good causes. The apostolic truth needed apostolic authority, and that required the use of an apostolic name. This was deceit in service of the truth.

Later still, other (non-apostolic) Christian leaders came to be cherished as authority figures: Clement of Rome, for example, or Ignatius of Antioch, and eventually Jerome, Augustine, and Chrysostom. And so sundry authors claimed those names as well for their own writings, lying about their identities to get their views heard. It happened a lot.

That, then, is one set of theses that I have tried to establish in the preceding chapters. Forgery occurred to a notable extent and it involved both well-known names and historically important writings, including a large number that became Scripture. As subsidiary theses I have tried to show that explanations for the phenomenon that at times seem ubiquitous, especially among Neutestamentlers, lack compelling evidence and are almost certainly wrong. This includes the claim that it was common practice in philosophical schools for students to write treatises in the names of their teachers, with impunity, as an act of humility, and the assertion that letters written in the names of such stalwarts as Peter and Paul can best be explained as having been produced by secretaries or coauthors, rather than the apostles themselves.

One other overarching conclusion is the corollary: forgery was indeed understood in antiquity to be a form of lying and deceit. This is seen not only in the negative terms used to describe writings produced by an author falsely claiming to be someone else, such as νόθα (bastards) and ψευδεπίγραφα (writings inscribed with a lie). It is also seen in the extensive discourse surrounding the activity, which castigated it as a form of lying. The true nature of these false writings was clearly recognized, as we have seen, by the greatest scholar of ancient forgery, Wolfgang Speyer, in words that bear repeating: "Every forgery feigns a state of affairs that does not correspond to actual events. In this vein, forgery belongs in the realm of lie and deceit." . . . "Only where the intent to deceive—that is to say: dolus malus—exists, does [a work] attain to the status of forgery. Forgery thus belongs in the same category as the lie, indeed as the intentional lie."[6]

6. "Jede Fälschung täuscht einen Sachverhalt vor, der den tatsächlichen Gegebenheiten nicht entspricht. Damit gehört die Fälschung in das Gebiet der Lüge und des Betrugs. . . . Nur wo Täuschungabsicht, also

I should stress again that forgery is not—and was not–simply an ancient form of transparent "fiction." The authors of forgery in almost every known instance meant to deceive their readers and the vast majority of times they appear to have succeeded. And so, "fiction" is not at all the right designation for this kind of practice.[7] Both in antiquity and today "fiction,"[8] involves a kind of contract between the author and the reader, in which the requirement of factual reporting is, by mutual assent, suspended. To revert to the helpful explanation of Michael Wood:

> Fiction is pure invention, any sort of fabrication. It is invention which knows it is invention; or which knows *and says* it is invention; or which, whatever it knows and says, *is known* to be invention. It is permissible or noble lying, licensed under quite specific cultural circumstances, and displays (sometimes) the linguistic or textual marks of its license. It is not lying at all, but exempt from all notions of truth and falsehood, licensed in quite a different way. . . .[9]

That is not what we are dealing with when considering forgeries. The reports of and discussions about the practice in antiquity consistently show that in fact there was no agreement between author and reader for the assumption of a false name. Instead, forgery was seen as a form of lying meant to deceive. As such it was closely related to other literary practices that we have mentioned only in

---

dolus malus, vorliegt, wird der Tatbestand der Fälschung erfüllt. Insofern gehört die Fälschung zur Lüge, und zwar zur vorsätzlichen Lüge"; *Literarische Fälschung*, pp. 3, 13.

7. If such a thing as "fiction" can be imagined for antiquity. On this, see the next note. In antiquity, of course, there were epic poems, Greek novels (as satirized in Lucian's "True Story"), epistolary novels, etc., and these *were* read differently from "histories."

8. For an argument that ancient writers and readers did not have anything that corresponded to our category of "fiction," see Christopher Gill, "Plato on Falsehood–Not Fiction," in Gill and Wiseman, eds., *Lies and Fiction*, pp. 38–87. Gill maintains that in modern ways of construing literature, we think of fiction as narrative that is imaginary, "made up" by the author. This is not a category for Plato. When he speaks of the myths being ΨΕΥΔΟΙ, he does not mean that they are made up; he means they teach lessons that are not true. That is Plato's principle category: Does something teach what one needs to learn in order to live rightly? And so he does not contradict himself when he condemns the ΨΕΥΔΟΙ of the poets but then tells his own myths (Er, the Cave, and so on). And when he urges the Noble Lie (which is true). Or when he invents dialogues. None of these things is the absolute embodiment of truth, since that can be reached and conveyed only through dialectical reasoning. But they are pathways to the truth, false in medium and in not being able to convey "truth" in its full and pristine state, but not false because they are made up, invented, imagined. I am in full agreement with this view of Plato. At the same time, it should not be overlooked that ancient persons did recognize that a history of Thucydides was not the same sort of writing as a novel by Achilles Tatius. Nowhere is that clearer than in Lucian's parody of history in his fictional work, "A True Story."

9. "Prologue," Gill and Wiseman, *Lies and Fiction*, p. xvi. Emphasis his.

passing throughout this study[10]: plagiarism,[11] falsification,[12] fabrication,[13] and false attribution.[14]

It is important at this stage to stress that even though I have insisted throughout the study that forgery is a form of literary deception, only in passing, at the outset, have I addressed the question of whether or not this kind of lying was ever considered morally acceptable. That, of course, is a different issue altogether.

Any normative evaluation of literary deceit should be the work of ethicists or, possibly, theologians—not historians. But the historian does have the obligation to consider how such activities would have been perceived in their own day. As it turns out, the (ancient) moral evaluation of lying is complicated, as might be expected when dealing with Christian authors who urge their readers to tell the truth, after lying about their own identity.[15] To make sense of this situation we need to consider the attitudes to lying and deception in the early church.

LIES AND DECEPTION IN EARLY CHRISTIANITY

The question about whether lies could be deemed moral was entertained by Speyer:

> As noted already, it is the intent to deceive that lies beyond any particular literary purpose that makes a pseudepigraphon a forgery. Forgery and lie agree in this regard, that they conceal the real situation and give the appearance of truth to a non-existent state of affairs. To this end, they use the means of dissimulation. Literary forgery is thus a special case of the lie, or rather: of deceit. This relationship between literary forgery and lie does not appear, however, to

---

10. See more fully pp. 43–67.

11. We have seen, for example, the problems with considering the Apostolic Constitutions and 2 Peter as plagiarized, even though they certainly take over other writings wholesale for the production of their own (though not under the author's own name).

12. The New Testament writings were widely falsified by scribes over the centuries, but they do not stand alone. We have seen the interpolations in the Pseudo-Ignatians and the Sibyllina (considering only these in our study, since they are closely related to forgeries in their respective corpora); other instances abound, as, for example, in the writings of Dionysius of Alexandria and Origen.

13. Many fabricated stories are not to be chalked up to malicious intent. But there are numerous episodes from the lives of Jesus that do not pass even ancient standards of veracity, whether stories about Jesus involving a census under Augustus when Quirinius was governor of Syria or involving his mischievous deeds as a five-year-old wunderkind. Stories about the apostles proliferated as well, as we have seen, whether made up as entertainment or for other more ideological reasons, such as Peter and the smoked tuna, Paul and the baptized lion, and John and the obedient bedbugs, just to stick with an animal theme.

14. I have not dealt at any length with false attribution here, even though it affects a number of the writings of the New Testament (the Gospels, 2 and 3 John), not to mention later writers (Pseudo-Justin, Pseudo-Tertullian, Pseudo-Chrysostom, and on and on). In many instances the attributions may have been made in full cognizance that there were no real grounds for making the ascriptions (the Gospel of Matthew); in other instances they were probably simply made by mistake (Pseudo-Justin).

15. See further pp. 546–47.

> have been examined closely in antiquity or the modern era. . . . We must ask, however, whether in antiquity any lie would have been judged unethical, or whether there were differentiations, and deception was considered permissible in certain cases.[16]

To ask what ancient persons—even orthodox Christians among the highly educated literary elite—thought about lying would be like asking this question of modern people. It depends on whom you ask. For the purposes of this sketch, I will map out two of the extreme positions, the well-known Augustinian view that it was never, ever right to lie, about anything, at any time, for any reason, whatsoever, and the lesser known but (at the time) more popular view represented by his contemporary John Cassian, that in fact there were instances where lying was not only acceptable but in fact the right thing to do.[17]

Augustine's Views of Lying

Augustine's views of lying can be found scattered throughout his writings, but come to clearest expression in his two treatises devoted to the subject, *De mendacio* and *Contra mendacium*.[18] The overarching point is the same in both treatises:

---

16. "Wie bereits bemerkt wurde, macht die Täuschungsabsicht, die jenseits eines literarischen Zwekkes liegt, ein Pseudepigraphon zur Fälschung. Fälschung und Lüge aber stimmen darin überein, daß sie einen wirklichen Sachverhalt verhüllen und den Schein der Wahrheit für einen nicht zutreffenden Tatbestand vortäuschen. Dazu benutzen sie das Mittel der Verstellung. Die literarische Fälschung ist somit ein Sonderfall der Lüge, näherhin des Betruges. Diese Verwandtschaft zwischen literarischer Fälschung und Lüge scheint jedoch weder im Altertum noch in der Neuzeit näher beachtet worden zu sein. . . . Es ist aber zu fragen, ob im Altertum jede Lüge als unsittlich verurteilt wurde, oder ob hier unterschieden wurde und Täuschung in gewissen Fällen als erlaubt galt"; *Literarische Fälschung*, p. 94

17. For important literature on lying in antiquity, see the classic studies of Franz Schindler, "Die Lüge in der patristischen Literatur," *Beiträge zur Geschichte des christlichen Altertums und der byzantinischen Literatur* (Amsterdam: Rodopi, 1969; originally published 1922); P. Wenzeslaus Sadok Mackowiak, *Die Ethische Beurteilung der Notlüge in der altheidnischen, patristischen, scholastischen, und neueren Zeit* (Zolkiew: Verlag der Dominakamer, 1933); Gregor Müller, *Die Wahrhaftigkeitspflicht und die Problematik der Lüge: Ein Längsschnitt durch die Moraltheologie und Ethik unter besonderer Berücksichtigung der Tugendlehre des Thomas von Aquin und der modernen Lösungsversuche* (Freiburg: Herder, 1962). In addition, see David Satran, "Pedagogy and Deceit in the Alexandrian Theological Tradition," in *Origeniana Quinta* ed. R. J. Daly (Leuven: Peeters, 1992), 119–24; Boniface Ramsey, "Two Traditions on Lying and Deception in the Ancient Church," *Thom.* 49 (1985): 504–33; and the studies cited in n. 18.

18. There are a number of important studies of Augustine's view of lying, all of them eclipsed by Paul J. Griffiths, *Lying: An Augustinian Theology of Duplicity* (Grand Rapids, MI: Brazos Press, 2004). See also Alan Brinton, "St. Augustine and the Problem of Deception in Religious Persuasion," *RelS* 19 (1983): 437–50; Marcia L. Colish, "The Stoic Theory of Verbal Signification and the Problem of Lies and False Statements from Antiquity to St. Anselm," in *L'Archéologie de Signe*, ed. L. Brind'amour and E. Vance (Toronto: Institut Pontifical d'Etudes Médiévales, 1983), pp. 17–43; Thomas D. Feehan, "Augustine on Lying and Deception," *AugStud* 19 (1988): 131–39; Feehan, "The Morality of Lying in St. Augustine," *AugStud* 21 (1990): 67–81; and Feehan, "Augustine's Own Examples of Lying," *AugStud* 22 (1991): 165–90.

under no circumstances is it permissible for a Christian to lie. You can imagine the most extreme position you want—that a white lie may prevent someone from being raped and tortured to death—and it is still not right to lie, no matter what.

De mendacio and Contra mendacium

De mendacio provides a long and nuanced discussion of what a lie actually is, followed by the question of whether it is ever appropriate or permissible for a Christian to tell a lie. For Augustine, a lie is the intentional discrepancy between what a person thinks to be true (whether or not she is right) and the contrary thing she says. A person "lies . . . who holds one opinion in his mind and who gives expression to another through words or any other outward manifestation" (ch. 3).[19] As Paul Griffiths puts it, for Augustine the mark of a *mendacium* is duplicity: that is, "a fissure between thought and utterance that is clearly evident to the speaker as she speaks. Lying words are spoken precisely with the intent to create such a fissure." So the speaker of the lie, the *mendax* has to believe that what she is saying is false, and to be intentionally saying it anyway (whether or not it really is false is beside the point).[20] Or more simply: "For Augustine, the lie is deliberately duplicitous speech, insincere speech that deliberately contradicts what its speaker takes to be true."[21]

Augustine is well aware of instances in the Bible where important figures lie with apparent approbation: Sarah and Jacob in Genesis, the Egyptian midwives at the beginning of Exodus. But he insists that these passages demand a figurative, not a literal, interpretation; and he finds no lies among Jesus or his followers in the New Testament. In his view, not only is there no biblical warrant for lying; there is no warrant whatsoever. He gets to this point by a kind of argumentum ad absurdum: no one would commend fornication in order to attain a greater good; and lying is condemned in Scripture just as much as fornication. One should not try to imagine a hypothetical situation in which a lie would ever bring about the ultimate, greatest good possible—for example, the eternal life of another. For one who proclaims the gospel with a lie undercuts the truth of the gospel, and if a person cannot trust a Christian who is telling a lie for the sake of his salvation, then he would have no grounds for trusting him with respect to the message of salvation itself: "When regard for truth has been broken down or even slightly weakened, all things will remain doubtful, and unless these are believed to be true, they cannot be considered as certain" (ch. 17). "When all aspects of the problem of lying have been considered, it is clear that the testimony of the Holy Scriptures advises that one should never lie at all" (ch. 42). "Whoever thinks, moreover, that there is any kind of lie which is not a sin deceives himself sadly when he considers that he, a deceiver of others, is an honest man" (ch. 42).

---

19. Translation of Mary Muldowny, *Augustine: Treatises on Various Subjects* FC, 16 (Washington, DC: Catholic University Press of America, 1952). All subsequent quotations of both this work and the *Contra mendacium* will be from this translation.

20. Griffiths, *Lying*, p. 25.

21. Ibid., p. 31.

Augustine's hard line continues in the *Contra mendacium*. This tractate was occasioned by a somewhat unusual situation. The heretical Priscillians had argued that lies were sometimes not only acceptable, but commendable. An orthodox leader, Consentius, was willing to pretend to accept Priscillian teachings (a kind of lie) in order to infiltrate the group and expose them as heretics. For Augustine, even such commendable ends do not justify the use of deception. As he asks rhetorically, "Therefore, how can I suitably proceed against lies by lying?" (ch. 1). Augustine goes on to maintain that if duplicitous concealment were licit, Christ would have told his sheep to dress in wolves' clothing, so as to discover the wolves; instead, they are told to beware of wolves in sheep's clothing (ch. 12). For Augustine, the teaching of Scripture is plain: God will destroy *all* who lie, not just some (see Psalm 5:6–7).

Moreover, if lying were ever appropriate, the martyrs to the faith would have been completely justified in lying to avoid torture and death. But they did not lie, for they realized that something is far worse than temporary torture and physical death: it is eternal torment and spiritual death, which comes to all those who willfully sin (ch. 3). And so, for Augustine, "Of course, it makes a difference for what reason, for what end, with what intention anything is done. But, those things which are clearly sins ought not to be done under any pretext of a good reason, for any supposedly good end, with any seemingly good intention" (ch. 18). His ultimate conclusion:

> You must hold and firmly defend the contention that in matters of divine religion we ought never to lie at all. Just as we do not seek out hidden adulterers by adultery or homicides by homicide or sorcerers by sorcery, so we should not seek out liars by lying or blasphemers by blasphemy. (ch. 41)

Similar Perspectives

It is sometimes overlooked that Augustine needed to argue so vociferously for his position on lying precisely because most Christians took a different view. As Griffiths points out, Augustine may have been the first thinker in the Christian religion to give a systematic treatment of the two big questions about lying: what a lie is, and whether it is ever permissible. But "few Christians agreed with him when he wrote."[22]

There were some who did, however. And so, Lactantius, writing against the poet Lucilius, who implied that whereas one should never lie to one's friends, it was acceptable to lie to one's enemies, could state:

> The other things which the worshiper of God ought to observe are easy when those virtues have been attained. For he would never lie for the sake of deceiving or harming. It is wrong for him who is eager for the truth to be false in

22. Ibid., p. 14.

> any respect and to depart from that very truth which he follows. In this way of justice and of all virtues, there is no place for a lie. . . . Nor will he ever commit the crime of having his tongue, "the interpreter of the mind," at variance with his feeling and intention.[23]

So too Eusebius, in the *Preparatio*:

> A mortal man who paid any little regard to virtue would never lie but would choose rather to reverence the truth; nor would he lay the blame of a lie upon any necessity of fate or course of the stars. But even if anyone were to bring fire or sword against his body, to compel him to pervert the word of truth, yet even against this he would reply in freedom's tone:
>
> "Come fire, come sword;
> Burn, and scorch up this flesh, and gorge thyself
> With my dark blood; for sooner shall the stars
> Sink down to earth, and earth rise up to heav'n
> Than fawning word shall meet thee from my lips." (6.6)[24]

John Cassian's Alternative Perspective

This hard-core view of lying as never, ever permissible ran up against a much more popular view, embraced by non-Christian and Christian authors alike, that there were indeed circumstances under which it was not only permissible but commendable to engage in lies and other forms of deceit. As Speyer and, especially, Norbert Brox have recognized, this ancient Christian attitude may well explain the willingness of many anonymous literati to forge documents in the names of others, lying about their identity in order to convey what they understood to be the truth.[25] This contrary view can be seen in a relatively clear form in a key passage of John Cassian's *Conferences*, in which he recounts a late sleepless night conversation in the desert between Abba Germanus and Abba Joseph (the words are those of Joseph; they appear to represent Cassian's own view as well, but whether they do or not is immaterial to the point).

Abba Joseph insists that it is sometimes the right thing to do to lie, but one must use supreme caution and circumspection:

> And so a lie is to be thought of and used as if it were hellebore. If it is taken when a deadly disease is imminent it has a healthful effect, but taken when

23. *Institutions* 6:18; translation of Mary Francis Macdonald, *Lactantius, The Divine Institutions*, FC (Washington, DC: Catholic University Press of America, 1964).

24. Translation of Edwin Hamilton Gifford (1903 tr.).

25. Speyer, *Literarische Fälschung*, p. 96; Brox, *Falsche Verfasserangaben*, pp. 83–104. See pp. 132–37 above.

> there is no urgent need it is the cause of immediate death. For we read that even men who were holy and most approved by God made such good use of lying that they not only did not commit sin thereby but even acquired the highest righteousness. If deceit were capable of conferring glory on them, would truth, on the other hand, have brought them anything but condemnation?[26]

Joseph cites the story of Rahab from the book of Joshua. Had she spoken the truth when asked where the Israelite spies were hiding, they could not have done her a favor later, and spared her family or her, and she would never, then, have become one of the progenitors of Christ himself (in fact, the messianic line then would have been broken). Contrast that with Delilah who disastrously spoke the truth and as a result "obtained everlasting perdition in exchange for this, and left to everyone nothing but the memory of her sin." Joseph's conclusion: "When some grave danger is connected with speaking the truth, therefore, the refuge of lying must be resorted to (yet in such a way that we are bitten by the healthful guilt of a humbled conscience.)" But that is acceptable before God, who ""perceives the inner devotion of the heart and judges not the sound of the words but the intent of the will, because it is the end of the work and the disposition of the doer that must be considered." In sum: "One person can be justified even when lying, whereas another can commit a sin deserving everlasting death by telling the truth."

A sharper contrast to the Augustinian view can scarcely be imagined (except one that insisted that lying was *always* the moral thing!). But Cassian was not inventing an ethics of lying out of whole cloth. On the contrary, he was standing in a long and noble line of ethical thinking that can be traced back for centuries. In pagan circles, it is most famously associated with the great Socrates himself.[27]

Pagan Advocacy for the Lie

According to Xenophon, Socrates taught that there were certain situations in which lying was not only permissible but appropriate. This is the case, for example, when a general "seeing that his army is downhearted, tells a lie and says that reinforcements are approaching, and by means of this lie checks discouragement among the men." So too, in a yet better known and much repeated example, lying is proper if "a man's son refuses to take a dose of medicine when he needs it, and the father induces him to take it by pretending that it is food, and cures him by

---

26. Translation of Boniface Ramsey, *John Cassian: The Conferences* (ACW; New York: Newman Press, 1997). All quotations of this work will be taken from this edition.

27. Among a host of studies, see esp. T. P. Wiseman, "Lying Historians: Seven Types of Mendacity," in Gills and Wiseman, eds., *Lies and Fiction*, pp. 122–46; Christopher Gill, "Plato on Falsehood"; Jane S. Zembaty, "Plato's Republic and Greek Morality on Lying," *JHP* 26 (1988): 517–45.

means of this lie" (*Memorab.* 4, 2, 14–18).[28] This idea of a "medicinal" lie became a commonplace in ancient ethical discourse. It recurs on Socrates's lips in Plato's "Republic."

Plato's own views of lying, as with most of his views on most things, are very difficult to ascertain, given the nature of his dialogues and the logic of his dialectical methods. But the various positions championed at one point or another in the dialogues—whether they are the historical Plato's actual views or others' that he sees either as false or only as partly true—are almost always views that were seen as "acceptable" to some of his ancient Greek readers.

There is a good deal of discourse on lying in the "Republic." For example, at 382c-d, Socrates declares that it is acceptable to lie to one's enemies, to one's friends in order to prevent them from doing harm to themselves, and in fables and myths designed to lead a person to the truth. Best known, however, is Socrates's proposal of the "noble lie" that was to help sustain the proper leadership and ordered society of his Republic. In building his case for the noble lie, Socrates begins by insisting that lying is sometimes the proper thing to do, with recourse to the idea of the medicinal lie:

> But further we must surely prize truth most highly. For if we were right in what we were just saying and falsehood is in very deed useless to gods, but to men useful as a remedy or form of medicine, it is obvious that such a thing must be assigned to physicians, and laymen should have nothing to do with it" [and who, for Plato, are the "physicians" who can dole out the medicinal lie? The enlightened rulers of the state, who are all trained in philosophy]. "The rulers then of the city may, if anybody, fitly lie on account of enemies or citizens for the benefit of the state: no others may have anything to do with it." (389b)[29]

Somewhat later, in a summary statement, Socrates reiterates: "It seems likely that our rulers will have to make considerable use of falsehood and deception for the benefit of their subjects" (459c-d). The noble lie itself is spelled out in 414–15. In this utopian Republic, the philosopher-kings who are the leaders need to propagate the lie that everyone in the state was formed within the earth by God, some of them with gold intermixed with their characters (these would be the ones appointed by God to be the rulers), others with silver (their helpers), and yet others, the majority, with brass or iron. On no account can a ruler have a mixture of brass or iron in his constitution.

As a kind of control over society, then, the rulers claim that they are inherently suited—made by God—to be rulers, and the artisans and farmers and the like, that is, the majority of the people, have been made with inferior characters.

---

28. Translation of E. C. Marchant and O. J. Todd, *Xenophon*, LCL (Cambridge, MA: Harvard University, 1923).

29. Translation of Paul Shorey, *Plato*; LCL (Cambridge, MA: Harvard University, 1937).

These then must be ruled by others of superior nature. The irony is that for Plato, this "lie" actually conveys the "truth." There really are some people who are constituted to be leaders: the philosophers who are able to sustain the hard training of dialectical reasoning so as to come to see the "truth." No one else can rule in the ideal state. And so, as Christopher Gill has stressed, "The noble lie is properly described as a 'lie' because what is involved is deliberate non-veracity; but the lie is clearly designed to propagate an idea which the argument presents as true, namely that each member of the ideal state should be placed in the class for which he or she is naturally suited." For Plato, says Gill, "lying, as in the case of the noble lie, may be the most effective way to propagate truth."[30]

The idea that there could be occasions when lies and other forms of deceit were legitimate is attested throughout the writings of pagan authors, often showing up in unexpected places, as in the "Philoctetes" of Sophocles, where Odysseus tries to convince Neoptolemus to take Philoctetes by deceit, since otherwise it would be impossible. Neoptolemus asks, "Then you think it brings no shame to speak what is false?" And Odysseus replies, "No, not if the falsehood yields deliverance" (ll. 108–09).[31] Centuries later Cicero can state with mild approbation that "rhetoricians are allowed to lie in their historical presentations" (*Brutus* 11.42). In a sharply contrasting context Heliodorus celebrates the virtue of the helpful lie, "For lying is good when it benefits those who speak the lie and does no harm to those who hear it" (*Ethiopica*, 1.26.6,).

Christian Advocacy of the Lie

What matters most for our purposes is that there was also a widespread Christian discourse, which Augustine found deeply irritating, that advocated the appropriate use of lies and deceit, in certain circumstances.

The Insistence on the Truth

As might naturally be expected, early Christian sources are full of exhortations to speak the truth. The author of Ephesians, as we have seen, can urge his readers: "Let each of you put aside the lie and speak the truth with his neighbor" (Eph. 4:25). I have already mentioned the irony, to be dwelt on at greater length in a moment, that this injunction occurs in a letter whose author lied about his own identity. The same irony occurs in the equally pseudonymous letter to the Colossians: "Do not lie to one another" (Col. 3.9). After the New Testament period comes a host of injunctions not to lie. In the orthonymous *Shepherd* of Hermas, for example, the following brief exchange appears between the Shepherd and Hermas:

30. Gill, "Plato on Falsehood," pp. 53, 55.

31. *The Philoctetes of Sophocles*. Edited with introduction and notes by Sir Richard Jebb (Cambridge: Cambridge University Press, 1898).

> Then he spoke to me again, "Love the truth and let all truth come from your mouth . . . For the Lord is true in his every word, and there is no lie in him. And so, those who lie reject the Lord and defraud him, not handing over to him the deposit they received. For they received from him a spirit that does not lie; if they return it to him as a liar, they defile the commandment of the Lord and become defrauders." (Commandments, 3.1–2)

So too Justin, allegedly writing to the emperor, points out: "You can be sure that we have spoken these things for your benefit, since we, when on trial can always deny [that we are Christians]. But we do not desire to live by lying" (1 *Apol.* 8.2). This, as we have seen, is a view later picked up by Augustine, who pointed out that the martyrs were a clear proof that it is never right to lie in order to reap a greater benefit, such as avoiding torture.

The Virtue of the Lie

Even though it is a "given" that Christian ethical teachings insisted on the truth, there are a startling number of authors who share the view of Cassian's Abba Joseph, that it is also sometimes a good thing to lie. We might start with Clement of Alexandria, who insists that the true "Gnostic" tell the truth but makes an exception for the so-called medicinal lie: "For [the Gnostic] both thinks and speaks the truth; unless at any time, medicinally, as a physician for the safety of the sick, he may deceive or tell an untruth, according to the Sophists" (*Strom.* 7.9).[32] That Clement does not see this simply as a bit of sophistry is evident from what follows. The apostle Paul was known, according to Clement, to have used deceit in two circumstances, when he circumcised Timothy after declaring that "circumcision made with hands profits nothing" and when he occasionally took upon himself the burdens of the Jewish Law in order to win Jews over to the faith, so that he, "accommodating himself to the Jews, became a Jew that he might gain all." Elsewhere, again, Clement uses the physician analogy to justify the use of deception (*Strom.* 7.53).

Origen, not surprisingly, argues in a similar vein. In the *Contra Celsum* he notes that Celsus had accused the Christians of making God a purveyor of deceit by coming to earth in the (false) appearance of being human. In this context Celsus alludes to Plato, "Deceit and lying are in all other cases wrong except only when one uses them as a medicine for friends who are sick and mad in order to heal them, or with enemies when the intention is to escape danger" (4.18).[33] For Celsus, then, the divine deceit at the incarnation was impermissible, because it did not meet the criterion of a justified lie. Origen demurs, arguing that God in fact came to earth as a man precisely to "heal" the human race, so that the incarnation deceit was completely justified.

---

32. Translation in Alexander Roberts and James Donaldson *ANF*, vol. 2.

33. Translation of Chadwick, *Contra Celsum*.

> Do you not say, Celsus, that sometimes it is allowable to use deceit and lying as a medicine? Why, then, is it unthinkable that something of this sort occurred with the purpose of bringing salvation? . . . There is nothing wrong if the person who heals sick friends healed the human race which was dear to him with such means as one would not use for choice, but to which he was confined by the force of circumstances. Since the human race was mad, it had to be cured by methods which the Word saw to be beneficial to lunatics. (4.19)

Elsewhere we learn that Origen supported the use of the strategic lie. The passage comes to us from the now-lost *Stromateis*, which fortunately are quoted, in parts, by Jerome. The most relevant portion comes from book six in which, according to Jerome, Origen "tries to adapt our Christian doctrine to the opinions of Plato"[34]:

> To God falsehood is shameful and useless, but to men it is occasionally useful. We must not suppose that God ever lies, even in the way of economy; only, if the good of the hearer requires it, he speaks in ambiguous language, and reveals what he wills in enigmas. . . . But a man on whom necessity imposes the responsibility of lying is bound to use very great care, and to use falsehood as he would a stimulant or a medicine, and strictly to preserve its measure.

He then instances the sanctioned lies told by the biblical characters of Judith, Esther, and Jacob and concludes: "From all this it is evident that if we speak falsely with any other object than that of obtaining by it some great good, we shall be judged as the enemies of him who said, 'I am the truth.'"

Jerome, however, attacks this view with a good bit of wit: "[Origen's] teaching is that the master may lie, but the disciple must not. The inference from this is that the man who is a good liar, and without hesitation sets before his brethren any fabrication which rises into his mouth, shows himself to be an excellent teacher" (*Adv. Rufin.* 1.18).

It is interesting to note, however, that Jerome elsewhere speaks approvingly of the use of Christian deception, in particular with respect to the famous incident in Antioch discussed by Paul in Galatians 2 (the view that prompted Augustine to write *De mendacio*): in Jerome's well-known position, Peter and Paul did not actually have a falling out. They put on a show, in a double act of dissimulation: Peter "pretended" to be subject to Jewish dietary laws for the sake of the brethren, knowing that he was not really subject to them, and Paul, cognizant of the true state of things, "pretended" to rebuke Peter in order to show the gentile Christians that he was on their side so as to keep from giving offense.[35]

---

34. Jerome, *Adv. Rufin.* 1.18.

35. Jerome's *Commentary on Galatians* ad loc. See his Epistle 112 to Augustine. I owe this reference to Maria Doerfler. See also Chrysostom's *Homily* 2 on Galatians. I owe this reference to Andrew Jacobs.

Origen provides a particularly interesting perspective on the permissible lie in his *Commentary on John*, where he is dealing with the historical discrepancies among the canonical Gospels. In his view, the evangelists changed historical data on occasion in order to convey spiritual truths: "For their intention was to speak the truth spiritually and materially at the same time, where that was possible, but where it was not possible in both ways, to prefer the spiritual to the material. The spiritual truth is often preserved in the material falsehood, so to speak" (10.4).[36] As an example of how this works, Origen appeals to the famous instance of Jacob lying, for a good cause, to his blind father Isaac, saying "I am Esau, your first born son." According to Origen, Jacob "was telling the truth in the spiritual sense . . . because he had a share of the birthright which was already perishing in his brother." And this is why contradictory statements about Christ in Scripture can both be true, because they participate in spiritual truths even if they contain material contradictions. Thus Christ can be called both man and not man; he can be both Son and servant.[37]

In addition to these rather abstract disquisitions on lying, we have several anecdotes about prominent church fathers in which, without any qualms, they used deceit when it served their purposes. One of the more amusing, worth quoting in full, involves Athanasius under pursuit, as narrated by Theodoret in his *Church History* (again, the historicity of the story does not matter for my point, as it shows an attitude toward deceit):

> Moved by these supplications Julian condemned Athanasius not merely to exile, but to death. His people shuddered, but it is related that he foretold the rapid dispersal of the storm, for said he "It is a cloud which soon vanishes away." He however withdrew as soon as he learnt of the arrival of the bearers of the imperial message, and finding a boat on the bank of the river, started for the Thebaid. The officer who had been appointed for his execution became acquainted with his flight, and strove to pursue him at hot haste; one of his friends, however, got ahead, and told him that the officer was coming on apace. Then some of his companions besought him to take refuge in the desert, but he ordered the steersman to turn the boat's head to Alexandria. So they rowed to meet the pursuer, and on came the bearer of the sentence of execution, and, said he, "How far off is Athanasius?" "Not far," said Athanasius, and so got rid of his foe, while he himself returned to Alexandria and there remained in concealment for the remainder of Julian's reign. (*H.E.* 3.5)[38]

---

36. Translation of Ronald Heine, *Origen: Commentary on the Gospel of John 1–10*, FC (Washington, DC: Catholic University of America, 1989).

37. See also Origen's *Homilies* on Jeremiah, 19.15 and 20.3, where he strains to explain Jer. 20:7: "You have deceived me, Lord, and I was deceived."

38. Translation of Blomfield Jackson, *NPNF*, series 2, vol. 3.

This is obviously a case where no lie was actually told. The humor of the story resides in the fact that, strictly speaking, Athanasius told the truth. But recall Augustine's view that a lie need not come only in words, but in "signs of whatever kind."

A second and better known account involves an autobiographical tale told by Chrysostom in Book One of *De sacerdotio*, a passage that Paul Griffiths has aptly termed "a hymn of praise to the lie."[39] According to Chrysostom's account, as promising young men, both he and Basil were being pursued in order forcibly to be ordained into the episcopacy. Chrysostom lied to Basil, promising to accept the ordination, and on those grounds Basil relented and did so himself. But Chrysostom did not; it was all a pretext. In its aftermath, Chrysostom engaged in a bit of Schadenfreude, to Basil's dismay: "But when he saw that I was delighted and beaming with joy, and understood that he had been deceived by me, he was yet more vexed and distressed" (1.6).[40]

Basil responds with a bitter lament: "I placed my very life, so to say, in your hands, yet you have treated me with as much guile as if it had been your business to guard yourself against an enemy" (1.7). In response, Chrysostom launches into a kind of encomium to deceit:

> What is the wrong that I have done thee, since I have determined to embark from this point upon the sea of apology? Is it that I misled you and concealed my purpose? Yet I did it for the benefit of thyself who wast deceived, and of those to whom I surrendered you by means of this deceit. For if the evil of deception is absolute, and it is never right to make use of it, I am prepared to pay any penalty you please . . . But if the thing is not always harmful, but becomes good or bad according to the intention of those who practice it, you must desist from complaining of deceit, and prove that it has been devised against you for a bad purpose. . . . For a well-timed deception, undertaken with an upright intention, has such advantages, that many persons have often had to undergo punishment for abstaining from fraud. (1.8)

Here we have Cassian's view instantiated and celebrated: lies are not harmful if the intention of the liar is good. Indeed, they are to be used when the circumstances call for it. Chrysostom does not stop there, however, but goes on to speak of two biblical instances of "good" deceit that saved the life of King David (1 Sam 19:12–18; 20:11), and to refer to doctors who employ the medicinal lie: "If any one were to reckon up all the tricks of physicians the list would run on to an indefinite length. And not only those who heal the body but those also who attend to the diseases of the soul may be found continually making use of this remedy" (1.8). He concludes with bold statements that are precisely at odds with the view of an Augustine:

---

39. Griffiths, *Lying*, p. 135.

40. Translation taken from W. R. W. Stephens in *NPNF*, series 1, vol. 7.

> For great is the value of deceit, provided it be not introduced with a mischievous intention . . . And often it is necessary to deceive, and to do the greatest benefits by means of this device, whereas he who has gone by a straight course has done great mischief to the person whom he has not deceived. (1.8)[41]

The Morality of Christian Forgery

At the outset of our study we saw that forgery, when it is explicitly discussed in antiquity, is roundly and emphatically condemned. Most readers did not consider this kind of lie to be acceptable, even if they did sanction other lies for other reasons. If someone's life could be saved by a white lie, all to the good (for many Christians); if someone could be delivered from pain and suffering, from rape or torture, then surely (for many Christians), lying could be justified. But with the literary texts written under the cloud of deceit, we are not dealing with matters of life and death. The issues may have seemed enormous to the writers of these texts. But most readers, at least, condemned the practice. Moreover, unlike fiction, forgery does not include a contract between author and reader where veracity is suspended for the sake of the text. Ancient Christian readers expected authors to name themselves, if they named anyone at all, and not to lie about who they really were.

And so, it is not difficult at all to see what someone standing in Augustine's camp would have thought of forgery. Augustine may well have been speaking for many (most?) other Christians, both of his own day and earlier, when he reflected on the need for Scripture, in particular, not to be implicated in lying and deceit:

> It seems to me that no good at all can come of our believing that the sacred texts contain anything false or incorrect—that is, that these men through whom the Bible was given to us and who committed it to writing set down anything that was not true in those books. It is one question whether a good man might at some time tell a lie, but it is another question altogether whether a writer of Holy Scripture might have intended to lie or deceive. No, it is not another question—it is no question at all. If you can point out at least one instance of the intentional falsehood within this holy citadel of authority, then anything in the Bible which strikes us as too hard to practice, or too difficult to believe in, can simply be explained away as a deliberate untruth. (*Epist.* 28.3)[42]

---

41. For divinely sanctioned use of deceit in the early Christian tradition, one need only think of the bizarre crucifixion scene narrated, or so we're told by Irenaeus, in the Gospel of Basilides, where Jesus, having pulled an identity switch with Simon of Cyrene, stands by and laughs while the Romans crucify the wrong man. The theme is reprised in the Pseudo-Clementines in the fateful switch of identity that Simon effects with Faustianus, a move that seriously backfires thanks to the clever intervention and manipulation of Peter.

42. Translation of Joseph W. Trigg, *Biblical Interpretation* (Wilmington, DE: Michael Glazier, 1988), p. 259.

Or, as he says elsewhere in another letter:

> [I]f it is the case that we admit into Holy Scripture claims which are untrue but which serve some profounder purpose—for the sake of religion, let us say—then how do we defend the authority of the Bible? What statement in the Bible will be strong enough to stand up against the wicked stubbornness of heresy? Anyone arguing with you can claim that in the passage you are citing the writer really intended something else, he had a higher purpose in mind" (*Epist.* 40.3)[43]

This is clearly a hard line when it comes to truth and deceit, and I see no reason to doubt that a large number of Christians would have agreed with it (whether the majority or not—who can say?). Augustine may have seen himself standing shoulder-to-shoulder with the author of Ephesians, who tells his readers that they are to "Fasten the belt of truth around your waist." Truth was all-important for this canonical writer. Early on he refers to the gospel as "the word of truth" (1:13); he indicates that the "truth is in Jesus" (4:21); and he declares that the "fruit of the light is found in the truth" (5:9). Most important, as we have seen, he insists that his readers "put aside the lie and speak the truth" to their neighbors (4:25). And yet the author lied about his own identity, claiming to be the apostle Paul when in fact he was someone else, living years later. What would Augustine and those who were like-minded have thought about this author, and his book, had they known the truth of its authorship? They would have called the author a liar and his book a deceit, and they would not have admitted it into the canon of Scripture.

But what did the author himself think? He must have known that he lied. But if he was like a large number of other Christians, he must have also thought that there were times when it was appropriate to lie, that the intention of the lie was more important than the fact of the lie, that sometimes it was the right thing to do to reject truth and embrace falsehood. Most Christians—and undoubtedly this unknown author himself—knew full well that throughout Scripture lies could further and promote the will of God. If Abraham had not lied about his wife Sarah, calling her his sister, he may well have been killed and the nation of Israel would never have come into being (Genesis 12). If Jacob had not deceived Isaac to receive the birthright, Israel would never have become heir of the promises of God (Genesis 27). If the midwives of Egypt had not lied about the hardiness of the Hebrew women giving birth, the nation may well have been destroyed and Moses would certainly never have come into existence (Exodus 1). If Rahab had not lied about the whereabouts of the Israelite spies, Israel may have never been able to take the Promised Land; if they did, she and her family would not have been spared, and she would not have been in the messianic line; in fact the line may well have ended prematurely at that point (Joshua 2). If Michal and Jonathan

43. Trigg, *Biblical Interpretation*, p. 263.

had not lied for David, he may well have been killed by Saul, before he produced the offspring that would lead to the coming of his greatest Son, the Messiah (1 Samuel 19–20). Jesus too was known to have used deceit, indicating that he was not going to the feast in Jerusalem while knowing full well that he was about to go (John 7). Even God could use deceit when he chose to do so, as declared in forthright terms by the prophet Jeremiah: "You deceived me and I was deceived" (20:7). And as shown, for example, in his declaration through Jonah that Nineveh was to be destroyed in forty days, when he knew full well that it was not to be.

Did forgers think that lying is sometimes not only right, but divinely sanctioned? That it is sometimes morally acceptable, even necessary, to lie and deceive others? That a greater good can sometimes result from a lie than from the truth? At an early stage of our study we considered the one instance of a Christian forger who discussed his motives for lying about his identity, Salvian of Marseille, who, among other things declared: "For this reason the present writer chose to conceal his identity in every respect for fear that his true name would perhaps detract from the influence of his book, which really contains much that is exceedingly valuable."[44] He had an important book to write, and no one would read it if it were attributed to a nobody like Salvian. And so he wrote it in the name of Timothy, in hopes that it would have a wide influence.

It may well be that other forgers—of both canonical and non-canonical texts—felt similarly. They may have believed that they had a high moral obligation to convey the truth as it had been revealed to them. They may have reasoned that they needed to have their words read as widely as possible. They may have realized that the best way to assure a broad and much-deserved influence was by hiding their identity behind that of a greater authority. They may have thought that they had a truth to convey, and they may have been willing to lie in order to convey it.

44. See the discussion on pp. 94–96.

BIBLIOGRAPHY

Aageson, James W. *Paul, the Pastoral Epistles, and the Early Church*. Peabody, MA: Hendrickson, 2008.

Achtemeier, Paul. *1 Peter*. Hermeneia. Minneapolis: Fortress Press, 1996.

Achtemeier, Paul J., Joel B. Green, and Marianne M. Thompson. *Introducing the New Testament, Its Literature and Theology*. Grand Rapids, MI: Eerdmans, 2001.

Aland, Kurt. "The Problem of Anonymity and Pseudonymity in Christian Literature of the First Two Centuries." *JTS* 12 (1961): 39–49.

Allard, M. Paul. "Une nouvelle théorie sur le martyre des Chrétiens de Lyon en 177 A.D." *Revue des questions historiques* 93 (1913): 53–67.

Allen, John L. "The Protevangelium of James as an Historia : The Insufficiency of the Infancy Gospel Category." SBLSP 30 (1991): 508–17.

Amelungk, Arnold. "Untersuchung über Pseudo-Ignatius." *ZWT* 42 (1899): 508–81.

Amsler, F. "État de la recherche récente sur le roman pseudo-clémentin." In *Nouvelles intrigues pseudo-clémentines—Plots in the Pseudo-Clementine Romance: Actes du deuxième colloque international sur la littérature apocryphe chrétienne (Lausanne, 30 août—2 septembre 2006)*, edited by Frédéric Amsler, Albert Frey and Charlotte Touati, pp. 25–45. Lausanne: Zèbre, 2008.

Anastassiou, A., and D. Irmer, eds. *Testimonien zum Corpus Hippocraticum*. Pt. 2, *Galen; vol. 1 Hippokrateszitate in den Kommentaren und im Glossar.* Göttingen: Vandenhoeck, 1997.

Arnold, Clinton. *Colossian Syncretism: The Interface between Christianity and Folk Belief at Colossae*. Tübingen: Mohr Siebeck, 1995.

Attridge, Harold W. *The Epistle to the Hebrews*. Heremenia. Philadelphia: Fortress, 1989.

Ayres, Lewis. *Nicaea and Its Legacy: An Approach to Fourth-Century Trinitarian Thinking*. Oxford: Oxford University Press, 2004.

Bagatti, Bellarmino. "Caphernaum." *MdB* (1983): 8–16.

Bahr, Gordon. "Paul and Letter Writing in the First Century." *CBQ* 28 (1966): 465–77.

Bailey, John A. "Who Wrote II Thessalonians?" *NTS* 25 (1979): 131–45.

Balz, Horst R. "Anonymität und Pseudepigraphie im Urchristentum: Überlegungen zum literarischen und theologischen Problem der urchristlichen und gemeinantiken Pseudepigaphie." *ZTK* 66 (1969): 403–36.

Bar-Ilan, Meir. "Illiteracy in the Land of Israel in the First Centuries CE." In *Essays in the Social Scientific Study of Judaism and Jewish Society*, ed. Simcha Fishbane et al. Hoboken, NJ: Ketv, 1992; vol. 2, 46–61.

Bardy, Gustave. "Faux et fraudes littéraires dans l'antiquité chrétienne" *RHE* 32 (1936): 5–23, 75–302.

Barlow, Claude W. *Epistolae Senecae ad Paulum et Pauli ad Senecam*. Horn, Austria: F. Berger, 1938.

Barnes, T. D. "A Note on Polycarp," *Journal of Theological Studies* 18 (1967): 433–437.

Barnes, T. D. "Review of Silvia Ronchey, *Indagine sul martirio di San Policarpo: Critica storica e fortuna agiografica di un caso giudiziario in Asia Minore*," *JTS* 43 (1992): 237–38.

Barrett, C. K. *The Acts of the Apostles*, ICC; 2 vols. Edinburgh: T&T Clark, 1998.

Barth, Markus. *Ephesians*. ABC 34. New York: Doubleday, 1974.

Barth, Markus, and Helmut Blank. *Colossians*. ABC 34B. New York: Doubleday, 1994.

Bauckham, Richard J. "The Acts of Paul as a Sequel to Acts." In *The Book of Acts in Its Ancient Literary Setting*, edited by Bruce Winter and Arthur Clark, pp. 105–152. Grand Rapids, MI: Eerdmans, 1993.

Bauckham, Richard J. "The *Apocalypse of Peter*: A Jewish Christian Apocalypse from the Time of Bar Kokhba." *Apocrypha* 5 (1994), 7–111; reprinted in Bauckham, *The Fate of the Dead: Studies on the Jewish and Christian Apocalypses* (Leiden: Brill, 1998), pp. 160–258.

Bauckham, Richard J. "The Ascension of Isaiah: Genre, Unity and Date." In *The Fate of the Dead: Studies on the Jewish and Christian Apocalypses*, edited by eidem, pp. 363–90. NovTSup 93. Leiden: Brill, 1998.

Bauckham, Richard J. *Jude, 2 Peter*. WBC, 50.Waco, TX: Word Books, 1983.

Bauckham, Richard J. *Jude and the Relatives of Jesus in the Early Church*. London: T&T Clark, 1990.

Bauer, Walter. *Orthodoxy and Heresy in Earliest Christianity*. Philadelphia: Fortress, 1971; trans. of *Rechtgläubigkeit und Ketzerei im ältesten Christentum*. Tübingen: Mohr Siebeck, 1934.

Baum, Armin Daniel. *Pseudepigraphie und literarische Fälschung im frühen Christentum*. WUNT 138. Tübingen: Mohr Siebeck, 2001.

Baum, Armin Daniel. "Semantic Variation within the *Corpus Paulinum*: Linguistic Considerations Concerning the Richer Vocabulary of the Pastoral Epistles." *TynBul* 59 (2008): 271–92.

Baur, F. C. *Die sogenannten Pastoralbriefe des Apostels Paulus*. Stuttgart: J. G. Cotta, 1835.

Beatrice, Pier Franco. "Forgery, Propaganda and Power in Christian Antiquity: Some Methodological Remarks." In *Alvarium: FS Christian Gnilka*, edited by Wilhelm Blümer, Rainer Henke, Markus Mülke, pp. 39–51. JAC 33. Münster: Aschendorffsche Verlagsbuchhandlung, 2002.

Becker, Adam H., and Annette Yoshiko Reed. *The Ways That Never Parted: Jews and Christians in Late Antiquity and the Early Middle Ages*. Minneapolis: Fortress, 2007.

Becker, Eve-Marie. "Von Paulus zu 'Paulus.'" In *Pseudepigraphie und Verfasserfiktion in frühchristlichen Briefen*, edited by Jörg Frey et al., pp. 363–86.

Becker, Eve-Marie. "Ὡς δι' ἡμῶν in 2 Thess 2.2 als Hinweis auf einen verlorenen Brief." *NTS* 55 (2009): 55–72.

BeDuhn, Jason. "The Historical Assessment of Speech Acts: Clarifications of Austin and Skinner for the Study of Religions." *MTSR* 12 (2000): 477–505.

Bellinzoni, A. J. *The Sayings of Jesus in the Writings of Justin Martyr*. Leiden: Brill, 1967.

Benko, Stephen. "The Libertine Gnostic Sect of the Phibionites According to Epiphanius." *VC* 21 (1967): 103–19.

Benko, Stephen. *Pagan Rome and the Early Christians*. Bloomington: Indiana University, 1984.

Bentley, Richard. "Dissertation upon Phalaris." In *The Works of Richard Bentley*, ed. Alexander Dyce, vol. 1, pp. 289–96. London: F. MacPherson, 1836; reprinted New York: Hildesheim, 1971.
Bernays, J. *Gesammelte Abhandlungen* 1 (1885), p. 250, as cited in Speyer, *Literarische Fälschung*, pp. 5–6.
Best, Ernest. *Ephesians*. ICC. Edinburgh: T&T Clark, 1998.
Best, Ernest. "Who Used Whom? The Relationship of Ephesians and Colossians." *NTS* 43 (1997): 72–96.
Bickel, Ernst. *Lehrbuch der Geschichte der römischen Literatur*, 2nd ed. Heidelberg: C. Winter, 1961.
Bickell, J. W. *Geschichte des Kirchenrechts*, vol. 1. Giessen: G. Heyer, 1843.
Bickerman, E. J. "Faux littéraires dans l'antiquité classique en marge d'un livre récent." In *Studies in Jewish and Christian History*, edited by eidem, pp. 196–211. Leiden: Brill, 1986.
Bigg, Charles. "The Clementine Homilies." In *Studia Biblica et Ecclesiastica: Essays Chiefly in Biblical and Patristic Criticism*, vol. 2, pp. 157–93. Oxford: Clarendon Press, 1890.
Bisbee, Gary. *Pre-Decian Acts of Martyrs and Commentarii*. HDR 22. Philadelphia: Fortress, 1988.
Bischoff, Bernhard. "Der Brief des Hohenpriesters Annas an den Philosophen Seneca—eine jüdisch-apologetische Missionsschrift (Viertes Jahrhundert?)" In *Anecdota Novissima: Texte des vierten bis sechzehnten Jahrhunderts*, pp. 1–9. Stuttgart: Anton Hiersemann, 1984.
Bludau, A. *Die Schriftfälschungen der Häretiker: Ein Beitrag zur Textkritik der Bibel*. Münster: Aschendorf, 1925.
Blum, Rudolf. *Kallimachos und die Literaturverzeichnung bei den Griechen*. Frankfurt: Buchhändler-Vereinigung, 1977.
Boeft, Jan den, and Jan Bremmer. "Notiunculae Martyrologicae V." *VC* 49 (1995): 146–64.
Boissier, G. "Le Christianisme de Sénèque." *Revue des deux mondes* 92 (1871): 40–71.
Boring, M. Eugene. "First Peter in Recent Study." *WW* 24 (2004): 358–67.
Bovon, François. "The Dossier on Stephen, the First Martyr." *HTR* 96 (2003): 279–315.
Bovon, François. "Mary Magdalene in the Acts of Philip." In *Which Mary? The Marys of Early Christian Tradition*, ed. F. Stanley Jones, pp. 75–90. Leiden: Brill, 2003.
Bovon, François. "The Synoptic Gospels and the Noncanonical Acts of the Apostles." *HTR* 81 (1988): 19–36.
Bowden, Hugh. "Oracles for Sale." In Peter Derow and Robert Parker, eds., *Herodotus and His World*, pp. 256–74. New York: Oxford University Press, 2003.
Bowman Thurston, Bonnie. "The Widows as the 'Altar of God.'" SBLSP 24 (1985): 279–89.
Boyarin, Daniel. *Border Lines: The Partition of Judaeo-Christianity*. Philadelphia: University of Pennsylvania, 2004.
Bradshaw, Paul. *The Search for the Origins of Christian Worship*, 2nd ed. New York: Oxford University Press, 2002.
Bremmer, Jan N. "Perpetua and Her Diary: Authenticity, Family, and Visions." In *Märtyrer und Märtyrerakten*, ed. W. Ameling, pp. 77–120. Stuttgart: Franz Steiner Verlag, 2002.
Bremmer, Jan N., ed. *The Pseudo-Clementines*. Leuven: Peeters, 2010.
Brinton, Alan. "St. Augustine and the Problem of Deception in Religious Persuasion." *RelSt* 19 (1983): 437–50.
Brock, Sebastian. "Eusebius and Syriac Christianity." In *Eusebius, Christianity, and Judaism*, ed. Harry Attridge and Gohei Hatta, pp. 212–34. Detroit: Wayne State University, 1992.
Bröcker, L. O. "Die Methoden Galens in der literarischen Kritik." *Rheinisches Museum für Philologie* 40 (1885): 415–38.
Brooks, James A. "Clement of Alexandria as a Witness to the Development of the New Testament Canon." *SecCent* 9 (1992): 41–55.

Brown, Milton P. "Notes on the Language and Style of Pseudo-Ignatius." *JBL* 83 (1964): 146–52.

Brown, Raymond. *The Birth of the Messiah: A Commentary on the Infancy Narratives in Matthew and Luke.* New York: Doubleday, 1977.

Brown, Raymond. *Community of the Beloved Disciple.* New York: Paulist, 1979.

Brown, Raymond. *The Epistles of John.* ABC. Garden City: Doubleday, 1982.

Brox, Norbert. *Falsche Verfasserangaben: zur Erklärung der frühchristlichen Pseudepigraphie.* Stuttgarter Bibelstudien, 79. Stuttgart: KBW, 1975.

Brox, Norbert. *Die Pastoralbriefe*, 4th ed. Regensburg: Pustet, 1969.

Brox, Norbert, ed. *Pseudepigraphie in der heidnischen und jüdisch-christlichen Antike.* Darmstadt: Wissenschaftliche Buchgesellschaft, 1977.

Brox, Norbert. "Pseudo-Paulus und Pseudo-Ignatius: einige Topoi altchristlicher Pseudepigraphie." *VC* 30 (1976): 181–88.

Brox, Norbert. "Quis ille auctor? Pseudonymität und Anonymität bei Salvian." *VC* 40 (1986): 55–65.

Brox, Norbert. "Situation und Sprache der Minderheit im ersten Petrusbrief." *Kairos* 19 (1977): 1–13.

Brox, Norbert. "Zu den persönlichen Notizen der Pastoralbriefe." *BZ* 13 (1969): 76–94; reprinted in *Pseudepigraphie in der heidnischen und jüdisch-christlichen Antike*, edited by eidem, pp. 272–94. Darmstadt: Wissenschaftliche Buchgesellschaft, 1977.

Brox, Norbert. "Zur pseudepigraphischen Rahmung des ersten Petrusbriefes." *BZ* 19 (1975): 78–96.

Buchheit, V. "Rufinus von Aquileja als Fälscher des Adamantiosdialogs." *ByzZ* 51 (1958): 314–28.

Buchholz, Dennis D. *Your Eyes Will Be Opened: A Study of the Greek (Ethiopic) Apocalypse of Peter.* Atlanta: Scholars Press, 1988.

Budge, E. A. W. "An Encomium on Saint John the Baptist." In *Coptic Apocrypha in the Dialect of Upper Egypt*, pp. 128–45, 335–51. Oxford: Oxford University Press, 1913.

Bujard, Walter. *Stilanalytische Untersuchungen zum Kolosserbrief: als Beitrag zur Methodik von Sprachvergleichen.* Göttingen: Vandenhoeck & Ruprecht, 1973.

Bundy, D. "The Pseudo-Ephremian *Commentary on Third Corinthians:* A Study in Exegesis and Anti-Bardaisanite Polemic." In *After Bardaisan: Studies on Continuity and Change in Syriac Christianity in Honour of Professor Han J. W. Drijvers*, ed. Gerrit J. Reinink and Alexander Cornelis Klugkist, pp. 51–63. Louvain: Peeters, 1999.

Burkitt, F. C. *Early Christianity Outside the Roman Empire.* Cambridge: Cambridge University Press, 1899.

Burkitt, F. C. *Early Eastern Christianity.* London: John Murray, 1904.

Burnet, Régis. "Pourquoi avoir écrit l'insipide épître aux Laodicéens?" *NTS* 48 (2002): 132–41.

Buschmann, Gerd. *Martyrium Polycarpi—eine formkritische Studie. Ein Beitrag zur Frage nach der Entstehung der Gattung Märtyrerakte.* BZNW 70. Berlin/New York: de Gruyter, 1994.

Byrskog, Samuel. "History or Story in Acts—A Middle Way? The 'We' Passages, Historical Intertexture, and Oral History." In *Contextualizing Acts: Lukan Narrative and Greco-Roman Discourse*, ed. Todd Penner and Caroline Vander Stichele, pp. 257–84. Atlanta: Society of Biblical Literature, 2003.

Calhoun, Robert Matthew. "The Letter of Mithridates: A Neglected Item of Ancient Epistolary Theory." In *Pseudepigraphie und Verfasserfiktion in frühchristlichen Briefen*, edited by Jörg Frey et al., pp. 295–330.

Callon, Callie. "Sorcery, Wheels, and Mirror Punishment in the *Apocalypse of Peter.*" *JECS* 18 (2010): 29–49.

Campbell, William Sanger. *The "We" Passages in the Acts of the Apostles: The Narrator as Narrative Character.* Atlanta: Society of Biblical Literature, 2007.

Campenhausen, Hans Freiherr von. "Bearbeitungen und Interpolationen des Polykarpmartyriums." SHAW 3 (1957): 5–48.

Candlish, J. S. "On the Moral Character of Pseudonymous Books." *Expositor* 4 (1891): 91–107 262–79.

Capelle, Bernard. "Les homélies 'De lectionibus euangeliorum' de Maximin l'arien." *RBén* 40 (1928): 49–86.

Capelle, Bernard. "Un homiliaire de l'évêque arien Maximin." *RBén* 34 (1922): 81–108.

Capelle, Bernard. "Le texte du 'Gloria in excelsis.'" *RHE* 44 (1949): 439–505.

Carey, Greg. "*The Ascension of Isaiah*: An Example of Early Christian Narrative Polemic. *JSP* 17 (1998): 65–78.

Casey, M. *Is John's Gospel True?* London: Routledge, 1996.

Cavallo, G., and H. Maehler. *Greek Bookhands of the Early Byzantine Period, A.D. 300–800.* London: University of London, Institute of Classical Studies, 1987.

Chambers, Edmund Kerchever. *The History and Motives of Literary Forgeries.* Burt Franklin Research & Source Works Series 508. Oxford: B. H. Blackwell, 1891; reprinted New York: Burt Franklin, 1970.

Chancey, Mark. *Greco-Roman Culture and the Galilee of Jesus.* Cambridge: Cambridge University Press, 2005.

Charles, J. Daryl. *Literary Strategy in the Epistle of Jude.* Scranton, PA: University of Scranton Press, 1993.

Clarke, Emma C., John M. Dillon, and Jackson B. Hershbell, trs. and eds. *Iamblichus: On the Mysteries.* Atlanta: Society of Biblical Literature, 2003.

Cludius, H. H. *Uransichten des Christenthums nebst Untersuchungen über einige Bücher des neuen Testaments.* Altona: Hermann Heimart, 1808.

Colish, Marcia L. "The Stoic Theory of Verbal Signification and the Problem of Lies and False Statements from Antiquity to St. Anselm." In *L'Archéologie de Signe*, edited by L. Brind'amour and E. Vance, pp. 17–43. Toronto: Institut Pontifical d'Etudes Médiévales, 1983.

Collins, John J. "The Development of the Sibylline Tradition." *ANRW* 2 20.1 (1987) 421–59.

Collins, John J. "Pseudepigraphy and Group Formation in Second Temple Judaism." In *Pseudepigraphic Perspectives: The Apocrypha and Pseudepigrapha in Light of the Dead Sea Scrolls*, edited by Esther G. Chazon and Michael Stone, pp. 43–58. Leiden: Brill, 1999.

Connolly, R. H. *Didascalia apostolorum: The Syriac Version Translated and Accompanied by the Verona Latin Fragments, with an Introduction and Notes.* Oxford: Clarendon Press, 1929.

Cook, David. "The Pastoral Fragments Reconsidered." *JTS* 35 (1984): 120–31.

Costa, C. D. N. *Greek Fictional Letters.* New York: Oxford University Press, 2001.

Côté, Dominique. "La fonction littéraire de Simon le magicien dans les Pseudo-Clémentines." *LTP* 57 (2001): 513–23.

Cothenet, Edouard. "Le Protévangile de Jacques: origine, genre et signification d'un premier midrash chrétien sur la Nativité de Marie." *ANRW* 2.25.6 (1988): 4252–69.

Courcelle, P. *Histoire littéraire des grandes invasions germaniques*, 3rd ed. Paris: Étude augustiniennes 1964.

Cribiore, Raffaella. *Gymnastics of the Mind: Greek Education in Hellenistic and Roman Egypt.* Princeton: Princeton University, 2001.

Cribiore, Raffaella. *Writing, Teachers, and Students in Graeco-Roman Egypt.* Atlanta: Scholars Press, 1996.

Crönert, W. *Kolotes und Menedemos.* Amsterdam: Adolf M. Hakkert, 1965.

Crossan, J. D. *The Cross That Spoke: The Origins of the Passion Narrative*. San Francisco: Harper & Row, 1988.

Crossan, J. D. "The Gospel of Peter and the Canonical Gospels. Independence, Dependence of Both?" *Forum*, New Series 1, 1 (1998): 7–51.

Cureton, William. *The Ancient Syriac Version of Saint Ignatius*. London: Rivington, 1845.

Czachesz, István. "The Grotesque Body in the *Apocalypse of Peter*." In *The Apocalypse of Peter*, edited by Jan Bremmer and István Czachesz, pp. 108–26. Leuven: Peeters, 2003.

Czachesz, István. "Torture in Hell and Reality: The *Visio Pauli*." In *The Visio Pauli and the Gnostic Apocalypse of Paul*, edited by Jan Bremmer and István Czachesz, pp. 130–43. Leuven: Peeters, 2007.

Daniélou, Jean. *The Ministry of Women in the Early Church*. London: Faith Press, 1961.

Daniels, Boyd Lee. "The Greek Manuscript Tradition of the Protevangelium Jacobi." Ph.D. dissertation, Duke University, 1956.

Davids, Peter H. *The Letters of 2 Peter and Jude*. Grand Rapids, MI: Eerdmans, 2006.

Davies, Stevan L. "Women, Tertullian and the Acts of Paul." *Semeia* 38 (1986): 139–43.

Davis, Stephen J. "A 'Pauline' Defense of Women's Right to Baptize? Intertextuality and Apostolic Authority in the Acts of Paul." *JECS* 8 (2000): 453–59.

de Jonge, M. *Pseudepigrapha of the Old Testament as Part of Christian Literature: The Case of the Testaments of the Twelve Patriarchs and the Greek Life of Adam and Eve*. Leiden: Brill, 2003.

de Labriolle, Pierre. *La réaction païenne: étude sur la polémique antichrétienne du Ier au VIe siècle*. Paris: L'artisan du Livre, 1934.

de Strycker, Emile. *La Forme la plus ancienne du Protévangile de Jacques*. Brussels: Société des Bollandistes, 1961.

de Zwaan, J. "Date and Origin of the Epistle of the Eleven Apostles." In *Amicitiae Corolla: A Volume of Essays Presented to James Rendel Harris, D.Litt., on the Occasion of His Eightieth Birthday*, edited by H. G. Wood, pp. 344–55. London: University of London Press, 1933.

Dechow, Jon. *Dogma and Mysticism in Early Christianity: Epiphanius of Cyprus and the Legacy of Origen*. Patristic Monograph Series, 13. Macon: GA: Mercer, 1988.

DeConick, April. *The Original Gospel of Thomas in Translation*. London: T&T Clark, 2006.

DeConick, April, and Jarl Fossum. "Stripped Before God: A New Interpretation of Logion 37 in the Gospel of Thomas." *VC* 45 (1991): 123–50.

Dehandschutter, B. "The Martyrium Polycarpi: A Century of Research." *ANRW* 2.27.1, (1933): 485–522.

DeMaris, Richard. *Colossian Controversy: Wisdom in Dispute at Colossae*. Sheffield: Sheffield University Press, 1994.

Denker, Jürgen. *Die theologiegeschichtliche Stellung des Petrusevangeliums: Ein Beitrag zur Frühgeschichte des Doketismus*. Europäische Hochschulschriften 23. Frankfurt: Peter Lang, 1975.

Dibelius, Martin. *James: A Commentary on the Epistle of James*. Translated by Michael W. Williams. Hermeneia. Philadelphia: Fortress Press, 1976.

Dieterich, Albrecht. *Nekyia; Beiträge zur Erklärung der neuentdeckten Petrusapokalypse*. Leipzig: Teubner, 1893.

Doering, Lutz. "Apostle, Co-Elder, and Witness of Suffering: Author Construction and Peter Image in First Peter." In *Pseudepigraphie und Verfasserfiktion in frühchristlichen Briefen*, edited by Jörge Frey et al., pp. 645–81.

Donelson, Lewis R. *Pseudepigraphy and Ethical Argument in the Pastoral Epistles*. Tübingen: Mohr Siebeck, 1986.

Draguet, R. "Un commentaire grec arien sur Job." *RHE* 20 (1924): 38–65.

Drake, Hal. *Constantine and the Bishops: The Politics of Intolerance*. Baltimore: Johns Hopkins University Press, 2002.

Drey, Johann Sebastian von. "Über die apostolischen Constitutionen, oder neue Untersuchungen über die Bestandtheile, Entstehung und Zusammensetzung, und den kirchlichen Werth dieser alten Schrift." *TQ* 11 (1829): 397–477.

Drijvers, Han J. W. "Adam and the True Prophet in the Pseudo-Clementines." In *Loyalitätskonflikte in der Religionsgeschichte, FS Carsten Colpe*, edited by Christoph Elsas and Hans Kippenberg, pp. 314–23. Würzburg: Königshausen und Neumann, 1990.

Drijvers, Han J. W. "Addai und Mani: Christentum und Manichäismus im Dritten Jahrhundert in Syrien." In *IIIo Symposium Syriacum, 1980: Les contacts du monde syriaque avec les autres cultures (Goslar 7–11 Septembre 1980)*, edited by René Lavenant, pp. 171–85. OrChrAn 221. Roma: Pontificium Institutum Studiorum Orientalium, 1983.

Drijvers, Han J. W. "Facts and Problems in Early Syriac Speaking Christianity." *SecCent* 2 (1982): 157–75.

Dubois, Jean-Daniel. "Contribution à l'interprétation de la Paraphrase de Sem." In *Deuxième journée d'études coptes*, pp. 150–60. Louvain: Peeters, 1986.

Dubois, Jean-Daniel, and Rémi Gounelle. "Lettre de Pilate à l'empereur Claude." In *Écrits apocryphes chrétiens*, vol. 2, edited by Pierre Geoltrain and Jean-Daniel Kaestli, pp. 357–63. Paris: Gallimard, 2005.

Duff, Jeremy N. "P46 and the Pastorals: A Misleading Consensus." *NTS* 44 (1998): 578–90.

Duff, Jeremy N. "A Reconsideration of Pseudepigraphy in Early Christianity." Ph.D. thesis, University of Oxford, 1998.

Dunn, James D. G. *The Epistles to the Colossians and to Philemon*. NIGTC. Grand Rapids, MI: Eerdmans, 1996.

Dunn, James D. G. *The Living Word*. Philadelphia: Fortress, 1988.

Edwards, Mark J. "The *Clementina*: A Christian Response to the Pagan Novel." *CQ* 42 (1992): 459–74.

Edwards, Mark J. "Ignatius and the Second Century: An Answer to R Hübner." *ZAC* 2 (1998): 214–26.

Edwards, Mark J., Martin Goodman, and Simon Price, eds. *Apologetics in the Roman Empire: Pagans, Jews, and Christians*. Oxford: Oxford University Press, 1999.

Ehrman, Bart D. *The Apostolic Fathers*. LCL 24. Cambridge, MA: Harvard University Press, 2003.

Ehrman, Bart D. *The Orthodox Corruption of Scripture: The Effect of Early Christological Controversies on the Text of the New Testament*, 2nd ed. New York: Oxford University Press, 2011.

Ehrman, Bart D., and Zlatko Pleše, *Apocryphal Gospels: Texts and Translations*. New York: Oxford University Press, 2011.

Eichhorn, J. G. *Einleitung in das Neue Testament*. 3 vols.. Leipzig: Weidmannischen Buchhandlung, 1804–1814.

Elliott, John H. *Home for the Homeless: A Sociological Exegesis of 1 Peter, Its Situation and Strategy*. Philadelphia: Fortress, 1981.

Elliott, John H. "Peter, First Epistle of." *ABD* 5. 269–78.

Elliott, John H. "Peter, Second Epistle of." *ABD* 5. 282–87.

Elliott, John H. "The Rehabilitation of an Exegetical Step-Child: 1 Peter in Recent Research." *JBL* 95 (1976): 243–54.

Epp, Eldon J. "Issues in the Interrelation of New Testament Textual Criticism and Canon." In *The Canon Debate: On the Origins and Formation of the Bible*, edited by Lee M. McDonald and James A. Sanders, pp. 485–515. Peabody, MA: Hendrickson, 2002; reprinted in E. Epp, *Perspectives on New Testament Textual Criticism: Collected Essays 1962–2004* (Leiden: Brill, 2005), 596–639.

Ewald, Heinrich. *Die Sendschreiben des Apostel Paulus*. Göttingen: Dieterisch, 1857.

Faivre, A. "Apostolicité et pseudo-apostolicité dans la 'Constitution ecclésiastique des apôtres': L'art de faire parler les origines," *RevScRel* 66 (1992): 19–67.

Fee, Gordon D. *The First Epistle to the Corinthians*. Grand Rapids, MI: Eerdmans, 1987.

Fee, Gordon D. *1 and 2 Timothy, Titus*. NIBCNT. Peabody, MA: Hendrickson, 1988.

Feehan, Thomas D. "Augustine on Lying and Deception." *AugStud* 19 (1988): 131–39.

Feehan, Thomas D. "Augustine's Own Examples of Lying." *AugStud* 22 (1991): 165–90.

Feehan, Thomas D. "The Morality of Lying in St. Augustine." *AugStud* 21 (1990): 67–81.

Feldman, Louis. *Jew and Gentile in the Ancient World: Attitudes and Interactions from Alexander to Justinian*. Princeton: Princeton University, 1993.

Feldman, Louis. *Josephus's Interpretation of the Bible*. Hellenistic Culture and Society 27. Berkeley: University of California Press, 1998.

Fenton, J. C. "Pseudonymity in the New Testament." *Theology* 58 (1955): 51–56.

Ficker, Gerhard. *Studien zu Vigilius von Thapsus*. Leipzig: Johann Ambrosius Barth, 1897.

Fideler, David R. "Introduction." In *The Pythagorean Sourcebook and Library: An Anthology of Ancient Writings Which Relate to Pythagoras and Pythagorean Philosophy*, compiled and translated by Kenneth Sylvan Guthrie. Grand Rapids: Phanes Press, 1987.

Fischer, Karl Martin. "Anmerkungen zur Pseudepigraphie im Neuen Testament." *NTS* 23 (1967): 76–81.

Fischer, Karl Martin, and Hans Martin Schenke. *Einleitung in das Neue Testament*. Berlin: Evangelische Verlagsanstalt, 1973.

Fitzmyer, Joseph A. *The Gospel According to Luke*, 2 vols. ABC. New York: Doubleday, 1981–1985.

Flower, Michael A. *The Seer in Ancient Greece*. Berkeley: University of California Press, 2008.

Fonrobert, Charlotte Elisheva. "The Didascalia Apostolorum: A Mishnah for the Disciples of Jesus." *JECS* 9 (2001): 483-509.

Foskett, Mary. *A Virgin Conceived: Mary and Classical Representations of Virginity*. Bloomington: Indiana University Press, 2002.

Foster, Paul. *The Gospel of Peter: Introduction, Critical Edition, and Commentary*. Leiden: Brill, 2010.

Foster, Paul. "The Writings of Justin Martyr and the So-Called Gospel of Peter." In *Justin Martyr and His Worlds*, edited by Sara Parvis and Paul Foster, pp. 104–21. Minneapolis: Fortress, 2007.

Frank, Nicole. "Der Kolosserbrief und die 'Philosophia': Pseudepigraphie als Spiegel frühchristlicher Auseinandersetzungen um die Auslegung des paulinischen Erbes." Pages 411–32 in *Pseudepigraphie und Verfasserfiktion in frühchristlichen Briefen*, edited by Jörg Frey et al., 2009.

Frenschkowski, M. "Erkannte Pseudepigraphie?" Pages 181–32 in *Pseudepigraphie und Verfasserfiktion in frühchristlichen Briefen*, edited by Jörg Frey et al., 2009.

Frey, Albert. "Protévangile de Jacques." In *Écrits apocryphes chrétiens*, vol. 1, edited by François Bovon and Pierre Geoltrain, pp. 73–80. Paris: Gallimard, 1997.

Frey, Jörg. "Autorfiktion und Gegnerbild im Judasbrief und im Zweiten Petrusbrief." In *Pseudepigraphie und Verfasserfiktion in frühchristlichen Briefen*, edited by Jörg Frey et al., 2009.

Frey, Jörg, Jens Herzer, Martina Janssen, and Clare K. Rothschild, eds. *Pseudepigraphie und Verfasserfiktion in frühchristlichen Briefen*. WUNT 246. Tübingen: Mohr Siebeck, 2009.

Fuchs, Rüdiger. *Unerwartete Unterschiede: Müssen wir unsere Ansichten über "die" Pastoralbriefe revidieren?* Wuppertal: R. Brockhaus Verlag, 2003.

Funk, Franz X. *Die Apostolischen Konstitutionen. Eine literar-historische Untersuchung*. Rottenburg: W. Bader, 1891.

Funk, Robert, Roy W. Hoover, and the Jesus Seminar, eds. *The Five Gospels: The Search for the Authentic Words of Jesus*. New York: Macmillan, 1993.

Funkelstein, Amos. *Perceptions of Jewish History.* Los Angeles: University of California Press, 1993.

Furnish, Victor Paul. "Colossians, Epistle to the." *ABD* 1090–96.

Furnish, Victor Paul. "Ephesians, Epistle to the." *ABD* 2.535–42.

Fürst, Alfons, Therese Fuhrer, Folker Siegert, and Peter Walter. *Der apokryphe Briefwechsel zwischen Seneca und Paulus.* Scripta Antiquitatis Posterioris ad Ethicam Religionemque pertinentia XI. Tübingen: Mohr Siebeck, 2006.

Gager, John G. *The Origins of Anti-Semitism: Attitudes Toward Judaism in Pagan and Christian Antiquity.* New York: Oxford University Press, 1983.

Gager, John G. "Some Attempts to Label the Oracula Sibyllina Book 7." *HTR* 65 (1972): 91–97.

Gamble, Harry Y. "Pseudonymity and the New Testament Canon." In *Pseudepigraphie und Verfasserfiktion in frühchristlichen Briefen,* edited by Jörg Frey et al., pp. 333–62.

Geffcken, Johannes. *Komposition und Entstehungszeit der Oracula Sibyllina.* Leipzig: J. C. Hinrichs, 1902.

Gero, Stephen. "The Infancy Gospel of Thomas: A Study of the Textual and Literary Problems." *NovT* 13 (1971): 46–80.

Gero, Stephen. "With Walter Bauer on the Tigris: Encratite Orthodoxy and Libertine Heresy in Syro-Mesopotamian Christianity." In *Nag Hammadi, Gnosticism, and Early Christianity,* edited by Charles W. Hedrick and Robert Hodgson, pp. 287–307. Peabody, MA: Hendrickson, 1986.

Gese, Michael. *Das Vermächtnis des Apostels: Die Rezeption der paulinischen Theologie im Epheserbrief.* WUNT 2.99. Tübingen: Mohr Siebeck, 1997.

Gibson, E. Leigh. "Jewish Antagonism or Christian Polemic: The Case of the Martyrdom of Pionius." *JECS* 9 (2001): 339–58.

Gill, Christopher. "Plato on Falsehood—not Fiction." In *Lies and Fiction in the Ancient World,* edited by Christopher Gill and T. P. Wiseman, pp. 38–87. Austin: University of Texas Press, 1993.

Glasson, T. F. "The Gospel of Thomas, Saying 3, and Deuteronomy XXX.11–14." *ExpTim* 78 (1976–77): 151–52.

Goppelt, L. *A Commentary on 1 Peter.* Grand Rapids, MI: Eerdmans, 1993.

Görgemanns, Herwig. "Epistolography." *Brill's New Pauly,* ed. Anne-Marie Wittke. Leiden: Brill, 2010.

Gottschalk, H. B. *Heraclides of Pontus.* Oxford: Clarendon Press, 1980.

Gounelle, Rémi. "Évangile de Nicodème ou Actes de Pilate." In *Écrits apocryphes chrétien,* edited by Pierre Geoltrain and Jean-Daniel Kaestli, pp. 251–59. Paris: Éditions Gallimard, 2005.

Gounelle, Rémi. "Rapport de Pilate, réponse de Tibère à Pilate, comparution de Pilate." In *Écrits apocryphes chrétiens,* vol. 2, ed. Pierre Geoltrain and Jean-Daniel Kaestli, pp. 303–4, 306–7. Paris: Gallimard, 2005.

Gounelle, Rémi, and Zbigniew Izydorczyk. *L'Évangile de Nicodème ou Les Actes fait sous Ponce Pilate.* Belgium: Brepols, 1997.

Grafton, Anthony. *Forgers and Critics: Creativity and Duplicity in Western Scholarship.* Princeton, NJ: Princeton University Press, 1990.

Grant, Robert M. "The Appeal to the Early Fathers." *JTS* 11 (1960): 13–24.

Grant, Robert M. *Heresy and Criticism: The Search for Authenticity in Early Christian Literature.* Louisville, KY: Westminster, 1993.

Grant, Robert M. "The Religion of Maximin Daia." In *Christianity, Judaism, and Other Greco-Roman Cults,* edited by J. Neusner, pp. 143–66. Leiden: Brill, 1975.

Grébaut, S. "Littérature éthiopienne ps. Clémentine. La seconde venue du Christ et la resurrection des morts." *Revue de l'Orient Chrétien* (1907): 139–51; (1910): 198–214, 307–23, 425–39.

Greschat, Katharina. "Justins 'Denkwürdigkeiten der Apostel' und das Petrusevangelium." In *Das Evangelium nach Petrus: Text, Kontexte, Intertexte*, edited by Thomas J. Kraus and Tobias Nicklas, pp. 197–214. TU 158. Berlin: de Gruyter, 2007.

Griffiths, Paul J. *Lying: An Augustinian Theology of Duplicity*. Grand Rapids, MI: Brazos Press, 2004.

Griffiths, Sidney. "The *Doctrina Addai* as a Paradigm of Christian Thought in Edessa in the Fifth Century." *Hugoye* 6.2 (2003).

Gryson, Roger. *The Ministry of Women in the Early Church*. Collegeville, MN: Liturgical Press, 1976.

Gudeman, Alfred. "Literary Frauds Among the Greeks." In *Classical Studies in Honor of Henry Drisler*, pp. 52–74. New York, London: Macmillan, 1894.

Gudeman, Alfred. "Literary Frauds Among the Romans." *Transactions and Proceedings of the American Philological Association* 25 (1894): 140–64.

Guerrier, Louis, and Sylvain Grébaut. *Le testament en Galilée de notre-Seigneur Jésus Christ*. Paris: Firmin-Didot, 1912.

Gunkel, Hermann. *Schöpfung und Chaos in Urzeit und Endzeit: eine religionsgeschichtliche Untersuchung über Gen. 1 und Ap. Joh. 12*. Göttingen: Vandenhoeck and Ruprecht, 1895.

Gunther, John J. "The Meaning and Origin of the Name 'Judas Thomas.'" *Mus* 93 (1980): 113–48.

Gunther, John J. *St. Paul's Opponents and Their Background*. Leiden: Brill, 1973.

Haefner, A. "A Unique Source for the Study of Ancient Pseudonymity." *Anglican Theological Review* 16 (1934): 8–15.

Häfner, Gerd. "Das Corpus Pastorale als literarisches Konstrukt." *TQ* 187 (2007): 258–73.

Hagedorn, Dieter. *Der Hiobkommentar des Arianers Julian*. Berlin: Walter de Gruyter, 1973.

Hahneman, Geoffrey Mark. *The Muratorian Fragment and the Development of the Canon*. Oxford: Clarendon Press, 1992.

Hall, Robert G. "The *Ascension of Isaiah*: Community Situation, Date, and Place in Early Christianity." *JBL* 109 (1990): 289–306.

Hammond Bammel, Caroline. "Ignatian Problems." *JTS* 33 (1982): 66–97.

Hannah, Darrell D. "The Ascension of Isaiah and Docetic Christology." *VC* 53 (1999): 165–96.

Hannah, Darrell D. "Isaiah's Vision in the Ascension of Isaiah and the Early Church." *JTS* 50 (1999): 80–101.

Hannah, Jack W. "The Setting of the Ignatian Long Recension." *JBL* 79 (1960): 221–38.

Hanson, Ann Ellis. "Galen: Author and Critic." In *Editing Texts, Texte edieren*, edited by Glenn W. Most, pp. 22–53. Göttingen: Vandenhoeck & Ruprecht, 1998.

Hanson, R. P. C. *Allegory and Event: A Study of the Sources and Significance of Origen's Interpretation of Scripture*. Richmond, VA: John Knox, 1959.

Harnack, Adolf von. *Apocrypha IV. Die apokryphen Briefe des Paulus an die Laodicener und Korinther*, 2nd. Ed. Berlin: de Gruyter, 1931.

Harnack, Adolf von. *Bruchstücke des Evangeliums und der Apokalypse des Petrus*. Leipzig: J. C. Hinrichs, 1893.

Harnack, Adolf von. *Die Chronologie der altchristlichen Litteratur bis Eusebius*. Leipzig: J. C. Hinrichs, 1897–1904.

Harnack, Adolf von. *Geschichte der altchristlichen Literatur bis Eusebius, vols. 1–2*. Leipzig: J. C. Hinrichs, 1958; original 1897.

Harnack, Adolf von. *Die Lehre der zwölf Apostel nebst Untersuchungen zur ältesten Geschichte der Kirchenverfassung und des Kirchenrechts. TU 2.1* Leipzig: J. Hinrichs, 1984.

Harnack, Adolf von. *Marcion: Das Evangelium vom fremden Gott; eine Monographie zur Geschichte der Grundlegung der Katholischen Kirche*. Leipzig: J. Hinrichs, 1924.

Harnack, Adolf von. "Review of James Westfall Thompson, 'The Alleged Persecution.'" *TLZ* 3 (1913): 74–77.

Harnack, Adolf von. "'We' and 'I' Passages in Luke-Acts." *NTS* 3 (1957): 128–32.

Harris, William. *Ancient Literacy*. Cambridge, MA: Harvard University Press, 1989.

Harrison, P. N. *The Problem of the Pastoral Epistles*. Oxford: Oxford University Press, 1921.

Haufe, Günter. "Gnostische Irrlehre und ihre Abwehr in den Pastoralbriefen." In *Gnosis und Neues Testament: Studien aus Religionswissenschaft und Theologie*, edited by Karl-Wolfgang Tröger, pp. 325–99. Güterslow: Gütersloher Verlagshaus Mohn, 1973.

Havelaar, Henriette W., ed. *The Coptic Apocalypse of Peter (Nag-Hammadi Codex VII, 3)*. Berlin: Akademie Verlag, 1999.

Heffernan, Thomas J. "Philology and Authorship in the *Passio Sanctorum Perpetuae et Felicitatis*." *Traditio* 50 (1995): 315–25.

Hengel, Martin. "Anonymität, Pseudepigraphie und 'Literarische Fälschung' in der Jüdisch-Hellenistischen Literatur." In *Pseudepigrapha I: Pseudopythagorica, Lettres de Platon, Littérature pseudépigraphique juive*, edited by Kurt von Fritz, pp. 231–308. Vandoeuvres-Genève: Fondation Hardt pour l'Étude de l'Antiquité Classique, 1972.

Hengel, Martin. *The Four Gospels and the One Gospel of Jesus Christ: An Investigation of the Collection and Origin of the Canonical Gospels*. London: SCM Press, 2000.

Hengel, Martin. "Der Jakobusbrief als antipaulinische Polemik." In *Tradition and Interpretation in the NT: Essays in Honor of E. Earle Ellis*, edited by G. Hawthorne and Otto Betz, pp. 248–78. Grand Rapids, MI: Eerdmans, 1987.

Henne, P. "La datation du Canon de Muratori." *RB* 100 (1993): 54–75.

Hercer, R. *Epistolographi Graeci*. Paris: A. F. Didot, 1873; reprinted Amsterdam: A. M. Hakkert, 1965.

Herzer, Jens. "Fiction oder Tauschung? Zur Diskussion über die Pseudepigraphie der Pastoralbriefe." In *Pseudepigraphie und Verfasserfiktion in frühchristlichen Briefen*, edited by Jörg Frey et al., pp. 489–536.

Herzer, Jens. *Petrus oder Paulus? Studien über das Verhältnis des Ersten Petrusbriefes zur paulinischen Tradition*. Tübingen: Mohr Siebeck, 1998.

Herzer, Jens. "Rearranging the 'House' of God: A New Perspective on the Pastoral Epistles." In *Empsychoi logoi—Religious Innovations in Antiquity: Studies in Honour of Pieter Willem van der Horst*, edited by Alberdina Houtman, A. F. De Jong, and M. Misset-Van De Weg, pp. 547–66. Leiden: Brill, 2008.

Hezser, Catherine. *Jewish Literacy in Roman Palestine*. Tübingen: Mohr Siebeck, 2001.

Hilgenfeld, A. "Die beiden Briefe an die Thessalonicher." *ZWT* 5 (1862): 225–64.

Hilgenfeld, A. "Das Petrus-Evangelium über Leiden und Auferstehung Jesu." *ZNW* 36 (1893): 439–54.

Hilhorst, Anthony. "The *Apocalypse of Paul*: Previous History and Afterlife." In *The Visio Pauli and the Gnostic Apocalypse of Paul*, edited by Jan Bremmer and István Czachesz, pp. 1–22. Leuven: Peeters, 2007.

Hilhorst, Anthony. "The *Epistola Anne ad Senecam*: Jewish or Christian?" in G. J. M. Bartelink et al., eds., *Eulogia. mélanges offerts à Antoon A.R. Bastiaensen à l'occasion de son soixante-cinquième anniversaire*, pp. 147–61. Steenbrugge: Abbatia S. Petri, 1991.

Hilhorst, Anthony. "Tertullian on the Acts of Paul." In *The Apocryphal Acts of Paul and Thecla*, edited by Jan Bremmer, pp. 150–63. Kampen: Pharos, 1996.

Hill, Charles E. "The Debate over the Muratorian Fragment and the Development of the Canon." *WTJ* 57 (1995): 437–52.

Hill, Charles E. "The *Epistula Apostolorum*: An Asian Tract from the Time of Polycarp." *JECS* 7 (1999): 1–53.

Hills, Julian. *Tradition and Composition in the Epistula Apostolorum*. Minneapolis: Fortress, 1990.

Hock, Ronald. *The Infancy Gospels of James and Thomas*. Santa Rosa, CA: Polebridge, 1995.

Hoehner, Harold W. *Ephesians: An Exegetical Commentary*. Grand Rapids, MI: Baker, 2002.

Holland, Glenn S. "'A Letter Supposedly from Us': A Contribution to the Discussion About the Authorship of 2 Thessalonians." In *The Thessalonian Correspondence*, edited by Raymond F. Collins, pp. 94–402. Leuven: Peters, 1990.

Holtzmann, Heinrich J. *Lehrbuch der historisch-kritischen Einleitung in das Neuen Testament*, 3rd ed. Freiburg: Mohr Siebeck, 1892.

Holtzmann, Heinrich J. *Die Pastoralbriefe, kritisch und exegetisch behandelt*. Leipzig: Englemann, 1880.

Honigman, Sylvie. *The Septuagint and Homeric Scholarship in Alexandria: A Study in the Narrative of the Letter of Aristeas*. London: Routledge, 2003.

Hooker, Morna. "Were There False Teachers in Colossae?" In *Christ and the Spirit in the New Testament*, edited by Barnabas Lindars and Stephen S. Smalley, pp. 315–31. Cambridge: Cambridge University Press, 1973.

Hopfner, Theodor. *Über die Geheimlehren von Jamblichus*. Leipzig: Theosophisches Verlagshaus, 1922.

Hornschuh, Manfred. *Studien zur Epistula Apostolorum*. Berlin: De Gruyter, 1965.

Hose, M. *Kleine griechische Literaturgeschichte*. Munich: C. H. Beck, 1999.

Hovhanessian, Vahan. *Third Corinthians: Reclaiming Paul for Christian Orthodoxy*. New York: Peter Lang, 2000.

Hübner, R. M. "Thesen zur Echtheit und Datierung der sieben Briefe des Ignatius Antiochien." *ZAC* 1 (1997): 44–72.

Hughes, Frank Witt. *Early Christian Rhetoric and 2 Thessalonians*. JSNTSup, 30. Sheffield: Sheffield Academic Press, 1989.

Hüneburg, Martin. "Paulus versus Paulus: Der Epheserbrief als Korrektur des Kolosserbriefes." In *Pseudepigraphie und Verfasserfiktion in frühchristlichen Briefen*, edited by Jörg Frey et al., pp. 387–409.

Hunzinger, Claus-Hunno. "Babylon als Deckname für Rom. und die Datierung des 1 Petrusbriefes." In *Gottes Wort und Gottes Land*, edited by Henning Graf Reventlow, pp. 67–77. Göttingen: Vandenhoeck & Ruprecht, 1965.

Izydorczyk, Z. *The Medieval Gospel of Nicodemus: Texts, Intertexts, and Contexts in Western Europe*. Medieval and Renaissance Texts and Studies, 158. Tempe: Arizona State University, 1997.

Jackson-McCabe, Matt. *Logos and Law in the Letter of James: The Law of Nature, the Law of Moses, and the Law of Freedom*. Leiden: Brill, 2001.

Jackson-McCabe, Matt. "The Politics of Pseudepigraphy and the Letter of James." In *Pseudepigraphie und Verfasserfiktion in frühchristlichen Briefen*, edited by Jörg Frey et al., pp. 599–623.

James, Montague R. "A New Text of the Apocalypse of Peter." *JTS* 12 (1910/11): 36–54, 362–83, 573–83.

Janssen, Martina. *Unter falschem Namen: Eine kritische Forschungbilanz frühchristlicher Pseudepigraphie*. Frankfurt: Peter Lang, 2003.

Janssen, Martina. "Antike (Selbst-)Aussagen über Beweggründe zur Pseudepigraphie." In *Pseudepigraphie und Verfasserfiktion in frühchristlichen Briefen*, edited by Jörg Frey et al., pp. 125–79.

Jewett, Robert. *The Thessalonian Correspondence*. Philadelphia: Fortress, 1986.

Johnson, Luke Timothy. *The First and Second Letters to Timothy*. ABC 35A. New York: Doubleday, 2001.

Johnson, Luke Timothy. "First Timothy 1,1–20: The Shape of the Struggle." In *1 Timothy Reconsidered*, edited by Karl Paul Donfried, pp. 19–39. Leuven: Peeters, 2008.

Johnson, Luke Timothy. *The Letter of James*. ABC 37A. New York: Doubleday, 1995.
Johnson, Luke Timothy. "II Timothy and the Polemic against False Teachers: A Reexamination." *JRelS* 6 (1978): 1–26.
Johnston, Steve. "La Correspondance apocryphe entre Paul et les Corinthiens: un Pseudépigraphe paulinien au service de la polémique anti-gnostique de la fin du II siècle." M.A. thesis, University of Laval, 2004.
Joly, Robert. *Le Dossier d'Ignace d'Antioche*. Université libre de Bruxelles, Faculté de Philosophie et Lettres 69. Brussels: Éditions de l'université de Bruxelles, 1979.
Jones, F. Stanley. "An Ancient Jewish Christian Rejoinder to Luke's Acts of the Apostles: Pseudo-Clementine *Recognitions* 1.27–71." *Semeia* 80 (1997): 223–45.
Jones, F. Stanley. *An Ancient Jewish Christian Source on the History of Christianity Pseudo-Clementine "Recognitions" 1.27–71*. SBL Texts and Translations 37, Christian Apocrypha Series 2. Atlanta, GA: Scholars Press, 1995.
Jones, F. Stanley. "Introduction to the *Pseudo-Clementines*." In *Pseudoclementina Elchasaiticaque inter Judaeochristiana: Collected Studies*. Edited by eidem. Orientalia Lovaniensia Analecta 203; Leuven: Peeters, in press.
Jones, F. Stanley. "Jewish Christianity of the *Pseudo-Clementines*." In *Companion to Second-Century Christian 'Heretics,'* edited by Antti Marjanen and Petri Luomanen, pp. 315–34. Leiden: Brill, 2005.
Jones, F. Stanley. "Marcionism in the Pseudo-Clementines." In *Poussières de christianisme et de judaïsme antiques*, edited by A. Frey and R. Gounelle, pp. 225–44. Prahins: Editions du Zèbre, 2007.
Jones, F. Stanley. "The Pseudo-Clementines: A History of Research." *SecCent* 2 (1982): 1–33, 63–96.
Jülicher, A. and E. Fascher. *Einleitung in das NT*, 7th ed. Tübingen: J. C. B. Mohr, 1931.
Kaestli, Jean-Daniel. "Mémoire et pseudépigraphie dans le christianisme." *Revue de théologie et de philosophie* 125 (1993): 41–63.
Kaestli, Jean-Daniel. "La place du Fragment de Muratori dans l'histoire du canon. À propos de la thèse de Sundberg et Hahneman." *Cristianesimo nella storia* 15 (1994): 609–34.
Karris, Robert J. "The Background and Significance of the Polemic of the Pastoral Epistles." *JBL* 92 (1973): 549–63.
Keim, Theodor. *Aus dem Urchristenthum: geschichtliche Untersuchungen*. Zurich: Orell Fsli, 1978.
Keith, Chris. *The Pericope Adulterae, the Gospel of John, and the Literacy of Jesus*. Leiden: E. J. Brill, 2009.
Kelley, Nicole. *Knowledge and Religious Authority in the Pseudo-Clementines: Situating the Recognitions in Fourth Century Syria*. Tübingen: Mohr Siebeck, 2006.
Kelley, Nicole. "Problems of Knowledge and Authority in the Pseudo-Clementine Romance of *Recognitions*." *JECS* 13 (2005): 315–48.
Keresztes, Paul. "The Emperor Antoninus Pius and the Christians." *JEH* 22 (1971): 1–18.
Kern, F. H. *Der Charackter und Ursprung des Briefs Jakobi*. Tübingen: Fues, 1835.
Kertelge, K. *Gemeinde und Amt im Neuen Testament*. München: Kösel, 1972.
Kiley, Mark. *Colossians as Pseudepigraphy*. Sheffield: JSOT Press, 1986.
Kirk, Alan. "The Johannine Jesus in the Gospel of Peter: A Social Memory Approach." In *Jesus in Johannine Tradition*, edited by R. T. Fortna and T. Thatcher, pp. 313–22. Louisville, KY: Westminster John Knox, 2001.
Klijn, A. F. J. "The Apocryphal Correspondence between Paul and the Corinthians." *VC* 17 (1963): 2–23.
Knight, Jonathan. *Disciples of the Beloved One: The Christology, Social Setting and Theological Context of the Ascension of Isaiah*. JSPSup 18. Sheffield: Sheffield Academic Press, 1996.

Knust, Jennifer. *Abandoned to Lust: Sexual Slander and Ancient Christianity.* New York: Columbia University, 2005.

Konradt, Matthias. "'Jakobus, der Gerechte': Erwägungen zur Verfasserfiktion des Jakobusbriefes." In *Pseudepigraphie und Verfasserfiktion in frühchristlichen Briefen,* edited by Jörg Frey et al., pp. 575–96.

Konradt, Matthias. "Der Jakobusbrief als Brief des Jakobus." In *Der Jakobusbrief: Beiträge zur Rehabilitierung der "strohernen Epistel,"* edited by Petra von Gemünden, Matthias Konradt, and Gerd Theissen, pp. 16–53. Münster: Lit Verlag, 2003.

Kopecek, Thomas A. "Review of Marcel Metzger, *Les Constitutions Apostoliques,* vol. 1." *JTS* 38 (1987): 209.

Koschorke, Klaus. *Die Polemik der Gnostiker gegen das kirchliche Christentum.* Leiden: Brill, 1978.

Kotrc, Ronald F., and K. R. Walters. "A Bibliography of the Galenic Corpus." *Transactions and Studies of the College of Physicians of Philadelphia* 5.1 (1979): 256–304.

Kraemer, Ross, and Shira L. Lander. "Perpetua and Felicitas." In *The Early Christian World,* vol. 2, edited by Philip Esler, pp. 1048–65. Routledge Worlds Series. London: Taylor & Francis, 2000.

Kraus, Thomas J., and Tobias Nicklas, eds. *Das Petrusevangelium und die Petrusapokalypse: Die griechischen Fragmente mit deutscher und englischer Übersetzung.* Berlin: de Gruyter, 2004.

Krauter, Stefan. "Was ist 'schlechte' Pseudepigraphie? Mittel, Wirkung und Intention von Pseudepigraphie in den Epistolae Senecae ad Paulum et Pauli ad Senecam." In *Pseudepigraphie und Verfasserfiktion in frühchristlichen Briefen,* edited by Jörg Frey et al., pp. 765–85.

Krentz, Edgar. "A Stone That Will Not Fit: The Non-Pauline Authorship of Second Thessalonians." In *Pseudepigraphie und Verfasserfiktion in frühchristlichen Briefen,* edited by Jörg Frey et al., pp. 439–70.

Krentz, Edgar. "Thessalonians, First and Second Epistles to the." *ABD* 6.517–23.

Krusch, B. "Reimser Remigius Fälschungen." *Neues Archiv Gesellschaft für ältere deutsche Geschichtskunde* 20 (1895): 531–37.

Lambert, David. "The Pseudonymity of Salvian's Timothy ad Ecclesiam." *StPatr* 38 (2001): 422–428.

Lambot, C. "L'écrit attribute à S. Augustin *Adversus Fulgentium Donatistam.*" *RBén* 58 (1948): 177–222.

Lampe, G. W. H. "The Trial of Jesus in the Acta Pilati." In *Jesus and the Politics of His Day,* edited by E. Bammel, pp. 173–82. Cambridge: Cambridge University Press, 1984.

Laub, Franz. "Falsche Verfasserangaben in neutestamentlichen Schriften: Aspekte der gegenwärtigen Diskussion um die neutestamentliche Pseudepigraphie." *TTZ* 89 (1980): 228–41.

Lechner, Thomas. *Ignatius adversus Valentinianos? Chronologische und theologiegeschichtliche Studien zu den Briefen des Ignatius von Antiochen.* VCSup, 47. Leiden: Brill, 1999.

Legras, Bernard. "La sanction du plagiat littéraire en droit grec et hellénistique." In *Symposion 1999 (Pazo de Mariñan, 6–9 septembre 1999),* edited by E. Cantarella and G. Thür, pp. 443–61. Cologne-Weimar-Vienne: Böhlau, 2003.

Leipoldt, Johannes. *Das Evangelium nach Thomas.* TU 101. Berlin: Akademie Verlag, 1967.

Lémonon, Jean-Pierre. *Pilate et le gouvernement de la Judée: textes et monuments.* Paris: J. Gabalda, 1981.

Leppä, Outi. *The Making of Colossians: A Study on the Formation and Purpose of a Deutero-Pauline Letter.* Göttingen: Vandenhoeck & Ruprecht, 2003.

Leutholf, J. *Ad suam Historiam Aethiopicam antehac editam Commentarius.* Frankfurt am Main, 1691.

Lewis, F. W. "Note on the Date of the First Epistle of Peter." *The Expositor* 5, 10 (1899): 319–20.

Liénard, Édmond. "Sur la Correspondance Apocryphe de Sénèque et de Saint-Paul." *RBPh* 11 (1932): 5–23.

Lienhard, Joseph. *Contra Marcellum: Marcellus of Ancyra and Fourth-Century Theology.* Washington, DC: Catholic University of America, 1999.

Lieu, Judith. *I, II, and III John: A Commentary*. NTL. Louisville, KY: Westminster John Knox, 2008.

Lightfoot, J. B. *The Apostolic Fathers: Clement, Ignatius, and Polycarp.* 5 vols. London: Macmillan, 1889–90.

Lightfoot, J. B. *St. Paul's Epistles to the Colossians and to Philemon.* London: Macmillan, 1904.

Lightfoot, J. B. *Saint Paul's Epistle to the Philippians,* 2nd ed. London: Macmillan, 1869.

Lincoln, Andrew T. *Ephesians.* WBC 42. Dallas: Word Books, 1990.

Lindemann, Andreas. "Antwort auf die 'Thesen zur Echtheit und Datierung der sieben Briefe des Ignatius von Antiochien.'" *ZAC* 1 (1997): 185–95.

Lindemann, Andreas. *Die Aufhebung der Zeit: Geschichtsverständnis und Eschatologie im Epheserbrief.* Gütersloh: Gerd Mohn, 1975.

Lindemann, Andreas. *Paulus im ältesten Christentum: Das Bild des Apostels und die Rezeption der paulinischen Theologie in der frühchristlichen Literatur bis Marcion.* Tübingen: Mohr Siebeck, 1979.

Lindemann, Andreas. "Zum Abfassungszweck des Zweiten Thessalonicherbriefes." *ZNW* 68 (1977): 35–47.

Lipsius, R. A. "Der Märtyrertod Polykarps." *ZWT* 17 (1874): 188–214.

Löhr, Winrich. "*Der Brief der Gemeinden von Lyon und Vienne (Eusebius, h.e. V, 1–2(4)).*" *Oecumenica et patristica,* 1989, pp. 135–49.

Looks, Carston. *Das Anvertraute bewahren: Die Rezeption der Pastoralbriefe im 2 Jahrhundert.* Munich: Hebert Utz, 1999.

Louw, Johannes P., and Eugene Nida, eds. *Lexical Semantics of the Greek New Testament.* Atlanta: Scholars Press, 1992.

Lüdemann, Gerd. "Anti-Paulinism in the Pseudo-Clementines." In *Opposition to Paul in Jewish Christianity,* edited by G. Lüdemann and Eugene Boring, pp. 169–94. Minneapolis: Fortress, 1989.

Luttikhuizen, Gerard P. "The Apocryphal Correspondence with the Corinthians and the Acts of Paul." In *The Apocryphal Acts of Paul and Thecla,* edited by Jan Bremmer, pp. 75–92. Kampen: Pharos, 1996.

Luttikhuizen, Gerard P. "The Suffering Jesus and the Invulnerable Christ in the Gnostic *Apocalypse of Peter.*" In *The Apocalypse of Peter,* edited by Jan Bremmer and István Czachesz, pp. 187–99. Leuven: Peeters, 2003.

MacDonald, Dennis Ronald. *The Legend and the Apostle: The Battle for Paul in Story and Canon.* Philadelphia: Westminster, 1983.

MacDonald, Margaret Y. *Colossians and Ephesians.* SP 17. Collegeville, MN: Liturgical Press, 2000.

MacDonald, Margaret Y. *The Pauline Churches: A Socio-Historical Study of Institutionalization in the Pauline and Deutero-Pauline Writings.* SNTSMS 34. Cambridge: Cambridge University Press, 1988.

Mackowiak, P. Wenzeslaus Sadok. *Die Ethische Beurteilung der Notlüge in der altheidnischen, patristischen, scholastischen, und neueren Zeit.* Zolkiew: Verlag der Dominakamer, 1933.

Malherbe, Abraham J. *The Letters to the Thessalonians: A New Translation with Introduction and Commentary.* ABC 32B. New York: Doubleday, 2000.

Manson, T. W. "St Paul in Greece." *BLJR* 35 (1952–53): 428–47.

Marjanen, Antti. "Thomas and Jewish Religious Practices." In *Thomas at the Crossroads: Essays on the Gospel of Thomas*, edited by Risto Uro, pp. 163–82. Edinburgh: T&T Clark, 1998.

Marrou, H. I. "Review of H. von Campenhausen, 'Bearbeitungen und Interpolationen des Polykarpmartyriums.'" *TLZ* 84 (1959): 361–63.

Marshall, I. Howard. *The Pastoral Epistles*. ICC. Edinburgh: T&T Clark, 1999.

Martin Hogan, Karina. "Pseudepigraphy and the Periodization of History in Jewish Apocalypses." In *Pseudepigraphie und Verfasserfiktion in frühchristlichen Briefen*, edited by Jörg Frey et al., pp. 61–83.

Martin, Troy. *By Philosophy and Empty Deceit: Colossians as Response to a Cynic Critique*. Sheffield: Sheffield Academic Press, 1996.

Martyn, J. Louis. *History and Theology in the Fourth Gospel*. New York: Harper and Row, 1968.

Marxsen, Willi. *Der zweite Thessalonicherbrief*. Zürich: Theologischer Verlag, 1982.

Masson, F. *Histoire critique de la république des lettres*. Tome X. Utrecht: Chès Guillaume à Poolsum, 1714.

Matthews, Chris. "Review of J. Wehnert, *Die Wir-Passagen der Apostelgeschichte*." *JBL* 110 (1991): 355–57.

Mayer, H. H. *Über die Pastoralbriefe*. Göttingen: Vandenhoeck & Ruprecht, 1913.

Mayerhoff, E. T. *Der Brief an die Colosser mit vornehmlicher Berüchsichtigung der drei Pastoralbriefe*. Berlin: Hermann Schültz, 1838.

McCant, Jerry. "The Gospel of Peter: Docetism Reconsidered." *NTS* 30 (1984): 258–73.

McDowell, D. *Aristophanes and Athens: An Introduction to the Plays*. New York: Oxford University Press, 1995.

McNabb, V. "Date and Influence of the First Epistle of St. Peter." *Irish Ecclesiastical Record* 45 (1935): 596–613.

Meade, David G. *Pseudonymity and Canon: An Investigation into the Relationship of Authorship and Authority in Jewish and Earliest Christian Tradition*. Grand Rapids, MI: Eerdmans, 1985.

Merkle, Stefan. "The Truth and Nothing but the Truth: Dictys and Dares." In *The Novel in the Ancient World*, edited by G. Schmeling, pp. 564–80. Leiden: Brill, 1996.

Merz, Annette. "The Fictitious Self-Exposition of Paul: How Might Intertextual Theory Suggest a Reformulation of the Hermeneutics of Pseudepigraphy?" In *The Intertextuality of the Epistles: Explorations of Theory and Practice*, edited by Thomas L. Brodie, Dennis Ronald MacDonald, and Stanley E. Porter, pp. 113–32. Sheffield: Sheffield Phoenix Press, 2006.

Merz, Annette. *Die fiktive Selbstauslegung des Paulus: Intertextuelle Studien zur Intention und Rezeption der Pastoralbriefe*. Göttingen/Fribourg: Vandenhoeck & Ruprecht/Academic Press, 2004.

Methuen, Charlotte. "Widows, Bishops and the Struggle for Authority in the *Didascalia Apostolorum*." *JEH* 46 (1995): 197–213.

Metzger, Bruce M. *The Canon of the New Testament: Its Origin, Development, and Significance*. Oxford: Clarendon Press, 1987.

Metzger, Bruce M. "Literary Forgeries and Canonical Pseudepigrapha." *JBL* 91 (1972): 3–24.

Metzger, Marcel. *Les constitutions apostoliques*. SC 320, 329, 336. Paris: Cerf, 1985, 1986, 1987.

Metzger, Marcel. "La theologie des Constitutions apostoliques par Clément." *RevScRel* 57 (1983): 29–49.

Meyer, Arnold. "Religiöse Pseudepigraphie als ethisch-psychologisches Problem." *ZNW* 35 (1936): 262–79; earlier in *Archiv für die gesamte Psychologie* 86 (1932): 171–90.

Meyers, Eric, and James Strange. *Archaeology, the Rabbis and Early Christianity*. Nashville, TN: Abingdon, 1981.

Michaelis, Wilhelm. "Pastoralbriefe und Wortstatistik." *ZNW* 28 (1929): 69–76.

Miller, James D. *The Pastoral Epistles as Composite Documents*. Cambridge: Cambridge University Press, 1997.

Minns, Denis. "The Rescript of Hadrian." In *Justin Martyr and His Worlds*, edited by Sara Parvis and Paul Foster, pp. 38–49. Minneapolis: Fortress, 2007.

Mirecki, Paul. "Peter, Gospel of." *ABD*, 5. 278–81.

Mirkovic, Alexander. *Prelude to Constantine: The Abgar Tradition in Early Christianity*. Frankfurt: Peter Lang, 2004.

Mitchell, Margaret M. "Corrective Composition, Corrective Exegesis: The Teaching on Prayer in 1 Tim 2, 1–15." In *1 Timothy Reconsidered*, edited by Karl Paul Donfried, pp. 41–62. Leuven: Peeters, 2008.

Mitchell, Margaret M. "The Letter of James as a Document of Paulinism?" In *Reading James with New Eyes: Methodological Reassessments of the Letter of James*, edited by Robert L. Webb and John S. Kloppenborg, pp. 75–98. London: T&T Clark, 2007.

Mitchell, Stephen. "Maximinus and the Christians in A.D. 312: A New Latin Inscription." *JRS* 78 (1988): 105–24.

Mitton, C. L. *The Epistle to the Ephesians: Its Authorship, Origin and Purpose*. Oxford: Oxford University Press, 1951.

Mitton, C. L. "The Relationship Between 1 Peter and Ephesians." *JTS* 1 (1950): 67–73.

Momigliano, Arnaldo. "The New Letter by 'Anna' to 'Seneca.'" *Athenaeum* 63 (1985): 217–19.

Montanari, Franco. "Zenodotus, Aristarchus and the Ekdosis of Homer." In *Editing Texts*, edited by Glenn W. Most, pp. 1–21. Göttingen: Vandenhoeck & Ruprecht, 1998.

Morgan, Teresa. *Literate Education in the Hellenistic and Roman Worlds*. Cambridge: Cambridge University Press, 1998.

Morton, A. Q., and J. McLeman. *Paul: The Man and the Myth*. New York: Harper & Row, 1966.

Moss, Candida R. "On the Dating of Polycarp: Rethinking the Place of the *Martyrdom of Polycarp* in the History of Christianity." *Early Christianity* 1 (2010): 539–74.

Muddiman, John. *The Epistle to the Ephesians*. Black's New Testament Commentaries. London: Continuum, 2001.

Mueller, Joseph G. *L'ancien testament dans l'ecclésiologie des Pères*. Turnhout: Brepols, 2004.

Mueller, Joseph G. "The Ancient Church Order Literature: Genre or Tradition?" *JECS* 15 (2007): 337–80.

Mülke, M. *Der Autor und sein Text: Die Verfälschung des Originals im Urteil antiker Untersuchungen*. Unterschungen zur Antiken Literatur und Geschichte 93. Berlin: Walter de Gruyter, 2008.

Müller, Carl Werner. "Die neuplatonischen Aristoteleskommentatoren über die Ursachen der Pseudepigraphie." *Rheinisches Museum für Philologie* 112 (1969): 120–26; reprinted in *Pseudepigraphie in der heidnischen und jüdisch-christlichen Antike*, ed. Norbert Brox, pp. 264–71.

Müller, Gregor. *Die Wahrhaftigkeitspflicht und die Problematik der Lüge: Ein Längsschnitt durch die Moraltheologie und Ethik unter besonderer Berücksichtigung der Tugendlehre des Thomas von Aquin und der modernen Lösungsversuche*. Freiburg: Herder, 1962.

Müller, Peter. *Anfänge der Paulusschule: Dargestellt am zweiten Thessalonicherbrief und am Kolosserbrief*. Abhandlungen zur Theologie des Alten und Neuen Testaments, 74; Zurich: Theologische Verlag, 1988.

Muretow, M. "Über den apokryphen Briefwechsel des Apostels Paulus mit den Korinthern." Theologische Boten (1896).

Murphy-O'Connor, Jerome. *Paul the Letter-Writer: His World, His Options, His Skills*. Collegeville, MN: Liturgical Press, 1995.

Murphy-O'Connor, Jerome. "2 Timothy Contrasted with 1 Timothy and Titus." *RB* 98 (1991): 403–18.

Mussies, Gerard. "Review of J. Wehnert, *Die Wir-Passagen der Apostelgeschichte.*" *Filologia Neotestamentaria* 6 (1993): 70–76.

Musurillo, Herbert. *The Acts of the Christian Martyrs.* Oxford: Clarendon Press, 1972.

Nagel, Peter. "Wenn ihr nicht den Sabbat zum Sabbat macht?" In *Sprachen Mythen, Mythizismen: Festschrift Walter Beltz*, edited by Armenuhi Drost-Abgarjan, Jürgen Tubach, and Mohsen Zakeri, pp. 507–17. Halle: Martin-Luther-Universität Halle-Wittenberg, 2004.

Najman, Hindy. *Seconding Sinai: The Development of Mosaic Discourse in Second Temple Judaism.* Leiden: Brill, 2003.

Nicklas, Tobias. "Die 'Juden' im Petrusevangelium (PCair. 10759). Ein Testfall." *NTS* 47 (2001): 206–21.

Nielsen, Charles Merritt. "The status of Paul and his letters in Colossians." *PRSt* 12 (1985): 103–22.

Nienhuis, David R. *Not by Paul Alone: The Formation of the Catholic Epistle Collection and the Christian Canon.* Waco, TX: Baylor University, 2007.

Norelli, Enrico. *L'Ascensione di Isaia: Studi su un apocrifo al crocevia dei cristianesimi.* Bologne: Centro editorial dehoniano, 1994.

Ohlig, K.-H. *Die theologische Begründung des neutestamentlichen Kanons in der alten Kirche.* Kommentare und Beiträge zum Alten und Neuen Testament. Düsseldorf: Patmos, 1972.

Osiek, Carolyn. "The Widow as Altar: The Rise and Fall of a Symbol." *SecCent* 3 (1983): 159–69.

Painter, John. *Just James: The Brother of Jesus in History and Tradition.* Edinburgh: T&T Clark, 1997.

Painter, John. *1, 2, and 3 John.* SP18. Collegeville, MN: Liturgical Press, 2008.

Parke, H. W. *Sibyls and Sibylline Prophecy in Classical Antiquity.* London: Routledge, 1988.

Parvis, Sara. "Justin Martyr and the Apologetic Tradition." In *Justin Martyr and His Worlds*, edited by eidem and Paul Foster, pp. 115–27. Minneapolis: Fortress, 2007.

Pearson, Birger A. "The Apocalypse of Peter and the Canonical 2 Peter." In *Gnosticism and the Early Christian World*, edited by James Goehring, pp. 67–74. Sonoma, CA: Polebridge Press, 1990.

Pearson, Birger. "Melchizedek." In *The Nag Hammadi Scriptures: The International Version*, Marvin Meyer, ed., pp. 597–98. San Francisco: HarperOne, 2007.

Peppermüller, Rolf. "Griechische Papyrusfragmente der *Doctrina Addai.*" *VC* 25 (1971): 289–301.

Perkins, Pheme. *The Gnostic Dialogue: The Early Church and the Crisis of Gnosticism.* New York: Paulist Press, 1980.

Perler, Othmar. "Die Briefe des Ignatius von Antiochien: Frage der Echtheit—neue, arabische Übersetzung." *FZPhTh* 18 (1971): 381–96.

Perler, Othmar. "Pseudo-Ignatius und Eusebius von Emesa." *Historisches Jahrbuch* 77 (1958): 73–82.

Pervo, Richard. *The Making of Paul: Constructions of the Apostle in Early Christianity.* Minneapolis: Fortress, 2010.

Pervo, Richard. "Romancing an Oft-Neglected Stone: The Pastoral Epistles and the Epistolary Novel." *Journal of Higher Criticism* 1 (1994): 25–47.

Pesce, Mauro. *Il "Martirio di Isaia" non esiste: L'Ascensione di Isaia e le tradizioni giudaiche sull'uccisione del profeta.* Bologna: Centro Stampa Baiesi, 1984.

Pfeiffer, Rudolf. *The History of Classical Scholarship from the Beginnings to the End of the Hellenistic Age.* Oxford: Clarendon Press, 1968.

Pilhofer, Peter. "Justin und das Petrusevangelium." *ZNW* 81 (1990): 60–78.
Pink, Karl. "Die pseudo-Paulinischen Briefe." *Bib* 6 (1925): 68–91, 179–200.
Piovanelli, Pierluigi. "'L'ennemi est parmi nous': Présences rhétoriques et narratives de Paul dans les *Pseudo-clémentines* et autres écrits apparentés." In *Nouvelles intrigues pseudo-clémentines—Plots in the Pseudo-Clementine Romance: Actes du deuxième colloque international sur la littérature apocryphe chrétienne (Lausanne, 30 août—2 septembre 2006)*, edited by Frédéric Amsler, Albert Frey, and Charlotte Touati, pp. 329–36. Lausanne: Zèbre, 2008.
Piovanelli, Pierluigi. "The Miraculous Discovery of the Hidden Manuscript, or the Paratextual Function of the Prologue of the Apocalypse of Paul." In *The Visio Pauli and the Gnostic Apocalypse of Paul*, edited by Jan Bremmer and István Czachesz, pp. 23–49. Leuven: Peeters, 2007.
Piovanelli, Pierluigi. "Les origines de l'Apocalypse de Paul reconsidérées." *Apocrypha* 4 (1993): 25–64.
Plisch, Uwe-Karsten. *The Gospel of Thomas: Original Text with Commentary*. Translated by Gesine Schenke Robinson. Stuttgart: Deutsche Bibelgesellschaft, 2008.
Plümacher, E. "Wirklichkeitserfahrung und Geschichtsschreibung bei Lukas: Erwägungen zu den Wir-Stücken der Apostelgeschichte." *ZNW* 68 (1977): 2–22.
Plummer, A. *The Epistles of S. John*. Cambridge: Cambridge University Press, 1886.
Poirer, Paul-Hubert. "The Writings Ascribed to Thomas and the Thomas Tradition." In *The Nag Hammadi Library After Fifty Years*, edited by J. D. Turner and A. McGuire, pp. 295–307. Leiden: Brill, 1997.
Pokorný, Petr. "Das theologische Problem der neutestamentlichen Pseudepigraphie." *EvT* 44 (1984): 486–96.
Popkes, Wiard. *Der Brief des Jakobus*. Leipzig: Evangelische Verlagsanstalt, 2001.
Popkes, Wiard. "James and Scripture: An Exercise in Intertextuality." *NTS* 45 (1999): 213–29.
Popkes, Wiard. *The Secretary in the Letters of Paul*. WUNT 2.42. Tübingen: Mohr Siebeck, 1991.
Pouderon, Bernard. *Les apologistes grecs du IIe siècle*. Paris: de Cerf, 2005.
Praeder, Susan Marie. "The Problem of First Person Narration in Acts." *NovT* 29 (1987): 193–218.
Pratscher, Wilhelm. *Der Herrenbruder Jakobus und die Jakobustradition*. Göttingen: Vandenhoeck & Ruprecht, 1987.
Prior, Michael. "Paul the Letter-Writer and the Second Letter to Timothy." *JSNT*: Supplement series. Sheffield: University of Sheffield Press, 1989.
Prostmeier, Ferdinand-Rupert. *Handlungsmodelle im ersten Petrusbrief*. Würzburg: Echer Verlag, 1990.
Prothero, Rowland E. *The Works of Lord Byron. Letters and Journals*, IV. New York: Scribner, 1900.
Pucci Ben Zeev, Miriam. "The Reliability of Josephus Flavius: The Case of Hecataeus' and Manetho's Accounts of Jews and Judaism: Fifteen Years of Contemporary Research (1974–1990)." *Journal of Jewish Studies* 24 (1993): 215–34.
Quinn, Jerome D. *The Letter to Titus*. ABC. New Haven, CT: Yale University, 1990.
Rainer, Jakobi. *Die sogenannte "Epistula Anne ad Senecam."* Torun: Wydawn. Uniwersytetu Mikołaja Kopernika, 2001.
Ramelli, Ilaria. "L'epistolario apocrifo Seneca-san Paolo: alcune osservazioni." *VetChr* 34 (1997): 299–310.
Ramsey, Boniface. "Two Traditions on Lying and Deception in the Ancient Church." *Thomist* 49 (1985): 504–33.
Reed, Jonathan. *Archaeology and the Galilean Jesus: A Re-examination of the Evidence*. Harrisburg, PA: Trinity Press International, 2000.

Reinmuth, Eckhart. "Die Briefe an die Thessalonicher." In *Die Briefe an die Philipper, Thessalonicher und an Philemon*, edited by N. Walter, E. Reinmuth, and P. Lampe, pp. 105–204. Göttingen: Vandenhoeck & Ruprecht, 1998.

Reumann, John. "The 'Itinerary' as a Form in Classical Literature and the Acts of the Apostles." In *To Touch the Text: Biblical and Related Studies in Honor of Joseph A. Fitzmyer, S.J.*, edited by M. P. Horgan and P. J. Kobelski, pp. 335–57. New York: Crossroad, 1989.

Reynolds, L. D., and H. G. Wilson. *Scribes and Scholars*. Oxford: Clarendon Press, 1991.

Richards, E. Randolph. *Paul and First-Century Letter Writing: Secretaries, Composition, and Collection*. Downer's Grove, IL: Intervarsity, 2004.

Richards, William A. *Difference and Distance in Post-Pauline Christianity: An Epistolary Analysis of the Pastorals*. New York: Peter Lang, 2002.

Rink, W. F. *Das Sendschreiben der Korinther an den Apostel Paulus und das dritte Sendscheiben Pauli an die Korinther*. Heidelberg: C. F. Winter, 1823.

Rist, M. "Pseudepigraphy and the Early Christians." In *Studies in New Testament and Early Christian Literature. Essays in Honor of A. P. Wikgren*, edited by David E. Aune, pp. 75–91. NovTSup. Leiden: Brill, 1972.

Rist, M. "III Corinthians as a Pseudepigraphic Refutation of Marcionism." *Iliff Review* 26 (1969): 49–58.

Rius-Camps, Josep. *The Four Authentic Letters of Ignatius*. Rome: Pontificium Institutum Orientalium Studiorum, 1979.

Robbins, Vernon K. "By Land and by Sea: The We-Passages and Ancient Sea Voyages." In *Perspectives on Luke-Acts*, edited by C. H. Talbert, pp. 215–42. Macon, GA: Mercer University, 1978.

Roberge, Michel, "The Paraphrase of Shem." In *The Nag Hammadi Scriptures: The International Edition*, Marvin Meyer, ed., pp. 437–47. San Francisco: HarperOne, 2007.

Rohde, J. "Pastoralbriefe und Acta Pauli." *Studia Evangelica*, ed. F. L. Cross, 5 (1968): 309.

Ronchey, Silvia. *Indagine sul martirio di San Policarpo: Critica storica e fortuna agiografica di un caso giudiziario in Asia Minore*. Nuovi Studi Storici, 6. Rome: Istituto Italiano per il Medio Evo, 1990.

Roose, Hanna. "'A Letter as by Us': Intentional Ambiguity in 2 Thessalonians 2.2." *JSNT* 29 (2006): 107–24.

Rordorf, Willy. "Hérésie et orthodoxie selon la correspondance apocryphe entre les Corinthiens et l'apôtre Paul." In *Orthodoxie et Heresie dans l'Eglise ancienne*, edited by H. D. Altendorf. *Cahiers de la Revue de Theologie et de Philosophie* 17. Freiburg: Revue de Theologie et de Philosophie, 1993.

Rordorf, Willy. "Tertullien et les Actes de Paul (à propos de bapt 17,5)." In *Lex Orandi Lex Credendi*, edited by Gerardo J. Békés and Giustino Farnedi, pp. 475–84. Rome: Editrice Anselmiana, 1980.

Rosenmeyer, Patricia A. *Ancient Epistolary Fictions*. Cambridge: Cambridge University Press, 2001.

Rothschild, Claire. *Hebrews as Pseudepigraphon: The History and Significance of the Pauline Attribution of Hebrews*. Tübingen: Mohr Siebeck, 2009.

Rouleau, Donald. *L'Épître apocryphe de Jacques (NH I, 2)*. Bibliothèque copte de Nag Hammadi, Section "Textes" 18. Québec: Les Presses de l'Université Laval; Louvain: Peeters, 1987.

Rowland, Christopher. *The Open Heaven: A Study of Apocalyptic in Judaism and Early Christianity*. New York: Crossroad, 1982.

Ruether, Rosemary. *Faith and Fratricide: The Theological Roots of Anti-Semitism*. New York: Seabury, 1974.

Ruinart, Theodore, ed. *Acta primorum martyrum sincere et selecta*. Paris: Muget, 1689.

Russell, D. H. *The Method and Message of Jewish Apocalyptic 200 B.C.—A.D. 100*. London: SCM, 1964.

Sanders, E. P. "Literary Dependence in Colossians." *JBL* 85 (1966): 28–45.

Sappington, Thomas. *Revelation and Redemption at Colossae*. Sheffield: JSOT Press, 1991.

Satran, David. "Pedagogy and Deceit in the Alexandrian Theological Tradition." In Origeniana Quinta, ed. R. J. Daily, pp. 119–24. Leuven: Peeters, 1992.

Saxer, Victor. "L'authenticité du 'Martyre de Polycarpe': Bilan de 25 ans de critique." *Mélanges de l'école française de Rome. Antiquité* 94 (1982): 979–1001.

Saxer, Victor. *Morts, Martyrs, reliques, en Afrique Chrétienne aux premiers siècles*. Paris: Éditions Beauchesne, 1980.

Schäublin, C. "Μήτε προσθεῖναι μήτ' ἀφελεῖν." *Museum Helveticum* 31 (1974): 144–49.

Scheidweiler, Felix, and Wilhelm Schneemelcher. "The Gospel of Nicodemus/Acts of Pilate and Christ's Descent into Hell." In *New Testament Apocrypha*, revised edition, transl. R. McL. Wilson, vol. 1, pp. 501–05. Louisville, KY: Westminster John Knox. 1991.

Schenk, Wolfgang. "Die Briefe an Timotheus I und II und an Titus (Pastoralbriefe) in der neueren Forschung (1945–1985)." *ANRW* 2. 25.4, pp. 3404–38.

Schenke, Hans-Martin. "Melchisedek (NHC IX, 1)." In *Nag Hammadi Deutsch*, 2nd ed., Hans-Martin Schenke, Hans-Gebhard Bethge, and Ursula Ulrike Kaiser, eds., pp. 474–76. Berlin: De Gruyter, 2010.

Schenke, Hans-Martin. *Das Thomas Buch (Nag Hammadi-Codexs II, 7)*. Berlin: Akademie-Verlag, 1989.

Schermann, T. *Eine Elfapostelmoral oder die x-Rezension der "beiden Wege."* Munich: Lentner, 1903.

Schindler, Franz. "Die Lüge in der patristischen Literatur." In *Beiträge zur Geschichte des christlichen Altertums und der byzantinischen Literatur*, edited by Albert Michael Koeniger, pp. 421–33. Amsterdam: Rodopi, 1969; originally published 1922.

Schleiermacher, Friedrich. *Über den sogenannten Ersten Brief des Paulus an den Timotheus: Ein kritisches Sendschreiben*. Berlin: Realschulbuchhandlung, 1807.

Schmeller, Thomas. *Schulen im Neuen Testament? Zur Stellung des Urchristentums in der Bildungswelt seiner Zeit*. Freiburg: Herder, 2001.

Schmidt, Carl. *Acta Pauli: Aus der Heidelberger Koptischen Papyrushandschrift Nr. 1*. Leipzig: J. C. Hinrichs, 1905.

Schmidt, Carl. *Gespräche Jesu mit seinen Jüngern nach der Auferstehung. Ein katholisch-apostolisches Sendschreiben des 2. Jh.* Leipzig: J. C. Hinrichs, 1919.

Schmidt, Darryl. "Syntactical Style in the 'We'-Sections of Acts: How Lukan Is It?" SBLSP 28 (1989): 300–308.

Schmidt, Darryl. "The Syntactical Style of 2 Thessalonians: How Pauline Is It?" In *The Thessalonian Correspondence*, edited by Raymond F. Collins, pp. 383–93. Leuven: Peeters, 1990.

Schmidt, Francis. "'Traqué comme un loup' A propos du débat actuel sur l'apocalyptique juive." *Archives de sciences sociales des religions* 53 (1982): 5–21.

Schmidt, Johann Ernst Christian. *Vermutungen über die beiden Briefe an die Thessalonicher*. Bibliothek für Kritik und Exegese des Neuen Testaments und älteste Christengeschichte 2, 3. Hadamar: Gelehrtenbuchhandlung, 1801.

Schmidt, Karl Matthias. *Mahnung und Erinnerung im Maskenspiel: Epistolographie, Rhetorik und Narrativik der pseudepigraphen Petrusbriefe*. Freiburg: Herder, 2003.

Schmidt, Karl Matthias. "Die Stimme des Apostels erheben: Pragmatische Leistungen der Autorenfiktion in den Petrusbriefen." In *Pseudepigraphie und Verfasserfiktion in frühchristlichen Briefen*, edited by Jörg Frey et al., pp. 625–44.

Schnackenburg, R. *The Johannine Epistles*. New York: Crossroads, 1992, ET of 7th German edition of 1984; original 1953.

Schoedel, William. *Ignatius of Antioch: A Commentary on the Letters of Ignatius of Antioch*. Hermeneia. Philadelphia: Fortress, 1985.

Schoedel, William. "Polycarp of Smyrna and Ignatius of Antioch." *ANTW* 2.27.1; pp. 272–358.

Schöllgen, Georg. "Der Abfassungszweck der frühchristlichen Kirchenordnungen: Anmerkungen zu den Thesen Bruno Steimers." JAC 40 (1997): 55–77.

Schöllgen, Georg. "Pseudapostolizität und Schriftgebrauch in den ersten Kirchenordnungen. Anmerkungen zur Begründung des frühen Kirchenrechts." In *Stimuli: Exegese und ihre Hermeneutik in Antike und Christentum. Festschrift Für Ernst Dassmann*, edited by George Schöllgen and Clemens Scholten, pp. 96–121. Münster: Aschendorffsche Verlagsbuchhandlung, 1996.

Schrörs, H. *Hinkmar, Erzbischof von Reims*. Freiburg im Breisgau, 1884.

Schütrumpf, Eckart. *Heraclides of Pontus: Text and Translations*. New Brunswick, NJ: Transaction, 2009.

Schutter, William. *Hermeneutic and Composition in 1 Peter*. Tübingen: Mohr Siebeck 1989.

Schwegler, Albert. *Das nachapostolische Zeitalter in den Hauptmomenten seiner Entwicklung*, 2 vols. Tubingen: Ludwig Friedrich Fues, 1846.

Scopello, Madeleine. "The Secret Book of James." Introduction. In *The Nag Hammadi Scriptures*, Marvin Meyer, ed., pp. 19–22. San Francisco: HarperOne, 2007.

Segal, Judah. *Edessa, the "Blessed City."* Oxford: Clarendon Press, 1970.

Sellin, Gerhard. *Der Brief an die Epheser*. *KEKNT* 8. Göttingen: Vandenhoeck & Ruprecht, 2008.

Sellin, Gerhard. "Die Häretiker des Judasbriefes." *ZNW* 77 (1986): 206–25.

Seufert, W. "Das Verwandtschaftsverhältnis des ersten Petrusbriefs und Epheserbriefs." *ZWT* 24 (1881): 178–97, 332–80.

Sevenster, J. N. *Do You Know Greek? How Much Greek Could the First Jewish Christians Have Known?* Leiden: Brill, 1968.

Shepardson, Christine. *Anti-Judaism and Christian Orthodoxy: Ephrem's Hymns in Fourth Century Syria*. Washington, DC: Catholic University of America Press, 2008.

Shimada, Kazuhito. "Is 1 Peter Dependent on Ephesians? A Critique of C. L. Mitton." *Annual of the Japanese Biblical Institute* 17 (1991): 77–106.

Shimada, Kazuhito. "Is 1 Peter Dependent on Romans?" *Annual of the Japanese Biblical Institute* 19 (1993): 87–137.

Silverstein, T. "The Date of the 'Apocalypse of Paul.'" *MS* 24 (1962): 335–48.

Simon, Marcel. *Verus Israel: A Study of the Relations Between Christians and Jews in the Roman Empire 135–425 AD*. New York: Oxford University Press, 1946; French original 1948.

Sint, Josef A. *Pseudonymität im Altertum: Ihre Formen und ihre Gründe*. Innsbruck: Universitätsverlag Wagner, 1960.

Smid, Harm R. *Protevangelium Jacobi: A Commentary*. Assen: van Gorcum, 1965.

Smith III, James D. "Reflections on Euzoius in Alexandria and Antioch." *StPatr* 36 (2001): 514–20.

Smith, Jonathan Z. "The Garments of Shame." *HR* 5 (1966): 217–38.

Smith, Morton. "Pseudepigraphy in the Israelite Tradition." In *Pseudepigrapha I: Pseudopythagorica, Lettres de Platon, Littérature pseudépigraphique juive*, edited by Kurt von Fritz, pp. 189–215. Vandoeuvres-Geneve: Fondation Hardt pour l'Étude de l'Antiquité Classique, 1972.

Smith, Terrence V. *Petrine Controversies in Early Christianity: Attitudes Towards Peter in the Christian Writings of the First Two Centuries*. WUNT 2.15. Tübingen: Mohr Siebeck, 1985.

Speyer, Wolfgang. *Bücherfunde in der Glaubenswerbung der Antike. Mit einem Ausblick auf Mittelalter und Neuzeit*. Göttingen: Vandenhoeck & Ruprecht, 1970.

Speyer, Wolfgang. *Die literarische Fälschung im heidnischen und christlichen Altertum: Ein Versuch ihrer Deutung*. München: Beck, 1971.

Speyer, Wolfgang. "Religiöse Pseudepigraphie und literarische Fälschung im Altertum." *JAC* 8/9 (1965–66): 88–125.

Spicq, Ceslas. *Saint Paul: les épîtres pastorales*. Paris: Gabalda, 1969.

Standhartinger, Angela. "Colossians and the Pauline School." *NTS* 50 (2004): 572–93.

Standhartinger, Angela. *Studien zur Entstehungsgeschichte und Intention des Kolosserbriefs*. Leiden: Brill, 1999.

Stanton, Graham. "Jewish Christian Elements in the Pseudo-Clementine Writings." In *Jewish Believers in Jesus*, edited by Oskar Skarsaune and Reidar Hvalvik, pp. 305–24. Peabody, MA: Hendrickson, 2007.

Steimer, Bruno. *Vertex Traditionis: Die Gattung der altchristlichen Kirchenordnungen*. Berlin: de Gruyter, 1992.

Stephenson, A. M. G. "On the Meaning of ἐνέστηκεν ἡ ἡμέρα τοῦ κυρίου in 2 Thessalonians 2,2." In *Studia Evangelica*, 4, edited by F. L. Cross, pp. 442–51. Berlin: Akademie-Verlag, 1968.

Stewart-Sykes, Alistair. *The Apostolic Church Order: The Greek Text with Introduction, Translation and Annotations*. Strathfield, Australia: St Pauls, 2006.

Stewart-Sykes, Alistair. "The Asian Context of the New Prophecy and of *the Epistula Apostolorum*." *VC* 51 (1997): 416–38.

Stewart-Sykes, Alistair. *The Didascalia Apostolorum*. Turnhout: Brepols, 2009.

Stirewalt, M. Luther. *Studies in Ancient Greek Epistolography*. Atlanta: Scholars Press, 1993.

Stone, Michael E. "Pseudepigraphy Reconsidered." *Review of Rabbinic Judaism* 9 (2006): 1–15.

Strange, James F. "Capernaum." In IDBSup, edited by K. Crim, pp. 140–41. Nashville, TN: Abingdon, 1976.

Strecker, Georg. *The Johannine Letters*. Translated by Linda Maloney. Hermeneia. Minneapolis: Fortress, 1996; German original 1989.

Streeter, B. H. *The Primitive Church: Studies with Special Reference to the Origins of the Christian Ministry*. New York: Macmillan, 1929.

Sumney, Jerry L. *"Servants of Satan," "False Brothers" and Other Opponents of Paul*. JSNTSup, 188. Sheffield: Sheffield Academic Press, 1999.

Sundberg, A. C. "Canon Muratori: A Fourth Century List." *HTR* 66 (1973): 1–41.

Syme, Ronald. *Emperors and Biography: Studies in the Historia Augusta*. Oxford: Clarendon Press, 1971.

Syreeni, Kari. "James and the Pauline Legacy: Power Play in Corinth?" In *Fair Play: Diversity and Conflicts in Early Christianity*, edited by Ismo Dunderberg, C. Tuckett, and Kari Syreeni, pp. 397–437. SuppINT, 103. Leiden: Brill, 2002.

Tardieu, Michel. "Commémoration gnostique de Sem." In *La commémoration: Colloque du centenaire de la section des sciences religieuses de l'École pratique des hautes études*, edited by Ph. Gignoux, pp. 219–23. Louvain: Peeters, 1988.

Tardieu, Michel. "Hérésiographie de l'Apocalypse de Pierre." In *Histoire et conscience historique dans les civilisations du Proche-Orient ancient: Actes du Colloque de Cartigny 1986*, edited by Albert de Pury. Les Cahiers du Centre d'étude du Proche-Orient ancien, 5. Leuven: Peeters, 1989.

Taylor, Archer, and Fredric John Moshe. *The Bibliographical History of Anonyma and Pseudonyma*. Chicago: University of Chicago Press, 1951.

Testuz, Michel. "La Correspondance apocryphe de saint Paul et des Corinthiens." In *Littérature et Théologie Pauliniennes*, edited by A. Descamps, pp. 217–23. Louvain: Desclée de Brouwer, 1960.

Thesleff, Holger. *An Introduction to the Pythagorean Writings of the Hellenistic Period*. Åbo: Åbo Academi, 1961.

Thompson, Bard. "Patristic Use of the Sibylline Oracles." *RR* 16 (1952): 115–36.

Thompson, James Westfall. "The Alleged Persecution of the Christians at Lyons in 177." *AJT* 16 (1912): 359–84.

Thompson, James Westfall. "The Alleged Persecution of the Christians at Lyons in 177, A Reply to Certain Criticisms." *AJT* 17 (1913) 249–58.

Thornton, Claus-Jürgen. *Der Zeuge des Zeugen: Lukas als Historiker der Paulusrseisen*. WUNT, 56. Tübingen: Mohr Siebeck, 1991.

Thornton, Claus-Jürgen. "Justin und das Markusevangelium." *ZNW* 84 (1993): 93–110.

Tigchelaar, Eibert. "Forms of Pseudepigraphy in the Dead Sea Scrolls." In *Pseudepigraphie und Verfasserfiktion in frühchristlichen Briefen*, edited by Jörg Frey et al., pp. 85–101.

Tigchelaar, Eibert. "Is the Liar Bar Kokhba? Considering the Date and the Provenance of the Greek (Ethiopic) *Apocalypse of Peter*." In *The Apocalypse of Peter*, edited by Jan Bremmer and István Czachesz, pp. 63–77. Leuven: Peeters, 2003.

Too, Y. L. *The Idea of Ancient Literary Criticism*. Oxford: Clarendon Press, 1998.

Torm, Friedrik. "Die Psychologie der Pseudonymität im Hinblick auf die Literatur des Urchristentums." *Studien der Luther Akademie*, Heft 2 (Gütersloh: Bertelsmann, 1932); pp. 7–55; reprinted in *Pseudepigraphie in der heidnischen und jüdisch-christlichen Antike*, ed. N. Brox, pp. 111–49.

Trilling, Wolfgang, ed. *Untersuchungen zum 2.Thessalonicher*. Leipzig: St. Benno, 1972.

Trilling, Wolfgang. "Zum Petrusamt im Neuen Testament: Traditionsgeschichtliche Überlegungen anhand von Matthäus, 1 Petrus und Johannes." *TQ* 151 (1971): 110–33.

Trout, Dennis. "Review of Ronchey, *Indagine sul martirio di San Policarpo: Critica storica e fortuna agiografica di un caso giudiziario in Asia Minore*." *Spec* 68 (1993): 251–53.

Trummer, Peter. "Corpus Paulinum—Corpus Pastorale: Zur Ortung der Paulustradition in den Pastoralbriefen." In *Paulus in den neutestamentlichen Spätschriften: zur Paulusrezeption im Neuen Testament*, edited by Karl Kertelge, pp. 122–45. Freiburg: Herder, 1981.

Turner, C. H. "Notes on the Apostolic Constitutions I-III." *JTS* 16 (1914–15): 54–61, 523–38; 31 (1930): 128–41.

Turner, John D. "The Book of Thomas and the Platonic Jesus." In *L'évangile selon Thomas et les textes de Nag Hammadi*, edited by Louis Painchaud and Paul-Hubert Poirier, pp. 599–634. Québec: Presses de l'Université Laval; Louvain: Peeters, 2007.

Ullmann, W. "Some Remarks on the Significance of the *Epistola Clementis* in the Pseudo-Clementines." *StPatr* 4 (1961): 330–37.

Uro, Risto. *Thomas: Seeking the Historical Context of the Gospel of Thomas*. London: T&T Clark, 2003.

Ussher, J. *In Polycarpionam epistolarum Ignationarum syllogen annotations*. Oxford: Leonard Lichfield, 1644.

Valantasis, Richard. *The Gospel of Thomas*. London: Routledge, 1997.

Vallée, Gerard. *A Study in Anti-Gnostic Polemics: Irenaeus, Hippolytus, and Epiphanius*. Studies in Christianity and Judaism, 1. Waterloo, Ontario: Wilfred Laurier University, 1981.

Van der Waerden, B. L. *Die Pythagorer: Religiöse Bruderschaft und Schule der Wissenschaft*. Zurich: Artemis, 1979.

Van der Waerden, B. L. "Die Schriften und Fragmente des Pythagoras." *Realencyclopädie der Classischen Altertumswissenschaft: Supplementband* 10 (1965): 843–64.

Van Minnen, Peter. "The Greek *Apocalypse of Peter*." In *The Apocalypse of Peter*, edited by Jan Bremmer and István Czachesz, pp. 15–39. Leuven: Peeters, 2003.

Van Stempvoort, P. A. "The Protevangelium Jacobi, the Sources of Its Theme and Style and Their Bearing on Its Date." In Studia Evangelica III., ed. F. Cross, pp. 410–26. Berlin: Akademie Verlag, 1964.

van Unnik, W. C. "De la règle ΜΗΤΕ ΠΡΟΣΘΕΙΝΑΙ ΜΗΤΕ ΑΦΕΛΕΙΝ dans l'histoire du canon." *VC* 3 (1949): 1–35.

van Unnik, W. C. "'Die Formel nichts wegnehmen, nichts hinzufügen' bei Josephus." In *Josephus als historischer Schriftsteller*, edited by eidem, pp. 26–49. Heidelberg: Schneider, 1978.

van Unnik, W. C. "Once More St. Luke's Prologue." *Neot* 7 (1973): 7–26.

Verheyden, Joseph. "The Canon Muratori: A Matter of Dispute." In *The Biblical Canons*, edited by J.-M. Auwers and H. J. De Jonge, pp. 487–556. Leuven: Peeters, 2003.

Verheyden, Joseph. "Some Reflections on Determining the Purpose of the 'Gospel of Peter.'" In *Das Evangelium nach Petrus: Text, Kontexte, Intertexte*, edited by Thomas J. Kraus and Tobias Nicklas, pp. 281–99. TU 158. Berlin: de Gruyter, 2007.

Vessey, Mark. "The Forging of Orthodoxy in Latin Christian Literature: A Case Study." *JECS* 4 (1996): 495–513.

Vielhauer, P. "On The Paulinisms of Acts." In *Studies in Luke Acts*, edited by Leander Keck and J. Louis Martyn, pp. 33–50. Nashville, TN: Abingdon, 1966.

Vögtle, Anton. *Der Judasbrief. Der 2 Petrusbrief.* Düsseldorf: Benzinger Verlag, 1994.

Voss, Isaac, ed. *Epistolae genuinae S. Ignatii martyris.* Amsterdam: Blaev, 1646.

Vouaux, Léon. *Les actes de Paul et ses lettres apocryphes.* Paris: Letouzey et Ané, 1913.

Wacholder, Ben Zion. "The Letter from Judah Maccabee to Aristobulus: Is 2 Maccabees 1:10b–2:18 Authentic?" *HUCA* 49 (1978): 89–133.

Wagner, Georg. "Zur Herkunft der Apostolischen Konstitutionen." In *Mélanges liturgiques offerts au R. P. dom Bernard Botte à l'occasion du cinquantième anniversaire de son ordination sacerdotale (4 juin 1972)*, edited by J.-J. von Allmen, pp. 525–37. Louvain: Abbaye du Mont César, 1972.

Wedderburn, A. J. M. "The 'We'-Passages in Acts: On the Horns of a Dilemma." *ZNW* 93 (2002): 78–98.

Wehnert, Jürgen. *Die Wir-Passagen der Apostelgeschichte: Ein lukanisches Stilmittel aus jüdischer Tradition.* Göttingen: Vandenhoeck & Ruprecht, 1989.

Wehrli, F. *Die Schule des Aristoteles*, Hefte VII, *Heracleides Pontikos*, 2nd ed. Basel: Schwabe, 1969.

Weijenborg, Reinoud. "Is Evagrius Ponticus the Author of the Longer Recension of the Ignatian Letters?" *Anton* 44 (1969): 339–47.

Weijenborg, Reinoud. *Les lettres d'Ignace d'Antioche.* Leiden: Brill, 1969.

Westcott, Brooke Foss. *A General Survey of the History of the Canon of the New Testament*, 4th ed. London: Macmillan, 1875.

Whiston, William. *Collection of Authentic Records Belonging to the Old and New Testament*, Part II. London: William Whiston, 1727.

White, Benjamin L. "Reclaiming Paul? Reconfiguration as Reclamation in 3 Corinthians." *JECS* 17 (2009): 497–523.

Wikenhauser, A. *Einleitung in das Neue Testament*, 6th ed., revised by Josef Schmid. Freiburg: Herder, 1973.

Wilder, Terry L. *Pseudonymity, The New Testament, and Deception: An Inquiry into Intention and Reception.* Lanham, MD: University Press of America, 2004.

Wilken, Robert. *John Chrysostom and the Jews: Rhetoric and Reality in the Fourth Century.* Berkeley: University of California, 1983.

Williams, Rowan. *Arius: Heresy and Tradition*, rev. ed. Grand Rapids, MI: Eerdmans, 2001.

Wilson, R. McL. *Colossians and Philemon.* London: T&T Clark, 2005.

Wimsatt, W. K. *The Verbal Icon: Studies in the Meaning of Poetry.* Lexington: University of Kentucky, 1954.

Wischmeyer, Wolfgang. "Die Epistula Anne ad Senecam: Eine jüdische Missionsschrift des lateinischen Bereichs." In *Juden und Christen in der Antike*, edited by J. Van Amersfoort and J. van Oort, pp. 72–93. Kampen: Kok, 1990.

Wiseman, T. P. "Lying Historians: Seven Types of Mendacity." In *Lies and Fiction in the Ancient World*, edited by C. Gill and T. P. Wisemann, pp. 122–46. Austin: University of Texas Press, 1993.

Wisse, Frederik. "The Epistle of Jude in the History of Heresiology." In *Essays on the Nag Hammadi Texts in Honour of Alexander Böhlig*, edited by Martin Krause, pp. 133–43. Leiden: Brill, 1972.

Wisse, Frederik. "The Nag Hammadi Library and the Heresiologists." *VC* 25 (1971): 205–23.

Wood, Michael. "Prologue." In *Lies and Fiction in the Ancient World*, edited by C. Gill and T. P. Wisemann, pp. xiii–xviii. Austin: University of Texas Press, 1993.

Woollcombe, K. J. "The Doctrinal Connexions of the Pseudo-Ignatian Letters." *StPatr* 6 (1962): 269–73.

Wrede, W. *Die Echtheit des zweiten Thessalonicherbriefs*. TU n.s. 9.2. Leipzig: J. C. Hinrichs, 1903.

Yoshiko Reed, Annette. "Heresiology and the (Jewish-)Christian Novel: Narrativized Polemics in the Pseudo-Clementine *Homilies*." In *Heresy and Identity in Late Antiquity*, edited by Eduard Iricinschi and Holger M. Zellentin, pp. 273–98. Tübingen: Mohr Siebeck, 2008.

Yoshiko Reed, Annette. "'Jewish Christianity' after the 'Parting of the Ways': Approaches to Historiography and Self-Definition in the Pseudo-Clementines." In *The Ways That Never Parted: Jews and Christians in Late Antiquity and the Early Middle Ages*, edited by Adam H. Becker and Annette Yoshiko Reed, pp. 189–231. Tübingen: Mohr Siebeck, 2003.

Yoshiko Reed, Annette. "'Jewish Christianity' as Counter-history? The Apostolic Past in Eusebius' *Ecclesiastical History* and the Pseudo-Clementine *Homilies*." In *Antiquity in Antiquity: Jewish and Christian Pasts in the Greco-Roman World*, edited by Gregg Gardner and Kevin L. Osterloh, pp. 173–216. Tübingen: Mohr Siebeck, 2008.

Yoshiko Reed, Annette. "Pseudepigraphy, Authorship, and the Reception of 'The Bible' in Late Antiquity." In *The Reception and Interpretation of the Bible in Late Antiquity: Proceedings of the Montréal Colloquium in Honour of Charles Kannengiesser, 11–13 October 2006*, edited by Lorenzo DiTommaso and Lucian Turcescu, pp. 467–90. Leiden: Brill, 2008.

Zahn, Theodore. *Geschichte des Neutestamentlichen Kanons* II/2. Leipzig: A. Deichert, 1892.

Zahn, Theodore. *Ignatius von Antiochien*. Gotha: Perthes, 1873.

Zembaty, Jane S. "Plato's Republic and Greek Morality on Lying." *Journal of the History of Philosophy* 26 (1988): 517–45.

Zervos, George. "Prolegomena to a Critical Edition of the Genesis Marias (Protevangelium Jacobi): The Greek Manuscripts." Ph.D. thesis, Duke University, 1986.

Zhmud, Leonid. *Wissenschaft, Philosophie und Religion im frühen Pythagorismus*. Berlin: Akademie Verlag, 1997.

Zmijewski, Josef. "Die Pastoralbriefe als pseudepigraphische Schriften—Beschreibung, Erklärung, Bewertung." *SNTSU* 4 (1979): 97–118.

Zohrab, J. *Astuatsashunch' Matean Hin Ew Nor Ktakarants'* (= Scriptures of the Old and New Testaments). Venice: Srboyn Ghazaru, 1805; reprinted Delmar: Caravan Books, 1984.

INDEX OF ANCIENT SOURCES

This index includes only **Ancient Sources**.

For general concepts, including a topical guide to ancient sources, refer to the **Subject** Index found on pages 591–622.

For modern scholars, refer to the **Modern Scholars** index found on pages 623–628.

BIBLICAL

OTHER

INDEX OF SUBJECTS

This **Subject** index includes general concepts, including a topical guide to ancient sources.
For specific ancient sources organized by book, chapter and verse, refer to the **Ancient Sources** index found on pages 575–589.
For modern scholars, refer to the **Modern Scholars** index found on pages 623–628.

INDEX OF MODERN SCHOLARS

This index includes only **Modern Scholars**.
For specific ancient sources organized by book, chapter and verse, refer to the **Ancient Sources** index found on pages 575–589.
For general concepts, including a topical guide to ancient sources, refer to the **Subject** index found on pages 591–622.

ELIZABETH I

AUTHOR'S NOTE

The four parts contained in this book, covering different aspects of the life and times of Queen Elizabeth I, were originally published – in the order in which they appear here – as individual books, which accounts for an occasional overlap in the subject matter.

Alison Plowden
2004

ELIZABETH I

ALISON PLOWDEN

SUTTON PUBLISHING

Dedication
To Joe Burroughs
In Happy and Grateful Memory

This edition first published in the United Kingdom in 2004
by Sutton Publishing Limited

Reprinted in 2007 by Sutton Publishing,
an imprint of NPI Media Group Limited
Cirencester Road · Chalford · Stroud · Gloucestershire · GL6 8PE

Previously published under the titles:
The Young Elizabeth
Danger to Elizabeth
Marriage with my Kingdom
Elizabeth Regina

Copyright © Alison Plowden, 2004

All rights reserved. No part of this publication may be reproduced, stored in a retrieval system, or transmitted, in any form, or by any means, electronic, mechanical, photocopying, recording or otherwise, without the prior permission of the publisher and copyright holder.

Alison Plowden has asserted the moral right to be identified as the author of this work.

British Library Cataloguing in Publication Data
A catalogue record for this book is available from the British Library

ISBN 978-0-7509-3242-4

Typeset in Photina.
Typesetting and origination by
NPI Media Group Limited.
Printed and bound in England.

Contents

Part One: The Young Elizabeth

The First Twenty-Five Years of Elizabeth I

Part Two: Danger to Elizabeth

The Catholics under Elizabeth I

Part Three: Marriage With My Kingdom

The Courtships of Elizabeth I

Part Four: Elizabeth Regina

The Age of Triumph, 1588–1603

Part One

The Young Elizabeth

Simplified Genealogical Table Showing the Descent of the House of Tudor

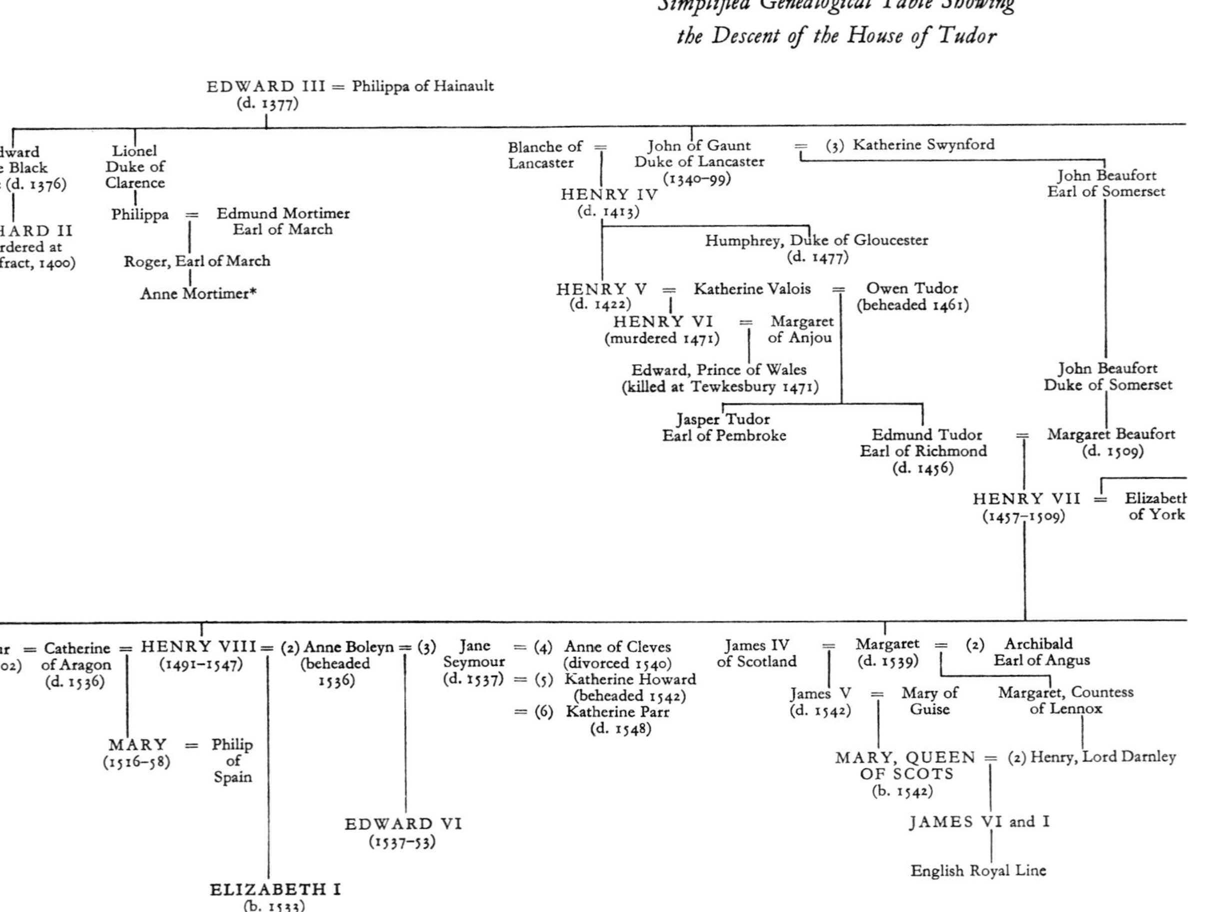

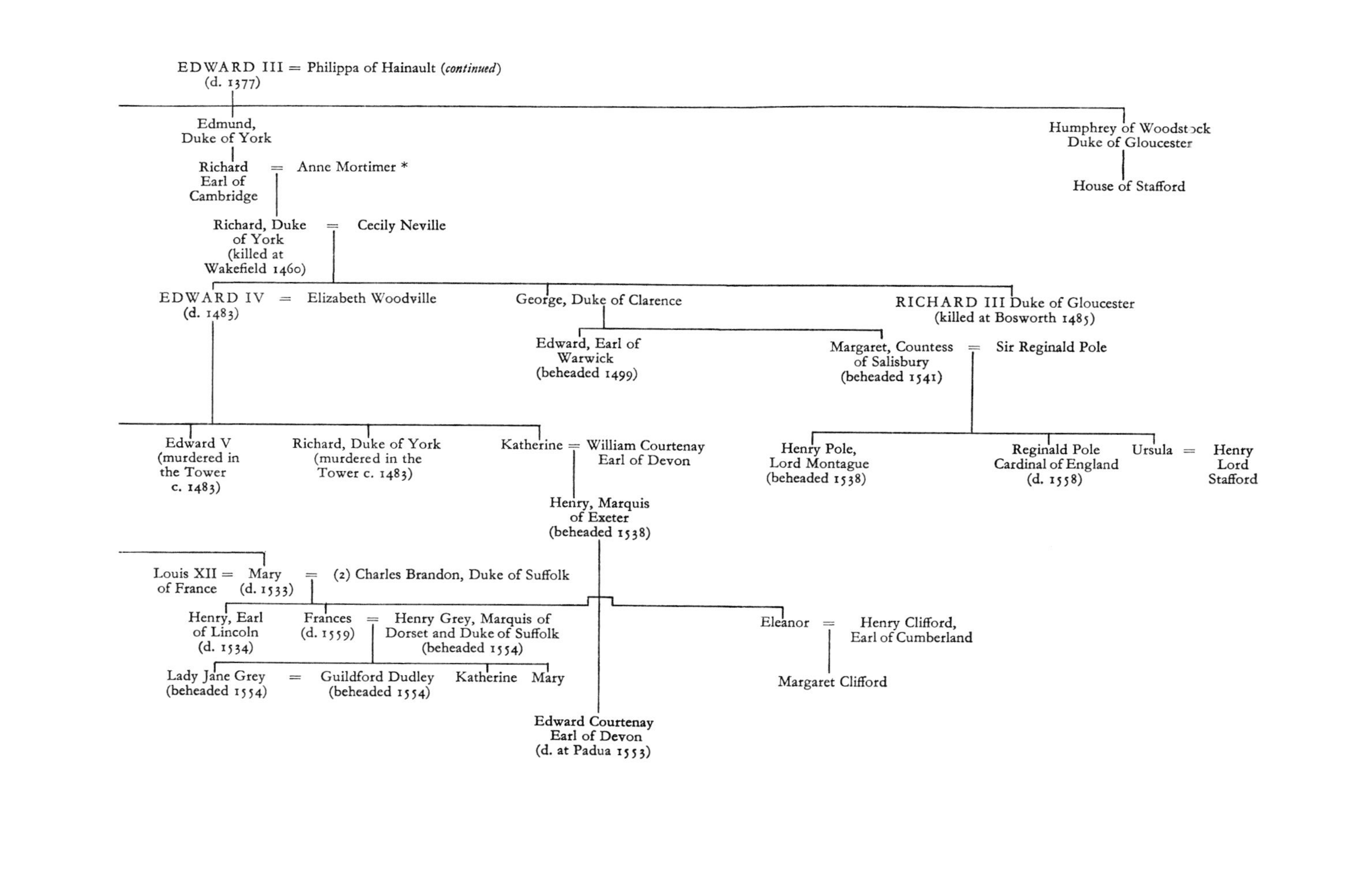

EDWARD III = Philippa of Hainault (*continued*)
(d. 1377)
Edmund, Duke of York
Richard Earl of Cambridge = Anne Mortimer *
Richard, Duke of York (killed at Wakefield 1460) = Cecily Neville
EDWARD IV (d. 1483) = Elizabeth Woodville
George, Duke of Clarence
RICHARD III Duke of Gloucester (killed at Bosworth 1485)
Humphrey of Woodstock Duke of Gloucester
House of Stafford
Edward, Earl of Warwick (beheaded 1499)
Margaret, Countess of Salisbury (beheaded 1541) = Sir Reginald Pole
Edward V (murdered in the Tower c. 1483)
Richard, Duke of York (murdered in the Tower c. 1483)
Katherine = William Courtenay Earl of Devon
Henry, Marquis of Exeter (beheaded 1538)
Henry Pole, Lord Montague (beheaded 1538)
Reginald Pole Cardinal of England (d. 1558)
Ursula = Henry Lord Stafford
Louis XII of France = Mary (d. 1533) = (2) Charles Brandon, Duke of Suffolk
Henry, Earl of Lincoln (d. 1534)
Frances (d. 1559) = Henry Grey, Marquis of Dorset and Duke of Suffolk (beheaded 1554)
Eleanor = Henry Clifford, Earl of Cumberland
Lady Jane Grey (beheaded 1554) = Guildford Dudley (beheaded 1554)
Katherine
Mary
Margaret Clifford
Edward Courtenay Earl of Devon (d. at Padua 1553)

Prologue

At three o'clock in the afternoon of Thursday, 29 May 1533, Queen Anne Boleyn, Marquess of Pembroke, 'most dear and well-beloved' wife of Henry VIII, embarked at Greenwich for the journey up-river to the Tower at the beginning of her coronation celebrations. She was escorted by an impressive contingent of the nobility and by the Lord Mayor and Aldermen, with all the crafts of the City of London in barges sumptuously decorated with banners and streamers and cloth of gold, and plentifully supplied with bands of musicians 'making great melody'.[1] According to one awed foreign spectator, there were so many boats and barges, and so many ladies and gentlemen that it was a thing to wonder at. He added that, although it was four English miles from Greenwich to London and the river was quite wide, nothing else could be seen all the way but boats and barges draped with awnings and carpeted. On arrival at the Tower, the Queen was greeted by a salvo of more than a thousand guns so that it seemed to the same foreigner 'verily as if the world was coming to an end'.[2] In fact, such was the gunners' enthusiasm, that not a single pane of glass survived either in the Tower or neighbouring St Katherine's.

On Saturday, the thirty-first, came the recognition procession through the City to Westminster, and no expense had been spared to make it a memorable occasion. The great cavalcade, shimmering with gold and crimson, silver and purple and scarlet, wound its way through freshly gravelled and gaily decorated streets. The Queen herself, dressed in white cloth of tissue and 'sitting in her hair' as one observer put it, rode in a litter of white cloth of gold drawn by two palfreys caparisoned to the ground in white damask. At every point of vantage along the route pageants and tableaux were presented, children spoke carefully rehearsed pieces in welcome and praise, and all afternoon the conduits and fountains ran with wine.

The climax of splendour was reached on the following day, Whitsunday, with the coronation ceremony itself when

> Queen Anne was brought from Westminster Hall to the Abbey of St Peter's with procession, all the monks of Westminster going in rich copes of gold with thirteen abbots mitred; and after them all the King's Chapel in rich copes with four bishops and two archbishops mitred, and all the Lords going in their Parliament robes, and the crown borne afore her by the Duke of Suffolk, and her two sceptres by two Earls, and she herself going under a rich canopy of cloth of gold, apparelled in a kirtle of crimson velvet powdered with ermines

> and a robe of purple velvet furred with powdered ermines over that, and a rich coronet with a caul of pearls and stones on her head, and the old Duchess of Norfolk bearing up her train, and the Queen's Chamberlain staying the train in the midst.[3]

In the Abbey itself, set in her 'seat royal' before the high altar, Anne Boleyn was anointed and crowned Queen of England by the Archbishops of Canterbury and York, 'and so sat crowned in her seat royal all the Mass and offered also at the said Mass'. Afterwards, at the banquet in Westminster Hall, she occupied the place of honour at the high table under the Cloth of Estate, served by the nobility of England, while the minstrels made 'goodly sweet harmony' in the background and the King looked on from a place which he had had made from which he could see without being seen.

This was Anne's moment of triumph – a moment which for six years she had worked and schemed to bring about, conducting a dangerous and difficult campaign with cold-blooded courage, tenacity and skill. It only needed now for the child she was so visibly carrying to be a healthy boy and her tremendous gamble – a gamble which had brought the former maid-of-honour to the second highest place in the land – would finally have paid off beyond all possibility of doubt.

1

A Gentleman of Wales

The story of Elizabeth Tudor began just over a hundred years before she was born. It began with a love story – with the romance of a young widowed queen and 'a gentleman of Wales'.

Katherine of Valois, called 'the Fair', daughter of the King of France, had been married to that notable warrior, King Henry V of England, hero of Agincourt, in June 1420 – a marriage designed to seal the Treaty of Troyes which was to inaugurate 'perpetual peace' between the two countries. Two years later, on the last day of August 1422, Henry died of dysentery at the Castle of Vincennes just outside Paris. Katherine became a widow shortly before her twenty-first birthday, and her son, 'Harry born at Windsor' who was destined to lose all the glory his father had gained, became King Henry VI at the age of nine months.

The youthful Queen Dowager, stranded in a foreign country and probably both bored and lonely, presently found diversion with one of the gentlemen of her household, Owen Tudor, her Welsh Clerk of the Wardrobe. 'Following more her appetite than friendly counsel and regarding more her private affections than her open honour', as the chronicler Edward Hall put it. Understandably perhaps, for Owen is described by Polydore Vergil as being 'adorned with wonderful gifts of body and mind', and by Hall as 'a goodly gentleman and a beautiful person garnished with many godly gifts both of nature and of graces'. Another (earlier) chronicle was less complimentary, referring to him tersely as a man of neither birth nor livelihood.

Years later, Owen's grandson, the first Tudor king, was to be somewhat embarrassed by certain 'reproachful and slanderous assertions' about the deficiencies of his pedigree, and felt it necessary to appoint a commission consisting of the Abbot of Valle Crucis, Doctor Owen Poole, canon of Hereford, and John King, herald, to enquire into the matter. After visiting Wales and consulting the bards and other authorities, these seekers after knowledge drew up their master's 'perfect genelogie' from the ancient Kings of Britain and Princes of Wales. The Tudors, they said, could prove lineal descent by issue male, saving one woman (an artistic touch), from Brute the Trojan – mythical first King of the Britons, who was supposed to have given his name to the land.

In actual fact, however, the founder of the family fortunes appears to have been Edynfed Fychan, who served the rulers of Gwynedd – the principality of North Wales – as seneschal or steward, from approximately 1215 to his death in 1246. Edynfed was evidently highly thought of by his employers, for they rewarded him with extensive grants of land in Anglesey and Caernarvon. He also acquired estates in West Wales, and he and his relatives were allowed the unusual privilege of holding their lands free from restriction, excepting homage and military service in time of war.

The conquest and subjugation of Wales by England in 1282 does not seem to have adversely affected Edynfed's descendants. On the contrary, by the middle of the next century, the seneschal's great-great-grandson, Tudur ap Goronwy, had emerged as a considerable landowner. Like a number of other Welsh magnates, he probably supported the English crown and Goronwy, eldest of five sons, served with the army in France. It was the unsuccessful revolt of Queen Glendower in the early 1400s which brought about the family's downfall. Through their mother, Tudur's sons were first cousins to Glendower. Old loyalties reasserted themselves and the remaining four brothers (Goronwy had died in 1382) threw in their lot with the rebel chieftain. The consequences were disastrous. Rhys, the middle brother, was executed in 1412 and all the family estates were confiscated, though the property at Penmyndd in Anglesey was later returned to Goronwy's heirs.[1]

Owen Tudor was the son of Maredudd, youngest of the brothers, who held some office under the Bishop of Bangor and was escheator of Anglesey. He was born most probably some time in 1400 and despite the ill-judged activities of his relations, later contrived to enter the English royal service. It is not known exactly how or when this happened, although he may have followed Glendower's son, who was officially pardoned in 1417 and became a Squire of the Body to Henry V. There is no evidence to support the tradition that Owen was present at the battle of Agincourt, but he may have been in France in 1421 on the staff of the distinguished soldier and diplomat Sir Walter Hungerford. Sir Walter was one of the executors of Henry V's will and in 1424 became steward to the infant Henry VI, so it is at least possible that he was the means of finding the promising young Welshman a job in the Queen's household.[2]

The circumstances surrounding Owen's courtship of the Queen Dowager are unfortunately obscure. As Clerk of the Wardrobe, his duties would have included guarding Katherine's jewels and buying and paying for the materials for her dresses – duties which no doubt provided plenty of opportunity for them to get acquainted. It is said that on one occasion he was called upon to dance before the Queen and her ladies. He overbalanced and fell into Katherine's lap, and her reaction to this familiarity led the onlookers to suspect there was something between them.

No record survives of when or where they were married; but, as Katherine bore her second husband three sons and one, possibly two, daughters before her death in 1437 and their legitimacy seems never to have been questioned, the ceremony cannot have taken place much later than 1429, the date generally assigned to it.

It would be fascinating to know more about the private life of this oddly assorted couple. Katherine's own early childhood had been unsettled, with a background of disruption and war. Her father, Charles VI of France, was subject to long and recurring fits of insanity, during which he was liable to tear his clothes, smash the furniture and imagine himself to be made of glass, so that he dared not move for fear of breaking. Her mother, Isabeau of Bavaria, acquired a considerable reputation for loose living and general bad character. She is said to have neglected her younger children to such an extent that for a time they went ragged and hungry. Katherine's short-lived marriage to Henry V was a matter of high politics and one hopes she found happiness with her Welshman.

Their wedding took place without the knowledge or consent of the Duke of Gloucester – Protector of the realm during the King's minority – and several accounts declare that it was not discovered until after Katherine's death. it is straining credulity somewhat to believe that the Queen Dowager could have successfully concealed at least four pregnancies, even if she was living away from the court. A more probable explanation seems that her unsuitable marriage was tolerated by tacit consent during her lifetime, rather than precipitate a scandal involving the King's mother. Owen may also have had influential friends, for in 1432 he was granted letters of denizenship which relieved him of some at any rate of the penal legislation then in force against the Welsh people. Towards the end of 1436, however, the family broke up. Katherine retired into the Abbey of Bermondsey, where she died the following January at the age of thirty-five – possibly giving birth to a daughter who did not survive. The Abbess of Barking took charge of the other Tudor children – Edmund and Jasper, then about six and five years old, Owen, who later became a monk, and a girl of whom nothing is known except that she, too, entered the religious life.

Their father's subsequent career contains all the ingredients of an old-fashioned adventure-story. Deprived of his wife's protection, he evidently thought it wiser to remove himself from the vicinity of the Duke of Gloucester. He was at Daventry when, not long after Katherine's death, a summons was issued by the Council requiring 'one Owen Tudor the which dwelled with the said Queen Katherine' to come into the King's presence. Suspecting a trap, Owen refused to obey unless he was given an assurance in the King's name that he might 'freely come and freely go'. According to a minute of the Privy Council's proceedings dated 15 July 1437, a promise to this effect was conveyed to him by a certain Myles Sculle, but

Owen was not entirely satisfied. He came to London 'in full secret wise' and took sanctuary at Westminster, where 'he held him many days'. This despite the fact that 'divers persons stirred him of friendship and fellowship to have comen out thereof, and some in especial to have disported him in [the] tavern at Westminster gate'. Owen, no doubt wisely, resisted these persuasions. However, some time later, hearing that the King was 'heavily informed of him', he suddenly appeared in the royal presence and

> declared his innocence and his truth, affirming that he had nothing done that should give the King occasion or matter of offence or displeasure against him, offering himself in large wise to answer as the Kings true liege man should to all things that any man could or would submit upon him. And so submitted himself by his said offer to abide all lawful answer.[3]

He was allowed to depart 'without any impeachment' but shortly afterwards was arrested and committed to Newgate. The Council felt it necessary to justify their action in a somewhat specious memorandum, saying that Owen's 'malicious purpose and imagination' were not known to the King or the Duke of Gloucester when the safe conduct was issued. They added piously that it was 'thought marvellous' that one of the King's liegemen should desire any such surety before coming to his presence, and anyway Owen had been allowed to go free – for a time.

Polydore Vergil says that he was committed to ward by order of the Duke of Gloucester, 'because he had been so presumptuous as by marriage with the Queen to intermix his blood with the noble race of kings', but there is nothing to support this assertion in the Privy Council minutes. In fact no specific charge is mentioned, but from the very meagre information which does exist it would appear that Owen was involved in some private quarrel – probably of a financial nature – with an unnamed adversary.

As entry in the Chronicle of London for the sixteenth year of the King's reign records that Owen 'brake out of Newgate against night at searching time, through help of his priest, and went his way, hurting foul his keeper; but at the last, blessed be God, he was taken again'.[4] This was probably in February. He was recaptured by Lord Beaumont and temporarily consigned to the dungeons of Wallingford Castle in Berkshire, but later returned to Newgate with his servant and the priest. On 4 March 1438, Lord Beaumont received twenty marks to cover his expenses, and the sum of eighty-nine pounds which was found on the priest was handed over to the Exchequer.[5] It would be interesting to know if this enterprising cleric was the same priest who had married Owen and Katherine.

When Henry VI reached his majority the fortunes of the Tudor family improved. The gentle, devout king took a constructive interest in the welfare of his Welsh relations and provided for the education of his two elder half-brothers. As soon as they outgrew the Abbess of Barking,

Edmund and Jasper were brought up 'chastely and virtuously' by discreet persons. Their father also received a pension of forty pounds a year which the king, moved by 'certain causes', paid out of his privy purse 'by especial grace'. Owen, who had finally been released from prison in 1439, was now a respected member of the royal household and presently found it convenient to adopt an English style patronymic, Owain ap Maredudd [or Meredith] ap Tudur becoming Owen Tudor.

On Christmas Day 1449 Edmund and Jasper Tudor were knighted. Four years later they were created Earls of Richmond and Pembroke respectively. The king was also apparently instrumental in providing a wife for the Earl of Richmond and in 1445 Edmund married twelve-year-old Margaret Beaufort – a union which was to have far-reaching consequences.

The Beaufort family was the result of a long-ago liaison between John of Gaunt, Duke of Lancaster, third son of Edward III, and Katherine Swynford, a lady of Flemish extraction who had been governess to the Duke's daughters. Their four children were indisputably born on the wrong side of the blanket, but after the death of his second wife John of Gaunt proceeded to make an honest woman of Katherine. His Beaufort progeny (so called after the castle in France where they were born) were legitimated by the Pope, by Letters Patent granted by Gaunt's nephew Richard II, and for good measure by Act of Parliament. The Beauforts grew rich and powerful – Cardinal Beaufort, the last survivor of Katherine Swynford's brood, had governed England with the Duke of Gloucester during Henry VI's long minority – and after the King and his heirs they represented the royal and ruling family of Lancaster. Margaret, heiress of her father, John, Duke of Somerset, great-granddaughter of John of Gaunt and later to develop into a remarkable personality in her own right, was a matrimonial prize by any standards – especially for the son of an obscure Welsh squire.

Their marriage coincided with the outbreak of that long-drawn-out dynastic struggle among the all too numerous descendants of Edward III, which is known to history as the Wars of the Roses. The quarrel had its roots in the *coup d'état* of 1399, when Henry Bolingbroke, John of Gaunt's eldest son, wrested the crown from his cousin Richard II; and it became progressively more bitter and more complicated – as family quarrels usually do. It was fought out on one side by the pathetic Henry VI's tigerish Queen, Margaret of Anjou; and on the other, first by the Duke of York and later his son, Edward, Earl of March, representing a senior branch of the royal house, but whose descent had twice passed through the female line.

Edmund Tudor did not live to see the outcome. Neither did he live to see his son. He died at Carmarthen early in November 1456, at the age of twenty-six, leaving his young wife six months pregnant. Jasper at once took his brother's widow under his protection, and Margaret Beaufort's child was born at Pembroke Castle on 28 January 1457. He was given, prophetically as it turned out, the royal English name of Henry but at the time the birth attracted little attention. Henry Tudor was said to be a delicate baby. His future looked uncertain.

Meanwhile the deadly power-game of York and Lancaster continued unabated. The Duke of York was killed at Wakefield in December 1460, but his son remained to carry on the struggle. Jasper Tudor, Earl of Pembroke, brave, energetic and loyal, was a leading supporter of the Lancashire cause; so, too, his father, quite an old man by this time. Nevertheless, Owen Tudor was present, fighting under Jasper's banner, at the battle of Mortimer's Cross near Wigmore on 2 February 1461. The Lancastrians were defeated by the young Earl of March, and Owen, not quite so spry as he had once been, was among those captured. He was brought to Hereford and executed there in the market-place. It seems he could not believe his luck had turned at last for, one old chronicle says, he trusted

> all away that he should not be headed till he saw the axe and the block, and when that he was in his doublet he trusted on pardon and grace till the collar of his red velvet doublet was ripped off. Then he said 'that head shall lie on the stock that was wont to lie on Queen Katherine's lap' and put his heart and mind wholly unto God and full meekly took his death.

Afterwards his head was displayed on the highest step of the market-cross and 'a mad woman combed his hair and washed away the blood of his face and she got candles and set about him burning more than a hundred.'[6] It was a sad but perhaps suitably bizarre end for the adventurous gentleman of Wales who had sired a dynasty of kings, whose great-granddaughter's descendants occupy the English throne to this day, and whose great-great-granddaughter was to be the most complex and fascinating personality ever to occupy it and give her name to a whole glittering epoch of English life.

1461 was a black year for the House of Lancaster. On 4 March the nineteen-year-old Earl of March was acclaimed as King Edward IV in Westminster Hall, and his victory over Queen Margaret at Towton at the end of the month confirmed his position. Margaret fled to Scotland, taking Henry VI and their young son with her. For a while she succeeded in keeping the fight alive, but four years later King Henry, reduced by this time to a wandering fugitive in the North Country, was betrayed to his enemies and deposited in the Tower. The Queen and the Prince of Wales sought refuge abroad. The Yorkists appeared triumphant.

Jasper Tudor, who had inherited all his father's slipperiness, escaped after Mortimer's Cross and was reported 'flown and taken to the mountains'. For the next few years he led the life of an underground resistance-leader, moving from one safe house to another in Wales, then turning up in Ireland, then Scotland, over to France, back in Wales again. 'Not always at his heart's ease, nor in security of life or surety of living' he remained unswerving in his devotion to the cause of Lancaster, and lost no opportunity, however slight, of stirring up trouble for the new regime.

The task of subduing Wales had been entrusted to William Herbert, himself a Welshman, who was rising in the councils of Edward IV. Pembroke Castle surrendered on 30 September 1461, and in February of the following year Herbert was granted the wardship and marriage of Henry Tudor then five years old. Whether or not the child actually came into the hands of his new guardian at this time is uncertain. Harlech Castle was still holding out for the Lancastrians and provided a convenient shelter for refugees – little Henry may well have been among them. But in 1468 Harlech was besieged, and despite an attempt by Jasper to come to its rescue the Castle finally surrendered on 14 August. Jasper got away again but William Herbert was rewarded with his earldom of Pembroke.

In the following year there was another reversal of fortune. Edward IV fell out with his powerful ally, Richard Neville, Earl of Warwick, 'the Kingmaker'. Warwick defected to the other side and in the summer of 1470 came to an arrangement with Queen Margaret, still chafing in exile. Edward, caught unawares, fled abroad in his turn, escaping capture by a hair's breadth. Once more the Lancastrians were in the saddle. The wretched, apathetic Henry VI was brought out of the Tower, dusted off and once more installed in the royal apartments at Westminster.

Another captive was set at liberty by the new turn of events. Jasper Tudor lost no time in recovering his young nephew. According to Polydore Vergil, he found him 'kept as a prisoner, but honourably brought up with the wife of William Herbert'. Jasper, again according to Vergil,

> took the boy Henry from the wife of the Lord Herbert, and brought him with himself a little after when he came to London unto King Henry. When the King saw the child, beholding within himself without speech a pretty space the haultic disposition thereof, he is reported to have said to the noblemen there present, 'This truly, this is he unto whom both we and our adversaries must yield and give over the dominion.'

'Thus,' added Vergil, 'the holy man showed it would come to pass that Henry should in time enjoy the kingdom.'

There was a long road to travel before this pious (and most probably apocryphal) prophecy was fulfilled. Without the help of a crystal-ball, not even the most optimistic well-wisher of Henry Tudor would have foretold in 1470 any other future for him than that of an honoured and profitable career in the service of Henry VI and his heirs. In fact, the Lancastrian revival was short-lived. Barely six months after his flight, Edward was back in England, re-proclaiming himself King. On Easter Day 1471, he defeated Warwick at the battle of Barnet which, appropriately enough, was fought in thick fog. The Kingmaker was killed and Henry VI, 'a man amazed and utterly dulled with troubles and adversity', was taken back to the Tower.

On the day that Barnet was being lost and won, Queen Margaret and her son landed at Weymouth, too late to save the situation. Together with the Lancastrian lords who had rallied to them, they marched up the Severn valley, hoping to join forces with Jasper Tudor and his Welshmen coming down from North Wales. But Edward, with his usual speed and tactical skill, intercepted them at Tewkesbury, an encounter which ended in disaster for the House of Lancaster. The last surviving male members of the Beaufort family lost their lives and the Prince of Wales, for whose sake his mother had struggled so long and so valiantly, was killed trying to escape. On 21 May, Edward IV re-entered London in triumph with the Queen, her spirit broken at last, a prisoner in his train. That same night 'between eleven and twelve of the clock' Henry VI was released from his earthly troubles with the help of a Yorkist sword.

When Jasper heard that Queen Margaret 'was vanquished in a foughten field at Tewkesbury and that matters were past all hope of recovery', he retired to Chepstow (where he had yet another narrow escape from capture and death). He had been unable to help the cause in battle but there was still one important service he could perform. In the person of his fourteen-year-old nephew was now represented the last surviving male of the Lancastrian line – the last slender hope for the future. At all costs Henry Tudor must be kept from falling into Yorkist hands. Margaret Beaufort had confided her son to Jasper's care – a trust which he faithfully performed – and now that there was no possibility of 'any comfort or relief to be had for the part of poor King Henry' she asked her brother-in-law to take the boy out of the country to safety.

Jasper made for Pembroke and was immediately besieged. But once again his luck held, and after eight days he was able to make his way through 'ditch and trench' with the help of one David Morgan. He then

> departed forthwith to a town by the sea side called Tenby, where having a bark prepared out of hand he sailed into France with his brother's son Henry Earl of Richmond, and certain other his friends and servants, whose chances being to arrive in Brittany he presented himself humbly to Francis, duke there, and reporting the cause of his coming, submitted himself and his nephew to his protection. The Duke received them willingly, and with such honour, courtesy and favour entertained them as though they had been his brothers, promising them upon his honour that within his dominion they should be from henceforth far from injury, and pass at their pleasure to and fro without danger.[7]

Nevertheless, the young Earl of Richmond was to have at least two very nasty moments during his exile. Edward IV made several attempts to persuade the Duke of Brittany to part with his guest – 'the only imp now left of King Henry VI's blood' – and on one occasion very nearly succeeded, sending ambassadors 'laden with great substance of gold' and with instructions to tell the Duke that he intended to arrange a marriage for young Henry which would unite the rival factions 'by affinity'. Duke Francis was convinced, either by the sight of the gold or the smooth-talking ambassadors, and delivered the Earl of Richmond into their hands, 'not supposing that he had committed the sheep to the wolf, but the son to the father'. Edward's ambassadors set off with their prize towards the coast, but Henry 'knowing that he was carried to his death, through agony of mind fell by the way into a fever'. (Or was he desperately playing for time, in much the same way as his granddaughter was to do in later years?) Fortunately the Duke was warned in time that 'the Earl of Richmond was not so earnestly sought for to be coupled in marriage with King Edward's daughter, as to have his head parted from his body with an axe.'[8] Henry was snatched back at St Malo and thereafter more closely guarded by his host – partly for his own safety and partly to appease the English government, who continued to pay the Bretons handsomely to keep him prisoner.

It cannot have been a very cheerful existence for the young man, helpless to defend himself, knowing that his life depended on the goodwill of a protector who might at any time be subjected to heavy financial and political pressures from outside (though, in fact, Duke Francis was to prove a good friend) and with little apparent prospect of ever being able to lead a normal life and enjoy even the fruits of his own earldom.

Then, suddenly, in April 1483, Edward IV was dead. His two young sons fell into the hands of his brother, Richard Duke of Gloucester, who proceeded to declare the King's marriage to have been defective and his children bastards. The Princes were lodged in the Tower and shortly afterwards disappeared permanently and mysteriously from sight. In June, Richard of Gloucester was King of England. He was not popular. In an age not noted for squeamishness many of his subjects were repelled by persistent rumours that he had his nephews murdered, and the future of the exile in Brittany looked unexpectedly brighter. Margaret Beaufort, now married for the third time to Lord Stanley, a powerful magnate generally regarded as a Yorkist supporter, set to work to build up a following for her son – no doubt beginning with her husband. She also quietly approached Edward IV's widow, Elizabeth Woodville, who had been stripped of her royal dignity by Richard, suggesting that a marriage between Henry Tudor and the widow's eldest daughter, Elizabeth, would solve a great many problems, by uniting the rival factions once and for all and ousting the usurper. The Queen and her daughter were agreeable. Other people, too, alarmed by the ferocity of the new King's behaviour, had begun to think in terms of Henry Tudor as a possible replacement. The Duke of Buckingham declared in his favour and messengers were sent to Brittany inviting the Earl of Richmond to come and claim his bride and his kingdom.

With the help of Duke Francis, Henry gathered a force of fifteen ships and 5000 mercenaries and embarked for England in October. But the rising was still-born. Richard fell on the conspirators with his usual violence. Buckingham was executed and even Margaret Beaufort had a narrow escape. Fortunately for her son, the winds had scattered his small fleet, driving it back on the coast of France. He himself got as far as Plymouth, but 'viewing afar of all the shore beset with soldiers' and realising that it would be suicidal to land, 'hoisted up sail' and returned to Brittany. But despite this setback, the tide was running in his favour. Fugitives from Richard's rule began to gather round him, and on Christmas Day 1483 Henry Tudor swore a solemn oath in the cathedral at Rennes 'that so soon as he should be King he would marry Elizabeth, King Edward's daughter'.

All the same, his troubles were not yet over. The following September he was to have a very narrow escape indeed. King Richard, like King Edward before him, had already done his best to ensure that Henry should at least be kept a permanent prisoner in his Breton sanctuary. But after the Buckingham episode the King, 'more doubting than trusting in his own cause, was vexed and tormented in mind with fear almost perpetually of the Earl Henry and his confederates' return; wherefore he had a miserable life'.[9] Determined 'to rid himself of this inward grief', Richard despatched another embassy to Brittany. Unfortunately, Duke Francis had 'become feeble by reason of sore and daily sickness' and the ambassadors were received by his treasurer, Peter Landois. They offered the yearly revenues of the earldom of Richmond, together with those of the other English nobles who had fled since the rising, in return for Henry's surrender. Peter Landois, a man 'of sharp wit and great authority', was ruling 'all matters as he list' in the incapacity of his master, and as a result had aroused considerable hostility among his own countrymen. According to Polydore Vergil, he felt that the King of England would be a powerful ally against his enemies at home, and for that reason and not any personal spite he agreed to betray Henry Tudor.

Once again the luck held. Henry heard about Landois's plans and, 'thinking it meet to provide for his affairs with all diligence', applied for and got a safe conduct from the King of France. He sent word to the faithful Jasper to get himself and the other English refugees across the frontier into Anjou without delay, and set about arranging his own escape. He gave out that he was going to visit a friend who lived near by;

> but when he had journeyed almost five miles, he withdrew hastily out of the highway into the next wood and donning a serving man's apparel he as a servant followed one of his own servants (who was his guide in that journey) as though he had been his master, and rode on with so great celerity that he made no stay anywhere, except it were to bait his horses, before he had gotten himself to his company within the bounds of Anjou.[10]

Not a moment too soon, for when Peter Landois, 'who wanted no subtlety', heard that Henry had gone

> he sent out horsemen incontinent every way to pursue, and if they could overtake him, to apprehend and bring the earl to him. The horsemen made such haste as that there was never thing more nigh the achieving than the overtaking of the earl; he was scarce an hour entered the bounds of France when they came thither.[11]

It is pleasant to know that Duke Francis recovered, and when he heard that 'Henry was so uncourteously entertained as that he was forced to fly out of his dominion' was very angry with Peter Landois, at least so Polydore Vergil says. It is also salutory to remember that the whole future of the dynasty and the very existence of Elizabeth Tudor may well have depended on that quick change in a Breton wood, and to dash to safety with barely an hour to spare.

The fugitives were welcomed in France and the exile began 'to have good hope of happy success'. By the following summer the time seemed ripe for another attempt on England. At best it was likely to be a desperate venture, and delay might be fatal. There was no knowing how much longer Elizabeth of York would be allowed to remain unmarried, the loyalty of the English refugees – many of them discontented Yorkists – could not be relied on for ever and France might yet prove inhospitable. Henry borrowed money, 'a slender supply' from the French King, and more where he could get it, and left Paris to start collecting a fleet. On 1 August 1485 – 'thinking it needful to make haste, that his friends should not be any longer kept in perplexity between hope and dread, uncertain what to do' – he sailed from the mouth of the Seine with 2000 armed men and a few ships, and 'with a soft southern wind' behind him. A week later he landed at Milford Haven and began his march up through Wales towards the Midlands, gathering support as he went. The local gentry came in to join him, less because he was the last Lancastrian than because he was Owen Tudor's grandson and Jasper's nephew. 'He was of no great statue', this unknown Welshman, the adventurer come to conquer if he could, 'his countenance was cheerful and courageous, his hair yellow like burnished gold, his eyes gray, shining and quick.'[12]

Henry had sent messages to his mother but he still did not know how the powerful Stanley family was going to react, and as he approached the English heartland he heard that King Richard 'with an host innumerable was at hand'. The final confrontation, the great gamble on which everything depended, took place on 22 August at the village of Market Bosworth, 'a little beyond Leicester'. After two hours' fierce fighting it was all over. The naked corpse of the last Plantagenet king had been carried ignominiously away, slung across the back of a horse, to be buried in the Franciscan Abbey at Leicester. The crown had been found in a hawthorn bush and placed on Henry Tudor's head by Lord Stanley.

The new King was twenty-eight. He had had no practical experience of government or of warfare. As he himself is supposed to have said, he had been either a prisoner or a fugitive since he was five years old. Apart from one brief visit in his boyhood, he had never set foot in England before. His hereditary title was not impressive and devolved entirely from his mother. If descent from Edward III through the female line was admitted, then there were Yorkist claimants alive with unquestionably better titles in law, not least Henry's intended bride, Elizabeth, eldest surviving child of Edward IV. But the majority of his subjects were less concerned with the legality of Henry VII's claim to the crown than with his ability to hold on to it. The dynastic struggles of the past thirty years had not unduly affected the life of the country as a whole. It had not been a civil war fought over some fundamental principle of the kind that tears a nation apart. Ordinary people had been able to conduct their affairs more or less undisturbed, while the great pursued a more than usually stimulating form of bloodsport. But, in an age when the government was the King, continued uncertainty as to who was likely to be occupying the throne next was unsettling. It was bad for business, bad for the orderly administration of justice, and bred dangerous habits of disrespect for the rule of law. The crown was weakened and impoverished, the nobility were becoming disagreeably powerful and England had lost prestige abroad. If the new dynasty could establish a strong central authority, it would be assured of support from the solid middle block of the population with a stake in stability and prosperity.

In January 1486, Henry redeemed the pledge given at Rennes two years before and married Elizabeth, King Edward's daughter. In the veins of the second and third generations of Tudor monarchs would flow the blood of Plantagenet, both York and Lancaster, of Valois and Mortimer, Neville and Woodville, of the lady from Flanders and the seneschal to the princes of Gwynedd.

Like her bridegroom, Elizabeth was very much a child of the warring factions. She had been twice hurried into sanctuary with her mother; had suffered the grief of the unexplained disappearance and sinister end of her two brothers, and all the other alarms and anxieties of Richard's reign. She was a pretty, fair-haired girl in her early twenties at the time of her marriage, sweet-tempered, docile and affectionate; generous to her less fortunate younger sisters and kind to her mother, who was by all accounts a rather tiresome woman with an unlucky talent for making enemies.

Henry allowed his wife no share in the executive power, but there is no indication that she ever expected it or resented the fact that he wore a crown which should rightfully have been hers. Elizabeth of York seems to have been perfectly content with the role of Queen Consort, and certainly nobly fulfilled her prime function, giving birth to eight children before her death in 1503. Only one son and two daughters survived into adult life, not a very good omen even in an age of high infant mortality, but it was enough to secure the succession.

Henry VII has been likened to a man who, starting from virtually nothing, built up a flourishing family business. His spirit, says Polydore Vergil, was distinguished, wise and prudent, his mind brave and resolute. John Stow thought him 'a prince of marvellous wisdom, policy, justice, temperance and gravity'. In private life he was a devoted son, an affectionate husband and a conscientious father. He was fond of music, a keen sportsman and generous to those in trouble. In spite of his early disadvantages, he was a cultured man, a patron of literature and the arts with a taste and talent for royal magnificence. His public abilities as king and statesman are beyond dispute, but he remains essentially a lonely figure – cold, secret and remote. His precarious youth had taught him to trust no one completely, to keep his own counsel and, above all, the importance of holding on to what he had won. He was admired, feared and respected by his contemporaries, but not loved. The first Henry Tudor lacked the precious gift of personal magnetism possessed in such abundance by his granddaughter Elizabeth, who in many other ways so closely resembled him, but he laid the foundation without which her achievement would have been impossible.

When he died the country was at peace. The crown was solvent. Despite some determined challenges, his dynasty was established and accepted. Reputable foreign monarchs were prepared to marry their children into it. There was a healthy male heir of full age ready to take over. Few men could have done more.

2

THE KING'S GREAT MATTER

On one point everybody was agreed: the youthful Henry VIII was a most magnificent specimen of manhood, who seemed to embody all the gifts and graces of the ideal Christian monarch. Where he succeeded to his father's throne in the spring of 1509 his contemporaries went wild with delight over this 'new and auspicious star', this 'lover of justice and goodness', their dazzling eighteen-year-old King. 'If you could see how all the world here is rejoicing in the possession of so great a prince,' wrote William Mountjoy to Desiderius Erasmus,

> how his life is all their desire, you could not contain your tears for joy. The heavens laugh, the earth exults, all things are full of milk, of honey and of nectar! Avarice is expelled the country. Liberality scatters wealth with bounteous hand. Our king does not desire gold or gems or precious metals, but virtue, glory, immortality.[1]

The country was ready for a change. In his last years Henry VII had become 'a dark prince, infinitely suspicious' and his subjects, forgetting the many solid benefits he had brought them, complained loud and bitterly about the shocking extortions of his tax collectors. In 1509 it really seemed as if a new era – 'called then the golden world' – had dawned, and few English kings have ever embarked on their reigns in such a general atmosphere of goodwill and buoyant optimism than the future father of Elizabeth Tudor – 'our natural, young, lusty and courageous prince and sovereign lord, King Harry the Eighth'.

As a physical type, the new King resembled his maternal grandfather, Edward IV, who was 'very tall of personage, exceeding the stature almost of all others' and 'of visage lovely, of body mighty, strong and clean-made. Howbeit in his latter days, with over-liberal diet, somewhat corpulent and burly. . . .' Descriptions which could equally well have been applied to his grandson. The descriptions of Henry's own appearance as a young man were lyrical. Piero Pasqualigo, the Venetian Ambassador Extraordinary, writing in 1515, declared that 'His Majesty is the handsomest potentate I ever set eyes on; above the usual height, with an extremely fine calf to his leg, his complexion very fair and bright, with auburn hair combed straight and short in the French fashion, and a round face so very beautiful that it would become a pretty woman.'[2] Four years later, Sebastian Giustinian, another Venetian, was just as complimentary. Nature could not have done more for the King, he said. He was much handsomer than any other sovereign in Christendom, very fair and his whole frame admirably proportioned.

Henry took after his grandfather Edward in other ways. The Yorkist king had been noted for his popularity and, as Polydore Vergil rather disapprovingly remarked, 'would use himself more familiarly among private persons than the honour of his majesty required'. Edward had fully realised the truth of the somewhat cynical observation that 'the common people oftentimes more esteem and take for greater kindness a little courtesy, than a great benefit'. Henry knew this too, whether consciously or not. He mingled freely with the common people, and when he chose to exert his charm he could be irresistible. Thomas More put his finger on it when he wrote to John Fisher: 'the king has a way of making every man feel that he is enjoying his special favour, just as the London wives pray before the image of Our Lady by the Tower till each of them believes it is smiling upon *her*'.[3]

Henry had also inherited the prodigious energy of his Plantagenet forbears, and to his admiring subjects there seemed no end to the skills and accomplishments of their glorious prince. According to the Venetians, he could draw the bow with greater strength than any man in England and jousted marvellously. He was a capital horseman, inordinately fond of hunting, and capable of tiring out eight or ten horses in one day. He was an enthusiastic tennis-player, 'at which game', wrote Sebastian Giustinian, 'it is the prettiest thing in the world to see him play, his fair skin glowing through a shirt of the finest texture'.[4] The King was, in fact, a first-rate all-round sportsman – wrestling, tilting, shooting, hawking, dancing, running at the ring, casting of the bar – whatever form of physical exercise he engaged in, he excelled at.

Nor was his prowess only athletic. Henry had plenty of native shrewdness and a good brain, when he stood still long enough to use it. He had been well educated. He was an enthusiastic amateur theologian. He spoke fluent French and Latin, some Spanish and a little Italian. He enjoyed the company of scholars and liked to display his own learning. A music-lover like his father, he was himself a talented musician. He played the lute, organ, virginals and harpsichord, could sing 'from book at sight' and composed two five-part masses, a motet and many instrumental pieces, rounds and part songs.

> Pastance with good company
> I love and shall until I die

he sang to his own accompaniment and, thanks to old Henry's careful counting of the pennies, 'such grace of plenty reigned' that young Henry was able 'to follow his desire and appetite' to his heart's content. With the unselfconscious absorption of a child, he threw himself into the delightful business of cutting a dash in the world. He received the Venetian ambassadors under a canopy of cloth of gold, wearing a doublet of white and crimson satin and a purple velvet mantle lined with white satin. Round his neck was a gold collar from which hung a diamond the size of a walnut, while his fingers 'were one mass of jewelled rings'. Mounted on a warhorse caparisoned in cloth of gold with a raised pile, he looked like St George in person. On board his new warship, named in honour of his sister Mary, he acted as pilot, wearing 'a sailor's coat and trousers made of cloth of gold, and a gold chain with the inscription "Dieu *est* mon Droit", to which was suspended a whistle, which he blew nearly as loud as a trumpet'.[5] He had a passion for dressing up – as Robin Hood; 'in Turkey fashion'; 'in white satin and green, embroidered and set with letters and castles of find gold in bullion'; in an abbreviated suit of 'blue velvet and crimson with long sleeves, all cut and lined with cloth of gold'.[6] 'Youth will needs have dalliance,' sang the King; and tournaments, pageants, banquets, revels and 'disguisings' followed one another in an unending, untiring stream, so that life was spent 'in continual festival'.

From across the centuries one's mind balks at the splendours, and superlatives, the super-human energy, the sheer prodigality and over-exuberance of it all. He was more than life-size, this amazing young man: a great, sumptuous, heraldic beast, rampant on a field of scarlet and gold, 'disposed all to mirth and pleasure', innocently exulting in his own magnificence. There were not many signs as yet of that other beast, the cold-hearted egotist, tricky, violent and cruel, which lurked behind the smooth pink and white countenance with its intermittent aureole of fluffy red beard. Some people caught a glimpse of it. George Cavendish, Thomas Wolsey's gentleman usher, watching his master's rise to power, noticed indulgently enough that the King 'loved nothing worse than to be constrained to do anything contrary to his royal will and pleasure'. Thomas More saw deeper. Even in the unclouded days when Henry used to send for him to discuss 'astronomy, geometry, divinity, and such other faculties'; and when 'for the pleasure he took in his company' would visit More at his house at Chelsea and walk in the garden with him, an arm flung round his shoulders, Sir Thomas had no illusions. He told his son-in-law, William Roper, that if his head could win the King a castle in France 'it should not fail to go'.[7]

One of Henry's first actions had been to get himself a wife. Barely six weeks after he came to the throne he married his brother's widow, the Spanish princess Catherine of Aragon,* daughter of those redoubtable

* I have spelt Catherine of Aragon's name with a 'C', coming as it does, from the Spanish 'Catalina'. For the other, numerous, Katherines who appear in this story, I have followed the English spelling at the time.

monarchs Isabella of Castile and Ferdinand of Aragon – *los Reyes Catolicos* – the Catholic Kings of Spain. Catherine had come to England in 1501, when she was fifteen, to be married to Arthur, Henry's elder brother, then Prince of Wales. Not quite five months after the wedding young Arthur was dead and, in order to preserve the Anglo-Spanish alliance, Catherine had been betrothed to Henry, then rising eleven years old, their marriage to take place when he was fifteen. Then Isabella of Castile died. The political situation in Spain looked less stable. Henry VII, always cautious, had hesitated, wondering if after all he might do better for his one remaining son. The marriage was postponed and Catherine remained a widow, a pawn in the game of dynastic politics and the victim of a not very edifying dispute over the payment of the second instalment of her dowry. For seven years she waited; stoically enduring the humiliating position of a guest who had outstayed her welcome. Cold-shouldered and neglected, dependent on the reluctant provision of her father-in-law, Catherine had no money to pay her servants, hardly enough money for food and clothes, but she refused to despair. She had come to England to be married, to serve Spain with her own body, and in England she would stay. Even in her teens Catherine of Aragon had a will of iron. In 1509 she got her reward. In the best tradition of all fairy tales, Prince Charming came into his own, rescued the forlorn princess and carried her off in triumph. It certainly looked like a happy ending.

Catherine was not startlingly beautiful but she was a good-looking girl, small and slender, with clear grey eyes and a mass of russet-coloured hair. She was also intelligent and thoughtful, and in the early days Henry relied on her a good deal, respecting her opinion and listening to her advice. Many of his most extravagant entertainments were planned, so he said, for her pleasure and Catherine never failed to be suitably appreciative. He wore her favour in the lists; heard vespers and compline every day in her chamber; read the latest books with her and hurried to bring her any titbits of news he thought would interest her.[8]

The King found his diversions, of course; that was to be expected. There was Elizabeth Blount who bore his bastard son in 1519. Later there was Mary Boleyn. There may well have been others. All the same, despite his highly coloured reputation, Henry was no Don Juan. By the standards of royal behaviour at the time, he was a faithful husband, at any rate in those early years, and Catherine repaid him with steadfast loyalty and devotion. Well bred, virtuous and dutiful, she had every quality of an ideal Queen Consort except the all-important one: she could not produce a healthy son.

The tragedy of the Queen's child-bearing began in 1510 with a still-born daughter. A son arrived on New Year's Day 1511, but lived only a few weeks. Time went by and more pregnancies ended in miscarriages, in babies born dead, babies who lived only a few days. Then, in February 1516, a child was born at Greenwich, alive and healthy. It was a girl, christened Mary. The King was philosophical, at least in public. 'We are both young', he said to a congratulatory ambassador; 'if it was a daughter this time, by the grace of God the sons will follow.' In the autumn of 1517 Catherine miscarried again. In November 1518 she was delivered of a still-born child. It was her last pregnancy.

By the early 1520s Henry was seriously worried about the succession. In June 1525 he created his bastard Henry Fitzroy, then six years old, Duke of Richmond – a semi-royal title. There was even talk of a marriage between Richmond and the legitimate heiress, Princess Mary. Henry's love affair with his wife had long since grown cold. Catherine was nearly forty now, her prettiness faded, her slender figure thickened and spread – although ambassadors still remarked on her beautiful complexion. Henry no longer needed her as audience and confidante. Her very nationality had become a liability, as English foreign policy, under the guidance of Thomas Wolsey, leaned more and more towards a French alliance. And there were no sons.

In the early spring of 1527, something or someone led the King to open his Bible and turn to the Book of Leviticus. There, in the twentieth chapter, he read: '. . . if a man shall take his brother's wife, it is an unclean thing . . . they shall be childless'. According to Henry's own account, once his attention had been drawn to these alarming words, he began to have qualms (that famous scruple which 'pricked' his conscience) soon to grow into an unalterable conviction that his marriage was against God's law; that for eighteen years he had been living in incestuous adultery with his brother's wife. And the fact that they were childless, or as good as childless, was surely, he reasoned, a sign of God's displeasure. After all, Henry asked himself, why else should God who had favoured him in all things, and whom he regarded very much in the light of a senior partner, deny him living sons? Obviously something must be done, and the King turned to Cardinal Wolsey, always so reliable, so devoted to his master's interests and anxious only to satisfy his royal will and pleasure. Wolsey, confronted with what was in effect a command to arrange the removal of the Queen with a minimum of scandal and inconvenience, did his usual efficient best to oblige and in May 1527 instituted the divorce proceedings, or, to be more exact, the nullity suit which was to have such incalculably far-reaching effects on the whole course of English life.

The first tentative steps in 'the King's great matter', as it was carefully referred to by those in the know, were taken in an atmosphere of elaborate secrecy; but it was not long before news of it leaked out. By midsummer the whole affair, as the Spanish ambassador scornfully remarked, was 'as notorious as if it had been proclaimed by the public crier'. By the end of the summer it was being freely rumoured that the pricking of the King's conscience was not the only spur prompting him to question the validity of his marriage to Catherine of Aragon. No one knows exactly when Henry first became enamoured of Anne Boleyn, but certainly by September what George Cavendish described as 'the long hid and secret love' between the King and Mistress Anne was a secret no longer.

The rise of the Boleyn family, who came originally and obscurely from Sall in Norfolk, had followed the classic pattern. Early in the fifteenth century, Geoffrey Boleyn, second son of a tenant farmer working some thirty acres of land, came up to London to seek his fortune. In 1428 he was admitted to the freedom of the City in the art of hatter, but subsequently changed his trade to become a mercer. In 1446 he was Sheriff of London and also of Middlesex. he married the daughter of Lord Hoo and Hastings, held the office of Lord Mayor in 1457 and before his death in 1463 had firmly established the family fortunes – acquiring the property of Blickling Hall in Norfolk from Sir John Fastolf and the manor and castle of Hever from the Cobhams of Kent. His son William had no need to concern himself with commerce. He was created Knight of the Bath at Richard III's coronation and was able to lead the pleasant life of a wealthy country squire. The Boleyns were now well on the way up the social ladder and William married into the noble Anglo-Irish family of Butler. His wife Margaret was the daughter and co-heir of Thomas Butler, last Earl of Ormonde. William Boleyn's son, Thomas, came to court to make his way in the royal service – one of the new men of the new dynasty. Thomas Boleyn had all the qualifications of a capable underling and by 1512 he was being entrusted with diplomatic missions abroad. He also made a useful marriage – to Lady Elizabeth Howard, one of the daughters of the second Duke of Norfolk. There were three surviving children of this marriage, George, Mary and Anne.

There has always been some confusion between the Boleyn sisters and controversy over Anne's date of birth. William Camden, the scholar and antiquarian, who held a post at her daughter's court and who, as a friend and confidant of William Cecil, had access to much first-hand information, gives it categorically as 1507. However, recent research, based on a new reading of an undated (and wildly misspelt) letter written by Anne to her father, has revived the case for an earlier date, around 1501, by placing her in the Netherlands at the court of Margaret of Austria in the spring of 1513. If this is correct, then it would make Anne well into her mid-twenties before she first caught the King's eye, and in her early thirties, unusually late for a first pregnancy, when Elizabeth was born.

It is certain that one of the Boleyn girls, identified only as Mademoiselle Boullan, did go over to the Netherlands, but this may have been Mary, the elder of the two, and certainly it was Mary who went to France in 1514 in the train of the King's sister when she was briefly married off to old Louis XII. Anne is also known to have spent some part of her girlhood at the French court, and it is possible that she, too, went over in 1514. Alternatively, it may not have been until 1519, when Thomas Boleyn was appointed ambassador, that she crossed the Channel to be 'finished' in the household of Queen Claude, wife of Francois I.

Whatever the true sequence of these events, she was back in England by the end of 1521. Her father had used his growing influence to get her accepted as one of Queen Catherine's maids of honour and she was present at the New Year revels, wearing a gown of yellow satin and a caul of Venice gold. Thomas Boleyn was planning a match for her with one of her Irish kinsmen – a project which, for reasons connected with the political situation in Ireland, had the active support of the King and Cardinal Wolsey. But the negotiations made slow progress and finally came to nothing. Meanwhile, Mistress Anne was looking round for a husband on her own account and her choice fell on Henry Percy, the twenty-year-old son and heir of the Earl of Northumberland. This rather slow-witted youth was attached to Wolsey's entourage and 'when it chanced the Lord Cardinal at any time to repair to the court, the Lord Percy would then resort for his pastime unto the Queen's chamber, and there would fall in dalliance among the Queen's maidens, being at the last more conversant with Mistress Anne Boleyn than with any other'.[9] The two young people soon reached an understanding, but any blossoming romance was ruthlessly blighted by Wolsey who, in a public scolding, reduced the unfortunate Percy to tears for so far forgetting himself and his position as to become entangled with 'a foolish girl yonder in the court', and warning him 'not once to resort to her company again' on pain of his father's and the King's severe displeasure.

George Cavendish believed that the King had already begun to 'kindle the brand of armours' for the lady in question and had ordered the Cardinal to intervene. With the benefit of hindsight this must have seemed a perfectly reasonable assumption, but there is no evidence to suggest that Henry had kindled any amorous feelings for Anne Boleyn in 1522. A less romantic but more plausible explanation is that Wolsey had simply acted to prevent an important nobleman's son entrusted to his care from being trapped into matrimony by a scheming young woman of no particular family. As for Anne, she showed her furious disappointment so openly that she was sent home in disgrace and, so far as is known, did not return to court until 1525 or early 1526.

It is a little hard to understand just what Henry saw in her. She was certainly not an especially beautiful girl. Her complexion is variously described as sallow or 'rather dark'. She had a slight deformity – a rudimentary sixth finger – on one hand and a mole, or strawberry mark, on her neck. The Venetian ambassador, a reasonably detached observer, wrote in 1532: 'Madam Anne is not one of the handsomest women in the world; she is of middling stature, swarthy complection, long neck, wide mouth, bosom not much raised, and in fact has nothing but the English King's great appetite, and her eyes, which are black and beautiful.'[10] Her eyes seem to have been her best feature; another ambassador remarked enigmatically that they 'invited to conversation'. She also had quantities of thick, glossy black hair. She sang well, played the lute and was a graceful dancer, but apart from her French education appears to have had no special advantages or accomplishments to distinguish her from many other young women of her time and class. She is said to have had a ready wit, but no record of it has survived. Nevertheless, attractive she undoubtedly was. Thomas Wyatt, the able and sophisticated courtier and poet, unquestionably found her so. Probably her fascination lay in that special quality of sexual magnetism which eludes description, defies portraiture and has very little to do with physical beauty. She also had a venomous temper, rapacious ambition and a definite tendency to hysteria. It proved a highly explosive mixture and Elizabeth Tudor's mother was to leave a trail of wrecked lives behind her.

Henry must presumably have started in serious pursuit of Anne Boleyn some time towards the end of 1526 and became 'so amorously affectionate that will bare place and high discretion was banished for the time'. But the King soon made the surprising discovery that Anne had no intention of becoming his mistress. Her sister Mary had already filled that position and gained little as a result. Thomas Boleyn's younger daughter, from her vantage point as maid-of-honour, had been able to watch the Queen's influence weakening and had begun to realise that if she kept her head and played her cards skilfully she might conceivably win for herself an uninmaginably greater prize. Whatever her faults, Anne had courage, vision and tremendous strength of will. Henry now in his mid-thirties, was still an extremely attractive man – foreign ambassadors were still writing eulogies about his angelic appearance. He also had the almost magical aura of his kingship, quite apart from the famous charm. It would have taken very considerable resolution to refuse to give him what he wanted; not to mention the tact and finesse needed to make him accept her rebuff without resentment. This is remarkable enough. Even more astonishing is the undoubted fact that she contrived to go on resisting (and enthralling) him for six years – sometimes repulsing, sometimes encouraging, meek, imperious, seductive, pettish by turns. In another age, Anne Boleyn might have found an outlet for her energy and talent on the stage. Her daughter Elizabeth certainly inherited her very considerable histrionic talent.

Henry was not used to being refused, and what he could not have he wanted with furious concentration. Having satisfied himself that Anne was only interested in marriage, he made up his mind with majestic simplicity to give her marriage. Here, he decided, was a woman worthy to be the mother of his sons. He did not, however, tell Wolsey about his matrimonial intentions when he first broached the subject of divorce in the spring of 1527. That September, when the Cardinal (who had been hoping to replace Queen Catherine with a French princess) saw what was in the wind, he was 'extremely annoyed at a circumstance which boded no good to him'. But Wolsey concealed his feelings. Anne Boleyn was not the only person in England who disliked him, and his position depended almost entirely on the King's goodwill. The King must therefore be given what he wanted.

In normal conditions this should not have presented insuperable problems. The ending of a marriage – especially a royal marriage – by a decree of nullity was by no means without precedent, and provided a reasonably viable case could be made out the Pope would be unlikely to disoblige so dutiful a son of the Church as the King of England. Unfortunately for Henry, conditions were not normal. In Italy, one of the interminable wars between France and the Habsburg empire was in progress, and in the early summer of 1527 Rome suffered occupation and sack by a Habsburg army. The Pope was virtually a prisoner of the Habsburg Charles V, the most powerful monarch in Christendom, Holy Roman Emperor, ruler of Spain, the Spanish Netherlands and a whole patchwork of German states. And Charles, who had a strong sense of family loyalty, was Queen Catherine's nephew. As soon as Catherine heard about her husband's intentions – and she heard about them sooner than he meant her to – she appealed energetically to her nephew for help, begging him to prevent any hearing of the case in England and especially any hearing of it by Wolsey. Henry was by now sending a procession of envoys to Rome, all badgering the Pope for a commission giving Wolsey full powers to hear the case and pronounce judgement on it without fear of reversal. The Holy Father shed tears and tore his beard. He temporised. He hesitated. Eventually, however, as the French advanced and the Emperor's army of occupation retreated in disorder, he agreed to send Cardinal Lorenzo Campeggio to England with a decretal commission authorising him and Wolsey jointly to enquire into the validity of the King's marriage and declare it null and void if the facts seemed to warrant it – a document so worded that it virtually directed the verdict in Henry's favour. But Campeggio was also given instructions not to let the commission out of his possession. He was to take no irrevocable action without reference to Rome. He was to delay matters as much as possible and, if possible, persuade the King to abandon the whole idea.

Campeggio arrived in London on 9 October 1528. He found Henry restive and impatient for action. He was not amenable to persuasion and appeared so completely satisfied with the justice of his cause that, after a long interview with him, Campeggio reported that he believed an angel descending from heaven would be unable to persuade him otherwise. Henry based his argument on the text in Leviticus and on the contention that the Pope who had originally issued dispensations for his marriage to Catherine (or any other Pope for that matter) had no authority to dispense the law of God. Catherine's main line of defence was simple. Her marriage to Prince Arthur had never been consummated, she told Campeggio. She had come to Henry *virgo intacta*. Therefore, the question of the Levitical prohibition and the Pope's powers to dispense it did not arise; although, as she pointed out, this had all been carefully gone into at the time of her second betrothal. She refused all bribes, all attempts to induce her to retire gracefully into a convent. She was unmoved by threats. She believed herself to be Henry's lawful wife. If she blasphemed against the sacrament of marriage, she would be damning her immortal soul and consenting to the damnation of her husband's. She would be admitting that she had lived in sin for nearly twenty years and that her daughter was a bastard. She would also leave the way open for Anne Boleyn. All her instincts as a woman, wife, mother and Queen were outraged.

By the following summer Campeggio had run out of delaying tactics. In June 1529 the legatine court, which was to consider the King of England's marriage, opened at Blackfriars and cited Henry and Catherine to appear. It was an extraordinary occasion, and one unprecedented in England. The King did not appear to notice that he was admitting the right of a foreign power to set up a court in his own realm and to summon him before it as a private individual. Nothing mattered, it seemed, if he could only get his divorce. Honest George Cavendish, watching the progress of events from his place in Wolsey's shadow, was deeply shocked. In his Life of his master, he lamented the wilfulness of princes against whose appetites no reasonable persuasions would suffice. 'And above all things', he went on, 'there is no one thing that causeth them to be more wilful than carnal desire and voluptuous affection of foolish love'.

On 18 June the Queen lodged a formal protest against the jurisdiction of the legatine court, and appealed to the Pope to advoke the case to Rome. Three days later she made her famous appeal to Henry himself. In the great hall at Blackfriars before both cardinals and the whole bench of bishops, she knelt at her husband's feet and begged him, for all the love that had been between them, to do her justice and right and to take some pity on her. 'And when ye had me at the first', she said, 'I take God to my judge that I was a very maid without touch of man; and whether it be true or no, I put it to your conscience.' There was silence. Henry looked straight ahead, stony-faced. Catherine finished her speech. She rose from her knees, curtsied and turned to go, ignoring the repeated summons from the court crier. 'And thus she departed out of that court without any further answer at that time or at any other, nor would never appear in any court after.'[11]

After Catherine had gone, Henry repeated the same speech he had already made several times to various audiences. How he valued the Queen's noble qualities and what an excellent, virtuous and obedient wife she had always been, but how greatly his conscience troubled him and how he feared himself in danger of God's indignation. How it behoved him to consider the state of the realm and the danger it would stand in for lack of a prince to succeed him. It was hardly necessary to remind his hearers again of the 'mischief and manslaughter' which had prevailed between the Houses of York and Lancaster in the time of their fathers and grandfathers. He had therefore thought it proper to 'attempt the law therein' to see if he might take another wife by whom God would send him male issue. He was not moved, he said, by any carnal concupiscence nor by any misliking of the Queen's person. It was an effective speech, moving and dignified. It was also sincere. Henry had long since convinced himself that he was acting in purest good faith. Not everybody, though, was similarly convinced. 'The common people being ignorant of the truth and in especial women and others that favoured the Queen, talked largely and said that the King would for his own pleasure have another wife.'[12] Catherine had always been popular with the common people, just as they always cordially hated Anne Boleyn.

At Blackfriars the Queen was declared contumacious and the proceedings continued in her absence. Catherine had been quite right when she said that she would never get a fair hearing before any court in England. Only one person – John Fisher, Bishop of Rochester – had the courage to speak cogently in her defence, and much of the court's time was taken up by a somewhat prurient attempt to prove that her first marriage had been fully consummated. It was all to no purpose, however, for the European scene was changing. On 21 June the French had been decisively defeated in battle. A week later the Pope came to terms with the victorious Emperor. In July he agreed to revoke the authority of the legatine court. The King of England's divorce case would now, after all, be decided at Rome.

It was the end of Wolsey. Predictably, he became the scapegoat for Henry's rage and disappointment. Scenting blood, his enemies gathered for the kill, and that autumn, Eustace Chapuys, the Emperor's new ambassador in London, reported that the downfall of the Cardinal was complete.

The King's domestic arrangements at this time were unusual. Anne now accompanied him wherever he went, and as George Cavendish remarked kept an estate more like a Queen than a simple maid. She had her own apartments at Greenwich and was receiving all the attentions due to a royal bride-to-be; while in another part of the palace Queen Catherine, outwardly unperturbed, continued to preside over the household, mending her husband's shirts and quietly attending to his comforts.

In December 1529, Thomas Boleyn, already Viscount Rochford, was further rewarded with the earldoms of Wiltshire and Ormonde. His daughter became Lady Anne Rochford. At a splendid banquet held to mark the occasion, Lady Anne took precedence even over the Duchesses of Suffolk and Norfolk and, according to the indignant Chapuys, 'was made to sit by the King's side, occupying the very place allotted to a crowned Queen, which is a thing never done before in this country. After dinner there was dancing and carousing, so that it seemed as if nothing were wanting but the priest to give away the nuptial ring and pronounce the blessing'.[13]

But the struggle for the divorce went on, and the ultimate prize seemed as far away as ever. Time was passing, as the Lady Anne did not scruple to remind her frustrated lover, while for his sake she sacrificed her youth and her chances of making an honourable marriage elsewhere. The case was still pending at Rome, and despite the pressure exerted by the Emperor's agents, despite repeated pleas from Catherine herself, the Pope remained inactive. Henry had already threatened schism if judgement were to go against him. If he carried out that threat, it would mean a loss to the Papacy in revenue and prestige which it could ill afford – especially at a time when heresy was spreading alarmingly in Europe. As long as the matter was left undecided, the King might hesitate to do anything rash. One of the disputants might die. Henry might tire of Anne. Few people had yet realised the exact nature of her hold on him. Her will was law, reported one ambassador. There were occasions when the King even seemed rather frightened of her. Her sharp tongue and arrogant behaviour had made her a lot of enemies, but Henry was still fascinated – almost, it sometimes appeared, against his will.

It was during the year 1530 that the King first began to evolve the plan which would solve both his marital problems and the financial difficulties now besetting him. If the Pope would not give him the divorce – and it was becoming pretty clear that he would not – then he must manage without the Pope, although remaining, at least in his own estimation, a good Catholic. If he were to take on himself the supreme religious power in his own realm, the clergy would come to realise that they could no longer look to Rome for protection and would be dependent only on the King. They would then be eager to do the King's bidding. The appearances of law could be maintained and the wealth of the English Church would be at the disposal of the crown.

Henry had found a new councillor by this time – Thomas Cromwell, once a rather shady underling of Cardinal Wolsey's – and this radical solution may have been his idea; certainly his was the executive genius which put it into practice. The idea itself somehow bears the stamp of the King's single-minded ruthlessness when it came to getting his own way. At all events, it was an idea which could hardly fail to appeal to him.

In July 1531 he finally separated from Catherine. Henry had gone on a hunting trip, accompanied as usual by Anne, and he sent a message ordering the Queen to leave the court before his return. Catherine replied calmly that she would go wherever her husband commanded, to the stake if need be. Sympathy for her plight among all classes of Englishmen and their wives (especially their wives) was now so strong that Eustace Chapuys thought very little encouragement would be necessary to produce a general uprising against the divorce. Despite government intimidation and bribery, this feeling was reflected in both houses of Parliament; but, although the members would do nothing directly to assist the King to get his divorce, it was easy to incite them to attack the Church. In May 1532, the clergy, already badly shaken by Wolsey's fall, lacking any effective leadership at home and with little support apparently forthcoming from Rome, abjectly surrendered all their ancient freedom from lay authority. To all intents and purposes, the English Church was Henry's to do what he liked with.

Only one obstacle now remained. William Warham, Archbishop of Canterbury, was an old man, ill and frightened, but there was a point beyond which he could not go. He would not defy the Pope's ban on any reopening of the 'great matter' in England, and the King must have the authority of Canterbury to give his divorce and remarriage even the appearance of legality. In August, Providence came to Henry's aid and death removed the Archbishop from the scene. Cromwell and Anne Boleyn knew the very man to replace him: Thomas Cranmer, once a chaplain in the Boleyn household, an inoffensive creature who could be relied on to do what he was told.

That October Anne, decked in Queen Catherine's jewels, was to accompany the King on a state visit to France, but before the ambiguous couple crossed the Channel an event of considerable significance had taken place. Anne at last surrendered the citadel of her body and gave Henry what he had been waiting for since 1526. Her sense of timing was impeccable. Had she yielded sooner, she might easily have lost everything. Had she insisted on waiting for Cranmer's installation, the King might have had too much time to think. Infatuated though he was, he had not been entirely unresentful of some of her high-handed ways, and serious doubts about her virtue were (not surprisingly) being expressed by a good many people. Now that divorce was within his grasp, Henry might well have reflected that another more tractable, more socially acceptable wife than Anne could also give him the sons he yearned for. But in September 1532 his gratification was complete. Anne had surrendered on her own terms and was accorded full honours of war. She marched out, as it were, with bands playing and colours flying, being created Marquess of Pembroke in her own right on the first of the month. A grant of a thousand pounds a year in land went with her new dignity, and remainder in lands and title to the heirs male of her body – the usual qualifying phrase 'lawfully begotten' being omitted from the Letters Patent. The significance of the omission is clear enough. Anne felt reasonably confident of final victory now, but even at this late stage she was taking no unnecessary chances. In the years to come her daughter was to display the same cautious hard-headedness, the same determination always to leave open a line of retreat.

3

'An Incredible Fierce Desire to Eat Apples'

On 22 February 1533 a very odd little episode took place at court and was promptly reported to Eustace Chapuys, the Emperor's ambassador, who made it his business always to be well informed of current gossip. It seemed that Anne Boleyn, Marquess of Pembroke, or 'the Lady' as Chapuys usually scornfully referred to her (at other times he used a blunter epithet) had emerged from her private apartments into the hall or gallery, where a large crowd was assembled. Seeing a particular friend among the company, 'one she loves well' – most likely it was Sir Thomas Wyatt – she called out to him in sudden excitement, apparently *à propos* of nothing, that 'for the last three days she had had such an incredible fierce desire to eat apples as she had never felt before, and that the King had said to her that it was a sign that she was with child, and she had said no, it was not so at all'. She then burst out laughing and disappeared abruptly back into her rooms, while the onlookers stared at each other 'abashed and uneasy'.[1] It is not difficult to imagine the scene – the ring of avidly curious faces, the awkward silence broken by that disconcerting shriek of laughter, the shut door and then a rising susurration of voices as the court fell happily on this juicy new titbit of scandal. Anne was, in fact, nearly three months pregnant by the time she made her somewhat unconventional announcement. She did not add that it was now nearly a month since she had been married to the King, or perhaps it would be more accurate to say had gone through a form of marriage with him, since Henry, in spite of everything, was still legally tied to his first wife. The secret had been well kept. Even Thomas Cranmer, Archbishop-elect of Canterbury, was not told, so he said, until a fortnight after the event. Eustace Chapuys, for all his excellent intelligence network, had heard nothing definite; though that devoted friend and tireless champion of Queen Catherine and her daughter was becoming increasingly worried by the way things were going.

Henry must have known that Anne was pregnant by about the middle of January, and from then on that one momentous fact transcended everything else in importance. Whatever happened, whoever had to suffer, no matter what drastic action had to be taken, the child – the longed-for son and heir – must be born in wedlock and there was no more time to lose. Already a Bill setting out the self-sufficiency of the English Church was being drafted for parliamentary approval. In future all spiritual causes, including, of course, the royal divorce, were to be settled within the jurisdiction of the state without appeal to any higher earthly authority, because in future no higher earthly authority would exist. But the breach with Rome was not yet complete. Before it became irreparable, one last vital favour must be wrung from the Pope. In spite of Chapuys's repeated and vehement warnings that Cranmer had the reputation of being 'devoted heart and soul to the Lutheran sect', that he was a servant of Anne's and would do nothing to displease the King, the Pope, astonishingly, allowed himself to be duped into accepting Cranmer's nomination to the see of Canterbury and on 26 March the Bulls authorising his consecration arrived in England. On 30 March the new Archbishop was installed with all the usual pomp of the ancient ceremony. On 11 April, less than a fortnight after he had sworn a solemn oath of allegiance to the Pope before the high altar, Cranmer defied the Pope's solemn decree imposing silence on all parties to the divorce *lite pendente*. In a letter which is almost comic in its crawling servility, he begged the King for licence 'to proceed to the examination, final determination and judgement' of his matrimonial difficulties. Licence was duly granted. It would certainly not have been proper, wrote Henry in reply, for Cranmer, as a subject, to meddle in 'so weighty and great a cause, pertaining to us, being your Prince and Sovereign' without prior permission. The King recognised no superior on earth and was not subject to the laws of any other earthly creature; 'yet', he continued kindly, 'because ye be, under us, by God's calling and ours, the most principal minister of our spiritual jurisdiction, within this our realm, who we think assuredly is so in the fear of God, and love towards the observance of His laws, to the which laws, we, as a Christian King, have always heretofore and shall ever most obediently submit ourself, will not therefore refuse . . . your humble request, offer, and towardness; that is, to mean to make an end, according to the will and pleasure of Almighty God, in our said great cause of matrimony'.[2] The fact that the Archbishop had received his preferment and authority at the hands of the Pope was now conveniently ignored. The unblinking dishonesty of these manoeuvres was also ignored. They would achieve the desired result, and that was all that mattered.

Any remaining shreds of reticence about the exact nature of Anne's status were now cast aside. On Easter Saturday, 12 April, she appeared in public for the first time in full royal state; going to Mass with trumpets sounding before her, 'loaded with diamonds and other precious stones' and wearing a gorgeous dress of gold tissue, with the Duke of Norfolk's daughter carrying her train. Henceforth Anne was officially prayed for as Queen, though this caused more than one congregation to walk out in protest, and the nobility, with the King's eye watchfully fixed on them, were required to pay their respects to her. According to Chapuys, now that the moment had come, 'all people here are perfectly astonished, for the whole thing seems a dream, and even those who support her party do not know whether to laugh or cry'.[3]

On the afternoon of 10 May, Cranmer opened his enquiry into 'the great cause of matrimony' at the small Augustinian priory of St Peter at Dunstable, chosen because it was well away from London and near enough to Ampthill, the secluded Bedfordshire manor where she was now living, to enable Catherine to attend without causing any commotion. In fact, the government hoped to get the whole business over and done with before too many people realised what was happening. Catherine, of course, refused to recognise the jurisdiction of Cranmer's court and ignored his summons to appear, no doubt to his enormous relief. On 23 May, to the surprise of no one, the Archbishop pronounced the King's first marriage to have been null and void from the beginning. By 28 May he had faithfully completed his task by finding his master's second marriage good and lawful; 'for', as he wrote, 'the time of the Coronation is so instant, and so near at hand, that the matter requireth good expedition to be had in the same'.[4] Thus the stage was set for the legitimate appearance of the child for whose sake the ancient framework of the canon law had been so ruthlessly manipulated. The King himself might be satisfied but many loyal subjects entertained serious doubts as to whether he did, in fact, have the power to interpret the law of God to suit himself.

When, on 31 May, Anne rode in state through the City of Westminster to be crowned, she is said to have complained that she saw 'a great many caps on heads, and heard but a few tongues'. According to one hostile witness, there were not ten people who greeted her with 'God save you!'[5] Chapuys, of course, thought the whole occasion 'a cold, meagre, and uncomfortable thing, to the great dissatisfaction not only of the common people, but also of the rest.'[6] The common people always enjoyed a good show, but the initials H.A. set up everywhere by the city authorities provoked some rude laughter. Ha ha! Ha ha! jeered the cynical Londoners and, in spite of the free drink running in profusion from the conduits all that day, the general reaction was one of obstinate distaste and a conviction that no amount of ceremony would ever make a Queen out of that 'goggle-eyed whore' Nan Bullen.

As for Catherine, still the true Queen to the vast majority of the English people, in loneliness, humiliation and apparent defeat, she was still fighting. That April, before Cranmer had even opened his court at Dunstable, she had been visited by a deputation headed by Anne Boleyn's uncle, the Duke of Norfolk. The substance of their message, reported Chapuys, was that Catherine must renounce her title of Queen and allow her case to be decided in England. By so doing she would not only prevent possible bloodshed, but would be treated 'much better than she could possibly expect'. In any case, Norfolk told her flatly, further resistance was useless, as the King had already married again. In future she was to be known as Princess Dowager and, unless she submitted, would have to manage on a greatly reduced allowance. Catherine's reply was predictable. 'The Queen', Chapuys's report continued, 'resolutely said that as long as she lived she would entitle herself queen; as to keeping house herself, she cared not to begin that duty so late in life.' She hoped her husband would allow her to retain her confessor, a physician, an apothecary and two maids. If even that seemed to much to ask, 'she would willingly go about the world begging alms for the love of God'.[7]

In the opinion of Chapuys, the King, although by nature kind and generously inclined, had been so perverted by Anne's malign influence that he no longer seemed the same man. Henry would listen to none of the ambassador's indignant remonstrances about Catherine's treatment, but when Chapuys was awkward enough to point out that he could not be certain of having children by his new wife the King exclaimed three times running: 'Am I not a man like others?' All the same, it is embarrassing for any man to find himself with two wives. A King and two Queens crowned and anointed in his realm runs a grave risk of looking foolish, or worse. So, in July, yet another attempt was made to bully Catherine into surrender. The King's commissioners found her 'lying on her pallet, because she had pricked her foot with a pin, so that she might not well stand or go, and also sore annoyed with a cough', but she was as indomitable as ever. When Catherine of Aragon had told the two Cardinals, Wolsey and Campeggio, five years earlier that she believed herself to be Henry's lawful wife and would submit to the Pope's judgement in the matter and to no one else's, she had meant just that. Now she restated her position yet once more, yielding not one inch of ground, and was faced with the meanest threat of all; that her obstinacy and 'unkindness' might well provoke the King to 'withdraw his fatherly love' from her daughter, 'which chiefly should move her', thought the commissioners hopefully, 'if none other cause did'. Catherine was grieved but unmoved. Her reply, as quoted in the official report, was a model of dignity and courage.

> As to the Princess, her daughter, she said that she was the King's true begotten child, and as God had given her unto them, so, for her part, she would render her again unto the King, as his daughter, to do with her as shall stand with his pleasure; trusting to God that she will prove an honest woman.[8]

Not for any consideration on earth, not even for her beloved only child, would the daughter of the Catholic Kings of Spain put her immortal soul in danger, or allow her honour to be impugned. Nothing and nobody would ever induce her 'to be a slanderer of herself and confess to have been the King's harlot these four-and-twenty years'.[9] When the commissioners, at her request, brought her the written account of their confrontation, Catherine called for a pen and furiously scratched out the words 'Princess Dowager' wherever they appeared.

The fine summer of 1533 wore on. Anne's time was approaching and preparations for her lying-in had begun. 'The King', wrote Chapuys,

> believing in the report of his physicians and astrologers, that his Lady will certainly give him a male heir, has made up his mind to solemnize the event with a pageant and tournament. . . . The King has likewise caused to be taken out of his treasure room one of the most magnificent and gorgeous beds that could be thought of. . . .

'Very fortunately for the Lady', continued the ambassador rather spitefully,

> the said bed has been in her possession for the last two months; otherwise she would not have it now, for it appears that she being some time ago very jealous of the King, and not without legitimate cause, made use of certain words which he very much disliked, telling her that she must shut her eyes and endure as those who were better than herself had done, and that she ought to know that he could at any time lower her as much as he had raised her.[10]

The coldness following this tiff had lasted several days but Chapuys felt obliged to add that it was only a 'love quarrel' of which 'no great notice should be taken'. Nevertheless it was a red light, a warning that the honeymoon was over.

By early September the court had moved to the delightful riverside palace of Placentia at Greenwich. Originally built as a royal residence by Humphrey, Duke of Gloucester, the same Duke of Gloucester who had once so harried Owen Tudor, it had become a favourite home of Owen's descendants. Henry himself had been born there. It was at Greenwich that he had married Catherine nearly a quarter of a century ago. His daughter Mary had been born and christened there, and at Greenwich on 'the seventh day of September, 1533, being Sunday, Queen Anne was brought to bed of a fair daughter at three of the clock in the afternoon'.[11]

Chapuys, though he said he considered the news of no great importance, could not conceal his malicious satisfaction. 'The King's mistress', he reported, 'was delivered of a girl, to the great disappointment and sorrow of the King, of the Lady herself, and of others of her party, and to the great shame and confusion of physicians, astrologers, wizards and witches, all of whom affirmed it would be a boy.'[12]

Henry's private feelings can only be guessed at. Throughout the long, bitter struggle for the divorce – in the course of which he had defied the Pope, insulted the Emperor and deeply offended so large a proportion of his subjects that even his apparently unassailable popularity had waned – he had been driven by that most primordial urge: the urge to beget a son and heir. And now he had failed to secure the succession; if anything he had made matters worse by introducing an element of doubt and confusion. The only saving grace was that Anne's useless daughter was at least healthy and gave promise that she might have healthy brothers. All the same, Henry was forty-two now. If and when he did have a son, there was a strong likelihood of another long minority and nobody was under any illusions about the kind of trouble that could lead to. Probably no royal birth in English history was quite such a grievous disappointment as Elizabeth Tudor's.

Still, a good face had to be put on it. A Te Deum for Anne's safe delivery was sung in St Paul's in the presence of the Lord Mayor and the Aldermen, and the christening took place on the afternoon of Wednesday, 10 September in the Friars' Church at Greenwich. The Mayor and Aldermen were there again in force, and the way between the palace and the church was hung with arras and strewn with green rushes. In the church, which was also hung with arras, 'divers gentlemen with aprons and towels about their necks' stood round the font, over which was hung a canopy of crimson satin fringed with gold so that 'no filth should come in', and 'a close place with a pan of fire' was provided 'to make the child ready in'. The procession, headed by eleven selected citizens of London, then formed up at the Palace. The three-day-old baby, wrapped in a mantle of purple velvet with a long train, was carried by the Dowager Duchess of Norfolk, flanked by the Dukes of Norfolk and Suffolk and followed by the Countess of Kent, the Earl of Wiltshire, who must surely have been a pardonably proud grandfather, and the Earl of Derby. 'When the child was come to the church door,' says Edward Hall in his Chronicle,

> the Bishop of London met it with divers bishops and abbots mitred, and began the observances of the Sacrament. The godfather was the lord Archbishop of Canterbury: the godmothers were the old Duchess of Norfolk and the old Marchioness of Dorset, widows, and the child was named Elizabeth.

The baby was then brought to the font and baptised,

> and this done, Garter chief King of Arms cried aloud, God of His infinite goodness, send prosperous life and long, to the high and mighty Princess of England, Elizabeth: and then the trumpets blew, then the child was brought up to the altar, and the Gospel said over it: and after that immediately the Archbishop of Canterbury confirmed it.[13]

The trumpets sounded again, suitably expensive gifts were presented, and refreshment wafers, comfits and hippocras was provided for the company. Then the procession reformed and trooped back to the palace by torchlight. After the infant Princess had been safety restored to her mother, the city fathers were thanked for their attendance and repaired to the cellar to wet the baby's head in a more sustaining beverage than hippocras before taking their barges to go home.

The faithful Chapuys duly reported to the Emperor that the christening of 'the little bastard' – he always referred to Elizabeth in the flattest terms – had been 'as dull and disagreeable' as the mother's coronation and that nowhere had there been 'the bonfires, illuminations, and rejoicings customary on such occasions'. The ambassador was most afraid of the consequences for the King's elder daughter, now seventeen years old and still officially heir to the throne. Immediately after Elizabeth's birth it had been proclaimed that Mary was no longer to be called Princess of Wales. There was also a rumour going round the court that her household and allowances were soon to be reduced. 'May God in His infinite mercy', wrote Chapuys, 'prevent a still worse treatment. Meanwhile,' he continued, 'the Princess, prudent and virtuous as she naturally is, has taken all these things with patience, trusting entirely in God's mercy and goodness. She has addressed to her mother, the Queen, a most wonderful letter full of consolation and comfort.'[14]

It was two years now since Mary had been allowed to see Catherine and, obliged to stand helplessly by, watching from a distance while her mother's predicament steadily worsened, she not unnaturally harboured thoughts of Anne Boleyn which were far from being either prudent or virtuous. Mary had always ranged herself beside her mother on the domestic battlefront as – quite apart from her strong natural loyalties and deep religious convictions – she was bound to do. For if Mary admitted the nullity of her parents' marriage she also admitted her own illegitimacy and denied her rights of inheritance.

Until the arrival of her half-sister, Mary had been left more or less alone, living quietly in the country chaperoned by her friend and Lady Governess, the Countess of Salisbury. Now all this was to be changed. On 20 September her newly appointed Chamberlain, Lord Hussey, reported to the Council that he had, as commanded, signified to the Princess the King's pleasure 'concerning the diminishing of her high estate of the name and dignity of Princess'. It was the first direct challenge and Mary met it boldly. She was astonished, she told Hussey, at his declaring such a thing 'alone, and without sufficient authorisation by commission or other writing from the King'. She knew herself to be the King's lawful daughter and heir and would not believe that he intended to diminish her estate 'without a writing from him'.[15] On 2 October Hussey received a letter from William Paulet, Comptroller of the King's Household, ordering Mary's removal from her pleasant house at Beaulieu, the manor of Newhall Boreham in Essex, because the King wished to lend it to, of all people, Anne Boleyn's brother George. Mary demanded to be shown Paulet's letter and there saw herself referred to baldly as 'the Lady Mary, the King's daughter'. Her title of Princess had disappeared. Apparently she was now no better than Henry Fitzroy, the King's bastard, or not as good – he at least bore the title of Duke of Richmond. Mary tried sending a letter to her father, hoping perhaps that a personal appeal might still reach him, 'for I doubt not', she wrote pathetically, 'but you take me for your lawful daughter born in true matrimony. If I agreed to the contrary I should offend God; in all other things Your Highness shall find me an obedient daughter.'[16]

Her only answer was an admonitory visit from a commission of three earls and Dr Simpson, Dean of the King's Chapel. They brought with them 'Articles' which were to be shown on the King's behalf to his daughter, the Lady Mary. The King, according to this document, was 'surprised' to be informed that his said daughter had so far forgotten her 'filial duty and allegiance' as to 'arrogantly usurp the title of Princess' and pretend to be heir apparent. The commissioners were 'commanded to declare to her the folly and danger of her conduct' and to point out that she 'worthily deserved the King's high displeasure and punishment by law'. However, if she conformed to his will, he might incline, 'of his fatherly pity', to promote her welfare.[17] Faithfully taking her tune from her mother, Mary would not conform and the battle between father and daughter was joined.

On 3 November, Chapuys wrote to the Emperor with his usual splutter of indignation that, 'not satisfied with having taken away from his own legitimate daughter the name and title of princess', the King was now threatening to send Mary to live as a maid-of-honour to 'his bastard daughter'.[18] The ambassador was genuinely appalled. Not merely would such a step be a brutal humiliation to the proud, sensitive girl accustomed all her life to being treated as the King's heir, but Anne Boleyn had already been heard to express herself with some violence on the subject of Mary and her obstinacy. If the King carried out his threat, she would be alone and unprotected in a household ruled by Anne's relations. There was no knowing what indignities she might be subjected to, or what 'perils and insidious dangers' might lie in wait for her in such a situation. Chapuys continued to remonstrate, to expostulate and to hint darkly at the undesirable consequences likely to result from the 'cruel and strange' treatment being accorded to the Emperor's cousin, but he got little satisfaction. The King was an honourable, virtuous and wise prince, incapable of doing anything not founded on 'justice or reason', Thomas Cromwell assured him blandly.

By the end of November, arrangements for the separate establishment to be set up for the little Princess Elizabeth had been completed. On 2 December it was formally recorded in the Acts of the Council that:

> Item, the King's Highness hath appointed that the Lady Princess shall be conveyed from hence towards Hatfield upon Wednesday the next week; and that Wednesday night, to repose and lie at the house of the Earl of Rutland, in Enfield; and the next day to be conveyed to Hertford* and there to remain with

* Hertford Castle had been the first choice of residence, later altered to Hatfield but not corrected in the document the second time.

such family in household, as the King's Highness hath assigned and established for the same.[19]

This was normal procedure. The court was not regarded as a suitable place for bringing up small children, who needed clean country air, free from plague and other infections, if they were to have an even chance of survival. The new household was put under the general charge of Anne Shelton and Alice Clere, both Anne Boleyn's aunts, while the 'Lady Mistress', with particular responsibility for the baby's health and well-being, was Margaret Bryan, also a connection of Anne's on the Howard side.

So, on or about 12 December, the three-month-old Elizabeth set out on her first 'progress', being carried through the City with some ceremony, in order, according to Chapuys, 'the better to impress upon the people the idea of her being the true Princess of Wales'. Escorting the party was the Duke of Norfolk who, once he had seen his great-niece safely installed at the old bishop's palace at Hatfield, descended on the unfortunate Mary and bundled her off at half-an-hour's notice to join the nursery establishment. When asked, on her arrival, 'if she did not like to see and pay her court to the Princess', Mary replied fiercely that 'she knew of no other princess in England but herself' and that 'the daughter of "Madam of Pembroke" was no princess at all'. If the King acknowledged the baby as his daughter, then Mary would call her 'sister', as she called Henry Fitzroy 'brother', but no more. Before he abandoned her to her hostile surroundings, Norfolk enquired if she had any message for the King. 'None', came the immediate retort, 'except that the Princess of Wales, his daughter, asks for his blessing.' Norfolk told her that he dared not take such a message. 'Then go away', cried Mary, her control snapping, 'and leave me alone.' According to Chapuys, 'she then retired to her chamber to shed tears, as she is now continually doing'.[20]

While one duke was bullying Mary, the other, Suffolk, had gone on a similar errand to Catherine, now at Buckden in Huntingdonshire. His orders were to take her to Somersham, an even more remote house situated in the middle of the Fen country and notoriously unhealthy. Catherine flatly refused to go, unless 'bound with ropes'. To agree to such a move, she said, would be tantamount to conniving at her own suicide. After a furious scene with Suffolk who, to do him justice, had little enthusiasm for his task, Catherine locked herself in her bedroom and refused to budge. 'If you wish to take me with you,' she told the harassed Suffolk through a hole in the wall, 'you must first break down the door.' The idea of the move to Somersham was quietly dropped, but not long afterwards Catherine was taken to Kimbolton Castle, a gloomy, semi-fortified, moated house half-a-day's ride from Buckden. There, refusing to acknowledge the existence of those newly appointed household officers who had been sworn to her as Princess Dowager, and whom she frankly regarded as jailers, she confined herself entirely to her own rooms, waited on by a few faithful Spaniards who still remained with her, and having her food cooked before her eyes as a precaution against poison.

At Hatfield, Mary was forced to eat all her meals in the crowded Great Hall without even the customary safeguard of a servant ordered to taste her food. She was made to yield precedence to her baby sister, and was not allowed out even to hear Mass. When Henry came to visit Elizabeth in January, Mary was kept out of sight. Chapuys believed this to be Anne's doing – that she was afraid the King's resolution might weaken if he were to see his elder daughter. Chapuys also heard that Anne had sent a message to Lady Shelton telling her to give Mary a box on the ears now and then 'for the cursed bastard she is'.

It is not easy to find any justification in human terms for Henry's protracted persecution of his discarded wife and elder daughter, whose only crime was their stubborn refusal to accept their relegation. All the same, it must in fairness be said that there was some political justification for the King's attitude. Catherine and Mary were fighting for what they believed to be their basic human rights, against what they believed to be the powers of darkness, and they were both the objects of very considerable popular sympathy. As long as they continued to resist, they would provide a natural rallying-point for the growing disaffection in the country. This applied especially to Mary – still the rightful heiress to the great majority of Englishmen. Her submission would be the most valuable and the heaviest pressure was now directed against her. For the next two and a half years Mary endured insult and neglect, personal sorrow and physical fear, the effects of which permanently ruined her health and spoilt her disposition, and turned a gentle, affectionate child into a bigoted, neurotic and bitterly unhappy woman.

In March 1534 the Pope at long last gave judgement on the King's divorce, and gave it in Catherine's favour. Almost simultaneously Parliament passed the Act of Succession, which finally satisfied Anne's marriage and entailed the crown on her children. It was now high treason to question the legality of the divorce by deed or writing. In order to drive the lesson home, every member of Parliament, 'all the curates and priests in London and throughout England', and indeed 'every man in the shires and towns where they dwelled' were required to swear a solemn oath 'to be true to Queen Anne and to believe and take her for lawful wife of the King and rightful Queen of England, and utterly to think the Lady Mary . . . but as a bastard, and thus to do without any scrupulosity of conscience'.[21] Anyone who refused the oath could be held guilty of misprision of treason.

Meanwhile the new heiress of England, in her cradle trimmed with crimson satin and fringe, grew and throve – untouched as yet by the storms brewing round her. The nursery was on the move again in the spring and William Kingston wrote to Lord Lisle on 18 April: 'Today the

King and Queen were at Eltham and saw my Lady Princess – as goodly a child as hath been seen. Her Grace is much in the King's favour, as goodly child should be, God save her.'[22] But while Henry fondled and played with the six-month-old Elizabeth at Eltham Palace, there were definite indications that the baby's mother was no longer in a similarly favoured position. A rumour had been circulating that she was pregnant again, but it proved a false hope and by midsummer it was noticed that the King was paying quite marked attentions to one of the maids-of-honour. Her name is not mentioned but it was probably Jane Seymour. When Anne, in a rage, tried to dismiss the girl from her service, Henry told her brusquely that 'she ought to be satisfied with what he had done for her; for, were he to begin again, he would certainly not do as much; she ought to consider where she came from, and many other things of the same kind'.[23] All these scrapes of gossip, lovingly collected and passed on by Chapuys, did not amount to very much in themselves, but before the end of the year, the situation was clear enough to any interested observer. Henry's passion had burnt itself out, leaving nothing but cold, sour ashes behind it, while Anne's growing sense of insecurity drove her on into making scenes which only exacerbated his irritation and distaste. She had developed an almost insane hatred of Catherine and Mary, especially Mary, and the elegant, fascinating, dark-eyed girl who had once so enslaved the King was becoming a shrill, nervous virago who could not always control her hysterical outbursts, even on public occasions. She once deeply offended a French ambassador who thought she was laughing at him.

Potentially serious though they were, Henry had more on his mind than his domestic disappointments during the autumn and winter of 1534. In November, he and Thomas Cromwell set the capstone on their programme of legislation codifying the breach with Rome, when the Act of Supremacy, declaring the King to be officially, explicitly and unconditionally Head of the Church in England came before Parliament. As from the following February it would be high treason 'maliciously' to deny this addition to the royal style. The Act was, as Sir Thomas More put it, 'like a sword with two edges, for if a man answer one way it will destroy the soul, and if he answer another it will destroy the body'. In the summer of 1535 John Fisher, Bishop of Rochester, and Thomas More, once Lord Chancellor of England – neither of whom shared the King's splendid confidence in his special relationship with the Almighty, and whose consciences could not allow them to accept Henry Tudor as their supreme earthly authority on spiritual matters – suffered the penalty of that treason. Although the most illustrious, they were by no means the only victims who considered the soul of more importance than the body. As he stood on the scaffold, Thomas More once again put the matter in a nutshell for them all. 'I die the King's good servant,' he said, 'but God's first.' The deaths of Fisher, a prince of the Church, and More, a scholar renowned and respected throughout the civilised world, sent a shockwave of revulsion round Europe. But Henry had learnt his own strength now (not long before, Thomas More had warned Cromwell, '. . . if a lion knew his own strength, hard were it for any man to rule him') and in future it would be impossible to rule him. Chapuys was seriously afraid that Catherine and Mary might be his next victims. Both, needless to say, had refused to take the Oath of Succession and neither was prepared to recognise the King as Head of the Church. Chapuys also continued to fear Anne's influence. Earlier in the year an ugly little story had been going round that Anne had bribed a soothsayer to tell the King that she would never conceive a son while Catherine and Mary lived.

In the second half of the summer Henry went on a progress through the south-western counties and the court paid a visit to the home of Jane Seymour's father in Wiltshire. The household of the Princess Elizabeth followed its usual routine, keeping regularly on the move on the circuit of royal manors round London – Hunsdon, Hatfield and Hertford, the More near Rickmansworth, on to Richmond, down-river to Greenwich or neighbouring Eltham on its windy hill. Sometimes the baby was visited by her parents – sometimes she was brought to visit them, decked out perhaps in one of the elaborate white or purple satin caps 'laid with a rich caul of gold' which her mother had ordered to be made for her. An important stage in her development was now felt to have been reached: a decision solemnly conveyed to Thomas Cromwell, chief Secretary of State, by William Paulet on 9 October. 'The King's Highness,' wrote Paulet, 'well considering the letter directed to you from my Lady Bryan and other my Lady Princess' officers, His Grace, with the assent of the Queen's Grace, hath fully determined the weaning of my Lady Princess to be done with all diligence.'[24]

The winter closed in. Chapuys could get no access to Mary and he heard rumours that the Oath of Succession was soon to be put to her again. There was also a whisper that Acts of Attainder, the same weapon which had been used against More and Fisher, would be prepared against both Catherine and Mary if they continued to refuse the Oath. Chapuys continued to hint at the reprisals which would be taken by his master should 'anything untoward happen to either of the ladies'; but the Emperor, though sympathetic, could do little in practical terms to alleviate the plight of his aunt and cousin. Over-burdened as he already was by the weight of his unwieldy territories, he would not add a war with England to his problems if he could help it. He sent a message from Naples on 29 December that, although 'the good ladies must be advised not to take the oath except at the last extremity', nevertheless if the danger seemed really imminent, rather than lose their lives, they should submit.

Catherine was not called upon to face such a decision. Her troubles were resolved by death in the first week of January 1536, but she died in her bed at Kimbolton – her spirit and her will unbroken. Henry did not attempt to conceal his relief. 'Thank God, we are now free from any fear of war!' he exclaimed. The day after the news reached the court, which was a Sunday, Chapuys reported:

> the King dressed entirely in yellow from head to foot, with the single exception of a white feather in his cap. His bastard daughter Elizabeth was triumphantly taken to church to the sound of trumpets and with great display. Then, after dinner, the King went to the hall where the ladies were dancing, and there made great demonstration of joy, and at last went to his own apartments, took the little bastard in his arms, and began to show her first to one, then to another, and did the same on the following days.[25]

The temptation to speculate on whether this was Elizabeth's first conscious memory is irresistible. She was nearly two and a half now and a bright, 'noticing' child. It seems just possible that she would be able to recall the events of that Sunday as one remembers a vague, bright dream of long ago. Certainly the occasion must have been indelibly printed on the retina of her unconscious mind: the braying of the trumpets; the smells of sweat and incense and hot wax; the bright lights and colours; the pale bur of upturned, admiring faces and the half-pleasurable, half-terrifying sensation of being swung up in her father's arms and carried in triumph round the room by that tremendous, godlike being.

It would be more than twenty years before Elizabeth Tudor rode in triumph again.

4

'ANNE SANS TETE'

Catherine of Aragon was buried in the Benedictine Abbey at Peterborough on Saturday, 29 January 1536, and by a curious irony of fate, on the very day of the funeral, 'Queen Anne was brought abed and delivered of a man child before her time, for she said that she had reckoned herself but fifteen weeks gone with child. It was said she took a fright, for the King ran that time at the ring and had a fall from his horse. . . .'[1] Anne tried, rather desperately, to put the blame on her uncle, the Duke of Norfolk, who, she said, had upset her by tactlessly breaking the news of the King's accident. This was held to be a lame excuse. According to gossip, it was not so much concern for her husband's safety as jealous rage over his continuing and marked attentions to Jane Seymour which had been the cause of the Queen's unlucky miscarriage – either that, or her own 'defective constitution'. Whatever the reason, it was a personal disaster for Anne, whose position was becoming increasingly precarious. Eustace Chapuys heard that the King had not spoken to 'his concubine' more than a dozen times in the past three months. Henry was also telling certain close friends, in the strictest confidence of course, that he had been tricked into his second marriage by charms and witchcraft, and therefore considered it to be null and void. Even more ominously, he was again referring to the evident signs of God's displeasure. If this was repeated to Anne, she would have known what it meant to be afraid. That she was aware, in part at least, of her danger is evident by the fact that she had been making overtures of friendship to Mary – overtures which were scornfully rejected.

When the King was told that Anne had miscarried of a son, he said, simply and terribly, 'I see that God will not give me male children.' He showed his wife no sympathy, saying only as he left her bedside, 'When you are up I will come and speak to you.'[2] By a certain rough justice Anne was now experiencing something of what her predecessor had suffered, but with none of Catherine's iron capacity for endurance to support her. During the pre-Lenten festivities, Henry left her behind at Greenwich while he went off to disport himself in London; 'whereas', as Chapuys noted, 'in former times he could hardly be one hour without her'. On 31 March the ambassador had an illuminating conversation with Thomas Cromwell, who remarked, with an ill-concealed smirk, that although the King was still inclined to sport with ladies he thought he would continue to live chastely in his present marriage. Chapuys was not deceived. It was obvious to any interested observer that the pale, prim Jane Seymour, carefully chaperoned and coached by her brother Edward, was being groomed for the role of third wife. It was also clear that Cromwell did not intend to lift a finger for Anne. All the same, Chapuys, who never missed an opportunity of doing anything that might even indirectly be of advantage to Mary, still thought it worth his while to present the Queen with two candles in church on Easter Tuesday. As he remarked in a letter to a friend, if he had seen any hope of the King's answer he would have offered not two but a hundred candles to the she-devil.[3]

But the sands were running out. Henry was already making definite enquiries about the possibility of a second divorce, but Chapuys heard that the Bishop of London, on being approached (and evidently considering discretion to be the better part of valour), had refused to commit himself. It was hardly likely, though, that Anne would be allowed to escape so lightly. Even divorced she would still be Marquess of Pembroke with a considerable income in her own right. She was not entirely without friends or influence and, with her child having once been officially recognised as the King's heiress, she would constitute a serious embarrassment to the government. Obviously a more final solution to the problem would have to be found. Henry would not initiate the necessary action himself, that was not his way, but Thomas Cromwell knew what was expected of him and his path proved a good deal smoother than Wolsey's had been. A word of warning in a receptive royal ear that treason was brewing and that it might be wise to hold a thorough investigation, and the matter was as good as settled. By 24 April, a special commission consisting of Cromwell himself, the Dukes of Norfolk and Suffolk, the Lord Chancellor Thomas Audeley, several earls (including the Earl of Wiltshire) and various assorted judges and officials had been set up, empowered to enquire as to every kind of treason by whomsoever committed. The commission wasted no time.

'On May Day', recorded Edward Hall in his Chronicle, 'were a solemn jousts kept at Greenwich, and suddenly from the jousts the King departed having not above six persons with him, and came in the evening from Greenwich into his place at Westminster. Of this sudden departing many men mused, but most chiefly the Queen. . . .'[4] Henry's abrupt retreat to Westminster was the signal and that night, alone at Greenwich – a place of ill-omen for her – cut off from any hope of escape or possibility of appeal, Anne could only wait. Next day she was arrested on a charge of adultery and 'about five of the clock at night' was brought up-river to the Tower – that same journey which she had made in triumph on the way to her coronation. This time her escort was a grim quartet, comprised of the Lord Chancellor, the Duke of Norfolk, Thomas Cromwell and William

Kingston, Constable of the Tower; 'and when she came to the court gate, entering in, she fell down on her knees before she said lords, beseeching God to help her as she was not guilty of her accusement, and also desired the said lords to beseech the King's grace to be good unto her, and so they left her their prisoner'.[5]

In fact William Kingston was left to cope with the prisoner, by now in a state of near collapse. She asked if she was to go into a dungeon and on being told, 'no, madam, you shall go into the lodging you lay in at your coronation', exclaimed, 'it is too good for me, Jesu have mercy on me'. She then, Kingston's report continued,

> kneeled down, weeping a good space, and in the same sorrow fell into a great laughing, as she has done many times since. . . . and then she said, Mr Kingston, do you know wherefore I am here? and I said nay. And then she asked me, when saw you the King? and I said I saw him not since I saw him in the tilt yard. And then, Mr Kingston, I pray you to tell me where my lord father is? And I told her I saw him afore dinner in the Court. O where is my sweet brother? I said I left him at York Place; and so I did. I hear say, said she, that I should be accused with three men; and I can say no more but nay, without I should open my body. And therewith opened her gown. O Norris, hast thou accused me? Thou art in the Tower with me, and thou and I shall die together; and, Mark, thou art here too. . . . And then she said, Mr Kingston, shall I die without justice? And I said, the poorest subject the King hath, hath justice. And therewith she laughed. . . .[6]

Anne had obviously been told that Henry Norris, one of the gentlemen of the Privy Chamber, and Mark Smeaton, the lute player, had been arrested; but Kingston did not have the courage, it seems, to tell her that her 'sweet brother' George, Viscount Rochford, was also a prisoner. Two days later Sir Francis Weston and William Brereton were brought to join the others. All five were accused of 'using fornication' with the Queen and of conspiring the King's death. On 5 May Sir Richard Page and Thomas Wyatt the poet completed the list.

Indictments were now drawn up charging the Queen, Rochford, Norris, Smeaton, Weston and Brereton. It was alleged that Anne, 'despising her marriage, and entertaining malice against the King, and following daily her frail and carnal lust, did falsely and traitorously procure . . . divers of the King's daily and familiar servants to be her adulterers and concubines'. She was also charged with having 'procured and incited her own natural brother' to violate her; and of having conspired with her lovers 'the death and destruction of the King . . . often saying she would marry one of them after the King died, and affirming that she would never love the King in her heart'.[7] According to the indictment, all these 'abominable crimes and treasons' had begun within a month of her daughter's birth.

A true Bill was duly returned by two juries, and on 12 May the four commoners were tried before a special Commission of Oyer and Terminer in Westminster Hall. They all pleaded not guilty, with the exception of poor, terrified Mark Smeaton. He was the only one who had confessed having intercourse with the Queen, but this admission had apparently been extorted from him by torture or the threat of it, and he was – it was generally agreed – not a gentleman. The proceedings were little more than a formality and all four were convicted and condemned to death.

The Queen herself and her brother were to be tried within the precincts of the Tower on the following Monday, 15 May, before a commission of the House of Lords, headed by the Duke of Norfolk. During the fortnight she had been in prison Anne's moods had fluctuated wildly. She had asked to have the sacrament in her closet so that she might pray for mercy, and, according to one of William Kingston's painstaking reports to Cromwell, 'one hour she is determined to die and the next hour much contrary to that'. She told Kingston that she had been 'cruelly handled as was never seen', but added 'I think the King does it to prove me; – and did laugh withal and was very merry'.[8] But when she appeared before her judges, she was controlled and dignified. She denied all the charges absolutely and, according to Chapuys, gave a plausible answer to each. Even after she had been convicted and heard the sentence, to be burnt or beheaded at the King's pleasure, pronounced by her uncle Norfolk 'she preserved her composure', saying she was ready for death and regretted only that the other prisoners, who were innocent and loyal to the King, were to die for her sake. She may have been trying to help her brother, whose own trial followed immediately. George indeed defended himself so ably that Chapuys heard that several of those present wagered ten to one he would be acquitted. They lost their money.

Was there, in fact, any substance in the charges? Anne had been in regular daily contact with the five men accused of being her lovers. She *could* have slept with any or all of them, but, apart from Smeaton's dubious confession, not a shred of direct evidence was ever produced to show that she did. It is hardly credible that she, who had been 'so cunning in her chastity' would have deliberately put at risk everything she had so laboriously gained. She may well have been indiscreet, even recklessly so. The date, October 1533, assigned to her first misconduct is significant. Anne's vanity craved attention and admiration. She throve on excitement and basked in the limelight. When, after those six heady years of royal courtship, she found herself being relegated to the role of brood mare, it was quite in character that she should have turned more and more to the company of the professional gallants about the court. She undoubtedly enjoyed and encouraged the sort of stylised love-play fashionable among young people in high society at the time – the heavy sighs and meaning glances, the exchange of tokens, extravagant compliments and flirtatious chatter. Anne seems, too, to have taken a perverse pleasure in egging her admirers on. She had asked Norris why he delayed his marriage and when he replied that 'he would tarry a time' she said, 'You look for dead men's shoes, for if aught came to the King but good, you would look to have me.' Norris did not respond as she apparently expected and she turned on him, saying 'she could undo him if she would'.[9] She certainly encouraged the wretched Smeaton to make sheep's eyes at her, and did much the same with Francis Weston. As for the charge of incest, this would appear to be merely frivolous and was based, according to Chapuys, on nothing more than the fact that Rochford had once been a long time in Anne's room with her. Brother and sister were known to be fond of each other, and most likely the accusation was simply used as a convenient pretext for getting rid of George who might otherwise have made a nuisance of himself.

The government, of course, was playing up the horrid scandal of the Queen's behaviour for all it was worth – and more. Cromwell told Stephen Gardiner that 'the Queen's incontinent living was so rank and common that the ladies of her privy chamber could not conceal it'. He added solemnly that 'besides that crime there brake out a certain conspiracy of the King's death, which extended so far that all we that had the examination of it quaked at the danger his Grace was in'.[10] John Hussey, in a letter to Lady Lisle dated 13 May, gave it as his opinion that anything which had ever been 'penned, contrived, and written' against women since Adam and Eve was 'verily nothing in comparison of that which hath been done and committed by Anne the Queen'. Hussey was ashamed, he said, that any good woman should give ear to it, although, he added honestly, he could not believe that all the rumours going about were true.[11]

The King, who was taking an active interest in the proceedings, believed them all – or said he did. Indeed, he said he believed that Anne had had to do with more than a hundred men. He had long been expecting something of this kind to happen and had written a tragedy on the subject which he carried about with him in his bosom, so the Bishop of Carlisle told Chapuys. One of the counts in the indictment against Anne had been that when the King became aware of her misdeeds, he 'took such inward displeasure and heaviness' that certain harms and perils had befallen his royal body; but Chapuys remarked that he had never seen 'prince nor man who made greater show of his horns or bore them more pleasantly'. The court, in fact, had seldom been gayer. Henry was seeing a lot of Jane Seymour, dining with her and sometimes staying until after midnight. Chapuys heard that on one such occasion, returning by river to Greenwich, the King's barge was filled with minstrels and musicians, playing and singing; 'which state of things', wrote the ambassador, 'was by many a one compared to the joy and pleasure a man feels in getting rid of a thin, old and vicious hack in the hope of getting soon a fine horse to ride.'[12] Although Anne had never been popular and few people felt any sympathy for her personally, it was generally considered that the King's behaviour was not quite in the best of taste.

Rochford, Norris, Smeaton, Weston and Brereton were executed on 17 May. The charges against Richard Page and Thomas Wyatt had been quietly allowed to drop and they were presently released. Two things had to be done before the Queen went to her death. The executioner from Calais, the only one of the King's subjects who knew how to behead with a sword, had to be summoned and Anne's marriage had to be annulled. This last office was performed by the ever-useful Thomas Cranmer. Cromwell had tried to find grounds for annulment by proving a pre-contract between Anne and young Percy, but received such a categorical denial from the now Earl of Northumberland that he was obliged it seems to fall back on – of all things – the King's previous adultery with his sister-in-law, Mary Boleyn. Why did Henry feel it necessary to divorce Anne as well as kill her? One of the reasons was apparently to bastardise her daughter. For one so set on establishing the succession, the King was prodigal in disposing of possible heirs. Chapuys heard it was to be declared that Elizabeth was not even the King's daughter, but begotten by Norris; however, Henry would not allow that. Elizabeth might be a bastard, but she was unquestionably his bastard and her paternity cannot be doubted. Cranmer pronounced his sentence of nullity on the seventeenth, and on 18 May Anne was to die for adultery, having never been a wife.

At the last moment there was a hitch, possibly due to the late arrival of the executioner. His importation seems to have been in the nature of a special favour and cost the Treasury £23 6*s* 8*d*. Although two days earlier Kingston had reported that 'at dinner the Queen said she would go to a nunnery and is in hope of life', she was now anxious to end it. She chafed at the delay and complained to Kingston, 'I thought to be dead by this time and past my pain'. He told her there would be no pain, it was so little. 'And then she said,' continued a puzzled Kingston, '"I heard say the executioner was very good, and I have a little neck", and put her hands about it, laughing heartily. I have seen many men and also women executed, and all they have been in great sorrow, and to my knowledge this lady has much joy and pleasure in death.'[13] Chapuys, too, heard that Anne was in high spirits that night and had said it would not be hard to find a nickname for her – she would be called 'la Royne Anne sans teste'.

Next day, Friday, 19 May, all was ready and 'at eight of the clock in the morning, Anne Boleyn, Queen, was brought to execution on the green within the Tower of London' where a select band of spectators was waiting. In spite of official instructions that all foreigners were to be excluded, by far the most vivid account of Anne's last moments is to be found in the Chronicle of Henry VIII, written by an anonymous Spaniard living in London. His chronicle is not always a reliable source, but on this occasion it has the unmistakable flavour of an eye-witness report. The Queen was wearing a night robe of damask with a red damask skirt and a netted coif over her hair, and 'was as gay as if she was not going to die'. According to established etiquette, the executioner asked forgiveness for what he had to do and then begged her to kneel and say her prayers.

> So Anne knelt, but the poor lady only kept looking about her. The headsman, being still in front of her, said in French, 'Madam, do not fear, I will wait till you tell me.' Then she said, 'you will have to take this coif off', and she pointed to it with her left hand. The sword was hidden under a heap of straw, and the man who was to give it to the headsman was told beforehand what to do; so, in order that she should not suspect, the headsman turned to the steps by which they had mounted, and called out, 'bring me the sword'. The lady looked towards the steps to watch for the coming of the sword, still with her hand on the coif; and the headsman made a sign with his right hand for them to give him the sword, and then, without being noticed by the lady, he struck off her head to the ground.[14]

Head and trunk were hastily stowed in a plain coffin – according to one report, a chest used for storing arrows – and buried with little ceremony in the choir of St Peter-ad-Vincula within the tower.

Some people remarked disapprovingly that the Queen had died 'very boldly' but Chapuys, who knew how to give credit when it was due, praised her courage and great readiness to meet death. In his despatch to the Emperor dated 19 May, he added: 'The lady who had charge of her has sent to tell me in great secrecy that the Concubine, before and after receiving the sacrament, affirmed to her, on the damnation of her soul, that she had never been unfaithful to the King.'[15]

'Who so list to hunt, I know where is an hind' Thomas Wyatt had once written, in a thinly veiled reference to Anne Boleyn, but:

> Who list her hunt, I put him out of doubt
> As well as I may spend his time in vain:
> And graven with diamonds, in letters plain
> There is written her fair neck round about:
> *Noli me tangere*, for Caesar's I am;
> And wild for to hold, though I seem tame.

This image of a deer appears more than once in Wyatt's poetry. Perhaps there was something doe-like about Anne, with her great dark eyes and swift, nervous movements. And Caesar had hunted her down the years, with cheerfully amorous enthusiasm, with obsession, with cold, revengeful fury, until he brought her to bay on a May morning on Tower Green, and his lust at last was sated, his guilt was purged and his vengeance complete. She was gone, that wild, strangely disturbing creature, her only legacy a red-headed little girl, now two years and eight months old.

There were several consequences of Anne's death. The most immediate being that

> on the 20th day of May the King was married* secretly at Chelsea, in Middlesex, to one Jane Seymour, daughter to Sir John Seymour, knight, in the county of Wiltshire . . . which Jane was first a waiting gentlewoman to Queen Katherine, and after to Anne Boleyn, late Queen, also; and she was brought to White Hall, by Westminster, the 30th day of May, and there set in the Queen's seat under the canopy of estate royal.[16]

Chapuys was hoping for great things from the new Queen's influence. She was thought to have remained faithful to the memory of her first mistress and had already shown herself friendly to Catherine's daughter. As for Mary, she clearly believed that things would be different now. On 26 May, a week after Anne's death, she wrote to Cromwell:

> Master Secretary, I would have been a suitor to you before this time, to have been a mean for me to the King's grace, my father, to have obtained his Grace's blessing and favour; but I perceived that nobody durst speak for me, as long as that woman lived, which now is gone, whom I pray our Lord of his great mercy to forgive. Wherefore, now she is gone, I am the bolder to write to you. . . .[17]

As her mother had done before her, Mary clung desperately to the belief that all her troubles were due to the malignity of 'that woman'. She totally failed to appreciate that her father's unlovable behaviour, for which Anne had so long been a convenient scapegoat, in fact had its origin in traits inherent in his own nature.

Guided by Thomas Cromwell, Mary now submitted abjectly enough. She made two copies of a letter sent to her by the Secretary in which she was prostrate before the King's most noble feet, his most obedient subject and humble child, who not only repented her previous offences but was ready henceforward to put her 'state, continuance, and living' in his gracious mercy. The copies, one sealed for the King and another open, were returned to Cromwell, together with a covering letter from Mary telling him that she had done the uttermost her conscience would suffer her. But when Cromwell read his copy he found a fatal reservation added to his draft. Mary was ready to submit to the King 'next to Almighty God'. This would not do. Another draft was sent down to her at Hunsdon and this time, tormented by neuralgia which gave her 'small rest day or night', Mary copied 'without adding or minishing'. Only one copy this time, because she 'cannot endure to write another'. Still it was not enough, and a commission – headed by that bird of ill-omen the Duke of Norfolk – was sent to visit her. They brought with them a document for her signature which explicitly acknowledged the King as Supreme Head of the Church and the nullity of her mother's marriage. When Mary refused to sign, the behaviour of the commissioners finally extinguished any lingering hopes

* This was the betrothal ceremony. The wedding took place at Whitehall on the thirtieth.

she may have had of an honourable reconciliation with her father. She was such an unnatural daughter, said one, that he doubted whether she was even the King's bastard. Another added pleasantly that if she was *his* daughter, he would beat her to death or strike her head against a wall until it was as soft as a boiled apple. They told her she was a traitress and would be punished as such. Finally they said she might have four days to think the matter over and ordered Lady Shelton to see that she spoke to no one, and was not left alone for a moment, day or night. In spite of this, Mary contrived to make two last frantic appeals for help, to Chapuys and to Thomas Cromwell.

But the ambassador, for so long her faithful friend and ally, saw that the time had come for surrender and advised her to yield. Trying to comfort her, he wrote that God looked more at the intentions than the deeds of men. As for Cromwell, he was badly frightened and told Chapuys that for several days he had considered himself a dead man. When the commissioners reported their failure with Mary, Henry flew into a towering rage, directed not only at his daughter but anyone who could be suspected of showing her any sympathy, or of encouraging her resistance. The Privy Council was in session from morning till night and the King forced the judges to agree that if Mary continued to defy him she could be proceeded against in law.

Cromwell made his feelings perfectly clear in his reply to Mary's appeal. 'How great so ever your discomfort is', he wrote, 'it can be no greater than mine, who hath upon your letters spoken so much of your repentance . . . and of your humble submission in all things, without exception and qualification.' He enclosed 'a certain book of articles' which she was to sign, and added,

> if you will not with speed leave all your sinister counsels, which have brought you to the point of utter undoing . . . and herein follow mine advice, I take my leave of you for ever, and desire you never to write or make means to me hereafter. For I will never think you other than the most ungrate, unnatural, and most obstinate person living both to God and your most dear and benign father.[18]

When Cromwell's letter reached her, Mary knew that she was beaten. For nearly three years she had fought gallantly to defend her principles and her good name – now, ill, alone and exhausted, she gave in. At eleven o'clock at night on a Thursday about the middle of June, she signed the 'book of articles' acknowledging 'the King's Highness to be supreme head in earth under Christ of the Church of England' and utterly refusing 'the Bishop of Rome's pretended authority'. She also acknowledged that her parents' marriage had been 'by God's law and Man's law incestuous and unlawful'.[19]

Her reward came on 6 July, when she was 'brought riding from Hunsdon secretly in the night to Hackney, and that afternoon the King and the Queen came thither, and there the King spake with his dear and well-beloved daughter Mary, which had not spoken with the King her father in five years afore'.[20] Two days later Chapuys wrote of this encounter:

> It is impossible to describe the King's kind and affectionate behaviour towards the Princess, his daughter, and the deep regret he said he felt at his having kept her so long away from him. . . . There was nothing but conversing with the Princess in private and with such love and affection, and such brilliant promises for the future, that no father could have behaved better towards his daughter.[21]

Henry's attitude allowed his unbounded relief at Mary's surrender. It is easy to dismiss him as a monster for his undeniably brutal treatment of her, but the political implications of the situation have to be remembered. There was serious unrest over the King's revolutionary religious policy, especially in the more backward and rural parts of the country, as the Pilgrimage of Grace was presently to demonstrate. Mary represented the old, familiar ways and had a considerable popular following. Until she herself had renounced her birthright, there was a strong possibility that she might have been used as a lever in an attempt to force Henry back to the paths of righteousness.

Mary rode back to Hunsdon with 'a very fine diamond ring' given her by Queen Jane and 'a check for about 1,000 crowns' from her father, but nothing could help her in the bitterness of her remorse. She begged Chapuys to ask the Pope to give a secret absolution for what she had done, but for one of her stubborn rectitude not even that could alter the fact that she had knowingly betrayed her religious faith and her mother's memory – the two things which meant most in the world to her. The memory of that betrayal, made by a frightened girl of twenty, was to haunt her for the rest of her life.

Meanwhile, the King's younger daughter was being bastardised and disinherited in her turn. Parliament had met in June and passed a second Act of Succession, ratifying the annulment of Henry's marriage to Anne Boleyn and officially declaring the issue of that marriage to be illegitimate. The succession was now vested in the offspring of Henry and Jane Seymour. Failing this, the King was given full powers to appoint any heir or heiress he chose at any time by Will or by Letters Patent. This unprecedented step shows how acute the problem of the succession was becoming. There was some talk of naming the Duke of Richmond. As the Earl of Sussex remarked, reasonably enough, if all the King's children were bastards, why not choose the boy? If Henry had any such plans they were frustrated, for young Richmond died on 22 July 1536, at the age of seventeen, 'having pined inwardly in his body long before he died', a victim of the tuberculosis to which the young Tudor males were so fatally susceptible. If the downfall of the House of Plantagenet had been too many sons, the likely cause of the downfall of the House of Tudor was by now all too apparent.

None of this, of course, not even the abrupt diminution of her own social status, as yet troubled the small Elizabeth overmuch. There is a story that Sir John Shelton, husband of Lady Shelton and steward or governor of the household at Hunsdon, made a formal announcement to the child regarding her new style. Elizabeth is supposed to have replied sharply: 'How haps it, Governor, yesterday my lady Princess, today but my lady Elizabeth?' Sir John, who seems to have been a rather tiresome individual, may well have made the announcement. The retort, even allowing for the unnerving precocity of sixteenth-century royal children, is a little difficult to credit. A far more convincing portrait is drawn by Margaret Bryan, the Lady Mistress, in her famous letter to Thomas Cromwell, written in August 1536. It also reflects the confusion currently reigning in the nursery. 'Now,' wrote Lady Bryan distractedly, 'as my lady Elizabeth is put from that degree she was in, and what degree she is at now I know not but by hearsay, I know not how to order her of myself, or her women or grooms.' The little girl was evidently growing fast, for 'she has neither gown nor kirtle nor petticoat, nor linen for smocks', not to mention such other necessities as nightgowns, nightcaps, 'body-stychets' and handkerchiefs. 'All these her Grace must take. I have driven off as long as I can, that, by my troth, I cannot drive it no longer.' Lady Bryan had been having trouble with the interfering John Shelton, who 'saith he be master of this house. What fashion that shall be', continued her ladyship tartly,

> I cannot tell, for I have not seen it afore. . . . Mr Shelton would have my lady Elizabeth to dine and sup every day at the board of estate. It is not meet for a child of her age to keep such rule yet. If she do, I dare not take it upon me to keep her Grace in health; for there she shall see divers meats, and fruits, and wine, which it would be hard for me to restrain her Grace from.

Lady Bryan sensibly wanted her charge to have 'a good mess of meat to her own lodging, with a good dish or two meet for her to eat of'. There were other problems, too, equally familiar to anyone who has ever looked after a small child. 'My lady hath great pain with her great teeth, and they come very slowly forth, which causeth me to suffer her Grace to have her will more than I would.' However, the Lady Mistress means to put this right as soon as possible. 'I trust to God and her teeth were well graft, to have her Grace after another fashion than she is yet, so as I trust the King's grace shall have great comfort in her Grace. For she is as toward a child and as gentle of conditions, as ever I knew any in my life, Jesu preserve her Grace.' Lady Bryan will guarantee Elizabeth's good behaviour at any time when 'it shall please the King's grace to have her set abroad' but afterwards she must be allowed 'to take her ease again'.[22] Lady Bryan got her way about meal times, for on 16 August John Shelton was writing to Cromwell: 'I perceive by your letter the King's pleasure that my lady Elizabeth shall keep her chamber and not come abroad.' But Sir John had his problems, too, and told Cromwell that unless he received the King's warrant for money for the household he would not be able to continue it. Especially as 'within seven or eight days provision must be made at the seaside for Lent store (presumably salt fish) and other necessities'.[23]

All the same, there is nothing to suggest that Elizabeth was ever deliberately made to suffer for her mother's disgrace, and no evidence that her household was reduced. The unfortunate state of her wardrobe was more likely due to oversight than any fixed policy of neglect. Also, of course, since Anne's death there was no longer anyone at court with a special interest in her welfare, or who would even think to remember that the child must be growing out of her clothes.

There is nothing to indicate either when or how Elizabeth heard what had happened to her mother. Most probably she was never officially told, but it would be very odd if, in the cheerfully crowded conditions which prevailed in manor-houses like Hunsdon and others where she spent so much of her early life, such an intelligent child did not overhear a good deal of talk not meant for her ears – talk that would be the more disturbing for being only dimly understood. All those fascinating tales of Anne's scandalous behaviour would lose nothing in the retelling, and as Elizabeth grew up she would never ben able to remember a time when she had not known that her mother was a bad woman, an adulteress, perhaps worse, for it was freely rumoured that Anne had hastened good Queen Catherine's death by giving her poison. In May Chapuys was reporting that the King, with tears in his eyes, had told his bastard son that he and his sister, meaning Mary, had had a narrow escape from the hands of 'that woman, who had planned their deaths by poison'. When Richmond died in July, it was said that Anne had indeed been poisoning him by some unspecified and diabolical means.

Elizabeth would also never be able to remember a time when she had not known that her mother had died because her father ordered it. There is no record that she ever mentioned Anne's name during her childhood, or ever asked any questions about her; but the necessary information was there, filed away in that acutely receptive brain – its implications registered long before the conscious mind could comprehend and deal with it.

5

THE KING'S DAUGHTER

The two disinherited princesses continued, for the most part, to share an establishment over the next five years. No doubt it was a convenient and economical arrangement. The sisters now stood on equal terms socially but Mary, as the elder, had regained a natural precedence. Several of her old friends and servants were being allowed to rejoin her and early in August Chapuys reported that 'the treatment of the Princess is every day improving. She never did enjoy so much liberty as she does now, nor was she ever served with such solemnity and honour as she is at present.' Although nothing had yet been formally settled, the ambassador was hoping that soon there would be a complete reversal of fortune with 'the little bastard' having to pay her court to the Princess of Wales.[1] Contrary to many people's expectations, however, Mary's title was not restored and her position, like Elizabeth's, remained in a state of ambiguity. Both were the King's daughters and were treated as such, and yet both were and continued to be bastards by Act of Parliament.

There is no reason to suppose that at this time Mary harboured any resentment towards the little girl who had been the cause of so much of her unhappiness – rather the contrary. She wrote to the King: 'My sister Elizabeth is in good health, thanks be to our Lord, and such a child toward, as I doubt not but your Highness shall have cause to rejoice of in time coming.'[2] All her life Mary was pathetically fond of children and her privy-purse accounts contain a number of entries relating to presents of pocket-money and other things for her small sister.

In October 1536, at the time of the ill-fated rising in the North known as the Pilgrimage of Grace, both sisters were summoned to court. According to an anonymous correspondent writing to Cardinal du Bellay, the Bishop of Paris, this was intended to 'soften the temper of the people'. More probably Henry wanted his daughters safely under his eye during a time of potential danger. Cardinal du Bellay's informant continued: 'Madame Marie is now the first after the Queen, and sits at table opposite her, a little lower down, after having first given the napkin for washing to the King and Queen . . . Madame Isabeau [Elizabeth] is not at that table, though the King is very affectionate to her. It is said he loves her much.'[3] Despite indications to the contrary, it is undoubtedly true that Henry *was* fond and proud of all his children and, provided of course they never showed any sign of having wills of their own, he was an affectionate even an indulgent father. As for his children, they were none of them – not even Mary with her first-hand experience of the dark side of his nature – immune from the astonishing force of his personality or the irresistible simplicity of his charm, and they repaid him with a genuine, if fearful, devotion, taking enormous pride in their remarkable parent.

In 1537 came the event for which Henry had been striving throughout the whole of the previous decade. At two o'clock in the morning of Friday, 12 October, Jane Seymour gave birth to a healthy son at Hampton Court Palace. Later that morning a solemn Te Deum was sung in St Paul's Cathedral and every parish church in London. The bells rang out, toasts were drunk and bonfires lit all over the City.

> Also the same night, at five of the clock, there was new fires made in every street and lane, people sitting at them banqueting with fruits and wine, the shalmes* and waits playing in Chepeside, and hogsheads of wine set in divers places of the City for poor people to drink as long as they listed; the mayor and aldermen riding about the city thanking the people, and praying them to give laud and praise to God for our prince; also there was shot at the Tower that night above two thousand guns, and all the bells ringing in every parish church till it was ten at the clock at night.[4]

Everyone joined in the party. Even the foreign merchants of the Steelyard lit bonfires and torches, 'and gave a hogshead of wine to poor people, and two barrels of beer also'. There must have been some notable hangovers in London on 13 October. Messengers rode out to 'all the estates and cities of the realm' spreading the glad news, and the whole country went hysterical with joy. After very nearly thirty years there was an indisputable male heir born in unquestionably lawful wedlock. It was certainly high time. Henry was forty-six now. He had put on a lot of weight and there were signs that even his magnificent physique was beginning to rebel against the demands he made on it.

The infant prince was christened Edward, in the chapel at Hampton Court on Monday, 15 October, and in the ceremonial procession to the font his four-year-old sister Elizabeth carried out her first official duty, bearing the chrisom (the heavily jewelled and embroidered baptismal robe) on her breast; although 'the same lady for her tender age was borne by the Viscount Beauchamp'. Viscount Beauchamp was the recently ennobled Edward Seymour, brother of Queen Jane. Another Seymour, Thomas, was also present – one of six gentlemen supporting the canopy carried over the Prince. Elizabeth would know both brothers all too well in

* A reed instrument.

later years. Her grandfather, the Earl of Wiltshire, was there too, still gamely hanging on, with a towel round his neck bearing the taper of virgin wax.

Thanks, no doubt, to Lady Bryan's careful training, the little princess apparently conducted herself with suitable decorum and in the return procession, relieved of her burden, she walked with her sister Mary, Lady Herbert of Troy bearing her train. Lady Herbert was the sister of a future step-mother, Katherine Parr. The Tudor children lived in a small, close-knit world.

Mary had officiated as godmother to the baby, the other sponsors being Archbishop Cranmer and the Duke of Norfolk – a more curiously assorted trio is hard to imagine.

Jane Seymour died on 24 October. According to Thomas Cromwell, her death was due to 'the neglect of those about her who suffered her to take cold and eat such things as her fantasy in sickness called for'.[5] A more likely cause is puerperal sepsis, which carried off so many women after childbirth. Her funeral took place at Windsor on 12 November, with Princess Mary as chief mourner. Jane was the first, in fact the only one, of Henry's wives to be buried as Queen. Perhaps this was fair. She was, after all, the only one who had fulfilled her side of the bargain to his satisfaction.

After the birth of his son, 'England's Treasure', Henry naturally had less attention to spare for his daughters. They were now little more than potentially useful assets on the international marriage-market; but, although their names occur from time to time in ambassadors' despatches in connexion with various rather half-hearted matrimonial projects, their value was considerably reduced by the King's obstinate insistence on their bastard state.

Elizabeth's life continued to follow much the same course as before, moving with her household round the same circuit of royal manors, sharing with either her sister or brother. There were sound practical reasons for this restless existence. In such large establishments, crowded with hangers-on and with only the most primitive sanitary arrangements, it was obviously a sensible precaution to vacate the premises at regular intervals to allow for a general 'sweetening' and cleaning up. Also, in days of slow and difficult transport, once the royal households had eaten up all the locally available provision, it was tactful as well as necessary to move on to pastures new. Another reason, of course, was to avoid contact with outbreaks of infectious disease, or to seek a healthy situation according to the time of year.

These were quiet and (to the best of anybody's knowledge) happy childhood years for Elizabeth, spent in pleasant places with affectionate friends around her. Although Margaret Bryan's time was now fully occupied supervising Prince Edward's nursery, Elizabeth was not neglected. There was Blanche Parry, the Welshwoman, who had seen her rocked in her cradle. There was Katherine Champernowne, who had been appointed a waiting gentlewoman in her household in June 1536, on the recommendation of Thomas Cromwell. Katherine was a Devonshire woman of good education and good, though impoverished, family. Four months after her appointment she was obliged to write rather plaintively to Cromwell, pointing out that she could not maintain her position to the King's honour without some yearly stipend and adding that she would be loath to charge her father, 'who has as much to do with the little living he has as any man'.[6] Presumably Mistress Champernowne got her stipend, for she was soon promoted to become Elizabeth's governess. In 1545 she married John Ashley or Astley, a first cousin of Anne Boleyn's, but she remained in the service of her princess, and the two were devoted to one another. And then, throughout these early years, there was always Mary, the kind grown-up sister and nearest substitute for a natural mother that the small Elizabeth was to know.

She was undoubtedly a most attractive child physically. Even Eustace Chapuys, who saw her with Edward in March 1538, and was hardly likely to be prejudiced in her favour, felt bound to admit that she was 'certainly very pretty'. Her other qualities, too, were becoming apparent. Her New Year's gift to her brother in 1539 was 'a shirt of cambric of her own working'. In December of that year, Thomas Wriothesley paid a visit to Mary at Hertford Castle, where both sisters were then in residence. He reported to Cromwell:

> When I had done with her Grace, I went then to my Lady Elizabeth's Grace, and to the same made the King's Majesty most hearty commendations, declaring that his Highness desired to her of her health and sent her his blessing. She gave humble thanks, enquiring again of his Majesty's welfare, and that with as great a gravity as she had been forty years old. If she be no worse educated than she now appeareth to me, she will prove of no less honour to womanhood than shall beseem her father's daughter.[7]

At six years old Elizabeth was evidently already well schooled in the elaborate code of politeness and subservience to her elders that all properly brought-up children were expected to observe. Her formal education would, of course, have been progressing for at least a year by this time, although little or nothing is known of its beginnings. Presumably she learnt to read and write under the supervision of Katherine Champernowne, and as her later achievements testify she was certainly well grounded in Latin at an early age. Perhaps Mary had some hand in this, for despite the fact that she never showed anything like the formidable intellectual capacities of her younger brother and sister she had received a thorough, classical training in the best Renaissance tradition.

Elizabeth's education was progressing in other directions too, as she began to become aware of the world around her – the world outside the nursery and the schoolroom. Travelling in her litter to and from Hertford or Enfield, Ashridge or Hatfield, Hunsdon or Havering Bower, or to visit her father at Greenwich or Hampton Court, through the green, well-wooded countryside as yet barely scarred by man, the horses throwing up clouds of white dust in summertime, slipping and straining in the mired ruts of winter, she was learning to return the greetings of countryfolk, who left their work in fields and gardens to watch the King's daughter and her company ride by. Passing through the little towns and villages round London she would see the housewives and schoolchildren, the tradesmen and their apprentices who came to their doors and windows to wave and cry 'God save you'. These were the English people, tough, vigorous, quarrelsome, independent, irrepressibly free-spoken, whose goodwill was to be the breath of life to Elizabeth all her life. A people, roughly three million of them, whose existence, despite their idyllic surroundings, were for the most part unimaginably hard, narrow and precarious in a world where only the fittest, and the luckiest, survived and where life was always balanced on a knife-edge with death. There were plenty of reminders of this for an observant child. A funeral procession or a blackened corpse rotting on a wayside gallows were familiar sights, and death, as Elizabeth already knew, was no respecter of rank or dignity.

On the road she would meet a fair cross-section of other traffic: drovers with their herds of cattle going to market at Smithfield and farmers with wagons piled high with produce, rumbling in to feed the ever-hungry capital; trains of pack-horses carrying grain or wool or finished cloth; a prosperous merchant on a buying trip; some great lord's steward on business for his master; a band of strolling players or tumblers; a laden packman trudging to the next village. Sometimes her escort would quicken to attention, forming a close hedge about her and her ladies, and then there would be the fearful thrill of catching a glimpse of a troop of 'sturdy beggars' on their way to terrorise some isolated hamlet or lonely farmhouse. The fact that in this 'fair field full of folk' there might be a number of dispossessed monks, and nuns too, turned out of their convents to seek a living as best they could; or that one no longer saw the black or grey habited figures of the itinerant preaching friars, or the cheerful, jingling parties of pilgrims travelling to one of the world-famous shrines – Our Lady of Walsingham or the Holy Blissful Martyr of Canterbury himself – would mean little to Elizabeth. She would never be able fully to understand the anguished distress which the dissolution of the monasteries and desecration of the shrines, now proceeding briskly under the aegis of Thomas Cromwell, caused to people like her sister Mary, who clung to the old ways. Very much a child – if not, in fact, *the* child – of the English Reformation, Elizabeth was little affected by these early manifestations of the social revolution going on around her.

This is not the place for any sort of detailed survey of the niceties of doctrinal change resulting from the break with Rome; but it should perhaps be remembered that the Henrician Reformation was essentially a movement initiated and controlled from above – as opposed to the progressive movement from below, which began to gather strength after the King's death and to work its way steadily to the surface throughout the remainder of the century. Henry's Church was very much his own creation and bears the unmistakable stamp of his own idiosyncratic personality.

It has been said that during his reign England remained Catholic without the Pope, but this is an oversimplification. Changes – part from that first fundamental one – were made, new ideas considered and experimented with. An English Bible was provided in every church. A simple, vernacular prayer book, the first official English Primer, was published and Cranmer was given royal permission to embark on a programme of major liturgical reform. Even the education of Prince Edward was entrusted to those whose opinions were distinctly left of centre. On the other hand it is true that Henry upheld, and (by means of the Act of Six Articles) saw to it that his subjects also upheld, belief in such basic tenets of Catholicism as transubstantiation, the celibacy of the clergy, the existence of purgatory and the need for auricular confession. Consistency was never a strong point of the Supreme Head of the new Church of England. He could (and did) prosecute both Lutherans and Catholics for their faith; but, in an age when religion and politics were for all practical purposes indivisible, the king found it useful to hold a balance between the parties of progress and reaction. He was well aware of the dangers that could result if either side became too powerful, and had no intention of allowing control to slip out of his hands.

By the end of 1539 Henry had been a widower for two years and was about to embark on the second half of his matrimonial marathon. After an intensive search for a bride through the courts of Europe – during which Hans Holbein the Younger had been kept busily employed providing portraits of no fewer than five princesses – the King's choice had fallen on a German girl, Anne, sister of the Duke of Cleves. A rather surprising choice, in view of the report from Nicholas Wotton that Anne occupied most of her time in needlework, could speak no language but her own, and neither sang nor played any instrument, 'for they take it here in Germany for a rebuke and an occasion of lightness that great ladies should be learned or have any knowledge of music'. Wotton added, 'I could never hear that she is inclined to the good cheer of this country'.[8] None of this makes her sound a particularly suitable bride for Henry VIII; and, contrary to the legend, Holbein's portrait did not depict a ravishing beauty. However, other reports were more encouraging and Anne of Cleves landed at Dover on 27 December 1539. The moment Henry set eyes on her he was grievously disappointed. This dull, shy, rather cow-like creature bore no resemblance to the paragon he had apparently been expecting. 'Alas', he grumbled, 'whom should men trust?' He felt he had been shamefully deceived by his ambassadors – it is always convenient to be able to blame someone else. To Thomas Cromwell he said: 'Is there none other remedy but that I must needs, against my will, put my neck in the yoke?' None immediately suggested itself. England needed friends abroad and Henry did not quite have the courage to send Anne back to her brother as substandard goods. The wedding took place on 6 January, the bridegroom still dragging his feet and complaining piteously to Cromwell that 'if it were not to satisfy the world and my realm, I would not do that I must do this day for none earthly thing'.[9] Not even for his realm, though, could he bring himself to consummate the marriage and some remedy had to be found. Especially as the royal eye had now been caught by one of the new Queen's maids of honour – pretty, vivacious Katherine Howard who, by a curious coincidence, was Anne Boleyn's cousin. In fact there is an element of farce in the way the King's second divorce parodied his first. Henry's conscience quickly got to work on the fact that Anne had once been tentatively betrothed to the Duke of Lorraine's son, and by midsummer enough legal confusion had been created to enable a nullity case to be got up. On 9 July 1540, Convocation duly pronounced the marriage to be null and void, and four days later an obedient Parliament confirmed the judgement of the clergy. Divorce was a good deal easier now and Anne accepted her relegation with a docility, an alacrity even, which quite surprised the King. She settled down to spend the remainder of her life in comfortable retirement in England, always sure of a good place in royal processions and becoming quite a friend of the family, particularly of Princess Mary.

On 28 July Henry married Katherine Howard, and that same day Thomas Cromwell was executed for high treason. Cromwell's fall bore a close resemblance to that of his former master, Cardinal Wolsey. Like Wolsey, his position had depended entirely on the King's favour. Like Wolsey, he had made enemies and, like Wolsey, his downfall was engineered from below by, among others, the Duke of Norfolk, who was fortunately able to provide another niece to dazzle the King and temporarily distract his attention from the bitter in-fighting going on in the Council.

To the King's small daughter it must sometimes have seemed as if stepmothers came and went with the seasons, but she would soon have learnt that it was not tactful to comment on this interesting phenomenon. According to Gregorio Leti (a not very reliable seventeenth-century biographer of Elizabeth) Katherine Howard made quite a pet of her young kinswoman, and on the day she first dined publicly as Queen under the Cloth of Estate, gave Elizabeth the place of honour opposite her at table, saying she was her cousin and of the same blood and lineage. Leti has been largely discredited as an authority, but on this occasion he may well have been telling the truth. Katherine's rise had been a dizzy one. From being a neglected orphan, dragged up by servants in her grandmother's house, she suddenly found herself, at the age of about nineteen, with the King, and the world, at her feet. A kind-hearted girl (all too kind-hearted as it turned out), she was revelling in her astonishing good fortune and ability to dispense treats.

Henry was entranced by her. He forgot his increasing age and girth and the painful ulcers on his legs, and enjoyed a brief Indian summer of renewed youth and vigour with his 'rose without a thorn'. Unluckily it quickly transpired that Katherine had been unchaste before her marriage and had begun to commit adultery soon after it. When the news was first broken to Henry by Cranmer on 1 November 1541, he refused to believe it. But the evidence was damning and the French ambassador reported in December that the King 'has changed his love for the Queen into hatred, and taken such grief at being deceived that of late it was thought he had gone mad, for he called for a sword to slay her he had loved so much'. When his rage wore off, 'he took to tears regretting his ill luck in meeting with such ill-conditioned wives'.[10] The wretched Katherine, too, was in a sorry state. Cranmer, who had been sent to try and get a confession out of her, found her in hysterics and approaching such a 'franzy' of remorse and terror that the kindly Archbishop was moved to pity and to fear for her reason. Although for a time Henry seems to have wavered, there was no mercy for Katherine Howard. She was not even accorded the courtesy of a trial. An Act of Attainder was passed against her and on 13 February 1542 she was beheaded on Tower Green and went to join her cousin Anne in the chapel of St Peter-ad-Vincula. Elizabeth was eight years old at the time of Katherine's disgrace. It was another object lesson for the child in the recurring connexion between royal marriage and sudden death.

After his last two unfortunate experiences, the King temporarily abandoned matrimony and turned his attention to more congenial matters, such as harrying the Scots and planning an invasion of France. His children continued to live quietly in the country. Elizabeth was now spending a good deal of her time in the company of her little brother, and according to the dramatist Thomas Heywood: 'Cordial and entire grew the affection betwixt this brother and sister; insomuch that he no sooner began to know her, but he seemed to acknowledge her, and she being of more maturity, as deeply loved him.'[11] Edward's education had now begun under the direction of Dr Cox, Provost of Eton, and Elizabeth apparently shared the services of her brother's tutors. Heywood, writing early in the next century, draws this rather charmingly artless picture of their routine when they were together.

> So pregnant and ingenious were either, that they desired to look upon books as soon as the day began to break. Their *horae matutinae* were so welcome, that they seemed to prevent the night's sleeping for the entertainment of the

> morrow's schooling. Besides, such were the hopeful inclinations of this princely youth and pious virgin, that their first hours were spent in prayers and other religious exercises. . . . The rest of the forenoon (breakfast-time excepted) they were doctrinated and instructed, either in language, or some of the liberal sciences; in moral learning, or other collected out of such authors as did best conduce to the instruction of princes. And when he was called out to any youthful exercise, becoming a child of his age, (for study without action breeds dullness) she in her private chamber betook herself to her lute or viol, and (wearied with that) to practise with her needle.[12]

The superhuman attainments of the princely youth and pious virgin (Edward was producing Latin prose by the time he was seven) become rather more understandable if one remembers that to these children Latin was not a dead thing confined within the pages of a grammar, but a living language for everyday writing and speaking, which they began to learn very soon after learning English, and which in its early stages was taught in a way not far removed from the latest 'direct' methods of teaching modern languages. Also, of course, they had the benefit of individual tuition by the cream of the available teaching talent, at a time when some of the best minds in the country were taking a special interest in the education of the young. All the same, there is no doubt that both Edward and Elizabeth were well above average intelligence, eager to learn and with enormous capacities for sheer, concentrated hard work.

On 12 July 1543, the King made his last and, in some ways, his most successful marriage. Katherine Parr was thirty-one, the daughter of a Northamptonshire knight who had already been twice married, and been twice widowed. She was a pretty woman, mature, cultured and sensible – and far from overjoyed at the honour done to her. Henry was no longer a very attractive proposition physically. Now in his early fifties, he had aged rapidly since the Katherine Howard *débâcle* and was becoming grossly fat, with suppurating, foul-smelling ulcers on both legs. His brain was still razor sharp but he was increasingly moody and suspicious, often morose and unpredictably bad-tempered. It is not surprising that Katherine Parr quailed at the prospect before her – especially as she was already more than half in love with Henry's brother-in-law, the dashing Thomas Seymour. But Tom Seymour knew better than to enter into amatory competition with his sovereign lord. As soon as the King's interest became clear, he melted rapidly into the background, leaving Katherine to shoulder the burden of another elderly husband. It is entirely to her credit that she shouldered it cheerfully, and gave Henry loyal and sympathetic companionship during the last years of his life.

In addition to being a good wife, Katherine Parr made an excellent step-mother, taking a serious and constructive interest in the welfare of the King's oddly assorted brood. She became very friendly with Mary – there was only four years difference in their ages – and the two younger children were soon devoted to her. But it was probably Elizabeth who benefited most from her influence. The princess had her tenth birthday that September and was growing up fast; a rather rootless little girl, who badly needed the affection and guidance of an older woman she could respect and admire. She still had Katherine Champernowne (soon to become Katherine Ashley) of course; but Kat, as Elizabeth called her, was always associated with nursery days and her charge was beginning to outstrip her intellectually. There was still Mary but, although the sisters remained on perfectly amicable terms, an invisible barrier was growing up between them as Elizabeth left babyhood behind her, a barrier rooted in the unhappy past. Elizabeth could never enter Mary's private territory and they would never be able to enjoy true intimacy. Also, as the pattern of the younger girl's education developed, the gulf inevitably widened. Edward and Elizabeth were beginning, inevitably, to represent the future, just as Mary must always be identified with the past. In Katherine Parr, Elizabeth was fortunate to find just the friend she needed, at a time when she most needed her.

The new Queen – always a lively person of intellectual Protestantism – played an active part in the reorganisation of the royal schoolrooms which took place during the first half of 1544, and not long after Edward's sixth birthday. In July, Sir John Cheke, Regius Professor of Greek at Cambridge and a leader of progressive religious opinion, was brought in to take over from Dr Cox, assisted by such other luminaries as Roger Ascham and Anthony Cooke (whose daughter later married William Cecil). A few months later, William Grindal, also a Cambridge man and a notable Greek scholar who had been Ascham's pupil, was appointed tutor to Elizabeth. Thus, from the age of eleven, her education became closely associated with the Cambridge humanists and her classical studies now began in earnest. She was learning French too by this time, and Italian. Her earliest surviving letter, dated 31 July 1544, was written to Katherine Parr in Italian – probably as an exercise, it certainly reads like one. 'Inimical fortune,' the ten-year-old princess complains to her step-mother,

> envious of all good and ever revolving human affairs, has deprived me for a whole year of your most illustrious presence, and, not thus content, has yet again robbed me of the same good; which thing would be intolerable to me, did I not hope to enjoy it very soon. And in this my exile, I well know that the clemency of your Highness has had as much care and solicitude for my health as the King's Majesty himself. By which thing I am not only bound to serve you, but also to revere you with filial love, since I understand that your most Illustrious Highness has not forgotten me every time you have written to the King's Majesty, which, indeed, it was my duty to have requested from you. For heretofore I have not dared to write to him. Wherefore I humbly pray your most Excellent Highness, that, when you write to his Majesty, you will condescend to recommend me to him, praying ever for his sweet benediction, and similarly entreating our Lord God to send him best success, and the obtaining of victory over his enemies, so that your Highness and I may, as soon as possible, rejoice together with him on his happy return.[13]

This letter has been held to mean that Elizabeth was for some reason in disgrace with her father at the time, but the evidence seems extremely slender. Henry had gone over to France on 14 July to superintend the siege of Boulogne and Katherine had been made Regent in his absence (an honour not accorded to a Queen Consort since the days of Catherine of Aragon), so she would have been fully occupied. Elizabeth, bemoaning her 'exile', must mean, if anything, that she has not seen the Queen during the current year, for she was certainly at court the previous December with Mary and Edward. Most probably she has only 'not dared' to trouble the King with letters while he is busy on such important matters abroad. At any rate, Henry, writing to his wife on 8 September, sends his 'hearty blessings' to all his children.

Family relations apparently continued to be entirely cordial, and on New Year's Day 1545 Elizabeth presented her step-mother with a translation into English prose of a very long and very dull poem by Margaret of Navarre, entitled *The Mirror of the Sinful Soul.* This laborious effort was accompanied by a letter declaring that since 'pusillanimity and idleness are most repugnant unto a reasonable creature' the writer has undertaken her task to the best of her 'small wit and simple learning' and hopes that the Queen will not find anything in it 'worthy of reprehension'. The whole was enclosed in an embroidered cover worked by the translator. Elizabeth seems to have developed the economical habit of making her own presents at an early age, but no doubt Katherine received it with suitable enthusiasm.

Elizabeth spent most of the closing years of her father's reign with Edward, working quietly at her lessons in such familiar surroundings as Ashridge and Hatfield. By the terms of the third and last Henrician Act of Succession, passed in 1544, she and Mary had been restored to their places in line for the throne, should Edward fail to produce heirs, or failing any new heirs by the latest royal marriage, and subject to certain conditions to be laid down by Henry in his Will or by Letters Patent. Neither princess was legitimised by the new Act, but something had been done to regularise their peculiar position.

The King's health was failing now. He had probably overtaxed himself riding a great courser at the siege of Boulogne and he certainly began to deteriorate visibly after his return from France in October 1544. His vast bulk had to be carried about indoors in a chair and he was subject to frequently recurring attacks of fever, deriving from the ulcers on his legs which caused him intense pain. Henry had suffered from a 'sorre legge' on and off ever since 1528 and it used to be thought that this trouble was of syphilitic origin. However, as there is no record that the King ever received the recognised treatment for venereal disease – a titbit which would hardly have escaped the notice of some sharp-eyed ambassador – and as no other symptoms ever appeared, either in himself or his children, the general consensus of medical opinion now is that the ulcers were varicose, resulting from varicose veins. In a heavy man, addicted to violent physical exercise, who refused to rest and was subjected to the savage therapeutics of his day, such a condition would naturally be exacerbated. Another, more recent, theory is that Henry may have been suffering from osteomyelitis, a chronic septic infection of the bone, following an injury received in one of his mishaps in the tiltyard.[14]

At the end of November 1546 Edward and Elizabeth were separated, he and his entourage going to Hertford Castle and she to Enfield. The parting seems to have been a sorrowful one and prompted a rather pathetic note (written, needless to say, in Latin) from the nine-year-old Prince.

> The change of place, in fact, did not vex me so much, dearest sister, as your going from me. Now, however, nothing can happen more agreeable to me than a letter from you; and especially as you were the first to send a letter to me, and have challenged me to write. Wherefore I thank you both for your good-will and despatch. . . . But this is some comfort to my grief, that I hope to visit you shortly (if no accident intervene with either me or you), as my chamberlain has reported to me.[16]

The visit did indeed take place and, although accident had intervened, it was not with either Edward or Elizabeth.

As the year wore away, it became obvious that the King was seriously ill. Katherine Parr was sent to keep Christmas at Greenwich, but Henry stayed at Westminster. He, who had once been the handsomest prince in Christendom, was now a swollen, rotting hulk, often in such pain that the Imperial ambassador reported he grew black in the face and speechless. But still his mind remained clear, and his indomitable will held on to life while he worked to perfect the safeguards he had devised for Edward's minority. It was less than seventy years since the little princes had disappeared in the Tower and Henry was under no illusions about the dangers that might lie in wait for his son. Towards midnight on Thursday, 27 January he lapsed into merciful semi-consciousness and in the early hours of Friday, the twenty-eighth, he died – his task completed to the best of his ability. He had ruled England for thirty-eight years and had grown from a young god into a father-figure of overwhelming proportions. He had done things which no English king before him had dared to do and had, incredibly, got away with them. Beneath his monstrous, sometimes preposterous, egotism, he had loved England and its people, although they had not always approved of him, had loved him in return. Indeed, his tremendous personality impressed itself so deeply on the national consciousness that it has passed into folk-memory, and to this day Bluff King Hal is one of the very few English monarchs who is still instantly recognisable.

Almost before the breath had left his body, many of his carefully-thought-out arrangements were being disregarded, as Edward Seymour, now Earl of Hertford, rode out to gain possession of the little King. Hertford brought Edward to Enfield to Elizabeth and there broke the news to brother and sister together. Both wept, clinging together in such a passion of tears that the onlookers watched in some awe, and presently joined in. Whether the children cried from genuine grief, from shock, or just in sympathy with each other it is impossible to say. Probably it was a mixture of all three. Edward, of course, had always been the apple of the King's eye and Elizabeth had never known direct experience of his wrath. He had been a remote figure, a god to be worshipped and propitiated from a distance, but at least he was the one person she could trust implicitly never to let anyone else harm her. For Edward and Elizabeth the sheet anchor had gone, and their world could be a hard place for fatherless children, even, perhaps especially, for royal children. This was the end of childhood for them both, and both knew it. Edward, the fair, pretty, clever boy, who already carried the seeds of the disease which was to kill him, must step into his father's enormous shoes. Elizabeth, she was thirteen and a half now, must begin a hard, lonely apprenticeship in which, she was soon to learn, she would have no one but herself to trust.

6

ELIZABETH'S ADMIRAL

In drawing up his will, Henry VIII had named sixteen executors who were to form a Council of Regency during Edward's minority. There was no mention of a Protector or Governor of the Realm, Henry being apparently reluctant to trust any one man with supreme power, and each member of the Council was to have equal precedence. This inner Cabinet was to be supplemented by a secondary body of assistant executors who could offer guidance and advice, but whose exact powers and status were not defined.

During his lifetime Henry had always been careful to maintain a balance between those members of the Privy Council who favoured his own peculiar brand of Catholicism, and those who urged further reform. After Cromwell's fall, some five years previously, the conservatives had, on the surface at any rate, seemed to gain the edge over the progressives – although the fact that the heir to the throne was being educated as a Protestant did not promise well for their future. Then, in the last months of the old King's life, the conservative party had suffered a virtual death-blow in the loss of its two most influential leaders: the Duke of Norfolk, the eminently dislikeable old man who had, nevertheless, always served King Henry with the grim loyalty of a savage watchdog; and Stephen Gardiner, Bishop of Winchester, a brilliant but tricky lawyer and diplomat.

The ruin of the Howard family seemed complete. Norfolk's arrogant soldier-poet son, the Earl of Surrey, was executed for treason on 19 January 1547, and Norfolk himself escaped a similar fate by a hair's breadth – he had been due to meet the headsman only a few hours after Henry's own death. Stephen Gardiner had fallen out of favour during the autumn of 1546, and when Henry was drafting the final version of his Will in December he struck the Bishop off the list of executors saying that 'he was a wilful man and not meet to be about his son'.

The reasoning which lay behind the assault on the Howards and the removal of Gardiner is by no means clear, but in each case the initiative came directly from the King. Henry may have doubted whether either Norfolk or Gardiner was entirely sound on the question of the Royal Supremacy. He may have feared a Roman counter-attack once his own strong hand had gone, possibly even open violence between the opposing factions. He was also, surely, too much of a realist not to have known that the progressives could not be restrained indefinitely and that with them, in the last resort, must lie the future greatness of the English nation. Henry's motives were frequently either obscure or obscured, but one thing is plain enough: before his death he himself had ensured that in his son's reign the balance of power would be decisively tilted in favour of the Protestants.

The sixteen members of the Council of Regency were all 'new' men, in the sense that none of them bore a title more than ten years old. They were all men who had risen to wealth and influence by their loyalty and service to the Tudor monarchy, and their unquestioning acceptance of the doctrine of Royal Supremacy. Only four of their number could be regarded as having any sympathies with Catholicism. The remainder either had no strong convictions or were declared Protestants. The outstanding figure among them was Edward Seymour, Earl of Hertford, the new King's maternal uncle and a rising star in the political firmament.

Edward Seymour not unnaturally saw himself as the obvious choice for Regent, and while Henry was still alive, speechless and barely conscious in his great bed at Whitehall, Seymour and his friend and ally, that experienced tactician, Secretary of State William Paget, paced the long gallery outside the royal bed-chamber, waiting for the end and discussing future arrangements. During their vigil several important matters were settled. It was agreed that Seymour should go at once to Hertford Castle to fetch the new King and bring him to London. In the meantime, Paget would keep Henry's Will in his own hands (temporarily suppressing any inconvenient portions of it) and would use his considerable authority and prestige to persuade the other executors that Seymour should be made Protector during his nephew's minority. In return, it was understood that Paget should act as Seymour's principal adviser in the new government. It was also agreed that until such time as the transference of power had been completed, the fact of Henry's death should be concealed.

This plan went smoothly into action, the only hitch occurring when Seymour, in his haste to set out to fetch Edward, inadvertently took with him the key of the chest containing the Will and was obliged to send it back to Paget from Hertford Castle, with a hurried note written 'between three and four o'clock in the morning' of 29 January.[1] Such indeed was the speed and efficiency of the whole operation that there was no time for opposition to form.

The executors – or the twelve of them who were in London – met together formally for the first time on Monday, 31 January, and Paget had little difficulty in getting them to disregard both the spirit and the letter of their late master's Will. They agreed

> that being a great number appointed to be executors with like and equal charge, it should be more than necessary, as well as for the honour, surety and

> government of the most royal person of the King our sovereign lord that now is, as for the more certain and assured order and direction of his affairs, that some special man of the number and company aforesaid should be preferred in name and place before others.

After this, by unanimous consent and 'upon mature consideration of the tenderness and proximity of blood' between the new King and the Earl of Hertford, the executors proceeded to bestow on Hertford 'the first and chief place among us, and also the name and title of the Protector of all the realms and dominions of the King's majesty that now is, and of the Governor of his most royal person'.[2]

The news of Henry VIII's death was now officially released and later that same day, 31 January, King Edward arrived in the capital, escorted by his uncle, and was lodged, according to established custom, in the Tower. The *coup d'état* had been a brilliant and painless success, though in fairness to the new Protector it should be said that he did have strong claims to an office normally considered essential during a royal minority. Edward Seymour was an able, sincere and well-meaning man. Whether he possessed the necessary strength and ruthlessness to defend his position against the competitors who would inevitably rise to assail it remained to be seen.

Katherine Parr had been left no say in the guardianship of her stepson, but it was agreed that the Princess Elizabeth should be placed in the Queen Dowager's care while she finished her education. This seemed an eminently suitable arrangement, and shortly after her father's death Elizabeth moved with her household to join the Queen, now installed at Chelsea, part of her jointure property.

Henry VIII had acquired the manor of Chelsea from Lord Sandys in 1536, and had built a new house there, on the site of the present Cheyne Walk, just to the east of the Albert Bridge. Completed about 1540 and supplied with water from a spring in Kensington, it was apparently intended as an extra nursery for the royal children. Elizabeth had been there in May 1541, when an item occurs in the account presented by Robert Kyrton, Master of the Barge, 'for serving my Lady Elizabeth from Suffolk Place to Chelsea'.[3] In 1547, this pleasant red-brick mansion overlooking the Thames at Chelsea Reach, was to see the beginning of the first, and in some ways the most momentous crisis of her life.

Whatever resentment Katherine Parr may have felt at being excluded from any further share in Edward's upbringing was soon forgotten in the excitement of a promising development in her private life. Her old suitor, Thomas Seymour, was renewing his attentions, and now all of a sudden it seemed to Katherine that 'the time is well abbreviated, by what means I know not, except the weeks be shorter at Chelsey than in other places'.[4]

The well-known, near-contemporary description of Thomas Seymour – 'fierce in courage, courtly in fashion; in personage stately, in voice magnificent, but somewhat empty of matter' – is accurate, as far as it goes. It does not add that he was also vain, greedy, selfish and dangerous. Utterly unscrupulous in his use of man, woman or child – especially woman or child – in any scheme which would further his own ends, Tom Seymour, the classic confidence-trickster, possessed just the kind of charm calculated to make him irresistible to his victims.

On 17 February, Edward Seymour had been created Duke of Somerset to match his new dignity, and in the general sharing-out of honours which took place before the coronation Thomas became Baron Seymour of Sudeley and was given the office of Lord High Admiral. He had been named as one of the assistant executors in Henry VIII's Will, which now ensured him a place on the Privy Council, but he was far from satisfied – regarding his elder brother's semi-regal state with savage envy. It seemed the height of injustice to Thomas Seymour that one of the King's uncles should enjoy all the fruits of their valuable relationship, while the other was apparently to be fobbed off with mere consolation prizes.

Labouring under an acute sense of grievance, therefore, the Lord Admiral set about considering ways and means of altering this distressing state of affairs. As an eligible bachelor in his late thirties, his obvious first step was to choose a wife whose position would improve his own status, and with astonishing effrontery he considered the Princess Mary and Elizabeth in turn. As Henry's daughters had been restored to the Succession with the explicit proviso that any marriages they might make must first be fully approved by the King and Council, Tom Seymour cautiously sounded some of his fellow councillors on the subject and was, not surprisingly, rebuffed. It was only after this that he turned back to the Queen Dowager whose feelings towards him, he was confident, had not changed.

He was perfectly correct in this assumption and Katherine, unaware of her lover's treacherous behaviour, was transparent with happiness. 'I would not have you to think that this mine honest good will toward you to proceed of any sudden motion of passion,' she wrote to him earnestly from Chelsea. 'For as truly as God is God, my mind was fully bent the other time I was at liberty to marry you before any man I knew.'[5] The Almighty, it seemed had withstood her will 'most vehemently' on that occasion, but now she was to have her reward for self-abnegation and could only say, with heartfelt sincerity, that 'God is a marvellous man.'

Katherine was thirty-four now but, not having been worn out with child-bearing, she was still young enough and attractive enough to be eager to snatch her chance before it was too late. The Admiral was impatient – he had no intention of being balked again – and some time that spring there was another secret wedding between a Queen Dowager of England and a bold, handsome adventurer. As on the previous occasion, no record survives of where or when the ceremony took place, but the evidence points to a date in April or early May.

The next step was to find a tactful way of breaking the news. Katherine wrote again to the Admiral, probably before the marriage had actually been solemnised: 'As I gather by your letter, delivered to my brother Herbert, ye are in some feat how to frame my lord your brother to speak in your favour.' The Queen had no intention of crawling to the Protector (or to his wife, whom she disliked). 'I would not wish you to importune for his good will', she told Tom, 'if it come not freely at the first; it shall be sufficient once to require it, and then to cease. I would desire you might obtain the king's letters in your favour, and also the aid and furtherance of the most notable of the council . . . which thing obtained, shall be no small shame to your brother and loving sister, in case they do not the like.'[6] In the meantime, however, it was necessary to be discreet. 'When it shall be your pleasure to repair hither,' wrote Katherine, 'ye must take some pain to come early in the morning, that ye may be gone again by seven o'clock; and so I suppose ye may come without suspect. I pray you let me have knowledge over-night at what hour ye will come, that your porteress may wait at the gate to the fields for you.'[7]

Tom Seymour had already taken one precaution of suborning a gentleman of the Privy Chamber, one John Fowler, to further his interest with the King and act as a go-between. He also wrote to Mary, asking her to favour his suit, but got little satisfaction from this quarter. Mary was plainly shocked and disappointed, 'considering whose wife Her Grace was of late', that Katherine should even be contemplating another marriage so soon. What Elizabeth thought is, characteristically, open to question. She was probably in the secret from the beginning. Even if Katherine had not confided in her, she must have heard about those mysterious comings and goings in the Chelsea fields during the small hours. The boisterous, loud-voiced person of the Admiral was not easy to conceal at any time, and the Queen's maids would have been agog with the excitement of it all.

The unreliable Italian, Leti, in his Life of Elizabeth, records that Mary sent her sister an urgent invitation to leave their unworthy step-mother's roof and make a home with her, but that Elizabeth refused. Although expressing her grief and affliction at seeing 'the scarcely cold body of the King, our father, so shamefully dishonoured', she considered neither she nor Mary were in a position to risk offending so influential a couple as the Queen and the Admiral and that their best course would be dissimulation. According to Leti, she justified this by pointing out that Henry's memory, 'being so glorious in itself, cannot be subject to those stains which can only defile the persons who have wrought them'. Besides which, the Queen has shown her so great affection and done her so many kind offers, that Elizabeth 'must use much tact . . . for fear of appearing ungrateful'.[8]

The invitation may have been sent and, if so, would surely have been gracefully declined – life at Chelsea, after all, promised to be more amusing than life buried in Essex with Mary – but the whole correspondence strikes a false note. Elizabeth was not a free agent to live where she chose and, whatever she thought, is hardly likely to have committed herself so far – even in a private letter to her sister. All the same, it is true that the text, if it is genuine, has been translated three times and may have suffered in the process. And it is quite possible that Elizabeth was somewhat piqued by her much-loved step-mother's precipitate remarriage. In view of subsequent events, it is reasonable to assume that she did not yet know about Tom Seymour's earlier matrimonial intentions towards herself. Leti again provides an elaborate apparatus of letters – an ardent proposal and an elegantly phrased refusal, both dated in February – but these are almost certainly inventions of his own. Nevertheless, it was not long before Katherine Ashley had heard the gossip about what would have happened if the Lord Admiral 'might have had his own will', and could not resist passing on this interesting piece of information to her charge.

The Queen paid a visit to court in May and seems to have discussed the whole question of her remarriage with the King, explaining that no disrespect was intended to his father's memory. Reassured on this point, Edward wrote to her on 30 May: 'since you love my father, I cannot but much esteem you; since you love me, I cannot but love you in return; and since you love the Word of God, I do love and admire you with my whole heart. Wherefore, if there be anything wherein I may do you a kindness, either in word or deed, I will do it willingly.'[9]

News that the marriage had actually taken place had leaked out by midsummer and the King was graciously pleased to give it his blessing. 'I will so provide for you both', he told Katherine magnificently, 'that hereafter, if any grief befall, I shall be a sufficient succour in your godly or praisable enterprises.' But the Lord Protector, as Edward noted laconically in his Chronicle, 'was much displeased'. However, the damage was done, and the outbreak of war with Scotland later in the summer helped to distract the Protector's attention from his brother's misdeeds.

The Admiral should have commanded the Fleet in the Scottish campaign, but he preferred to remain at home to pursue certain projects of his own. He and Katherine, and Elizabeth, were now all living together – sometimes at Chelsea, sometimes further out in the country at Hanworth, another of the Queen's dower houses, and sometimes at Seymour Place, Tom's London residence. Katherine was relaxed and happy. Tom, having achieved one of his objectives, was in high good humour and the domestic atmosphere was gay and informal.

Remarkably informal, in fact, for it was at Chelsea, 'incontinent after he was married to the Queen', that the Lord Admiral began his semi-jocular pursuit of his wife's step-daughter. He

> would come many mornings into the Lady Elizabeth's chamber, before she were ready, and sometimes before she did rise. And if she were up, he would

> bid her good morrow, and ask how she did, and strike her upon the back or on the buttocks familiarly, and so go forth through his lodgings; and sometime go through to the maidens and play with them, and so go forth.

If Elizabeth was still in bed, 'he would put open the curtains, and bid her good morrow, and make as though he would come at her. And she would go further into the bed, so that he could not come at her.' All good clean fun perhaps, and certainly quite a new experience for Elizabeth. There was one morning when the Admiral went rather too far and 'strove to have kissed her in her bed' but Mrs Ashley, who was present, 'bade him go away for shame'.[10]

When the household moved to Hanworth, Tom would 'likewise come in the morning unto her grace', but found Elizabeth up and dressed, except for two occasions when the Queen came with him 'and there they tickled my lady Elizabeth in the bed, the Queen and my lord Admiral'. Another time, in the garden at Hanworth, 'he wrestled with her and cut her gown in an hundred pieces, being black cloth'. When Mrs Ashley scolded the princess, 'her grace answered, she could not do with all, for the Queen held her, while the Lord Admiral cut it'.[11]

Years later, Henry Clifford, writing the biography of his mistress, Jane Dormer, who had been one of Mary's favourite maids of honour, remarked of Elizabeth that 'a great lady who knew her well, being a girl of twelve or thirteen, told me that she was proud and disdainful, and related to me some particulars of her scornful behaviour, which much blemished the handsomeness and beauty of her person'.[12] Clifford can, in general, be regarded as a hostile witness, but Elizabeth always had a healthy idea of her own importance and may well have been inclined to stand on her dignity. All the same, she seems to have responded readily to teasing and for a few carefree weeks during the summer of 1547 she expanded and behaved more naturally and childishly than at any time since she was a baby. Unfortunately, however, the opportunity had come too late. At almost fourteen Elizabeth was no longer a child. Tom Seymour was a very personable man, and his thinly disguised advances naturally excited her adolescent vanity and soon began to provoke an experimentally coquettish response.

Mrs Ashley was worried. Tongues were beginning to wag. There was more romping at Chelsea, when Elizabeth, 'hearing the privy lock undo' and knowing that meant the Admiral was coming, 'ran out of her bed to her maidens, and then went behind the curtain of the bed, the maidens being there; and my lord tarried to have her come out'.[13] It was after this episode that the governess waylaid his lordship in the gallery to tell him that 'these things were complained of and that my lady was evil spoken of'. Tom was unrepentant. He meant no evil, he said, and swore, by God's precious soul, that he was being slandered and would himself complain to the Lord Protector.[14] Seeing that 'she could not make him leave it', Mrs

Ashley took her troubles to the Queen, who 'made a small matter of it', but said she would come with her husband in future. 'And so', according to Mrs Ashley, 'she did ever after,'[15] or for a time, at least. There were other occasions, 'at Seymour Place, when the Queen lay there' when the Admiral used 'to come up every morning in his nightgown, barelegged in his slippers'. These days, however, Elizabeth was usually up and 'at her book', so Tom had to content himself by looking in at the gallery door and bidding her good morrow before going his way. Even so, Mrs Ashley told him severely, it was an unseemly sight to come visiting a maiden's chamber so improperly dressed; 'with which he was angry, but he left it'.[16]

It is difficult to see what, if anything, the Admiral hoped to achieve by these rather questionable antics. Probably they had started simply as his idea of a joke – no doubt it gave him a pleasant sense of power to be on slap-and-tickle terms with Henry VIII's daughter – and were continued out of bravado after the joke had gone stale. For it had gone stale. Elizabeth was becoming self-conscious and Katherine, in spite of her apparent casualness, was not entirely happy about the situation. There had been a curious little incident at Hanworth, when the Queen told Mrs Ashley that 'my lord Admiral looked in at the gallery window and saw my lady Elizabeth cast her arms about a man's neck'. When Mrs Ashley taxed the princess with this, she 'denied it weeping, and bade ask all her women', but the governess knew such an accusation could not be true, 'for there came no man but Grindal, the Lady Elizabeth's schoolmaster'. She began to wonder, rather uneasily, if the Queen was growing jealous of her step-daughter and had invented the story of a strange man as a warning to Mrs Ashley to 'take more heed and be, as it were, in watch betwixt her and my Lord Admiral'.[17]

In spite of all these distractions, Elizabeth was making good progress under Grindal's tuition, and Roger Ascham did not know 'whether to admire more the wit of her who learnt, or the diligence of him who taught'.[18] Ascham was anxious to further his acquaintance with Elizabeth and took care to cultivate Mrs Ashley, writing tactful letters of congratulation on her labour and wisdom in so diligently overseeing that noble imp, her charge. He sent Elizabeth an Italian book and a book of prayers, had her pens mended, and asked to be commended to 'all that company of godly gentlewomen' who surrounded the Queen Dowager.[19]

The godly gentlewomen by this time included the ten-year-old Lady Jane Grey. She had been placed in the Queen's household by her ambitious parents, and the Admiral had persuaded her father, the Marquess of Dorset, to put her future in his hands. As the granddaughter of Henry VIII's younger sister Mary, who had married the Duke of Suffolk, Jane Grey stood close enough to the throne to be a valuable potential asset; for Henry, using the powers given him by Parliament, had bequeathed the Succession, in default of heirs from any of his own children, to the Suffolk line. Tom

Seymour was not quite sure yet how he could best turn the custody of Lady Jane to his advantage, but he was full of 'fair promises' and dropped hints to the Dorsets about a possible marriage for her with the King.

Edward was, of course, the most important of the three children whom the Admiral hoped to make use of in the various undesirable ploys he had under consideration, and he lost no opportunity of ingratiating himself with the boy by flattery and gifts of pocket money.

The young King was beginning to feel a trifle overburdened with uncles. The Protector was proving a strict guardian. A 'dry, sour, opinionated man', according to Van der Delft the new Imperial ambassador, he kept Edward so strait that he could not have money at his will, and the King had conceived a perfectly dispassionate dislike for his 'uncle of Somerset'. The Admiral, on the other hand, was jovial and open-handed. Edward had no objection to the open-handedness and was in the habit of sending his uncle Tom terse demands for cash via the useful John Fowler, but he soon became irritated by the Admiral constantly urging him to assert himself, and trying to involve him in the Seymour family squabbles.

There was an acrimonious dispute in progress that autumn over some pieces of the Queen Dowager's jewellery held by the Protector. Katherine claimed they had been personal gifts from King Henry, but Somerset refused to give them up, saying they were crown property. As these items included her wedding-ring, Katherine's annoyance was understandable. Somerset had also installed a tenant, against her wishes, in one of her manors. The normally sunny-tempered Katherine was furious and threatened to 'utter her choler' to His Grace. Family relations were not improved by the attitude of the Protector's wife. The Duchess of Somerset, 'a woman for many imperfections intolerable but for pride monstrous',[20] was bitterly resentful of the fact that Katherine, as Queen Dowager, took precedence over her at state functions, and made no secret of her feelings on the subject of presumptuous wives of younger sons.

The first session of Parliament in the new reign was held in November, and the Admiral, imbued with a fresh sense of his wrongs, stamped about shouting that 'if I be thus used, they speak of a black Parliament, by God's precious soul I will make this the blackest Parliament that ever was in England'. When his cronies tried to restrain him, he exclaimed defiantly that he could better live without the Protector than the Protector without him, and that if anybody went about to speak evil of the Queen he would take his fist to their ears, from the highest to the lowest.[21]

Tom had tried to persuade Edward, now considerably in his debt financially, to sign a letter to be presented to 'the lords of the Parliament House' requesting them to favour a suit which the Admiral meant to bring before them. This suit was Tom Seymour's pet scheme to have the offices of Protector of the Realm and Governor of the King's person divided between his brother and himself. Edward, however, took the advice of his tutor, Sir John Cheke, who warned him seriously on the dangers of becoming compromised in the Admiral's intrigues, and wisely refused to sign anything he might be made to regret. The Admiral, frustrated, took to prowling the corridors of St James's Palace, remarking wistfully that he wished the King were at home with him in his house, and speculating on how easy it would be to steal the boy away under the Protector's nose.

Elizabeth paid a visit to court in December, but although she and Edward remained genuinely fond of each other their relationship had changed considerably since that day, less than a year ago, when they had cried together so bitterly over the news of their father's death. The respect exacted by a Tudor king, even one just ten years old, was formidable. An Italian visitor, Petruccio Ubaldini, thought the whole business somewhat exaggerated. Commenting on the elaborate formalities which took place when one of the King's sisters dined in the royal presence, he remarked,

> she may neither sit under a canopy nor on a chair, but must sit on a mere bench which is provided with a cushion, and so far distant from the head of the table and the King, that the canopy does not overhang her. The ceremonies observed before sitting down at table are truly laughable. I have seen, for example, the Princess Elizabeth drop on one knee five times before her brother, before she took her place.[22]

But Elizabeth had been brought up to regard the person of the sovereign with an almost superstitious reverence, and would see nothing in the least laughable about kneeling to her little brother who was also the King. At any rate she seems to have enjoyed her visit, for she asked to be allowed to stay over Christmas, and Mary was invited to join the family party.

Perhaps Elizabeth was rather glad to escape briefly from the increasingly charged atmosphere of her step-mother's household, and found reassurance in the ordered formality of the court. There was plenty of congenial male company among the group of young noblemen who surrounded the King, and she would have been able to renew her acquaintance with at least one old playmate – Robert Dudley, a dark, handsome boy just her own age whom she had known on and off since she was seven or eight. There was a long-standing connexion between the Tudors and the Dudleys, dating back to the days when Robert's grandfather had been one of Elizabeth's grandfather's hated tax-gatherers. His father had risen in the service of Elizabeth's father, and now created Earl of Warwick, was one of those members of the Privy Council standing watchfully in the shadows behind the Lord Protector.

Elizabeth returned to either Chelsea or Hanworth in January and presently suffered the loss of her tutor, William Grindal, who died of plague during that month. Elizabeth had no hesitation in her choice of a replacement. On 12 February, Roger Ascham wrote to his friend John Cheke, telling him that the princess 'is thinking of having me in the place of Grindal. . . . I was with the illustrious lady during these last days: she signified to me her pleasure and I did not try to make any bargain for my own advantage, but at once declared that I was ready to obey her orders.' It was not quite so simple as that, for Katherine and the Admiral, who were away in London, favoured appointing a man called Goldsmith, and Ascham was anxious not to appear pushing. He urged Elizabeth to follow her guardians' judgement and to think only of 'bringing to perfection that singular learning of which Grindal had sown the seeds'. However, he told Cheke, 'when the Lady Elizabeth comes to London, she will talk over this matter with the Queen and the Lord Admiral; nor do I think they will settle anything without you'.[23]

Whether as a result of her own determination, or through the growing influence of John Cheke with the Privy Council, Elizabeth got her way. Ascham obtained leave of absence from St John's College, Cambridge, where he was a Fellow, and took up his new post in the spring of 1548.

Roger Ascham, a Yorkshireman in his early thirties, had already published *Toxophilus*, his famous treatise on archery, and was acquiring an international reputation for scholarship. He was not entirely strange to royal circles, having been called in by Cheke on several occasions to teach Edward the penmanship of which he was a notable exponent, and had played a considerable part in forming Elizabeth's exquisitely legible Italianate handwriting; but he must have found a household dominated by the ebullient personality of Tom Seymour something of a contrast to Cambridge. Still, there were enough kindred spirits devoted to 'godly learning' in the Queen Dowager's establishment to make Roger Ascham feel at home. He was already on familiar terms with Mrs Ashley and her husband, and soon struck up a friendship with John Whitney, a young gentleman-in-waiting with whom he shared a bed. There was also Lady Jane Grey, already fast developing into a formidable paragon of Protestant erudition; her tutor, John Aylmer; the Queen's younger sister, Ann Parr; and, of course, Elizabeth herself who fulfilled Ascham's highest expectations as a pupil. He taught her Latin and Greek by his famous method of double translation, presenting her with passages of Demosthenes or Cicero, to be turned first into English and then back into their original languages. The mornings were usually devoted to Greek, beginning with a reading from the Greek New Testament, and followed by selected orations of Isocrates or one of Sophocles' tragedies. Ascham thought that from these sources the princess would 'gain purity of style, and her mind derive instruction that would be of value to her to meet every contingency of life'. In the afternoons they went on to Latin, and Elizabeth read almost the whole of Cicero and a 'great part' of Livy under Ascham's supervision. To these authors he added various works of St Cyprian and Melanchthon's Commonplaces, which he considered 'best suited, after the Holy Scriptures, to teach her the foundations of religion, together with elegant language and sound doctrine'.[24] It sounds an indigestible diet for a fourteen-year-old girl, but Elizabeth apparently throve on it, eagerly absorbing a carefully balanced mixture of classical ethics and Christian piety. Katherine Parr had not forgotten her zeal for 'true religion' of the reformed variety – though it was noticeable that the Lord Admiral had developed a habit of remembering urgent business elsewhere when it was time for family prayers.

Roger Ascham cannot have been more than two months in his new, intellectually stimulating surroundings when the volcano which had been simmering beneath the surface of the Queen Dowager's household for the past year suddenly erupted. Katherine was now carrying Tom's child, and a first pregnancy for a woman in her mid-thirties was no light matter in the sixteenth century. Whatever her good intentions, the Admiral's wife was no longer in any condition for chaperoning horseplay – especially in the early morning. We do not know exactly what happened to bring matters to a head, but it seems to have been something rather less innocent than hide-and-seek round the bed-curtains. According to a hearsay account given eight months after the event: 'the Queen, suspecting the often access of the Admiral to the Lady Elizabeth's grace, came suddenly upon them, when they were all alone (he having her in his arms). Wherefore the Queen fell out, both with the Lord Admiral and with her grace also. And hereupon', this same account continues, 'the Queen called Mrs Ashley to her, and told her fancy in that matter; and of this there was much displeasure.'[25]

Katherine was understandably hurt and angry, and she cannot be blamed for venting her feelings on Mrs Ashley, who does appear to have been guilty of some negligence. Quite apart from her personal distress, Katherine must also have been badly frightened. The Protector had so far shown himself remarkably forbearing towards his brother's various indiscretions, but the Queen knew that if any harm were to come to Elizabeth, a virgin of the blood royal, while in their charge, both she and her husband would find themselves in a very ugly situation. Katherine was also clearly thinking of Elizabeth herself, whose whole life could be ruined by a scandal now. At all costs that must be avoided and for everyone's sake the princess must be put out of the Admiral's reach as quickly and as quietly as possible. Arrangements were therefore made for Elizabeth and her household to leave Chelsea in the week after Whitsun 1548 for Cheshunt (or Cheston) to stay in the house of Sir Anthony and Lady Denny.

Tom Seymour's conduct towards a girl fully young enough to be his daughter living under his wife's protection was, of course, inexcusable; but Elizabeth cannot be entirely exonerated. At best she had been thoughtless, at worst stupid, and cruelly ungrateful to a woman who had loved and trusted her. That she knew she had behaved badly, and recognised the tact and generosity Katherine had shown in extricating her from an embarrassing predicament, is evident from a distinctly chastened note in the first letter she wrote to her step-mother from Cheshunt:

> Although I could not be plentiful in giving thanks for the manifold kindness received at your Highness' hand at my departure, yet I am something to be borne withal, for truly I was replete with sorrow to depart from your Highness, especially leaving you undoubtful of health: and, albeit I answered little, I weighed it more deeper, when you said you would warn me of all evils that you should hear of me; for if your Grace had not a good opinion of me, you would not have offered friendship to me that way, that all men judge the contrary. But what may I more say, than thank God for providing such friends to me; desiring God to enrich me with their long life, and me grace to be in heart no less thankful to receive it than I now am glad in writing to show it; and although I have plenty of matter, here I will stay, for I know you are not quiet to read. From Cheston, this present Saturday. Your Highness' humble daughter, Elizabeth.[26]

There had obviously been an uncomfortable interview with Katherine during which Elizabeth had had to digest a number of unpalatable home-truths on the subject of light and unseemly conduct. There is, of course, no record of what passed between them on that occasion, but, according to the ever-helpful Leti, Katherine told her step-daughter: 'God has given you great qualities. Cultivate them always and labour to improve them, for I believe that you are destined by heaven to be Queen of England.' She may well have said something of the sort – perhaps offering an olive branch after certain realisation of what she stood to lose. It cannot have been an entirely new idea to Elizabeth. She was far too acute not to have already thought of it for herself, but perhaps it was the first time anyone had put such a thought into words, and coming from someone like Katherine it would have made a deep impression. After all, looked at dispassionately, was it so far-fetched? True, Edward seemed sturdy enough, but he was being subjected to abnormal stresses and strains for a child of his age, and had yet to pass through the adolescent years which had proved fatal to several male members of his house – his uncle Arthur, his bastard half-brother the Duke of Richmond, his first cousin the Earl of Lincoln. Then there was Mary, over thirty now, still unmarried and in poor health. Even if she were to marry at once, with her mother's history behind her the chances of her bearing children looked remote. The Tudors had not so far shown themselves either a fruitful or a long-lived stock. Henry VII had died at fifty-two, his younger daughter at thirty-eight. Even that magnificent physical specimen Henry VIII had only survived to fifty-five, and he had been an old man for some years before his death.

All the evidence points to the fact that certainly by her mid-teens the conviction that she would one day be Queen of England had taken firm root in Elizabeth's mind. It became a goal to work towards – a vision to sustain her through the difficult and frightening decade that lay ahead.

7

'The Peril that Might Ensue'

Thanks to the Queen's prompt and sensible action, any immediate danger of scandal touching the princess and the Admiral had been averted. Indeed, the arrangements for Elizabeth's move were so skilfully handled that even her own household did not know the real reason for it. The Dennys may have been in the secret, but they were old friends of the family and could be trusted to be discreet. Sir Anthony Denny had been a favourite of Henry VIII, and a gentleman of his privy chamber. Lady Denny was one of those pious matrons who had been closely associated with the Queen during Henry's lifetime, and in this emergency Katherine evidently considered her the most suitable person available to take over responsibility for Elizabeth. Matters were made easier by the fact of Katherine's advancing pregnancy, for it was known that she was preparing to retire to Sudeley Castle down in Gloucestershire to await the birth of her baby.

Any unpleasantness between the Queen Dowager and her husband about what had happened was quickly smoothed over, and if Katherine felt any lingering resentment she kept it to herself. No doubt she was pinning her hopes on the coming child. If Tom had a son to think of it might steady him – make him settle down and forget all the wild whirling schemes revolving in his head.

Certainly Tom needed something to steady him. It was part of his duties as Lord Admiral to suppress the gangs of pirates which preyed on shipping in the English Channel, but instead it appeared that the Lord Admiral was well on the way to becoming a pirate himself. According to a number of justifiably irritated merchants and sea-captains, he was actually encouraging the marauders, allowing them to use his property in the Scilly Isles as a haven and taking a cut of their loot. But Tom Seymour had more important things on his mind than piracy, for he was still cherishing his ambition to wrest the guardianship of the King out of his brother's hands. If he was ever to achieve that ambition he would need powerful friends, and to buy those friends he would need money – a great deal of money. It seemed a wise move, therefore, to enlist the services of Sir William Sharington, vice-treasurer of the Bristol Mint. William Sharington had been appointed to this office in 1546, and since that time had enriched himself and his associates by such undesirable practices as the clipping and debasing of coin, and the buying-up and minting of considerable quantities of church plate. The Admiral now promised protection from the possible consequences of this form of private enterprise, if Sharington would provide him with the funds he needed. It was good always to have a mass of money ready, remarked Tom vaguely, for then 'a man might do somewhat withal'. Another time he said, 'God faith, Sharington, if we had £10,000 in ready money, that were well.' The Admiral had been reckoning how much it would cost to 'find 10,000 men a month' and boasting that 'he had more gentlemen that loved him than my Lord Protector had', but he was noticeably evasive when questioned directly about his future plans.[1]

He did not take his wife into his confidence either, but Katherine was quite intelligent enough to have guessed a good deal of what was in his mind. Although she loyally supported Tom in his personal quarrels with the Protector, she tried to lower the temperature when she could, and was understandably eager to divert his attention from any more dangerous pranks.

Katherine was particularly anxious that nothing should prevent their going down to Gloucestershire together. The baby had quickened now, and she wrote from Hanworth to her 'sweetheart and loving husband' who had been delayed in London on business: 'I have given your little knave your blessing, who like an honest man stirred apace after and before; for Mary Odell being abed with me had laid her hand upon my belly to feel it stir. It hath stirred these three days every morning and evening, so that I trust when you come, it will make you some pastime.'[2] This evoked a characteristic reply. The Admiral, 'perplexed' as usual that he could not have justice from those who should have been partial to him, was nevertheless much revived to hear that 'my little man doth shake his poll, trusting, if God should give him life to live as long as his father, he will revenge such wrongs as neither you nor I can at this present'. And the expectant father added some helpful obstetric advice: 'I do desire your Highness to keep the little knave so lean and gaunt with your good diet and walking, that he may creep out of a mouse-hole.'[3]

The Queen Dowager and her husband set out for Sudeley on Wednesday, 13 June, accompanied by a princely retinue and taking little Jane Grey with them. Jane's parents had been growing impatient, as no sign of the brilliant marriage promised for her materialised, and had tried to get her back. But the Admiral was too much for the Marquess of Dorset, being 'so earnest with him in persuasion' that Dorset could not resist him – especially perhaps as the persuasion included a substantial sum of money lent without security – and Jane stayed with Katherine, who had grown very fond of the child.

Katherine also saw to it that she and Tom maintained normal friendly relations with Elizabeth in her exile at Cheshunt. The princess had written a curiously dignified little note to the Admiral, in reply apparently to an apology of his at not being able to do her some small service:

> My lord, you needed not to send an excuse to me. For I could not mistrust the not fulfilling of your promise to proceed for want of good will, but only opportunity serveth not. Wherefore I shall desire you to think that a greater matter than this could not make me impute any unkindness in you. For I am a friend not won with trifles, nor lost with the like.[4]

Elizabeth was obviously feeling out of things and missing Katherine badly. She wrote to her on 31 July:

> Although your Highness' letters be most joyful to me in absence, yet considering what pain it is to you to write, your Grace being so great with child and so sickly, your commendation were enough in my lord's letter. I much rejoice . . . with my humble thanks, that your Grace wished me with you, till I were weary of that country. Your Highness were like to be cumbered if I should not depart till I were weary of being with you; although it were the worst soil in the world, your presence would make it pleasant.

She is anxious that the Admiral 'shall be diligent to give me knowledge from time to time how his busy child doth', and ended with a rather sad little attempt at a joke, 'if I were at his birth, no doubt I would see him beaten for the trouble he has put you to'.[5]

Elizabeth had not been well herself. As a little girl she had always been remarkably robust, and there is no record of her even suffering from any of the usual childish ailments. But now began that period of ill-health which was to last intermittently for the remainder of her teens. According to Mrs Ashley, 'she was first sick about mid-summer'. There is no description of the exact nature of this illness, which was to recur in the autumn and become serious enough for one of the King's physicians, Dr Bill, to be sent down to Cheshunt to attend her. In the absence of more definite information, it seems reasonable to assume that it was connected with the onset of Elizabeth's menstrual cycle, aggravated in a highly strung, sensitive girl by the effects of depression and emotional disturbance.

Katherine's baby was born on 30 August. It was a girl, christened Mary. The Admiral apparently felt no disappointment over the child's sex, and at once wrote enthusiastically to his brother with the good news. The Protector had been in the middle of a long, reproachful letter, urging Tom to mend his ways, but he added a kindly postscript: 'We are right glad to understand by your letters that the Queen, your bedfellow, hath had a happy hour; and, escaping all danger, hath made you the father of so pretty a daughter.'[6]

Tragically, however, these congratulations were premature. Katherine developed a high fever, the dreaded symptom of puerperal sepsis, and in her delirium all the carefully buried hurt of the past few months rose to the surface. 'I am not well handled,' she told her friend (and step-daughter by an earlier marriage), Elizabeth Tyrwhit, 'for those that be about me careth not for me, but standeth laughing at my grief; and the more good I will to them, the less good they will to me.' She was holding on to Tom's hand as she spoke and when he exclaimed, 'Why, sweetheart, I would do you no hurt', Katherine said, 'very sharply and earnestly', in his ear, 'No, my lord, I think so; you have given me many shrewd taunts.' Tom, distressed and somewhat embarrassed, lay down beside her on the bed in an attempt to calm her 'with gentle communication'. But Katherine was not to be pacified and rambled on that she would have given a thousand marks to have had her full talk with the physician on the day she was delivered, but 'durst not for displeasing of you'.[7] The possible implications of all this were not lost on the bystanders and inevitably a whisper began to circulate that the Queen had been poisoned.

Katherine died on 5 September 1548, and with her death was extinguished one of the most attractive personalities of the age. She was buried in the chapel at Sudeley with all the ceremonial due to a Queen Dowager of England, and ten-year-old Jane Grey officiating as chief mourner.

For a little while the Admiral seemed genuinely stricken and 'so amazed' that he had small regard to himself or his doings. For all his faults Tom was not a deliberately cruel man. The unhappiness he had caused his wife had been due more to sheer selfish thoughtlessness than any fixed desire to wound, and a servant of his, coming to Cheshunt, told Mrs Ashley that the Admiral 'was a heavy man for the Queen'.

Mrs Ashley, of course, was all agog. Knowing what she did about his lordship's earlier plans, she was already beginning to hear wedding-bells. Elizabeth was 'sick in her bed' again, and in what seems to have been a somewhat unfortunate attempt to cheer her up the governess observed archly, 'your old husband that was appointed unto you after the death of the King now is free again. You may have him if you will.' No, said Elizabeth. 'Yes,' persisted Mrs Ashley, 'yes, you will not deny it if my Lord Protector and the Council were pleased therewith.' After all, why not? The Admiral had been worthy to marry a Queen, and was 'the noblest man unmarried in this land.' But the response was disappointing, for 'her Grace would ever say, nay by her troth'.[8]

Mrs Ashley wanted the princess to write to the Admiral 'to comfort him in his sorrow', but Elizabeth remained unco-operative. She would not do so, she said shortly, 'for it needs not'. Her own feelings about Katherine's death she kept to herself. Sometime in October the household moved from Cheshunt to Hatfield – no doubt to the relief of the Dennys, for the accommodation of Elizabeth and her considerable retinue over the past five months must have put a severe strain on their resources – and John Seymour, escorting the princess on her journey, brought a message from Tom recommending him to her and enquiring 'whether her great buttocks were grown any less or no?' which certainly sounds as if he was quite his old self again.

In any case, the widower could not allow himself the luxury of mourning – there were too many urgent matters requiring his attention. In the confused period after Katherine's death, the Dorsets had insisted on removing their daughter; but Jane Grey was too valuable a property to lose without a struggle, and the Admiral was afraid (or so he said) that the Protector meant to marry her to his own son. He went to see the Dorsets and, according to the Marquess, 'was so earnestly in hand with me and my wife that in the end, because he would have no nay, we were contented she should again return to his house'.[9] Tom had reassured the anxious parents that not only the Queen's gentlewomen but also 'the maids which waited at large' should remain to attend on Jane, and that his own mother 'would be as dear unto her as though she were her own daughter'.[10] More to the point, he made Dorset another loan and renewed his promise that 'if he might once get the King at liberty' a royal marriage would be arranged. The Dorsets – chronically short of money, weak, greedy and not over-endowed with common sense – fell once again into the trap.

The Admiral was now openly canvassing support for his schemes for putting an end to the Protectorate. He asked Dorset what friends he could count on in his part of the world, and advised him to make much of the prosperous yeomen and freeholders, 'for they be men that be best able to persuade the multitude'. 'Go to their houses', urged Tom, 'carrying with you a flagon or two of wine and a pasty of venison, and use a familiarity with them, for so shall you cause them to love you and be assured to have them at your commandment.'[11] He repeated this ingenuous advice to his brother-in-law, William Parr, Marquess of Northampton, and the young Earl of Rutland, telling Rutland that he would like to see the King 'have the honour and rule of his own doings'.

The Admiral did not appear to notice how lukewarm was the response, and, when Rutland had the temerity to remark that he thought his power would be much diminished by the Queen's death, brushed this aside impatiently, saying the Council never feared him so much as they did now. He continued to express his dissatisfaction with his brother's regime to anybody who would listen, and never tired of looking at 'a chart of England' which he had, and declaring how strong he was, 'how far his lands and dominions did stretch . . . and what shires and places were for him'.[12]

More sinister, though, than all this rather meaningless talk was the close proprietary interest that Tom Seymour had begun to take in the Princess Elizabeth and her affairs. Mrs Ashley, who had fallen completely under his spell, chattered away happily to Elizabeth about his intentions, how he was sure to come wooing before long, and all about the exciting possibilities which that opened up. Poor Katherine Ashley has come in for a good deal of criticism over her conduct at this time, and certainly she was not very wise. All the same, it must be remembered that she was by no means the only person to be taken in by Tom. She seems to have genuinely believed that Henry VIII would have approved the match and that it would be a good thing for her beloved princess. It was time Elizabeth had a husband. Mrs Ashley could not bear to think she might become a lonely old maid like her sister Mary. The Admiral, too, would be able to protect her – Mrs Ashley could not be expected to realise how very precarious in fact his position was.

Elizabeth did need someone to protect her. Death had removed the Queen, her only powerful and disinterested friend, and in her household of over a hundred people there was no married woman of rank to whom she could turn for advice or guidance. In the circumstances she kept her head wonderfully well, but she was not entirely proof against the relentless propaganda-campaign she was being subjected to. Mrs Ashley's husband, an observant and sensible man, warned his wife several times 'to take heed, for he did fear that the Lady Elizabeth did bear some affection to my Lord Admiral. She seemed to be well pleased therewith, and sometime she would blush when he were spoken of.'[13]

In the outside world, gossip linking the Admiral's name with the princess grew insistent, and more than one person attempted to warn Tom of the risk he was running. At the end of November, as they rode together to Parliament behind the Protector, Lord Russell, the venerable Lord Privy Seal, said seriously: 'My Lord Admiral, there are certain rumours bruited of you which I am very sorry to hear.' He was informed, he went on, that the Admiral was hoping to marry with either the Lady Mary or the Lady Elizabeth and added, 'my lord, if ye go about any such thing, ye seek the means to undo yourself and all those that shall come of you'. Tom naturally wanted to know 'the authors of that tale' and 'seemed to deny that there was any such thing attempted of his part, and that he never thought to make any enterprise therein'.

Two or three days later, however, again finding himself next to Lord Russell in the procession riding from the Protector's house to Westminster, the Admiral reopened the subject himself. 'Father Russell,' he said, 'you are very suspicious of me. I pray you tell me who showed you of the marriage that I should attempt?' Russell, very properly, refused to name his sources and renewed his warning that Tom should 'make no suit for marriage' with either of the princesses. This time the Admiral persisted. 'It is convenient for them to marry,' he said, 'and better it were that they were married within the realm than in any foreign place. . . . And why might not I, or another, made by the King their father, marry one of them?' He got an unequivocal answer. If he or any other within the realm attempted such a match, declared the Lord Privy Seal, he would 'undoubtedly procure unto himself the occasion of his utter undoing' – and Tom above all others, 'being of so near alliance to the King's Majesty'.

Both Henry VII and Henry VIII, Russell pointed out, though wise and noble princes, had been well known for their suspicious natures. What was more likely than that Edward would take after his father and grandfather in this respect? If one of his uncles married one of the heirs to his crown, he would be bound to think the worst, 'and, as often as he shall see you, to think that you gape and wish for his death'. There was another thing: 'And I pray you, my lord, what shall you have with any of them?' 'Three thousand a year,' said Tom promptly and was as promptly disabused. Whoever married the princesses, Russell told him, would get no more than 'ten thousand pounds in money, plate and goods, and no land. And what', enquired the Lord Privy Seal, 'should that be to maintain his charges and estate, matching himself there?' 'They must have the three thousand pounds a year also,' said the Admiral. 'By God, they may not!' 'By God,' roared Tom, 'none of you all dare say nay to it!' But old Lord Russell was not to be intimidated. 'By God, for my part I will say nay to it; for it is clean against the King's will!'[14]

Mary and Elizabeth had each been left lands to the value of £3000 a year by their father, and the Admiral, who apparently would not be warned, now began to make detailed enquiries into Elizabeth's finances. Her steward, or 'cofferer', Thomas Parry, came up to London shortly before Christmas and Tom Seymour took the opportunity to have several conversations with him. He wanted to know all about the state and size of the princess's household; the whereabouts and profitability of her lands; what terms she held them on; and, especially, whether or not her title to them had yet been confirmed by Letters Patent. She could get her lands exchanged for better ones, he told Parry, and wished they were situated in Wales or the West Country, significantly where most of his own strength lay. He went on to ask about her housekeeping expenses and to compare them with 'what was spent in his own house'.

It was partly a question of houses which had brought Parry to town. Elizabeth wanted to visit her brother, but Durham House, where she had been accustomed to stay when she came up to London, was now being used as a Mint. When the Admiral heard about this difficulty, he was eager to help. The princess must have his own house whenever she wanted it. He would like to see her, too. Perhaps when she moved to Ashridge – it would not be far out of his way when he went into the country. As for Durham House, Elizabeth should go to the Duchess of Somerset and 'make suit' to the Protector to grant her a suitable town-residence, and agree to the exchange of her lands before her Patent was sealed.

Parry was much impressed. When he returned to Hatfield, he told Elizabeth all about my lord's 'gentle offers' and the suggested visit. As she seemed to take this 'very gladly and to accept it very joyfully and thankfully', Parry was emboldened to ask whether, if the Council approved, she would marry the Admiral? He got small satisfaction. 'When that comes to pass,' said Elizabeth, 'I will do as God shall put into my mind.' Then she wanted to know what Parry meant by asking her such a question, 'or who bade him say so'. Nobody, the steward assured her hastily, nobody bade him say so – it was just that from the tone of the Admiral's conversation it had seemed 'he was given that way rather than otherwise'. As for his advice that she should go cap in hand to the Duchess of Somerset, Elizabeth would not believe it at first and, considering Tom's freely expressed dislike of his sister-in-law, it does seem odd to say the least. But when Parry said yes, by his faith, she was annoyed. 'Well, I will not do so,' she exclaimed crossly, 'and so tell him.' No Tudor was going to be driven to ask favours of a Seymour. 'I will not come there,' said the Tudor princess, 'nor begin to flatter now.' She asked if Mrs Ashley knew of the Admiral's talk with Parry and ordered him to be sure to tell her. 'For I will know nothing but she shall know of it. In faith, I cannot be quiet until ye have told her of it.' The fifteen-year-old Elizabeth fully realised, even if nobody else did, the danger of becoming involved in anything that looked like secret negotiations.

Mrs Ashley had also been on a trip to London. She saw John Cheke's wife and Lady Tyrwhit, who told her it was being said that the Admiral was keeping the Queen's maidens together to wait on the Lady Elizabeth after they were married. Mrs Ashley then had to endure a highly unpleasant interview with the Protector's wife, during which the Duchess of Somerset 'found great faults' with her for having allowed Elizabeth to go with the Admiral in a barge on the Thames one night (this excursion must presumably have taken place the previous Christmas), and 'for other light parts'. 'She was not worthy to have the governance of a King's daughter,' said the Duchess, and threatened that 'another should have her place'.[15]

Mrs Ashley came back to Hatfield considerably subdued and began to tell Elizabeth that she might have to wait 'till the King's majesty came to his own rule', for it looked as if 'my Lord Protector's grace nor the Council would not suffer a subject to have her'; and not to set her mind on the marriage 'seeing the unlikelihood of it'.[16] Mrs Ashley, in fact, was becoming a little frightened. She had not altogether liked the sound of the Admiral's behaviour recently; if he was planning to do anything without the Council's consent, it would be disastrous for all concerned, and especially for herself.

But in spite of her newly acquired circumspection, Mrs Ashley presently enjoyed a cosy gossip with Thomas Parry on the subject uppermost in both their minds. This conversation took place on the day before Twelfth Night 1549 and, judging by its general tone, was accompanied by something guaranteed to keep out the cold and loosen the tongue.

Parry remarked on the goodwill which he had noticed 'between the Lord Admiral and her Grace'. Oh, said Mrs Ashley, it was true. 'I would wish her his wife of all men living,' sighed the governess. 'Yes, he might bring it to pass at the Council's hands well enough.' But, she told Parry, she had had such a 'charge' from the Duchess of Somerset that she dared not speak of it; 'and so fell again in praising the Admiral'.

Parry observed that for all that he had heard much evil report of the Admiral, 'that he was not only a very covetous man and an oppressor, but also an evil jealous man; and how cruelly, how dishonourably and how jealously he had used the Queen'. Nonsense, said Mrs Ashley, 'I know him better than ye do, or those that so report him.' No, he would make but too much of Elizabeth, and she knew it. As for the stories about the Admiral's jealousy, 'I will tell you,' went on Mrs Ashley with one of those rare flashes which illuminate a landscape: 'As he came upon a time up a stairs to see the Queen, he met with a groom of the chamber upon the stairs with a coal basket coming out of the chamber; and because the door was shut, and my lord without, he was angry and pretended that he was jealous.'

The Admiral loved Elizabeth 'but too well, and had so done a good while' confided Mrs Ashley, and forgetting all discretion she proceeded to tell Parry about the Queen's jealousy, how Elizabeth had been discovered in the Admiral's arms and had had to be sent away to Cheshunt.

Something in the steward's reaction, perhaps the eagerness of his 'Why, hath there been such familiarity indeed between them?' brought Mrs Ashley up short, for she 'seemed to repent that she had gone so far' and begged him several times never to repeat what she had said, 'for her Grace should be dishonoured for ever and she likewise undone'. Of course not, said Parry, of course not, he would 'rather be pulled with horses'.[17]

A couple of days later Parry was in London again and saw the Admiral briefly in his room at the court. It was an unsatisfactory interview, for it seemed to the cofferer that his lordship was either 'in some heat, or very busy, or had some mistrust of me'.[18] Tom Seymour had, in fact, come very nearly to the end of the road. The Protector had heard about his proposed visit to Elizabeth, and said with unwonted sternness that he would clap his brother in the Tower if he went anywhere near the princess. More serious was the fact that William Sharington's malpractices were at last coming to light. Sharington's house had been searched on 6 January and evidence discovered of his dealings with the Admiral. Tom was summoned to give an account of himself to the Protector in private, but with astonishing pigheadedness he refused to go until it should be more convenient for him.[19]

After this there was nothing for it but to lay the whole matter before the Council. The Council had put up with a good deal from the Admiral, but reports of his 'disloyal practices' were growing too numerous and too circumstantial to be ignored any longer. Finally, after 'divers conferences had at sundry times' it was unanimously decided at a meeting held on 17 January 1549 'to commit the said Admiral to prison in the Tower of

London, there to remain till such further order be taken with him as the case . . . shall require'.[20]

At the last moment Tom seems to have come to some realisation of his danger. He told the Marquess of Northampton on the day before his arrest that the Council had been having great secret conferences, and, although he knew the matter touched him, he could learn nothing of it.[21] Walking in the gallery of his house with Lord Dorset after dinner on 17 January, he said that the Earl of Rutland had accused him, and he showed himself 'to be much afraid to go to the Council'. He would not go, he declared, without some pledge that he might return home again. Dorset's brother, Thomas, who was also present, observed with irritating good sense: 'Knowing yourself a true man, why should you doubt to go to your brother, knowing him to be a man of much mercy? Wherefore, if you will follow my advice, you shall go to him; and if he list to have you, it is not this house that can keep you, though you have ten times so many men as you have.'[22]

In spite of having boasted that, by God's precious soul, he would thrust his dagger into whosoever laid hands on him, when the Council's agents came for him that night the Admiral went quietly, protesting his innocence and swearing that no poor knave was ever truer to his prince.

Within the next couple of days John Harington, the Admiral's confidential servant, William Sharington and the serviceable John Fowler of the Privy Chamber had followed him to the Tower, and a party headed by Lord St John, Great Master of the Household, Anthony Denny and Sir Robert Tyrwhit was despatched to Hatfield. Mrs Ashley and Thomas Parry were taken away for questioning, and Robert Tyrwhit was left behind to obtain a statement from the Princess Elizabeth concerning her own guilty knowledge of the Admiral's subversive activities.

When Elizabeth was told that her governess and her steward had been arrested, 'she was marvellous abashed and did weep very tenderly a long time' demanding to know whether they had confessed anything or not. This sounded promising, and Robert Tyrwhit was not anticipating any great difficulty in his assignment. But when the princess summoned him, saying she had forgotten to tell Lord St John and Denny of certain matters which she would now open to him, it turned out to be no more than a letter she had written to the Admiral requesting some favour for her chaplain and asking him to credit her trusty servant, Parry, her cofferer, in all other things. This, said Elizabeth, had only meant that she wanted the Admiral's help in getting Durham House back. Oh, and there was one other thing. Mrs Ashley had written to the Admiral telling him he had better not visit the princess 'for fear of suspicion', and when Elizabeth heard about this she had been much offended and advised Mrs Ashley not to write so, 'because she would not have her to take upon her the knowledge of any such thing'.

Tyrwhit was disappointed. Elizabeth must clearly be made to realise that she was in no position to play games. 'After all this,' he wrote to the Protector, 'I did require her to consider her honour and the peril that might ensue, for she was but a subject.' Having allowed Anne Boleyn's daughter to digest this ominous piece of advice, he continued,

> I further declared what a woman Mistress Ashley was . . . saying that if she would open all things herself, all the evil and shame should be ascribed to them and her youth considered both with the King's Majesty, your Grace and the whole Council. But in no way she will not confess any practice by Mistress Ashley or the cofferer concerning my Lord Admiral; and yet I do see it in her face that she is guilty, and do perceive as yet she will abide more storms ere she accuse Mistress Ashley.

Tyrwhit felt he had every reason to believe that Elizabeth was being deliberately obstructive, for when Thomas Parry had heard the 'sudden news that my Lord Great Master and Master Denny was arrived at the gate' he had rushed to his chamber and said to his wife: '"I would I had never been born, for I am undone", and wrung his hands and cast away his chain from his neck and his rings from his fingers'.[23] If that did not sound like guilt, reasoned Robert Tyrwhit, what did?

On the following day, 23 January, he wrote again to the Protector. He had had another interview with Elizabeth, but was obliged to admit: 'All I have gotten yet is by gentle persuasion, whereby I do begin to grow with her in credit.' The princess had told him how the Admiral had kindly offered to lend her his house in London 'for her time being there to see the King's Majesty', and had repeated most of the conversation she had subsequently had with Parry. It was not much, but, wrote Tyrwhit hopefully, 'this is a good beginning, I trust more will follow.' All the same, he ended, 'I do assure your Grace, she hath a very good wit, and nothing is gotten of her but by great policy'.[24]

Elizabeth needed all the wit and self-control she could muster. She was in a tight corner and knew it. She was now not merely alone, she was surrounded by enemies and spies. She was being called upon to answer the kind of charge, based chiefly on backstairs gossip, which is always most difficult to refute. She faced continual interrogation, designed to trap her into admissions which would have ruined her good name for ever and probably cost her any chance of succeeding to the throne. Her liberty might well be at stake, and, for all she knew of the political situation in London, perhaps even her life. And she was still only fifteen years old

Robert Tyrwhit now resorted to that time-honoured device of showing Elizabeth a letter from the Protector, pretending 'with a great protestation' that he would not for a thousand pounds have it known that he had done so. Elizabeth thanked him for his kindness, but was not deceived. A false friend, Lady Browne, was introduced into the household in the hopes that the princess might be persuaded to confide in her sympathetic ear. But on 28 January, after more than a week of concentrated effort, Tyrwhit had nothing further to report. 'I do verily believe', he wrote to Somerset, 'that there hath been some secret promise between my Lady, Mistress Ashley and the cofferer, never to confess till death; and if it be so, it will never be gotten of her, but either by the King's Majesty, or else by your Grace.'[25]

The Protector had now taken a hand in the game and written to Elizabeth himself. Tyrwhit was slightly cheered to note that she 'hath been more pleasant since the receipt thereof than she hath been at any time since my being here'. Not surprisingly, for Elizabeth had seen her chance, and in her reply to Somerset she took it with both hands. His lordship had counselled her 'as an earnest friend' to declare all she knew of the matter and Elizabeth was perfectly willing to oblige. Out it all came again – the matter of her chaplain, the Admiral's offer of his house, Parry's report of his conversations with the Admiral, Mrs Ashley's letter to the Admiral, some (though not all) of Mrs Ashley's badinage. There had been no secret understanding of any sort. 'As concerning Mrs Ashley, she never advised me unto it, but said always (when any talked of my marriage) that she would never have me marry, neither in England nor out of England, without the consent of the King's Majesty, your Grace's, and the Council's.' Elizabeth herself, of course, would never have agreed to such a thing without the Council's consent. 'And as for Katherine Ashley or the cofferer, they never told me they would practice it. These be the things which I both declared to Master Tyrwhit', she continued, 'and also whereof my conscience beareth me witness, which I would not for all earthly things offend in any thing; for I know I have a soul to save, as well as other folks have.' But if she should remember anything else, she would either write it herself, 'or cause Master Tyrwhit to write it'. Elizabeth ended with an indication of the sort of tactics which were being employed against her.

> Master Tyrwhit and others have told me that there goeth rumours abroad which be greatly against my honour and honesty (which above all other things I esteem), which be these; that I am in the Tower; and with child by my Lord Admiral. My lord, these are shameful slanders, for the which, besides the great desire I have to see the King's Majesty, I shall most heartily desire your lordship that I may come to Court after your first determination, that I may show myself there as I am.[26]

This famous letter, polite but businesslike, written in a beautifully neat schoolgirl hand, is by any standards a masterpiece of its kind. Elizabeth had wasted no paper on protestations of innocence or outraged modesty. She had defended herself and her servants against unwarrantable accusations with courage and dignity, and more than hinted that she would expect an apology.

Unfortunately, however, not everyone possessed the qualities of

Elizabeth Tudor. Parry and Mrs Ashley both made detailed confessions with which, on 5 February, Tyrwhit was able to confront the princess. 'She was much abashed and half breathless,' he reported, 'and perused all their names and particularly', although, as Sir Robert added scornfully, she knew both Mrs Ashley's hand and the cofferer's 'with half a sight'. Parry had been the first to break, he told her. Mrs Ashley would say nothing until she and Parry were brought face to face, when the steward stood fast to all he had written and 'she seeing that, she called him false wretch and said that he had promised he would never confess it to death'. Then, commented Elizabeth simply, 'it was a great matter for him to promise such a promise, and to break it'. Tyrwhit went on, 'I will tomorrow travail all I can, to frame her for her own surety and to utter the truth.'[27]

But by the next day Elizabeth had had time to recover from her embarrassment and to think. It had been acutely humiliating to see the details of those merry romps at Chelsea and Hanworth set out in writing for all to read. They made her look more like a giggling servant girl than a princess. That was bad enough, but it was not remotely treasonable. Parry and Mrs Ashley did not show up in a particularly good light either, but that was all. There was nothing in their statements to implicate any of them in actual treason; no evidence that either they, or Elizabeth, had ever been involved in a secret matrimonial plot. When Robert Tyrwhit returned to the attack, the princess allowed him to take down her formal 'confession' but, apart from a few additional details, it contained absolutely nothing new. 'They all sing the same song,' wrote the exasperated Tyrwhit, 'and so I think they would not do, unless they had set the note before.'[28]

In spite of Elizabeth's spirited defence of Mrs Ashley, the Council had come to the conclusion that the governess had 'shown herself far unmeet' to occupy her position and appointed Elizabeth Tyrwhit, Sir Robert's wife, instead, hoping that the princess would 'accept her service willingly'. The princess did nothing of the kind. She was furious and showed it. 'Mrs Ashley was her mistress,' she said, 'and she had not so demeaned herself that the Council should now need to put any more mistresses unto her.' Lady Tyrwhit replied tartly that 'seeing she did allow Mrs Ashley to be her mistress, she need not be ashamed to have any honest woman to be in that place'. But Elizabeth 'took the matter so heavily, that she wept all that night and lowered all the next day'. Sir Robert felt sure he knew the reason for these tantrums. 'All is no more,' he wrote in yet another of his reports to the Protector, 'she fully hopes to recover her old mistress again. The love she beareth her is to be wondered at. I told her if she would consider her honour and the sequel thereof, she would, considering her years, make suit to your Grace to have one, rather than to make delay to be without one one hour.' However, the princess could not 'digest such advice in no way' and Tyrwhit, who had plainly had just about enough, added that in his opinion she needed not one governess but two.[29]

The Protector had now replied to Elizabeth's letter, and Tyrwhit had offered more advice on drafting a suitable reply which Elizabeth again 'would in no wise follow, but writ her own fantasy. She beginneth now a little to droop', he went on, 'by reason she heareth that my Lord Admiral's house be dispersed. And my wife telleth me now that she cannot bear to hear him discommended but she is ready to make answer therein; and so she hath not been accustomed to do, unless Mistress Ashley were touched, whereunto she was very ready to make answer vehemently.'[30]

On 21 February Elizabeth wrote 'her own fantasy' to the Duke of Somerset. She understood that he had taken her previous letter 'in evil part' and thought she was altogether too sure of herself. The princess was sorry, but the Protector had asked her to be plain with him and she had only told the truth. Regarding her complaint about the rumours being spread of her 'lewd demeanour', Elizabeth did not see that 'your Grace has made any direct answer at this time'. 'Howbeit,' she continued, 'you did write "that if I would bring forth any that had reported it, you and the Council would see it redressed". Which thing, though I can easily do it, I would be loath to do, because it is mine own cause.' It was not for Elizabeth herself, she indicated, to be forced to bring counter-charges to clear her name. That would only get her the evil will of the people which thing she would be loath to have. However,

> if it might seem good to your lordship and the rest of the Council to send forth a proclamation into the countries that they refrain their tongues, declaring how the tales be but lies, it should make both the people think that you and the Council have great regard that no such rumours should be spread of any of the King's Majesty sisters, (as I am, though unworthy) and also that I should think myself to receive such friendship at your hands as you have promised me. . . . Howbeit, I am ashamed to ask it any more, because I see you are not so well minded thereunto.[31]

This letter was another masterly piece of tactics, in which Elizabeth had neatly out-manoeuvred the Protector and regained the initiative by putting him subtly in the wrong. In fact, she knew by this time that, although the war was by no means over, her own immediate battle had been won. The cost had been great, how great she could not yet know, but the challenge had been met and met with fortitude. During the past month she had grown from a girl into a woman and, for better or worse, she would never be the same again.

8

SWEET SISTER TEMPERANCE

If the Government had expected that Elizabeth would prove a star witness in the case against Tom Seymour, they had certainly been disappointed; but, as it turned out, there was no shortage of other people only too eager to turn King's evidence.

William Sharington had thrown himself on the Protector's mercy and made a full and abject confession. John Fowler, too, sought safety in offering a circumstantial account of the part he had played in assisting Tom's efforts to win his nephew's affection. Those surreptitious gifts of pocket money, so gratefully accepted at the time, were now produced as evidence of treasonable intent. The Lords Dorset, Rutland and Northampton all came forward with statements about their dealings with the Admiral. Even the King obligingly remembered certain conversations he had had with his uncle over the past two years. The only person, in fact, who made any attempt to speak up for Tom was his friend, John Harrington.

The Council met on 22 February to consider the result of their enquiries and came to the conclusion that 'the Lord Admiral was sore charged of divers and sundry Articles of High Treason, great falsehoods and marvellous heinous misdemeanours against the King's Majesty's person and his Royal Crown'.[1] It looked an open and shut case, but Tom himself had so far made no confession. It was therefore decided that the Lord Chancellor and the rest of the Council should 'repair unto the Tower, and there propound and declare unto the said Lord Admiral the said heinous Articles which were objected unto him . . . to the intent that he should, if he could, clear himself of them, or show some excuse or pretence, if he had any, whereby he could think to purge himself of them'.[2]

Thirty-three Articles, or charges, had been drawn up in a form of indictment and, on the following day, this was solemnly read aloud to the Admiral in the Tower. Tom remained uncooperative, refusing to make any answer 'except he had his accusers brought before him, and except he were brought in upon trial of arraignment, where he might say before all the world what he could say for his declaration'.[3] He would not budge from this position, and the Council were finally obliged to depart empty-handed, leaving him 'in his old custody'.

On 24 February the lords reported their failure to the Protector and it was agreed that the law should now be allowed to take its course, and 'specially for so much as these things have chanced to be revealed in the time of His Majesty's High Court of Parliament, and the Parliament should have the determination and order thereof'.[4] In other words, that the proceedings should take the form of an Act of Attainder. First, however, the matter must be laid before the King and his consent obtained. Later that same day, 'after the King's Majesty had dined', the Council assembled in his presence, the Lord Chancellor declared 'the heinous facts and treasons of the Admiral', and made a formal request for permission to proceed against him 'according to the order of justice and the custom of the realm in like cases'. One by one the members of the Council cast their votes in favour. Last of all came the Lord Protector who, 'declaring how sorrowful a case this was unto him, said that he did yet rather regard his bounden duty to the King's Majesty and the Crown of England than his own son or brother, and did weigh more his allegiance than his blood, and therefore he could not resist nor would not be against the Lords' request, but as his Majesty would, he would most obediently be content'.[5] Now it was the King's turn. 'We do perceive', announced the eleven-year-old Edward, 'that there is great things which be objected and laid to my Lord Admiral, mine uncle, and they tend to treason, and we perceive that you require but justice to be done. We think it reasonable, and we will well that you proceed according to your request.'[6] At these words, 'coming so suddenly from his Grace's mouth of his own motion', the Council, much relieved by the King's commendably unsentimental attitude, 'were marvellously rejoiced, and gave his Highness most hearty praise and thanks'.[7]

The gravamen of the long and repetitive list of charges against the Admiral was that he had intended to overthrow the legally constituted government of the country, and had taken deliberate steps to put his plans into action. There can be little doubt on the evidence that, technically, he was guilty of treason, but whether such a recklessly inefficient conspirator had ever represented any serious danger to the state is at least questionable.

When he realised that he was not going to have an open trial and that he could expect no rescue operation from his brother or his nephew, Tom Seymour finally agreed to make some sort of answer. He had already vehemently denied meaning any hurt to the Protector, or planning to take the King from him by force. Now he admitted that he had given Fowler and others secret presents of money for the King, and that he had 'sought out certain precedents' for dividing the office of Protector and Governor of the King's person but, he said, he had become 'ashamed of his doings and left off that suit and labour'. He also admitted that he had tried to persuade Edward to sign a memorandum to be presented to Parliament, favouring a change in his guardianship. Having gone thus far, Tom suddenly bade his interrogators to be content, saying plainly that 'he would answer no more before them'.[8] He could not be prevailed upon to break his silence again. The whole of that ebullient, energetically self-confident façade seems to have collapsed into apathy and introspection.

The Bill declaring the Admiral to be 'adjudged and attainted of high treason' had passed both Houses of Parliament by 5 March. It now lay with the Protector to take the final decision on his brother's fate. There was silence for nearly a week while, presumably, the unfortunate Somerset wrestled with his conscience. Then the Earl of Warwick, who was quietly waiting for the Seymour brothers to destroy each other, applied some discreet pressure on his colleagues, and on 10 March the Council waited on the King and asked permission to proceed 'without further troubling or molesting in this heavy case either his Highness or the Lord Protector'. Edward, with Somerset at his side, thanked the lords for the great care they had taken for his surety, and gave the necessary permission. On 15 March the Admiral was warned to prepare for his execution. On the twentieth he was led out on to Tower Hill, there to suffer the same fate which had befallen another Queen Dowager's widower, in the market square at Hereford eighty-eight years previously. Unlike Owen Tudor, though, Tom Seymour left no legacy for posterity. His infant daughter, stripped of her inheritance and abandoned to the reluctant care of the dowager Duchess of Suffolk, disappeared into obscurity and is generally believed to have died in childhood.

It is said that Tom spent his last night on earth writing to the princesses, urging them to beware of the Protector's influence with the King, and 'enforcing many matters against him to make these royal ladies jealous of him'. The Admiral entrusted these missives, laboriously inscribed with a pen improvised from 'the aglet of a point that he plucked from his hose', to a servant who had sewn them into the sole of a velvet shoe; but as he mounted the scaffold his muttered reminder to the man to 'speed the thing that he wot of' was overheard, and the letters were discovered and destroyed.[9]

Tom met his end calmly, but not, it seems, in the articulately repentant frame of mind considered proper on such occasions. This led Bishop Latimer to remark, in a sermon not noticeably pervaded with the spirit of Christian charity, that 'he died very dangerously, irksomely, horribly' and to conclude that God had clean forsaken him. 'Whether he be saved or no,' continued the Bishop, 'I leave it to God, but surely he was a wicked man, and the realm is well rid of him.'[10]

When Elizabeth was told the news down at Hatfield, she is reputed to have said: 'This day died a man with much wit, and very little judgement.' The authority is Leti who could never leave an occasion unimproved, but it cannot have come as any surprise to Elizabeth by this time to hear that Tom was dead and she may well have prepared some suitably dispassionate public reaction. What had she really felt about him? The detailed testimony of eye-witnesses makes it plain that she had never been indifferent. He had undoubtedly roused and stimulated her nascent sexual awareness, and she had some affection for him as a friend; although, had she seen more of him, she must soon have become bored by his essential shallowness and irritated by his stupidity. The reality of Tom's attentions seems to have half-excited, half-repelled her. In the abstract, of course, they acquired the glamour of forbidden fruit, inspiring private fantasies and public blushes and sidelong looks. However, from the evidence available, it seems perfectly safe to say that Elizabeth had never for a moment entertained the idea of a runaway marriage. She may sometimes have yearned for the Admiral's embraces, but if anything had been needed to drive home the lesson that physical love brought danger, terror and violent death the consequences of her first tentative experiment in this field, coming just at the age of puberty, had certainly provided it. Elizabeth knew now, at the deepest level of consciousness, that sexual fulfilment was forbidden to her. She could play with physical desire, circle round it, approach it as close as she dared with a sort of delicious defiance but there was a point beyond which she might never, could never go. It was always to be the same type of man who roused this desire – handsome, showy, athletic. She once remarked brutally of a would-be suitor that, like her father, she loved a man who was a man and not one who would sit at home all day among the cinders. She loved, in fact, the kind of man who reminded her of Tom Seymour – the kind of man who reminded her of her father.

Elizabeth had learnt a more immediately useful lesson during the month of February 1549. Her own innate intelligence and political sense had kept her out of really serious trouble, but now the necessity of cultivating habits of caution and dissimulation, of concealing her true feelings at all costs, had been forcibly instilled. It became part of her nature to face the world from behind a mask, by no means always the same mask, but always one which exactly suited the purpose of the moment. At this particular moment, in the spring of her sixteenth year, Elizabeth's purpose was to repair her damaged reputation. She had got the promise of a proclamation from the Protector, but she knew the smear left by her connexion with the Admiral would not easily be removed. There were plenty of people who still vividly remembered the fall of Anne Boleyn and who would be only too glad of an opportunity to rake up old scandals. There were plenty of people to say that of course blood will out, like mother like daughter, and no smoke without a fire. Gossip sizzled pleasurably. One specially hoary chestnut going the rounds concerned the midwife summoned mysteriously at dead of night and taken blindfold to a strange house, where she delivered a child which was then 'miserably destroyed'. The approved conduct for midwives who found themselves in such a situation was to snip a piece from the bed-curtains when no one was looking. In the current version of the legend, however, the midwife seems to have omitted to take this sensible precaution and could only swear afterwards that her patient had been 'a very fair young lady'.[11] But everybody who had a friend who knew someone whose aunt or cousin had heard the midwife's tale from her own lips could make an informed guess as to the fair young lady's identity.

Elizabeth was well aware that she had a long campaign ahead of her, and her first step was to get Katherine Ashley out of prison. She had three reasons for requesting her governess's release she told the Protector in a letter dated 7 March

> First, because that she hath been with me a long time, and many years, and hath taken great labour and pain in bringing me up in learning and honesty; and, therefore, I ought of very duty to speak for her. . . . The second is, because I think that whatsoever she hath done in my Lord Admiral's matter, as concerning the marrying of me, she did it because knowing him to be one of the Council, she thought he would not go about any such thing without he had the Council's consent thereunto; for I have heard her many times say 'that she would never have me marry in any place without your Grace's and the Council's consent'. The third cause is, because that it shall, and doth make men think, that I am not clear of the deed myself; but that it is pardoned to me because of my youth, because she that I loved so well is in such a place.[12]

Elizabeth ended with a plea for Mr Ashley, 'which, because he is my kinsman, I would be glad he should do well'.

Elizabeth seems to have become more or less reconciled to Lady Tyrwhit, who remained in the household for a while, but Mrs Ashley was released, and was back with her princess probably by the autumn. So, too, was Thomas Parry and this despite the fact that Sir Robert Tyrwhit, who had been going through the cofferer's accounts, had discovered that Parry's sins were not confined to meddling in affairs of state, but his books were 'so undiscreetly made that it doth well appear he had little understanding to execute his office'. Elizabeth, it seemed, had been overspending and would have 'to abate her charges'. She had immediately requested that Parry's place should not be filled. One of his clerks could easily take over, she said, and that would save her £100 a year.[13] Clearly, though, her motive was not economy but a determination to keep the post vacant. It is also clear that Elizabeth harboured no resentment against Mrs Ashley or Parry for their betrayal of her. She knew something of the pressures they had been subjected to and did not blame them for succumbing. Once Elizabeth gave her love or trust it was not lightly withdrawn, but above all she was a realist. Katherine Ashley and Parry were her friends and whatever their imperfections she needed them and wanted them with her, and would protect them so far as she was able.

After his return Parry sometimes served the princess in the capacity of secretary. In September she received a courtesy visit from the Venetian ambassador, who spent a day at Hatfield, hunting and talking with her Grace, 'at sundry times'. Parry, at Elizabeth's request, at once wrote to inform the Protector; 'not for that the talk did import weight, but that her Grace will neither know nor do in matters that either may sound or seem to be of importance without doing of my Lord's Grace to understand thereof'.[14] Parry's letter was addressed to his distant kinsman, the Protector's secretary, young Mr William Cecil. This is not the first recorded instance of Elizabeth's connexion with the man who was to be so closely associated with her that it is virtually impossible to think of them separately. A letter written by Mrs Ashley, dated August 1548 and with a postscript in Elizabeth's own hand, shows that friendly relations existed between them even then.

About a fortnight after the Venetian ambassador's visit to Hatfield, Cecil's master suffered political eclipse. The year 1549 had been marked by a general and increasing popular discontent. This was partly economic in origin, caused by rising prices and widespread unemployment; and partly due to the reaction of a largely conservative population against sweeping religious innovations now being introduced by the government. The discontent erupted into two quite serious revolts, one in the West Country and one in Norfolk. The ruling classes were alarmed by the Protector's mild attitude to these demonstrations which, although it earned him the title of the Good Duke among the common people, did not endear him to the nobility and gentry. His increasing arrogance and refusal to take advice was also alienating many of his colleagues on the Council. His friend, William Paget, who had played such a large part in engineering his elevation, warned him bluntly 'that unless your Grace do more quietly show your pleasure in things wherein you will debate with other men, and hear them again graciously say their opinions, when you do require it, that will ensue whereof I would be right sorry, and your Grace shall have first cause to repent. . . . Howsoever it cometh to pass I cannot tell', Paget went on,

> but of late your Grace is grown in great choleric fashions whensoever you are contraried in that which you have conceived in your head. A king which shall give men occasion of discourage to say their opinions frankly, receiveth thereby great hurt and peril to his realm. But a subject in great authority, as your Grace is, using such fashion is like to fall into great danger and peril of his own person.[15]

But the Protector, it seems, was no longer willing to face the realities of the political sense, or to accept the position of *primus inter pares* which had originally been envisaged for him. His image, too, had been fatally damaged by the Admiral's death – just as the Earl of Warwick had known it would be. Somerset's coldly correct attitude towards his brother's attainder and execution had disgusted many people, who now stigmatised him as 'a bloodsucker and a ravenous wolf'.

In mid-September Warwick returned to London, after successfully and ferociously suppressing the rebellion in Norfolk, and judged the time was now ripe for a move to dislodge the Protector.

> Suddenly, upon what occasion many marvelled, but few knew, every Lord and Councillor went through the City weaponed, and had their servants likewise weaponed, attending upon them in new liveries, to the great wondering of many; and, at the last, a great assembly of the said Councillors was made at the Earl of Warwick's lodging, which was then at Ely Place in Holborn, whither all the confederates in this matter came privily armed, and finally concluded to possess the Tower of London.[16]

Somerset was at Hampton Court with the King, attempting ineffectually to raise support, when he learnt that the 'London Lords', as the opposition had become known, intended to pay him an unfriendly visit. On 6 October, between nine and ten in the evening, he routed Edward out of bed and bundled him off to seek sanctuary at Windsor Castle – an unnerving experience for which the King never really forgave his uncle. But the London Lords, under the skilful and determined leadership of the Earl of Warwick, were too strong for him. A few days later the Protector had surrendered and been conveyed under arrest to the Tower. It was not, as might have been expected, the final disaster. The Duke still had a considerable popular following, both in London and the country at large, and Warwick was far too astute to risk overreaching himself at this stage. Somerset was presently released, even temporarily regaining a seat on the Council, but his reign was over and his end merely postponed.

The Lords had addressed a somewhat specious letter of explanation and justification of their proceedings to the heiress-presumptive, Princess Mary, and thought it worth while to send a duplicate to her younger sister. Elizabeth probably welcomed the news, guessing that this shift at the seat of power was likely to be to her advantage. She needed something to distract her thoughts for, although her emotional involvement with Tom Seymour may not have gone very deep, reaction after the strain she had undergone was inevitable. She was not at all well, suffering from catarrh and what sounds like severe attacks of migraine. References to 'my evil head', 'the pain in my head' and even to 'a disease of the head and eyes' recur in her letters over the next few years.

In spite of her headaches and other troubles, Elizabeth did not abandon her studies. After the parting from Katherine Parr she had, in fact, clung to Roger Ascham with something like desperation. So much so that Ascham began to find her demands on his time a trifle irksome. He wrote to a former pupil at St John's in July 1548 that he would willingly have paid a visit to his friends at Cambridge on the occasion of the last meeting of the Senate, had not his illustrious mistress prevented him. This may have been due to the fact that there had recently been a sense of plague at his old college and Elizabeth was not risking the loss of another tutor or simply, as Ascham rather plaintively put it, 'because she never lets me go away anywhere'. He was hoping, he said, to return to the University for good at Michaelmas, 'if I can get my lady's permission which I can hardly hope, for she favours me wonderfully'. This plan came to nothing – either permission was not forthcoming, or Ascham had had second thoughts. 'Many men', he observed, 'who have become courtiers, praise their former life of retirement, but have not courage to leave the splendour of a court: I cannot promise anything about myself, but I think somewhat about it.'[17] He did, however, spend Christmas at Cambridge, returning to Hatfield just as the storm over the Admiral was about to break. He was not personally involved and remained with Elizabeth throughout the crisis, but in the misfortunes of his friends the Ashleys, he had plenty of opportunity to observe at first hand the sort of pitfalls which lay in wait for courtiers.

In January 1550 he himself suffered 'shipwreck', as he described it, 'overcome by court violence and wrongs'. In a letter to John Cheke he complained fluently of the injuries done him, as a result of which, through no fault of his own, he had either been forced to resign or had been dismissed from the princess's service. The details of this episode remain obscure, but there had evidently been intrigue against him in the household – the chief troublemaker being Thomas Parry, who was probably jealous of Ascham. Elizabeth, too, seems to have developed a coolness towards her tutor, and in her nervy irritable state had allowed herself to be influenced by malicious tale-bearing.

Whatever the cause of the temporary rift between them, Roger Ascham did not blame his 'illustrious Lady', for the following April he addressed his famous letter in praise of the princess to Johann Sturm, Rector of the Protestant University of Strasbourg. 'She has just passed her sixteenth birthday', he wrote,

> and shows such dignity and gentleness as are wonderful at her age and in her rank. Her study of true religion and learning is most energetic. Her mind has no womanly weakness, her perseverance is equal to that of a man, and her memory long keeps what it quickly picks up. She talks French and Italian as well as English; she has often talked to me readily and well in Latin, and moderately so in Greek. When she writes Greek and Latin, nothing is more beautiful than her hand-writing. She is as much delighted with music as she is skilful in the art. In adornment she is elegant rather than showy, and by her contempt of gold and head-dresses, she reminds one of Hippolyte rather than of Phaedra. . . . Whatever she reads she at once perceives any word that has a doubtful or curious meaning. She cannot endure those foolish imitators of Erasmus, who have tied up the Latin tongue in those wretched fetters of proverbs. She likes a style that grows out of the subject; chaste because it is suitable, and beautiful because it is clear. . . .

'I am not inventing anything, my dear Sturm,' he concluded, 'it is all true: but I only seek to give you an outline of her excellence, and whilst doing so, I have been pleased to recall to my mind the dear memory of my most illustrious lady.'[18]

This is a remarkable encomium, coming from a scholar of Ascham's reputation. In writing to Sturm he had no particular reason to flatter Elizabeth, except in so far as the achievements of his former pupil must of necessity reflect some glory on himself, and his admiration seems genuine. 'I teach her words,' he had told his friend John Aylmer, 'and she me things. I teach her tongues to speak, and her modest and maidenly looks teach me works to do. For I think she is the best disposed of any in all Europe.'[19]

Elizabeth continued for the most part to live very quietly in the country, dividing her time between Hatfield and Ashridge. Her retired existence is traditionally ascribed to the fact of her still being in disgrace following the Seymour scandal. This tradition does not, however, stand up to close examination, for it was perfectly well known in government circles that no sort of case had ever been established against her. Her own indifferent health and the dangerously unsettled state of the political scene are much more likely causes for her avoidance of the limelight – not, in fact, that her rustication was as complete or as prolonged as is sometimes stated. It is true that she did not come to London again until after the Protector's fall, but it is hardly surprising that Somerset, beset on every side, should have discouraged visits from a potential powerfully young woman who had no reason to feel well disposed towards him. On 19 December 1549, however, Van der Delft, the Imperial Ambassador, informed his master that: 'The Lady Elizabeth, sister to the King, arrived at Court the other day, was received with great pomp and triumph, and is continually with the King.'[20]

After her return to Hatfield, Elizabeth maintained a dutiful correspondence with her brother. Edward asked to have a portrait of her, and complying with this request she wrote somewhat sententiously:

> For the face, I grant, I might well blush to offer; but the mind I shall never be ashamed to present. For though from the grace of the picture the colours may fade by time, may give by weather, may be spotted by chance; yet the other nor time with her swift wings shall overtake, nor the misty clouds with their lowerings may darken, nor chance with her slippery foot may overthrow. Of this, although yet the proof could not be great, because the occasions hath been but small; notwithstanding, as a dog hath a day, so may I perchance have a time to declare it in deeds, where now I do write them but in words. And further I shall most humbly beseech your Majesty, that when you shall look on my picture you will witsafe to think, that as you have but the outward show of the body afore you, so my inward mind wisheth, that the body itself were oftener in your presence.[21]

In spite of her bodily absence, Elizabeth kept a close watch on her interests. During the first half of 1550, possibly as a result of her

Christmas visit, her financial position was put on a firmer footing when the King, in fulfilment of Henry VIII's Will, formally granted his sister lands to the value of £3000 a year. But when Elizabeth discovered that Hatfield was to be given to the Earl of Warwick she protested vigorously. The old palace, once the property of the Bishops of Ely, pleasantly situated on a wooded hill with the River Lea winding through its grounds, is traditionally associated with Elizabeth's girlhood, and, although until now she does not appear to have spent more time there than at the other royal manors in the Home Counties, she seems to have had a special affection for it. At any rate, she was not prepared to give it up without a struggle. On 22 June it was recorded in the minutes of the Privy Council that: 'Where the Lady Elizabeth's Grace desired to have the house, parks and lands of Hatfield of the Earl of Warwick she to have the same in exchange for as much lands of hers in value again to the said Earl.'[22] The princess relinquished a manor in Lincolnshire and everyone, presumably, was satisfied.

Elizabeth was naturally careful to keep on friendly terms with Warwick and that autumn Jehan Scheyfve, who had now replaced Van der Delft as the Emperor's ambassador in London, picked up an odd little rumour which he thought worth passing on. 'I have heard from a safe source', he wrote, 'that my lord Warwick is about to cast off his wife and marry my Lady Elizabeth, daughter of the late King, with whom he is said to have had several secret and intimate personal communications; and by these means he will aspire to the Crown.'[23] There is no reason to suppose that there was a word of truth in this particular item of gossip, but it throws an interesting glimmer of light on the kind of thin ice Elizabeth was learning to tread. She was seventeen now, an age when it was unusual for a sixteenth-century princess to be still unmarried, or at least unbetrothed. There were, as there always had been, foreign suitors under consideration. Those whose names occur in the early fifties were a French duke and the eldest son of the King of Denmark, but nothing came, or seemed at all likely to come, of their pretensions. The future was altogether too uncertain.

Early in 1551 Elizabeth made another of her carefully spaced public appearances. On 21 January, Jehan Scheyfve reported her arrival in London a few days previously, accompanied by a great suite of gentlemen and ladies and escorted by one hundred of the King's horse. 'She was most honourably received by the Council', wrote Scheyfve, 'who acted thus in order to show the people how much glory belongs to her who has embraced the new religion and is become a very great lady.'[24]

If anyone was now officially out of favour it was the King's elder sister and the Emperor's cousin, which accounts for the acid note in Scheyfve's despatches. The religious question was again becoming acute, and the wretched Mary was once more being hounded for her beliefs – this time by her brother's ministers. Two years earlier the Act of Uniformity had established the new English Prayer Book – the result of Cranmer's programme of liturgical reform begun in the last reign – as the only service book of the Church of England. It came into official use on Whitsunday, 1549, and it meant the end of the ancient Latin Mass. When Mary saw the very foundation and cornerstone of her faith being threatened, she appealed frantically to the Emperor for help, and Charles had responded more energetically than usual. He instructed his ambassador to obtain a guarantee from the Protector that Mary should be allowed to hear Mass undisturbed in her own household for as long as she chose. After some argument, Van der Delft had extracted a verbal promise from Somerset that the princess could do as she thought best until the King came of age. There the matter might have rested. Mary was an old friend of the Somersets, the Duchess had once been one of her mother's maids and the Duke was a man of his word. Unfortunately, however, the Earl of Warwick was not a man to be bound by anyone's word. He found it convenient to form an alliance with the extreme Protestants – men far to the left of Cranmer – and by the summer of 1550 Mary's position had become so intolerable to her that, for the second time in her life, she wanted only to escape from England and seek sanctuary with the Emperor. The battle of the Princess Mary's Mass continued to rage intermittently for the rest of Edward's life, poisoning the relationship between brother and sister, and finally reducing Mary to practising her religion in fear, behind locked doors.

Elizabeth at least had no problems of this nature to contend with and her own relationship with her brother remained unclouded to the end. Indeed, it was later said that 'there was between these two princes a concurrency and sympathy in their natures and affections, together with the celestial conformity in religion which made them one, and friends; for the King ever called her his sweetest and dearest sister, and was scarce his own man, she being absent, which was not so between him and the Lady Mary'.[25] It suited Protestant hagiographers, writing in the seventeenth and eighteenth centuries, to present an idealised picture of two such notable stalwarts of the Protestant faith as Edward and Elizabeth, and in doing so they both exaggerated and oversimplified the situation. Edward was genuinely fond of his elder sister, and genuinely troubled over the difficulties caused by her religious fervour which presented a mirror image of his own; but he naturally felt more at ease with Elizabeth, so much nearer to him in age and sharing so much more of his background and upbringing.

Elizabeth had by now virtually succeeded in obliterating any unfortunate impression created by the Seymour affair – at any rate among those predisposed in her favour. She adopted a severely plain style of dressing, which no doubt suited her admirably, and John Aylmer remarked approvingly on her maidenly apparel – so dramatically contrasted to the noblemen's wives and daughters who went 'dressed and painted like peacocks'. Even after the visit to court in 1551 of Mary of Guise, Queen

Dowager and Regent of Scotland, on her way back from France, had awakened a new interest in French fashions, Elizabeth would alter nothing 'but kept her old maiden shamefacedness'.[26] She was setting the fashion herself for high-born Protestant maidens; and Jane Grey, receiving a mouth-watering present from Mary of a dress of 'tinsel cloth of gold and velvet, laid on with parchment lace of gold', is said to have complained: 'What shall I do with it?' 'Marry, wear it,' answered one of her ladies in surprise. 'Nay,' said Jane, never noted for her tact, 'that were a shame to follow my Lady Mary against God's word, and leave my Lady Elizabeth, which followeth God's word.'[27]

It was inevitable that the Protestant faction should look hopefully towards Elizabeth, although she never made a parade of her beliefs – merely conforming without unnecessary comment. She always had a strong sense of public decorum, and, as much as many Catholics, may have disliked the current excesses of the anti-ritualists, the spoliation of the parish churches and the coarse derision being hurled at the old worship; but, if so, she kept her opinions to herself. As well as her carefully unadorned appearance, her quiet, modest demeanour was winning her the reputation of having 'a marvellous meek stomach', and Edward is said to have called her 'his sweet sister Temperance'.

After her New Year visit of 1551, sweet sister Temperance left London again for Hertfordshire, resolutely avoiding any involvement in the controversy over Mary and her Mass, or indeed any involvement in anything even remotely controversial. She maintained her connexion with William Cecil, and had appointed him Surveyor of her landed property at a salary of £20 a year. Cecil, shortly to become Sir William, now held the influential post of Principal Secretary to the Earl of Warwick, and Elizabeth obviously relied on him to hold a watching brief on her interests at court. Thomas Parry, forwarding a letter from Elizabeth to Warwick, which was to be delivered by Cecil, observes in his covering note: 'Her Grace commanded me to write this: "Write my commendations in your letter to Mr Cecil, that I am well assured, though I send not daily to him, that he doth not, for all that, daily forget me; say, indeed, I assure myself thereof."' Elizabeth was still having to use Parry as a secretary, and he goes on: 'I had forgotten to say to you that her Grace commanded me to say to you, for the excuse of her hand, that it is not now as good as she trusts it shall be; her Grace's unhealth hath made it weaker, and so unsteady, and that is the cause.'[28]

Elizabeth's household books for the period October 1551 to September 1552 show how simply she was living. On 13 February 1552, she received a visit from the King's drummer and fife and John Heywood's troupe of child actors which cost her altogether £7 9*s* 0*d*. In April she paid Beaumont, the King's servant, ten shillings 'for his boys which played before her grace'. There are some other scattered entries in August:

For Farmor that played on the lute	30*s*
More the harper	30*s*
My lord Russell's minstrels	20*s*

But apart from these musical interludes the household seems to have spent nothing on entertainment. Elizabeth paid £26 0*s* 0*d* for velvet coats and £78 18*s* 0*d* for liveries for her yeomen, but her own expenditure on clothes was moderate. A pair of silk-lined upper-bodies cost her 2*s* 8*d* in October 1551. On the thirty-first of the month Anthony Brisquet's account for 'a piece of wrought velvet containing twenty yards and a half and a half quarter', and another ten yards or so of black velvet for a pair of sleeves, two French hoods and partlets came to £43 *7s 2d*. Rafe Hope was paid nine shillings and eightpence on 8 November 'for lining of her grace's kirtles'. Elizabeth Slannying received £8 15*s* 3*d* on 1 April for 'certain damask and crimson satin' and, later in the month, £79 0*s* 0*d* for velvet, silk and other necessaries to her grace's use. Cauls and linen cloth cost only 22*s* 4*d*, and Warren, the tailor, charged £21 10*s* 0*d* for 'making diverse robes for her grace'. Other miscellaneous items in the Chamber and Robe Accounts give a fascinating insight into the trivialities of daily life. Mrs Ashley spent twelve shillings on six ells of holland for towels, and one and fourpence on thread. Forty-four and ninepence was paid 'to him that made her grace a table of walnut tree', and five shillings 'to a poor woman which brought six chickens and two capons'. Brooms from the chamber cost three shillings, and Elizabeth paid seventeen shillings for lute strings. She was not particularly open-handed, for her total expenditure on alms given 'at sundry times to poor men and women' over this period amounted to no more than £7 15*s* 8*d*, and she only spent £32 3*s* 10*d* on gilt plate for New Year's gifts in 1552. Thomas Parry was getting no opportunity to feather his nest these days, for every page of his accounts was meticulously signed and countersigned by Elizabeth and her chamberlain, Walter Buckler.[29]

But, in spite of her economies at home, she knew when it paid to put on a good show. In March 1552 she came up to town for what was to prove her last state visit to Edward, having demanded and got the loan of St James's Palace for herself and her suite. Henry Machyn, the undertaker, recorded in his diary that:

> The 17th day of March rode through London unto St James in the field, the King's place, the King's sister, my Lady Elizabeth, with a great company of lords and knights and gentlemen, and after her a great number of ladies and gentlewomen to the number of two hundred on horseback, and yeomen. The 19th day of March [she] came from St James through the park to the Court, and from Park gate unto the Court was strewn with sand fine, and afore her came dukes, lords and knights, and after ladies and gentlewomen a great company, and so she was received into the Court goodly.[30]

There had been some significant political developments since Elizabeth's last appearance at court. John Dudley, Earl of Warwick, was now Duke of Northumberland, and the last act of the Seymour tragedy had been played out. Dudley had found it impracticable to spare his defeated rival indefinitely, and on 22 January, three years almost to the day after Tom's execution, Somerset had suffered a similar fate on Tower Hill. In January 1551 Jehan Scheyfve had told the Emperor that Warwick was 'the man who governs absolutely' and now the new Duke, although he never officially adopted the title of Protector, wielded as much, if not more, influence over the King as ever Somerset had done. Northumberland favoured a more athletic and open-air regime for his charge, and Edward had grasped the opportunity to prove his manhood with pathetic eagerness. Elizabeth may not have liked or trusted John Dudley – few people did – but the King seemed well and happy in his care. When she said good-bye to Edward, after what appears to have been quite a short visit, Elizabeth, percipient as she was, can hardly have guessed that she would never see her brother again.

9

The Queen's Sister

At the beginning of April 1552, Edward developed a rash and a high temperature. He himself recorded in his Chronicle 'I fell sike of the mesels and the smallpokkes.' This would surely have been a lethal combination and the trouble was probably a sharp attack of measles. He recovered quickly and was able to reassure Elizabeth, for she wrote on the twenty-first to congratulate him on his 'good escape out of the perilous diseases'. 'And that I am fully satisfied and well assured of the same by your Grace's own hand,' she went on, 'I must needs give you my most humble thanks, assuring your Majesty, that a precious jewel at another time could not so well have contented, as your letter in this case hath comforted me.'[1]

The King was able to take part in the St George's Day celebrations at Westminster Abbey on 23 April, wearing his Garter robes. On the thirtieth the court moved to Greenwich, where Edward ran at the ring and attended a 'goodly muster of his men at arms' on Blackheath. On 27 June, still in good spirits, he left London to make a progress through the south and west, but people noticed that he was looking pale and thin. That unlucky bout of measles, coming just at the most dangerous age for Tudor boys, followed by a strenuous summer had fatally weakened him. When he returned to Hampton Court, a few days before his fifteenth birthday, tuberculosis was already established. By Christmas it had become obvious that the King was far from well, and a more than usually elaborate programme of festivities was arranged to distract attention from this uncomfortable fact. Mary came to court at the end of January, but found Edward in bed with a fever and unable to see her for three days.

Elizabeth had sent word that she, too, was 'determined about Candlemas to come to see the King's Majesty'. She was still trying to get Durham House back, although she had apparently been offered the great mansion which the Duke of Somerset had built for himself in the Strand as a town residence. She could not have her things ready there in time, she declared, and again applied for the loan of St James's Palace. Northumberland, remarking appreciatively that he was sure her Grace would have done no less though she had kept Durham House still, stalled her. He did not want Elizabeth at court just then and her visit was postponed. John Dudley was worried about the future. If the King were to die, the edifice of his own power, so carefully built up over the past four years, would collapse overnight, for at best he could expect total political extinction from Mary and her friends. He was doing all he could to conceal the gravity of Edward's illness but, despite reassuring bulletins issued from the court, it was impossible to stop the rumours spreading. Jehan Scheyfve reported at the end of April: 'I hear from a trustworthy source that the King is undoubtedly becoming weaker as time passes, and wasting away. The matter he ejects from his mouth is sometimes coloured a greenish yellow and black, sometimes pink like the colour of blood.'[2]

Elizabeth must have heard some of these disquieting stories and was far too intelligent not to realise that she was being deliberately prevented from seeing her brother. Some time in the spring of 1553 she made a determined effort to reach him and actually set out on the journey to London. Half-way there she was intercepted by a messenger, supposedly from the King, who 'advised' her to turn back. After that there was nothing she could do but return to Hatfield and wait upon events. She continued to write to Edward, but it was unlikely that any of her letters reached him. Once he knew the King was dying, Northumberland had gone to considerable pains to separate him from his sisters. It was essential that no external influences should be brought to bear on the boy, and also that neither of the princesses should learn of certain interesting plans being made for their future.

The secret seems to have been well kept, although, as time passed, and Edward grew steadily worse, the court and City seethed with speculation, for no one expected the Duke would give up his dictatorship without a fight. Scheyfve at first believed that he meant to use Elizabeth as his instrument; either by marrying her to his eldest son, after first causing him to divorce his wife, or else – again – 'that he might find it expedient to get rid of his own wife and marry Elizabeth himself'. In fact, Northumberland had devised a simpler and more radical scheme. Edward, like his father, would dispose of the Crown by Will, disinheriting both his sisters in favour of his cousin Jane Grey. Mary and Elizabeth were to be declared unfit to succeed because both were (a) illegitimate, (b) related to the King by half-blood only, and (c) liable to marry foreign princes who would gain control of the government and thus 'tend to the utter subversion of the commonwealth'.

The question of whether or not or both Henry VIII's daughters could properly be regarded as having been born in wedlock was just the kind of nice point guaranteed to keep lawyers and theologians happily occupied for a lifetime. The other two grounds cited for their exclusion were constitutionally merely frivolous. As for Jane Grey's claim, it was true that Henry had settled the Crown, in default of heirs from his own children, on the descendants of his youngest sister; but, if Mary and Elizabeth were to be disabled, the next heir was Jane's mother Frances. Apart from all this, no Will made by Edward could have any validity while the 1544 Act of Succession, 35 Henry VIII, remained on the Statute Book. But, from Northumberland's point of view, the legality of the plan mattered less than the speed and efficient with which it was carried out. Once the princesses were safely in his hands and Jane established on the throne, he had little doubt of being able to persuade Parliament to repair any constitutional deficiencies. So, on Whitsunday, 21 May 1553, fifteen-year-old Jane Grey was married, much against her own will but with the eager connivance of her deplorable parents, now Duke and Duchess of Suffolk, to Northumberland's son, Guildford Dudley. It only remained to draft the necessary document and bully or cajole the rest of the Council into acquiescence.

Although Northumberland must bear a considerable share of the blame, the prime mover in this ingenious attempt to set aside the provisions of the 1544 Act was undoubtedly Edward himself. He believed just as rigidly as Mary did that his was the only way of salvation for himself and for his people, for whose salvation, he had always been taught, he was personally responsible under God. Conviction of this kind overrode all other considerations, and as soon as he began to realise that he might not live to provide heirs of his own body, Edward knew that if he valued his immortal soul, he must take every precaution to safeguard the work of godly reform. Why he was so determined to rule out the Protestant Elizabeth as well as the Catholic Mary has never been fully explained, but it would obviously be difficult to justify the exclusion of one princess and not the other, and Elizabeth might easily be forced by circumstances into marrying a Catholic. The 'Device for the Succession' went through several drafts, but by the middle of June it was ready in its final form and the Privy Councillors had, more or less reluctantly, appended their signatures before the end of the month.

Northumberland had worked fast but he was only just in time. The last of the Tudor kings died on 6 July 1553, and that night a fearsome thunderstorm broke over London, as if presaging other storms to come. For the first time in nearly three-quarters of a century England was faced with a disputed succession and all the unpleasant consequences which that inevitably entailed. Also, the very contingency which Henry VIII had laboured so murderously to avoid was now at hand; for the first time since the days of Matilda of unhappy memory, England was to be ruled by a woman.

Northumberland, choosing his moment carefully, had already despatched letters to Mary and Elizabeth summoning them to Edward's deathbed. These letters must have reached their destinations about the fourth or fifth of July; and Mary, then at Hunsdon, obediently set out on the journey. She had got as far as Hoddesdon on the London road when, on the evening of 6 July, she received an anonymous warning that the summons was a trap. This warning may have come, as he later claimed, from Nicholas Throckmorton. It is just as likely that its author was William Cecil. Elizabeth, warier or better informed than her sister, never set out at all. There is no record that she, too, received a specific warning, but it would surely be odd if certain unobtrusive travellers had not been riding the road to Hatfield during the past few weeks carrying letters or, more probably, verbal messages from Master Secretary Cecil to the Lady Elizabeth. William Cecil had already been fortunate enough to survive one change of regime, but he was a careful man, and no doubt took steps to provide himself with as much insurance as possible.

As soon as she realised that the *coup d'état* was under way, Elizabeth, according to most accounts, gave out that she was too ill to go to London and prudently retired to bed. All the same, the next fortnight must have been an extremely anxious time for her. If Northumberland won, and on the face of it the odds seemed heavily in his favour, she knew that the most she could expect at his hands would be marriage to some obscure Protestant princeling – a marriage which would take her out of England and give her a husband with no power to insist on her rights. According to Camden, the Duke sent emissaries to the princess offering large financial rewards if she would surrender her claim to the throne. It seems unlikely that Northumberland would have wasted time on such an obviously pointless errand, but, if the story is true, Elizabeth made the only answer possible – 'that they must first make their agreement with her elder sister, during whose lifetime she had no claim or title to resign'.

Mary, meanwhile, had fled, first to Kenninghall in Norfolk, and subsequently to Framlingham Castle, accompanied only by six loyal members of her household, and narrowly evading capture by a party of horse under the command of Robert Dudley, sent out in pursuit of her. The King's death was kept secret for three days, but when it became apparent that Mary had, temporarily at least, slipped through his fingers Northumberland was obliged to proceed without her. On 9 July Nicholas Ridley, Bishop of London, in a sermon at Paul's Cross, referred to both princesses as bastards, and Bishop Latimer, never one to mince words, declared it would be better that God should take away the ladies Mary and Elizabeth, rather than by marrying foreign princes they should endanger the existence of the Reformed Church. On 10 July Jane Grey was summoned to Syon House and officially informed of the contents of Edward's Will. Her protests were ignored, and later that day she was brought in state to the Tower, her formidable mother bearing her train and Guildford Dudley, resplendent in white and silver, preening himself at her side. At seven o'clock in the evening 'was made a proclamation at the Cross in Chepe by three heralds and one trumpet with the King's sheriff of London, Master Garrard, with divers of the guard for Jane the Duke of Suffolk's daughter to be Queen of England, but', added the chronicler ominously, 'few or none said God save her'.[3]

The Duke of Northumberland was not a man to take public opinion into account, but this was to prove a fatal omission. The English people had always had a soft spot for Mary and, even more to the point, they loathed the whole tribe of Dudley as greedy, tyrannical upstarts. Richard Troughton, the bailiff at South Walshen in Lincolnshire, hearing of Mary's flight from his friend James Pratt, as they stood together by the cattle drinking-place called hedgedyke, was moved to exclaim: 'Then it is the Duke's doing and woe worth him that ever he was born, for he will go about to destroy the noble blood of England. I wish this dagger at the villain's heart with my hand at it, as hard as I can thrust, face to face and body to body, whatsoever may become of me. May God's plague light upon him and may God save the Queen's majesty and deliver her grace from him.'[4] John Dudley might control the capital, the fortress of the Tower with its armoury and its Mint, he might have the Council in his pocket; but Richard Troughton spoke for England, and England had had more than enough of John Dudley and was not prepared to stand by while King Harry's daughter was cheated out of her natural inheritance.

On 9 July Mary had written defiantly to the Council from Kenninghall. It seemed strange, she said, that they had failed to inform her of 'so weighty a matter' as her brother's death and added that she was not ignorant of their consultations to undo the provisions made for her preferment, although she was still prepared to believe in their loyalty. Her letter ended with a command that her right and title was to be proclaimed in her City of London.

The news that Mary meant to show fight came as an unwelcome surprise to her enemies, but not even the most optimistic of her well-wishers believed she had any chance of winning. At the Imperial embassy, where Jehan Scheyfve had recently been reinforced by three envoys extraordinary, there was only gloom. The ambassadors scarcely thought it worth their while to pass on to the Emperor Mary's desperate pleas for help, and could think of nothing better to do than beg the Council to be good to her. But the Duke knew on what a fragile foundation his power really rested, and every day that Mary remained at large undermined it further. Already disquieting news was coming in of the support rallying to her. The Earls of Bath and Sussex had joined her, together with quite a few substantial gentlemen and their tenantry, not to mention 'innumerable companies of the common people'. On 12 July a muster was proclaimed in Tothill Fields to collect an army 'to fetch in the Lady Mary' and that night, says Henry Machyn, 'was carried to the Tower three carts full of all manner of ordnance, as great guns and small, bows, bills, spears, morris-pikes, harness, arrows, gunpowder and victuals'.[5] On Friday, 14 July, 'the great Duke of Northumberland with other lords and knights with a great power of horsemen with artillery and munitions of war departed from London towards Norfolk to suppress the rebels, as he took them which had taken the

Lady Mary's part'.[6] But as the impressive cavalcade passed through Shoreditch, the Duke was heard to say 'to one that rid by him, "The people press to see us, but not one sayeth God speed us"'.[7]

Northumberland had been manoeuvred into taking the field himself by his fellow councillors, but although he had the reputation of being 'the best man of war in the realm' on this occasion his genius seems to have deserted him. He allowed his followers to waste precious time burning and looting and falling out over the spoils, and his soldiers began to remember pressing engagements elsewhere. In the Tower, his associates, relieved of his hypnotic presence, began to suffer from cold feet. When they heard that the crews of the royal ships, sent to lie off Yarmouth to cut off Mary's escape route to the Continent, had gone over to her in a body, it became a question of not whether but when the Council would do the same. On 18 July the decision was taken and on the nineteenth, between five and six o'clock in the afternoon, they proclaimed Queen Mary 'Queen of England, France, and Ireland, and all dominions, as the sister of the late King Edward VI and daughter unto the noble King Henry VIII'. This time, reported an anonymous correspondent in the City, 'the number of caps that were thrown up at the proclamation were not to be told. The Earl of Pembroke threw away his cap full of angels. I saw myself money was thrown out at windows for joy. The bonfires were without number, and what with shouting and crying of the people, and ringing of the bells, there could no one hear almost what another said, besides banquetings and singing in the streets for joy.'[8]

That night, while the citizens were still drinking the health of Queen Mary and destruction to the Dudleys in the wine and beer flowing in every street, the Earl of Arundel and William Paget slipped away, riding post into Norfolk to explain to the new Queen that the Privy Council had always remained her true subjects in their hearts, but until now had seen no possibility of declaring their loyalty 'without great destruction and bloodshed'. There seems to be no record of how or when the news reached Hatfield, but it was not long before Elizabeth heard of her sister's triumph and wrote to congratulate her. On 29 July she came riding through Fleet Street to Somerset House accompanied, according to Henry Machyn, by two thousand horsemen all in green garded with white velvet or satin taffeta.

Mary was now making her way slowly down to the capital and on the following day Elizabeth set out to meet her. She passed through the City 'at twelve of the clock in the forenoon, being Sunday, and rode out at Aldgate towards the Queen's Highness, accompanied with a thousand horses of gentlemen, knights, ladies and their servants'.[9] It was some time since the sisters had last met, possibly not since Christmas of 1547, but they had continued to correspond and, on the surface at any rate, remained good friends. Mary greeted Elizabeth affectionately, kissed all the ladies in her sister's train, and the two processions formed up for the Queen's entry into London.

The royal party reached Whitechapel at seven o'clock in the evening of 3 August, and Mary paused only to change her dress before resuming her triumphal progress. At Aldgate, which was 'goodly hanged with cloths', she was received by the Lord Mayor and his aldermen and then passed on into the City, with the Earl of Arundel, who had successfully made his peace, riding ahead bearing the sword and Elizabeth following immediately behind the Queen. They must have made a poignant contrast, those two daughters of Henry VIII, as they rode together through the gaily decorated streets, with the citizens cheering themselves hoarse on every side, the trumpets sounding before them and the church bells ringing in their ears. Mary, dressed in purple velvet and satin heavy with goldsmith's work, a baldrick of gold, pearl and stones round her neck and a rich billament of stones and great pearl on her hood, was thirty-seven years old. As a girl she had been pretty, small and finely made, with the delicate pink and white complexion which often goes with red hair. Now she was painfully thin and, although dispassionate foreign observers still described her as 'fresh-coloured', the long years of unhappiness, ill-health and unkindness had left their indelible mark upon her. Elizabeth would be twenty in a month's time. She was never, even in the full bloom of youth, strictly beautiful, but the Venetian ambassador considered her face and figure 'very handsome' and her bearing regally dignified. There can be no doubt that to very many people in those welcoming crowds of Londoners she represented all the hope for England's future.

When the Queen's procession reached the Tower, she was met at the Gate by four kneeling figures – the old Duke of Norfolk, who had lain there under sentence of death ever since King Henry died; Stephen Gardiner, Bishop of Winchester, who had spent most of Edward's reign in prison; Somerset's termagant Duchess and young Edward Courtenay, now virtually the only surviving member of the ancient royal line of Plantagenet. Mary raised them all and kissed them, saying 'these are my prisoners'. There were certain other inmates of the Tower currently enjoying Her Majesty's hospitality who were not in evidence on that auspicious occasion – the Duke of Northumberland and his brood of sons, and Jane Grey, whose palace had now become her prison.

The Queen remained at the Tower for about a fortnight and then the court moved to Richmond. These first few weeks of the new reign were a difficult period of adjustment for Elizabeth. Accustomed, ever since she had begun to grow up, to thinking of her sister as 'poor Mary' – bullied, downtrodden and neglected, dismissed by Northumberland and his like as a weepy, neurotic old maid – she must now get used to the idea of Mary as Queen. Elizabeth never seems to have found the least difficulty in according her younger brother the exaggerated respect due to royalty. All the evidence points to the fact that she never really found it easy to do the same for her elder sister.

While her brief, incredulous flush of happiness lasted, Mary showed Elizabeth a flattering degree of attention, holding her by the hand whenever they appeared in public together and always giving her the place of honour at her side, but this satisfactory state of affairs was inevitably short-lived. Mary had inherited all her mother's pride, courage and stubbornness – none of her father's subtlety and political acumen. A 'good' woman, narrow in outlook, limited in intelligence, fanatical in the religious beliefs which for so long had been her only solace, and still carrying that terrible burden of guilt, she was to prove a dangerous person to deal with – and especially dangerous for Elizabeth. Mary had never borne malice to the child who had been the innocent cause of so much of her sufferings, but she soon made it clear that she could neither like nor trust the young woman – the past and their mothers' ghosts lay too heavily between them. Added to this, there was now a poisoning element of sexual jealousy in their relationship. Mary's friends had naturally been in the forefront of those ready to believe the worst of Anne Boleyn's daughter four years ago, and it would be strange indeed if Mary had not heard and been influenced by the stories circulating at that time. No least breath of scandal had ever touched Mary's name, no man had ever come near her, her virtue was unassailable; but, as one of her biographers has remarked, even a good woman can regret things which she ought not.[10] The Queen, looking at her young half-sister's demurely inscrutable countenance, must on occasion have been assailed by some highly regrettable pangs of envy and curiosity. None of this could be acknowledged, of course, but there was one issue between them which would soon have to be brought into the open, and that was the prickly question of Elizabeth's religious faith.

Mary had not the least doubt that her unexpected victory had been due entirely to the personal intervention of the Almighty, not that it was now her duty to lead her people back into the fold of the true Church. On this point, she told the Emperor's ambassador, she felt so deeply that she was hardly to be moved. Unfortunately, however, she had misjudged the mood of the country almost as disastrously as Northumberland had done. Living in rural retreat, surrounded by her Catholic household, she had, not surprisingly, failed to realise how strongly a nationalistic form of Protestantism had taken hold – especially among the artisan classes in London and the south-east – during the past few years; and had completely misinterpreted the rapturous welcome she had received. The people were thankful to be rid of Northumberland and delighted to see the true line of succession re-established. They had no intention of returning meekly to the dominance of Rome. Within a month of the Queen's accession there had been unmistakable and violent demonstrations of this feeling in the streets of London.

For a time Mary clung to her hopes for a peaceful reconciliation. Her 'determination and pleasure' uttered to the Council on 12 August was that she did not mean to 'compel or constrain other men's consciences', but trusted that God would put into their hearts a persuasion of the truth.[11] Shortly afterwards a proclamation was issued in which the Queen expressed the hope that the religion which she herself had professed from infancy would now be quietly and charitably embraced by all her subjects.

Mary had never made any secret of her beliefs and, although it was still officially illegal, Mass was now being openly celebrated at court – not once, as the Emperor was informed at the end of August, but six or seven times a day with the Councillors assisting. There was, however, one notable absentee, for the Queen's sister and heiress had not so far put in an appearance. The religious problem was a particularly delicate one for Elizabeth. The Protestant party was already turning to her as their figurehead and white hope for the future, and, so far as it is possible to tell, her own private inclinations lay with the Protestant right wing. Elizabeth was not the stuff of which martyrs are made and had no intention of becoming one if she could help it, but it would not do to alienate her friends. Added to this, if she apostatised too ardently, she would be tacitly admitting her own illegitimate birth. On the other hand, she dared not offend the Catholics too deeply, and Mary's attitude was beginning to show that she would soon have to make some gesture to placate them. Early in September the gesture was made, an event which, as Simon Renard of the Imperial embassy reported sardonically to his master, 'did not take place without a certain amount of stir'.

Alarmed by her sister's sudden coldness, Elizabeth had asked for a private audience, which was held in one of the galleries at Richmond Palace with a door or half-door separating the participants. Elizabeth fell on her knees and shed tears. She saw only too clearly, she said, that the Queen was not well disposed towards her and could think of no other cause except religion. She might, however, be excused on this point as she had been brought up in the way she held and had never been taught the doctrine of the ancient faith. She begged Mary to send her books 'contrary to those she had always read and known hitherto' so that she might see if her conscience would allow her to be persuaded; 'or that a learned man might be sent to her, to instruct her in the truth'. These requests were granted and Elizabeth apparently found her conscience easily persuadable, for on 8 September, the day after her twentieth birthday, she accompanied the Queen to Mass. The effect of this from the Catholic point of view was somewhat marred by the fact that 'she tried to excuse herself, saying she was ill and complained loudly all the way to Church that her stomach ached, wearing a suffering air'.[12] Simon Renard had no illusions about the true worth of Elizabeth's conversion and Antoine de Noailles, the French ambassador, told the King of France on 22 September, 'everyone believes that she is acting rather from fear of danger and peril from those around her than from real devotion'.[13]

The religious difficulty was only part of the quagmire surrounding Elizabeth and waiting hungrily for her least false step. Mary, accustomed all her adult life to relying on her mother's relations for support and advice, now turned as naturally and trustfully to Simon Renard as once she had turned to Eustace Chapuys; and Renard, the shrewd and skilful diplomat who had taken over as the Emperor's resident ambassador, was dedicated to cementing the important English alliance with Spain and the Empire. The Queen listened eagerly to the sage counsel passed on by her cousin's ambassador. She was to move cautiously at first in matters of religion and refrain from taking too harsh a revenge on her enemies. But Mary had no desire for revenge and only three of the Northumberland conspirators, the Duke himself and two of his closest confederates, were executed. In Renard's opinion the same fate should properly have overtaken Jane Grey, but here Mary proved unexpectedly intractable. 'As to Jane of Suffolk, whom they had tried to make Queen,' he reported, 'she could not be induced to consent that she should die.' Jane had written to Mary, admitting she had done wrong in accepting the Crown but vehemently denying that she had either consented or been a party to Northumberland's intrigues. Mary believed her and told Renard that her conscience would not permit her to have Jane put to death. The ambassador pointed out that 'power and tyranny had sometimes more force, especially in affairs of state, than right or justice' but the Queen was immovable. Nevertheless, she promised to be careful and to take all the necessary precautions before setting the usurper free! Renard could only shrug up his shoulders and hope, without much conviction, that Mary would not regret her astonishing clemency.[14] But, however much he might deplore Jane's preservation, he regarded Elizabeth as potentially even more dangerous. The Queen's heretical heir would be an obvious focal point for all discontent, both religious and political, and her name recurs in his despatches with relentless iteration. He told the Emperor, in a curiously felicitous phrase, that she had a spirit full of enchantment (*qu'est ung esprit plain d'incantation*) and was greatly to be feared.[15] He told the Queen at every opportunity not to trust her sister 'who might, out of ambition, or being persuaded thereto, conceive some dangerous design and put it to execution, by means which it would be difficult to prevent, as she was clever and sly'.[16]

The over enmity of Simon Renard was formidable enough by itself, but Elizabeth knew she had as much or more to fear from his rival, Antoine de Noailles, who professed to be her friend. The French ambassador's chief business was to prevent, if possible, too close an alliance between England and Spain. Such an alliance could only be hostile to France, and as rumours began to spread that the Queen of England was contemplating marriage with the Emperor's son, Philip, French alarm increased. There was another compelling reason for the King of France's close interest in

English affairs – a reason represented in the person of the young Queen of Scots, now nearing her twelfth birthday, who was being brought up at the French court as the intended bride of the Dauphin. Mary Stuart was the granddaughter of Margaret Tudor, Henry VIII's elder sister, who had married James IV of Scotland. In spite of Henry's Will, which arbitrarily excluded the Scottish line, by all the laws of primogeniture Mary Stuart had an excellent claim to the English crown. No slur had ever been cast on her birth, and many people felt she had every right at least to be regarded as the heiress presumptive. The King of France was naturally attracted by the prospect of seeing his future daughter-in-law become queen of both the island kingdoms and, if some sufficiently lethal form of dissension could be stirred up between the Tudor sisters he was not unhopeful of the outcome. De Noailles was an accomplished intriguer and could be relied upon to do his best in this direction.

Mary was already beginning to entertain grave doubts as to the purity of Elizabeth's motives in attending Mass, and 'asked her if she firmly believed what the Catholics now believed and had always believed concerning the holy sacrament'. She begged her 'to speak freely and declare what was in her mind'.[17] Oddly enough Elizabeth might have been wiser, at this stage, to have done just that. Mary's own sincerity was patent and she could respect genuine scruples of conscience in others. Unfortunately, however, the gulf between the sisters was now so wide that no trust or confidence was possible. Elizabeth told the Queen that she was considering making a public declaration 'that she went to Mass and did as she did because her conscience prompted and moved her to it; that she went of her own free will and without fear, hypocrisy or dissimulation'.[18] Mary could not believe her and the suspicion that Elizabeth was deliberately using the religious faith which the Queen held sacred as a political weapon did nothing to improve her opinion of the girl.

All the same, by using these somewhat dubious methods, Elizabeth succeeded in maintaining a foothold at court and in securing her proper place at Mary's coronation, which took place on 1 October. She was paired with that old friend Anne of Cleves, still living in England in comfortable and respected retirement. They rode together 'in a chariot covered with cloth of silver' in the procession through the City from the Tower, and later both dined at the Queen's table at the banquet in Westminster Hall.[19] But even at the coronation festivities Renard was watching Elizabeth closely and reported that she appeared to be conspiring with the French ambassador. Apparently the Princess had complained to de Noailles about the weight of her coronet and he answered brightly that she must have patience, for soon this crown would bring her a better one.[20]

Mary's first Parliament met on 5 October and proceeded to repeal the divorce of Henry VIII and Catherine of Aragon, pronouncing their marriage to have been lawful and valid. Mary can hardly be blamed for wanting to vindicate her mother's memory and doing what she could to right that old wrong, but it was embarrassing for Elizabeth to have her bastard state thus emphasised. In fact, and contrary to Renard's expectations, the re-establishment of Mary's legitimacy did not affect her own position *vis-a-vis* the succession. Under the peculiar powers granted to Henry VIII by Parliament, as long as the 1544 Act of Succession remained in force, Elizabeth was still next in line to the throne if Mary died childless. So far, the present Parliament, although willing to oblige the Queen up to a point, had shown no disposition to interfere with this arrangement, but Elizabeth could have no illusions about what her sister might do if the opportunity presented itself. In one hysterical outburst that autumn, Mary had cried out that it would be a scandal and a disgrace to the kingdom to allow Elizabeth to succeed, for she was a heretic, a hypocrite and a bastard.[21] On another occasion the Queen went so far as to say that she could not even be sure that Elizabeth was King Henry's bastard. Her mother had been an infamous woman and she herself 'had the face and countenance' of Mark Smeaton, the lute-player.[22] No doubt all this was faithfully repeated to the Princess, and on 25 October de Noailles reported that 'Madame Elizabeth is very discontented, and has asked permission to withdraw from this Court'.[23]

Permission was refused, and Simon Renard, who saw heretical plots behind every bush and the hands of Elizabeth and de Noailles in all of them, urged the Queen to send her sister to the Tower without more ado. Mary would not go as far as that, but in November she was foolish enough to insult Elizabeth publicly, by giving precedence to the Countess of Lennox and the Duchess of Suffolk at state functions. To be made to follow Margaret Douglas, daughter of Margaret Tudor's second marriage to the Earl of Angus, or the Duchess of Suffolk, mother of the convicted traitor Jane Grey, was too much for Elizabeth's temper. There was something perilously close to an open quarrel, and Elizabeth showed her feelings by sulking in her own apartments. Mary's friends cut her, but the younger element at court – especially the younger male element – openly sided with the Princess.

Renard heard rumours that she was entertaining de Noailles in secret, and although Elizabeth had no difficulty in clearing herself from this accusation the atmosphere had become so strained that she renewed her demands to be allowed to retire into the country. As things turned out, she might have done better to have stayed where she was, but her desire to escape from the intolerable situation at court is very understandable.

This time leave was granted, and at the beginning of December the sisters met to say good-bye. Mary had been given a good talking-to by Renard, who told her she would have to make up her mind what to do about Elizabeth. If she would not put her in the Tower, then, for reasons of policy, she must treat her with at least outward civility. His words had some effect for, although he wrote 'I have much difficulty in persuading the Queen to dissemble', Mary made a heroic effort and gave Elizabeth an expensive parting-present of a sable hood. Her dislike of her younger sister had by now grown into a near obsession. Renard observed that 'she still resents the injuries inflicted on Queen Catherine, her lady mother, by the machinations of Anne Boleyn, mother of Elizabeth', and it is tempting to speculate whether there was something about Elizabeth at this time which reminded Mary with especial vividness of the hated Anne – something which made all that long pent-up bitterness come welling uncontrollably to the surface. All the courtesies, however, were observed at their leave-taking and de Noailles heard that there had been a complete reconciliation. According to Renard, Elizabeth 'addressed a petition to the Queen, asking her not to believe anyone who spread evil reports of her without doing her the honour to let her know and give her a chance of proving the false and malicious nature of such slanders'.[24]

Before she was allowed to leave London, the Princess received a visit from the Earl of Arundel and William Paget, who 'spoke to her frankly and said what they thought salutary for her to hear, namely that if she left the straight road and intrigued with the heretics and French, she might have reason to regret it'.[25] If Elizabeth found anything ironic in this homily from two gentlemen, neither of whom was exactly noted for following the straight road himself, she gave no sign of it and merely repeated her assurance 'that as for religion she was not acting hypocritically but according to the dictates of her conscience'. She would show her good intentions by her way of living, she told them. She would take priests into her household, dismiss any of her servants who might be suspect and 'do all in her power to please the Queen'. On the day of her departure Renard himself, anxious to leave no stone unturned, went to see her and 'spoke seasonable words calculated to counteract the effects of French intrigues'. 'Nevertheless,' he assured the Emperor, 'care was being taken to have her every action observed.'[26]

Elizabeth was bound for Ashridge, which lay close to the Great North Road, and Renard was highly suspicious of a request previously made by de Noailles 'to have posting-houses on the road to Scotland'. De Noailles had told the Council that this was for the convenience of his colleague, the Sieur d'Oysel, when he passed through England on his way north to take up the post of French ambassador in Scotland; but Simon Renard felt convinced that it was all part of some dark scheme being hatched with Elizabeth's connivance.

As Elizabeth rode out of the capital, her purest emotion was probably relief at getting away. She knew it could only be a temporary respite, the storm signals were too unmistakable, and she was well aware that she was still surrounded by spies; but she could relax her vigilance just a little, while she prayed to be delivered from her friends.

10

'We Are All Englishmen'

The bulk of the work of Mary's first Parliament had consisted of repealing various treason Acts passed during the two preceding reigns, and sweeping away the whole of the Edwardian religious settlement. With this, for the time being, the Queen had to be content, although her ultimate objective, as revealed to Parliament by Stephen Gardiner, Bishop of Winchester and now Lord Chancellor, was to return unconditionally to the authority of Rome. The solid conservative core of the nation as represented in the House of Commons was willing enough to return to the *status quo* which had existed at King Henry's death – in other words, to a form of Anglo-Catholicism. Further than that they were not so far prepared to go, and Mary found she was still saddled with the unwanted title of Head of the Church. The spirit of national pride and independence fostered by Henry's defiance of the Pope was a powerful driving-force and, even more to the point, a large number of family fortunes had been founded on the spoils of the Reformation. Certainly no holder of Church lands was now going to part with a foot of his plunder without a bitter struggle.

If the Queen was dissatisfied, so too was the Protestant left wing, a noisy and well-organised minority which manifested its opposition to her policy by acts of hooliganism in the churches, physical assaults on priests and the dissemination of a shower of highly inflammatory anti-Catholic propaganda. It was not, however, the religious dispute *per se* which brought about the first and most narrowly contested trial of strength between Mary and her people. By the beginning of November 1553, it had become generally known that the Queen seriously intended marriage with Philip of Spain, who was not merely a foreigner and a Catholic but the representative of the most formidable Catholic power bloc in Europe. It looked as if all Northumberland's direst predictions were going to be fulfilled, and public reaction was sharp and immediate. The Protestant pressure groups redoubled their efforts; both Houses of Parliament sent a joint deputation to the Queen begging her to marry an Englishman and there were grave misgivings within the Privy Council itself.

No one, of course, questioned that the Queen must marry and the sooner the better. The idea of a single woman attempting to rule such a turbulent nation as England was not to be thought of, especially as Mary had already shown that she possessed neither the taste nor the aptitude for government. Obviously she must have a husband to support her and undertake, as Simon Renard delicately put it, 'those duties which were not the province of ladies'. In the opinion of many people and in particular of the Lord Chancellor, the Queen's wisest choice of consort would have been Edward Courtenay, 'the last sprig of the White Rose'. Courtenay, a good-looking, charming but rather weak-witted young man now in his mid-twenties, was a grandson of one of Edward IV's daughters and had spent nearly half his life in prison for that very reason. Mary was prepared to be kind to him – she created him Earl of Devon and arranged that he should be given special opportunities to make up for the time he had wasted in prison – but she made it perfectly clear that she had no intention of marrying him, or indeed any other Englishman. Her desire for Philip, although politically, and as it turned out, personally disastrous, was natural enough in the circumstances. The fact that the Prince of Spain happened to be the most brilliant match available weighed less with Mary than the fact that he was a Spaniard and one of her mother's kin. Having been skilfully and patiently piloted by Renard through the shoals of her maidenly shrinking, self-doubt and indecision, Mary was now more than half in love – a heady emotion for one of her naturally affectionate temperament who had so far always schooled herself to an almost nun-like renunciation of the flesh.

One of the reasons which had been officially advanced in favour of the Queen's marriage was to secure an heir to safeguard the succession but, although nobody was tactless enough to say so, few people seriously believed that Mary would ever bear a child. Mary herself was not so sure. After all, God had already worked one miracle for her. Why should He not work another and give her a son to guarantee the continued success of her mission? For, with Philip at her side, surely nothing could prevent her from bringing England safely back to Rome. She did not reach her decision lightly, but when on 29 October, after many weeks of heart-searching, tears and prayer, Mary finally gave her word to Renard she had convinced herself that it was God's will for her to marry Philip and after that, of course, she was immovable.

The Lord Chancellor was the only person with sufficient prestige and authority to try to make the Queen understand the sort of trouble she was storing up for herself and for the country, but unfortunately there was always a fatal element of awkwardness and reserve in their relationship. Mary could not forget that Stephen Gardiner had once been one of her father's most trusted and able instruments in the struggle for the divorce, and Gardiner was especially hampered on this occasion by his known personal fondness for Courtenay. As Mary snappishly remarked, was it suitable that she should be forced to marry someone simply because a bishop had made friends with him in prison? Gardiner could only reiterate that the people would never stomach a foreigner who would make promises that he would not keep. The Queen retorted that if her Chancellor preferred the will of the people to her wishes, then he was not keeping *his* promises. The Chancellor, with his past experience of Tudor obstinacy, gave in, saying it was too dangerous to meddle in the marriages of princes. With the parliamentary delegation, Mary took an even higher tone. It was none of their business, she told them, to dictate to her on such a matter. She could be trusted to remember the oath she had taken at her coronation and always to put her country first. Anyway, she added in a burst of petulance, if they forced her to marry against her will, she would not live three months and they would only be defeating their own ends.[1] In fact, as the Queen indicated defiantly to all and sundry, she meant to have Philip or nobody.

Across the Channel, the French, seeing themselves threatened with encirclement, were full of despondency. Mary's ambassador, Nicholas Wotton, had been instructed to tell the King of France that, no matter whom she married, she intended to continue to live in peace and amity with him, but that cynical monarch was not convinced. 'It is to be considered', he remarked to Wotton, 'that a husband may do much with his wife; and it shall be very hard for any wife to refuse her husband any thing that he shall earnestly require of her.' Wotton had been abroad in the world, continued the King, and knew how subtle and crafty the Spaniards were, so that whatever good intentions Mary might profess now it was very doubtful whether she would be able to keep to them in the future.[2] Indeed, the fear that England would be dragged into war with France was one of the most serious objections to the Spanish marriage, and, as it turned out, a fear which was to prove only too well founded.

Meanwhile, in London, de Noailles had not given up hope that even now the marriage might be prevented. Although the Emperor, throughout the delicate process of negotiation, was doing his utmost to avoid treading on English corns – an alliance which would give him command of the sea route between Spain and the Netherlands was worth any amount of diplomacy – the English people in their present mood of suspicion and xenophobia preferred to believe the various horrific rumours being carefully spread by interested parties; that a horde of Spaniards all armed to the teeth would shortly land on their coast; that England was to be reduced to the status of a province of the Empire and the Pope's authority forcibly reimposed. The country was clearly ripe for mischief and de Noailles thought he knew best how to put the finishing touches to it. Mary might have refused to have young Courtenay, but there was still Elizabeth. 'From what I hear,' he told the King of France in December, 'it only requires that my Lord Courtenay should marry her, and that they should go together to the counties of Devonshire and Cornwall. Here it can easily be believed that they would find many adherents, and they could then make a strong claim to the crown, and the Emperor and Prince of Spain would find it difficult to suppress this rising.' Elizabeth and Courtenay should certainly have made a virtually irresistible combination, but de Noailles was too clear-headed not to see at least one of the snags. 'This misfortune', he continued, 'is that the said Courtenay is of such a fearful and timid disposition that he dare not make the venture. . . . There are many, of whom I know, who would be ready to give him encouragement and all help in carrying out some plan to his advantage, and I do not see what should hinder him, except his weakness, faint-heartedness and timidity.'[3] The ambassador seems to have taken Elizabeth's co-operation for granted but if she ever had any idea of raising rebellion against her sister, of which there is no proof whatever, the timorous Courtenay was the last person with whom she would have been likely to throw in her lot.

Nevertheless, ambitious plans for armed resistance against the proud Spaniard and 'the coming in of him or his favourers' were now being laid. They were still maturing when, on 2 January 1554, the Emperor's envoys, led by Count Egmont, arrived 'for the knitting up of the marriage' between the Queen and the Prince of Spain. Egmont and his coadjutors landed at Tower Wharf to the salute of 'a great peal of guns' from the Tower batteries, and on Tower Hill a reception committee headed by Courtenay was waiting to conduct them ceremoniously through the City. They got no welcome from the watching crowds, for 'the people, nothing rejoicing, held down their heads sorrowfully'. On the previous day the embassy servants had been pelted with snowballs, but at least nothing was actually thrown at the distinguished visitors.[4]

On 12 January the marriage treaty was finally signed and its terms, as outlined by the Lord Chancellor two days later in an eloquent oration to the lords, nobility and gentlemen in the presence chamber at Westminster, should have been generous enough to satisfy the most exacting Englishman. But unfortunately the rising tide of panic and prejudice could no longer be stemmed by reasoned argument. The mindless rallying-cry 'We still have no foreigner for our King' had temporarily driven out common sense, and Gardiner's announcement, according to one chronicler, was 'heavily taken of sundry men, yea and thereat almost each man was abashed, looking daily for worse matters to grow shortly after'.[5] Within a week word reached London that Sir Peter Carew was up in Devonshire 'resisting the King of Spain's coming'. Almost simultaneously the Council heard that Sir Thomas Wyatt, son of the poet, and a number of others were up in Kent 'for the said quarrel in resisting the said King of Spain . . . and partly for moving certain councillors from about the Queen'. About this time, according to the same account, 'Sir James Crofts departed to Wales, as it is thought to raise his power there', and news also came in that the Duke of Suffolk had mysteriously disappeared from his house at Sheen.[6]

The rising had originally been timed for March, to coincide with Philip's actual arrival, but someone had let the secret out. It was generally believed that Courtenay, always the weak link in the chain, had taken fright and confessed to Gardiner or else that the Chancellor, becoming suspicious and alarmed for his protégé, had somehow extracted the story from him. The other conspirators, not knowing to what extent their plans had been betrayed and too deeply committed to draw back, were forced to move prematurely. The movement in the West Country was virtually still-born. It had always depended very largely on Courtenay's presence and the prestige of his name, without him, its morale rapidly collapsed and Peter Carew fled to France. In Kent, however, things looked serious. Thomas Wyatt had taken Rochester Bridge, and the crews of the royal ships lying in the Medway had gone over to him with their guns and ammunition.

While these stirring events were taking place, Elizabeth remained lying close at Ashridge. Earlier in the month Mary had written to her asking for news and received a letter in reply saying that Elizabeth was not at all well. She had been troubled, she said, with such a cold and headache as she had never felt before, and for the past three weeks had had no respite from the pain in her head and arms. Then came the outbreak of armed rebellion, and rumours began to circulate that Ashridge was being provisioned for a siege. Gardiner's agents picked up a report that the Princess intended moving to Donnington Castle, a semi-fortified house near Newbury in Berkshire, and on 26 January, the day after Wyatt entered Rochester, Mary wrote again to her sister:

> We tendering the surety of your person, which might chance to be in some peril, if any sudden tumult should arise, either where you now be, or about Donnington, whither (as we understand) you are bound shortly to remove, do therefore think it expedient you should put yourself in readiness with all convenient speed to make your repair hither to us, which, we pray you, fail not to do, assuring you, that as you may more surely remain here, so shall you be most heartily welcome to us. And of your mind herein we pray you return answer by this messenger.[7]

Velvet gloves were still being worn, but the hint of steel in the invitation was unmistakable. Elizabeth returned a verbal answer. She was too ill to travel, she said. The officers of her household felt it prudent to follow this up with a letter addressed to the Lord Chancellor. 'Albeit we attend here on my Lady Elizabeth's Grace, our mistress,' they wrote,

> in hope every day of her amendment, to repair towards the Queen's Highness, (whereof we have, as yet, none apparent likelihood of health,) yet, considering this dangerous world, the perilous attempts and the naughty endeavours of the rebels . . . we do not forget our most bounden duty, nor yet our readiness in words and deeds to serve Her Highness by all the ways and means that may stand in us, both from her Grace, our mistress, and of our own parts also.[8]

There, for the moment, the matter rested; during the next fortnight the Queen and Council were too busy coping with a major crisis on their doorstep to have any leisure to spare for Elizabeth.

A hastily collected force, consisting of men of the Queen's guard and the City train bands, had been sent down to Kent; but the Londoners and a fair proportion of the guard promptly defected to the rebels with rousing cries of 'We are all Englishmen!' In the words of one Alexander Brett, they preferred to spend their blood 'in the quarrel of this worthy captain, Master Wyatt' and prevent at all costs the approach of 'the proud Spaniards' who, as every right-thinking Englishman knew, would treat them like slaves, despoil them of their goods and lands, ravish their wives before their faces and deflower their daughters in their presence.[9]

Thus reinforced, Wyatt resumed his advance on the capital. From Blackheath on 30 January he announced his terms: the custody of the Tower with the Queen in it, the removal of several councillors and their replacements to be chosen by him. London was in a turmoil and everything depended on the loyalty of the citizens, which appeared doubtful to say the least. It was Mary herself who saved a very ugly situation. Like all her family, she showed to the best advantage in a crisis which demanded a display of physical and moral courage. Disregarding advice that she should seek her own safety, she rode into the City on 1 February and made a fighting speech in the crowded Guildhall that not even Elizabeth could have bettered. Her audience rose to her, and when Wyatt reached Southwark two days later he found the bridge heavily defended against him. A period of uneasy stalemate followed, during which the Lord Mayor and the sheriffs got into armour and commanded the householders to be ready 'in harness to stand everyone at his door, what chance soever might happen'. It was a long time since London had been besieged and 'much noise and tumult was everywhere' as shops were shuttered, market stalls hastily dismantled and weapons and armour unearthed from store and prepared for use. The Queen had refused to allow the Tower guns to be turned on the rebels in case any of the innocent inhabitants of Southwark should suffer, and finally, on Shrove Tuesday, 6 February, Wyatt withdrew his men from 'the bridge foot' and marched down-river to Kingston, where they crossed to the northern bank before turning eastwards again. But the steam had gone out of them by now. They were tired and hungry, and too much time had been wasted. Still they came on through the western suburbs. There was some skirmishing with the royalist forces under the command of the Earl of Pembroke around St James's and Charing Cross, and some panic at Whitehall when, in the general confusion, a cry of treason was raised within the precincts of the palace as a rumour spread that Pembroke had gone over to the enemy. 'There', remarked one observer, 'should ye have seen running and crying of ladies and gentlewomen, shutting of doors, and such a screeching and noise as it was wonderful to hear.' But still the Queen stood fast and 'many thought she would have been in the field in person'.[10] Wyatt and a handful of followers got through Temple Bar and on down Fleet Street, but found Ludgate barred and defended against them. As they turned back they realised that they had become separated from the main body of their army and Pembroke was coming up to cut off their retreat. A few minutes later it was all over and Wyatt had yielded to Sir Maurice Berkeley at Temple Bar.

Once the immediate danger had passed and the rank and file of the insurgents were being rounded up and crammed into makeshift prisons, the government was able to turn its attention to unravelling the threads of the conspiracy. Before the end of January, Gardiner, believing with some justification that de Noailles was involved up to his neck, had resorted to highway robbery on one of the ambassador's couriers. As a result indisputable evidence emerged that de Noailles had known all about the plot and the names of the plotters for at least two months. Even more interesting, the Lord Chancellor's men discovered a copy of Elizabeth's last letter to the Queen on its way to the French King by diplomatic bag. From this it seemed reasonable to assume that the Queen's heir was in correspondence with the emissaries of a foreign power. Whether she had been actively involved in the recent disturbance remained to be proved, but although Wyatt had never openly invoked her name there could be no doubt that she, if anyone, had stood to gain from his success. At all events, it was time she came to London to give an account of herself. Mary was already suspicious of the convenient illness Elizabeth was still using as an excuse for skulking in the country, and two of the royal physicians, Drs Owen and Wendy, were despatched to examine the patient and report on her condition. On 10 February, the medical team was reinforced by a commission consisting of Lord William Howard, the Lord Admiral and Elizabeth's maternal great-uncle, Sir Edward Hastings and Sir Thomas Cornwallis.

According to a highly coloured and quite unsubstantiated account by that enthusiastic martyrologist John Foxe, their orders were to bring the Princess back with them 'either quick or dead'. Holinshed says they arrived late at night and insisted on forcing their way unbidden into her bedroom. The commissioners themselves reported more soberly to the Queen on the following day that 'immediately upon our arrival at Ashridge, we required to have access unto my Lady Elizabeth's Grace; which obtained, we delivered unto her your Highness' letter; and I, the Lord Admiral, declared the effect of your Highness' pleasure'. The doctors had given it as their opinion that Elizabeth could be moved 'without danger of her person' and the commission therefore that that 'we might well proceed to require her in your Majesty's name (all excuses set apart) to repair to your Highness with all convenient speed and diligence'. They found the invalid 'very willing and conformable' but still fighting a determined rearguard action, for 'she much feared her weakness to be so great that she should not be able to travel and to endure the journey without peril of life'. Elizabeth knew that the peril lay not in the journey but its destination and begged a further respite, 'until she had better recovered her strength'. It was, however, politely but firmly made clear that the time for such delaying tactics had passed, and she gave in with becoming meekness, agreeing to set out on the following day.[11]

Although, for obvious reasons, she was making the most of it, there is no doubt that her illness was genuine. When her escort 'had her forth' at nine o'clock in the morning of Monday, 12 February, 'she was very faint and feeble and in such case that she was ready to swound three or four times' before they could get her into the Queen's litter which had been brought to carry her. From the description of her symptoms – her face and limbs were so distended that she was laid to be 'a sad sight to see' – Elizabeth appears to have been suffering from acute nephritis, or inflammation of the kidneys, and it has been suggested that she may have had an attack of scarlet fever of which this form of Bright's Disease is often a complication.[12] But her physical discomfort can scarcely have compared with her mental anxiety. The situation she had been dreading ever since Mary's accession was now at hand and there could be no disguising the fact that she stood in deadly danger. The litter jolting its way slowly but inexorably through the frost-rutted Hertfordshire lanes might well be taking her towards a traitor's death.

In deference to his charge's fragile condition, Howard had planned the thirty-mile journey to Westminster in very easy stages, expecting it to last five days; but he had reckoned without Elizabeth's talent for procrastination and it was 22 February before the cortège was able to leave Mr Cholmeley's house at Highgate and descend into the City. Simon Renard reported that Elizabeth, who was wearing unrelieved white for the occasion, 'had her litter opened to show herself to the people' and the people themselves, clearly expecting the worst, came flocking gloomily to gaze on the swollen, pallid countenance of their Princess. According to Renard, she appeared 'proud and haughty', an expression which in his opinion was assumed to mask the vexation she felt.[13]

Elizabeth's feelings on that dismal Thursday afternoon can only be guessed at, but the sights which greeted her as she was carried through Smithfield and on down Fleet Street can have done nothing to raise her spirits. The government had had a bad fright and the work of exemplary justice was proceeding briskly. Gallows had been erected throughout the City, in Bermondsey, at Charing Cross and Hyde Park Corner, and all the gates into London were decorated with heads and dismembered corpses.[14] The great were suffering with the simple. Courtenay was back in the Tower. The Duke of Suffolk, who owed his life and liberty after Northumberland's *coup* entirely to the Queen's generosity, had tried to raise the Midlands against her and was now awaiting execution. Mary had also reluctantly been brought to agree that Jane Grey would have to die. Innocent she might be of any complicity in Wyatt's rebellion but the very fact of her existence had come to represent an unacceptable doubt. Diminutive, freckle-faced Jane, who was not yet seventeen, had followed her young husband to the block on the day Elizabeth left Ashridge – a piece of news which more than any other must surely have brought home her own nearness to the abyss. If Mary could be persuaded to kill Jane of whom, despite her heresy, she had always been rather fond, there seemed even less chance that she would be in any mood to spare the sister she so overtly distrusted.

When Elizabeth reached Whitehall the portents were bad. She had already been separated from most of her household. The Queen refused to see her and she was lodged in a part of the Palace from which, said Renard, neither she nor her remaining servants could go out without passing through the guard. There she stayed for nearly a month, a prisoner in fact if not in name, while determined efforts were made to build up the case against her. Renard could not understand the delay in sending her to the Tower, since, he wrote, 'she has been accused by Wyatt, mentioned by name in the French ambassador's letters, suspected by her own councillors, and it is certain that the enterprise was undertaken for her sake. Indeed, Sire,' he told the Emperor in some exasperation, 'if she does not seize this opportunity of punishing her and Courtenay, the Queen will never be secure.'[15]

It is impossible, at this distance in time, to say just how deeply Elizabeth had in fact been implicated in the rebellion. There was some circumstantial evidence – enough, it must be admitted, to justify an enquiry. But it soon turned out to amount to very little in real terms. Wyatt, who was being rigorously interrogated, admitted having sent Elizabeth two letters; one advising her to retreat to Donnington, where she could have defended herself until the insurrection had succeeded; the other informing her of his arrival at Southwark. Francis Russell, the Earl of Bedford's son, confessed to acting as postman but the replies, if any, had been verbal and non-committal. Sir James Crofts, one of the conspirators now in custody, had been to see Elizabeth at Ashridge, and according to a report from Mr Secretary Bourne dated 25 February had incriminated William Saintlow, a member of her household. But William Saintlow, examined by the Council, 'stoutly denied' knowing anything of Wyatt's plans, 'protesting that he was a true man, both to God and his prince'.[16] 'Crofts is plain and will tell all,' wrote Bourne hopefully, and Renard, in a despatch dated 1 March, declared that Crofts had 'confessed the truth, written his deposition, and admitted in plain terms the intrigues of the French ambassador with the heretics and rebels'.[17] Possibly the wish was father to the thought – in actual fact Sir James, although 'marvellously tossed', does not appear to have revealed anything of importance. Even the discovery of that letter in de Noailles's postbag was not in itself evidence against Elizabeth. There was nothing to prove that she herself had given it to de Noailles or had permitted anyone else to do so.

While it is difficult to believe that she had been entirely ignorant of the conspiracy, it is equally hard to credit that she had either approved or been actively involved. On the other hand, she could scarcely have betrayed the men who, however wrong-headed, believed themselves to be her friends, and had they been successful, she would have found it impossible to stand aside. There can be little doubt that one of the first consequences of such a success would have been the removal of Mary and an attempt to replace her by putting Elizabeth and Courtenay jointly on the throne. Since everything we know about Elizabeth leads to the conclusion that this was the last day she would ever have chosen to come into her inheritance, her most likely course is the one which, in the light of the available evidence, she may be said to have pursued – to try to know as little as possible and hope to keep out of it.

On 15 March Wyatt was brought to trial and convicted. The next day, which was the Friday before Palm Sunday, Elizabeth received a visit from Stephen Gardiner and nineteen other members of the Council, who 'burdened her with Wyatt's conspiracy' as well as with the 'business made by Sir Peter Carew and the rest of the gentlemen of the West Country'. It was the Queen's pleasure, they told her, that she should go to the Tower 'while the matter were further tried and examined'. Elizabeth was aghast. She denied all the charges made against her, 'affirming that she was altogether guiltless therein', and said desperately that she trusted the Queen's Majesty would be a more gracious lady unto her than to send her to 'so notorious and doleful a place'. Stony-faced, the deputation indicated that there was no alternative, the Queen was fully determined, and they trooped out 'with their caps hanging over their eyes'. Barely an hour later four of them were back again. Her own servants were removed and six of the Queen's people appointed to wait on her, so that 'none should have access to her grace'. A hundred soldiers from the north in white coats watched and warded in the Palace gardens that night, and a great fire was lit in the Hall, where 'two certain lords' kept guard with their company.[18]

It is not difficult to imagine the twenty-year-old Elizabeth lying awake in the darkness, listening to the tramp of feet beneath her window and knowing that the net was closing round her. Within a few hours, short of some miracle, she would be in 'that very narrow place' the Tower, from which few prisoners of the blood royal had ever emerged alive. But, on the following morning, when the Earl of Sussex and another lord whom Foxe tactfully omits to name (he was probably the Marquess of Winchester, the same who as Lord St John had once ridden down to Hatfield with Robert Tyrwhit), came to tell her that the barge was waiting and the tide now ready 'which tarrieth for nobody', Elizabeth made it clear she had by no means given up the fight. It was a time for clutching at straws. She asked to wait for the next tide and was refused. Then, if she might not see the Queen, she begged at least to be allowed to write to her. Winchester said he dared not permit such a thing, adding that in his opinion it would do Elizabeth more harm than good. But Sussex, suddenly kneeling to the prisoner, exclaimed that she should have liberty to write, and, as he was a true man, he would deliver her letter to the Queen and bring an answer 'whatsoever came thereof'.[19]

Writing-materials were hastily produced, and with her court hovering in the background Elizabeth sat down to begin what might well prove to be the most important letter of her life. Her pen flowed easily over the first page, in sentences which she must have been polishing during the watches of the night. 'If any ever did try this old saying', she wrote,

> that a King's word was more than another man's oath, I most humbly beseech your Majesty to verify it in me, and to remember your last promise and my last demand, that I be not condemned without answer and due proof, which it seems that now I am; for that without cause proved I am by your Council from you commanded to go into the Tower, a place more wonted for a false traitor than a true subject. . . . I protest afore God, who shall judge my truth, whatsoever malice shall devise, that I never practised, counselled nor consented to anything that might be prejudicial to your person any way, or dangerous to the state by any means. And I therefore humbly beseech your Majesty to let me answer afore yourself, and not suffer me to trust to your councillors; yea, and afore that I go to the Tower, if it is possible; if not, afore I be further condemned. . . . Let conscience move your Highness to take some better way with me, than to make me condemned in all men's sight afore my desert [be] known.

It might be dangerous to remind Mary of Tom Seymour and yet she had to risk it. 'I have heard in my time', she went on,

> of many cast away for want of coming to the presence of their Prince; and in late days I heard my Lord Somerset say that if his brother had been suffered to speak with him, he had never suffered; but the persuasions were made to him too great, that he was brought in belief that he could not live safely if the Admiral lived, and that made him give his consent to his death. Though these persons are not to be compared to your Majesty, yet I pray God as evil persuasions persuade not one sister against the other. . . .

So far so good – she had reached the end of the page – but the strain was telling and as she turned over mistakes and corrections began to come thick and fast. Perhaps Sussex was at her elbow by this time, urging her to make an end. 'I humbly crave to speak with your Highness,' scribbled Elizabeth,

> which I would not be so bold to desire if I knew not myself most clear as I know myself most true. And as for the traitor Wyatt, he might peradventure write me a letter, but on my faith I never received any from him. And for the copy of my letter sent to the French king, I pray God confound me eternally if

ever I sent him word, message, token or letter by any means. And to this my truth I will stand to my death.

She had said all she could say, but more than half her second sheet was left blank – an open invitation to some forger to add a last-minute confession or damaging admission – so Elizabeth scored the page with diagonal lines, before adding her final appeal at the very bottom. 'I humbly crave but only one word of answer from yourself. Your Highness's most faithful subject that hath been from the beginning and will be to my end, Elizabeth.'[20]

She might have saved herself the trouble. Mary flew into a royal rage when the letter was brought to her. She roared at the Council that they would never have dared to do such a thing in her father's time and wished, in a triumph of illogicality, that he were alive again if only for a month.[21] All the same, Elizabeth had won twenty-four hours respite for she had contrived to miss the tide. The great boat-shaped starlings which supported the piers of old London Bridge restricted the flow of the river and turned the water beneath it into a mill-race. 'Shooting the bridge' was a hazardous business at the best of times, but when the tide was flooding it became impossible – there could be a difference of as much as five feet in the level of the water on either side. The government had no intention of courting a riot by taking the Princess through the streets, but the bridge would not be navigable again until midnight and the danger that a rescue attempt might be mounted under cover of darkness seemed too great to risk. It was therefore reluctantly decided to wait for daylight.

At nine o'clock on the morning of Palm Sunday Sussex and Winchester came for her again. This time there was no question of any reprieve. 'If there be no remedy', said Elizabeth dully, 'I must needs be contented.' As she was hurried through the damp gardens to the riverside, she looked up at the windows of the Palace, perhaps in a faint hope of seeing Mary, but there was no sign. Even now she seems to have been half-expecting a miracle, for she cried out that she marvelled much at the nobility of the realm who would suffer her to be led into captivity 'the Lord knew whither, for she did not'.[22] No miracle was forthcoming and she embarked at the Privy Stairs with the two peers, three of the Queen's ladies and three of her own, her gentleman usher and two grooms. The barge was cast off and rowed away downstream. The nightmare – the horror which had been lying in wait for Elizabeth in the dark places of her mind all her conscious life – was a nightmare no longer. It was actually happening in the bleak daylight of a wet Sunday morning. Not quite eighteen years ago her mother had travelled on this same river to the same destination. It would surely be a crowning irony if Thomas Wyatt, whose father had loved Anne Boleyn, was now to drag Anne's daughter down with him.

In their haste to be rid of their uncomfortable charge, Sussex and

Winchester had misjudged the tide and there was a tense moment under the bridge when the barge 'struck upon the ground, the fall was so big and the water so shallow'. Then they were through and the grey, ghost-ridden bulk of the Tower loomed ahead. It was the end of Elizabeth's journey. Here her mother had died with the five young men accused of being her lovers. Her mother's cousin – poor, silly, wanton Katherine Howard – had come this way by water from Syon House. There were so many others – Tom Seymour and Tom's brother; Northumberland, 'that great devil'; Suffolk, the weak fool; her own cousin, Jane Grey, with whom Elizabeth had once shared lessons and gone to Christmas parties and who had met the executioner with such perfect courage – this had been the end of the journey for them all.

Now the boatmen were shipping their oars and tying up at the Water Gate – Traitor's Gate. And still Elizabeth was struggling. At first she refused to land, she was no traitor, besides she would be over her shoes in water. The two lords had gone on ahead, but when they were told the prisoner would not come Winchester turned back and told her brutally that she could not choose. He offered her his cloak, which she rejected 'with a good dash' and then, with one foot on the stairs, exclaimed: 'Here landeth as true a subject, being a prisoner, as ever landed at these stairs; and before Thee, O God, I speak it, having none other friends but Thee alone!' If that were so, said Winchester, unimpressed, it was the better for her. A company of soldiers and Tower warders were drawn up on the landing-stage and Elizabeth took the opportunity of making another little speech for their benefit. 'O Lord,' she said, 'I never thought to have come in here as prisoner; and I pray you all, good friends and fellows, bear me witness that I come in no traitor, but as true a woman to the Queen's majesty as any is now living; and thereon will I take my death.' She was rewarded by a voice from the ranks crying 'God preserve your Grace!' and, turning to the Lord Chamberlain, Sir John Gage, she asked if all these harnessed men were for her. 'No, madam' was the reply, and another voice added helpfully that it was the use so to be, when any prisoner came thither. But Elizabeth was not going to have her effect spoilt. 'Yes,' she insisted mournfully, 'I know it is so. It needed not for me, being, alas! but a weak woman.' A few steps further on she suddenly stopped and sank down 'upon a cold stone'. 'Madam, you were best to come out of the rain,' said the Lieutenant of the Tower, 'for you sit unwholesomely.' 'It is better sitting here than in a worse place,' answered Elizabeth, 'for God knoweth, I know not, whither you will bring me.' This was too much for her gentleman usher, who burst into tears and was promptly rounded on by his mistress demanding to know what he meant 'so uncomfortably to use her, seeing she took him to be her comforter, and not to dismay her'. Especially, she added sharply, since she knew her truth to be such that no man had cause to weep for her. Then, her courage restored, or perhaps having played out the scene to her satisfaction, she got up from her wet stone and swept on into the Tower.

She was lodged in the Bell Tower, and Winchester and Sir John Gage began at once to 'lock the doors very straitly' and to discuss further security arrangements. But the Earl of Sussex, who had throughout shown himself more compassionate – or more long-sighted – intervened. They would be wise, he pointed out, not to be over-zealous and to remember that Elizabeth was 'the King our master's daughter' as well as being the Queen's sister. 'Therefore,' said Sussex, 'let us use such dealing that we may answer it hereafter, if it shall so happen; for just dealing is always answerable.' This significant reminder that their prisoner might yet become their Queen seems to have gone home, and the escort departed a trifle thoughtfully.[23]

Elizabeth might have been cheered if she had known just how deeply the government was divided on the subject of her future, and that it was only after heated discussion and because no one would accept the responsibility of her safe-keeping that the decision to send her to the Tower had been taken. Sussex told her that several members of the Privy Council 'were sorry for her trouble' and, he himself was sorry he had lived to see this day; but now, abandoned in the prison which seemed only too likely soon to become her grave, there was little comfort to be gained from mere sympathy and her spirits sank to a very low ebb. Years later she was to tell a foreign ambassador how, having no hope of escape, she had planned to beg the Queen, as a last favour, to have a French swordsman brought over for her execution as had been done for Anne Boleyn – anything rather than suffer the clumsy butchery of the axe.

11

Elizabeth, Prisoner

In spite of all the passions it had aroused; in spite of the fact that it had already led to one of the most serious rebellions against the authority of the crown in living memory, and that popular opposition still rumbled ominously, preparations for the royal wedding continued to go forward. Count Egmont, who had slipped unobtrusively away while the trouble was at its height, returned to England early in March, bringing with him the ratification of the marriage treaty, and on the sixth Philip and Mary had been formally betrothed in the binding form of *verba de praesenti*, with Egmont standing proxy. In fact, all that was lacking now was the presence of the bridegroom, but Simon Renard, only too conscious of his heavy responsibilities, had begun to have serious misgivings about the wisdom of allowing the Prince to hazard his precious person in a country so ungrateful for the honour bestowed on it – at least as long as Elizabeth and Courtenay were alive to provide figure-heads for future insurrections. In Renard's opinion a more than suspicious negligence was being shown over bringing these two 'great persons' to trial, and could only conclude that 'delays were being created in the hope that something may crop up to save them'.[1]

Renard saw the Queen on Easter Sunday and took advantage of the occasion to express some of his doubts on the subject of Philip's future safety. He indicated, in the most tactful manner, that until 'every necessary step' had been taken he would not feel able to recommend the Prince's coming to her country. The blackmail was implicit and Mary replied, with tears in her eyes, that 'she would rather never have been born than that any harm should be done to his Highness'.[2] She promised to see to it that Elizabeth's and Courtenay's trials were over before his arrival.

However, it was continuing to prove unexpectedly difficult to collect enough evidence against either of the suspects even to begin proceedings. As far as Courtenay was concerned, the circumstances were certainly suspicious and there had certainly been a good deal of loose talk; but he had not apparently actually *done* anything. He had not gone down Devonshire. He had not at any time taken up arms against the Queen. He had not attempted to escape. The plan to marry him to Elizabeth had been openly suggested by William Paget, a member of the Privy Council, the previous autumn; but Courtenay had rejected it, on the grounds that it would be beneath the dignity of one of his unblemished lineage, and there was no evidence that he had ever had any secret correspondence with her. Renard suspected that Stephen Gardiner was deliberately shielding his young friend, but had there been any direct proof against Courtenay it is unlikely that the Chancellor's influence could have saved him. As for Elizabeth herself, nothing fresh had so far come to light. Wyatt was being kept alive in the hope that he might yet be induced to incriminate her further, but although he is said to have signed a statement to this effect no such document has ever come to light.

About a week after her committal to the Tower, the Princess was visited by Gardiner and some other members of the Council, who 'examined her of the talk that was at Ashridge, betwixt her and Sir James Crofts, concerning her removing from thence to Donnington Castle, requiring her to declare what she meant thereby'. In spite of her vehement protestations of innocence, Elizabeth seems to have been a little touchy on the subject of Donnington. She began by saying that she did not even remember owning a house of that name but then, perhaps seeing that this would not do, she pulled herself together and admitted that she did have such a place, but had never been there in her life and could not remember anyone suggesting that she should. She was then confronted with James Crofts and asked by Gardiner what she had to say to him? Elizabeth replied calmly that she had little to say to him, or 'the rest that were then prisoners in the Tower'. 'But my lords', she went on, 'you do examine every mean prisoner of me, wherein, methinks, you do me great injury. If they have done evil, and offended the Queen's majesty, let them answer it accordingly. I beseech you, join not me in this sort with any of these offenders.' Having regained command of the situation, she proceeded to dispose of the subject of Donnington. She remembered now, she said, that there had been some talk between James Crofts and certain officers of her household about the possibility of her moving there, but what was that to the purpose? Surely she had a perfect right to go to one of her own houses at any time?

It was at this point that the Earl of Arundel, who was a member of the examining body, unexpectedly fell on his knees exclaiming, 'Your Grace saith true, and certainly we are very sorry that we have so troubled you about so vain matters.' Elizabeth took her cue at once. 'My lords, you do sift me very narrowly,' she said, with a sad, reproachful dignity, 'but well I am assured you shall not do more to me than God hath appointed; and so God forgive you all.'[3] Since Arundel was one of the leaders of the pro-Spanish faction on the Council and therefore counted as one of her enemies, his outburst must have encouraged Elizabeth considerably. Exactly what lay behind his sudden change of heart remains obscure but he may have begun to feel, like Sussex, that it would be wise to think of the future. In fact, he later became one of the most determined of her

English suitors, so perhaps Elizabeth was already fishing for men's souls 'with so sweet a bait that no one could escape her network', and perhaps Arundel was among the first of those poor fish 'who little knew what snare was laid for them'.[4]

The Lord Chancellor, on the other hand, after a period of hesitation, had apparently made up his mind that the Princess would have to be sacrificed. He told Renard at the beginning of April that 'as long as Elizabeth lived he had no hope of seeing the kingdom in peace'. Renard himself continued to impress on the Queen how essential it was to have Elizabeth and Courtenay tried and executed to make England safe for Philip; but he was irritated to discover that, as matters stood, the laws of England did not provide penalties applicable – at any rate to Elizabeth. The Queen assured him that fresh proof against the Princess was coming in every day 'and there were several witnesses to assert that she had gathered together stores and weapons in order to rise with the rest and fortify a house in the country, whither she had been sending her provisions'.[5] The house in the country was, presumably, Donnington, but this apparently promising line of enquiry had already turned into a blind alley, and Elizabeth swore that any defensive preparations made at Ashridge were simply as a protection against the Duke of Suffolk, who had been in the neighbourhood at the time. Unpalatable though it might be to some, the fact remained that the government were no nearer to making out a case against her than they had been two months earlier.

Meanwhile, even in the Tower, life settled down into a daily routine. To begin with there had been some housekeeping problems. Elizabeth had to provide (and pay for) her own and her attendants' food, and the officers of her household responsible for making such provision found they had to deliver their mistress's diet into the hands of 'common rascal soldiers' at the outer gate of the fortress. This seemed to Elizabeth's people both dangerous and unsuitable and they accordingly waited on the Lord Chamberlain to protest, 'beseeching his honour to consider her Grace and to give such order that her viands might at all times be brought in by them which were appointed thereunto'. They got short shrift from Sir John Gage, who declared that the Princess was a prisoner to be served with the Lieutenant's men like any other, and he saw no reason why she should be given preferential treatment. The deputation took offence at these 'ungrateful words', whereupon Sir John lost his temper and 'sware by God (striking himself upon the breast), that if they did either frown or shrug at him, he would set them where they should see neither sun nor moon'. However, representations were made at a higher level, with the result that Elizabeth's servants were given permission to bring her food in and cook and serve it themselves. The Lord Chamberlain, who was also acting Constable of the Tower, did not at first take kindly to having his authority set aside but when, after some skirmishing in the kitchen, he contrived to secure the services of the Princess's cook for himself as well, matters went more smoothly. 'And good cause why,' observed John Foxe sardonically, 'for he had good cheer and fared of the best, and her Grace paid well for it.'[6]

After about a month's close confinement and 'being very evil at ease therewithal', Elizabeth began to agitate for some fresh air and exercise. At first she was only allowed to walk in the Queen's lodgings, 'the windows being shut and she not suffered to look out at any of them', but presently this licence was extended to include a small garden, 'the doors and gates being shut up'.[7] There were other slight diversions in the shape of the five-year-old son of the Keeper of the Wardrobe, who brought the Princess posies of spring flowers, and two little girls – Susanna, who was 'not above three or four years old', and another who came to give the captive a tiny bunch of keys, so that she might unlock the gates and go abroad.[8] These touching visits were, however, brought to an abrupt end by the Lord Chamberlain, in case the children might be used to convey other, less innocent, messages.

The Tower was crowded with political prisoners at this time, and stringent measures were in force to prevent any unauthorised person from speaking to, or even seeing, the Princess. As well as several officers of her own household, there were a number of old friends among her fellow inmates. John Harington, who had once been Tom Seymour's man, was now undergoing one of those periodic spells in jail which were an occupational hazard for anyone connected with the great, and Elizabeth's childhood playmate Robert Dudley and his surviving brothers were still suffering the consequences of their father's ill-judged activities of the previous summer. A long-standing tradition maintains that, despite all official precautions, Elizabeth and Robert Dudley managed to meet in prison and lay the foundations of their peculiar, life-long relationship. If this is true, it must at least have helped to alleviate the gloom and boredom of their incarceration.

Thomas Wyatt was finally executed on 11 April. On the scaffold he explicitly exonerated both Elizabeth and Courtenay from having had any guilty knowledge of the rebellion, and although the government attempted to suppress or deny it the news spread rapidly and joyfully through the City. It was now clear that there was no chance whatever of getting a legal conviction against the Princess. Barely a week after Wyatt's execution Nicholas Throckmorton was acquitted of a charge of treason by a London jury, and there were renewed demonstrations against both the Queen's religion and her marriage. A dead cat, dressed as a priest, was found hanging on the gallows in Cheapside. Pamphlets were scattered in the streets – one adjuring all Englishmen to stand firm and keep out the Prince of Spain – another, so Renard reported angrily, 'as seditious as possible and in favour of the Lady Elizabeth'. There had also been the scandalous but ingenious affair of 'The Voice in the Wall' which, when addressed with the words 'God Save Queen Mary' remained silent, but responded to 'God Save the Lady Elizabeth' with an emphatic 'So be it'. This remarkable phenomenon attracted admiring crowds until the Voice was unmasked as a servant girl, cunningly concealed in an empty house.

Quite apart from the inflamed state of public opinion, the Council itself was split from top to bottom. On 22 April Renard sent the Emperor a vivid word-picture of the situation. 'Since I last wrote', his despatch began, 'quarrels, jealousy and ill-will have increased among the Councillors, becoming so public that several of them, out of spite, no longer attend the meetings. What one does, another undoes; what one advises, another opposes; one strives to save Courtenay, another Elizabeth; and such is the confusion that one can only expect the upshot to be arms and tumult.' Renard believed that the Queen would be persuaded to pardon Courtenay altogether, and, as for Elizabeth, 'the lawyers can find no sufficient evidence to condemn her'. 'Even if there were evidence,' he went on, 'they would not dare to proceed against her because her relative, the Admiral, has espoused her cause, and controls all the forces of England.'[9] There had already been some high words between Lord William Howard and John Gage on the subject of Elizabeth, and the influential Lord Admiral certainly opposed any undue show of severity towards his great-niece.

Elizabeth owed her apparently miraculous preservation to a number of factors – her own unfathomable discretion, the surprising strength of her popularity, government weakness and lack of direction – but most of all she owed it to her sister. Early in March the Queen had told Renard bitterly that 'Elizabeth's character was just what she had always believed it to be' but, in spite of her personal dislike of the girl and in spite of the pressure being exerted on her most vulnerable flank, Mary remained true to her principles. Her conscience had insisted on a painstaking examination of all the evidence, and although she herself remained highly sceptical, as long as the case remained 'not proven', Elizabeth would continue to be given the benefit of any doubt.

The fear of judicial execution might have receded, but Elizabeth knew she was by no means out of the wood. Renard had not abandoned his efforts to get her removed before Philip's arrival, and if she could not be put to death there were other – though admittedly less efficient – ways of disposing of her. In the present mood of the country any attempt to persuade Parliament to disinherit her would obviously be pointless, but there was still marriage; not, of course, marriage to an Englishman, but one of the Emperor's vassals who could be trusted to keep her safely under control. Emmanuel Philibert, Duke of Savoy and Prince of Piedmont, seemed the most suitable candidate and his name was to become wearisomely familiar to Elizabeth as time went by.

Other less obvious but equally nerve-wracking fears kept her awake at night and dogged her through the long, monotonous days. Mary's always precarious health had not been improved by the strain of the past few months and there were those among her friends with little to hope for from her successor. Thoughts of some desperate act which could not be undone must have passed through several minds. Elizabeth took what precautions she could against poison and a rumour went round that a warrant for her immediate execution, 'subscribed with certain hands of the Council', had been delivered to the Lieutenant of the Tower, but honest John Brydges, fortunately noticing that the Queen's signature was missing, refused to act upon it.

Then, on 5 May, Sir John Gage was relieved of his office as Constable and 'one Sir Henry Bedingfield placed in his room'. Bedingfield marched in to take over command of the Tower bringing with him a hundred men in blue liveries, and Elizabeth's reaction to this 'sudden mutation', at least as described by John Foxe, clearly illustrates her state of mind. The arrival of Sir Henry, being 'a man unknown to her Grace and therefore the more feared', seems to have induced a fit of panic. She demanded to be told 'whether the Lady Jane's scaffold were taken away or no?' Reassured on this point, but still not entirely satisfied, she went on to ask who Sir Henry Bedingfield was and whether, 'if her murdering were secretly committed to his charge, he would see the execution thereof?'[10]

In the circumstances, Elizabeth's alarm was understandable but it proved groundless. Henry Bedingfield was no ogre. A stolid country squire in his mid-forties from Oxborough in Norfolk, he was a staunch Catholic and one of those gentlemen who, with their tenantry, had gone to Mary's aid when she was standing embattled at Framlingham the year before. He was also, ironically enough, son of Edmund Bedingfield who had been Catherine of Aragon's custodian during her last sad years at Kimbolton Castle. As Elizabeth's jailer, Sir Henry has naturally come in for a lot of hard words from such vigorous Protestant partisans as John Foxe, but in actual fact he seems to have performed an unenviable task, if not with much tact or imagination, at least with resolute and incorruptible integrity.

The question of the Princess's future had become something of an embarrassment to the government. She could not be left in the Tower indefinitely but she was still under too much of a cloud to be set free. Neither would it be 'honourable, safe nor reasonable' to expect the Queen to receive her at court. Some face-saving formula would have to be found and Mary fell back on the time-honoured expedient of sending her sister to live under restraint in a remote country house. After a period of some indecision, the manor of Woodstock – once a hunting-lodge favoured by the Plantagenets – had been chosen, although Renard would have preferred a castle in the North, where the people were Catholics.

Having been officially consigned to Bedingfield's charge, Elizabeth left the Tower on Saturday, 19 May, at one o'clock in the afternoon and was taken by river to Richmond. Antoine de Noailles, although in disgrace with the Queen for dabbling in Wyatt's treason, was still taking a close interest in the Princess and had picked up a rumour that two envoys from the Emperor were to meet her at Richmond on the following day and would 'lay before her the proposals for her marriage with the Duke of Savoy'. In order to try to find out more about what was going on, de Noailles sent one of his agents to follow Elizabeth 'under the pretext of carrying her a present of apples', but he had been misinformed. There were no envoys at Richmond, and Bedingfield got an early opportunity to prove his zeal by seizing the messenger and stripping him to his shirt.[11] Fortunately there was nothing on him but the apples, though it was possibly as a result of this incident that the Princess was again separated from her own people 'which were lodged in out-chambers'. Whether she still harboured suspicions of Bedingfield's intentions or was just sick of the whole dreary business, Elizabeth – at any rate according to Foxe – seems to have thought herself in some special danger, for she called to her gentleman usher as he left her 'and desired him with the rest of his company to pray for her: "For this night", quoth she, "I think to die"'.[12]

However, the night, though 'doleful', passed quietly and next morning the cavalcade set off for Woodstock. Elizabeth, who was riding in a warped and broken litter, did not hesitate to say that she was being led 'like a sheep to the slaughter'; but in fact the journey soon turned into something suspiciously like a triumphal progress. Bedingfield, conscientiously reporting from Sir William Dormer's house at West Wycombe at the end of the second day, told the Council that: 'Her grace passed the town of Windsor with much gazing of people unto Eton College, where was used the like, as well by the scholars as other; the like in villages and fields unto Wycombe where most gazing was used, and the wives had prepared cake and wafers which, at her passing by them, they delivered into the litter. She received it with thanks until by the quantity she was accombered . . . and desired the people to cease.'[13] The next day, at Aston, the church bells were rung for her and that night was spent at Lord William's house at Ricote, where 'her grace was marvellously well entertained'. In fact Bedingfield considered that Lord Williams had rather overdone his hospitality to one who was, after all, 'the Queen's majesty's prisoner and no otherwise' and warned that there might be 'after-claps' of royal displeasure; but his lordship replied sharply that 'he was well advised of his doings', adding 'that her grace might and should in his house be merry'.[14]

All the rest of the way, through the Oxfordshire villages of Wheatley and Stanton St John, Islip and Gosford, the country people crowded the roadside to cheer the Princess as she passed with cries of 'God save your Grace', and Bedingfield must have breathed a sign of relief when he finally got his charge to Woodstock. The house itself turned out to be in a state of considerable dilapidation. Elizabeth was accommodated in the gatehouse, where four rooms had been prepared for her, but Sir Henry was disquieted to find that only three doors in the whole building could be locked and barred. To do him justice, he was as nervous of possible assassins getting in, as of his prisoner getting out.

Elizabeth was to spend nearly ten months in detention at Woodstock under conditions which, though irksome, were hardly intolerable. Bedingfield was responsible for seeing 'that neither she be suffered to have conference with any suspected person out of his hearing, nor that she do by any means either receive or send any message, letter or token to or from any manner of person'. However, the Queen's instructions were that her sister was to be treated 'in such good and honourable sort as may be agreeable to our honour and her estate and degree'.[15] Elizabeth had a respectable number of servants to wait on her. She was able to walk in the 'over and nether gardens' and the orchard, and was also to be allowed any books, within reason, to help pass the time. All the same, it was not a very stimulating existence and, once the Princess had recovered from her initial distrust of Bedingfield, she could not resist teasing him with demands for all sorts of small indulgences. Sir Henry, never quite sure whether she was in earnest or not and 'marvellously perplexed whether to grant her desires or to say her nay', took refuge in clinging tenaciously to the letter of his instructions and insisting on referring every detail to London. He was not above getting in an occasional sly dig on his own account. Elizabeth had been asking for that suspiciously heretical object, an English Bible, and Bedingfield offered her instead some Latin books which he had by him, 'wherein, as I thought,' he reported blandly, 'she should have more delight, seeing she understandeth the same so well'. Elizabeth retaliated by accusing him of failing to pass on any of her requests to the Council and then refused to speak to him.[16] However, there does not seem to have been any real malice on either side and the relationship between prisoner and custodian came to be based on a grudging but mutual respect.

Although she may have derived a certain amount of amusement from baiting Sir Henry, Elizabeth had a more serious underlying purpose. The events of the past few months had plainly demonstrated the importance of public opinion as a weapon in her armoury; but memories were short and she was evidently afraid that, buried in the country, she might be forgotten and that Renard would seize the opportunity to have her shipped abroad. In spite of Bedingfield's care, she may have got wind of a scheme, currently being propounding by the Emperor, to send her to Brussels to the court of his sister, the Dowager Queen of Hungary. At any rate, Elizabeth had no intentions of allowing the authorities to forget her, and on 12 June Bedingfield apologised to the Council for the fact that he was being 'enforced, by the importunate desires of this great lady, to trouble your lordships with more letters than be contentful to mine own opinion'.

Elizabeth was now nagging for permission to write to the Queen herself and eventually got it, although it does not appear to have done her much good. Mary's only response was to send Bedingfield a terse note, telling him that she did not wish to receive any more of her sister's 'disguised and colourable letters'. This having been faithfully reported to Elizabeth, she demanded that Bedingfield should write to the Council on her behalf. When he refused, she told him that she was being worse treated than any prisoner in the Tower and, on second thoughts, worse than the worst prisoner in Newgate.

She was ill again towards the end of June with a recurrence of her nephritis, being 'daily vexed with swelling in the face and other parts of her body'. She wanted the Queen's physicians to be sent down to Woodstock, but for various reasons they were not available. Dr Owen wrote to Bedingfield explaining that her grace's body was 'replenished with many cold and waterish humours, which will not be taken away but by purgations meet and convenient for that purpose'. However, apparently it was not the right time of year for such ministrations and Elizabeth would have 'to take some patience'. In the meantime, Owen sent a diet-sheet for her to follow which 'would preserve her grace from the increase of such humours', and recommended the services of Dr Barnes and Dr Walbeck, 'two honest and learned men remaining at Oxford'. But, although she continued to be 'very evil at ease', the Princess indignantly refused to make any strangers privy to the estate of her body and preferred, she said, to commit it to God.[17]

So the battle went on. In July the Queen agreed to allow Elizabeth 'to write her mind' to the Council via Bedingfield. The letter granting this concession was dated the seventh, but it was three weeks before the prisoner condescended to take advantage of it. 'My Lady Elizabeth,' wrote Bedingfield at last,

> this present 30th of July, required me to make report of her grace's mind as her suit to your honours, to be means to the Queen's majesty on her behalf to this effect. To beseech your lordships all to consider her woeful case, that being but once licensed to write as an humble suitress unto the Queen's highness, and received thereby no such comfort as she hoped to have done, but to her further discomfort in a message by me opened, that it was the Queen's highness's pleasure not to be any more molested with her grace's letters. That it may please the same, and that upon every pity, considering her long imprisonment and restraint of liberty, either to charge her with special matter to be answered unto and tried, or to grant her liberty to come unto her highness's presence, which she sayeth she would not desire were it not that she knoweth herself to be clear even before God, for her allegiance.

Elizabeth ended her appeal by requiring Bedingfield 'to move chiefly' those members of the Council who had been executors 'of the Will of the King's majesty her father' and requesting that the Queen would at least allow some of them to visit her and hear her state her case in person. 'Whereby she may take release not to think herself utterly desolate of all refuge in this world.'[18] Deferentially phrased though it was, the mention of King Henry's Will was a shrewd reminder that, outcast and disgraced though she might be, Elizabeth still remained the heiress-presumptive.

Meanwhile, having delayed for as long as he decently could, Philip of Spain had finally arrived in England. He disembarked at Southampton on 20 July and five days later he and Mary were married in Winchester Cathedral amid scenes of great splendour. Philip, a good-looking young man of twenty-seven, privately considered himself a sacrifice on the altar – literally – of political expediency, but in public he and his train was studiously polite. On 18 August the Queen brought her bridegroom in triumph to London. The gallows had been removed and decorates more suitable to the occasion substituted. The citizens, well primed with free drink, were in a benevolent mood and, although there was plenty of jealousy and backbiting behind the scenes at court, and the Spaniards complained they were being charged twenty-five times the proper price for everything in the shops, on the surface things went reasonably well.

Elizabeth may have hoped that Mary would soften towards her, now that she had achieved her heart's desire, but Mary, apparently absorbed in gaiety, made no sign and Elizabeth had to possess herself in patience as best she could. According to the story preserved by Foxe and Holinshed, it was at Woodstock that she scratched 'with her diamond in a glass window very legibly' the famous couplet:

> Much suspected of me,
> Nothing proved can be:
> Quoth Elizabeth, prisoner.

It seems uncharacteristic of Elizabeth that she would have gone so far as even to admit anything *could* have been proved. More credible is the old tale that she envied the freedom of 'a certain milkmaid singing pleasantly' in the Park, saying that 'her case was better and life more merrier'.[19] Once, in a fit of pious resignation, she wrote on the flyleaf of her edition of the Epistles of St Paul: 'I walk many times into the pleasant fields of the Holy Scriptures, where I pluck up the goodlisome herbes of sentences by pruning, eat them by reading, chew them by musing, and lay them up at length in the high seat of memorie, by gathering them together, that so having tasted their sweetness I may less perceive the bitterness of this miserable life.'[20]

She was by no means always so resigned, however, and Bedingfield continued to be harassed by the various whims and importunities of 'this great lady', as he persistently referred to her. Elizabeth complained bitterly about the Council's failure to respond to her appeal and pestered Bedingfield to let her write again herself. When he refused to take the responsibility without first going through the usual channels, she told him that their lordships would smile in their sleeves at his 'scrupulosity'. But, after the necessary permission had been laboriously obtained and Bedingfield had doled out pen, ink and paper, the Princess changed her mind and made him write at her dictation, declaring haughtily that she was not accustomed to communicate with the Council except through a secretary and overriding his rather feeble protests.

Elizabeth's general tiresomeness was, in some ways, the least of Sir Henry's worries. He lived in daily dread of leaks appearing in his security system, and the activities of Thomas Parry in particular were a constant source of anxiety. As the Princess's cofferer, Parry was responsible for feeding and paying her household, and had set up his headquarters at the sign of The Bull in Woodstock village. The Bull, in Bedingfield's opinion, was 'a marvellous colourable place to practise in'. Elizabeth's servants were always finding excuses for slipping off there and it was becoming, Sir Henry was gloomily convinced, a haunt and resort for all her undesirable friends. As time went by, with no release in sight for anyone, other pressing problems began to arise. The house would have to be put into a better state of repair before the winter if they were not all to freeze to death. Already, in early October, the nights were becoming too long and cold for the Queen's soldiers to continue their watch 'standing upon the hill' and they would have to be brought within the gates. The men's pay, too, was a month in arrears, and the inhabitants of Woodstock were making it clear that unless some ready money was forthcoming soon they would cut off supplies. But, in spite of the heart-rending pictures drawn by Bedingfield of the plight of the soldiers and the poor folk of Woodstock, the government was very slow to respond and eventually he was forced to advance money to the local people out of his own pocket, to avoid, as he put it, 'their daily exclaiming'.[21]

On 28 October Dr Owen and Dr Wendy came down to see Elizabeth and took some blood from her arm and foot. 'Since which time,' reported Bedingfield, 'thanks be to God, as far as I see or hear, she doeth reasonably well.'[22] Probably the enforced period of rest and quiet had done her as much good as anything. At any rate, no more is heard about headaches or kidney trouble. The Council, however, remained deaf to her repeated appeals for her case to be reopened. The Queen was apparently determined to wring some admission of guilt and contrition from her sister before she would consider restoring her to liberty. The winter closed in and the household at Woodstock settled down grimly to wait out the contest of Tudor stubbornness.

In London, events were taking place which had temporarily pushed the problem of Elizabeth's future into the background. Mary believed she was pregnant, and on 12 November she and Philip together opened the Parliament which, if all went well, would see the re-establishment of

Rome's authority over the Church in England. On 24 November, Cardinal Pole, the first papal Legate to set foot on English soil since the days of Wolsey and Campeggio, came up-river from Gravesend. He brought with him the Pope's absolution for her excommunicated country, and as Mary greeted him she felt certain 'that the babe had quickened and leapt in her womb'.[23] Reginald Pole, who had been living in exile for nearly thirty years, was another offshoot of the Plantagenet tree, the son of Mary's old friend and governess the butchered Countess of Salisbury, and he was a reminder of happy childhood days as well as being the symbol of her future hopes.

A few days later the reconciliation with Rome had been effected. Parliament, in an orgy of emotional remorse, voted a 'supplication' and, as both Houses knelt 'in the Great Chamber of the Court at Westminster' to receive absolution from the Bishop of Winchester, England was taken back into the bosom of the Catholic Church. The negotiations leading up to this remarkable moment had been going on throughout the autumn, while watertight arrangements were devised to safeguard the property rights of all holders of Church lands. Once that was done, the Commons, who had been carefully chosen from 'the wise, grave and Catholic sort', were ready to undo the Reformation and restore the old laws and penalties against heresy.

As the time of Mary's delivery approached, the question of Elizabeth came once more into prominence. Stephen Gardiner was frankly of the opinion that any attempts to eradicate Protestantism in England would amount to no more than stripping the leaves and lopping the branches as long as the root of the evil – Elizabeth herself – remained untouched. Now was the time, he urged, to frame a Bill to disinherit her once and for all, but there was no enthusiasm for this project and it was quietly dropped. Philip's approach to the problem was a good deal more pragmatic. A measure had been passed which would give him the Regency if Mary died in child-birth and her child survived. But what if neither mother nor child survived? In the resulting chaos, he and his Spaniards would find themselves isolated among a hostile population and Elizabeth might then be a useful hostage. Anyway, he wanted the whole matter of the succession put on a regular basis. Elizabeth could not be left in limbo for ever and, according to Bedingfield, she was conducting herself like a good Catholic these days. Far better, reasoned Philip, to make a friend of this unknown young woman at a time when she was likely to be suitably grateful for his support. She could then be married to a Prince subservient to Spain, and the future of the English alliance would be secured.

On or about 20 April 1555, Bedingfield at last received a summons to convey his charge to Hampton Court, where the Queen had gone to prepare for her lying-in. Her journey from Woodstock was made in typical blustery spring weather, and on the first day out the party encountered violent gusts of wind which got under the ladies' skirts and more than once blew the Princess's hood from her head. She wanted to take shelter in a near-by gentleman's house to repair the ravages but Bedingfield, with his usual inflexibility, refused to allow even this slight deviation from his itinerary, and Elizabeth was obliged to do up her hair under a hedge as best she could.[24]

After three over-night stops – the last being at The George at Colnbrook, where about sixty of her gentlemen and yeomen had come to catch a glimpse of her – she entered Hampton Court 'on the back side'. She was still a closely guarded prisoner, but according to a French report Philip paid her a private visit three days after her arrival and the Queen sent a message telling her to be sure and wear her best clothes for the occasion.[25] Nearly another fortnight went by, and then she was waited on by the Lord Chancellor, the Earls of Arundel and Shrewsbury and the Secretary Petre. Elizabeth greeted them with the words: 'My lords, I am glad to see you; for methinks I have been kept a great while from you, desolately alone.' Gardiner went on his knees to her and begged her to submit herself to the Queen. If she did so, 'he had no doubt that her majesty would be good to her'. Elizabeth answered sharply that she would rather lie in prison all the days of her life. She wanted no mercy from the Queen, 'but rather desired the law, if ever she did offend her majesty in thought, word or deed'. Besides, she went on, 'in yielding, I should speak against myself and confess myself to be an offender, which I never was, towards her majesty, by occasion whereof the King and the Queen might ever hereafter conceive of me an evil opinion. And therefore I say, my lords, it were better for me to lie in prison for the truth, than to be abroad and suspected of my prince.'

Next day, Gardiner returned to the attack. The Queen marvelled, he told her, 'that she would so stoutly use herself, not confessing that she had offended'. It made it look as if she thought she had been wrongfully imprisoned. No, replied Elizabeth, the Queen must deal with her as she felt it right. 'Well,' said Gardiner, 'her majesty willeth me to tell you that you must tell another tale ere that you be set at liberty.' Elizabeth would only repeat that she would rather stay in prison 'with honesty and truth' than go free under a cloud. 'And this that I have said I will stand unto,' she declared, 'for I will never belie myself.' Gardiner tried another tack. Dropping on his knees again, he said: 'Then your grace hath the vantage of me, and other the lords, for your wrong and long imprisonment.' 'What vantage I have', answered the Princess, 'you know; taking God to record I seek no vantage at your hands for your so dealing with me. But God forgive you and me also.'[26]

It looked like stalemate. There was silence for a week. Then, without any warning, at ten o'clock one night, came a summons for Elizabeth to go at once to the Queen. She had been angling for a personal interview for over a year, but now the moment had arrived she was understandably shaken. It was probably to cover her nervousness, in case it might be misconstrued, that she asked her attendants to pray for her, saying 'she could not tell whether ever she should see them again or no'.

Susan Clarencieux, Mary's close friend and Mistress of the Robes, had come to fetch her, and escorted by Bedingfield, with her ladies following and her gentleman usher and grooms of the chamber going before to light the way. Elizabeth walked the short distance across the garden in the summer night till she reached the foot of the staircase which led to the Queen's lodging. There the procession halted. Bedingfield and the others waited outside while Elizabeth, accompanied only by Susan Clarencieux and one of her own ladies, went up the stairs to her sister's bedroom. Without waiting for Mary to speak, she knelt and once again proclaimed her innocence. She was a true subject and begged the Queen so to judge of her. She would not be found the contrary, whatsoever reports had gone of her. 'You will not confess your offence', said Mary out of the shadows, 'but stand stoutly to your truth. I pray God it may so fall out.' 'If it doth not,' answered Elizabeth, 'I request neither favour nor pardon at your majesty's hands.' 'Well,' came the somewhat ungracious rejoinder, 'you stiffly still persevere in your truth. Belike you will not confess but that you have been wrongfully punished.' 'I must not say so, if it please your majesty, to you.' 'Why then,' persisted the Queen, 'belike you will to others.' 'No, if it please your majesty, I have borne the burden and must bear it. I humbly beseech your majesty to have a good opinion of me, and to think me to be your true subject, not only from the beginning, but for ever, as long as life lasteth.'

Looking at the supple figure kneeling before her in the candlelight, Mary knew she had lost the battle of wills. She must accept, however reluctantly, Elizabeth's movingly worded assurances of loyalty and make her peace with Anne Boleyn's daughter. There is a tradition that Philip was present at their meeting, hidden behind a curtain – a tradition based perhaps on the report that Mary made some remark in her husband's language. The interview ended with a few 'comfortable' words from the Queen, but, added John Foxe darkly, 'what she said in Spanish, God knoweth'.[27]

12

'A Second Person'

About a week after that nocturnal interview with Mary, Elizabeth said goodbye to Henry Bedingfield – it would probably be difficult to say whether prisoner or jailer was the more relieved – and his departure marked the end of a period of close restraint which had lasted just over fifteen months. The Princess remained at Hampton Court still under a limited form of surveillance, not appearing in public outside her own rooms. She was, however, able to set up her own household again, and some of the courtiers were given permission to visit her, although, commented the Venetian ambassador, 'they all avail themselves of it with great reserve'.[1]

In the circumstances, such caution was hardly surprising. At no time since the days of the Wars of the Roses had England been in such a nervous and unsettled state. The government was weak, divided and unpopular. The uncertain outcome of the Queen's impending childbed, bringing with it the dread of another minority, dominated this time by a Spanish regency, hung like a fog blotting out the future. To make matters gloomier still, the religious persecution which has left such an indelible stain on the memory of Mary's reign had now begun. The first heretics went to the stake in February 1555, and the burnings were to continue intermittently for the next three years. In all some three hundred people, including sixty women, suffered this peculiarly horrific form of death. It was not, however, by contemporary standards, an especially vicious campaign (by contemporary Continental standards it was mild), and it has to be remembered that in the eyes of the government Protestantism had, with justification, become synonymous with sedition, treason and open rebellion. It nevertheless remains an unpleasant episode – one of its least attractive features being the fact that the vast majority of the victims were humble people. The better-to-do Protestants either conformed just sufficiently to satisfy the authorities' not very exacting standards, or else went abroad more or less unhindered. From the point of view of what it hoped to achieve, the Marian persecution was a total and monumental failure in tactics. By giving the Reformers their martyrology, it also gave them respectability in the eyes of many to whom they had formerly appeared as little more than a gang of violent, loud-mouthed trouble-makers. The deaths of the Bishops Hooper, Latimer and Ridley who, with

Thomas Cranmer, were virtually the only sufferers of note, did indeed light such a candle in England as, with God's grace, never was put out. Apart from a certain native distaste for religious persecution *per se*, Catholicism, in the current political climate, began to become ineradicably associated with foreign oppression in the minds of Englishmen, and now were sown the seeds of an implacable fear and hatred of Rome and all its works. These seeds, carefully watered by the outpourings of such men as John Foxe (the Protestants always did have the edge in the propaganda war), blossomed and burgeoned over the remainder of the century and, indeed, over three centuries to come.

As Head of State, Mary must, of course, bear ultimate responsibility for the acts committed in her name, but how far she personally initiated the persecution which earned her her unenviable nickname remains in some doubt. In many ways she was the most merciful of her family. Certainly towards her political enemies her leniency bordered on recklessness. Even the retribution visited on the Wyatt rebels was soon being tempered by the Queen's clemency, a clemency which extended beyond the rank and file. Edward Courtenay, after a period of incarceration at Fortheringay Castle, had been released shortly before Elizabeth was brought up from Woodstock, and sent to travel abroad. However doubtful his guilt, he would not have been so fortunate under Henry VIII. There had been a general spring-cleaning, too, at the Tower and the remaining prisoners left over from both the Northumberland and Wyatt affairs were pardoned and dispersed to their homes. Henry VIII would never have taken such a risk; neither would his younger daughter. Treason against herself Mary was ready to forgive, but heresy smacked of treason against God and that was another matter. The heretics were also imperilling their immortal souls and infecting others by their example. To Mary it would have been an unforgivable dereliction of duty – the duty so clearly laid upon her by the Almighty – if she had not tried by every means at her disposal to save her unhappy subjects from themselves.

It was against this background of uncertainty and fear, made even more depressing by a wet summer when the corn failed to ripen, that the tragic farce of the Queen's false pregnancy played itself out. By April all was ready for the arrival of the 'young master'. Midwives, nurses and rockers were in attendance, the cradle prepared and waiting, and the court crowded with noble ladies come to assist at the Queen's delivery. At daybreak on 30 April, a rumour circulated in the capital that Mary had given birth to a son the night before 'with little pain and no danger'. So circumstantial was the report that it was generally believed and, before anyone could stop them, the citizens had shut up shop and surged into the streets in search of the customary free food and drink. Bonfires were lit and 'there was great ringing through London, and in divers places Te Deum Laudamus sung'.[2] It was afternoon before messengers returning from Hampton Court brought the dispiriting news that not only had there been so safe delivery, but that it was not even imminent.

The days lengthened into weeks, weeks into months, gossip in the alehouses grew more and more ribald and eventually the fact had to be faced that there was no 'young master' or mistress either, and had never been one. The amenorrhea and digestive troubles to which Mary had always been subject, possibly, too, an incipient tumour, had combined with her desperate longing which – according to the omniscient Venetians – even produced 'swelling of the paps and their emission of milk' to create that pathetic self-deception.

For Elizabeth the tension of those early summer months must have been especially trying. If, against all the odds, Mary were now to bear a child, then, of course, her own prospects would be ruined and she would probably be reduced to accepting whatever marriage Philip and the Queen chose to arrange for her. Anxiety about the future apparently drove her surreptitiously to consult the famous astrologer, Dr Dee. Someone laid information, and Dee and three of Elizabeth's servants were arrested for having conspired to calculate 'the King's and Queen's and my Lady Elizabeth's nativity'. Elizabeth herself contrived to avoid direct involvement. Perhaps the report that both the informant's children had been stricken 'the one with present death, the other with blindness', discouraged too close an investigation.[3]

Elizabeth also took the opportunity to embark on a cautious flirtation with Philip, while Mary remained lurking miserably in the increasingly foetid atmosphere of the Palace. The Princess was as interested in her brother-in-law's friendship as he in hers, and there is evidence to suggest that he found her physically attractive. Two years later, when the Venetian ambassador, Giovanni Michiel, was compiling a detailed report on his tour of duty in England for the Senate, he observed that 'at the time of the Queen's pregnancy, Lady Elizabeth . . . contrived so to ingratiate herself with all the Spaniards, and especially with the King, that ever since no one has favoured her more than he does'. So much so that, in Michiel's opinion, it implied 'some particular design on the part of the King towards her'.[4] Years later still, according to the account of William Cecil's son Thomas, Philip himself was heard to admit that 'whatever he suffered from Queen Elizabeth was the just judgement of God, because, being married to Queen Mary, whom he thought a most virtuous and good lady, yet in the fancy of love he could not affect her; but as for the Lady Elizabeth, he was enamoured of her, being a fair and beautiful woman'. As for Queen Elizabeth, she was to boast cheerfully that since their enmity had begun with love no one need think they could not get on together at any time she chose. The Queen was never afflicted with false modesty about her conquests, real or imaginary, though it is not likely on this occasion that she expected to be taken seriously. All the same, there is something curiously poignant in the picture of those two life-long antagonists – the elegant, fair-haired little Prince, heir to half the thrones of Europe but always careful of his dignity, as if to compensate for his unfortunate lack of inches, and the pale, red-headed girl of doubtful birth and dubious reputation, whose regality was yet instinctive and unconscious – walking together in the gardens of Wolsey's sumptuous red-brick mansion or under the dripping trees in the Park in the intense greenness of that far-off English summer, Elizabeth exerting herself to charm as only she knew how and acutely aware of Philip's enigmatic gaze upon her.

By the end of July, the situation at Hampton Court was becoming too embarrassing to continue any longer. Something had to be done to put a stop to the daily processions and prayers for the Queen's delivery, and on 3 August the court moved away to Oatlands in a tacit admission that Mary had given up hope. Elizabeth did not accompany them. According to Michiel, she was given permission to withdraw with all her attendants to a house distant three miles from her Majesty's. He added that she was not expected to return, 'as she is completely free'.[5] There had been more talk of sending her to Brussels but, when it was pointed out to the Emperor that any attempt to take the Princess Elizabeth out of the kingdom 'would certainly cause too great disturbance and most certain mischief', the plan was dropped without further comment.

Philip, however, was making definite preparations for his own departure. He had spent over a year in a country he disliked, among people who had not hesitated to slight him at every opportunity. He had been unfailingly kind and considerate to a wife more than ten years older than himself who did not attract him and could not produce an heir. He considered he had done as much as could reasonably be expected of him. Mary, having just come through the most appallingly humiliating experience any woman could suffer, now had to come to terms with the fact that the husband she adored with all the strength of her passionate, affection-starved nature, was determined to leave her. For a while she struggled against the inevitable, but Philip assured her patiently that he still loved her, explained that he had urgent business to attend to in his father's dominions and promised he would only be away for a few weeks. Mary had no alternative but to believe him and she gave in. He was to embark at Dover as soon as the escorting fleet was ready, and at the end of August the court went down to Greenwich to see him off. On the twenty-sixth, King and Queen rode in state through the City to Tower Wharf where 'they took their barge' to complete the journey by river. After all the conflicting rumours which had been flying about, many people believed Mary to be dead and, when she appeared now for the first time since her long retirement, the London crowds, whose unpredictability was the despair of all foreign observers, ran wild with joy at the sight of her.[6] Elizabeth was also bound for Greenwich but she had no part in the triumphal procession, making the trip entirely by water, according to de Noailles in a plain barge with only a few attendants. Philip left for Dover on 29 August but before he went, again according to de Noailles, he particularly commended Elizabeth to Mary's good will and was soon writing from the Low Countries to repeat what was virtually a command to handle her sister with kid gloves, as well as secretly leaving similar instructions with the Spaniards who remained in London.[7]

The Queen intended to stay at Greenwich until her husband's return, and Reginald Pole was given lodgings in the Palace, so that he might 'comfort and keep her company, her Majesty delighting greatly in the sight and presence of him'.[8] Elizabeth also stayed at Court, although it is doubtful whether her presence caused Mary any particular delight. Appearances, however, were being carefully kept up. The Queen, in deference to Philip's wishes, dutifully choked back her antipathy and treated her sister graciously in public, only conversing with her about 'agreeable subjects'. Elizabeth, too, was on her best behaviour. At Woodstock she had gone to confession and received 'the most comfortable Sacrament'. Now she attended Mass regularly with the Queen, and on 4 September joined in a three-day fast to qualify for indulgence from Rome. To the outward eye her Catholicism seemed beyond reproach – the time for doctrinal hair-splitting was long past – but many people, Simon Renard for one, remained unconvinced.

In spite of the Queen's laborious amiability, the atmosphere at Greenwich cannot have been very enlivening. Mary spent a good deal of her time weeping in corners, where she thought she was unobserved. Cardinal Pole treated Elizabeth with cold reserve, and the other members of the court were still a trifle wary of being seen too frequently in the Princess's company. In the circumstances, she probably took particular pleasure in renewing her acquaintance with one old friend. After a period of diplomatic service abroad, Master Roger Ascham was back in England. Being one of those Protestants who had found it prudent to conform to the new scheme of things, he now held the position of Latin Secretary to the Queen, and was able to resume his sessions with his old pupil. In September 1555 he wrote to his friend Sturm with all his old enthusiasm: 'The Lady Elizabeth and I read together in Greek the orations of Aeschines and Demosthenes on the Crown. She reads it first to me, and at first sight understands everything, not only the peculiarity of the language and the meaning of the orator, but all the struggles of that contest, the decrees of the people, the customs and manners of the city, in a way to strike you with astonishment.'[9]

Meanwhile, a dismal summer had turned into a dismal autumn. On 29 September 'was the greatest rain and floods that ever was seen in England'. Men and cattle were drowned. Worse still, 'cellars both of wine and beer and ale' in London and elsewhere were flooded out and a great deal of other valuable merchandise was lost.[10] October came in with no sign of Philip's return, and Mary had to leave Greenwich for St James's for the opening of Parliament. Elizabeth was given permission to go back to the country, and on 18 October she passed through the City on her way to Hatfield. The people turned out to give her a rousing send-off but, heartened though she always was by the evidence of her popularity, Elizabeth had no desire to give the Queen any unnecessary cause for offence and, according to de Noailles, she sent some of her gentlemen into the crowds 'to calm and restrain them'.[11]

Settled once more at Hatfield, she began to take up the threads of her old life. Katherine Ashley was back with her. So was Thomas Parry, and Roger Ascham came out to see her and read with her whenever he could get leave of absence. If it does not sound a particularly exhilarating programme for an energetic young woman of twenty-two, Elizabeth knew that time was on her side. She seems to have been perfectly content to wait, concentrating on keeping out of trouble and perhaps making a few tentative preparations for the future. Although no documentary proof has survived, it seems highly probable that she was now unobtrusively resuming her contacts with William Cecil. After all, he was still her Surveyor. Cecil, living quietly at his house in Wimbledon, was another of the prudent conformers and, although he held no office under Mary, the government had found itself obliged from time to time to make use of his services and experience on an *ad hoc* basis. Like the Princess, William Cecil had demonstrated a remarkable talent for survival. Like her, he was content to wait for better days.

All things considered, from Elizabeth's point of view, the situation looked a good deal brighter than it had done at the time of her previous retreat from court. She had made a powerful ally in Philip, Simon Renard was no longer dropping poison into Mary's ear – he had left England in September. But, in any case, Renard was coming round to Philip's way of thinking in regard to Elizabeth. Another gap appeared in the ranks of her enemies that November with the death of Stephen Gardiner. Although 'wily Winchester' had, in fact, scarcely lived up to his title of 'bloody Bishop', luridly depicted by John Foxe as dedicated to hunting down the rightful heiress by fair means or foul, it is not likely that Elizabeth greatly regretted his departure from the scene. But, although 'some hope of comfort' was appearing 'as if out of a dark cloud', her troubles were not yet over. Indeed, as the winter wore on, the events of two years before began to repeat themselves with sinister exactitude.

Mary, left to struggle single-handed with a suspicious and refractory House of Commons, was making little headway. She was acutely short of money, but Parliament's normal reluctance to grant a subsidy was on this occasion not unnaturally exacerbated by the Queen's conscientious determination to relinquish that part of her income which derived from the first fruits and tenths of benefices appropriated by Henry VIII after the breach with Rome. A Bill directed against the English Protestant refugees abroad was defeated and Mary dared not even raise the project closest to her heart and Philip's – that his courtesy title of King should now be made a reality by coronation. But the Commons knew it was in her mind, and fears that this might prove a first step towards letting 'the absolute rule of the realm' pass into Philip's hands stiffened their generally unco-operative attitude. The members, too, remained preternaturally sensitive on the subject of Church property and Church revenues. The merest suggestion that any of this might be surrendered was enough to set alarm bells ringing, and Spanish and Popish influence was seen behind the most harmless measures. De Noailles was once more busily stirring the pot of suspicion and resentment; the only too evident weakness of the crown encouraged malcontents and hotheads; and by the early spring of 1556 the smell of conspiracy was once more in the air.

The Dudley plot as it became known, after one of its ringleaders, Henry Dudley, a distant connexion of the Duke of Northumberland, resembled Wyatt's in that its avowed intention was 'to send the Queen's Highness over to the King [but more likely to dispose of her in a more permanent fashion] and to make the Lady Elizabeth Queen and to marry the Earl of Devonshire to the said lady'.[12] Unlike the Wyatt rebellion, however, it relied heavily on French assistance and on the English *émigrés* being sheltered by the King of France. The Dudley conspirators, too, numbered a good many dubious characters – soldiers of fortune, restless exiles, unpaid royal officials and professional troublemakers – who were moved less by genuine reasons of patriotism than by hopes of personal profit. Nevertheless, the movement was symptomatic of a deep-rooted and widespread discontent, and the fact that it came to nothing does not mean that the threat it represented was not real and immediate. Too many people were involved in the actual plot for it to remain a secret for long. One of its many ramifications was a scheme to raid the Exchequer where the Queen's hard-earned subsidy now reposed, and it was at this point that the first leak was sprung when, early in March, one Thomas White went to Cardinal Pole and told all he knew. The first arrests were made on 18 March, and as the Council began painfully to thread their way through a maze of confessions and depositions the names of Elizabeth's friends started to appear with ominous frequency. As for the Princess herself, the conspirators apparently regarded her hopefully as 'a jolly liberal dame, and nothing so unthankful as her sister'. Inevitably Elizabeth was the lodestone which drew 'the affections and wishes of the majority'. She was young and healthy. She would bear sons. Above all, she was an Englishwoman through and through. Inevitably, as Giovanni Michiel was later to remark, 'never is a conspiracy discovered in which either justly or unjustly she or some of her servants are not mentioned'.[13]

In April 1556 the Venetian picked up a report that there was a plan to send Elizabeth to Spain – a plan linked perhaps with the bizarre proposal originally put forward the previous autumn to marry her to Don Carlos, Philip's ten-year-old son by his first wife. Later in the month, Michiel heard that the idea of sending Elizabeth abroad was being 'earnestly canvassed' by the queen in person, who, he wrote, 'conceives that by removing her bodily from hence, there will be a riddance of all the causes for scandal and disturbances'. He added that Elizabeth was saying plainly she would never marry, 'even were they to give her the King's son or find any other greater Prince'.[14]

So far there was no suggestion that the Princess was personally implicated in the Dudley conspiracy. It is true that in February, while the plot was still hatching, the Constable of France had sent a letter to de Noailles instructing him to be careful and 'above all, restrain Madame Elizabeth from stirring at all in the affair of which you have written to me; for that would be to ruin everything'.[15] Fortunately for Elizabeth this letter was not intercepted, but even if it had been it would not have been direct proof against her. The French, it seems, were still taking a good deal for granted where she was concerned.

All the same, the scent was beginning to lead the Council's bloodhounds uncomfortably close. Some time in May, Somerset House, still her London residence, was searched and a coffer full of seditious, anti-Catholic literature discovered. These were the tracts, ballads and broadsheets which continued to cause the government considerable annoyance, and their ownership was traced to no less a person than Katherine Ashley. Mistress Ashley, Elizabeth's Italian master Baptista Castiglione, Francis Verney (one of those gentlemen whose visits to The Bull at Woodstock had caused Bedingfield so much anxiety), and a fourth person were arrested for questioning. Katherine Ashley denied any knowledge of the conspiracy. Her mistress's feelings were such, she declared, that it would be as much as her place was worth to harbour any evil thoughts of the Queen. But all those 'writings and scandalous books' were apparently hers and the governess spent three months in the Fleet prison. She was once more dismissed from her post and ordered not to see Elizabeth again on her release. Castiglione seems to have cleared himself but Francis Verney was tried and convicted of treason, although subsequently pardoned.

It was the official attitude adopted towards Elizabeth herself which showed how much times had changed. Apart from the obvious danger of public disorder if any arbitrary action was taken against the Princess, Mary would not move without first consulting Philip. Michiel reported to the Doge on 2 June that a special courier had been hastily despatched to Brussels. 'It being credible', he wrote, 'that nothing is done, nor does anything take place, without having the King's opinion about it and hearing his will.'[16] It was presumably according to Philip's will that Sir Edward Hastings and Francis Englefield were sent to Hatfield bearing a kind message from the Queen, assuring her sister of her good will and using 'loving and gracious expressions, to show her that she is neither neglected nor hated, but loved and esteemed by her Majesty'. Michiel added significantly that this had been very well taken by the whole kingdom. The messengers were also instructed to condole with Elizabeth on the loss of her servants, but to point out that their arrest had been necessary in view of the licentious lives they were leading, 'especially in matters of religion'; and the fact that some of them were undoubtedly involved in the conspiracy was exposing her 'to the manifest risk of infamy and ruin'.[17]

The words were honeyed, but Mary did take the opportunity of reorganising the household at Hatfield. 'A widowed gentlewoman' was supplied in place of Mrs Ashley, and Sir Thomas Pope, 'a rich and grave gentleman of good name both for conduct and religion', installed as Governor. Although Sir Thomas himself 'did his utmost to decline such a charge', Elizabeth accepted him with good grace.[18] Thomas Pope was a very different proposition from Henry Bedingfield. For one thing, he was no stranger, having been a member of the household at Ashridge in 1554. He was also a witty, cultivated man, the founder of Trinity College, Oxford, and a pleasant companion whose presence would relieve her of responsibility.

Throughout the remainder of the summer, a hot dry one this year with a four-month drought, the aftermath of the Dudley plot continued to smoulder beneath the surface. In July a feeble attempt was made to stir up the dying embers when a Suffolk schoolmaster named Cleobury created some local disturbance by pretending to impersonate Edward Courtenay and proclaiming 'the Lady Elizabeth Queen and her beloved bedfellow, Lord Courtenay, King'. Thomas Pope was instructed to acquaint the Princess with 'the whole circumstance', so that 'it might appear how little these men stood at falsehood and untruth to compass their purpose and how for that intent they had abused her Grace's name'.[19] Elizabeth promptly improved on the occasion by writing to Mary in her most windy and high-flown style. 'When I revolve in mind (most noble Queen)', she began, 'the old love of paynims to their prince, and the reverent fear of Romans to their senate, I can but muse for my part, and blush for theirs, to see the rebellious hearts and devilish intents of Christians in name, but Jews in deed, toward their anointed king.' She ended by wishing 'that there were as good surgeons for making anatomies of hearts, that might show my thoughts to your Majesty, as there are expert physicians of the bodies. . . . For then, I doubt not, but know well, that whatsoever other should suggest by malice, yet your Majesty should be sure by knowledge; so that the more such misty clouds offuscate the clear light of my truth, the more my tried thoughts should glister to the dimming of their hidden malice.'[20] This choice specimen of her sister's epistolary art – a closely written page in Elizabeth's most elegant hand – can scarcely have failed to irritate Mary profoundly.

The Queen was enduring a miserable summer. She seldom appeared in public and trusted only a tiny handful of royal Catholic councillors. As one of her frequent envoys to Brussels had told Philip the previous December, 'when she looks round and carefully considers the persons about her, she hardly knows one who has not injured her or who would fail to do so again, were the opportunity to present itself'.[21] Nicholas Heath, the new Lord Chancellor, was a poor substitute for Gardiner, and Mary was coming to lean more and more on Reginald Pole, the frail, middle-aged, idealistic scholar who had become Cardinal Archbishop of Canterbury in March. She yearned for Philip, but still there was no sign of his return. The old Emperor, preparing to bow off the stage and spend his last years in the monastery of Yuste, had now handed over all his burdens, save the Empire and Burgundy, to his son. Philip, as King of Spain, Naples and Sicily and Lord of the Netherlands, would have less time than ever to spare for England in the future. He was not pleased by his wife's failure to secure him the crown matrimonial and sent only promises – promises repeatedly and cynically broken – in reply to her self-abasing pleas that he should come back to her. Mary's last birthday had been her fortieth and, as the months passed, she could only rage and despair by turn while her stubborn hopes of bearing children were mocked by her husband's absence.

In September 1556 one of the anxieties shared by the Tudor sisters was removed by the death, in Padua, of Edward Courtenay. The disappearance of that sad, shadowy figure, chosen by popular acclaim to be Elizabeth's husband, was apparently a signal for Philip to renew his efforts to arrange her marriage to Philibert of Savoy. The Princess paid a visit to court that winter. On the twenty-eighth day of November, recorded Henry Machyn, 'my good lady Elizabeth's grace' came riding through Smithfield and Old Bailey and on down Fleet Street to Somerset House, handsomely escorted by 'a great company of velvet coats and chains, her Grace's gentlemen' and upwards of two hundred horsemen wearing her own livery of red trimmed and slashed with black velvet.[22]

Her arrival caused a flurry of interest among the members of the diplomatic corps, all of whom were eager to find out whether Elizabeth was in town on business or pleasure. Giovanni Michiel heard that she had not been sent for, but had herself 'with great earnestness solicited to come'. She got, as usual, a rapturous welcome from the Londoners and although none of 'the Lords or gentlemen of the Court' had ventured to go out and meet her, many of them had since been to pay their respects at Somerset House.[23] Antoine de Noailles was no longer at the French embassy. After the Dudley fiasco England had become rather too hot for him and he had been replaced by his younger brother François, the Bishop of Acqs. The Bishop was longing to send a message to the Princess to enquire whether her patience was exhausted and if she had any plans for the following summer; but she was so closely surrounded that he hesitated to risk discovery which, he remarked, was only too probable with people who were incapable of concealing anything, and prudently decided to wait 'until God should give him a better opportunity'.[24]

Elizabeth duly went to see the Queen and was received, according to Michiel, 'very graciously and familiarly'. She even had an interview with Cardinal Pole – apparently the first time they had met, in spite of having been near neighbours at Greenwich for more than a month in 1555. Everything seemed to be going smoothly. Michiel planned to pay the Princess a courtesy visit, and it was generally thought that she would stay over the Christmas festivities. Then, on 3 December, less than a week after she had come to London, Elizabeth and her entourage were riding through the City again on their way back to Hatfield. The Venetian intelligence service was usually excellent but on this occasion Michiel had no comment to offer, except that the Lady Elizabeth departed so suddenly that he had had no time to call on her, and his visit would have to be reserved for another occasion.[25]

The solution of the mystery was to be provided by no less a person than the King of France, in a conversation some three weeks later with Giacomo Soranzo, Venetian ambassador to the French Court. On being asked by Soranzo if he had any 'advices' from England, the King said he had been told that the Queen had sent for the Lady Elizabeth and proposed to marry her to the Duke of Savoy. The Princess had responded by bursting into floods of tears, saying that she had no wish for any husband and her afflictions were such that she only wanted to die. She wept so bitterly that tears came to Mary's own eyes, but all the same the interview had ended painfully. Faced with her sister's obduracy, the Queen had dismissed her from the court and 'purposed assembling Parliament to have her declared illegitimate and consequently incapable of succeeding to the crown'.[26]

Elizabeth's refusal to marry the Duke of Savoy is perfectly understandable. Naturally she would resist to the uttermost any attempt to tie her hands in this way before she ever came to the throne. Her aversion to the idea of marriage in general is also surely not very difficult to understand. All her life, ever since she had been a small child listening to her maids as they gossiped over their sewing, she had heard story after story and seen illustration after illustration of what women could be made to suffer at the hands of men: Mary's mother and her own; Jane Seymour, who had endured a labour lasting three days and two nights giving birth to the heir; even poor, dull Anne of Cleves, contemptuously rejected and condemned to a life of arid chastity, however full of creature comfort. There had been Katherine Howard's terrible end, and Katherine Parr betrayed by Tom Seymour and then killed bearing his child. If any further warning were needed, she had now before her eyes the dreadful example of how marriage was destroying Mary, a reigning queen. But Elizabeth had not forgotten the lessons she had learnt before she was sixteen; with that ice-cold brain and steely inner core of pride and self-knowledge to support her, she was to be able to say – and mean – that never would she trust her body or her soul to any man.

Nevertheless, the violence of her reaction on this particular occasion was uncharacteristic and a little surprising. If Michiel was right and Elizabeth had invited herself to court, it is possible that she had become a trifle overconfident and was taken off-balance by Mary's sudden, determined assault. But she must have known that the Queen, much as she wanted to please Philip, no longer had the power to force her into marriage or otherwise dispose of her against her will – the threat to disinherit her was an empty one and both knew it. Elizabeth had so far successfully evaded all matrimonial entanglements, and now that her position was stronger than it had ever been she had only to stand firm and keep her head to go on evading them. Were all those tears and protestations just histrionics, or were they symptomatic of some deeper emotional upheaval? If the French ambassador can be regarded as a reliable witness, it appears that there was rather more involved than yet another routine refusal to get married, for according to the Bishop of Acqs a very curious incident indeed took place during Elizabeth's visit to London. In a letter to a friend, written in December 1570, the Bishop related how the Countess of Sussex, who was attached to the Princess's household, had come to see him twice, secretly and in disguise, to tell him that Elizabeth's servants were urging her to extricate herself from her problems by fleeing the country and had asked him if he could arrange to get her across to France. The Bishop, however, so he says, strongly advised against such a desperate course of action. Elizabeth should remember and profit by her sister's example at the time of Northumberland's attempt to deprive her of her inheritance, and stay where she was whatever happened. When the Countess came again, he said flatly that if the Princess ever hoped to succeed to the throne she must on no account leave England. He boasted, in fact, that by following his advice Elizabeth owed her crown to him.[27]

If this astonishing story is true, and on the face of it there seems little reason why Francois de Noailles should have gone to the trouble fourteen years later of inventing such a circumstantial account, it reveals Elizabeth in a state of very considerable emotional upheaval. Certainly in normal circumstances she would not have needed anyone to tell her that flight, and to France of all places, must inevitably have led to total disaster. Was it simply that she had temporarily lost confidence in her own judgement and her ability to deal with Mary? Or was she suffering from a sudden, uncontrollable revulsion of feeling, now that the prize which for so long had lain glittering before her as if at the end of a dark, endless tunnel – the sort of prize one dreams of and struggles for but yet somehow never quite believes in – was at last becoming a reality? Perhaps some change in her ageing, unhappy sister's appearance over the past year had brought it home to Elizabeth, with a sudden blinding flash of realisation, that quite soon now, possibly even within a matter of months, she would be Queen of England and just for a little while she was afraid. On the other hand, the whole hare-brained scheme may have been the invention of the Countess of Sussex who, undeterred, went over to France, presumably to explore the situation on the spot, and was closely questioned by the Privy Council about her doings when she returned.[28] We are never likely to know for certain just what did lie behind this episode, but it is sobering to remember that Antoine de Noailles was not likely to have behaved in such a statesmanlike fashion as his brother apparently did, and Elizabeth might well have found the trap closed on her before she had had time to repent. In the event, she was able to go back to sanctuary at Hatfield and recover from whatever nervous crisis had overwhelmed her.

She was undoubtedly feeling the strain of her position as the *de facto* but so far officially unrecognised heiress-presumptive, and it is natural enough that she should have known moments of exhaustion and despair. Once, in later years, she was to refer briefly to that period of her life when she had been 'a second person'. She had tasted of the practices against her sister, she remarked enigmatically, and had herself been 'sought for divers ways'. In 1556 she was still assimilating the hard lessons of the world about her – the hardest and most important being that one who aspired to take, and keep, the highest place could not afford to give way to moments of human weakness, however natural. Fortunately for England and for herself, Elizabeth learnt that lesson and only on rare occasions was she tempted to forget it.

13

ENGLAND'S ELIZABETH

In March 1557 Mary's prayers were answered and Philip came back to England after an absence of nineteen months. The chief reason for his visit was to use his wife's devotion as a lever to force her reluctant countrymen into active embroilment in the perennial Franco-Spanish quarrel – jus as the King of France and every other opponent of the Spanish marriage had always feared sooner or later that he would. Philip was also increasingly anxious to settle the question of Elizabeth's future. His sister, the Duchess of Parma, and his cousin, the Duchess of Lorraine, crossed the Channel with him, and the Venetian ambassador in France heard that 'the cause of their ladyships' going was that on their return they might bring with them "Madama" Elizabeth of England to give her for wife to the Duke of Savoy'.[1]

Philip succeeded in his first objective but, in spite of Mary's eager assistance and the fact that a considerable proportion of the Privy Council were accepting pensions from him, the task was not easy. He might even have failed if there had not been another particularly foolish attempt to disturb the Queen's peace that spring. Towards the end of April, Thomas Stafford – another of those disgruntled Englishmen who were being petted and paraded at the French court – together with a small force of the raff and scaff of the exiles collected with beat of drum off the back streets of Rouen, was landed from a French ship on the Yorkshire coast. Stafford, a scion of the noble House of Buckingham and descended of the old blood royal on both sides, seized the town of Scarborough and proceeded to issue an inflammatory proclamation. He and his companions had come, he said, 'with the aid and help of all true Englishmen, to deliver our country from all present peril, danger and bondage, whereunto it is like to be brought by the most devilish device of Mary, unrightful and unworthy Queen of England'. He accused the Queen of 'showing herself a whole Spaniard and no Englishwoman in loving Spaniards and hating Englishmen' and raked up all the old bogeys about oppression by proud, vile and spiteful Spaniards.[2] But this time the cynical French policy of deliberately fomenting civil unrest and anti-Spanish feeling had overreached itself. Home-grown rebellions were one thing. Invasion – even by other Englishmen – was another. Local support for Stafford proved minimal and the whole silly affair was quickly put down by the Earl of Westmorland. It had caused a good deal of alarm in the North, however, as a sizeable French army was known to be quartered just over the border in Scotland and it undoubtedly smoothed Philip's path for him. On 7 June England declared war on France, and a month later Philip had gone. This time, as if she realised she would not see him again, Mary went with him to Dover down to the water's edge.

That other piece of business which the King had hoped to see concluded was making no progress and Elizabeth remained undisturbed. In April, the Bishop of Acqs had sent her a warning via the Marchioness of Northampton that there was a plan to take her to Flanders and marry her to Savoy. Elizabeth thanked him and sent a message in reply that she would rather die before either of these things should come to pass.[3] The visit of the two duchesses does not appear to have been a great success. The Queen did not take to them and, as far as we know, Elizabeth did not even meet them. At any rate, they had both returned home by the beginning of May. Philip, however, had not given up, and during the summer of 1557 he made another determined effort to get Elizabeth married to his friend and dependant Emmanuel Philibert, and recognised by the Queen as heir to the throne. Philip had long since resigned himself to the fact that Elizabeth would succeed her sister. She might be a doubtful quantity in many ways, but she was still infinitely preferable to Mary Queen of Scots; from Philip's point of view almost any successor would have been preferable to the King of France's daughter-in-law. He therefore sent his confessor, Francisco de Fresneda, to try again to persuade the Queen to push the marriage through without further delay, and if necessary without the consent of Parliament. De Fresneda had instructions to explain that it was for 'all the considerations both of religion and piety, and of the safety of the realms, and to prevent the evils which might occur were the Lady Elizabeth, seeing herself slighted, to choose . . . to take for her husband some individual who might convulse the whole kingdom into confusion'.[4]

But opposition to this sensible plan was by no means all on Elizabeth's, or Parliament's side, as de Fresneda soon discovered. According to a secret report relayed by one of the Venetian ambassadors, apparently on good authority: 'For many days during which the confessor treated this business, he found the Queen utterly averse to giving the Lady Elizabeth any hope of the succession, obstinately maintaining that she was neither her sister nor the daughter of the Queen's father, King Henry. Nor would she hear of favouring her, as she was born of an infamous woman, who had so greatly outraged the Queen her mother, and herself.'[5] Philip, naturally exasperated by his wife's behaviour, made his displeasure plain; but Mary, although miserable in the knowledge that she was alienating whatever affection he still felt for her, remained impervious to blackmail. In a long, anguished, self-exculpatory letter written about this time, she promised not to be stubborn or unreasonable; she would listen 'with a true and sincere heart' to any persons her husband thought fit to appoint to speak to her about the affair but, she added, 'that which my conscience holds, it has held for this four and twenty years'.[6] It was four and twenty years since Elizabeth's birth and, for all Mary's rationalisations and excuses, this apparently obscure phrase probably contains the nub of the matter. As little as Simon Renard did she believe in Elizabeth's conversion, but not even the argument that a Catholic husband would keep her sister in the fold could move her. Old wrongs cast long shadows and to Mary, now facing the ruin of all her hopes, the bitter past was as real as the bitter present. Once she had acknowledged Elizabeth as her legitimate successor, she would have publicly admitted that Anne Boleyn and her daughter had won. Not even for Philip, not even for the Church, could Catherine of Aragon's daughter bring herself to do that.

Philip was busy with the war and once again the question of Elizabeth's future had to be shelved. Giovanni Michiel left England early in 1557, but in his final report he included a detailed account of the Princess on whom the eyes of all Europe were now turning. 'My Lady Elizabeth', he wrote,

> is a young woman whose mind is considered no less excellent than her person, although her face is comely rather than handsome, but she is tall and well formed, with a good skin, although sallow. She has fine eyes and above all a beautiful hand of which she makes a display; and her intellect and understanding are wonderful, as she showed very plainly by her conduct when in danger and under suspicion. As a linguist she excels the Queen, for besides Latin she has no slight knowledge of Greek, and speaks Italian more than the Queen does, taking so much pleasure in that from vanity she will never speak any other language with Italians. She is proud and haughty, as although she knows that she was born of such a mother, she nevertheless does not consider herself of inferior degree to the Queen, whom she equals in self-esteem. . . . She prides herself on her father and glories in him; everybody saying that she also resembles him more than the Queen does.[7]

Elizabeth was still making do on the income of £3000 a year as provided by her father's Will, but this was no longer really adequate for her needs. Michiel remarked that she was always in debt, and would have been much more so had she not been careful to keep the numbers of her household within bounds. This was not easy, since there was scarcely a lord or gentleman in the kingdom who had not tried to enter her service or place a son or brother in it, 'such being the love and affection borne her'. However, went on the ambassador, 'when requested to take servants she always excuses herself on account of the straits and poverty in which she is kept, and by this astute and judicious apology she adroitly incites a tacit compassion for herself and consequently yet greater affection, as it seems strange and vexatious to everybody that being the daughter of a King she should be treated and acknowledged so sparingly.'[8]

Elizabeth might not hesitate to turn her straitened circumstances to good account but, in fact, even if their relationship had been different, there was not much that Mary could have done to help her. The crown itself was frighteningly short of money and, although this was not really the Queen's fault, the military adventure she had now embarked on had added an additional burden which the country was ill-equipped to carry. The war in France had begun well with an Anglo-Spanish victory at St Quentin, but then the tide turned, and 1558 opened with disaster. On 10 January came the news that Calais had fallen 'the which was the heaviest tidings to London and to England that ever was heard of'. The town of Calais and the Pale, some 120 square miles of French territory, although no longer of any very great strategic importance, represented the last outpost of England's cross-Channel empire and possessed considerable sentimental value – recalling as it did the glorious days of Crécy and Agincourt, of the Black Prince and King Harry V. Its loss was a national humiliation on a grand scale.

For Mary it was to be followed by yet another personal grief. During the Christmas holidays, with a dreadful pathos which still comes raw and shocking across the centuries, she had told Philip that she was pregnant again, having kept the news a secret for nearly seven months 'in order to be quite sure of the fact, lest the like should happen as last time'.[9] Did she really believe it, or was it just a final desperate attempt to bring her husband back to her? It did not bring him but Count de Feria was despatched to England, ostensibly bearing congratulations but more likely to find out if there was, in fact, any possibility of another pregnancy. There was not, as de Feria presently reported.

Elizabeth paid a short visit to London at the end of February 'with a great company of lords and noblemen and noblewomen'. In all probability this was the last occasion on which she appeared in public before her accession and the last time she saw her sister.[10] De Feria wondered whether he should go to see her while she was in town, but decided against it for fear of upsetting the Queen and having been given no definite instructions on the matter.[11]

There was a brief flare-up on the matrimonial front in April, when the Protestant King of Sweden sent an ambassador to propose a marriage between Elizabeth and his eldest son, Eric. Gustavus Vasa, however, so far forgot the proprieties as to address himself directly to the Princess without first observing the formality of asking the Queen's permission – a social gaffe which gave Elizabeth all the excuse she needed for sending the envoy about his business. When news of this affair reached Mary she worked herself into a state of violent agitation, apparently fearing that Philip would blame her for having allowed such an unsuitable proposal even to be suggested, and that he might make it the occasion for renewing his presence on her to come to a decision about her sister. Sir Thomas Pope was ordered to speak to Elizabeth to try and discover from her own lips what her attitude to the Swedes really was, and also if she had any plans about marriage in general. Elizabeth reiterated her settled preference for a spinster's life, and with regard to the Swedish offer declared that she had liked both the message and the messenger so well that she hoped never to hear of either of them again. Thomas Pope, probing a little further, ventured to remark that he thought 'few or none would believe but her Grace would be right well contented to marry, so there were some honourable marriage offered her by the Queen's highness, or with her Majesty's consent'. He got nothing out of Elizabeth, however, beyond the calm reply: 'What I shall do hereafter I know not, but I assure you, upon my truth and fidelity, and as God be merciful unto me, I am not at this time otherwise minded than I have declared unto you. No, though I were offered the greatest prince in all Europe.' Sir Thomas of course, did not take her seriously for a moment. As he commented in his report, 'the Queen's majesty may conceive this rather to proceed of a maidenly shamefacedness, than upon any such certain determination'.[12] It is unlikely that Mary believed in Elizabeth's expressed determination to stay single any more than Thomas Pope did, but after hearing from Hatfield de Feria was able to tell Philip that the Queen had calmed down, although she was still taking a passionate interest in the affair.[13]

De Feria remained in England for several months charged with the thankless task of trying to wring further supplies of men and money for the French war out of an obstructive and apathetic Privy Council. He did, however, make the journey into Hertfordshire to see Elizabeth in June, and the encounter was apparently satisfactory to both parties.[14]

It was a restless, uneasy summer. The sense of great changes impending rumbled in the air like distant thunder and every man's mind was 'travailed with a strange confusion of conceits, all things being immoderately either dreaded or desired'. The Queen was now a very sick woman. She could not sleep and suffered from long, stupent fits of melancholy and a 'superfluity of black bile'. Early in September she had a high fever, a new symptom for her, although the doctors maintained there was no cause for alarm.[15] But as the autumn approached excitement mounted. Rumour ran riot and 'every report was greedily both inquired and received, all truths suspected, diverse tales believed, many improbable conjectures hatched and nourished'.[16] The English people had suffered, more or less patiently, a decade of weak, factious government, internal dissension and bad housekeeping. Above all now they wanted peace, stability and the sort of leadership which would enable them to get on with their own concerns, undistracted by fear of strangers without or civil strife within. After their current experience of that unnatural phenomenon, a woman ruler, considerable uncertainty prevailed in some circles as to whether 'the succeeding Prince' would be able to give them that stability. In the words of the historian John Hayward, 'the rich were fearful, the wise careful, the honestly-disposed doubtful, the discontented and desperate, and all such whose desires were both immoderate and evil, joyful, as wishing trouble, the gate of spoil'. The inarticulate masses, though, just waited stoically and longed for 'their Elizabeth'.

Elizabeth was ready now, receiving visitors and quietly completing her preparations. There were no more nerve storms, no more fears or hesitations. During these last two years of comparative tranquillity she had been able to recover from the stress and strain of her teens and early twenties; to digest the experiences of that hectic period; to mature and develop. By the late summer of 1558 all her astonishing faculties were tuned to concert pitch and she stood in the wings, waiting composedly for her cue to step out into the dazzle of the spotlight and take her place upon the stage. Her twenty-fifth birthday came and went. The trees in Hatfield Park turned to red and yellow, and at St James's Palace Mary's life was drawing to its close.

By 22 October the news reaching Philip in Flanders had become sufficiently serious for him to send de Feria back to England 'to serve the Queen during her illness'. The Venetians heard that the Count's mission was to make a last-minute attempt to get Elizabeth suitably married and induce the Queen 'to give her the hope of succeeding to the Crown'. De Feria reached London on 9 November, but his instructions were already out of date and he was received, so he said, 'as a man who came accredited with the Bulls of a dead Pope'. Three days earlier the Privy Council, taking advantage of one of Mary's more lucid intervals, had spoken to her 'with a view to persuading her to make certain declarations in favour of the Lady Elizabeth concerning the succession'. Mary was too tired to struggle any longer, and on the day before de Feria's arrival the Comptroller and the Master of the Rolls had gone down to Hatfield to inform Elizabeth that the Queen was willing she should succeed in the event of her own death, but asked two things of her; that she would maintain the old religion as Mary had restored it and pay the Queen's debts.[17]

Realising that there was nothing more to be done at St James's, de Feria lost no time in joining the throng of courtiers already taking the Hatfield road. Elizabeth received him well, but not quite so cordially as she had done before. However, she invited him to supper and seemed pleased to see him. She went on to speak of her gratitude for Philip's good offices in the past and for his assurances of continued friendship. But when the ambassador, not very tactfully, began to indicate that she owed the recognition of her claim not to the Queen or the Council but to Philip, Elizabeth pulled him up sharply. She expressed considerable indignation at the treatment she had endured during her sister's reign and declared that she owed her crown not to Philip or even to the nobility 'but to the attachment of the people of England, to whom she seemed much devoted'. De Feria proceeded to offer much the same sort of advice about caution and moderation as Renard had once given Mary but, although Elizabeth remained perfectly amiable, discussed several of the Councillors with him, and even laughed with him about the idea of her marrying the Earl of Arundel, she gave little away and de Feria was left with an uneasy suspicion that she meant to be governed by no one. She was very vain, he reported, very acute and clearly an enthusiastic admirer of her father's methods and policies. He was afraid she would be unreliable on religious matters, for she appeared to favour those councillors who were suspected of heresy and he was told that all her ladies were similarly inclined. In fact, remarked de Feria bitterly, there was not a traitor or heretic in the country who had not risen, as if from the tomb, to welcome her accession.[18]

The Queen died at six o'clock in the morning of Thursday, 17 November, and later that same day, closing a chapter with unusual tidiness, the Cardinal of England, Reginald Pole, died too at Lambeth. There was little pretence of public mourning, and it is not likely that Elizabeth felt any personal grief for her sister. In spite of some sentimental stories that there had been a reconciliation between them during the last months of Mary's life, all the reports of the diplomatic observers indicate that they continued to dislike each other to the end, and really there was no reason why it should have been otherwise. A deputation led by that serviceable pair, the Earls of Pembroke and Arundel, brought the news to Hatfield, and Elizabeth is said to have fallen on her knees, exclaiming: 'A Domino factum est illud et est mirabile in oculis nostris!'[19] That afternoon the citizens of London rang the church bells 'and at night did make bonfires and set tables in the streets, and did eat and drink and make merry for the new Queen Elizabeth'.[20] Holinshed's Chronicle, admittedly with the benefit of hindsight, waxes lyrical on the subject of the accession.

> After all the stormy, tempestuous and blustering windy weather of Queen Mary was overblown, the darksome clouds of discomfort dispersed, the palpable fogs and mists of most intolerable misery consumed, and the dashing showers of persecution overpast; it pleased God to send England a calm and quiet season, a clear and lovely sunshine, a quietus from former broils . . . and a world of blessings by good Queen Elizabeth.

The transition to the new reign had been accomplished with remarkable smoothness. Mary notwithstanding, Elizabeth had long been generally accepted as the heir, but she had taken certain precautions and would have been ready to fight for her throne if necessary. Fortunately there was no need. In some ways she had been lucky. The death of Reginald Pole was, of course, an unexpected advantage, but after the disastrous humiliation of the French war there were few Englishmen ready to contemplate inviting Mary Stuart across the Channel and there was no other obvious alternative to whom the Catholics might have rallied. All the same the change-over was facilitated by the statesmanlike behaviour of the Lord Chancellor, Nicholas

Heath. Parliament was then in session and, on the morning of 17 November, Heath sent for the Speaker and 'the knights and burgesses of the nether house' to come immediately to the Lords. He proceeded to announce the news of Mary's death and went on:

> Which hap as it is most heavy and grievous unto us, so have we no less cause another way to rejoice with praise to Almighty God for that He hath left unto us a true, lawful and right inheritrice to the crown of this realm, which is the Lady Elizabeth, of whose lawful right and title we need not to doubt. Wherefore the lords of this house have determined with your assents and consents, to pass from hence into the palace, and there to proclaim the said Lady Elizabeth Queen of this realm without further tract of time.[21]

There were no dissenting voices and the Chancellor, by his prompt action, had not only ensured Elizabeth's solemn recognition by Parliament before it was automatically dissolved by the death of the reigning monarch; but, as himself a leading Catholic, had secured the loyalty of any doubtful members of his party for the new sovereign.

Elizabeth spend the next few days holding court at Hatfield and consolidating her position. Nicholas Throckmorton, who had achieved the distinction of being acquitted of treason shortly after the Wyatt rebellion, had sent a long memorandum of advice to the new Queen in which he counselled her to move warily at first, so that neither 'the old or the new should wholly understand what you mean'. It was the sort of advice which Elizabeth was superbly equipped to follow. On 20 November she held her first Council meeting, and William Cecil was sworn in as Principal Secretary of State. Thus virtually the first act of the reign was to inaugurate a partnership which was to last for forty years, and must surely count as the most famous and successful in English history. Elizabeth's words to her old friend and new Secretary on that auspicious occasion are well known but still bear repeating. 'I give you this charge', she said,

> that you shall be of my Privy Council and content to take pains for me and my realm. This judgment I have of you that you will not be corrupted by any manner of gift and that you will be faithful to the state; and that without respect of my private will you will give me that counsel which you think best and if you shall know anything necessary to be declared to me of secrecy, you shall show it to myself only. And assure yourself I will not fail to keep taciturnity therein and therefore herewith I charge you.[22]

Other old friends were remembered during that exciting week. Fat Thomas Parry was knighted, given the post of Controller of the Household and made a member of the Privy Council. Kate Ashley became chief Lady of the Bedchamber, and her husband Keeper of the Jewel House. Robert Dudley was created Master of the Horse, a position which entailed close attendance on the Queen.

On 23 November Elizabeth set out for London where she stayed at the Charterhouse; 'in which removing and coming thus to the City, it might well appear how comfortable her presence was to them that went to receive her on the way and likewise to the great multitudes of people that came abroad to see her Grace'.[23] Five days later, on Monday, 28 November, the Queen, wearing purple velvet with a scarf about her neck, the trumpets blowing before her and 'all the heralds in array', rode in procession to the Tower, while the City literally exploded with joy all around her.[24] The entry into the Tower can scarcely have failed to be a highly charged moment for the Queen, and for her Master of the Horse riding close behind her. Elizabeth summed up the situation with masterly simplicity, saying to those about her: 'Some have fallen from being Princess of this land to be prisoners in this place; I am raised from being prisoner in this place to be Prince of this land. That dejection was a work of God's justice; this advancement is a work of His mercy.'[25]

She remained in residence at the great fortress palace for nearly ten days, still feeling her way, holding Council meetings and taking the first cautious steps in the mystery of her craft. In spite of the general atmosphere of optimism and rejoicing, few English monarchs have ever had to contend with so many dangers and difficulties in the first few months of their reigns. Armagil Waad, Clerk of the Council under Edward, had drawn up a succinct list of some of the most pressing problems facing the new administration:

> The Queen poor, the realm exhausted, the nobility poor and decayed. Want of good captains and soldiers. The people out of order. Justice not executed. All things dear. Excess in meat, drink and apparel. Divisions among ourselves. Wars with France and Scotland. The French king bestriding the realm, having one foot in Calais and the other in Scotland. Steadfast enmity but no steadfast friendship abroad.[26]

On the political front at home the religious question loomed large and threatening. Already 'the wolves were coming out of Geneva' as the Marian exiles prepared to return home eager to build the new Jerusalem. On this especially sensitive issue Elizabeth was moving with especial care, but it was obvious that a new settlement would have to be worked out as soon as possible. The Protestants, who regarded her as their saviour, the 'new star' which the Lord had caused to arise, and who had supported her in her darkest days, could not be disappointed now; but her Catholic subjects must not be driven to desperation and neither must the Catholic powers of Europe be too deeply offended. Abroad, the barometer pointed to storm. Young Mary of Scotland was openly quartering the royal arms of England on her shield and once those two colossi, Philip II of Spain and Henri II of France, had settled their differences, which they were now in the process of doing, it seemed only too likely that they would proceed to dismember England between them at their leisure. All over Europe bets were being laid that the new Queen of England would not keep her rickety throne for six months.

If the new Queen of England was at all daunted by the prospect before her, she certainly did not show it. The Court moved to Whitehall for Christmas and was apparently given over to merry-making. De Feria, who was becoming progressively more disenchanted with the new regime, had told Philip in November that Elizabeth was 'very much wedded to the people and thinks as they do, and therefore treats foreigners slightingly'. In December he was complaining querulously:

> It gives me great trouble every time I write to your Majesty not to be able to send more pleasing intelligence, but what can be expected from a country governed by a Queen, and she a young lass who, although sharp, is without prudence and is every day standing up against religion more openly? The kingdom is entirely in the hands of young folks, heretics and traitors, and the Queen does not favour a single man whom her Majesty who is now in heaven would have received.[27]

But however much de Feria might regret the lowered moral and social tone of the court, he was obliged to admit that Elizabeth seemed 'incomparably more feared than her sister, and gives her orders and has her way as absolutely as her father did'.

Already the Queen was giving clear promise of her matchless abilities as a ruler, and already she was capturing the devotion of her subjects. The warmth and spontaneity of the welcome she had received, even from those 'whose fortunes were unlike either to be amended or impaired by change', had exceeded her expectations and during those early weeks she worked singlemindedly to foster and promote that love affair with the English people which was to be such a great source of her strength. 'If ever any person had either the gift or the style to win the hearts of people', wrote John Hayward,

> it was this Queen; and if ever she did express the same, it was at that present, in coupling mildness with majesty as she did, and in stately stooping to the meanest sort. All her faculties were in motion, and every motion seemed a well guided action; her eye was set upon one, her ear listened to another, her judgment ran upon a third, to a fourth she addressed her speech; her spirit seemed to be everywhere, and yet so entire in herself, as it seemed to be nowhere else. Some she pitied, some she commended, some she thanked, at others she pleasantly and wittily jested, contemning no person, neglecting no office; and distributing her smiles, looks and graces so artificially, that thereupon the people again redoubled the testimonies of their joys; and afterwards, raising everything to the highest strain, filled the ears of all men with immoderate extolling their Prince.[28]

In one sense, the consummation of the marriage between Queen and people can be said to have taken place at her coronation procession; in another, it only marked the beginning of the continuing drama to be played out on both sides for nearly half-a-century. On 12 January 1559 Elizabeth went by river from Whitehall to the Tower – not quite five years since the last time she had made that particular journey. Now, as she was rowed downstream, surrounded by her court and attended by the Lord Mayor and aldermen and all the crafts of the City in barges decorated with streamers and banners of their arms, the spectacle reminded an Italian observer of Ascension Day at Venice, when the Signory went out to espouse the sea.[29] To the crowds lining the river banks and clinging perilously to every vantage point on London Bridge, it was the living embodiment of a fairy tale, the perfect illustration of a moral – of virtue rewarded, the Cinderella princess coming to her own. Two days later, on Saturday 14 January, at two o'clock in the afternoon, the Queen mounted an open litter trimmed to the ground with gold brocade and her great cavalcade, 'richly furnished and most honourably accompanied, as well with gentlemen, barons and other the nobility of this realm as also with a notable train of goodly and beautiful ladies', set off from the Tower to make the recognition procession through the City. No one looking at the jewels and gold collars, at the cloth of gold and crimson velvet, at the Queen herself, 'dressed in a royal robe of very rich cloth of gold with a double-raised stiff pile', would have guessed that the Treasury was empty, that there was a huge foreign debt and that Sir Thomas Gresham was already in Antwerp raising further loans on his country's virtually non-existent credit. These uncomfortable facts were not allowed to obtrude. Elizabeth, like her father and grandfather knew when it paid to put on a splendid show, and now if ever was the time to dazzle friend and enemy alike.

It was a cold day with flurries of snow in the air and muddy underfoot, but no such minor discomforts as wet feet could spoil the unalloyed success of the occasion. Everywhere the Queen was greeted with 'prayers, wishes, welcomings, cries, tender words and all other signs which argued a wonderful earnest love of most obedient subjects towards their sovereign'. And Elizabeth responded 'by holding up her hands and merry countenance to such as stood far off, and by most tender and gentle language to those that stood nigh unto her Grace, did declare herself no less thankfully to receive her people's good will than they lovingly offered it unto her'. All along the route, at Fenchurch Street and Gracious Street, Cornhill and Cheapside, St Paul's, Fleet Street and Temple Bar, there were pageants, presentations and loyal orations in Latin and English. Even Anne Boleyn had been rehabilitated, and in a tableau representing the Queen's lineage was placed next to Henry VIII 'apparelled with sceptre and diadem'. Everywhere Elizabeth had an appropriate word of thanks and appreciation. Her reply to the Recorder of London, who offered her a purse of crimson satin richly wrought with gold and containing a thousand gold marks, was considered especially pithy. 'Whereas your request is that I should continue your good lady and Queen', she said, 'be ye assured that I will be as good unto you as ever Queen was to her people. No will in me can lack, neither do I trust shall there lack any power. And persuade yourselves, that for the safety and quietness of you all, I will not spare if need be to spend my blood.'

No incident was too small for her comment and attention. 'About the nether end of Cornhill' an old man who turned his head away and wept was pointed out to her, but Elizabeth was not dismayed and exclaimed, 'I warrant you it is for gladness.' In Cheapside she was seen to smile 'for that she heard one say "Remember old King Henry the eight"'. 'How many nosegays did Her Grace receive at poor women's hands?' demanded Holinshed's Chronicle rhetorically. 'How oftentimes stayed she her chariot when she saw any simple body offer to speak to her Grace?' She kept a branch of rosemary, given to her with a supplication by a poor women at the Fleet Bridge, in her litter all the way to Westminster, 'not without the marvellous wondering of such as knew the presenter and noted the Queen's most gracious receiving and keeping the same'.

As well as her gentle condescension to the 'base and low', it was noted with approval that the Queen showed no signs of forgetting her debt to the Almighty, who had 'so wonderfully placed her in the seat of government'. When she was presented with an English Bible at the little conduit in Cheapside, she took it in both hands, kissed it and laid it upon her breast 'to the great comfort of the lookers on', who felt that God would undoubtedly preserve a princess who took her beginning so reverently.[30] Temple Bar had been decorated with images of the giants Gog and Magog and there the City which, 'without any foreign person, of itself beautified itself' and had spared no expense in the process, reluctantly parted with the resplendent golden figure of the Queen. And so, as the short winter day closed in, borne along on the great warm wave-crest of her subjects' joyful approbation England's Elizabeth came home to Westminster by torchlight for her crowning.

If one were to try to draw up a balance sheet of all the qualities Elizabeth owed to her progenitors, one might say she inherited her fine eyes, sharp features and sharp tongue from her mother; together with Anne Boleyn's considerable ability as an actress, her bourgeois determination to drive a hard bargain and her hysterical tendencies. From her father, with his strong Plantagenet streak, came the red gold hair, physical energy, family pride, self-confidence, vanity, personal magnetism and sure political instinct. From her grandfather, that wise and prudent prince who in some ways she resembled most of all, came the cold, calculating brain, shrewdness in statecraft, opportunism and exact knowledge of the value of money – not to mention an unswerving resolution to hold on to her sceptre against all comers. Perhaps, too, beneath it all, there was an element of the earthy, peasant cunning of those Welsh hill farmers from whom had sprung the seneschal to the rulers of Gwynedd.

How much did she owe to all the varied men and women who had filled the crowded canvas of her girlhood? A store of memories and twenty-five years of experience from which she had learnt discretion, self-discipline, patience and self-reliance; to know herself and her fellows and a strong distaste for the practice of making windows into men's souls. But whatever Elizabeth Tudor drew from her ancestry and her background, she had a magic that was all her own which made her the steely, subtle, enigmatic genius, the Faerie Queen who enthralled, baffled and infuriated her contemporaries for forty-five years and has enthralled, baffled and infuriated every enquirer for four centuries since. Even those among her contemporaries who knew her best never really understood her. Perhaps Robert Cecil came nearest the mark when he said of the Queen that she 'was more than a man, and (in troth) sometimes less than a woman'. And yet Gloriana always knew exactly how to use her femininity to disarm criticism and whistle justly irritated councillors back into puzzled subjection. She kept her secret then. She keeps it now, and is likely to go on keeping it for all time. The one thing that can be said of her with absolute certainty is that she loved England and England's people with a deep, abiding, selfless love. When de Feria remarked that she seemed 'wedded to the people' he spoke no more than the literal truth, and it is one of the happy accidents of history that she and they came together at exactly the right moment for them both.

Part Two
Danger to Elizabeth

Prologue

THIS LADY AND PRINCESS

'This lady and princess is a notable woman.'
Francis Knollys, Carlisle, 11 June 1568

At seven o'clock in the evening of Sunday, 16 May 1568 housewives in the 'lytle prety fyssher town' of Workington, which lay near the mouth of the River Derwent on the coast of Cumberland, were indoors preparing supper; but those people still out and about enjoying the Sabbath air had been able to watch the progress of a small vessel edging into the harbour and tying up at the quayside. The unexpected visitor turned out to be a rough little craft of the type used for inshore fishing and carrying coals and lime across the Solway Firth, but the idlers on the waterfront could see at a glance that her passengers – sixteen of them in all – were neither colliers nor Galloway fishermen. Although tired and travel-stained, these were clearly people of consequence – among them an unusually tall young woman, muffled in cloak and hood, who stumbled and fell as she came ashore.

The strangers sought shelter for the night at Workington Hall, their spokesman (he was John Maxwell, Lord Herries) giving out that he had carried off an heiress whom he was hoping to marry to the son of his old friend Sir Henry Curwen; but by the time darkness had fallen the whole neighbourhood was buzzing with the news that the tall young woman was none other than the already legendary Mary Queen of Scots, deposed and imprisoned by her ungrateful subjects and now fleeing for her life. Henry Curwen happened to be away from home but one of his servants, a Frenchman, had recognised the Queen as soon as she crossed the threshold and told a member of her entourage that he had formerly seen Her Majesty in a better plight than now.

The reasoning which lay behind Mary's rash decision to throw herself on the protection of her cousin, Elizabeth of England, remains obscure. It was a decision taken, as she herself later admitted, against the advice of her best friends. In the six and a half years which had passed since her return to her northern kingdom it was by no means the first time that the Queen of Scots had refused to listen to advice. Certainly the stubborn determination to go her own way was characteristic enough, as was her gambler's instinct to stake all on a single throw.

During her brief period of freedom – it was just over a fortnight since she had escaped from Lochleven Castle with the assistance of Willy Douglas – Mary had sent Elizabeth a full account of her predicament. Now she wrote again from Workington Hall on Monday, 17 May, ending with a moving plea for help: 'I entreat you to send for me as soon as possible, for I am in a pitiable condition, not only for a Queen but even for a gentlewoman, having nothing in the world but the clothes in which I escaped, riding sixty miles the first day and not daring to travel afterwards except by night, as I hope to be able to show you, if it please you to have compassion on my great misfortune and permit me to come and bewail them to you.'

Mary can scarcely have finished this letter before she was ceremoniously waited on by a deputation of local gentry, who conducted her a few miles inland to the town of Cockermouth. There Sir Richard Lowther, deputy governor of Carlisle, 'made his attendance' upon her and it was agreed that she should spend that night in the house of a well-to-do merchant, one Master Henry Fletcher. When Mary told the Queen of England that she had nothing but the clothes she stood up in, she had, it seems, been speaking the literal truth. Richard Lowther noted that 'her grace's attire is very mean, and as I can learn, hath not any better, neither other wherewith to change'. Henry Fletcher is said to have presented his guest with thirteen ells of crimson velvet, and a black cloth gown was hastily made up for her on credit.

Anxious not to be outdone in matters of hospitality, Richard Lowther 'ordered her charges at Cockermouth to be defrayed', and himself provided horses to carry her and her train on the remainder of the journey to Carlisle. Lowther was not at all certain about the protocol governing the reception of refugee queens who had made their own realms too hot to hold them – especially a queen who represented the sort of political dynamite that Mary Stuart did – and he begged Sir William Cecil for instructions. Meanwhile, he intended to keep the fugitive safe at Carlisle Castle with such entertainment as he could provide 'on such sudden'.

Mary had been considerably cheered by the kindness of her welcome. The warm-hearted (and predominantly Catholic) North Country folk were touched by her plight, besides being naturally curious to catch a glimpse of so romantic a figure as the Queen of Scots, and they came flocking in to Carlisle to pay their respects. Mary's naturally buoyant spirits rose and, in a letter dated 20 May, she told the Earl of Cassilis that she expected to be back in Scotland at the head of an army, French if not English, by the middle of August.

By 20 May the news of her arrival had reached London. It cannot have been entirely unexpected. Queen Elizabeth had known for at least a week about her cousin's escape from captivity and the possibility that Mary might be driven to cross the border must certainly have occurred to her. Elizabeth Tudor had in the past been given small reason to feel any personal affection for Mary Stuart but, as she had already made abundantly clear to the Scots, she held strong views on subjects who, whatever the provocation, forced their sovereign to abdicate, held her prisoner and threatened her very life. According to the French and Spanish ambassadors, Elizabeth's first impulse had been to take Mary's part and receive her at Court, but a majority on the Council quickly overruled their mistress's instinctive desire to show solidarity with the afflicted Queen of Scotland. 'Although these people are glad enough to have her in their hands,' wrote the Spanish ambassador, 'they have many things to consider. If they keep her as in prison, it will probably scandalise all neighbouring princes, and if she remain free and able to communicate with her friends, great suspicions will be aroused. In any case,' added Guzman de Silva with studied understatement, 'it is certain that two women will not agree very long.'

The English Council, only too conscious of the many things they had to consider, at once 'entered into serious deliberation' as to what should be done with the Queen of Scots – Elizabeth's Catholic, *de facto* if unacknowledged heir, who had 'heretofore openly challenged the crown of England, not as a second person after the Queen's majesty, but afore her'.

At the age of twenty-five Mary had already succeeded in leaving a quite considerable trail of havoc behind her. Widely suspected of complicity in the assassination of her second husband at Kirk o'Field the year before, she had not improved matters by marrying again, three months later, 'the principal murderer' James Hepburn, Earl of Bothwell. It was this unconventional course of action which had led to her downfall and Scotland was now controlled by her bastard half-brother, the Earl of Moray, ruling in the name of her infant son and the Protestant Kirk. Moray, strongminded and capable, showed every sign of being able to provide his countrymen with some much needed stability and, if he was left undisturbed, of pursuing a policy of peaceful co-existence with England. He had, after all, been accepting an English pension for some years.

In the circumstances, therefore, Mary's sudden eruption into their midst presented the English government with an embarrassing problem. 'If she were detained in England,' says William Camden, 'they reasoned lest she (who was as it were the very pith and marrow of sweet eloquence) might draw many daily to her part which favoured her title to the crown of England, who would kindle the coals of her ambition, and leave nothing unassayed whereby they might set the crown upon her head. Foreign ambassadors would further her counsels and designs; and the Scots then would not fail her, when they should see so rich a booty offered them.' Besides this, Camden observed, 'the trust of keepers was doubtful'.

If Mary were to die in England, even though from natural causes, it would be made a 'matter of calumniation' and Elizabeth would be 'daily molested with new troubles'. If she were allowed to go over to France, her powerful kinsmen there would stir up a hornets' nest on her behalf in both Scotland and England. On the other hand, for Elizabeth to attempt to restore her to her Scottish throne by force of arms would be to invite civil war in Scotland, disruption of the precious, none too secure 'amity' with that country, and a possible revival of the old Franco-Scottish alliance which had been the cause of so much ill-feeling and bloodshed in the past. In any case, it was unthinkable that a Catholic monarch should be re-imposed on a Protestant kingdom with the help of other Protestants. At the same time, it had to be remembered that Mary had sought refuge in England of her own volition, trusting in Elizabeth's many previous – and public – promises of help. She could not now with any appearance of decency be handed back to her enemies.

It was a situation calling for the most careful handling in the long term, but some action had to be taken quickly. On 22 May, therefore, Elizabeth sent her Vice-Chamberlain, Sir Francis Knollys, an old and trusted friend, to take charge at Carlisle. He found Mary recovering rapidly from the rigours of her escape and flight, and full of an articulate sense of grievance over the wrongs she had suffered in Scotland. Knollys, an ardent left-wing Protestant, was immediately impressed by her charismatic personality and her other formidable qualities. She had 'an eloquent tongue and a discreet head', he reported, 'and it seemeth by her doings she hath stout courage and liberal heart adjoined thereto.'

After an uneasy fortnight in her company, Knollys saw no reason to change his opinion. 'This lady and princess is a notable woman,' he wrote on 11 June. 'She seemeth to regard no ceremonious honour beside the acknowledging of her estate regal. She showeth a disposition to speak much, to be bold, to be pleasant, and to be very familiar. She showeth a great desire to be avenged of her enemies. She showeth a readiness to expose herself to all perils in hope of victory. She delighteth much to hear of hardiness and valiancy, commending by name all approved hardy men of her country, although they be her enemies, and she concealeth no cowardice even in her friends. The thing that most she thirsteth after is victory, and it seemeth to be indifferent to her to have her enemies diminished either by the sword of her friends, or by the liberal promises and rewards of her purse, or by division and quarrels raised among themselves: so that for victory's sake pain and peril seemeth pleasant to her: and in respect of victory, wealth and all things seemeth to her contemptible and vile. Now what is to be done with such a lady and princess?' enquired Francis Knollys, with a certain rhetorical flourish, of his friend William Cecil.

No one, least of all either of the rival queens, could have foretold that it would be eighteen years before history provided its inexorable answer to that question.

14

A WISE AND RELIGIOUS QUEEN

'We have a wise and religious Queen'
John Jewel, London, 22 May 1559

When Elizabeth Tudor succeeded to her sister's throne in November 1558 she was the same age as Mary Stuart at the time of her flight into England, but Elizabeth at twenty-five was still very much of an unknown quantity. This was partly due to the fact that she had spent most of the previous five years either in prison or living in rural retirement under some form of surveillance, and partly to the habits of discretion and dissimulation acquired during her precarious adolescence. However, as it became obvious that the ailing, unhappy Mary Tudor would leave no other heir, international curiosity about the young Elizabeth had intensified, and in 1557 the Venetian ambassador included a detailed description of the Princess in his report on his tour of duty in England. Her face, wrote Giovanni Michiel, was comely rather than handsome, but she was tall, well-formed and with a good skin, although sallow. She had fine eyes and very beautiful hands which she took care to display.

Even in her early twenties, the pale, sharp-featured, red-haired Elizabeth had never been able to compete with her Scottish cousin's fabled beauty, but she possessed other attributes which were to prove of greater value in the long-drawn-out battle between them. As early as 1557, Michiel could comment respectfully on the excellence of her mind and on the wonderful intellect and understanding she had shown when facing danger and suspicion. She was proud, too, and haughty, he declared, in spite of the fact that her birth was regarded as illegitimate by most of Christian Europe and that her mother, the great-granddaughter of a London mercer, had once been commonly referred to as that goggle-eyed whore Nan Bullen. Nevertheless, Elizabeth it seemed did not regard herself as being of inferior degree to her half-sister the Queen, whose mother had been a Spanish princess of irreproachable lineage and virtue. 'She prides herself on her father and glories in him', wrote Michiel, adding that her resemblance to Henry VIII was remarked by everybody.

Elizabeth's greatest source of strength in the dismal days of her sister's reign had always been her immense popularity, especially with the Londoners, and her accession was greeted with a spontaneous outburst of public rejoicing which had seldom been equalled. The uninhibited warmth of her welcome cannot be explained away by mere desire for a change, or relief that the transition had been accomplished peacefully. In the decade which had passed since King Henry's death, the nation had suffered from the rule of greedy, factious juntas during the minority of Edward VI and the unpopular, inefficient government of a Queen accused of loving Spaniards and hating Englishmen. Mary Tudor had indeed leaned heavily on Spanish advisers and on her Spanish husband, who had ended by dragging the country into a ruinous war with France, culminating in the loss of Calais, last outpost of England's once great Continental empire.

Some people doubted whether another woman ruler would be much of an improvement, but there seems to have been a widespread, intuitive feeling that Henry VIII's younger daughter was a genuine chip off the old block. Elizabeth was at least a full-blooded Englishwoman, unencumbered by foreign ties. Most important of all, she was young and healthy and with any luck would bear healthy sons. That apart, in the winter of 1558, she looked like being England's last hope of peace and good government for a long time to come, and one senses an undercurrent of rather desperate optimism in the cheers, the pealing bells and salutes of guns which greeted the new Queen as she rode in procession through the City to the Tower on 28 November.

Among the legacy of problems Elizabeth had inherited from her sister were a restive, divided kingdom, an empty Treasury and a mountain of debt. The international situation, too, looked grim, with 'steadfast enmity but no steadfast friendship abroad'. Technically England was still at war with France – 'the French King', in Armagil Waad's picturesque phrase, 'bestriding the realm, having one foot in Calais and the other in Scotland'. The first task facing the new administration, therefore, was to make peace on the best terms it could get, and it did not seem as if they would be very good. As well as possessing all the military and strategic trumps, the French held a strong political card in their control of young Mary Stuart, granddaughter of Henry VIII's elder sister Margaret who had married James IV of Scotland.

In the eyes of the Catholic world which, of course, had never recognised the King of England's famous divorce, Mary had a far better legal claim to the English throne than Henry's daughter, born during the lifetime of his first wife. Elizabeth had, after all, been bastardised and disinherited by her own father in a still unrepealed Act of Parliament, and her present title was based on another Act of 1544 restoring her to the succession. The English Catholics, led by the Lord Chancellor, Nicholas Heath, had accepted her on the strength of her parliamentary title. The French, however, were less convinced of either Henry's or Parliament's competence to manipulate the natural laws of inheritance, and in December 1558 Lord Cobham reported from Brussels that they 'did not let to say and talk openly that Her Highness is not lawful Queen of England

and that they have already sent to Rome to disprove her right'. A few weeks later, Sir Edward Carne was writing from Rome that 'the ambassador of the French laboreth the Pope to declare the Queen illegitimate and the Scottish Queen successor to Queen Mary'.

The King of France had every reason to take a close interest in this matter, since Mary Stuart, who had been brought up in France, was now married to the Dauphin while her mother, Mary of Guise, ruled Scotland with French support. If the Queen of Scots' right to the English throne could be established, it opened up a tempting prospect of French hegemony. So at least it seemed to several experienced English politicians, among them Nicholas Wotton, one of the Commissioners at the preliminary peace talks being held at Cercamp.

Wotton was pessimistic about their prospects of coming away with anything more than 'a piece of paper only containing the words of a treaty of peace', and he wrote to William Cecil gloomily outlining the various causes which moved him to doubt the sincerity of the French. These included 'the ancient and immortal hatred they bear unto us . . . the pretence they make now by the Scottish Queen's feigned title to the crown of England; the occasion and commodity they have now to invade us by land on Scotland side . . . the most dangerous divisions in religion among ourselves . . . the poor state the crown of England is in for lack of money, which I fear they understand too well; the lack of good soldiers, captains and of all kind of munition that we have; the nakedness of all our country, having almost never a place well fortified to sustain a siege; the great commodity which they look to have thereby, if they may subdue England to them; for, bringing once that to pass, (which God forbid) and having England, Scotland and Ireland, no doubt they would look shortly after to be monarchs of almost all Europe; and so were they like to be indeed.' Wotton also regarded Mary Stuart's ambitious Guise relations with the gravest misgivings, 'considering that the House of Guise's greatness and authority dependeth chiefly upon the great commodity that France hath and looketh to have by this marriage of Scotland. And therefore, whatsoever they shall say, sing or pipe, their meaning and intent can be none other but to seek all the means possible to increase the power and honour of their niece the Queen of Scots and of her posterity.'

The fact that the sixteen-year-old Mary was now quartering the royal arms of England with her own and was styled Queen of England in official documents, appeared to reinforce Wotton's forebodings. As it turned out, however, the King of France was not so much interested in embarking on military adventures on behalf of his daughter-in-law as in using her potential status as a lever to extort concessions from the English Commissioners. For example, when the question of the restitution of Calais was raised at the conference table, the French were able to enquire blandly: to whom should Calais be restored? Was not the Queen of Scotland true Queen of England?

This sort of talk naturally infuriated Queen Elizabeth, but she and her advisers knew that without Spanish assistance there was not the slightest chance of recovering Calais. They also knew – as did the King of France – that Philip II, King of Spain, Naples and Sicily, Lord of the Netherlands and widower of Mary Tudor, while showing no disposition to help England in the matter of Calais, would go to considerable lengths to prevent France from interfering in the matter of the succession. Philip might be a zealous Catholic, but he was also a practical statesman who infinitely preferred to see an English queen of doubtful orthodoxy on the English throne, than one half-French by birth and wholly French in sympathy.

Nevertheless, although for the time being, Mary Stuart's very Frenchness was paradoxically a safeguard, the question of her claim remained a source of anxiety and possible danger. The 'auld alliance' between France and Scotland had been a running sore in England's side for generations. It was unfortunate that just now, when the body politic seemed least able to deal with it, this complaint should be present in an acute form.

The other immediate task facing the new Queen of England and her government was the particularly delicate one of making a religious settlement at home. Ironically enough, it had been to ensure her own birth in wedlock that Elizabeth's father, a quarter of a century earlier, had separated England from the body of the Roman Church and had thus helped to destroy the unity of Christendom – that seamless garment of common discipline and belief which had covered the whole of mediaeval Western Europe. Henry's Reformation had been a deliberate political act and, although explicitly denying the authority of the Pope, his Church retained many of the basic tenets of Roman Catholicism.

As long as he lived, the old King had ridden both conservative spirits and more radical reformers with a tight rein, but after his death the radicals quickly took the bit between their teeth. Doctrinal and liturgical innovations followed one another thick and fast. Old rites and ceremonies were abolished, the clergy were permitted to marry, heresy laws were swept away, it was ordained that the laity should henceforward communicate in both kinds, and on Whitsunday 1549 Cranmer's first English Book of Common Prayer became the official and obligatory order of service in every parish church. Based on the old Sarum use, Cranmer's prayer book was still something of a compromise between old and new and worded loosely enough to be acceptable, it was hoped, to both old and new. The new liturgy was, however, rejected by certain ungrateful and reactionary West Countrymen as 'a Christmas game', while others of a more progressive turn of mind did not scruple to refer to it as 'a Popish dunghill'. Three years later a second, more radical version was introduced. The Prayer Book of 1552 completed the process of transforming the sacrifice of the ancient Latin Mass into a communion or commemorative service. The words of the administration: 'Take and eat this in remembrance that Christ died for thee, and feed on him in thy heart by faith with thanksgiving' could no longer be interpreted, even by the most elastic conscience, as anything but a denial of the Real Presence.

Then, in 1553, Edward VI, enthusiastically hailed by the reformers as 'a young Josiah', died in his sixteenth year and Mary Tudor, after unexpectedly defeating the *coup d'état* in favour of Lady Jane Grey, succeeded to the throne. Henry VIII's elder daughter had never made any secret of her devout Catholicism. Indeed she had suffered for it repeatedly, both at her father's hands and the hands of her brother's ministers. She made no secret either of the fact that she believed herself to have been specially called by God to save her unhappy and deluded subjects from the forces of darkness.

There can be no question about Mary's sincerity, but her gallant rearguard action was foredoomed to failure. Had she been content merely to restore the Anglo-Catholic settlement of her father's day, she might well have succeeded. The Protestant left-wingers, although noisy and well-organised, represented as yet only a small minority of the nation, a great bulk of which would have been glad enough to return to the more seemly ritual of the Henrician Church – as in fact was demonstrated by the Parliament of October 1553. Unfortunately this could not satisfy one of Mary's uncompromising spirit. The following year it seemed as if she had won her victory when, on 30 November, England was officially absolved from the sin of schism and received back into the bosom of Mother Church. The Edwardian ecclesiastical legislation had already gone, the married clergy had been ordered to put away their wives and Mass was again being celebrated in all its old panoply; now the mediaeval heresy laws were revived once more and all the Henrician statutes denying papal authority repealed.

But Mary's victory proved a hollow one. The contemporary habit of obedience to the sovereign's will was strong. It was not strong enough to persuade any of those who had profited from the plunder of the Reformation to part with an inch or a pennyworth of their loot. Watertight safeguards for the holders of Church property had had to be devised before Parliament was prepared to accept the Pope's forgiveness. Worse than this, it soon became depressingly clear that the Queen was losing the battle for hearts and minds. Many prominent Protestants found it prudent to go abroad to wait for better times but many others, in less fortunate circumstances, were showing a disconcerting readiness to suffer for their faith. Serious heresy hunting began in February 1555 and continued spasmodically until Mary's death; by which time nearly three hundred men and women, nearly all of them humble people and nearly all of them from London and the south-eastern counties, had been burnt alive.

It is often predicated that the persecution of a minority for the sake of an ideology is invariably a self-defeating exercise; this is a fallacy. There have been instances in history when persecution has been extremely successful. In order to succeed, however, such persecution must be carried out with utter conviction and single-minded ruthlessness. It must also have at least passive support from the bulk of the population in the country concerned. The Marian persecution fulfilled neither of these conditions and therefore had the inevitable effect of strengthening the persecuted. The Edwardian reformers, hitherto quite widely regarded as a loud-mouthed gang of troublemakers, grew immeasurably in dignity and stature and, in Bishop Latimer's immortal words to Ridley as they stood bound to the stake in the dry ditch outside the walls of Oxford, they did indeed light such a candle, by God's grace, in England as never was put out.

In the sixteenth century violent and painful death was too much of a commonplace to be regarded with the same revulsion as it is today, but on those people who witnessed the fortitude of their neighbours – poor widows, journeymen and apprentices, agricultural labourers, weavers, clothworkers, artisans and tradesmen – dying in agony for what they believed to be God's truth, the burnings made an impression disproportionate to the numbers who actually suffered. From the ashes of the Marian martyrs rose the phoenix of that bitter, ineradicable fear and hatred of Rome which had begun to spread its wings even before John Foxe published his famous best-seller, and which was to brood over the national consciousness for centuries to come.

Although public sympathy for Mary's victims was immediate, it has also to be remembered that for every Protestant who took his conscience to the more congenial climate of Germany or Switzerland, or who lit a candle of martyrdom in the local market-place, there were many thousands more who stayed at home, going about their business, obeying the law and keeping their opinions to themselves. The most notable of these conformers was the heir to the throne. During Edward's reign Elizabeth had come in for a good deal of praise from Protestant divines who commented approvingly on her 'maiden shamefastness' and devotion to godly learning; and, as the Holy Roman Emperor's ambassador reported rather sourly on the occasion of one of her visits to Court, 'she was most honourably received by the Council who acted thus in order to show the people how much glory belongs to her who has embraced the new religion and is become a very great lady.' Elizabeth, however, was not the stuff of which religious martyrs are made. After little more than a token show of resistance she had asked for instruction in the Catholic faith and was soon accompanying the Queen to Mass. She unblinkingly assured her anxious sister that 'she went to Mass and did as she did because her conscience prompted and moved her to it; that she went of her own free will and without fear, hypocrisy or dissimulation'. While she was living under restraint at Woodstock, her custodian reported that she had received 'the most comfortable sacrament', and after her release she had joined the rest of the Court in a three-day fast to qualify for indulgence from Rome.

To the outward eye Elizabeth's Catholicism was difficult to fault, and yet somehow nobody had ever believed for a moment in her conversion. Count de Feria, the King of Spain's ambassador who arrived in England in the autumn of 1558, had an interview with her a few days before Mary's death and reported to Philip that he was afraid the new Queen would be unreliable over religion. She appeared to favour those councillors who were suspected of heresy and he was told that all her ladies were similarly inclined. In fact, it seemed to the ambassador that there was not a traitor or heretic in the country who had not risen, as if from the tomb, to welcome her accession.

This jubilation was not confined to England. In such centres of advanced Protestant thought as Strasbourg, Frankfurt, Zurich, Basle and Geneva, the English exiles were already packing their bags preparatory to returning home to assist in rebuilding the walls of Jerusalem. To these enthusiasts the removal of Mary Tudor came as a sign from heaven comparable to the deliverance of the children of Israel from Egyptian bondage, and Sir Anthony Cooke, William Cecil's father-in-law and once tutor to Edward VI, wrote hopefully from Strasbourg on 8 December to the Swiss reformer Heinrich Bullinger: 'If the Queen, mindful of the great mercy she has received, will but place her confidence in God; if she will daily say unto the Lord, Thou art my fortress, my rock, and my refuge, there will neither be wanting to herself the spirit of a Judith or a Deborah, nor wisdom to her councillors, nor strength to her army.'

De Feria in London continued to take a gloomy view of the situation, and on 14 December he told Philip that the Queen was every day standing up against religion more openly. The kingdom, he wrote, was entirely in the hands of young folks, heretics and traitors. The old people and Catholics were dissatisfied but dared not open their lips. Elizabeth seemed incomparably more feared than her sister and gave her orders and had her way as absolutely as her father had done. Certainly, remembering some of King Henry's ways, this hardly looked a good augury for Rome.

Nevertheless, in spite of de Feria's pessimism, Elizabeth was in no hurry to show her hand and refused to be drawn about her intentions by either side. Shortly after the accession an amnesty was granted to some classes of offenders and a bold courtier reminded the Queen that there were four or five more innocent men in prison, 'the four evangelists and the apostle Paul, who have long been shut up in the prison of an unknown tongue'. The prisoners would have to be asked first if they wanted to be let out, retorted Elizabeth. When de Feria took the first available opportunity to beg her to be very careful about religious affairs, she answered demurely 'that it would indeed be bad for her to forget God who had been so good to her', and with this 'equivocal' reply the ambassador had to be content.

A number of Protestants had been included in the newly constituted Privy Council and Protestant influence was growing in Court and government circles, but the weeks passed and England remained officially a Catholic country, in full communion with Rome, with the doctrines and rites of the Church still being carefully observed. There were certain obvious advantages to be derived from keeping it that way. The Pope would be only too pleased to rectify the little matter of the Queen's illegitimacy in return for assurances of her continued orthodoxy. The menace of Mary Stuart would be effectually neutralised and England assured of the friendship and protection of Spain. Yet it seemed unthinkable that Elizabeth, idol of the Protestant Londoners, who owed her very existence to the English Reformation, could be contemplating such a course. There is, in fact, no evidence that she ever did contemplate it. The grass within the Roman fold might look temptingly green, but Elizabeth was far too astute a politician not to sense the quagmire which lay beneath it: even if it had been in her nature to be content to acquiesce in the undoing of her father's work, to accept her throne at the Pope's hands, and to allow her country to sink to becoming a client state of the Hapsburg empire.

She gave the world its first definite clue as to the course she meant to follow on Christmas Day 1558 by sending a message to Owen Oglethorpe, Bishop of Carlisle, ordering him not to elevate the Host at High Mass. The bishop, reported de Feria, answered stoutly 'that Her Majesty was mistress of his body and life, but not of his conscience, and accordingly she heard the Mass until after the gospel, when she rose and left, so as not to be present at the canon and adoration of the Host which the bishop elevated as usual'. The Queen's next move was to issue a proclamation forbidding all preaching and teaching, thus silencing hotheads on both sides and putting an end to 'unfruitful dispute in matters of religion'. The proclamation laid down that the gospel, epistle and ten commandments were to be recited in the vernacular 'without exposition or addition'. There was to be no other 'public prayer, rite, or ceremony in the church, but that which is already used and by law received; or the common litany used at this present in Her Majesty's own Chapel, and the Lord's Prayer and the Creed in English; until consultation may be had by parliament, by Her Majesty, and her three estates of this realm, for the better conciliation and accord of such causes as at this present are moved in matters and ceremonies of religion.' After this it was obvious that the forthcoming session of Parliament would be a crucial one.

But even before Parliament met, the Queen had given further and unmistakable signs of what her policy was likely to be. During her triumphant procession through the City on the day before the Coronation she was presented with an English Bible which she ostentatiously kissed and clasped to her breast. The Coronation ceremony itself was performed by Owen Oglethorpe – the only bishop who could be persuaded to officiate – and again Elizabeth withdrew before the elevation of the Host. Neither did she receive communion, which was administered in one kind only according to the Catholic rite.

On 25 January, after an early dinner, the Queen went in state to Westminster for the opening of Parliament wearing a robe of crimson velvet, with an ermine cape 'like the one worn by the Doge of Venice', and on her head 'a cap of beaten gold covered with very fine oriental pearls'. 'On arriving at Westminster Abbey,' wrote an Italian observer, 'the Abbot, robed pontifically, with all his monks in procession, each of them having a lighted torch in his hand, received her as usual, giving her first of all incense and holy water; and when Her Majesty saw the monks who accompanied her with the torches, she said, "Away with those torches, for we see very well"; and her choristers singing the litany in English, she was accompanied to the high altar under her canopy. Thereupon, Dr Cox, a married priest who has hitherto been beyond the sea, ascended the pulpit and preached the sermon, in which, after saying many things freely against the monks, proving by his arguments that they ought to be persecuted and punished by Her Majesty, as they were impious for having caused the burning of so many poor innocents under pretext of heresy, on which he expatiated greatly; he then commenced praising Her Majesty, saying among other things that God had given her this dignity to the end that she might no longer allow to tolerate the past iniquities; exhorting her to destroy the images of the saints, the churches, the monasteries, and all other things dedicated to divine worship; proving by his own arguments that it is very great impiety and idolatry to endure them; and saying many other things against the Christian religion.' Dr Cox thundered on for an hour and a half and it is scarcely surprising that the Spanish ambassador should have reported on 31 January that the Catholics were 'very fearful of the measures to be taken in this Parliament'.

With the benefit of four hundred years of hindsight, Elizabeth's actions during the first few months of 1559 have an air of inevitability about them. But in the political climate of the time it seemed an astonishingly bold, even foolhardy proceeding for a young, inexperienced Queen whose title to her throne would not stand up to too close an examination, deliberately to cut off her small, ramshackle kingdom once again from the community of Christendom. The Continental Catholic Church was now beginning to shake off its late mediaeval torpor and was gathering its still formidable resources to combat the creeping plague of heresy. Once those two colossi France and Spain had settled their differences, England might well find herself alone in a ring of hostile powers.

Elizabeth was playing a dangerous game, but national unity and national independence were prizes worth gambling for and this was just the kind of diplomatic poker she excelled at. Besides, she could feel reasonably confident that political considerations would continue to outweigh Philip's crusading fervour. It had always been a cardinal principle of Hapsburg foreign policy to maintain an alliance with England. Philip's father had, after all, swallowed a quite remarkable number of insults from Elizabeth's father to safeguard his maritime communications with the Netherlands. Even when peace was concluded between France and Spain the old mutual distrust would remain – it might even been possible to foster it – and both countries had enough problems of their own to keep them occupied at home with any luck for some little time to come.

All the same, Elizabeth knew she was trying Philip pretty high. Since his marriage with Mary Tudor he had felt a special responsibility for the English Catholics, and de Feria reminded him at frequent intervals that they were looking to him for protection. It would also be embarrassing at the least for one who liked to regard himself as the eldest son of the Church to be seen to be openly condoning heresy, however compelling his worldly reasons. Elizabeth quite saw the King of Spain's difficulty and did her best to make things easier for him by leaving, or at any rate appearing to leave, the door of reconciliation if not open, at least ajar. She had refused his half-hearted offer of marriage, no doubt greatly to his relief, but she allowed him to suggest his equally orthodox cousins, the Austrian Archdukes Ferdinand and Charles, as possible alternatives, and she continued to move with circumspection over the religious settlement.

She told de Feria on one occasion that she wanted to restore religion as her father had left it and became 'so disturbed and excited' that the ambassador at last said soothingly that he did not consider she was heretical. Another time she declared that she did not mean to call herself Head of the Church. On yet another occasion she said she wanted the Lutheran Augustanean or Augsburg confession to be maintained in her realm, and when de Feria marshalled arguments to dissuade her, she shifted her ground again, telling him that it would not be the Augsburg confession but something else like it. According to de Feria, she then went on to say that she herself differed very little from the Catholics, 'as she believed that God was in the sacrament of the Eucharist, and only dissented from three or four things in the Mass'.

One way and another the Queen was contriving to create enough uncertainty about her intentions, both religious and matrimonial, to give Spain an excuse for staying friendly, although de Feria was personally convinced that she was going to perdition and complained mournfully about the difficulties he was experiencing in negotiating with a woman so naturally changeable. Philip, however, continued to be nervous of possible French machinations and while de Feria lost no opportunity of trying unsuccessfully to impress Elizabeth with a proper sense of her dependence on his master, his instructions remained doggedly conciliatory. The King was for some time to cling pathetically to the belief that his unpredictable sister-in-law could be controlled if she could only be persuaded into marriage with one of his archducal cousins.

Meanwhile Parliament had embarked on the work of a stormy and momentous session. The first measure introduced by the government was a bill confirming the Queen's title. Unlike her sister in similar circumstances, Elizabeth did not take the trouble to have her birth re-legitimised. Advised by Nicholas Bacon, she took her stand firmly on the 1544 Act of Succession and on the principle 'that the Crown once wore quite taketh away all defects whatsoever'. Another government measure was a bill restoring clerical first fruits and tenths to the Crown. These had first been annexed from the Pope by Henry VIII and subsequently renounced by Mary. The bill made rapid progress in the Lords, although the spiritual peers all voted against it – an unwelcome portent of the unco-operative attitude to be adopted by the Marian bishops. On 9 February the Commons began the first reading of a bill 'to restore the supremacy of the Church of England to the Crown of the realm', and it was at this point that the government began to encounter serious opposition to its plans.

During the two months which had passed since her accession, Elizabeth had been presented with several detailed memoranda of advice on religious matters. All except one – the anonymous 'Device for the Alteration of Religion' which urged the immediate setting-up of a national Protestant Church and the avoidance of 'a cloaked papistry or a mingle-mangle' – were in favour of caution. The lawyer Richard Goodrich, much as he hated Rome, was even prepared to accept the retention of papal supremacy for a time. It is now generally believed that the Queen had made up her mind to proceed by stages – thus following the precedents set by her father and sister – and that to begin with she had intended to go no further than an Act of Supremacy, in which a clause permitting communion in both kinds for the laity was to be inserted as a sop to Protestant opinion. A Catholic order of service would thus have been maintained, at any rate until the next Parliament, by which time those bishops who refused to take the Oath of Supremacy could have been removed and foreign reaction assessed more accurately.

If this was, in fact, the Queen's intention, she and her advisers had seriously misjudged the mood of the House of Commons in general, and the determination and tactical skill of the returned Marian exiles in particular. There was a caucus of at least a dozen of these earnest individuals sitting in the Commons led by Anthony Cooke, Nicholas Bacon and Francis Knollys – all men of ability and influence and all impatient of playing politics with the Word of God.

'We are now busy in parliament about expelling the tyranny of the Pope and restoring the royal authority and re-establishing true religion,' wrote Anthony Cooke to Peter Martyr on 12 February. Busy they certainly were. When the Supremacy bill emerged from its committee stage it had been virtually redrafted. Although the actual text has not survived, it would appear from other evidence that the second Edwardian Act of Uniformity, the 1552 Prayer Book and the Act allowing the clergy to marry – a matter of close personal interest to the *émigré* Protestant divines, most of whom had wives – were all resuscitated and provision made to stiffen the penalties for refusing the Oath of Supremacy. The bill in its amended form was sent up to the Lords on 25 February and there followed a fortnight's pause, during which time presumably the Queen and Council considered what action to take.

Elizabeth was not yet prepared to climb down. Like all her family she strongly resented being hustled, and at this stage she was still apparently hoping to move gradually towards a far more conservative settlement than that envisaged by her obstreperous House of Commons. At all events, the bill was given a second reading by the Lords on 13 March and then went into committee, where it was stripped of its amendments and restored more or less to its original form. Although this was undoubtedly done on instructions from above, it was the House of Lords and especially the bishops who got the blame. 'The Queen,' wrote John Jewel, another returned exile, 'though she openly favours our cause, yet is wonderfully afraid of allowing innovations . . . She is, however, prudently and firmly and piously following up her purpose, though somewhat more slowly than we could wish.'

The militants in the Commons did not wait for the emasculated Supremacy bill to be returned to them. On 17 March they launched a counter-attack, introducing a measure of their own 'that no persons shall be punished for using the religion used in King Edward's time'. This demand for non-conformity ran directly counter to government policy and its sponsors could scarcely have expected to get it through the Lords. It seems to have been intended both as a propaganda gesture and a warning to the government on the strength of left-wing feeling in the Lower House. Outside Parliament Protestant propagandists were keeping up an active campaign against official pusillanimity. According to the Mantuan envoy, they were 'clever, loquacious and fervent, both in preaching and in composing and printing squibs and lampoons, or ballads as they entitle them, which are sold publicly'. The shocked Italian considered these of 'so horrible and abominable a description' that he wondered their authors did not perish by act of God. The Almighty, however, was to remain strictly neutral in the contest being carried on in his name.

Nevertheless, as Easter approached and with it the expected dissolution of Parliament, it began to look very much as though the activists were going to lose this particular round. The pressure group in the Commons was not yet prepared to risk open defiance of the government, and anyway if they had refused to accept royal supremacy without a Protestant service, they would have been left with continued papal supremacy, and that was not to be contemplated. Accordingly they passed the bill as re-amended and by 22 March it was ready for the royal assent. The Queen had intended to go to Westminster on Good Friday, 24 March, and de Feria noted with some satisfaction that the heretics were very downcast. Then, at the last moment, Elizabeth changed her mind. Instead of ending the session, she adjourned Parliament until 3 April and thus dramatically foreshortened the whole course of her religious policy.

Exactly what had brought about this apparent *volte-face* is not known, but several reasons can be surmised. The reformers had powerful allies on the Council and no doubt some pretty intensive lobbying had been going on at Court. The unexpectedly aggressive unity displayed by the House of Commons had probably also led to second thoughts about the political wisdom of leaving the question of public worship more or less in abeyance. Added to this, the intransigent behaviour of the bishops (who had voted against royal supremacy in the Lords) made it plain that the government was going to have to rely on the ministers among the returning exiles to lead their reorientated Church. Another important contributory factor was the news which had reached London on 19 March that the English Commissioners had concluded a reasonably satisfactory peace treaty with France at Câteau Cambresis. These were all solid, practical considerations in helping the Queen to come to a decision, but Elizabeth possessed an almost uncanny flair for gauging the drift of public opinion. Once she had sensed that the country at large wanted the matter settled and would be ready to accept a moderate form of Protestantism, it seems as if she made up her mind to act.

During the Easter recess a public disputation was staged between a contingent of Protestant leaders – all except one returned exiles, all except one future bishops – and a contingent of Catholic bishops and theologians. This disputation was a propaganda exercise pure and simple; its object, according to John Jewel, being to deprive the Catholic bishops of any excuse for saying they had been put down only by the power and authority of the law – in other words, that they had never been given a chance to put their case. The result was a foregone conclusion. The Catholics refused to accept the conditions of debate imposed upon them, as the government had known they would. The proceedings came to an abrupt end and the Protestants were able to make useful capital out of the apparent obstinacy and obscurantism of the Catholics. However, when Parliament reassembled, the Queen made it clear that although she had yielded in principle, she was not prepared to go all the way with the radical party. The Supremacy bill was now redrafted for a third time.

Elizabeth had decided, just as she told de Feria she would, not to accept the title of Supreme Head of the Church. She was instead to be styled Supreme Governor – a fine distinction possibly, but it was nevertheless a rejection of Henry VIII's caesaro-papalism and came as a relief to radicals and conservatives alike. Masculine prejudice did not find it easy to reconcile the idea of a woman occupying such a position with the views forcibly expressed by St Paul; neither did Elizabeth's own tastes run to the sort of personal intervention in matters of dogma and ritual which her father had found so stimulating. Not that she intended to give her bishops a free hand. Her influence was to make itself decisively felt, but she preferred to exercise it indirectly.

The Supremacy bill in its final form had a relatively smooth passage through both Houses of Parliament; it was over the new bill for the Uniformity of Common Prayer and Service in the Church and Administration of the Sacraments, that the last round in the battle for the Elizabethan settlement was fought. Again, when the Queen told de Feria that she wanted the confession of Augsburg, or something like it, maintained in her realm and that she herself believed in a Real Presence, there is every likelihood that she was speaking the plain truth. (It is ironical that so often when Elizabeth was being most sincere, she was taken least seriously.) She had after all been brought up in the High Anglicanism of the latter part of her father's reign; she had been educated by the Cambridge humanists and strongly influenced by the intellectual Lutheranism of her last step-mother, Katherine Parr. Elizabeth may have been a politique to her fingers' ends, but that is no justification for saying she had no religious convictions.

A Protestant order of service grounded on the 1549 Prayer Book and retaining some at least of the externals of Catholic practice would not only have chimed in with the Queen's personal preferences, but would also have opened up a prospect of alliances with Lutheran states abroad and compromise with conservatives at home. Unfortunately for such hopes, the inescapable fact remained that the Church of England could not be made a going concern without the active co-operation and assistance of the returning radical exiles, and they would accept nothing less than the 1552 Prayer Book. Many of them, indeed, would have liked to move still further to the left. During the diaspora they had had the opportunity of seeing at first-hand some of the 'best-reformed' Churches abroad – that is those modelled on the Swiss pattern – and they had all drunk more or less deeply of the heady waters of Calvinism. Fortunately for the government's peace of mind, the 'wolves' from Geneva itself did not, in fact, arrive home in time to take any direct part in the settlement. Elizabeth would certainly not have tolerated any attempt to impose a system which would seriously have undermined the principle of royal supremacy. There was no room in her Church for ministers of religion claiming a mandate straight from heaven, neither had she forgiven John Knox, that sturdy disciple of Calvin, for his singularly tactless remarks on 'the monstrous regimen of women'.

When the Queen agreed to negotiate on the basis of the second Edwardian Prayer Book, she had gone every inch of the way she intended to go and still hoped to salvage something from the wreck of her original plans. In the event, she won several small but significant victories. The phrase: 'The body of our Lord Jesus Christ, which was given for thee, preserve thy body and soul into everlasting life', taken from the 1549 Prayer Book, was prefaced to the administration of the communion in eucharistic belief. The so-called 'Black Rubric' of 1552 which explicitly denied the existence of a Real Presence was deleted, as was the offensive reference to 'the tyranny of the Bishop of Rome'. Elizabeth also insisted on the inclusion of a proviso concerning the retention of church ornaments and vestments which was to lead to a controversy of quite remarkable bitterness. But this lay in the future. When Parliament finally dispersed on 8 May 1559 a compromise had been hammered out, not – as has sometimes been said – between Catholicism and Protestantism, but rather between the Queen's and the Commons' conceptions of Protestantism.

As is usually the way with compromises, no one was particularly pleased. Elizabeth had been outmanoeuvred by the revolutionary tactics of the clique in the Commons and was irritated and alarmed by their success – certainly she was to resist all further attempts at encroachment by the left-wing with bulldog tenacity. The left-wingers, for their part, felt they had achieved little more than a 'leaden mediocrity'. John Jewel in particular regretted the survival of so much of 'the scenic apparatus of divine worship'. He was saddened that those in authority should have clung to the old-fashioned notion that 'the Christian religion could not exist without something tawdry', although he loyally excepted the 'wise and religious' Queen from this reproach. Foreign Catholic observers, on the other hand, did not hesitate to voice their conviction that all questions of religion in the island kingdom would henceforward go to ruin. De Feria's informants told him that everything was now even worse than it had been in King Edward's time, and he wrote to Philip in a fit of petulance that England had fallen into the hands of a woman who was a daughter of the devil, and the greatest scoundrels and heretics in the land.

What the people of England thought about their new Church is more difficult to discover, but all the evidence points to the conclusion that the silent majority accepted it with a placidity bordering on indifference. A cynical foreigner had once remarked that the English would turn Mohammedan if commanded by their prince, and it seems fair to postulate that a nation which had to all intents and purposes been content to change its religion three times in the space of thirty years was not unduly preoccupied with the quality of its spiritual life. The committed Protestants, whose vigour and efficient organisation did so much to gain their party its victory in 1559, still represented a very small section of the total population – at a generous estimate the Marian martyrs and exiles put together only account for some 1200 souls. The fact that their strength was concentrated in London, the south-east and the great seaports – the most prosperous and forward-looking parts of the country – had of course helped considerably in the conduct of their campaign. So had the undoubted fact that the Marian counter-reformation had failed to kindle any spark of enthusiasm amongst the laity as a whole. This seems to have been very largely due to the ineptitude with which it was presented and carried out. Mary Tudor's politically disastrous Spanish marriage, coinciding as it did with one of England's periodic attacks of xenophobia, had polluted the whole of her regime with the taint of foreign interference and oppression. Fairly or unfairly, Roman Catholicism was not to lose that taint for centuries.

There were, of course, committed Catholics in both Houses of Parliament, but lacking leadership or active support in the country they could make little headway against their opponents in the Commons. In the Lords, the depleted ranks of Mary's bishops – notably Heath of York and Scott of Chester – fought a losing battle with courage and dignity, but without government backing their position had been hopeless from the start.

All the same, even after the Acts of Supremacy and Uniformity the situation remained fluid and the lines had not yet been drawn. Despite the Queen's disappointing lack of godly zeal, the radicals had by no means given up hope of improving and consolidating their position. Despite her repeated protestations of reluctance, the conservatives were optimistic that she would soon be marrying a Catholic. No reasonable man ungifted by second sight could have been expected to foresee the astonishing epic of the Virgin Queen, or that the Church of England – which did not look an especially sturdy infant – would prove so tenacious of life. In 1559 neither side was willing or able to push matters to a crisis, but equally neither side believed for a moment that the final victory had been won.

15

There is Nothing to be Done

'There is nothing to be done, but everything to endure, whatsoever God may will.'
Nicholas Heath, London, May 1559

The ease with which the English Catholics surrendered to the forces of reform has long been a source of sorrow to Catholic historians. It even came as something of a surprise to the Protestant reformers. 'The ranks of the papists have fallen almost of their own accord,' wrote John Jewel with a touch of awe. At first sight, the apparently spontaneous collapse of the Old Faith does seem a little odd, especially in view of the fact that de Feria, never one for looking on the bright side, had told King Philip in March 1559, 'I am sure that religion will not fall, because the Catholic party is two thirds larger than the other.' But in another dispatch, written two months later, the ambassador provides two important clues to the mystery. 'The Catholics are in a great majority in the country,' he declared, 'and if the leading men in it were not of so small account things would have turned out differently. It is quite impossible that the present state of affairs can last.'

The situation of the Catholics in 1559 was, in fact, not unlike that of a once-great political party which, having held office for generations, suffers an overwhelming defeat at the polls and retreats exhausted to lick its wounds in decent privacy while waiting for better days to return. Looking back over the upheavals of the past three decades, it was not unreasonable to assume that better days would return. After all, none of the three previous religious revolutions had survived the monarchs who had presided over them. The style of government in the sixteenth century depended to an enormous extent on the personality of the sovereign – especially in England with its tradition of a strong monarchy – and life in the sixteenth century was notoriously uncertain. Elizabeth might die. (She very nearly did die of smallpox in 1562.) If she lived, she would soon be getting married – her frequently expressed preference for a single life being very properly ignored by all sensible men – and when she married it was difficult to see how she could avoid choosing a Catholic consort.

Since the death of Edward Courtenay in Padua four years earlier, there was no Englishman of sufficiently exalted rank to make him acceptable to his fellows, and abroad there was as yet no Protestant ruling house which could be compared in importance with the English one. Mary Tudor had indignantly refused to demean herself by marrying a subject and it seemed unlikely that her younger sister would have any less an idea of her dignity. In one of her frequent conversations with de Feria on the subject he reported that she spoke like a woman who would only accept a great prince.

Elizabeth was very well aware of her value in the international marriage market and zestfully exploited the advantages attached to being the most eligible spinster in Europe, turning the apparent disability of her sex into a diplomatic weapon which for the next twenty years she was to wield with deliberate, ruthless feminine guile. However, it is scarcely surprising that her male contemporaries should have failed to recognise such an unnatural and unwomanly purpose, and during the early sixties the Catholics in England were able to cling to the comforting conviction that the facts of life would soon be catching up with the Queen. Her 'Catholic husband' (the Archduke Charles of Austria remained for some time the most favoured candidate) would then take up the reins of government while Elizabeth was occupied with her real business of bearing children.

From the point of view of the English Catholics in the early sixties, though, it was fatally unfortunate that they possessed no leaders with the foresight to realise that time might not after all be on their side, and who might have rallied the faithful to resist during that crucial period before the new national Church had become embedded in the national life. By the early seventies, when such leaders did begin to come forward, it was too late. This absence of initiative illustrates perhaps more clearly than anything else just how far Catholicism had decayed in mid-sixteenth century England. On the other hand, of course, it also saved England from the religious wars which were to ravage France.

Due in large measure to the ruthless policies pursued by her father and grandfather, Elizabeth had no over-mighty Catholic subjects to contend with. The Duke of Norfolk, England's premier nobleman and only duke, although sympathetic towards Catholicism was officially a Protestant; besides, Thomas Howard, while commanding the affection and respect of his friends, was no leader of men. In 1559, therefore, the only focal point to which the Catholic laity could turn for guidance and inspiration was the hierarchy appointed by Mary Tudor. But here again, although the surviving Marian bishops were, in the opinion of Count de Feria, excellent men who had borne themselves bravely and piously, there was no outstanding personality among them. Their titular head, Reginald Pole, Cardinal Archbishop of Canterbury and the chief instrument of Mary's counter-reformation, had died on the same day as his Queen – as though to emphasise the fact that an era had ended. Even if he had lived, it is more than doubtful whether Pole, a frail, blue-blooded, middle-aged scholar who had spent most of his life in exile and understood the English people as little as Mary had done, could have influenced the course of events.

After his death, the leadership of the Catholic party had devolved on Nicholas Heath, but no crusading fire burnt in the veins of the Archbishop of York. Before de Feria left England in May 1559, he had visited Heath to ask his advice on what ought to be done for the cause of religion. 'There is nothing to be done,' the archbishop is said to have replied, 'but everything to endure, whatsoever God may will.' This may have shown a very proper spirit of Christian resignation. It was emphatically not the spirit which wins battles for souls. Nicholas Heath had been Mary's Lord Chancellor – the statesman whose prompt action had secured Parliamentary recognition of Elizabeth's title on the day of her sister's death. He would do nothing which might endanger the peace and unity of the nation, but he would not compromise his conscience by subscribing to the Oath of Supremacy or attending the new Protestant service. Nor would any of his brother bishops who were all, according to de Feria, firmly and steadfastly determined to die for their faith.

While Elizabeth had no intention of obliging any would-be candidates for martyrdom, their lordships' attitude was naturally a disappointment – especially as several of them had proved pliant enough under her father and brother – and the government seems to have made some effort to persuade them to change their minds. At the end of June, Alvaro de Quadra, de Feria's successor at the Spanish embassy, reported that five bishops had been summoned before the Council and proffered the Oath 'with great promises and threats'. Another attempt was made a few days later, after which they were released on bail of £500 each and ordered not to leave London until further notice. The support of even a few of the old hierarchy would have been valuable in giving the Anglican Church a broader base and in helping to undermine right-wing opposition, but the Queen could not afford to wait for long – her laws had to be seen to be obeyed – and by the end of the summer all the Catholic bishops (with the exception of Kitchin of Llandaff who conformed) had been removed from office.

Opinions as to the harshness or otherwise of their subsequent treatment differ according to point of view. John Strype, the eighteenth-century Protestant historian, observed that they were never burdened with any capital pains, 'nor yet deprived of any of their goods or proper livelihoods, but only removed from their ecclesiastical offices, which they would not exercise according to the laws'. On the other side, the contemporary Catholic writer Edward Rishton insisted gloomily that after being deprived of their dignities and 'committed either to prison or to the custody of divers persons', the bishops were all worn out by the weariness of their miserable treatment. The truth, as is usually the case, seems to have lain somewhere between these two extremes. Mary's bishops, together with a number of other senior members of the Catholic clergy, all suffered some degree of financial loss, personal inconvenience, humiliation and loss of liberty; but it also has to be remembered that they were all disobeying the law of the land, and there are indications that each case was decided more or less on its merits.

Nicholas Heath, a public figure respected in both camps, was allowed 'after a little trouble' (three years in the Tower to be exact) to retire to his house at Chobham in Surrey where he lived unmolested, even, it is said, receiving occasional friendly visits from Elizabeth herself. 'An example of gentleness never matched in Queen Mary's days,' remarks Strype with an air of righteousness. That rugged individual Edmund Bonner, Bishop of London, was a different proposition. Bonner's enthusiasm for the pursuit of heretics in the previous reign had earned him an unpleasant, though probably rather exaggerated reputation for cruelty even among Catholics. As a result, he was so hated by the Londoners that he ran the risk of being lynched when he appeared in public. In the spring of 1560 he was committed to the old Marshalsea prison in Southwark where, although Strype assures us he 'lived daintily' and had the use of the garden and orchards when he was minded to walk abroad and take the air, he stayed until his death nine years later.

Owen Oglethorpe, Ralph Bayne of Coventry and Lichfield, and Cuthbert Tunstal of Durham all died before the end of 1559 of an apoplexy, the stone, and old age respectively. John White of Winchester, who had got into trouble very early on for preaching a provocative sermon at Queen Mary's funeral and would needs preach in his 'Romish pontifical vestments', spent some months in the Tower, but was released when he became ill, and died of a quartan ague at his sister's house in Hampshire in January 1560. Most of the other bishops did varying terms in gaol for 'obstinately' absenting themselves from public worship and actively opposing the new dispensation. Thomas Thirlby of Ely, 'a person of nature affable' but who also manifested an unfortunate tendency to preach against the Reformation, was later released into the custody of Dr Parker, Elizabeth's first Archbishop of Canterbury, and remained an involuntary house guest at Lambeth for ten years. Thomas Watson of Lincoln, described by Camden as being 'learned in deep divinity but surely with an austere gravity' and by Strype as 'altogether a sour and morose man', survived until 1584 but spent the rest of his life either in prison or in the custody of one or other of the new bishops. Released for a while in 1574, he came under suspicion of being 'too conversant' with 'certain Romish emissaries' and was sent to the concentration camp which had been set up to house refractory Catholics at Wisbech Castle near Ely.

For the rest, Gilbert Bourne of Bath and Wells ended his days with his friend Dean Carewe. James Turberville of Exeter, 'an honest gentleman but a simple bishop', was restricted to certain limits after his release from prison but allowed to live in his own home. David Poole of Peterborough, 'an ancient grave person and quiet subject', never actually went to prison but he, too, was ordered to remain within a three-mile limit of London and the suburbs. Cuthbert Scott, 'a rigid man', spent four years in the Fleet gaol and then skipped his bail and escaped to the Low Countries. Richard Pate of Worcester also went abroad, as did Thomas Goldwell of St Asaph. Goldwell, who had once shared Reginald Pole's exile, died in Rome in 1585, the last survivor of the old hierarchy.

The sixteenth century was not a comfortable epoch for anyone in holy orders and bishops, by the very nature of their office, found themselves in the front line of battle. Nearly all the Marian bishops had known previous experience of deprivation, imprisonment, exile and anxiety. All of them had done the state some service during the course of their careers, and when the final test came they were no longer young men: Heath and Bonner were both nearly sixty, Cuthbert Tunstal was well into his eighties, Thomas Thirlby over fifty. Their steadfastness, therefore, does them more credit, but given the climate of the times and remembering what had happened to such conscientious objectors as Fisher of Rochester and the monks of the Charterhouse under Henry VIII – not to mention the fate of the Protestant bishops under Mary – it is difficult to agree that they were treated with particular severity.

1559 was a busy year. While the cases of the individual bishops were still pending, the government was pressing ahead with its plans for establishing the Church of England. The new Prayer Book came into use officially on Midsummer Day and by August a series of visitations had been organised, the Queen's Commissioners setting out on a tour of all the dioceses of England and Wales to enforce nationwide obedience to the provisions of the Acts of Supremacy and Uniformity, as well as the newly issued Royal Injunctions which dealt, among other things, with such important matters as the replacing of stone altars by communion tables. The commissioners were also supplied with a list of fifty-six 'Articles of Inquiry' – an alarmingly detailed questionnaire covering every aspect of clerical character and conduct.

In view of the pious example set by their former episcopate, it cannot be said that the rank and file of the clergy put up a very impressive defence of their faith. A great deal of patient research and scholarship has been devoted to this subject, but again conclusions tend to differ quite widely according to point of view. Catholic historians estimate that between six and seven hundred beneficed clergy out of a total of eight thousand were deprived of their livings for refusing to accept the new order. Protestants, beginning with Camden, put the number of non-conformers at between two and three hundred out of a total of nine thousand, although John Jewel maintained that 'if inveterate obstinacy was found anywhere, it was altogether among the priests'. In the absence of reliable statistics (it is not even known for certain how many priests there were in England and Wales in 1559) the discrepancy between the two estimates is never likely to be satisfactorily resolved.

What is certain, however, is that the overwhelming majority of parish priests did conform, at least outwardly, and really this is scarcely surprising. They were most of them poor men and they wanted to eat. They had become accustomed by this time to being told what to do by the central government, whatever its complexion, and their standard of education was generally low, a fact vigorously bemoaned by the new hierarchy. Nor was illiteracy the worst of the shortcomings uncovered by the Visitors. According to Strype, not only were superstition, absenteeism and corruption rife, but many parsons, vicars and curates had got into the habit of haunting taverns and alehouses, giving themselves to drinking, rioting and playing at unlawful games. Another frequent accusation made against incumbents ('almost in every parish' says Strype) concerned fornication, keeping other women besides their wives and having bastard children.

No doubt this was a time for the settling of scores and the Visitors also heard the complaints of many clergymen 'that had been turned out of their livings under Queen Mary for being married, whom they restored'. Queen Elizabeth never became entirely reconciled to the idea of clerical marriage and popular prejudice was against it, but the reformers got their way – although it was laid down that in future a would-be parson's wife must be honest, sober and approved by the bishop and two justices of the peace. What with hardly knowing from one year to the next if they were legally married or not and having to put up with disparaging remarks from old-fashioned parishioners, the pioneer generation of vicarage ladies led a precarious and harassed existence.

In spite of the regrettable tendency of so many clergy to neglect their cures for the more congenial pastimes of ale-swilling and bastard-begetting, John Jewel felt able to allow himself a certain cautious optimism when he returned to London at the end of October after his trip through the western group of dioceses. 'We found everywhere the people sufficiently well disposed towards religion, and even in those quarters where we expected most difficulty,' he wrote. 'It is however hardly credible what a harvest, or rather what a wilderness of superstition had sprung up in the darkness of the Marian times. We found in all places votive relics of saints, nails with which the infatuated people dreamed that Christ had been pierced, and I know not what small fragments of the sacred cross. The number of witches and sorceresses had everywhere become enormous. The cathedral churches were nothing else but dens of thieves, or worse, if anything worse or more foul can be mentioned.'

Allowing a certain amount of natural exaggeration by the new Protestant brooms, there can be no doubt that they found the Church in a bad way. In those sees which had been left vacant by Reginald Pole abuses of various kinds flourished unchecked, and the convulsions of the past ten years had not been exactly conducive to good order and management anywhere. The low morale of the clergy was reflected in an acute shortage of parish priests – so acute, in fact, that the authorities were obliged to continue to employ many of the old priests whose conformity was doubtful to say the least, and to fill the gaps with laymen pressed into service as readers.

Strype says that 'these readers had been tradesmen, or other honest, well-disposed men, and they were admitted into inferior orders to serve the church in the present necessity by reading the common prayer and the homilies, and orders unto the people'. This expedient was defended on the grounds that it was better to supply some small cures with 'honest artificers exercised in the scriptures' – at any rate until the universities were able to produce enough men of learning to fill their places – rather than leave the people either with no pastor at all or to the care of ignorant 'mass-mongers', a popish Sir John Mumblemattins, Dr Dicer or Mr Card-player.

James Pilkington, the new Bishop of Durham, was thoroughly depressed by the 'negligent forgetfulness of God' which he saw all around him. 'Worldly wise men,' he wrote, 'see so many things out of order, and so little hope of redress, that they cannot tell which to correct or amend first; and therefore let the whip lie still, and every one to do what him list, and sin to be unpunished.' Certainly the new hierarchy had a formidable task before it, and the new Archbishop of Canterbury had to contend with indifference from the masses, who were understandably losing respect for the institutions of public worship – according to Bishop Pilkington the churches were half empty on Sundays, even when there was the added attraction of a sermon, while 'the ale-house is ever full' – as well as active hostility from the militant left wing and passive resistance from the right. It was a prospect to make the boldest quail and Matthew Parker, a moderate, scholarly man of retiring disposition who had once been Anne Boleyn's chaplain, did quail. He had to take the job on, however, and turned out to be an inspired choice. It was due very largely to his tact and patience that by the end of the 1560s the Anglican Church had taken hold, and by the seventies and eighties was strong enough to withstand determined attacks from both within and without.

The question of just how many of the English people could properly be counted as Catholics in 1559 will again probably never be answered with real accuracy. Much detailed research has been done and is still being done into local records but no statistics, however detailed, can show the way into the human heart. Catholic sympathisers, both native and foreign, continued to insist naturally enough that their party was in the majority. Nicholas Sander, the English Catholic apologist, in a report drawn up for Cardinal Moroni some time in the spring of 1561, declared that 'the English common people consist of farmers, shepherds and artisans. The two former are Catholic. Of the others none are schismatics except those who have sedentary occupations, as weavers and shoemakers, and some idle people about the court. The remote parts of the kingdom are still very averse from heresy as

Wales, Devon and Westmorland, Cumberland and Northumberland. As the cities in England are few and small, and as there is no heresy in the country, nor even in the remoter cities, the firm opinion of those capable of judging is that hardly one per cent of the English people is affected.'

Sander, of course, is a highly prejudiced witness but he may not have been so very far out in his estimate. Technically, every Englishman and woman over the age of thirty-five had been baptised and brought up in the Church of Rome. It was still only fourteen years since Henry VIII's death and his Church had retained so many of the elements of Catholic practice that the ordinary layman might have been excused for hardly noticing the difference. The Edwardian revolution had lasted a bare six years before the pendulum swung back again, so that the great majority were still far more accustomed to the Catholic form of service than to any other. It was also true that in the more remote and conservative parts of the country people had as yet scarcely begun to think of themselves as 'Catholics' or 'Protestants'. Terms like 'papist', 'heretic', 'mass-monger' and 'schismatic', which were freely banded about among the initiates in London, had little currency in the Yorkshire Dales, the Welsh mountains or the Cumberland fells where life was harder and more primitive and the farmers and shepherds, unlike all those sedentary weavers and shoemakers in the south-east, had little surplus energy to spare for the heady intellectual delights of theological debate.

Nevertheless, all the evidence points to the fact that committed Catholics were in a small minority. It has been argued that after the defection of the priesthood and with it the disappearance of their church as an organised body, the laity had little choice but to conform to the new scheme of things. This is true, but it can also be argued *a posteriori* that if the laity in general had been less apathetic the priesthood might have stood firm. Certainly an untried Queen and government could never have imposed a Protestant settlement on a nation of convinced Catholics. In the event, the great majority of the laity, like the priesthood, did conform, at least outwardly. They continued to attend their parish church partly in order to keep out of trouble with the law, partly from sheer force of habit and, habit being what it is, gradually became absorbed as communicating members of the new Church.

There were positive as well as negative reasons for this. Many people much preferred to worship in their native tongue – a significant number of Catholics had been reluctant to part with their English bibles during Mary's reign. Also no reasonable man could deny that some measure of reform was long overdue. The moribund state of the Church of Rome in the first half of the sixteenth century was by no means confined to England, but by the time that revivifying force known to history as the Counter-Reformation had crossed the Channel, the process of absorption had gone too far and the English people had finally turned their backs on Rome.

Perhaps the strongest underlying cause of this rejection was the fact that Roman Catholicism had become un-English. For reasons connected with both history and geography, England's ties with Rome had never been quite as binding as those of other European countries, and English Protestantism at the grass roots level was closely connected with the growth of nationalism. The mediaeval polity of Church and State existing side by side as interdependent but separate bodies, each exacting their own due measure of allegiance, had been destroyed by Henry VIII. It was Henry who first equated Roman Catholicism with treason, introducing the novel concept that allegiance to the Bishop of Rome – that is to a foreign power – could no longer be regarded as compatible with the subject's duty of allegiance to the Crown.

The perplexity facing patriotic Elizabethan Catholics in 1559 was neatly summarised in the Oath of Supremacy by which everyone holding office in Church or State had to 'utterly testify and declare in my conscience that the Queen's highness is the only supreme governor of this realm . . . as well as in all spiritual or ecclesiastical things or causes, as temporal, and that no foreign prince, person, prelate, state or potentate has, or ought to have, any jurisdiction, power, superiority, pre-eminence or authority ecclesiastical or spiritual within this realm; and therefore I do utterly renounce and forsake all foreign jurisdictions, power, superiorities and authorities, and do promise that from henceforth I shall bear faith and true allegiance to the Queen's highness, her heirs and lawful successors.' This oath, rejecting as it did the spiritual authority of Rome, was one which no true Catholic could conscientiously swear, but the stigma of implied disloyalty attached to refusing it was to prove too much for most Englishmen.

The Old Faith did not disappear. It went underground as other old faiths had done before it; those who clung to the old ways from conviction or from affection being divided roughly into three groups. At one end of the scale were the irreconcilables like Sir Richard Shelley, the last prior of the English Knights of Malta, Sir John Gage, who had been Queen Mary's Lord Chamberlain, and Sir Francis Englefield, one of her most devoted servants. These men, who could not accept the authority of a Protestant state and – perhaps even more to the point – could not bring themselves to accept Anne Boleyn's daughter as their Supreme Governor in matters spiritual, sought refuge abroad, some in Spain and some in Italy. More serious was the exodus from the universities. Edward Rishton declared that 'the very flower of the two universities Oxford and Cambridge, was carried away as it were by a storm and scattered into foreign lands'. Rishton was overstating the case but Oxford was certainly to prove a fertile breeding ground for Catholic thought and already had a bad reputation among the reformers. John Jewel, writing to his friend Bullinger in 1559, lamented that whatever had been planted there by

Peter Martyr had now been 'so wholly rooted out, that the Lord's vineyard was turned into a wilderness'. Jewel could not recommend sending any Protestant youths to be educated at the senior university in case they should be corrupted by popery and return home 'wicked and barbarous'.

The scholars who fled from Oxford and to a lesser extent from Cambridge in the early sixties gathered in various towns in Northern France and the Spanish Netherlands, but their chief centre was Louvain near Brussels which had a long-standing connection with the family and friends of Sir Thomas More. Like their counterparts in Mary's reign, the Elizabethan exiles were a minority of a minority, probably never exceeding more than a few thousand; also like their Marian counterparts, they were men of ability and initiative who exerted an influence out of proportion to their numbers and who represented a considerable loss to their native land, for the Elizabethan refugees were to be condemned to a lifetime of exile. Not that the colony at Louvain was content to wait in idleness. Under the leadership of Nicholas Sander and his principal lieutenants and fellow-Wykehamists, Thomas Stapleton and Thomas Harding, they were to miss no opportunity of attempting to further their cause by whatever means appeared most promising. They at once embarked on a vigorous propaganda campaign and between the years 1559 and 1570 produced getting on for sixty books, tracts and broadsheets stating the Catholic case and refuting the arguments of their Protestant opponents. Titles such as *Harding Against the Apology of the English Church*; Sander's *The Rock of the Church Wherein the Primacy of St. Peter and of His Successors the Bishops of Rome is Proved out of God's Word* and Sander's *Rock of the Church Undermined by W. Fulke*; not to mention Sander's *Treatise of the Images of Christ and of his Saints: and that it is unlawful to break them and lawful to honour them* and Thomas Stapleton's *Counterblast to Mr. Horne's Vain Blast against Mr. Feckenham . . . touching the Oath of Supremacy* became the ammunition for a series of briskly conducted paper skirmishes.

This war of words kept its participants happily employed and at least had the advantage of not actually hurting anyone. All the same, the Elizabethans were fully alive to the power of propaganda and by the mid-sixties the importation of 'seditious and slanderous books' into England had begun to cause the government a measure of concern. As most of this undesirable literature was apparently finding its way in through the Port of London, the bishop, John Aylmer, received a directive from the Queen in January 1566 ordering him 'specially to have regard thereunto'. Aylmer was authorised to appoint 'one or more persons of discretion . . . to resort to our custom house of London, as any ship or vessel shall come in from time to time, and there to sit with our customers and other officers for the search and perfect understanding of the state of such books'. Despite the vigilance of the port authorities, the output of the printing presses at Louvain and other places in the Netherlands continued to be smuggled in and found a ready market among English Catholics, for whom it represented virtually their only contact with the outside world.

In 1565 John Jewel wrote that 'the Popish exiles are disturbing us and giving us all the trouble in their power' but, in fact, during the first dozen years of Elizabeth's reign the exiles had little more than nuisance value. In the early days the government adopted what might be described as a 'good riddance' policy towards them, even allowing them to take money out of the country. Francis Englefield was given permission to live abroad, providing he undertook not to reside in Rome itself, and Thomas Stapleton remained legally a prebendary of Chichester Cathedral until 1563. Later, as attitudes hardened, it was to be a different story.

Among the Catholics who stayed at home, either by choice or necessity, two distinct sub-divisions had begun to emerge by the middle of the 1560s. The first and largest consisted of those who attempted, not unreasonably in the circumstances, to have things both ways. They were to become known as 'Church papists' by the Protestant establishment and as 'schismatics' by their more resolute co-religionists; they attended services at the parish church often enough to avoid unwelcome notice from the authorities, while continuing to practise their own religion as and when they could. The hard core Catholics – or 'recusants' – rejected this form of compromise, and it was they who suffered the brunt of the approaching storm.

A graphic general picture of the sort of shifts to which the faithful were resorting is provided by Edward Rishton. 'At the same time,' he wrote, 'they had Mass said secretly in their own houses by those very priests who in church publicly celebrated the spurious liturgy, and sometimes by others who had not defiled themselves with heresy; yea, and very often in those disastrous times were on one and the same day partakers of the table of our Lord and of the table of devils, that is, of the blessed Eucharist and the Calvinistic supper. Yea, what is still more marvellous and more sad, sometimes the priest saying Mass at home, for the sake of those Catholics whom he knew to be desirous of them, carried about him Hosts consecrated according to the rite of the Church, with which he communicated them at the very time in which he was giving to other Catholics more careless about the faith the bread prepared for them according to the heretical rite.'

All the same, in those early days even strict Catholics saw no harm in simply being present at the Protestant service. The thin end of the wedge dangers inherent in this attitude were soon obvious, and in the summer of 1562 a deputation of English Catholics, lacking any other guidance, approached the Spanish ambassador to ask for a ruling on whether or not it was lawful for them to attend their parish church. De Quadra referred the matter to Rome and in due course it was considered by a committee of the Council of Trent. The answer which came back that October was definite: no Catholic might lawfully be present at the heretical service, not even to avoid the penalties for recusancy. For some this was the parting of the ways. The Duke of Norfolk's mother-in-law had been 'accustomed to have the Protestant service read to her by a chaplain in her house and afterwards to hear Mass said privately by a priest. But as soon as she understood the unlawfulness of this practice, she would never be present at the Protestant service any more.' Others, for example the eminent lawyer Edmund Plowden, were able to hold for a few more years that the Pope had not yet explicitly condemned the Protestant ritual.

It is generally accepted – at least by Protestant historians – that the English Catholics were treated with comparative leniency by the Elizabethan government until attempts to overthrow it, sponsored by international Catholicism, forced it to adopt harsher measures. Certainly the penal legislation passed at the beginning of Elizabeth's reign was mild enough by sixteenth-century standards – mild in comparison with that of Mary's reign and mild in comparison with that of the 1580s. At the same time it was severe enough, even in 1559, to prove quite a powerful deterrent, at least on paper.

Anyone who refused to take the Oath of Supremacy was deprived of office and barred from holding office for life. The Oath could be administered to all ecclesiastics, judges and mayors, to anyone taking holy orders or university degrees, to all office-holders under the Crown. Non-jurors, therefore, faced loss of livelihood, and for conscientious Catholic youth the way to advancement was closed. The Act of Supremacy also laid down that anyone who 'by writing, printing, teaching, preaching, express words, deed or act' maintained and defended the spiritual or ecclesiastical jurisdiction of any foreign prince or prelate (i.e. the Pope) could lose all his goods and chattels for a first offence, lose all his property and go to prison for life for a second offence, and suffer the penalties of high treason for a third offence.

By the terms of the Act of Uniformity, any beneficed clergyman who refused to use the new Prayer Book, who used any other form of service – in other words, who said Mass – or who spoke 'in derogation' of the Prayer Book, could lose a year's income and go to prison for six months for a first offence, lose all his benefices and go to prison for a year for a second offence, and suffer life imprisonment for a third offence. Any layman who spoke in derogation of the Prayer Book, or who caused any clergyman to use any other form of service – in other words, who heard Mass – could be fined 100 marks and 400 marks respectively for a first and second offence (the mark was worth thirteen shillings and fourpence), lose all his goods and go to prison for life for a third offence. Anyone absent from church on Sundays and holy days without a sufficient reason could be fined twelve pence for each offence or suffer 'censure of the church'. This could involve lesser or greater excommunication which, in its turn, could involve the loss of certain civil rights. For example, an excommunicated person's evidence was considered worthless in a court of law – a serious handicap in a litigious age.

While none of these penalties was exactly comparable to burning at the stake, and while they were by no means systematically or universally enforced, their mere presence on the Statute Book was an uncomfortable weight on the minds of those people they were intended to deter – clergymen, country gentlemen and justices of the peace, squires and small landowners. These were the leaders of the local community whose example would be followed by their tenants and dependants. These were the people least able to face with equanimity the prospect of a prison sentence, the loss of a modest property, or a career and reputation. It is small wonder, therefore, that the majority were prepared to pay lip service at least to the Church of England.

Lip service was really all that was required of the majority. 'The Queen and her ministers,' observed Edward Rishton, 'considered themselves most fortunate in that those who clung to the ancient faith, though so numerous, publicly accepted, or by their presence outwardly sanctioned in some way the new rites they had prescribed. They did not care so much about the inward belief of these men, or if they did, they thought it best to dissemble for a time.' Elizabeth was not, in fact, particularly interested in her subjects' inward beliefs which, as long as they did not affect their outward conduct, she regarded as being their own business. Her government claimed, and was to continue to claim, that provided the Queen's subjects obeyed the law, they would not suffer molestation 'by way of examination or inquisition of their secret opinions in their consciences'.

One modern Catholic historian has summed up the position in words not so very different from Edward Rishton's. 'The Queen's subjects may continue to be Catholics so long as they pretend to be Protestants, and to live as Protestants and to use the new rites as though they are Protestants. They do not need to believe anything of what they profess to believe.' This may have been doubtful ethics, but it was sound political common sense.

The Queen's distaste for the practice of making windows into men's souls and the fact that her subjects were to be exempt from inquisition of their secret opinions in their consciences did not, however, mean that she was prepared for a moment to allow them liberty of conscience. No sixteenth-century state could have contemplated such a course and expected to retain any semblance of national unity. When, in 1561, the Emperor Ferdinand asked Elizabeth to let the English Catholics have the use of at least one church in every city in which 'without molestation or hindrance' they might celebrate the divine offices and sacraments, he received a polite but firm refusal which can scarcely have surprised him very much.

'This request,' wrote the Queen, 'is of such a kind and beset with so many difficulties that we cannot without hurt alike to our country and our own honour, concede it. . . . To found churches expressly for diverse rites, besides being only repugnant to the enactments of our Supreme Parliament, would be but to graft religion upon religion, to the distraction of good men's minds, the fostering of the zeal of the factious, the sorry blending of the functions of church and state, and the utter confounding of all things human and divine in this our now peaceful state: a thing evil in itself, of the worst example pernicious to our people, and to those themselves in whose interest it is craved, neither advantageous nor indeed without peril.' Oddly enough, the King of Spain thought it a poor plan, too, as it might give the Queen an opportunity of identifying the most devout and then punishing them!

There might be no question of giving the Catholics their own places of worship, but Mass continued to be quite widely available for those who knew where to look for it: in quiet country houses where a sympathetic gentleman had given shelter to a deprived priest; in remote districts where, once the Queen's Visitors had ridden away, priest and people continued to do just as they had always done; in London in the chapels of the French and Spanish embassies, where from time to time government agents arrived to take the names of those present.

The Spanish embassy at Durham House was (not without reason) an object of particular suspicion to the English government and a caretaker was installed to make a note of comings and goings. The Council, however, was by no means satisfied with this arrangements and in January 1563 took advantage of a disturbance at the embassy, caused by an armed quarrel between two Italians, to increase their surveillance. 'At the hour when certain people were coming hither to hear Mass,' reported de Quadra indignantly, 'some locksmiths were sent, without any respect or consideration, to change the locks and keys on the doors and hand the new keys to the custodian.' The Council was unimpressed by the ambassador's protests at this violation of his diplomatic immunity. He had allowed his house to become a resort of criminals, they said; a breach of the peace might have resulted endangering the lives of innocent passers-by and, anyway, there had been complaints from the neighbours.

The Council had complaints of its own, too, which it proceeded to set out in detail. 'It is a notorious fact,' de Quadra was informed, 'that by the back door leading to the water there has been for a long time past public access to your house given to a great number of persons, subjects of Her Majesty the Queen, both citizens of London and elsewhere, who come every Sunday and feast day to hear your Mass, which has been a means of keeping them obstinate in their disobedience and disregard for the laws of this realm. In order that these persons might not be recognised when they resorted to your house on such days, the doors of the hall towards the street are closed and the custodian himself detained outside.' Worse than this, it could be proved that 'certain traitors' had been slipping in and out of the embassy by the river door and had been encouraged and advised by the ambassador.

Certainly, the previous year, on de Quadra's own admission, the Irish rebel Shane O'Neill 'and ten or twelve of his principal followers . . . received the holy sacrament in my house with the utmost secrecy'. He was also using his servants to bring in consecrated oils from the Netherlands, 'as Catholics come to me for them'. The English government clearly had a shrewd idea of what was going on, for their reply continued: 'To speak plainly, it is believed that, under cover of religion, your lordship is the cause of a large number of Her Majesty's subjects being disposed to sedition and disobedience who otherwise would have been good and loyal.'

The Spanish ambassador was not, in fact, the only person encouraging the Queen's Catholic subjects in disobedience. In 1564, the bishops were ordered to consult the leading figures in their dioceses known to be reliable Protestants and with their assistance to conduct a survey of justices of the peace, classifying them according to their religious proclivities. The bishops' labours revealed that opposition to the Government's policy was strongest in the north and west – the dioceses of Carlisle, Durham, York, Worcester, Hereford and Exeter containing the largest numbers of 'hinderers of religion'. There were pockets of resistance, too, in Staffordshire, Buckinghamshire and, in fact, wherever the most influential local family clung to Catholicism. Out of a total of 852 justices listed by the bishops, 264 were marked as unfavourable or at best indifferent, while 157 were actively hostile.

It was naturally difficult to enforce the law on a nationwide basis when approximately half the local magistrates were either persistently turning a blind eye to infringements or committing infringements themselves. They were clearly many occasions when the justice of the peace knew very well that the middle-aged man living in a neighbour's house and being passed off as a tutor or perhaps a poor relation was one of those 'popish and perverse priests which, misliking religion, have forsaken the ministry and yet live in corners'. Clearly there were many villages where the inhabitants knew very well that if you knocked on the side door of a certain house at a certain time, you would find Mass being discreetly celebrated in an upper room with, most probably, the justice of the peace among the worshippers – even if later that same day he might be seen sitting in the family pew at the parish church, listening unblinkingly to a godly Protestant sermon.

Queen Elizabeth undoubtedly knew this too, but on the whole she was apparently not dissatisfied with the progress of her religious settlement; at any rate no drastic measures were taken as a result of the bishops' survey. Justices of the peace with the requisite legal and local knowledge did not, after all, grow on trees and in several cases the bishops themselves had been obliged to recommend that the services of some 'noted adversaries of religion' be retained because there was no one suitable to replace them.

So far as it is possible to generalise, it seems fair to say that throughout the 1560s the Catholic population was allowed a good deal of rope. Every now and then and then an example would be made. For instance, in 1561 Sir Edward Waldegrave and his wife, Sir Thomas Wharton and several other prominent Catholics were sentenced to the statutory penalty for hearing Mass. Every now and then an embassy chapel would be raided and the congregation arrested en bloc.

In March 1568, the current Spanish ambassador, Don Diego Guzman de Silva, was telling King Philip that the Catholics in England were numerous but much molested and that news had recently arrived from the Duchy of Lancaster, 'where nearly all the people are Catholics', that many people of position had been arrested for refusing to take the Protestant communion or to attend the services and also, so he heard, because Mass was celebrated in their houses. But apart from these occasional drives – noticeably directed at the most prominent people in a given neighbourhood – the Queen at least was content to leave her Catholic subjects in peace, providing they kept their activities within decent bounds and, most important, providing there was no immediate prospect of any foreign intervention on their behalf.

Elizabeth seems to have been hoping that when the old generation of priests on whom the English Catholics were forced to rely had died out, and when a new generation of schoolchildren reared on sound Protestant principles (after 1563 all schoolmasters were required to take the Oath of Supremacy) had grown up, the problem would go away by itself. The fact that it did not was due in large measure to two people. One was Mary Stuart, Queen of Scotland. The other was William Allen.

16

A Beginning Has Been Made

'. . . by God's goodness a beginning has been made.'
Jean Vendeville, Douai, October 1568

In the year 1568 two events took place which were effectually to destroy the English government's hopes of reaching a peaceful solution to the problem of their Catholic minority. The first of these events was Mary Stuart's escape from her Scottish prison and flight across the Solway Firth. The second was the renting of a modest house in the university quarter of Douai to accommodate a handful of English theological students under the directorship of Dr William Allen. The Queen of Scots' dramatic descent on the coast of Cumberland naturally attracted most attention at the time, but the less well-publicised activities of Dr Allen were to have equally if not more far-reaching results.

The Allens of Rossall Grange in the County of Lancaster were typical of those ancient gentry families, intensely, innately conservative, who clung stubbornly to the old ways; families as rooted in their native soil as the oak trees growing on their demesnes, who were to suffer not only the physical and material consequences of their steadfastness to the faith of their ancestors, but who more tragically were to become increasingly divorced from the mainstream of English national life. William Allen was born in 1532 – the year which saw the death of the last pre-Reformation Archbishop of Canterbury, the year in which Henry VIII and Thomas Cromwell were putting the finishing touches to their plans for the break with Rome. Young William was educated at home, in a sheltered, happy family atmosphere, where there was no room for any new-fangled ideas and where the seven Allen children imbibed all the comfortable convictions, prejudices and old-fashioned piety of their parents, untouched as yet by the social upheaval going on around them.

William was only four at the time of the so-called Pilgrimage of Grace – that ill-fated movement of popular revulsion against the new order by the conservative North Country – and the Allens were not personally involved in the rising. But the hanging of the abbot of the nearby Cistercian house of Whalley in front of his own monastery, together with two of his monks – one of whom was William Haydock of the Haydocks of Cottam Hall, close friends and neighbours of the family at Rossall Grange – can only have impressed the young Allens with the truth of their parents' teaching that an evil force had been let loose in the world.

In 1547, the year of King Henry's death, William Allen went up to Oriel College, Oxford. Unlike Cambridge, Oxford had never become a centre of advanced thought, and Oriel College in particular was regarded as being a stronghold of popery. William's tutor was a Welshman, Dr Morgan Philipps, an ardent Catholic nicknamed 'the Sophister' because of his skill in disputation. The fifteen-year-old boy made rapid progress under Philipp's guidance and although the three years he spent reading for his BA was a time of uncertainty and stagnation in the university, his studies do not seem to have been unduly affected, nor is there any record of his coming into conflict with the reforming authorities.

In 1554, the year of the Wyatt rebellion and Mary Tudor's marriage to Philip of Spain, William Allen, already a Fellow of his College, took his Master of Arts degree. Two years later he was appointed Principal of St Mary's Hall and elected to the office of Proctor. It was in this year, 1556, that Thomas Cranmer was at last brought out of Bocardo gaol to be burnt at the stake for heresy. It would be interesting to know whether Allen was among the crowd of spectators outside St Mary's Church on that wet March morning. All Oxford was there, so it seems likely enough. It would also be interesting to know what his feelings were as one of the chief architects of the English Reformation made his last, and probably most telling contribution to the future of English Protestantism.

Now that the nation had been officially taken back into the bosom of Mother Church, Allen's own future looked bright. He was a man who responded to the discipline and security of academic life. He possessed all the attributes of brains, energy, good looks and personal charm. He was well-born, well-connected, well-liked and respected. His orthodoxy was irreproachable. He was, in fact, just the kind of recruit that a renascent Catholic establishment in England was going to need. At the age of twenty-four William Allen could reasonably hope that an honoured and profitable career of service to his country and his Church lay before him.

Then came the new Queen, closely followed by the new Queen's religious settlement. Allen's faith was not of the kind which admitted compromise. There could be no question of his taking the Oath of Supremacy and in 1560 he resigned his post at St Mary's Hall, although he stayed on at Oxford for a time. The conservative element in the university remained strongly entrenched – according to Nicholas Sander, 'on the Visitors going to the Colleges severally, they did not obtain oath or subscription from one in twenty' – and it was still possible for even such a well-known and recalcitrant Catholic as William Allen to live and study privately without being molested. But by the following year the climate had become so uncongenial that Allen joined that 'flower of the two universities' which was being scattered into foreign lands and crossed over to Flanders, where he made a welcome addition to the English colony at Louvain.

Louvain was a famous university town where there was every facility for study, and Allen would have found many of his friends already established there. In fact, the exiles, with all the Englishman's passion for club life and facility for creating a little bit of home in the most unpromising surroundings, had lost no time in organising themselves into two communities, christened Oxford and Cambridge. William Allen played his part in the propaganda campaign, writing his *Treatise on Purgatory* which defended the Catholic practice of saying prayers for the dead. In order to support himself, he took on the job of tutoring young Christopher Blount – the same who forty years later was to die on the scaffold for his part in the Essex rebellion. Allen also went on with his theological studies, trying to keep usefully occupied during what he hoped would be a period of only temporary set-back.

Nevertheless, those early months of exile were a bitterly unhappy time. His lodgings at Louvain were a poor substitute for Oriel College; the flat, insipid landscape of Flanders not to be compared with the hills of his native North Country or the sight and smell of Morecambe Bay lapping the edges of the Rossall estate. Nor was tutoring and the writing of tracts much compensation for the brilliant career which had been snatched away from him. Some time that year Allen's pupil became ill with what is ominously described as 'an atrophy, or perishing away of his body'. Allen was similarly afflicted, but in his case the trouble seems to have been largely psychosomatic in origin – a fact recognised by the Flemish doctor who told him he must go home if he wanted to save his life. So, in the late summer or autumn of 1562, William Allen returned unobtrusively to England to 'lie hidden among his own people'.

The reunion with his family and the invigorating Atlantic breezes soon restored him to health, but in other directions there was little comfort to be found. The people of Lancashire were still predominantly Catholic, but Allen was shocked and saddened by the evidence of apathy and decay he saw everywhere about him. He at once embarked on a one-man crusade, visiting his friends and kinsmen in the vicinity of Rossall – the Haydocks at Cottam, Thomas Hoghton, John Westby at Mowbreck Hall, John Talbot at Salesbury and Edward Osbaldeston – doing his best to stiffen their resistance to the new laws. But Allen was too well-known a local figure to be able to stay close to his home for long, and presently he shifted the field of his operations to the Oxford area, where he moved about from one 'safe house' to another and where, as he later told his friend Dr Vendeville: 'I demonstrated by irrefragable notes and tokens the authority of the Church and the Apostolic See, and I proved by popular but invincible arguments that the truth was to be found nowhere else save with us Catholics.'

As he travelled about the country, Allen became increasingly worried over the number of Catholics 'who believed the faith in their hearts and herd mass at home when they could' but who 'frequented the schismatical churches and ceremonies, some even communicating in them'. Worse than this, he, like Edward Rishton, had come across many instances of priests who said mass secretly and then 'celebrated the heretical offices and supper in public, thus', wrote Allen, 'becoming partakers often on the same day, O horrible impiety! of the chalice of the Lord and the chalice of devils'. These pernicious practices had, of course, arisen from 'the false persuasion that it was enough to hold the faith interiorly while obeying the Sovereign in externals, especially in singing psalms and parts of scripture in the vulgar tongue, a thing which seemed to them indifferent and, in persons otherwise virtuous, worthy of toleration'.

William Allen set his face firmly against such complacency. According to his biographer, Nicholas Fitzherbert, he went 'vehemently to exhort at various meetings and to enforce with many arguments that so great was the atrocity of this crime that whosoever was contaminated by it could on no account remain in the Catholic communion'. Allen knew that the recent ruling from Rome forbidding the faithful to attend Church of England services had not been entirely well received – 'many worldly-wise men' giving it as their opinion that in the circumstances any attempt to enforce strict ecclesiastical discipline would only result in considerably reducing the number of Catholics who did still 'hold the faith interiorly'. Allen had no patience with this defeatist attitude and fifteen years later he was to write: '. . . we have now more confessors and genuine Catholics than with all our indulgence and connivance we then had concealed Christians; a class of men, moreover, whose inward faith would have furthered neither their own salvation nor that of others, while their outward example would have led many to ruin; and thus, without giving a thought to the damnable sin of schism, or to the restoration of the true religion, but flattering themselves with their good will and pleading in excuse for their unlawful acts the Sovereign's laws, they would have plunged themselves and theirs, unrepentant, into the miserable abyss of destruction'. Thus, in a nutshell, William Allen summed up the basic, irreconcilable conflict between the laws of his God and his Queen.

Allen was to spend two and a half years in England labouring at his self-appointed task; writing and circulating his 'notes, rules or motives for distinguishing with certainty the Catholic faith from heresy' (which were later to be published at Douai in expanded form), rallying the faint-hearted, admonishing back-sliders and bringing as many wandering sheep as he could reach back into the fold. 'He both kept to their duty the family in which he resided,' says Fitzherbert, 'and often visited Oxford which was near and there soon converted not a few.'

It is a commentary on the generally relaxed attitude of the early sixties that Allen, who had lived in Oxford for fourteen years and would have been known by sight to the majority of the citizens, was apparently able to go about openly encouraging people to break the law. All the same, he evidently felt it would be unwise to push his luck and after a time sought shelter under the hospitable roof of the Duke of Norfolk. In spite of the fact that he had once been tutored by the redoubtable John Foxe of martyrology fame, Thomas Howard had many Catholic connections and his East Anglican estates offered sanctuary to a number of those 'stragling doctors and priests who have liberty to stray at their pleasure within this realm and do much harm secretly and in corners'.

It is said that Allen subsequently went back to Oxford, but now the relatives of one of his young converts were after his blood; one man in particular, who knew his face, having undertaken to find him and denounce him to the magistrates. This man, so the story goes, actually sat opposite to Allen at dinner at an inn and either providentially failed to recognise him or was suddenly struck by remorse and remained silent. There is a distinct flavour of St Elizabeth and the roses about this episode, but it may well reflect the healthy English dislike of laying information and also something of the astonishing indifference of the English – until they begin to feel personally threatened.

William Allen left for the Low Countries again in the spring of 1565. He made his way to Malines where he was at last ordained priest and was appointed lecturer in theology at the Benedictine college in the city. At the age of thirty-three he had become a man with a mission in life – from now on there would be no more time for homesickness. His *Certain Brief Reasons concerning Catholic Faith* had already appeared in print. In May 1565 his *Treatise on Purgatory* was published at Antwerp, to be followed in 1567 by further treatises on such controversial matters as the authority of the priesthood to remit sins, the duty of confession and 'the Churches meaning concerning Indulgences, commonlie called the popes pardons'.

In 1567 in England there were signs of a general stiffening of attitudes on both sides of the religious divide. The Catholics had by this time shed most of their dead wood and the Established Church, having survived the critical years of its infancy, was growing in stature and self-confidence. The government still clung to its gradualist policy, but the obstinate survival, even resurgence, of Catholicism in parts of the North was giving cause for concern, especially in view of the remarkable events currently taking place in Scotland. Strype records that 'religion in Lancashire and the parts thereabouts went backwards, papists about this time showing themselves to be numerous, Mass commonly said, priests harboured, the Book of Common Prayer and the church established by law laid aside, many churches shut up and cures unsupplied, unless with such popish priests as had been ejected'.

William Allen's work in his native county had been followed and supplemented by a visit from his fellow Lancastrian and fellow exile

Laurence Vaux, who came to spread the militant word of the new Pope; and now reports were reaching London of groups of gentlemen taking oaths not to attend the Protestant communion and of leading families becoming reconciled to Rome. Slowly but inexorably the tragedy was beginning to unfold.

In February 1568 a writ went out under the Queen's name to Edward Holland, Sheriff of Lancashire. 'Whereas we have been credibly informed,' it ran, 'that certain persons, who having been late ministers in the Church were justly deprived of their offices of ministery for their contempts and obstinacy, be yet or lately have been secretly maintained in private places in that our county of Lancaster (whose names are here subscribed) where they do not only continue their former doings in contempt, as it seemeth, of our authority and good orders provided for an uniformity, but also do seditiously pervert and abuse our good subjects to our no small grief: like as we think it convenient for the service of Almighty God and for the love we bear to our good and obedient subjects to have such evil members rooted out to the end the good may the better prosper: so we have thought good to will and command you forthwith upon the receipt hereof, to the end that none may pretend ignorance herein, to take order and cause to be openly published in the chief market towns of that our county in times and places of most resort thither, that our pleasure is to have the said persons and every of them apprehended and committed to ward.' The list of the half-dozen wanted men subscribed was headed by 'Allen who wrote the late book of Purgatory'.

By the time the warrant for his arrest was out in Lancashire, William Allen was in Rome. He had made the journey apparently hoping there might be an opening for him as chaplain at the English Hospice in the city, but the job did not materialise and later that spring Allen returned to Flanders in the company of his friend Jean Vendeville. Both men were in a despondent frame of mind. Dr Vendeville had spent the winter in Rome trying to interest the Pope in an ambitious project for the conversion of all infidels, but Pius V had more immediate matters on his mind and Vendeville had failed to get a hearing. As they travelled across Europe together, he poured out his disappointment to William Allen and William Allen promptly seized what looked like a heaven-sent opportunity to try and divert this missionary zeal into more practical channels by propounding a scheme of his own – a scheme which may well have been in his mind ever since his trip to England.

Allen and his fellow propagandists had found it convenient to lay the blame, at least in public, for the dismal collapse of English Catholicism on 'the terrible rigour of the law'. But Allen had had personal experience of the degree of latitude being allowed to even such a determined proselytiser as himself. He was far too intelligent a man not to have realised that it was not persecution but isolation – the absence of leadership and hope for the future – which had demoralised the English Catholics. Quite as clearly as Queen Elizabeth he could see that once the old generation of priests had died out, 'no seed would be left hereafter for the restoration of religion, and that heresy would thus obtain a perpetual and peaceful possession of the realm'. Unless, of course, something was done to prevent it.

He therefore suggested that a college should be founded where the exiled scholars, then scattered in various towns throughout the Low Countries, 'might live and study together more profitably than apart'. In this way, he hoped, their energies might be concentrated and conserved, so that a body of learned men would always be ready and waiting 'to restore religion when the proper moment should arrive'. Such a college would also provide a much needed centre and refuge for future exiles and offer a means of snatching from the jaws of death 'as many souls of our countrymen as in a very few years might be educated in this society of ours'.

Allen does not at this stage seem to have envisaged the active missionary work for which Douai was to become so famous. On the contrary, he felt it would be hopeless to attempt anything 'while the heretics were masters'. His plan was simply to keep the flame alight and be prepared to seize whatever opportunity might be offered by the death of the Queen or some other similar cataclysm. But Dr Vendeville, who took up the idea with enthusiasm, did envisage it. His thoughts, as Allen put it, took a wider range and he saw no reason why, after a few years preparation, the students should not be employed in promoting the Catholic cause in England 'even at the peril of their lives'.

As soon as the two men got back to Belgium, Dr Vendeville went into action on his friend's behalf. The recently established university at Douai in the province of Artois, now in northern France but then forming part of the King of Spain's Burgundian heritage, seemed the most promising site for the new venture. Vendeville himself held the position of Regius Professor of Canon Law and was able to win the support of the Chancellor, Dr Galen. William Allen was appointed Public Catechist which gave him some standing in the university, but the most pressing need was money, and Vendeville set about raising the necessary funds by appealing to 'four or five devout and pius men who possessed the means and from their piety seemed unlikely to refuse'. He also petitioned the Duke of Alva for a grant of 300 crowns, with what success is not recorded.

The idea of an English college did not meet with universal approval, but Vendeville refused to be discouraged and by October he was able to write to Dr Viglius, President of the Council of the Netherlands, that 'by God's goodness a beginning has been made; for from St Michael's feast a house has been rented of sufficient size, and very convenient, nigh to the theological schools, and there are already living in it five or six Englishmen of great ability and promise, some of whom are men, while others are youths of twenty-three or twenty-four, and also two of our countrymen'.

If it was Jean Vendeville's practical enthusiasm which brought the English College at Douai into being, its immediate and continuing success was undoubtedly due to the character of its first president. William Allen was a born schoolmaster, with the gift of inspiring genuine personal affection as well as respect. Political refugees are a notoriously touchy and cantankerous breed and the English Catholic exiles were no exception to this rule, but Douai was to remain noticeably free from the internecine feuds which afflicted later foundations. John Pitts, himself a one-time student, was to write: 'Allen presided over everything, and with wonderful dignity, constancy and authority governed the whole college, yea, through the college almost all the Catholics of our nation, and by his firm and prudent rule kept them all to the fulfilment of their duties in the greatest charity, peace and concord.' Dr Worthington, another student in the early days of the college, recalled that 'there was no need of any written law to keep the members in discipline . . . If a question arose about anything, it was decided by the president, Allen, whose will was a law to all. . . . He alone prescribed the laws of study and piety. He taught his people by example, word of mouth and in every way. Everyone depended on his will like sons, and that too most readily.' Dr Humphrey Ely, the Welsh priest, added to the generally idyllic picture when he wrote that the students at Douai lived 'very quietly without rigorous rules and penances . . . governed and ruled by the countenance and look of one man whom all from highest to the lowest did love and highly reverence'.

William Allen had had the commonsense to realise that it would be impossible to attempt to subject his students – men of widely differing ages and backgrounds – to conventional college discipline. 'A little government there is and order,' he was to write, 'but no bondage nor straitness in the world. There is neither oath nor statute nor other bridle nor chastisement; but reason and every man's conscience in honest superiority and subalternation each one towards others.' This wise and liberal policy paid handsome dividends. It was work after Allen's heart and in later years, when his feet were set on murkier paths, he always remembered Douai with affectionate nostalgia.

Not that it was easy; apart from the battle with the common adversary, Allen, like all successful pioneers, had to contend with jealousy and prejudice from his own side. But his most urgent problems were connected with money, or rather lack of it. During the first seven years of its existence the college was entirely dependent on voluntary contributions, supplemented after 1570 by its President's salary as Professor of Divinity at the university. Even when a regular allowance began to come from Rome money continued to be a problem, for Allen steadfastly refused to turn away anyone who came to his door. As a result, conditions at Douai were spartan – so much so that the two Belgians who formed part of the original intake soon took themselves off – but to the zealous and idealistic a life of poverty made its own appeal. In 1575, a visitor reported seeing nearly sixty men and youths of the greatest promise seated at three tables, 'eating so pleasantly a little broth, thickened merely with the commonest roots, that you could have sworn they were feasting on stewed raisins and prunes, English delicacies'.

The living may have been plain, but the thinking at Douai was high. Although Allen wrote that 'our students, being intended for the English harvest, are not required to excel or be great proficients in theological science' and laid down that, above all, 'they must abound in zeal for God's house, charity and thirst for souls', he did not make the mistake of underrating the opposition. He knew that if the new generation of priests he was hoping to create were to have any chance of reversing current trends in England, they must be educated and trained to meet and beat the enemy on his own ground.

'In the first place,' he told Jean Vendeville in a long apologia for the college and its work, written about 1578, 'since it is of great consequence that they should be familiar with the text of holy Scripture and its more approved meanings, and have at their fingers' ends all those passages which are correctly used by Catholics in support of our faith or impiously misused by heretics in opposition to the church's faith, we provide for them, as a means by which they may gain this power, a daily lecture on the New Testament, in which the exact and genuine sense of the words is briefly dictated to them. . . .

'At suitable times they take down from dictation with reference to the controversies of the present day all those passages of holy Scripture which make for Catholics or are distorted by heretics, together with short notes concerning the arguments to be drawn from the one and the answers to be made to the other. A disputation is held once a week on these passages, in which the students defend in turn not only the Catholic side against the texts of Scripture alleged by heretics, but also the heretical side against those which Catholics bring forward, that they may all know better how to prove our doctrines by argument and to refute the contrary opinions.'

On Sundays and feast days the advanced students took it in turn to preach a sermon in English, 'in order to acquire greater power and grace in the use of the vulgar tongue, a thing on which the heretics plume themselves exceedingly and by which they do great injury to the simple folk'. Allen was well aware of the importance of this advantage which the heretics, 'however ignorant they may be in other points', had over the more learned Catholics, 'who having been educated in the universities and the schools do not commonly have at command the text of Scripture or quote it except in Latin'. 'Our adversaries, on the other hand,' wrote Allen, 'have at their fingers' end all those passages of Scripture which seem to make for them, and by a certain deceptive adaptation and alteration of the sacred words, produce the effect of appearing to say nothing but what comes from the Bible.'

As well as realising the need for a Catholic version of the Bible in English – a need which Douai was later to supply – Allen knew it was vital that his students should not only be able to preach fluently and persuasively to the 'unlearned' in their own language, but should also have no difficulty in holding their own in any scriptural quoting match. (It was a favourite scoring point of the reformers to demonstrate that there was no justification for Catholic dogma in Holy Writ.) Every day, therefore, at dinner and supper, three or four chapters of the Bible were read aloud and before they left their places at table the students heard 'a running explanation' of one chapter of the Old and another of the New Testament, this being in addition to daily private study beforehand. By this method the Old Testament was gone through twelve times and the New Testament sixteen times during the three years which the course at Douai normally lasted, and it proved, not surprisingly, to be 'a great help towards acquiring a more than common familiarity with the text'.

But although he was prepared to take on the opposition at their own game where necessary, in drawing up his training programme William Allen never lost sight of the fundamental issues. Since the budding missionaries were to be employed in administering the sacraments and hearing confessions, they had to be carefully instructed in the catechism and pastoral matters. They must also know as much as possible about ecclesiastical penalties and censures, and 'of the way to deal with their people in such cases'. It was Allen's ambition not merely to restore 'a real and true observance of church discipline' among the afflicted English Catholics, but to see every aspect of the Faith – especially the power and authority of the Pope – 'better known and more devoutly and purely honoured than it used to be; for it is the exceeding neglect and contempt with which this was treated by pastors and people alike that God had punished with the present miserable desolation'. This was, of course, the only possible, the only bearable explanation.

Even the most optimistic well-wishers of the small experiment begun at Douai on 29 September 1568 knew that results, if any, could not be expected for some time. The startling reappearance on the scene of Mary Queen of Scots was another matter altogether. The fact that Queen Elizabeth's Catholic subjects now had not only a potential leader but a potential alternative to their present sovereign actually in their midst was to produce immediate, if unfortunate results, and for nearly twenty years was to cast an ever darkening shadow across English political life.

The relative positions of the two Queens had changed radically during the past decade. Elizabeth had survived the first critical years of her reign and come safely through a major crisis in her emotional life. 'Queen Elizabeth,' wrote an admiring Venetian, 'owing to her courage and to her great power of mind . . . declines to rely upon anyone save herself, although she is most gracious to all.' Her stature as a ruler had increased slowly but steadily and at thirty-four she was firmly established on her throne – a force to be reckoned with in international affairs.

Mary's fortunes, by contrast, had fluctuated violently. In November 1558 she had stood on the threshold of a career which promised to be of unexampled brilliance. By the following summer, the freakish death of Henri II had brought her to the French throne beside her youthful husband – a Queen twice over at sixteen and a half. By December 1560 the sickly Francois II was dead, leaving 'as heavy and dolorous a wife as of right she had good cause to be'. The Venetian ambassador, Michel Surian, took a sympathetic view of Mary's altered circumstances. 'The thoughts of widowhood at so early an age,' he wrote, 'and of the loss of a consort who was so great a King, and who so dearly loved her, and also that she is dispossessed of the Crown of France, with little hope of recovering that of Scotland which is her sole patrimony and dower, so afflict her that she will not receive any consolation, but, brooding over her disasters with constant tears and passionate and doleful lamentations, she universally inspires great pity.'

Not quite universally, though, for Nicholas Throckmorton, Queen Elizabeth's representative in Paris, could only regard Mary's dispossession from the French crown as providential. 'And yet, my lord,' he warned Robert Dudley, 'this I trust shall be no occasion to make her Majesty less considerate, or her counsel less provident, for assuredly the Queen of Scotland, her Majesty's cousin, doth carry herself so honourably, advisedly, and discreetly, as I cannot but fear her progress.'

When Throckmorton saw Mary on 31 December, she had recovered her spirits and begun to take stock of her situation. Her ten-year-old brother-in-law was now King of France and effective power had passed into the hands of the Queen Mother, that formidable matriarch Catherine de Medici, whose chief preoccupation lay in defending the rights of her remaining Valois sons against the predatory House of Guise. As a childless dowager Mary's immediate usefulness to her Guise relations was at an end and their star had gone into temporary eclipse. Meanwhile, the new Regent was making no particular secret of the fact that she would prefer the Queen of Scots' room to her company. All the same, Mary could have stayed on in France, living in comfortable retirement on her dower lands while awaiting future developments. Not surprisingly, this unexciting course held no appeal for a full-blooded, optimistic young woman of eighteen.

Mary had been brought up to regard her Scottish kingdom as a mere appanage of France (at the time of her marriage she had signed a secret deed of gift making over Scotland, and, incidentally, her rights to the English succession unconditionally to the crown of France in the event of her death without heirs), but in the early spring of 1561 Scotland appeared in a rather different light, offering a challenge and a promise of adventure with perhaps more glittering triumphs to come. The only question was, would Scotland have her back?

Two years earlier the Protestant nobility, banded together under the title of the Lords of the Congregation and egged on by John Knox, newly returned from the fountain-head at Geneva, had risen in revolt against the Catholic and alien government of the Queen Regent, Mary of Guise. 'Everything is in a ferment in Scotland,' wrote John Jewel happily to Peter Martyr. 'Knox, surrounded by a thousand followers, is holding assemblies throughout the whole kingdom. The old Queen has been compelled to shut herself up in garrison. The nobility, with united hearts and hands, are restoring religion throughout the country, in spite of all opposition. All the monasteries are everywhere levelled with the ground: the theatrical dresses, the sacrilegious chalices, the idols, the altars, are consigned to the flames; not a vestige of the ancient superstition and idolatry is left. What do you ask for? You have often heard of drinking like a Scythian; but this is churching it like a Scythian.' Unfortunately, though, the military capabilities of the Lords of the Congregation did not match their iconoclastic fervour and they were forced to turn to the Queen of England for help. 'If the occasion is lost,' Kirkcaldy of Grange told William Cecil, 'ye may thirst for, yet not find another.'

The English Secretary of State scarcely needed reminding that this might well be a unique opportunity to get the French out of Scotland, neither did his mistress. Both, however, fully realised the risks involved. To interfere in Scottish internal affairs would be a direct violation of the four-month-old Treaty of Câteau-Cambresis and would be to invite retaliation by one of the greatest military powers in Europe. If things went badly, Elizabeth could easily find herself with a victorious French army sitting on the border and only the Catholic North Country between it and the vulnerable, undefended South. Cecil, always a careful man, weighed up the pros and cons and finally came to the conclusion that the game was worth the candle. The Queen agreed with him, up to a point, and in August 1559 Sir Ralph Sadler was sent north with £3,000 in gold to be distributed among the rebels under conditions of elaborate secrecy.

Thus, within a year of her accession, Elizabeth first found herself cast in the role of Protestant champion. It was never a role she enjoyed as, quite apart from the risk and expense it invariably carried with it, she never lost her reservations about the ultimate wisdom of encouraging other people's rebels. In the cast of Scotland, these reservations were strengthened by the fact that she could not stand John Knox and his revolutionary Calvinism at any price. The long-suffering Cecil soon discovered that the mere mention of the name of Knox was enough to provoke and explosion.

As the winter drew on, it became distressingly apparent that the Scots were not going to be able to dislodge the Regent and her three thousand or so French veterans from their stronghold at Leith without more visible assistance than surreptitious subsidies, but here Elizabeth balked. Cecil, now irrevocably committed to a policy of intervention, had to resort to threats of resignation to shift her. In December, a fleet under the command of William Winter was despatched to lie in the Firth of Forth, with orders to annoy the French and blockade the garrison at Leith. At the same time, any action Winter took was to appear to come 'of his own head and of himself, as though he had no commission therefore' from the Queen. William Winter performed his delicate task with skill and imagination, and has the distinction of being the first Elizabethan naval commander to weigh anchor with instructions of this kind.

It was beyond even Elizabeth's ingenuity to disclaim responsibility for an army, but by the time her land forces did eventually arrive under the walls of Leith in the spring of 1560, a number of external factors were beginning to make it look as if God might be a Protestant after all. Storms in the Channel the previous autumn had scattered and partially destroyed a French fleet carrying reinforcements for Scotland. The French government was now having serious trouble with its own heretics and in consequence had become demonstrably less eager to embroil itself with the Scottish variety. The death in June of that gallant warrior Mary of Guise took the heart out of the resistance of Leith, and news that Philip of Spain had been heavily defeated by the Turks in the Mediterranean removed any immediate fears of interference from that quarter.

William Cecil, therefore, found himself in an unexpectedly strong position at the peace talks which opened in Edinburgh on 19 June, and during the course of a fortnight's hard bargaining extracted a series of major concessions from the French Commissioners acting on behalf of the young Queen and her husband. Among other things, it was agreed that all French troops should be withdrawn from Scotland, the fortifications at Leith dismantled and that in future the country should be governed by a council of Scottish nobles. France also formally recognised the Queen of England's right to occupy her own throne and undertook that the King and Queen of France would give up their provocative use of the English royal arms and title. The burning question of religion was tactfully left in abeyance but when the Scots Parliament met in August they at once proceeded to abolish the Pope's authority and adopt a Calvinistic form of Protestantism as the national religion. Thomas Randolph, the English agent in Edinburgh, told Cecil that he had never seen 'so important matters sooner dispatched, or agreed to with better will'.

In these circumstances it was hardly surprising that the Lords of the Congregation should regard the prospect of the return of their Catholic sovereign with something less than enthusiasm. 'I believe here will be a mad world!' remarked William Maitland of Lethington. 'Our exactness and singularity in religion will never concur with her judgement; I think she will hardly be brought under the rule of our discipline, of the which we can remit nothing to any estate or person.'

Mary, as Queen of France, had refused to ratify the Treaty of Edinburgh and in the autumn of 1560 had expressed herself forcibly on the proceedings in the Scottish Parliament to Nicholas Throckmorton. '"My subjects of Scotland do their duty in nothing, nor have they performed one point that belongeth to them. I am their Queen," quoth she, "and so they call me, but they use me not so. They have done what pleaseth them, and though I have not many faithful there, yet those few that be there of my party, were not present when these matters were done, nor at this assembly. I will have them assemble by my authority, and proceed in their doings after the laws of the realm, which they so much boast of, and keep none of them. . . . I am their sovereign, but they take me not so. They must be taught to know their duties."'

In the spring of 1561 she was no longer in a position to take this high tone and had the sense to realise it. Guided by the advice of those experienced operators her Guise uncles to 'repose most upon them of the reformed religion' and who now held power, she set herself out to charm the English and Scottish envoys who came to France to look her over. It was noticeable that since her widowhood she had stopped using the English royal arms, but all the efforts of Nicholas Throckmorton and the Earl of Bedford to get her to ratify the Treaty of Edinburgh were unsuccessful. She must first take the advice of the Estates and nobles of her own realm, said Mary demurely. It was only right and proper that they should be consulted before she took such an important step. She hoped Queen Elizabeth would understand and repeatedly declared her earnest desire to live in peace and amity with her 'good sister and tender cousin'.

To the Scots she indicated that she was ready to let bygones be bygones and accept the status quo in Scotland. Not, of course, that she could have done anything else but she did it gracefully, insisting only that she must be given the right to practise her own religion in private. 'I will be plain with you,' she told Throckmorton. 'The religion that I profess I take to be most acceptable to God, and indeed neither do I know, nor desire to know, any other. Constancy doth become all folks well, but none better than Princes and such as have rule over realms, and especially in the matter of religion. I have been brought up in this religion, and who might credit me in anything if I should show myself light in this case?' Having made her position clear, adding rather pointedly that she was 'none of those who would change their religion every year', Mary repeated that she had no intention of constraining her subjects in matters of conscience and trusted in return that no one would attempt to constrain her. This sounded reasonable enough – evidently Mary Stuart was no Mary Tudor –

and as it began to dawn on the Scots that their Queen's dynastic potentialities would now work in favour of Scotland rather than France, they cheered up and got ready to welcome her home.

Mary in fact was winning golden opinions all round and Nicholas Throckmorton's despatches were full of her virtue and discretion, her good judgement, her 'wisdom and kingly modesty' and her willingness to 'be ruled by good counsel'. It may not have been entirely tactful to praise one Queen to another in quite such glowing terms, but Throckmorton had not yet forgiven his mistress for the acute embarrassment she had caused him the previous autumn when, for a few nerve-wracking weeks, it had looked very much as if she meant to marry a man strongly suspected of having done away with his wife.

Elizabeth, for her part, was clearly disconcerted and not a little alarmed by the siren-like propensities being displayed by her eighteen-year-old cousin. If Mary could so captivate Nicholas Throckmorton, a hardheaded diplomat and man-of-the-world, there was no knowing what sort of havoc she might create among the hot-headed, restless Scottish warlords. Who could tell how many simple men might be 'carried away with vain hope, and brought abed with fair words'?

When Mary made a formal application for the Queen of England's safe conduct for her journey, her envoy met with a flat refusal. Let the Queen of Scots first ratify the Treaty of Edinburgh, as she was in honour bound to do. Then would be the time to start talking about passports. This was a pretty devastating public snub, but irritatingly Mary kept both her nerve and her temper. She was only sorry, she said, that she had demeaned herself by asking for something she did not need. The English had not been able to prevent her voyage to France thirteen years ago. They could not prevent her from returning home now. Mary only wanted to be friends but, she told Nicholas Throckmorton, it was beginning to look as if the Queen of England was more interested in 'the amity of her disobedient subjects than of their Sovereign'. Elizabeth had called her young and inexperienced. Yet, said Mary, she hoped she knew how to behave uprightly towards her friend and kinsfolk and would not allow *her* passion to betray her into using unbecoming language of another Queen and her nearest kinswoman. She was not without allies, she added pointedly, and Elizabeth would find she was not to be bullied.

In the first round of the personal contest between the cousins, Mary had won on points. Elizabeth, realising that she had over-reacted and was getting bad publicity as a result, did finally send the safe conduct with its implicit offer of an amicable meeting – a meeting which might have had such incalculable results – but it was too late. Mary had already sailed for Scotland. The long journey to Fotheringay had begun.

For the next two years all Mary's efforts in the field of foreign policy were directed towards obtaining formal recognition of her status as heiress presumptive to the English throne. Within a fortnight of her return home, Maitland of Lethington, ablest of her Scottish councillors, was despatched to London with instructions to approach the Queen of England on the subject. He met with no success but, in the course of several interviews, Elizabeth talked very freely about her attitude to Mary and the whole delicate matter of the succession.

She knew that Mary was 'of the blood of England', her cousin and next kinswoman, so that she was bound by nature to love her. 'And as my proceedings have made sufficient declaration to the world,' she went on, 'that I never meant evil towards her person nor her realm, so can they that knew most of my mind bear me accord that in time of most offence and when she, by bearing my arms and acclaiming to the title of my crown, had given me just cause to be most angry with her, yet could I never find in my heart to hate her, imputing rather the fault to others than to herself. As for the title of my crown, for my time I think she will not attain it, nor make impediment to my issue, if any shall come of my body. For so long as I live, there shall be no other Queen in England but I.' As for the succession, that was a matter she would not meddle in. It was like the sacrament of the altar. Some thought one thing, some another and 'whose judgement is best, God knows'. If Mary's right was good, Elizabeth would do nothing to prejudice it. 'I for my part,' she told Maitland, 'know none better, nor that myself would prefer to her.' Neither, in fact, could she think of any serious competitor.

At their next meeting, the Queen returned to the same thorny topic. 'I have always abhorred to draw in question the title of the crown,' she said feelingly, 'so many disputes have been already touching it in the mouths of men. Some that this marriage was unlawful, some that someone was a bastard, some other, to and fro, as they favour it or mislike it.' 'Howsoever it be,' declared Elizabeth Tudor, summing up the whole tangle in masterly fashion, 'so long as I live, I shall be Queen of England. When I am dead, they shall succeed that have most right.' If that person was Mary, well and good. If someone else could show a better right, then it was not reasonable to ask Elizabeth to do them 'a manifest injury'.

Maitland had argued that settling the succession on Mary would cement the friendship between them. Elizabeth did not agree. 'Think you that I could love my winding sheet?' she enquired brutally. There was another consideration – the most weighty of all. 'I know the inconstancy of the people of England,' remarked their Queen, 'how they ever mislike the present government and have their eyes fixed upon the person that is next to succeed, and naturally men be so disposed. *Plures adorant solem orientem quam occidentem*.' Many a politician to his sorrow has since learnt the truth of that piece of Elizabethan wisdom.

The Queen went on to illustrate her point by favouring Maitland with one of her infrequent references to her own early days. 'I have good experience of myself in my sister's time,' she said, 'how desirous men were that I should be in [her] place and earnest to set me up. And if I would have consented, I know what enterprises would have been attempted to bring it to pass, and now perhaps the affections of some are altered. As children dream in their sleep of apples, and in the morning when as they wake and find not the apples they weep; so every man that bore me good will when I was Lady Elizabeth . . . imagineth with himself that immediately after my coming to the crown every man should be rewarded according to their own fantasy, and now finding the event answer not their expectation it may be that some could be content of new change, in hope to be then in better case.'

At the age of twenty-eight Elizabeth saw things clearly and saw them whole, without bitterness but without illusion, either about herself or her fellow men. 'No princes' revenues be so great that they are able to satisfy the insatiable cupidity of men,' she observed. 'And if we, either for not giving to men at their discretion or yet for any other cause, should miscontent any [of] our subjects, it is to be feared that if they knew a certain successor of our crown they would have recourse thither; and what danger it were, she being a puissant princess and so near our neighbour, ye may judge. I deal plainly with you, albeit my subjects I think love me as becomes them, yet is nowhere so great perfection that all are content.'

Maitland did his best to persuade her to change her mind. He was sure, he said, that Mary would be only too pleased to agree to whatever safeguards Elizabeth liked to name. Elizabeth was unimpressed. She 'still harped on that string: saying "It is hard to bind princes by any security where hope is offered of a kingdom"'. In private conversation she would admit that she considered Mary to be her natural and lawful successor. She was fully prepared to be friendly and would like to meet her 'good sister and cousin' as soon as it could be arranged. She was ready to have the Treaty of Edinburgh reviewed and to modify the clause which bound Mary to abstain from using and bearing the English royal arms and title 'at all times coming'. She would be quite content if Mary would agree not to bear the arms of England or style herself Queen of England during Elizabeth's lifetime or that of her children. Further than this she would not go. She would not make the Queen of Scots her heir 'by order of Parliament' and nothing Maitland could say would budge her.

No one, of course, had the bad taste to say so aloud, but the possibility that once Mary had received public and Parliamentary recognition of her right to the reversion of the English crown, the temptation to hasten the processes of nature might be too much for her (or for those of her friends who could feel they would be serving the Church of Rome at the same time) must have been in Elizabeth's mind. Something of the sort had certainly been in William Cecil's mind when, in the spring of 1561, he had drawn up a memoranda of certain precautions he and his colleagues wished their mistress to observe: 'We think it very convenient,' wrote the Secretary of State, 'that your Majesty's apparel, and especially all manner of things that shall touch any part of your Majesty's body bare, be circumspectly looked unto; and that no person be permitted to come near it, but such as have the trust and charge thereof.

'Item: That no manner of perfume either in apparel, or sleeves, gloves or suchlike, or otherwise that shall be appointed for your Majesty's savour, be presented by any stranger or other person, but that the same be corrected by some other fume.

'Item: That no foreign meat or dishes being dressed out of your Majesty's Court be brought to your food, without assured knowledge from whom the same cometh; and that no use be had hereof. . . .

'Item: It may please your Majesty to give order who shall take the charge of the back doors to your chamberer's chambers where laundresses, tailors, wardrobers and such use to come; and that the same doors may be duly attended upon as becometh and not to stand open but upon necessity. . . .'

Cecil had his moments of disenchantment with Elizabeth – 'God send our mistress a husband and by time a son, that we may hope our posterity shall have a masculine succession' he wrote to his friend Nicholas Throckmorton at a time when she was being particularly trying – but he and a number of others closely associated with the new regime were only too acutely conscious of how much depended on the fragile thread of one woman's life. The Queen's near fatal attack of smallpox in the autumn of 1562 brought this danger home to the country at large for the first time and led to a determined but fruitless attempt by both Houses of Parliament to persuade Elizabeth to marry and to name her successor, although none of the members showed any enthusiasm for the claims of the Queen of Scots.

The Queen of Scots had by no means given up hope of cajoling the Queen of England into changing her mind, and throughout the early sixties she worked hard and by no means unsuccessfully to build up an atmosphere of trust and goodwill. Then, in February 1565, she first set eyes on another of her cousins, Henry Stuart, Lord Darnley, a handsome baby-faced youth of nineteen, and fell head over heels in love. Prudence, politics and statecraft alike were thrown to the winds. Mary in the grip of physical passion was no longer willing 'to be ruled by good counsel'. She quarrelled fatally with her illegitimate half-brother James Stewart, now Earl of Moray, and had apparently ceased to care if she offended Queen Elizabeth. Her old admirer Nicholas Throckmorton was shocked at the change in her and William Cecil feared the worst.

After Mary herself Darnley, by the accepted laws of primogeniture, stood closest to the English throne, and Cecil not unnaturally considered that an alliance between them could only comfort and encourage 'all such as be affected to the Queen of Scots either for herself or for the opinion of her pretence to this crown or for the desire to have a change of the form of religion in this realm'. 'The general scope and mark of all their designs,' he wrote, 'is, and always shall be, to bring the Queen of Scots to have the royal crown of this realm. And therefore, although the devices may vary amongst themselves for the compass hereof . . . yet all their purposes, drifts, devices and practices shall wholly and only tend to make the Queen of Scots queen of this realm and to deprive our sovereign thereof.'

But there was no stopping Mary and by July she had embarked on her disastrous second marriage. From then on the home life of the Queen of Scotland became different indeed from the general run of well-regulated royal households. None of the professional Scotland-watchers stationed at Berwick and in Edinburgh itself were in the least surprised when the egregious Darnley met his spectacularly messy end at Kirk o'Field, but his widow's subsequent career, culminating in her marriage to the Earl of Bothwell, a divorced man, according to the rites of the Protestant church, was watched with horrified astonishment by the outside world.

Mary's friends abroad could scarcely believe their eyes. The Venetian ambassador in Paris was of the opinion that Catholicism had now no hope of ever raising its head in Scotland again. The King of France and his mother told Mary's ambassador she 'had behaved so ill and made herself so hateful to her subjects' that they were unable to give her either help or advice. The Pope decided to have nothing more to do with her, 'unless by and by he shall discover in her some sign of improvement in life and religion'. The Holy Father, in fact, was moved to remark that he found it difficult to say which of the two queens in Britain was the worst.

It has been suggested that Mary may have been subject to attacks of porphyria, the hereditary disorder which caused the intermittent madness of her descendant George III. Certainly this is the most charitable explanation. Mary's contemporaries, however, could only suppose that the Queen of Scotland had allowed her illicit passion to run away with her and 'by yielding to spite and appetite' had conclusively demonstrated, as one Venetian delicately put it, 'that statecraft is no business for ladies'. But it was not long before the reaction began to set in. Mary Stuart at large and defiantly flouting every convention in the book was one thing. Mary Stuart in adversity, insulted, imprisoned, threatened and forced to abdicate by her own subjects, was quite another.

'Although she have merited all the evil she now endures,' wrote Michel Surian reflecting on the misfortunes of the Queen of Scots, 'yet does she deserve some measure of pity, since all are apt to err, not to say a lady, and a young lady, and meet for pleasure as she was.' Mary's escape from Lochleven helped to hasten the process of rehabilitation. 'With regard to her flight,' reported Giovanni Correr from Paris, 'it is judged here, by those who know the site and how strictly she was guarded, that her escape was most miraculous.'

Mary had also written to her uncle the Cardinal of Lorraine 'a letter . . . which should move every hard heart to have compassion upon her. The first lines express that she begs pardon of God, and of the world, for the past errors of her youth, which she promises to amend for the future. Then she acknowledges her release solely from His Divine Majesty, and returns him most humble thanks for having given her so much strength in these her afflictions; and she declares that she has never swerved in the least from her firm purpose to live and die a Catholic, as she now intends to do more than ever.' Thus by the time the Queen of Scots landed on the Queen of England's doorstep the romantic legend of the misprized heroine had already begun to flourish. With the Queen of Scots nothing succeeded like failure.

There can be no doubt of Mary's courage, her resourcefulness, her invincibly optimistic outlook, her personal charm and her ruthless egotism – all qualities which were to make her infinitely more dangerous as a homeless fugitive in her cousin's realm than she had ever been as a neighbouring sovereign.

17

All The North is Ready

'All the north is ready and only awaits the release of the Queen of Scotland.'
Guerau de Spes, London, 17 September 1569

Fifteen hundred and sixty-nine was a year of crisis for the Queen of England – a year when, in the words of John Strype, the clouds began to gather over her head and her peace seemed 'to be much threatened by Popish combinations'. Certainly the outlook was unsettled, both at home and abroad. In France religious civil war still raged intermittently. Elizabeth made no attempt to intervene – she had burnt her fingers at that game six years before – but the embattled Huguenots were receiving a good deal of unofficial aid from sympathisers across the Channel. In present circumstances the regime of Charles IX and Catherine de Medici was not looking for trouble but in the general turmoil there was always a danger that it might be overthrown by the ultra-Catholic Guises, who had a considerable popular following, especially in Paris. The Guise faction, led by Mary Stuart's influential relations, was dedicated to the extermination of heresy in general and to the promotion of the Queen of Scots' cause in particular. It represented an obvious menace to Elizabeth and rumours of plots were always coming out of France. In the summer of 1568 Captain François, an Italian secret agent otherwise known as Franchiotto, sent a warning to Cecil that these rumours should not be taken too lightly and advising the Queen to look well to her food, bedding and other furniture, in case an attempt was made to poison her.

There was trouble of a more immediate nature brewing across the North Sea where the Low Countries, England's old allies and trading partners, were in revolt against their Spanish sovereign. Unlike his father the Emperor, King Philip had never taken much interest in his Dutch and Flemish territories – legacy of that strange, long-ago marriage of his grandmother Juana of Castile to Philip of Burgundy – regarding them chiefly as a useful source of revenue. The nobility of the seventeen provinces resented the loss of their ancient liberties under his increasingly heavy-handed rule; the merchants and burghers resented his taxation. But the conflict had been sparked off by the spread of a militant form of Protestantism in the north and east and in Antwerp, commercial capital of Northern Europe. Philip might be obliged to tolerate heresy in other countries for reasons of political expediency; in no circumstances whatever would he tolerate it in his own dominions, and in 1567 he despatched the notorious Duke of Alva and an army of 10,000 'blackbeards' to carry out a policy of blood and iron in the disobedient provinces.

The thought of this kind of force no more than a day's sail from its own coastline was not a comforting one for the English government, especially as Anglo-Spanish relations began to deteriorate rapidly at the end of the sixties. There had been a good deal of unpleasantness over the expulsion by King Philip of Elizabeth's ambassador Dr John Man who, among other things, had been ill-mannered enough to refer to the Pope as 'a canting little monk' at a Madrid dinner party. The new Spanish ambassador who arrived in London late in 1568 was also singularly unfitted for his task. It was unfortunate, therefore, that Don Guerau de Spes at once had to deal with an incident which called for diplomatic skill and tact of a high order.

Some time in November four small coasters laden with bullion for Alva's army were driven by bad weather and French pirates to take shelter in Plymouth. The temptation thus offered to a queen perennially short of ready cash was hardly to be resisted. Elizabeth made no attempt to resist it – not when she discovered that the money could still technically be regarded as the property of the Genoese bankers who were lending it to Philip. The Genoese had no objection to transferring their business to another client. Philip and the Duke of Alva were predictably annoyed. When Alva, egged on by hysterical reports from de Spes, retaliated by placing an embargo on English trade in the Low Countries, he was even more annoyed to find that this hurt him more than Elizabeth. It also provided him with an illuminating demonstration of how completely an unfriendly England, assisted by Dutch and Huguenot privateers, could disrupt his communications with Spain, and the Duke, cursing de Spes, was obliged to open time-consuming negotiations with a blandly impenitent Elizabeth.

On paper, the King of Spain should have had no difficulty in dealing with the Queen of England as she deserved. In practice, the affair of the treasure ships was a classic and not unfamiliar example of the way in which a small nation, lucky enough to occupy a strategic position on the map, is able to tie tin cans on the tail of a giant.

All the same, some conservative members of the English Council looked askance at this form of brinkmanship and while England continued to harbour a Trojan horse in the shape of Mary Queen of Scots, it might well prove an expensive luxury. As early as July 1568 the then Spanish ambassador, Guzman de Silva, had reported, 'the Queen of Scots certainly has many friends, and they will increase hourly, as the accusations of complicity in the murder of her husband are being forgotten and her marriage with Bothwell is now being attributed to compulsion and fear.

This view is being spread,' added de Silva, 'and friends easily persuade themselves of the truth of what they believe.' How right he was!

Guerau de Spes, writing to Philip in January 1569, described Mary as 'a lady of great spirit', gaining so many friends where she was that 'with little help she would be able to get this kingdom into her hands'. Later in the same despatch he wrote gleefully: 'the Queen of Scotland told my servant to convey to me the following message – "Tell the ambassador that if his master will help me, I shall be queen of England in three months and mass shall be said all over the country"'.

William Cecil, reviewing the state of the realm about this time in a memorandum divided into the headings Perils and Remedies, saw the general situation in thoroughly gloomy terms. At the top of his list of perils came 'a conspiration of the Pope, King Philip, the French king and sundry potentates of Italy to employ all their forces for the subversion of the professors of the gospel'. It was always Cecil's nightmare that sooner or later the Catholic powers would combine against Elizabeth. The fact that they had not already done so was, in his opinion, sheer good luck and Cecil did not believe in trusting to luck. The French Huguenots did occasionally win a battle or a temporary measure of toleration, but their destruction looked like being only a matter of time. It was hardly probable that the Calvinists in the Low Countries could survive Alva's calculated reign of terror and already the pressure on Philip's other flank by the Turks in the Mediterranean was diminishing. As soon as France and Spain were free of internal problems, they would turn their joint attention to England – where Mary Stuart was waiting for them.

Cecil's remedies included a more vigorous application of the law governing religious uniformity, a programme of aid for the rebels in both France and the Low Countries, and the establishment of a defensive Protestant alliance with Denmark, Sweden and the German Lutheran princes. He also recommended that the country's defences should be strengthened, especially along the south and east coasts, and that the navy should be put on a war footing.

The English Secretary of State was never one for looking on the bright side but he was unquestionably a highly experienced, highly intelligent observer of the international political scene and clearly he placed no reliance whatever on the possibility of peaceful co-existence between the two ideologies. Cecil was no warmonger, but by the end of the sixties he saw Western Europe in terms of two armed camps with a final confrontation of might against right as inevitable and perhaps not long delayed.

In fact, the troubles of 1569 came from within rather than without and before the year's end they had culminated in the first and, as it turned out, the only serious armed rebellion of Elizabeth's reign. The Rising in the North or the Rising of the Northern Earls, as it is variously known, was not primarily an affair of Catholics versus Protestants, but it rapidly became an affair of old versus new and its success could only have benefited the Catholic cause. It had its origins in a suggestion that the Queen of Scots might be married to the Duke of Norfolk, first put forward in the autumn of 1568 by a well-meaning body of opinion which was not happy about keeping Mary in England, to all intents and purposes a State prisoner. Elizabeth was not happy about keeping Mary in England either – she found it both expensive and embarrassing – but unless and until some formula could be hammered out by which the Queen of Scots could be restored to her throne without prejudicing the Earl of Moray's government, there seemed no alternative.

Running parallel with the unofficial plan for Mary's future, but soon to become inextricably involved with it, was a Cecil-Must-Go movement gathering strength among the nobility, nominally headed by Norfolk. The conservative peers could see the same dangers from abroad that Cecil did, but they favoured a policy of appeasement – the return of Alva's bullion and all Spanish merchandise currently being detained in English ports, the cutting off of all aid to the French rebels, the release of the Queen of Scots and recognition of her status as heir presumptive. They were also, of course, jealous of the Secretary's power and influence. The reason why Cecil escaped the fate of Thomas Cromwell lay in the fact that the present Duke of Norfolk was not the man his grandfather had been and Queen Elizabeth was emphatically not the kind of monarch her father had been. She might drive her loyal servants to the verge of nervous breakdown, but she was not in the habit of throwing them to the wolves.

Nevertheless, it was an uneasy summer for the Queen and her Secretary of State. The Norfolk marriage scheme may, at its inception, have been an honest if somewhat naïve attempt to find a solution to the problem of Mary by subjecting her to a trustworthy and suitably high-ranking English husband; but it is noticeable that none of its promoters – least of all the bridegroom elect – could quite bring themselves to mention it to Elizabeth. Elizabeth soon got to hear about it, though, and was under no illusions as to who would be the dominant partner in such a union, or of what its consequences would be to herself. She told the Earl of Leicester in September that if it took place she would be in the Tower within four months and ordered Norfolk on his allegiance to deal no more in the matter. 'But,' wrote Guerau de Spes hopefully, 'I do not believe the Duke will desist from his enterprise in consequence. A stronger guard has been placed around the Queen of Scotland,' he went on, 'although I have understood that she will nevertheless soon find herself at liberty, and this country itself greatly disturbed. All the north is ready and only awaits the release of the Queen of Scotland.'

Vague but disquieting rumours had been coming in from the north for some weeks and when, at the end of September, the Duke of Norfolk suddenly bolted to his East Anglian estates, Elizabeth not unnaturally took alarm. 'I do not know what will happen' de Spes told King Philip on the 30th; 'but I understand, considering the number of the Duke's friends in England, he cannot be ruined, except by pusillanimity, and the Queen of Scotland has sent to urge him to behave valiantly and not to fear for his life which God would protect'. In fact, the shifty Norfolk who, without exactly meaning to, had become deeply involved with Mary and the dubious activities of such right-wing Catholics as the Earls of Northumberland and Westmorland, had lost his nerve. Elizabeth ordered him back to Court. He sent excuses, pleading illness. The Queen told him to come anyway, by litter if necessary, and a few days later he obeyed.

De Spes, who had been busy stirring the pot all summer, reported that 'the earls of Northumberland, Westmorland, Cumberland, Derby and many others, all Catholics, are much grieved at this cowardice, if such it can be called, of the Duke of Norfolk, and they have sent Northumberland's servant, who spoke to me before on the matter, to say that they will by armed forces release the Queen [of Scots] and take possession of all the north country, restoring the Catholic religion in this country'.

Norfolk had sent a message to the northern earls warning them not to go ahead with these enterprising plans and, for all their large talk, both Northumberland and Westmorland would have been glad enough of an excuse to back down. But Elizabeth, now thoroughly roused, summoned them to Court to give an account of themselves. The Earl of Sussex, President of the Council of the North and more than doubtful about the loyalty of his local levies should it come to a fight, advised against positive action. As the man on the spot he wanted to be allowed to 'nourish quiet' until the winter, when dark nights, wet weather and bad roads could be trusted to take the heat out of the situation. Sussex may well have been right. Unfortunately, though, Elizabeth had her doubts – unfairly as it turned out – about *his* loyalty and in any case she was in no mood to leave sedition to breed unchecked.

When the royal command reached Northumberland and Westmorland they were driven into a corner. Both had everything to lose and the example of Norfolk, now in the Tower, was scarcely encouraging; but they had gone too far to be able to refuse the Queen's challenge without forfeiting every shred of credibility. Northumberland's friends and servants, says William Camden, 'being now prepared for rebellion, seeing him thus wavering and fearful, called upon him at unawares in the dead of the night, crying that . . . his enemies were at hand with an armed power to carry him away prisoner.' They urged him not to betray the religion of his fathers at a moment when the Catholics were ready to rise all over England. The Countess of Westmorland wept and exclaimed dramatically, 'We and our country were shamed for ever, that now in the end we should seek holes to creep into.'

Neither of the earls was proof against this form of blackmail, and to the sound of church bells being rung backwards 'to stir up the multitude' they issued proclamations declaring themselves 'the Queen's true and faithful subjects', but: 'Forasmuch as divers disordered and evil disposed persons about the Queen's majesty have, by their subtle and crafty dealing to advance themselves, overcome in this our realm the true and Catholic religion towards God; and by the same abused the Queen, disordered the realm and now, lastly, seek and procure the destruction of the nobility: we therefore have gathered ourselves together to resist by force . . . to see redress of these things amiss, with restoring of all ancient customs and liberties to God's church and this noble realm; lest, if we should not do it ourselves, we might be reformed by strangers, to the great hazard of the state of this our country.'

The rebel forces went first to Durham, 'where they rent and trampled underfoot the English bibles and books of Common Prayer which they found in the churches. From thence they went small journeys, celebrating Mass in all places where they came, trooping together under their colours (wherein were painted in some the Five Wounds of Christ, in others the chalice), Richard Norton an old gentleman with a reverend gray head, bearing a Cross with a streamer before them.' These activities, faintly echoing the long-ago Pilgrimage of Grace, were no doubt a comfort to all those honest Catholics who had flocked to the banner of the Five Wounds. They were not, however, the most effective method of exploiting the rebels' brief initial advantage for, until reinforcements could be rushed from the Midlands and the South, the Earl of Sussex dared not risk an open engagement.

'There be not in all this country ten gentlemen that do favour and allow of her Majesty's proceedings in the cause of religion', wrote Sir Ralph Sadler to Cecil from York on 6 December, 'and the common people be ignorant, full of superstition and altogether blinded with the old popish doctrine, and therefore do so much favour the cause which the rebels make the colour of their rebellion, that though their persons be here with us, I assure you their hearts, for the most part, be with the rebels. . . . If the father be on this side, the son is on the other, and one brother with us, the other with the rebels.'

The situation could easily have turned ugly but, in the event, the prophecy of that hard-faced realist the Duke of Alva was fulfilled and the business did all end in smoke. There was no general rising of the English Catholics – even local support proved disappointing, the rebel forces mustering no more than about 5,000 horse and foot – and as the royal army advanced inexorably northward the rebels wavered, broke and fled. Apart from a shortlived flare-up under the leadership of Leonard Dacres the following February, stamped out in the only pitched battle of the whole campaign, the rising was over by the end of the year and the painful process of retribution had begun.

If the Northern rebels had been better led and better equipped, if they had been able to release Mary Stuart, if help had come from abroad, above all if they had received more popular support, the story might have had a different ending. As it was, the failure of the Rising in the North only served to emphasise the fact that the old, turbulent, baronial England was dead and that the future belonged to the new men – the lawyers and businessmen, the sober civil servants and bureaucrats – denizens of an increasingly urbanised, increasingly settled and commercialised society. The long arm of the central government could now reach at will into the remoter corners of the realm and make itself obeyed; the putrefying corpses hanging 'for a terror' in every town and village which had sent men to join the rebel army drove this depressing point home with grim finality.

The Northern Earls themselves sought refuge across the border, traditional sanctuary of English dissidents. But here, too, thanks largely to Elizabeth's careful cultivation of the Earl of Moray, times were changing. The Scots caught the Earl of Northumberland and presently handed him over, for a consideration. Westmorland 'at length escaped with some Englishmen into the Netherlands, where he led a very poor life, even to his old age, living upon a very slender pension from the Spaniard.' No longer would Neville or Percy or Dacres rule their territories like petty kings – the day of the over-mighty subject was done at last.

Although the underlying causes of the rebellion lay in a complex web of personal and economic jealousies, the two earls had naturally chosen to present their cause in the light of a disinterested bid for a return to religious orthodoxy. Government propaganda, equally naturally, presented them as ungrateful traitors to their sovereign and disturbers of 'the public and blessed peace of the realm'. 'As to the reformation of any great matters,' observed the royal proclamation issued on 24 November, 'they were as ill chosen two persons, if their qualities were considered, to have credit, as could be in the whole realm. For they were both in poverty; one having but a very small portion of that which his ancestors had left; and the other having wasted almost all his patrimony. The Queen therefore saw in what sort they went about to satisfy their private lack of ambition, through the persuasion of the number of desperate persons associated as parasites with them.'

A statement put out by the Earl of Sussex four days later had been equally scathing about the 'popish holiness' assumed to give false colour to manifest treason and to mislead the Queen's subjects. In fact, the most heartening conclusion which the government was able to draw from the events of 1569 was the manifest reluctance of the Queen's subjects to be misled. Out of a possible total of at least 60,000 men of fighting age in the Northern counties, the rebels had never been able to raise more than 7,000 at most. The remainder, with true native caution, had waited to see which way the cat would jump. It was ironic, therefore, that this resounding display of inertia by the English Catholics should have provided the occasion for the launching of the long-delayed thunderbolts from Rome.

During the first half-dozen years of Elizabeth's reign, while hopes of her marriage and conversion were still being entertained, the Vatican had leaned over backwards to be conciliatory and a campaign conducted by the English exiles during the early sixties for her immediate excommunication met with little support. But after the death of the genial Pius IV in 1565, the beginnings of a hard line papal policy became discernible. Pius V, a former Dominican friar nicknamed Brother Woodenshoe, was an ascetic, a theologian and a man of strict moral principles who disapproved of playing politics with the Word of God just as strongly as any left-wing member of the House of Commons.

The distressing antics of Mary Stuart during the first years of his pontificate had caused Pius to hesitate to smooth her path to the English throne, but by 1569 Elizabeth's excommunication was once more a live issue. The Pope sent a secret emissary to England that summer to sound the feelings of the native Catholics and he apparently brought back an encouraging report. Then, early in November, the first rumours that the nobility were preparing to rise against their heretic sovereign reached Rome. According to various garbled 'newsletters' coming in from the Netherlands and Germany, the Duke of Norfolk (curiously transmogrified into the Earl of Suffolk) was already married to the Queen of Scots; an insurgent army numbering 18,000 foot and 4,000 horse, all desperate men vowed to live and die for the Church of God, was in the field; there were disturbances in Wales and Ireland and 'opinion prevailed that the people would soon with one accord declare themselves for the Catholic faith and unite with the rest'. In February 1570 the Pope received an appeal for support from the Earls of Westmorland and Northumberland which had been despatched the previous November, and Nicholas Sander in Louvain assured him that if the papacy would only make a bold gesture, England would shortly be restored to the fold. Pius hesitated no longer and before the end of the month he had signed the bull *Regnans in Excelsis*. It was an uncompromising document.

'He that reigneth on high,' it ran, 'to whom is given all power in Heaven and in Earth, hath committed his One, Holy, Catholick and Apostolick Church, out of which there is no Salvation, to one alone upon Earth, namely to Peter, the chief of the Apostles, and to Peter's successor the Bishop of Rome, to be by him governed with plenary Authority. Him alone hath he made Prince over all People and all Kingdoms, to pluck up, destroy, scatter, consume, plant and build; that he may preserve his faithful people . . . in the Unity of the Spirit and present them spotless and unblamable to their Saviour. In Discharge of which Function, We, who are by God's goodness called to the government of the aforesaid Church, do spare no Pains, labouring with all earnestness, that Unity and the Catholick Religion . . . might be preserved sincere. But the number of the Ungodly hath gotten such Power, that there is now no place in the whole World left which they have not assayed to corrupt with their utmost Doctrines; and amongst others, Elizabeth, the pretended Queen of England, the Servant of Wickedness, lendeth thereunto her helping hand, with whom, as in a Sanctuary, the most pernicious persons have found a Refuge. This very Woman, having seized on the Kingdom, and monstrously usurped the place of Supreme Head of the Church in all England, and the chief Authority and Jurisdiction thereof, hath again reduced the said Kingdom into a miserable and ruinous Condition, which was so lately reclaimed to the Catholick Faith and a thriving condition.

'. . . We, seeing the Impieties and Wicked actions are multiplied one upon another, as also that the Persecution of the Faithful and Affliction for Religion groweth every day heavier and heavier through the Instigation and by means of the said Elizabeth, and since We understand her heart to be so hardened and obdurate that she hath not only contemned the godly Request and Admonitions of Catholick Princes concerning her Cure and Conversion, but also hath not so much as suffered the Nuncios of this See to cross the Seas for this purpose into England, are constrained of necessity to betake ourselves to the Weapons of Justice against her. . . .

'Being therefore supported with His authority whose pleasure it was to place Us (though unable for so great a Burthen) in this Supreme Throne of Justice, We do out of the fullness of our Apostolick Power, declare the aforesaid Elizabeth as being an Heretick and a Favourer of Hereticks, and her Adherents in the matters aforesaid, to have incurred the Sentence of Excommunication, and to be cut off from the Unity of the Body of Christ. And moreover We do declare her to be deprived of her pretended Title to the Kingdom aforesaid, and of all Dominion, Dignity and Privilege whatsoever; and also the Nobility, Subjects and People of the said Kingdom, and all others who have in any sort sworn unto her, to be for ever absolved from any such Oath, and all manner of Duty of Dominion, Allegiance and Obedience: and We also do by Authority of these Presents absolve them, and do deprive the said Elizabeth of her pretended Title to the Kingdom and all other things before named. And We do command and charge all and every the Noblemen, Subjects, People and others aforesaid, that they presume not to obey her, or her Orders, Mandates and Laws: and those which shall do the contrary, We do include them in the like Sentence of Anathema.'

For an organisation not normally noted for the speed of its reactions, the Vatican had on this occasion moved with commendable despatch – the whole process being completed within a period of three weeks. Even so, by the time copies of the bull could be circulated, the only visible signs of the Rising of the Northern Earls were the gallows disfiguring the countryside, and if Pius had seriously expected to release an upsurge of Catholic militancy in England, he was disappointed. Nor did the Catholic princes of Europe display any particular enthusiasm for the papal initiative. In fact, it caused the most Catholic prince of them all to take serious umbrage.

'His Holiness has taken this step without communicating with me in any way,' wrote Philip of Spain to Guerau de Spes, 'which certainly has greatly surprised me, because my knowledge of English affairs is such that I believe I could give a better opinion upon them and the course that ought to have been adopted under the circumstances than anyone else. Since, however, His Holiness allowed himself to be carried away by his zeal, he no doubt thought that what he did was the only thing requisite for all to turn out as he wished, and if such were the case, I, of all the faithful sons of the Holy See, would rejoice the most. But I fear that not only will this not be the case, but that this sudden and unexpected step will exacerbate feeling there and drive the Queen and her friends the more to oppress and persecute the few good Catholics still remaining in England.'

There were obvious difficulties in the way of telling the English people about their Queen's altered status and this unenviable task was finally undertaken by John Felton, a well-to-do Catholic living in Southwark, who in the early hours of 15 May 1570 nailed a smuggled copy of *Regnans in Excelsis* to the Bishop of London's door. Popular reaction was predictable. Patriotic ballads, broadsheets and pamphlets flooded the market. A particularly glutinous form of mud, compounded of personal insult and biblical quotation in about equal parts, was flung enthusiastically in the direction of Rome, much opportunity for merry sport being afforded by the convenient double meaning of the word 'bull'. *A disclosing of the great Bull and certain calves that he hath gotten and specially the Monster Bull that roared at my Lord Bishop's Gate* was an example of this genre.

The Bishop of Salisbury, in his rather more sonorously phrased *View of a Seditious Bull*, likened it to Pandora's box 'full of hurtful and unwholesome evils'. He found it to be 'a matter of great blasphemy against God and a practice to work much unquietness, sedition and treason'. 'For,' he went on, 'it deposeth the Queen's majesty from her royal seat and teareth the crown from her head: it dischargeth all us her natural subjects from all due obedience: it armeth one side of us against another: it emboldeneth us to burn, to spoil, to rob, to kill, and to cut one another's throat.' After making an attack on the institution of the papacy in general ('Where did Christ make this commission to Peter only? where be the words? in what scripture? in what gospel or epistle? Where did Christ ever say to Peter, I commit the government of the church to thee alone?'), John Jewel addressed himself to matters of more immediate importance. How dared the Pope, that 'wilful and unlearned friar', how dared he say that Queen Elizabeth was no lawful Queen? Elizabeth, the right inheritor of the houses of York and Lancaster, accepted by the nobility and joyfully acknowledged by all the commons of the realm; Elizabeth who was to her people 'as a comfortable water in a dry place, as a refuge for the tempest, and as the shadow of a great rock in a weary land'. The bishop felt it unnecessary to remind his public of the blessings of peace, but he did so all the same. They had only to look at neighbouring lands such as France and Flanders to see the ruined homes, the burning cities, the bloodshed, the widows and the fatherless children. 'But God, even our God, gave us Queen Elizabeth; and with her gave us peace, and so long a peace as England hath seldom seen.'

The bull was not merely an unwarrantable interference in the affairs of another nation; by its call for civil disobedience it struck at the very roots of society. 'What shall we do then for laws of common peace,' demanded Jewel, 'and of holding our possessions and goods to our private use, and so maintaining the good estate of our neighbours; for paying our rents to landlords, and custom and tribute where custom and tribute are due?' The Pope had said, 'Let not any obey these laws.' Was this fatherly counsel? Or was it the road to anarchy and misery? Had Christ ever set himself up against the temporal ruler? Had not Peter said, 'It is the will of God that you obey your prince'? Had not Paul required the Roman to obey Nero, 'the most wicked ruler that ever reigned'? Had not the prophets willed the children of Israel to pray for the life of Nebuchadnezzar, even though he 'fired and rased their city, sacked their sanctuary and spoiled their temple'?

Bishop Jewel was in no doubt as to the answers to all these questions. 'Remember,' he thundered in his peroration, 'if thou obey thy prince as God hath commanded thee, thou art accused by the Pope; or, if thou disobey thy prince as the Pope requireth thee, thou art condemned by the judgement of God. Remember that the Pope hath conference with traitors in all countries, that he raiseth subjects against their princes, that he causeth princes to plague their subjects . . . that he suffereth Jews and harlots to live in wealth and peace with him at Rome, and yet will not suffer a christian and lawful prince to live in the peace of her own country at home; that he is the procurer of theft and murder, of rebellion and dissension in the land; that he hath sent in a bull to show his meaning, and to work our disquiet, so bold and vain and impudent a bull, and so full fraught with blasphemy and untruth as never before him did any. Let these things never be forgotten: let your children remember them for ever.' And remember them they did – for centuries.

At the time, condemnation of the Pope's action was pretty well universal. In England 'the most part of the moderate sort of Papists secretly misliked this Bull, because there had been no Admonition preceded according to Law, and foreseeing also that thereby a great heap of mischiefs hung over their heads.' Informed Catholic opinion abroad regretted not so much the excommunication itself as the fact that the bull had been published without adequate arrangements – indeed without any arrangements at all – for putting it into effect. As the Bishop of Padua presently remarked to the Cardinal of Como, there was not much point in turning the key of Peter with one hand unless the other wielded the sword of Paul. By resorting to sanction which he was powerless to enforce Pius appeared to have committed a political blunder of unusual proportions; he had done nothing to improve the already parlous state of Catholicism in England and, at the same time, had seriously damaged the prestige of the papacy. This leads rather naturally to the question – why on earth did he do it?

It seems to be generally accepted that the Pope acted in good faith on the basis of inaccurate and out of date information; that he genuinely believed the English Catholics were both able and eager to throw off the heretic yoke and only hesitated to act lest, by taking the law into their own hands, they might endanger their souls. Clearly Pius was convinced that speed was of the essence – the bull itself bears every evidence of hasty drafting and certain formalities normally required by canon law were omitted from the proceedings. Clearly, too, his intelligence service left much to be desired. This in itself is surely a little odd. True, sixteenth-century international communications were slow and not infrequently impeded, but institutions like the great Italian banking houses and city states such as Venice were usually extremely well informed – they went to considerable trouble and expense to ensure that they were. Nor was England at this time in any sense an iron curtain country. Apart from little local difficulties like that with the Duke of Alva, trade and diplomatic relations with Catholic Europe went on uninterrupted and traffic moved freely in and out of English ports.

One is led to the conclusion that the Pope, impatient for an excuse to assert himself, preferred to listen to unconfirmed and prejudiced reports. In other words, he believed what he wanted to believe – a not uncommon human foible but perhaps an unfortunate one in the spiritual leader of Western Christendom. But although it is easy enough to condemn him for being precipitate, bigoted and stupid, it is also quite possible to see his predicament. For twelve years the papacy had patiently pursued a policy of wait and see towards the Queen of England with no visible results save a steady deterioration of its cause. By failing to seize an apparently golden opportunity when it was offered, Pius might lay himself open to the charge of having allowed some four million souls to go to eternal damnation without lifting a finger to save them. Even if the expected rising failed, a gesture would at least have been made; the surviving Catholics could feel they had not after all been abandoned by Rome. They might be emboldened to try again and succeed. The Catholic Powers might yet be shamed into assisting them.

So Pius appears to have reasoned, but the English government naturally found it hard to credit that he would have taken such a step without the prior knowledge and at any rate tacit approval of France and Spain. *Regnans in Excelsis* might be dismissed in London as 'a vain crack of words that made a noise only'; its implications nevertheless remained profoundly disturbing and suspicions that 'some monster was a-breeding' were inevitably heightened.

By his unequivocal declaration that orthodox Catholicism and allegiance to the Queen of England were not longer compatible, the Pope had given Elizabeth every excuse for treating all her Catholic subjects as potential traitors. But apart from a certain stepping-up in the number of prosecutions, due largely to the aftermath of the Northern Rising, there were few tangible signs of any further hardening of official attitudes during the summer of 1570, and in June the Queen issued a reassuring public statement, read on her behalf by Lord Keeper Bacon in the Star Chamber.

'Whereas certain rumours are carried and spread abroad among sundry her Majesty's subjects that her Majesty hath caused, or will hereafter cause, inquisition and examination to be had of men's consciences in matters of religion; her Majesty would have it known that such reports are utterly untrue, and grounded either of malice, or of some fear more than there is cause. For although certain persons have been lately convented before her Majesty's council upon just causes, and that some of them have been treated withal upon some matter of religion; yet the cause thereof hath grown merely of themselves, in that they have first manifestly broken the laws established for religion in not coming at all to the church, to common prayer and divine service. . . .

'Wherefore her Majesty would have all her loving subjects to understand that, as long as they shall openly continue in the observation of her laws and shall not wilfully and manifestly break them by their open actions, her Majesty's meaning is not to have any of them molested by an inquisition or examination of their consciences in causes of religion; but will accept and entreat them as her good and obedient subjects. And if any shall otherwise by their open deeds and facts declare themselves wilfully disobedient to break her laws; then she cannot but use them according to their deserts, and will not forbear to inquire of their demeanours and of what mind and disposition they are, as by her laws her Majesty shall find it necessary.

'Of all which, her Majesty would have her subjects in all parts of her realm discreetly warned and admonished not to be abused by such untrue reports, to bring them any wise to doubt of her Majesty's honourable intention towards them . . . being also very loath to be provoked by the overmuch boldness and wilfulness of her subjects to alter her natural clemency into a princely severity.'

By offering her Catholic subjects what amounted to a bargain – freedom to practise their religion in private in exchange for public observance of the Anglican rite – Elizabeth was merely restating her personal attitude to the whole religious controversy: an attitude which can be stigmatised as displaying cynical disregard for Christian belief or admired for its humanity and good sense. To restate it so openly in the political climate of 1570 remains an act of courage and faith. But then Elizabeth always valued national unity at a much higher price than theological purity and never really believed that any significant number of her people would rise against her on the orders of a foreign bishop. Whether she would be able to maintain her liberal stand in the face of a nervous Council and a belligerent House of Commons was another matter. In time of ideological war humanity and good sense are usually the first qualities to fly out of the window.

Elizabeth's experience of Parliament to date had not caused her to feel any particular affection for that institution and it was only with reluctance that she agreed to summon it again in the spring of 1571. This was the first occasion on which every member had to take the Oath of Supremacy before taking his seat. It was the first occasion, therefore, when not a single committed Catholic was present at Westminster and the Commons soon revealed itself to be in a singularly unecumenical frame of mind. The left-wing Protestants, or Puritans as they were beginning to be labelled, backed by the younger, more radical clergy, had grown in strength and self-confidence and were becoming increasingly difficult to control.

Their loyalty and patriotism could hardly be faulted but their attempts to interfere in matters which the Queen considered none of their business infuriated her. Apart from her personal predilection for a bit of decent ceremony, she regarded demands for further Church reform – curtailment of the powers of the episcopacy, the abolishing of copes and surplices, doing away with wedding rings and kneeling at communion – to be a direct attack on her prerogative, an attack she would resist to the uttermost. The left-wingers were also pressing for more stringent enforcement of the Uniformity laws, but a bill which would have made it compulsory for everyone to come to communion and receive the sacrament at least once a year, although it had the support of the bishops and the Privy Council, was vetoed by the Queen.

There was no trouble over a government measure to make it a treasonable offence to bring papal bulls or similar documents into the country. By the same act, anyone who imported or received Agnus Dei, rosaries 'or such like vain and superstitious things', became liable to lose his life and property. Another bill was passed making it high treason to write or signify that Elizabeth was not the lawful Queen, or that she was a heretic, schismatic, tyrant, infidel or usurper. This was the other half of the government's answer to *Regnans in Excelsis*. It was given its first reading in the Commons on 9 April and one Thomas Norton, 'a man wise, bold and eloquent', was quickly on his feet to remind the House 'that her Majesty was and is the only pillar and stay of all our safety'. The 'care, prayer and chief endeavour' of Parliament must therefore be for the preservation of her life and estate. He liked the bill but thought it did not go far enough. He wanted, in fact, to extend its provisions to exclude from the succession anyone who 'hath [made] or hereafter shall make claim to the crown of England during her Majesty's life, or shall say she hath not lawful right, or shall refuse to acknowledge her to be undoubted Queen'.

Norton's 'addition' was clearly aimed at the Queen of Scots and he had a good deal of support in both Houses, but Elizabeth rejected it. 'This being brought unto us,' she told the assembled Lords and Commons at the end of the session, 'we misliked it very much; being not of the mind to offer extremity or injury to any person. For as we mind no harm to others, so we hope none will mind [it] unto us. And therefore, reserving to every his right, we thought it not good to deal so hardly with anybody as by that bill was meant.'

Parliament was dissolved on 29 May, not without a few pointed remarks from the Queen about the arrogance and presumption of certain members who had wasted everyone's time with 'frivolous and superfluous speech' and by 'meddling with matters neither pertaining unto them nor within the capacity of their understanding'. Nevertheless, she had succeeded for the time being in preserving a measure of indulgence for loyal conservatives and in restraining left-wing exuberance. If the Commons had known what she and William Cecil already knew – or guessed – about the activities of a certain Roberto Ridolfi, her task would have been more difficult.

Although labyrinthine in its ramifications, the objectives of the so-called Ridolfi Plot were straightforward enough – to take Elizabeth alive or dead, to free the Queen of Scots and set her on the throne with the Duke of Norfolk as her consort and, of course, to restore the Catholic religion; three remarkable feats which were to be accomplished by the native Catholics led by Norfolk and assisted by a Spanish army from the Netherlands. It is hardly surprising that a scheme so unrealistic in conception and based on almost total ignorance of actual political and geographical conditions should be regarded with a certain amount of scepticism today. Indeed, one Catholic historian has made out a detailed case to show that Ridolfi may have been acting as an *agent provocateur* in the pay of William Cecil – a case which, however, remains and is likely to remain 'not proven'. It is tempting now either to laugh off Ridolfi's machinations or to try and find some hidden meaning beneath such an apparently incredible set of circumstances. But at a time when England faced a potentially hostile Europe (since the assassination of the Regent Moray in January 1570 not even Scotland was assured) and when the government was suffering from that uncomfortably itchy feeling between the shoulder blades which afflicts those who fear a stab in the back from potential traitors within, the situation would have had a very different flavour.

Ridolfi himself was a member of an influential Florentine banking family with longstanding English connections and had been living and working in London for the past ten years. Lately, though, he had begun to find plotting a more stimulating occupation than banking. He had certainly had a finger in the pie of the Northern Rising and in October 1569 he had been arrested and confined for a time in the house of no less a person than Francis Walsingham. Ridolfi succeeded in convincing Walsingham of his innocence – an achievement which is regarded as highly suspicious in some circles – and was let off with a caution. There may have been no more to it than that. Rather than antagonise important Italian banking interests, the authorities may have preferred to give him the benefit of the doubt. They may have hoped that given enough rope he would hang himself and others. Ridolfi may have come to a mutually advantageous arrangement with his captors. Whatever the truth of the matter, he at once returned with unabated zest to performing the functions of unofficial papal nuncio and conspirator-in-chief – for which his legitimate business activities provided excellent cover.

In March 1571, his work in England completed, Ridolfi left for Rome, taking with him letters of credence and detailed 'Instructions' from the Queen of Scots and the Duke of Norfolk. On the way, he called at Brussels to see the Duke of Alva, who was notably unimpressed by the talkative Italian and his impracticable schemes. But in Rome and later in Madrid, Ridolfi had nothing to complain of in the welcome he received. He brought the Pope just the sort of news that Pius wanted to hear and when he continued his journey to Spain at the end of May, Ridolfi carried a letter from the Holy Father charging and imploring the Catholic King 'to repose in him unhesitating faith'.

Philip's co-operation was all-important. The Pope could provide blessings, absolutions and moral support for the invasion of England. He might even provide some cash. But no soldiers would embark at the ports of Flanders without the King of Spain's word. The King of Spain, therefore, was worthy of Ridolfi's best persuasive efforts, and Ridolfi's best efforts were very persuasive. Seldom or never, he told Philip, did such an opportunity befall a Christian prince to store up treasure in heaven by doing God's work on earth at so little cost to himself. Vast numbers of Englishmen were not yet abandoned by the grace of God and loathed the life they were being forced to lead. They could no longer endure the unjust laws, the perfidy, the welter of schism and heresies which prevailed in their country. The self-styled Queen was already distraught and suspicious, a prey to terror and vacillation. It would all be so easy. The English ports were open and undefended. The Queen of Scots' party was great and powerful. The insurgent nobility were the greatest and most powerful in the land and were ready to lead the way. They were only asking for a supporting force – a few men, a few arms, a little money. The

Queen of Scots would be grateful for ever and would use her influence to prevent any future trouble with France. She would also be willing to send her son to Spain to be brought up a Catholic under Philip's eye. In any case, quite apart from all the material benefits which would accrue, what work could be more just and acceptable to God than to defend a widow, aid a child and succour the oppressed?

Philip, cautious at first, became steadily more enthusiastic and soon Ridolfi was writing letters to Mary and Norfolk to tell them that the business was as good as settled. The only spoilsport in the game of let's pretend as played in Rome and Madrid that summer was the Duke of Alva, who placed no reliance whatever on the English Catholics and could see himself with horrid clarity being forced to take part in a disastrous fiasco – a sixteenth-century Bay of Pigs. As for Ridolfi – 'A man like this,' wrote the Duke scornfully, 'who is no soldier, who has never witnessed a campaign in his life, thinks that armies can be poured out of the air, or kept up one's sleeve, and he will do with them whatever fancy suggests.' Alva seems also to have been the only person to spell out the undoubted fact that the first consequence of failure would be the permanent destruction of Mary Stuart – the best, indeed the only hope for the future of Catholicism in the British Isles.

But Ridolfi's triumphal progress round Europe had not passed unnoticed in London, and to Alva's unspeakable relief before the point of no return had been reached the inevitable happened. In April Charles Bailly, a servant of Mary's ambassador the Bishop of Ross, was arrested as he landed at Dover and found to be in possession of prohibited books. Bailly carried something more incriminating than books, but the official in charge at the port – he was Lord Cobham – was sympathetic towards the English refugees in Flanders and allowed a packet of letters to be sent on to their recipient. All the same, the Council had its suspicions and subsequently discovered, by means of a stool-pigeon that Bailly was corresponding with his master in code. Pressure was applied and 'after much ado' Bailly revealed the key, but still the identities of the principles referred to remained a mystery. Then, about the end of August, the fortunate curiosity of a Welsh draper conveying a parcel to Shrewsbury provided the vital clue – the Duke of Norfolk had been caught in the act of sending money and letters to the Queen of Scots' partisans. Now at last the government was able to move in for the kill.

Norfolk himself, who had been released from the Tower and allowed to live under surveillance in his own house, was re-arrested on 7 September. His servants were rounded up for questioning and the whole sorry affair began to come into the open. Letters were found under mats and the 'alphabets' of codes hidden under the roof tiles at Howard House. The Council's representatives heard about 'writings' smuggled in and out in bottles of drink with specially marked corks and of other messages wrapped in black paper and thrown into 'a little dark privy-house' to be retrieved when the coast was clear. In the light of these new developments, the Bishop of Ross was re-examined and, after it had been forcibly pointed out to him that neither his cloth nor his ambassadorial status would protect him in a crisis of this nature, his lordship in a cold sweat told all he knew. It turned out to be a good deal.

Although Norfolk had retained just enough sense not to sign letters for Ridolfi, there can be no reasonable doubt that he had fallen in with at least part of that enterprising individual's suggestions. There is no doubt at all that, despite his solemn undertaking to the Queen, he had continued to correspond with Mary, to lend her money and to advise her not only about her plans for escape but on the terms of the treaty she was negotiating with Elizabeth. The Duke, in fact, had been riding a tiger for the past three years and was lucky to have lasted so long. By the end of November the case against him was complete and on 16 January 1572 he was brought to trial, convicted and condemned.

As for Mary, her own ambassador had not hesitated to implicate her in the plot. Mary herself naturally denied all charges of conspiracy but, while it has to be remembered that the Bishop of Ross was almost indecently anxious to save his skin and that some of the documentary evidence is not above suspicion, it is a little hard to believe in the Queen of Scots' lilywhite innocence. After all, why should she have been innocent? Mary was a fighter and an inveterate optimist. She considered herself to be unjustly imprisoned. As a Catholic she now had moral justification for regarding Elizabeth as an usurper to be deposed by force, and Ridolfi's schemes were exactly calculated to appeal to her gambling instincts. 'Ah, the poor fool will never cease until she lose her head,' exclaimed the King of France after reading the report of his ambassador in London.

Nevertheless, there seemed no immediate prospect of this happening. Elizabeth was angry. She abandoned her policy of negotiation with Mary and significantly allowed the Earl of Moray's version of the Darnley affair, together with the much disputed Casket Letters, to be published for the first time. Mary's household was cut down and her confinement became more rigorous, at least temporarily. But this was apparently as far as the Queen of England meant to go. Even Norfolk was still alive. Three times the warrant for his execution had been signed. Three times Elizabeth had revoked it at the last moment. Her well-wishers were in despair at this display of feminine weakness. 'The Queen's majesty hath been always a merciful lady and by mercy she hath taken more harm than by justice' wrote Cecil, or Lord Burghley as he now was, to Francis Walsingham after the first of these postponements. 'God's will be fulfilled and aid her Majesty to do herself good' he wrote after the second one.

Lord Burghley's nervous system was not improved when Elizabeth succumbed to a short but violent attack of food poisoning towards the end of March. He and the Earl of Leicester spent three nights at her bedside and it is not difficult to imagine the kind of thoughts passing through their heads during this vigil. Thomas Smith put the general feeling into words when he wrote from the embassy in Paris to thank Burghley for his bulletins and for 'calling to our remembrance and laying before our eyes the trouble, the uncertainty, the disorder, the peril and danger which had been like to follow if at that time God had taken from us that stay of the Commonwealth and hope of our repose, that lantern of our light next God'.

No doubt this scare stiffened the Council in their resolve to call another Parliament. Strong pressure must have been brought to bear on the Queen to get her to agree and certainly it was an unusual step to summon the members to Westminster so late in the year. It was May before they could be assembled and summer was not a healthy time to be in the plague-ridden capital. However, 'the cause was so necessary and so weighty as it could not otherwise be'. A committee of both Houses immediately met to discuss this weighty cause – the future of the Queen of Scots – and after listening to its report the Commons proceeded to make it crystal clear what they wanted done about Mary. In the words of Richard Gallys, member for New Windsor, they wanted to 'cut off her head and make no more ado about her'. With scarcely a dissenting voice the clamour grew for a final solution to the problem of that sower of sedition and disturber of the peace, that notorious whore, adulteress and murderess, that monstrous and huge dragon.

It is easy now to condemn this baying for blood as vindictive and hysterical but the Parliament of 1572 did not see it in that light. The sober knights and burgesses gathered in the Palace of Westminster could see their whole way of life, their peace and prosperity, the future peace and prosperity of their children and grandchildren being put at risk for the sake of a scruple. They knew what was happening in France and the Low Countries. Enough people living in the south and east had heard enough first-hand atrocity stories from Flemish, Dutch and Huguenot refugees to make their blood boil and their flesh creep – and much stories lost nothing in the re-telling. Fears of Popish plots, of the invading armies of anti-Christ breathing fire and slaughter may have been exaggerated, but they were very understandable. The vast majority of Englishmen knew that everything they held dear depended, quite literally, on Elizabeth's life, and every Elizabethan knew that in the midst of life they were in death.

The Queen knew this too, but she was unmoved by all the urgent and piteous pleas being addressed to her. She was grateful for so much concern for her safety but she was unmoved. Even the numerous precedents for the putting to death of wicked kings cited from the Old Testament failed to impress her. 'Partly for honour, partly for conscience, for causes to herself known' she would not consent to a Bill of Attainder against the Queen of Scots. To the consternation and near despair of her faithful Lords, Commons and Council, she would not even agree to a bill excluding Mary from the succession. Norfolk had to be sacrificed, Parliament would not be baulked entirely of its prey, but Mary survived.

For the second time Elizabeth, by her deliberate, personal intervention, had saved the life of her mortal enemy. From a distance of four hundred years one can only wonder at the astonishing force emanating from this woman, isolated in a world of men, who was prepared to back her own instinct, intuition and judgement against the will of the nation as expressed by both Houses of Parliament, against the combined weight of her Council, against every reasonable argument of expediency, prudence and ordinary common sense. But Elizabeth Tudor intended to play the game of statecraft by her rules or not at all. In her way she was as great a gambler as Mary Stuart. The size of the stakes did not appear to dismay her in the least.

18

GOD IS DAILY GLORIFIED

'God is daily glorified and served in our country with great increase of the Catholic faith.'
William Allen, Cambrai, 10 August 1577

The public image of Catholicism had suffered serious damage as a result of *Regnans in Excelsis* and the disclosures of the Ridolfi Plot. Both had provided the Protestant cause with first-rate propaganda material and sober Protestant citizens shuddered at the thought of their narrow escape from Alva's blackbeards. Mary Stuart ceased to be regarded as a somewhat forlorn figure, a queen torn from her throne, a mother torn from her child, a prisoner to be secretly pitied, and became instead the ungrateful 'bosom serpent' of Francis Walsingham's telling phrase, a snake in the grass who had been ready to welcome an invading army into the country – a crime no Englishman would readily forgive. The Queen of Scots in particular and the Catholic religion in general were now firmly associated in the popular imagination with subversion, treachery and foreign interference. Then, at the end of August 1572, came news from France which confirmed every Protestant fear and prejudice.

The Massacre of St Bartholomew's Day is one of history's more spectacular horror stories and provides a depressingly familiar example of mob savagery. Ironically enough the occasion of this particular demonstration was an apparent *rapprochement* between Charles IX and his Huguenot subjects, sealed on 18 August by the marriage of the King's sister and the Huguenot prince, Henri of Navarre. Both *rapprochement* and marriage had been engineered by the King's mother, that optimistic politique Catherine de Medici, who needed allies to play off against the predatory Guise family. But Catherine had become seriously alarmed by the influence which the veteran Huguenot leader, Admiral Coligny, was establishing over her neurotic and unstable son, and feared that he was about to involve Charles in a Huguenot relief expedition to the Netherlands.

The Italian Queen would go to any lengths to protect her position as the power behind the throne and decided with devastating practicality that Coligny must go, confidently entrusting the Guises with the actual task of disposal. This should have been carried out on 22 August, but at the crucial moment the Admiral stooped to adjust a slipping overshoe and the assassin's bullet missed its mark, shattering the victim's arm. Charles sent his own physicians to attend Coligny, came personally to enquire, and promised a full investigation into the outrage. His mother, realising that her own complicity would be bound to emerge, hastily counterattacked. She persuaded Charles that his own life was in grave danger from a Huguenot conspiracy and that his only recourse was to sanction the immediate and wholesale murder of the Huguenot notables so conveniently assembled for the Navarre wedding.

Catherine anticipated no difficulty in putting a policy of overkill into action. The Parisians were predominantly and hot-temperedly Catholic and the presence of several thousand angry and suspicious Protestants was doing nothing to lower the temperature in the capital. Although the wedding festivities had ended, the streets remained unusually full of people showing an odd reluctance to go back to work and numbers of armed men could be observed mingling with the crowds.

Across the river in the Faubourg St Germain, Queen Elizabeth's ambassador, that dour Kentish gentleman and devout Protestant, Francis Walsingham, his wife and daughter and their guest Philip Sidney waited nervously for news. In the small hours of 24 August the distant sound of church bells may have disturbed a wakeful member of the Walsingham family and during the morning rumours of a disturbance of some kind near the Louvre began to trickle through; but it was not until groups of terrified Protestants, both English and foreign, began to seek sanctuary at the embassy that they learnt the full horror of the situation. Those church bells had been a signal for Catholic to fall upon Huguenot. Paris was like a sacked city, the streets littered with corpses, the very gutters, according to some accounts, running with blood.

That night the beleaguered occupants of the English embassy huddled together in fear, praying for deliverance and expecting an unpleasant form of death at any moment. They were, in fact, lucky to escape. A mob which has tasted blood is no respecter of diplomatic immunity and the French government had quickly lost control of the monster it had unleashed. The slaughter spread to the provinces and altogether it is estimated that about ten thousand Huguenots or suspected Huguenots – men, women and children – lost their lives. Until now the atrocity score in the struggle between idolatry and heresy taking place in France had been roughly equal, but after St Bartholomew the Catholics gained an undeniably winning lead.

Reaction from abroad varied. Te Deums were sung in Rome which was illuminated as for a great victory. The Pope ordered commemorative medals to be struck and the King of Spain sent his personal congratulations to the King of France. The Dutch insurgent leader William of Orange, on the other hand, declared that Charles would never be able to cleanse himself of the bloody deed and even Ivan the Terrible was moved to enter a protest.

The first news of the massacre reached England on 27 August from Huguenot refugees pouring across the Channel into Rye and other ports in the south-east. The French ambassador was astonished at the depth of feeling it aroused. The English, he reported, were expressing 'extreme indignation and a marvellous hatred against the French, reproaching loudly broken faith, with great execration of excesses and so many kinds of outrages, mixed with words of defiance by those who bear arms'. Even after the matter had been explained to them La Mothe Fénelon was pained to see that the islanders showed no signs of moderating their opinions, 'holding that it was the Pope and the King of Spain who kindled the fire in France . . . and that there is something evil afoot from all three of them against England'. The Bishop of London put a widespread fear into words when he wrote to Lord Burghley on 5 September, 'These evil times trouble all good men's heads and make their hearts ache, fearing that this barbarous treachery will not cease in France but will reach over unto us. Neither fear we the mangling of our body, but we sore dread the hurt of our head, for therein consisteth our life and safety.'

News of the death of Admiral Coligny in the general holocaust on St Bartholomew's Day brought a special sense of foreboding to England. It was not merely that Coligny had been a wounded man trusting to the protection of the French King which made his murder so shocking. He was the second Protestant leader to die by assassination in less than three years. In the autumn of 1572 the writing on the wall looked plain enough and one immediate repercussion was a renewed outcry against Mary Stuart. No one suggested that Mary had been in any way responsible for events in Paris, although it was being remembered that Mary's relations had led the killer pack (Henri of Guise had personally supervised the despatch of Coligny). Mary's intentions, innocent or otherwise, were becoming less and less relevant. It was the mere fact of her existence within the Protestant state which was becoming more and more intolerable, 'as nothing presently is more necessary than that the realm might be delivered of her'. 'If the sore be not salved,' wrote Francis Walsingham ominously, 'I fear we shall have a Bartholomew breakfast or a Florence banquet.' The Bishop of London recommended that the Scottish Queen's head should be cut off forthwith and even gentle Archbishop Parker offered much the same advice.

Top-secret contingency plans were, in fact, being made to send Mary back to Scotland where, it was hoped, the Regent Mar and his party might be 'by some good means wrought . . . so they would without fail proceed with her by way of justice, so as neither that realm nor this should be dangered by her hereafter'. As it turned out the Scots demanded too high a price for doing the Queen of England's dirty work and, no doubt fortunately for Elizabeth's reputation at the hands of latter-day moralists, this somewhat sinister plan came to nothing. That it was seriously considered is an indication of the near-panic created in government circles by the events in France.

England and France had recently signed a defensive treaty, but to those not privileged to read the minds of Catherine de Medici and her son, the attempted extermination of the Huguenots and the re-emergence of the Guises looked at first very much like the beginning of a concerted Catholic attack on Protestantism everywhere. Certainly it revived that perennial nightmare of a hostile league of Catholic powers which was to recur in a more or less acute form throughout Elizabeth's reign. This nightmare has been ridiculed by modern Catholic historians as a mere propaganda bogey, invented and nurtured by Protestant leaders to frighten their followers and keep their ardour alive. We know now that it was indeed a chimera, that no such Papal League ever existed, even on paper. But anyone who has lived through the years since the Second World War also knows just how powerfully fear and suspicion can work on the minds of governments and peoples when the passions aroused by rival ideologies are poisoning international relations. In such conditions threats of encirclement and aggression do not need to be actual to be real.

In view of the various political crises of the late 1560s and early 1570s, it might have been expected that the lot of the English Catholics would have altered dramatically for the worse, but there seems no evidence that this was so. Had the Catholic minority showed any signs of responding to the call of *Regnans in Excelsis* no doubt the story would have been different. No such signs were forthcoming. The bull itself contained enough legal flaws to offer loopholes to all but the most tender consciences and it could plausibly be argued that as long as Elizabeth remained the *de facto* queen, her Catholic subjects could safely go on obeying her laws – or at any rate most of them.

Pockets of resistance remained. In July 1574, Lancashire was being described as 'the very sincke of Poperie', and despite periodic drives by the Earl of Derby and the Bishop of Chester, the region was to continue to present the authorities with an especially intractable problem. East Anglia, where families such as the Huddlestons, Walpoles and Bedingfields kept the flame alight, was another trouble spot. In December 1571 the Bishop of Norwich received orders from London to carry out a purge of recusants in his diocese and the following February addressed a letter to a certain Mr Townsend of Braken Ashe.

'I have been often advertised,' wrote his lordship, 'that you, and my lady your wife, do absent yourselves from church and hearing divine service and the receiving of the sacrament. I have hoped still that my favourable forebearing, together with your duties in this behalf, would have moved you to have conformed yourselves. And yet I hear, and thank God for it, that for your own part you come on very well and shall by God's grace increase daily. But touching my lady, I hear she is wilfully bent, and little hope as yet of her reformation, to the displeasure of Almighty God, the breach of the Queen's majesty's laws, my danger and peril to suffer so long, and an evil example and encouragement to many others.' The bishop had been very patient with the Townsends, but now, he went on, 'My duty and place of calling, together with my conscience to Godward, cannot suffer me to know such disorder and to suffer the same any longer. And therefore I desire you both from henceforth to frequent the church and the receiving of the sacrament as becometh Christians: so as I may be certified forthwith both of the one and the other; which I look for. Otherwise, this is most assured, I will not fail to complain of you both to her Majesty's Council.'

Although the headmasterish tone of the bishop's letter concealed a real enough threat, it was still not precisely comparable to persecution as understood by his French and Spanish counterparts. Queen Elizabeth's government sensibly preferred to use mental rather than physical pressure wherever possible. One Catholic who could be persuaded to attend the Protestant service – even one like Sir Thomas Cornwallis who ostentatiously read 'some Lady psalter or portasse' throughout the proceedings – was worth fifty martyrs from a propaganda point of view. The Queen herself certainly thought so, although her well-wishers often felt she carried her low-profile policy too far.

The Bishop of London had long suspected that the Portuguese ambassador was abusing his diplomatic privilege by admitting the general public to his private family mass and on 1 March 1572 Edwin Sandys ordered the sheriff, Mr Pipe, to raid the embassy in Tower Street and arrest any of the Queen's subjects found 'committing idolatry'. The ambassador appears to have put up a spirited resistance, offering 'to shoot dags' at the intruders. During the general uproar, the congregation was able to melt away and the sheriff's officers only succeeded in bagging four Irish law students. The aftermath of this affair was even more disappointing, for the ambassador rushed off to Court to complain, getting his story in first so that the Queen took his part and 'was somewhat offended with these proceedings'. The bishop, much aggrieved, wrote to Lord Burghley, 'Truly, my lord, such an example is not to be suffered. God will be mighty angry with it. It is too offensive. If her Majesty should grant it, or tolerate it, she can never answer God for it. God's cause must be carefully considered of. God willeth that his ministers purge the church of idolatry and superstition. To wink at it is to be partaker of it.'

In the opinion of such sturdy left-wingers as Edwin Sandys, the Catholic envoys were no more than spies lurking in the realm to practise mischief and the sooner they were all packed off 'to serve their god Baal at home' the better it would be. But it was not only in embassy chapels that mass was said in London. On Palm Sunday 1574, fifty-three people, 'whereof the most part were ladies, gentlewomen and gentlemen', were rounded up at illegal Catholic services in various parts of the city – in

Lady Morley's chamber at Aldgate, at the Lady Guildford's in Trinity Lane, Queenhithe, at 'Mr. Carus his house beside Limehouse'. According to Dr Gardiner, Dean of Norwich, writing to his bishop from the Court: 'The priests gloried in their doings, and affirmed that there were five hundred masses in England said that day.' The dean went on to utter a warning against complacency. 'The days be dangerous. The Devil is busy to lull men asleep in security, and to be negligent in their offices that require vigilant pastors, to such time as he may by policy plant ignorance and idolatry to be commended with cruelty. The greatest diligence is too little and the least spark of careless negligence is too much.'

Just as it is impossible to say with any degree of accuracy how many Catholics in the early seventies were still practising their religion in defiance of the law, it is impossible to compute how many priests ordained before 1559 were still at work among them. Apart from those who had so horrified William Allen and Edward Rishton by partaking on the same day of the chalice of the Lord and the chalice of devils and the 'stragling doctors' who had found shelter in the houses of sympathisers, there were others going from place to place 'disguised in apparel, either after the manner of servingmen or of some other artificers' maintaining the Queen's subjects in 'superstition and error'. Dr Humphrey Ely of St John's College and a close friend of William Allen knew of 'many ancient priests of Queen Marie's days that stood firm and stable in their faith, and drew daily some out of the mire of schism by preaching and teaching'. William Allen himself paid tribute to the labours of the Marian priests who had 'by the secret administration of the sacraments and by their exhortations confirmed many in the faith and brought back some who had gone wrong'. But the numbers of these ageing men, which can never have been more than a few hundred, were being steadily eroded by natural wastage, and as long as no replacements were forthcoming, a religion like Catholicism which depended so heavily on its priests must eventually wither and die. This was the logic on which the Elizabethan government had based its policy, and it goes some way towards explaining the intense official vexation when replacements did start to filter through from abroad and when it began to look as though the fruits of fifteen years of patience had been wasted.

The activities of the exiles in Flanders had not gone unnoticed. The Parliament of 1571 had passed an Act Against Fugitives over the Sea, which laid down that anyone who had gone abroad without permission since the beginning of the reign and who did not return in a contrite spirit within six months was to forfeit his goods and chattels and the profits of his estates. In a scrupulous attempt to avoid the appearance of religious persecution, the Act included a provision for the relief of the 'desolate wife and children' of any man who had gone into exile 'by reason of blind zeal and conscience only' and who was not accused of being involved in treason. The steady trickle of Catholic books and propaganda tracts which, despite the efforts of the customs authorities, was still finding its way into the country continued to be a source of annoyance, but in 1574 the government felt confident enough to release conditionally several prominent Catholics who had been in prison since the early sixties. By a curious irony this was the very year in which the first Douai-trained missionaries arrived in England.

Contrary to many people's expectations, the college at Douai had not only survived, it had prospered. By the mid-seventies, less than ten years after its foundation, there were eighty students at the seminary and their numbers increased steadily. The chief problems continued to be financial ones, especially after 1571 when the wealthier exiles could no longer draw on their English revenues and as it became more and more difficult for Catholics at home to send money overseas. But William Allen was not a man to let anything so paltry as lack of funds interfere with his work for souls or to allow it to discourage anyone 'whom Christ had touched with the thought of taking holy orders'. 'None were rejected,' wrote Dr Ely, 'had they money or had they none, brought they commendations or brought they none. After they had been tried there awhile, such as were not found fit (which God knoweth were but few) were graciously and courteously dismissed with money in their purses.'

The fame of Douai was spreading and it was becoming, just as Allen had always hoped it would, a powerhouse for the revival and refreshment of English Catholicism in general. Some of those who passed through its ever open doors were gentlemen's sons, 'who were studying humanities, philosophy or jurisprudence, and who either of their own accord or through the exhortations of Catholic relations and friends, had been moved by the fame of the seminary to seek here a Catholic education'. These lay students paid for their board and lodging and remained 'until, according to their age and condition, they had been duly catechised and reconciled to the Church by penance for their previous life and schism'. 'There came at the same time,' records William Allen, 'not a few who were simply heretics, and even heretical ministers and preachers, all of whom being moved to penance through our instructions and conversation were not only sincerely reconciled to the Church, but after a year or two spent under the college discipline desired to become priests, and when they had obtained their wish zealously devoted themselves to the English harvest.'

A steady stream of visitors was also soon penetrating to Douai. As well as those who had business with the students, travellers on their way to France or Italy would come to see a friend at the seminary or simply out of curiosity to have a look at a place 'about which there was already much talk'. The majority of these callers were, by Douai standards, either 'devoid of all religion' or at the least serious backsliders, but all would be welcomed and pressed to stay for a few days. Those without means would be offered a month's free board and instruction in 'the chief heads of the Catholic religion'. Allen lost no chance, however slight, of reconciling a soul to God, no opportunity of publicising the aims and work of his foundation. This policy played havoc with his budget but it paid dividends in other ways. Many who came to stare or to scoff, returned home deeply impressed by what they had seen, and, wrote Allen, 'persuaded many others to leave all and come to us at Douai, or at least to come once to hear and see us, as some heretics had done'.

As part of its publicity campaign, the college issued invitations to 'the more learned heretics' in England who had been misled by bad education, 'praying them to make for once a trial of our mode of life and teaching, and promising them, so long as they remained with us, such courteous entertainment as befitted their dignity'. There is no record of any response to these hopeful offers, but some contact was established between Douai and the remnants of the Catholic priesthood at home. Allen was anxious that these weary labourers in the Lord's vineyard should come over to the college for a refresher course and specialised instruction suitable for 'the necessities of the present time' such as his own students were receiving. This was a good deal easier said than done but one Marian priest, Father John Peel, did make the pilgrimage in 1576 and there may have been others. At any rate, the knowledge that someone somewhere was interested in keeping the flame alight must have encouraged those members of the older generation still active in the field.

It was four and a half years before William Allen saw the first tangible results of his hard work when he presented four of his students at the Easter ordination held in Brussels. Another six were ordained in 1574 and it was in that year that the first pioneers left for England. They were Louis Barlow, Henry Shaw, Martin Nelson and Thomas Metham. Seven more crossed over in 1575, eighteen in 1576, fifteen in 1577 and by the end of the decade a hundred priests had been sent out from Douai. Very little seems to be known about these earliest missionaries or how they set about their task but, at least according to their own accounts, their success was immediate and spectacular.

'The number of Catholics increases so abundantly on all sides,' wrote Henry Shaw to Allen in 1575, 'that he who almost alone holds the rudder of the state [presumably Lord Burghley] has privately admitted to one of his friends that for one staunch Catholic at the beginning of the reign there were now, he knew for certain, ten.' John Payne, writing the following summer, declared that the numbers of those being reconciled to the Church increased daily and he added: 'the heretics are as much troubled at the name of the Anglo-Douai priests, which is now famous throughout England, as all the Catholics are consoled thereby'. Early in 1577, Allen heard from people coming over to France that 'the numbers of those who were daily restored to the Catholic Church almost surpassed belief' and that 'one of the younger priests lately sent on the mission had reconciled no fewer than eighty persons in one day'.

Some allowance should be made for wishful-thinking in these reports and it has to be remembered that the missionaries were to a certain extent preaching to the converted, in the sense that they naturally gravitated to Catholic houses and Catholic neighbourhoods, finding shelter among sympathisers. But these young men were a different breed of priest to the old ignorant 'mass monger', 'the popish Sir John Mumblematins' who all too often had done little more than gabble his unintelligible Latin prayers over a largely uncomprehending and indifferent congregation. The Douai priests, highly trained, highly educated and burning with the thirst for souls, were both able and willing to answer awkward questions, discuss and resolve problems and expound points of doctrine. Most important of all, they were manifestly ready to practise what they preached, to accept hardship and death 'for the deliverance of the Church and their brethren'. They came too late and too few to reverse the Protestant tide, but they did succeed in breathing new life into the dying embers of English Catholicism.

By no means all the Catholic hierarchy approved of the initiative taken by William Allen and in 1577 he found himself defending his ex-students to Father Maurice Chauncy, Prior of the English Carthusians at Bruges, who, with a remarkable failure to grasp the realities of the current situation, had apparently objected to the secular disguises adopted by the Douai priests in their battle 'to win the souls of their dearest countrymen'. Allen had no illusions about the dangers, spiritual as well as physical, to which the missionaries were exposed. Once they arrived in England they were on their own and would certainly need 'to pray instantly and fast much and watch and ward themselves well, lest the needful use of sundry enticements to sin and necessary dissimulation in things of themselves indifferent, to be fit for every company, bring them to offend God, and so while they labour to save others themselves become reprobate'.

Allen fully realised the vulnerability of those 'who had taken upon them to be guides of other men's lives and belief' – especially those whose declared aim was to persuade other men to abandon a comfortable compromise and deliberately invite trouble on themselves for the sake of a principle. He knew the Douai priests would be watched lynx-eyed for the slightest lapse. He had no illusions, but he clearly found it difficult to be patient when armchair critics like Father Chauncy carped at his *protégés*. 'Most men mark their misses,' he wrote, 'and few consider in what fears and dangers they be in, and what unspeakable pains they take to serve good men's turns to their least peril. I could reckon unto you the miseries they suffer in night journeys in the worst weather that can be picked, peril of thieves, of waters, of watches, of false brethren; their close abode in chambers as in prison or dungeon without fire and candle lest they give token to the enemy where they be; their often and sudden rising from their beds at midnight to avoid the diligent searches of heretics; all which and divers other discontentments, disgraces and reproaches they willingly suffer.' These 'pains' Allen considered were surely penance enough for the 'feathers' of their secular dress and pains which, he added tartly, few men pitied or rewarded as they should.

Another of the criticisms being levelled at the missionaries was that they were too young and too inexperienced for the responsibilities they were being called upon to carry. Allen might have pointed out that the 'English harvest' was essentially an undertaking for younger man, who would not only have the necessary physical stamina but who would know how to appeal to the all-important younger generation. He was, however, intensely conscious that it was an undertaking for handpicked men. None of the candidates he had presented for ordination had been under twenty-five, he told Father Chauncy. All the priests he had sent to England had been 'thirty years old or not far under and many of them much more'. All of them, it went without saying, were 'of irreprovable life and conversation and of very good testimony'.

In fact, the consistently high reputation of the Douai priests was a tribute to Allen's judgement and the quality of the training he provided. In 1577 he could thank God that he had not yet heard of any 'enormous crimes or notorious offences by any of them all, nor that any is so ill and inconstant to fall, by fear or force, to deny their faith or to schism or heresy'. It was true that some had 'unadvisedly uttered in their sudden fear some places and persons of their resort and catholic exercise'. Allen was sorry about this, but then the missionaries were only human. There were bound to be those who would crack under interrogation or nervous strain and betray the names of their contacts. In the circumstances, he could only be grateful that no one had fallen any further from grace. He admitted that his students, being not all 'of settled age, experience and discretion', might be more likely to make mistakes but he had had to work with the material available to him. 'And though they were never so old,' he went on, 'would there be no faults spied among them, think you? Would all such live and teach and deal in those matters without all offence, trow you? It were to be wished, but it is not to be hoped. The busy enemy to all good intentions, the devil, can cast impediments enough among the oldest that be, to make their labour less profitable and less grateful to the people.'

It was easy enough, Allen implied, to wring one's hands about the state of England from a safe distance. His venture might be inadequate. He did not pretend for a moment that it was perfect, but at least as a result of the travails of the Douai priests 'God is daily glorified and served in our country with great increase of the Catholic faith'. Many of those secret Catholics, the so-called Church papists who had hitherto conformed 'for worldly fear', were now being emboldened to confess their faith openly and 'abhor all communion and participation with the sectaries in their service and sacraments'. As well as this, wrote Allen, 'there is daily such joyful resort of many to this side the seas to learn their belief and to take experience of the

Church's discipline by our said priests' special exhortation, that it is wonderful to strangers and comfortable to us to behold'. For his part, he would have considered his 'poor pains and desires' well rewarded if every one of his missionaries had succeeded in saving only one soul from perdition but, he concluded with a touch of pardonable smugness, 'I have assured intelligence every one gaineth full many.'

A few months after William Allen had despatched his broadside in the direction of Father Chauncy, Douai gained added respectability in the eyes of the Catholic world by acquiring its first martyr – the distinction falling to one of those wandering heretical sheep whose painful search for truth had led them into Allen's fold. Cuthbert Mayne was a West Countryman, born in the parish of Sherwell near Barnstaple in 1544. Brought up as a Protestant by a parson uncle, who wanted his nephew to follow in his footsteps and inherit his own fat benefice, the boy was educated at Barnstaple Grammar School and then Oxford, where he was ordained and appointed chaplain to St John's College at a time when, as he later lamented, 'he knew neither what ministry nor religion meant'. Mayne, an attractive and intelligent young man, soon became influenced by the prevailing pro-Catholic atmosphere of Oxford.

Just as Cambridge in the thirties and forties had been a hotbed of advanced Protestant ideas, so Oxford in the sixties and seventies was flirting dangerously with Rome. This was not really surprising. The Church of England as set up in 1559 had been essentially a political compromise and therefore could scarcely be expected to appeal to earnest, high-minded youth, sheltered from and impatient of political realities. The fact that Catholicism was anti-establishment added to its appeal among undergraduates, while William Allen's success in improving its intellectual image had attracted many of the younger Fellows – Cuthbert Mayne must certainly have spent some of his time sitting at the feet of Edmund Campion, the brilliant tutor at St John's.

Sooner or later all these restless spirits had to face the decision of whether or not they were going to settle down and accept the law of the land. In the end most did accept it. It was one thing to attend an occasional illicit Mass in a 'safe house' near Oxford and indulge in the stimulating luxury of theological dissent in the cosy common room of one's own college – quite another deliberately to abandon family, career, livelihood and possessions to go out into the cold for conscience sake. But by the beginning of the seventies Edmund Campion had chosen the hard way. So had Gregory Martin, also a St John's man, and Thomas Ford, another member of the circle and a close friend of Cuthbert Mayne. Mayne himself still hesitated, unhappy but apparently not yet able to summon the courage to make the break, and there is no doubt that it needed courage as well as conviction. While he hovered on the brink, he continued to correspond with his friends overseas and before long the inevitable had happened.

Mayne was away from Oxford, probably visiting his uncle, when he received a warning that some of these letters had been intercepted and that the Bishop of London was about to take an unfriendly interest in him. His decision had been made for him, and early in 1573 he 'took shipping on the coast of Cornwall' and found his way to Douai. Two years later he was ordained for the second time and in April 1576 joined the ranks of the missionaries, crossing to England in the company of John Payne. The two priests separated on the night of their arrival and Mayne set off for the West. He had apparently brought letters of introduction to Francis Tregian of Wolveden or Golden in Cornwall. At any rate he found sanctuary in the household, being passed off as the steward.

The Tregians were a comparatively new family but wealthy and well-connected. Francis Tregian's father had married a daughter of the Arundells of Lanherne, aristocratic, influential and obstinately Catholic. Tregian himself was married to a daughter of Lord Stourton whose widow had married an Arundell. The Tregian estates extended widely between Truro and Launceston and his position as 'steward' gave Mayne excellent cover for his journeys about the countryside, saying Mass and reconciling the lapsed. He was later to admit that he had often been with his master to Sir John Arundell's at Lanherne, sometimes staying for as much as a week or a fortnight.

In this small, closed community it must soon have been common knowledge that there was a priest at work among the Catholics, but Mayne was able to carry on his ministry undisturbed for over a year. This state of affairs was probably not unconnected with the fact that the sheriff of Cornwall in 1576 was an easy-going old gentleman, unwilling to cause unpleasantness among his neighbours – an illustration of how difficult it could be to enforce the law at local level when the local justices were too idle, too timorous or too sympathetic to take action. In November, however, came an ominous change for Cuthbert Mayne and his hosts when Richard Grenville of Stowe took over as sheriff. Grenville, of Revenge fame, was a tough, thrusting, vigorous character with no inhibitions about causing unpleasantness, and determined to deal with the active Catholic cell within his territory. All the same, it was not until the following summer that he was in a position to take action.

In June 1577 the Bishop of Exeter was holding a visitation at Truro and Grenville took the opportunity of asking his help in smoking out the seminary at Golden. A force of nearly a hundred men – the sheriff himself, several justices of the peace and their servants, and the bishop's chancellor, who was to lend ecclesiastical authority to a search party proceeding without a warrant – accordingly set out on 8 June. It seems odd that no advance warning of this formidable little army riding the dusty lanes from Truro should have reached Golden, but Francis Tregian's security arrangements appear to have been lax to the point of non-existence. Just before the sheriff's posse arrived, Mayne had been in the garden, where, says the account later prepared by William Allen, 'he might have gone from them'. Instead, he unwisely returned to his room and locked himself in.

Meanwhile, Francis Tregian had met Grenville on the threshold and an altercation developed about his right of entry. According to Allen's informant, who may well have been an eye-witness: 'As soon as they came to Mr. Tregian's house, the Sheriff first spake unto him saying that he and his company were come to search for one Bourne, which had committed a fault in London, and so fled to Cornwall and was in his house as he was informed. Mr. Tregian answering that he was not there, and swearing by his faith that he did not know where he was, further telling him that to have his house searched he thought it a great discourtesy, for that he was a gentleman as he was, for that he did account his house as his castle: also stoutly denying them, for that they had no commission from the Prince.' But Francis Tregian was no match for Richard Grenville. 'The Sheriff being very bold, because he had a great company with him, sware by all the oaths he could devise that he would search his house or else he would kill or be killed, holding his hand upon his dagger as though he would have stabbed it into the gentleman. This violence being used, he had leave to search the house.'

As it turned out, not much searching took place. Evidently someone had already told Grenville all he needed to know about the domestic arrangements at Golden, for he made straight for Mayne's room and hammered on the door. 'As soon as the Sheriff came into the chamber, he took Mr. Mayne by the bosom and said unto him "What art thou?" and he answered "I am a man". Whereat the Sheriff, being very hot, asked whether he had a coat of mail under his doublet, and so unbuttoned it and found an Agnus Dei case about his neck, which he took from him and called him a traitor and rebel with many other opprobrious names.'

The sheriff now had all the justification he needed for his high-handed proceedings. To be in possession of an Agnus Dei (a small wax disc made from the Paschal candles, bearing the imprint of a lamb and blessed by the Pope) was a penal offence under the Act of 1571 and Mayne was certainly very foolish to have allowed himself to be caught wearing one. His books and papers were also seized and Richard Grenville added a chalice and vestments to the haul before bearing his prisoner off to the bishop at Truro. Mayne was later transferred to the gaol in Launceston Castle where 'he was confined to a filthy and dark underground prison, loaded with heavy irons, chained to his bedposts, allowed no books or writing materials . . . and not permitted to see anyone except in the presence of a gaoler'. Francis Tregian, as befitted a gentleman of substance, was granted bail.

Cuthbert Mayne came up for trial at the Michaelmas Sessions before Judges Manwood and Jefferys. He was indicted on five counts: traitorously obtaining from the See of Rome a certain printed instrument containing a pretended matter of absolution of divers subjects of the realm; traitorously publishing a certain printed instrument obtained from the See of Rome; upholding, maintaining and setting forth the ecclesiastical power, authority and jurisdiction of a foreign prelate, the Bishop of Rome; bringing a certain vain sign and superstitious thing called an Agnus Dei into the realm and giving it to Francis Tregian; and, finally, saying a certain public and open prayer called a private Mass and ministering the Sacrament of the Lord's Supper after a papistical manner. Mayne was convicted on all five counts and condemned to death – the first two charges automatically carrying the penalty for high treason.

Among the papers found at Golden had been a Bull of Absolution issued by Pope Gregory for the Jubilee Year of 1575 and which had now expired. Mayne's defence was that he had bought a copy in a printer's shop at Douai and must have packed it up accidentally with his other belongings before coming to England. He pointed out that anyway it was now merely a void paper 'of no force and out of all use'. He denied ever 'publishing' it. Since the Bull was now out of date, there was some doubt in the judges' minds as to whether it did actually come within the meaning of the Act, and sentence was respited while further advice was sought. Although, as a result of his own extraordinary carelessness, Mayne could technically be regarded as a traitor, in normal circumstances he might have expected to receive the benefit of the doubt on a tricky point of law. Circumstances, however, were far from normal. The government was irritated and alarmed by the arrival of the new priests, and determined to make an example. On 12 November orders came from the Council that the execution was to proceed without further delay.

All the same, on the day before he died, a sustained attempt was made to persuade Cuthbert Mayne to recant – an apostate priest would be infinitely more valuable than a dead priest. But he was not to be tempted by offers of life and liberty. Whatever doubts and hesitations he may once have felt were long behind him now. Weakened by the rigorous conditions of his imprisonment, with nothing before him but a particularly unpleasant form of death, Mayne demonstrated the terrible, immovable strength that comes from utter conviction. His teachers at Douai had done their work well.

The Queen, he told his examiners, never was, nor is, nor ever shall be Head of the Church of England. No one who called himself a Catholic might 'in any wise receive the Sacrament, come to the Church or hear the schismatical service which it established in the same here in England'. He believed that the people of England might be won back to Roman Catholicism by the 'secret instructors' already in the country and those who would be coming in the future. He refused to give any information about these secret instructors but hoped they and others would 'use secret conference to withdraw the minds of the subjects of the realm from the religion established in the same'. He went on to affirm 'that if any Catholic prince took in hand to invade any realm to reform the same to the authority of the See of Rome, that then the Catholics in that realm invaded by foreigners should be ready to assist and help them'. Here was the heart of the matter. It was not for these opinions that Cuthbert Mayne had been condemned, but they were why he had been condemned.

The sentence on him – hanging, disembowelling and dismembering – was duly carried out in Launceston market-place and the remains of the first of the Douai martyrs were thoughtfully distributed over North Devon and Cornwall – to Barnstaple, Bodmin, Wadebridge and Tregony. As well as Mayne and Francis Tregian (who was subjected to the pains of praemunire for harbouring, aiding and abetting the priest and who was to remain in prison until 1601), a number of prominent Cornish recusants had been rounded up and fined and a potentially dangerous Catholic remnant rooted out. The Council was understandably pleased with the High Sheriff, and Richard Grenville received the accolade at Windsor that October at the end of an eventful year of office.

Less than three months after Mayne's death, a second missionary priest suffered at Tyburn. This was John Nelson, a Yorkshireman of good family who had gone over to Douai in 1573 at the unusually mature age of forty. He came back to England in November 1576 and like Mayne remained at liberty for just over a year. He was arrested in London late in the evening of Sunday, 1 December 1577 as he was saying Matins for the next day and was committed to Newgate on suspicion of papistry. The Oath of Supremacy was put to him in prison and was refused. Although suggestive, this in itself was not necessarily an offence, since it had not been proved that Nelson came within any of the categories who could be compelled to take it. When, however, he was questioned about his reasons for refusing, he replied that he had never heard or read that a lay prince could have that pre-eminence. When asked who then, in his opinion, was Head of the Church, his answer was unequivocal, 'the Roman Pontiff, as being Christ's Vicar and the lawful successor of St. Peter'. When asked his opinion of the religion now established in England there could, therefore, be only one reply, that it was schismatical and heretical. This line of questioning could lead to only one end: was the Queen, as Governor of the Church of England, herself a schismatic?

Nelson seems to have tried to evade the open trap by replying that he could not tell, not knowing her mind with regard to the support and promulgation of schism. His questioners had no intention of letting him off the hook. The Queen, they told him, was a wholehearted supporter of Protestantism. After this there could, again, be only one reply. 'If she be the setter forth and defender of this religion now practised in England, then is she a schismatic and a heretic.' Having thus brought himself within the scope of the Treasons Act of 1571, Nelson's fate became a foregone conclusion. At his trial the evidence was clear. Indeed he made no attempt to deny it and met his death on 3 February 1578 with constancy and courage.

The third victim of the government's new hard-line policy was a layman, Thomas Sherwood. A Londoner by birth and son of a pious, middle-class Catholic family (his mother, Elizabeth, was the sister of Francis Tregian), Thomas went into his father's drapery business on leaving school, but 'being more devoted to a religious course of life than to a worldly, he obtained from his parents leave to pass the seas and come to Douai'. He did not, however, enter the college at once but came back to London to settle his affairs and 'to procure some competent means to maintain him for some time at his study'.

This was to prove his undoing. He spent a good deal of his time in the house of Lady Tregony or Tregonwell and her son – either fearing that his mother would get into trouble as a result, or out of jealousy – denounced Sherwood as a Papist. He was arrested one morning in November 1577 while walking down Chancery Lane and brought before Thomas Fleetwood, the Recorder of London, well known for his anti-Catholic zeal. During the course of his first examination Sherwood, like Nelson, denied the Royal Supremacy and went on to say that if the Pope had indeed excommunicated Elizabeth, he thought she could not be lawful Queen. This brought Sherwood, like Nelson, within the scope of the 1571 Act. Unlike Nelson though, Sherwood was presently handed over to the Lieutenant of the Tower and confined in an especially noisome dungeon 'amongst the rats'. His friends were not allowed the customary privilege of providing him with bedding and extra food and he was racked on several occasions in an attempt to discover the names of his associates and the houses where he had heard Mass. It was also hoped that he might perchance 'bolt out some other matters or persons worthy to be known'.

This appears to have been the first use of torture – later to become a highly controversial issue – to extort information from Catholics and Sherwood may well have been singled out for such treatment because of his close connection with the Tregians. But although an undersized young man (he was twenty-seven at the time of his death) and unsupported either by priestly vows or the thorough-going indoctrination supplied at Douai, Thomas Sherwood betrayed no 'matters or persons worthy to be known'. Indeed, he displayed all the desperate, pathetic gallantry of which the human spirit can be capable. The story goes that when he was warned by a sympathetic gaoler that he was to be racked again, he answered 'merrily and with a cheerful countenance . . . "I am very little and you are very tall. You may hide me in your great hose and so they shall not find me"'. According to the report which presently reached Douai, 'in all his torments his cry had been, "Lord Jesus, I am not worthy to suffer these things for Thee, much less receive those rewards which Thou has promised to such as confess Thee",' and it was said that even the Recorder Fleetwood shed tears at the sight of his sufferings.

Sherwood was tried at Westminster on 3 February 1578 charged with upholding the authority of the Pope; denying the Royal Supremacy; declaring that Elizabeth was not lawful Queen; and diabolically, maliciously and traitorously affirming 'in the presence and hearing of divers faithful subjects of the said Lady our Queen . . . that our said Queen Elizabeth . . . is a schismatic and an heretic, to the very great scandal and derogation of the person of our said Lady the Queen and the subversion of the state of this realm of England'. His conviction followed speedily and he was condemned to the dreadful traitor's death: 'that the aforesaid Thomas Sherwood be led by the aforesaid Lieutenant unto the Tower of London, and thence be dragged through the midst of the city of London, directly unto the gallows at Tyburn, and upon the gallows there be hanged, and thrown living to the earth, and that his bowels be taken from his belly, and whilst he is alive be burnt, and that his head be cut off, and that his body be divided into four parts, and that his head and quarters be placed where our Lady the Queen shall please to assign them'.

Catholic historians and hagiographers have naturally made the most of the sufferings inflicted on the missionary priests and unfortunates like Thomas Sherwood, but when one remembers the sort of fate normally reserved for heretics and other religious deviants in Catholic countries at the time, they are perhaps not in the best position to throw stones. Hanging, drawing and quartering – to us an unimaginably obscene form of death – was nothing new. It had been the accepted end for traitors in England since mediaeval times and was to continue, at least in theory, until the eighteenth century. In practice, the victim was frequently allowed to hang until he was dead, unless his crime was considered to be extra heinous or unless the authorities wanted to make an example. The thought of any living, breathing creature being subjected to these and other horrors for whatever reason must arouse extreme revulsion now among all civilised people – it aroused revulsion among the tenderhearted then. But in an age without the benefit of anaesthetics or pain-killing drugs, physical discomfort and physical pain of an acute kind were commonplaces of daily life. It followed, therefore, that physical punishments had to be drastic to be effective and that something rather special had to be devised as a deterrent for traitors – generally regarded as society's most dangerous enemies.

No one ever suggested that Cuthbert Mayne, John Nelson or Thomas Sherwood were traitors in any but a technical sense – it was their connection with Douai and thence with Rome which made them politically dangerous. By the calculated ferocity of its reaction, the government showed just how seriously it took the threat of a Catholic revival at home, at a time when the international situation was steadily approaching crisis point.

19

If These Fellows Stand Thus Immovable

'If these fellows stand thus immovable before such Princes in Rome, what will they do in England before the heretics?'
Robert Parsons, Rome, March 1579

For the English government the 1570s was a decade of intense diplomatic activity, labyrinthine in its complexity. In the conduct of her foreign policy, the Queen of England has frequently been accused of tergiversation, indecision and plain bloodymindedness – both by her contemporaries and by historians trying to grope their way through the baffling palisade she erected to conceal her intentions. While Elizbeth must surely have been a most infuriating female to serve and to negotiate with, it is now possible to see that her underlying purpose was paradoxically not only extremely simple but unwavering in its aim – to keep her people, her kingdom and her throne peaceful, prosperous and secure. In order to achieve that aim and to stay dryshod in the quicksand of European politics, Elizabeth was prepared to shift her ground as often as seemed necessary. In fact, the more confusion and uncertainty she could create in the minds of others, the more freedom of action she retained for herself. Flexibility was the keynote of her policy. Among its cardinal principles were always to leave open as many options as possible, never to be manoeuvred into some exclusive commitment and, above all, to keep out of other people's bloody and self-destructive faction fights.

The diplomatic poker game as played by Elizabeth Tudor demanded strong nerves and unremitting concentration. The fact that it also demanded subtlety, subterfuge and histrionic ability of a high order only added to its zest. There can be no doubt that Elizabeth enjoyed the game for its own sake – certainly her skill as a player has never been equalled. Its justification is that it paid off. While the Spanish Empire went slowly bankrupt, France tore herself to pieces and the Low Countries became a desert, England remained solvent, united and increasingly powerful. When war did come it affected only a tiny minority of the population and provided a not uncongenial outlet for the energies of those who might well have got into mischief at home. No foot of English countryside was laid waste. No English farmstead was burnt down, no English town looted or put to the sword, no Englishman, woman or child slaughtered by an invading army.

This was Elizabeth's achievement, and if it has laid her open to accusations of selfishness and deceit she would have thought the price cheap. She had started, of course, with several built-in advantages. Still 'the best match in her parish', she unblushingly employed the weapon of courtship twice during the seventies and early eighties. She was unhampered by any masculine urge to prove virility by conquest. Most important of all, she was unhampered by those rigid ideological convictions which caused such untold misery throughout her century.

The Queen's cold-bloodedly secular approach to politics was often a source of sorrow to her well-wishers. Francis Walsingham, who had succeeded Lord Burghley as Principal Secretary in 1573, believed there could be no coexistence with the Catholic powers, for 'Christ and Belial can hardly agree'. To Walsingham and others of his way of thinking, the only safe and moral method of dealing with Philip of Spain was to recognise him as an enemy and treat him as such. 'What juster cause can a Prince that maketh profession of the Gospel have to enter into wars,' wrote Walsingham, 'than when he seeth confederacies made for the rooting out of the Gospel and religion be professeth?' But Elizabeth was not interested in wars, just or otherwise. Her only interest in confrontations, whether between Christ and Belial or between herself and Spain, lay in seeking the surest way of avoiding them. Slowly but inexorably the position of Protestant champion was to be forced upon her, but Elizabeth, who undertook foreign adventures only with extreme reluctance, never accepted the role of crusader.

The issue which dominated her diplomacy throughout the 1570s was the future of the Netherlands – a matter of immense importance to England from a strategic as well as a commercial point of view. The prospect of a Spanish victory leaving a Spanish army in undisputed possession of the invasion ports of Flanders represented a threat to English security which no English government could be expected to accept. It was true that at the beginning of the decade there seemed no immediate danger of this particular nightmare coming true. The forces of the revolted Dutch provinces under the leadership of William of Orange were frequently down but somehow never entirely out. William did have the advantage of sea-power which cushioned him to some extent from the effects of disaster on land. All the same, his position in general looked pretty desperate and very few people would have been prepared to bet on his future, unless he got outside help and got it quickly.

To the simple-minded it might have seemed that William of Orange would need to look no further than Elizabeth of England for assistance in embarrassing the King of Spain, but although a number of far from simple-minded persons were urging this very course upon her, Elizabeth was currently showing a more friendly face towards Spain than towards William. There were several cogent reasons for this apparently surprising attitude. Apart from her ineradicable dislike for the dangerous and unethical practice of lending official recognition to other sovereigns' rebels (unofficial aid was another matter altogether), Elizabeth had a low opinion of the Dutch in general, regarding them as grasping, quarrelsome, untrustworthy and Calvinist. She had no illusions about what it would cost to finance a foreign war, and no illusion about the limitations of her resources. She was also well aware that those who clamoured loudest for action against Anti-Christ would be the first to grumble when it came to paying the bills. By careful management and good housekeeping, she had just succeeded in freeing herself from debt and her credit was excellent. She had no intention of losing that priceless advantage if she could help it. Words were a great deal cheaper than armies and the thrifty Queen would continue to use them for as long as possible.

Elizabeth had no desire to see either a Spanish or an Orange triumph. Even less did she want to see France, that inveterate enemy of Spain, go on a fishing expedition in those troubled waters. What she wanted was a negotiated settlement by which all foreign troops would be evacuated from the Netherlands and the provinces restored to their traditional civil rights and liberties. In return, the Netherlanders would remain under Spanish suzerainty and Philip would have the right to impose Catholicism as the state religion. It was, after all, generally accepted that a prince should impose one form of belief on his subjects in the interests of national unity and was a right which Elizabeth exercised herself. Such a settlement could only benefit Europe at large and England in particular, removing the threat to her south-eastern coastline and allowing trade and commerce to function normally again. To one of Elizabeth's essentially pragmatic nature, this was the obvious solution to an irritating and unnecessary problem and one which she pursued with astonishing pertinacity.

She was undeterred by repeated failure, unmoved by all appeals to sentiment on behalf of the embattled Dutch Protestants, by the openly-voiced disapproval of an influential section of public opinion at home, and by the near despair of councillors who were convinced that the enemy's only interest in peace talks lay in keeping England off guard. She was still doggedly pursuing it when her own troops were fighting in Flanders, when the Spanish invasion fleet was preparing to weigh anchor in Lisbon harbour. Nothing and nobody, in fact, could shake her faith in the axiom that 'to jaw jaw is better than war war'. From every commonsense point of view, of course, she was right, but by her stubborn insistence on regarding the problem in purely political terms she failed to take enough account of the depth and bitterness of Dutch hatred and distrust of Spain, or the inflexibility of Philip's resolve not to yield one inch of ground to his rebel subjects. As a sensible woman and practical sovereign, Elizabeth naturally found it had to take seriously the King of Spain's pronouncement that he would rather rule over a desert than a nation of heretics. It would have made little difference if she had and perhaps it was just as well that she didn't, for by refusing to be discouraged so long as any spark of hope remained she both postponed and minimised England's involvement in this sixteenth-century Vietnam war.

The Queen began to mend her fences with Spain in the aftermath of the St Bartholomew's massacre, when it looked as though the French alliance would have to be written off. In April 1573 she reached an agreement with the Duke of Alva by which trade with the Netherlands, suspended since the crisis of 1568, was restored for a period of two years and negotiations were started on the claims of both sides for compensation over the seizures of property. Other negotiations followed, and in March 1575 a further agreement was concluded with Alva's successor, Don Luis Requesens. This confirmed, under certain conditions, the privileges of English merchants in Antwerp and also conceded that Requesens would expel the English Catholic exiles from their refuge in the Netherlands, for some time a sore point with Elizabeth. In return, Elizabeth closed her ports to William of Orange and forbade her subjects, officially at any rate, to succour the Dutch rebels until they returned to their natural obedience.

This looked a promising beginning and in 1576 events in the Netherlands seemed to offer an opening for just the sort of settlement Elizabeth had in mind. A mutinous Spanish army, unpaid and temporarily leaderless, went on the rampage, and the resultant reign of terror in Flanders produced such intensity of anti-Spanish feeling that the Flemings and Brabanters temporarily joined with the Dutch and Zeelanders in demanding the expulsion of Spain. The new Spanish Governor, Don John of Austria, faced by a united and hostile front was forced (in the intervals of planning the invasion of England and offering himself as a bridegroom to the Queen of Scots) to adopt a conciliatory attitude. For a time things looked really hopeful. Don John set himself out to charm; while from the side-lines the Queen of England urged the State General for God's sake not to lose any occasion for obtaining peace and threatened Don John that if he attempted to renew the conflict she would help the provinces with all the might and power she could.

In the end, the victor of Lepanto had to come to terms, promising to evacuate the Spanish garrisons and to respect the provinces' civil liberties. As a result he was received in Brussels in May 1577 amid scenes of much rejoicing. Only William of Orange held aloof – implacably hostile, immovably suspicious. As it turned out, his distrust of Spanish fair words proved fully justified. In July, Don John threw off the irksome restraints that had been imposed upon him and, on the not improbable pretext that his life was in danger, seized Namur with a company of Walloons, making such unconciliatory declarations as swearing to avenge his honour by bathing in the blood of traitors. The war was on again, the new-born settlement drowned in Flanders mud.

Don John died of plague the following year and was succeeded by Alexander Farnese, Duke of Parma, by far the ablest of Philip's generals but hamstrung like all his predecessors by shortage of cash and poor communications with Spain. Meanwhile, the affairs of William of Orange went from bad to worse and back again to bad. In 1579 the Catholic Walloon provinces made a separate peace with Spain, but in the north William – assisted by grudging subsidies from England and some not very helpful forays by France – grimly carried on the struggle. And so it went on, and on, and famine, pestilence and atrocity stalked the land.

Although Artois in the south had not been directly affected by the war, it was inevitable that the political upheavals in the Netherlands would sooner or later have repercussions on the seminary at Douai. Until the mid-seventies the English college continued to flourish, with recruits flowing in as fast or faster than they could be accommodated. In August 1575 Pope Gregory had conferred extensive discretionary powers of absolution and dispensation on William Allen, authorising him to delegate these faculties to such of his missionaries as he thought fit. Also in 1575 the Pope granted the college an official allowance of one hundred gold crowns a month which went some way towards alleviating its chronic financial problems, and by Michaelmas 1576 there were a hundred and twenty students in the college.

Trouble, however, was already brewing. After the 'Spanish Fury' in November of that year, the anti-Spanish fury in the Netherlands began to spill over on to any foreigners who could be suspected of pro-Spanish sympathies. So sensitive was the situation that, it was said, even a cheerful expression on the face of an English exile was liable to be interpreted as a sign of rejoicing over local misfortunes. The college itself was subjected to a campaign of harassment by the municipal authorities and the inmates had to submit to the indignity of having their rooms searched for arms. They had to give their names to the magistrates at frequent intervals and every member of the college was called on to renew his oath of allegiance to the university and town of Douai. On top of these irritations, rumours began to circulate that English government agents, men of 'sinister aspect and well-mounted', had been seen loitering in the vicinity with intent to kidnap or assassinate William Allen.

In the circumstances it was hardly surprising that many of the students felt it would be prudent to remove themselves for a while, and within three months their numbers had fallen dramatically. Allen himself went on a trip to Paris, partly as a precaution for his own safety and partly to explore the possibilities of finding a French sanctuary for his flock should the climate at Douai deteriorate still further. In the spring of 1577, after

Don John had made his peace with the Netherlanders under the terms of the unfortunately named Perpetual Edict, conditions improved for a time. Allen returned from France and the numbers in residence at the college rose again to a hundred and fifteen. By mid-summer, though, the situation had taken another turn for the worse. The students were warned to be especially careful not to give the townspeople any excuse for taking offence or exciting murmurs against them. Even so, the atmosphere once more became acutely uncomfortable. Professors and students were liable to insult when they ventured into the town – Dr Humphrey Ely was called a traitor to his face – and one morning in August a visiting Englishman was greeted with some surprise by a passing local and asked if all the English had not been killed the previous night.

William Allen reviewed his evacuation plans and he and the senior members of his staff made several reconnaissance trips to the city of Rheims, where the French government had offered them hospitality. Allen was reluctant to leave the dominions of the King of Spain, whom he regarded as the natural protector of the English Catholics, but if a move became unavoidable Rheims had obvious advantages. It contained a famous university and was within reasonable travelling distance of Douai. It was also ruled by the ultra-Catholic Guise family who, as relations of the Queen of Scots, could hardly fail to be friendly towards the exiles. Mary herself had written to Allen that summer, warmly praising his work and telling him not to hesitate to use her name if it would help him in any way.

Matters came to a head early in 1578. The Duke of Parma's victory over the states at Gembloux at the end of January caused a resurgence of patriotic nationalism. A new governor and new magistrates appointed by William of Orange took office at Douai, and it was freely predicted that the English would soon be expelled bag and baggage. On 11 February the governor paid a visit to the college asking searching questions about the number and ages of the students and how they were supported. On 22 March, the day before Palm Sunday, a proclamation was issued commanding all the English residents except the old men, women and children and university professors to leave the town within twenty-four hours. The expulsion order, in fact, only applied to the students at the seminary, young and able-bodied men capable of bearing arms, but students and staff migrated in a body.

Thanks to Allen's foresight and careful staffwork the seminary was able to settle down in the new quarters at Rheims with the minimum of disruption, and on 27 May there were fifty-five students on the roll – forty-four living in college and the remainder in the town. They had received a flattering welcome from the Cardinal Archbishop, Louis of Guise, as well as from the university and municipal authorities, but even here there was a good deal of ill-feeling among the local people. At Douai the English had become unpopular because they were regarded as pensioners and partisans of Spain. At Rheims they were unpopular because they were English.

Gregory Martin, writing to Edmund Campion in August, observed, 'It is most uncertain whether we shall remain here in quiet and permanently, though the family of Guise is very favourable to us, because the name itself of Englishman begets suspicion in the French.' Allen also had second thoughts about the wisdom of their move, and in September he made enquiries about the chance of some other home in Belgium. Louvain was suggested, but Louvain, not for the last time in its history, had been devastated by war. Plague was rife in the town, the university had virtually disappeared and horses were being stabled in the burnt-out colleges. Clearly the Netherlands were out of the question until the political and military situation had quietened down. The English would have to stick it out where they were and put up with the widely held belief that they crept out at night to make plans of the fortifications. As it turned out, they were to stay for nearly twenty years.

Although the unsettled conditions of the past two years had not been exactly conducive to a programme of concentrated study, the work of the college suffered only temporary interruption and was in fact soon to be extended by the establishment of another English college in Rome itself. In common with most other European countries, pre-Reformation England had maintained a hostel for its pilgrims in the Holy City and as early as 1559 or 1560 there had been some talk of converting this institution into a seminary for English priests. The proposal, however, had languished in the Vatican's pending tray until the success and reputation being gained by William Allen at Douai stirred certain individuals, in particular Dr Owen Lewis, on of the Welsh exiles, to emulatory zeal. When Allen visited Rome in 1575, the setting up of another factory of labourers for the English vineyard was among the subjects discussed and certainly it had become a matter of some urgency – with numbers now topping the hundred mark, Douai was bursting at the seams.

It was therefore agreed that Allen should send his overflow to be accommodated at the hostel and during the next three years several batches of recruits arrived from Douai and Rheims. As a result of intensive lobbying by Owen Lewis, Cardinal Moroni, official 'protector' of the English nation, advised the Pope to appoint the warden of the old hospice, another Welshman, Dr Maurice Clenock, to be rector of the new foundation. Two Jesuit fathers moved in to help him and the *Venerabile Collegium Anglorum de Urbe* was formally inaugurated at Christmas 1578.

The early history of the English college in Rome clearly shows how much Douai had owed to the personality of William Allen. Dr Clenock was an elderly man and quite unequal to the task of running a college of forty students. He also appears to have been unfortunately lacking in both tact and commonsense, 'so there arose many complaints and many suspicions of a lack of right and fair administration and various accusations of more indulgent treatment being meted out to Welshmen than to Englishmen in the distribution of the things of the house'. Encouraged by Archdeacon Lewis and his nephew Hugh Griffin (a natural trouble-maker by the sound of him), the Welsh seem to have taken the view that the new seminary had been founded 'for the peculiar benefit of their race'. National feelings were soon running high and the English, who formed the great majority of the student body, became so irritated that they petitioned Cardinal Moroni for the removal of Dr Clenock and for the management of the college to be made over entirely to the Jesuits.

Cardinal Moroni was not accustomed to being told his business by students, Drs Clenock and Lewis were long-established and respected members of the Roman community and in any case the Cardinal could hardly be expected to appreciate the finer points of Celtic and Anglo-Saxon hostility. He attempted to dismiss the petitioners without more ado, 'making a sharp reprehension unto them for their stir' and threatening them with expulsion 'except they admitted quietly the government appointed'. But the English students, penniless exiles though they might be, were not going to put up with that sort of treatment. His Eminence was therefore treated to some plain North Country speaking by their representatives, much to the surprise of the standers-by who 'did wonder to see such liberty of speech before so great a personage'. It seems to have surprised the Cardinal as well, for he changed his tune, promising the students 'to consider better their matter' and asking them 'to give him in writing both the defects of Mr Maurice in particular and the manner of government which they desired'.

The affair was soon the talk of Rome. The apparent fearlessness of the English in demanding their rights gave rise to much admiring comment. 'If these fellows stand thus immovable before such Princes in Rome,' it was asked, 'what will they do in England before the heretics?' Some people declared that although they had previously doubted reports of the bold answers made by priests captured in England, now they could believe anything of them. But while public sympathy was largely on the side of the dissidents, a first-class row was brewing over the future of the English college, with the Welsh faction supported by Cardinal Moroni accusing the Jesuits of trying to make a take-over bid. On the other side it was being said that Dr Clenock was trying to increase his party by inviting Welshmen, however unsuitable, from all over Europe to enter the college. Hints were also dropped that the Welsh students had no intention of ever making the journey to England.

The battle was still raging when four of the students, led by Richard Haydock, William Allen's nephew, went on their own initiative to lay their troubles before the Pope. But, so the story goes, Cardinal Moroni 'showed his anger and aversion, and persuaded Pope Gregory, who seemed inclined to give way to the scholars' petitions, to reject the frequent memorials which they presented'. In any event, Clenock was confirmed in his office, whereupon the Welsh became so overweening that knives were flourished in the refectory and open brawling was only averted by the two Jesuits on the staff – at least according to a Jesuit account. Something clearly had to be done about a situation rapidly getting out of hand and the authorities ordered the four ringleaders of the revolt to leave the college, presumably in the hope that this would intimidate the rest. The English, however, accepted the challenge with enthusiasm and in the best trade union tradition they marched out in a body – an event which caused Hugh Griffin to give a leap in the college hall saying 'Who now but a Welshman?' The homeless students spent that night in the house of a sympathetic compatriot and next morning appeared on the streets to beg alms for their journey back to Rheims.

It was the beginning of Lent – Ash Wednesday in fact – and the streets were full of pious citizens on their way to church. 'When the news spread that so many young men of great expectations, some of them even being priests, were purposing and proposing to return to England, there to risk their lives for the Catholic faith, braving the fury of the heretics, there was a great stir in men's minds'. The Lenten preachers took up the students' cause and from pulpit after pulpit 'the necessities of these scholars were commended to the charity of the faithful'. The warm-hearted, sentimental Italians responded eagerly and it was soon obvious that there would be no lack of charity. It was also obvious that the Pope would have to take action. That afternoon, therefore, when the students went to take their leave of him, the Holy Father greeted them with tears and smiles, and after an affecting scene of reconciliation sent them back to the college escorted by a papal chamberlain, promising to meet their demands in full. The rebels had conducted their campaign with considerable tactical skill and won a notable victory over the Roman establishment. The long-term consequences, however, were not so happy, for the seeds of a bitter quarrel which was to react disastrously on English Catholicism had been sown in fertile ground.

The Society or Company of Jesus, which took over responsibility for the English college on 23 April 1579 and which now for the first time became actively associated with the English mission, had started life in 1534 as a small group of priests dedicated to practical social work among the poor, the heathen and the illiterate. Their founder, the crippled Spanish ex-soldier turned soldier of Christ, also dreamed of restoring the Catholic Church to the position of pre-eminence it had occupied in the Middle Ages. Ignatius Loyola believed in the military virtues of discipline, efficiency and obedience, and although his ultimate aim may have been to put the clock back, he was not afraid to use modern methods, to adapt the old monastic ideal to meet the needs of the times. Loyola's new society was in no sense enclosed – in fact he dispensed altogether with the normal obligation of a religious order to recite the office in choir. The Society of Jesus was to provide front line troops for the Church and therefore its members must be free at all times to go about in the world, fighting the Church's battles wherever they were to be found. Loyola had passed through a phase of extreme religious asceticism, but he was to prove himself a born leader, a hard-working, intelligent administrator, and when he died in 1556 his army had become a highly-trained, well-organised body of men over a thousand strong.

Jesuit missionaries had followed the *Conquistadores* to America and had penetrated as far as China and Japan in the east. Jesuit schools were already deservedly famous. Jesuit fathers held key positions in the Catholic universities of Europe and on the councils of many European rulers. They kept representatives at the Imperial Diet in Germany; they were said to have the ear of Philip of Spain, to be whispering advice to Catherine de Medici in France. It was as palace politicians that the Jesuits made enemies, both inside and outside the Church, but it was on their proficiency as schoolmasters that their real power was based. From teaching the children of the illiterate poor, they had progressed to teaching the children of the aristocracy, to the all-important task of forming the minds of each successive generation of the international Catholic establishment.

Although the Superiors of the Order had, in fact, been somewhat reluctant to add yet another commitment to an already long list, training candidates for the English mission was to provide the Society of Jesus with an opportunity to exercise their skill on some of the finest material available. As one contemporary writer pointed out, even in Catholic countries there were many who entered the priesthood only for honour and gain, but the pupils at the English seminaries, 'among whom are noblemen and eldest sons not a few', had already accepted the loss not only of their natural heritage but of any other earthly reward. When, after a period of probation, the young men at the college in Rome took an oath to be ready and willing to receive holy orders in God's good time and to return to England for the salvation of souls 'whenever it shall seem good to the superior of this college to order me to do so', they were, in nine cases out of ten, consciously and cheerfully signing their own death warrants.

Human nature being what it is, not quite everyone who came to Rome did so from the highest motives. There were those who made the pilgrimage out of restlessness, curiosity, or simply to see if there was anything to be got out of it. Among these 'tourists' was one Anthony Munday, an enterprising stationer's apprentice who, in 1578, broke his indentures and left England with a friend named Thomas Nowell. Although Munday declared that he had been moved only by an urge for self-improvement, a 'desire to see strange countries, as also affection to learn the language', he was later in a position to provide the government with valuable information about the inmates of the English college. He became, in fact, a useful witness for the Crown at the trials of Edmund Campion and of other priests he had known at Rome. It was after this, when certain unsympathetic people began to show signs of doubting his word and to hint that he had never been out of England, that Munday first published the graphic account of his adventures.

He and Nowell had crossed the Channel to Boulogne, but on the road to Amiens were robbed of their money and most of their possessions by 'despoiling soldiers'. In the town they were befriended by an old English priest who gave them a night's lodging and provided them with letters of introduction to William Allen at Rheims. The travellers sold their cloaks for two French crowns and set out on their journey. Three or four miles from Amiens, however, they sat down 'on the side of a hill' to consider the situation. Munday, who always represented himself as a staunch Protestant, had decided it would be a waste of time to go to Rheims, and brushing aside his companion's feeble expostulations about their destitute state and the dangers they were likely to encounter, persuaded Nowell to come with him to Paris instead. In Paris they first paid a visit to the English ambassador, who 'bestowed his honourable liberality' on them and sensibly advised them to go home. But on leaving the embassy and walking into the city, Munday and Nowell fell in with some English gentlemen who showed themselves 'very courteous' in offering them money, lodging and other necessaries.

Through these new friends, Munday records, 'we became acquainted with a number of Englishmen more who lay in the city, some in Colleges and some at their own houses: where using daily company among them, sometime at dinner and sometime at supper, we heard many girds and nips against our country of England, her Majesty very unreverently handled in words and certain of her honourable Council undutifully termed'. The visitors heard a lot of talk about a projected invasion of Ireland by an army of Spaniards; how the famous Dr Sander 'under the Pope's standard, would give such an attempt there as soon after should make all England to quake'; and how other Englishmen had gone to the Pope for more aid 'at whose return, certain noblemen Englishmen, then being in those parts . . . would prosecute the matter with such speed as might be'. This agreed in almost every point with the gossip they had picked up from the priest at Amiens, which made Munday 'to doubt, because in every man's mouth her Majesty's style was aimed at, in such manner as I tremble and shake to think on their words'.

He and Nowell were being 'very earnestly persuaded' to join the ranks of expatriates and to travel on to Rome where, they were assured, they would be entertained in style. 'We were soon entreated to take the journey on us,' wrote Munday, 'because we thought if we could go to Rome and return safely again into England we should accomplish a great matter, the place being so far off and the voyage so dangerous.' If nothing else, it would give them a story to dine out on for the rest of their lives. Being now accepted as members of the club, the travellers were showered with money and with letters of introduction to Owen Lewis and Maurice Clenock, 'then the Rector of the English Hospital or College in Rome'. They left Paris some time in the autumn and made the dangerous voyage without mishap. According to Munday there were friendly Englishmen 'almost in every city by the way', an illuminating comment on the extent of the network of Catholic exiles now established in Europe.

Munday and Nowell reached Rome at the beginning of February 1579. They were given a kind welcome by Dr Clenock and besieged by the students with so many questions 'that we knew not which to answer first'. Munday, however, was soon buttonholed by one of the priests and carried off into the garden for a private conversation. In Paris he had been mistaken for the son of a Catholic gentleman, whom he discreetly omits to name, and had turned this fortunate accident to good account. Now it transpired that the priest knew his supposed 'father' well and a sweating Munday began to find the situation distinctly uncomfortable. He knew none of the people he was being asked about and 'was put to so hard a shift that I knew not well what to say'. Fear of exposure sharpened his wits and he managed to extricate himself by explaining that it was a long time since he had been at home, as he had been sent to London and Paris to study. All the same, when the bell rang, he remarked that 'the priest was not so ready to go to his supper as I was glad for that time to break off company'.

Munday was in Rome while the Anglo-Welsh quarrel was at its height, but the most interesting part of his narrative is the detailed account he gives of daily life at the English college. The students slept four or six to a room, but 'every man hath his bed proper to himself, which is two little trestles with four or five boards laid along over them, and thereon a quilted mattress as we call it in England, which every morning after they are risen, they fold up their sheets handsomely, laying them in the midst of the bed and so roll it up to one end, covering it with the quilt that is their coverlet all the night time'. The students' day was governed by the sound of the bell. After the rising bell came a bell for private prayer, 'when as every one presently kneeling on his knees, prayeth for the space of half an hour: at which time, the bell being tolled again, they arise and bestow a certain time in study, every one having his desk, table and chair to himself very orderly, and all the time of study silence is used of everyone in the chamber, not one offering molestation in speech to another'. After the study period came breakfast, which consisted of a glass of wine and a quarter of a manchet loaf. After breakfast, signalled by another bell, the students walked two by two to the Roman college or Gymnasium Societatis Jesu, where they spent the morning attending lectures in divinity, logic and rhetoric; then back to their own college to walk up and down in the garden talking, until the bell called them to dinner.

'The custom is' wrote Munday, 'that daily two of the students take it by turns to serve all the others at the table, who to help them have the butler, the porter and a poor Jesuit that looketh to all the scholars' necessaries. . . . As to their fare, trust me it is very fine and delicate, for every man hath his own trencher, his manchet, knife, spoon and fork laid by it, and then a fair white napkin covering it, with his glass and pot of wine set by him.' The meal consisted of four courses – an 'antepast' which might be Spanish anchovies or stewed prunes and raisins, followed by 'a certain mess of potage of that country manner' made of 'divers things' whose names Munday could not remember but which he considered to be 'both good and wholesome'. Then came two more courses, one boiled, the other stewed, roasted or baked, and dinner – which was accompanied by readings from the Bible and martyrology – ended with cheese and some 'preserved conceits', figs, almonds, raisins, a lemon and sugar, a pomegranate 'or some such sweet gear, for they know that Englishmen loveth sweetmeats'. After an hour's recreation came more study and more lectures and then a collation of bread and wine as at breakfast (Munday had no complaints about the food).

In the early evening there were exercises in disputation and then the students were free again until supper time. 'After supper, if it be winter time, they go with the Jesuits and sit about a great fire talking, and in all their talk they strive who shall speak worst of her Majesty, of some of her Council, of some bishop here, or such like: so that the Jesuits themselves will often take up their hands and bless themselves to hear what abominable tales they will tell them. After they have talked a good while, the bell calleth them to their chambers, the porter going from chamber to chamber and lighteth a lamp in every one: so when the scholars come, they light their lamps, lay down their beds and go sit at their desks and study a little till the bell rings, when every one falls on his knees to prayers. Then one of the priests in the chamber, as in every chamber there is some, beginneth the Latin litany, all the scholars in the chamber answering him, and so they spend the time till the bell rings again, which is for every one to go to bed.'

Discipline in the college was strictly enforced. The student who failed to 'turn up his bed handsomely', was late on his knees for prayers, missed the daily Mass or forgot to put a peg against his name on the board 'to give knowledge who is abroad and who remaineth within', had to perform public penance at dinner time. 'Either to kneel in the midst of the hall on his bare knees and there to say his beads over; or to say certain Pater Nosters and Ave Marias; or to stand upright and have a dish of potage before him on the ground and so to bring up every spoonful to his mouth; or to lose either one or two or three of his dishes appointed for his dinner; or to stand there all dinner time and eat no meat.' Munday observed ruefully that he had been forced to do all these penances during his stay at the college, 'for that I was always apt to break one order or other'.

Heavier penances were meted out in the confessional and for the more spectacular of these the penitent appeared, either at dinner or supper, 'clothed in a canvas vesture down to the ground, a hood of the same on his head, with two holes where through he hath sight, and a good big round place bare against the midst of his back. In this order he goeth up and down the hall, whipping himself at that bare place, insomuch that the blood doth trickle on the ground after him.' Munday would have nothing to do with this practice, which he considered to be unscriptural, but he was not the only one to disapprove. 'When a man doth it at the first,' wrote Dr Humphrey Ely, 'he is so far ordinarily from amendment that in his heart he doth grutch and repine at his superiors for the giving of it. But when he is used three or four times to do it, then he maketh a very scoff and mocking or may game of it. So far is it from a true penance as it engendreth . . . both hatred and mockery.'

Anthony Munday did not stay the course at the college for long. It was no part of his intention to be drawn into regular membership, besides which the climate of Rome could at any time have turned unhealthy. He left after a few months in an odour of goodwill, being entrusted with messages and holy pictures to be delivered to Catholics at home. But the numbers of young Englishmen between the ages of eighteen and twenty-five, physically sound and of blameless reputation who had forsaken families, friends, even in some cases brides, to seek the road to Calvary showed no signs of decreasing. As the Jesuits tightened their hold, supervision of every aspect of the students' lives and thoughts became closer. Contact with the outside world was reduced to a minimum. Private reading was limited to devotional books and lives of the saints, correspondence was censored, personal friendships restricted and discouraged. On the practical level every last detail of the college rule was directed to total sublimation of the ego into a conscious and deliberate preparation for self-immolation. Even the walls of the house were covered with pictures of the scaffold and torture-chamber and the college itself earned the respectful sobriquet of *Seminarium Martyrum.* Every normal emotion of human love, ambition and patriotism was harnessed to this end.

The students were taught in all seriousness that they alone had been chosen by Divine mercy – an elect and sacrificial few – to save their countrymen from the pains of eternal damnation by the example of their teaching; their example and their suffering. In this context physical martyrdom became unimportant, except insofar that it must be willingly and cheerfully embraced. To drive this lesson home, the Spiritual Exercises, originally formulated by Ignatius Loyola, were used to help the initiate to exercise his will by contemplation to the extreme point where fantasy and reality became indistinguishable. 'To see in imagination the length, breadth and depth of hell. . . . To beg for a deep sense of the pain which the lost suffer. . . . To see the vast fires and the souls enclosed, as it were, in bodies of fire. To hear the wailing, the howling, cries and blasphemies against Christ our Lord. . . . With the sense of smell to perceive the smoke, the sulphur, the filth and corruption. To taste the bitterness of tears, sadness and remorse of conscience. With the sense of touch to feel the flames which envelop and burn the souls.'

Whatever may be thought of this system of training – or brainwashing – as applied to impressionable, idealistic youth, it was certainly efficient in producing the required result. Not surprisingly though, in that highly-charged emotional atmosphere the English college at Rome continued to be subject to bitter internal feuds and jealousies. In order to extend their control over their charges' private thoughts and opinions, the Jesuits unwisely resorted to the time-honoured but questionable practice of introducing *Angeli custodes*, or to put it more bluntly, spies among the student. These 'guardian angels' would 'speak liberally' against the college authorities and lead their companions on 'to complain of their government and usage towards them, of their apparel, meat and drink, and against the straight keeping of them in, and against whatsoever they think is not well done in the college'. Having accumulated enough evidence, the informers would then 'carry the whole discourse straight to the Rector'. 'If such spies were at Oxford,' commented Humphrey Ely, 'they would be plucked in pieces.' Another cause of ill-feeling was the fact that the Society of Jesus not unnaturally sought recruits for the Order from the ranks of the English students. This soon led to complaints that these novices were given favoured treatment and helped to fan the flames of the smouldering quarrel between secular and Jesuit factions – a quarrel which was eventually to divide the college once again into 'two hostile camps'.

From Rheims, William Allen had followed the progress of the early troubles at Rome with close attention. He was naturally anxious that the new foundation should be a success and also that nothing should happen to alienate the Pope's support – both moral and financial. Allen was acutely aware of the danger of internal dissension and of the 'marvellous scandal and inconvenience' it could so easily breed. 'My first care was that it should take no hold in our company,' he told Owen Lewis in 1579, 'where I thank God at this day they live as sweetly together without all differences or respect of nations or other distraction as ever I knew any such number in my life. And yet so to hold it, because we well perceived the common inclinations of Adam to like and whisper underhand for their own against others of other countries, great moderation and dexterity was necessary I assure you.' In view of the rapidly disintegrating situation, Allen's relief when the Jesuits took over was understandable and made 'a double Easter' at Rheims. Whether or not he foresaw future difficulties, he could only be glad that the continuation of the second English college was now assured. The community at Douai and later at Rheims had flourished without oaths and statutes, stringent rules and regulations or degrading physical punishments because there had been no need for them. These were men drawn together by a common ideal, sustained by the vision and determination of a single, much-loved leader. But Allen knew that was not enough. If the English mission was ever to make a lasting and significant contribution to the survival of English Catholicism, it must expand. Its amateur days were over. It was time for the professionals to move in

Allen had another, more specific, reason for being pleased at the new turn of events. As an intellectual *élite*, the Society of Jesus was naturally attracting some of the best minds among the younger generation. As a first-rank corps in the battle for the counter-reformation it was also attracting some of the most fervent souls. Allen had seen a number of his own pupils, perhaps most notably the outstanding Edmund Campion, join the Society. He would not stand in their way, but until now a recruit won by the Jesuits had meant a labourer lost by the English harvest. William Allen hoped that this need no longer be so – it certainly seemed a pity to be sending English members of the Society as missionaries to the Indies when there was work for them so much nearer home, and this was a point which soon occurred to the English students at Rome.

Father Robert Parsons, the English Jesuit who had had a good deal to do with stage-managing the students' revolt, had his ear to the ground (he usually did) and quickly picked up 'a certain murmur' which, according to Humphrey Ely, would in time have grown into open sedition, if by Father Parsons' wisdom and industry it had not been prevented. 'The cause was this', wrote Ely. 'Our scholars, having obtained their desire and falling to their studies, used very zealously all the godly exercises of mortification, in such sort as some one or two of them became so contemplative that they would needs be Jesuits. Which when their companions understood, they began to mislike of those spirits, alleging that the College was founded for the education of virtuous and learned priests to help their country and not to bring up men to enter into religion and leave the harvest at home. Whereupon Father Parsons procured Dr. Allen's coming up to Rome, who obtained of the Pope to command the General of the Jesuits to send of his religious into England, the which appeased all this murmur. For (quoth the scholars) let as many now enter the Society as will, for when they have been sufficiently brought up therein they shall be sent into England. And thus each party was pleased; the fathers for that they might receive of the scholars into their Society without grudge or mislike, and the scholars because such as entered, most of all (if not all) should be in time employed for their country.'

Allen's third visit to Rome in the summer of 1579 turned into something of a personal triumph. The Pope treated him as an honoured guest and when Allen remarked how he had longed to see the students of His Holiness at Rome, Gregory replied 'They are thine, Allen, not mine'. All this was very gratifying and the ostensible purpose of his visit – to act as peace-maker and heal by his presence any lingering resentment between the factions at the college – was duly carried out in a moving address to the assembled students. But even more important, negotiations with the Superiors of the Society of Jesus were brought to a successful conclusion and it was agreed that Robert Parsons and Edmund Campion should be the pioneers of the Order in the English mission field. When Allen returned to France in February 1580 he had reason to feel a modest degree of optimism. In the eleven years which had passed since the renting of that house in Douai, he had himself sent a hundred labourers into the vineyard. Now he not only had the very human satisfaction of knowing that his work was being supported and appreciated but also that it would be carried on.

20

THE ENTERPRISE IS BEGUN

'The expense is reckoned, the enterprise is begun.
It is of God, it cannot be withstood.'
Edmund Campion, Hoxton, 19 July 1580

It has been said that the first Jesuit mission or, to be more precise, the first batch of missionaries to include Jesuit fathers in their number, marked the beginning of the 'heroic' period of the English Mission. Certainly it marked the beginning of a new, more bitterly contested phase of the ideological struggle. If the image of the Jesuit priest flitting through the corridors of power aroused complicated emotions of jealousy and suspicion among the members of longer established, less enterprising Catholic orders, the feelings it evoked in Protestant circles were not in the least complicated. To the English government, perennially (some would say morbidly) preoccupied with the dangers of subversion from within and encirclement from without, the Society of Jesus embodied everything they feared and hated most about Roman Catholicism. By the early 1580s the bogeyman of the 'pollyticke Jesuit' had become ineradicably established in the official mind as public enemy number one of the Protestant state. Official reaction to the news that Jesuits were actually planning to set their cloven hooves on English soil was therefore excitable.

In spite of their highly-coloured reputation, the Superiors of the Order had been far from eager to involve themselves in the English harvest. The Society of Jesus was a closely-knit, highly organised body – therein lay its strength, and its weakness. The Jesuit General and his advisers knew that under present conditions in England it would be virtually impossible to maintain either organisation or discipline. They hesitated to send their members into such outer darkness and, according to Robert Parsons, 'found divers difficulties in the matter in respect of the novelty thereof, especially about their manner of living there in secular men's houses in secular apparel . . . as how also their rules and orders for conservation of religious spirit might there be observed'. Apart from the spiritual dangers to be overcome, England was a political hot potato which would need the most delicate handling if the missionaries were not to lay themselves open to charges of plotting and intrigue – thus damaging both the Society and the cause it served.

However, having once committed themselves, the Jesuits began preparing for the task which lay ahead with their usual efficiency and attention to detail. Full instructions were drawn up for the guidance of the pioneers, who were to keep to the rules of the Society as far as circumstances would permit and 'so behave that all may see that the only gain they covet is that of souls'. They were to be very careful about the company they kept, associating only with Catholics and preferably reconciled Catholics of high rank. It was emphasised that the principle aim of the mission was 'the preservation and augmentation of the Faith of the Catholics of England' and the fathers were to avoid contact with heretics altogether. They must not carry about anything forbidden by English law – no amateurish mistakes such as Cuthbert Mayne had made – or letters which might compromise them. Most important of all, 'they must not entangle themselves in affairs of State' or write to Rome about political matters. They were not to speak against the Queen, or allow others to do so in their presence, 'except perhaps in the company of those whose fidelity has been long and steadfast and even then not without strong reasons'. In a later version of the instructions, issued the following year, this proviso was omitted and the official prohibition on talking politics became absolute.

Before the missionaries actually set out on their journey, there was one thing which the Jesuits wanted settled – the debatable question of the continued force of *Regnans in Excelsis*. Were pious Catholics in England really obliged to consider themselves under interdict if they recognised and obeyed (in civil matters at least) their deposed and schismatic Queen? During the eleven years which had passed since Pius V loosed the papal thunderbolts in Elizabeth's direction, none of William Allen's pupils had apparently thought it necessary to seek a ruling on this point. In typically English fashion the problem had been quietly swept under the carpet and left there. Such a solution was not acceptable to the logical Latin minds which ruled the Society of Jesus and they accordingly extracted an *Explanatio* from Pope Gregory, laying down that although the provisions of the bull still applied in full to Queen Elizabeth and her heretical supporters, while things remained as they were it in no way bound the English Catholics, 'except when public execution of the said bull shall become possible'. In other words, it seemed that the Queen's Catholic subjects might continue to accept her as their *de facto* sovereign unless and until means could be found to overthrow her. The Jesuits would have been wiser to have left well alone, for when in due course this interesting piece of information found its way into the hands of the English government, they showed no signs of gratitude for the respite thus thoughtfully granted.

Edmund Campion who, with Robert Parsons, was to form the spearhead of the Jesuit advance, reached Rome from Prague on 5 April 1580 and on the 18th, after an audience with the Pope, the party was ready to set out. It was, in fact, quite a large party. In addition to Parsons, Campion and Ralph Emerson, a Jesuit 'coadjutor' or lay-brother, five young graduates of the English college (including Ralph Sherwin, one of the leaders of the student revolt) were making the journey. There were also four elderly English priests dating from the Marian era who had been chaplains at the hospice, and such notable names among the first generation of exiles as Laurence Vaux, Edward Rishton and Dr Nicholas Morton. The most senior of the travellers, however, was Thomas Goldwell, once Bishop of St Asaph and almost the last survivor of the Marian hierarchy.

On 18 April a Welsh friend of Humphrey Ely living in Rome wrote to him at Rheims with the news that 'my lord of St. Asaph and Mr Dr Morton are gone hence, some say to Venice, some to Flanders, and so further, which if it be true you shall know sooner than we here. God send them well to do whithersoever they go, and specially if they be gone to the harvest. . . . This day depart hence many of our countrymen thitherward, and withal good Father Campion.' This letter was intercepted by an English spy who promptly forwarded it to Francis Walsingham, but it would not have greatly taxed the powers of any spy to send advance warning to London. The departure of the missionaries was about as secret as that of a hopeful Cup Final team. The whole of the English colony in Rome came to see them off, and scenes of solemn and affectionate farewell took place at the Ponte Molle.

The first destination was Rheims, which Campion and Parsons reached at the end of May and where they heard for the first time that theirs was not the only expedition which had been despatched against the heretics with a papal blessing. There had for some time been talk of armed intervention in Ireland, Anthony Munday had heard all about it in Paris in 1578, and in that year Sir Thomas Stukeley, Devonian, rogue, vagabond and soldier of fortune, had sailed from Civita Vecchia with a ship, six hundred men and a quantity of arms provided by the Pope at a cost, according to a wistful Cardinal of Como, of 'thousands and thousands of crowns'. But Stukeley, one of those comic opera characters who flourished in the sixteenth century, got no nearer to Ireland than Lisbon. There he and his men were diverted to North Africa by the King of Portugal, and Sir Thomas was killed at the Battle of Alcazar.

But Pope Gregory, who was the spiritual heir of Pius V in more ways than one, did not abandon the idea of stirring up trouble in Ireland – that at least never presented any difficulty – and presently found another candidate in the person of James Fitzmaurice, first cousin of the Earl of Desmond. Irish internal politics, then as now, were a quagmire into which outsiders ventured at their own risk, but to anyone looking for an opportunity to embarrass the English government the temptation was understandable. A full-scale rebellion would divert English forces and English money from assisting continental Protestants. It would leave England open to attack along her south-eastern approaches. Ireland might also serve as a springboard for invasion from the west.

Fitzmaurice was a native Irishman, an ardent Catholic, an ardent enemy of England, and could command the support of the Desmond clan. He seemed to have a fighting chance and in the opinion of Nicholas Sander – the most articulate and irreconcilable of the English exiles – it was a chance well worth taking. When Fitzmaurice with a handful of men landed at Dingle Bay on 17 July 1579 he was accompanied by Sander in the capacity of papal nuncio. If any further confirmation of the Vatican's involvement was needed, Fitzmaurice provided it in proclamations declaring that the Pope had deprived Elizabeth of her unjust possession of her kingdom and that he – Fitzmaurice – was the Pope's captain come to unseat a tyrant 'which refuseth to hear Christ, speaking by his vicar'. In the event, the landing was a failure. Fitzmaurice was killed quite early on and although Sander kept the insurrection alive for a time, the English had no particular difficulty in dealing with it. Sander himself ended as a hunted fugitive, dying in 1581 of exhaustion and exposure.

The Irish *débâcle* was the Vatican's second major tactical blunder in its campaign against Elizabeth. By a futile demonstration of hostility, Gregory had only succeeded in irritating his opponents. More seriously – since the English government could hardly be expected to appreciate the distinction between the Pope wearing his temporal hat and his spiritual one – he had gone a long way towards destroying the credibility of the missionary priests as a non-political force. None realised this more clearly than the missionary priests themselves. 'Though it belonged not to us to mislike this journey of Dr. Sander, because it was made by order of his superiors,' wrote Robert Parsons, 'yet were we heartily sorry, partly because we feared that which really happened, the destruction of so rare and worthy a man, and partly because we plainly foresaw that this would be laid against us and other priests, if we should be taken in England, as though we had been privy or partakers thereof, as in very truth we were not, nor ever heard or suspected the same to this day. But as we could not remedy the matters, and as our consciences were clear, we resolved through evil report or good report to go on with the purely spiritual action we had in hand; and if God destined any of us to suffer under a wrong title, it was only what he had done, and would be no loss, but rather gain, in his eyes who knew the truth, and for whose sake alone we had undertaken the enterprise.'

In spite of these brave words, both Parsons and Campion felt some very natural doubt as to whether there was now any point in going on, especially since they had been told that their arrival was expected and the ports being watched for them. But after discussing the matter with William Allen and the Jesuit fathers at St Omer, they decided it was too late to turn back and that further delay would probably only increase the danger. One of the travellers who did decide to turn back was old Thomas Goldwell, whose nerve had understandably failed. Allen was disappointed, because he was becoming increasingly aware of the need for someone on the spot to exercise overall control of the priests at work in England. But it was obviously unrealistic to expect a man of Goldwell's age (he was in his eightieth year) to withstand the rigours of life underground and certainly it was better that the bishop 'should yield to fear now than later on, at the other side'. The remaining members of the party, which had been reinforced by more priests from Rheims, now split up to find their way across the Channel in twos and threes by separate routes. Nearly all were to end in prison or on the gallows but after the defection of Thomas Goldwell, public interest focused exclusively on Edmund Campion and Robert Parsons. Both were men of outstanding ability but circumstances and history were to deal with them very differently.

Edmund Campion, born in 1540, was the son of a London bookseller. His father had planned to apprentice him to a merchant, but one of the London companies – most probably the Grocers – took an interest in the clever boy and he was sent instead to the new foundation of Christ's Hospital. Campion achieved his first public distinction at the age of thirteen, when he was chosen to speak a Latin oration on behalf of the London grammar schoolchildren on the occasion of Queen Mary's triumphant progress through the City. Still sponsored by the Grocers' Company, he went on to St John's College, Oxford. Unlike Allen, he was not a committed Catholic at this stage of his career and took the Oath of Supremacy when it was required of him in 1564 apparently without a serious misgiving. He was soon making a name for himself as a tutor and lecturer. Like William Allen, Campion was a born teacher and attracted a devoted following among the undergraduates, known as the 'Campionists'. He was appointed proctor and public orator, and in the latter capacity scored a notable success when the Queen visited Oxford in 1566. Elizabeth praised his eloquence and recommended him to the patronage of the Earl of Leicester, Chancellor of the University. Leicester is said to have sent for Campion to ask what he could do for him and to have urged him not to be too modest, for it was not only the Queen's command but his own inclination to befriend him. 'Ask what you like for the present,' declared the chancellor expansively. 'The Queen and I will provide for the future.' Lord Burghley (or William Cecil as he then was) also made a favourable note of the promising young Fellow of St John's.

At the age of twenty-six, therefore, Edmund Campion had the world at his feet. In addition to his persuasive intellectual gifts, he was blessed with the sort of sweetness of nature which disarms jealousy – at any rate no one at Oxford seems to have grudged him his triumphs. Tragically, though, Campion's conscience was beginning to stir. He had made friends with Richard Cheney, Bishop of Gloucester, one of the more right-wing members of the Elizabethan hierarchy, and had allowed himself to be ordained as a deacon, but the further he progressed in the study of theology the more unsettled he became. Finally, in 1569, he left Oxford for Ireland to take a post as a private tutor, hoping in due course to find congenial employment at the reconstituted University of Dublin. This plan came to nothing and Campion filled in his time by writing a history of Ireland which he dedicated to the Earl of Leicester. He returned home early in 1571 and, so Robert Parsons says, was present at the trial of Dr Storey – one of the original exiles who had been kidnapped in somewhat dubious circumstances and brought back to England to be executed as a traitor.

Whether it was this episode which made up Campion's mind for him, or whether he had succumbed to the persuasion of his friend Gregory Martin who had gone over to Douai some years previously, he now left England for the second time. He spent two years under the tutelage of William Allen and then set off on foot to Rome where he joined the Society of Jesus. He was sent to the University of Prague by his superiors and occupied the position of Professor of Rhetoric – scarcely, it might be thought, the most rewarding fulfilment for a man who Lord Burghley himself had described as 'one of the diamonds of England'.

It is difficult for the twentyfirst-century mind to comprehend a man like Edmund Campion and it is tempting to try and explain him in terms of guilt complexes, death wishes, or plain inability to face the stresses and responsibilities of the career of public service which had undoubtedly been his for the asking. Robert Parsons makes a revealing remark in his biography of his friend. Speaking of the time when the Jesuits were competing for services of their new recruit, he says that Campion was 'incredibly comforted with this battle of the provincials for possession of his body, because he saw that he was no more his own man, but in the hands of others who, under God, would dispose of him better than he could do for himself'. But however one attempts to rationalise such a man he remains elusive and, in spite of his noble reputation, subtly unsympathetic. Robert Parsons, though he was harshly judged by his own contemporaries and has had a bad press from historians ever since, is paradoxically more likeable – perhaps because as a human being he is immediately recognisable.

Robert Parsons (or Persons) was a West Countryman born in 1546 in the village of Nether Stowey on the edge of the Quantock Hills. He says himself that his parents 'were of humble worldly condition but honourable and of somewhat better rank than their neighbours around'. It is thought that his father was a blacksmith and as such would have been a figure of importance in the rural community. Young Robert was one of a family of eleven and 'scarcely was he out of childhood when he was given over to an elder brother, a merchant, to learn business'. But, again according to Parson's own account, 'it happened by the seeming providence of God that his brother lost nearly the whole of his fortune, and sent Robert back home to his parents'. The local vicar now took a hand. 'He was pleased with Robert's disposition, and also somewhat moved by the consideration that this was the first child that he had baptized after his entry into the parish.' He therefore persuaded Robert's father to send him to the grammar school at Stogursey, offering to pay part of the expenses. (The early careers of both Campion and Parsons provide an interesting illustration of the ways in which clever boys of comparatively humble birth were helped to rise in the world.)

Robert and another of his brothers spent a year at Stogursey and then went on to the larger free school at Taunton. Robert was unhappy there, and at the age of fifteen decided he had had more than enough of education. He wrote home complaining bitterly about his teacher's severity and offering a number of cogent reasons why he should be allowed 'to give over his book'. According to the recollections of yet another of the Parsons brothers, his father was ready to be persuaded by this 'fine and smooth letter', but his mother would not hear of it. She had set her heart on seeing Robert become a scholar and personally rode the seven miles to Taunton to ensure that he stayed. After the failure of this bid for freedom, Robert seems to have settled down. 'He fell to his book very heartily and became the best in the school, and so continued as long as he was there.'

When he was eighteen he progressed to Oxford, studying logic at St Mary's Hall and becoming a Fellow of Balliol in 1568. Like so many of the younger Oxford men, he had begun to flirt with Catholicism and Edmund Campion, who was proctor that year, offered to help him to evade the Oath of Supremacy. But his efforts were unsuccessful and, says Parsons in his autobiography, 'wicked and ambitious youth that I was, not to lose my degree, I twice pronounced with my lips that abominable oath, though at heart I detested it'. Like Campion he was a successful tutor, but his career at Oxford ended under a cloud, and in 1573 he was expelled from Balliol 'even with public ringing of bells'. Later, when Robert Parsons had become a target for official vilification, it was put about that he had been found to be illegitimate and therefore ineligible for his Fellowship; also that he was suspected of misappropriating college funds. Parsons himself claimed that he was the victim of a conspiracy and had resigned 'both freely and perforce'.

The most likely explanation seems to be that he had become generally disliked by his colleagues, who combined to get rid of him. Unlike Campion, Parsons was an abrasive personality of the kind which easily makes enemies – especially in the touchy atmosphere of a college common room. One of his fellow dons described him as 'a man wonderfully given to scoffing, and that with bitterness, which was the cause that none of the company loved him'. William Camden, who also knew him at Oxford, says he was 'fierce natured' and has left a felicitous picture of him in his student days 'much noted for his singular impudency and disorder in apparel, going in great barrel hose, as was the fashion of hacksters of those times, and drawing also deep in a barrel of ale'. It is all a very familiar pattern – the brilliant 'scholarship boy' with a chip on his shoulder, the lonely young man driven to use his bitter, sarcastic tongue to conceal the frightening insecurity within.

After his ignominious departure from Oxford, Parsons decided to go to Padua to study medicine. He had a little money from the sale of a piece of land given him by the father of one of his pupils and left England in the early summer of 1574. He was in no sense a religious refugee, but while he waited at Antwerp for company on the road through Germany, he was persuaded to visit Louvain where he made his first acquaintance with the Society of Jesus and spent several days going through the Spiritual Exercises. The experience moved him deeply and he might have stayed if he had not already sent his money on to Italy. In the end he travelled to Padua as planned and early the following year went on a trip to Rome, afterwards regretting that he 'had attended more to see profane monuments of Caesar, Cicero and other such like, than to places of devotion'. Back in Padua, he set up house with two English law students, bought a supply of medical books and some clothes from the wardrobe of an English nobleman who had recently died in Venice. But somehow the idea of becoming a doctor had lost its appeal and Parsons spent the next few months in an agony of indecision about his future.

'Many cogitations passed my mind,' he wrote, 'what course it were best for me to take, sometimes thinking to steal away out of Padua and to go to the Alps and there to put myself into some remote and solitary monastery or cell, never to converse more with men; some other times purposed to live a secular life, but yet retired and given to study'. Robert Parsons would certainly not have made a successful hermit. He needed the stimulus of the world, even if he sometimes found it difficult to get on with its inhabitants. In May 1575 he left Padua on foot for Rome – a self-imposed penance for, as he plaintively remarked, he was 'no good goer a-foot and the weather was hot'. However, he stuck it out and having at last made up his mind what he wanted to do with his life, entered the jesuit novitiate on 25 June, the day after his twenty-ninth birthday.

The Society of Jesus seems to have quickly appreciated his executive as well as his intellectual abilities – at any rate there was never any question of sending him off to some distant corner of Europe. Given polish and self-confidence by Jesuit training, Parsons stayed in Rome, cutting his political teeth on the gritty problems of the English college and becoming a persuasive advocate of the English Mission. When it came to choosing the pioneers, he was an obvious candidate and, although junior to Campion both in age and religion, was put in charge of the party.

If even half the rumours flying round St Omer in June 1580 were true, it was obvious that the task of getting the three Jesuits safely into England was not going to be easy. Robert Parsons therefore consulted the leader of the English community, a Mr George Chamberlain, who had a reputation for being discreet and well-qualified to give advice. It was decided that Parsons should go on ahead by the short sea-route to Dover, 'under the habit and profession of a captain returned from the Low Countries'. If all went well, Campion would follow disguised as a merchant in precious stones with Ralph Emerson as his servant. Although there was no official expeditionary force in the Netherlands as yet, quite a number of the Queen's subjects – some from conviction but probably more out of a taste for rough games – were fighting with the Dutch rebels on a freelance basis. The mercenary captain on his way to or from the wars was therefore a familiar enough sight at the Channel ports and George Chamberlain undertook to provide a military coat of buff leather suitably embellished with gold lace and a hat with a feather.

Parsons adopted his new personality with enthusiasm. 'Such a peacock, such a swaggerer,' wrote Campion, 'that a man needs must have very sharp eyes to catch a glimpse of any holiness and modesty shrouded beneath such a garb, such a look, such a strut.' None of this was precisely in accordance with the instructions of the Superiors in Rome who, while recognising that the missionaries would be obliged to dress as laymen, had laid down that such dress 'ought to be of a modest and sober kind, and to give no appearance of levity and vanity'; but Parsons took a certain ironic pleasure in the appropriateness of the disguises chosen. Their mission was, after all, one of warfare, albeit spiritual warfare, and they were bringing with them the 'jewel' of the Faith.

Parsons sailed from Calais some time after midnight on 16 June and reached Dover without incident. Nor did he experience any difficulty with the immigration authorities, who 'found no cause of doubt in him, but let him pass with all favour, procuring him both horse and all other things necessary for his journey to Gravesend'. No one, it seemed, suspected the dark, rugged-featured, swaggering soldier and Parsons was quick to follow up his advantage. He asked a friendly official to look out for his friend Mr Edmunds, a merchant with urgent business in London, and left a letter to be forwarded to St Omer, telling Campion that if he made haste he could help him to sell his jewels. Parsons then went on his way to Gravesend which he reached late that night, just twenty-four hours after leaving Calais. He got himself a place on a boat taking a convivial party of musicians up river but, feeling it would be unwise to prolong the acquaintance, he hailed a passing wherry which landed him in Southwark about four o'clock in the morning of the 17th.

Parsons was now in the heart of enemy territory and soon discovered that 'the greatest danger of all seemed to be in London itself'. Innkeepers were suspicious of lone travellers on foot and his military appearance, which had occasioned no surprise at the seaports, was uncomfortably conspicuous in the capital. As Parsons trudged around Southwark looking for a lodging, he became conscious of curious glances cast in his direction and realised that he was courting disaster by staying on the streets. It seems odd that although it was now six years since the first missionaries had begun to work in England, there were still no sort of organisations for meeting and helping incoming priests. There were, however, places where a Catholic would be certain of finding friends, and after walking up and down for half the day Robert Parsons 'resolved to adventure into the prison of the Marshalsea and to ask for a gentleman prisoner there named Mr. Thomas Pound'. This was not quite such a desperate step as it sounds – though it provides an illuminating comment on the Elizabethan prison system. In general, the 'better sort' of Catholics in gaol for simple recusancy were able to live in reasonable comfort – that is, as long as they could pay for their comforts – and the Marshalsea was a five star prison. It was expensive but the wealthier inmates could receive visitors, send messages and even sometimes get out for a while. Mr Pound, however, was in residence and delighted to welcome Father Parsons.

After dinner he was able to introduce him to another visitor, Mr Edward Brooksby, who bore him off to a 'safe house' in the City. Here Parsons met again a young man he had known in Rome. This was George Gilbert who, although brought up a Protestant, had been converted to Catholicism while travelling abroad – Parsons had actually stood godfather to him. Gilbert at once attached himself to his sponsor and was to become the forerunner of a group of enthusiastic young gentlemen – all scions of well-to-do families – who took it on themselves to act as guides, couriers and bankers for the missionary priests. As news of Parsons' arrival spread along the grapevine, he was showered with invitations and, after making arrangements for the reception of Campion and Emerson, he left London to 'employ himself in the best manner he could to the comfort of Catholics' in the surrounding countryside.

Meanwhile, Campion and Emerson were preparing to leave St Omer. Unlike Parsons, Campion had little relish for the business of dressing-up. 'You may imagine the expense,' he wrote to the Jesuit General on 20 June, 'especially as none of our old things can be henceforth used. As we want to disguise our persons, and to cheat the madness of this world, we are obliged to buy several little things which seem to us altogether absurd.' Campion had no illusions about the dangers which lay ahead. 'It is a venture which only the wisdom of God can bring to good,' he wrote, 'and to his wisdom we lovingly resign ourselves.' As soon as Parsons' letter arrived, Campion and Emerson set off for the coast and sailed from Calais on the evening of 24 June. At Dover they immediately ran into trouble – in fact it looked for a time as though their mission would be ended before it had begun. There was a security scare on at the port and the Customer had received orders to examine all incoming travellers with extra care 'for that it had been understood that certain priests had come that way into England of late days'. To make matters worse, the Council had been tipped off that William Allen's brother Gabriel was coming over and Campion apparently fitted his description. Both Campion and Emerson were brought before the Mayor of Dover as suspicious characters and were told they would be sent up to London under guard. Then, as they waited despondently in an antechamber, they were suddenly dismissed without explanation and told to be on their way. After this remarkable reprieve the two Jesuits reached London without further incident, travelling by river as Parsons had done, and as they stepped ashore were met by a Mr Thomas James who came up to Campion saying, 'Mr Edmunds, give me your hand; I stay here for you to lead you to your friends.'

Parsons had left instructions that Campion should wait for his return to London and spend the time doing all he could for the comfort of the Catholics. Campion was at once surrounded by the young men of George Gilbert's circle who begged him to preach for them. Through the good offices of Lord Paget they were able to use the great hall of Lord Norreys' house at Smithfield and here, on 29 June, three days after his arrival, Campion addressed a considerable audience. He had not lost his gift of oratory and the congregation was profoundly moved, but although the doors were guarded by gentlemen volunteers 'of worship and honour' such an event could hardly be kept secret. Campion was high on the wanted list and the government would have liked to catch him in the act of preaching. Agents were therefore sent out on the streets with orders to 'sigh after Catholic sermons and to show great devotion and desire of the same, especially if any of the Jesuits might be heard'. But Campion, though impatient of security measures, had enough sense not to be trapped by quite such obvious methods and when Parsons returned to London early in July, he found his friend had 'retired for his more safety into a certain poor man's house in Southwark'. Even so, the hunt was becoming uncomfortably hot. Already several priests out of the recent larger than usual draft from Rome and Rheims had been captured. 'The searches,' wrote Parsons, 'grew to be so eager and frequent at this time and the spies so many and diligent as every hour almost we heard of some taken, either upon suspicion or detection against them.'

Parsons needed no warning that the sooner he and Campion were away the better, but before they left town he was anxious to hold a conference with the more influential Catholic priests and laymen in the capital; partly to remove any misconceptions about the nature of their mission, and partly to ensure general conformity of teaching on such tricky matters of Church discipline as whether it could ever be regarded as permissible for a Catholic to be present at an Anglican service. The assembly, which met at St Mary Ovaries, became known as the Synod of Southwark, and Parsons opened the proceedings by making a solemn declaration on oath that neither he nor Campion had had any prior knowledge of Sander's Irish adventure. He went on to reaffirm that their purpose was apostolic – 'to attend to the gaining of souls without knowledge or intention in the world of matters of state'.

The question of church-going, a matter of close personal interest to all the laymen present, was then discussed. The government's requirements in this respect could scarcely be described as onerous, for Parsons told the rector of the college in Rome of some Catholic gentlemen then in prison who were offered their freedom 'if they would attend the churches of the heretics once a year only, making a declaration in advance that they came not for the sake of religion or of approving the doctrine there, but merely to yield external obedience to the Queen'. A lady of high birth had also apparently been told she would be released from gaol if she would agree 'merely to pass through the middle of the church whilst the heretics were holding service there, making no stay and giving no sign of reverence'. These offers, Parsons noted with satisfaction, had been virtuously refused and he went on to tell another story of the kind which makes one despair for the human race. A boy of ten years old had been tricked into entering a church by walking in a bridal procession. When he realised he had fallen into schism he was inconsolable until a few days later 'he chanced to meet' Robert Parsons. 'Whereupon he ran to me and falling at my feet begged me with a flood of tears that he might make confession of his sins, promising that he would be racked with every kind of torment rather than again consent to so great a sin.'

Other Catholics of a more practical turn of mind were arguing that if it could be made clear that they attended an occasional service only from obedience to the law and to save themselves and their families from harassment, they could surely not be accused of schism. Unfortunately, it was not as simple as that. The Roman Church held that by the public act of appearing at the heretical service, Catholics were giving countenance to the Elizabethan Settlement which exalted a temporal sovereign at the expense of the Pope. Whether they took part in the service or not was beside the point. This was an issue on which there could be no compromise and the Synod of Southwark, like the Council of Trent before it, stood firm. It was agreed that the missionary priests would continue to 'teach and insinuate unto Catholics in all places' that even a token attendance at the parish church must be regarded as an act of the highest iniquity and impiety. This, plus the fact that attendance at the parish church was beginning more and more to represent an act of allegiance to the state, did nothing to make life easier for the great majority of English Catholics doing their best to be loyal to their Queen and their religion.

After going on to discuss such matters as the correct observation of fast days and in which parts of the country priests could most usefully be employed, the assembly broke up. It was none too soon, for two members of the circle – Henry Orton, Parsons' companion on his recent tour, and a priest named Johnson – had actually been denounced and arrested while on their way to Southwark. The traitor on both occasions was a man called Charles Sledd or Slade, once a hanger-on at Rome who was now turning his memory for faces to profitable account. 'I am not surprised at the Apostle complaining so bitterly of false brethren,' wrote Parsons; 'here they are most troublesome to us and more deadly than anything else.' Parsons and Campion had had at least two very narrow escapes in less than a month. It was high time to be away from the poisoned atmosphere of London and on 18 July they set off on their travels, going by night for greater security. They paused at the village of Hoxton on the eastern outskirts of the City and here they were followed by Thomas Pound, who had contrived to bribe his way temporarily out of the Marshalsea.

Thomas Pound had been visited by a brilliant idea. If, as seemed only too probable, either or both of the Fathers were captured, the government propaganda machine would certainly represent them as traitors and stirrers-up of rebellion and they would be given no opportunity of stating their side of the case. Let them, therefore, write declarations now, setting out the true meaning and purpose of their coming. Pound would keep the documents safe and would have them published only if necessity arose. It seemed a sensible suggestion and Campion is said to have written his statement, addressed to the Lords of the Council, in less than half an hour. It was duly handed over to Pound but, either from carelessness or trustfulness, Campion had omitted to seal it. Pound, who has been described as very fervent 'but somewhat abounding in singularities', could not resist the temptation to read it and was at once thrown into such transports that he was obliged to show it to several close friends. Manuscript copies were made and passed from one 'safe' man to another so that, of course, it was not long before it reached some very unsafe men indeed.

'My charge is, of free cost to preach the Gospel,' Campion had written, 'to minister the Sacraments, to instruct the simple, to reform sinners, to confute errors – in brief, to cry alarm spiritual against foul vice and proud ignorance wherewith many my dear countrymen are abused.' He reiterated that he was expressly forbidden to meddle 'with matters of state or policy' and went on to ask 'with all humility, and under your correction, three sorts of indifferent and quite audience. The first before your honours; wherein I shall discourse of religion so far as it toucheth the commonwealth and your nobilities. The second, whereof I make most account, before the doctors and masters and chosen men of both universities; wherein I undertake to avow the faith of our Catholic Church by proofs invincible, scriptures, councils, fathers, histories, natural and moral reason. The third, before the lawyers spiritual and temporal; wherein I will justify the said faith by the common wisdom of the laws standing yet in force and practice.'

Campion would be loth, he declared, to say anything which might sound like 'an insolent brag or challenge', especially as he considered himself 'being now as a dead man to this world'. He was, however, perfectly confident of victory, because he knew 'that none of the Protestants, nor all the Protestants living, nor any sect of our adversaries . . . can maintain their cause in disputation'. In fact, 'the better furnished' his opponents, the more welcome they would be, and Campion was ready to cast his bait for the biggest fish of all. 'Because it hath pleased God to enrich the Queen my sovereign lady with noble gifts of nature, learning and princely education, I do verily trust, that if her highness would vouchsafe her royal person and good attention to such a conference . . . or to a few sermons which in her or your hearing I am to utter, such a manifest and fair light, by good method and plain dealing, may be cast upon those controversies, that possibly her zeal of truth and love of her people shall incline her noble grace to disfavour some proceedings hurtful to the realm, and procure towards us oppressed more equity.'

Whatever happened the fight would be carried on 'by those English students whose posterity shall not die, which, beyond the seas, gathering virtue and sufficient knowledge for the purpose, are determined never to give you over, but either to win you to Heaven or to die upon your pikes. And touching our Society,' wrote Campion, 'be it known unto you, that we have made a league – all the Jesuits in the world, whose succession and multitude must overreach all the practices of England – cheerfully to carry the cross that you shall lay upon us, and never to despair your recovery while we have a man left to enjoy your Tyburn, or to be racked with your torments, or to be consumed with your prisons. The expense is reckoned, the enterprise is begun. It is of God, it cannot be withstood. So the faith was planted, so it must be restored.'

Looked at dispassionately, Campion's Bragge as it quickly became known, is a quite astonishing mixture of naivety and arrogance. It is not difficult to imagine the sort of reception a similar threat of conversion made by a Protestant divine at large in his dominions would have been given by King Philip of Spain. The first reaction of Queen Elizabeth's government was one of studied but heavy breathing calm. In mid-July an official proclamation was issued in the Queen's name restating her determination 'to maintain her honour and glory by retaining her people in the true profession of the Gospel and free from the bondage of Roman tyranny'. Any who harboured 'unnatural affections' were warned 'not to irritate her Majesty to use the rod or sword of justice against them . . . from which, of her own natural goodness, she hath a long time abstained'. Her Majesty was aware of the danger threatened by rebels and traitors overseas, not to mention their sympathisers at home, who were seeking foreign aid to overthrow her. She was also aware that these same rebels and traitors were spreading tales about how the Pope and the King of Spain meant to invade England to 'dispose of the Crown and of the possessions of the subjects of the realm at pleasure', with the result that some were 'emboldened to persist in their undutifulness, some to be afraid to continue dutiful'.

But the Queen thanked God that she had 'such a strength as, in comparison, never any king of the realm hath had the like, to overcome all foreign malice to her and to the state of true Christian religion'. She therefore urged all her good people to 'continue in the true and dutiful service of Almighty God . . . and also to remain constant in courage with their bodies and substance to withstand any enterprise that may be offered to this realm'. They should not be influenced by any 'false rumours' and do their best to help the authorities to round up 'all such spreading like rumours'.

The proclamation carefully avoided any specific mention of the Jesuits Lord Burghley, who had been responsible for drafting this somewhat long-winded document, saw no reason to advertise the fact that they had slipped through his defensive outworks, but there was a noticeable tightening-up of security that summer as the newly arrived Spanish ambassador, Bernardino de Mendoza, reported to King Philip in July. 'All the Catholics in London,' he wrote, 'and the whole of the country, who had been released on bail, or had given sureties to appear when summoned, have been ordered to surrender themselves in the London prisons within twenty days, under pain of death. A great number of them have already done so, and it is a subject of heartfelt gratitude to God that they bear with joy and confidence this travail and persecution, such as they have never been afflicted with before.' Whether Mendoza's last statement is strictly accurate or not may be doubtful, but the time of tacit toleration for the Catholic minority was now fast running out. No one could any longer pretend that Catholicism was withering away of its own accord. In the words of one London preacher who believed in calling a spade a spade, 'the Papists and Jesuites, with other the riffe raffe and scumme of this Realme are nowe seen to appeare, who before this tyme have beene hidden in the dytches and channelles of England'.

It was a nervous summer, made more nervous by rumours of Spanish reinforcements on their way to Ireland and a fresh spate of highly circumstantial reports from abroad about the dreaded Papal League. A letter was sent to the Earl of Huntingdon, President of the Council of the North (always a black spot), authorising him to pursue a more stringent policy. Plans were drawn up for the stricter segregation of Catholic prisoners, especially 'the principal persons of most mark', and preparatory steps were taken towards strengthening the anti-recusancy laws. The twelve pence fine for non-attendance at church had remained unchanged since the beginning of the reign and a committee of judges, Queen's Counsel, 'together with some well-learned civilians', was set up to consider 'how by canon and common law a greater penalty might lawfully be set upon wilful and usual recusants that come not to the church at all'. In the autumn of 1580, however, the government was concentrating its efforts on the most effective counter-measure of all – that of catching the missionary priests.

21

And Christ Their Capitaine

'. . . It is that noble traine,
That fight with word and not with sword,
And Christ their capitaine.'
The complaint of a Catholic for the death of M. Edmund Campion

After a brief stay at Hoxton, Parsons and Campion separated, arranging to meet again in London at the end of September. Parsons then set off on a circuit of the Midlands and part of the West Country, while Campion went on a less ambitious trip into Berkshire and Oxfordshire. The idea of these missionary tours was a new one and reflects the increased efficiency of organisation and method which the Jesuits brought to the English harvest, as well as the energy and foresight of Robert Parsons. The Douai priests, operating individually, had for the most part returned to their own part of the country, or at any rate had stayed in one place or one district where their labours, however devoted, affected only a comparatively small circle. Parsons saw that to achieve maximum results, every missionary must reach as many people as he could in the probably all too short time at his disposal, and to do that he must travel. In order to make such travel on any useful scale a feasible proposition, it would be essential for the priests to have the support of a network of reliable helpers with a wide range of contacts among Catholics and Catholic sympathisers, and Parsons had already taken the opportunity of channelling the fervour of the newly converted George Gilbert into the task of recruiting the nucleus of an underground army. The prospect of acting as aides to the heroic fathers and sharing something of the danger and excitement of their work naturally appealed strongly to idealistic Catholic youth, and by the time Parsons and Campion landed in England Gilbert had collected a number of volunteers from among his own friends – all with plenty of spare and time and spare cash to devote to the cause.

While they were inevitably accused of aiding and abetting the priests in subversive activities, there is no evidence that these lay assistants, or 'sub-seminaries' as they became known, ever formed a political group in the accepted sense – although the names of some of them, such as Francis Throckmorton, Anthony Babington and Chideock Tichborne, were later to recur in a rather less innocent context. All these young men came of good family – indeed it was during Elizabeth's reign that native English Catholicism first acquired its close connection with the upper classes or, to put it more crudely, the specialised snob appeal which it has not entirely lost to this day. There was undoubtedly an element of class-consciousness – a feeling that Calvinism was no religion for a gentleman – in the missionaries' somewhat obsessive concern with the high rank of their supporters, and Campion's contemptuous dismissal of the Marian martyrs as 'a few apostates and cobblers' has a somewhat distasteful ring about it today.

At the same time, this apparent snobbism was based on sound practical considerations. The priests were in no position to make direct contact with the general public and the mission was only possible with the assistance – active or passive – of the gentry. The newer nobility, whose fortunes had been made out of the loot of the Reformation, were naturally predominantly Protestant, as were the bourgeoisie, merchants and artisans to whom the Elizabethan Settlement had brought peace, stability and freedom to get on with their lives with the minimum of clerical interference. It was among the remnants of the ancient nobility and to an even greater extent the older gentry families, often untitled, who owed neither their lands nor their position to an upstart royal house that the missionaries found shelter. These families, who had been part of the local scene for centuries, commanded an influence over their neighbours out of all proportion to the size of their estates or fortunes and their patronage was therefore the most valuable. It was, in fact, the constancy and clannishness of a handful of squires and small landowners which kept the faith alive, and in their houses that Parsons and Campion were welcomed as they travelled through England that faraway summer on their gallant but hopeless attempt to put the clock back.

'I ride about some piece of the country every day,' wrote Campion. 'The harvest is wonderful great. On horseback I meditate my sermon; when I come to the house, I polish it. Then I talk with such as come to speak with me, or hear their confessions. In the morning, after Mass, I preach; they hear with exceeding greediness and very often receive the sacrament, for the ministration whereof we are ever well assisted by priests, whom we find in every place, whereby both the people is well served, and we much eased in our charge. . . . I cannot long escape the hands of the heretics; the enemies have so many eyes, so many tongues, so many scouts and crafts. I am in apparel to myself very ridiculous; I often change it, and my name also. I read letters sometimes myself that in the first front tell news that Campion is taken, which, noised in every place where I come, so filleth my ears with the sound thereof, that fear itself hath taken away all fear. My soul is in mine own hands ever.' Neither Campion nor Parsons was under any illusion about the risks they and their hosts were running. According to Campion, 'at the very writing hereof, the persecution rages most cruelly. The house where I am is sad; no other talk but of death, flight, prison, or spoil of their friends; nevertheless they proceed with courage.' 'We never have a single day free from danger,' remarked Parsons but unlike Campion, who had considered himself as a dead man from the moment he left Rome, Parsons took a more optimistic view of their chances of survival, feeling that the dangers were not so great as to make capture unavoidable. Indeed, he hoped they might escape 'for many years, or at any rate months'.

Both men were united in begging their Superiors in Rome to send reinforcements as soon as possible and neither had any doubt about the worthwhile nature of their work. 'Very many, even at this present,' wrote Campion, '[are] being restored to the Church, new soldiers give up their names, while the old offer up their blood; by which holy hosts and oblations God will be pleased, and we shall no question by Him overcome. . . . There will never want in England men that will have care of their own salvation, nor such as shall advance other men's; neither shall this Church here ever fail so long as priests and pastors shall be found for their sheep, rage man or devil never so much.' 'The hope of a harvest is excellent,' wrote Parsons, 'for we are so spoilt by the Catholics and kept so busy that we have neither time nor strength sufficient. I am forced two or three times every day on this my tour to give discourses to men of rank, and they are touched by the spirit of God and are most ready for any distinguished service. More often than not they put at my disposal their persons and all their chattels, and their zeal and fervour is worthy of astonishment.' This letter, which was written on 5 August to the rector of the English college in Rome, ends with another appeal for reinforcements. 'I beg your Reverence to get for me from his Holiness and from our Father General the help of men of the Society, men of learning, not fewer than three of four.'

Meanwhile the journeys continued. 'We passed through the most part of the shires of England,' Parsons recorded, 'preaching and administering the sacraments in almost every gentleman and nobleman's house that we passed by, whether he himself were a Catholic or no, if he had any Catholics in the house'. The usual procedure in a doubtful place was to claim hospitality by posing as a friend or kinsman of some member of the household known to be a Catholic. When this was impracticable, the priest was introduced as the travelling companion of one of George Gilbert's young men. The Catholics would then arrange for him to be quartered 'in some part of the house retired from the rest', where a temporary chapel was set up. There he could change out of his lay disguise and there, when everybody else was in bed, as many of the local faithful who could manage it would gather to ask his blessing, lay their problems before him and make confession. In the early morning Mass would be celebrated and a sermon or exhortation delivered and then the priest, dressed once more in his sober riding clothes, took the road again. It seems likely that in most cases the master of the house must have been perfectly well aware of what was going on under his roof but, providing the visit was kept short and discreet, was prepared to be conveniently unobservant.

In houses where the whole family was Catholic, things became a little easier. The visiting father could stay longer, move about more freely and preach to a wider audience. But neither the priest nor his hosts could ever relax completely, for there was danger as well as protection to be found in the large, hospital establishments kept up by the average landed gentleman. While the arrival of a couple of additional house-guests would not necessarily attract any particular attention, in places where too many people were in the secret there was always a very real risk that careless talk might rouse the suspicions of an inquisitive neighbour, or that some disgruntled servant or dependant might seize the opportunity to pay off an old grudge and make a bit of extra money by laying information to the authorities.

Robert Parsons has left us an unforgettable description of what it felt like to be part of such a household when a priest was being entertained. ‘Sometimes,’ he wrote, ‘when we are sitting at table quite cheerfully, conversing familiarly about matters of faith or piety (for this is the most frequent subject of conversation), it happens that someone knocks on the front door a little more insistently than usual, so that he can be put down as an official. Immediately, like deer that have heard the huntsman and prick up their ears, all stand to attention, stop eating and commend themselves to God in the briefest of prayers. No word or sound of any sort is heard until the servants come to report what the matter is. If it turns out that there is no danger, we laugh at our fright.’

Many Catholic families had already taken the precaution of providing secret places where a wanted man could be hidden in case of emergency. As time went on the construction of such hides became a highly skilled and specialised craft – Nicholas Owen, son of an Oxford carpenter, being its most noted practitioner. But in the early days the hiding places were often amateurish affairs and known to too many people, so that the priests would prefer to take refuge in woods and thickets, lying in ditches or even holes in the ground. The atmosphere, as Parsons noted, was reminiscent of the primitive church. Services were held in attics and cellars, in barns and caves and, not surprisingly in such circumstances, the emotional temperature was high. ‘No one is found in these parts to complain that services last too long. If at any time Mass fails to last nearly an whole hour, this is not much to the taste of many of them.’ Everywhere the missionaries and especially the Jesuits went they were greeted with rapture, importuned with requests for sermons, blessings and advice, begged to stay as long as possible and released only with great reluctance. Campion hardly liked to touch on the ‘exceeding reverence all Catholics do unto us’, while Parsons wrote that he would never come to an end if he began to talk about the zeal and fervour of the Catholics.

All this was highly gratifying from the point of view of the mission, but the unremitting physical and mental strain imposed on the individual priests was killing. No human being could have withstood it for long without a breakdown and after about two and a half months on the road Parsons returned to London. He had intended to look for a suitable lodging where Campion could join him, but when he discovered that the 'Bragge' was still the main topic of dinner-table conversation with its author heading the government's wanted list, he realised that this plan would have to be abandoned. He got off a hasty warning which reached Campion at Uxbridge, fifteen miles away, in time for him to find a haven in the house of a Mr William Griffiths. Here Parsons and some of the other priests who had come over from Rome that summer presently foregathered and were able to spend a few weeks unwinding and comparing notes – relating 'one to the other the mercies that God had showed them in the time of their being abroad in the country, what shires, towns, houses they had visited, what success they had had, what perils they had escaped, what disposition they found in themselves and others for the time to come'.

It was agreed, among other things, that a recruiting drive for the foreign seminaries should be started in the universities and two priests were detailed to work among the undergraduates. Parsons had decided to send Campion up to Lancashire where, surrounded by a predominantly sympathetic population, his chances of survival might be better. He also wanted him to write something in Latin which could be circulated at Oxford where Campion's memory was still green, and in the Catholic houses of the North he would have greater leisure for literary composition and more 'commodity of books'.

After the party at Uxbridge broke up, Parsons himself went back to London. He was fully aware of the risk he was running and laid his plans accordingly. 'Though I have many places in London where I can stay,' he wrote to his friend Father Agazzari in November, 'yet in none of them do I remain beyond two days, owing to the extremely careful searches that have been made to capture me. I think, however, that by the Grace of God I am sufficiently safe from them owing to the precaution I take, and am going to take, of being in different places from early morning till late at night.' But as the pressure on the Catholic laity increased Parsons knew that he might not always be able to rely on his friends for shelter and he acquired a house of his own on the north bank of the Thames near Blackfriars which he used as his headquarters, as a storage place for books, vestments and the other paraphernalia of his trade, and as a refuge for other priests in time of need.

From his base in the capital Robert Parsons had, in fact, now taken over effective control of the Mission's operations. Such was the reputation of the Society of Jesus and the force of his own personality, that the secular priests co-operated willingly and seemed only to ready to follow his lead. All the same, Parsons was feeling the strain of his position and told

Agazzari that the burden was more than he could easily support without fresh help. Apart from the purely practical considerations, he was anxious to consolidate the predominance of Jesuit over secular priest and continued to press for a new draft of at least five men from the society. One of these, he stipulated, should be a Spaniard, a first-rate man and especially qualified to resolve complicated questions of conscience. He also wanted fresh reserves from the English college – a supply of 'numerous soldiers, courageous for the battle'. Until these reinforcements arrived, Parsons was prepared to carry on as best he could. After celebrating Mass and preaching, sometimes twice in one day, 'I struggle with almost unending business', he wrote. 'This consists mainly in solving cases of conscience which occur, in directing other priests to suitable places and occupations, in reconciling schismatics to the Church, in writing letters to those who are tempted at times in the course of this persecution, in trying to arrange temporal aid for the support of those who are in prison and in want. For every day they send to me, laying bare their needs. In short, the burdens of this kind are so many that, unless I perceived clearly that the honour of God required what we are doing, and that very badly, I should not hesitate to say that I am weary.'

Weary though he might be, during that winter Parsons was to add yet another task to his already overwhelming work-load. In spite of all the government's efforts to suppress it, book-running – the illegal importation of works of Catholic propaganda and devotion from Continental presses – was still going on, but Parsons had conceived the bold idea of publicising the Mission's activities by setting up his own underground press in or near London. The technical problems involved in putting this idea into practice were formidable – a suitably private place had to be found to house the press, printers and binders recruited and supplies of paper and type got together without arousing suspicion. Although never a man to minimise technical problems, Parsons was not easily discouraged by them, and during the course of November 1580 he set about contriving ways and means. Through the good offices of one of George Gilbert's young men, he got the loan of Mr Brooksby's house at Greenstreet, lying between the then outlying suburban villages of East Ham and Barking. Another of his contacts, the printer Stephen Brinkley, came with seven workmen to manage the press and Parsons himself was the author of the first work to be printed – *A Brief Discourse containing certain reasons why Catholics refuse to go to Church.*

Even so, there were, as Parsons remarked, 'very great difficulties in carrying out the project'. To start with, all the equipment had to be carried the six or seven miles from London, and the press itself had to be worked so that Mr Brooksby should remain in ignorance of what was going on. Then the local parish authorities began to cause trouble. Ironically enough they wanted to know why the occupants of Greenstreet House did not come to church. Parsons and the faithful George Gilbert, who was with him, had one very bad scare when a rumour reached them that the press had been discovered, due, so Parsons believed, to 'an incautious purchase of paper'. One of Brinkley's men was arrested and, to make matters worse, Parsons had begun to have serious doubts about the reliability of his servant, Robert Alfield. But at last the book was ready for distribution and the press could be dismantled.

No sooner had this been done than the first official counterblasts to Campion's Bragge appeared on the streets. Brinkley, coming to report that all was safe, found Parsons worried and depressed. Neither of the two replies to Campion – one written by the Puritan William Charke and the other by a more orthodox churchman Meredith Hanmer – were particularly startling, but both contained accusations which wanted answering. Brinkley offered to set up the press again, but there was now nowhere to put it and Parsons was increasingly anxious about the intentions of the servant Alfield. The situation was saved by Francis Browne, brother of Lord Montague, who offered the loan of a house and servants. Parsons was able to send Alfield away on a visit to his father, and ten days later appeared *A Brief Censure upon two books written in answer to Mr. Edmund Campion's offer of a disputation*. Another book or pamphlet produced by the secret press was *A Discoverie of John Nichols* – an exposure by Parsons of a somewhat dubious individual, originally a Protestant minister, who had spent some time at the English college in Rome and who was now being much petted and paraded by the government as a notable convert to Protestantism.

The difficulties of this form of publishing did not, of course, end with printing and binding. The books had to be distributed 'so that what is written may reach the hands of all'. The usual method was to make up parcels of fifty or a hundred copies at some central clearing house and pass them on to the missionary priests, who circulated them among the faithful on their travels. This, however, was not the only way in which they were brought to the notice of the public. According to Parsons, as soon as one of the regular searches for proscribed literature was under way, numbers of young gentlemen would be standing 'ready to distribute other copies at night in the dwellings of the heretics, in the workshops as well as in the palaces of the nobles, in the Court and about the streets, so that the Catholics alone may not be charged with being in possession of them'. No doubt this prank appealed strongly to the young gentlemen, but it would have done nothing to endear them to the authorities, trying unsuccessfully to track down the source of this new material being produced under their noses. For although Parsons and Brinkley tried to camouflage their activities – the *Brief Discourse* alleged itself to have been printed at Douai – any knowledgeable printer could recognise English paper and English type.

A very much harder line was now being taken against all Catholics and in his letter to Agazzari of 17 November, Parsons reported that 'the violence of the persecution, which is now inflicted on the Catholics throughout the whole kingdom, is most intense and it is of a kind that has not been heard of since the conversion of England. Everywhere there are being dragged to prison, noblemen and those of humble birth, men, women and even children . . . and in proclamations as well as in discourses and sermons they are made infamous in the eyes of the people under the name of traitors and rebels.' This new wave of severity, in which a considerable number of the better-known recusants were being round up and gaoled without the option, was due in part to the troubles in Ireland – Mendoza told Philip of Spain in October that over the past six weeks 'more than five hundred Catholic English gentlemen have been imprisoned for fear that they might rise in consequence of the news from Ireland' – in part to a fresh crisis situation beginning to build up in Scotland and in part, of course, to the disturbing resurgence of confidence visible among the Catholics themselves.

The government's biggest guns were trained on the priests who had brought this resurgence about and on the laymen suspected of association with them, but in spite of increasingly fierce proclamations about the consequences which could be expected by those caught maintaining, harbouring, and succouring jesuits and other seminary priests, and the revival currently being enjoyed by the ancient trade of informer, the two most wanted men in the country continued to prove irritatingly slippery customers. Campion, 'the wandering vagrant', after a slow and difficult journey had reached the comparative sanctuary of the north-west. Parsons, 'the lurking wolf', going about his business in the capital, seemed to bear a charmed life. Ralph Sherwin was taken on 13 November, the very day after he had been staying with Parsons, and Edward Rishton and a group of gentlemen from Lancashire were arrested when the Red Rose public house in Holborn was raided. Parsons was expected at this gathering, in fact he was on his way, but although he knew the district well and had been there only a few days before, he failed to find the house – possibly because he enquired for it by its other name, the Red Lion. Next day he heard that the door had been shut and 'the secretary Walsingham's men within it that were sent to apprehend me'. A little later he was visiting a house in Tothill Fields when the searchers arrived and only escaped 'by running into the haymow'.

When Parliament met on 16 January 1581, the fact had to be faced that the Queen's gradualist policy was no longer working. Those of her advisers who had never concealed their disapproval of this policy were not sorry to have been proved right. Everyone was agreed that the anti-Catholic legislation which, in general outline, had remained unaltered since 1559, must now be strengthened. The only area of disagreement lay in the nature and extent of the changes and it soon became evident that Elizabeth was not going to be stampeded into panic measures. She would certainly have had little sympathy with the Puritan divine who was gloomily convinced that the world was going mad and Anti-christ resorting to every extreme 'that he may with wolf-like ferocity devour the sheep of Christ'. The Queen clung to her belief that consciences were not to be forced and to her refusal 'to make windows into men's hearts and secret thoughts'. Ten years earlier she had vetoed a bill making it compulsory to take the Anglican communion at stated intervals. In 1572 and 1576 she had squashed attempts to reintroduce it, and she would have nothing to do with it now.

But if interfering with men's secret thoughts was one thing, permitting foreign interference and open defiance of her laws was quite another, as Sir Walter Mildmay, one of the government's spokesmen in the Commons, made clear. After referring to the 'implacable malice of the Pope and his confederates' which so far, thanks to the 'almighty power of God', had proved ineffectual, Sir Walter went on to warn his audience that 'seeing our enemies sleep not, it behoveth us also not to be careless'. The enemies of the Protestant state would if they could 'procure the sparks of the flames that have been so terrible in other countries to fly over into England and kindle as great a fire here'. Meanwhile, the Pope was resorting to underhand methods of encouraging dutiful subjects to defy their Queen. 'The obstinate and stiff-necked Papist is so far from being reformed as he hath gotten stomach to go backwards and to show his disobedience, not only in arrogant words but also in contemptuous deeds. To confirm them herein, and to increase their numbers, you see how the Pope hath and doth comfort their hollow hearts with absolutions, dispensations, reconciliations and such other things of Rome. You see how lately he hath sent hither a sort of hypocrites, naming themselves Jesuits, a rabble of vagrant friars newly sprung up and coming through the world to trouble the Church of God; whose principal errand is, by creeping into the houses and familiarities of men of behaviour and reputation, not only to corrupt the realm with false doctrine, but also, under that pretence, to stir sedition.' As a result, not merely the old, hard-core recusants but 'many, very many' who had previously been willing to conform were now refusing to come to church, and this, of course, was the really worrying thing.

Having outlined the problem, Sir Walter turned to the question of a solution. The Queen, he pointed out, had been extraordinarily patient over a long period, but since the Catholics had not responded to 'favourable and gentle manner of dealing' it was time 'to look more narrowly and straitly to them, lest . . . they prove dangerous members . . . in the entrails of our Commonwealth'. This represented the feeling of the entire House. Indeed, the Commons' only complaint was that the Queen had been patient for far too long. A committee, consisting of all the Privy Councillors and fifty-seven members of the Lower House, was appointed and began work immediately on drafting a bill entitled 'For obedience to the Queen's Majesty against the see of Rome', which received its first reading on 8 February. The Commons were then informed that the Lords were also considering a bill along the same lines as their own, but a good deal milder in its provisions.

Since both Houses were united in their desire to see more stringent penalties imposed on Catholic recusancy, they agreed to join forces. If, as seemed only too probable in the light of past experience, the Queen were to baulk at the last moment, Parliament's only hope of putting pressure on her lay in presenting a common front. After several meetings between the representatives of both Houses, a longer and amended version of the Commons' bill emerged and was read for the first time on 18 February. Among other things, it made the saying of Mass a felony and therefore subject to the death penalty. Anyone hearing Mass would now become liable to six months in gaol for a first offence and the pains of praemunire – loss of all goods and imprisonment during the Queen's pleasure – for the second. The recusancy fines were raised from the old flat rate of twelve pence to a staggering £20 for a first offence, £40 for the second, £100 for the third and after that praemunire.

If the bill had passed into law in this form and if it had been rigorously enforced, it would undoubtedly have gone a long way towards eradicating Catholicism in England by making life intolerable even for its peaceful and loyal adherents. This, as Professor Neale has pointed out, was undoubtedly what it was planned to do. There seems no reason to doubt, either, that this is what the three great advisory bodies – Council, Lords and Commons – wanted to happen. Certainly there is no indication that there were any dissenting voices. It did not happen because the Queen would not have it, or so all the available evidence suggests. After 18 February there was silence for nine days – a period presumably taken up with intensive consultations at Court. Then came another flurry of meetings between the parliamentary committees and on 4 March a third version of the bill was laid before the Commons. It was this version which presently reached the Statute Book as the 'Act to retain the Queen's Majesty's subjects in their due obedience' and which represented the limits Elizabeth was prepared to go to.

The bill as enacted was a good deal harsher than any previous anti-Catholic legislation but the earlier drafts had been significantly toned down. The section dealing with the missionaries and their undesirable activities was framed as an extension of the Act of 1571, which had made it a treasonable offence either to reconcile or be reconciled to Rome through the influence of *Regnans in Excelsis* or any similar pronouncement. This statute was now to apply to the missionary priests and their converts. In future, any person attempting to 'absolve, persuade or withdraw' any of the Queen's subjects from their 'natural obedience', or who persuaded them *'for that intent'* to leave the Church of England for the Church of Rome were to be adjudged as traitors. Any person who allowed himself to be so persuaded, or who promised obedience to the 'pretended authority of the See of Rome' was to suffer as in cases of high treason. Anyone aiding, abetting or concealing such persons would be guilty of misprision of treason. The addition of the words 'for that intent' in the final draft of the bill emphasised the Queen's stubbornly secular approach to the whole problem and allowed for some elasticity in the interpretation of the law – at least this is probably what she intended. In practice, however, it seems to have made little difference to those who were tried under the Act, since the courts persisted in regarding the fact of reconciliation to Rome as automatically involving a withdrawal of allegiance. This is certainly what the Commons had intended and in view of the Pope's attitude was not entirely unreasonable.

The most dramatic difference between the Act as originally envisaged by Parliament and the Act which received the royal assent lay in the sharp distinction drawn between the crime of becoming a Catholic (or rather of becoming one again) and the crime of being a Catholic. The former, to all intents and purposes, was now the treason of adhering to the Queen's enemies; the latter could still be compounded for with fines and imprisonment. For saying the Mass the price had risen to a fine of two hundred marks and a year in gaol, for hearing Mass a fine of one hundred marks and a year in gaol, for the luxury of refusing to go to church a fine of £20 a month. Anyone over the age of sixteen who was absent for twelve months must produce two sureties in the sum of at least £200 until such time as they did conform. This was galloping inflation in the cost of salvation and could quickly prove ruinous when enforced, but it was a good deal better than it had been before the Queen's intervention.

Another bill passed by the 1581 session of Parliament was the Act against seditious words and rumours uttered against the Queen's most excellent Majesty. Hitherto the penalty for slandering the sovereign had been the loss of both ears and three months in gaol, but with the option of a fine in lieu of ears. The new bill withdrew the option and increased the term of imprisonment to last during the Queen's pleasure. To repeat such an overheard slander (as distinct from inventing one) had previously involved one ear and one month in gaol, again with the option of a fine instead of an ear. Now that option was to disappear as well, and the term in gaol increased to three years. A repetition of either offence would now become a felony. Under the old law the punishment for writing or printing a slander against the sovereign had been the loss of the right hand, as the Puritan hero John Stubbs had recently discovered. Under the new law this, too, became a felony. Oddly enough, opposition to this savage measure came from the Commons. Not that they objected to the savagery, but they could see that it would be a two-edged weapon – one which could be turned against outspoken critics from the Puritan left as easily as against the Catholic right. In Professor Neale's felicitous phrase, 'they had visions of an earless *élite* of godly men, languishing for years in prison'.

The House therefore set about amending the bill and scaling down the penalties. Thomas Norton, that scourge of popery, inserted a clause which would have made it a seditious rumour to affirm that the doctrine taught by the Church of England was heretical or schismatic. If Norton had succeeded in getting this clause past the Queen he would, in theory at least, have imposed an ideological orthodoxy as rigid as that of any modern totalitarian state. In fact, of course, he did not. After a period of deadlock and a good deal of huffing and puffing between the Lords and Commons, a compromise was arrived at. Norton's addition had to be sacrificed, but the Commons succeeded in restoring the optional fines and in reducing the terms of imprisonment to six months and three months respectively. Second offences remained felonies, as did the writing or printing of slanderous material, but the left-wingers were able to get in a qualifying 'with malicious intent' which, they hoped, would protect all but the rashest of the godly. The only response the missionaries could make to the challenge of the new legislation was to redouble their efforts, in an attempt to increase their flocks to the point where no prison could hold them. It was a forlorn hope but Robert Parsons' letters are full of the cheerful resignation with which the Catholics of England faced the prospect of increased hardship and 'perpetual imprisonment'.

In the spring of 1581 the drama of the first Jesuit mission had begun to move towards its climax. Parliament rose on 18 March and about a week later Parsons received the manuscript of Campion's book. This work, which contained 'Ten Reasons for the confidence with which Edmund Campion offered his adversaries to dispute on behalf of the Faith' and which is usually referred to as the *Decem Rationes*, ran to about 200,000 words. The main thread of Campion's argument – and the one least likely to endear him to his adversaries – was that the Protestants knew their position to be intellectually indefensible and were therefore obliged to depend on brute force rather than reasoned disputation. Since the book was intended for a learned public, it bristled with quotations and references. Parsons, knowing that Campion had been working almost entirely from memory and that the smallest error would be joyfully pounced on, commissioned one of his lay contacts, Thomas Fitzherbert of Swynnerton, to verify the text as far as he could without arousing suspicion. Even taking this precaution, and knowing the dangers involved, Parsons decided that Campion ought to come south to superintend the printing of this important and complicated piece of work, but as an added safeguard he was to stay at public inns instead of Catholic houses on the journey.

Meanwhile, Parsons turned to grapple with the problem of setting up the secret press again. Stephen Brinkley offered to act 'as prefect of the printers' for the third time and a priest, William Maurice, began to buy paper and other essentials. But the greatest difficulty, as always, was to find a safe base for their operations. At last, 'having searched very diligently', Parsons was put in touch with a widow willing to lend her house 'which stood in the middle of a wood, twenty miles from London'. This was Stonor Park near Henley and Parsons and his team moved in towards the end of April. They were only just in time, for one evening not long afterwards, Father William Hartley, one of the priests deputed by the Uxbridge conference to work at the university, happened to mention while visiting Stonor that he had heard in Oxford that the servant of Roland Jenks, a Catholic bookbinder, had gone over to the enemy and betrayed his master.

This was a bad blow, as Parsons had very recently employed Jenks at his house at Blackfriars. First thing next morning he sent a messenger to London, but he was too late – the house had already been raided and its contents seized. Worse than the loss of his property was the news that during the search Alexander Bryant, a Douai priest and close friend of Parsons, had been found hiding in a nearby house and arrested. Bryant's special connection with Parsons was evidently known to the authorities, for he was at once singled out for special treatment. After a week in prison, where he was deprived of food and drink, Bryant was transferred to the Tower and tortured with unusual severity – as well as being repeatedly racked, needles were thrust under his nails in an attempt to wring from him 'by the pain and terror of the same' details of the whereabouts of Parsons and the secret press.

Campion had arrived from the north when the news of Bryant's sufferings reached Stonor, and he and Parsons sat up together nearly all one night discussing what they would do if they were taken. With incredible fortitude Bryant had remained silent and the printing of the *Decem Rationes* proceeded without incident, although slowly because of the limited supply of type available. It was ready by the end of June and William Hartley undertook the dangerous business of distributing it at Oxford. In a feat of considerable daring and ingenuity several hundred copies were planted on the benches in St Mary's Church, where a formal Academic Exercise was being held, and not surprisingly caused a sensation.

As soon as Hartley had reported the success of his mission, the party at Stonor broke up. Campion was ready to leave on 11 July, intending to return to Lancashire where he had left his books and belongings and then to make his way to Norfolk. First, though, he wanted Parsons' permission to accept an urgent and long-standing invitation to visit Lyford Grange, which lay in the Vale of the White Horse between Wantage and Abingdon. The mention of Lyford set alarm bells ringing in Parsons' head. Ever since the capture of Alexander Bryant he seems to have had a presentiment that time was running out and Lyford was just the sort of place most likely to prove a death trap. Its owner, Mr Yate, a noted recusant was in gaol and his mother lived in the house with a community of eight ex-Brigittine nuns. There were two priests, Father Ford and Collington, in constant attendance, so Campion's visit was scarcely necessary from the spiritual point of view.

On the other hand, it was not easy to refuse. Mr Yate had written to Campion from prison, begging him to go and see his mother and Campion himself was very persuasive. He may well have pointed out that neither he nor Parsons were in England for their health but to bring aid and comfort to the oppressed Catholics whatever the circumstances. Parsons' every instinct told him that Campion should get out of the neighbourhood of Oxford as soon as possible, and it went badly against the grain of his practical commonsense to put the whole of their mission at risk for the sake of a piece of sentiment. But in the end he gave way, only stipulating that the visit to Lyford should not last more than one night. As an added precaution, he put the lay-brother, Ralph Emerson, in charge, ordering him to see that this programme was carried out. The two friends then said goodbye and Parsons returned to London, although he would now be without the invaluable support of George Gilbert. The hunt had grown too hot for that enterprising young gentleman and Parsons had been forced to send him abroad to safety.

Contrary to Parson's forebodings, Campion's overnight stay at Lyford passed off quietly. His hostess and her companions were, of course, in a flutter of delight at seeing him and reluctant to let him go, but Campion kept his promise and immediately after dinner on Wednesday, 12 July, he and Emerson rode away, accompanied by Father Collington, one of Mrs Yate's resident chaplains who was to escort them on the first stage of their journey. All might have been well if, later that day, a party of Catholics had not arrived to call on the ladies. There was bitter disappointment when they discovered how narrowly they had missed the treat of hearing the glamorous Father Campion. Then someone had a bright idea. The travellers could not have gone far. Surely it would be possible to catch up with them and beg Campion to return, just for a few days? Thomas Ford, the other priest at Lyford, who should have known better, set off at once on this extremely ill-advised errand. He found Campion at an inn near Oxford where already a considerable number of people with more enthusiasm than sense had come out from the university to meet him and try and persuade him to preach.

When Ford's proposition was put to him, Campion explained that he was acting under obedience and that Ralph Emerson was now his superior. Everyone present then combined to make an impassioned assault on Ralph. Father Parsons, they pointed out, had not realized there would be such a large company in urgent need of spiritual consolation; he certainly could not have intended that so many hungry souls should be sent empty away. Sturdy little Ralph Emerson was not proof against this sort of argument. Before he knew where he was, he found himself agreeing to ride on alone to Lancashire to attend to the unfinished business there, thus sparing the Father the dangers and fatigue of the journey. Campion should stay at Lyford, where he would be among friends, until the following Sunday, and then go direct to Norfolk to wait for Ralph in another 'safe' house.

But on the following day, as Campion and the other two priests retraced their steps along the narrow Berkshire lanes, through the fields of standing corn, someone else was planning to pay a visit to Lyford. George Elliot was not untypical of that class of person who found in the laying of information a ready-made solution to their personal and financial problems. Although neither his character nor past career would bear too close an inspection – he is said to have been in prison facing a charge of murder when he wrote to the Earl of Leicester offering his services – Elliot had at one time been a Catholic and had worked in various Catholic households, both useful qualifications for a priest-catcher. In its campaign against the missionary priests, the government was obliged to rely heavily on informers and could not afford to be over-fussy about their antecedents – at least someone in Elliot's position would have a strong motive for giving satisfaction. Accordingly he was let out of gaol to begin a startlingly successful career as one of those 'false brethren' who constituted by far the greatest single danger to the Catholic population.

Whether or not it was pure chance that Elliot should have been pursuing his avocation in and round Oxford just at the time when Campion was in the neighbourhood is uncertain, but after 12 July anyone with any Catholic connections could scarcely have failed to pick up his scent. Quite apart from this, Lyford, just as Robert Parsons had foreseen, was an obvious target for one of Elliot's profession. When he presented himself there on Sunday 16 July, following his usual simple but effective routine of posing as a devout member of the faithful eager to hear Mass, he gained admission without difficulty; Mrs Yate's cook, who had known him in the days when he had been steward to Mr Roper of Orpington, whispering that he would be lucky enough to hear Father Campion preach. Elliot just had time to send his companion, one David Jenkins, to find a magistrate before proceeding decorously to the chapel, where a congregation of some sixty people was assembled. He sat through the Mass and Campion's sermon on the all too appropriate text 'Jerusalem, Jerusalem, thou that killest the prophets'. Elliot, Judas Elliot, as he was to become known, then took his leave with more haste than courtesy, refusing a pressing invitation to stay to dinner.

This in itself should have aroused suspicion but in the general euphoria of the moment no one seems to have taken any particular notice of the stranger's abrupt departure – besides Father Campion would be setting out for Norfolk as soon as he had eaten. Considering the identity of her guest,

Mrs Yate's security arrangements were remarkably casual. Only one look-out had been posted, and while the company was still at the dinner table he came panting in with the horrifying information that the house was surrounded by armed men. Campion wanted to be allowed to take his chance outside. He might even now be able to slip through the cordon and in any case if he were taken, the searchers would probably be satisfied. But his hosts would not hear of such a thing and the three priests were hustled away into a secret place opening out of one of the upper rooms just as the first hammering fell on the front door.

To begin with the search party, which was made up of local men dragged from their normal Sunday pursuits, showed no great enthusiasm for their task. They found nothing and were only too willing to call off the hunt. Once outside, they had no hesitation in giving Elliot a piece of their collective mind for wasting their time on a fool's errand and making trouble for them with their neighbours. But Elliot was not going to be cheated of his triumph by a parcel of ignorant yokels. Did they really expect to find Campion, the notorious Jesuit and traitor, hiding under a bed or keeping company with the rest of the family, he demanded scornfully? Or were they perhaps all secret papists, conspiring to aid the Queen's enemies? This was fighting talk, but when Elliot flourished his royal warrant and insisted on a more thorough search being made the magistrate, much as he may have resented taking orders from this jumped-up jack-in-office, had no choice but to obey. At their second attempts the posse uncovered several likely hiding places, but no priests. It was growing dark by this time and operations were suspended until the following day, Elliot and a select band of helpers remaining on guard.

Mrs Yate had her bed made up in a room close to the priests' hole and when all was quiet Campion came out to speak to her and some of her companions – nobody at Lyford can have felt like sleeping that night. The noise disturbed the searchers, who came to investigate, but Campion was able to get back unseen. Next morning it all began again – the examining of every cupboard, closet and chimney, tapping the wainscot for hollow sounds, hacking at suspicious plaster, tearing up the floorboards, but still nothing. Not even the most zealous priest-catcher could complain of lack of co-operation now and tension in the house mounted unbearably as it began to look as if the miracle was going to happen. Then, just as Elliot prepared sulkily to admit defeat, someone – was it Elliot himself? – looked up and noticed a chink of light over the stairwell in a place where no chink of light should have been. A section of the wall was opened up with a crowbar and there were the three priests in a space just large enough for them to lie side by side.

Humphrey Forster of Aldermaston, Sheriff of Berkshire for the year 1581, had been away from home that eventful weekend, but the news that Campion was taken brought him hurrying to Lyford. The sheriff seems to have been a trifle embarrassed by the size of the fish which had been landed and he sent to the Council for instructions on how to proceed. After three days, during which time Campion remained at Lyford being treated with careful respect by his captors, orders arrived that the male prisoners – in addition to the three priests, nine laymen were in custody – should be brought to London under strong guard. The journey took them through Abingdon and Henley, where Robert Parsons had once more taken refuge. He was dissuaded from going in person to see the procession pass by but sent his servant Alfield, who reported that Campion seemed well and in good spirits. The third and last halt was at Colnbrook and then came the ride through London to the Tower. The authorities were naturally eager to show off their prize to his maximum disadvantage and Campion was placed at the head of the cavalcade, 'on a very tall horse, without cloak on his back, his arms tied behind his loins, and his feet confined by a rope beneath his horse's belly. . . . Around the hair of his head they encircled an inscription written in great big capital letters: EDMUND CAMPION, THE SEDITIOUS JESUIT.' Although the great majority of the people who lined the streets found this spectacle eminently satisfactory, there was a more thoughtful element who were not entirely happy at seeing a man of Campion's calibre and reputation for scholarship being treated like a common criminal, or his case so blatantly pre-judged.

In the four months which elapsed between his arrest and trial, Campion was alternately offered life, liberty and preferment if he would change his religion, and racked to extort confessions and names. According to the rack-master, who should have been a connoisseur in such matters, Campion did not possess quite the iron physical courage of Alexander Bryant and some information was wrung from him. At a Council meeting held on 4 August a letter was drafted to Sir Henry Nevill and Ralph Warcoppe instructing them 'to repair unto the Lady Stonor's house and to enter into the same, and there to make diligent search and enquire for certain Latin books dispersed abroad in Oxford at the last Commencement, which Edmund Campion upon his examination hath confessed to have been there printed in a wood, and also for such other English books as of late have been published for the maintenance of popery, printed also there as it is thought by one Parsons, a Jesuit, and others; and further, for the press and other instruments of printing, etc., thought also to be there remaining.'

In the raid on Stonor the press was seized and the priest William Hartley, the printer Stephen Brinkley and four of his assistants, and a member of the Stonor family arrested and carried off to London. But Robert Parsons' phenomenal luck still held. He had just left Stonor to visit a house near Windsor and when news of this latest disaster reached him, he retreated to Michelgrove in Sussex. There he was unexpectedly offered an opportunity of crossing to France with a party of Catholic refugees. Parsons had to make a difficult decision and make it quickly. He was now on the run and if he stayed in England his capture could only be a matter of weeks, perhaps days. Once across the Channel, he would be able to make a detailed report to his Superiors without fear of his letters falling into the wrong hands. He could also discuss the needs of the Mission with William Allen in person, and Parsons was becoming more and more convinced that the Jesuit mission could not be maintained 'unless there were someone to be agent beyond the seas for many matters'. Then there was the secret press. Parsons believed that the value of keeping up a steady flow of Catholic books could not be underestimated and it might well be months before production could be started again in England. He had two or three manuscripts in preparation, and in France he could get on with the work of printing without delay. Of the reinforcements he had begged from the Society in Rome, Fathers Heywood and Holt had now arrived and should be able to carry on for a while. From the practical point of view, the arguments in favour of his going, for a time at least, were overwhelming. On the other hand, Parsons knew that it would look as if he were deserting his post and was worried about the possible effect on morale. All the same, the issue was never in doubt. Edmund Campion could serve the cause by dying nobly a martyr's death. Robert Parsons' vein of earthy, peasant commonsense told him that he could serve it best by staying alive.

He left England sometime between 13 and 21 August and was to devote the rest of his life to working unceasingly for the hopeless dream of the Great Enterprise. He never did return and died at last, in 1610, far from the green hills of his native West Country, a lonely, embittered man with the sour taste of failure in his mouth.

22

All My Joints to Tremble For Fear

'It makes my heart leap for joy to think we have such a jewel.
It makes all my joints to tremble for fear when I consider the loss of such a jewel.'
George Ireland, the House of Commons, February 1585

The execution of Edmund Campion is generally accepted today as an act of judicial murder. Certainly there can be little doubt that Campion and the thirteen others arraigned with him in Westminster all were not guilty as charged and that their trial was rigged as ruthlessly as in any modern 'purge', but in 1581 the English government was less concerned with observing the niceties of fair play than with questions of national survival. There had, in fact, been some indecision in government circles over the best way of proceeding against Campion – by far their most important capture so far. In the first draft of the indictment he was charged with having traitorously pretended to have power to absolve the Queen's subjects from their natural obedience, with the intention of withdrawing 'the said subjects of the said Queen from the religion now by her supreme authority established within this realm of England to the Roman religion, and to move the same subjects of the said Queen to promise obedience to the pretensed authority of the Roman See to be used within the dominions of the said Queen'. Before the trial came on, however, these charges were dropped and it was decided instead to invoke the old Treason Statute of 1352.

Another, far more wholesale indictment was drawn up charging William Allen and Robert Parsons in their absence, Edmund Campion and (presumably as an afterthought since their names were added in the margin) the dozen assorted priests then in custody and the layman Henry Orton with having conspired together in Rome and Rheims to imagine, contrive and compass not merely the deposition of the Queen but her death and final destruction. They were also accused of having planned 'to incite, raise and make sedition' in the realm, 'to procure and set up insurrection and rebellion' against the Queen, and 'to change and alter according to their will and pleasure the government of the said realm, and to invite, procure and induce divers strangers and aliens . . . to invade the realm and to raise, carry on and make war against the said Queen'.

The reasons which lay behind this somewhat startling change of plan are conjectural but they were probably not unconnected with Elizabeth's extreme sensitivity over measures which could be construed as religious persecution for its own sake and her equally extreme reluctance to do so. Added to and arising from this was the official determination to discredit the missionary priests – especially those fabled monsters the Jesuits – as thoroughly as possible in the public mind. If the government had stuck to its original plan and prosecuted Campion under the 1581 Act now on the statute book, they would have had a better case in law and it would probably have been the wiser decision, but it made very little difference in the end. His life was equally forfeit either way, and either way the Catholic propaganda machine was bound to present him as a martyr for religion.

Campion himself certainly had no doubts on the matter. When the customary question, whether he had anything to say why sentence should not be passed, was put to him by the Lord Chief Justice, he replied: '. . . if our religion do make us traitors, we are worthy to be condemned; but otherwise are and have been as true subjects as ever the Queen had. In condemning us you condemn all your own ancestors – all the ancient priests, bishops and kings – all that was once the glory of England, the island of saints, and the most devoted child of the See of Peter. For what have we taught, however you may qualify it with the odious name of treason, that they did not uniformly teach? To be condemned with these old lights – not of England only, but of the world – by their degenerate descendants, is both gladness and glory to us. God lives; posterity will live: their judgement is not so liable to corruption as that of those who are now going to sentence us to death.'

Campion's death provoked a positive barrage of pamphlets, tracts and 'True Accounts' which kept the printers working overtime on both sides of the Channel. It also brought into sharp focus the perennial argument as to whether the English Catholics and the missionary priests were being persecuted for their religion, as the Catholics maintained; or whether they were being punished as ordinary law-breakers and traitors respectively, as the English government maintained. This is an old controversy and an unfruitful one, based as it is on the false premise that religion and politics could be treated as separate issues. If this ever had been possible in the past, *Regnans in Excelsis* and papal intervention in Ireland had effectively put an end to any hope that it might become possible again in the foreseeable future.

In any ideological conflict, however, public opinion is of paramount importance. This was as true of the sixteenth century as of the twenty first, and in 1583 the English government felt impelled to issue an explanation and justification of its use of torture in the interrogation of captured priests – a matter which was being made much of by Catholic propagandists, despite the fact that no contemporary Catholic regime had a particularly clean record when it came to the use of physical barbarity on prisoners. *A Declaration of Favourable Dealing by Her Majesty's Commissioners for the Examination of Certain Traitors* was probably written by Thomas Norton, one of the commissioners concerned with the examination of Edmund Campion. It pointed out that torture was legal in certain cases and affirmed that it was never applied in matters of conscience, but only to uncover treasonable practices. Nor was it used 'at adventure', but only where there were reasons for believing the prisoner was concealing evidence. Also in 1583 appeared *The Execution of Justice in England, not for Religion but for Treason*, a twenty-page pamphlet written by Lord Burghley and spelling out the official attitude to the missionary priests.

Burghley's own religious convictions were slightly left of centre but in *The Execution of Justice* his approach, like the Queen's, was strictly secular and political. England's quarrel was not with Roman Catholicism as such but with the Pope's claims of supremacy in temporal matters. No national ruler, whatever his creed, who lived in the real world could accept the right of another state to interfere in any way with the exercise of his sovereign power. No national ruler did accept it. Even the Catholic Mary Tudor had forbidden the entrance of certain papal bulls and had refused to allow the Pope to replace her favourite Cardinal Pole. Burghley regarded the excommunication of Elizabeth as a declaration of war, the invasion of Ireland as an act of unprovoked aggression. *Regnans in Excelsis* had invited the Queen's subjects to rebel against her – indeed it had laid a duty on them to do so. The fact that the *Explanatio*, which had recently fallen into the government's hands, temporarily absolved the English Catholics of that duty made things no better – it merely enabled them to continue to enjoy the benefits accruing to loyal subjects while waiting for a favourable opportunity to rise up and bite the hand that was feeding them.

The principal result of the *Explanatio*, although curiously enough Lord Burghley failed to exploit this valuable propaganda point, was to cast serious doubt on the credibility of all Catholic protestations of loyalty, such as those made by Edmund Campion on the scaffold. As far as the Jesuit and seminary priests were concerned, Burghley maintained they were being prosecuted not because they were Roman Catholics, not even because they were unable to give satisfactory answers to the so-called Bloody Questions – did they believe that the Pope had power to depose the Queen? – in the event of a foreign invasion to enforce the deposition, would they fight on the Pope's side? – but because they were traitors found guilty under the normal processes of the law. The missionaries were Englishmen born who had chosen to transfer their allegiance to the Queen's avowed enemies. They were infiltrating the realm in disguise, using their religious proselytising as a cloak to conceal their real purpose, which was to sow sedition, win subjects from their allegiance and practice conspiracies 'for the procurement and maintenance of the rebellion and wars against her Majesty and her realm'.

In reply to those critics who objected that since the priests had come unarmed as simple scholars and schoolmasters it would have been enough to correct them without 'capital pain', Burghley asked: 'Shall no subject that is a spial and explorer for the rebel or enemy against his natural prince be taken and punished as a traitor because he is not found with armour or weapon, but yet is taken in his disguised apparel, with scrolls and writings, or other manifest tokens, to prove him a spy for traitors, after he hath wandered secretly in his sovereign's camp, region, court or city?' The Lord Treasurer had no doubt in his own mind that, if 'reason and experience' were to be used in dealing with such adversaries, 'all these and suchlike are to be punished as traitors', because no right-minded person could deny that 'the actions of all these are necessary accessories and adherents proper to further and continue all rebellions and wars'. And if anyone maintained that 'none are traitors that are not armed', then 'they will make Judas no traitor that came to Christ without armour, colouring his treason with a kiss'.

The Catholic answer to *The Execution of Justice* appeared in the following year. In *A True, Sincere and Modest Defence of English Catholics*, William Allen was at pains to refute accusations of treachery against the mission and to insist on its irreproachably non-political character. He had little difficulty in demolishing the case against Edmund Campion and argued that no priest could properly be convicted under the old treason laws, but only under those passed since 1559 which made matters of conscience into treason. He also dismissed all assertions that the English Catholics were not being persecuted for their faith as 'a very notorious untruth', challenging anyone to deny that 'most prisons in England be full at this day and have been for years, of honourable and honest persons not to be touched with any treason or other offence in the world' except their faith. As far as *Regnans in Excelsis* was concerned, Allen maintained that neither he nor the English Catholics at large had ever 'procured our Queen's excommunication; we have sought the mitigation thereof; we have done our allegiance notwithstanding; we have answered, when we were forced unto it, with such humility and respect to her Majesty and council, as you see, no man can charge us of any attempt against the realm or the prince's person'.

At the same time, Allen admitted his belief in the justice of spiritual supremacy over temporal and that the Pope had the right, in certain circumstances, to depose a reigning sovereign. 'Therefore,' he went on, 'let no man marvel that in case of heresy the Sovereign loseth his superiority and right over his people and kingdom: which cannot be a lawful Christian state or commonwealth without due obedience to Christ's and the Church's laws.' There was nothing new about this. The papacy had claimed the right of deposition for centuries and had occasionally exercised it with varying degrees of success but, wrote William Allen, to claim, as Burghley had done, that while Popes were 'suffered to make and unmake kings at their pleasure' no monarch could sit securely on his throne was nonsense – 'a bugge fit only to fright babes'. No Catholic prince, against whom the same power could equally be applied, was in the least worried by it. Allen omitted to add, however, that no Catholic prince was currently in the least danger of being deposed. *The True and Modest Defence* ended with an eloquent plea for some measure of toleration for the English Catholics, conveniently ignoring the fact that there was no toleration for Protestants in Catholic countries, except in those cases where the executive was too weak to prevent it.

Neither side, of course, was being completely honest. In their anxiety to create a favourable public image neither side could afford to be completely honest. As a result, neither the picture of the sinister, lurking priest indoctrinating the gullible with superstitious nonsense and poisoning their minds against their lawful sovereign in such time as he could spare from plotting murder and treachery; nor that of a saintly, disinterested priesthood administering spiritual consolation to an oppressed majority before being cruelly and unjustly butchered represents anything like the truth. The truth, as usual, lay somewhere in the large grey area between these starkly black and white alternatives.

The basic dishonesty of the official English attitude lay in its stubborn insistence that the Catholics, both lay and priestly, were not in any sense being persecuted for their religious beliefs. In an age when it was axiomatic that religious disunity was the first step on the road to national disunity and from thence to civil war and anarchy, religious deviants of all kinds inevitably suffered for their beliefs. At a time when national security was being threatened by international Catholicism, pressure on the native Catholic population inevitably intensified. At least in England persecution remained on a political basis, though this was a matter of regret to those who equated Roman Catholicism and all its works with Anti-Christ.

The basic dishonesty of the Catholic position lay in its determined attempt to have things both ways – its vocal indignation that such men as Edmund Campion should be smeared with 'the odious name of traitor', while at the same time refusing to face the uncomfortable fact that no orthodox, believing Roman Catholic could logically accept the bastard, heretic and excommunicated Elizabeth as his lawful sovereign. A very few, notably Nicholas Sander, did have the sort of three-o'clock-in-the-morning courage which could look squarely at the problem and then make the choice of allegiance which conscience dictated. The rest either postponed a decision until circumstances had made it for them, or else slid gratefully through whatever legalistic loopholes the Vatican was able to provide. In the event, after the normal, illogical fashion of the human race, the vast majority of those Englishmen who also happened to be Roman Catholics were and remained loyal subjects of the crown – thus vindicating the

Queen's confidence that habits of national and personal loyalty would always prove stronger than loyalty to any creed.

As front-line combatants in the battle for hearts and minds, the missionary priests occupied a special category and although the vast majority of them were undoubtedly as uninterested and uninvolved in politics as they professed to be, it was neither reasonable nor realistic to expect the English government to regard them in isolation from the wider political scene. It is, in fact, possible to over-sentimentalise the missionary priests. While their courage and their devotion is not in question, they were all grown men who came to England of their own free will with the openly avowed intention of propagating and practising a system of belief and a form of worship forbidden by law, all of them knowing exactly what they could expect if they were caught. It also needs to be remembered that although only a very few were traitors in the accepted sense – in the sense of being actively engaged in plotting the destruction of the state by direct means – indirectly the success of their mission must necessarily have led to the overthrow of the Protestant constitution. William Allen, though he tried conscientiously to keep his various interests in watertight compartments, was by the early eighties deeply committed to plans for overthrowing the Protestant state by whatever direct means appeared to offer the best chance of success. Had a Catholic army ever managed to establish a bridgehead on English soil, the priests would not have been able to stand aside. They were ear-marked for the important role of directing the consciences of Catholics – in other words, of helping to organise the rising of English Catholics which would be a vital part of any attempt to enforce *Regnans in Excelsis*.

It is not, therefore, surprising that the Protestant state regarded the missionaries as a fifth column 'who privily felt the minds of men, spread abroad that princes excommunicate were to be deposed, and whispered in corners that such princes as professed not the Romish religion had forfeited their regal title and authority. . . . that the Bishop of Rome hath supreme authority and absolute power over the whole world, yea even in temporal matters; that the magistrates of England were no lawful magistrates . . . yea, that whatsoever was done by the Queen's authority since the time that the Bull declaratory of Pius Quintus was published against her, was by the laws of God and man altogether void and to be esteemed as of no validity'. Of course the Protestant state over-reacted, but states which feel themselves threatened have a habit of over-reacting, especially to danger which appears to come from within the body politic.

Lord Burghley summed the matter up neatly enough when he remarked that 'where the factious party of the Pope . . . do falsely allege that a number of persons whom they term as martyrs have died for defence of the Catholic religion, the same in very truth may manifestly appear to have died (if they so will have it) as martyrs for the Pope'. If the

Elizabethan establishment had had the courage and far-sightedness to content itself with merely restraining and deporting the missionaries; if the papacy had had the wisdom and far-sightedness to confine its efforts to win England back to Rome by spiritual means alone, both sides would have emerged from the struggle with a cleaner record. But over an issue so clouded with emotion, an issue which, beneath all the long words, the justification and rationalisation, was concerned with such basic human drives as fear, anger and aggression, any attempt to pass moral judgements on either side is a somewhat pointless exercise.

Conditioned as we are to thinking of the Elizabethan era as one of the most notable success stories of history, it is fatally easy to forget that that was seldom the way it looked to thinking Elizabethans, and at the beginning of the 1580s thinking Elizabethan observers of the international scene had more excuse than usual for feeling pessimistic about the future. The decade had opened with the Spanish annexation of Portugal, an event which alarmingly increased the already alarming power and wealth of Spain. It gave King Philip control of the entire Iberian peninsula, with the use of Portuguese ports and the Portuguese navy. It gave him the revenues of Portugal's colonial empire in the east to add to those of his own colonial empire in the west. It made him, on paper at least, the richest and most powerful monarch the world had ever seen. In France the increasing influence and popularity of the Holy League, an ultra-Catholic and pro-Spanish faction led by Mary Stuart's cousin the Duke of Guise, boded no good to Protestants anywhere but to English Protestants in particular it threatened danger in an acute form.

Trouble was brewing even nearer home in Scotland, where Mary Stuart's son James, having reached his teens, was becoming another factor to be reckoned with. In 1579 a dispute over the title and estates of the Lennox earldom brought James's cousin Esmé Stuart, the seigneur d'Aubigny, an ardent Catholic and client of the Duke of Guise, across from France – ostensibly to stake his claim to the Lennox patrimony but actually bearing an unadvertised commission from his patron to win young James's affection and revitalise the French party in Scotland. Not surprisingly, young James, who had been brought up according to sound Calvinistic principles, found the companionship of this good-looking, Frenchified kinsman an altogether delightful novelty. Within a matter of months d'Aubigny, or the Duke of Lennox as he soon became and his henchman, Captain James Stewart, later Earl of Arran, had established their ascendancy. Within a couple of years they had engineered the downfall of the unlikeable but reliably pro-English Regent Morton and the eclipse of the English party which had held power in Edinburgh ever since the last remaining adherents of Mary Stuart had been eradicated in the aftermath of St Bartholomew.

This ominous turn of events on the other side of the vulnerable postern gate aroused the liveliest suspicions in London but Elizabeth, preoccupied with the hectic courtship she was currently conducting with the French King's brother, was unwilling to attempt the eviction of Lennox by force. She could not afford to offend France while she was bargaining for an alliance to counter-balance the weight of Spain; nor would she risk alienating Scottish national feelings and perhaps driving the adolescent James irretrievably into the arms of his mother's relations. Thrifty as ever, she was equally reluctant to try bribery on a scale likely to be effective – at least not until she could feel assured of an adequate return for her money. For the time being, therefore, there was little to be done but listen unconvinced to Lennox's private protestations of goodwill and watch his flirtation with the Elders of the Kirk while awaiting developments. From her past experience of the way in which Scottish affairs were not infrequently conducted, the Queen of England may have felt that it would not be long before there were developments of an interesting nature north of the Border.

To the political wing of the English Catholic exiles, lacking similar valuable experience, the apparent success of the Duke of Lennox opened up a wide range of exciting possibilities. In October 1581, Robert Parsons, now established with his printing press at Rouen, wrote to the General of the Jesuits '. . . the greatest hope we have lies in Scotland, on which country depends the conversion not only of England but of all the lands in the North. For the right to the kingdom of England belongs to the Queen of Scotland and her son (after the death of this woman who now reigns) and some hopes have now begun to be conceived of this son of hers, especially now that the Earl of Morton has been executed, if sufficient contact were made with him while he still gives evidence of great obedience to his mother and before he is confirmed in heresy'. Even before he was obliged to leave England Parsons had sent one of the missionaries, Father Watts, up to Scotland to carry out a preliminary reconnaissance. Watts' first report was encouraging. He had been received by several of the nobility and had even been presented to James.

By the time this report arrived Parsons had crossed to France and the Spanish ambassador in London had taken a hand. Watts was instructed to go back to Scotland 'to try to get a private interview with d'Aubigny, and tell him that, if the King would submit to the Roman Catholic Church, many of the English nobles and a great part of the population would at once side with him and have him declared heir to the English crown and release his mother'. Watts proceeded cautiously – he was not entirely sure of Lennox with his French connections nor of the sincerity of the Scottish nobles. Towards the end of October he told Mendoza that the best argument to bring about James's conversion – apart, of course, from its being the true road to salvation – was to show him 'that it was the only means by which he could become a powerful King, uniting the crowns of Scotland, England and Ireland' and this, as Mendoza remarked in a dispatch to Philip, could only be achieved 'by his gaining the sympathy of so mighty a monarch as your Majesty'.

Whether James would rise to the bait or not remained in doubt but throughout the winter of 1581–2 plans were being laid for a Catholic *coup d'état* in Scotland to be followed by an invasion of England by the way of the border. The threads of this elaborate conspiracy stretched from Mendoza at the Court of St James's to Mary Queen of Scots in her prison at Sheffield Castle, from Lennox at Holyrood across the North Sea to the Duke of Guise, Robert Parsons, William Allen and the Spanish and papal representatives in France, while two Jesuit fathers, Holt and Creighton, commuted between London, Edinburgh and Paris bearing letters and messages, promises and suggestions. Progress was slow at first – there was a good deal of mutual distrust to be overcome, distances were considerable and the need for secrecy meant that no corners could be cut – but in April 1582 Father William Creighton arrived from Scotland with a letter for Juan Bautista de Tassis, Spanish ambassador in Paris, from the Duke of Lennox.

Lennox, encouraged by Creighton's confident assurances of support, had finally agreed to commit himself to the 'design' which the Pope and the King of Spain had in hand 'for the restoration of the Catholic religion and the liberation of the Queen of Scotland' – providing he was guaranteed adequate backing, and he had listed his requirements in a memorandum to be passed on by Creighton to the appropriate quarters. Lennox's ideas of what constituted adequate backing were optimistic – an army of 20,000 men, preferably Spaniards, Italians, Germans and Swiss, paid for eighteen months, together with a number of pioneers, plenty of munitions and artillery plus the sum of 20,000 crowns. When de Tassis was visited by Creighton and Robert Parsons he at once raised his eyebrows at the size of these demands but was hastily reassured that Lennox would leave such matters to be settled by the Duke of Guise, who was of the opinion that six to eight thousand infantry would be ample. Guise himself was full of enthusiasm for the project and proposed making a diversionary landing on the coast of Sussex 'to put the whole kingdom into confusion'.

Robert Parsons went on to tell de Tassis that the English Catholics were eager for the design to be carried out, and that if arms were taken up in Scotland 'with a well grounded prospect of success', they would come flocking to join the invading army. The North and 'all that part which borders upon Scotland' was full of Catholics, and if the Pope would name some influential person for the great bishopric of Durham (Parsons had William Allen in mind) he would be able to raise the people. There were many other persons who would do the same in other districts, since England was 'so full of Catholics that it could not be believed'.

Having just spent over a year in England, Parsons could reasonably be accepted as an authority but de Tassis, who seems to have possessed rather more commonsense than his colleague in London, was not entirely convinced. 'When I asked him what security they have for all this,' he wrote to Philip, 'and whether any of the principal men had formed a confederation for this object and given each other some security of signatures, as the custom is, he answered me that he knew all this from what many of them had declared when he had treated with them of their consciences.' If the ambassador thought this an evasive answer, he was careful not to actually say so and, having received no briefing from Spain, listened to his visitors 'with a friendly countenance', trying 'neither to divert them in any way from what they propose, nor yet to give them encouragement' but showing himself 'desirous, as a Christian, that everything should succeed as they are planning it'.

Apparently undismayed by this, the two Jesuits went away to spend the next six weeks putting the final touches to the invasion plan. Several conferences were held in which the Duke of Guise, William Allen, the Archbishop of Glasgow, Mary Stuart's agent in Paris, the papal nuncio and even the sceptical de Tassis took part. Snags such as the fact that the mercenary army to be landed in Scotland, whether six or twenty thousand strong, existed only on paper; that the Duke of Guise, despite his soubriquet of King of Paris, was not King of France, and that Henri III, poor creature though he might be, would certainly warn Queen Elizabeth of any Guisard plot against her the moment he heard about it, were brushed aside. But even the most optimistic of the conspirators could not ignore the fact that no action of any kind would be possible until the Pope and the King of Spain had been persuaded to disgorge something more substantial than fair words. Accordingly, at the end of May, Creighton set off for Rome and Parsons for Lisbon, where Philip was then in residence.

Before anything concrete had resulted from either of these missions, the inevitable happened in Scotland. Discreetly prodded by the English government, the Kirk and the Protestant lords decided that Lennox had had a long enough run for his money. On 22 August James was kidnapped by the earls of Angus, Gowrie and Mar in the so-called Raid of Ruthven, and James Stewart, Earl of Arran, was arrested. Lennox holed up for a time in the fortress of Dumbarton but was finally obliged to apply to Queen Elizabeth for a safe conduct to return to France by way of England. The Duke was out of the game and by the following spring he was dead.

The Raid of Ruthven came as a bad blow to the Franco-Spanish plotters, but they were not discouraged for long. On 4 May 1583, de Tassis was reporting to Philip, 'It appears to me that Hercules (code name for the Duke of Guise), seeing matters in Scotland altered, and with but small probability of promptly assuming a position favourable for the plans that had been formed, has now turned his eyes towards the English Catholics, to see whether the affair might not be commenced there. . . . I understand that he has the matter in such train as may ensure his success, and in such case it would be very necessary that he should have at hand the funds for immediate wants, and particularly for one object which I dare not venture to mention here, but which if it be effected will make a noise in the world, and if not, may be safely mentioned another time.'

In a letter to the Cardinal of Como dated two days before, the papal nuncio Castelli had been rather more explicit. 'The Duke of Guise and the Duke of Mayenne,' he wrote, 'have told me that they have a plan for killing the Queen of England by the hand of a Catholic, though not one outwardly, who is near her person and is ill-affected towards her for having put to death some of his Catholic relations. This man, it seems, sent word of this to the Queen of Scotland, but she refused to attend to it. He was however sent hither, and they have agreed to give him, if he escapes, or else his sons, 100,000 francs. . . . The Duke asks for no assistance from our Lord [the Pope] for this affair; but when the time comes he will go to a place of his near the sea to await the event and then cross over on a sudden into England. As to putting to death that wicked woman, I said to him that I will not write about it to our Lord the Pope (nor do I) nor tell your most illustrious lordship to inform him of it; because, though I believe our Lord the Pope would be glad that God should punish in any way whatever that enemy of His, still it would be unfitting that His Vicar should procure it by these means. The Duke was satisfied; but later on he added that for the enterprise of England, which in this case would be much more easy, it will be necessary to have here in readiness money to enlist some troops to follow him.' Castelli reported that Guise estimated his requirements at 100,000 to 80,000 crowns, adding, 'God grant that with this small sum that great kingdom may be gained'.

The Cardinal of Como replied on 23 May: 'I have reported to our Lord the Pope what your lordship has written to me in cipher about the affairs of England, and since his Holiness cannot but think it good that this kingdom should be in some way or other relieved from oppression and restored to God and our holy religion, his Holiness says that, in the event of the matter being effected, there is no doubt that the 80,000 crowns will be, as your lordship says, very well employed.' In the event, of course, this projected 'deed of violence', as de Tassis cautiously phrased it in another dispatch to Philip at the end of June, was not mentioned again. Philip was disappointed, but not surprised.

It was not the first time that this particular method of solving the English problem had been suggested. Three years earlier, the Welshman Humphrey Ely had visited Madrid on behalf of a group of anonymous English noblemen, to seek a ruling from the papal nuncio there as to whether or not they would incur sin by carrying out a plan to murder the Queen. The nuncio, Cardinal Sega, gave it as his opinion that they need have no qualms, adding that in any case he was sure the Pope would grant them a retrospective absolution. However, to make assurance doubly sure, he referred the matter to Rome, at the same time asking for absolution for himself if it was felt that he had gone too far. On 12 December 1580, the Cardinal of Como, who as papal Secretary of State could speak with peculiar authority, conveyed the official feeling on the subject of assassination in a letter to Sega. 'Since that guilty woman of England rules over two such noble kingdoms of Christendom,' he wrote, 'and is the cause of so much injury to the Catholic faith, and loss of so many millions souls, there is no doubt that whosoever sends her out of the world with the pious intention of doing God service, not only does not sin but gains merit, especially having regard to the sentence pronounced against her by Pius V of holy memory. And so, if those English nobles decide actually to undertake so glorious a work, your lordship can assure them that they do not commit any sin. We trust in God also that they will escape danger. As far as concerns your lordship, in case you have incurred any irregularity, the Pope bestows upon you his holy benediction.'

Quite apart from the dubious moral position of a spiritual leader who condones murder as being a justifiable means to a desired end, Pope Gregory was committing yet another of the numerous tactical errors made by the papacy in its campaign against Elizabeth. The English government was not, of course, in a position to tap the confidential correspondence of papal nuncios, but it had other sources of information and was in little doubt that the Holy Father would cheerfully have pinned a medal on anyone who succeeded in killing the Queen. In 1581 a renegade priest named Tyrrel confessed to having personally heard the Pope say that such a deed would be 'a good work', although it should be carried out without bringing discredit on his reputation.

Popes, being human, can be wrong-headed – they are not normally fools and it was outstandingly foolish to hand over to one's enemy, gift-wrapped, such a first-class propaganda weapon. The explanation lies partly in the fact that the Vatican was still relying on reports and recommendations supplied by the English exiles – both of which were more remarkable for wishful thinking than for accuracy. A memorandum of 1583, attributed to William Allen, presented a picture of England where two-thirds of the population were Catholic sympathisers, either open or secret, living in fear and slavery, who would 'seize the first opportunity to help chastise their adversaries, whose intolerable yoke they hate more than if they were Turks' and who had learned 'to detest their domestic heretic more than any foreign prince'. Another such document of 1582, attributed to Robert Parsons, declared that all the Catholics in England would welcome Mary Stuart as their Queen and went on to state unblushingly that there was never a prince as universally hated in England as Elizabeth. If Gregory believed even half these reports he had some reason for thinking that murder might well prove the quickest and cheapest method of achieving results.

Meanwhile, throughout the summer and autumn of 1583, plans for the reconstructed 'holy enterprise' were being worked out in Paris.

Although James regained his freedom of action in June and had recalled the Earl of Arran, Parsons and Allen both advised that, while the state of Scotland and the King's religious intentions remained so uncertain, a direct invasion of England offered the best chance of success. A Spanish force of about 5,000 men, drawn from the Duke of Parma's army in the Netherlands, commanded by the Duke of Guise and accompanied by all the English exiles, was to land at the Pile of Fouldrey on the Lancashire coast where it would be joined by a further force of 20,000 native Catholics. It would then proceed to liberate Mary Stuart and, unspecified but implicit, dispose of Elizabeth Tudor in some convenient but permanent fashion. This, in outline, was the scheme laid before the Pope by Robert Parsons in September, and William Allen wrote to Rome urging 'that now was the time for acting, that there had never been a like opportunity, nor would such a chance ever recur'. The Pope was sympathetic and ready to be co-operative, but he would not produce any cash until he was certain of the King of Spain. Without the King of Spain's word not a soldier would embark and the King of Spain, while paying lip-service to the idea, remained notably lukewarm. At last, in October, he definitely withdrew his support and the whole house of cards collapsed.

Ever since the spring of 1580 the English government, and especially Principal Secretary of State Francis Walsingham, had been watching the situation in Scotland and France with close attention and considerable anxiety. Walsingham, whose nose for such matters was acutely sensitive, was convinced that 'some great and hidden treason not yet discovered' was being hatched, but although he worried at the problem for nearly three years, using every source of information – official and unofficial – that was open to him, hard news proved surprisingly hard to come by. Rumours there were in plenty, and enough clues to confirm suspicions that a conspiracy involving Mary Queen of Scots, the Catholic faction in Scotland, the Jesuits, the Papacy and either France or Spain – perhaps both – aimed at destroying Elizabeth and setting Mary on the throne did indeed exist.

In October 1581 a letter from Mary to the Archbishop of Glasgow in Paris was intercepted and revealed that she knew all about certain 'designs' of her cousin the Duke of Guise. It did not, unfortunately, reveal what those designs were. In May of the following year one of Mendoza's messengers, disguised as a dentist, was picked up near the border. The 'dentist', who was probably Father Watts, managed to bribe his way out of trouble, but left behind a looking-glass with letters addressed to the Duke of Lennox hidden in the back. In March 1583, the Jesuit Holt was arrested in Scotland at the instigation of Walsingham's agents but, much to Walsingham's annoyance, was released by the Scots before anything useful could be got out of him.

By piecing together such scraps of information as he had been able to collect, Walsingham had come to the conclusion that the key to the puzzle would be found in France. In a sense, of course, he was right but, rather surprisingly for one with his intimate knowledge of French affairs, he failed to take account of the antipathy which existed between the Guise faction and the King of France. Not realising that the conspirators were taking a good deal of trouble to keep Henri III and his ambassador in ignorance of their intentions, Walsingham settled down to watch the French embassy like puss at a mousehole. Although the immediate results of this surveillance were disappointing, it was information received from a member of the embassy staff which finally put the Secretary of State on the right track by drawing his attention to the suspicious behaviour of one Francis Throckmorton, who was one of the Queen of Scots' chief agents and who seemed curiously shy of being seen by daylight. Walsingham therefore extended his operations to include a watch on Throckmorton's movements and by early November 1583 had collected enough evidence to justify an arrest. Throckmorton was taken at his house by Paul's Wharf where a number of incriminating papers were also seized.

At his preliminary examination before the Council he tried to brazen things out, but later, after two sessions on the rack, he broke down and confessed all he knew. It was not everything – he had not been in on the conspiracy from the beginning and had acted chiefly as a subordinate carrying out orders from abroad – but it was quite enough to enable Walsingham to set about unravelling the mystery which had defeated him for so long. It was also enough to show him that it was the Spanish, not the French, ambassador who had been abusing his diplomatic privileges and in the New Year Bernardino de Mendoza was summoned before the Council and informed that he was no longer *persona grata* with the Queen. His departure, in a flurry of mutual umbrage, did not, in fact, have much effect on Anglo-Spanish relations – certainly his presence in England had done nothing to improve them. What did bring the inevitable confrontation perceptibly closer was another, this time successful, murder plot. On 1 July 1584, William of Orange was shot three times at close range as he was going up the stairs of his house in Delft by a Burgundian, Balthazar Gerard, generally believed to have been an agent of the King of Spain.

With the death of Orange, Dutch resistance, already under severe pressure from the efficient and energetic Duke of Parma, would almost certainly collapse – unless help came from outside – and Elizabeth was brought face to face with the issue she had been successfully evading for nearly twenty years. Should she stand aside and see the remainder of Flanders, Holland and Zeeland swallowed up, and the whole of the North Sea coastline with the great ports of Antwerp and Flushing fall into Spanish hands; or should she embroil herself in a Continental war which would not only cost her a great deal of money she could ill afford, but provide the King of Spain with a cast-iron *casus belli* any time he cared to use it?

While the Queen and her Council wrestled with the political and financial problems raised by William's death, other people were looking at it from a more personal angle. Two of the great Protestant leaders – Admiral Coligny and the Prince of Orange – had been murdered in cold blood by Catholic fanatics. Now only Elizabeth was left. But for how long? The previous October a young Catholic gentleman named Somerville, or Somerfield, had set out for London from Warwickshire with the declared intention of shooting the Queen and seeing her head set on a pole, 'for she was a serpent and a viper'. There is no reason to believe that Somerville was part of any larger scheme and no doubt he was more than a little mad, but that did not necessarily make him any the less dangerous, as the twentyfirst century has every reason to know. It only needed one madman, one fanatic armed with knife or pistol, to get within range for a few seconds and the whole elaborate structure of Elizabethan England would have been destroyed, literally, at a stroke. There would be no Parliament – it was automatically dissolved by the sovereign's death – no Council, no lords lieutenant, on judges, no magistrates, no royal officials of any kind – their commissions all expired with the sovereign. There would, in fact, have been no authority anywhere until the heir-at-law took possession of the throne – and that heir was the Queen of Scotland.

To a nation still digesting the alarming disclosures of what has become known for convenience sake as the Throckmorton Plot, news of the assassination in Delft came as a forcible reminder not of how much depended on Elizabeth's life – the nation had been living with that uneasy knowledge and worrying about it at intervals for twenty-six years – but of how terrifyingly that life might be cut off, and of whom would stand to benefit. To brush aside the Queen's danger just because she happened to survive is to miss the point entirely. The danger was real enough; there were enough shady characters slipping to and fro between England and the Continent during those years with little to lose and everything, including a martyr's crown, to gain by a single 'deed of violence'. Elizabeth was not assassinated but she certainly *could* have been. That she escaped was due in part to the remarkable ineptitude of her ill-wishers, in part to the unsleeping vigilance of Francis Walsingham.

The Council, who knew more than most about the inside story, took the threat very seriously indeed and regarded it as so immediate that they were not prepared to wait for Parliament to act. In September 1584 they embarked on dramatic and unprecedented measures to try and safeguard the Queen by removing the principal motive for her murder. To this end an association of 'natural-born subjects of this realm of England' was to be set up, dedicated to avenging with their 'whole powers, bodies and lives' any attempt on the life of their 'most gracious sovereign lady Queen Elizabeth'. The bond which members of this association were to sign went through several drafts, but in its final form – the form in which it was circulated through the towns and shires that autumn and winter – it was a straightforward invitation to lynch law. The signatories, and there were tens of thousands of them, bound themselves by their solemn oath and 'in the presence of the everlasting God' not merely never to accept any pretended successor 'by whom or for whom any such detestable act shall be attempted or committed', but 'to prosecute such person or persons unto death and to act the utmost revenge upon them'. In other words, in the event of Elizabeth's untimely end, Mary Stuart was to be killed out of hand – whether she had been an accessory before the fact or not.

The Bond of Association was a naked appeal to the most primitive instincts of its signatories, a statement of intent to meet violence with violence, and, as undoubtedly its authors hoped it would, it had the effect of hardening and canalising national feeling. When Parliament met at the end of November, members found some difficulty in containing their loyalty, their patriotism and their fury. Sir Walter Mildmay, speaking on the 28th, scarcely needed to remind his audience that 'through the goodness of Almighty God by the ministry of this our gracious Queen we have enjoyed peace now full twenty-six years, the like whereof, so long together, hath not been seen in any age; the commodities whereof may appear sufficiently by comparing the blessedness of this our happy peace with the miserable state of our neighbours, long afflicted with cruel wars'. Nor did he need to chill their blood any further by spelling out the consequences of a successful 'sacred enterprise', further details of which had just come to light from documents found in the possession of Father Creighton, captured at sea by the Dutch acting on a tip-off from Walsingham. Quite as clearly as Sir Walter members of the House of Commons could visualise the 'devastation of whole countries, sacking, spoiling and burning of cities and towns and villages, murdering of all kind of people without respect of person, age or sex, and so the ruin, subversion and conquest of this noble realm'.

Against this looming horror a double line of defence was planned – first to provide for the Queen's safety by making it clear in the strongest possible terms that the Catholic heiress would not survive to enjoy an inheritance seized for her by violent means and, second, to extirpate once and for all those 'malicious, raging runagates' the Jesuits and seminary priests. The passage of the Act for the Queen's Safety resolved itself, in outline, into a struggle between a majority of the Commons who wanted the Bond of Association to be given the force of law on the one hand, and on the other, the Queen herself who 'would not consent that anyone should be punished for the fault of another' or that anything should reach the statute book 'that should be repugnant to the Law of God or the Law of Nature, or grievous to the conscience of any of her good subjects, or that should not abide the view of the world, as well enemies as friends'.

Apart from the ethical considerations involved, Elizabeth was clearly anxious that nothing should be done which might prejudice the ultimate right of Mary's Stuart's son to the reversion of the English crown. As the Bond of Association was worded, any person that might any way claim by or from a 'pretended successor' would have been included in the wholesale vendetta. Looking into the future, it seems that Elizabeth had already begun to regard James as her natural heir. In the short term it would obviously have been extremely unwise to take legislative action which might have the effect of driving him into the arms of the Catholic powers. But the House of Commons – whose feelings for the Queen are probably best summed up in words of a member for a Wiltshire borough who was moved to exclaim, 'It makes my heart leap for joy to think we have such a jewel. It makes all my joints to tremble for fear when I consider the loss of such a jewel.' – were thinking with their hearts and not their heads. They were obsessed with one basic issue – or rather two interrelated basic issues – how best to protect their 'jewel' and how best to protect themselves if they should lose her.

A compromise still had to be hammered out when, early in February 1585, came the shock revelations of the 'Parry Plot'. Sir Edmund Neville, himself strongly suspected of sympathising with the enemy, accused one William Parry, Doctor at Law, with having propounded to him an amiable scheme for collecting a party of ten horsemen 'to set upon the Queen as she rode abroad to take the air, and to kill her'. Dr Parry had at one time been employed by Lord Burghley as a secret service agent and in that capacity had gone abroad to try and penetrate 'the dangerous practices devised and attempted against her Majesty by her disloyal subjects and other malicious persons in foreign parts'. In the course of his duties he had, so he said, encountered Thomas Morgan, one of Mary Stuart's agents in France, who suggested to him that he should undertake Elizabeth's murder. Parry had replied that this 'might easily be done, if it might appear to be lawful', and had then written off to Rome requesting papal approval for his 'Design' and a plenary pardon. He returned to England in January 1584 and at once made a full report to the Queen, who heard him 'without being daunted', and proceeded to grant him various marks of favour. Certain of his past misdeeds were forgiven and he was actually sitting in the Parliament of 1584 as member for Queensborough. In December, though, he had electrified the House by making a speech in defence of the Jesuits, for which error of taste he had been committed to the serjeant's ward by his outraged colleagues and only released after his own abject apologies and the Queen's personal intervention.

When Parry was arrested he began by denying 'with great and vehement protestations' that he had been planning the Queen's destruction, but after a confrontation with Edmund Neville and a further night's reflection he decided to make a full confession, without the added incentive of torture. He admitted all the facts but swore that his intentions had been of the best, that he had never meant any harm to come to the Queen – on the contrary, he had been trying to uncover further dangerous designs against her life. Precisely what Dr Parry's intentions were, remain unclear. Some of the early part of his story is corroborated by independent evidence and he may have been speaking the truth, in which case his only crime was over-enthusiasm. But he was no longer in the government service and it was dangerous to the point of being suicidal for a private individual even to mention a murder plot to anyone without authority from above. Also, if he was acting the part of *agent provocateur* on his own initiative, it seems odd that he did not unburden himself to Francis Walsingham in private, as he was given every opportunity to do at his first examination. Perhaps, as Holinshed's Chronicle grimly suggests, he had been practising 'at sundry times to have executed his most devilish purpose and determination; yet covering the same so much as in him lay with a veil and pretence of great loyalty unto her Majesty'.

William Parry remains something of an enigma. 'A man of very mean and base parentage but of a most proud and insolent spirit, bearing himself always far above the measure of his fortune after he had long led a wasteful and dissolute life', he was a typical product of the strange twilight world which existed just beneath the surface of Elizabethan society – a world of spies, adventurers and soldiers-of-fortune living on their wits, ready to sell their services and their souls to the highest bidder, resorting to straightforward crime when times were bad, hobnobbing with the great when their luck was in. Parry may have been suffering from delusions of grandeur. He may have been a double agent. He may quite simply have wanted money. We are never likely to know for certain.

To the general public, by far the most startling disclosure of the Parry Plot was the letter addressed to Parry by the Cardinal of Como and produced in evidence at his trial. This remarkable document, the English translation of which, printed by Holinshed, corresponds with the Italian draft preserved in the Vatican archives, added still more fuel to the furnace of popular fury. '. . . his Holiness doth exhort you to persevere, and to bring to effect that which you have promised' the Cardinal had written. 'And to the end you may be so much the more holpen by that good Spirit which hath moved you thereunto, he granteth unto you his blessing, plenary indulgence, and remission of all your sins, according to your request. Assuring you, that beside the merit that you shall receive therefore in heaven, his holiness will further make himself debtor, to acknowledge your deservings in the best manner that he can. . . . Put therefore your most holy and honourable purposes in execution, and attend your safety.'

The discovery of a potential assassin in their very midst raised the already feverish temperature of the Commons, and two overwrought members petitioned the Queen to allow them to devise an especially horrible kind of penalty to fit Parry's 'most horrible kind of treason'.

Elizabeth thanked them for their concern, but refused their request. She would not agree to any dealing other than 'the ordinary course of law'. Nor had this most recent scare in any way modified her resolve not to be stampeded into allowing the law of the jungle to become the law of England. The Queen had strong feelings about the necessity of observing proper decorum in the public conduct of affairs, and by legalising murder she would achieve nothing except to advertise her insecurity to the world; no Act of Parliament, however draconian, was ever going to deter the kind of mentality set on winning the halo of a tyrannicide. Neither would Elizabeth have anything to do with the proposals, painstakingly drafted by Lord Burghley, providing for an Interregnum in case of her sudden death. These proposals included provision for a sovereign parliament – a revolutionary concept which revolted the Queen. And again, as her coldly sceptical mind would have told her, no such arrangements, however painstakingly worked out, would have the slightest hope of averting civil war if she died before the Catholic heiress.

The Act for the Queen's Safety as finally passed was a much emasculated version of the notorious Bond. In the event of invasion, rebellion or plot against the state, a panel of commissioners, privy councillors and others, was empowered to hold an enquiry into the facts. Then, and only then, might the members of the association pursue and wreak vengeance upon any person judged by the commissioners to have been privy to such an outrage. In the event of a successful attempt on the Queen's life, the 'pretended successor', unnamed but no prizes were being offered for guessing her identity, was to be declared disabled. The heirs of such a successor were exempted unless, of course, also judged 'assenting and privy'. There would be no Interregnum, no Grand Council or sovereign parliament, nothing, in fact, to prevent the country from sliding into anarchy and darkness.

There can be no question but that Elizabeth knew the risk she was running, both for herself and for England; that if an assassin's bullet found her while Mary Stuart still lived, she would leave behind a reputation for criminal negligence which nothing would ever erase. But, as so often before, she preferred to back her own judgement, her own instinctive flair, against all the sound, logical advice she was being offered. Stubbornly she preferred to trust in God, or providence, to hope to ride out the storm, to gamble on survival. She had, after all, been gambling on survival since her teens. As so often before, events, or luck, were to prove her judgement, or instinct, a better guide than the soundest, most logical advice available.

The Act for the Queen's Safety served its purpose. It provided a respectable legal framework for the subsequent proceedings against Mary Stuart. It did nothing to prejudice the final, peaceful accession of James, and it kept him quiet in the meantime. But in 1585 it needed a strong head not to succumb to the prevailing atmosphere of panic, an iron will to resist the pressure of emotional blackmail. Fortunately for England's reputation among the nations and before posterity, Elizabeth Tudor's courage and self-confidence were equal to the occasion. Years before she had told an obstreperous House of Commons, 'I will never by violence be constrained to do anything', and she had meant just precisely what she said.

23

So Long as That Devilish Woman Lives

'So long as that devilish woman lives, neither her Majesty must make account to continue in quiet possession of her crown, nor her faithful servants assure themselves of safety of their lives.'
Francis Walsingham, London, January 1572

The second piece of business which engaged the attention of the Parliament of 1584–5 was a bill against Jesuits, seminary priests and other such like disobedient persons. In the opinion of Thomas Digges, the member for Southampton, 'these hellhounds cladding themselves with the glorious name of Jesus, and such wretched souls as they bewitch with their wicked doctrine' were the only real danger to the Queen, since, as he wrote in a Discourse in the subject, 'they are fully persuaded her Majesty's life is the only stay why their Roman kingdom is not again established here'. Thomas Digges was by no means alone in his opinions and there were those who wanted the bill to include a clause 'that whosoever should teach the Romish religion should be as a traitor, because between the Queen and the Pope there can be no communion'. This motion was, however, rejected. It would confuse treason with heresy and give colour to the Catholic accusation that the Protestants were trying to stamp out Catholicism by foul means because they could not confine its doctrine in a fair fight.

The Act which presently received the royal assent was designed to keep the missionary priests within bounds by 'letting them find how dangerous it shall be for them to come here or once to put their foot on land within any her Majesty's dominions'. It laid down that any priest ordained by the authority of Rome since the first year of the Queen's reign must leave the country within forty days. Any such priest who disobeyed this order or who came into England in future would automatically be guilty of high treason. Any layman who 'willingly and wittingly' received, comforted or maintained a priest would not be guilty of felony; any 'home Papist' who sent money to the English colleges and seminaries abroad would become liable to the penalties of praemunire; anyone sending a child to be educated at a Catholic school abroad could be fined £100 for each offence;

anyone knowing the whereabouts of a priest who failed to lay information within twelve days could be fined and imprisoned at the Queen's pleasure.

The government took immediate advantage of the forty-day moratorium by rounding up a number of priests being held in custody and sending them into exile, among them Father Jasper Heywood, who had taken over from Robert Parsons as superior of the Jesuits in 1581, two other Jesuits, Fathers Bosgrave and Hart, and Edward Rishton, one of the party which came from Rheims in 1580. The new law was the logical expression of the fear of a threatened society of the enemy within its gates – a fear which most contemporary Western societies have experienced to some degree. But this latest attempt to expel from the state such members who acknowledged allegiance to a power dedicated to its overthrow did not have any immediately noticeable deterrent effect on the missionary priests. As long as there continued to be a supply of determined men irrevocably committed to the task of saving other men's souls, and equally immutably convinced that not only were they helping to atone for their country's sins in the eyes of God but also incidentally earning their own eternal reward by their sufferings on earth, no man-made law ever would deter them.

William Allen's brother Gabriel, returning to Rheims from England in March 1583, reported that during the three years he had been away 'never a day passed but he had the opportunity of hearing Mass'. Gabriel Allen had spent a month in London waiting for a passage to France and had visited nearly all the Catholic prisoners, both lay and priestly, excepting those in the Tower which he wisely 'did not venture to go near'. In prisons like the Marshalsea, he told his brother, the inmates were able to say Mass every day and visitors were allowed in from time to time for conference, confession or communion. More surprisingly, the priests were 'allowed to go out every day to different parts of the city, and attend to the spiritual needs of the Catholics, on condition that they return to the prison at night'.

Gabriel's experience reinforced William Allen's long-held conviction that no attention should be paid to those faint hearts who cried aloud or whispered that the priests should be reserved 'for more seasonable times'. 'We have not to wait till things are better,' he wrote energetically, 'but to make them better, and we must buy back happier times from the Almighty . . . by zeal, labour and blood, especially that of priests.' And so the priests continued to offer themselves as willing sacrifices. Just as no Act of Parliament could terrify them, no physical barriers existed which could keep them out – there were too many stretches of lonely coastline where a ship's boat could be beached on a dark night.

During the first half of the 1580s the organisation of this cross-Channel 'underground railway' was in the capable hands of Robert Parsons, working in conjunction with William Allen at the college at Rheims. 'We have shared the business between us,' wrote Parsons to the Spanish Jesuit Pedro de Ribadeneira in September 1584, 'he sending me priests from the Seminary, and I arranging, to the best of my power, for their safe transport to England. To do this and a number of other things required for the equipment of this spiritual war, I am obliged to maintain a modest establishment at Rouen, which is a most convenient town on account of its nearness to the sea, so that from there some can make trips to the coast to arrange for boats to convey people across (for they cannot use either the public boats or the ordinary ports that are well known).' Just how many priests Parsons was handling does not appear to be recorded but, according to his own estimate, there were nearly three hundred missionaries labouring in the vineyard at this time. Of these the vast majority were secular priests – the number of Jesuits either at work or in prison in England at any one time during the 1580s could be counted on the fingers of one hand.

Two members of the Society who did pass through the 'modest establishment' at Rouen were Father William Weston and Ralph Emerson, who embarked at Dieppe on 8 September 1584, together with Henry Hubert, a layman and an old friend of Weston's. William Weston, born at Maidstone in 1550, was yet another Oxford man whose conscience had taken him on the well-trodden pilgrim road to Rome via Douai. His early years in the priesthood were spent in Spain and he was at Seville when the summons 'to go to England and work there for the salvation of souls' reached him. Ralph Emerson was, of course, the former companion of Edmund Campion who had escaped capture at the time of Campion's arrest. He had since been in Scotland with the Jesuit William Holt and was now returning to England to distribute a consignment of 'books, written in English, both on spiritual and devotional matters, and on matters of controversy' – the writing, printing and dissemination of which remained one of Robert Parsons' special concerns.

Despite the intense alarm and resentment building up over the political activities of the Society of Jesus, the fact remained that the Jesuit Mission in England had recently diminished almost to vanishing point. Jasper Heywood had not been a great success as Superior and during the first eight months of 1584 there appears to have been only one inexperienced priest still at liberty. The ever practical Superiors of the Order questioned whether, in present circumstances, any useful purpose would be served by sending over more suitably qualified men, always in short supply, but the combined pressure exerted by William Allen and Robert Parsons had persuaded the Father General to make another effort. Parsons thought highly of William Weston and was hopeful that 'he would win much success'. Being, however, a firm believer in the maxim that God helps those who help themselves, he had gone to considerable trouble, borrowing money for the purpose, to ensure that his colleague's mission should get off to the best possible start.

'Father William Weston and Ralph left here ten days ago with all they required for going on board,' he wrote to the General on 15 September. 'I arranged for a special boat to be at their disposal and managed also that an English gentleman [this was Henry Hubert or Hubbard], who was staying here and has properties on the English coast, should enter the country with them, for the sole purpose of guiding them safely to his house: afterwards he and his servant will come back. They are very well equipped for the journey – that is to say, they are well primed with information, well clothed, have seventy crowns in their purse . . . and all their expenses are paid until they reach the boat. The cost of the boat and the gentleman's expenses I am also paying. We are obliged to do all this so that they may cross safely, as I hope in God they will do, since the gentleman will go with them as far as London, where there are many houses now fitted up to receive them.'

The journey, thus efficiently provided for, went smoothly and Weston sent Parsons a letter from the boat in such good spirits that he broke into Greek verse. The party made landfall on the East Anglian coast, between Yarmouth and Lowestoft, where Hubert's estates lay, and Weston and Hubert went ashore to take shelter in a safe house in the neighbourhood. 'In the meantime,' Weston was to write in the autobiography which describes his adventures, 'Ralph stayed in the boat with our baggage – it was our plan to send him a horse secretly, under cover of night, and collect our possessions. . . . This was done very quickly. So far all had gone well, and he joined us with his valuable burden safe and entire. The next day, after we had made arrangements for their conveyance by river, Ralph put the cases of books aboard a light boat and sailed with them to Norwich – the starting-place for the freight-waggons and carriers that take the merchandise of the district to London. Meanwhile we got on our horses, and making our way by comfortable stages, arrived in London ahead of him.'

In London Henry Hubert, who had taken every precaution to keep his return from France a secret, got a nasty fright when an acquaintance came up to him and greeted him by name 'in the open street', but Weston, whose face was not known, felt brave enough to go to the carrier terminus at Bishopsgate to await Emerson's arrival. In the end, to his great relief, he ran into him in the middle of the road. Ralph himself was safe but his news was bad – the precious cases of books had been detained by a suspicious official and the difficult decision of whether to take the coward's way out and abandon them or run the obvious risk of trying to reclaim their property now had to be faced. 'Whatever we did, we were in trouble,' Weston wrote. After a good deal of anxious discussion, Ralph's devotion to duty won the day and, feeling that if necessary he could 'bribe his way through', he went back to the inn where the books were impounded, only to find that the worst had already happened. The cases had been opened and the moment Emerson appeared he was arrested and taken before the magistrates. He was questioned closely about the books but luckily no one seems to have suspected his connection with William Weston. All the same, Ralph, who was to spend the next twenty years in prison, was now definitely out of the picture and his 'misadventure' came as a bad blow to his companions, who had been relying on him to vouch for them to their fellow Catholics.

Parsons had given Weston an introduction to a Mrs Bellamy, who had once sheltered him at her house near Harrow, and he and Hubert now decided to ride out and see her. Weston had some 'tokens' to prove his identity, but even when these had been handed over, 'secretly, as had to be done on such an occasion', he met with blank denial. Mrs Bellamy did not know what her visitor was talking about, she had never set eyes on Father Parsons, had never even heard of him. Weston saw that nothing was to be gained by persisting. 'Besides,' he wrote, 'I suspected I might be treading on unsafe ground, and feared that we might have made a mistake either about the house or about the lady, or that the situation might have altered, as it so often does in the present troubled state of the country. So giving the rein to our horses, Henry and I rode off, taking a different road from that by which we had come.' It was just as well that they did take this simple precaution, for it subsequently transpired that there had been a spy in Mrs Bellamy's house who followed them to try and discover their identity.

Back in London, the two men took stock of their position. It was not encouraging. Both fully realised the danger of staying too long at a public inn where awkward questions might be asked at any moment. In fact, their chances of survival were negligible unless they could make contact with the Catholic underground, and their recent experience with Mrs Bellamy had been a frightening indication of the prevailing mood of acute suspicion of all strangers. One other possible line of approach remained open. When Henry Hubert fled to France he had left his pregnant wife behind and had been told that she had gone into hiding at a friend's house until her child was born – a device often resorted to by Catholic mothers-to-be in order to avoid the necessity of presenting their babies for baptism at the parish church.

Although they were not even certain that Mrs Hubert was still in the same retreat, it seemed worth trying to find her and, as Hubert himself was by this time scared of his own shadow – 'every house and building appeared suspect and unsafe to him' – William Weston set off alone to make enquiries. At first he was greeted with the same distrust and flat denial. No one at the house had heard of Mrs Hubert, she was not there and never had been. However, 'from one or two indications', Weston felt fairly certain that he had come to the right place and 'became rather more daring'. Eventually his persistence paid off and as soon as the family were convinced of his *bona fides*, they lavished on him 'every courtesy and attention their kindness could suggest'. Henry Hubert was fetched for a reunion with his wife while Weston was taken in charge by a fellow priest and given facilities to start work.

William Weston was to remain at liberty for just under two years, during which time he fulfilled all Parsons' hopes by 'doing wonders and . . . giving great edification to all'. His most notable convert was Philip Howard, Earl of Arundel and son of the Duke of Norfolk executed for his part in the Ridolfi Plot. Probably his most notable exploit was when he penetrated into the Tower with, not surprisingly, 'a feeling of great trepidation', to spend a whole day in conference with Jasper Heywood shortly before the latter's banishment. William Weston was a brave man and a modest one, although he had a somewhat dubious enthusiasm for exorcising evil spirits. After several narrow escapes he was finally captured in London on 3 August 1586, but fortunately for the continuity of the Jesuit Mission, Fathers Garnet and Southwell had arrived three weeks earlier and were able to take over.

Garnet and Southwell, like Parsons and Campion before them, formed a powerful combination of talent. Southwell, the poet, had all Campion's charm, his other-worldly sweetness of nature, his eagerness for martyrdom (or unhealthy preoccupation with death), and his felicity of language. 'Our ship may be tossed about and grind upon the rocks,' he wrote to the Rector of the English college in Rome in December 1586, 'but it cannot go to pieces or be sunk. We live on in the midst of storms, with but little security for the body. Yet, if they do carry us off, they will only be taking us to life and to rest. Even in shipwreck we shall be blessed. . . . Christ's soldiers fight under most favourable terms; for if the enemy defeat them he crowns them, and if he let them alone, he is himself defeated: while they are in life they save the souls of others, and in death they win salvation for their own souls . . . in the midst of dangers it is marvellous what joy of heart I feel, reflecting under whose name and in what cause I am enlisted. For though the flesh be weak, and this corruptible body drag down the soul, still our blood if shed will ransom souls. . . . Assuredly it is not unpleasant to die that virtue may spring to life in many souls, and vices receive their deathblow.' In fact, Southwell evaded capture for six years and was not executed until 1594.

Henry Garnet, a Derbyshire man, whose special interests were music and mathematics, proved an even more slippery and resourceful customer than Parsons had been and survived for a record twenty years, only coming to grief in the aftermath of the Gunpowder Plot. Like Parsons he operated a secret press. Like Parsons he organised an efficient system for meeting and helping new priests as they came in from France and Flanders before posting them to districts where they were most needed. As a result, he wrote, 'many persons who saw a seminary priest hardly once a year, now have one all the time and most eagerly welcome any others no matter where they come from'.

Another Jesuit, arriving in the crisis year of 1588 and who might (in some respects) be described as the James Bond of the missionary priests, was John Gerard. Gerard, landing on the Norfolk coast with three companions one wet November night, made effective use of his knowledge of the technical terms of hunting and falconry as a cover – especially when in the company of those Protestant gentlemen 'who had practically no other conversation except, perhaps, obscene subjects or rant against the saints and the Catholic faith'. He proved an exceptionally tough and enterprising campaigner, but was eventually caught in the spring of 1594 as a result of information received. Taken to the Tower, he was tortured by 'the manacles' – that is, hung up by the wrists – in an attempt to get him to betray Garnet's whereabouts among other things, and Gerard, in his autobiography, has left a detailed description both of the mechanics of this particular form of persuasion and of what it felt like.

'They took me to a big upright pillar,' he wrote, 'one of the wooden posts which held the roof of this huge underground chamber. Driven in to the top of it were iron staples for supporting heavy weights. Then they put my wrists into iron gauntlets and ordered me to climb two or three wicker steps. My arms were then lifted up and an iron bar was passed through the rings of one gauntlet, then through the staple and rings of the second gauntlet. This done, they fastened the bar with a pin to prevent it slipping, and then, removing the wicker steps one by one from under my feet, they left me hanging by my hands and arms fastened above my head.' Gerard was a tall, heavy man and the tips of his toes still touched the floor. As he had been suspended from the highest staple in the pillar, the earthen floor beneath him had to be scraped away. 'Hanging like this,' he went on, 'I began to pray. The gentlemen standing around asked me whether I was willing to confess now. "I cannot and I will not," I answered. But I could hardly utter the words, such a gripping pain came over me. It was worst in my chest and belly, my hands and arms. All the blood in my body seemed to rush up into my arms and hands and I thought that blood was oozing out from the ends of my fingers and the pores of my skin. But it was only a sensation caused by my flesh swelling above the irons holding them. The pain was so intense that I thought I could not possibly endure it.'

He did, however, more than once, without uttering a syllable the authorities wanted to hear. Some people, as has been remarked, are torturable and some are not. Gerard's career, in fact, was far from over. After recovering from his ordeal, he achieved the rare distinction of escaping from the Tower. He remained at work in England until 1606 when he was smuggled out of the country by the Spanish ambassador, and died in Rome at a ripe old age on 27 July 1637.

In spite of the Act of 1584, by no means all the missionaries captured after this date were executed as traitors. Weston, for example, survived to tell the tale of his adventures and his twenty years in prison (he was released and deported in James's reign, as was Ralph Emerson), and there were communities of priests in most of the London prisons, as well as at special centres like Wisbech, living as guests of her Majesty under far from intolerable conditions by contemporary standards. Those with the necessary funds could and did bribe their warders and they were generally able to practise their religion, say or hear Mass regularly and receive visitors. Gerard, referring to the time he spent in the Clink, makes the illuminating remark that 'after a few months we had, by God's grace, everything so arranged that I was able to perform there all the tasks of a Jesuit priest, and provided only I could have stayed on in this prison, I should never have wanted to have my liberty again in England'. Not all prisoners, of course, were so fortunate or so well organised, but few sixteenth-century governments would have gone to the trouble and expense of keeping such potentially dangerous enemies of the state alive under any conditions.

Apart, however, from the obvious undesirability of giving the Catholic cause too many martyrs – the alacrity and cheerfulness with which the victims went to the scaffold was liable to move some standers-by to speculate 'that such an extraordinary contempt of death cannot but proceed from above' – neither the Queen nor the nation (with the exception of the lunatic fringe), would have tolerated a bloodbath on the standard Continental pattern. The statistics show that, roughly speaking, the number of deaths went up and down with the political barometer. In 1581, four priests were executed; in 1582, eleven priests; in 1583, two priests and two laymen; in 1584, six priests and three laymen; in 1585, two priests and two laymen; in 1586, twelve priests and three laymen; in 1587, six priests; and in 1588, the Armada year, twenty-one priests and ten laymen. There was another peak in the early 1590s, also a time of acute international tension, but after that executions fell off noticeably. It is estimated that altogether some two hundred and fifty people died as a more or less direct result of their religious proclivities during the forty-four years of Elizabeth's reign, and this includes about fifty who died in prison. It was enough, but it was no bloodbath in any sixteenth-century book.

No statistics, of course, can measure individual human suffering, such as those of the priests who fell into the clutches of that legendary monster and sadist Richard Topcliffe, 'old and hoary and a veteran in evil', who for a time held a special licence from the Council to torture suspects in private in his own house. All the same, in circumstances which naturally tend to bring such individuals from out of the woodwork, it is surprising and gratifying to know that Topcliffe, who enjoyed his work, was the exception rather than the rule. According to the accounts of the priests themselves, prison officials were often openly sympathetic and found the whole business nauseating. Nevertheless it went on – a necessary weapon it was felt – and the twentyfirst century has little to teach the sixteenth when it comes to the techniques of breaking down a prisoner's resistance.

'Some,' wrote Robert Southwell in his *Humble Supplication to her Majesty*, 'besides their tortures, have been forced to lie continually booted and clothed many weeks together, pined in their diet, consumed with vermin, and almost stifled with stench. Some have been watched and kept from sleep, till they were past the use of reason, and then examined upon the advantage, when they could scarcely give account of their own names.' Apart from the rack, which could dislocate the victim's joints by stretching him between wooden rollers, and the manacles, the most common forms of physical torture seem to have been 'Little Ease', a dungeon so constructed that its inmate could neither stand nor lie, and 'The Scavenger's Daughter', an iron ring which rolled victims into a ball and so crushed them 'that the blood sprouted out at divers parts of their bodies'. Some, too, as Robert Southwell delicately put it, 'have been tortured in such parts, as is almost a torture to Christian ears to hear it'. Not unnaturally, much useful information was obtained by these methods.

While the brunt of the attack was borne by the priests, the laity – or at any rate that section of the laity which was actively involved with the Mission – could suffer acutely from harassment, anxiety and mental stress, as evidenced by William Weston's early adventures. In general, though, it was their property and their liberty which were at risk rather than their lives, and contemporary Catholic propagandists weaken their own case by hysterical overstatement. Despite the fact that the penal laws had become progressively more severe, the situation had not altered fundamentally. Even in the seventies and eighties those Catholics who managed to avoid drawing undue attention to themselves and, above all, kept out of politics, do not appear to have experienced worse inconvenience than that of any disadvantaged minority in any society.

Among the professional classes, probably as good an example as any is that of the lawyer Edmund Plowden, who never made any secret of his religious opinions but who remained much esteemed among his colleagues and published two volumes of reports or 'Commentaries' which became a standard legal text book. As treasurer of his Inn, the Middle Temple, he had much to do with the building of the Middle Temple Hall and earned a respectful posthumous tribute from William Camden. 'In England died this year [1584] no man more worthy to be remembered than Edmund Plowden, who as he was singularly well learned in the Common Laws of England, whereof he deserved well by his Writings, so for Integrity of Life he was second to no man of his Profession.' At the same time, Plowden never became a serjeant-at-law, never in fact advanced beyond the status of 'un Apprentice de la Comen Ley', when in happier circumstances a man of his quality could have confidently expected to hold high office. He could, so the tradition goes, have become lord chancellor, if only he had not been a Catholic.

Few known recusants escaped the notice of the authorities at some time in their lives – Edmund Plowden was no exception. Some were bound over in their own recognisance to be of good behaviour and appear before the Council when summoned; some were confined within narrow geographical limits; but even those who went to gaol were occasionally released, either temporarily or permanently, on compassionate or other grounds. Sir John Southworth was let out in March 1586 to go to Bath to take the waters, but he was alleged to have broken the terms of his parole by associating with Catholics and was re-arrested in May. John Talbot of Grafton was allowed to leave the house in Surrey where he was confined to go to his home in Worcestershire to settle some private business, and William Tyrwhitt in Kent received a similar licence for a journey to Lincolnshire. In 1585, Lady Lovell and her son were released from prison and granted immunity from further prosecution on the intervention of the Queen herself. There were many petitioners for clemency, and the degree of success they achieved seems to have depended on the amount of influence they or their relatives could command and, of course, on the nature of their offence.

If the penal laws had ever been rigorously and uniformly enforced, the picture would have been very different and life would have become intolerable for the most well-behaved and peaceable Catholics. This, however, was probably never the government's intention – it was certainly never the Queen's – and even if it had been, the thing could not have been done. The executive could pounce punitively on an isolated centre of disaffection in any part of the country at need, as in 1569, and from time to time individual bishops or lords lieutenant would mount search and destroy missions in selected areas, but the sort of administrative machinery necessary for keeping all of the Catholic population under an iron hand all of the time simply did not exist.

The fine of twenty pounds a month for non-attendance at church is a case in point. If this had been levied on anything like a systematic basis, it would quickly have bankrupted the small gentry families which formed the solid core of Catholic recusancy. In 1586 a report on the working of the 1581 Act brought to light the disturbing facts that some recusants were escaping indictment altogether through the corruptness of juries, and that some 'being indicted are winked at by justices in respect of kindred or friendship'. Others were going untouched through the inefficiency, deliberate or otherwise, of clerks of assize and sheriffs 'who do not their duties in orderly sending out process, or in forbearing to apprehend the offender, when they may, or in committing some error or other whereby the execution of the law is deferred'. As a result of this deplorable state of affairs, the report concluded gloomily, 'many are encouraged to offend and to make small account of the pains set down against them'. In 1587 Parliament made an attempt to close the more obvious loopholes, but even so it has been estimated that less than two hundred people were actually paying the dreaded monthly fine during the period 1581 to 1593.

Generalisations about the English Catholics under Elizabeth are not made any easier by the fact that no one really knows how many of them there were. Estimates, or rather informed guesses, vary from between two and three per cent by one authority to from 750,000 to 1,000,000 by another, out of a total population of three and a half to four millions at the end of the reign. It does seem, though, that the spiritual revival brought about by the efforts of the Douai and Jesuit missionaries had reached and passed its peak by 1584. What might be termed the 'second wave' of the Jesuit invasion went some way towards stabilising the situation – in the 1590s the government was sufficiently alarmed by the numbers of priests still being sheltered in private houses to bring in further anti-Catholic legislation – but by the second half of the 1580s the continual pressure, the continual sense of insecurity, the threat as well as the actuality of imprisonment with all its attendant discomforts and inconveniences, the threat as well as the actuality of crippling fines and distraint on lands and chattels, were having their inevitable effect.

There were other forces at work too. Civil disobedience never sat easily on the shoulders of what was an essentially law-abiding section of the community and, as the international crisis worsened, the imputation of disloyalty hurt a class with a long and honourable record of service to king and country worst of all. It is scarcely surprising, therefore, that even those Catholics who had clung most staunchly to the faith of their ancestors should have begun to seek a compromise way out of the agonising dilemma they were trapped in, and that the slide into outward conformity should have gathered momentum. Especially as the Catholic community became more and more rent by internal dissension. Those unfortunates whose consciences, fears of hell fire, or plain stubbornness would not allow them release simply lay low and waited out the siege as best they could, trying to avoid prosecution by such stratagems as temporarily leaving home, cultivating local officialdom (churchwardens and even searchers could often be either bribed or overawed), and pleading excuses like ill-health or being 'out of charity' with a neighbour to avoid going to church. In many places, especially in country districts, Catholics and Protestants lived quite comfortably together, but the saying 'a Catholic always pays his debts', which became current at this time, was probably due not so much to superior moral rectitude as to the fact that no Catholic who might at any time have to depend heavily on the goodwill of his neighbours, could afford to make a single unnecessary enemy.

With so many imponderables to be taken into account, the only honest answer to the question 'what was it like to be a Catholic during Elizabeth's reign?' must be 'it depended'. It depended on an individual family's degree of commitment to their religious faith, on their standing in the community, on the climate of local opinion, on the zeal or lack of it shown by the local ecclesiastical and civil authorities, and, of course, on the international situation. This seldom remained static for long, and by the end of 1585 there had been a number of developments. On the credit side, Anglo-Scottish relations, after six years of instability, were once again on a firm basis. King James, having finally made up his mind on which side his bread was buttered, had signed a treaty with Elizabeth agreeing not to attack England and to go to her assistance if she were attacked. In return, James accepted an annual pension of £4,000 from the English crown (he had wanted £5,000 but Elizabeth refused to part with a penny more), and a tacit assurance that nothing would be done by Parliament to prejudice his right to the succession.

Also on the credit side, though this was not immediately apparent, Elizabeth's arch-enemy, Pope Gregory XIII, had died to be replaced by Sixtus V, who was privately sceptical about the chances of the Holy Enterprise and who disapproved of assassination as a weapon of war. In France, too, things had changed. Elizabeth's former suitor, the Duke of Anjou, was dead and, as Henri III for the most obvious of reasons would never father children, the Huguenot leader, Henri of Navarre, had now become heir to the French throne. This was too much for the Duke of Guise and his Holy League, and in January 1585 the concluded a secret treaty with Spain by the terms of which Guise became King Philip's pensioner to the tune of 50,000 crowns a month in return for his promise to ensure, by whatever force of arms proved necessary, that Henri of Navarre should never enjoy his inheritance.

It was spring before the English government first got wind of the Treaty of Joinville and it needed nobody to explain that if this meant the bellicose duke would now be kept busy at home, it also meant that Philip now had nothing to fear from French interference in whatever foreign adventures he might be contemplating. It meant, in fact, that France and Spain had reached the sort of understanding which England had most reason to fear: especially as by the end of the year a state of open, if undeclared warfare existed between England and Spain. In May, Philip had seized all English shipping in Spanish ports. In August, Elizabeth had at last stepped over the brink by taking the Dutch under her protection and despatching an expeditionary force to the Netherlands. In September, that enthusiastic private entrepreneur Francis Drake was unleashed to 'annoy the King of Spain' on his own coast as only he knew how, before going off to pay another of his unwelcome visits to the Caribbean. By the winter, the King of Spain had become sufficiently annoyed to begin giving serious consideration to plans for solving the English problem once and for all, and instructed his veteran naval commander, the Marquis of Santa Cruz, to draw up detailed estimates of the forces that would be required for such an undertaking.

One other thing which happened in 1585 was the departure to Rome of William Allen and Robert Parsons. Ostensibly the purpose of Allen's journey was to discuss the increasingly serious financial position of the seminary at Rheims, and that of Parsons to prepare for taking his final vows in the Society of Jesus. No doubt these were both perfectly valid reasons, but they did not prevent both men from concentrating their energies over the next three years on working to promote a Spanish invasion of England by all the means at their joint disposal. William Allen had travelled a long and stony road since that autumn day in 1568, when he had started his modestly optimistic venture at Douai for the reconversion of his countrymen by peaceful persuasion.

By the early spring of 1586, the international situation could hardly have looked much blacker from the point of view of William Allen's countrymen. With the King of France apparently the helpless puppet of the King of Spain's hired bullies, with the King of Spain's army in the Netherlands apparently sweeping all before it, England, not for the last time in her history, stood alone with nothing but the hard-pressed Dutch rebels and the equally hard-pressed French Huguenots between her and an inexorably advancing Spanish tide which would soon be lapping the shores of Western Europe from Gibraltar to the Elbe. No one in England realised all the grim implications of this situation more clearly than Francis Walsingham, who maintained listening posts in every European capital.

In some cities Francis Walsingham has the reputation of a sixteenth-century Lavrenti Beria. Somewhat closer inspection reveals the disappointing reality of a conscientious, over-worked and under-staffed government official, frequently in poor health and much given to physicking himself, who combined the functions of Home and Foreign Secretaries with those of head of MI5 and the Special Branch. It is on his performance in the latter capacities that Walsingham's notoriety depends but, in fact, there were probably never more than about a dozen full-time professional agents on his pay-roll at any given moment. Reliable spies, always in short supply, tended to come expensive and it was not until 1582 that Walsingham first began to receive any sort of regular budget for this side of his work. It started at a grudging £750 per annum and was gradually increased to £2,000 by 1588, two years before his death. In the early days most of the cost of maintaining a secret service is said to have come from its founder's own pocket.

Nevertheless, by the mid-eighties, Francis Walsingham had built up a formidable and far-reaching intelligence network. He drew his information from a wide range of sources. Much of it came in through normal diplomatic channels. Queen Elizabeth's representatives in France and elsewhere were all expected to set up their own intelligence services (this was an important part of the job for the ambassadors of every first-class power), and there was always at least one servant or secretary or minor official in every Court or great man's household ready to part with gossip and sometimes even with hard news if the price was right. Walsingham could also rely on the friendly offices of Dutch, French and German Protestant leaders. As well as those official and semi-official sources, he made use of an unknown but quite considerable number of free-lance news-gatherers scattered all over Europe. These included merchants, traders, businessmen, commercial agents, licensed travellers and petty functionaries who would pass on any interesting items which happened to come their way.

From a list drawn up after his death, it seems that Walsingham was in the habit of receiving information from twelve places in France, nine in Germany, four in Italy (he had even penetrated the English college at Rome), four in Spain, three in the Low Countries and from as far afield as Constantinople, Algiers and Tripoli. In addition to his foreign network he had four regular agents in England, engaged on tracking the movements of the Jesuit and seminary priests. One way and another, it would probably be no exaggeration to say that very little went on in Catholic circles either at home or abroad during the 1580s which did not, sooner or later, come to the notice of that 'most subtle searcher of secrets', Sir Francis Walsingham.

By modern standards Queen Elizabeth's secret service was a pitifully haphazard and amateurish affair. Its agents, both full and part-time, were a floating population of greatly varying ability and trustworthiness, working individually and often, without doubt, working for both sides. Many of their reports were sheer guesswork, many were very likely sheer invention. The service owed its remarkable record of success to the skill and flair which enabled Francis Walsingham to sort out the mass of apparently unrelated material which flowed through his office, piece it together and make from it a coherent whole. It was a task which needed not only endless patience but an instinct for spotting and interpreting the single relevant fact or sentence in an agent's report. Walsingham had the patience. He developed the instinct slowly by unremitting hard work and concentration, helped by the fact that he was motivated throughout by a deep sense of the righteousness of his cause – sincere convictions were after all no means a Catholic monopoly. Walsingham held distinctly left-wing views which, despite the valuable services he rendered her, was why the Queen never really liked him. He was noted by William Camden to be 'a most sharp maintainer of the purer religion', and he undoubtedly believed that in his labours he was fighting Anti-Christ and all his works.

High on the list of these works Walsingham numbered Mary Queen of Scots. 'So long as that devilish woman lives,' he had written to Leicester in January 1572, 'neither her Majesty must make account to continue in quiet possession of her crown, nor her faithful servants assure themselves of safety of their lives.' Nothing which had happened since the unravelling of the Ridolfi Plot had caused Walsingham to alter that opinion. The unravelling of the Throckmorton Plot, his own first major *coup*, left him in no doubt that Mary had been as deeply involved in the one as in the other. Francis Throckmorton, like the Duke of Norfolk before him, had learned on the scaffold that he who supped with the Queen of Scotland needed a long spoon indeed, but the Queen of Scotland herself was apparently once more to escape unscathed the consequences of her misdeeds – almost, but on this occasion not quite.

Ever since the first few months after her arrival in England Mary had been living under the guardianship of George Talbot, Earl of Shrewsbury, in one or other of that much-tried nobleman's mansions in the North Midlands. Her freedom of movement had, it is true, been restricted, but she was served by a retinue of her own servants and friends more than thirty strong, and dined as befitted a queen beneath a cloth of estate, her 'diet' and entertainment costing Queen Elizabeth £52 a week and, according to Shrewsbury, a good deal more out of his own pocket. No other viable solution to the problem (apart from the one favoured by the House of Commons) had suggested itself over the years, but during the early eighties Elizabeth, in the search for a solution to the problem of James, had made a prolonged and apparently genuine effort to find some way by which mother and son might be reunited and reign jointly in Scotland. The negotiations foundered, as they were bound to do, on the two Queens' ineradicable mutual distrust and on the virtual impossibility of devising adequate safeguards against Mary's repudiation of any undertakings given while a prisoner the moment she regained her liberty. Mary was outwardly all complaisance – indeed the initiative for this round of peace talks had come from her – but that did not prevent her from taking an equally active interest in the progress of the Guise/Mendoza plans to free her by force of arms and place her in her own right on another and infinitely more attractive throne.

Just how seriously the Queen of England and her advisers took these negotiations with Mary, or whether they ever really believed in James's much vaunted (by Mary and her friends) 'devotion' to his mother and her cause is difficult to say. Elizabeth may have hoped that by using the bait of the succession it would be possible, now that James was reaching maturity, to proposition him into taking over responsibility for his volatile parent. But James himself presently put an end to any such optimistic thoughts by making it perfectly plain that he was not interested in sharing his throne with anybody, and that his only concern about his mother's future was that England should continue to bear the odium and expense of keeping her safely out of the way. The arrest of Francis Throckmorton and Father Creighton, the assassination of Orange, and the breaking of the Parry murder plot all combined to extinguish the last spark of hope of reaching a negotiated settlement with the Queen of Scots. The curtain had come down and already the scene shifters were setting the stage for the last act of her tragedy.

To Francis Walsingham one of the most disturbing revelations of the Throckmorton affair had been the extent of Mary's foreign correspondence and the ease with which she was apparently able to send and receive uncensored letters in the large and laxly organised Shrewsbury establishments. By the summer of 1584 a reverberating three-cornered row between the earl, his formidable countess (better known as Bess of Hardwick), and their royal guest in which, at least so far as the two ladies were concerned, no holds of any kind were barred, had provided an unexceptionable excuse for making a change.

After an interim period of six months a new custodian was appointed and Mary quickly discovered that her circumstances had altered in more ways than one. Sir Amyas Paulet was no great nobleman, though he was accustomed to high society, having been Queen Elizabeth's ambassador in France. More important he was a man of strict Puritanical principles and a close and trusted friend of Francis Walsingham. He treated Mary with scrupulous respect but, like John Knox before him, was immune to her famous charm and unmoved by tantrums. Paulet took his responsibilities very seriously and wrote to Walsingham in July: 'Whereas it hath pleased her Majesty to commit unto me the charge, as well as the safe keeping of this Queen, I will never ask pardon if she depart out of my hands by any treacherous slight or cunning device, because I must confess that the same cannot come to pass without some gross negligence or rather traitorous carelessness. . . . My conscience beareth me witness,' he went on, 'and my doing I hope shall testify for me, that as I have been very careful and curious to perform every syllable contained in my instructions with all preciseness and severity, so I have done all my endeavour to make these people and their friends to know that if it were possible I would not be deceived by them.'

Paulet's instructions had been drafted by Walsingham and were extremely detailed – there was to be no communication between Mary's household and his own, except in his presence; none of Mary's servants were to leave the house without a guard; no strangers were to be admitted on any pretext whatever, and special attention was to be paid to the comings and goings of 'laundresses, coachmen and the like'. 'I have (I thank God) reformed no small number of abuses of dangerous consequence,' wrote Paulet, 'and experience doth inform me daily of other such new faults as might carry great peril, which I omit not to redress by little and little as I may.' Throughout the spring and summer of 1585 Walsingham and Paulet were engaged in methodically stopping the earths. By the autumn they felt satisfied that Mary had been effectively isolated from her undesirable friends, and in the New Year Paulet was able to report that it was impossible for a piece of paper as big as his finger to be conveyed without his knowledge. Walsingham had completed the first part of his plan. It was now time to put stage two into operation, and the Secretary of State had the means ready to his hand.

In December 1585, a Catholic exile named Gilbert Gifford had come over from France entrusted by Thomas Morgan with the task of trying to find a way of evading Paulet's unceasing vigilance and reopening a secret channel of communication with Mary. Gifford was arrested on his arrival at Rye and at once sent up to Walsingham in London. He may or may not have already been in Walsingham's employment – to a suspicious mind his appearance looks just a little too pat to be entirely coincidental. At any rate he spent some time in secret conference with the Secretary and, so far as is known, raised no difficulties when certain suggestions were put to him.

Walsingham, it appeared, was as interested as Thomas Morgan in setting up Mary's private post office again. This time, though, it would be a supervised private post office. The arrangements discussed between Gifford, Walsingham and Walsingham's confidential secretary, Thomas Phelippes, were ingenious but essentially simple. The Queen of Scots was now established at Chartley Manor in Staffordshire, and beer for the household was delivered once a week from the town of Burton. With the connivance of the brewer, letters could be carried in and out in a watertight box small enough to be inserted into the bunghole of a beer barrel. Gifford's part was to collect Mary's personal mail from the French Embassy, where it arrived by diplomatic bag. He passed it on to Thomas Phelippes, an expert linguist and genius with codes. While Phelippes copied and deciphered the letters, Gifford travelled by leisurely stages to Chartley where the originals were returned to him by Paulet. Gifford handed the letters to the brewers and the brewer, unknown to Gifford, took them back to Paulet who checked that nothing had been added to the package. It was then delivered as arranged. The outgoing post would work in reverse order. The trap looked foolproof. Walsingham hoped it would prove a death trap.

The first trial delivery was made on 16 January 1586 and went without a hitch. Mary, naturally delighted to have made contact once more with the world of intrigue which was her life-line, and fatally unsuspicious, gave orders that the backlog of clandestine correspondence which had been piling up at the French embassy should be sent on to her forthwith. Eighteen years ago Francis Knollys had written of the Queen of Scotland, 'she hath courage enough to hold out as long as any foot of hope may be left unto her'. She had not changed.

To begin with the person who derived most benefit from this unusual postal service was the brewer of Burton, code-named 'the honest man'. He was, of course, being handsomely paid for his trouble by both sides but, as a man of sound business instincts, it soon occurred to him to raise the price of his invaluable beer. Paulet considered 'the honest man's' demands both peremptory and unreasonable, but had to give in to them 'or lose his service'.

Meanwhile, an exceptional amount of overtime was being worked in Walsingham's office as letters, twenty-one packets of them 'great and small', some of which had been waiting delivery for nearly two years, started to flow out of the French ambassador's private coffers. There were letters from the Queen of Scots' agents in the Low Countries, from Thomas Morgan and the Archbishop of Glasgow in Paris, from Charles Paget and Sir Francis Englefield, both prominent figures in the exiled community, from Robert Parsons, from the Duke of Guise and the Duke of Parma. They provided a complete picture of everything Mary's partisans in Europe had been doing and saying on her behalf since the time of the Throckmorton Plot. It was the sort of windfall any secret service chief dreams of, but although it filled many gaps in his knowledge and gave him much interesting information to be filed away for future use, it did not in general terms tell Walsingham anything that he had not already known or guessed.

By the middle of May, Mary's replies were coming back. In them she made it perfectly clear that she was completely identified with the purpose of the Enterprise, that she would welcome an invasion and was willing and eager to seize her cousin's throne. They provided helpful corroborative evidence that Mary had no scruples about conspiring against the state, but again they told Walsingham very little that he and his mistress did not already know. From past experience the Secretary also knew that the only hope of getting Elizabeth to proceed against Mary would be to confront her with irrefutable proof that the Queen of Scots had brought herself within the scope of the 1585 Act. From past experience of Mary and her friends he had little doubt that sooner or later such proof would be forthcoming. In the meantime, the beer barrels were providing him with a first-rate listening post.

The genesis of the Babington Plot, like that of most of its predecessors, is complicated and more than somewhat obscure. As usual a good many equivocal personalities were involved, and in the labyrinth of spy and counter-spy, double agent and *agent provocateur*, it is far from clear at this distance in time who was double-crossing who. It is evident that this was often far from clear at the time. In outline, though, the plot was the same mixture as before – a rising of English Catholics, aided by an invading army financed jointly by Spain and the Pope, to release Mary, depose Elizabeth and replace her by Mary, and re-establish the Catholic faith.

Two things, however, give this particular affair a distinctive character. One was the fact that the assassination as well as the deposition of Elizabeth was an integral part of the plan from the beginning. (Some conspirators had been less explicit on this point, but whether any conspirators, having once succeeded in deposing Elizabeth, would then have gone to the trouble or the risk of keeping her alive is hardly worth debating.) The other fact was that this time Elizabeth's government, thanks to its increasingly efficient secret service, was in a position to follow developments from an early stage.

The two chief protagonists in England were a priest named John Ballard and Anthony Babington. Both Ballard and Babington were already known to Walsingham who had begun to keep an eye on their movements in May. Ballard was in the habit of associating with a group of ardent young Catholic gentlemen who hung about the fringes of the Court, and the most prominent figure in this group was Anthony Babington – a young man of good family with a good deal more money than sense, handsome, gay, charming, conceited and cowardly. He had first made Mary's acquaintance in the days when he had been a page in the Earl of Shrewsbury's household and had since acquired the reputation among Mary's friends in France of being one of her staunchest adherents. He was, therefore, the obvious person to organise the actual rescue operation and act as her liaison officer.

Towards the end of June 1586, Mary received a letter from Thomas Morgan through the beer barrel post advising her to write a friendly letter to Babington. This she promptly did and Babington's reply contained a lengthy exposition of the plans afoot for her liberation. As far as Walsingham was concerned the most interesting paragraph came towards the end. 'For the despatch of the usurper,' wrote Babington, 'from the obedience of whom we are by the excommunication of her made free, there be six noble gentlemen all my private friends, who for the zeal they bear unto the Catholic cause and your majesty's service will undertake that tragical execution. It resteth that according to their good deserts and your majesty's bounty their heroical attempt may be honourably rewarded in them if they escape with life, or in their posterity and that so much I may be able by your majesty's authority to assure them.'

This was what Walsingham had been waiting for. Everything now depended on Mary's reply and Thomas Phelippes was sent up to Chartley to be ready to decipher it the moment it emerged from the beer barrel. First came a brief acknowledgement with the promise of more to follow. 'We attend her very heart at the next,' reported Phelippes. On 17 July it came. It was a very long letter. After warmly commending Babington and his suggestions in general terms, Mary proceeded to offer the conspirators much sound practical advice on how 'to ground substantially this enterprise and to bring it to good success'. She had, after all, become quite an expert on such matters by now. She also knew that if anything went wrong this time, the consequences were likely to be disastrous, not only for Babington and his friends, but for herself. In the circumstances, she was understandably anxious that there should be no security leaks and that no detail of the preliminary staff work should be overlooked. 'Affairs being thus prepared,' she went on, 'and forces in readiness both without and within the realm, then shall it be time to set the six gentlemen to work, taking order, upon the accomplishing of their design, I may be suddenly transported out of this place, and that all your forces in the same time be on the field to meet me in tarrying for the arrival of the foreign aid, which then must be hastened with all diligence.'

If this did not sign Mary's death warrant then nothing would, but Walsingham, in his natural anxiety to make a clean sweep of the culprits, either instructed or allowed Phelippes to add a postscript asking for 'the names and qualities of the six gentlemen' before the letter was sent on to its destination. He thus provided useful ammunition for all those partisans of Mary who were later to insist that she had been framed.

As it happened it was a waste of effort, for Babington never replied. Already events were slipping out of his precarious control and he contemplated flight. On 2 August Walsingham decided it would be dangerous to wait any longer and the arrests began. Babington himself was taken in the house of that same Mrs Bellamy who had once sheltered Father Parsons and been so suspicious of William Weston. By the end of September the fourteen known conspirators had been tried, condemned and executed amid heartfelt rejoicing on the part of the citizenry of London – rejoicing manifested by 'public bonfires, ringing of bells, feastings in the streets, singing of psalms and such like'. All that now remained was to ensure that the 'wicked murderess' herself, the 'bosom serpent', the 'monstrous and huge dragon' came to her just deserts. This, as no doubt Francis Walsingham and his colleagues had foreseen, proved a good deal easier said than done. It took, in fact, six months of concentrated hard work, with Elizabeth fighting a determined rearguard action throughout and trying everyone's patience to its limit.

'I would to God,' Walsingham was moved to lament at once point, 'her Majesty could be content to refer these things to them that can best judge of them, as other Princes do.'

Mary's trial finally came on at Fotheringay Castle in October before a panel of thirty-six distinguished commissioners, as provided by the Act for the Queen's Safety. She defended herself with courage, eloquence and dignity. She denied, as she was bound to do, all knowledge of the conspiracy but, in the face of Babington's evidence and that of her own secretaries (who had had no hesitation in betraying their mistress), quite apart from the other evidence so patiently amassed by Walsingham, her denials were regarded as no more than a matter of form. The commissioners would have proceeded to judgement, had they not been suddenly called back to London by royal command. There, in the Star Chamber, all the evidence was solemnly passed in review, Mary's two secretaries, Nau and Curle, were produced and repeated the statements they had previously given in writing. After this the assembled commissioners unanimously gave their sentence, finding the Queen of Scots 'not only accessory and privy to the conspiracy but also an imaginer and compasser of her Majesty's destruction'.

Two further formalities now had to be observed – the sentence must be publicly proclaimed, as laid down in the 1585 Act, and Elizabeth must sign the warrant for Mary's execution. Parliament had already been summoned, 'to make the burden better borne and the world abroad better satisfied', as Lord Burghley put it, and after two postponements the session opened on 29 October. It was an extraordinary session. All normal business went by the board while both Houses, united as seldom before and seldom since, combined to exert the last ounce of pressure on their obstinate sovereign lady. Elizabeth had won some notable battles of will with Parliament in the past and she could no doubt have won again – when she had made up her mind on a matter of principle she was immovable – but on this occasion her battle was with herself. It was not until the beginning of December that she finally agreed to have the sentence published under the Great Seal and once more bonfires were lit, bells rung and psalms (and most probably other things as well) sung in the streets of London. Another two months, though, had gone by before Elizabeth could bring herself to sign the warrant and the Queen of Scots went to her predestined end in the Great Hall at Fotheringay.

That Elizabeth's indecision and distress during this period were both genuine and agonising there need be no question. But her extreme, apparently perverse reluctance to authorise the execution of her deadliest enemy is, on the face of it, difficult to comprehend. So difficult, in fact, that some people have dismissed it as mere play-acting. Possibly there was some play-acting. Elizabeth always was a consummate actress, 'a princess who can act any part she pleases', and she knew she was presenting the Catholic world with a first-rate propaganda weapon.

'What will they not now say,' she exclaimed, 'when it shall be spread that for the safety of her life a maiden Queen could be content to spill the blood even of her own kinswoman?'

Elizabeth suffered from a most un-Tudor-like squeamishness when it came to spilling the blood of her kinsfolk, but it is not really likely that humanitarian considerations were weighing very heavily on her this time. Mary had been a nuisance and a source of anxiety for nearly thirty years. For nearly fifteen years she had been a source of ever-increasing danger both to England and to Elizabeth.

'I am not so void of judgement as not to see mine own peril,' the Queen had told Parliament in November, 'nor yet so ignorant as not to know it were in nature a foolish course to cherish a sword to cut mine own throat; nor so careless as not to weigh that my life daily is in hazard.'

All the same, if she could have found a way even then of keeping Mary alive, she would undoubtedly have done so. Once Mary was dead, Philip of Spain would have no excuse left for postponing the Enterprise. With Mary on the English throne, the Guise family would become all-powerful and their attitude to Spain was not likely to remain subservient; but once Mary was dead, Philip need have no qualms that he would be spending Spanish blood and Spanish gold to bring about the close Anglo-French alliance it had always been the cornerstone of his policy to avoid. To the Catholic King himself, to the Duke of Parma commanding a magnificent fighting instrument in the Netherlands, to Pope Sixtus in Rome, to the clamorous English expatriates all over Europe, it would then indeed appear 'God's obvious design' to bestow upon him the crowns of England and Scotland. Elizabeth, looking into a future dark with the threat of war and the terror of the unknown, had every reason to hesitate before she removed the cause of any lingering doubt in Philip's mind about the Almighty's intentions.

Probably, though, more than all the solid political considerations, more than her inherent dread of committing herself to any irrevocable course of action, more than any scruples of compassion for her cousin and sister queen, the aspect of Mary's end which upset Elizabeth most and lay beneath her irrational, hysterical reaction after the deed had been done, was the superstitious revulsion of one who has violated a sacred mystery. To the sixteenth-century mind there was something unutterably atrocious in the notion of subjecting God's anointed to earthly trial and judicial execution. To one of Elizabeth's background and temperament it was the ultimate tabu – hence her desperate, eleventh-hour attempt to shift the terrible responsibility onto the shoulders of men who had, after all, taken a solemn oath to pursue the 'pretended successor' unto death, once she had been found guilty by due process of the law.

The rights and wrongs of the Queen of Scots have been exhaustively rehearsed over the centuries – literally rivers of ink and forests of paper have been consumed in the process. But Elizabeth Tudor and Mary Stuart were trapped by history in a life-and-death struggle over which they had very little control – cousins fore-doomed to enmity by their blood and birth. It is, therefore, as futile to blame Elizabeth for her treatment of Mary as it is to blame Mary for her endless intrigues; to blame her for being the sort of woman she was – constitutionally incapable of ever seeing anyone's point of view but her own. That Mary had coveted Elizabeth's throne since the days when she quartered the English royal arms with her own is not really in question. Just how deeply she was involved in the plots to seize that throne by violence will no doubt always remain a matter of debate. But by 1586 Mary's guilt or innocence had long ceased to have any relevance. The mere fact of her existence was now intolerable and England quite simply could no longer hold the rival queen. Her presence had become a gangrenous sore which the nation must slough off or perish. This was the tragedy of Mary Stuart.

24

Epilogue: There is Only One Christ Jesus

'There is only one Christ Jesus and one faith: the rest is dispute about trifles.'
Elizabeth I, Queen of England

If the defeat of King Philip's invincible Armada proved to the satisfaction of Queen Elizabeth's subjects that God was an Englishman (as indeed they had always suspected), it also proved, to the relief of the other European nations, that he was not a Spaniard. Although the indecisive running battle in the Channel did not really prove anything else, this in itself was enough to take the heat out of the long struggle for power which had been fought in the freezing Flanders mud, on the waters of the Spanish main, in the fever-ridden swamps of Central America, and in manor houses hidden in the green depths of the English countryside. But to the English Catholics the heat and the heart had gone out of the fight sixteen months before the sails were sighted off the Lizard. They could have accepted and welcomed the peaceful accession of Mary Stuart with clear consciences, but no one except the extreme right-wing lunatic fringe would for a moment have accepted Philip of Spain – despite his descent from John of Gaunt. After 1587 the struggle became simply one for survival; a struggle to hand on the tiny, obstinate spark of faith to each succeeding generation until the memory of old wrongs and old fears had faded and Englishmen at last realised that the two creeds could live together side by side without threatening each other with extinction, or – to put it more brutally – until they realised that it is no longer mattered very much.

It is tempting and easy for a materialistic age to dismiss the whole conflict as a useless, sterile waste of time, but to do so is surely to miss the point entirely. The men and women of sixteenth-century England did not regard it as a waste of time. To them the reality of the living God was a vital part of their lives, even if many of them were content to keep him for Sundays and to worship him as the Establishment thought best. To us perhaps the worst aspect is the terrible, unnecessary human suffering, the waste of lives, the tragedy of a situation in which men who could have fulfilled themselves by rendering valuable services to the community were instead condemned to be butchered on the scaffold, to rot in prison or eat their hearts out in exile.

William Allen, who misunderstood the mood of his own countrymen so profoundly that he could issue a bitter personal attack on the Queen on the eve of the Armada, urging his fellow Catholics as they valued their immortal souls not to fight for 'an infamous, depraved, accursed, excommunicate heretic, the very shame of her sex and princely name; the chief spectacle of sin and abomination in this our age; and the only poison, calamity and destruction of our noble Church and Country', understood very well the nature of his own predicament. 'Thou knowest, good Lord,' he wrote, 'how often we have lamented together, that for our sins we should be constrained to spend either all, or most, of our serviceable years out of our natural country, to which they are most due, and to which in all ages past they should have been most grateful; and that our offices should be acceptable, and our lives and services agreeable to strangers, and not to our dearest at home.' But neither Allen and the other exiles, nor the victims of rope and knife and rack, ever for a moment believed their sorrows and torments were a waste.

Deeply as many individual Catholics suffered, it is as well to remember that it might all have been very much worse. All the seeds of religious hysteria were present, and if the Queen had for one moment relaxed her iron grip on the fanatical left-wing element, which was strong – especially in the eighties – in the House of Commons and within the Church of England itself, then there might well have been some very nasty scenes indeed. As it was, at no time, not even when a Catholic invasion fleet was in the Channel, within sight of the coast, were the English Catholics ever in danger of Protestant mob violence. In spite of a continual jeremiad that the Queen's fatal tendency to lenience, her wilful blindness to the full extent of the papist menace would certainly bring disaster upon her and upon the godly, Elizabeth continued to refuse to regard her subjects as Protestants and Catholics. To her they were all Englishmen, good, bad and indifferent. She was right, of course, and when the moment of crisis came, they rose to her as Englishmen, first, last and always. Perhaps the saddest irony of all is that when the defeat of the Sacred Enterprise was spread abroad the English students in the college at Rome cheered aloud at the news.

Of course it was all a tragic waste, but no one living in the twentyfirst century should need to be told that when man's aggressive instincts become sublimated in devotion to a cause, when passions become mixed with politics, the result is inevitably suffering, bloodshed and, above all else, waste. The pity of it is that more people could not have agreed with Queen Elizabeth when she remarked, 'There is only one Christ Jesus and one faith: the rest is dispute about trifles.'

Part Three

Marriage With My Kingdom

Yea, to satisfie you, I have already joyned my self in Marriage to an Husband, namely, the Kingdom of England. And behold (said she, which I marvell ye have forgotten,) the Pledge of this my Wedlock and Marriage with my Kingdom.

And therewith she drew the Ring from her Finger, and shewed it, wherewith at her Coronation she had in a set form words solemnly given her self in Marriage to her Kingdom.

William Camden, *Annals of the Reign of Queen Elizabeth*

PROLOGUE

On or about 28 August 1556 a young Englishman, with his hawk on his wrist, took a gondola out of Venice hoping to enjoy a day's sport among the islands. But the bad luck which had dogged Edward Courtenay, Earl of Devonshire, throughout his life pursued him even across the Venetian lagoon. A violent squall of wind and rain caught him on the tiny, shelterless island of Lio and the young man in his light summer clothes was quickly soaked to the skin. A gondola was useless in such conditions, and the Earl and his party were fortunate to be picked up by a Venetian naval craft cruising in the area.

Edward Courtenay was travelling abroad at his sovereign's command rather than his own inclination. He took no part in the social round of Venice, keeping himself resolutely to himself and admitting to his friendship only a small group of those gentlemen eager to make much of the romantic English milord. Five days after his adventure on the lagoon, which had brought on an attack of malaria, the Earl of Devonshire had a fall on the stairs of his house and decided to move to Padua. The University of Padua was famous for its medical school, and an invalid could expect to receive the most up-to-date treatment from the city's doctors.

Most people travelled the twenty-five miles from Venice by water, patronising horse-drawn barges which plied up and down the River Brenta. But Edward Courtenay, either from obstinacy or impatience, 'took the worst way and came by a certain waggons called coches' – a form of transport which, in the opinion of Peter Vannes, Queen Mary's agent in Venice, was 'very shaking and uneasy'. Vannes was himself temporarily resident in Padua to avoid the plague which reigned in Venice during the summer months. News of the Earl of Devonshire's arrival reached him late on Saturday night, and next morning he hastened to pay his respects to the distinguished visitor. Vannes found the Earl very weak and feverish after his uncomfortable journey, and although two of the best available physicians were summoned to his bedside his condition deteriorated rapidly. The last representative of the old royal house of England, whose grandmother had been a Plantagenet princess, lay alone in his lodgings, gripped by 'a continual great hot ague', nursed only by his servants, too ill to see anyone but Peter Vannes and the Italian doctors.

The end came on 18 September. Vannes reported that he believed the Earl of Devonshire had died a good Christian who could hope for God's mercy. He had listened meekly to spiritual exhortation, lifted up his eyes and knocked himself on the breast in token of repentance of his sins; but by this time 'his tongue had so stopt his mouth, and his teeth so cloven together', that he had been unable to receive the sacrament.[1]

Knowing that news of Edward Courtenay's death would come as a considerable relief to at least one European power and as a serious disappointment to another, Peter Vannes took the precaution of securing sworn statements from the Earl's servants, from the physicians who had attended him and the surgeons who had carried out the post-mortem examination that to the best of their knowledge he had died from natural causes.[2] Vannes was also saddled with the responsibility of making the funeral arrangements, which he hoped to contrive 'with as much sparing and as much honour as can be done'. In the event, there was more sparing than honour. Vannes was currently suffering from such an acute attack of penury – the chronic affliction of sixteenth-century ambassadors – that he described himself as being 'next door to going a-begging', and Mary Tudor proved unresponsive to suggestions that she should pay for the obsequies of a kinsman she had small reason to regret.[3]

Half a century later, an English tourist exploring St Anthony's Church in Padua was deeply shocked when a plain wooden coffin containing the mortal remains of Edward Courtenay, Earl of Devonshire, was pointed out to him stacked casually in the cloister and 'having neither epitaph nor any other thing to preserve it from oblivion.'[4] It was then five years since the House of Tudor had followed the House of Plantagenet off the stage, and the name of Edward Courtenay had long since been forgotten. Worthy Thomas Coryat, gazing on the sight of a noble Englishman so ignobly buried, was struck by compassion and remorse. He was not aware that he was also looking at the last resting-place of a man who, as the predestined bridegroom of Elizabeth Tudor, might so easily have altered the whole course of English history.

25

THE KING'S LAST DAUGHTER

When Anne Boleyn gave birth to a girl between the hours of three and four o'clock on the afternoon of Sunday, 7 September, 1533, Catholic Europe sniggered behind its hands over the devastating snub which Providence had dealt the King of England and his concubine. Messire Eustace Chapuys, the Holy Roman Emperor's ambassador at the Court of St James's, did not attempt to conceal his malicious amusement.[1]

Te Deum for Queen Anne's safe delivery was sung in St Paul's Cathedral in the presence of the Lord Mayor and Aldermen of the City of London, and the 'high and mighty Princess of England, Elizabeth', was given a splendid christening in the Friar's Church at Greenwich.[2] Over these proceedings, however, there hung a faint but palpable air of defiance. No amount of pompous ceremony and displays of official rejoicing could conceal the embarrassing fact that the flamboyantly masculine Henry VIII had once more failed to get a legitimate son. In his quest for a male heir, Henry had repudiated his blameless first wife and offended her influential relatives; he had challenged the Pope and resigned from the Church of Rome; he had ruthlessly manipulated the accepted laws of God and man to suit his own ends – and all he had got for his pains was another daughter.

In 1533 the break with Rome was not yet irrevocable. In July, Pope Clement had solemnly condemned the King's separation from Catherine of Aragon, denounced his second marriage and framed (but not published) a bull of excommunication.[3] In November, at a meeting with the Pope arranged under the auspices of the King of France, Henry's representatives made what seemed a deliberately provocative appeal against the threatened excommunication to a future General Council of the Church.[4] But still the way to reconciliation was not finally barred. For years now Clement had temporised and delayed in the matter of the King of England's divorce. If he could have devised some face-saving formula, he would, even at this eleventh hour, have used it thankfully. As for Henry, if he had been offered a settlement on his own terms, he might, even now, have accepted it. The King's position was not unlike that of a man who has quarrelled with the committee of his club and left to set up a rival establishment, but who, at the same time, cherishes a sneaking desire to be invited to return.

The invitation never came. On 23 March 1534 the Pope was finally forced to give a ruling on the divorce. Twenty-two cardinals in secret consistory pronounced in favour of Queen Catherine – declaring her marriage to be lawful and valid, and optimistically enjoining the King to take her back as his wife.[5] Later that year Parliament at Westminster passed the Act of Supremacy, 26 Henry VIII, recognising the King, his heirs and successors, without qualification, as 'the only supreme head in earth of the church of England', with all the 'honours, dignities, pre-eminences, jurisdictions, privileges, authorities, immunities, profits and commodities . . . belonging and appertaining'.[6] After this, nothing short of unconditional surrender by one party or the other could heal the breach between England and Rome.

The King's divorce, the Great Matter which had occupied Henry's thoughts and energies almost exclusively for the past seven years, had come to overshadow every aspect of English domestic and foreign policy, and had had the effect of forcing the country further and further into the arms of France. France might remain the ancestral enemy, Spain the traditional ally, the Netherlands – now a Spanish apanage – the trading partner on which England's economic prosperity depended; but unfortunately Charles V – ruler of Spain, Lord of the Netherlands, the Franche-Comte and Austria, King of Naples, Sicily and Sardinia, suzerain of the Habsburg fiefs in Germany and northern Italy, and Holy Roman Emperor – also happened to be the nephew of the discarded Queen of England. Charles, with the cares of half Europe on his shoulders, menaced by advancing Turkish hordes in the east, harassed by heresy in Germany and by French territorial ambitions in Italy, was naturally reluctant to add war with England to his problems. Common decency and the obligations of family honour compelled him to protest at the humiliation of his aunt, and to promote her cause by all the diplomatic means at his disposal. More than that he had not, so far, been prepared to do. At the same time, the Empire represented the greatest power-bloc in Europe and the Emperor could, if sufficiently provoked, make things very uncomfortable for the King of England. It had, therefore, seemed a necessary precaution to strengthen English ties with France. In 1532 a new defensive treaty was negotiated between the two countries and in September of that year the *entente cordiale* was sealed by a meeting between the two kings – Henry and François – at Boulogne.[7]

Their alliance was based on mutual self-interest. Henry needed a promise of French assistance in case of an Imperial attack. He also needed friends in Rome, especially since he had dispensed with the invaluable services of Cardinal Wolsey. François needed English support in his perennial feud with the Emperor – with English help he could close the Channel and cut sea-borne communications between Spain and the Netherlands. To embarrass Charles, he was prepared to side with Henry in his battle for the divorce, and French cardinals were instructed to use their influence at the Vatican on his behalf. The King of France was not, however, prepared to offend the Pope and certainly not, as Henry appears to have believed, to join England in schism. François needed papal backing for his Italian ploys and in 1533 acquired the Pope's niece, Catherine de Medici, as a daughter in law. He was, in fact, attempting to perform the increasingly difficult feat of running with the King of England while hunting with the Pope.

Then, in the autumn of 1534, Clement VII died, to be succeeded by Paul III. Though an Italian, the new Pope was said to be 'a good Frenchman'. He was also said to have been pro-Henry in the matter of the divorce and soon after his election began asking for advice on 'what means he should take to win back the King of England'.[8] François, always an optimist, began to hope that here might be an opportunity to realise his long-cherished ambition to weld England, the papacy and perhaps even the German Protestant states into a grand alliance directed against the hegemony of the Empire. In terms of practical politics this had never been a particularly realistic scheme, and in 1534 it was probably less so than ever, but the Emperor was sufficiently disturbed by the general trend of events to make some friendly overtures to François and to send the Count of Nassau on a special mission to France. The English government maintained an attitude of elaborate unconcern although, in the opinion of Eustace Chapuys, Nassau's visit was 'a flea in their ear'. English immunity from fears of Imperial vengeance depended largely on the continued animosity between France and the Empire, and Henry was haunted by a suspicion that François would not hesitate to stab his ally in the back any time it suited him.

It was common gossip that the Count of Nassau had come to discuss 'great affairs and marriages' with the King of France, but no one seemed to know any details. The details were, in fact, being carefully concealed, for Nassau had brought a top-secret proposition from Charles that François should suggest a match between Mary Tudor, Catherine of Aragon's only surviving child, and his own third son, the Duke of Angoulême. It was true that Mary had recently been bastardised and disinherited by Act of Parliament, but in the eyes of Rome, and therefore of all orthodox Catholics, she was still the legitimate English heiress. This was to be pointed out to François, together with a reminder of the various financial and political advantages to be gained by himself and his son, and a hint that if he co-operated with the Emperor, the thing could be carried through whether the King of England was willing or not. In other words, France and the Empire could jointly exert enough pressure on Henry to force him to restore his elder daughter to her proper place in the succession.[9]

Charles naturally took a close interest in his young cousin, who was currently being bullied and threatened by her father and step-mother, and made to yield precedence to her baby half-sister. The Emperor was not without human feelings and, besides, Mary was a potentially valuable weapon in his dynastic armoury. If the King of France could be induced to make an offer for her without revealing the Emperor's interest, it might kill three Imperial birds with one stone; it would divert François from further Italian adventures, drive a useful wedge into the Anglo-French alliance – Henry could scarcely miss the wounding implication that not even his closest ally recognised his do-it-yourself divorce – and might also provide an escape-hatch for Mary.

Unhappily for these amiable intentions, the only effect of Nassau's cautiously worded approach was to impress François with a sense of the Emperor's disquiet and to strengthen his hopes of being able to make a successful challenge. A few weeks after the Count's departure, a mission led by Philippe Chabot, sieur de Brion and Admiral of France, crossed the Channel for high-level talks in London. De Brion at once passed on Charles's suggestion of a French marriage for Mary – a suggestion which Henry had no hesitation in ascribing to the Emperor's malice and his intent to 'dissolve the amity' between François and himself. At the same time, the King resisted French proposals designed to involve him in the Habsburg–Valois vendetta. Instead, he put forward a proposal of his own. If François could obtain from Pope Paul a reversal of Clement's 'unjust and slanderous' verdict on the divorce, Henry would consider formally renouncing the title of King of France, still borne by the kings of England, and would also be willing to open negotiations for a marriage between the Princess Elizabeth and the Duke of Angoulême.[10] Thus the twelve-year-old duke achieved the distinction of becoming the first in a long line of Elizabeth Tudor's suitors and Elizabeth, at the age of fourteen months made her debut on the international political stage.

In spite of much outward cordiality, the French were disappointed by Henry's reluctance to be drawn into their net and by his evident determination not to give an inch in dealing with the Pope. According to Eustace Chapuys, de Brion left for home in a mood of disenchantment, and certainly his departure was followed by a somewhat ominous silence. Henry, who seems to have been expecting a prompt reply to his flattering offer, grew so impatient that de Morette, the resident French ambassador, began to avoid the Court, but it was not until the end of January 1535 that de Brion's secretary, Palamedes Gontier, returned to London to resume discussions. The King received him informally, leaning against a sideboard as Gontier opened the subject of the Angoulême marriage with a discreet enquiry about the prospective bride's exact legal status – a matter of some interest to her prospective father-in-law. François assumed that, having given Elizabeth the title of princess, Henry intended to assure it to her and treat her as his only heiress; but, said Gontier, his king felt that in the circumstances steps ought to be taken which would 'deprive lady Mary of any occasion or means of claiming the Crown'.[11]

Henry hastened to allay any French misgivings by explaining 'what had been done by Parliament' – that is, by the 1534 Act for the Establishment of the King's Succession. This was the Act which had ratified the divorce proceedings conducted under the aegis of Thomas Cranmer at Dunstable in May 1533. It declared Henry's marriage to Catherine of Aragon 'utterly void and annulled' and settled the succession on children born of the Anne Boleyn marriage, naming 'the Lady Elizabeth, now princess', as heiress presumptive. To make assurance doubly sure, it further laid down that the King's subjects were to 'make a corporal oath' to 'truly, firmly and constantly . . . observe, fulfil, maintain, defend and keep . . . the whole effects and contents of this present act' or incur the penalties of misprision of high treason.[12] This oath, Henry assured Gontier, had now been taken throughout the kingdom, adding pleasantly that everyone took Mary for the bastard she was. Elizabeth had been quickly proclaimed his sole heiress and there was no question of Mary ever becoming Queen or claiming any right to the crown. He went on to point out that, if François would only persuade the Pope to agree that his first marriage was null and void, all doubts would cease.[13] This was not strictly true, for the French had already been taking legal advice as to whether or not Mary could still be considered legitimate, even if her parents' marriage *was* invalid.[14]

Palamedes Gontier did not, however, feel it necessary to mention this to Henry, but turned instead to financial matters, indicating that the King of France would be obliged if the annual pensions being paid to England under the terms of the Treaty of Amiens were remitted as part of Elizabeth's dowry. The King of England 'took this ill'. Considering that he had, of his own accord, offered the heiress of a kingdom 'of most certain title, without remainder of querel to the contrary', to a younger son, all the obligation was on the French side and 'they ought rather to give him something than ask'. Such looking of a gift horse in the mouth, together with the long delay in giving him an answer, made him think 'there was a practice going on elsewhere'.[15]

Having got over these preliminary skirmishes, Gontier was passed on to the King's advisers, and during the month he spent in England the rough draft of a marriage treaty was drawn up and arrangements made for a further meeting between the representatives of both sides to be held at Calais at Whitsun, so that the Bishop of Faenza, papal nuncio in France, thought the matter could reasonably be expected to take effect.[16]

But, unknown to the Bishop, some devious cross-currents were moving beneath the surface. Thomas Cromwell, the King of England's hard-headed secretary and man of business, placed little long-term reliance on the French connection. Cromwell, who had already set in train the complicated administrative machinery for nationalising the resources of the Catholic Church in England, knew there was not going to be any accommodation with the Pope, that, in fact, the open hostility of the Pope could not be long delayed. He also knew that France, a Continental power with important interests in Italy, would never break her ties with Rome and that, if it came to a showdown, England could not rely on her support. By far the most logical alliance for England was still with the Emperor, and Cromwell, unhampered by illusions, ideals or old-fashioned notions of honour and filial piety, found it hard to credit that Charles could seriously mean to go on denying himself the obvious advantages of English friendship just for the sake of a surely expendable aunt and cousin. As early as February 1535, Master Secretary was remarking to Eustace Chapuys that it would be better to be talking of a marriage between the Spanish prince – the Emperor's eight-year-old son Philip – and the King's last daughter.[17] This unlikely suggestion was apparently intended as a joke, and the ambassador took it as such, but a month later Cromwell brought the subject up again – only to drop it hastily at the sight of Chapuys' frosty expression, saying wistfully that he suspected the Emperor would not hear of it out of respect for his cousin.[18]

Meanwhile, negotiations with France continued. The Calais meeting duly took place at the end of May, but ended in stalemate. The English commissioners, headed by the Duke of Norfolk, had been instructed to press their opposite numbers to agree that young Angoulême should come to England immediately to complete his education, although the formal betrothal would not be solemnised until Elizabeth was seven years old.[19] The French, not unnaturally, jibbed at the idea of parting with their bridegroom before the bride was of full marriageable age and, according to the Bishop of Faenza, François refused disdainfully to send his son to be a hostage in England.[20] But this was a negotiable point, and the rock on which the talks foundered seems to have been Henry's 'exorbitant demand' that François should make a public declaration binding himself to uphold the validity of the Anne Boleyn marriage against all comers.[21] The King of France was quite prepared to do his best to persuade the Pope to re-open the King of England's case with a view to revoking Clement's 'false and unreasonable' judgement on the divorce;[22] for such a revocation would not only place Henry under a heavy obligation to France but, more important, would also go a long way towards realising her king's dreams of detaching the papacy from its dependence on the Empire. But François could only move through conventional channels. He neither could nor would reject or even question the Pope's right of jurisdiction in matters of Canon Law. By July, therefore, the Angoulême marriage negotiations had petered out and the Anglo-French *entente* was showing distinct signs of strain.[23]

Fortunately for Henry, developments in Italy in the autumn of 1535 portended the imminent renewal of Franco-Imperial hostilities and considerably increased his opportunities for engaging in the exhilarating diplomatic sport of playing one great power off against the other. In October, Cromwell was telling Chapuys about attempts by certain 'malicious

1. Elizabeth I in her Coronation robes, 15 January 1559, by an unknown artist
(National Portrait Gallery, London)

GRANDPARENTS

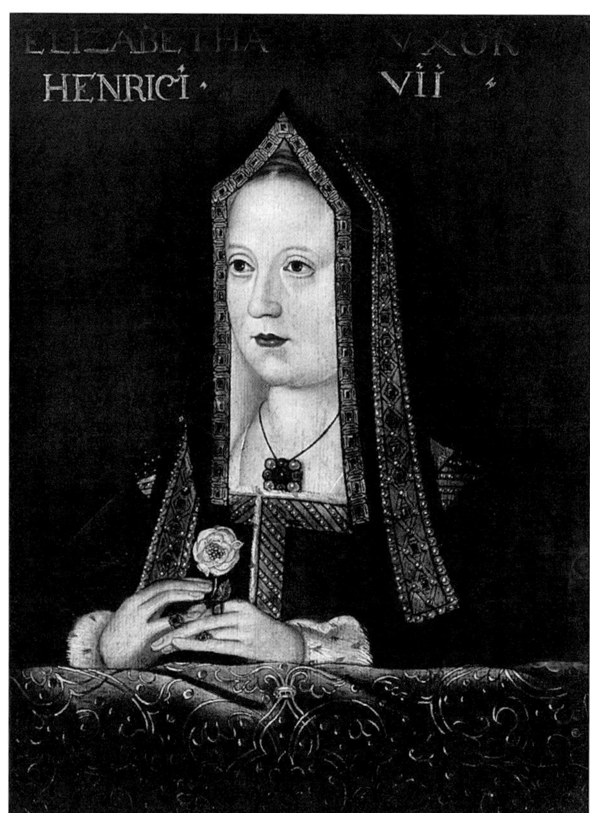

2. Elizabeth of York by an unknown artist *(National Portrait Gallery, London)*

3. Henry VII's tomb effigy by Pietro Torrigiano *(Westminster Abbey, London/Bridgeman Art Library)*

4. Anne Boleyn, a drawing by Holbein *(c. The British Museum)*

5. Henry VIII by Joos van Cleeve *(The Royal Collection c. 2004 Her Majesty the Queen)*

6. Edward VI, portrait by an unknown artist *(The Royal Collection c. 2004 Her Majesty the Queen)*

7. Mary I, 1544, a portrait by Master John *(National Portrait Gallery, London)*

8. The Lord Admiral, Thomas Seymour
(National Portrait Gallery, London)

9. The Old Manor at Chelsea
(c. The Guildhall Library)

10. The Old Palace, Hatfield
(from the Illustrated London News, *1846).*

11. Mary Queen of Scots; artist unknown *(Victoria and Albert Museum, London)*

12 William Allen S.J. (from 'Lodge's British Portraits', 1823 (engraving), English School, (19th century) / Private Collection (Ken Welsh / www.bridgeman.co.uk)

13. Robert Parsons S.J. by an unknown artist *(National Portrait Gallery, London)*

14. Father and son Lord Burghley and Robert Cecil
(By courtesy of the Marquess of Salisbury)

15. Francis Walsingham, The Principle Secretary of State (*National Portrait Gallery, London)*

16. Philip II of Spain *(Kunsthistorisches Museum, Vienna)*

17. William of Orange (the Silent) (1533-84) Stadholder of the Netherlands, 1555-56 (oil on canvas), Moro, Giacomo Antonio (c.1519-c.1576) / (Gemaldegalerie, Kassel, Germany, Lauros / Giraudon / Bridgeman Art Library / www.bridgeman.co.uk)

18. Robert Dudley, Earl of Leicester; artist unknown *(National Portrait Gallery, London)*

19. Eric XIV of Sweden *(Mary Evans Picture Library)*

20. Archduke Charles von Hapsburg of Austria *(Mary Evans Picture Library)*

21. Henry of Anjou *(Mary Evans Picture Library)*

22. François, Duke of Alençon (Elizabeth's Frog) *(Mary Evans Picture Library)*

23. Robert Devereaux, Second Earl of Essex in a portrait by Marcus Gheeraerts the younger around 1597 *(National Portrait Gallery, London)*

24. Elizabeth I, Armada portrait, c.1588 (oil on panel), English School, (16th century)
(Private Collection, / www.bridgeman.co.uk)

25. Queen Elizabeth I (1533-1603) being carried in Procession, c.1600 (oil on canvas), Peake, Robert (fl.1580-1626) (attr. to) / Private Collection, / www.bridgeman.co.uk)

26. Sir Robert Cecil, 1st Earl of Salisbury by John De Critz *(National Portrait Gallery, London)*

27. Portrait of Sir Walter Raleigh, Anonymous *(National Portrait Gallery of Ireland, Dublin, Ireland, / www.bridgeman.co.uk)*

28. Sir Francis Drake by Jodocus Hondius *(National Portrait Gallery, London)*

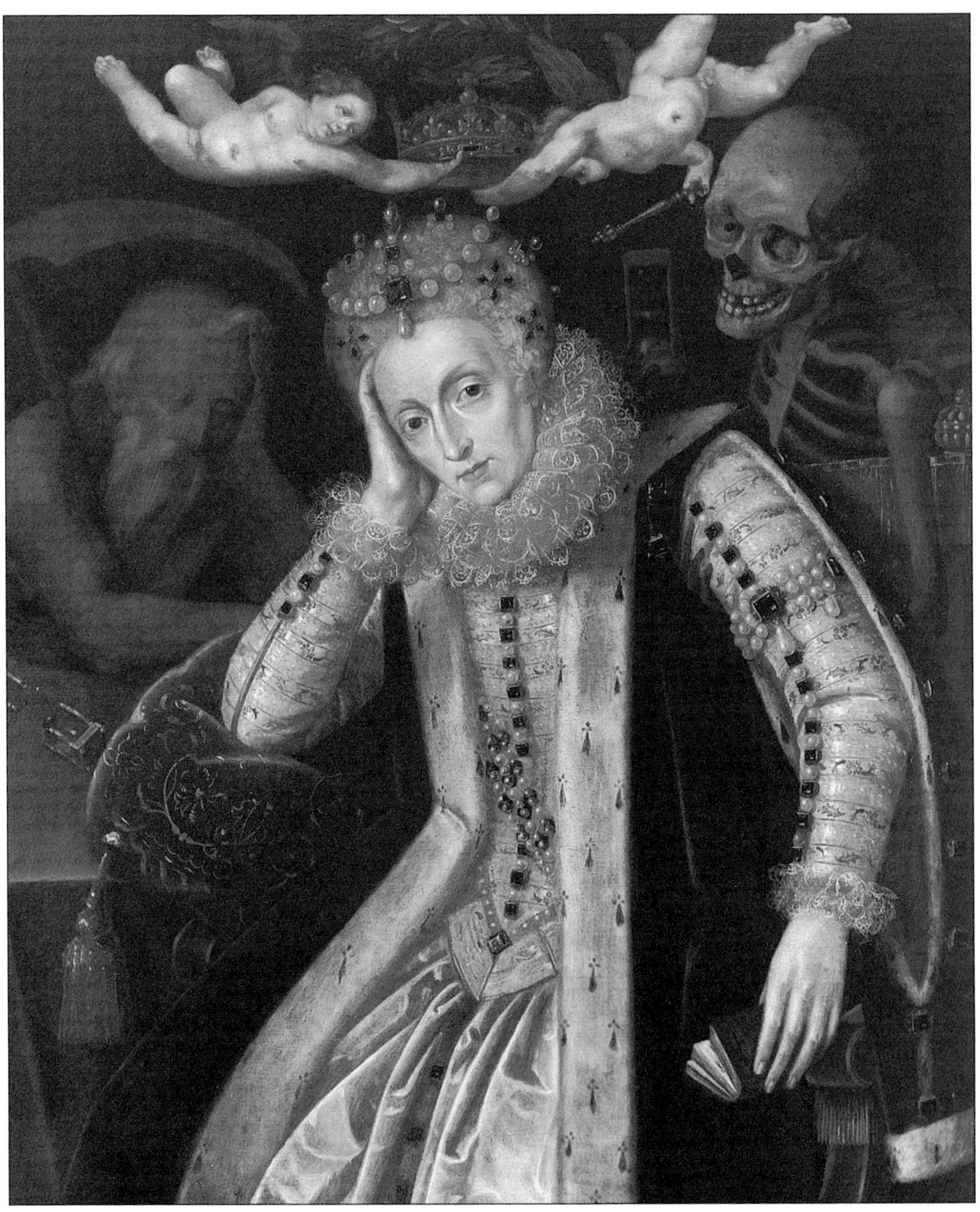

29. 'Elizabeth I with Time and Death' by an unknown artist
(Methuen Collection, Corsham Court: photograph Courtauld Institute of Art)

and badly-intentioned parties' to make mischief between their respective masters, and that Henry was thinking of sending 'a very great and most honourable embassy' to the Emperor to discuss a renewal of their old friendship and confederacy.[24] Cromwell had also reverted to his idea of an alliance cemented by the marriage of Elizabeth and the Prince of Spain, working the subject into conversation with elaborate casualness and always making the suggestion timidly, 'like one offering a coin to an elephant'.[25]

During the Christmas holidays Chapuys had a long audience with the King, who walked the ambassador up and down with an arm round his neck explaining how invaluable English support would be to the Emperor should war break out again in Italy. But, Henry went on, if Charles did not soon respond to his overtures, he would be obliged to listen to the French, who were overwhelming him with the most flattering offers.[26] When Chapuys tried to pin him down, saying that all the time he and Cromwell had been discussing the possibility of a new understanding no tangible proposal had been made, Henry himself spoke of the marriage of his 'little daughter'. Although Chapuys was too old a hand not to see through Henry's game, and found the thought of a marriage between the English king's bastard and the Holy Roman Emperor's heir almost too preposterous to be mentioned, he nevertheless told his master that perhaps the proposal should not be rejected out of hand, in case England was driven back irretrievably into the French orbit.[27]

During the first half of 1536 the situation on both the international and the domestic fronts underwent a radical change. By the spring a French army had invaded northern Italy, and the Emperor had less time than ever to spare for England. In any case, the chief personal bones of contention between Henry and himself were now beginning to disappear. Catherine of Aragon died in January and, on 2 May, Anne Boleyn was arrested and taken to the Tower. A fortnight later she was arraigned before a commission of lords on a charge of treason against the King's own person. The result of the trial was, of course, a foregone conclusion and Anne was beheaded on Tower Green at eight o'clock in the morning of Friday, 19 May, 'when she had reigned as Queen three years, lacking fourteen days, from her coronation to her death'. But Henry was not content with merely killing the woman for whom he had so recently been prepared to turn the world upside down. Two days before her execution, 'at a solemn court kept at Lambeth by the Lord Archbishop of Canterbury and the doctors of the law, the King was divorced from his wife Queen Anne . . . and so she was discharged and was never lawful Queen of England'.[28]

The dissolution of the King's second marriage necessitated a second Act of Succession, passed in the summer of 1536, by which Parliament once again ratified a decision by Thomas Cranmer on Henry's matrimonial affairs and once again bastardised and disabled his heiress. The two-year-old Elizabeth thus joined her half-sister in social limbo, the natural consequence being a drastic reduction of her value in that area where sixteenth-century princesses were alone considered to be of value – the international marriage-market.

Such wholesale dissipation of his potential assets worried the King's more frugal advisers, and in the spring of 1537 an *aide-mémoire* drawn up for a council meeting noted that: 'The King has two daughters, not lawful, yet king's daughters, and as princes commonly conclude amity and things of importance by alliance, it is thought necessary that these two daughters shall be made of some estimation, without which no man will have any great respect to them'. As Mary, now twenty-one, would be 'more apt to make a present alliance', it was suggested that the King should either legitimise her or else 'advance her to some certain living decent for such an estate, whereby she may be the better had in reputation'. A similar course could then be taken with regard to Elizabeth and in this way Henry might, by means of his elder daughter, 'provide himself of a present friend and have the other in store hereafter to get another friend'.[29]

Needless to say, no part of this ingenuous plan was ever carried out. It was probably never even discussed. The legitimacy or otherwise of the princesses was a touchy subject at the best of times, but especially so just then in the aftermath of the Pilgrimage of Grace. That October, Queen Jane Seymour succeeded (though it killed her) in presenting the King with a male heir unquestionably born in wedlock, but Henry continued to adopt an uncompromising take-it-or-leave-it attitude towards his daughters' suitors. In any case, now that he was a widower again, he had a far more tempting piece of merchandise to offer and at once embarked on an extensive programme of consumer research.

Although there is a strong flavour of *opéra bouffe* about the King of England's heavy-footed pursuit of love round the courts of Europe during the years 1538 and 1539 – a pursuit which finally netted the despised Anne of Cleves – his underlying purpose was serious enough. The King of France and the Emperor, both at least temporarily exhausted by their increasingly pointless and increasingly expensive hostility, were showing definite signs of coming to an understanding. Such an understanding might well lead to England's isolation; at a time of domestic unrest, ominously linked with the names of certain surviving members of the old royal house, it might well lead to something worse. Dread of the Catholic powers combining to attack the heretic island under colour of a papal crusade, in the expectation of internal support as well as of rich pickings for themselves, first became acute in the late 1530s and influenced English foreign policy for the rest of the century. Henry's marriage-mongering was therefore designed primarily to prevent a new alignment of the great powers or, failing that, to prevent his exclusion from any new Continental alignment.[30]

With this end in view, either a French or an Imperialist bride would do equally well, and the King's first choice fell on a Frenchwoman, the widowed Mary of Guise. But, when the lady was irritatingly snapped up by James of Scotland, Henry turned his attention to the Emperor's niece, the young Duchess of Milan – and certainly the far-reaching Habsburg family provided greater scope for the multiple marriage-schemes he now began to evolve.

The first suggestion was for a double wedding – Henry to the Duchess of Milan and Mary to Dom Luis of Portugal. This idea was presently expanded to include the other two Tudor children, Prince Edward being offered to the Emperor's daughter and Elizabeth either to one of his nephews, sons of the Kings of Hungary, or alternatively to a son of the Duke of Savoy.[31] Charles von Habsburg and Emmanuel Philibert, Prince of Piedmont, were later to become familiar figures in the Elizabethan matrimonial scene, but in 1538 not even Henry could expect his younger daughter – bastard of a notorious adulteress – to be in much request among foreign royalty in search of eligible brides, and by October he was lumping Elizabeth together with his niece, Margaret Douglas, and Mary Howard, widow of his base-born son, in a special bargain offer – all three girls to be bestowed by the Emperor's advice 'upon such of the princes of Italy as shall be thought convenient'.[32]

Just how seriously Henry took schemes of this nature is hard to say, but in any case he was, as usual, asking too high a price for his goods. He had not been able to prevent Charles and François from signing a ten-year truce in the summer of 1538 and, predictably, neither monarch was now so interested in an English alliance. In 1539 the international situation became so threatening that Henry was forced to look for friends among the non-aligned German Lutheran princes, and by the end of the year found himself trapped in his distasteful fourth marriage.

But the crisis was short-lived. Cracks soon began to appear in the papering-over of Habsburg–Valois animosity, and by the beginning of 1541 France and the Empire were at loggerheads once more, thus once more opening up England's freedom of diplomatic manoeuvre. Since there were no longer any personal obstacles in the way of an Anglo-Imperial alliance and since, for both economic and sentimental reasons, English public opinion favoured the Emperor, France was now obliged to make the running if she wanted to avoid being left out in the cold. In June, therefore, François instructed his ambassador to assure the Duke of Norfolk that he had 'no greater desire than to live in perpetual amity with England'. If Norfolk showed any disposition to enquire how this amiable intention might be furthered, Charles de Marillac was to reply that he had heard that when the Duke was last in Calais 'some question of marriages' had been under discussion, and that these were the surest bonds to strengthen amity between princes. He could then add – quite casually, of course – that the King of England had a daughter, 'her who is held legitimate', and François a son, M. d'Orléans, to whom he intended to give the Duchy of Milan, and that this would be one of the greatest matches in Christendom 'by means of which great things could be accomplished both for France and England'. Marillac was to suggest that Norfolk might care to think the matter over, while at the same time being careful to maintain the convention that it was all his own idea, and one that he would not like his master to know he had even mentioned.[33]

There were two flaws in this interesting scheme, one being that François was under the mistaken impression that Elizabeth was still regarded as legitimate by the English. The other concerned the Duchy of Milan, the rival claims to which constituted one of the chief bones of contention between François and Charles. France plus Milan plus England would certainly have formed a powerful combination, but unfortunately Milan was currently firmly in the Emperor's possession. Another snag was the fact that M. d'Orléans was already married. But since his wife, Catherine de Medici, had so far proved barren there was talk of divorcing her.

It was August before the Duke of Norfolk gave the French ambassador his cue to broach the subject of the Orléans marriage and appeared so receptive to an initial approach that Marillac felt justified in asking how it could best be arranged and which of King Henry's daughters should be proposed for the honour. Although Mary was better qualified by age and seniority, no French prince – and especially not Henri d'Orléans, who was François' eldest surviving son and his heir – could ever marry a bastard, so perhaps it might be better to choose the younger sister in spite of her regrettable maternity. The Duke's reaction was immediate and for that reason, thought Marillac, unfeigned. The younger of the two was not to be spoken of, he said roundly. For one thing she was only seven years old, and her mother's reputation was such that 'it was quite decided to consider her illegitimate, as the Act of Parliament declared'. In any case, Norfolk refused to become involved. Anne Boleyn had been his niece and, if he attempted to advance Elizabeth's cause, he would be laying himself open to accusations of 'seeking to aggrandise his own house'.[34]

Such sensitivity seems a little curious in a man who had recently married another of his nieces to the King, but Norfolk was not, as he hastened to assure Marillac, opposed to a French alliance in principle. The Lady Mary was available, and the Duke readily undertook 'to forward matters so that a good end might be expected'.[35] Negotiations did, in fact, begin and dragged on for several months – always to be frustrated by Henry's rigid insistence on the immutable nature of Mary's illegitimacy. Not even by implication would he allow the annulment of his first marriage to be questioned.

Meanwhile the King was busy angling for an alliance with the Emperor, and in 1542 Elizabeth's name was again briefly linked with the Prince of

Piedmont. Eustace Chapuys saw on objection to this. Such a connection, he thought, would help to detach England from France.[36] But the whole tide of events during the 1540s was taking England away from France, and an Anglo-Imperial treaty was concluded in February 1543. It was not, however, to be sealed by a marriage. Henry, it appeared, did not intend actually to part with his daughters if he could help it; they were too useful to him as bargaining-counters in the endless horse-trading of dynastic diplomacy, as bribes to be dangled in front of recalcitrant allies.

Mary, now in her mid-twenties, her youth slipping emptily away, had already realised that as long as her father lived 'there would be nothing to be got but fine words', and was bitterly resigned to being only the Lady Mary, 'the most unhappy lady in Christendom'.[37] Elizabeth, at nine years old and not yet understanding all the bleak implications of a spinster's fate, was old enough and intelligent enough to have begun to observe the developing pattern of her sister's life and her own. A sixteenth-century princess was conditioned to expect an arranged marriage at an early age, to serve her country's interests abroad with her own body. There was nothing new or remarkable about that. But to see herself being cynically hawked in the market-place without serious intention was another matter. It was not playing fair. If Elizabeth did indeed say to Robert Dudley about this time 'I will never marry', it may have been a child's statement of simple fact rather than of intent.

In 1543, Henry's younger daughter was once again featured in the shop-window as the centre of political interest moved to Scotland, where a crisis situation had been building up over the past two years. Scottish friendship with France, dating back to the early fourteenth century, had always been a source of inconvenience and sometimes danger to her southern neighbour. Henry VIII had hoped to break the 'auld alliance' by marrying his daughter Margaret to King James IV, but even this did not prevent James in 1513 from adhering to the time-honoured custom of attacking through England's back door while English forces were engaged across the Channel.

At the beginning of the 1540s it looked as if the bloody lesson of Flodden Field had been lost on Margaret Tudor's son. As he grew to manhood James V turned his face obstinately towards France, choosing first one French wife and then another. Influenced by the powerfully pro-French Cardinal Beaton, he snubbed his English uncle's friendly overtures and rejected the anti-papal propaganda disseminated by Henry. Scotland remained a Catholic country, potentially if not actually hostile – a state of affairs made more than ordinarily explosive by the fact that the King of Scots stood very close to the English throne. The King of England was no longer a young man, and his health had begun to deteriorate. Prince Edward was still little more than a baby, and Henry had himself removed his daughters from the succession. If he could not soon separate James from his foreign friends and secure the vulnerable land-frontier, the danger from possible future consequences scarcely needed spelling out. In 1541 border incidents were already proliferating, and by the autumn of 1542 England and Scotland were at war.

Within a matter of weeks a dramatic series of events had changed the situation out of all recognition. The Scots had suffered total and humiliating defeat at Solway Moss, the melancholic James had turned his face to the wall and died, and a week-old baby girl had succeeded to the Scottish throne. Now, if ever, was the time for a bold stroke of dynastic diplomacy. A marriage between the five-year-old heir to the English throne and the infant Mary Queen of Scots would unite the two countries with England as the dominant partner and certainly seemed to offer the best chance of a permanent solution to the whole intractable problem of Anglo-Scottish relations. 'I would she and her nurse were in my lord Prince's house,' remarked one Englishman less than a fortnight after Mary's birth.

To begin with, at least, the omens looked favourable. The Scots were ready to make peace, the Franco-Catholic party had fallen into disarray, and in January 1543 the Scottish Council named James Hamilton, Earl of Arran, as regent or governor. Arran was generally considered to be well disposed towards England, but the Hamiltons were themselves of royal Stuart blood; Arran was, in fact, the heir presumptive, and it was known that he had hoped to marry the little Queen to his own son. It would, therefore, be necessary to offer him a consolation prize and, in April, Sir Ralph Sadler, the English diplomat sent by Henry to handle negotiations in Edinburgh, was instructed to tell him that the King had a daughter called the Lady Elizabeth 'endowed with virtues and qualities agreeable with her estate'. If Arran proved sincere in his friendship, Henry meant to condescend to her marriage with his son, and would 'bring up and nourish his said son' as a son-in-law at the English court.[38]

When these tidings were conveyed to him, reported Sadler, 'the Governor understanding the great honour your Majesty did offer unto him in that behalf, put off his cap and said, "he was most bound of all men unto your Majesty, in that it pleased the same, being a prince of so great reputation in the world, to offer such alliance and marriage with so poor a man as he is, for the which he should bear his heart and service to your Majesty next unto his sovereign lady during his life".'[39] Three days later Arran told Sadler that he would willingly 'accept and embrace' Henry's proposal, and on 6 May he sent the Earl of Glencarne and Sir George Douglas to London with instructions 'humbly to desire the King to accomplish the contract of marriage betwixt the Lady Elizabeth and James Lord Hamilton, son and heir apparent to us, James Earl of Arran, governor and second person of Scotland; not doubting but the King shall provide for the said lady and her part according to the state of such a princess'.[40]

Meanwhile, progress towards accomplishing the other and more important Scottish marriage-contract was less satisfactory for, with his customary insensitivity, Henry had presented a shopping-list of demands calculated to confirm the worst fears of a nation notoriously touchy and suspicious of English intentions. Although the treaty finally signed at Greenwich in July met the Scots rather more than half-way, the damage had been done and the pro-French faction led by Cardinal Beaton and the Queen-Dowager, Mary of Guise, was rapidly regaining its former ascendancy. Arran continued to feed Sadler with fair words, but he was not a strong character and his position had become untenable. In September, to Henry's unspeakable disgust, he threw in his lot with the Cardinal and a rare opportunity for creating a peaceful and united Great Britain had vanished into the northern mist.

The King of England spent most of the next eighteen months trying to win by fire and sword what he had failed to achieve at the conference table. In the spring of 1544 he sent the Earl of Hertford on a punitive expedition to Scotland and that summer embarked on a war with France which, although undertaken in conjunction with the Emperor, was chiefly designed to cut the Scots off from their Continental allies.

The capture on 14 September of the strategic port of Boulogne by the English army went some way towards gaining this objective by cutting the short sea-route to Edinburgh. Henry had personally superintended the siege of Boulogne, and its fall gave him a good deal of simple pleasure. To the French it was a serious loss which they immediately exerted their best efforts to recover. As early as October, Cardinal du Bellay was suggesting to William Paget that Henry might care to give his younger daughter to 'some Prince of France' together with Boulogne, and François might afterwards exchange other lands in France for it. Unsurprisingly Paget was not impressed by this hopeful plan. It would, he remarked, be a great dowry and offer no compensation for the cost of winning it.[41]

Henry clung to Boulogne, but by the beginning of 1545 found himself uncomfortably short of friends. He had fallen out with his Imperial ally and, since France and the Empire had made a separate peace, François would now be in a position to concentrate all his forces against England. Henry, therefore, turned once more to Germany, sending his unofficial envoy, Christopher Mundt, on a visit to the Landgrave of Hesse with instructions to propose an offensive and defensive alliance with the Protestant League. Mundt, and Walter Buckler who went with him, were to say that the King was surprised that none of the German princes had so far sought 'to enter with us by marriage or otherwise'. They were 'to set forth the qualities' of the King's two daughters – either of whom would, of course, be a catch 'for a prince of the greatest honour' – and suggest the King of Denmark's brother as a possible bridegroom.[42]

The King of Denmark, when this flattering offer was relayed to him, was polite but not notably enthusiastic – the Protestant League had problems enough of its own at that particular moment – and Henry, facing the prospect of a French counter-offensive, was obliged to mend his fences with the Emperor. All the old triple-marriage proposals were trotted out again – Mary to the Emperor himself, Prince Edward to the Emperor's daughter and Elizabeth to Philip of Spain. Elizabeth's claims in particular were pressed when Henry got wind of 'a practice in hand' for a French marriage for Philip.[43]

After a period of intense diplomatic activity the Anglo-Imperial *entente* was patched up, but no betrothals followed. The Emperor, who was just then gathering his forces for an onslaught on German Protestantism, seemed unaccountably uninterested in welcoming the Tudors into the great Habsburg clan, and when Henry died in January 1547 he left his daughters unsought, unpromised and fancy-free – their future a matter for speculation.

26

THE NOBLEST MAN UNMARRIED IN THIS LAND

Elizabeth Tudor was rising thirteen and a half when her father died. The portrait painted by an unknown artist some time between 1542 and 1547 shows a pale flat-chested girl in a red dress. Her carroty-coloured hair is parted in the middle and tucked smoothly under a French hood. Her eyes, dark and watchful in the immature but unmistakable Tudor countenance, give nothing away. She holds a book in her incredibly long fingers. Beside her another book lies propped open on a reading-stand. She looks the very image of the studious young lady whose 'maiden shamefastness' was considered so praiseworthy by sober Protestant divines like John Aylmer. She looks, in fact, as if butter wouldn't melt in her mouth.

Until 1547, Elizabeth's life had been spent almost entirely in one or other of the royal manor-houses which lay in a rough semi-circle to the north of London, sometimes sharing an establishment with her elder sister, sometimes with her brother. Apart from those infrequent occasions when she was summoned to court to play her part with the rest of the royal family in some state function, she had lived quietly in the country, working at her lessons, aware of the great world which lay on the periphery of her existence but not yet personally involved in it. Now all this was to be changed. The year 1547 marked the end of childhood – the beginning of a long life spent at the epicentre of the great world.

Henry had left his daughters in a peculiar constitutional position. Both remained bastards by Act of Parliament but, bastards or not, both had now been restored to their places in the succession. In 1536, Parliament had granted the King power to bequeath the crown by will in order to meet the then very real possibility that he might die without any legitimate heirs at all. The birth of Prince Edward had relieved the worst of this anxiety, but in 1544 the situation was still sufficiently uncertain to make a third Act of Succession seem a necessary precaution. In the event of Edward's death without heirs, and failing any further heirs born of the King's sixth marriage, this Act settled the succession first on Mary and then Elizabeth, subject to conditions to be laid down in their father's will or by his letters patent. In his will, a complicated and much discussed document, Henry confirmed his daughters' rights to the reversion of the crown on condition that neither of them married without 'the written and sealed consent' of a majority of the surviving members of the Privy Council appointed by the same will to rule during Edward's minority. If either Mary or Elizabeth failed to observe this condition, she would forfeit her chance of succeeding.[1]

Looked at from a personal point of view, both sisters were left in a peculiarly uncomfortable position – both were orphaned and unmarried in a society where the Law, with few exceptions, regarded women as the extension of either husband or father; both were shadowed by the reproach of bastardy and yet both, by reason of their royal blood and their father's will, might well become objects of dangerous interest to practitioners of the sort of cut-throat politics likely to prevail in a country suddenly bereft of strong leadership.

Of the two princesses, Elizabeth was the most vulnerable. Mary was at least an adult, with an adult's experience and capacity for judgement. Elizabeth, at thirteen, was still a child, although in the eyes of the Law she had reached maturity and was of full marriageable age. Unlike her sister, she had no relatives, either at home or abroad, with the power to exert themselves on her behalf. The Boleyn family had disappeared as completely as if it had never been, and Elizabeth's noble kinsfolk, the Howards, were in eclipse – the Duke of Norfolk being in the Tower under sentence of death. Her natural protector, of course, was her brother, but at nine years old King Edward could scarcely be expected to provide much in the way of support. For the time being, at any rate, effective power over the government, over the King and the King's sisters lay in the hands of the King's maternal uncle, Edward Seymour, Earl of Hertford, now created Duke of Somerset.

The question of Elizabeth's immediate future had been settled by the beginning of March 1547 when François van der Delft, the current Imperial ambassador, reported from London that the Queen-Dowager was shortly going to reside in the suburbs with Madam Elizabeth, daughter of the late King. Madam Elizabeth, he added, would remain always in the Queen's company.[2] On the face of it, this seemed a sensible and humane arrangement. The Queen-Dowager was the obvious person to take charge of the King's sister and Katherine Parr, in many ways the most sympathetic of Henry's wives, had already proved herself a conscientious and affectionate step-mother. The household she established in the cheerful, modern, red-brick mansion overlooking the Thames at Chelsea was joined by nine-year-old Jane Grey, eldest of King Henry's English great-nieces, as well as by Elizabeth and offered all the facilities of an exclusive boarding-school. No one could reasonably have forseen the danger that was to intrude itself into these decorous surroundings.

Trouble, inevitably in the circumstances, came in masculine shape. The Queen Dowager was serious-minded and pious, an active patron of the

New Learning and advanced Protestant thinkers. But, for all that, Katherine was no prig. She had already been obliged to nurse more than one elderly husband. Now, in her mid-thirties and still a very pretty woman, she considered she had earned the right to a little personal happiness, and some time in the late spring of 1547 she married Thomas Seymour, younger brother of the Duke of Somerset and another of King Edward's maternal uncles.

The newly wedded pair were old friends. Thomas had in fact been courting Katherine at the time when King Henry's eye was attracted by the charming Lady Latymer – a development which brought their relationship to an abrupt conclusion. As Lady Latymer, Katherine Parr had been a rich and desirable widow. As Queen-Dowager, she was even richer and still more desirable – a first-rate matrimonial prize for any younger son, even if he did happen to be the King's uncle. Nevertheless, a rumour soon got round that Thomas Seymour, always more noted for optimism than common sense, would have preferred one of King Henry's daughters to King Henry's widow. Elizabeth's governess, Katherine Ashley, falling into conversation with the bridegroom in the park at St James's, remarked that she had 'heard one say that he should have married my lady'. 'Nay', answered Thomas, 'I love not to lose my life for a wife. It has been spoken of, but that can never be. But', he went on, 'I will promise to have the Queen'. 'It is past promise,' said Mrs Ashley, who had evidently been keeping an ear to the ground, 'as I hear you are married already.'[3]

Thomas Seymour had been named as an assistant executor of Henry's will, which gave him a seat on the Council. He had now been elevated to the peerage as Baron Seymour of Sudeley and presented with the office of Lord High Admiral, but he was very far from satisfied. It seemed to him the height of injustice that one brother should rule the country in vice-regal state, enjoying both the prestige of the title of Lord Protector and the material benefits accruing from custody of the King, while the other was excluded from all but a fraction of the sweets of power. It was a state of affairs which the Lord Admiral intended to alter just as soon as he was in a position to challenge the Protector on equal terms.

As eligible bachelor, his obvious first step was to make the best marriage available, and having failed – not very surprisingly – to get himself considered as a husband for Princess Elizabeth he wasted no time in renewing his attention to Katherine Parr. The Dowager, unaware of her lover's treachery, needed little persuasion. It is true that she spoke of a two-years delay, but Thomas Seymour was not risking the loss of his second choice and made short work of her scruples about unseemly haste. All the same, their marriage was kept secret until Katherine had been able to see the King and explain that no disrespect was intended to his father's memory. Young Edward, who was genuinely fond of his stepmother and becoming increasingly dependent on his uncle's gifts of pocket money, was graciously pleased to give them his blessing and offer to be 'a sufficient succour' in their godly and praisable enterprises; but the Lord Protector considered this particular enterprise neither godly nor praisable and was 'much displeased' when the news leaked out.[4] However, no actual offence had been committed – it was not a crime to marry the Queen-Dowager – and by midsummer the Admiral had moved in with his wife.

The boisterous loud-voiced personality of Thomas Seymour blew like a gale through the cosy ultra-feminine atmosphere of the Queen's household, rapidly dispelling all resemblance to a girl's boarding-school. He took no interest in the New Learning or in advanced Protestant thought, his over-riding interest in the advancement of Thomas Seymour leaving very little room for anything else. Vain, greedy and shallow, he was, nevertheless, an extremely attractive man physically with a commanding presence and plenty of surface charm. The Admiral wanted to be liked – to be considered a good fellow, generous, open-handed, everybody's friend, was an important part of his image – but his total self-absorption made him a dangerous friend, especially to the weak, the foolish, the innocent and the inexperienced whom he both fascinated and exploited without ever actually meaning them any harm. He was to cause his wife great unhappiness and come close to ruining the Princess Elizabeth without actually meaning either of them any harm.

There was probably no deliberate malice behind his teasing pursuit of the Princess – all those early-morning romps in her bedroom at Chelsea and Hanworth and Seymour Place during the summer and autumn of 1547 were innocuous enough in themselves. At the same time, a moment's thought would have shown most men that such rowdy goings-on might easily be misunderstood and damage the reputation of a nubile young woman. Unfortunately, the Admiral was not given to looking at any situation from anyone's point of view but his own, and when Mrs Ashley attempted to remonstrate, he roared that by God's precious soul he meant no evil and would not leave it. The Lady Elizabeth was like a daughter to him, he added, conveniently forgetting that only a few months earlier he had been hoping she might be a wife to him.[5]

An Italian life of Elizabeth, published in the seventeenth century and more remarkable for its imaginative than its historical qualities, prints a turgid correspondence between Seymour and the Princess, dated February 1547 and consisting of a formal proposal of marriage and an equally formal refusal. These letters are almost certainly without foundation in fact and it is unlikely that Elizabeth knew anything about the Admiral's intentions at that time. According to her own account, she first heard of them from Mrs Ashley, who unwisely told her that 'if my lord might have had his own will' he would have had her before he married the Queen.[6] This knowledge added extra spice to games of hide-and-seek round the bed-curtains, rousing all the nascent sexual awareness of an adolescent girl and giving her a delicious sense of power. One way and another it was a situation fraught with undesirable possibilities; but when Mrs Ashley, unable to control either the Admiral or her charge, went to the Queen for help Katherine was inclined 'to make a small matter of it'. However, she promised to chaperon her husband's marauding expeditions in future, and so she did for a time at least.[7]

Whether it was her stepmother's intervention, or a consciousness of her new fourteen-year-old dignity, Elizabeth seems to have lost her taste for slap-and-tickle. When the household moved to Seymour Place in London, she took to getting up earlier, so that when the Admiral came surging in, still in his nightgown and slippers, 'to bid her good morrow', he would find the Princess up and dressed and 'at her book'.[8] Their relationship, inevitably, was changing, and what had begun as a joke in rather doubtful taste was now ceasing to be a joke of any sort.

There had been an ominous little episode at Hanworth, when the Queen told Mrs Ashley that 'my lord Admiral looked in at the gallery window and saw my lady Elizabeth cast her arms about a man's neck'. The Princess denied this accusation tearfully, but Mrs Ashley knew there could be no truth in it, 'for there came no man but Grindal, the Lady Elizabeth's schoolmaster', and he was evidently quite unembraceable. All the same, the governess was worried and began to wonder if the Queen was becoming suspicious and had intended the story as a hint that she should take better care of her charge 'and be, as it were, in watch betwixt her and my Lord Admiral'.[9] Mrs Ashley was also warned by her husband, who told her several times 'to take heed, for he did fear that the Lady Elizabeth did bear some affection to my Lord Admiral'.[10]

All this illustrates clearly enough the kind of danger to which the bastardised and orphaned Elizabeth was exposed. During King Henry's lifetime no man would have dreamt of approaching either of his daughters – no man ever did dream of approaching Mary. But then Mary's mother had been a princess of impeccable virtue and lineage, and in the days before the divorce, when she had been the Princess of England, Mary's governess was Margaret, Countess of Salisbury, a lady of the highest breeding whose royal Plantagenet blood finally brought her to the block. Elizabeth's governess, on the other hand, had originally entered her service in 1536 as a waiting-gentlewoman. Katherine Ashley, *née* Champernowne, was a good-hearted woman devoted to her princess, but although she came from a perfectly respectable old Devonshire family she lacked – in an intensely status-conscious world – the authority and prestige of aristocratic birth. Even Katherine Parr, Elizabeth's official guardian, was neither noble nor royal in her own right. As the Lord Protector's wife spitefully remarked, she had been but Latymer's wife before King Henry raised her 'in his doting days', and was now married to a mere younger son. Katherine possessed intelligence, kindliness and much generosity of spirit but she did not, unfortunately, inspire the sort of dread necessary to protect a self-willed Tudor princess from predators like Thomas Seymour.

The volcano which had been rumbling below the surface of the Queen-Dowager's household for nearly a year finally erupted in the spring of 1548, when 'the Queen, suspecting the often access of the Admiral to the Lady Elizabeth's grace, came suddenly upon them, when they were alone (he having her in his arms). Wherefore the Queen fell out, both with the Lord Admiral and with her grace also.'[11] Katherine's anger is understandable. To find herself betrayed by the husband she loved and the girl she had mothered was enough to try her patience to its limit, particularly when she was five months pregnant with her first child. The Queen found some relief by sending for Mrs Ashley and giving that lady a piece of her mind, but she could not afford the luxury of giving way to her feelings for long. Gossip, once started, would be unstoppable and a public scandal would be appallingly damaging to all concerned.

Clearly, though, the two households could no longer remain under one roof and arrangements were made for Elizabeth to pay an extended visit to Sir Anthony and Lady Denny, old and trusted friends of the Royal family, at their house at Cheshunt. The Princess and her entourage set out immediately after the Whitsun holiday and, thanks to Katherine's self-control and good sense, no one, except Mrs Ashley and possibly the Denny's, who could be relied on to keep their mouths shut, knew the real reason for the move.

The Queen and her stepdaughter parted on affectionate terms, and Elizabeth's gratitude is manifest in her 'bread-and-butter' letter to Katherine. 'Although I could not be plentiful in giving thanks for the manifold kindness received at your Highness' hand at my departure,' she wrote, 'yet I am something to be borne withal, for truly I was replete with sorrow to depart from your Highness, especially leaving you undoubtful of health; and, albeit I answered little, I weighed it more deeper, when you said you would warn me of all evils that you should hear of me; for if your Grace had not a good opinion of me, you would not have offered friendship to me that way, that all men judge the contrary.'[12]

Although any immediate danger of scandal had been averted, the episode had left its mark and Elizabeth was ill that summer – the first recorded instance of her suffering from even a minor indisposition. In her later teens and early twenties she was to be afflicted by well-documented and recurrent attacks of migraine, catarrh and nephritis, but this particular illness is not described. It may have been the result of emotional disturbance coinciding with puberty; but the possibility that it was the result of a miscarriage – induced or otherwise – cannot be dismissed out of hand. We know – or, rather, we can deduce – that at one time in her life Elizabeth's periods were irregular and scanty, but there is no reason to suppose that she did not develop normally. In the sixteenth century girls of fourteen were generally considered fully mature – many were married by that age, some were already mothers. We know, from the accounts of eye-witnesses, that Elizabeth was physically attracted by Thomas Seymour – it would probably not be too much to say that she believed herself in love. We know that Seymour was a man of strong appetites with few scruples about taking what he wanted. We are also told that he and Elizabeth found opportunities of being alone together. An experienced, self-indulgent man and a susceptible inexperienced girl can make an explosive mixture. It would not be unbearably surprising if they had lost control of themselves.

According to Mrs Ashley, the Princess 'was first sick about mid-summer' – that is, approximately six weeks after she reached Cheshunt – and it is perhaps not without significance that Katherine Ashley and Joan Denny were sisters. If Elizabeth was, or was feared to be, in the early stages of pregnancy, it is at least possible that between them the two matrons could have concealed her condition, and perhaps taken steps to end it.

All this, of course, is conjecture. We are never likely to know for certain whether or not Elizabeth remained *virgo intacta*, and on the evidence that exists she must continue to be given the benefit of the doubt. At the same time, it's worth remembering that, if she ever did lose her celebrated virginity, this was about the only period of her life when it might have passed undetected.

Whatever the nature of her illness in the summer of 1548, it persisted for some weeks and she was still 'sick in her bed' with Mrs Ashley in close attendance when news of Katherine Parr's death in childbirth reached Cheshunt. For Mrs Ashley this changed everything, and she at once began to tell Elizabeth that her 'old husband' was free again, and she could have him if she liked. 'Nay,' said Elizabeth. 'Yes,' said Mrs Ashley, 'yes, you will not deny it if my Lord Protector and the Council were pleased therewith.' 'Why not?' persisted the governess, with splendid disregard for political realities. The Admiral had been worthy to marry a queen and was now 'the noblest man unmarried in this land'. Elizabeth continued to say 'nay, by her troth', but she could not quite conceal her interest. Playing the parlour game of 'drawing hands', 'she chose my lord and chased him away', and when Mrs Ashley told her 'that she would not refuse him if the Lord Protector and the Council did bid her' she answered 'yes, by her troth'.[13]

In the privacy of the household Elizabeth might allow herself the indulgence of blushing and smiling over the Admiral, and showing 'a glad countenance' when, as frequently happened, he formed the topic of conversation; in public her discretion was absolute – an example which Thomas Seymour would have done well to copy. But Seymour was growing increasingly impatient of discretion, and in London that autumn gossip linking his name with the Princess had begun to reach government circles.

Riding with the Admiral 'towards the Parliament House' at the end of November, the Lord Privy Seal, Lord Russell, took the opportunity of tackling him on the subject, warning him bluntly that, if he 'made means' to marry either Mary or Elizabeth, he would be courting disaster. Taken off his guard, the Admiral hedged and 'seemed to deny that there was any such thing attempted of his part'; but a few days later, again finding himself next to the Lord Privy Seal in the procession to Westminster, Seymour took the offensive himself. It was convenient for the princesses to marry, he said, and it would surely be better if they found husbands at home instead of in some foreign place. 'And', he went on, 'why might not I, or another, made by the King their father, marry one of them?' Lord Russell told him. Any Englishman who attempted to marry either of the princesses would 'procure unto himself the occasion of his utter undoing'; but Thomas Seymour, 'being of so near alliance to the King's majesty', would be writing his own death warrant. The Tudor monarchs, though wise and noble princes, were noted for their suspicious minds. If one of his uncles married one of the heirs to his throne, young Edward would certainly take occasion to have that uncle in great suspect 'and, as often as he shall see you, to think that you gape and wish for his death' – a thought which once rooted in the royal head would grow and flourish. Then there was the financial aspect. Under the terms of their father's will, both Mary and Elizabeth were to receive lands to the value of £3000 a year and marriage portions of £10,000 in money, plate and goods. How far would that go, demanded Russell, to maintain a man's charges and estate, matching himself there? They must have the three thousand a year as well, said the Admiral. 'By God! but they may not,' said Russell. 'By God! none of you all dare say nay to it!' But old Lord Russell had the last word. 'By God! for my part I will say nay to it, for it is clean against the King's will!'[14]

After this, even the most optimistic suitor should have been convinced that he stood no chance of getting official blessing, but Thomas Seymour was not easily discouraged. He was, it seems, impossible to discourage. Certainly he would not be warned. Elizabeth had wisely refused to correspond with him; and Seymour, perhaps fortunately, was not much of a letter-writer. Instead, he used the Princess's steward, Thomas Parry, as a go-between; and when Parry came up to London shortly before Christmas he had a long session with the Admiral, who was showing a close, almost a proprietorial interest in Elizabeth's affairs. The Admiral wanted to know how many servants she kept, what houses and lands had been assigned to her, and whether her title to them had yet been confirmed by the King's letters patent. It had not, and the Admiral told Parry that she could get her lands exchanged for better lands, preferably 'westward or in Wales'. He went on to ask about her housekeeping expenses and to compare them with his own.[15]

Elizabeth had now left Cheshunt and was established with a retinue of about a hundred and forty people in the old bishop's palace at Hatfield. She wanted to come to London, said Parry, to see her brother, but Durham House in the Strand which had previously been at her disposal was being used as a mint and she had nowhere to stay. The Admiral at once offered the loan of Seymour Place, adding that he would like to see the Princess himself – perhaps something could be arranged when she moved to Ashridge, which would be on his way when he went into the country.

Parry returned to Hatfield well primed with messages, and as his mistress appeared to receive them 'very joyfully and thankfully' he ventured to ask whether, if the Council approved, she meant to marry the Lord Admiral. 'When that shall come to pass,' said Elizabeth, 'I will do as God shall put into my mind.' Anyway, what did Parry mean by asking such a question? 'Who bade him say so?' The steward retreated hastily, explaining that nobody had bade him say anything, but it had seemed as if my lord 'was given that way rather than otherwise'. Elizabeth then wanted to know if Mrs Ashley had been told about the Admiral's 'gentle offers' and ordered Parry to be sure to pass on everything that had been said, 'for I will know nothing but she shall know of it'.[16]

But Mrs Ashley had also been to London and had heard all the gossip about the Admiral's gentleness towards the Lady Elizabeth; how he would soon be coming to woo her and had even kept Queen Katherine's maids together, so that they would be ready to wait on his new bride. Mrs Ashley, though, was not quite so sanguine as she had once been. She had had an unpleasant quarter of an hour with the Protector's formidable wife, who had rebuked her for being too friendly with the Admiral and told her she was not worthy to have the governance of a king's daughter.[17] Somewhat depressed by this experience, she warned Elizabeth that it might not be possible for the Admiral to get his way 'till the King's majesty came to his own rule', for it looked as if the Protector and the Council 'would not suffer a subject to have her'. In fact, she had better not set her mind on the marriage, seeing the unlikelihood of it, but be content to hold herself at the appointment of my Lords of the Council.[18]

This was good advice; but all the same Mrs Ashley could not quite bring herself to give up her romantic dreams, and towards the end of the Christmas holiday she and Thomas Parry enjoyed a good gossip on the all-absorbing topic of the Lord Admiral and the Lady Elizabeth. Parry commented on the goodwill between them, which he had gathered 'both from him and her Grace also'. Oh yes, said Mrs Ashley, it was true, but she had had such a 'charge' from the Duchess of Somerset that she dared not speak of it. All the same, promoted by Parry, she did speak of it, and at length. She would wish the Princess to marry the Admiral 'of all men living' and thought he might bring the matter to pass at the Council's hands well enough. When Parry remarked that he had heard 'much evil report' of the Admiral, that he was not only a covetous man and an oppressor, but also a jealous man who had used the Queen very cruelly, Mrs Ashley flared up in defence of her favourite. 'I know him better than you do,' she exclaimed, 'or those that so report him.' He would 'make but too much of her Grace' and she knew it. 'He loves her but too well,' went on the governess, 'and has done so a good while.' It was the Queen, poor soul, who had been jealous, and Mrs Ashley told Thomas Parry all about Katherine Parr finding her husband with Elizabeth in his arms.[19]

It was less than a fortnight after this remarkable conversation that the bubble burst. On 17 January 1549 the Admiral was arrested at Seymour Place. Next day the government began to round up his cronies – including Katherine Ashley and Thomas Parry – while, at Hatfield, Sir Robert Tyrwhit arrived to extract a confession from the Princess Elizabeth.

When Elizabeth was informed that her governess and her steward had been arrested, she burst into tears and seemed 'marvellous abashed', but she did not confess. There was, apparently, nothing to confess. She had once written a note to the Admiral requesting a favour for one of her chaplains. She had asked him, through Parry, to help her recover the use of Durham House and he had kindly offered the loan of Seymour Place instead. When he suggested paying her a visit in the country, Mrs Ashley had written saying he had better not come 'for fear of suspicion'. Elizabeth had been annoyed about this and told her governess not to become involved in such matters, but there had never been the slightest question of a secret understanding with my lord. Mrs Ashley had never advised it – quite the contrary, in fact – and Elizabeth herself would never have considered any proposal of marriage without the full consent of the King, the Protector and the Council. She did not believe either Mrs Ashley or Parry had been engaged in any 'practice' to get her married without consent – certainly they had never told her they would do so.[20]

It was all very unsatisfactory. Robert Tyrwhit could see by the Princess's face that she was guilty, but he also perceived 'she would abide more storms ere she accuse Mistress Ashley'. 'I do assure your Grace, she hath a very good wit,' he wrote to the Protector, 'and nothing is gotten of her but by great policy.' During the weeks that followed he tried every trick of the interrogator's trade to break her resistance, and failed. The fifteen-year-old Elizabeth remained impervious to threats, was not deceived by promises or the blandishments of false friends, and reacted strongly to even more disagreeable methods. When Tyrwhit told her it was being said that she was already in the Tower and with child by the Lord Admiral, the Princess declared flatly that these were shameful slanders and, in a famous letter to the Protector, demanded that she should be allowed to come to court and 'show myself there as I am'.[21]

Tyrwhit himself, having practised unsuccessfully with my lady's grace 'by all means and policies' to persuade her to confess more than she had already done, was driven to the conclusion that there had been some secret promise between my lady, Mistress Ashley and the cofferer never to confess until death; but Thomas Parry and Katherine Ashley were not made of such stern stuff as the Tudor princess. Both cracked under pressure and, on 5 February, Tyrwhit was able to confront Elizabeth with their statements. The details of those frolics at Chelsea and elsewhere looked extraordinarily unfunny set down in black and white by some clerk's scribbling pen; none of it reflected much credit on those concerned, but it was not evidence of conspiracy. The Princess's servants had exposed her to embarrassment and a certain amount of moral censure; they had not implicated her in any treasonable activity, and this she was quick to realise. Apart from a few unimportant details, Tyrwhit got nothing further out of her.

The Admiral's activities were a very different matter. His undercover courtship of Elizabeth had been only one strand, albeit an important one, in the complicated web of subversion in which he was now enmeshed. Apart from the accusation that before he married the Queen he had gone about to marry the Lady Elizabeth and since that time had 'by secret and crafty means . . . practised to achieve the said purpose of marrying the said Lady Elizabeth', there were thirty-two charges against him in the list drawn up by the Privy Council.[22] There can be no reasonable doubt that Thomas Seymour would have liked to marry Elizabeth, that he would have liked to overthrow his brother's government and had actively plotted to achieve both these ends; but whether it was fair to deduce that 'following the example of Richard III he wished to make himself King' is another matter.[23] The younger Seymour was a basically unstable character who had allowed personal jealousy to become an obsession. Such an inept conspirator scarcely represented a very serious danger to the State. He did, however, represent a serious nuisance which could no longer be safely tolerated, and by 5 March a bill declaring him 'adjudged and attainted of high treason' had passed all its stages in both Houses of Parliament.

At Hatfield, Elizabeth heard that my Lord Admiral's household had been dispersed, and knowing what that meant she began 'a little to droop'. Robert Tyrwhit reported that 'now she cannot bear to hear him discommended but she is ready to make answer therein; and so she hath not been accustomed to do, unless Mistress Ashley were touched'.[24] There could, of course, be only one end to the Admiral's story and, when news of his execution arrived, the Princess's only comment is said to have been: 'This day died a man of much wit but little judgement.' It was as apt an epitaph as any.

Elizabeth's emotional involvement with Thomas Seymour may not have gone very deep. Nevertheless, it had been a frightening and deeply shocking experience which she had faced with a courage and strength of will astonishing in a girl of fifteen. Now she buried the terror and the shock – at a cost of how much psychological damage can only be guessed

– and began grimly to pick up the pieces. As it turned out, she was helped in the task of refurbishing her public image by external events. That autumn a *coup d'état* stage-managed by John Dudley, Earl of Warwick, toppled the Lord Protector more efficiently than anything the Admiral's amateurish efforts could have hoped to achieve. The new régime bore the Princess Elizabeth no personal animus and in December she paid a visit to court where, according to the Emperor's ambassador, she was received with great pomp and triumph and was continually with the King.[25]

The unfortunate episode of Thomas Seymour might be officially regarded as closed, but Elizabeth's future remained as uncertain as ever. In November 1550 the new Imperial ambassador, Jehan Scheyfve, picked up a rumour 'that my Lord of Warwick is about to cast off his wife and marry my Lady Elizabeth . . . with whom he is said to have had several secret and intimate personal communications; and by these means he will aspire to the crown'.[26] Although Scheyfve was confident that his information had come from a 'safe source', there is no corroborative evidence to substantiate it. Brilliant, rapacious and essentially crooked, the Earl of Warwick had won his own way to the top and was to go to considerable lengths to stay there, but in 1550 he had more immediate problems on his mind, and there were more feasible bridegrooms in view for the Princess Elizabeth.

In the field of foreign affairs England was now reaping the sour fruit of Henry VIII's impetuous policies in Scotland, where his celebrated 'rough wooing' of the little Queen, unwisely pursued by Protector Somerset, had had the predictable result of driving the embattled Scots back into the 'auld alliance' with France. François had not long survived his old sparring partner the King of England, and Henri II – less absorbed by dreams of Italian conquest than his father had been – was readier to commit himself in the north. As he listened to the siren voices of the Duke of Guise and the Cardinal of Lorraine urging him to go to the aid of their sister the Scottish Queen-Mother and their niece the Queen of Scots, Henri could also reflect that Mary Stuart was a great-granddaughter of Henry VII, with an undeniable place in the English succession. The King, in fact, can scarcely be blamed for seeking to exploit a situation so fraught with interesting possibilities. In June 1548 a force of 6,000 French troops landed at Leith, and in July the French ambassador offered the Scottish Estate his master's unstinted protection against the English invader. In return, the Scots were to surrender their Queen, who would be taken at once to France and in due course be married to the Dauphin. The Scottish lords listened to the reassuring chink of French gold in their pockets, thought with satisfaction of English discomfiture, and agreed. On 29 July the five-year-old Mary went on board a French galley and was spirited away round 'the back of Ireland'. France and Scotland, not England and Scotland, had become one country, and in future England would have to live with the knowledge that her hereditary enemy would walk through her back door virtually at will.

Matters were not improved by the fact that England's nominal ally, Charles V, was currently engaged in a losing battle to control heretic Germany and in no position to come to her assistance. Apart from this, relations between the allies had become increasingly strained over the English government's attempts to force the Princess Mary to comply with its new religious laws and, in March 1551, Jehan Scheyfve threatened the Council with the Emperor's grave displeasure if his cousin was deprived of the opportunity to hear mass.[27]

In the circumstances, the Earl of Warwick had little option but to cultivate the French, and the price of friendship was naturally high. Boulogne had already been ceded. Now England was obliged to relinquish all claims to the Queen of Scots as a bride for Edward VI. It was agreed that Edward should be betrothed instead to the French princess, Elisabeth of Valois, and in the summer of 1551, amid an ostentatious exchange of embassies and civilities, the Duke of Guise was putting forward possible suitors for the English Princess Elizabeth. His suggestions included his own brother and, according to Scheyfve, the Princess 'very hastily but with great care had her portrait painted just before the gentleman left for France, so that they might take the picture with them'. Such a marriage, the ambassador went on, would certainly go to prove that England and France intended to observe close friendship and alliance although, he was pleased to note, not a few Englishmen of rank were saying it was all too sudden and vehement to last.[28]

Another Guise proposal, made through the Florentine merchant Anthony Guidotti, was the Duke of Ferrara's son, 'one of the goodliest young men of all Italy'. Then there was the Duke of Florence's son, who was only eleven years old. 'If this party were liked,' wrote Guidotti persuasively, 'it were an easy matter to be concluded without any excessive dote.'[29] Yet another European prince whose name was being linked with Elizabeth's in 1551 was the King of Denmark's eldest son and, in November, Scheyfve heard that the Council was opening negotiations with the Danes, as it considered this match would be better than a French one 'because of religion and other reasons'.[30]

The Ferrara marriage came up again in March 1553 when Sir Richard Morysine, the English envoy in Antwerp, reported that he had been approached on the subject by Francisco d'Este, the young man's uncle. D'Este had asked for a description of the Princess, and Morysine replied tactfully that, even if God had made her a poor man's daughter, 'he did not know that prince that might not think himself happy to be the husband of such a lady'.[31] Morysine was also able to report that he had received a letter out of Saxony giving him to understand that Duke Hans Frederick's second son would, 'if he durst, bear a great affection to the Lady Elizabeth's grace'.[32]

But, as so often in the past, nothing came of any of these widely varied and mostly tentative proposals, and Elizabeth at nineteen remained an eligible spinster. England, hamstrung by the French presence in Scotland, her population restive and her currency devalued, did not cut a very impressive figure on the European scene during the early fifties, and the European princes preferred to await developments before committing themselves to firm alliances – so much depended on when, or if, Edward VI attained his majority. In the spring of 1552, just as he was approaching the dangerous age for Tudor boys, Edward had succumbed to a severe attack of measles. He seemed to make a good recovery and resumed his normal activities, but the damage had been done and by the autumn tuberculosis was already established. By the spring of 1533 he was dying and, in spite of an official news-blackout, London seethed with speculation.

The political power of John Dudley, now Duke of Northumberland, was still unchallenged and his influence over the King unbroken. His numerous brood of sons filled the Privy Chamber and people grumbled, though not too loudly, about Dudley greed and Dudley arrogance. The Lords of the Council grumbled to each other about the way in which the Duke – he was the first Englishman unconnected with the blood royal to bear such a title – summoned them daily to his house to wait upon his pleasure and reminded each other privately that his father had died a convicted traitor. Not that this was necessarily a social disgrace – the highest in the land quite frequently died as convicted traitors – but John Dudley's father, although descended from a respectable baronial family, had been a mere lawyer and one of Henry VII's hated tax gatherers. John Dudley himself had no illusions about his unpopularity, or about his probable fate after Edward's death, and as soon as he realised that this would not be long in coming he began to put certain contingency plans into operation.

No one expected Northumberland to retire gracefully, but no one seemed very certain exactly what he intended to do. Jehan Scheyfve was in no doubt that the Duke and his party would try to prevent Mary from succeeding. 'They are evidently resolved to resort to arms against,' he wrote, 'with the excuse of religion among others.' It was after this that the issue became clouded.

At Whitsun, M. de l'Aubespine, a secretary frequently employed by the French king on high-level diplomatic missions, arrived in England. The reason for his visit was surrounded 'with the greatest mystery', but Scheyfve reported that it was being said he had come to offer the King of France's services to the Duke of Northumberland in the event of King Edward's death, and whether it might not be possible to make a closer alliance with England by arranging a French marriage for Elizabeth. Another story going the rounds was that, 'if the Duke of Northumberland felt himself well supported, he would find means to marry his eldest son, the Earl of Warwick, to the Lady Elizabeth, after causing him to divorce his wife . . . or else that he might find it expedient to get rid of his own wife and marry the said Elizabeth himself, and claim the crown for the house of Warwick as descendants of the House of Lancaster'.[33]

Although ideally Northumberland might well have chosen to use Henry VIII's Protestant daughter as his instrument in furthering the pretensions of the house of the Dudley, his knowledge of the lady would certainly have told him that she was likely to prove a highly unsatisfactory cat's-paw. Elizabeth had always been careful to keep on good terms with the Duke, but there is no evidence whatever that she would even have considered linking her fortunes with a man so universally disliked and distrusted, or indeed that he ever approached her on the subject. Northumberland had no time to waste on persuasion, or divorce, and he had already settled on his victim. At Whitsun, the hapless Jane Grey was married to the last remaining unmarried Dudley son, Guildford, and Edward was now being helped to make a new will – or rather to alter his father's will.

Failing heirs from his own children, Henry had settled the crown on the descendants of his younger sister, who had married the Duke of Suffolk – arbitrarily excluding the Stuart descendants of his elder sister. Edward's 'Devise for the Succession' arbitrarily excluded Mary and Elizabeth in favour of fifteen-year-old Jane Grey, granddaughter of Mary Tudor, Duchess of Suffolk.[34] The legality of the Devise was – to say the least – doubtful, but Northumberland was understandably less concerned with legality than with self-preservation, and when the King died, on 6 July 1553, Northumberland immediately had Jane proclaimed as Queen.

On paper the Duke's position looked unassailable. He controlled the capital, the fortress of the Tower with its armoury and mint, and the Council followed him like sheep – apparently hypnotised by his powerful personality. The rightful heiress was a lone woman of thirty-seven, in poor health, without friends, money or influence. No one believed she had a chance, not even the Emperor, who could only advise his ambassadors to try to influence Northumberland on Mary's behalf and to win his confidence.[35]

Neither the Emperor nor the Duke was in the habit of paying much attention to public opinion, and consequently the ignominious collapse of the *coup* and Mary's overwhelming victory took them almost equally by surprise. The English people had quite simply had enough of Northumberland and his kind. They rose in an unprecedented spontaneous demonstration of loyalty for the true Tudor line and of revulsion against the upstart tribe of Dudley, and the great Duke was swept away. It looked like a miracle. Mary herself – unfortunately, as it turned out – had no doubt at all that it was the personal handiwork of God.

27

Le plus beau gentilhomme d'Angleterre

The sixteenth century was an age of queens, but Mary Tudor was England's first queen regnant (unless you count the long-ago Matilda of unhappy memory); and the islanders, delighted though they were over Mary's triumph, did not for a moment expect her to rule alone. Even before the Queen, travelling slowly down from East Anglia, had reached the capital, speculation as to the identity of the man she would choose to be her husband was already rife.

There was no doubt about the preference of all those who had an opininon on the subject – they wanted the Queen to marry an Englishman. One of the reasons put forward in King Edward's Devise to justify the exclusion of his sisters from the succession was that they might marry abroad and bring foreigners into the realm, an eventuality which could only 'tend to the utter subversion of the commonwealth'.[1] This was about the only point made by the Devise which struck any answering chord in the population as a whole. But, after all, why should the Queen marry a foreigner when there was an eminently suitable Englishman available? Edward Courtenay, grandson of Edward IV's youngest daughter and that monarch's only surviving male descendant, was surely the obvious candidate for the post of king-consort. 'There is much talk here to the effect that he will be married to the Queen, as he is of the blood royal,' reported the Emperor's ambassadors on 22 July.

The Courtenay family had in the past been given good reason to regret their royal blood. They'd been arrested in the November purge of 1538, when the threatening noises coming from the Catholic powers had prompted Henry and Thomas Cromwell to round up all the remaining offshoots of the Plantagenet tree they could lay their hands on. Edward Courtenay's father, the Marquis of Exeter, had been executed that December, together with the kinsmen Henry Pole and Edward Neville. His wife and twelve-year-old son were left in the Tower and, although Gertrude, Marchioness of Exeter, was presently 'pardoned' and released, young Edward had stayed in gaol for very nearly fifteen years – until the evening of 3 August 1553 when Queen Mary Tudor rode through the main gateway of his prison, the guns of the fortress booming a welcome, and raised him from his knees and kissed him and formally set him free.[2]

Despite the fact that no one yet knew for certain what the Queen's intentions were, Edward Courtenay had now become a figure of international importance and, as such, a focus of international interest. He had, it seemed, made good use of his captivity, devoting himself 'to all virtuous and praiseworthy studies', so that he could speak several languages and had also learnt to become proficient on 'various instruments of music'. There was in him, too, 'a civility which must be deemed natural rather than acquired by the habit of society' – the Imperial envoys were forgetting that the society to be found in the Tower was apt to include the best breeding in the land – and his bodily graces were in proportion to those of his mind.[3] No portrait of Edward Courtenay appears to have survived, but all foreign observers were agreed that he was uncommonly handsome. '*Le plus beau et plus agréable gentilhomme d'Angleterre*,' commented the French ambassador, Antoine de Noailles; and another Frenchman was to note in his memoirs: '*Il estoit l'un des plus beaux entres les jeunes seigneurs de son age*.'

At first glance, therefore, this beautiful, accomplished, well-mannered, high-born young man looked like the answer to any royal maiden's prayer and, from Mary Tudor's point of view, Edward Courtenay should have possessed other special advantages. He had remained faithful to the old religion, and there were long-standing ties of loyalty and affection between their families. The Marquis and Marchioness of Exeter had been close friends of Mary's mother – if Eustace Chapuys can be trusted, the Marquis had been ready to join an armed demonstration of sympathy for Queen Catherine during the early 1530s – and Mary was always conscious of an obligation towards those very few members of the aristocracy who'd been prepared to risk her father's murderous displeasure for her own and her mother's sake. The widowed Marchioness had now become one of the Queen's most intimate ladies-in-waiting, usually sharing her bedroom, but whether Mary was planning to extend a similar privilage to her friend's son was still a matter for conjecture.

It was, though, a matter which the Emperor, who was taking a close personal interest in his cousin's plans, wanted cleared up as quickly as possible. Charles V was naturally eager to grasp what might be a unique opportunity to forge a permanent link between England, Spain and the Netherlands; and, with this end in view, he was prepared to suggest his heir, Prince Philip, now a widower of twenty-six, as a bridegroom for Mary Tudor. Charles wasn't worried about other foreign competition, but he recognised that his son had a potentially dangerous rival in Edward Courtenay, and Simon Renard of the Imperial embassy was instructed to drop a hint to the Queen that such an inexperienced young man was scarcely a fit match for her. Renard might perhaps mention the rumours that Courtenay was already beginning to give himself airs and how it was being whispered that he'd been seen visiting houses of ill-fame in the city. At the same time, wrote Cardinal Granvelle, the Emperor's right-hand man in Brussels, the ambassador must be very careful not to go too far - at least until Mary's intentions were more clearly known - for, if she did take it into her head to have Courtenay, nothing would stop her, if she was like other women, and she would then always hold Renard's words against him.[4]

Simon Renard was far too shrewd a diplomat to risk jeopardising such delicate negotiations through lack of tact in the early stages, but by the middle of August he felt reasonably confident that the Queen 'had no wish to wed an Englishman'. 'As far as I can judge,' he told Granvelle on the fifteenth, 'she wishes his Majesty to suggest someone, believing he will name a person agreeable to her; and I am in hopes that if his Majesty were inclined to propose our Prince it would be the most welcome news that could be given to her.'[5] It was, however, necessary to be certain, and at the next opportunity Renard returned to the subject of Courtenay 'and the common rumour about his marriage to the Queen'. Mary brushed this aside. She had scarcely seen Courtenay since the day she had pardoned him and, in any case, there was no one in England she wanted to marry. Hadn't the Emperor, she asked, selected some suitable person yet? The Queen could hardly have given Renard a better opening and within a few minutes Philip's name had entered the conversation in the most natural way in the world. Seizing his opportunity, the ambassador began to expatiate on his Highness's great good sense, judgement, experience and moderation, adding hopefully that the Prince was already 'an old married man' with a seven-year-old son. Philip was actually a year younger than the despised Edward Courtenay, but Renard, knowing Mary's sensitivity about her own advancing age, contrived to skate round this awkward fact, it seemed, though, as if the Queen was hardly listening. She had never, she told Renard with painful honesty, known that thing which was called love, 'nor harboured thoughts of voluptuousness'; she had never even thought of marriage until now, when God had been pleased to raise her to the throne. She left it all to the Emperor, whom she regarded as a father. He would have to take the initiative and deal with the Council for her, as she could not face the prospect of discussing such a delicate personal matter with them.[6]

It was unfortunate, but not surprising, that Mary should have disliked and distrusted so many of the men with whose help, for better or worse, she now had to govern the country. Nearly all of them were associated in some way with past humiliations; nearly all had been prepared to bow before the recent violent wind of religious change; and nearly all were more or less heavily compromised by their connection with the Duke of Northumberland. The Duke himself had paid the price of unsuccessful treason, but his erstwhile accomplices remained. Since a novice queen could not afford to alienate the Crown's most influential and experienced servants, she'd been obliged to accept their apologies and explanations; but for advice and support Mary turned, as she had always done, to her cousin Charles, and Simon Renard, as her cousin's surrogate, was rapidly becoming her closest confidant and friend.

To have won the Queen was a triumph for Imperial diplomacy, but neither Renard nor his master was deluding himself that the Spanish marriage would be easy to negotiate. Such a project would inevitably stir up strong feeling both in England and elsewhere – elsewhere, in this instance, meaning France. Antoine de Noailles was not one of Mary's favourites – he had, after all, been another of Northumberland's cousins – and the Frenchman, excluded now from the inner circle at court, had spent August trying to find out what the Imperialists were up to. He got his first definite clue early in September, when he heard from a friend in the royal household that the Emperor had already formally offered his son to Mary. The news was premature but it confirmed all de Noailles' forebodings. The sort of alliance being planned between the Queen of England and her Habsburg relations could only result in France's encirclement and it was, therefore, the plain duty of France's ambassador to bestir himself to prevent it.

De Noailles wasted no time. Having despatched a rather panicky warning to Paris that Mary and Philip might be found in bed together before anyone realised what was happening, he at once set about opening channels of communication with Courtenay and his friends, with leading members of the Protestant party – with any Englishman, in fact, with any influence to exert who could be guaranteed to oppose the importation of a foreign king. Using this varied assortment of allies, the ambassador began to organise a vigorous and highly effective anti-Imperialist scare campaign, but he also employed the more conventional diplomatic approach of waiting on the Lord Chancellor, Stephen Gardiner, Bishop of Winchester, to endeavour to impress on him the obvious practical and political disadvantages of a Spanish marriage. If, de Noailles pointed out reasonably enough, the Queen wanted a husband at her side to support her and perhaps give her children, then Philip could hardly be a more unsuitable choice. A prince with so many prior commitments abroad would not be able to stay in England, and Mary would probably be lucky if she saw him for as much as a fortnight in the whole of her life. Apart from this, she and the country would inevitably be dragged into the Emperor's unappeasable quarrel with France – a quarrel in which they had no interest and from which they could expect no profit.[7]

Stephen Gardiner found himself in the embarrassing position of agreeing wholeheartedly with everything de Noailles said, while at the same time distrusting him profoundly. As an Englishman, a patriot and politician, the Chancellor instinctively recoiled from too close an involvement with any foreign power-bloc. As a Catholic who had spent most of the previous reign in prison for his religious beliefs, he was afraid that any chance of achieving a peaceful reconciliation with Rome, such as he and Mary both desired, would vanish overnight if once he became associated in the public mind with the taint of foreign interference. He knew the French would not hesitate to play on Protestant fears and prejudices in their efforts to kill the Spanish marriage, and he also knew that, once roused, the closely related passions of nationalism and religious fanaticism could quickly boil over into violence – already there had been some ominous anti-Catholic demonstrations in London.

But, until the Emperor came into the open, there wasn't a great deal Gardiner could do. He did, however, go to see the Queen, taking with him a group of pro-Courtenay councillors – Robert Rochester, Francis Englefield and Edward Waldegrave – to ask her to think seriously about marriage and naming Courtenay as a desirable and acceptable match. Gardiner was, on paper at least, her principal adviser and the other three were old friends, loyal and devout Catholics who'd stood by her and suffered with her in the past. But even in this company Mary's reserve held. Courtenay was very young, she remarked dismissively. Only time would show what he was made of.[8]

Renard, meanwhile, had been waiting for instructions. These finally arrived towards the end of September. He was to seek a private interview with the Queen and make the Emperor's offer of Prince Philip in strict confidence, at the same time asking her to 'set aside the ceremony and concealments which are practised by strangers when dealing with matters of this nature'. Charles wanted a plain answer from his cousin 'as to her own inclination' for, if she didn't like the idea, he would prefer it not to go any further.[9]

It was nearly another fortnight before Renard was able to act. In spite of his privileged position, it wasn't always easy to see the Queen in private. His colleagues at the embassy, including his predecessor Jehan Scheyfve, who was still in England, were inclined to be jealous; and Mary herself was busy with her coronation, which took place on 1 October, and with the opening of Parliament on the fifth. At last, on Tuesday the tenth, an assignation was made and a servant came late that evening to lead the ambassador to the Queen's inner sanctum at Westminster.

The moment the proposal had actually been spoken aloud, Mary's immediate and instinctive reaction was to draw back. She couldn't make up her mind so quickly. It was such an important step and would be for all her life. She didn't know how the people would take it – the Emperor knew what they were like – or whether the Council would consent. Then, she really knew very little about Philip. She had heard he was not so wise as his father. He was very young and, if he were disposed to be amorous, 'such was not her desire', not at her time of life and having never harboured thoughts of love.[10]

Renard settled down patiently to reassure her, much as he might have gentled a nervous thoroughbred. Philip's nature was so admirable, so virtuous, prudent and modest as to appear 'too wonderful to be human', and this was no exaggeration. He was so stable and settled that he could no longer be considered young – he was nearly thirty, after all – and, besides, the Queen must remember that an older man might not be able to give her a child. The Emperor had 'maturely examined her requirements' and had been unable to think of a more fitting person. It would be a great marriage, too, both for herself and her country; Philip being so puissant a prince to whom the kingdom could turn confidently for protection and succour. Of course, certain people would have reasons of their own for disliking the match. 'The Queen and her Council', said Renard impressively, 'would do well to remember that she had four certain and open enemies; the heretics and schismatics, the rebels and partisans of the late Duke of Northumberland, the French and Scots, and the Lady Elizabeth, who would never cease to trouble her while they had the means, and even rise against her and her government.'[11]

Ever since his arrival in England, Renard had been keeping a watchful eye on the Queen's half-sister, who, he was convinced, was deep in the counsels and intrigues of the heretics and rebels. He also suspected the Princess of being in touch with the French ambassador, though he'd so far been unable to prove it. He warned Mary frequently, and unnecessarily, not to trust her sister and discussed wistfully with the Emperor the possibility of shutting Elizabeth up in the Tower or, alternatively, of persuading Parliament to disinherit her. A more immediately practicable solution to the problem of the Protestant heiress (Elizabeth was now accompanying the Queen to mass, but her suffering air robbed the gesture of much of its effect as far as the Catholic party was concerned), would be to marry her off to a reliable Catholic husband, and it was being suggested in some quarters that, if the Queen didn't want young Courtenay for herself, she might pass him on to the Princess.

This idea seems to have been circulating as early as the previous August, when the Imperial ambassadors were reporting, without naming their sources, that Elizabeth showed signs of taking a great interest in Courtenay.[12] But Courtenay himself, in conversation with the Queen early in October, had been careful to disclaim any desire for 'so exalted an alliance'. If the Queen wished him to marry, then he would much prefer 'some simple girl' to Elizabeth, who was a heretic, too proud and 'of too doubtful lineage on her mother's side'.[13] These words were evidently repeated – at any rate, Renard wrote on the nineteenth that Courtenay was in disgrace with the Lady Elizabeth 'for having spoken otherwise than she had looked for about *amourettes* said to have existed between them'.[14]

Ten days later, after much heart-searching and prayer, Mary gave Renard her solemn word in the presence of the Holy Sacrament that she would marry Philip and 'love him perfectly'.[15] The Queen's decision was, of course, a major step forward; but Renard and his ally on the Council, William Paget, now had somehow to win over the anti-Spanish councillors led by Stephen Gardiner, and it was in this context that the question of a marriage between Elizabeth and Courtenay began to be seriously discussed. As Paget explained to Renard, although Parliament had willingly reversed Henry VIII's divorce from his first wife and relegitimised the Queen, this did not, contrary to all reasonable expectations, in any way affect Elizabeth's right to the succession – a right which, in Paget's opinion, would be very difficult to take away without causing the sort of trouble everyone was most anxious to avoid. Besides this, the next heirs, according to King Henry's will, were the Suffolk girls – Lady Jane Grey, currently in prison awaiting her trial for the treason of usurping the throne, and her younger sisters – all of them Protestants and none of them exactly likely to commend herself to the Emperor. Worse still, if Henry's will were disregarded and the normal laws of inheritance followed, the crown would go to Mary Queen of Scots, now a pretty and promising ten-year-old shortly to become the King of France's daughter-in-law.

If Mary Tudor were to have children, then naturally these difficulties would disappear of their own accord; but Mary Tudor would be thirty-eight before her marriage could be consummated and no one personally acquainted with her and her long history of ill-health could honestly rate her chances of successful motherhood at more than remote. William Paget knew better than to say this aloud, but he was surely thinking of the future – his own and England's – when he suggested that the next Parliament should be asked to confirm Elizabeth as heiress presumptive, on condition she married Courtenay. In the short term, as he pointed out to Renard, this would disarm the pro-Courtenay faction on the Council and satisfy Elizabeth's numerous supporters in Parliament and elsewhere. Elizabeth and Courtenay themselves would be conciliated, the nobility would be pleased, and popular opposition to the idea of the Spanish marriage would be allayed. Looking further ahead, dangerous uncertainty over the succession would be removed and, with any luck, French intrigue discouraged by this setback to their candidate's hopes.[16]

It sounded persuasive, but Renard remained unconvinced. To unite two such doubtful quantities at such a sensitive moment seemed to him to be taking a quite unacceptable risk. Another obstacle was Mary's unconcealed dislike and distrust of her sister. Elizabeth, she said flatly, was a heretic, a hypocrite and a bastard; it would be a disgrace to the kingdom to allow her to succeed on any terms.[17] Nevertheless, the scheme continued to be aired at intervals through the autumn, being finally vetoed by the Emperor in a letter dated Christmas Eve.[18]

Throughout that autumn, though, it was the Queen's matrimonial plans which were getting all the attention. 'In the beginning of

November', commented a contemporary chronicler, 'was the first notice among the people touching the marriage of the Queen to the King of Spain', and the news struck dismay into the hearts of Courtenay's supporters. Renard heard that they were planning to ask Parliament 'to speak to the Queen about the match, begging her not to wed a foreigner and expressing a fear that if she does so the people simply will not stand it'.[19] The only Englishman who might, even at this late stage, have been able to make Mary see the sort of trouble she was storing up for herself was Stephen Gardiner, and it was particularly unfortunate in the circumstances that so little trust or communication should have existed between them. Mary could not forget that the Bishop had once been one of her father's most active agents in the matter of her mother's divorce; and Gardiner, faced with a stubborn emotional woman who had already given her confidence elsewhere, seems to have lost his nerve. Against Renard he could marshal his arguments with cogency and force; to Mary he could only object lamely, 'And what will the people say? How will they put up with a foreigner who will promise things he will not keep?' The Queen retorted that her mind was made up and, if her chancellor preferred the will of the people to her wishes, then he was not keeping *his* promises.[20] Stephen Gardiner was no longer a young man, he was already a sick man and, with his past experience of Tudor wilfulness in matrimonial matters, he was understandably uneager for a battle. He was also hampered in this instance by his known personal fondness for Courtenay, to whom he'd become much attached when they were in the Tower together. As the Queen snappishly remarked, was it suitable to expect her to marry someone just because the Bishop had made friends with him in prison?[21] Gardiner gave it up. His first loyalty was to his sovereign and, if she really wanted Philip, then he would abide by her choice.

Having vanquished the Chancellor, Mary proceeded to make short work of the Speaker of the Commons. Her marriage was entirely her own affair and it was no business of Parliament to attempt to dictate to her on such a personal matter. In any case, if they forced her to take a husband who would not be to her liking, they would cause her death, for she would not live three months and would have no children, and then, indicated the Queen, they would be sorry![22]

Gardiner's surrender and Mary's reception of the parliamentary delegation made it clear that all hope of preventing the Spanish marriage by constitutional methods was at an end; but opposition in the country at large was mounting steadily, and Antoine de Noailles had by no means given up hope that it might yet be possible to confound the Imperialists. The Princess Elizabeth had left court early in December for her country house at Ashridge, and on the fourteenth of the month de Noailles told the King of France: 'From what I hear it only requires that my Lord Courtenay should marry her and that they should go together to the counties of Devonshire and Cornwall. Here it can easily be believed that they would find many adherents, and they could then make a strong claim to the crown, and the Emperor and the Prince of Spain would find it difficult to suppress this rising.'[23]

Elizabeth and Courtenay (he had recently been created Earl of Devonshire) should certainly have made a powerful combination. Indeed, the romantic appeal of such a handsome well-matched young couple, both of the English blood royal, ought to have been irresistible. But, wrote de Noailles, 'the misfortune is that the said Courtenay is of such a fearful and timid disposition that he dare not make the venture . . . There are many, of whom I know, who would be ready to give him encouragement and all help in carrying out some plan to his advantage, and I do not see what should hinder him, except his weakness, faintheartedness and timidity.'[24] The disappointing truth was that, for all his good looks, pretty manners and patrician breeding, Courtenay had turned out to be a poor creature, self-indulgent, irresponsible and vain, with a vicious streak beneath the charm; one who would agree amiably to the suggestions of his more strongminded friends and then carry tales to the Queen. He was obviously untrustworthy and in a crisis would undoubtedly lose such nerve as he possessed; but de Noailles, who had to work with the available material, continued to hope that, properly handled, he would make a useful tool.

As for Elizabeth, the ambassador seems to have taken her cooperation for granted, though on what grounds it's impossible to say with any certainty. It was highly unlikely that the Princess ever took him into her confidence. She was far too shrewd not to have seen through his flattering eagerness to promote her cause; not to have realised that, although France's immediate objective might be to stop the Spanish marriage at all costs, her long-term cross-Channel interests were bound up in the person of the young Queen of Scots. It would clearly have been pointless to try to create a party for Mary Stuart in the England of 1553 but, if Henry VIII's daughters could be goaded or tricked into destroying one another, then the prospects of seeing England and Scotland united under the sovereignty of his half-French great-niece would look a great deal more hopeful.

Elizabeth had long since learnt to keep her own counsel, yet it's difficult to believe that she was unaware of the plans being made for her future. Of the dozen or so gentlemen now busily engaged in conspiring to depose the Queen, to marry the Princess to Edward Courtenay and place them jointly on the throne, at least three were personally acquainted with her or with members of her household, and one of their leaders, James Crofts, assured de Noailles that he was 'very familiar' with the Princess and her servants. Crofts, who actually paid a visit to Ashridge about this time, used Elizabeth's name freely in his communications to the ambassador, describing her determination to resist any attempt by the Emperor to marry her to one of his nominees and her hopes of gaining the crown, 'especially if the matters undertaken for her come to a successful end'.[25]

Whether Crofts was speaking with authority, or whether he was simply trying to convince the French that the conspiracy had a solid 'foundation', we have no means of knowing. We do know that Elizabeth strongly resented her sister's hostile and at times insulting treatment of her, and de Noailles may well have been right when he reported that 'she was most desirous of freeing herself from control', but this doesn't necessarily mean that she approved of the steps being contemplated by her friends. Certainly in later life she never showed the slightest sign of wishing to rule jointly with anyone and, if she was really hoping to gain the crown by force, the chicken-hearted Courtenay was surely the last person she would willingly have chosen for a partner. Not a scrap of reliable evidence survives to indicate that they ever corresponded, ever made contact at a personal level or indeed ever met at all, except formally and in public. It therefore seems pretty safe to assume that the '*amourettes*' said to have existed between them existed only in Simon Renard's imagination, and that Elizabeth's reputed eagerness to wed Courtenay and ride westwards with him was based on the wishful thinking of men like James Crofts. One thing is quite certain: the Princess had no intention of showing her hand unless and until the conspiracy had succeeded in its object of removing Mary. What she might have done then remains anybody's guess.

The rising intended to save England from the rule of the proud Spaniards who, as all right-thinking Englishmen knew, would ravish their wives, deflower their daughters, despoil them of their goods and lands, and then cut their throats, was to have been a four-pronged attack, with armed revolt in the west country, led by Peter Carew with Courtenay himself as figurehead; in Wales, led by James Crofts; in Leicestershire, under the command of Jane Grey's father, the Duke of Suffolk; and in Kent, under Sir Thomas Wyatt. The outbreak of violence had been planned to coincide with Philip's expected arrival in the spring of 1554, but things began to go wrong early in January, when the Council suddenly summoned Peter Carew to London. Carew defied the order, and Stephen Gardiner, worried about the way Courtenay's name kept cropping up in connection with reports of impending trouble in the west, and afraid that his young friend had been getting into bad company, took the opportunity of having a serious talk with him. The upshot, according to de Noailles, was that 'this young fool of a Lord Courtenay' promptly revealed everything he knew about 'the enterprise of Peter Carew and his companions'.[26]

But even before Courtenay's betrayal the conspirators, realising they'd lost the element of surprise, had decided to go ahead – it was a case of now or never. The movement in Devonshire had always depended heavily on Courtenay's presence, on the prestige of his name and his strong family connections with the area. Without him it died at birth, and Peter

Carew was obliged to leave hurriedly for France. It was only in Kent that the rebel forces came anywhere close to success; and Thomas Wyatt's men, marching on the capital to the battle cry of 'We will have no foreigner for our King', came very close indeed to success. They failed because, in the last resort, the sober citizens of London found that old habits of loyalty and obedience to the sovereign – not to mention a natural repugnance at the thought of possible danger to their property – outweighed their detestation of the sovereign's affianced husband. The rebellion failed to prevent the Spanish marriage and served to confirm Mary and Gardiner in their belief that the heretics would stop at nothing to defeat the cause of true religion. It was the death of sixteen-year-old Jane Grey and might have been the death of Elizabeth Tudor.

Before the end of February both Elizabeth and Courtenay were in custody – he back in the Tower, she confined to her apartments at Whitehall. The 'Queen', wrote Simon Renard, 'is advised to have her thrown into the Tower, as she has been accused by Wyatt, mentioned by name in the French ambassador's letters . . . and it is certain that the enterprise was undertaken for her sake.'[27] Renard believed that unless Mary seized this heaven-sent opportunity to get rid of her sister she would never be secure again, and he was therefore exasperated to discover that 'the law as laid down by the English Parliament did not inflict the capital penalty on those who had consented to treason if they had committed no overt act'.[28]

By the middle of March he had begun to despair of the English. Religion was unsettled, the Queen's own councillors were at odds, the people fickle, treacherous and implacably hostile to foreigners. God might have granted victory over the rebels this time, but disaffection still seethed below the surface and it seemed to Renard that a suspicious negligence was being shown in high places over the business of bringing Elizabeth and Courtenay to trial. It even looked as if delays were being deliberately created 'in the hope that something may crop up to save them'.[29]

Two days after writing this thoroughly gloomy despatch in which, for the first time, he questioned the wisdom of allowing Philip to hazard his precious person among the ungrateful islanders, Renard was relieved to hear that the Council had at last taken the decision to commit the heir to the throne to the most notorious prison in the land.[30] But it was a decision taken only after heated argument and in the teeth of vigorous opposition, and when Renard next saw the Queen he took the opportunity of expressing his anxiety about the whole security situation. Philip, he reminded her, was forbidden by the terms of the marriage contract to bring an armed guard with him and would therefore be entirely dependent on his wife for protection. If anything were to happen to him, the consequences would be very serious, and Renard felt in duty bound to lay his doubts before the Queen so that, as he delicately put it, 'she might be pleased to take every necessary step'. Mary did not pretend to misunderstand her friend and mentor. She replied with tears in her eyes that she would rather never have been born than that any harm should come to his Highness, and promised to see to it that Courtenay's and Elizabeth's trials were over before he arrived.[31]

Renard continued, in his own words, to work unceasingly to make the Queen of England understand how essential it was to take very precaution and to have the trials and executions of all criminals, especially Courtenay and Lady Elizabeth, concluded before Philip's arrival. Mary continued to assure him that she was doing everything in her power, and there seems no reason to suppose that she would not unhesitatingly have sacrificed her sister had she been in a strong enough position to do so. But Wyatt had not, after all, accused Elizabeth, nor had James Crofts, although 'marvellously tossed'. Even her servant William Saintlow, who had actually been seen with Wyatt's army, resolutely refused to incriminate his mistress. Elizabeth herself denied everything and, since she had written no letters, made no promises, had not apparently done anything, it looked as if there was no case for her to answer. The Council, an unwieldy and increasingly factious body, remained deeply divided on the subject of her future – or lack of it. 'What one advises, another opposes,' wrote Renard; 'one strives to save Courtenay, another Elizabeth; and such is the confusion that one can only expect the upshot to be arms and tumult.'[32]

Thomas Wyatt was executed on 11 April and, in his last moments, publicly exonerated both Elizabeth and Courtenay from any complicity in the rebellion. The news spread joyfully through the city and after that, of course, any attempt to bring the Princess to trial would have been the signal for a popular uprising far more serious than anything which had gone before. So, what was to be done with her? As early as the end of March, William Paget had begun to suggest that, if it turned out to be impossible to put Elizabeth to death, then the best way of arranging matters might be to marry her to a foreigner – the Prince of Piedmont was his candidate this time – and settle the succession on her and her husband if the Queen died childless – a proposition to which Renard thought it better to make no immediate reply.[33]

Meanwhile, some decision had to be taken. The Princess couldn't very well be set free at once (Renard believed that, if she were, the heretics would probably proclaim her Queen), but already she was being allowed out to walk in the Tower gardens and she couldn't be left in prison much longer. Courtenay's friends were working on the Queen to persuade her to pardon him and it seemed as if he, too, was going to get off scot free – although Renard remained convinced that, in his determination to shield his protege, Stephen Gardiner had suppressed evidence which might have convicted both Courtenay and Elizabeth, and it's certainly true that an intercepted despatch of de Noailles', containing an account of Courtenay's crucial interview with the Chancellor in January, had conveniently gone missing.[34]

Eventually a face-saving formula was arrived at. It was agreed to send Courtenay to rusticate at Fotheringay Castle and, on 19 May, Elizabeth, demurely inscrutable as ever, departed for the disused royal residence at Woodstock under the escort of Sir Henry Bedingfield, a loyal and incorruptible Catholic gentleman from Norfolk, who was charged with the not very enviable task of keeping her out of harm's way and out of mischief until a more satisfactory solution to the problem of her future could be found.

The Princess's celebrated incarceration had lasted just under two months and, while it had undoubtedly been a frightening and upsetting experience, it may also have contained a few lighter moments. There's a longstanding tradition that she managed to see something of one of her fellow prisoners – her old friend Robert Dudley who, with his three surviving brothers, still languished in the Beauchamp Tower under sentence of death for his part in the family's enterprising activities during the previous summer. Elizabeth occupied a room in the neighbouring Bell Tower and, in spite of the strict security precautions being enforced in the crowded fortress, it's not impossible that the two could have contrived to meet. The tradition which maintains that this was the time when they fell in love is a good deal more doubtful. They had known each other since they were children – as he climbed to power the Duke of Northumberland had missed no opportunity of introducing his numerous progeny to the attention of the royal family, and Elizabeth and Robert were almost exactly the same age. He was, therefore, no new figure of romance, and at a time when Elizabeth needed all her wits and her self-control for staying alive she was unlikely to have further complicated her situation or dissipated any energy on flirtation.

Whatever the truth of the matter, Elizabeth may well have drawn comfort from the knowledge of Robert's nearness, and there's nothing like having been in gaol together for cementing the bonds of friendship. When the Princess was sent to Woodstock, Robert remained behind – until the following October, when he and his brothers were finally pardoned and released and sent home with instructions to stay there and behave themselves. Home for Robert Dudley was with his young wife Amy and his father-in-law, John Robsart, on the latter's East Anglian estates. But the routine of country life had little to offer a restless ambitious younger son with his way to make in the world; and in 1557, when, as all opponents of the Spanish marriage had always predicted would happen, England was drawn into Spain's quarrel with France. Robert grasped at the chance to rehabilitate himself. He did well in the fighting at St Quentin, and in March 1558 was sent home with despatches for the Queen at Greenwich. The same month the attainder on the family was lifted. Robert and his brothers and sisters were 'restored in blood' – an important step on the way towards more dramatic manifestations of royal favour.

28

No Alliance More Advantageous than That with the Duke of Savoy

Having postponed his arrival for as long – or rather longer than – he decently could, Philip of Spain finally disembarked at Southampton on Friday, 20 July 1554, and to the crowds of curious sightseers who trampled over one another in their eagerness to catch a glimpse of him, the bloodstained ogre of the Protestant propaganda machine was revealed as a slim dapper young man, rather below average height with blue eyes and yellow hair and beard which, some observers considered, made him look like a Fleming.[1]

Philip had come primed with instructions to be affable and to show himself to the people, to be lavish with presents as well as with smiles, to 'caress the nobility' and take them hunting with him – in short, to make every effort to placate and propitiate the rude, heretical English.[2] To a prince very well aware of his importance as an international figure, and who was in the habit of concealing his natural shyness with strangers under a stiff reserved manner, such advice was no more palatable than the prospect of a middle-aged bride in a hostile country. But Philip was a dutiful son and realised quite as fully as his father the inestimable value of an alliance which would not only secure the sea-route to the Netherlands and help safeguard those wealthy Habsburg possessions against a predatory France but which might also, if all went well, permanently tilt the balance of power in Habsburg favour. If such an alliance was worth bedding a woman whom Philip sardonically described as his 'dear and well-beloved aunt', then it was certainly worth any amount of synthetic affability. He did his best – kissing all the Queen's ladies on the mouth after the English custom which, he tactfully declared, was a good one, laboriously learning a few words of the language and even, heroically, calling for some English beer and drinking it.[3]

The royal wedding took place in Winchester Cathedral on 25 July, the Queen in a trance of happiness keeping her eyes fixed on the sacrament throughout the hour-long nuptial mass. The fact that Philip was the greatest match in Christendom had always mattered far less to Mary Tudor than the fact that he was of her mother's kin, a true Catholic who would help her bring her people back to Rome. All that mattered now was the fact that he was there beside her, that she was already hopelessly, helplessly in love. When the religious ceremonies were over, the couple adjourned to the Bishop's Palace for a sumptuous wedding breakfast eaten off gold plate to the strains of music. This was followed by dancing, in which Philip's Spanish gentlemen led the English ladies on the floor and the King and Queen danced together 'after the German fashion'. Then, at last, after a quiet supper in their private apartments, Stephen Gardiner blessed the marriage bed and the newly wedded couple were left alone. 'What happened that night,' wrote an anonymous Spaniard in a letter home, 'only they know. If they give us a son our joy will be complete.'[4]

A few weeks later Mary brought her bridegroom to London, travelling in easy stages via Basing, Reading and Windsor, with Philip always at her side, ready to help her mount and dismount, unfailingly polite and attentive. 'Their Majesties are the happiest couple in the world and more in love than words can say,' gushed a member of Philip's suite, and the Spaniards were full of praise for their master's exquisite manners, for the Queen, although a dear good creature and a perfect saint, dressed badly, was older than they'd been led to expect and was not at all beautiful, being small and flabby with no eyebrows.[5]

To everyone's relief the entry into the capital passed off without incident. Renard reported that the people had been favourably impressed by Philip's appearance and their present opinion seemed to be that he was a handsome prince 'of benign and humane countenance and likely to turn out a good ruler'.[6] There was, inevitably, a fair amount of jealousy and backbiting. The Spaniards complained that they were being palmed off with inferior accommodation, were not allowed to do anything for their prince, were insulted when they ventured on to the streets and horribly overcharged in shops and inns; while the English grumbled that it was they who were kept kicking their heels in Philip's antechamber, that London was overrun by foreigners who made them feel like strangers in their own homes and that the Queen seemed to care nothing for her own subjects but only for Spaniards and bishops.[7] There were faults and nasty prejudices on both sides, and the atmosphere was often edgy and strained, but considering what had gone before things might have been a great deal worse.

There were two important developments on the political front that autumn – by the end of September, Mary believed herself to be pregnant and, by the end of November, England had once more become a Roman Catholic country. Both these interesting events were, in the long term, capable of altering the course of history. In the short term, both served to highlight the perennial problem of the Princess Elizabeth. Stephen Gardiner had never made any secret of his conviction that all attempts to eradicate English Protestantism would amount to no more than stripping the leaves and lopping the branches as long as the root of the evil – the heretical heiress presumptive – remained untouched. Back in the spring he had told Simon Renard that 'as long as Elizabeth lived he had no hope of seeing the kingdom in peace' and now he was insisting that a bill to bastardise and disinherit her should be introduced during the current session of Parliament. But there was little support for the Chancellor. Even Renard believed it would be a mistake to attack Elizabeth now – for one thing it would be bound to stir up trouble in the country and for another it might soon be unnecessary.[8] William Paget, always an influential figure, was taking the line that, since the Queen was with child, Elizabeth no longer mattered very much and the safest way of disposing of her would be to marry her off to 'some poor German prince'. The Emperor was inclined to agree – certainly marriage did seem the only possible solution – but with the stipulation that the poor German prince in question should have domains far enough inland to prevent his ever becoming a nuisance to England, and the Margrave of Baden was mentioned as a likely candidate.

Another idea might be to marry the Princess in Spain – to the Duke of Segorbe's son, for instance, whose lands were situated on the Mediterranean coast; but the obstacle here was that, being 'defiled' by heresy, Elizabeth or her servants might meddle in matters which the Inquisition would have to take seriously and the result would be scandal.[9] The thought of Elizabeth Tudor becoming a Spanish duchess and scandalising the Holy Office is sufficiently intriguing, but the Emperor was probably only thinking aloud – at any rate, nothing more was heard of this interesting scheme.

In the meantime, another suitor had decided to try his luck in person. Emmanuel Philibert, Duke of Savoy, was a poor relation of the Habsburg clan and, since losing his duchy in the everlasting dispute with France, had become entirely dependent on Habsburg patronage. To a professional soldier in reduced circumstances the prospect of marrying the English princess was naturally an enticing one, and in November 1554, the Duke was planning to sail to England and 'pluck the fruit of the hopes that are now blossoming there'.[10] He did, in fact, cross the Channel and seems to have stayed at Somerset Place, Elizabeth's London house. But he did not see the Princess, who was still at Woodstock, and left again shortly after Christmas a disappointed man.

Emmanuel Philibert, though, had his supporters. In the spring of 1555, Simon Renard prepared a long memorandum on English affairs for Philip, who was already beginning to wonder how soon he could get away, and inevitably a good deal of this document was concerned with the twin problems of Elizabeth and the succession. 'Supposing', wrote Renard, 'the Queen is not with child and dies without issue, there will certainly be strife and the heretics will espouse the cause of the Lady Elizabeth.' If

Elizabeth was set aside, he reminded Philip again, the next heir would be the Queen of Scotland. But, if Elizabeth were to succeed, England would undoubtedly relapse into heresy and very likely into a new alliance with France – unless something was done to prevent it. 'If Elizabeth is married to an Englishman,' Renard went on, 'she will prevail upon her husband to adopt the new religion, even if he is a Catholic. If a foreign husband is found for her, it will be necessary to make sure that he is constant and faithful to your Majesty.'[11]

After nearly two years in England, Renard had come to realise that it would be virtually impossible to upset Henry VIII's will, and that Elizabeth's right to the succession would have to be recognised. Therefore, he argued, 'there would seem to be no alliance more advantageous for her than that with the Duke of Savoy'. It would be better than marrying the Princess in Germany or Spain, since the Duke could act as Philip's lieutenant in England, helping the Queen to cope with the burden of government during her husband's unavoidable absences. Then, when Philip returned, he might go over to Flanders and take Elizabeth with him, thus helping to promote international understanding. Renard believed that the marriage would be popular and that the sooner it was arranged the better. In any case, he urged Philip to see Elizabeth before he left the country and warn her to behave herself, in which case he might promise to remember her and to 'do what is suitable for her'.[12]

This last piece of advice, at least, the King took and, at the end of April, Elizabeth was summoned to Hampton Court, where the royal household had gone to prepare for the Queen's confinement. Courtenay had been released from Fotheringay and sent to travel abroad – to the Imperial court in Brussels in the first instance, so that his activities could be supervised – but Philip wanted Elizabeth under his own eyes. He may have been motivated in part by natural curiosity, but he was also taking out insurance against an uncertain future. If Mary died in childbirth, a fate which frequently overtook young strong women, and if the baby (always supposing there was a baby) died with her, Philip and his small retinue of Spaniards would find themselves isolated among a hostile population. In such circumstances it would be useful to have a hostage, perhaps even an ally. The Venetian ambassador went so far as to remark that Philip's safety and security would depend more on Elizabeth than any other person, and it was being widely speculated that the King might be contemplating a marriage with his sister-in-law if the Queen were to die.[13]

Elizabeth, though, was still officially in disgrace and she arrived at court 'very privately', entering the palace by a back way, still under the escort of Sir Henry Bedingfield and accompanied by a mere handful of her own people. She remained isolated in her apartments for nearly another month but, according to French and Venetian sources, the King and Queen both saw her in private. According to the Protestant historian John Foxe, who provides a detailed account of the occasion, Elizabeth was summoned to her sister's bedroom late one evening towards the end of May and a reconciliation was patched up between them.[14] Foxe declares that Philip was present, hidden behind a curtain; but, whether this is true or not, the reconciliation and Elizabeth's return to at least a limited amount of favour had undoubtedly been engineered by Philip. A correspondent writing to Edward Courtenay in Brussels on 25 May was able to assure him that 'my Lady Elizabeth is at her full liberty' and that she had seen the Queen twice.

It was a restless uneasy summer. 'Everything in this kingdom depends on the Queen's safe deliverance,' wrote Renard in June and if, against all the odds, Mary did give birth to a healthy child, then the Habsburgs would have absorbed England as efficiently and cheaply as in the previous generation they had absorbed Spain, and the rich Burgundian inheritance of the Netherlands in the generation before that. So, at least, it appeared to most thinking Englishmen in the spring and summer of 1555 and the thought was not a pleasant one. Not even the most committed Catholic could summon up any enthusiasm at the prospect of seeing his country fall victim to yet another dynastic takeover bid by the Habsburgs family. Small wonder, then, that Renard noticed some strange expressions on the faces of the people round him. Even those he had previously counted as allies now seemed to have 'a masked appearance'.[15]

Early in the morning of 30 April a rumour reached London that the Queen had been delivered of a male child during the night 'with little pain and no danger'. Despite lack of official confirmation the report was so circumstantial that it was generally believed. Church bells were rung through the city, bonfires lit in the streets and free wine provided for all comers. Whatever its implications, the birth of a prince was automatically an occasion for rejoicing. But rejoicing was premature, as were prophecies of doom. There was no prince, not even any sign of his imminent arrival. On 24 June, Renard reported that the Queen's doctors had proved to be two months out in their calculations and that she would not be delivered for another eight or ten days. July came in and still the empty cradle waited, but Mary stubbornly refused to give up hope. Sir John Mason in Brussels was ordered to contradict the now widespread gossip that the Queen was not pregnant at all and to assure the Emperor's court that she was near her time. The doctors and midwives were still talking about miscalculation and hinting that the Queen might not be delivered until August or even September, but only the pathetic Queen believed them.

By the beginning of August something had to be done to bring Mary back to reality and put an end to what was rapidly becoming an acute embarrassment. Apart from anything else, the Queen's long seclusion and her refusal to transact any business were bringing the work of government to a virtual halt. So, on the third of the month, the court moved away to the royal hunting lodge at Oatlands where there would be no accommodation for the noble ladies who had flocked to the palace to support the Queen through her ordeal and who had been living there at her expense all summer. In order to save as much face as possible, it was given out that Hampton Court needed cleansing (and so it must have done after four months of crowded occupation), but everyone recognised the move for what it was – Mary's tacit admission of defeat. As the Venetian ambassador put it, the pregnancy seemed to have ended in wind. In fact, the amenorrhoea and digestive troubles which had afflicted Mary ever since her unhappy adolescence, together possibly with incipient cancer of the womb, had combined with her desperate yearning to bear Philip's child to produce this tragic self-deception.

Elizabeth did not accompany her sister and brother-in-law to Oatlands, but she had every reason to be pleased with the way events were moving. She had regained her freedom of action, and the fear of seeing her inheritance fall to some little half-Habsburg intruder had receded. She also now felt reasonably confident that she could rely on Philip's protection. The Princess had not wasted these months at Hampton Court. While Mary hid herself away in the stuffy foetid atmosphere of the palace, often sitting on the floor for hours at a time with her knees drawn up to her chin, Elizabeth had been busy laying the foundations of a useful friendship with the prince of Spain. Two years later, the retiring Venetian ambassador noted in his report to the Doge and Senate that 'at the time of the Queen's pregnancy, the Lady Elizabeth . . . contrived so to ingratiate herself with all the Spaniards, and especially with the King, that ever since no one has favoured her more than he does; for not only would he not permit, but opposed and prevented the Queen's wish to have her disinherited and declared a bastard by Act of Parliament . . . which, besides affection, implies some particular design on the part of the King with regard to her'.[16]

Philip's designs with regard to Elizabeth could undoubtedly have been summed up in a single question: how best could the English heiress be made to serve Habsburg interests? With every week that passed it was becoming more and more obvious that Elizabeth would, in due course, succeed her sister, and now that he had made her acquaintance, Philip could view the future in a rather more optimistic light. The Princess appeared to have seen the error of her ways and was behaving herself like a good Catholic. In spite of Simon Renard's gloomy forebodings, Philip believed that this demure, flatteringly deferential young lady might yet be turned into an asset. The right husband would have to be found for her – that went without saying – but there was no immediate hurry. Elizabeth would do nothing without consulting the brother-in-law who had taken such a kindly interest in her affairs and she was still full young, not quite twenty-two. Besides, in August 1555, Philip had other things on his mind. All sorts of problems urgently needing his attention were piling up abroad and, in any case, he was itching to escape from the uncongenial scene of his disappointing and unfruitful marriage. But before he left England at the end of the month he took the precaution of telling the Queen that he wanted Elizabeth to be treated with consideration and, according to the French, followed this up by writing to Mary from Flanders 'commending the princess to her care'.

Elizabeth had gone down to Greenwich with the rest of the court to see Philip off and stayed there for about six weeks. She was still very much on her best behaviour, going to mass with the Queen every day; while Mary, mindful of her husband's instructions, was trying hard to conceal her 'evil disposition' towards Anne Boleyn's daughter under a mask of synthetic amiability. Both sisters probably found all this a considerable strain and, when the Queen returned to London in October for the opening of Parliament, Elizabeth seized the opportunity to apply for permission to go back to the country – permission which was eagerly granted.

The winter passed with no sign of Philip's return – and no sign, either, that he had made up his mind about Elizabeth's future. There were various reports of vague plans for sending her over to Spain but, although the Queen was said to be strongly in favour, fears of the outcry which would be caused by any attempt to take the heir to the throne out of the country caused them to be abandoned – at least, according to the Venetians.[17] There was a somewhat bizarre scheme to marry the Princess to Philip's son, Don Carlos, but – again according to Venetian sources – Elizabeth was now saying plainly that she would not marry 'even were they to give her the King's son'.[18] Since Don Carlos was only ten years old and rumoured to be not quite right in the head, this reaction seemed understandable. Rather more plausible were the reports that the Emperor was planning a match between the Queen of England's sister and his nephew Ferdinand of Austria. When the King of France heard about this, he threatened to marry his son's fiancée, Mary Queen of Scots, to Edward Courtenay – anything to prevent the House of Austria from establishing itself permanently in England.[19]

Edward Courtenay had now left Brussels and was on his way to Italy, but during the spring and early summer of 1556 his name was once more being linked with the Princess Elizabeth. In March details of the Dudley conspiracy – so called after one of its ringleaders, Sir Henry Dudley, a distant connection of the Duke of Northumberland – began to come to light. In outline, the plot 'to send the Queen's Highness over to the King and to make the Lady Elizabeth Queen and to marry the Earl of Devonshire to the said lady' bore a close family resemblance to the aims of the Wyatt conspirators. But, although their activities were symptomatic of a deep-rooted and widespread discontent with Mary's policies, plus strong resentment over the generally held belief that the Queen loved foreigners and hated Englishmen, Dudley and his friends (who included a number of distinctly gamy characters) never commanded any worthwhile support among the 'substantial gentry'. This levelheaded and influential section of the community reflected that the Queen was an ailing childless woman who had passed her fortieth birthday and made up its collective mind to wait for nature to take its course.

This was certainly the attitude being adopted by the heir to the throne; but as Giovanni Michiel of the Venetian embassy pointed out, 'never is a conspiracy discovered in which either justly or unjustly she or some of her servants are not mentioned'.[20] On this occasion four of Elizabeth's servants, including Mrs Ashley, her old friend and governess, were mentioned loudly enough to be arrested, but there was no question now of proceeding against the Princess herself. The country would not have stood for it and neither would Philip of Spain. Instead, two gentlemen of the royal household were sent down to Hatfield bearing a kind message from the Queen, assuring her sister of her continued goodwill and using 'loving and gracious expressions, to show her that she is neither neglected nor hated, but loved and esteemed by her Majesty'. Michiel added significantly that this had been very well taken by the whole kingdom.[21] All the same, Mary did seize the opportunity to reorganize the household at Hatfield. A 'widow gentlewoman' was installed to replace Mrs Ashley, and Sir Thomas Pope, 'a rich and grave gentleman, of good name both for conduct and religion', appointed to be the Princess's governor. Elizabeth accepted these changes with a good grace. Thomas Pope, a witty cultivated man, the founder of Trinity College, Oxford, made a pleasant enough companion and his presence would, she knew, act as a safeguard.

It was a long hot summer with everywhere the consciousness of sullen revolt simmering just below the surface. In July a Suffolk schoolmaster called Cleobury caused a local flare-up by attempting to impersonate Edward Courtenay and proclaiming 'the Lady Elizabeth Queen and her beloved bedfellow, Lord Courtenay, King'.[22] In the circumstances, therefore, the news of her beloved bedfellow's death that September probably came as a profound relief to Elizabeth Tudor. As for Edward Courtenay, although the conspirators declared he had not been privy to their plans, the last few months of his shadowed life had been shadowed still further by the repercussions of the Dudley affair. There were rumours that he'd been offered 30,000 crowns to go to France and rumours among the English dissidents being harboured by Henri II that he would soon be coming to join them. There were rumours that the Duke of Ferrara was working to persuade him to serve France against England; rumours of a Spanish plot to have him murdered; rumours that he was planning to return home and take up arms against the Queen. Everywhere he went the unfortunate young man's footsteps were dogged by rumour, by suspicion and by spies. 'You will do very well to watch him [Courtenay] carefully and find out everything he is up to,' wrote Philip to his agent in Venice.[23] No wonder Courtenay lived so quietly, almost as if he hoped that by doing nothing, saying nothing, going nowhere he might become invisible to all those watching eyes. When death found the last of the Plantagenets in Padua, perhaps he was not sorry to be released.

The Spaniards made little attempt to hide their relief, and the Venetians wondered if Philip would now return to England. As Federico Badoer wrote rather enigmatically from the Netherlands, he might take this opportunity to 'better arrange such things as are desired by him, and which as yet he has been unable to obtain'.[24] Philip did not return, although Mary was still begging and praying him to come back to her; but, at the end of November, Elizabeth paid a brief visit to London. According to the gossip at the French court, the Queen had summoned her in order to press her to accept the Duke of Savoy. Elizabeth, it seems, had burst into tears and declared she would rather die. Whereupon the Queen, seeing that her sister 'still persisted in this opinion of not choosing to marry', had packed her off back to Hatfield with renewed threats to have her disinherited.[25]

Finally, in March 1557, Philip did return to England, bringing with him his sister and his cousin, the Duchesses of Parma and Lorraine. This promptly led to speculation that the ladies had come for the purpose of escorting 'Madama' Elizabeth back to Flanders to be married to the Duke of Savoy.[26] The French ambassador thoughtfully sent Elizabeth warning of this scheme, for which the Princess thanked him but declared again that nothing would induce her to consent to such a thing. In fact, the real purpose of Philip's visit was to embroil his wife's reluctant subjects in war with France. By the beginning of July, his mission accomplished, he was gone and Mary never saw him again.

But, in spite of all his other preoccupations, Philip had not forgotten about Elizabeth and during that summer he made what was probably his first really serious effort to settle his sister-in-law's future and the future of the English alliance. He instructed his confessor, Francisco de Fresneda, a man 'very dear to the Queen', to discuss the whole matter with her and to urge her to arrange Elizabeth's marriage with the Duke of Savoy without further delay. Fresneda was to explain how necessary this was for considerations of religion and piety, for the safety of the realm and to prevent all those evils which might ensue if Elizabeth, feeling herself slighted, were to choose a husband 'who might convulse the whole kingdom into confusion' – in other words, a husband hostile to the Habsburg interest.

Philip also wanted Mary to put an end to any remaining uncertainty about the succession by formally recognising Elizabeth as her heir, but here he came up against the blank wall of Mary's bitter obsessive jealousy of her half-sister. According to the Venetians – and their intelligence service was usually reliable – 'For many days during which the confessor treated this business, he found the Queen utterly averse to give Lady Elizabeth any hope of the succession, obstinately maintaining that she was neither her sister nor the daughter of the Queen's father, King Henry; nor would she hear of favouring her, as she was born of an infamous mother who had so greatly outraged the Queen her mother and herself.'[27]

It had long been an open secret among the diplomatic corps that the Queen's 'evil disposition' towards the Lady Elizabeth was due quite simply to the fact that Elizabeth was Anne Boleyn's daughter – a living reminder of Mary's sufferings at the time of her parents' divorce. Now this sad sick woman, faced with the realisation that her beloved husband was thinking only of a future in which she would have no share, was being asked publicly to admit that that future would belong to Anne Boleyn's daughter. She would not do it; and Philip, to whom the old feuds of the Tudor family were a mere irrelevance, was not unnaturally profoundly irritated by this new evidence of perversity on the part of his useless barren wife. But Philip was more than usually busy just then, with the French war and with taking over from his father – the old Emperor had decided to spend his last days in a monastery – so England would just have to wait, and once more the problem of Elizabeth was shelved.

Nevertheless, it continued to nag at the back of his mind, and it continued to nag at Simon Renard who, although he had left England in the autumn of 1555, still took a proprietary interest in English affairs. In March 1558 the ex-ambassador prepared another of his appreciations on the subject of the English succession, reminding Philip yet again of the undesirable consequences likely to follow Mary's death unless 'timely measures' were taken. Despite her careful Catholic observance, Simon Renard had never believed for a moment in the sincerity of Elizabeth's apparent conversion, and her principal supporters were all equally suspect. 'If she succeeds and marries an Englishman,' he wrote, 'religion will be undermined, everything sacred profaned, Catholics ill-treated, churchmen driven out, those monasteries which have been restored will again suffer, churches will be destroyed, affairs which had taken a favourable turn will once more be compromised . . . Moreover, the ancient amity, good neighbourliness and understanding that have so far been maintained, albeit with difficulty, between England and your Majesty's realms, will not only be impaired but disappear altogether.'[28]

Renard was still strongly of the opinion that the best – indeed, the only – solution to the problem was for Philip to find a husband for the Princess abroad and he still believed the Duke of Savoy was the only man who 'would appear to answer all requirements'. He was, however, very much afraid that his master had left it too late. Emmanuel Philibert himself had cooled off and was looking elsewhere for a wife, though he might still be attracted by the prospect of a seat on the English throne. As for Elizabeth, Renard had heard that 'she and the leading men of the realm would refuse a foreign match' and the Princess was in too strong a position now to be coerced. In spite of Mary's desperate last-ditch resistance, everyone knew that it was probably no more than a matter of months before Elizabeth Tudor became Queen of England.

Philip, of course, was not the only European sovereign taking an interest in her future, and in April the Protestant King of Sweden sent an ambassador to propose a marriage between the English heiress and his eldest son, Eric. The Swedes, however, were rash enough to address themselves to the Princess without first observing the formality of asking the Queen's permission – a breach of protocol which gave Elizabeth all the excuse she needed for sending the envoy about his business. All the same, when Mary got to hear about it, she worked herself into a great state of agitation, apparently afraid that Philip would blame her all over again for her opposition to the Savoy marriage and that he might take this opportunity to renew his pressure on her to come to a decision about her sister. Sir Thomas Pope was therefore instructed to speak to Elizabeth to try to find out what she really felt about the Swedish proposition and also if she had any plans about marriage in general. Elizabeth reiterated her settled preference for a spinster's life – an estate she liked so well 'as to persuade myself there is not any kind of life comparable to it'. As far as the Swedes were concerned, she could only say that she sincerely hoped she would never hear of them again. Probing a little further, Thomas Pope ventured to remark that he thought 'few or none would believe but that her Grace could be right well contented to marry; so that there were some honourable marriage offered her by the Queen's highness, or by her Majesty's assent'. But Elizabeth was not to be drawn. 'What I shall do hereafter I know not,' she answered calmly, 'but I assure you, upon my truth and fidelity, and as God be merciful unto me, I am not at this time otherwise minded than I have declared unto you; no, though I were offered the greatest prince in all Europe.' This was no way for a healthy young woman of twenty-four to be talking and, like a sensible man, Sir Thomas Pope didn't take such nonsense seriously for a moment. As he commented in his report, 'the Queen's majesty may conceive this rather to proceed of a maidenly shamefacedness, than upon any such certain determination'.[29] Whether or not Mary believed that Elizabeth meant what she said, she was calmer after hearing from Hatfield though, as Count de Feria, over from Brussels for a few months, told Philip, she continued to take a passionate interest in the affair.[30]

Poor Mary, she had always taken a passionate interest in marriages, in babies and christenings. If only things had been different she'd have been delighted to have found a husband for her sister, to have fussed over the details of her trousseau, given her good advice and stood godmother to her first child. But Mary Tudor had been called upon to face many sorrows, many injustices and disappointments; perhaps the one thing she could not have faced would have been to see Elizabeth make a successful marriage and bear the children Mary had craved with all the strength of her starved and passionate nature. Even so, if she had guessed that many people suspected Philip was only waiting for her death to marry Elizabeth himself and that this was the cause of his curious lethargy in the matter of her future, Mary might have tried to force the girl into the arms of Emmanuel Philibert and she might even have succeeded.

Years later there was a piece of gossip going round that Philip had been heard to attribute his sufferings at the hands of Queen Elizabeth to the judgement of God because 'being married to Queen Mary, whom he thought a most virtuous and good lady, yet in the fancy of love he could not affect her; but as for the Lady Elizabeth, he was enamoured of her, being a fair and beautiful woman'. It seems highly improbable that the prudent Philip was ever heard to say anything of the kind, but it's not impossible that he had been physically attracted to his sister-in-law – and he was a man of strong physical appetites, however rigorously he learnt to suppress them. One way or another during the mid-1550s there were enough cross-currents of sexual jealousy, of guilt, desire and old bitter resentment in the relationship of this peculiar threesome successfully to militate against the pragmatic approach advocated by Simon Renard – to prevent the sensible arranged marriage of the English heiress to some Habsburg nominee ever getting beyond the discussion stage. And it's worth remembering that, if the project had been tactfully presented and pursued at all seriously during the period between the death of Edward Courtenay and the disastrous French war which finally wrecked Philip's credit in England, Elizabeth might have found it very difficult to stand out against the pressure which could have been exerted on her. A lot of ifs and a good deal of speculation, but the fact remains that a unique variety of circumstances, both political and personal, had combined to enable Elizabeth to reach her twenty-fifth birthday still single and still unfettered to any foreign interest.

By the early autumn of 1558 it was becoming obvious that Mary's illness was approaching its final stages. By 22 October the news reaching Philip in Flanders had become sufficiently alarming for him to send Count de Feria back to England. The Venetians heard that 'the matter to be treated by him is the marriage of Miladi Elizabeth, to keep that kingdom in any event in the hands of a person in his Majesty's confidence', and that the Count's instructions 'purport that he is to try and dispose the Queen to consent to Lady Elizabeth being married as her sister, and with the hope of succeeding to the crown'.[31] De Feria arrived in London on 9 November, but whatever instructions he may have brought with him were already out of date and he was received, as he put it, like 'a man who came accredited with the Bulls of a dead Pope'. Three days earlier Mary had finally given in and recognised Elizabeth's right to succeed her, and now she was sinking fast. It didn't take de Feria long to realise that there was nothing more he could usefully do at St James's and by 10 November he was travelling the already crowded road to Hatfield.

Elizabeth received him amiably enough and invited him to supper. She spoke gracefully of her gratitude for Philip's kind offices towards her in the past, but she would have no truck with his ambassador's attempt to persuade her 'that the announcement of her succession was not owing either to the Queen or to the Council, but to Philip'. Elizabeth Tudor made it plain that she owed her crown to no foreign monarch, not even to the nobility of the realm, although they had all pledged their loyalty, but to 'the attachment of the people of England, to whom', commented de Feria, 'she seemed much devoted'. The Princess and the ambassador sent on to discuss the characters of various English notables who came up in the course of conversation and laughed together over the idea of her marrying the middle-aged Earl of Arundel, one of the more preposterous of her English suitors. De Feria took the opportunity of sounding her on the subject of marriage generally and was told she was aware that Philip had wanted her to marry the Duke of Savoy but that Mary's popularity had suffered by marriage with a foreigner. De Feria tried to offer the same sort of advice about caution and moderation that Simon Renard had once offered Mary, but the interview left him with a distinct impression that the queen-elect meant to be governed by no one. She was very vain, he wrote, and very acute and appeared to be an enthusiastic admirer of her father's methods and policies.[32]

Barely a week later Mary Tudor was released from her earthly troubles. As the news spread through London the church bells were rung and by afternoon the November dusk was being illuminated by bonfires as the citizens set tables in the streets and 'did eat and drink and make merry for the new Queen Elizabeth'.[33]

29

I Am Already Wedded to an Husband

The new Queen Elizabeth made her state entry into London on 28 November, riding from the Charterhouse through streets gay with banners and lined with cheering crowds; the trumpets brayed before her, the City waits blew enthusiastically down their various instruments, church bells pealed and the Tower guns thundered a salute such as 'never was heard afore'. Elizabeth's popularity – especially with the Londoners – had been her chief source of strength in recent times, but she was not likely to have forgotten that, only five years before, these same crowds had given her sister an equally rousing welcome. Nor is it likely that she would have failed to realise how much of her own popularity was due to the general dislike of Mary's régime, or that beneath all the cheering, the pealing of bells and the roar of the cannon there lurked a rather desperate optimism.

In the decade which had passed since King Henry's death England had suffered from the rule of greedy factious juntas and the weak, incompetent government of an inept and unlucky queen. The resultant dismal chaos – economic, political and social – filled most thinking men with gloom. 'I never saw . . . England weaker in strength, men, money and riches,' commented one; while another drew up a stark and succinct memorandum of the most urgent problems facing the new administration: 'The Queen poor, the realm exhausted, the nobility poor and decayed. Want of good captains and soldiers. The people out of order. Justice not executed. All things dear. Excess in meat, drink and apparel. Divisions amongst ourselves. Wars with France and Scotland . . . Steadfast enmity but no steadfast friendship abroad.'[1] Armagil Waad did not add – he scarcely needed to – that what England needed now was a strong and able ruler – someone with the personality to unite the nation and the tough-mindedness to re-establish the authority of the Crown; someone with the statesmanship to provide a period of peace and stability at home, while clearing up the economic mess, and restoring prestige abroad.

After their recent unfortunate experience of petticoat government by no means all Englishmen were convinced that the country would be any better off under another woman head of state, but Elizabeth was the last of King Henry's children and she looked like being the last hope of the Tudor dynasty. The bogey of a disputed and uncertain succession, caused by an unprecedented shortage of male heirs in the direct line, had overshadowed English political life for more than half a century and there can be very little doubt that, in the opinion of the vast majority of her subjects, by far and away the most valuable service their new Queen could render them would be to marry and bear sons – sturdy English sons to guard their future and their children's future.

In the circumstances, Elizabeth's matrimonial intentions were of the closer personal interest to her own countrymen, but the importance of the Queen of England's marriage extended far beyond the domestic sphere. England might currently be a trifle down-at-heel but she remained potentially a rich country and, in any case, nothing could alter the strategic value of her position on the map. In the struggle for supremacy between the two great European power-blocs, whoever commanded the English alliance would always keep the edge over his rival; and for Philip, with his extended and vulnerable lines of communication, a friendly or at least a neutral England continued to be an essential factor in his diplomacy.

On the face of it, the international situation at the end of 1558 should have favoured Philip. England was still officially at war with France, and France still harboured Mary Queen of Scots, almost sixteen now and married seven months previously to the Dauphin. The Queen of Scots had an undoubted claim to be regarded as heir presumptive to the English throne and, in the eyes of all those orthodox Roman Catholics who had never recognised King Henry's famous divorce, she had a strong claim to be regarded as the rightful Queen, rather than Elizabeth, born during the lifetime of her father's first wife. The King of France had gone so far as to have his daughter-in-law proclaimed queen of England on Mary Tudor's death; young Mary Stuart and her husband were already quartering the English royal arms with their own, in what would appear to be a deliberately provocative gesture; while rumours were circulating that the French intended to urge the Pope to declare Elizabeth 'a bastard and a heretic and therefore ineligible to the Crown'.[2] Add to this the fact of a strong French presence in Scotland, still being ruled by Mary's mother, the Queen-Dowager; the loss of Calais, last outpost of England's once great Continental empire, in the recent disastrous war; and it would seem that the English must of necessity turn to Spain for protection against the threat from France. So it would seem, and yet, on 21 November, de Feria wrote to Philip from London: 'The new Queen and her people hold themselves free from your Majesty and will listen to any ambassadors who may come to treat of marriage.'[3]

De Feria was only too well aware how important it was that 'this affair' should go through Philip's hands, but he foresaw difficulties 'except with great negotiation and money'. Negotiations, though, could not even begin until the identity of a Spanish candidate had been settled. The Duke of Savoy was now definitely a non-starter. According to de Feria, the English would not hear his name mentioned as they feared, reasonably enough, that 'he will want to recover his estates with English forces and will keep them constantly at war'. Archduke Ferdinand remained as a possible alternative but new complications had arisen here. Charles V had died in September and that German electors had chosen to confer the title of Emperor on his brother, father of the hopeful Ferdinand and the other, younger Archduke, Charles. It would never do for the Austrian Habsburgs to start getting ideas about their station, so if Ferdinand were lucky enough to be preferred it would have to be made perfectly clear that he was receiving 'the titbit', as de Feria put it, at his Spanish cousin's hands. And what of that highly eligible widower, Philip himself? The court at Brussels was buzzing with gossip about the King's intention to have 'Miladi' Elizabeth for himself but, cautious as ever, he showed no immediate signs of coming to the point – in spite of de Feria's confident assurances that if the Queen decided to marry out of the country 'she will at once fix her eyes on Your Majesty'.

Three weeks later the ambassador had become rather less optimistic. Already English affairs seemed to be sliding out of his grasp. The Queen was a sharp-witted young woman, but flighty and altogether too sure of herself. The government was now entirely in the hands of the heretical younger generation and all Queen Mary's reliable Catholic friends were being eclipsed. Spaniards were as unpopular as ever, and de Feria found himself cold-shouldered by the court, so that it was increasingly difficult for him to find out what was going on. He believed, shrewdly enough, that his best course would be to get a foot into the palace and see more of the Queen 'as she is a woman who is very fond of argument'. But, he went on, 'everybody thinks that she will not marry a foreigner and they cannot make out whom she favours, so that nearly every day some new cry is raised about a husband'.[4]

De Feria warned Philip that, in the present confused and excited climate of opinion, he could see no disposition, on the part of either the Queen or the Council, to consider 'any proposal on your Majesty's behalf'. All that could be done for the moment was to work on individual councillors to put them off the general ideas of marrying the Queen to an Englishman. Though, even when they had made up their minds to accept a foreigner, the ambassadors believed they would look more favourably on Ferdinand than Philip 'because they think he will always reside in the country and will have no quarrel with France'.[5] As for Elizabeth herself, de Feria knew no more than the next man what her real intentions were, but he hoped it might be possible to reach her by appealing to her vanity. 'We must begin by getting her into talk about your Majesty,' he wrote, 'and run down the idea of her marrying an Englishman and thus to hold herself less than her sister who would never marry a subject.' It could be pointed out how badly it would look if she chose one of her own countrymen (and luckily there was hardly a man among them worth mentioning) when there were such great princes available. The Queen of England could also be reminded of the rival claims of the Queen of Scots and of her urgent need for a powerful male protector. But, having succeeded in putting her in a suitably receptive frame of mind, de Feria could proceed no further without instructions from his master. 'If she inclines to your Majesty,' he observed rather plaintively in a long despatch dated 14 December, 'it will be necessary for you to send me orders whether I am to carry it any further to throw cold water on it and set up the Archduke Ferdinand, because I do not see what other person we can propose to whom she would agree.'[6]

Philip, though, was not to be hurried – not even de Feria's cry that 'one fine day we shall find this woman married and I shall be the last man in the place to know anything about it' could stir him into precipitate action – and it was the second week of January before he finally made up his mind to declare himself. In a matter of such grave importance, as he solemnly reminded the ambassador, 'it was necessary for me to take counsel and maturely consider it in all its bearings before I sent you my decision'. But even now it was a decision so hedged about with misgivings and conditions and made with such obvious reluctance as surely to dispose of any sentimental notions that Philip was cherishing a secret passion for his late wife's sister. On the contrary, the King could see the 'many great difficulties' which would present themselves with horrid clarity and proceeded to enumerate them to de Feria with a certain gloomy relish. He would not be able to spend much time in England – with his increased responsibilities perhaps less even than he had spent before. Another Anglo-Spanish marriage alliance 'would appear like entering upon a perpetual war with France' – a war in which the French would possess a useful weapon in the person of the Queen of Scots. In addition to this, another English wooing would involve him in crippling expense at a time when his exchequer was 'so utterly exhausted as to be unable to meet the most necessary ordinary expenditure, much less new and onerous charges'.[7]

On the other hand, Philip, that most Catholic of monarchs, could not lose sight of 'the enormous importance of such a match to Christianity and the preservation of religion which has been restored in England by the help of God'. Elizabeth's regrettable unsoundness over religion was only too well-known, and ever since her accession de Feria had been bombarding his master with dire warnings about the growing power and influence of the heretical faction. So, in view of the ethical and political importance of keeping England in the Roman fold, the King of Spain was resolved to set aside all objections and 'to render this service to God and offer to marry the Queen of England'. In return for this honour the Queen would, of course, have to undertake to remain a Catholic herself and promise to 'maintain and uphold' the faith in her kingdom by whatever means might seem necessary to her husband. 'In this way,' remarked Philip more than a little smugly, 'it will be evident and manifest that I am serving the Lord in marrying her and that she has been converted by my act.'[8]

Whether, after her sister's recent experience, either Philip or de Feria seriously expected Elizabeth would accept such a proposal is impossible to say but, having received the instructions he had been agitating for, the ambassador made no immediate attempt to follow them up. Philip had been insistent that this delicate matter must first be broached to the Queen alone, and obviously a propitious moment would have to be chosen – especially as de Feria still had really no idea about what she was thinking. Elizabeth was currently very much occupied with her coronation and its attendant festivities and with preparations for the opening of her first Parliament, which was to take place at the end of January, and de Feria had seen her only once, 'in the little chamber leading out of the privy chamber'. He did not bring up the marriage question then because, although the Queen had chatted to him 'very gaily', she was suffering from a heavy cold and, in any case, he thought it would be wiser to wait until Parliament had raised the subject, which Elizabeth informed him they were planning to do.[9]

Parliament got down to serious business during the first week of February, and on the afternoon of the sixth a deputation of members and Privy Councillors, headed by the Speaker, waited on the Queen and presented her with a petition urging her to take some man to be her husband. The deputation did not presume to be specific about his identity but it did point out in some detail the advantages which would accrue – the principal one, of course, being that the Queen might by marriage bring forth children and thus ensure her own immortality, and this, the Speaker of the Commons assured her fervently, was 'the single, the onely, the all-comprehending prayer of all English-men'.[10]

There are two accounts of the Queen's reaction to this, the first of numerous encounters she was to have with her anxious Commons on the subject of marriage. William Camden, who had access to some useful sources of confidential information through his friendship with William Cecil, says she told the Speaker that as a private person she had always chosen to remain single and, now that responsibility for governing the country had been laid upon her, she felt it would be 'inconsiderate folly' to add the distractions of marriage to a public career. In any case, she already had a husband – the kingdom of England – and, to emphasise her point, the Queen took her coronation ring from her finger and flourished it before her audience. 'Behold (said she, which I marvell ye have forgotten,) the Pledge of this my Wedlock and Marriage with my Kingdom . . . And do not (saith she) upbraide me with miserable lack of Children: for every one of you, and as many as are English-men, are Children and Kinsmen to me.'[11]

The official version of the Queen's reply, its text worked over and finally approved by the Queen herself, was not released for another four days and contains no mention of this classic piece of Elizabethan byplay. But in essence the two accounts agree. The Queen had so far remained unmarried by deliberate personal choice and hoped to continue in that way of life with which she was so thoroughly acquainted. If time or circumstances or both should cause her to change her mind, then she would be at pains to select a consort who could be trusted to be as careful for the preservation of the realm and people as she was herself. But Elizabeth made it clear that she regarded this as being an area very much within her own province and one in which she would tolerate no outside interference, however well-meant. As far as the succession was concerned, she reminded Parliament with characteristic hard-headedness that they could not be certain any children of hers would necessarily turn out well – on the contrary, they might 'grow out of kind and become perhaps ungracious'. For her own part, she would prefer to leave it to Providence, trusting that with God's help 'an heir that may be a fit governor' would make his appearance in due course. She herself would be quite content if, in the end, 'a marble stone shall declare that a Queen, having reigned such a time, lived and died a virgin'.[12]

This was not, on the face of it, a very satisfactory response to their petition and there was an abortive attempt by some members of the Commons to take the matter further by appointing a committee to discuss what authority should be vested in 'that person whom it shall please the Queen to take to husband'.[13] On the whole, though, this, the first of Elizabeth's 'answers answerless', was accepted with a good grace. No one, of course, took all that talk about living and dying a virgin in the least seriously, but the Queen was a young and desirable woman and she was entitled to be a little coy. Indeed, it was only right and proper that she should display a certain maidenly reluctance and, provided she didn't take too long over it, no reasonable man grudged her the opportunity to look around and survey the field.

Actually, when one got down to cases, the field was not all that extensive. As with Mary, most people would have preferred the Queen to marry at home, but in the spring of 1559 even the most enthusiastic xenophobe had to admit that the choice was limited to the point of virtual non-existence. Unless you counted the Earl of Arundel, an unimpressive widower in his late forties, or Sir William Pickering, diplomat and courtier and a great success with the ladies, there was really no one of suitable age and rank. The young Duke of Norfolk might have done (apart from being England's premier nobleman and only Duke, he was the Queen's cousin on her mother's side), but unfortunately he was already married. If only Edward Courtenay had not been so careless as to get himself carried off by fever in Italy, the story would have been very different. If Courtenay had survived, Elizabeth would have found it hard to evade matrimony. Probably she would not even have tried – the perils of refusing such an obviously pre-ordained match would have been too great – and the whole course of English history might have been changed. But Courtenay was dead and it was no use regretting the might-have-been. The Queen of England would have to look further afield for a husband, and anyone with a knowledge of the political realities was more or less resigned to the prospect of a foreign consort.

By the middle of February, de Feria had finally got round to making Philip's proposal and had been put off with 'fair words'. Elizabeth never had the smallest intention of accepting the King of Spain – it would have been the fastest way she could have chosen of committing political suicide – but de Feria was determined not to give this tiresome chit of a girl the satisfaction of being able to boast that she had refused the greatest prince in Christendom. He therefore cut short her objections and evasions and protestations about not wishing to marry, and it was finally agreed between them that he would have 'no answer that was not a very good one'. There the matter rested, but the ambassador was not optimistic, for, as he told Philip, he knew that the heretics who surrounded the Queen would take every opportunity to turn her against the idea.[14]

There were two other envoys in London that winter with marriage in mind. The Swedes had wasted no time in renewing the suit of their crown prince, but they seemed to have no idea of the social niceties to be observed in such matters. When the Swedish ambassador was brash enough to press the Queen for a reply to the letter sent to her the year before – the same which had caused Queen Mary so much anguish – he was told pretty sharply that this was no way for one monarch to approach another, especially a lady, and especially over a proposal of marriage. The letter in question had been written to the Princess Elizabeth. If the King of Sweden still wanted to offer his son, then he must address himself to the Queen of England in proper form. Elizabeth did not know whether Prince Eric was prepared to leave his country to marry her, but she would not leave hers for any consideration in the world.[15]

The other hopeful matchmaker was Count von Helfenstein, sent by the Emperor ostensibly to deliver his master's congratulations to the new Queen on her accession, but more importantly to try to discover what the prospects might be for the Habsburg Archdukes. The Emperor, like Philip, was concerned about the future of the Catholic religion in England, for he had heard disquieting rumours that the Queen was imbued with 'the new views of the Christian faith'. If this were so, it would probably put Ferdinand out of the running, as he was unassailably orthodox – there was also the little matter of his morganatic wife, Philippine Welser. Charles, being younger, was less set in his ways but his anxious father was naturally reluctant to expose him to the dangers of heretical infection and possible forfeiture of eternal salvation, unless, of course, the political advantages looked really worth having; nor did the Emperor want to risk offending Philip by seeming to poach on his preserves. Von Helfenstein was therefore instructed to say nothing about a marriage until he had seen how the land lay and had reported back to Vienna.[16]

The Count landed at Dover on 20 February and was given full V.I.P. treatment. He saw the Queen on the twenty-fifth when Elizabeth received him in her friendliest manner, asking after the health of the Emperor and his family, enquiring about the state of affairs in Germany, where Von Helfenstein himself came from, and whether he had had an easy journey, so that the Good Count was quite bowled over by her charms and wrote enthusiastic letters home in praise of her prudence and poise, her great-mindedness and 'all other heroic virtues'. He was also able to report that open curiosity was being displayed in English political circles about the Archdukes. 'There was no one there', he wrote on the day after his audience with the Queen, 'who did not, as vulgar parlance has it, prick up his ears and listen with great admiration and, as it were, silent reverence when I spoke or answered about the ages, the morals, the talents of Your Imperial Majesty's sons, as on these points frank and exhaustive enquiries were frequently made of me. For many thought that one of them would soon become consort of the Queen and rule her and England.' The broadest hints were dropped by the Earl of Sussex, who was acting as the Count's host, and even by the Queen herself that if he had anything private to say to her this could easily be arranged. The Count, obedient to his instructions, was careful not to commit himself but he was certainly given every reason to believe that a proposal was both expected and would be favourably received.[17]

As far as the religious question was concerned, von Helfenstein had made zealous and painstaking enquiries, but had 'observed nothing that deviates from the old Catholic creed'. Mass was still being said and fast-days kept, 'so there is great hope that, if they get a Catholic King, all religious questions may easily be settled by authority of the sovereign'. At the same time, the Count felt obliged to admit that, despite all his subtlety, he had been unable 'clearly to fathom' what the Queen's intentions were. 'From the very beginning of her reign,' he wrote, 'she has treated all religious questions with so much caution and incredible prudence that she seems both to protect the Catholic religion and at the same time not entirely to condemn or outwardly reject the new Reformation.'[18]

The burning of heretics, which had cast such a pall of gloom over the latter part of Mary's reign, had of course ceased and there had been a few minor innovations; but, at the end of February 1559, England was still officially a Catholic country and Count von Helfenstein was by no means the only person unable clearly to fathom Elizabeth's intentions with regard to the highly sensitive issue of religion. The concensus of government opinion was in favour of making haste slowly, and the Queen herself would pretty certainly have preferred to settle for a return to royal supremacy and an order of service based on the 1549 Prayer Book – in other words, to a modified form of the national Catholicism evolved by Henry VIII. It was, however, already clear that this would not satisfy the militant Protestants. These were still very much in a minority, but they formed a well-organised and articulate pressure-group, represented in the House of Commons by an influential choir of M.P.s eager to demonstrate that they wished to return not to the days of Henry VIII but to those of 'the young Josiah' his son.

For a time the government firmly resisted backbench attempts to force through a more radical solution to the problem; and as Easter approached, and with it the expected dissolution of Parliament, it looked very much as though the militants were going to lose the battle. Then, at the last moment, the Queen changed her mind. She adjourned the session, and when it re-assembled on 3 April a settlement along the lines of the second Edwardian Prayer Book, in which the mass had finally been transformed into a service of communion or commemoration, was officially put forward. Elizabeth had been taken aback by the strength of feeling and the determination manifested by the radical element in the Commons, but other factors had contributed to her sudden change of front. For one thing, the surviving Catholic bishops had proved irritatingly obstinate, all of them voting against the Supremacy Bill in the Lords. This meant that the Elizabethan Church would have to rely on Protestant divines, many of whom had taken refuge in such havens of advanced thought as Strasbourg and Geneva during Mary's reign and none of whom were prepared to accept anything less than the 1552 Prayer Book – some, indeed, would have liked to go further. Another development which undoubtedly influenced the Queen was the fact that a peace treaty had now been signed between England, France and Spain at Cateau-Cambrésis.[19]

Elizabeth's own religious inclinations were conservative – when she told de Feria that she believed in a Real Presence and only dissented from two or three things in the mass she was probably speaking quite sincerely. Certainly she disliked bigoted Protestants every bit as much, if not more, than bigoted Catholics and she had no time at all for the Calvinist breed of minister – the very name of John Knox was anathema to her. But she was far too astute not to see the dangers of attempting arbitrarily to impose a universally unpopular settlement, not to understand that the days when the nation would unquestioningly accept the sovereign's ruling on matters of salvation had gone for ever. Too many people now had read the Bible for themselves and had tasted the emotional and intellectual thrills of scriptural interpretation. Elizabeth, first-born child of the English Reformation, naturally came down on the Protestant side but she had been pushed further than she wanted to go and, despite their famous victory, the radical party did not get things all their own way – there was some disappointment among the returning exiles over the Queen's lack of godly zeal and her insistence on the retention of so much of 'the scenic apparatus of divine worship'. Nevertheless, when Parliament finally dispersed at the beginning of May, England was indisputably a Protestant country and the Anglican order of service, in very much the same form as it exists today, had become the only legal form of worship.

All this, of course, put an end to the Spanish courtship – as early as March, Elizabeth, in a rather excitable conversation with de Feria, had declared that she could not marry Philip 'as she was a heretic' and Philip, no doubt privately much relieved, had not waited for a formal refusal. In April he took the opportunity of sealing the new peace treaty by marrying the French princess Elisabeth, and the English Elizabeth remarked with a wistful air that the King of Spain could not, after all, have been so very much in love with her if he was not prepared to wait even four months![20]

De Feria knew the Queen well enough by this time not to take her seriously, but Philip was almost morbidly anxious that Elizabeth should not regard his marriage as a slight, or take it into her head that everything was now over between them. On the contrary, he wrote, de Feria was 'to assure her positively that this will not be so, but I am and shall remain as good a brother to her as before and as such shall take very great interest in what concerns her, and will try to forward her affairs as if they were my own'.[21] Philip was still hoping to draw England into the Habsburg net and had finally made up his mind to throw the full weight of his influence behind whichever of his archducal cousins seemed most likely to find favour. In a letter to de Feria dated 12 April he painstakingly outlined the obvious advantages of an Austrian marriage – advantages which the ambassador was to explain to the Queen at the earliest opportunity. Since neither Ferdinand nor Charles possessed a state of his own, her husband would be free to remain at her side and help her bear the burden of government. She would also acquire a host of powerful and affectionate relations who would welcome her into the family with open arms and give her all the protection she was ever likely to need; she would rise in the estimation of her own subjects and no one, at home or abroad, would dare to molest or offend her.[22] Naturally enough, it did not occur to Philip that the young Queen of England might regard the business of government not as a burden but as an absorbing challenge which she had no desire to share, or that she might have reservations about the prospect of all those affectionate Habsburg in-laws. After so many months and years of procrastination and indecision, the King had set his heart on this method of solving the Elizabeth problem and de Feria was urged to do his utmost to see that negotiations were brought to a speedy and successful conclusion.

De Feria himself, despite a gloomy conviction that the English and their queen were already at least half-way along the road to perdition, was prepared to concede that a marriage with Archduke Ferdinand appeared 'not a bad expedient' – if not, indeed, the only possible one. He accordingly made contact with Augustin Gyntzer, Count von Helfenstein's secretary, who had recently arrived in London with more friendly letters from the Emperor and a full-length portrait of Ferdinand, assuring him of wholehearted Spanish support and offering good – and, one suspects, rather patronising – advice on the best way to proceed. (De Feria was determined that, whatever happened, the Germans should be given no opportunity to claim credit for carrying off the prize independently.) The ambassador also went to see the Queen, finding her as usual full of fair words and graceful evasions of the issue. As he wrote to Philip on 18 April, 'to say the truth I could not tell your Majesty what this woman means to do with herself, and those who know her best know no more than I do.'[23]

In this same despatch, de Feria makes the first recorded public reference to the scandalous affair of the Queen's increasingly close, perhaps intimate, relationship with her old playmate Robert Dudley. 'During the last few days,' he observed, 'Lord Robert has come so much into favour that he does whatever he likes with affairs and it is even said that her Majesty visits him in his chamber day and night. People talk of this so freely that they go so far as to say that his wife has a malady in one of her breasts and the Queen is only waiting for her to die to marry Lord Robert. I can assure your Majesty that matters have reached such a pass that I have been brought to consider whether it would be well to approach Lord Robert on your Majesty's behalf, promising him your help and favour and coming to terms with him.'[24] Ten days later, after a querulous complaint about the difficulty of trying to negotiate anything with a woman so naturally changeable, and about the blindness, bestiality and general lack of understanding displayed by those around her, the ambassador went on: 'They talk a great deal about the marriage with Archduke Ferdinand and seem to like it, but for my part I believe she will never make up her mind to anything that is good for her. Sometimes she appears to want to marry him, and speaks like a woman who will only accept a great prince, and then they say she is in love with Lord Robert and never lets him leave her.'[25]

About a week after this, on 8 May, the Acts of Supremacy and Uniformity, twin cornerstones of the Elizabethan Religious Settlement received the royal assent and de Feria could only conclude that England had fallen into the hands of a woman 'who is a daughter of the devil, and the greatest scoundrels and heretics in the land'. The ambassador was already agitating for his recall and thankfully received permission to take his leave of the devil's daughter as soon as Parliament had risen. De Feria was an experienced and normally skilful diplomat but there could be no disguising the facts that his current mission had been a dismal and humiliating failure. He had totally failed to influence the course of events, failed to make any headway in negotiating the all-important English marriage and, worst of all in his opinion, failed to prevent the triumph of the heretics. In short, a raw young woman in her twenties had made rings round him and all he wanted to do now was to remove himself and his bride (he had recently married Jane Dormer, one of the late Queen's favourite maids) from the contaminating atmosphere of the godless island and never, never think about English affairs again. In his last despatch from London, dated 10 May, he reported that William Pickering, who had been strongly tipped as a possible bridegroom for the Queen, had returned home after a prolonged absence on the Continent. Elizabeth made quite a fuss of him, seeing him privately while Lord Robert was away on a hunting trip, and according to de Feria the London bookmakers were giving odds of four to one that he would soon be king. 'If these things were not of such great importance and so lamentable,' commented de Feria, 'some of them would be very ridiculous.'[26]

In fact, there is absolutely no evidence to suggest that Elizabeth ever seriously considered Pickering as a husband. He was an attractive man and amusing company, but that was all. Pickering himself naturally made the most of his brief ascendancy, entertaining lavishly, dining in solitary state to the accompaniment of a band of musicians and generally throwing his weight about. The Queen grew rather bored with him, and after a few months he had faded from the scene. The Swedes were still at court, bestowing expensive presents on all and sundry and getting laughed at for their pains, and there was no sign yet of any formal proposal from the Emperor. 'Meanwhile,' wrote the Italian gossip Il Schifanoya, 'my Lord Dudley is in very great favour and very intimate with her Majesty.'[27]

My Lord Robert Dudley, mounted on a snow-white steed, had been among the first to pay homage to the new Queen at Hatfield the previous November and she had rewarded him with the post of Master of the Horse, his 'beauty, stature and florid youth' together with his skill in riding a managed horse being apparently powerful recommendations. Good horsemanship and a fine presence were certainly both recommendations for this office, but it was no sinecure. The Master of the Horse was responsible for keeping the court adequately supplied with transport; for the buying, training, breeding and welfare of riding and carriage horses, pack horses and mules, horses capable of dragging heavy wagons over impossible roads, horses which could be trusted in crowds and processions. Robert always took this side of the job very seriously and worked hard at it, but his public and ceremonial duties were equally important and, involving as they did close attendance on the Queen on all state occasions, even more congenial. As for Elizabeth, she never made any secret of the pleasure she took in Robert's company and by the summer of 1559 it was beginning to look as if the Queen – who could have taken her pick of the bachelors of Christendom – had chosen to set her heart on the one man she could not have.

30

If the Emperor So Desires Me for a Daughter

On Friday, 26 May 1559, Caspar von Breuner, Baron of Stubling, Fladnitz and Rabenstein, arrived in London with powers to make the Queen a formal proposal of marriage on behalf of the Emperor's youngest son, Archduke Charles – Ferdinand having now definitely scratched from the English matrimonial stakes.

Von Breuner showed no signs of wishing to act independently of Spain. On the contrary, he immediately sought the assistance and hospitality of the Spanish embassy and 'was so determined to stay that there was no resisting him'. Don Alvaro de Quadra, Bishop of Aquila, who had taken over Count de Feria's thankless task, quickly summed up the good Baron as 'not the most crafty person in the world' and, bearing in mind his master's anxiety for the success of the Austrian mission, decided he had better be on hand during von Breuner's initial encounter with Elizabeth.

On the following Sunday afternoon, therefore, the two envoys went together to the palace, where they found the Queen 'very fine in her presence chamber looking on at the dancing'. De Quadra presented the Baron, begging Elizabeth to hear him out and decide the matter with 'the wisdom and prudence which God had given her', before standing aside with the air of one determined to give a junior colleague every chance to show what he could do. As it happened, the ambassador was able to fill in the time by having a useful chat with William Cecil on the subject uppermost in both their minds. The Secretary of State seemed distinctly lukewarm over the Austrian match, thinking, so de Quadra believed, that Ferdinand was about to be proposed 'as he is the only one that these people have any knowledge of and they have quite made up their minds that he would upset their heresy'. After mentioning all the flattering offers which the Queen had been receiving lately, Cecil went on to express polite regrets that religious difficulties had made a marriage with Philip impossible to arrange and de Quadra seized the opportunity to dispel any fears the Secretary and his friends might have that they had incurred his master's anger by their change of religion. He therefore answered 'without any reproach or complaint', merely remarking that what had been done certainly seemed 'very grave, severe and ill-timed' and hoping that a reform of those abuses at the court of Rome which had so scandalised the provinces would presently lead to a reconciliation, for surely God would not allow so noble and Christian a nation as England to remain separated in faith from the rest of Christendom to its own grave peril.[1]

This deliberately conciliatory policy towards the schismatic island was prompted in part by Philip's continuing need to keep the English alliance in being, and in part by his optimistic conviction that before long circumstances would force Elizabeth to marry into the Habsburg family. The King of Spain was to cling to this conviction for nearly ten years, but on that Sunday afternoon in May 1559 the prospects were not bright and Caspar von Breuner emerged from the Queen's presence in near-despair. Elizabeth was deeply honoured that the Emperor, whom she regarded as her dear lord and cousin, had deemed her worthy to marry one of his sons, and her own council and loyal subjects were daily and hourly begging and exhorting her to marry whom she would, so that they might hope for heirs. Whenever it should be possible, she would not only fulfil their wish but, if necessary, hazard her life in their service. She would also like to oblige the Emperor and recompense his paternal love and friendship with her own possessions and those of the Crown. But now, although she had often been desired in marriage, she could swear by the salvation of her soul that she had never set her heart upon, nor wished to marry, anyone in the world. She found her celibate life so pleasant and was so accustomed to it that she would rather go into a nunnery or suffer death than marry against her will. At the same time, she would not like it to be assumed that she had forsworn marriage entirely. She was only human and not insensible to human emotions and impulses, and when it became a question of the weal of her kingdom, or it might be for other reasons, she might change her mind.[2]

It was hardly surprising that the Baron, inexperienced in Elizabeth Tudor's normal methods of dealing with proposals of marriage, should have despaired – and this was de Quadra's cue to intervene. He accordingly went back to the Queen and seems for the first time to have made it clear that Charles and not Ferdinand was the proffered bridegroom. He did this, so he said, to clear the ground and find out whether Elizabeth was sincere about not wishing to marry or whether, as he suspected, was simply determined not to marry a Catholic. If de Quadra really expected to find out anything so definite, he was disappointed, but he did succeed in arousing the Queen's interest. She had probably already heard the rumours that Charles was not such a committed Catholic as the rest of his family – there had even been rumours that he might be thinking of leaving the Roman Church. All the same, she soon 'went back again to her nonsense and said she would rather be a nun than marry without knowing with whom and on the faith of portrait painters'. Someone had told her that Charles had an enormous head, even bigger than the Earl of Bedford's, and she was taking no risks. 'We continued at this for some time wasting words,' reported de Quadra, but the Queen was firm in her resolution not to marry, 'except to a man of worth whom she had seen and spoken to'. Did de Quadra think the Archduke would come to England so that she could have a look at him? De Quadra thought that no doubt the young man himself (Charles was just twenty) would come willingly, but whether the Emperor would agree to send his son on approval was something else again. 'I do not know whether she is jesting, which is quite possible, but I really believe she would like to arrange for this visit in disguise', wrote the ambassador. Finally von Breuner was recalled, and it was agreed that he and de Quadra should lay the Emperor's proposition before a committee of senior members of the Council. The Queen promised to listen to their advice, although she reiterated her resolve not to trust in portraiture and to 'see and know the man who was to be her husband'.[3]

The session with the Council took place on the following afternoon and seemed satisfactory, as far as it went – at least it made a welcome change to be dealing with sensible men who understood how these matters were arranged. But, when von Breuner saw the Queen again, it was obvious that no progress had been made. She did not wish to marry – at any rate, not yet. She might change her mind some time in the future or God, with whom all things were possible, might change it for her. It was not, as Elizabeth readily admitted, a satisfactory answer but she hoped the Emperor would accept it as honest and sincere. Von Breuner did not attempt to hide his disappointment and hinted a little stiffly that, in view of the encouraging reception given so recently to Court von Helfenstein, he thought the Emperor would be surprised and hurt. However, he would, of course, send his master a detailed account of what had passed and hoped soon to be able to tell him about it in person.

This was going too fast. The Emperor was in altogether too much of a hurry, complained the Queen. She would be writing to him herself and her letter and von Breuner's reports could quite well go by courier, so that the Baron could stay on in England for a while if he wished. It looked like a gleam of hope and during the course of two interviews, on 30 May and 3 June, the Baron did his utmost to get Elizabeth to say whether she wished to go on with 'this marriage business' or not, and whether there was really any point in his remaining. It was not for her, answered Elizabeth demurely, to dictate to the Emperor's ambassador. He must do as he thought best. She could not explicitly say that she would marry 'within a short time', or even if she would marry at all, for her heart had not yet spoken. Nevertheless, she contrived to make it clear that she wanted von Breuner to stay.[4]

Von Breuner himself did not know what to think. His instinct warned him that he was being made a fool of but, on the other hand, women, especially young women, were notoriously capricious. If Elizabeth was just playing hard to get – and surely she couldn't seriously mean to refuse the Archduke? – it would be criminal folly to risk losing such a prize by being over-hasty. So the Baron decided to persevere, encouraged by the fact that the Queen seemed to have taken a fancy to him. This was an impression which the Queen proceeded to foster and, during the ensuing week, von Breuner got the full treatment. After supper on 10 June he had taken a boat out on the Thames and encountered Elizabeth, who was also taking the air on what one assumes to have been a balmy summer evening. As soon as she saw the Baron, she summoned him over, invited him into the Treasurer's barge and then had her own boat rowed alongside and played to him on her lute. She invited him to breakfast next morning and out on the river again that evening in the royal barge, when she made him take the helm and was altogether 'very talkative and merry'. The talk, naturally, was all about Archduke Charles, Elizabeth asking endless questions but still harping on her determination to be wooed at first hand. Von Breuner tried unsuccessfully to argue her out of this unreasonable demand and continued to press her for a straight answer, which he didn't get. However, he was by this time so dazzled by the flattering attentions being showered on him that he hastened to assure the Queen that the Emperor would certainly not break off negotiation.[5]

Elizabeth had her reasons for wishing to prolong von Breuner's visit. The political situation in Scotland was once again boiling up to a crisis and the presence of the Imperial envoy on a matrimonial mission might become a useful weapon if things got really difficult. The Scottish Protestant party – the Congregation of Jesus, as it styled itself – had been growing in strength over recent years and was now in open revolt against the alien and Catholic rule of the Queen-Dowager, Mary of Guise. But, although the Congregation had been reinforced by the return of John Knox, that rugged enemy of Rome, to his native land, it was soon distressingly apparent that no amount of Calvinistic fervour would by itself be sufficient to dislodge the Regent and her garrison of French veterans from the fortress of Leith. The Lords of the Congregation had, therefore, appealed to the Protestant Queen of England for help.

Neither the Protestant Queen nor her Secretary of State needed reminding that here, at long last, might be England's opportunity to drive the French out of Scotland and put an end to the menace of the 'auld alliance' once and for all. But it was by no means as simple as it sounded. Elizabeth, not surprisingly, detested the revolutionary doctrine preached by the Scottish reformers that subjects had a positive duty to overthrow and spit upon any earthly prince who failed to obey the law of Christ – that is, of course, the law of Christ as interpreted by John Calvin and his disciples. Equally unsurprisingly, she cherished an implacable hatred for John Knox, whose anti-feminist opinions as expressed in his recently published *Blast . . . Against the Monstrous Regiment of Women* were enough to raise the hackles of any self-respecting female head of state. Apart from these considerations, and her instinctive reluctance to be seen lending aid and comfort to another sovereign's rebels, Elizabeth knew very well that to interfere in Scotland's internal affairs would be to invite retaliation from the greatest military power in Europe. The risk of such an adventure ending with a victorious French army poised on England's vulnerable land-frontier was too real to be disregarded.

At the beginning of July the situation was rendered even more explosive by the sudden death of King Henri II of France in a tilt-yard accident. The French throne passed to Henri's son François, an unhealthy child of fifteen, and François' wife, the sixteen-year-old Mary Queen of Scots; effective power passed into the hands of the Queen of Scots' maternal uncles, the Duke of Guise and the Cardinal of Lorraine, a pair of sharp-clawed predators who were not likely to stand aside while their sister, the Queen-Regent, was driven out of Scotland by a rabble of heretics. Once disembarked at Leith, a French expeditionary force would make short work of the Congregation of Jesus – and then what? Henry II, while naturally eager to wring the last drop of political advantage out of his daughter-in-law's claims to the English crown, had been on the whole a reasonable man with whom it was possible to do business. The Guise family had no such reputation. Would they be able to resist the temptation to fling their army across the border and down through the predominantly Catholic North Country into the undefended English heartland, seize and dispose of the bastard Elizabeth and add yet another kingdom to their niece's collection? The answer seemed only too probably that they would not. Small wonder, then, that Elizabeth, faced with her first major crisis after only eight months on her none-too-secure throne, should have hesitated to embroil herself openly with the Scots, hesitated indeed to do anything which might set a match to the powder-keg.

Certain things, however, she could do, and messages of encouragement and consignments of gold began to go north under conditions of the greatest secrecy. There was, of course, always another weapon available to Elizabeth Tudor. Bishop de Quadra heard that, when she was told François intended to have himself proclaimed King of England, she retorted sharply that she would take a husband who would give the King of France some trouble and do him more harm than he expected.[6] There was no secret about the identity of the husband in question. He was James Hamilton, Earl of Arran, the same to whom Henry VIII had offered to match his younger daughter back in 1543. The Scots leaders were pressing for a marriage between these two 'chief upholders of God's religion', both as a present bulwark against French aggression and as a possible future means of 'uniting England and Scotland together'; for after his father, now dignified by the French dukedom of Chatelherault, young Arran was the Scottish heir presumptive.[7]

Elizabeth, as usual, was not committing herself but she was taking a close interest in Arran's welfare. The Earl was currently abroad. He'd been living in France as a hostage for his father's good behaviour, James Hamilton senior being a notoriously untrustworthy character; but, when trouble broke out in Scotland, Arran had sensibly ignored a summons to Paris and was now in hiding in Switzerland. Elizabeth sent Thomas Randolph, an expert on Scottish affairs, to organise his escape, and in due course the Earl was successfully smuggled across the Channel disguised as a merchant. All this, naturally, was kept as quiet as possible, but rumours that Arran was already in either England or Scotland were circulating as early as the beginning of July, and de Quadra expected news of the marriage to break at any moment, for he believed the Queen would scarcely risk receiving the fugitive and offending the French at such a critical juncture unless the matter was settled and 'he was to be something more than a guest'.[8]

De Quadra should have known the Queen better. Arran actually reached London on 28 August and was secreted in William Cecil's house at Westminster. On the twenty-ninth he had a very private interview with Elizabeth at Hampton Court and two days later, still under Randolph's escort, he left for Scotland where, it was hoped, he would take over the leadership of the revolt and provide it with a popular figurehead. But no more was said about a marriage, and de Quadra cheered up again. It certainly looked to any reasonable diplomat as if Elizabeth must now accept Archduke Charles and a Spanish-Imperialist alliance to protect her against France – especially in view of the martial preparations going forward in that country. Elizabeth herself, well aware of the need to keep Philip friendly (and she had tried him fairly hard over the religious settlement), apparently felt it was time to offer the patient von Breuner some further encouragement and, on 7 September, de Quadra had interesting news for the Duchess of Parma in Brussels. It seemed that he and the Baron had had a visit from Lady Mary Sidney, one of the Queen's Bedchamber Women and sister of the favourite, Robert Dudley. According to Lady Sidney, now was the moment to press the Archduke's suit again. They must not mind what the Queen said, 'as it is the custom for ladies here not to give their consent in such matters until they are teased into it'. But, declared Lady Sidney, it would only take a few days and the Council would press the Queen to marry. The ambassador might be sure she would never dare to say such a thing if it were not true and she was acting now with the Queen's consent. Her Majesty would not raise the subject herself, but she definitely wanted the Archduke to come to England.[9]

Puzzled but impressed, de Quadra did a little checking. He had a word with Lord Robert, who assured him that in this as in all things he was at the disposal of King Philip to whom he owed his life – a tactful reference to his release from the Tower in the autumn of 1554. The ambassador also talked to the Treasurer of the Household, fat Thomas Parry, who had been with Elizabeth since before the days of the Seymour scandal and might safely be supposed to be fully in her confidence. Parry confirmed Lady Sidney's story, adding significantly that 'the marriage had now become necessary'. There was a rumour going round about a plot to poison the Queen and kill Lord Robert while they were both being entertained by the Earl of Arundel at Nonesuch, and de Quadra believed that this and the threatening international situation had combined to force Elizabeth into a decision.[10] However, when von Breuner bustled happily down to Hampton Court to seek audience with the Queen, he got smartly snubbed for his pains. It wasn't until de Quadra saw her in London three days later that any progress was made.

After a long preliminary skirmish over old ground – she didn't want to marry the Archduke or anybody else, if she married at all it would only be to a man she knew, but she didn't want Charles to come to England as she would not bind herself even indirectly to marry him – de Quadra made one more effort to pin her down, remarking reasonably enough that if they could not arrive at some sort of compromise they were simply wasting words. Let her begin, he went on, with the premise that she had to be married, as that could not now be avoided, and since she would not marry a man she had not seen let her agree to the Archduke's coming on a visit without her being bound any more than she was at present; let the Emperor be told of this, so that if he decided to send his son on those terms it might be done without further loss of time. After some more beating about the bush there was a pause and Elizabeth suddenly said: 'Shall I speak plainly and tell you the truth? I think that if the Emperor so desires me for a daughter he would not be doing too much by sending his son here without so many safeguards. I do not hold myself of so small account that the Emperor need sacrifice any dignity in doing it.'

'By these words and her manner of saying them', wrote de Quadra, 'I understood that she made no difficulty as to the conclusion of the business but only in the procedure to bring it about.' This looked like a giant step forward, but it was clear that the initiative must come from the Emperor. On no condition would Elizabeth herself ask Charles to come. It was not fit for a queen and a maiden to summon anyone to marry her for her pleasure – she would rather die a thousand deaths. In the circumstances, de Quadra felt justified in saying that, once the Emperor was satisfied his son would be welcome and that a visit might be 'convenient and advantageous', he was sure the matter could be arranged. A little more persuasion and Elizabeth had admitted that she would be glad to see the Archduke and was asking what languages he spoke. There followed a very pleasant conversation on the subject 'in a vastly different mood from her other conversations about her not wishing to marry' and, if it had not been for the risk of arousing the suspicions of the standers-by, de Quadra would have kissed her hand. He was still on delicate ground, though, for when he began to ask if Charles should come in public or privately Elizabeth drew back. She didn't want to be pressed any further. The Archduke must do as he thought fit; she didn't want to know anything about it. It must be clearly understood that she was not committing herself to marriage and had still not yet resolved to marry at all. But this, as de Quadra triumphantly pointed out, was after she had agreed to the visit. He did not think these protestations need cause any alarm, as they were 'certainly nothing but ceremony'. He conceded that he might easily be deceived himself, but went on, 'I do not believe that Lady Sidney and Lord Robert could be mistaken, and the latter says he never thought the Queen would go so far.'[11]

In any case, she really had no choice. Everyone knew she could not afford to delay her marriage much longer (most people believed it would take place by Christmas) and, whatever she said, by consenting to receive the Archduke at all Elizabeth *was* committing herself. Vain and fickle she might be, but not even she would have the gall to bring an Emperor's son half-way across Europe on a wild-goose chase and risk giving such mortal offence to the House of Habsburg. De Quadra quite realised it could be objected that, given these premises, all this uproar about seeing the Archduke before making up her mind was pointless – the Queen might just as well accept the inevitable and start negotiating the marriage treaty without wasting any more valuable time. 'I can only answer', he wrote, 'that in pure reason that is so, but, as she is a woman, and a spirited and obstinate woman too, passion has to be considered.' However tiresome to the logical masculine mind, feminine whims and fancies could not be ignored and would have to be pandered to if the main objective was to be achieved. De Quadra felt certain that the arguments in favour of sending Charles to London on Elizabeth's conditions far outweighed anything that could be said in favour of his staying away. Once the bridegroom-elect was actually on the spot the Queen would not be able to dismiss him, even if she wanted to – popular demand and pressure from the Council would be too strong – and in a long and detailed despatch the King of Spain's ambassador urged the Emperor to take the risk.[12]

Charles von Habsburg was by no means the only suitor competing for the Queen's favour that autumn. The King of Denmark's ambassador was parading about the court wearing a crimson velvet heart pierced by an arrow embroidered on his gown 'to demonstrate his King's love for Queen Elizabeth'; and Eric of Sweden, apparently impervious to discouragement, had sent his younger brother, the Duke of Finland, to plead his cause. The Duke landed at Harwich towards the end of September and turned out to be a pleasing young man, 'very courteous and princely, and well spoken in the Latin tongue'. He was free with his money too, and once he had got over an initial tendency to 'high looks and pontificiality' took enthusiastically to English ways. The Queen seemed to like him – he was often at Court and always well received. Some people began to whisper that he might be successful in a courtship on his own account, but 'how he shall speed, God knoweth and not I,' sighed William Cecil. The Scots had by no means given up hope for their candidate, the Earl of Arran, and a couple of outsiders, the Duke of Holstein and the Duke of Saxony's brother, hovered optimistically on the fringes of the crowd.

The Secretary of State, surveying this 'controversy of lovers' with a jaundiced eye, was moved to remark to his friend Ralph Sadler that he 'would to God the Queen had one and the rest were honourably satisfied'. The queen would not have agreed. The present situation suited her very nicely, and when the French ambassador visited her one Sunday afternoon early in November he found her with the Duke of Finland on one side and the Emperor's ambassador on the other watching a tournament in which Lord Robert Dudley and her cousin, Henry Carey, were challenging all comers.

Antoine de Noailles had sought an audience to urge the Queen not to be alarmed by the reinforcements being sent to Scotland. His master was obliged to assist the Queen-Regent in her present predicament, but the ambassador would swear on oath that the King of France had no unfriendly intentions towards England. Elizabeth conceded that the Regent might feel herself threatened but thought the King of France was exaggerating the danger. He must not be surprised if, in view of the warlike preparations he was making (which seemed to her far greater than the occasion warranted), she mobilised her fleet and put the coastal defences in a state of readiness, for this was always the custom when England's neighbours armed.[13] The conversation remained perfectly affable in tone and, although de Noailles had well-founded suspicions about Elizabeth's undercover dealings with the Scottish rebels and her part in engineering the Earl of Arran's escape, there was no getting past her blandly smiling guard. When it came to playing diplomatic poker, Elizabeth Tudor, even in her twenties had no equal – a fact which was already becoming recognised in international circles. If she was worried by the various problems currently besetting her – the increased French presence in Scotland and how best to counter it, England's acute military and financial weakness, the necessity of making up her mind to marriage and all the extra difficulties that was going to bring in its wake – she concealed her anxiety admirably. The court was very gay that second winter of the reign and the Queen, at the centre of a hectic social whirl of banquets, balls and hunting parties, appeared to have no concern in the world except to enjoy herself.

But no one could fail to notice (no one did fail to notice) that, while she was ready to be civil to the Duke of Finland, to go to considerable trouble to have a private interview with the Earl of Arran, to flirt rather absentmindedly with William Pickering and to discuss with every indication of seriousness the possibility of marriage with Archduke Charles, it was the tall, arrogantly handsome figure of Lord Robert Dudley who was most often to be seen at her side. Not surprisingly this was now giving rise to a good deal of ill-natured gossip, and Sir Thomas Challoner, *en poste* in Brussels, had heard enough to cause him to write worriedly to his friend William Cecil that, although he counted the slander most false, a young princess could not be too careful 'what countenance or familiar demonstration she maketh more to one than another'.[14] He would not say so, even in a private letter to a trusted confidant, but Thomas Challoner, a man of sense and experience, was clearly very much afraid that Elizabeth, whose future as a wife and mother was of such vital importance to England ('for without posterity of her highness what hope is left unto us?'), might be wasting her time and ruining her good name by having an affair with a married man.

Rumours of a similar nature had been reaching the Emperor in Augsburg, and Caspar von Breuner received instructions to make searching enquiries into this matter, which was of close personal interest to the Habsburg family. But, despite his best efforts, he did not succeed in making any very startling discoveries. 'I have employed as my agent', he reported on 6 August, 'a certain François Borth, who is on very friendly terms with all the ladies of the bedchamber and all other persons who have been about the Queen and have brought her up since childhood. They all swear by all that is holy that her Majesty has most certainly never been forgetful of her honour. And yet it is not without significance that her Majesty's Master of the Horse, my lord Robert, is preferred by the Queen above all others, and that her Majesty shows her liking for him more markedly than is consistent with her reputation and dignity.'[15]

Von Breuner had picked up a story that Katherine Ashley, now the Queen's 'most intimate Lady of the Bedchamber', had recently fallen at her old pupil's feet and implored her in God's name to marry and put an end to all these disreputable rumours, 'telling her Majesty that her behaviour towards the said Master of the Horse occasioned much evil-speaking'. A curious echo here of ten years before – of another time when Mrs Ashley had feared that her lady would be 'evilly spoken of'. Elizabeth, it seems, had replied that if she showed herself gracious towards her Master of the Horse 'he had deserved it for his honourable nature and dealings'. According to von Breuner's account, she had gone on to say that she failed to understand why anyone should object, 'seeing that she was always surrounded by her ladies of the bedchamber and maids of honour, who at all times could see whether there was anything dishonourable between her and her Master of the Horse'. 'If,' declared the Queen with a touch of defiance, 'if she had ever had the will or had found pleasure in such a dishonourable life . . . she did not know of anyone who could forbid her; but she trusted in God that nobody would ever live to see her so commit herself.' Von Breuner heard that Lord Robert was married to a fine lady 'from whom he has always had nothing but good', but ever since the Queen's accession he had never been away from court, and the fact that they were constantly together under the same roof was, in the Baron's opinion, feeding suspicion.[16]

Elizabeth might insist that she and Robert Dudley were just good friends, and nobody had yet been able to prove the contrary, but suspicion remained and gossip was growing uglier. In November, Bishop de Quadra informed King Philip that he had been told 'by a certain person who is accustomed to give me veracious news that Lord Robert has sent to poison his wife. Certainly,' continued the ambassador, 'all the Queen has done with us and with the Swede, and will do with the rest in the matter of her marriage, is only keeping Lord Robert's enemies and the country engaged with words until this wicked deed of killing his wife is consummated.'[17] De Quadra was in a rage, for he now believed that he had been deliberately tricked by the Queen and her favourite. He'd noticed that Lord Robert was 'slackening in our business' and that Lady Sidney, hitherto so encouraging, had begun to avoid his company. He had therefore gone to the Queen to try to find out what was going on. The Archduke, he told her, might be already on the road and, since all her conditions had been complied with, he thought it was time he and von Breuner were given some assurance in the matter. But Elizabeth would only repeat yet again that she was not thinking about marrying, although she might change her mind when she saw the Archduke. De Quadra, determined not to be put off any longer, said that this hardly justified her implicit invitation, whereupon the Queen remarked airily that she only wished to meet Charles and get to know him in case she felt inclined to marry at some future time. It was at this point that the ambassador lost his temper and began to quote Lady Sidney, but if he expected to disconcert Elizabeth Tudor he was disappointed. Some member of her household may have said such things, she agreed calmly, and no doubt with good intentions, but without any commission from her.[18]

It's not surprising that de Quadra should have been angry. Not merely had six months' patient stalking of the quarry apparently gone for nothing, but he himself had been to make to look a fool. He exonerated Mary Sidney, who had, he thought, been her brother's dupe – a suspicion borne out by a distinct coolness between them at this time – but he was now more than ready to hope for the worst as far as the Queen and Lord Robert were concerned: he'd been told some amazing things about their intimacy which he would never have believed, only he found Lord Robert's enemies on the Council were making no secret of their evil opinion of it. Lord Robert had numerous enemies by this time, especially among the older aristocracy who favoured the Austrian match, and the Duke of Norfolk had been heard to say that if the favourite 'did not abandon his present pretensions and presumption he would not die in his bed'. De Quadra was of the opinion that this general hatred of Robert would continue, 'as the Duke and the rest of them cannot put up with his being

King'.[19] As for the Queen, the ambassador did not pretend to understand her and had given up all hope of her affairs.

Caspar von Breuner, who finally left England in December, thought that much of Elizabeth's stubbornness and generally wilful behaviour was to be blamed on her unfortunate upbringing, 'for sometimes she was regarded as legitimate and at other times not . . . She has been brought up at Court, then sent away, and to crown all she has even been held captive.' Now that she had finally come to the throne, 'like a peasant on whom a barony has been conferred', she had become so puffed up with pride that she imagined she was without peer and might do as she pleased. 'But herein she errs,' wrote the good Baron severely, 'for if she marry the said my lord Robert, she will incur so much enmity that she may one evening lay herself down as Queen of England and rise the next morning as plain Mistress Elizabeth.'[20]

Both de Quadra and von Breuner were convinced that the Queen had been deliberately using them 'and the other envoys who are sojourning here on matrimonial business' partly as a threat to scare the French and partly as a shield against her own subjects. 'For, as long as we are here,' remarked von Breuner shrewdly enough, 'she can put off the vulgar mob who daily beg and implore her to marry, with the plea that she must have leisure to occupy herself with the requests of so many potentates, to the weal and advantage of her realm.' Certainly it was blindingly obvious by the last weeks of 1559 that Elizabeth had no serious intentions towards any of her current crop of suitors. But what *were* her intentions? No one seemed to know. Did she really mean to remain a spinster? Or could two successive Spanish ambassadors have been right when they declared she was only waiting for her lover's wife to die to marry him?

Few men were ever more consistently vilified in their own lifetimes than Lord Robert Dudley. Outside his immediate family circle, his contemporaries, almost without exception, loathed and detested him – a loathing which cannot be entirely explained away by jealousy – and people simply could not understand what the Queen saw in this upstart son of a convicted traitor. The historian William Camden, who knew them both, could only offer a tentative astrological explanation – that the undoubted conjunction and affinity of their minds was caused by 'a hidden conspiracy and consent of their stars'.

Actually, of course, Robert possessed a number of attributes calculated to appeal to Elizabeth. He was very good-looking – 'tall and singularly well-featured and all his youth well favoured, of a sweet aspect but high-foreheaded'. He dressed well too, and knew how to display himself to the best advantage, making a splendid ornament for the court. This was useful when there were foreign visitors to be impressed and always important in an age when outward show had so much inner and symbolic value. Looks mattered to the Queen, and she had high standards of male beauty, but looks were not everything. Robert was a fine athlete, excelling in all the popular manly sports and war-games; and Elizabeth, like her father, always loved a man who *was* a man. She told von Breuner in the early days of their acquaintance that she would expect her husband to take part in warlike exercises and not 'sit at home all day among the cinders'. Robert was a good dancer – also very important to the Queen, who loved dancing. He was intelligent and had been well-educated, though Roger Ascham once regretted that he took more interest in Euclid's pricks and lines than in the classics. He was amusing company, witty, sophisticated, accustomed all his life to moving in the highest social and political circles. But perhaps what mattered most was the fact that he and Elizabeth had grown up together, talked the same language, shared the same jokes, the same background and experience – had even been in gaol together. With Robert, as with no one else, Elizabeth could drop her guard, relax, unwind and be herself. And Elizabeth, who lived so much of her life strung up to concert pitch, needed someone she could relax with.

She rewarded her old friend generously during that first year. In May 1559, Robert, together with the Duke of Norfolk, the Marquis of Northampton and the Earl of Rutland – three senior peers of the realm – was made a knight of the Garter. He was given 'a capital mansion' known as the Dairy House down at Kew, as well as other landed property and several sums of ready cash to meet current needs. He became Lieutenant of Windsor Castle and also got an extremely valuable licence to export woollen cloth free of duty. The Queen was apparently indifferent to gossip. If she enjoyed the company of her Master of the Horse in her off-duty hours and wanted to present him with some solid tokens of her regard, that was her business. Thirteen months on the throne had changed Elizabeth from the repressed, unhappy creature, nervously picking her way through the traps and pitfalls – political, religious and matrimonial – which had crowded her footsteps during her sister's reign into a spirited, vital young woman, increasingly confident of her ability to govern and determined to choose her own friends and arrange her private life without interference.

31

Lord Robert Would Be Better in Paradise

By February 1560 there could be no disguising the fact that the Austrian marriage project was moribund. Despite all de Quadra's persuasive efforts of the autumn, the Archduke had not set out on his journey – no Habsburg ever did anything in a hurry. A number of people, including Count von Helfenstein who had returned to London in January in a final effort to breathe new life into the negotiations, thought this was a pity. The King of Bohemia and the Duke of Bavaria both spoke out in favour of the visit being made – the latter had even offered to accompany Charles and to contribute 100,000 crowns towards his travelling expenses. But the Emperor was determined to extract some sort of understanding from Elizabeth before allowing his son to leave for London, and the result was deadlock. The Duke of Finland, on the other hand, was getting ready to go home and, although brother Eric threatened to come courting in person, no one believed there was the least likelihood of a Swedish marriage. De Quadra believed that the Queen's tricks were finding her out, for if both her Austrian and Scandinavian suitors deserted her 'not only will the French despise her but her own people as well and, in the event of the Scotch business turning out badly for her, as it probably will, she will be left helpless'.[1]

It was certainly true that 'the Scotch business' did not look particularly promising at the beginning of 1560. The Earl of Arran had proved a serious disappointment, both as a military commander and as leader of a popular-front movement – he was, in fact, already showing signs of the mental instability which later became hopeless insanity – and the Congregation's repeated failure to make any noticeable headway against the forces of the Queen-Regent was driving Elizabeth into more and more open intervention on their behalf. An English fleet under the command of William Winter had sailed for the Firth of Forth in December to blockade the port of Leith, and the Duke of Norfolk was on his way north with orders to levy an army in preparation for a possible assault by land. Robert Dudley, however, remained at home, still in high favour, and de Quadra heard he had been boasting that 'if he live another year he will be in a very different position from now. He is laying in a good stock of arms,' went on the ambassador, 'and is every day assuming a more masterful part in affairs. They say that he thinks of divorcing his wife.'[2]

Considering she was destined to become the heroine of an internationally reverberant scandal, exceedingly little is known about Amy Dudley, born Amy Robsart, only legitimate child and heiress of a substantial Norfolk landowner. She and Robert probably first met in July 1549 when he was campaigning in East Anglia with his father at the time of Jack Kett's rebellion. Amy was then eighteen, Robert about a year younger, and there is some evidence that they fell in love – at least, William Cecil believed they did and he was in as good a position to know as anyone. They were married in June 1550 with King Edward VI among the wedding guests, for these were the years of Dudley ascendancy, but there is no record even then that Amy ever enjoyed any share of her in-laws' new grandeur. Country bred, barely literate and utterly unused to high society, she seems to have made no attempt to keep up. Was she perhaps content to worship her godlike husband from afar, grateful for such crumbs of his company as he chose to bestow on her? When the crash came she visited him in the Tower, and during the period of eclipse between his release from prison and the outbreak of the French war in 1557 he was able to live comfortably enough down in Norfolk on John Robsart's money. But the life of a country gentleman was emphatically not for Robert Dudley, and the moment an opportunity presented itself he was off again into the wide dangerous world where he was so much at home. There were no children to keep the marriage together and in any case such a union, based on nothing but physical attraction, was probably foredoomed to failure. Certainly by the beginning of 1559 any passion on Robert's side was long spent. With a new, perhaps unimaginably glittering future opening before him, his wife had become an encumberance to be kept out of sight and as far as possible out of mind.

Not that there was ever an open breach between them. The fact that Amy never came to court was of little significance by itself. The wives of the Queen's officers were not encouraged to put themselves forward and there was no accommodation for them in the overcrowded royal residences – unless, of course, they happened to hold some position in their own right. The unusual thing about the young Dudleys' domestic arrangements was the fact that they had no home of their own. Most of the principal court officials rented a town house where they could join their wives and entertain their friends in their off-duty hours. Most rising men would also have acquired a country place where they could play the local magnate and lord it over their less fortunate neighbours. Robert did neither of these things. He remained in constant attendance on the Queen, as he was more or less forced to do if he wanted to keep the life-giving sunshine of her favour, while Amy lived as a kind of superior paying guest with various friends or connections of her husband. She spent most of 1558 and 1559 at Denchworth near Abingdon in the house of a Mr Hyde, brother-in-law of Anthony Forster who was Robert's 'treasurer' or steward. It's possible that she preferred this kind of life, which relieved her of all housekeeping responsibilities, and there's no suggestion that she was ever in any sense a prisoner. The account books show that she moved around quite freely. She came up to London once or twice to see Robert, and he paid an occasional flying visit to Denchworth. She was attended as befitted a lady of rank and spent quite a lot of money on clothes. Sometime before midsummer 1560 she moved from Denchworth to Cumnor Place, which lay just off the main road between Abingdon and Oxford and had been leased by Anthony Forster from William Owen, son of the late George Owen, at one time physician to the royal family. Cumnor, once a monastic building, was not large and, as well as the Forsters, Mrs Owen was still occupying part of it. So when Lady Robert Dudley moved in with her servants, her personal maid Mrs Pirto, and a Mrs Odingsells, the widowed sister of her former host Mr Hyde who had apparently come along to keep her company, space must have been at a premium. It hardly seems a very suitable arrangement for the wife of such a prominent man, but whether Amy went to Cumnor because she wanted to, or whether she simply fell in with a plan made by other people, is one of the many points on which we have no information.

Round about this time the situation in Scotland was finally beginning to resolve itself. The Duke of Norfolk had crossed the border at the end of March and, although the attack on Leith mounted on 7 May resulted in ignominious failure, other factors were now working in England's favour. For one thing, the French were experiencing the first stirrings of the civil unrest which was later to tear the country apart; storms in the North Sea the previous winter had scattered or destroyed many of the ships carrying reinforcements to the Regent, and the government in Paris, reluctant to risk a direct confrontation with the English fleet in the Forth, felt itself unable to send any further assistance. The garrison at Leith was therefore starved out, and the death of that doughty warrior Mary of Guise took all the remaining heart out of the fight. France was ready to discuss terms, and William Cecil went north to represent Queen Elizabeth at the conference table.

Cecil was away for two months and during his absence the Queen's relationship with Robert Dudley is often said to have reached some sort of mysterious climax. In fact all that actually seems to have happened is that Elizabeth took advantage of the Secretary's sojourn in Scotland to enjoy a brief holiday from business herself and was out all day and every day hunting and riding with, naturally, her Master of the Horse. Like all the Tudors, Elizabeth was fantastically addicted to fresh air and exercise, and under Robert's tuition she was developing into a keen and fearless horsewoman. Indeed, as Robert told the Earl of Sussex, she was planning to send into Ireland 'for some hobbys for her own saddle, especially for strong, good gallopers which are better than her geldings'. Gossip, of course, continued unabated, and old Annie Dow of Brentwood got into trouble with the magistrates for spreading stories that Lord Robert had given the Queen a child. But people had been gossiping about the Queen and Lord Robert for more than a year now; there was nothing new in that. All the same, when Cecil returned to court at the end of July he was, for the first time, seriously alarmed about the Dudley affair – although his concern was probably caused not so much by the Queen's attitude to Robert Dudley as by her attitude to William Cecil.

Cecil had come home pardonably pleased with himself, for in the course of several weeks of hard bargaining in Edinburgh he had succeeded in extracting a series of important concessions from the French commissioners acting on behalf of the young Queen of Scots and her husband. It had, for example, been agreed that all French troops would be evacuated forthwith and the fortifications at Leith and Dunbar dismantled. It was also agreed that the government should be handed over to a Scottish Council, while England and France once more solemnly pledged themselves to observe a policy of non-interference. Finally, the French undertook that Mary would in future abstain from using the title and insignia of Queen of England. The religious question was carefully avoided but, as Cecil had confidently anticipated, the Scots wasted no time in adopting a Calvinistic form of Protestantism now they were free to do so and, whatever Queen Elizabeth's opinion of the Calvinists might be, even she must admit that they would make more desirable next-door neighbours than the French Army. It was never wise to be too sure of anything in Scottish affairs, but it did really look as if the foundations of a durable peace had been laid and the bogey of invasion from the north banished for good.

The Treaty of Edinburgh was a personal triumph for William Cecil and he could reasonably expect, if not a hero's welcome, at least some form of grateful recognition for his services. Instead the Queen virtually cut him dead and, to make matters worse, it looked as if he was going to be out of pocket as well. Exactly why Elizabeth treated her unfortunate Secretary in this unkind fashion is not very clear, but she may have been rather piqued by his success. Cecil had, from the beginning, been an enthusiastic advocate of intervention in Scotland and it was Cecil who had carried the policy through against all the Queen's misgivings. Events had proved him right and the Queen wrong, a situation no Tudor liked to be found in, and she probably just wished to make it understood that Cecil need not think he was infallible. But Cecil himself, who had not yet learnt to understand all his mistress's little ways, was deeply distressed and had no hesitation in laying the blame at Robert Dudley's door. There was, not surprisingly, no love lost between the Secretary and the Master of the Horse. Each feared and resented the other's influence, and each would have liked to dislodge the other from his privileged position in the Queen's confidence.

On 30 August the court moved down to Windsor and it was there, some time during the weekend of 7–8 September, that William Cecil chose to unburden himself to, of all people, the Spanish ambassador. De Quadra told the Duchess of Parma, in a letter dated 11 September, that after exacting many pledges of strict secrecy, Cecil said the Queen was conducting herself in such a way that he thought of retiring. 'He said it was a bad sailor who did not enter port if he could when he saw a storm coming on, and he clearly foresaw the ruin of the realm through Robert's intimacy with the Queen, who surrendered all affairs to him and meant to marry him. He said he did not know how the country put up with it, and he should ask leave to go home, although he thought they would cast him into the Tower first. He ended by begging me in God's name to point out to the Queen the effect of her misconduct, and persuade her not to abandon business entirely but to look at her realm; and then he repeated twice over to me that Lord Robert would be better in Paradise than here.' Cecil also told de Quadra that 'Robert was thinking of killing his wife, who was publicly announced to be ill, although she was quite well and would take very good care they did not poison her'.[3]

It is generally assumed that this remarkable outburst was a piece of calculated indiscretion on Cecil's part; that, knowing Elizabeth would be unlikely to listen to him in her present mood, he had turned to de Quadra in the hope that an outsider might be able to bring her to her senses and persuade her to bring her faithful Secretary in out of the cold. This seems as good an explanation as any, for Cecil seldom said or did anything without a reason. De Quadra, naturally fascinated by what appeared to be an authentic glimpse behind the scenes, made suitably shocked noises and promised to speak to the Queen, though he felt bound to remark that she had never taken his advice in the past. But, before the Bishop could intervene, the bombshell had burst. According to de Quadra, the very day after his conversation with Cecil the Queen told him as she returned from hunting 'that Robert's wife was dead or nearly so' and asked him not to say anything about it. Some people have taken this to infer that Elizabeth told King Philip's envoy about Amy's death before it occurred, thus tacitly admitting guilty knowledge of murder. But, if that were the case, de Quadra is curiously uninformative about dates. We know he arrived at Windsor on Friday the sixth and wrote to Brussels on the following Wednesday, by which time the Queen had 'published' the news; but the ambassador nowhere gives the date of his interesting little chat with William Cecil. However, since the messenger from Cumnor reached the Castle during the morning of Monday, 9 September, it can reasonably be placed at some time during Sunday the eighth – the very day of the tragedy.

By a rather odd coincidence a member of Lord Robert's entourage, a kinsman of his named Thomas Blount, had left Windsor that Monday morning bound for Cumnor. Blount had not gone far before he encountered one Bowes, riding for his life in the opposite direction, who told him that their lady was dead 'by a fall from a pair of stairs'. A little surprisingly Blount did not turn back for further instructions but, leaving Bowes to break the news at Windsor, he continued on his journey. Nor did he hurry on to reach Cumnor that day. Instead, he put up for the night at Abingdon because, as he presently informed his master, he was desirous to hear 'what news went abroad in the country'. While he was at supper he therefore called for 'mine host' and, without revealing his identity, asked 'what news was thereabout'. The landlord was naturally full of 'the great misfortune' which had befallen only three or four miles from the town – how my Lord Robert Dudley's wife was dead by falling down a pair of stairs. He was unable to supply any details and when Blount remarked that 'some of her people that waited on her' should be able to say what had happened, he was told no, apparently not, for they were all at the fair in Abingdon 'and none left with her'. Her ladyship, it seemed, had risen up early and 'commanded all her sort to go to the fair and would suffer none to tarry at home'.[4]

It sounded rather an odd story, but Thomas Blount would soon be making his own enquiries on the spot and just at the moment he was more interested in what was being said about Amy's death than in any second-hand information the landlord could give him. What was mine host's own opinion, he asked, and what was 'the judgement of the people'? Some were disposed to say well and some evil, answered mine host cautiously. For himself, he judged it a misfortune because it had taken place in an honest gentleman's house.[5]

Blount had needed no telling that, in the circumstances, 'the judgement of the people' was going to be all-important and the same thought was uppermost in the mind of the newly bereaved widower at Windsor, who wrote frantically to his 'Cousin Blount' on the Monday evening: 'The greatness and suddenness of the misfortune doth so perplex me until I do hear from you how the matter standeth, or how this evil should light upon me, considering what the malicious world will bruit, as I can take no rest. And, because I have no way to purge myself of the malicious talk that I know the wicked world will use, but one which is the very plain truth to be known, I do pray you as you have loved me, and do tender me and my quietness, and as now my special trust is in you, that you will use all the devices and means you can possibly for the learning of the truth, wherein have no respect to any living person.'[6]

But truth was to prove an elusive commodity. In his first report from Cumnor, Blount could only tell Lord Robert that the tale he had already heard from Bowes and from the landlord of the inn at Abingdon was confirmed by the household and by Amy's maid, Mrs Pirto, who, according to Blount, 'doth dearly love her'. Everyone agreed that her ladyship had insisted on sending all her servants out on the day of her death 'and was so earnest to have them gone to the fair, that with any of her sort that made reason for tarrying at home she was very angry'. She had even quarrelled with Mrs Odingsells, who at first refused to go because Sunday was no day for a gentlewoman to be seen gallivanting in the town. Amy had answered that Mrs Odingsells could do as she liked, but all her people should go and 'was very angry'. This was obviously considered uncharacteristic behaviour, and Blount remarked, 'Certainly, my lord, as little while as I have been here, I have heard divers tales of her that maketh me to judge her to be a strange woman of mind.' He had talked to the devoted Pirto, who should surely have known her mistress best, and went on: 'In asking Pirto what she might think of this matter, either chance or villainy, she said by her faith she doth judge very chance, and neither done by man or by herself.' Her lady, said Pirto, 'was a good virtuous gentlewoman, and daily would pray upon her knees'. Nevertheless, Pirto did let fall the possibly significant information that she had more than once heard the dead woman pray to God to deliver her from desperation. Blount pounced on this – then she might have had 'an evil toy' on her mind? 'No, good Mr Blount,' cried Pirto, 'do not judge so of my words; if you should so gather I am sorry I said so much!' It was not conclusive, of course – 'it passeth the judgement of man to say how it is' – but, all the same, Blount evidently believed that suicide could not be ruled out.

Robert had been insistent that the coroner's jury should be chosen from 'the discreetest and most substantial men . . . such as for their knowledge may be able to search thoroughly the bottom of the matter, and for their uprightness will earnestly and sincerely deal therein'. Blount was now able to tell him that the jury was already chosen and its members seemed to be 'as wise and as able men, being but countrymen, as ever I saw'. 'And for their true search,' he went on, '. . . I have good hope they will conceal no fault, if any be; for as they are wise, so are they, as I hear, part of them very enemies to Anthony Forster. God give them, with their wisdom, indifferency, and then be they well chosen men.'[7]

This sounded a trifle ominous, but for the moment there was no more to be done. The Queen had sent Robert away to his house at Kew while the matter of his wife's death was investigated, and while the country thrummed with shocked speculation over this melodramatic climax to eighteen months of scandal-mongering the widower waited in painful suspense, being measured for mourning clothes and writing more anxious letters to Thomas Blount at Cumnor: 'Until I hear from you again how the matter falleth out in very truth, I cannot be in quiet.' He sent an urgent message to the jury that they were to do their duty without fear or favour and 'find it as they shall see it fall out'. There is no record that Robert ever expressed even a passing regret over his wife's death or showed any interest in Blount's guarded references to her 'strange mind'. He was quite simply obsessed with the necessity of proclaiming his own innocence by making it clear that he had nothing to hide and would welcome the fullest possible enquiry.[8]

Sometime during that frightening week Robert had received a visit of condolence from no less a person than Mr Secretary Cecil and wrote to him afterwards: 'I thank you much for your being here; and the great friendship you have showed toward me I shall not forget . . . I pray you let me hear from you what you think best for me to do (for the sooner you advise me, the more I shall thank you). Methinks I am here all this while as it were in a dream, and too far from the place where I am bound to be . . . I pray you help him that sues to be at liberty out of so great a bondage. Forget me not, though you see me not, and I remember you and fail you not.'[9] Why it was that William Cecil had chosen to throw out a lifeline to the man he apparently regarded as his most dangerous enemy and whom he had recently been accusing of contemplating the murder which perhaps had now been committed, is something else which is by no means clear. But Cecil, a practised exponent of the art of political survival, was always a careful man who believed in taking out as much insurance as possible.

The Secretary's show of friendship had been a gleam of light and Robert received further comfort from Blount's second report, written on Friday, 13 September. It seemed that, although they had taken great pains to learn the truth, the jury – somewhat to their regret, in Blount's opinion – could find 'no presumptions of evil'. 'And,' Blount went on, 'if I judge aright, mine own opinion is much quieted; the more I search of it, the more free it doth appear unto me. I have almost nothing that can make me so much as think that any man should be the doer thereof, as, when I think your lordship's wife before all other women should have such a chance, the circumstances and as many things as I can learn doth persuade me that only misfortune hath done it and nothing else'.[10]

The inquest, as Blount had predicted, presently returned a verdict of misadventure and, on 22 September, Amy was buried in the church of St Mary the Virgin at Oxford with all the funeral pomp and ceremony due to her position. Officially the incident was closed, but few people believed that 'the very plain truth' or anything like it had been uncovered. How did Amy Dudley die? Had she been murdered by Robert's hired assassins – poisoned first, it was whispered, or stifled, and then arranged with a broken neck at the foot of that fatal staircase to make her death look like an accident? Had she committed suicide, driven to despair by the knowledge of her mortal illness, her husband's callous neglect and the terrible rumours which must have reached her? Or was the jury's verdict a true one after all? Modern medical research has revealed that in fifty per cent of cases of advanced breast cancer secondary deposits are present in the bones. The effect of such deposits in the spine is to make it extremely brittle – so brittle that the slightest stumble, even, as in Amy's case, the mere act of walking down a flight of stairs, could result in a spontaneous fracture of the vertebrae.[11] This suggestion, first put forward by Professor Ian Aird in 1956, is now generally accepted as the most likely explanation of the mystery and would certainly account for the curious fact that, although she had apparently suffered a fall violent enough to break her neck, the dead woman's headdress was undisturbed. But it still doesn't explain Amy's unusual behaviour on the day of her death. Why was she so determined to be alone that Sunday? Had she been planning to take her own life, or could she perhaps have been expecting a visitor? The question marks remain and, while it is only fair to remember that not one shred of hard evidence was ever produced to implicate Robert in murder, perhaps it is hardly surprising that in the autumn of 1560 the idea that such a suspiciously convenient death could have been accidental was greeted with widespread and cynical disbelief.

Nevertheless, by the end of September Robert was back at court, a free man in every sense of the word, and the world at large waited fascinated to see what would happen next. Bishop de Quadra, that disillusioned observer of the island scene, was not committing himself. He was not sure if the Queen intended to marry Robert at once or even if she would marry at all, as he did not think her mind was sufficiently fixed. But, as he told the Duchess of Parma, 'with these people it is always wisest to think the worst'.[12]

In France they were not merely thinking the worst, they were gleefully anticipating it, and the young Queen of Scots, so it was said, had exclaimed: 'So the Queen of England is to marry her horse-keeper, who has killed his wife to make room for her!' A remark which pretty well summed up opinion at the French court and elsewhere. Nicholas Throckmorton, Elizabeth's ambassador in Paris, was frantic with anxiety. 'I wish I were either dead or hence,' he wrote on 10 October, 'that I might not hear the dishonourable and naughty reports that are made of the Queen and the great joy among the French princes for the success they take it they are like to have in England – not letting to speak of the Queen and some others that which every hair of my head stareth at and my ears glow to hear. I am almost at my wits' end and know not what to say. One laugheth at us, another threateneth, another revileth the Queen. Some let not to say: "What religion is this that a subject shall kill his wife and the Prince not only bear withal but marry with him?" If these slanderous bruits be not slaked, or if they prove true, our reputation is gone forever, war follows and utter subversion of the Queen and country.'[13]

At home, there was one man prepared to disregard gossip and scandal and all those nasty low-minded foreigners – a man prepared to keep his eye on the object, on the urgent and fundamental reason for the Queen's marriage. Thomas Radcliffe, Earl of Sussex, loathed Robert Dudley and could hardly bring himself to be civil to him in public, but he wrote to

William Cecil that October: 'I wish not her Majesty to linger this matter of so great importance, but to choose speedily; and therein to follow so much of her own affection as [that] by the looking upon him whom she should choose, her whole being may be moved by desire; which shall be the readiest way, with the help of God, to bring us a blessed Prince.' If there had been other 'rightful inheritors' Sussex would not have advised such a desperate course, but seeing that Elizabeth was the country's 'ultimum refugium', and that 'no riches, friendship, foreign alliance or any other present commodity can serve our turn without issue of her body', he was ready to put aside his own feelings and prejudices and urge that 'if the Queen will love anybody, let her love where and whom she lists . . . And whomsoever she shall love and choose, him will I love, honour and serve to the uttermost.'[14]

Sussex found no supporters for this humane and generous attitude. Not even for the sake of a blessed prince would the English tolerate an upstart and a wife-murderer as their king, and Nicholas Throckmorton could hardly bring himself to contemplate the disastrous consequences of a Dudley marriage – 'the Queen our Sovereign discredited, condemned and neglected; our country ruined, undone and made prey'.

Throckmorton, writing to Cecil on 28 October, seems to have been genuinely afraid that the matter might be 'already determined, and so far past as advice will not serve', and yet two weeks earlier Cecil had told de Quadra that the Queen had now definitely decided not to marry Lord Robert.[15] Had she, at any time since the beginning of September, really considered it seriously? It is impossible to be absolutely certain, but the overwhelming probability is surely that she had not. If Amy had died peacefully in her bed, the Queen's decision might just conceivably have been different. But Amy dead as the result of a mysterious 'misadventure' presented just as insuperable an obstacle as Amy alive, and the verdicts of a dozen coroner's juries would not alter that. In any case, did Elizabeth need to marry Robert when she could have everything she apparently wanted from him – his daily companionship, his undivided attention and devotion – without marriage? Might there not, in fact, from the Queen's point of view, be a good deal to be said for keeping things as they were? As consort Robert would acquire independent power and status, as well as certain ungainsayable rights. As favourite, however much latitude she chose to allow him, he must in the last resort remain her creature, her servant and plaything.

This, of course, presupposed the situation which Elizabeth's contemporaries found so incomprehensible and which was admittedly an unusual one – an intimate relationship between a virile young man and a nubile young woman which yet was not based on physical love. For the answer to the question whether Elizabeth and Robert Dudley were lovers in the obvious sense is that they were almost certainly not. Such a thing could not have been concealed in the climate of the late fifties and early sixties when every aspect of the Queen's personal affairs was attracting the closest scrutiny of matchmaking ambassadors. Gossip that 'Lord Robert did swyve the Queen' and that she had borne him a child naturally continued, but there is not a shred of evidence to support it and Bishop de Quadra, who like all envoys of first-rate powers maintained a network of paid informers within the royal household, had seen no sign of such a thing and did not believe it.

As the weeks passed with no further alarming developments the crisis began gradually to go off the boil; but Nicholas Throckmorton, in his anxiety that the Queen should fully understand what foreign reaction to a Dudley marriage would be, sent his secretary, young Mr Jones, over to England to convey an urgent personal warning. Jones saw Elizabeth towards the end of November and reported that when he came 'to touch near the quick' the Queen stopped him. '"I have heard of this before," quoth she, "and my ambassador need not have sent you withall."' She then went on to explain that the whole matter of Amy Dudley's death had been carefully investigated 'and found to be not that which was reported'. Lord Robert had been at court at the time 'and none of his people at the attempt at his wife's house [which sounds rather as though Elizabeth suspected foul play of some kind]; and it fell out as should touch neither his honesty nor her own honour'.[16]

Jones was considerably reassured as a result of this interview. He thought the Queen did not look well – 'surely the matter of my Lord Robert doth much perplex her,' he told Throckmorton, 'and is never like to take place'. Talk of it had abated and, although Robert was still in high favour, favour should not, it seemed, be taken for granted. The Queen had promised him the earldom of Leicester, an honour which he greatly coveted, but Jones heard that when the letters patent for the creation were brought for Elizabeth's signature she had taken her penknife and 'cut them asunder', saying that the Dudleys had been traitors for three descents. Robert sulked and reproached her for her unkindness, but Elizabeth was in a teasing mood and would not relent, though she patted his cheek and said playfully, 'No, no, the bear and ragged staff [a reference to the Dudley crest, filched from the Neville family] are not so soon overthrown.' All the same, when some of Robert's friends urged her to marry him, she would only 'pup with her lips' and say she could not marry a subject; that would make her no better than the Duchess of Norfolk, for men would come asking for my lord's grace. It was pointed out that she could make her husband a king, but 'no,' said the Queen, 'that she would in no wise agree to'.[17]

And there the matter rested. William Cecil, now back in his accustomed place at the Queen's right hand, told Throckmorton at the end of December that, 'whatsoever reports and opinions be, I know surely that my lord Robert himself hath more fear than hope, and so doth the Queen give him cause'. But Robert had by no means given up hope and, in January 1561, de Quadra received a visit from his brother-in-law, Henry Sidney. After a good deal of beating about the bush Sidney finally came to the point which was, of course, a Dudley–Tudor alliance. Since de Quadra knew 'how much inclined the Queen was to the marriage' he was surprised that the ambassador had not thought of suggesting to King Philip this opportunity of winning Lord Robert's support for, if a hand were extended to him now, 'he would thereafter serve and obey your Majesty like one of your own vassals'.

De Quadra received this remarkable proposal with a good deal of reserve. What he had so far heard of the matter, he told Sidney, was of such a character that he had hardly ventured to write two lines to Spain about it nor, for that matter, had either the Queen or Lord Robert said a word to him that he could write. He had no means of guessing the Queen's thoughts and, although his master was always anxious to be helpful, his advice had been consistently disregarded in the past. Sidney was obliged to admit this was true but, reported de Quadra, he went on to say 'that if I was satisfied about the death of Robert's wife, he saw no reason why I should hesitate to write the purport of this conversation to your Majesty, as, after all, although it was a love affair yet the object of it was marriage . . . As regards the death of the wife, he was certain that it was accidental, and he had never been able to learn otherwise, although he had enquired with great care and knew that public opinion held to the contrary.'

Henry Sidney then began to drop broad hints that Elizabeth was anxious to take steps to remedy the religious disorders in the country, a task in which Lord Robert would willingly help her. But now, with popular suspicion so strong against him, so that 'even preachers in the pulpits discoursed on the matter in a way that was prejudicial to the honour and interests of the Queen', their marriage and any subsequent easing of the Catholics' position had become politically impossible. If, however, the Queen could be assured of the King of Spain's support, things would be very different and she and Robert would do everything they could to restore religion without delay.

De Quadra regarded Sidney as an honest and sensible man, but felt obliged to remind him of 'what happened with his wife in the matter of the Archduke when the Queen had deceived both of us'. The ambassador was determined not to be caught a second time. All the same, he told Philip: 'I have no doubt that if there is any way to cure the bad spirit of the Queen, both as regards religion and your Majesty's interests, it is by means of this marriage, at least while her desire for it lasts.'[19]

On 13 February, Sidney came to see de Quadra again, bringing Robert with him. Robert was in his most winning mood. He repeated everything his brother-in-law had said and promised that, if only Philip would advise the Queen to marry him, he would be the King's servant for life. De

Quadra was still wary. He was not going to risk involving his master in what might easily turn out to be some kind of trick – not at least without more definite information. But what he could do was to see Elizabeth again and urge her yet once more to marry and settle down. Then, if Robert's name should come up, he would speak of him 'as favourably as he could wish'.[20]

This interview took place two days later and the Queen responded coyly to De Quadra's kite-flying. 'After much circumlocution,' he wrote, 'she said she wished to confess to me and tell me her secret in confession, which was that she was no angel, and did not deny that she had some affection for Lord Robert for the many good qualities he possessed, but she certainly had never decided to marry him or anyone else, although she daily saw more clearly the necessity for her marriage, and to satisfy the English humour it was desirable that she should marry an Englishman, and she asked me to tell her what your Majesty would think if she married one of her servitors.' De Quadra replied that he did not know and had not thought of asking, but he felt sure the King would be pleased to hear of her marriage, whoever she chose, as it was so important for the welfare of her kingdom. He also felt sure that Philip would be happy to hear of Lord Robert's good fortune, as he had always understood that the King had a great affection for him and generally held him in high esteem. The Queen, commented de Quadra, 'seemed as pleased at this as her position allowed her to be'. She said that when the time came she would speak to de Quadra again and would do nothing without Philip's advice and approval.[21]

The ambassador got the impression that she would have liked to go even further but, although he felt he had been right to allow her 'this little pleasure and hope', he did not relax his guard. In spite of Robert's repeated assurances that it was only 'timidity' and fear of what people would say which was holding Elizabeth back, and his solemn promises that once their marriage had taken place everything, including religion, would be placed in Philip's hands, de Quadra was not convinced. He had a nasty feeling that the whole ploy might in some way be designed to discredit Philip and the Catholic cause. Certainly he had seen no signs as yet of any relaxation in the official attitude towards his co-religionists. On the contrary, he reported that the sees of the dispossessed Catholic bishops had now been given to the greatest heretics, 'which is a very bad sign for the fulfilment of Lord Robert's promises'. In fact, the English Catholics were becoming disturbed by de Quadra's apparently growing friendship with Lord Robert, so that the ambassador, who maintained discreet contact with their leaders, felt obliged to reassure them privately that he was working in their interests and towards a restoration of the old faith.

Several weeks passed with no further developments, and de Quadra told Philip that Robert was 'very aggrieved and dissatisfied that the Queen should defer placing matters in your Majesty's hands' and had even fallen ill with annoyance! Then, about the middle of March, William Cecil paid a visit to the Spanish embassy. It would be of great assistance to the Queen, he said, if the King of Spain could be persuaded to write to her advising her not to delay her marriage any longer and suggesting that, if she could not bring herself to accept any of her foreign suitors, she had better choose a gentleman of her own country whom Philip would befriend. This was all very well, but when de Quadra tried to find out if Cecil was speaking with authority or simply putting forward a plan of his own the Secretary hedged. The Queen was a modest maiden and reluctant to get married at all. It would not help to try to force her to propose these means and expedients herself, 'which would make her look like a woman who sought to carry out her desires and went praying people to help her.'[22]

Cecil went on to explain that, since Elizabeth was resolved not to do anything without the goodwill of her subjects, she wanted Philip's letter as an excuse for calling together a representative committee from both Houses of Parliament to lay the matters before them 'and with the accord of these deputies to arrange the marriage with Robert'. To present Robert Dudley to Parliament as the King of Spain's candidate would surely be the fastest way to kill the project stone dead, and de Quadra knew that Robert himself was violently opposed to such a course. 'The sum of it all', wrote the ambassador on 25 March, 'is that Cecil and these heretics wish to keep the Queen bound and subject to their will and forced to maintain their heresies.'[23]

This was quite possibly the very impression that Elizabeth intended to create. Exactly who was fooling whom in the elaborate charade being acted for de Quadra's benefit during the early part of 1561 is not entirely clear, but its underlying purpose was undoubtedly political and not unconnected with the reconvening of the Council of Trent. After a ten-year adjournment, this Great Council of the Church was about to make one last effort to repair the fractured unity of Christendom, and Pope Pius IV had made known his intention of inviting the Queen of England to send representatives to the negotiating-table. Elizabeth, acutely conscious of her country's vulnerable and isolated position, had always been careful in her dealings with the European Catholics never to seem to shut the door entirely on the possibility of reconciliation; while the Vatican, prompted by Philip, had so far been equally careful not to say or do anything which might antagonise her too severely. But if she refused to admit Abbé Martinengo, the papal nuncio now on his way to England bearing a papal olive-branch, it would be tantamount to a formal declaration that she had not only shut but finally locked the door on Rome. Certainly de Quadra regarded the reception of the Abbé as an important test of the Queen's good faith. The ambassador had no real idea what the outcome would be, but he thought there was still a chance that, with Philip's support, Elizabeth might be prepared to make a stand and free herself from 'the tyranny of the heretics'. Robert had recently been given new and more salubrious quarters next to the Queen's at Greenwich –

a gesture which had apparently restored his health and spirits – and de Quadra himself took lodgings at Greenwich so as to be on hand when the nuncio arrived.[24]

Then, suddenly, the whole house of cards collapsed. During the second week of April there was a series of arrests among prominent Catholic sympathisers in London and, to his unspeakable annoyance, the Spanish ambassador found that he was being accused of complicity in a dangerous Catholic conspiracy against the Queen. Even worse, it was now being openly said that Philip had promised to help Elizabeth to marry her lover if she would agree to turn Catholic – just the kind of damaging talk de Quadra had been most anxious to avoid. The Queen soothed him slightly by assurances that she personally did not hold him responsible, but the nuncio's visit was off. In present circumstances it could only be regarded as provocative and might lead to unacceptable disturbance and disquietude. Besides, England could not agree to take part in the General Council as at present constituted. If a genuinely representative assembly, open to all Christian princes and independent of the Pope, were ever to be held in the future, then the Queen would be pleased to send ambassadors and learned men to explain and defend the Anglican viewpoint.[25]

Elizabeth's own sympathies always inclined towards the conservative and traditionalist, and her well-known prejudice against Calvinist and Puritan bigotry was often interpreted as undue leniency to the Catholic faction; but at the same time it is surely unthinkable that she ever for one moment seriously contemplated a return to Rome. It is equally unthinkable that Elizabeth Tudor ever for one moment even considered the abject course of begging Spanish protection to enable her to make a marriage which would have caused the deepest offence to every section of her own people. It therefore looks very much as if she deliberately took advantage of Lord Robert's consuming ambition and lack of any particular religious conviction to gain a political point. In short, that she tricked him into believing that she might for his sake be persuaded to surrender her freedom of action and to forfeit her subjects' love and respect.

Elizabeth was all her life a politician to her fingers' ends and it would have been entirely typical of her to use her nearest and dearest as a political weapon if she thought it necessary for her country's good. This was a fact which her nearest and dearest would simply have to live with. Elizabeth seldom or never gave anything for nothing. She was investing a good deal of emotional and material capital in Robert Dudley and she demanded a full and fair return. If this sometimes involved being made to look like a knave and a fool, then he must accept it as the price of his unique position as the Queen's 'brother and best friend'.

32

Without a Certain Heir, Living and Known

In spite of their recent disappointment, Robert's dreams of winning the crown matrimonial and de Quadra's of using him to detach the Queen from the 'gang of heretics' who surrounded her proved remarkably tenacious of life. On 24 June, Robert gave a grand water-party on the Thames. De Quadra was among the guests and at one point during the afternoon found himself alone with Robert and Elizabeth on the deck of the vessel from which they were to watch the festivities. 'They began joking,' he wrote, 'which she likes to do much better than talking about business. They went so far with their jokes that Lord Robert told her that, if she liked, I could be the minister to perform the act of marriage and she, nothing loath to hear it, said she was not sure whether I knew enough English.' The ambassador let them have their fun and then tried to talk some sense into them. If they would only listen to him, they could extricate themselves from the tyranny of councillors like Cecil and his friends, and restore the country to peace and unity by reinstating the Catholic religion. (Like all Philip's envoys, de Quadra tended to overestimate the strength of Catholic feeling in England.) Once this was done, he went on, they could be married as soon as they liked and, with the King of Spain behind them, could snap their fingers at anyone who dared to object. De Quadra told Philip that he intended to persevere along these lines, for by keeping in with the Queen he would 'not only maintain her friendliness towards your Majesty, but have still some hopes of persuading her'.[1]

The Queen did not disillusion him. The longer Philip could be made to believe that her amorous desires might eventually overcome her fear of the heretics and lure her back into the orthodox fold, the better she would be suited – especially at a time when there might well be more trouble brewing north of the border. The young King of France had died the previous December and Mary Queen of Scots, a widow at eighteen, would now become a matrimonial prize second only to the Queen of England. This in itself was worrying, and so was the fact that Mary was about to return to her own kingdom, for who could tell what havoc the pretty creature might create among the volatile Scottish warlords? Who could tell how many simple men might begin to reflect, once she was back in their midst, on their queen's claims to her neighbour's throne and be 'carried away with vain hope and brought abed with fair words'? Mary herself was eloquent in her desire to be friends with her 'good sister and tender cousin' Elizabeth, but she was still refusing to ratify the Treaty of Edinburgh and Elizabeth was not impressed by fair words.[2]

The end of the summer brought the Queen another tiresome and possibly dangerous complication nearer home, when it came out that Lady Catherine Grey – heiress presumptive if the provisions of Henry VIII's will were to be regarded as binding – had married the Earl of Hertford without observing the courtesy of informing her sovereign lady. The matrons of the court had for some time been casting suspicious glances at Lady Catherine, and by August she was 'certainly known to be big with child' – a mishap which, in William Cecil's opinion, was a proof of God's displeasure. For the unhappy Lady Catherine, however, God's displeasure was of less immediate concern than Queen Elizabeth's, and of that the proof was unmistakable.

Elizabeth had never cared much for any of her Grey cousins and had never bothered to conceal her poor opinion of the Protestant heiress – a fact already noted with interest in certain quarters. Now she was furious at this evidence of flagrant deceit, disrespect and perhaps worse. Although it was no longer a punishable offence merely to marry a member of the royal family without the sovereign's consent, the Queen, with her own experience of the intrigues liable to surround the heir to the throne still fresh in her memory, suspected there was more to this tale of romance than met the eye. The young couple were therefore hustled into the Tower, pending an investigation of the circumstances surrounding their marriage, and Elizabeth's temper was not improved when Lady Catherine presently gave birth to a healthy son.

The affair occupied a good deal of attention during the autumn, but exhaustive enquiries failed to reveal anything more sinister than a quite astounding degree of irresponsibility on the part of the newly-weds. All the same, the Queen took a lot of convincing. Catherine's choice of husband had been particularly tactless, for Lord Hertford was a Seymour, son of the late Lord Protector Somerset, and the Seymours, as Elizabeth had good cause to know, had a long record of political ambition, besides being closely connected with the royal house. Elizabeth also knew that Catherine had a considerable following, that a number of influential people (including William Cecil) would have liked to see her officially recognized as the heiress presumptive. She was, after all, an Englishwoman born, a Protestant, and now she had proved her ability to bear sons. But anything which touched on the succession touched the Queen on her most sensitive spot. It was a matter which she regarded as coming entirely within the royal prerogative and over which she would tolerate no interference – even well-meant interference.

No evidence of conspiracy having come to light, Elizabeth proposed to deal with Catherine Grey by having her marriage declared invalid (or non-existent) and her infant a bastard. Since the clergyman who had performed the secret ceremony at Hertford's house the previous December had disappeared without trace and the only other witness, the bridegroom's sister, Jane, had since died, this did not seem likely to present any insuperable difficulty – especially as Catherine had characteristically lost the only piece of documentary evidence she had possessed, a deed of jointure given her by her husband. The case was handed over to the ecclesiastical authorities and the culprits remained in gaol where, thanks to the indulgence of their guards, they later compounded their offence by producing another son.[3]

Any inclination Elizabeth might have felt to forgive her cousin's indiscretions was not increased by the fact that there was widespread sympathy for the plight of the young Hertfords. Their romantic story had touched the imagination of a sentimental public and it was generally held that their inability to prove their marriage was more their misfortune than their fault. Besides, it was argued, the solution to the difficulty lay in the Queen's own hands. She had only to do the obvious sensible thing – get married and start a family herself – and any threat to her security posed by Catherine Grey would vanish like snow in summer.

But there was no sign that the Queen intended to do the obvious sensible thing. On the contrary, for there were not even any negotiations currently in progress. Archduke Charles had gone into cold storage; Elizabeth had long since refused the Earl of Arran, to the annoyance and disappointment of the Swedish Protestants; and she had now finally sent Eric of Sweden, the most persistent of her foreign suitors, about his business in a bluntly worded letter which admitted of no misunderstanding.[4]

Lord Robert, on the other hand, was still her constant companion and the horrid possibility of a Dudley marriage was by no means a dead issue. Robert himself revived it in January 1562 by renewing his request that the King of Spain should be asked to write to the Queen in his favour. This time there were no large promises about restoring the Catholic faith, but Robert did drop a hint that the French were making him 'great offers'. De Quadra replied that, since Elizabeth already knew his king was anxious to see her wedded and had a high opinion of Lord Robert, it seemed unnecessary to ask him for a personal letter. There was no doubt about Philip's goodwill – the problem, observed the ambassador, lay rather in persuading the Queen to act and he offered to raise the subject with her again.

When de Quadra saw Elizabeth she told him that, whatever the world might think, she was 'as free from any engagement to marry as the day she was born'. However, she had quite made up her mind not to accept any man she did not already know and realised this might mean she would have to marry an Englishman, 'in which case she thought she could find no person more fitting that Lord Robert'. She would like all friendly princes, but especially Philip, to write advising her to take Robert so that, if she ever felt disposed to it, people could not say she had married him to satisfy her own desires but instead had followed the advice of her princely friends and relatives. This, she added hastily, was what Robert wanted. She asked nothing for herself but did not see that Philip risked anything by complying with Robert's request, even if the marriage never took place.

But de Quadra had smelt a large rat. He believed all this anxiety to extract a letter from Philip was simply so that it could be used for propaganda purposes to show the English Catholics that the King of Spain no longer cared about their fate; that he was prepared to countenance the Queen's marriage, even to such a dubious character as Robert Dudley, just to keep her sweet and without demanding any preconditions on their behalf; that, in short, Philip was ready to remain friendly with the heretic regime under almost any circumstances. The ambassador, therefore, tried to turn the matter off 'in a joking way', telling Elizabeth not to dilly dally any longer but satisfy Lord Robert at once, as she knew how glad his king would be.[5]

Reports that the Queen had followed de Quadra's advice were current during the summer, and in June there was an especially circumstantial story going about that she and Robert had been secretly married during a visit to the Earl of Pembroke's house. (Pembroke was by way of being a friend of Robert's.) It was all over town that the wedding had actually taken place – and not only in town. The Queen herself told de Quadra with a certain amount of glee that her own ladies had asked her if they were now to kiss Lord Robert's hand as well as hers. She also told him, 'with an oath', that if she had to marry an Englishman it would only be Robert, and Robert was saying the Queen had promised to marry him, 'but not this year'.[6]

And so it went on. De Quadra got into trouble with the Council for passing on the secret-wedding story, an accusation he indignantly denied. He had never told anyone that the Queen was married, he said, and was only sorry that he could not do so truthfully. De Quadra was not alone in this regret. Many serious-minded Englishmen were becoming increasingly disturbed by the Queen's obstinate, apparently frivolous refusal to look ahead. She would be twenty-nine on her next birthday – more than time she settled down. Indeed, if she was to have children, there was really no time to be lost.

While the serious-minded continued to worry about the future in a general way, and to tell one another that something ought to be done to settle the succession, the reality of the danger which threatened England's security was dramatically brought home even to the most thoughtless. During October the Queen was in residence at Hampton Court when she succumbed to a virulent strain of smallpox which had already infected several of the ladies of her circle. The rash would not come out, Elizabeth's fever mounted and she was soon desperately ill. Cecil, summoned from London at midnight, reached the palace in the small hours of the sixteenth, and as the Queen lay unconscious, perhaps dying, the Council went into emergency session to discuss the horrifying crisis which faced the country.

According to de Quadra, out of the fifteen or sixteen members present, 'there were nearly as many different opinions about the succession to the Crown'.[7] In fact, the Council seems to have been split more or less down the middle. One group, which almost certainly included William Cecil, wanted to follow King Henry's will and name Lady Catherine Grey; others, 'who found flaws in the will', pressed the claims of Henry Hastings, Earl of Huntingdon, who could boast double descent from Edward III and was known to be a reliable Protestant. The Earls of Bedford and Pembroke supported Huntingdon, and so – although they were not council members – did the Duke of Norfolk and Lord Robert Dudley. Huntingdon was married to Lord Robert's sister Catherine, and de Quadra thought that Robert would be ready to back his brother-in-law by force of arms. A third and smaller group, led by the old Marquis of Winchester who had already survived the alarums and excursions of three reigns, urged against too much haste and suggested referring the matter to a committee of jurists, who could examine the rights of the various claimants and advise the Council accordingly. No one, it seemed, within the precincts of Hampton Court had mentioned the name of Mary Queen of Scots, and de Quadra reported that the Catholics, too, were divided – some favouring the Queen of Scots, others preferring her aunt, Margaret Lennox, who had been born in England and was considered to be 'devout and sensible'.[8]

While the Council was still deliberating, Elizabeth recovered consciousness and, in her confused and feverish state, begged the anxious throng at her bedside to make Robert Dudley protector of the kingdom, with a title and an income of £20,000 a year. She swore, in what she believed might be her last moments, that although she loved and had always loved Robert dearly, 'as God was her witness, nothing improper had ever passed between them', and asked that the groom who slept in his room should be given a pension of £500 a year. 'Everything she asked was promised,' reported de Quadra, 'but will not be fulfilled.'[9]

Only one thing emerged with any certainty out of the terror and confusion of that dreadful day; if the Queen had died – and she was 'all but gone' – she would have left a vacuum which would rapidly have filled with political anarchy, with bitter faction-fighting and most probably civil war. To the unspeakable relief of the Council, the nobility and the country at large, the Queen recovered. She even escaped the dreaded disfigurement of smallpox and within a surprisingly short space of time she was up and about again and once more in full command. But the nation had had a fright it would not soon forget and, before the end of November, de Quadra heard that groups of gentlemen were meeting under the auspices of the Earl of Arundel to discuss the succession. When Elizabeth heard about this she was furious and was said to have wept with rage. She summoned Arundel and they appear to have had a first-class row, the Earl telling her that, if she wanted to govern the country by passion, he could assure her that the nobility would not allow it. The succession was a matter which affected them vitally and they had every right to be concerned.[10]

As well as a mutinous nobility, Elizabeth now had to face another Parliament – something she would have avoided if she possibly could, knowing what opportunities that would provide for bringing organized pressure to bear on her. Unhappily she could not avoid it. She needed money. The Scottish adventure of 1560, although it had given value for money, had been expensive and now England was involved in another, equally expensive but far less well-judged foray on behalf of the French Huguenots. So the writs went out in November and, by the second week of January 1563, the members were gathering at Westminster with one thought uppermost in all their minds.

The first indication of the general mood came even before the official opening of the session, in the sermon preached at Westminster Abbey by Alexander Nowell, Dean of St Paul's, during the preliminary church service. Dr Nowell, never one to mince his words, reminded his hearers that, just as Queen Mary's marriage had been a terrible plague to all England, so now the want of Queen Elizabeth's marriage and issue was like to prove as great a plague. 'If your parents had been of your mind, where had you been then?' he demanded of the Queen sitting below him in the congregation. 'Or what had become of us now?' This was plain speaking and the Dean went on to ram his point home. 'When your Majesty was troubled with sickness, then I heard continual voices and lamentations, saying: "Alas! What trouble shall we be in? . . . For the succession is so uncertain and such division for religion! Alack! what shall become of us?"'[11]

What indeed? And the fears of the nation, as reflected by its elected representatives, were succinctly expressed in a petition presented to the Queen by the Speaker of the House of Commons on 28 January. They foresaw with awful clarity 'the unspeakable miseries of civil wars, the perilous intermeddlings of foreign princes with seditious, ambitious and factious subjects at home, the waste of noble houses, the slaughter of people, subversion of towns . . . unsurety of all men's possessions, lives and estates' if the sovereign were to die without a known heir, and pointed out that 'from the Conquest to this present day the realm was never left as now it is without a certain heir, living and known'.[12] The Commons still wanted Elizabeth to marry, of course, but it was significant that, since the 'great terror and dreadful warning' of her illness, the emphasis of their anxiety had shifted. Whether she married or not, they wanted the succession to be settled – *now*.

The Lords' petition, delivered a couple of days later by the Lord Keeper,

Nicholas Bacon, still put marriage first and begged 'that it would please your Majesty to dispose yourself to marry, where it shall please you, to whom it shall please you, and as soon as it shall please you'. But their lordships, too, were acutely worried about the succession and understandably so in a society where, as they grimly reminded the Queen, 'upon the death of princes the law dieth'. All the continuity of order and government depended on the peaceful transition from one reign to another, for with the death of the sovereign Parliament was automatically dissolved and could only be summoned again by the authority of the Crown. Nor would there be any council, judges, magistrates or royal officials of any kind – their commissions, too, automatically expired with the Crown. Without a known heir, ready and waiting to take over, the country would lapse into chaos where 'strength and will' must rule, with all the suffering, bloodshed and destruction that implied. It was a prospect calculated to terrify the stoutest hearted and the Lords ended with an urgent plea for immediate and serious consideration of the problem, so that 'good effect and conclusion may grow hereof before the end of the session of this Parliament'.[13]

Replying to the Commons, Elizabeth told them that she knew she was as mortal as the next woman. There was no need to keep reminding her about it. Nor was there any need to remind her of her responsibilities. She knew that she must seek to discharge herself of the 'great burthen' God had laid upon her. She quite understood the members' anxiety and did not take it amiss, but they could hardly expect an off-the-cuff answer 'in this so great and weighty a matter' which would need much thought and 'further advice'. In any case, they surely knew her well enough by now to trust her to look after them and to be 'neither careless nor unmindful' of their future welfare. 'And so I assure you all', she concluded 'that, though after my death you may have many stepdames, yet shall you never have a more natural mother than I mean to be unto you all.'[14]

If de Quadra is to be trusted, the Queen expended less tact on the Lords. According to him, she was very angry 'and told them that the marks they saw on her face were not wrinkles, but the pits of smallpox, and that although she might be old God could send her children as he did to St Elizabeth, and they [the lords] had better consider well what they were asking, as, if she declared a successor, it would cost much blood to England'.[15]

In spite of the depth of feeling on the subject, the succession was not openly debated, nor, in spite of a good deal of private agitation, was it officially referred to again until Parliament was prorogued at Easter. Then, in the presence of both Houses, Nicholas Bacon read a message from the Queen, written in her own hand and containing what might be construed as a conditional promise to get married in the not too distant future. Elizabeth still preferred spinsterhood for herself 'as a private woman, yet', she went on, 'do I strive with myself to think it not meet for a Prince. And if I can bend my liking to your need, I will not resist such a mind.' As regards the succession, she would not be drawn, taking refuge behind a baffling smoke-screen of words whose only discernible meaning seemed to be that the Queen did not feel the time was ripe for a decision. 'But', her latest 'answer answerless' concluded, 'I hope I shall die in quiet with *nunc dimittis*, which cannot be without I see some glimpse of your following surety after my graved bones.'[16]

A large part of Elizabeth's lifelong reluctance to have a named heir was rooted in her own experience during Mary's reign, but that was not the whole story. Always the keynote of her political philosophy was to keep things fluid – never, if humanely possible, to allow a situation to coalesce to the point where a decision had to be taken. People who made decisions also made mistakes, they limited their own freedom of action and they drove other people into making decisions – and mistakes. In the matter of the succession the Queen believed, and she was probably right, that any attempt to 'solve' the problem would have encouraged rather than disarmed faction and controversy. Perhaps more to the point, she did not regard it as a matter which was properly open to arbitrary settlement. The crown was not, after all, a piece of real estate to be bestowed according to personal or political convenience. The issue might have been clouded by religious passion and by King Henry's unfortunate will, but no one could deny that, out of the dozen or so persons of royal descent alive in the 1560s, Mary Queen of Scots had far and away the strongest hereditary claim to be recognised as heiress presumptive.

Elizabeth herself never denied it. She had already told the Scottish Secretary of State, William Maitland of Lethington, in private conversation that she considered Mary, her cousin and next kinswoman, to be her natural and lawful successor. 'I for my part', she said, 'know none better, nor that myself would prefer to her.' But she would not, despite everything Mary and Maitland could say or do to persuade her, agree to make the Queen of Scots her heir 'by order of Parliament'. When Maitland had urged that settling the succession on Mary would only cement the friendship between the two queens, Elizabeth promptly disabused him of any such sentimental notion. 'Think you that I could love my winding sheet?' she asked with brutal frankness. She had no illusions about the 'natural inconstancy' of men and nothing could shake her conviction that, the moment 'a certain successor' had been named, every restless, discontented or disappointed spirit in the kingdom, everyone with a real or imagined grievance, would turn towards the heir as towards the rising sun 'in hope then to be in better case'. 'So long as I live,' declared Elizabeth Tudor, 'I shall be Queen of England. When I am dead, they shall succeed that have the most right.'[17]

There, in the autumn of 1561, the matter had rested and there the

Queen would infinitely have preferred to leave it. Her instinct was to do nothing, to go on gambling on her own survival until such time as a natural solution to the problem presented itself. But in the spring of 1563 things looked rather different and Elizabeth was undoubtedly troubled over what to do for the best. She could sympathise with her people's fears about the future and was far from insensitive to the pressure being exerted on her. Perhaps, too, her recent brush with death had shaken her more than she cared to admit. One thing was certain – if any way out of the present *impasse* were to be found, it would have to involve the Queen of Scots. Nothing, it appeared, was ever going to persuade Elizabeth even to consider the claims of any other contender in the succession stakes.

Mary was twenty now and had been a widow for just over two years. This was not a state of affairs likely to continue for ever and a great deal, if not everything, would depend on the identity of her second husband. There had been talk of a Spanish or Habsburg alliance for the Scottish Queen – the name of that useful stand-by Archduke Charles had been mentioned, and so had Philip's psychopathic son Don Carlos – but Elizabeth did not think Mary would marry to disoblige her, or at least not while she still had any hope of cajoling her into changing her mind about the succession. So, if a suitable, really trustworthy husband could be found, then maybe something could be arranged. Elizabeth had evidently begun to think along these lines quite early in the year, for it was in March, while Parliament was still sitting, that she first broached the matter to Maitland of Lethington, who happened to be in London again.

The plan itself – that Mary should agree to accept a consort of Elizabeth's choice in return for a promise of recognition as Elizabeth's heiress – might indeed have offered a possible solution, or at any rate a basis for negotiation. Unfortunately, Elizabeth's choice appeared so preposterous as to put the whole scheme right out of court from the start. De Quadra, who had the story from the Scottish Secretary himself, passed it on to Philip in a despatch dated 28 March. It seemed that the Queen had told Maitland 'that if his mistress would take her advice and wished to marry safely and happily she would give her a husband who would ensure both, and this was Lord Robert, in whom nature had implanted so many graces that if she wished to marry she would prefer him to all the princes in the world'. William Maitland was a shrewd politician and practised diplomat, but the very thought of that shop-soiled and controversial widower, Robert Dudley, sharing the throne of Scotland caused him to gag almost visibly. All the same, he managed to respond with a nicely barbed compliment. It was certainly a great proof of the love the Queen of England bore his queen if she was willing to give her a thing she prized so much, but he felt sure that Mary, even if she loved Lord Robert as dearly as Elizabeth did, would not wish to deprive her cousin of the joy and solace she derived from his company. Elizabeth did not take the hint. It was a pity, she mused, that Ambrose Dudley (Robert's elder brother, now restored to the dignity of Earl of Warwick) did not possess Robert's charm and good looks, for then she and Mary could each have had one of them. This was too much for Maitland. If the Queen of England could make tasteless jokes on such a serious subject, then so could he. Elizabeth had better marry Robert herself 'and then when it should please God to call her to himself, she could leave the Queen of Scots heiress both to her kingdom and her husband' – that way Lord Robert could hardly fail to have children by one or other of them.[18]

Maitland could not believe that Elizabeth was serious, but apparently she was – at any rate, she kept returning to her bizarre suggestion. Thomas Randolph, the English agent in Edinburgh, was instructed to let Mary know that, if she would leave her marriage in Elizabeth's hands, the Queen would be as good as a mother to her and at last, in the spring of 1564, Randolph, much to his embarrassment, received orders to propose Lord Robert officially to the Queen of Scots.

Mary's public reaction was polite but unenthusiastic. Was it comformable to Elizabeth's promise to treat her as a daughter, to offer to match her to a subject? she asked. Supposing Elizabeth were to get married herself and have children, what would Scotland have gained then? However, she promised to think the matter over and discuss it with her advisers.[19] In private, she was highly sceptical and more than inclined to take offence. If the proposal had been accompanied by a guarantee of recognition of her right to the reversion of her cousin's throne, the Queen of Scots might have swallowed her natural umbrage at being offered her cousin's discarded lover – the notorious horsekeeper no less. But it was never Elizbeth's way to give guarantees and Mary could not rid herself of the suspicion that she was being hoaxed, that this was some kind of tease designed to make her look foolish before the world and perhaps spoil her chances of making a more worthy marriage. Mary was not alone in her suspicions and many people since have found it extremely difficult to accept that Elizabeth ever really meant to part with her favourite man – and not merely part with him but hand him over to another woman, younger, prettier and her most dangerous rival.

Had she ever meant it seriously? Where Elizabeth is concerned it is never wise to be too certain of anything and her thought processes could be as convoluted as her prose style. But the original idea, born out of a genuine dilemma, had obviously been worth exploring. It would at least demonstrate that the Queen was not shutting her eyes to the problem, that she was honestly trying to find a solution; it would show the Scots that she was prepared to take a constructive interest in their queen's future and it might buy valuable time. Such a marriage would remove the threat of another foreign power establishing itself on England's back doorstep and would bring the youthful Mary firmly under English control.

In the last resort what mattered to Elizabeth was the security of her throne and the peace and unity of her realm. If she could have been assured that her peculiar plan would achieve these ends, there is no real reason to assume that she would not have gone through with it, whatever the personal sacrifice involved.

She certainly continued to behave as though she meant it. When the Scottish courtier and diplomat James Melville came south in September 1564, Elizabeth told him that, if she had ever wanted to take a husband, she would have chosen Lord Robert. 'But being determined to end her life in virginity, she wished that the queen her sister should marry him, as meetest of all other and with whom she could find in her heart to declare the queen second person rather than any other.' For, she explained, if Mary were matched with Robert Dudley, 'it would best remove out of her mind all fear and suspicion to be offended by usurpation before her death; being assured that he was so loving and trusty that he would never give his consent nor suffer such thing to be attempted during her time'.[20] Robert was at last to get his peerage, to make the Queen of Scots 'think the more of him', and Melville had to stay and witness his investiture as Earl of Leicester and Baron Denbigh. The new earl conducted himself with very proper gravity and decorum throughout the ceremony but the Queen, helping to put on his robes, rather spoilt the solemn effect by putting a hand down his neck 'to tickle him smilingly'.[21]

Discussion of the marriage continued in a rather desultory fashion. Maitland and some others were coming round to the idea, but Mary remained lukewarm and, although she professed herself willing to be guided by Elizabeth over her choice of husband, it was clear that the Queen of Scots would not commit herself until she had seen the colour of the Queen of England's money. In other words, she wanted a definite undertaking, signed and sealed, about the succession. But Elizabeth, who preferred to deal obliquely, in hints, allusions and tacit understandings, would not oblige.

Given the fog of distrust which hung heavily between the two sides, there was probably never much real chance of reaching an agreement, and another obstacle lay in the attitude of the bridegroom-elect. The Earl of Leicester was not at all grateful for the kind plans being made for his advancement. On the contrary, he viewed them with consternation. He did not in the least wish to marry the Queen of Scots and be banished to the barbaric north. He wanted to stay at home and marry the Queen of England and, if Mary can be believed, he wrote to her secretly some time that winter to tell her that the project was nothing but a trick intended to discourage other suitors.

Nevertheless, another suitor was about to make his appearance on the scene. Henry Stuart, Lord Darnley, was Mary's first cousin – his mother, Margaret Lennox, being the daughter of Margaret Tudor's second marriage who had herself married into a collateral branch of the Stuart family. Mary and Darnley were therefore doubly related and the young man, through his combined Tudor, Stuart and Hamilton ancestry, stood very close to both the English and Scottish thrones. The cousins' names had been briefly linked during the first weeks of Mary's widowhood, and the Countess of Lennox, an ambitious and doting mamma, had been scheming unsuccessfully to make a match between them ever since. Queen Elizabeth knew this and it has always been something of a mystery why, in the circumstances, she allowed Lord Darnley to travel to Scotland in February 1565 – apparently accepting the not very convincing excuse that his presence there was necessary for the settling of some family business. In fact, so odd did it seem that some people later wondered if Elizabeth had had a sinister purpose. It is pretty well impossible now to unravel the dense cocoon of intrigue enveloping the whole affair, but it seems highly probable that Robert Dudley was working with the Lennox family behind Elizabeth's back and that it was he who talked her into letting Darnley go.

The Queen may have been genuinely deceived but, in view of her preternaturally sensitive antennae for matters of this kind, it is not very likely. More credibly, she may well have come to the conclusion by this time that her own plan was not going to work out – she told the Spanish ambassador that it failed because Robert had not consented – and she may even have decided that she could not, after all, bear to part with him. At the same time, she obviously could not expect to prevent Mary from marrying altogether. Darnley was technically her subject, having been born and brought up in England, and encouraged by Robert she may have seen him as a possible alternative. Mary had not so far shown any signs of interest in her young relative – Darnley was three years her junior and, apart from his breeding and rather girlish good looks, was of no particular account – but if she were now to take a fancy to him, then perhaps a marriage might be arranged. On suitable terms, of course. It would, at least, be preferable to another foreign connection.

But, if Elizabeth was reasoning along these lines, she failed to reckon with Mary's obstinacy when it came to getting her own way or with the strength of her biological urges. The Queen of Scots suffered from none of her English cousin's mysterious hang-ups on the subject of marriage. At twenty-one she was a warm-blooded, very normal young woman, impatient for love. Her first reaction to Darnley was favourable – he was 'the lustiest and best proportioned long man' she had seen – and before many weeks had gone by the Queen and her cousin were inseparable.

Mary did not guess that beneath the surface of this tall handsome princeling, with his pretty manners and courtly accomplishments, lay a spoilt, loutish, unstable youth with all the makings of a vindictive bully. Since her return home the young Queen of Scotland had often been lonely. She missed the brilliance and the civilised gaiety of the French court, and she had had to put up with a good deal of John Knox's conversation. Darnley crossed her path at a time of mounting disappointment and frustration and it is not in the least surprising that she should have seen him as an answer to prayer. But it was extremely unfortunate that she should have allowed her infatuation to blind her to all considerations of statecraft, of caution or even of plain common sense. Opposition to the match, of which there was plenty, only hardened her resolve and she quarrelled disastrously with her powerful kinsman, the Earl of Moray, who had so far guarded and guided her through the bloodstained jungle of Scottish politics. Nor, it seemed, did she any longer care if she offended Queen Elizabeth.

Queen Elizabeth was – or, at least, professed to be – deeply offended and promptly clapped the intriguing Lady Lennox into the Tower; but a suspicion persisted that she, or some other 'great person', had deliberately sent Darnley to Scotland in the hope of trapping Mary into an unhappy and demeaning marriage. William Cecil regarded the projected union of these two strong contenders for the English succession with deep misgiving – believing that it would inevitably comfort and encourage 'all such as be affected to the Queen of Scots, either for herself or for the opinion of her pretence to this crown or for the desire to have a change of the form of religion in this realm'.[22]

Thomas Randolph in Edinburgh believed that Mary had been bewitched and frankly despaired of her future, finding her 'so altered with affection towards Lord Darnley that she hath brought her honour in question, her estate in hazard, her country to be torn in pieces! I see also', he went on, 'the amity between the countries like to be dissolved, and great mischiefs like to ensue. To whom this may chiefly be imputed, what crafty subtlety or devilish device hath brought this to pass, I know not, but woe worth the time! (and so shall both England and Scotland say) that ever the Lord Darnley did set foot in this country.' Darnley's overweening arrogance was already making him intolerable to all honest men, but Mary, transported by love, would heed no warning, listen to no advice. Randolph could only speculate gloomily on what would become of her or what her life with such a husband would be and was moved to genuine pity for 'the lamentable estate of this poor Queen'.[23] She was so changed, he wrote, that she hardly seemed the same woman. 'Her majesty is laid aside – her wits not what they were – her beauty another than it was; her cheer and countenance changed into I wot not what.'[24]

Few people would have predicted a happy outcome for the marriage solemnised in the Chapel Royal at Holyrood House on 31 July 1565; but equally no one foresaw that it would end so soon and so melodramatically, or that it would have such far-reaching long-term consequences for both England and Scotland.

33

Talk is All of the Archduke

So for better or worse, the Queen of Scots was married while the Queen of England was still a maid and, at over thirty, in danger of becoming an old maid. Surely, people asked themselves, surely she must now recognise the urgent necessity of acquiring a husband before it was too late to provide the country with an heir no one could dispute? And in 1565 it did look rather as though Mary Stuart's marriage was forcing Elizabeth to reconsider her position. But in fact she had been reconsidering her position, or at least seeking to reopen certain avenues of approach, for nearly two years. Sooner or later she would have to face Parliament again and, if she was to avert a major confrontation with that increasingly vociferous body, would have to show that some attempt was being made to redeem the promise given to both Houses at Easter 1563.

In the autumn of 1563, therefore, William Cecil had been given the go-ahead to start the first cautious moves towards a possible resumption of negotiations with the Habsburg family. It all had to be done with exquisite tact. On no account must Elizabeth appear too eager and thus lose her initial advantage in the ritual dance of diplomatic courtship. On the contrary, elaborate precautions must be taken to conceal her interest in the affair. So Cecil wrote to Strasbourg to Dr Christopher Mundt, for many years the English government's agent and general go-between in German affairs. Mundt contacted the Duke of Württemberg, a close friend of the Imperial family, mentioning that, for various reasons, he personally believed this might be a propitious moment for raising the English marriage project again; and the Duke wrote to the Emperor, mentioning that he had recently received a visit from his old acquaintance Dr Mundt who, amongst other things, had discussed with him how 'the action of a marriage between Your Imperial Majesty's son, the Archduke Charles and the Queen of England, might best be resumed'.[1]

Although he was too much of a gentleman to say so, the Emperor probably had little difficulty in making an accurate guess as to the real origin of this new initiative. His reaction was guarded but sufficiently favourable to encourage the Duke of Württemberg to send an envoy to London in January 1564 – ostensibly to take the Queen a present of Lutheran books but actually to explore the situation on the spot and report accordingly. This individual, a Frisian who rejoiced in the name of Ahasverus Allinga, found the court at Windsor and on the day after his arrival had a very private interview with Elizabeth at which only Cecil and two maids of honour were present.

After listening patiently to a long harangue on the manifold advantages of marriage in general and marriage to the Archduke in particular, the Queen remarked that it was unnecessary to advance so many reasons at present, 'for she would never be induced by any appeals to reason but only by stern necessity, as she had already inwardly resolved that if she ever married it would be as Queen and not as Elizabeth'. There followed a somewhat inconclusive argument about whose fault it was that negotiations had been broken off last time. Elizabeth blamed the Emperor who, as she said, was behaving like an old woman and complained that he had treated her very badly over the matter of his son's visit to England. What did emerge with absolute clarity was that the Queen remained as determined as ever to have a good look at Charles before she committed herself to anything, and that the first move towards reopening negotiations would have to come from the Emperor. Elizabeth could not begin again 'without covering herself with ignominy' and was certainly not going to fall into the trap of declaring that she wanted to marry the Archduke. If she were to follow her own inclinations, she would far rather be a beggarwoman and single than a queen and married. Only necessity, she repeated, would ever induce her to marry.[2]

After this, Ahasverus Allinga was, not surprisingly, so discouraged that he told Cecil he could see no point in pursuing discussions any further. Not at all, replied the Secretary. The Queen had told him how much she had enjoyed the conversation and he believed she was by no means disinclined to the marriage. Allinga went home to Württemberg, no doubt to ponder on the peculiar mating habits of the English, and there for the moment the matter rested. Then, in July, the Emperor Ferdinand died – an event which might provide the opportunity for making a fresh start.

That autumn the talk in London was all of the Archduke, of how an important embassy would soon be going to offer condolences and congratulations to the new Emperor (he was Maximilian, eldest of Ferdinand's three sons), and at the same time to reanimate the Austrian marriage. But somehow argument and confusion over who should be sent to Vienna prolonged themselves into October, and in early November Christopher Mundt was writing again to Württemberg to tell the Duke that the Queen of England had been expecting Maximilian to return his father's insignia of the Garter, as was customary. It seemed that the neglect of this courtesy had caused Elizabeth to delay sending her own emissaries, and Mundt warned that these unfortunate hesitations and misunderstandings might prove fatal to the happy outcome of a connection so honourable to Christendom and greatly desired by the English nobility.[3]

The Queen gave her nobility another nasty fright in December by falling 'perilously sick' with an attack of enteritis. She recovered quickly but, as William Cecil told his crony Sir Thomas Smith, ambassador in Paris, 'for the time she made us sore afraid'. Cecil had always been in the forefront of those urging matrimony on the reluctant Elizabeth, praying that God would direct her heart to procure a father for her children. Now he prayed that the Almighty would take an even closer interest in the matter and 'lead by the hand some meet person to come and lay hand on her to her contentation'. If that were to happen, he told Smith, he could wish himself more health to enjoy the benefits he trusted would follow. 'Otherwise, I assure you, as now things hang in desperation, I have no comfort to live.'[4]

Cecil seems to have believed, although the wish may have been father to the thought, that the Queen was now thinking seriously about a foreign alliance, and during the early part of 1565 another project came under discussion. This time the suggested bridegroom was Charles IX of France but, apart from the other obvious difficulties, the fact that the King of France was fifteen years old to Elizabeth's thirty-one did not really make it seem a very likely proposition. Elizabeth herself remarked drily that people would say she was marrying her grandson. However, the Queen was never averse to being courted and, in view of the current trend of affairs in Scotland, even the most improbable-sounding Anglo-French connection could be turned to use. So there was much solemn confidential talk about young Charles' remarkable precocity, about an exchange of portraits, perhaps a secret exchange of visits. But, although these conversations were carried on with every outward appearance of serious intent, and were spun out over the best part of six months, the Austrian Archduke remained unchallenged in his apparently permanent position as the Queen of England's chief suitor.

In May 1565 another Imperial envoy arrived in London. The outward purpose of Adam Zwetkovich's visit was to take advantage of the proffered opening and return the late Emperor's Garter insignia. In reality, as everyone knew, he had come to make one more attempt to revive the marriage negotiations. Always provided, so his instructions ran, that he was satisfied with regard to the Queen's unspotted virtue – the Habsburgs still had misgivings about the real nature of her relationship with Robert Dudley.

Robert, of course, was the joker in the pack. If Elizabeth married the Archduke (or anyone else, for that matter), his unique position as her 'brother and best friend' would be gone, and even the fact that he now had his earldom and a seat on the Council would not compensate for its loss. Let him once be ousted from his place at the Queen's side and his enemies would close in for the kill. He could therefore be expected to fight the Austrian marriage tooth and nail. On the other hand, the Queen might yet decide to marry him after all, and there were those who believed that his chances were as good now in the spring of 1565 as they had ever been.

Robert himself alternated between hope and despair. He told the Spanish ambassador that the Queen would never marry him 'as she has made up her mind to wed some great Prince, or at all events no subject of her own'. Then, suddenly changing direction, he said he thought the Queen of Scots' marriage would mean that his business might be more easily arranged, as the reason Elizabeth had refused him before was because of her fear that Mary meant to marry some powerful foreign prince.[5]

There was a new Spanish ambassador in London by this time. Bishop de Quadra had died in the plague summer of 1563 and his replacement, Dan Diego Guzman de Silva, was proving to be a perceptive and sympathetic character with a nice sense of humour who, alone of King Philip's envoys to Elizabeth's court, made a genuine effort to promote the cause of Anglo-Spanish understanding. The Queen and William Cecil both liked and trusted him; and Robert, of course, had wasted no time in getting on terms with him. Unlike his predecessor, de Silva was being careful to avoid too close an involvement in the tangled web of the Austrian marriage and had already resisted an attempt on the part of the English government to use him as an intermediary, wisely refusing to enter into any negotiations 'without some firm assurance that the affair would be carried through'. This assurance had not been forthcoming and de Silva strongly suspected that there was no serious intent behind the recent resurgence of interest in the Archduke – that it was, in fact, simply a diversion. From his various conversations with the Queen, with Robert and from hints reaching him from other sources, the ambassador had come to believe that 'Lord Robert's affair is not off', while he had many reasons for being doubtful about the Archduke. He therefore made up his mind to adopt a strictly neutral attitude – doing what he could to advise and assist the Emperor's ambassador, while at the same time keeping Robert in play, 'helping him in such a way that if ever his marriage to the Queen should come off, he will be bound to continue friendly'.[6]

To the outward eye Robert's relations with the Queen seemed as intimate as ever. There was a well-publicised incident in March 1565 when he and the Duke of Norfolk were playing tennis, Elizabeth looking on, and Robert took the Queen's napkin out of her hand to wipe his sweaty face. Norfolk, outraged by the sight of this casual familiarity, had to be restrained from hitting his opponent over the head with his racquet, but Elizabeth was apparently unperturbed and her wrath lighted on the Duke.[7] There were, however, liberties which Robert was not allowed to take – witness that other, equally famous occasion when one of his henchmen attempted to take a high hand with a member of the royal household. This led to a furious telling-off. 'God's death, my lord, I have wished you well, but my favour is not so locked up for you that others shall not participate thereof . . . and if you think to rule here, I will take a course to see you forthcoming. I will have here but one mistress and no master.'[8] Robert took the warning. He knew Elizabeth too well to make that sort of mistake twice and, according to one commentator, 'his feigned humility was long after one of his best virtues'.

Robert might be good at managing the Queen, and was probably as close to her as any other human being, but not even he could read her mind. Early in June, de Silva heard that the Earl of Leicester had again become more hopeful about his marriage and was moving in the matter. 'It looks as if the Queen favoured it also,' he went on, 'and the French ambassador has been pointing out to her the objections to the Archduke's match, saying that he is very poor and other things of the same sort to lead her away from the project.'[9] The Emperor's ambassador was getting a similar message and told the Earl of Sussex that he believed the Queen was determined never to marry or that, if she did, she would take no one but the Earl of Leicester. Sussex who, like Norfolk and William Cecil, strongly supported the Austrian marriage, pooh-poohed the idea – the Queen had promised the kingdom she would marry, and if she refused the Archduke there was no one else. All the same, round about this time Cecil was facing up to the fact that it looked very much as if Elizabeth still meant to have Robert Dudley in the end. The objections to such a match were the same as they had always been. Nothing would be gained for the country 'either in riches, estimation or power'. On the contrary, Robert was heavily in debt and would think of nothing but enriching himself and his friends, which would inevitably lead to bitter dissension and faction. He was 'infamed' by the death of his wife and, if he and the Queen were to marry now, not only would all the old scandals be revived but it would be thought that 'the slanderous speeches of the Queen and the Earl have been true'. Added to this, Cecil believed Robert was likely to prove an unkind and jealous husband.[10]

Then, in July, the weather suddenly changed and the court realised with fascinated interest that Elizabeth was treating her old friend with marked coolness. More than that, for the first time since the eclipse of William Pickering, she was bestowing smiles and favours on another Englishman, Thomas Heneage, one of the gentlemen-in-waiting and 'a young man of pleasant wit and bearing and a good courtier'. Robert did not conceal his annoyance, and angry words passed between the two men. De Silva thought at first that it was 'all make believe and simply devised to avoid jealousy', especially as Heneage was 'a great intimate' of Robert's, but he heard later that the trouble had started with Robert paying court to the pretty young Viscountess of Hereford, born Lettice Knollys and a cousin of the Queen's, apparently in an attempt to test the strength of the Queen's affection for him. Elizabeth had retaliated by taking up Thomas Heneage, and Robert had asked leave to go away to his own place to stay 'as other noblemen do'. The result was a violent quarrel between the Queen and her best friend. 'The Queen was in a great temper,' reported de Silva, 'and upbraided him with what had taken place with Heneage and his flirting with the Viscountess in very bitter words.' Heneage was sent away and Robert sulked in his lodgings for several days. Finally, the Earl of Sussex and Cecil smoothed things over, although, as de Silva remarked, 'they are no friends of Lord Robert in their hearts'. Robert was sent for, and he and Elizabeth shed tears and made it up.[11]

It all sounded trivial enough, but the episode rankled and during the Twelfth Night festivities in January 1566 there was another furious altercation between Heneage and the Earl of Leicester. According to the gossip retailed at the French court, the Queen was once more very angry with Lord Robert, saying 'that if by her favour he had become insolent he should soon reform, and that she would lower him just as she had at first raised him'. But, the same correspondent added, it was also being said that she would shortly proclaim him a duke and marry him![12] A few weeks later Elizabeth herself told de Silva that, if only Robert were a king's son, she would marry him tomorrow. 'She is so nimble in her dealings,' remarked the Spaniard, 'and threads in and out of this business in such a way that her most intimate favourites fail to understand her, and her intentions are therefore variously interpreted.' Nevertheless, de Silva saw no reason to change his own view that, although the Queen loved the business of being courted and having all the world running after her, she would end by marrying Robert or no one – an opinion which was coming to be shared by other European observers.[13]

Meanwhile, negotiations over the terms of a marriage contract with the Archduke were continuing. In general both sides accepted the precedents for the marriage of an English queen regnant established by Mary Tudor – the laws of England and the rights of Englishmen to remain sacrosanct, and neither the Queen nor any children of the marriage to be taken out of the realm without the consent of the realm – but there was still plenty of scope for argument over other matters. For example, who was going to pay for the Archduke's keep? The Emperor maintained that his brother's household expenses should be charged to the English exchequer but the English, remembering those rumours so assiduously spread by the French ambassador that Charles had no money of his own, were making it a condition that the Queen's husband must now become a burden on the taxpayer. Then there was the question of status. The Habsburgs were demanding that the Archduke should at once be crowned king and rule jointly with Elizabeth, also that he should retain his footing in England in the event of her death – terms which found little favour on the English side.[14]

These, though, were bargaining-points capable of being resolved by negotiation. More serious was the great religious divide. The English insisted that Charles must conform to the rites and observances of the Anglican Church, while the Emperor was equally definite that his brother must be allowed the full, free and open practice of Roman Catholicism. Elizabeth herself was now saying flatly that she could not possibly marry anyone who did not share her religious persuasion, for two persons of different faiths could never live peaceably in one house. When it was pointed out to her that she had always known Charles was a Catholic, she answered that on the contrary she had always been led to believe he was not set in his ways and would be willing to change his opinions.[15] The Queen was apparently ready to use the religious difficulty as an excuse for rejecting the whole plan, but others felt that even this obstacle might be overcome. The Earl of Sussex told Adam Zwetkovich he thought the matter could be arranged if the Archduke would agree to accompany the Queen to church in public and hear mass privately in his own apartments.[16]

On the other outstanding issue – that old bone of contention, the Archduke's visit to England – neither side had shifted from its previously entrenched position. Elizabeth told Zwetkovich that she would take no man she had not seen. She had already said this a thousand times, she remarked irritably, and was still and ever would be of the same mind. She wanted Charles to come incognito, hinting that if they took a fancy to each other everything else would be plain-sailing. If they did not – and she would never give the Archduke cause to curse portrait-painters and envoys as Philip had done when he first set eyes on Queen Mary – then it could be given out that it had not been possible to agree on the articles of the marriage contract and no one need be any the wiser.[17]

Elizabeth considered this perfectly reasonable, but the Emperor could not approve a plan which he clearly regarded as thoroughly feminine and frivolous and 'entirely novel and unprecedented' among kings and queens. He also feared a trap – that the English would wait until the Archduke had arrived and then put forward a preposterous set of conditions which he would not be able to accept. In any case, there could be no question of secret visits or suchlike romantic nonsense – the union of realms and princes was a serious matter. When the Archduke went to England it would be 'with all befitting ceremony' and not until negotiations over the terms of the contract had been satisfactorily completed.[18] In other words, the Habsburgs were still determined to bind the Queen in advance, while she was equally determined not to be bound to anything – not until she had seen Charles with her own eyes would she start taking an interest in the small print. She would not even consider a suggestion by Adam Zwetkovich that she should send some distinguished personage to have a look at the Archduke and report back to her. Surely she would take the word of such an old and trusted friend as the Earl of Leicester, for instance? The ingenuous plan was rejected, but Zwetkovich still took the precaution of warning Vienna that Charles should henceforward be careful to wear his best clothes on all occasions and only be seen riding 'fiery steeds' – especially important this, as a reputation for dashing horsemanship would do him more good with the English than the possession of millions in gold.[19]

Elizabeth continued to nag about the visit, asking de Silva at frequent intervals if he thought the Archduke would come. One day in early August, when she was walking in the park at Windsor with both the Spanish and Imperial ambassadors, the subject came up again and de Silva could not resist the opportunity to do a little teasing. Had the Queen, he asked solemnly, noticed anyone she had not seen before among the gentlemen who accompanied the Emperor's ambassador and himself, as perhaps she was entertaining more than she knew? Elizabeth was momentarily taken in. She looked quickly at the faces round her, went quite white and became so agitated that de Silva could not keep a straight face and gave the game away by laughing. The Queen recovered her composure and remarked that it would not be at all a bad way for the Archduke to come, if his dignity would allow it. 'I promise you plenty of princes have come to see me in that manner,' she added airily.[20] In fact, probably nothing would have been more embarrassing for the Queen than if Charles had taken her at her word and come courting in person.

On 14 August, Adam Zwetkovich was dismissed with 'an honourable answer' and a personal letter from Elizabeth to the Emperor. Zwetkovich himself apparently felt satisfied that progress had been made, and William Cecil believed 'the Queen's Majesty, thanked be God, is well disposed towards marriage'. He told Thomas Smith that 'common opinion is that the Archduke Charles will come, which if he do and will accord with us in religion and shall be allowable for his person to her Majesty, then . . . we shall see some success'.[21] Guzman de Silva remained sceptical. He was being careful to stay friendly with the Earl of Leicester and still thought that 'if any marriage at all is to result from all this it will be his'.

In the spring of 1566 attention was temporarily diverted from the Queen of England's matrimonial prospects to the startling events beginning to unfold themselves in Scotland. Mary Stuart's marriage was already going badly. As early as the previous October, Thomas Randolph had been reporting 'jars' between the Queen of Scots and her husband, and by the New Year the rift gaped for all to see. Darnley, furiously disappointed at being refused the crown matrimonial, was drinking heavily and neglecting his wife for the whores of Edinburgh, while Mary, who was now carrying his child, treated him with cold contempt. On 13 February, Randolph wrote: 'I know now for certain that this Queen repenteth her marriage – that she hateth Darnley and all his kin'.

The Queen of Scots' domestic problems were rendered even more explosive by the favours Mary was lavishing on her private secretary and constant companion, the Piedmontese musician David Riccio. John Knox and the elders of the Calvinist kirk saw him as a papist snake-in-the-grass; the nobility furiously resented the low-born foreign interloper and Darnley believed, or was easily persuaded to believe, that 'that villain Davy' had done him 'the most dishonour that can be to any man'. In fact, despite the scurrilous rumours going about that he was the real father of her child, there is no more reason to suppose that David Riccio was ever Mary Stuart's lover than there is to suppose that Robert Dudley was ever Elizabeth Tudor's, but her obvious preference for his cheerful and uncritical society, though understandable, was in the circumstances extremely unwise. Six years earlier Caspar von Breuner had wondered why no Englishman could be found to stab milord Robert with a poniard. In Scotland, as its queen should surely have guessed, men did not suffer from such inhibitions and no one was particularly surprised when, at about eight o'clock in the evening of Saturday, 9 March, a gang of thugs, admitted by Darnley, burst into Mary's private apartments at Holyrood Palace, interrupting a decorous little supper party. Riccio was dragged screaming into an adjoining room and savagely stabbed to death, while the Queen, who had been forcibly restrained from going to his aid, was, so she afterwards alleged, threatened with a loaded pistol.

Scottish national pride had been salved by the slaughter of the wretched Italian, but the murder was only an incidental part of a plan to imprison the Queen in Stirling Castle and set up Darnley as the puppet king of a new régime untainted by popery. It was a plan which might well have succeeded had not the conspirators seriously underestimated the Queen's recuperative powers. She herself believed they had hoped she would miscarry and die, but for a delicately nurtured young woman six months pregnant who had just been subjected to an experience of nightmarish horror and fear, Mary displayed astonishing qualities of resilience, courage and self-command. Concealing her revulsion, she worked on Darnley all the following day to persuade him that he, as much as she, was in deadly danger. By the Monday evening she had contrived a means of escape and by dawn on Tuesday, 12 March, after a wild ride through the night, she and her husband were safe at Dunbar. With Darnley's desertion and the Queen once more a free agent, the *coup d'état* collapsed and Mary survived to bear her child, Prince James Charles, at Edinburgh Castle on 19 June.

In England the shocking events of that March weekend were regarded with disapproval and, early in April, Queen Elizabeth received Guzman de Silva wearing a portrait of the Queen of Scots hanging from a gold chain at her waist. Had she been in Mary's place, she told him energetically, she would have seized her treacherous husband's dagger and stabbed him with it, but added hastily that the Emperor must not think she would ever treat the Archduke in such a way![22]

Elizabeth had been given yet another object lesson in the perils and pitfalls of royal marriage but she could not avoid the issue for long. That autumn the much postponed confrontation with Parliament was due to take place with the succession still unsettled, the Queen still unmarried and in the embarrassing position of having to ask for money in time of peace. The problem of the succession had not grown any easier over the last three years. On the contrary, it was if anything even more highly charged than before and there were now signs of an organised campaign of agitation to have the matter 'proceed in Parliament' whether the Queen liked it or not.

In spite of her continued disgrace and imprisonment, Catherine Grey's claim to be recognised as heir presumptive still commanded strong support among the increasingly influential and militant left-wing Protestants – a faction powerfully represented in the House of Commons. On the other hand, the Queen of Scots' position had been greatly strengthened by the birth of her son – already being hailed in some quarters as the future King of England – and she was not likely to stand aside while another successor was nominated; indeed she demanded the right to send commissioners to London to represent her if the matter were to be raised in Parliament. Add to this Queen Elizabeth's well-known determination not to name any successor at all, and there seemed every prospect of a first-class political row in the offing.

Both houses assembled at Westminster on 30 September but the government, uncomfortably aware of the gathering storm, hesitated to precipitate it. Instead, at a council meeting on 12 October, they made a somewhat forlorn attempt to soften up the Queen. The Duke of Norfolk, acting as spokesman for the nobility, reminded her as tactfully as he could of the petitions presented by the Lords and Commons in 1563. So far no action had been taken because they still awaited her final answer, but now all those who had the welfare of the country at heart most humbly begged that she would allow Parliament to discuss both the succession and her marriage. Elizabeth was not impressed. The succession was her business, she retorted, and she wanted no one's advice on how to handle it. She had no intention of being buried alive like her sister. She remembered only too well how people had flocked to her at Hatfield in the last months of Mary's reign and wanted no such journeyings during her lifetime. As for Parliament, she bade the members do their duty and with that she brought the proceedings to a close.[23]

It did not sound hopeful and when, a week later, the subsidy bill had finally to be presented to the Commons the storm broke. The Lower House, or at any rate a well-organised and belligerent pressure group within the Lower House, was no longer prepared to be put off with promises and in the subsidy bill had seen a weapon which could be used to coerce the Crown. There would be no supplies until those far more urgent and important issues, the succession and the Queen's marriage, had been disposed of. Government efforts to cool the situation met with no success and the reply to one councillor who urged a little more patience was uncompromising: 'We have express charge to grant nothing before the Queen gives a firm answer to our demands. Go to the Queen and let her know our intention, which we have in command from all the towns and people of this Kingdom, whose deputies we are.'[24] After a bad-tempered debate which lasted two days and during which, according to the Spanish ambassador, the members even came to blows, it was then decided to make another approach to the Lords with a view to renewing joint pressure on the Queen. 'These heretics', commented Guzman de Silva, 'neither fear God nor obey their betters.'[25]

Elizabeth was very angry and possibly a little taken aback over this open insubordination. She told de Silva that the Commons had offered to vote her £250,000, if she would allow the nomination of Catherine Grey as her successor to be discussed, but she had refused. Apart from the fact that she had no intention of allowing Parliament to meddle in the matter at all, she was not going to make bargains. The money she was asking for was for the common good, to strengthen the Navy and to suppress trouble in Ireland, and it should be given freely and graciously. De Silva sympathised with her predicament but pointed out that if she married the Archduke all this trouble would automatically come to an end. She was aware of that, replied the Queen, and meant to send a message to the Emperor within a week 'signifying that her intention was to accept the marriage'. De Silva's information was that negotiations with Vienna were virtually at a standstill, but he kept his scepticism to himself.[26]

On Monday, 21 October, a committee of the Commons formally requested the Lords to join them in another petition to the Queen. Their lordships were just as worried about the general situation but, as befitted a more conservative and responsible body, they shrank from a head-on collision with their sovereign lady. Before answering the Commons, therefore, an imposing deputation headed by the Lord Treasurer, the old Marquis of Winchester now over eighty years old, waited on the Queen in her Privy Chamber. One by one they reminded her yet again of the need to provide for the future in good time. Parliament was being reduced to expensive futility by the present stalemate and one by one the peers begged the Queen to declare her will in the matter of the succession – either that or dissolve Parliament and let everyone go home before things got any worse. Elizabeth's answer gave no hint of concession. The Commons, she declared, were no better than rebels and would never have dared to treat her father in such a way. As for the Lords, they could do as they pleased and so would she. The succession was far too serious to be left to such a light-witted assembly and she was thinking of taking advice from the best legal brains in the country.[27]

Three days later the House of Lords agreed to combine with the Commons in their suit to the Queen. Elizabeth felt herself cornered and reacted accordingly. De Silva heard that she had called the Duke of Norfolk a traitor or something very like it and that, when the Earl or Pembroke tried to remonstrate, she told him he talked like a swaggering soldier. As for the Marquis of Northampton, who was also present, the

Queen remarked that he had better remember the arguments which got him married again while he had a wife living, instead of mincing words with her. Nor was the Earl of Leicester immune. Elizabeth said she had thought that, if all the world abandoned her, he would not, and, when Robert hastily protested his readiness to die at her feet, she retorted crossly that that had nothing to do with the matter. Then, having ordered them all to get out of her sight and stay out of it, she flounced off to pour her grievances into the receptive ear of the Spanish ambassador who, in her present state of almost total isolation, seemed the only friend she had. The Queen, reported de Silva, was especially incensed against the Earl of Leicester and asked what de Silva thought of such ingratitude from one to whom she had shown so much kindness and favour that even her honour had suffered. However, she was glad now to have such a good opportunity for sending him away and the Archduke would be able to come without any suspicion.[28]

Meanwhile the Commons were staging what amounted to a sit-down strike – after nearly a month virtually no government business had been transacted. Several behind-the-scenes attempts to reach a settlement had failed – according to de Silva, the Queen appeared to think it would be 'an affront to her dignity to adopt any compromise' – and tension was mounting. By 4 November the joint committees of the Lords and Commons were ready to make a new approach to the Palace and William Cecil optimistically assured the Spanish ambassador that he was sure everything would soon be favourably settled. De Silva himself thought the Queen 'will give them fair words with regard to the marriage and will defer the succession for a future time and the whole matter will thus be quieted for the present'.[29] They both underrated the Queen. There were to be no more fair words. Elizabeth was about to take the offensive.

On the morning of 5 November she commanded a delegation of thirty members from each House to appear before her that afternoon. The Speaker was expressly excluded. On this occasion the Queen intended to do all the speaking herself. After some stinging remarks about unbridled persons in the Commons whose mouths had never been snaffled by a rider and certain members of the Lords who might have been expected to know better, she burst out: 'Was I not born in the realm? Were my parents born in any foreign country? Is not my kingdom here? Whom have I oppressed? Whom have I enriched to other's harm? What turmoil have I made in this Commonwealth that I should be suspected to have no regard to the same? How have I governed since my reign?'

After this Elizabeth turned to the matter in hand. She had already said she would marry and would never break the word of a prince, spoken in a public place, for her honour's sake. She could only say again that she would marry as soon as she conveniently could, adding 'and I hope to have children, otherwise I would never marry'. As for the succession, she made another reference to her experiences during Mary's reign when she had 'tasted of the practices' against her sister and had herself been 'sought for divers ways'. There were individuals now sitting in the Commons, she observed, who knew exactly what she was talking about. But none of them had had personal experience of what it was like to be 'a second person', or any notion of what it would mean for her as Queen to have an impatient heir presumptive breathing down her neck. It was not convenient to settle the succession, 'nor never shall be without some peril unto you and certain danger unto me'. However, if she ever did see a suitable opportunity to name an heir, then she would 'deal therein for your safety, and offer it unto you as your Prince and head, without request; for it is monstrous that the feet should direct the head'.

One thing Elizabeth made abundantly clear. 'Though I be a woman, yet I have as good a courage, answerable to my place, as ever my father had. I am your anointed Queen. I will never be by violence constrained to do anything.' And she went on, 'I thank God I am endured with such qualities that if I were turned out of the realm in my petticoat, I were able to live in any place in Christendom.'[30]

When an expurgated version of this remarkable piece of Elizabethan rhetoric was passed on to the full House of Commons, it was received in stony silence. Two days later someone suggested that the House should proceed with its controversial suit for the limitation of the succession regardless of the Queen's attitude. The Queen retaliated by forbidding any further discussion of the matter, ordering the members to 'satisfy themselves with her Highness's promise of marriage'. This led to another revolt – Paul Wentworth, a leader of the militants, going so far as to raise the question of whether the Crown had any authority to prevent the Commons from debating a matter of urgent public concern.

By the middle of November the main issue at stake was no longer the succession or the Queen's marriage but royal violation of Parliament's 'accustomed lawful liberties', and it was beginning to look as if a serious constitutional crisis might be impending. The Queen had allowed temper and something very like panic to ride her and in consequence had got herself into an untenable position. Only two courses of action were now open to her. Either she must dissolve Parliament forthwith, which would not only mean doing without her much-needed cash but would also be a damaging admission of defeat for a sovereign who took justifiable pride in her warm relationship with her subjects – either that or she must surrender. Elizabeth surrendered and on 25 November she lifted her embargo. This sensible action, which was 'most joyfully taken of all the House', took the heat out of the situation, but it was not quite enough by itself and two days later the Queen sent another message to the Commons offering to sacrifice one-third of the subsidy payment. This time the bait was irresistible. The succession debate was dropped and the subsidy bill got its reading.

The battle was over – apart from one final skirmish. Subsidy bills normally carried preambles and a group of irreconcilables among the radicals conceived what seemed to them the brilliant idea of recording the Queen's promises to marry and to settle the succession as soon as a suitable opportunity arose in the preamble of the present bill. They would thus, they hoped, compel their artful mistress to honour her verbal assurances by incorporating them in the solemn and public apparatus of an Act of Parliament. It was an ingenious ploy but it failed. When Elizabeth saw the draft text she scribbled a furious comment in the margin. 'I know no reason why any my private answers to the realm should serve for prologue to a subsidies book. Neither yet do I understand why such audacity should be used to make without my licence an act of my words.' The draft was scrapped and in its final form contained only a pious hope that the succession would be settled at some future time.[31]

The Queen might be said to have won on points. The succession remained a contest open to all comers but at least the decision remained in her hands and, in spite of all her promises, the prospect of a royal wedding seemed as remote as ever. Elizabeth did, though, make one more move in the direction of the Habsburgs by sending the Earl of Sussex to Vienna during the summer of 1567.

After making the Archduke's acquaintance, Sussex was able to assure the Queen that she need have absolutely no qualms about his personal appearance. He was of a good height, his hair and beard a light auburn colour, 'his face well-proportioned, amiable, and of a very good complexion, without show of redness or over paleness; his countenance and speech cheerful, very courteous and not without some state; his body well-shaped, without deformity or blemish; his hands very good and fair; his legs clean, well-proportioned, and of sufficient bigness for his stature; his foot as good as may be'. Altogether, upon his duty to her Majesty, honest Sussex could say that he had not found 'any thing to be noted worthy misliking in his whole person'. So much for all those stories that the Archduke had an oversized head! He spoke fluent Spanish and Italian as well as Latin and, of course, his native German. He seemed popular with his own people; was reported to be wise and liberal and had proved his courage in the recent war with the Turks. He delighted in hunting, riding, hawking and all the manly exercises. Sussex had seen him run at the ring and was able to commend his horsemanship unreservedly. He was fond of music and took an interest in such intellectual matters as astronomy and cosmography.

The Earl was also able to nail the slander that Charles was a poor man. On the contrary, he was a great prince with wide territories in south-eastern Austria and Croatia, where he could ride for nearly three hundred miles without leaving the boundaries of his own estates. He drew large revenues from gold, silver and lead mines, as well as from the customs duties on grain and wine, and lived in 'great honour and state'.[32]

But unhappily all this splendour and excellence was not for sale, since

Charles was quite definitely not prepared to change his religion. He would, he told Sussex, do anything else to please Queen Elizabeth, but no consideration in the world would induce him to abandon the Catholic faith of his ancestors. He would promise not to admit any Englishman to his chapel; he would be careful never to say or do anything to prejudice the Church of England; he would even, if necessary, be present with the Queen at an occasional Anglican service; but in return he insisted that he must be given proper facilities in a decent public place of worship where he and his household could attend mass freely and openly, for he did not intend to be reduced to practising his religion in secret. Until this had been clearly conceded he could not come to England, and that was his final and unalterable decision.[33]

These convenient scruples of conscience on Charles's part gave Elizabeth an unexceptionable excuse for bringing the long farce of their courtship to a close. She could not, she explained, allow the laws of her country to be broken, not even – or perhaps especially not – by her own husband. She too had a conscience, and in any case she prized the continuance of a peaceable reign more highly than all the favours which the princes of the world and all kingdoms could confer on her. Charles could have a room in the palace fitted up as a chapel where he and his personal attendants could have a private mass, but in no circumstances would she allow him the use of a public church with its music, choristers 'and all the other solemnities usual in the chapels of princes, such as the Archduke would wish to have'.[34]

It would never have done, of course. An arrangement which might have been reluctantly tolerated in 1559 or 1560 would have provoked an insupportable alienation of feeling in the atmosphere of the late sixties, which were seeing a steady hardening of attitudes on both sides of the ideological divide. A Catholic consort, however tactful, however discreet he might honestly try to be, would inevitably become a focal point for lobbying and intrigue by all those English Catholics and crypto-Catholics who were still hoping for better times. A nest of papists openly practising their idolatrous abominations under the protection of the Queen herself would cause instant and furious offence to all law-abiding Protestants, while the radicals would not hesitate to make their displeasure felt in the crudest terms. Elizabeth was perfectly well aware that all those 'Protestant gentlemen' in the Commons who had been so impudently urging her to hurry up and get married would be the first to take exception to her Catholic husband.

So, in a civil exchange of letters early in 1568, the Austrian marriage project finally died. Two years later, when she was once more under severe political pressure, Elizabeth had the gall to try to revive it yet again; but the joke was now definitely over as far as the Habsburgs were concerned, and good patient Charles, released from his ten-year bondage, was courting the Duke of Bavaria's daughter. He lived on till 1590 and became, ironically enough, something of a persecutor of Protestants.

34

TO MARRY WITH FRANCE

The 1560s drew to a close in an atmosphere heavy with the sense of impending crisis. In Scotland young Darnley was dead – murdered in the house at Kirk o'Field with, there is really very little reason to doubt, the prior knowledge and consent of his wife. Few people privately would have blamed the Queen of Scots for choosing this drastic solution to her marital difficulties – Darnley had proved himself impossible as a husband and was becoming an increasingly dangerous nuisance all round – but even in sixteenth-century Scotland appearances had to be kept up. When Mary showed not the slightest interest in bringing the killers to justice but instead was regularly seen in the company of the Earl of Bothwell who, there is no reason at all to doubt, had been personally involved in the assassination, her days of queenship were numbered and her spectacular rampage of self-destruction during the spring of 1567 brought its inevitable nemesis. By the summer Bothwell had been driven into exile and Mary had been deposed by her outraged subjects; her infant son had been proclaimed as King James VI and she herself imprisoned in Lochleven Castle.

That the nobility would have taken an even shorter way with her had it not been for the furious reaction of the Queen of England is something else which cannot reasonably be doubted. Elizabeth, in common with every other western European head of state, had been horribly shocked by Mary's recent conduct; but an anointed queen was still an anointed queen and not to be insulted, threatened and put in fear of her life by subjects, no matter what the provocation. This she made clear beyond any possibility of misunderstanding to the new Scottish government. Her own councillors openly deplored their mistress's unfortunate determination to protect her cousin from the natural consequences of her misdeeds. They deplored it even more when, a year later, Mary escaped from her island prison and presently landed up on the coast of Cumberland, a refugee with nothing but the clothes she stood up in. 'I fear that our good Queen hath the wolf by the ears,' lamented the Archbishop of Canterbury, and how right he was. The presence of the *de facto* Catholic heiress on English soil (and the recent death of Catherine Grey had left her with no serious competitor) was to prove a violent and eventually an intolerable irritant to the Protestant body politic.

It also presented the Protestant Queen with a socially embarrassing, personally dangerous and politically insoluble problem.

It was no coincidence that less than eighteen months after Mary's arrival the first and, as it turned out, the only serious domestic rebellion of Elizabeth's reign broke out. The rising in the predominantly Catholic north country was due as much to social and economic as to political and religious grievances, but its best-remembered incident remains the descent of the rebels on Durham Cathedral, where they defiantly celebrated mass and 'rent and trampled underfoot the English bibles and books of Common Prayer'. The dissidents made no further headway towards their declared objective of restoring the true and Catholic religion, and never got within miles of releasing the Queen of Scots from the Midlands mansion where she was currently residing as the involuntary house-guest of the Earl and Countess of Shrewsbury. In fact, the movement soon collapsed, being suppressed without difficulty and with a good deal of savagery. Just the same, the Earl of Sussex, as Lord President of the North, had lived through some anxious days while waiting for reinforcements to reach him from the south, for he dared not rely on the loyalty of his local levies, and the rising served as a warning to the central government not to take national unity for granted – especially now that the Catholic population had so seductive a figurehead and potential leader in their very midst.

Mary Stuart's legendary beauty and charm, together with the romantic story of her escape from Lochleven and natural human sympathy for her present predicament, were by this time rapidly effacing the memory of the antics which had brought that predicament about, and by the end of the sixties the rehabilitation of the Queen of Scots was virtually complete. In January 1569, Don Guerau de Spes, who had taken over from de Silva as Spanish ambassador in London, described Mary as 'a lady of great spirit' and told King Philip that she was gaining so many friends in England that 'with little help she would be able to get this kingdom into her hands'.[1]

If the situation at home looked unsettled, abroad it was definitely menacing. Relations with Spain had been deteriorating rapidly during the past two years of the decade and not only for ideological reasons. Spain's determination to claim a monopoly of the vast wealth and trading potential of her American empire was becoming the cause of considerable ill-feeling; and the nasty episode at San Juan de Ulloa in September 1568, when an English fleet seeking shelter in the harbour was treacherously set upon by order of the local Spanish viceroy, sowed the seeds of an implacable hatred and distrust of all things Spanish in the hearts of the English mercantile and seafaring community.

A more immediate cause for concern existed much nearer home – just across the North Sea, in fact, where the Netherlanders, England's traditional allies and trading partners, had risen in revolt against Spanish rule. The Dutch and Flemish nobility resented the loss of many of their ancient liberties under Philip's heavy-handed régime, the merchants and burghers resented his taxation, but armed conflict had been touched off by the spread of a militant form of Calvinism in the north and east and in Antwerp, commercial capital of northern Europe. Philip might be forced to tolerate heresy in other countries for reasons of political expediency, but in no circumstances would he tolerate it within his own dominions, and in 1567 he had despatched the notorious Duke of Alva with an army of ten thousand 'black-beards' to pursue a policy of blood and iron in the disaffected provinces. Dutch resistance, under the dour leadership of William of Orange, proved unexpectedly tenacious, but no one could be in much doubt as to the eventual outcome and England faced the all too likely prospect of seeing a victorious and unemployed Spanish army camped within a day's sail of her all too vulnerable south-eastern coastline.

It was not a comforting thought – especially not in February 1570 when the Pope, apparently acting on inaccurate and out-of-date reports inspired by the Northern Rising, finally came down off the fence and issued his long-threatened bull of excommunication against the heretical and bastard Queen of England, depriving her of her 'pretended title' and absolving her Catholic subjects from their allegiance. Although this papal thunderbolt might be dismissed in London as 'a vain crack of words that made a noise only', its implications were deeply disturbing and the perennial Protestant dread that 'some monster was a-breeding' – that a league of Catholic powers dedicated to the extirpation of the gospel was in the making – inevitably grew sharper.

In the midst of all these perils the Queen of England stood as though in a spotlight, the target of enemies from both within and without the realm. In her late thirties Elizabeth Tudor had matured into an elegant, vigorous, self-confident woman who had won the respect, if not always the approval, of her fellow-sovereigns. But she was still single and unprotected by family ties with any other royal house; still childless when she would soon be past the normal childbearing age. To the society in which she lived, the Queen's freely expressed aversion to the holy state of matrimony, her stubborn refusal to accept her proper role as wife and mother, remained totally incomprehensible and more than a little shocking. As she herself once remarked to Guzman de Silva: 'There is a strong idea in the world that a woman cannot live unless she is married, or at all events that if she refrains from marriage she does so for some bad reason'.[2]

That Elizabeth's innermost reason for refraining from marriage had to do with childhood traumas seems at least a plausible theory. After all, had not her father killed her mother and her mother's cousin for crimes perhaps only dimly understood, but yet demonstrably connected with sexual guilt? It would scarcely be surprising if, by the time she was eight years old, a conviction that for the women of her family there existed an inescapable correlation between sexual intercourse and violent death had taken root in her subconscious mind – a conviction which could only have been strengthened by her own adolescent experience at the hands of Thomas Seymour. On a less speculative level, the adult Elizabeth Tudor had watched the shame and misery of unrequited physical passion ravage her sister, another reigning queen. Of one thing she could be certain – that to surrender to passion, to surrender her body to a man, any man, would diminish if not destroy her power, both as a woman and as a queen; and, if it is possible to be certain of any one thing about Elizabeth Tudor, it is that she lived and throve on the exercise of power over men.

The row with Robert Dudley which had blown up during the 1566 Parliament rumbled on into the following spring. In May 1567, Robert was having a good moan about royal ingratitude and general unreasonableness, and seeing no future for himself but a cave in a corner of oblivion. This time it was Nicholas Throckmorton (who had once been so afraid that Robert would run off with the Queen but was now one of his closest friends) who acted as peacemaker, and Elizabeth rather grudgingly agreed to make it up. By the summer they were back on their old cosy footing, but the hectic courtship, the blazing rows and tearful reconciliations of the sixties seemed to be over, giving place to a steadier, altogether more businesslike partnership. Robert, although never a popular figure, was becoming accepted as a permanent feature of the Elizabethan landscape – a sort of unofficial grand vizier through whose hands an enormous amount of patronage flowed and with whom it was wise to keep on good terms. Apart from his personal influence, the Earl of Leicester was now an important member of that charmed inner circle of the Queen's intimates who governed the country under her supervision and were honoured with pet names. As William Cecil was her Spirit, so Robert was her Eyes.

His public duties and responsibilities increased with the years (as well as everything else, he was still Master of the Horse), but Robert Dudley never forgot or neglected the very special relationship on which his career was founded. In July 1575, he entertained the Queen at Kenilworth, the Warwickshire estate she had bestowed on him twelve years earlier. The royal visit lasted for three exhausting ostentatious weeks – three weeks of plays, masques, pageants, feasts, revels, hunts, bear-baiting and firework displays, presented against a backdrop of idyllic countryside through a succession of hot, still summer days. The Princely Pleasures of Kenilworth cost Robert a small fortune but they established him beyond question as a great man who knew how a queen should be treated. Elizabeth accepted the tribute and the hospitality graciously enough, but she almost certainly preferred the small informal house-parties arranged for her at country houses like Rycote in Oxfordshire, home of the Norris family, where she could relax quietly with Robert and a few close friends. She was apparently quite content with the peculiar compromise she had evolved –

a compromise which kept him constantly at her side, her consort in all but name, her lover in all but physical fact.

If, by the early seventies, Elizabeth had organised her private life to her own satisfaction, that did not mean she had abandoned the public game of political courtship – far from it. She had so far always avoided aligning herself too closely with either of the two great European power-blocs, preferring to follow the classic pattern of English foreign policy of playing one off against the other. Now, however, with the shadow cast by Spain growing ever longer and darker, some form of Anglo-French *rapprochement* seemed inevitable.

The idea that this might be achieved by a marriage between the Queen of England and the French king's younger brother Henry, Duke of Anjou, had been in the wind since 1568 but was first openly suggested in the autumn of 1570. In December the French ambassador, de la Mothe Fénélon, had a long conversation on the subject with the Earl of Leicester and found him apparently all in favour. Fénélon then saw the Queen, who received him dressed in her best and in her most sprightly mood. She told him that if she ever did decide to marry it would only be to a prince of some important royal house, and when the ambassador mentioned Anjou's name her reaction was sufficiently encouraging for him to write to the French Queen-Mother, Catherine de Medici, saying that he thought it was time for an official proposal to be made.[3]

Meanwhile, Elizabeth had brought the matter up with her own council. Someone said doubtfully that the Duke was rather young and added that 'it would be well to consider deeply before they broke entirely with the House of Burgundy'. The other members, according to the Spanish ambassador, 'were silent, surprised to see her so set upon this marriage which they had always thought was merely a fiction'.[4] Considering that Anjou was nineteen years old to Elizabeth's thirty-seven and had the reputation of being an adherent of the ultra-Catholic party in France, their surprise was understandable. But 'I perceive her Majesty more bent to marry than heretofore she hath been', wrote Leicester to Francis Walsingham, the new English ambassador in Paris, on 14 February and at this stage of the game the eagerness seemed to be rather on the English side than the French.

Relations between the two countries were traditionally cool, when not actively hostile, and were now further complicated by the problem of the Queen of Scots. The King of France was in honour bound to protest at the restraint of his former sister-in-law and had been lending at least token support to her party in Scotland; while Elizabeth, on her side, was known to be lending moral and some financial support to the embattled French Protestants. If any sort of *entente* was to be arrived at, it would be based purely on mutual self-interest and not on any warmth of mutual trust or friendship. The Queen of England needed a counter weight to balance the threat from Spain and the Papacy. The French royal family, as represented by the young Valois King Charles IX and his strong-minded Italian mother, needed a counterweight to balance the threat to their freedom of action from the encroaching Guise family and their party of pro-Spanish Catholic ultras.

The most recent religious civil war in France had just ended more or less in a draw and the Queen-Mother was anxious to keep things that way – peace based on a measure of toleration for the Huguenots appearing to offer the best chance of keeping herself and her son on the top of the pile of warring factions. But, to achieve this desirable state of affairs, Catherine urgently needed to find a 'harbourage' for her second son. Anjou, ambitious, unstable and, since the end of the civil war, unemployed, would be easy prey for the Guises. Left to hang about at home, he would be at best a nuisance, at worst a serious menace to Valois domestic tranquillity. In the circumstances, therefore, the English marriage seemed to offer a solution to many of the Queen-Mother's problems – not only would France acquire a strong ally against Spain, but the House of Valois would also be buttressed against the House of Guise and her son (and Anjou was her favourite) would be handsomely provided for and kept out of mischief. The trouble was that Catherine could not be certain that Elizabeth was in earnest and she hesitated to commit herself to a formal proposal, knowing that as soon as the matter became official the advantage of being the one sought would pass to the Queen of England – and all Europe knew just how ruthlessly the Queen of England could exploit that advantage.

At last, in March 1571, Catherine took the plunge, setting out four major conditions as a basis for negotiation – Anjou and his household were to have full freedom to exercise their religion; on the day after the wedding he was to be crowned and rule jointly with Elizabeth; he was to be paid an annual allowance of £60,000 out of the English exchequer; and, if Elizabeth died first without leaving heirs, he was to enjoy both his title and his allowance for the rest of his life. Elizabeth was prepared to agree that her husband should rule with her as Philip had done with Mary and also that he should be called king, but she would not admit his right to be crowned. She agreed to provide him with a suitable allowance but not a life pension. Again, though, these were bargaining-points and, as before, it was the religious question which soon isolated itself as the main obstacle. Elizabeth offered to excuse the Duke from attendance at the Anglican service but was firm in refusing to allow him the exercise of his own religion, even in private.

This did not sound encouraging, and any prospects of reaching a compromise were not improved by Anjou's own lukewarm attitude towards the marriage. His Catholic friends were naturally doing all they could to stiffen his resistance, telling him that, apart from being a heretic, the Queen of England was old and probably barren. Gossip at the French court that Anjou had better marry Queen Elizabeth, who was an old woman with a sore leg, and then give her a 'potion' so that he would be free to wed the younger and prettier Queen of Scots and rule over both kingdoms soon reached Elizabeth's ears and annoyed her very much. It was true that she had been suffering from an ulcer on her leg which had been slow to heal but, she told the French ambassador crossly, it was a pity he had not been present at the Marquis of Northampton's ball where he could have seen her dance and would have been able to assure the Duke that he was in no danger of marrying a cripple.[5]

Negotiations continued throughout the summer, but everything really turned on whether either side could make concessions over the religious issue. Both sides, however, seem to have been imbued with the idea that, if they stood firm, the other would eventually give way. Certainly Elizabeth was sticking rigidly to her refusal even to allow Anjou a private mass. She remarked, characteristically enough, that she failed to see why he could not worship according to the Church of England rite without damage to his conscience – after all, the service was not so very different from the Roman one – and offered to have the Book of Common Prayer translated into Latin for him if that would help.[6] On the French side, Catherine de Medici told Francis Walsingham that, while she could understand Elizabeth's problems in marrying a Catholic, hinting that in due course her son might be willing to be converted, they could not in any circumstances agree to an unconditional surrender. She and the King, though, were obviously eager that the marriage should go through, if only to get Anjou out of the country and away from the Guises, and Walsingham was of the opinion that Monsieur was nowhere near so convinced a Catholic as he liked to make out. Walsingham also believed that the French probably *would* give way rather than lose Elizabeth altogether, but the English ambassador, himself something of a Protestant zealot, may have been over-influenced by the optimistic assurances of his Huguenot friends who were naturally working hard to promote the English alliance.

Opinion in England was generally in favour of the marriage, in spite of the religious difficulty. William Cecil, now Lord Burghley, certainly favoured it and so did the Earl of Sussex – both of them believing that a husband and a major European alliance were the only sure means of protecting the Queen from the dangers threatening her on every side. Nicholas Bacon, the Lord Keeper, had contributed a long memorandum on the subject, carefully balancing the pros and cons and pointing out that, by marrying Anjou, Elizabeth would be 'delivered of the continual fear of the practices with the Queen of Scots'; that the King of Spain would be made 'more comfortable'; that the Pope's malice would 'vanish like smoke'; and the Emperor would have the Queen in more estimation. It was noticeable, though, that Bacon said nothing about the 'matter of religion' which, as he admitted, was the weightiest consideration of all.[7]

The Earl of Leicester maintained his outwardly favourable stance, but Lord Burghley felt certain that it was Leicester who was behind the Queen's unwontedly hard Protestant line; that it was Leicester who had been whispering to the French to stand fast over Monsieur's mass and the Queen would compromise in the end. As for Elizabeth, no one, not even Burghley or Leicester, could say for certain whether she was serious or not. With the benefit of hindsight it is not difficult to guess that she was hoping to use the French marriage just as she had used the Austrian marriage – as a delaying tactic, a diplomatic ploy to create uncertainty and keep the Catholic powers off balance. Count, now the Duke, de Feria was most probably right when he wrote in May 1571 that the Queen was simply teasing Spain 'with inventions and fears that she will marry in France.' 'She will no more marry Anjou than she will marry me,' declared Elizabeth's old adversary bluntly.[8] All the same, in June, Alvise Contarini, the Venetian ambassador in Paris, was reporting to the Signory that 'the negotiation for the marriage between the Queen of England and Monsieur d'Anjou still continues. The Court is at Gaillon and the English ambassador has been granted a long and most gracious audience by the Queen-Mother who, for the great love which she bears her son, is doing her best to bring the affair to a conclusion; and although there are many reasons to the contrary, and amongst others the disparity of age and the difference of religion, it is nevertheless the opinion of many that the negotiation will be successful.'[9]

But, by July, Walsingham had pretty well come to the conclusion that the marriage was off. Anjou had turned obstinate and neither his mother nor his elder brother had been able to persuade him to agree to go to England without a public assurance that 'he might enjoy his religion there'. Catherine was very much annoyed but had not yet given up hope of changing her son's mind – or Elizabeth's. With this end in view a special envoy, Paul de Foix, a former French ambassador at the Court of St James's, went over to London in August; but, although he was warmly received, he failed to shift the Queen on the religious issue. When he returned to France in September, the Venetian ambassador heard that the marriage scheme was now definitely off but that a 'good understanding' had been established between the two countries.[10]

The marriage, though, was not yet quite dead. Events that autumn were to revive interest in it, at any rate on the English side. De Foix was still having talks in London as details of the Ridolfi Plot – so called after Roberto Ridolfi, Italian banker-cum-conspirator and builder of castles in the air – began to come to light. The aims of the plot were fourfold: to seize Elizabeth alive or dead, release the Queen of Scots, set her on the English throne with the now widowed Duke of Norfolk as her consort and, of course, restore the Catholic religion. These interesting feats – at least according to the blueprint Ridolfi had been offering for Philip of Spain's approval – were to be accomplished by the English Catholics led by Norfolk, in conjunction with an army provided by the Duke of Alva from the Netherlands.

The Mary–Norfolk marriage plan was not a new one. It had first been suggested early in 1569 and may, in its original form, have been an honest, if naïve, attempt to find a solution to the problem of the Queen of Scots by subjecting her to a suitably high-ranking and trustworthy English husband. Just the same, it was noticeable that none of its promoters, least of all the bridegroom-elect, could quite bring himself to mention it to Elizabeth. But Elizabeth had soon got to hear about it and had squashed it flat – she was under no illusions as to who would be the dominant member of such a partnership or what would be the consequences for herself. In spite of his categorical denials that he had ever sought to marry 'so wicked a woman, such a notorious adulteress and murderer', the Queen sensed a shiftiness in Norfolk which roused her suspicions and when, just before the outbreak of the northern rebellion, he suddenly bolted for his East Anglian estates, she ordered him back to London and incarcerated him in the Tower.

But the Duke was an important public figure, popular and respected. His integrity had always been taken for granted, and the idea that he could have been dabbling in treason seemed unthinkable. In the summer of 1570 he made a solemn submission to Elizabeth, binding himself on his allegiance never to have anything to do with the Queen of Scots again, and in August he was allowed to go home. But his promises were not worth the paper they were written on. In September 1571 he was caught in the act of sending money to Mary's partisans in Scotland, ciphers were found hidden under the roof tiles in his London house and it soon became only too clear that he had been in regular correspondence with Mary herself, lending her money, exchanging presents with her, even advising her on how to conduct the current round of negotiations with Elizabeth for her possible release and restoration.

The alarming revelations of the Ridolfi Plot made a deep impression on the public mind and served as a grim reminder of England's dangerous isolation. They strengthened the case of those who were urging the necessity of an alliance with France at almost any price and, for a time at least, it looked as if Elizabeth would be driven in this direction. Certainly she was now prepared to make a major concession in an effort to resuscitate the Anjou marriage by indicating that she would, after all, be willing to allow the Duke to practise his religion in private. Francis Walsingham, as the man on the spot, thought this was a mistake. His information was that the marriage project was beyond revival, 'the Duke of Anjou utterly refusing the match, all being granted that he desires'. Walsingham could find no one willing to deal any further in the matter and he was afraid that the Queen would be laying herself open to a damaging rebuff if she persisted.[11]

There remained the possibility of a defensive league without a marriage and, in December, Elizabeth sent Sir Thomas Smith, an old hand at dealing with the French, to see if, Walsingham regardless, the marriage could be revived and, failing that, to open negotiations for a simple treaty of friendship. The unhappy Smith had very bad crossing and was so sick 'that life and death were to him but one' but on reaching Calais he was gently entertained and soon felt better. He was received at court by King Charles on 4 January and two days later saw the Queen-Mother. Catherine repeated that the only obstacle to the Anjou marriage was the religious one but went on to say that her son had grown so devout that he was becoming quite 'lean and evil-coloured' from fastings and vigils. When Smith asked if the Duke would be content with a private mass in his own apartments, Catherine had to admit that he would not; he was now demanding public high mass with full ceremonial and would accept nothing less. 'Why, madame,' exclaimed Smith in disgust, 'then he may require also the four orders of friars, monks, canons, pilgrimages, pardons, oils and creams, relics and all such trumperies. That in no wise can be agreed.'[12]

This conversation marked the effective end of the Anjou courtship but not the end of the French marriage project. Catherine de Medici had yet another son and now she asked Smith if he thought the Queen of England might fancy him instead. Unfortunately, the Duke of Alençon was younger still, only seventeen, and while Anjou had been a tall, reasonably good-looking youth Alençon was undersized and disfigured by smallpox. But Catherine, who took a severely practical view of matrimony, remarked that if Elizabeth was disposed to marry at all 'she saw not where she might marry so well, and pointed out that without a marriage she could not see any league or amity being so strong or so lasting'. Smith quite agreed with her. It was an axiom of the times that 'the knot of blood and marriage was a stronger seal than that which was printed in wax, and lasted longer, if God gave good success'.[13]

Thomas Smith had always been in the forefront of those urging marriage on Elizabeth and apparently he could see nothing out of the way in a more than twenty-year disparity of age. He wrote home eagerly recommending the new proposal; Alençon might be young, dwarfish and pock-marked but he was less papistical and less pigheaded than his brother. He was also, it seemed, likely to be 'more apt for the getting of children' – perhaps Smith had been hearing about Anjou's homosexual tendencies. At any rate, the ambassador clearly hoped that here at last might be the solution to an intractable problem and was even ready to face more Channel crossings in such a good cause, though he were never so sick for it.[14]

But Elizabeth was not enthusiastic. She considered she had been shabbily treated over the Anjou affair and was disposed to take offence. The French need not think she was going to marry any old prince they happened to have handy. Burghley explained tactfully to Fénélon that, the Queen's natural repugnance to the idea of marriage having been overcome by Anjou's remarkable qualities, it would need a lot of persuasion to bring her to the point of accepting a substitute, and Fénélon warned Catherine that she might be wiser to conclude a treaty with England first and talk about marriage later.

The Queen-Mother took the hint, but some time in March she and Thomas Smith had another talk on the subject. After discussing Elizabeth's danger from the Queen of Scots (it had not escaped French notice that Mary was turning to Spain for help), Catherine exclaimed impatiently: 'Jesu, doth not your mistress, Queen Elizabeth, see plainly that she will always be in such danger till she marry? If she marry into some good house, who shall dare attempt aught against her?' Again, Smith was in complete agreement. Treaty or no treaty, he remained totally convinced that Elizabeth's only true safeguards would be marriage and children. If she had even one child, 'then all these bold and troublesome titles of the Scotch Queen or others, that make such gaping for her death, would be clean choked up'. But why stop at one child, cried Catherine, why not five or six? 'Would to God,' answered Smith, 'she had one.' 'No,' the Queen-Mother persisted, 'two boys, lest the one should die, and three or four daughters to make alliance with us again and other princes, to strengthen the realm.' 'Why then,' said Smith, 'you think that Monsieur le Duc shall speed?' With that Catherine laughed and said 'she desired it infinitely and trusted to see three or four at the least of her race, which would make her indeed not to spare sea and land to see her Majesty and them'. After all, if Elizabeth had been able to fancy Anjou, why not Alençon who was 'of the same house, father and mother, and as vigorous and lusty or rather more' – especially now that his beard had begun to sprout.[15]

While the Italian matriarch was making these optimistic plans, negotiations for an Anglo-French treaty of perpetual friendship were proceeding and on 19 April 1572 the draft protocol was signed at Blois. It was primarily a defensive alliance and not, as Francis Walsingham and his radical friends would have liked, an offensive league against Spain. It did not bar the way to a possible future renewal of the Burgundian connection, nor did it in any way commit England to involvement with French intervention in the Netherlands – something which Charles IX, persuaded by the great Huguenot leader Admiral Coligny, was now beginning seriously to contemplate. Even more usefully, France had now to all intents and purposes recognised the *de facto* government of little King James of Scotland under the pro-English Regent the Earl of Mar – thus virtually abandoning Mary Stuart to her fate.

Having got pretty well everything she wanted, Elizabeth showed even less interest in the Alençon match, but the French were not giving up. In June a high-powered embassy, headed by the Duke de Montmorenci came over to London to ratify the Treaty of Blois and to make the Queen a formal offer of marriage on behalf of the young Duke. Elizabeth received them graciously, entertained them lavishly and invested Montmorenci with the Garter, but she was lukewarm about the proposal. Alençon was too young, too short and really she did not feel she could stomach those pockmarks. However, as usual, she did not close the door. The embassy was dismissed with thanks and a promise that she would think the matter over and send her answer within a month. Lord Burghley was instructed to ask Francis Walsingham for a full report about Alençon, 'of his age in certainty, of his stature, of his condition, his inclination to religion' and so on.[16]

Walsingham, who was as much in favour of the marriage as Thomas Smith, did his best. Alençon was seventeen years old; he was wise and stalwart, of a tractable disposition, commendably free from French light-mindedness and in religion 'easily to be reduced to the knowledge of the truth'. Walsingham, however, could not conceal the fact that the young man was nothing to look at. Those wretched pockmarks were not a very serious disfigurement, since they were 'rather thick than great and deep' and that sprouting beard would help to cover them. But they were still definitely visible, and Walsingham feared that to the well-known 'delicacy of her Majesty's eye' they would prove an insurmountable obstacle.[17] So did Lord Burghley, in spite of Fénélon's assurances that he knew of a doctor who could remove this defect by a sure and simple remedy.

In July, Catherine de Medici sent one of her son's friends, M. la Mole, to England to plead his cause. La Mole was an attractive young man whose charm and gallantry were much to Elizabeth's taste. She entertained him at Warwick Castle, had him to supper, played the spinet to please him and invited him to watch a firework display, but she was not committing herself to anything. She told Fénélon that she had discussed the matter with her council but was still very much perplexed. The disparity of age and the difference in religion presented serious problems and, in any case, she could not possibly decide until she had seen Alençon for herself. Fénélon replied that the King and the Queen-Mother would be delighted to arrange this, if only they could be assured that her Majesty was really in the mind to marry. To date her attitude had been so doubtful that they hesitated to go further. But Elizabeth was firm. She must see the Duke and be certain that they could love each other before making any sort of commitment. It was Charles of Austria all over again.

La Mole went home in August without, apparently, having achieved anything very much; but he had made an excellent impression in official circles, and Lord Burghley, ever optimistic, told Walsingham that 'as it seemeth, the Queen's Majesty is come nearer to the matter than I hoped for'. But the Queen's Majesty had her suspicions that all these French attentions were designed to trap her, through marriage, into an anti-Spanish crusade in the Netherlands which would ultimately benefit only the King of France. She distrusted Catherine de Medici as strongly as Catherine distrusted her and had very little faith in the stability of Charles IX's government.

Elizabeth's doubts were soon to be tragically justified, for before any further progress could be made in the marriage negotiations the violent forces of sectarian hatred simmering just below the surface of sixteenth-century French society had erupted in a particularly horrible manner. The spark which ignited the explosion of St Bartholomew's Day is generally held to have been the Queen-Mother's jealousy of Admiral Coligny and his growing influence over the weak impressionable king; but what began as an effort to curb the undesirable ascendancy of the Huguenot Party by murdering its leader ended in a bloodbath. In Paris the Catholic mob is estimated to have slaughtered between three and four thousand Huguenots. The killing spread to the provinces and altogether something like ten thousand men, women and children were butchered during the last week of August 1572.

News of the massacre roused Protestants all over Europe to a deep and bitter anger more than tinged with fear. In England especially, where a stream of terrified refugees poured across the Channel into the south-coast ports, public opinion was profoundly shocked. A great wave of anti-Catholic, anti-French feeling surged through the country and any notion of a French marriage for the Queen had become unthinkable. Even the future of the French alliance looked distinctly precarious as preachers thundered for revenge from their pulpits, indignation meetings were held on street corners calling for the repudiation of the Treaty of Blois and the expulsion of the French ambassador, and anyone who did not join in the general outcry was in danger of rough handling from his neighbours. 'It is incredible', wrote Fénélon, sadly contemplating the ruin of his work, 'how the confused rumours . . . of the events in Paris have stirred the hearts of the English who, having heretofore shown a great affection for France, have suddenly turned to extreme indignation and a marvellous hatred against the French . . .'[18]

Events in Paris had put Queen Elizabeth in an awkward position. For the past two years her foreign policy had been based on the French connection and in the present international situation she could not risk an open break with her new friends. On the other hand, she certain could not give any appearance of condoning the massacre of her co-religionists. She therefore received Fénélon, after keeping him in suspense for three days, and listened in chilly silence while he presented his government's version of the 'accident' of St Bartholomew's Day. It seemed that an assassination plot had been discovered among the Huguenot leaders gathered in Paris for the wedding of the King's sister to the Huguenot Prince Henry of Navarre – a plot already so far advanced that the lives of the royal family were in imminent danger and this emergency forced the King into sanctioning a counter-attack which had, no doubt, led to some very regrettable occurrences. But there was no question of any change of policy towards the Huguenots in general and no intention of revoking their edicts of toleration. King Charles sincerely hoped that the Anglo-French *entente* would not be affected and he, for his part, intended to stand by the alliance.

Elizabeth heard Fénélon out and then remarked that this was a different story from the one she had been told by her own ambassador. She was bound to accept Charles's explanation as that of a monarch and a gentleman but she hoped he would now do all in his power to make amends for so much blood so horribly shed, if only for the sake of his own honour, now so blemished in the eyes of the world.[19] 'I can assure you, madame,' Fénélon told Catherine de Medici, 'that the late accident has wounded the Queen and her subjects so deeply that only a very skilful surgeon and a very sovereign balm can affect a remedy.'

Catherine was only too anxious that such a balm should be applied without delay. The monster she had so unwisely let loose on St Bartholomew's Day had seriously upset the delicate balance of power in France and the Duke of Guise was now to be seen striding about the streets of Paris wreathed in smiles. The Queen-Mother therefore, in spite of all that had happened, began to push the Alençon marriage again. It was true that Alençon, unlike either of his brothers, had played no part in the massacre and had indeed spoken out against it, but in the circumstances Catherine cannot surely have expected much of a response. She certainly did not get it. The recent slaughter of Protestants had filled Elizabeth's mind with doubts and she could come to no decision until she saw how the King of France meant to treat his Huguenot subjects in future. In any case, as she wrote reasonably enough to Walsingham, 'if that religion of itself be so odious to him that he thinks he must root out all the possessors of it, how should we think his brother a fit husband for us? Or how should he think that the love may grow, continue and increase betwixt his brother and us, which ought to be betwixt the husband and the wife?'[20] But Catherine still persisted, although her ingenuous suggestion that a meeting between Elizabeth and Alençon might be arranged on some neutral ground – say, the island of Jersey – was coldly rejected.

By the summer of 1573 the renewal of the civil war, precipitated by St Bartholomew's, had died down again and a truce was once more arranged. This peace, said the Queen-Mother, had been made largely to please Elizabeth and Alençon had been one of its prime movers. She and the King were now prepared to let the Duke come to England to be inspected with no strings attached. They were even ready to yield over the religious question – the Queen of England might rule in this matter at her pleasure.

But, if Catherine expected, by these blanket concessions, to drive Elizabeth into her son's arms, she underestimated that lady's inventive powers. The Queen was now rather averse to a meeting. She was afraid she would not like the Duke when she saw him – he would have to give her an undertaking not to be offended if she rejected him.

Matters continued in this way for several months – the French importuning Elizabeth for an answer, Elizabeth always retreating yet always contriving to leave just a little room for hope – until the early spring of 1574 when France at last began to lose interest. The political situation was changing again and Charles IX was dying – the judgement of God said the Protestants, though his early death was more likely due to the effects of congenital syphilis which riddled the Valois family. By that summer it seemed as if yet another Elizabethan courtship had faded into the mist.

35

A Frog He Would A-Wooing Go

What is conveniently known as the second Alençon courtship opened in 1578 and continued intermittently into the early 1580s. Like all Elizabeth's foreign flirtations with matrimony, it was initiated and prolonged for purely political reasons. What marks it out from its predecessors is the undoubted fact that, for a period of several months during the summer of 1579, Elizabeth managed to convince almost everyone – including perhaps herself – that this time she really was in earnest; that after all those years of obstinate and apparently contented spinsterhood she really did genuinely want to marry an ugly little Frenchman more than twenty years her junior.

Except that they had become considerably more complex and more menacing, the problems facing the Queen in the late seventies were basically much the same as those of the late sixties. On the home front, Mary Queen of Scots, that perennial threat to the government's peace of mind, was still a state prisoner, still intriguing incessantly with her friends abroad, still hoping against hope that her Guise relations, or the Pope, or Philip of Spain, or all three together would one day succeed in getting her out of the Earl of Shrewsbury's custody and on to Elizabeth's throne. Since Elizabeth flatly refused to consider the solution to the problem of Mary favoured by the House of Commons after the discovery of the Ridolfi Plot – to cut off her head and make no more ado about her – and since the prospect of finding a formula by which she could safely be returned to Scotland looked as remote as ever, there seemed nothing for it but to continue to keep her under restraint in England and hope to frustrate her more flamboyant schemes.

A new complication at home was the apparent revival of English Catholicism under the leadership of missionary priests, trained in seminaries in Douai and Rome, who had begun to infiltrate the country by the middle of the decade. In spite of the somewhat hysterical publicity they attracted, the missionaries came too late and too few to do much more than blow on the embers of a dying fire and coax the spark of faith into a tiny flame. By themselves they could never have caused much more than a minor irritation to the Protestant state. But taken in conjunction with the papal bull of excommunication, with the lack of a Protestant heir and the presence of a vigorous Catholic claimant on English soil, they represented a potentially serious danger which could not be ignored, and as a result many brave and sincere men suffered the unpleasant form of death normally reserved for more obvious traitors.

Abroad, European politics were still dominated by the growing might of Philip's empire. In the years immediately following the holocaust of St Bartholomew, when it seemed as if the French alliance would have to be written off, Elizabeth had succeeded, at least temporarily, in mending her fences with Spain. In 1578, Elizabeth and Philip were still just about on speaking terms, but few informed observers of the international scene believed that a confrontation could be postponed indefinitely. Harassed by the depradations of English privateers on his American trade, and increasingly convinced that he would never suppress his Dutch rebels while they continued to receive handouts from Elizabeth, even the slow-moving Philip would sooner or later use the Pope's interdict as an excuse for dealing with the heretical Queen as she deserved.

It was the war in the Netherlands which led more or less directly to the resumption of the Alençon courtship. Elizabeth, to the sorrow of her more radical Protestant advisers, did not like the Dutch. She lent them enough money to keep the rebel forces in being, but regarded them as greedy, quarrelsome, unreliable and Calvinist. In present circumstances, William of Orange and his brother Count Louis were performing a useful service by tying Philip down in a costly and unprofitable war of attrition, but Elizabeth was determined that her own involvement should be kept to a minimum. In the long term she was interested in a negotiated settlement, for in the long term England's national security and economic prosperity depended heavily on a peaceful and prosperous Netherlands. She was therefore alarmed and irritated when the French King's brother began to take an interest in Dutch affairs. Least of all did she want to see another round of the perennial Habsburg–Valois quarrel fought out on her own doorstep; besides which it had always been a cardinal point of English foreign policy to keep the French out of the Low Countries.

But when, in the spring of 1578, it became apparent that Alençon was playing a lone hand Elizabeth's attitude changed. If the Duke could be lured by the bait of marriage she ought, with any luck, to be able to control his future activities and use him to serve her purposes by making trouble for Philip without involving her too closely. It would certainly be considerably cheaper than the alternative course of paying the Dutch to send him away. It would also be safer, for if Philip should turn nasty the threat of approaching Anglo-French nuptials would serve to put the frighteners on.

Alençon himself was nothing loath, and indeed the first approaches seem to have come from him. Charles IX having died childless, the French throne was now occupied by Henry of Anjou, Elizabeth's former reluctant suitor, and the Valois family pattern was repeating itself. Alençon, restless, ambitious and dissatisfied with his lot, was on bad terms with his brother and rapidly becoming as much of a domestic nuisance as ever Anjou had been. His attempts to carve a career and a patrimony for himself in the Netherlands had not so far met with any noticeable success and he knew he could expect no help from home. The Queen of England was still, as Francis Walsingham put it, 'the best marriage in her parish' and even to become her official suitor would give him useful additional status. If she could be cajoled into financing his plans for his own self-aggrandisement, so much the better, and the Duke began to write winning letters assuring the Queen of his entire devotion and willingness to be guided by her in all his doings.[1]

By late summer the courtship was once more a live issue, although at this stage no one seriously supposed that it would lead to anything more than another prolonged bout of negotiations. The character of the affair began to change early in 1579 when Alençon sent his best friend, Jean Simier, to England with full powers to negotiate and conclude the marriage contract and also, it would appear, instructions to do his best to sweep Elizabeth off her feet, for Simier, who proved to be the epitome of every Englishman's idea of a gallant Frenchman – 'a most choice courtier, exquisitely skilled in love toys, pleasant conceits and court dalliances' – at once embarked on an ardent proxy wooing. Presumably he and his master reckoned that such an approach would be irresistible to a middle-aged spinster and it looked, for a time at least, as if they might have guessed right.

Elizabeth was charmed with Simier. He was rapidly admitted to the ranks of those privileged few known by royal nicknames, becoming the Queen's Monkey in a punning reference to his own surname. He was allowed to capture 'trophies' in the shape of gloves and handkerchiefs – even to mount a daring raid on the royal bedchamber and carry off one of the royal nightcaps. But, although Elizabeth blossomed under the life-giving ran of Simier's admiration (the French ambassador told Catherine de Medici that the Queen seemed quite rejuvenated and more beautiful than she had been fifteen years before), and appeared in some danger of losing her heart, she showed absolutely no signs of losing her head. Not all her new friend's skill in love toys or pleasant conceits could induce her to make any commitment. She told the current Spanish ambassador, Bernardino de Mendoza, that it was a fine thing for an old woman like her to be thinking of marriage and more than hinted that she was only encouraging Alençon to get him out of the Netherlands. In any case, she said, nothing could be settled until he had been over to see her.[2]

But by this time most people thought he would come and that he would not come in vain. Elizabeth herself had promised him that his honour would not suffer and Catherine de Medici was urging her son to take the plunge. 'I am sure', she wrote on 29 March, 'she [Elizabeth] will not be so ill advised as to let you return discontented, for she knows the wrong she would do in abusing the brother of so great a king.'[3] Gilbert Talbot told his father, the Earl of Shrewsbury, in a letter written from the court on 4 April that for the past five days the Privy Council had been continuously in session from eight o'clock in the morning until dinner time, 'and presently after dinner and an hour's conference with her Majesty, to council again and so till supper time. And all this,' he went on, 'as far as I can learn, is about the matter of Monsieur's coming hither, his entertainment here and what demands are to be made unto him in the treaty of marriage . . . and I can assure your lordship it is verily thought this marriage will come to pass of a great sort of wise men.'[4]

A committee of the Council had now begun to negotiate with Simier on the basis of the proposals put forward by the French when the Anjou marraige had been under consideration eight years previously, but it was clear that no real progress would be made unless and until Alençon himself came to England. In any case, the councillors were deeply divided over the advisability of the whole project. The Earl of Leicester and Francis Walsingham (now back at home as Principal Secretary of State) were both strongly opposed, while Lord Burghley and the Earl of Sussex were in favour. The arguments in favour of the Queen's marriage were basically the same as they had always been – the obvious advantages of an alliance with a major foreign power sealed by family ties and the hope of an undisputed heir to the throne. The old arguments against – that the only possible husband for the Queen was a foreigner and a Catholic – were now reinforced both by the deepening of the ideological divide and by fears that Elizabeth's life would be endangered if she were to become pregnant – she would be forty-six on her next birthday.

Leicester's objections were probably mainly personal but, as was shortly to become apparent, he was hardly in a position to complain. Walsingham's opinion, set out in a closely reasoned memorandum, was coloured by his deep distrust of all the Catholic powers. While not minimising the dangers facing the Queen at home and abroad, he believed that her best policy would be to trust in the Protestant God and keep clear of any entanglement with the representatives of anti-Christ. Alençon might not be a bigoted Catholic, but he was still a Catholic and as heir presumptive to the French throne would hardly be willing to jeopardise his inheritance by abjuring his religion. However compelling the political case for the marriage, Walsingham, after St Bartholomew, was convinced that every right-thinking Englishman would far rather Elizabeth stayed single than see her ally herself to a nasty unhealthy set of foreigners like the Valois and perhaps risk her life in childbirth.[5]

Against this, Sussex and Lord Burghley clung to the old-fashioned belief that any husband would be better than none and Burghley pooh-poohed the idea that the Queen was too old to have a child. The proportions of her body were excellent and she suffered from no physical impediment such as smallness of stature or largeness of body, 'nor no sickness, nor lack of natural functions in those things that properly belong to the procreation of children' he wrote in one of his careful *aides-mémoire* to himself. In the judgement of her doctors and those women who knew her estate in such matters and were most intimately acquainted with her body, there was no reason at all why she should not safely bear children for some time to come. Indeed there was every reason to believe that her Majesty was 'very apt for the procreation of children'. Burghley even thought that the therapeutic effects of sexual intercourse might cure Elizabeth's neuralgic pains and improve her health and spirits generally, for she would be spared 'the dolours and infirmities as all physicians do usually impute to womankind for lack of marriage, and specially to such women as naturally have their bodies apt to conceive and procreate children'.[6]

But Burghley seems to have been pretty much alone in his optimistic assessment of Elizabeth's childbearing prospects, and the Queen's closest advisers remained divided and hesitant in the face of the Queen's unexpected enthusiasm. According to Mendoza, writing early in May, she was now expressing 'such a strong desire to marry that not a councillor, whatever his opinion may be, dares to say a word against it'.[7] Nevertheless, at a full council meeting held a few days later, opinion was almost universally hostile. Again according to Mendoza, the new Lord Chancellor, Thomas Bromley, pointed out 'how bad this talk of marriage was, both for the Queen and the nation, since no succession could be hoped from it, and great confusion might be caused by the coming hither of Catholics, and above all Frenchmen, who were their ancient enemies'. Simier was then summoned and told that several of Alençon's demands – including coronation immediately after the marriage, a life pension of £60,000 and the garrisoning of a port by French soldiers for his own protection – were totally inadmissible.

At this the normally suave Simier lost his temper and, slamming his way out of the room, went straight to the Queen. She listened to him 'with much graciousness and many expressions of sorrow that her councillors disapproved of her marriage which she desired so much', and proceeded to assume a settled air of lovelorn melancholy. Mendoza heard that she had 'twice said when she was retired in her chamber "they need not think that it is going to end in this way; I must get married"'.[8]

There was much coming and going of envoys from France over the next few weeks, with the result that Alençon abated most of his preconditions – though he was still insisting on the private exercise of his religion. The negotiations were on again and Simier was ordered 'to use every possible means to attract and satisfy the lords and gentry of the kingdom', for which purpose money would be available. 'Simier has begun to do this already,' commented Mendoza on 14 May, 'and has given two grand banquets this week to the Council.'[9]

But in spite of the free food, and in spite of a lavish scattering of bribes and expensive presents, the opposition was not appeased. There were two rather amateurish attempts to assassinate Simier during the summer, both of which were blamed on the Earl of Leicester's party. It was after the second of these that a justifiably irritated Simier, who had been keeping his ear to the ground since his arrival in England, decided that the time was ripe to strike back at his most dangerous adversary and chose a propitious moment to pass on to the Queen an interesting piece of information about her precious Robert Dudley. He had, it seemed, been secretly married for nearly a year to Lettice, the widowed Countess of Essex – the same Lettice who, as Viscountess Hereford, had been the cause of so much ill-feeling back in the sixties.

If the Frenchman had hoped to provoke an explosion of wrath against the opponents of the marriage and smooth the way for Alençon's visit, he certainly succeeded brilliantly. The Queen, according to William Camden's account of the matter, 'grew into such a chafe that she commanded Leicester not to stir out of the palace of Greenwich and intended to have committed him to the Tower of London, which his enemies much desired. But the Earl of Sussex, though his greatest and deadliest adversary, dissuaded her. For he was of opinion that no man was to be troubled for lawful marriage, which estate amongst all men hath ever been held in honour and esteem.'[10]

Good faithful old Sussex managed to calm Elizabeth down and prevent her from making a fool of herself in public, but her rage against Robert was still terrible. Not only had he deceived and betrayed her, but he'd also had the unspeakable gall to oppose her own marriage when all the time he was married himself! As for Robert, after a brief period of house arrest at Court, he retreated to his house at Wanstead and wrote mournfully to Lord Burghley of his grief at the Queen's bitter unkindness after twenty years' faithful service. 'And,' he went on, 'as I carried myself almost more than a bondsman many a year together, so long as one drop of comfort was left of any hope, as you yourself, my Lord, doth well know, so being acquitted and delivered of that hope, and, by both open and private protestations and declarations discharged, methinks it is more than hard to take such an occasion to bear so great displeasure for.'[11]

It might seem hard that, having refused him herself, Elizabeth should now be creating such an uproar over Robert's marriage. But, as Robert very well knew, this was not an area ruled by logic. He had always occupied a unique position – the Queen's own creation and her special property. It was a position which had always carried its drawbacks as well as many solid material advantages, and while he could still dream of one day founding a royal Dudley dynasty he had been prepared to put up with any number of drawbacks. Now that old dream was finally dead and buried and it was time, more than time, to think of the future. Robert still loved Elizabeth in his own way, a relationship such as theirs could not have survived as it did without a solid basis of mutual affection and respect, but, as he stoutly told Lord Burghley, he was not prepared to be her slave. He wanted a wife and he wanted a son to carry on his name. This, of course, was a perfectly legitimate aspiration and one which Robert had evidently reasoned he should now be in a strong enough place to achieve without losing the Queen altogether. But, knowing the Queen's autocratic and naturally possessive temperament, he can hardly have expected to achieve it without an almighty row – hence his reluctance to make the matter public and face the inevitable consequences.

Meanwhile Elizabeth was showing a determinedly sprightly face to the world as she got ready to welcome her latest suitor – for Alençon was at last on the point of leaving for England to try his luck in person. 'She is burning with impatience for his coming,' commented Mendoza rather sourly, 'although her councillors have laid before her the difficulties which might arise . . . She is largely influenced by the idea that it should be known that her talents and beauty are so great, that they have sufficed to cause him to come and visit her without any assurance that he will be her husband.'[12]

The Duke reached Greenwich in the early hours of 17 August and later that day Elizabeth dined with him privately in Simier's rooms. His presence in the palace was supposed to be a secret, which put councillors and royal servants in the embarrassing position of having to pretend to be deaf and blind, but one thing was clear from the outset – from a personal point of view the visit was proving a triumphant success. Alençon might be a funny little man with a pock-marked complexion and a bulbous nose, but he was also charming, intelligent and witty. He became the Queen's Frog and the French ambassador hastened to inform Catherine de Medici that 'the lady has with difficulty been able to entertain the Duke, being captivated, overcome with love. She told me she had never found a man whose nature and actions suited her better.'[13] Mendoza, too, was obliged to admit to Philip that 'the Queen is delighted with Alençon and he with her, as she has let out to some of her courtiers, saying that she was pleased to have known him, was much taken with his good parts and admired him more than any man. She said that, for her part, she will not prevent his being her husband.'[14]

A grand ball was held at Greenwich on Sunday the twenty-third at which Elizabeth danced much more than usual, constantly waving and smiling at the Duke, who watched the proceedings not very adequately hidden behind a curtain. But for all this showing off, and for all the billing and cooing going on at the Palace, there had so far been, as Mendoza did not fail to point out, no sign 'that any resolution has been arrived at' and King Philip remained highly sceptical, convinced that the whole thing was mere pretence. Nevertheless, the party which opposed the marriage had taken grave alarm. 'Leicester,' reported Mendoza on 25 August, 'is in great grief.' Robert had recently had an interview with the Queen, after which his emotion was remarked, and that same evening a meeting of the opposition took place at the Earl of Pembroke's house, the Sidneys and various other friends and relatives of the Dudley clan being present. According to Mendoza, 'some of them afterwards remarked that Parliament would have something to say as to whether the Queen married or not. 'The people in general', he added hopefully, 'seem to threaten a revolution about it.'[15]

Alençon went home on the twenty-ninth and, although he and the Queen immediately began a hectic exchange of love letters, it seemed that no promises had yet been given. Meanwhile popular expressions of hostility to the marriage were growing. As far back as April, Gilbert Talbot had noted that the preachers were busy 'to apply their sermons to tend covertly against this marriage, many of them inveighing greatly thereat'; and during August, probably while Alençon was still at Greenwich, the Puritan writer John Stubbs published his famous pamphlet *The Discovery of a Gaping Gulf whereunto England is like to be swallowed by another French Marriage.*

Stubbs did not mince his words. The Queen was too old now to think of marriage and it was all a devilish French trick to push the matter so eagerly just at a time when childbearing was likely to be most dangerous to her. If only she would honestly consult her most faithful and wise physicians, they would tell her how fearful was the expectation of death. As for Alençon, he was rotten with debauchery – 'the old serpent himself in the form of a man come a second time to seduce the English Eve and to ruin the English Paradise'. If his mass was once allowed into the country it would be 'as wildfire that all the seas could not quench' and would seriously imperil the true Protestant faith.[16]

John Stubbs was not the only man to commit his objections to paper. Philip Sidney, Robert Dudley's beloved and brilliant nephew, also wrote earnestly to the Queen, begging her not to alienate the affection of her loyal Protestant subjects – 'your chief, if not your sole, strength' – by marrying a Frenchman and a papist, one whom even the common people knew to be the son of 'a Jezebel of our age'.[17]

Sidney had at least had the tact to address himself to the Queen's private ear and he escaped with an angry scolding. But Stubbs' provocative diatribe, which was attracting wide publicity, roused Elizabeth to real fury. She issued a fierce proclamation against the dissemination of all such lewd and seditious libels and ordered the arrest of Stubbs and his printer. They were prosecuted, ironically enough, under a statute originally framed to protect Philip of Spain when he was Mary's consort and sentenced to lose their right hands. The execution was carried out in the presence of a silently sympathetic crowd but it did not stifle the growing radical agitation which was beginning ominously to resemble that which had preceded Mary's marriage.

However, it seemed that Elizabeth meant to go ahead with her plans. Early in October she summoned the Council to discuss the matter and give her its considered advice, but after a series of meetings, one of which lasted without a break from eight in the morning till seven o'clock at night, it was clear that a majority of the members were still very unhappy about the whole thing. Their objections were summed up in a minute in Lord Burghley's hand, dated 6 October and headed 'Causes of Misliking of the Marriage'. These included the fact that Alençon was a Frenchman, 'the people of this realm naturally hating that nation', and the fact that he would in all probability shortly succeed his ailing and childless brother as King of France, with the obvious complications that would entail. Then there was 'the doubt that her Majesty either shall not have children, or that she may be endangered in child-birth'. Much as everyone wanted an heir to the throne, no one wanted to see the Queen risk her precious life. Her constitution was, after all, so good that, without courting the perils of marriage, she seemed 'like to live long'. Also, as someone pointed out, there was no guarantee that Monsieur would prove a kind and considerate husband. On the contrary, the huge discrepancy in their ages and their difference in religion hardly augured for 'a hearty love of her Majesty'. The difference in religion, of course, remained 'the greatest inconvenience' to those council members who foresaw that Alençon's Catholicism 'shall be a comfort to all obstinate Papists in England and a discomfort to all the subjects of good religion'.[18]

In spite of the weight of opinion against him, Lord Burghley still favoured the French marriage – at least, he painted a gloomy picture of the dangers to the realm from the unsettled succession (especially as Elizabeth grew older), from the pretensions of Mary Stuart and from foreign aggression if the Queen did not marry. Probably, though, the argument which influenced him most strongly was that Elizabeth herself appeared to want the marriage so much. Eventually it was decided that this was a matter on which the Council as a body could not advise – each individual member would state his position if required and each would do his best to carry out her wishes – but the Queen would have to make up her own mind first.

When this message was conveyed to the Queen on the morning of 7 October by a four-man committee headed by Lord Burghley, it got a stormy reception. Elizabeth burst into tears and reproached her faithful councillors bitterly for doubting that there could be any better safeguard for the realm than 'to have her marry and have a child of her own body to inherit and so to continue the line of King Henry VIII'. Since this was precisely what her faithful councillors had been urging her to do throughout all the years when it might have been physically practicable –

advice which she had consistently refused to accept – such reproaches must have seemed unreasonable to put it mildly, though none of those present ventured to say so. The Queen went on to curse herself for her 'simplicity' in allowing the matter to be debated at all, but she had expected, so she said, to have had 'a universal request made to her to proceed in this marriage'. Then, being too upset to continue, she dismissed the committee until the afternoon.

When they returned, the conversation was resumed along much the same lines, the Queen showing 'her great misliking' of anyone who opposed her marriage. As for the religious difficulty, 'she did marvel that any person would think so slenderly of her, as that she would not for God's cause, for herself, her surety and her people, have no straight regard thereto as none ought to make that such a doubt, as for it to forbear marriage and to have the Crown settled in her child'.[19]

After this remarkable display, there was nothing for the committee to do but report back to the full Council her Majesty's 'earnest disposition for this her marriage'. 'And thereupon,' recorded Lord Burghley, 'after long consultations had, all the Council accorded upon a new offer to be made to her Majesty of all our assents to offer our service in furtherance of this marriage, if so it shall please her.'[20]

The offer was duly made next day 'by the mouth of the Lord Chancellor', but was not received in any very gracious spirit. 'Her Majesty's answers were very sharp in reprehending of all such as she thought would make arguments against her marriage . . . and though she thought not meet to declare to us whether she would marry Monsieur or no, yet she looked at our hands that we did so much desire her marriage and to have children of her body, as we should have with one accord have made special suit to her for the same.'[21]

In spite of having apparently got what she wanted, Elizabeth remained in an exceedingly bad temper. She was still not speaking to the Earl of Leicester and had quarrelled furiously with Francis Walsingham, whom she suspected of being behind much of the popular agitation against the marriage. According to Bernardino de Mendoza, she was 'so cross and melancholy that it was noticed by everyone who approached her'.

Meanwhile, Simier, who had now been hanging about for nearly a year, was getting impatient and badgering the Queen for a decision. On 9 November they were closeted together for several hours and on the following day she summoned the principal councillors to her chamber 'and told them that she had determined to marry and that they need say nothing more to her about it, but should at once discuss what was necessary for carrying it out'.[22] This sounded like hard news at last but, as Mendoza told Philip a fortnight later, 'these people change so constantly in whatever they take in hand, that it is difficult to send your Majesty any definite information'.[23] Elizabeth had apparently changed her mind overnight and a messenger on his way to Alençon was stopped at Dover and recalled.

The Queen was now talking about getting every councillor to give his opinion of the marriage in writing. When Simier heard of this and protested at what looked like a deliberate delaying tactic, she complained that the Council leaked like a sieve. Her next move was an attempt to persuade that much-tried body to write a collective letter to Alençon urging him to come back to England as soon as possible, 'whereupon they replied that it was not for them but for her to do that'. They also, according to Mendoza, told her that someone of greater standing than Simier should be sent to complete the negotiations. The result was more trouble with Simier's wounded feelings and eventually, towards the end of November, a small committee, from which both Leicester and Walsingham were excluded, was set up to finalise the draft of the marriage contract. This was completed within a few days and conceded to Alençon and all his household the right to hear mass in their private chapel.[24]

But even now Elizabeth had been careful to leave herself an escape-route. She could not marry without her subjects' consent and must therefore be granted a two months' breathing-space during which she would do her very best to win them over to the idea. If she failed, then the engagement was to be regarded as broken off.[25]

Simier left for France on 24 November, laden with expensive presents and handsomely escorted. In December, Elizabeth talked to Mendoza on the subject of her marriage and 'referred to it so tenderly as to make it clear how ardently she desired it'. In January she had become perceptibly less enthusiastic. Leicester and Walsingham were both back at court by this time, and significantly the Queen was now herself raising the religious barrier. She wrote sorrowfully to her Frog telling him that in spite of all her efforts it seemed the English would never accept his mass, so, if he could not give it up, perhaps they had better forget about marriage and remain just good friends.

Had she ever been really serious? A number of learned historians have believed that she was, at least for a time, and have seen her as an ageing lonely woman snatching desperately at an eleventh-hour chance of marriage and motherhood. Well, maybe, and yet it is somehow very difficult to visualise Elizabeth Tudor, that supremely successful career woman, surrendering herself to a man fully young enough to be her own son; being willing, as Philip Sidney put it, to deliver him the keys of her kingdom and live at his discretion. At the same time, there has to be some explanation of her uncharacteristic behaviour during the summer and autumn of 1579. She was, of course, approaching if she had not already begun the menopause and this, combined with the emotional shock of Leicester's marriage, may well have thrown her temporarily off balance. There are other possible explanations. For more than twenty years Elizabeth had been using the courtship ploy at every opportunity, likely and unlikely, in her relations with foreign countries and, apart from the obvious advantages it gave her in the diplomatic poker game, there can be little doubt that she also derived more complicated satisfactions from the elaborate teasing of her prospective bridegrooms – satisfactions to do with the exercise of sexual power and the gratification of sexual vanity. As little as any other woman did the Queen enjoy being reminded of the passing years, but at forty-six she knew well enough that the time for playing her favourite game was coming to an end and, like any great actress making perhaps her last appearance in a role which has made her famous, she would naturally want the occasion to be a memorable one. It was ironical, too, that in this her final courtship Elizabeth should for the first time have found a supporting case worthy of her talents. Unlike the comically boorish Scandinavians, the stodgy Germanic Charles von Habsburg and sulky Anjou, young Alençon had been only too willing to enter into the spirit of the thing. He and Simier were both finished products of a society which regarded the making of courtly love as an art form and, bearing in mind the value of the prize they were after, neither grudged the expenditure of his best efforts. It was all a new and intoxicating experience for Elizabeth and perhaps it is hardly surprising that she should have allowed herself to be carried away. The illusion of renewed youth and beauty died on the morning on 7 October as she looked into the worried faces of some of her oldest friends and the awakening, it seemed, was bitter.

Illusion might be dead, but the Alençon courtship was still very much alive. The Queen was back at her old tricks of blowing hot and cold and driving sober statesmen like Francis Walsingham to distraction. 'I would to God,' he moaned, 'her Highness would resolve one way or the other touching the matter of her marriage.' Walsingham liked the idea no more than he had ever done, but he was terrified that Elizabeth would play fast and loose once too often and end up by offending the French past repair. 'If her Majesty be not already resolved touching her marriage,' he wrote to the Earl of Sussex, 'it will behove her to grow to some speedy resolution therein, for the entertaining of it doth breed her greater dishonour than I dare commit to paper, besides the danger she daily incurreth for not settling of her estate, which dependeth altogether on the marriage.'[26]

Walsingham's alarm was understandable, for as the year 1580 unfolded the international scene could hardly have looked much bleaker from England's point of view. Spain's annexation of Portugal that summer gave Philip control of the entire Iberian peninsula. It gave him the use of the fine Portuguese navy and the revenues of Portugal's colonial empire in the east to add to those of his own empire in the west, making him – on paper at least – the richest and most powerful monarch the world had ever seen. Across the North Sea, Alexander of Parma, the new Spanish commander in the Netherlands, was having a considerable run of success against the Dutch rebels, and now trouble threatened even nearer home, across the Scottish Border, where Mary Stuart's son was growing up. Unfortunately, young James's adolescent revolt against the restraints of his strictly Calvinist upbringing was taking the form of an ominous desire to hobnob with his mother's Guise relations – and that connection boded no good to Protestant England. In Protestant England itself, 1580 saw the arrival of the first Jesuit missionary priests, Fathers Campion and Parsons, and their startling, if short-lived, success among the Catholic minority caused acute alarm in government circles.

It was certainly no time for the Queen to make a single unnecessary enemy and, if ever she had needed friends, surely she needed them now. But Elizabeth refused to be deflected – she would go her own way just as she had always done. She was angling now for a new league with France without marriage, just as she had done ten years earlier, but this time the King of France and the Queen-Mother stood firm. They were determined to pin down the elusive virgin, to saddle her with responsibility for the volatile Alençon and ensure that she paid her full share of the price of war with Spain. As for Alençon himself, he was in the classic position of all adventurers in pursuit of an heiress and could not afford to take offence. He grumbled over the Queen's inconstancy but he had not lost hope, and the Queen took care that he should not. In April 1581, when one of her garters fell off during the famous visit to Sir Francis Drake on board the *Golden Hind* at Deptford, she allowed the French ambassador to 'capture' it as a trophy for the lovelorn Frog.[27]

Failing marriage, Alençon's plan was to coax or blackmail Elizabeth into giving him money. He was already deep in debt, having borrowed lavishly on his expectations, and had now just about reached the end of his resources. If he could not get more backing from somewhere soon, he would have to abandon his ambitions in the Netherlands and return empty-handed to his brother's unfriendly court. In the summer of 1581 the Queen finally opened her purse to the extent of lending her impecunious suitor £30,000, which was better than nothing but still nothing like enough, and Frog came to the conclusion that his best chance of getting more would be to go a-wooing again. He landed at Rye on 31 October and received a warm welcome. All the old routine of dalliance was resumed, Elizabeth making an enormous fuss of her prince frog, her little Moor, her little Italian and, according to gossip relayed by the Venetians, visiting him very morning while he was still in bed to take him a cup of broth; while Frog himself yearned eloquently to be allowed into her bed to show what a good companion he could be.

Mendoza reported that the French ambassadors and the Duke's own companions 'look upon the marriage as an accomplished fact, but the English in general scoff at it, saying that he is only after money . . . It is certain', went on Mendoza in a letter to Philip dated 11 November, 'that the Queen will do her best to avoid offending him, and to pledge him in the affairs of the Netherlands, in order to drive his brother into a rupture with your Majesty, which is her great object, whilst she keeps her hands free and can stand by looking on at the war.'[28]

What is certain is that Elizabeth was doing her utmost to inveigle the King of France into agreeing to share the cost of supporting Alençon and a good deal of hard bargaining was going on behind the screen of slightly farcical love-making. But Henri III refused to commit himself to anything until he was sure of the Queen and, although Mendoza heard from a reliable source that 'when the Queen and Alençon were alone together she pledges herself to him to his heart's content, and as much as any woman could to a man', she would not allow anything to be said publicly.

Matters came to a head on the morning of 22 November, when Elizabeth and her Frog were walking together in the gallery at Whitehall, Leicester and Walsingham being also present. Again according to Mendoza's account: 'the French ambassador entered and said that he wished to write to his master, from whom he had received orders to hear from the Queen's own lips her intention with regard to marrying his brother. She replied, "You may write this to the King: that the Duke of Alençon shall be my husband", and at the same moment she turned to Alençon and kissed him on the mouth, drawing a ring from her own hand and giving it to him as a pledge. Alençon gave her a ring of his in return, and shortly afterwards the Queen summoned the ladies and gentlemen from the presence chamber in the gallery, repeating to them in a loud voice in Alençon's presence what she had previously said.'[29]

The Queen could scarcely have gone further in her efforts to convince the French of her good faith. 'The standers-by', says William Camden, 'took it that the marriage was now contracted by promise' (a promise to marry made before witnesses constituted a legally binding contract), and the episode naturally created a considerable stir. When William of Orange heard about it he had the bells rung in Antwerp, while at home 'the courtiers' minds were diversely affected; some leaped for joy, some were seized with admiration, and others were dejected with sorrow'.[30] Camden goes on to say that the Queen quickly regretted her rash words and spent a sleepless night in 'doubts and cares' among the lamentations of her gentlewomen, but despite all appearances the Queen had, in fact, committed herself to very little. If the French took her up on her promise she had only to protest that she'd been misunderstood and raise her terms to even higher levels. (She was already demanding conditions which the King was expected to refuse.) Alternatively, she could call Parliament in the confident expectation of a Commons' veto on her marriage to a Catholic. In either case she would be able to cast the blame for failure on other shoulders. It's in the highest degree unlikely that she made her declaration unadvisedly – carried away 'by the force of modest love in the midst of amorous discourse'. The Indian summer madness of 1579 had long since faded and now, at least so she told the Earl of Sussex in

December, Elizabeth hated the idea of marriage more every day for reasons which she would not divulge to a twin soul.

That Alençon had taken her seriously, even for a moment, is almost equally unlikely. The Duke was nobody's fool and had probably known for some time that the marriage was a non-starter. However, the Queen had now given him a useful card which he proceeded to play by sitting tight and indicating quite plainly that she would have to make it worth his while to go away quietly. And it's difficult to blame him. Elizabeth had made shameless use of him and she owed him something. The poor Frog may also have been growing tired of his rootless, precarious gambler's existence. It was pleasant to live comfortably and free at the English court, and the prospect of going back into the cold clearly became less and less inviting. Of all Elizabeth's suitors it is possible to feel more than a little sorry for François, Duke of Alençon.

After some indecision and a good deal of haggling, Elizabeth finally offered him a 'loan' of £60,000 – half to be paid fifteen days after he had left the country and the other half fifty days after that. Still he would not go and showed signs of turning awkward, pointing out reasonably enough that the Queen had openly pledged herself to him and, if she turned him out now, he would become the laughing-stock of the world. The Queen advanced him £10,000 and still he lingered, hoping to extort better terms. At last, just as the situation threatened to become embarrassing, he had to accept the fact that the holidays were over and, after some last-minute delays, he left London on 1 February 1582. The Queen went with him as far as Canterbury and a rather sardonic Leicester was deputed to see him safely off the premises. The farewells were affectionate, Elizabeth protesting tearfully that she would give a million to have her dear Frog swimming in the Thames again and telling all and sundry that he would be back in six weeks to marry her – if only the King of France would keep his side of the bargain. In private she is said to have danced for joy in her bedchamber.

The Queen had reason to feel relief and some satisfaction. She had succeeded in extricating herself comparatively cheaply from a potentially dangerous predicament. There had been no rupture with France; Alençon might yet cause Philip some trouble in the Netherlands and Elizabeth had gained nearly three years' valuable time. As it turned out, Alençon accomplished very little in the Netherlands – indeed, he was to prove more of a nuisance to the hard-pressed Dutch than to anyone else – and when he died of fever in June 1584 he had long outlived his usefulness to the Queen of England. Nevertheless, Elizabeth apparently mourned him deeply, shedding tears for three weeks on end and unblushingly informing the French ambassador that she regarded himself as a forlorn widow. Perhaps she did feel a mild pang. Beneath all the nonsense and the play-acting she had liked Alençon. He had been her last fling and at least he had amused her for a season.

36

ENVOI

There were no more foreign suitors after the Duke of Alençon and most people were thankful for it. The English had long since resigned themselves to the extinction of the line of King Henry VIII and had become accustomed to the phenomenon of their Virgin Queen. To a nation growing increasingly prosperous and increasingly confident of its ability to survive no matter what, with the assured assistance of the Protestant God, an uncertain future seemed a small enough price to pay for freedom from foreign interference and foreign entanglements. Unmarried, the Queen belonged to every Englishman, and very few Englishmen would now have had it any other way. Indeed, it's difficult to see how it could ever have been any other way. In the absence of an acceptable native-born or foreign Protestant consort, it would have been impossible for Elizabeth to have married without splitting the country in half.

Once she had recovered from the emotional *crise* of 1579, Elizabeth herself showed no real signs of regret that her courting days were over – perhaps she too was rather thankful than otherwise. She had come to terms with the fact of the Earl of Leicester's marriage by simply ignoring it, and the new Countess was kept carefully out of her sight. Since the Queen continued to make regular use of Leicester's house at Wanstead for council meetings and conferences, this must have led to a good deal of inconvenience. But, in spite of the domestic problems caused by Elizabeth's refusal to recognise the existence of Lady Leicester, and although the longed-for son and heir, born at the end of 1579, lived only four years, Robert and Lettice seem to have been happy together and Robert proved a surprisingly uxorious husband, 'doting extremely upon marriage'.

He was not to have much leisure to enjoy it. The second half of the 1580s was a stormy period for everyone in English public life, but especially for Robert Dudley. After the assassination of William of Orange, Elizabeth had been reluctantly obliged to take a more active part in the Dutch struggle for survival, and in the autumn of 1585 Robert was appointed commander-in-chief of an expeditionary force of about five thousand men being sent to the Netherlands.

Trouble began when, after giving him a royal welcome, the Dutch Estates offered the Earl of Leicester the Supreme Governorship of the

United Provinces. Trouble increased dramatically when he accepted – it was an offer of power and prestige calculated to turn stronger heads than his. It was equally calculated to enrage the Queen, who had already refused an offer of Dutch sovereignty herself and who was, in any case, still determined to keep her involvement to an absolute minimum. When the news reached her she was angrier with her old friend than perhaps she had ever been before. 'We could never have imagined,' she wrote, 'had we not seen it fall out, that a man raised up by ourself and extraordinarily favoured by us above any other subject of this land, would have in so contemptible a sort broken our commandment in a cause that so greatly touched our honour.' An extra edge was added to Elizabeth's fury by gossip that Lady Leicester was planning to join her husband, taking with her 'such a train of ladies and gentlemen, and such rich coaches, litters and side saddles as her Majesty had none such and that there should be such a court of ladies as should far surpass her Majesty's court here'. This tale, so Robert was informed, had roused her Majesty 'to extreme choler and dislike of all your doings there, saying with great oaths she would have no more courts under her obeisance but her own, and would revoke you from thence with all speed'.

Robert, as usual, was in despair over the Queen's attitude and her refusal even to listen to his explanations. 'At the least,' he complained, 'I think she would never have so condemned any other man before she heard him.' But the Council, alarmed at the possible effect on the conduct of the campaign if Elizabeth carried out her threat to recall its general in disgrace, combined to smooth things over. Gradually the Queen calmed down and was finally prepared to admit that perhaps Robert had not really meant to disobey her, that he'd believed he was acting for the best, though mistakenly. She would not allow him to keep his governorship, but there was no more talk of recalling him and by the following summer he had once more been forgiven. 'Now will I end,' she wrote in a private letter dated July 1586, 'that do imagine I talk still with you and therefore loathly say farewell to my two Eyes, though ever I pray God bless you from all harm and save you from all foes, with my million and legion of thanks for all your pains and care.'

Robert, absent in the Netherlands, missed the fearful explosion of royal temperament which followed the execution of the Queen of Scots that winter and was considered fortunate by his colleagues, riding the storm in London; but he was home again before the end of 1587, ready to take up the onerous post of Lieutenant and General of the Queen's Armies and Companies being hastily mustered to defend the country against invasion. King Philip's long-threatened Enterprise against England had at last become an imminent reality and during the crisis summer of 1588, with a Spanish fleet expected hourly in the Channel, Elizabeth was showing an alarming disposition to go down to the south coast to meet the enemy in the front line. It was to divert her mind from such an unsuitable exploit that Robert suggested she should instead spend a few days visiting his headquarters at Tilbury, to see the camp and the forts and hold a review of the citizen army which had been concentrated to the east of London to meet an attack from Parma across the North Sea. The Queen took up the idea with enthusiasm and, during her famous visit to the army at Tilbury, Robert walked bare-headed at her bridle-hand. It was to be the last time he escorted her in public and it was fitting that it should have been the greatest occasion of them all. He had grown stout, red-faced and rather bald; she had taken to wearing a crimped orange wig and over-painting her face, and they were both middle-aged. But none of that mattered. The old strong bond of a lifetime's shared experience, which reached its peak on that glorious emotional day at Tilbury, would be broken now only by death.

In the middle of August, while the Armada was being beaten up the coast towards Scotland, Robert broke camp and returned to London. He wasn't at all well - the last few months had been an appalling strain – and had promised himself a short holiday. He spent a few quiet days with the Queen, dining with her every day, and then left for the country, intending to take the waters at Buxton. On the way he sent Elizabeth a note from Ryecote, the Oxfordshire manor-house where they had often stayed together in the past. He wanted to know how his gracious lady was – she had been suffering a few twinges lately – 'it being the chiefest thing in this world I do pray for, that she should have good health and long life. For my own poor case,' he went on, 'I continue still your medicine and find it amends much better than with any other thing that hath been given me. Thus hoping to find a perfect cure at the bath, I humbly kiss your foot. From your old lodging at Rycott this Thursday morning, ready to take my journey . . .'

He got as far as Cornbury, a few miles from Oxford, and there, on 4 September, he died – possibly from cancer of the stomach. In the general rejoicing which followed the defeat of the Armada, the disappearance of this great landmark of the Elizabethan scene passed almost unnoticed and generally unmourned. At a time when her people expected to see her bathed in the radiance of victory, the Queen could not afford the luxury of private grief but she took that brief note scribbled at Ryecote and put it by her. Fifteen years later it was found in the little coffer she kept at her bedside. Across it she had written: 'His last letter.'

The Queen continued obstinately to ignore the existence of the widowed Countess of Leicester – apart, that is, from hounding her for repayment of Robert's considerable debts to the Crown – but she could not, even if she had wanted to, ignore the widow's son. Robert Devereux, Earl of Essex, has often been described as the darling of Elizabeth's old age but it would probably be more accurate to describe him as one of its greatest headaches. Essex, still in his early twenties, was extremely good-looking and, when he chose to be, charming company. He was also spoilt, ambitious and headstrong. Unlike his stepfather, he never learnt the art of putting his passions in his pocket. Unlike Leicester, he had not grown up with Elizabeth and he made the fatal mistake of underestimating her. In his youthful arrogance and impatience he came to see her as a tiresome old woman who, if she could not be cajoled, would have to be bullied – a miscalculation which led inexorably to tragedy.

The war with Spain still dragged on, and in 1596 the Earl of Essex distinguished himself in a brilliantly successful raid on the port of Cadiz. He returned to a hero's welcome – his youth, his striking good looks, his open-handedness and his martial enthusiasm all combined to make him a favourite with the London crowds – but he was by no means universally popular. At Court two distinct and increasingly hostile factions were emerging: on the one side Essex and most of the younger element, eager for military profit and glory, who looked to him as their natural leader; on the other, what might be described as the peace party, headed by old Lord Burghley and his sober son, Robert. Elizabeth did her best to keep a balance. She was undoubtedly very fond of Essex – rather in the manner of an indulgent aunt with a wild but irresistibly attractive young nephew – but it was soon noticed that while the Earl seemed able to get anything for himself, including plenty of expensive presents, the Queen would give nothing to his friends. She had no intention of allowing him to build up too large a following, no matter how he coaxed. Essex was not used to being refused, and when he failed to get what he wanted by cajolery he would sulk and storm. These tactics led to rows, with Elizabeth swearing angrily that she would break him of his will and pull down his great heart.

One of the Earl's more sensible friends, the long-headed young lawyer Francis Bacon, tried to warn him of the risks he was running. 'A man of a nature not to be ruled,' wrote Bacon; 'of an estate not grounded to his greatness; of a popular reputation; of a military dependence: I demand whether there can be a more dangerous image than this represented to any monarch living, much more to a lady and of her Majesty's apprehension?' There would be no surer way to frighten and offend the Queen than by appearing to be too powerful or too popular, and Bacon urged his patron to break with his military followers, or at least to seem to do so, and seek advancement by peaceful means. This was excellent advice, but unhappily Essex was incapable of taking it. His unquiet spirit could find no fulfilment in the sort of career his stepfather had settled for and although the Queen, who found it difficult to be angry with him for long, continued patiently to try to tame him into becoming a useful servant of the Crown, the task was hopeless.

The last act of the Essex tragedy was played out during the winter of 1600, the year after his disastrous failure in Ireland. By this time a sick and despairing figure and probably more than a little mad, he was making wild plans to seize the court and the Queen, force Elizabeth to restore him to favour and, above all, to get rid of his arch-enemy Robert Cecil. The Queen and Robert Cecil watched and waited. Then, on Saturday, 7 February 1601, some of the more foolish members of the Essex faction bribed William Shakespeare's company of actors to put on a special performance of *Richard II*, the play in which a king is deposed and killed. That night Essex was summoned to appear before the Council. He refused to go, and next morning he and about two hundred of the rabble attempted to raise the City, running armed through the Sunday streets crying that a plot was laid for his life and England sold to the Spaniard. But the citizens stayed indoors and by evening it was all over.

The Earl of Essex was brought to trial, convicted of high treason and executed before the end of the month; but, although the Queen sorrowed for the death of a once brilliant and beautiful young man, she never hesitated over its necessity. Her sweet Robin, whom she had tried to love and tried perhaps to mould into a substitute for that other Robin now more than ten years in his grave, had committed two unforgiveable sins. He had set out to turn her own Londoners against her, and he would have touched her sceptre. When the young Elizabeth had told William Maitland of Lethington, 'as long as I live I shall be Queen of England', she had meant just precisely what she said.

The Queen had two more years to live – busy, active years with no respite from the burden of public care which she had borne for nearly half a century. To the very end she remained in full control of her situation, allowing no man to rule her, and, by her own special brand of magic, keeping the goodwill of all her husbands – the people of England.

Part Four

Elizabeth Regina

Early before the day doth spring,
Let us awake my Muse and sing:
It is no time to slumber,
So many joys this time doth bring,
As time will fail to number.

But whereto shall we bend our layes?
Even up to Heaven, againe to raise
The Maid, which thence descended:
Hath brought againe the golden days,
And all the world amended.

Rudeness itself she dothe repine,
Even like an Alchemist divine,
Gross times of iron turning
Into the purest forms of gold:
Not to corrupt, till heaven waxe old,
And be refined with burning.

John Davies,
Hymns of Astrea

Prologue

THE YEAR EIGHTY-EIGHT

The Spanish fleet did float in narrow seas,
And bend her ships against the English shore,
With so great rage as nothing could appease,
And with such strength as never seen before.

It was late in the afternoon of Friday, 19 June 1588 when Captain Thomas Fleming brought the bark *Golden Hind* scudding under full sail into Plymouth Sound. The Lord Admiral Charles Howard and a group of his senior officers were out on the Hoe relaxing over an after-dinner game of bowls when Fleming came panting up to report that the Spanish Armada had been sighted that morning off the Scillies and Sir Francis Drake, so the story goes, remarked that there was time enough to finish the game and beat the Spaniards too. The story may well be true. The wind was blowing from the south-west and at three o'clock the tide had begun flooding into the Sound. Until the ebb, round about ten in the evening, the English battle fleet was effectively immobilised and there could have been plenty of time to finish a leisurely game of bowls.

But all through that night Plymouth harbour seethed with activity as the crews sweated at their gruelling task of towing the heavy warships put on the ebb tide, and by daybreak the bulk of the fleet was riding at anchor behind Rame Head. All through that night, too, the beacon fires flung the news from hill-top to hill-top – leaping along the south coast from the Lizard to Beachy Head, up to Bristol and South Wales, across the Sussex Downs to the Surrey hills and the heights of Hampstead and into the Midland shires:

Till Belvoir's lordly terraces the sign to Lincoln sent,
And Lincoln sent the message on, o'er the wild vale of Trent;
Till Skiddaw saw the fire that burst on Gaunt's embattled pile,
And the red glare on Skiddaw roused the burghers of Carlisle.

The long nervous wait was over and England was as ready as she would ever be to meet the onslaught of Spain. Sir Walter Raleigh and his cousin Richard Grenville commanded in the vulnerable West Country and Sir

John Norris, responsible for coastal defences from Dorset to Kent, had detached three thousand men to guard the Isle of Wight, regarded as another key point. In Essex, which would be in the front line if the Duke of Parma's army, now embarking at Dunkirk, succeeded in making the crossing, the Earl of Leicester was gathering fourteen thousand foot and two thousand horse; while in Kent Lord Hunsdon had raised another eight thousand. The inland counties were also doing their bit, if a little reluctantly – the imminence of danger by seaborne invasion was naturally harder to impress on men who had never seen the sea. But Sir Henry Cromwell on a visit to London was so struck by the sense of urgency round the capital, by the sight of guarded ferries and crossroads and of men drilling with musket and caliver on every open space, that he wrote home to Huntingdon in a strenuous effort to convey the immediacy of the crisis and ordering all captains and leading gentlemen to stay at their posts, ready to march at an hour's warning.

A notably easy-going and unmilitaristic nation was doing its best and no one questioned the courage and resolution of the islanders as they prepared that long-ago summer to defend their lives and liberty, their homes and their religion. Equally, no one with any military experience could doubt that an encounter between Parma's Blackbeards – hard-bitten veterans of a dozen bloody campaigns commanded by the best general in Europe – and Queen Elizabeth's untrained, sketchily equipped citizen army would result in anything but a massacre. The business must be settled at sea, or the country would go down in fire and slaughter, famine, pestilence and persecution. Fortunately, the seamen, although fully conscious of the awesome nature of their responsibility, had every confidence in their ability to hinder the enemy's quiet passage into England. Francis Drake, writing to the Queen from Plymouth in April, assured Her Majesty that he had not in his lifetime 'known better men and possessed with gallanter minds than the people which are here gathered together, voluntarily to put their hands and hearts into the finishing of this great piece of work'. The navy, in fact, was itching to get to grips with the Armada.

The two fleets first sighted one another west of the Eddystone about three o'clock in the afternoon of Saturday 20 July and during that night the English succeeded in recovering the weather gauge. In other words, they stood out to sea across the enemy's bows and, by a very nice piece of seamanship indeed, worked their way round to the seaward and windward flank of the advancing Spaniards. So, on the morning of Sunday the 21st, began the pursuit up the Channel. At the outset both sides had received some unpleasant surprises. The Spaniards by the realisation that they were opposed by ships faster and more weatherly than any they had seen before, and the English by the sheer size of the Armada and the great defensive strength of its crescent-shaped formation.

Even with their superior fire-power and manoeuvrability, they knew that unless they could break that formation, it would be impossible to do it serious damage.

On the following day the Armada lost two capital ships, though neither as a result of enemy action. One blew up after a fire started in the magazine. The other lost her rudder and had to be abandoned. On Tuesday the wind veered. The English fleet temporarily lost the advantage of the weather gauge and a somewhat confused battle was joined off Portland Bill, the English trying to weather the Armada's seaward wing, the Spaniards trying to grapple and board their irritatingly nimble adversaries. Meanwhile, Martin Frobisher in the *Triumph*, the biggest ship in either fleet, together with five middle-sized London merchantmen, had become separated from the main body of the fleet on the shoreward side and was being attacked by Don Hugo de Moncada's galleasses – a hybrid form of sailing ship cum galley. Whether Frobisher was really in difficulties or was attempting to lure the galleasses into a trap has never been made clear but, as the wind veered again to the south, Howard in the *Ark Royal*, followed by the *Elizabeth Jonas*, the *Galleon of Leicester*, the *Golden Lion*, the *Victory*, the *Mary Rose*, the *Dreadnought* and the *Swallow*, stormed down to the rescue, pouring broadside after broadside into the *San Martin de Portugal*, the Spanish admiral's flagship, as he went. 'At which assault', reported Howard, 'after wonderful sharp conflict, the Spaniards were forced to give way and to flock together like sheep.'

On Wednesday there was a lull. The English had been using up their ammunition at an unprecedented rate and were obliged to send urgently to Portsmouth 'for a new supply of such provisions'. Howard was not particularly pleased by the way things were going. Whenever the fleets had come to blows the English had had the advantage, but the Armada was now well on its way towards the rendezvous with Parma, still maintaining strict formation and still relatively intact. But on board the *San Martin*, the Duke of Medina Sidonia also had his problems. He, too, was running short of ammunition and was increasingly worried by the fact that so far he had been unable to make any contact with the Duke of Parma.

On Thursday there was another indecisive skirmish off the Isle of Wight and on Saturday 27 July the Armada suddenly dropped anchor off Calais. The English promptly followed suit and for the next twenty-four hours the two fleets lay within culverin shot of each other. Medina Sidonia had made up his mind not to go any further until he had heard from Parma and at once dispatched an urgent message to Dunkirk asking for forty or fifty flyboats to be sent without delay, 'as with this aid', he wrote, 'I shall be able to resist the enemy's fleet until Your Excellency can come out with the rest and we can go together and take some port where the Armada may enter in safety.' No one, it seemed, had yet explained to Medina Sidonia that the only flyboats operational in the neighbourhood of

Dunkirk were the Sea Beggars, tough little craft of the embryonic Dutch navy commanded by Justin of Nassau, which had come down from the Scheldt Estuary and were now efficiently blockading the Flemish coast. The Spanish fighting ships drew twenty-five to thirty feet of water, which they would not find at Dunkirk, or Nieuport, the other port of embarkation, and as long as Justin continued to keep Parma's army penned up in its shallow, sandy harbours, the all important junction of the invasion force and its escort was – short of a miracle – going to be impossible.

Meanwhile, Charles Howard had been joined by the squadron of thirty-odd ships left to guard the mouth of the Thames, and that Saturday night the whole English navy, a hundred and fifty sail great and small was assembled in the Straits of Dover. No one seems to have told Howard that the Dutch were in position and, hag-ridden by the fear that Parma might turn up at any moment, he was determined to lose no time in flushing the Armada out of Calais Roads. The obvious way to do this was with fireships and about midnight on Sunday, eight small craft 'going in a front, having the wind and tide with them, and their ordnance being charged' were set on fire and let loose.

Fire was, of course, one of the greatest dangers a wooden sailing ship had to fear, and panic swept through the crowded anchorage as the Armada cut its cables and scrambled out to sea in the darkness. The fireships, although they did no actual damage, had achieved something which the English fleet had not yet been able to do and had broken up the Spaniards' formidable crescent formation. All the same, and due in large part to the stubborn courage and leadership of the Duke of Medina Sidonia, the scattered ships rallied, collected themselves and by Monday morning were ready to do battle once more.

Sir William Winter, second in command of the squadron which had been waiting off the North Foreland, told Francis Walsingham that 'about nine of the clock in the morning we fetched near unto them being then thwart of Gravelines, and they went into the proportion of a half-moon. The fight continued until six of the clock at night, in the which time the Spanish army bare away north-north-east as much as they could; keeping company one with another, I assure Your Honour, in very good order.' This was the fiercest fight and the nearest thing to a set battle which had taken place since the Armada had entered the Channel, but although the Spaniards had, for the first time, taken a real beating, Charles Howard was still not very happy. Sending an anxious plea to Walsingham for more victuals and munition, he wrote: 'Ever since morning we have chased them in fight until this evening late and distressed them much; but their fleet consisteth of mighty ships and great strength'. And he added a postscript. 'Their force is wonderful great and strong; and yet we pluck their feathers little and little.' Francis Drake was rather more optimistic. 'God hath given us so good a day in forcing the enemy so far to leeward as

I hope to God the Prince of Parma and the Duke of Medina Sidonia shall not shake hands this few days.'

God was certainly playing his part and, as Francis Drake always firmly believed, he was apparently a Protestant God, for during that night the wind blew hard from the northwest, driving the unhappy Armada remorselessly towards the shoals and banks of the Dutch coast. The *San Mateo* and the *San Felipe* went aground on the banks off Nieuport and Ostend to be snapped up by the Sea Beggars, and by dawn on Tuesday, 30 July it seemed as if the whole fleet must be pounded to death on the Zeeland Sands while the English looked on from a safe distance. Then, suddenly, the wind veered again and next day Drake wrote exultantly to Walsingham: 'We have the army of Spain before us and mind, with the grace of God, to wrestle a pull with him. There was never anything pleased me better than the seeing the enemy flying with a southerly wind to northwards. God grant you have a good eye to the Duke of Parma; for with the grace of God, if we live, I doubt it not but ere long so to handle the matter with the Duke of Sidonia as he shall wish himself back at St Mary Port among his orange trees.' As they set off in pursuit, still worried by shortages of food and ammunition, neither Drake nor Howard yet realised that they had seen the last of the Invincible Armada.

During those momentous ten days which were to settle the fate of western Christendom, Queen Elizabeth, 'not a whit dismayed', was in London, taking no notice of the specially picked force of two thousand men who were guarding her precious person and showing an alarming inclination to go down to the south coast and meet the enemy in person. It was largely to divert her Majesty's mind from such an unsuitable excursion that the Earl of Leicester had suggested she should pay a visit to his camp at Tilbury and so 'comfort' the army concentrated to the east of the capital, 'at Stratford, East Ham and the villages thereabout'. Elizabeth took the idea up eagerly. In fact, by this time the crisis was over and the battered Armada was being driven into the North Sea, but William Camden wrote: 'Whereas most men thought they would tack about again and come back, the Queen with a masculine spirit came and took a view of her Army and Camp at Tilbury, and riding about through the ranks of armed men drawn up on both sides of her, with a leader's truncheon in her hand, sometimes with a martial pace, another while gently like a woman, incredible it is how much she encouraged the hearts of her captains and soldiers by her presence and speech to them.'

The visit was a roaring success. The Queen had come down the Thames by barge to Tilbury, where she was received by Leicester and his officers, and greeted by a salvo of cannon fired from the port. She then got into her coach and set off to inspect the camp to a martial accompaniment of drums and fifes. A contemporary versifier, who rushed into print with a very long (and very bad) poem entitled *Elizabetha Triumphans*, probably captured the spirit of the occasion as well as anybody:

Our peerless Queen doth by her soldiers pass,
And shows herself unto her subjects there,
She thanks them oft for their (of duty) pains,
And they, again, on knees, do pray for her;
They couch their pikes, and bow their ensigns down,
When as their sacred royal Queen passed by.

Leicester's belief that the Queen's presence would be good for morale was undoubtedly fully justified.

The soldiers which placed were far off
From that same way through which she passed along,
Did hollo oft, 'The Lord preserve our Queen!'
He happy was that could but see her coach . . .
Thrice happy they who saw her stately self,
Who, Juno-like, drawn by her proudest birds,
Passed along through quarters of the camp.

Elizabeth spent the night at a nearby manor house, and next day came back to Tilbury to see a mock battle and to review her troops. Bare-headed and wearing a breastplate, she rode along the lines of men escorted only by the Earl of Leicester, the Earl of Ormonde, bearing the sword of state, and a page who carried her white-plumed helmet. She had dismissed her bodyguard for, as she was presently to say, she did not desire to live to distrust her faithful and loving people. Such fear was for tyrants. She had always so behaved herself that, under God, she placed her chiefest strength and safeguard in the loyal hearts and goodwill of her subjects.

Her dazzled and adoring amateur army did not see a thin, middle-aged woman with bad teeth and wearing a bright red wig perched on the back of an enormous white gelding. Instead they saw the personification of every goddess of classical mythology they had ever heard about, every heroine from their favourite reading, the Bible. They saw Judith and Deborah, Diana the Huntress and the Queen of the Amazons all rolled into one. But they also saw their own beloved and familiar Queen.

Her stateliness was so with love-show joined,
As all there then did jointly love and fear.
They joyed in that they see their Ruler's love:
But feared lest that in aught they should offend
Against herself, the Goddess of the land.

It was in this hectic emotional atmosphere that Elizabeth made her famous Tilbury Speech. She had not come among them for her 'recreation and disport' she told the soldiers, 'but being resolved, in the midst and heat of the battle, to live or die amongst you all, to lay down for my God, and for my kingdom, and for my people, my honour and my blood, even in the dust. I know I have the body of a weak and feeble woman, but I have the heart and stomach of a king, and of a king of England too, and think foul scorn that Parma or Spain, or any prince of Europe should dare to invade the borders of my realm; to which, rather than any dishonour shall grow by me, I will myself take up arms, I myself will be your general, judge and rewarder of every one of your virtues in the field. I know already for your forwardness you have deserved rewards and crowns; and we do assure you, in the word of a prince, they shall be duly paid you.'

Small wonder that her audience rose to her with 'a mighty shout' and when the Queen had gone back to London, a little disappointed perhaps that she had not after all been called upon to take arms herself, Leicester wrote to the Earl of Shrewsbury: 'Our gracious mistress hath been here with me to see her camp and people, which so enflamed the hearts of her good subjects, as I think the weakest person among them is able to match the proudest Spaniard that dares land in England.'

The year '88 which, it had long been prophesied, would see many 'most wonderful and extraordinary accidents', had seen a small island, only half an island in fact, triumphantly defy and repulse the assault of the greatest power in Europe and may surely be said to mark the high noon of the Elizabethan epic. It had also marked the consummation of a unique love affair between ruler and people. But no nation can live for long in such a white-hot passion of love and pride, and even as Elizabeth Tudor rode through the camp at Tilbury her world was changing. Economic pressures and other pressures and aspirations, as yet barely recognised or understood, of a society still emerging from an age of old certainties and dogmas were building up beneath seemingly solid ground, until – within the lifetimes of children already toddling in Armada summer – they were to erupt in a manner which effectively killed the old certainties for ever.

37

A Most Renowned Virgin Queen

Sacred, imperial, and holy is her seat,
Shining with wisdom, love, and mightiness:
Nature that everything imperfect made,
Fortune that never yet was constant found,
Time that defaceth every golden show,
Dare not decay, remove, or her impair;
Both nature, time, and fortune, all agree,
To bless and serve her royal majesty.

A little before noon on Sunday, 24 November 1588, the head of a very grand procession indeed emerged from the courtyard of Somerset House, turned right into the Strand and set off past St Clement Danes and Essex House towards Temple Bar and the City. It was an awesome spectacle, for the greatest names in the land were on their way to church to give thanks to the Almighty for their recent glorious deliverance from invasion and conquest by the mighty power of Spain.

Everybody who was anybody was in town that Sunday morning. Behind the heralds and the trumpeters and the gentlemen ushers rode the nobility, the privy councillors, the judges and bishops and all the great officers of state, the scribes and the men of war, all the brilliance and dignity, all the glamour and gallantry and professional expertise of the Elizabethan establishment: old Lord Burghley and sombre Secretary Walsingham; the Lord High Admiral Howard of Effingham and Lord Chancellor Christopher Hatton, Hunsdon and Pembroke, Knollys and Egerton, that dazzling all-rounder Sir Walter Raleigh and Archbishop Whitgift, the Queen's 'little black husband'.

After the Queen's men came the Queen herself, surrounded by the gentlemen pensioners and riding in an open chariot throne drawn by two white horses. Four pillars at the back end of this contraption supported a canopy 'on the top whereof was made a crown imperial', while in front two smaller pillars accommodated a lion and a dragon. Next came the Master of the Horse, the young Earl of Essex, leading the royal palfrey, and a contingent of ladies of honour with the yeomen of the guard in their gorgeous red and gold liveries, halberds in their hands, brought up the rear.

At Temple Bar the city musicians were in position over the gateway, ready to strike up a welcoming tune, and the Lord Mayor and his brethren, the scarlet-robed Aldermen, waited to greet Her Majesty and escort her through Fleet Street and up Ludgate Hill to St Paul's. According to long-established custom, the way was lined by the city companies in their livery hoods and wearing their best clothes, all standing in order behind railings draped with blue cloth and all 'saluting her highness as she proceeded along'. Lesser mortals seized what points of vantage they could from which to cheer the Queen and gape at the grand folk in her train.

The procession reached Paul's Church between the hours of twelve and one, and was received at the great West Door by the Bishop of London with more than fifty other members of the clergy drawn up in support, all in their richest copes and vestments. Descending from her chariot, the Queen at once fell on her knees and there and then 'made her hearty prayers to God' before being conducted down the long west aisle of the cathedral, where the banners captured from the Armada ships hung on display, while the litany was changed before her. She then crossed the transept and took her place in the gallery in the north wall of the choir, facing the open air pulpit cross, to hear the Bishop of Salisbury preach a sermon 'wherein none other argument was handled but that praise, honour and glory might be rendered unto God, and that God's name might be extolled by thanksgiving'. Elizabeth did not normally share her subjects' inordinate enthusiasm for sermons, but on this occasion she listened with gracious attention to the eloquent Dr Pierce and when he had finished she herself addressed the assembled congregation, 'most Christianly' exhorting them to give thanks – the people responding with a great shout, wishing her a long and happy life to the confusion of her enemies. Her obligations to a benevolent deity having been thus handsomely discharged, the Queen processed back through the church the way she had come and went to dine in state at the bishop's palace.

This solemn ceremony marked the climax of a series of public holidays, thanksgiving services, sermons, bonfires and other victory celebrations; but although the nation rejoiced, there was little euphoria and less complacency. The thousands who thronged the churches that autumn had needed no urging to give thanks to God as they reflected soberly on the providential nature of their escape from the King of Spain's invincible Armada, and no thinking person believed that this would be the end of the matter. Certainly the Queen did not. One crisis, perhaps the greatest, had been met and overcome, but as she brought a highly satisfactory day to its close, repeating her triumphal journey through the city streets back to Somerset House, the November dusk ablaze with a 'great light of torches', she harboured no illusions about the nature of the hazards which lay ahead.

Elizabeth Tudor was fifty-five now (the same age as her father had been when he died) and had just celebrated the thirtieth anniversary of her accession. By the standards of her day she was already well past middle-age, but if she was daunted by the prospect of beginning a new career as a war-leader so late in life, she gave no sign of it in the presence of her loving people. To a casual glance that spare, wiry figure and high-nosed profile had altered amazingly little over the past thirty years and the Queen's carefully cultivated public image was still, convincingly, that of a woman in her prime. She had once nearly died of smallpox and on at least two occasions since had been ill enough to cause serious anxiety, but she had always possessed great recuperative powers and in her mid-fifties her general health seems to have been excellent; even the ulcer on her ankle which had troubled her on and off for nearly ten years had healed at last. Physically she was as active as ever, dancing six or seven galliards in a morning and walking and riding with undiminished energy; while anyone rash enough to suppose that her mental powers might have begun to decline quickly discovered his mistake. She had kept up her lifelong habit of devoting some part of almost every day to study or serious reading and, as her godson, John Harington, records: 'Her highness was wont to sooth her ruffled temper with reading every morning, when she had been stirred to passion at the council, or other matters had overthrown her gracious disposition. She did much admire Seneca's wholesome advisings when the soul's quiet is flown away, and I saw much of her translating thereof.'

Unfortunately, the soothing properties of Seneca were not always efficacious. When stirred to passion, her Highness was still quite capable of filling the air with good round oaths and was subject on occasion 'to be vehemently transported with anger'. Elizabeth in a rage could be heard several rooms away and she was not above throwing things, or boxing the ears of the nearest maid of honour. 'When she smiled', wrote Harington, 'it was a pure sunshine that every one did choose to bask in; but anon came a storm from a sudden gathering of clouds, and the thunder fell, in wondrous manner, on all alike.' The Queen's bark, however, was usually worse than her bite and these tension-relieving explosions were always kept in the family. No outsider ever saw her other than graciously smiling or regally dignified.

But if, in 1588, Queen Elizabeth appeared to be at the peak of her form – tough, vigorous and autocratic, her appetite for the pleasures and problems of life seemingly unquenchable – time had not dealt so kindly with her contemporaries. Lord Burghley, now in his late sixties, was still in harness but increasingly burdened by the weight of his years and infirmities. Francis Walsingham was a sick man and most of the older generation of councillors and courtiers were nearing the end of their careers. Death, indeed, had already torn one gaping hole in that charmed circle of intimates whom the Queen honoured with pet names, and the procession to St Paul's had been the first great pageant of the reign in which the flamboyant figure of Robert Dudley, Earl of Leicester, had not figured prominently.

Leicester, as commander-in-chief of the home forces, had spent a strenuous summer helping to organise England's land defence and, although he was much the same age as the Queen, he hadn't worn as well as his mistress. Paunchy and red-faced, his white hair receding fast, little trace remained of the dark, slightly sinister good looks which had once earned him the opprobrious label of Gypsy. When the invasion scare was finally over and his headquarters at Tilbury had been dismantled, the Earl came back to London and was present at a grand military review held at Whitehall on 26 August, watching with the queen from a window while his young stepson ran two tilts against the Earl of Cumberland. Next day he left for the country, intending to take the waters at Buxton. He stopped en route at Rycote Manor near Oxford, home of the Norris family where he and Elizabeth had often stayed together in the past, and from there he scribbled one of his affectionate little notes to the Queen. A week later he was dead, 'of a continual fever'.

In the excitement of the time, the disappearance of this great landmark of the Elizabethan scene went unmourned and almost unnoticed by the general public. Leicester had never been liked. 'He was esteemed a most accomplished courtier', observed William Camden, 'a cunning time-server and respecter of his own advantages . . . But whilst he preferred power and greatness, which is subject to be envied, before solid virtue, his detracting emulators found large matter to speak reproachfully of him, and even when he was in his most flourishing condition spared not disgracefully to defame him by libels, not without mixture of some untruths. In a word, people talked openly in his commendation, but privately he was ill spoken of by the greater part.'

People, of course, had always resented his special relationship with the Queen (in some quarters he was still blamed for her failure to get married), and he'd recently become a prime target of the Catholic propaganda machine. *Leicester's Commonwealth*, the familiar title of a book published anonymously in Antwerp in 1584, had not only raked up the old scandal of his first wife's death but accused its victim, in exuberant and imaginative detail, of pretty well every iniquity known to man – from fornication and covetousness to murder and treachery. In spite of official attempts to suppress it, this little masterpiece of character assassination enjoyed an immediate runaway success with that numerous section of the community who'd always suspected the Earl of being a bad lot and were only too happy to see their prejudices confirmed in print. So much so that, at least according to the chronicler John Stow, 'all men, so far as they durst, rejoiced no less outwardly at his death than for the victory lately obtained against the Spaniard'.

For the Queen it was a grievous loss and Camden noted that she took it much to heart. Elizabeth had first known Robert Dudley when they were both children and ever since she came to the throne he had been one of her closest and most constant companions, her 'brother and best friend', and more than that, it had often been whispered. One of the Spanish government's secret agents in London picked up a story that the Queen was so grieved that she had shut herself up in her chamber for several days, refusing to speak to anyone, until finally Lord Burghley and some of the other councillors were obliged to have the doors broken open. This report is not confirmed by any other source, and sounds both improbable and uncharacteristic. Elizabeth had learnt to conceal her innermost feelings before she was out of her teens, and as she grew older she 'either patiently endured or politely dissembled' her greatest griefs of mind and body. Besides this, September 1588, when the magnitude of the victory lately obtained against the Spaniard was just beginning to dawn on her subjects, was emphatically not the moment for the Queen to parade a private sorrow which would be shared by no one. But she kept that note from Rycote. Fifteen years later it was found in the little coffer which always stood at her bedside. Across it she had written: 'His last letter.'

Meanwhile, Robert Dudley's death had created a vacancy on the committee of England's most exclusive club and some people thought this would work to the advantage of Sir Christopher Hatton, another close friend of longstanding and the only member of Elizabeth's inner circle who had stayed single for her sake. But although she never forgot old friends, the Queen had already found another Robert in Leicester's twenty-year-old stepson, Robert Devereux, second Earl of Essex. In many ways the choice was an obvious one. Nobly-born, brilliant and beautiful, Essex was plainly marked out to become a leader of the rising generation and, as such, one whom an ageing sovereign would be wise to keep under her eye and attached to her interest. Apart from that, Elizabeth was fond of the boy, who had undoubted claims on her favour. Fatherless from the age of nine (the first earl having died on royal service in Ireland), young Robert had been one of the Queen's wards and his mother, born Lettice Knollys, was the Queen's cousin.

Essex made his debut at Court when he was sixteen, under the sponsorship of his stepfather, and the following year he went with Leicester to the Netherlands to see something of the world and gain some martial experience. He did well in the fighting round Zutphen, where Philip Sidney received his deathwound, and Sidney, that beau ideal of Elizabethan youth, bequeathed his best sword to his 'beloved and much honoured Lord, the Earl of Essex'.

When Essex returned to England in December 1586, he had just passed his nineteenth birthday and the shy adolescent had developed into a mettlesome young blood, impatient to make a name for himself. He certainly made an immediate impact on the social scene for, as well as his striking good looks and impressive connexions, he was fortunate enough to be endowed with the gift of pleasing, 'a kind of urbanity or innate courtesy', which captivated the Queen and won him a popularity enjoyed by few other public figures of the time; the Londoners in particular taking him to their hearts and gazing with sentimental approval on this 'new adopted son' of royal grace.

Elizabeth was seldom given to sentiment and even more rarely visited by maternal yearnings, but she never lost her eye for an attractive man and Essex, with his engaging youthfulness, his cozening ways and eager devotion, offered a welcome addition to her court. Soon his tall, red-headed figure was seen everywhere at her side, and when her insomnia was troublesome she would keep him with her into the small hours, chatting or playing cards. He was, of course, still far too raw and inexperienced to be trusted with any serious responsibility, but he possessed breeding, courage and style, all attributes which the Queen looked for in her young men, and there seemed no reason to doubt that he would go far.

Even in these early days, though, Essex had his ups and downs, and in July 1587 he first betrayed a glimpse of the paranoid tendencies which would end by destroying him. During the course of her summer progress that year, the Queen paid a short visit to the Earl of Warwick, Leicester's elder brother, and Lady Warwick rather unwisely insisted on including Essex's sister Dorothy in her houseparty. Four years earlier Dorothy Devereux had made a runaway marriage in somewhat unsavoury circumstances to a man of considerably inferior rank and, as a result, had become *persona non grata* at Court.

The Warwicks were old and privileged friends, and kind Lady Warwick was no doubt counting on the Queen's fondness for Essex to smooth over any unpleasantness. But Elizabeth refused to meet Lady Dorothy and gave orders that she was to stay in her own rooms, a slight which Essex had no hesitation in blaming on the evil machinations of Walter Raleigh, whom he regarded as his most dangerous rival. After supper that evening he attacked the Queen for putting such a disgrace on his sister and himself 'only to please that knave Raleigh'. How could he give himself to the service of a mistress who stood in awe of such a man, he demanded, and proceeded to pour out a tirade of abuse against Raleigh – the scene gaining an added flavour from the fact that Sir Walter, in his capacity as Captain of the Guard, was on duty at the door and could hear everything that was said. The Queen was annoyed. She refused to listen to a word against Raleigh and the quarrel rapidly degenerated into a lively exchange of personalities, Elizabeth making some pungent comments on the manners and morals of her young friend's female relatives in general and his mother in particular. (She had reluctantly forgiven Leicester for marrying the widowed Countess of Essex, but she never forgave her cousin Lettice.)

Essex shouted that he would not endure to see his house disgraced and his sister should no longer remain to disquiet her Majesty. As for himself, he 'had no joy to be in any place', but nothing would induce him to stay where his affection was spurned for a wretch like Raleigh. Unimpressed, the Queen turned her back on him to resume her interrupted conversation with Lady Warwick and, though it was almost midnight by this time, Essex stormed away to rout his sister out of bed. Since some kind of grand gesture was now clearly called for, he made up his mind to return to the Netherlands and embrace a soldier's career. He would probably be killed and then people would be sorry! As it happened, of course, he got no further than the port of Sandwich before a royal messenger caught up with him and fetched him back – an eventuality he had doubtless been banking on.

In his own account of this rather foolish episode, Essex told a friend that he had been driven to act as he did by 'the extreme unkind dealing with me', a phrase which was to become his constant refrain, although, in fact, the Queen showed remarkable forbearance towards his tantrums. In November she finally yielded to the persuasions of the Earl of Leicester and bestowed his long-held and prestigious office of Master of the Horse on his stepson. The following year Essex was appointed cavalry commander of the army concentrated round Tilbury and created a Knight of the Garter – meteoric progress for a youth not yet twenty-one.

He continued to make his presence felt about the Court, where his obsessive jealousy of anyone who seemed to threaten his position as *jeune premier* led him to pick a quarrel with Charles Blount, another likely young man whose prowess in the tiltyard had attracted favourable notice. Essex got the worst of the duel fought in Marylebone Park and when the Queen heard of his discomfiture she snorted that, by God's death, it was high time someone took him down and taught him better manners or there would be no rule with him! One way and another, her red-haired protégé looked like becoming something of a problem child, but Elizabeth was not unduly perturbed. She liked a man to show some spirit and, in any case, she had more important matters on her mind just then.

After Lord Howard of Effingham finally abandoned his pursuit of the Spanish fleet off the Firth of Forth early in August, there had been a period of uncertainty, almost of anticlimax. Although it had been harassed in the Channel and badly mauled in the engagement off Gravelines, the Armada still represented a formidable fighting unit and for weeks Europe seethed with rumour and speculation. The Spaniards had put into a Scottish haven to refit and were only waiting for a favourable wind to return to the attack. There had been a great battle off the Scottish coast with at least fifteen English galleons sunk. The survivors had taken refuge in the Thames estuary and Drake (in European eyes Francis Drake *was* the English navy) had been wounded, killed, taken prisoner, had fled and vanished in the smoke. More level-headed and better-informed observers, notably the Venetians, were of the opinion that the Armada, driven northwards into hostile, dangerous waters and already seriously short of provisions and ammunition, would have been in no condition to fight any sort of battle. On the contrary, it would probably be as much as it could do to salvage the remains of the fleet by sailing home round Ireland and, as the reports which presently began to filter across the Irish Sea made plain, it had indeed been a desperate business of *sauve qui peut.*

The realisation that King Philip's long-heralded crusade against the heretical islanders had ended in total and humiliating failure may have taken some time to penetrate, but when it did finally sink in Queen Elizabeth's international prestige rocketed. The King of France, who had his own reasons for welcoming a Spanish defeat, did not hesitate to praise 'the valour, spirit and prudence' of the Queen of England, declaring that her recent achievement 'would compare with the greatest feats of the most illustrious men of past times'. Alone and unaided she had repulsed the attack of so puissant a force as Spain and triumphed over a fleet which had been the wonder of the world. The Venetian ambassador in Paris commented that the English had now proved they were the skilled mariners rumour reported them to be, for while they had always been on the enemy's flank they had not lost a single ship. The Queen, for her part, had kept her nerve throughout and had neglected nothing necessary for the occasion. 'Her acuteness in resolving on her action', continued Giovanni Mocenigo admiringly, 'her courage in carrying it out, show her high-spirited desire of glory, and her resolve to save her country and herself.' Even the Pope, who seldom missed an opportunity to annoy the King of Spain, lavished praises on the Queen. What a matchless woman she was! Were she only a Catholic she would be his best beloved. While as for Drake – what courage! What a great captain!

Now, of course, everyone was waiting to see what the Queen, and Francis Drake, would do next, for now, if ever, was surely the moment for a counter-attack – perhaps another of those brilliant smash-and-grab operations which had become synonymous with the name of El Draque. The Venetian ambassador in Spain, in a despatch datelined Madrid, 22 October, remarked that no small trouble would arise if Drake were to take to the sea and sail to meet the Peruvian fleet, or make a descent on the shores of Spain, where he would find no obstacle for his depredations. He might even destroy a part of those Armada ships which had managed to survive the dreadful journey home and were now lying scattered and helpless in various places along the coast, many of them quite unguarded and some in harbours which had no forts.

The idea of meeting the Peruvian fleet had already occurred to Elizabeth, and as early as the end of August she had summoned Drake to Court to discuss 'the desire that her majesty had for the intercepting of the king's treasure from the Indies'. In normal circumstances Drake would have required no encouragement to set off on a treasure hunt but, as he felt obliged to point out, after their hectic summer the Queen's ships were all in urgent need of refitting, and since the American silver fleet usually arrived round about the end of September there would scarcely be enough time to get a suitable force ready for sea. This was perfectly true. It was also true that Francis Drake, now standing at the peak of his remarkable career, had a rather more ambitious exploit in mind.

Ever since 1580, when the King of Spain had annexed the kingdom of Portugal, together with the wealth of its eastern empire and its first-rate ocean-going navy, the possibility of embarrassing him by supporting the rival claimant to the Portuguese throne had been explored by various people on more than one occasion. The dispossessed Dom Antonio, Prior of Crato and bastard nephew of the last native king of Portugal (or, as some unkind persons maintained, bastard son of a Lisbon merchant), had spent the greater part of his exile in England – a sad little man with a straggling beard who, like most exiles, painted an optimistic picture of the strength of his party at home and was lavish with promises to anyone who seemed even remotely interested in his cause. Drake, acutely conscious of the strategic importance of Lisbon, had always been interested in Dom Antonio's cause and in conference with the Queen he put forward a plan for a landing in Portugal based on the capture of Lisbon, whose population, if Dom Antonio was to be believed, would rise as one man to welcome its rightful king.

In his designs on the Portuguese mainland, Drake found a powerful ally in Sir John Norris, veteran of the war in the Netherlands and generally regarded as England's most distinguished professional soldier. Black John Norris and his comrades could see in the prospect of an expedition to Portugal those opportunities for profit and glory so conspicuously absent from the apparently endless slogging-match being fought over the dismal wastes of Flanders, Brabant and Zeeland, and they very naturally threw the whole weight of their influence behind it. The seizure of Lisbon would also open up the chances of putting into operation another plan long-cherished by the sailors, especially John Hawkins, for establishing a permanent presence in the Azores, those vital off-shore islands belonging to the Portuguese crown, which lay across the sea routes from both America and the East. Such a project had not been feasible while a Spanish navy commanded the whole western coastline of the Peninsula, but things were different now.

England's reply to the Armada – at least according to the scheme devised by her men of war and laid before the Queen and Council during the first fortnight of September 1588 – was thus to be a two-pronged assault on what might be described as the soft underbelly of the Spanish empire. The advantages of having a friendly government in Portugal hardly needed to be spelt out. Even if the expedition did no more than spark off a popular revolt – and there was some independent evidence to suggest that the Portuguese were growing increasingly restive under the heavy-handed rule of King Philip's viceroy – it should still be enough to force the King to divert men and materials from the Netherlands, that other scene of popular revolt against his rule, and with any luck keep him occupied at home for a considerable time to come. As for the other half of the proposed enterprise, the Venetian ambassador in Madrid told the Doge and Senate in December that 'those who understand declare that if Drake were to go now to the Azores, he would not only ruin the whole of the India traffic but could quite easily make himself master of those islands; especially as the garrison is said to be dissatisfied; and if the Azores were captured that would be the end of the Indies, for all ships have to touch there'. And if Philip could be cut off from the life-giving stream of silver flowing in from the mines of Central America, then he might indeed be rendered permanently harmless, the king of figs and oranges wistfully envisaged by Sir Walter Raleigh.

In theory, and as persuasively presented by Drake and Norris, it looked a good plan – just the sort of bold offensive stroke which the hawks around the Queen had been urging on her for years. It was certainly an audacious plan – rather too audacious perhaps for a small country with no standing army and little recent experience as a military power. It would also depend heavily on imponderables like the weather and the attitude of the Portuguese people. But the Queen could see as well as anyone that here was an opportunity which might never come her way again and she was ready to have a go – surprisingly ready in the context of the European situation as a whole. The trouble, of course, was money. It would cost a great deal of money to finance an undertaking on this scale and Elizabeth quite simply did not have the necessary cash at her disposal.

In the autumn of 1584 she had possessed reserves of 'chested treasure' amounting to three hundred thousand pounds, reserves prudently set aside for a rainy day while the going was good. But the cost of military aid for the Dutch rebels had, over the past three years, added up to nearly four hundred thousand pounds and the cost of defending England against the Armada had come to more than two hundred thousand. Since the ordinary revenues of the Crown, even when supplemented by Parliamentary grants, were nothing like enough to meet outgoings of this kind, the Queen had been obliged to draw heavily on her savings and by the autumn of 1588 they had dwindled to a mere fifty-five thousand pounds which, at current rates of expenditure, would barely see her through another six months. Nor was there any prospect of current rates of expenditure being reduced in the foreseeable future. True, it should now be possible to cut down on home defence, but the navy would soon be pressing for a new ship-building programme and the Queen dared not pull out of the Netherlands, where Philip's formidable lieutenant the Duke of Parma still commanded the army which had been intended for the invasion of England.

Everyone who knew anything about such matters knew that all the skill and courage of the English mariners, all the superior manoeuvrability and fire-power of their ships, might very easily have gone for nothing if, after the battle of Gravelines, the Armada had had the use of a deep-water port in which to refit and revictual; a port where it could have rendezvoused with Parma before carrying out its primary task of convoying his bargeloads of seasoned troops across the Channel. So long as Parma remained in Flanders it would continue to be vital to secure the mouth of the Scheldt estuary against any future armadas and that meant continued aid for the Calvinist Dutch of Holland and Zeeland. It also meant that the towns of Flushing and Brill, Ostend and Bergen-op-Zoom must remain in friendly hands whatever the cost.

There were other inescapable calls on the Queen of England's purse. Money was needed for Ireland and for Scotland, where it was important to keep King James in a good temper by paying his pension regularly. Moreover, events in France strongly suggested that Elizabeth might soon find herself having to subsidize her friends in that country as well. One way and another, she was beginning to be seriously worried about the financial situation and had started to explore the possibility of raising a foreign loan. No wonder she'd been so interested in ambushing Philip's treasure fleet – the quickest and most satisfactory form of foreign borrowing that could have been devised.

Drake and Norris quite understood the Queen's predicament and they had accordingly worked out an ingenious scheme by which rather more than two-thirds of the cost of the Portugal Expedition, as it came to be known, would be put up by private shareholders. If the Queen would contribute twenty thousand pounds and six of her 'second sort' of ships victualled for three months, plus a train of siege artillery for dealing with the defences of Lisbon, then Drake and Norris Incorporated undertook to raise forty thousand pounds and twenty or so armed merchant ships to make up the fleet. They further promised that if Elizabeth would appoint a treasurer and pay five thousand pounds into the kitty straight away, she would not be asked for another penny piece until the other 'adventurers' had given sureties for the whole of their forty thousand. The two commanders were to have the Queen's commission to recruit six thousand men for foreign service, while the remainder, two to three thousand in the original estimates, would be borrowed from the force of seven thousand more or less trained and experienced troops maintained by the Crown in the Netherlands under the terms of the Anglo-Dutch treaty of 1585. The Dutch would also be asked to provide transports, more siege guns and gunpowder.

The practice of waging war by join stock company may seem fantastic (and it did seem both fantastic and immoral to a whole generation of nineteenth century historians), but the logical Elizabethans could see nothing unreasonable in appealing to the business instincts of the Queen's wealthier subjects who, while they would have jibbed at paying higher taxes, could easily be persuaded to invest in a project which offered the chance of a handsome return. In any case, it was certainly the only method by which such an operation could have been financed in the time available.

It was not, of course, an ideal method – the most obvious snag being the fact that, when the two conflicted, commanders with their backers' interests to consider would naturally be more inclined to concentrate on taking prizes than on purely strategic objectives, and this was a snag which the Portugal Expedition encountered in its very early stages. The Queen and Council were still examining the small print of the prospectus when news began to come in from Spain that the battered survivors of the Armada, fifty or more capital ships, were limping home, not to Lisbon or the other western ports where the expedition could have finished them off at leisure, but to the nearest available refuges, Santander and San Sebastian deep in the Bay of Biscay. This was an unfortunate complication. It would be difficult and perhaps dangerous for Drake to have to take his fleet so far to leeward and then out again on the long windward beat to Cape Finisterre, but to Elizabeth the destruction of those ships was a matter of paramount importance and altered her whole concept of the enterprise.

The Queen has often in the past been accused of lacking any grasp of generalship, and of consistently impeding her gallant soldiers and sailors by her cheeseparing habits, her reluctance to take risks and her inability to make up her mind. This is an old canard, only recently beginning to be contradicted by modern scholarship, and one which arose, at least in part, from the fact that Elizabeth's war aims were always rather different from those of her gallant soldiers and sailors. Unlike Walter Raleigh and his fire-eating friends, the Queen had no particular desire to see Philip's great empire 'beaten in pieces', an eventuality likely to create as many problems as it solved. What she wanted – had always wanted – was to see the Netherlands restored to its old dominion status and given a measure of religious toleration, while remaining under the protection and sovereignty of Spain. She wanted an agreed share of trade with the New World for English merchants and, above all, relief from the constant burdensome dread of Spanish aggression. In short, she wanted a sensible, unexciting settlement of a foolish and wasteful quarrel.

Elizabeth may not have been a tactical expert, but she brought to the conduct of the war the same shrewd judgement and long experience of men and affairs which served her so well in other directions, and every instinct told her that the quickest way – probably, indeed, the only way – of forcing Philip to the negotiating table would be to destroy his naval strength once and for all. The King was a stubborn man and every report coming in from abroad spoke of his resolute determination to avenge his honour and go on serving God's cause. He meant to rebuild his shattered fleet – if necessary he would sell the very candlesticks on his dinner table – and return to the attack at the earliest possible moment. Those fifty odd ships in the Biscayan ports therefore represented both an invaluable asset and a unique opportunity. With all his resources, it had taken Philip the best part of seven years to assemble his first Armada. He'd lost half of it in the Enterprise of England and if the remaining half could be destroyed while it still lay immobilised, unrigged, unmanned, unarmed and defenceless, he might very well never be able to assemble another. For with no Spanish navy to interfere, it should be a comparatively simple matter not only to cut off the King's American revenues but also the supplies of grain and munitions, timber and cordage coming in from France, the Netherlands and the Baltic – at least until he was ready to see sense and start talking.

This is certainly how it looked to the Queen of England, and all the available evidence suggests that, if she had been in a position to call the tune, she would have scrapped the plan to restore Dom Antonio, which was bound to be a chancy business at best, and instead gone straight for the enemy's jugular vein. Unfortunately, though, the Queen was paying less than half the piper's wages and could hardly expect Drake and Norris to abandon their cherished Portuguese adventure altogether, but she did make it very clear that Lisbon was now to be regarded as no more than a sideshow. The expedition was to go first to the ports of Guipuzcoa, Galicia and Biscay and do their best endeavour either to take or destroy all the ships of any importance they found there. Only then might they go on to Lisbon and intercept the shipping in the Tagus, but they were not to attempt a landing unless they had real grounds for believing that Dom Antonio's supporters were as numerous 'and stand so well affected towards him as he pretendeth, and that there will be a party of the Portugal nation that will be ready to aid the king and join with his forces against the Spaniard'. Elizabeth was clearly worried that Drake was placing too much reliance on his protégé's optimistic assurances and might run himself and his fleet into a trap. If all went well at Lisbon, they might stay just long enough to see the new king settled in and then go on their other important task in the Azores; but, in her Instructions, the Queen again emphasised that 'before you attempt anything either in Portugal or the said Islands, our express pleasure and commandment is you shall first distress the ships of war in Guipuzcoa, Biscay and Galicia'.

The expedition had intended to sail in February 1589 – it was important that the troops drawn from the Netherlands should be back in time for the summer campaigning season and every month that passed gave Philip more time to repair and refit his ships of war – but a series of misunderstandings with the Dutch, always notoriously touchy and difficult to deal with, caused several weeks delay. Then the drafts from overseas were held up by freezing weather at the ports and after that the fleet itself was penned up in Plymouth Sound for a full month by persistent southwesterly winds, so that it was mid-April before they finally got away. By this time the Queen had been let in for considerably greater expense than she'd budgeted for (more than double the expense as it turned out), and the size of the expeditionary force had swollen to very nearly double the original estimate, which, of course, had played havoc with the logistical calculations.

The vast majority of these extra mouths so improvidently taken on the strength by Drake and Norris were 'gentlemen and divers companies of voluntary soldiers offering to be employed in this action' – among them being no less a person than the Earl of Essex, who had defied the Queen's prohibition and slipped away from Court to join Sir Roger Williams on board the *Swiftsure*. Like the rest of the volunteers, Essex was motivated by a mixture of enthusiasm, restlessness and greed, but in his case acute financial difficulties added an extra spur. 'If I should speed well, I will adventure to be rich', he wrote in one of the letters he left behind in his desk; 'if not, I will never live to see the end of my poverty.' This chance to recoup his fortunes and perhaps win some useful glory into the bargain had seemed too good to miss; but Elizabeth was furious and some historians, with a lack of perception only matched by their vulgarity of mind, have accused her of being more concerned with missing the company of her fancy man than over the shoddy provisioning of her army.

Such a flagrant disregard of her wishes by one so close to her was naturally hurtful – 'our great favours bestowed on you without deserts, hath drawn you thus to neglect and forget your duty; for other constructions we cannot make of these your strange actions' – but to a woman engaged in a lifelong struggle to stay on top in a world which took male superiority for granted, open insubordination of this kind had far more serious implications. In any case, for a nobleman of Essex's standing, who also held a responsible office in the Household, to go absent without leave and attempt to depart the realm without the sovereign's licence, was an insult to the Crown which no self-respecting monarch could have overlooked.

The Queen therefore fired a threatening salvo across the bows of her generals down in Plymouth. Sir Roger Williams was to be relieved of his command forthwith and placed under close arrest until her further pleasure was known, as they would answer for the contrary at their peril; 'for as we have authority to rule, so we look to be obeyed, and to have obedience directly and surely continued unto us'. If Essex had now come into their company, he was to be sent back to London at once, 'all dilatory excuse set apart'; and a posse headed by the truant's grandfather was despatched to the West Country. But this time Essex did not mean to be caught. Making the journey in a record thirty-six hours, he had gone straight to Falmouth where Roger Williams, a bloody-minded little Welshman generally believed to be the original of Shakespeare's Captain Fluellen, was waiting for him, and the *Swiftsure* promptly put to sea.

The fact that the second-in-command of the land forces of such an important undertaking apparently thought nothing of taking himself, his noble stowaway and one of the Queen's ships off on a private marauding expedition down the coast of Spain, only rejoining the main body at Lisbon when things looked like getting interesting, illustrates as clearly as anything can the extraordinary difficulty of imposing any sort of effective central control. Indeed, the whole history of the Portugal Expedition is an illustration of the government's inability to control the rugged individualism of its servants, for when the fleet did at last set sail it made not for San Sebastian or Santander, where forty Armada galleons were still slowly refitting, but for Corunna – or the Groyne as the English called it – Drake having got wind of a valuable prize in the vicinity. In fact, they found the harbour almost deserted. One warship and some half-dozen other assorted vessels were destroyed and the army stormed and sacked the lower town, spreading alarm and despondency in the surrounding countryside and seizing a large quantity of stores. (Any complaints about shortage of victuals after Corunna can only have been due to slackness and inefficiency on the part of the officers.) All this could, or should, have been accomplished in a couple of days but Norris and the sappers, for reasons best known to themselves, proceeded to waste a precious fortnight in a fruitless attempt to take the fortified upper town, while the rest of the army predictably got drunk on the local wine and went down with the local dysentery. Then, after the troops had finally been re-embarked on 8 May, the expedition set course straight for Lisbon.

The excuses subsequently offered for this piece of disobedience included unfavourable winds (always a useful one at sea) and lack of heavy guns to deal with shore batteries (the promised siege train never having materialised). But Elizabeth had already heard from William Knollys, who'd been with the fleet as far as Corunna, that there had been eight days fair wind for the Bay of Biscay prior to the descent on the Groyne and she was not impressed, remarking sourly that Drake and Norris 'went to places more for profit than for service'.

The Queen was, in fact, far from satisfied by the way things were going and she wrote to her commanders reminding them that: 'before your departure hence you did at sundry times so far forth promise as with oaths to assure us and some of our council that your first and principal action should be to take and distress the king of Spain's navy and ships in ports where they lay, which if ye did not, ye affirmed that ye were content to be reputed as traitors'. These were strong words, and Elizabeth ended by urging both men not to be 'transported with an haviour of vainglory which will obfuscate the eyes of your judgement'.

Whether it was vainglory or, more likely, the profit motive which obfuscated the judgement of Drake and Norris, there are strong reasons for assuming that they had always privately considered Lisbon as their main objective and, oaths regardless, had never intended to make more than a token gesture in the Biscayan area. After all, if they pulled off the more spectacular part of their mission, nobody was going to remember those semi-derelict galleons at Santander.

Nevertheless, when the expedition arrived off Cascaes at the mouth of the Tagus, it muffed its best and probably only real chance of success by a mixture of irresolution, faulty intelligence and plain ineptitude. The Spanish governor, having received ample warning of the English approach, had naturally used the time to take what precautions he could, but Cardinal Archduke Albert, with barely seven thousand troops, many of them unreliable Portuguese, under his command, might have found it hard to withstand a determined assault undertaken jointly by the fleet and the army, and bold action might also have encouraged the Portuguese to come out for Dom Antonio. Instead, it was decided to land the army at Peniche, nearly fifty miles north of Lisbon, presumably with the idea of carrying out a reconnaissance in France, while Drake took the fleet back to Cascaes, promising to meet Norris in the Tagus.

This loss of contact was to prove disastrous. The army encountered no opposition to speak of on its march down the coast but, apart from a handful of barefoot peasants and a gentleman bringing a basket of cherries, it gathered no support to speak of either. The heat, the aftermath of their excesses at Corunna and a virulent form of Portuguese tummy was playing havoc among the inexperienced amateur troops and by the time they reached the outskirts of Lisbon, Norris had only about six thousand men fit for duty. He had no artillery, such heavy guns as there were being still on the ships, there was obviously not going to be any internal revolt and, worst of all, Drake had not come upriver in support. No general could have risked an attack in such circumstances and on 29 May, despite Dom Antonio's pleas, Norris began to retreat to Cascaes. It was a grievous disappointment all round and nobody had made their fortunes. Plunder had been forbidden as long as there was any hope of the Portuguese playing their part, although, as one of those present observed wistfully, 'had we made enemies of the suburbs of Lisbon, we had been the richest army that ever went out of England'. According to John Norris's brother, Edward, the soldiers found a wonderful store of riches in merchandise, spices and victuals, 'but for lack of carriage they were forced to leave all behind them'.

It was at Cascaes at the beginning of June that the expedition had its first and only stroke of luck when Drake at last picked up the prize he'd been hoping to take at Corunna – sixty ships from the Baltic ports, some laden with grain and marine stores, and other in ballast, intended, so it was thought, to reinforce King Philip's 'decayed navy'. This was better than nothing, but it was nothing like enough, and after six largely wasted weeks the expedition still had to justify itself. On 5 June it was decided to abandon Lisbon. The prizes were sent home with the worst of the dysentery cases, and the Earl of Essex, having distinguished himself by a few flamboyant and perfectly useless gestures, such as wading ashore shoulder high through the waves at Peniche and offering his personal challenge to the gates of Lisbon, condescended to go with them. The fleet then set course for the Azores, but a strong southerly gale intervened and they never even sighted the Islands, let alone any treasure ships. Blown back on to the coast of Spain, Drake landed at Vigo and sacked the town, finding a great store of wine 'but not any thing else'. By now there were only about two thousand men in a fit state to fight; the ships, including the Queen's *Revenge*, were feeling the strain, and time was running out. Drake, with twenty of the best ships, made a last desperate effort to reach the Azores, but once again the weather turned nasty with southerly gales and storms. The great Portugal Expedition scattered before them and by the beginning of July the last stragglers had come trailing dejectedly and rather bad-temperedly back to Plymouth.

38

God's Handmaiden

All English hearts rejoyce and sing,
That feares the Lord and loves our Queene;
Yield thanks to God, our heavenly King,
Who hytherto her guide hath been.
With faithfull hartes, O God! we crave
Long life on earth her grace may have!

By no stretch of the imagination could the Portugal Expedition be regarded as a success. 'That miserable action' thought the rear-admiral, William Fenner, and John Norris was afraid that her Majesty would 'mislike the event of our journey', although, as he rather plaintively pointed out, 'if the enemy had done so much upon us, his party would have made bonfires in most parts of Christendom'. It was true that, if nothing else, the expedition had shown up the weakness of Spain's defences, demonstrating English ability to descend on the coast of the peninsula more or less as they pleased. Colonel Anthony Wingfield, hastening into print with his account of the Portugal Voyage, could boast that they had 'won a town by escalade, battered and assaulted another, overthrown a mighty prince's power in the field, landed our army in three several places of his kingdom, marched seven days in the heart of his country, lien three nights in the suburbs of his principal city, beaten his forces into the gates thereof, and possessed two of his frontier forts'.

According to the Venetian ambassador, the events of May and June 1589 had caused Philip great anxiety, 'not so much on account of the loss he suffers as for the insult which he feels that he has received in the fact that a woman, mistress of only half an island, with the help of a corsair and a common soldier, should have ventured on so arduous an enterprise, and dared to molest so powerful a sovereign'. But while the King undoubtedly smarted at this further humiliation – a complete black-out on news from Corunna and Lisbon was imposed in Madrid – the fact remained that little or no permanent damage had been done, and in August Tomasco Contarini could tell the Doge that a Spanish fleet of forty great and twenty smaller ships, although seriously undermanned, had left Santander for Corunna. In the same despatch he reported the safe arrival at the Azores of five ships of the India fleet, including one especially rich vessel from the

Moluccan Spice Islands, and towards the end of November word came from the Duke of Medina Sidonia that the American treasure ships, belated but unscathed, were anchored at Seville. A literally golden opportunity of bringing the war to an end had gone and was not likely to recur.

In the circumstances, the Queen of England kept her temper remarkably well. In public she was gracious, assuring Drake and Norris 'for both your comforts that we do most thankfully accept of your service and do acknowledge that there hath been as much performed by you as true valour and good conduction could yield'. Essex, needless to say, had already been forgiven. In spite of everything, Elizabeth found it very difficult to stay angry with him for long and even Roger Williams escaped further castigation – England possessed few enough experienced professionals in the military field. But while the Queen had too much common sense to indulge in useless recrimination, or to undermine the nation's confidence in its heroes, the expensive failure of the Portugal Expedition – especially its failure to go to Santander – continued to rankle and it was probably not entirely coincidental that Sir Francis Drake spent the next five years on the beach.

No more large-scale operations on the Spanish mainland were contemplated, at least for the time being. Instead, the English reverted to that element where they were most at home, the sea, and to the game they played so much better than anyone else. Before the war – or, more accurately, in the days when it was still possible and politic to pretend the war did not exist – the name of the game had been piracy, a matter for private enterprise surreptitiously abetted by the Crown. Now things were different. The sea-dogs had turned respectable and the Crown was asserting its right to confiscate the cargoes of neutral vessels trading with Spain. This was a new concept of war at sea and led to a flood of protests from such irritated neutrals at Denmark, Poland and Germany. But the Queen held firm. 'Her Majesty thinketh and knoweth . . . that whenever any doth directly help her enemy with succours of any victual, armour or any kind of munition to enable his ships to maintain themselves, she may lawfully intercept the same.'

The Channel blockade was, of course, an official matter, the concern of a naval squadron stationed in the Downs with instructions to stop and search any vessel whose master failed to produce a pass issued by the Lord Admiral. Out in the Atlantic, though, off the Azores and westward to the Spanish Main along King Philip's colonial trade routes there was still plenty of room for the individual privateer, and privateering was the growth industry of the eighties and nineties. Most of it, and most of the profits, passed into the hands of syndicates of hard-headed businessmen in London, Bristol and Plymouth dealing in prize cargoes of relatively prosaic commodities like hides and sugar, ginger and cochineal; but the age-old romantic lure of the treasure hunt, the unquenchable hope of one day seizing some great carrack stuffed with gold and jewels, silks, ivory and spices such as would make a man rich beyond his dreams, operated powerfully on all sorts and conditions of the Queen's subjects. Outstanding among them were men like Walter Raleigh and the Earl of Cumberland, both of whom financed and led their own expeditions, but nearly all the leading figures at Court put money into privateering ventures – even the sober Robert Cecil was not immune to the prevailing fever. Some people, notably the merchant bankers of the City of London, did very nicely out of privateering, which in a good year brought in prizes worth up to £300,000, and the seaport towns of the south and west prospered on the pickings; but many a likely lad ran off to sea to make his fortune only to die miserably far from home of typhus or scurvy or some other nastiness, and many an optimistic gentleman ruined himself and his family trying to get in on the act.

The Queen herself was often a shareholder in prize-hunting forays, more than once going into partnership with the Earl of Cumberland, and in 1590 a dozen royal ships, commanded by Martin Frobisher in the *Revenge* and John Hawkins in the *Mary Rose*, spent the summer in Spanish waters lying in wait for the American flota. Their presence created something of a panic, especially among the merchants of London and Seville; while from the colonial administrators in Puerto Rico and Havana, where privateers had already picked up a couple of silver ships, came anguished complaints that the English were daring them at their very doors. The English, reported a Dutch observer in the Azores, are become lords and masters of the sea and need care for no one. As it turned out, Frobisher and Hawkins enjoyed a negative success. They saw nothing of the treasure fleet for the simple reason that Philip had been driven to cancel that year's sailing, a confession of weakness which resulted in widespread failures among the Italian banking houses, a mutiny by Parma's unpaid troops in the Netherlands and still further delay in Spain's naval recovery.

Meanwhile, the focus of the land war was shifting. In July 1589 the last of the Valois kings was assassinated, an event which set alarm bells ringing in London. Henry III may never have been a conspicuous success either as a man or a monarch, but he had always somehow contrived to resist the pressures of the reactionary pro-Spanish elements around him and to preserve a tenuous link of friendship with Elizabeth. His death seemed likely to lead to a renewal of the civil wars which had ravaged France intermittently over the past forty years and, worse, to Spanish intervention; for the heir to the throne was the Huguenot leader, Henry of Navarre, and the prospect of a Protestant king would surely push the fanatics of the Catholic ultra party into extreme measures. The Catholic League was heavily subsidised by Spain and a Leaguer victory, with the consequent addition of France to Philip's clientage, was not something which the Queen of England could regard with equanimity. Henry of

Navarre, an experienced, hard-bitten warrior, could be relied on to fight for his rights, but unfortunately he was also stony broke. Without money from somewhere soon, he would be unable to continue the struggle for Paris and the north, where the League was strongest, and would probably be forced to withdraw south of the Loire, leaving the Channel coast and the Channel ports open to England's enemies.

So, when a special envoy from the new king appeared at Court in August with an urgent appeal for assistance, Elizabeth responded with uncharacteristic promptitude and on 7 September the sum of twenty thousand pounds in cash was handed over at the Lord Treasurer's house in Covent Garden. Henry could scarcely believe his eyes. When the Queen's gold reached him, he is reported, credibly enough, to have said that he'd never seen so much money in his life. It was nothing like enough, of course, and within a year the loan had trebled. In the autumn of 1589 a small expeditionary force under the command of Peregrine Bertie, Lord Willoughby, embarked at the port of Rye to spend three uncomfortable months campaigning with Henry's forces. Other contingents were to follow, and over the next five years Elizabeth spent getting on for four hundred thousand pounds altogether in aid to the King of France. In 1589, too, she'd had to find an extra six thousand for the King of Scotland to help him put down his Catholic rebels and set up house for his Protestant Danish bride.

Old Lord Burghley reflected the difficulty his generation sometimes experienced in adjusting to a situation which had transformed England's ancestral enemies into her most valued allies when he wrote to the Earl of Shrewsbury: 'My lord, the state of the world is marvellously changed, when we true Englishmen have cause for our own quietness to wish good success to a French king and a King of Scots.' Burghley, who seldom missed an opportunity to moralise, added, 'this is the work of God for our good, for which the Queen and us all, are most deeply bound to acknowledge his miraculous goodness, for no wit of man could otherwise have wrought it'.

For her part, the Queen may well have wished the Almighty could so have arranged matters that her friends were not invariably penniless. By 1590 the last of her peace-time savings had gone and already she was being driven to such distasteful expedients as extracting forced loans, or 'benevolences', from her wealthier subjects and selling off crown lands – £125,000 worth in 1590 alone. It was financial necessity which drove her to call another Parliament in the autumn of 1588. The session should have opened in November, but some sharp-eyed individual pointed out that the last instalment of the subsidy vote in 1587 was still being collected and to ask, as the government would have to do, for another grant of double the size before payment of the old was complete would scarcely be tactful. The assembly had therefore been postponed until February.

The Queen got her double subsidy. These were exceptional times – the House of Commons could see that – and, being a responsible, patriotic body of men, they had no wish to appear ungenerous. Only Henry Jackman, member for Calne in Wiltshire, seems to have spoken against the supply bill. In his view the danger of invasion, 'the principal and almost only persuader for the bill', was no longer imminent, 'the teeth and jaws of our mightiest and most malicious enemy having been so lately broken'. Higher taxation, on top of the recent burden imposed on the counties by home defence and having to contribute to the loan now being raised, would, he argued, breed discontent among the people and, worse, create a dangerous precedent 'both to ourselves and our posterity'.

The member for Calne may have gathered little open support, but he undoubtedly voiced the private misgivings of many of his colleagues, who clung to the old-fashioned belief that taxation should be no more than an occasional nuisance imposed to meet extraordinary expenditure in time of national emergency. The mediaeval habit of regarding government officials as the sovereign's personal servants and all the ordinary costs of government as the sovereign's personal responsibility died very hard; but in an increasingly complicated and expensive world, such pleasantly domesticated notions of public finance were becoming less and less realistic.

The Queen's income was derived principally from the revenues of the crown lands, supplemented by the monarchy's traditional perquisites of feudal and customs dues, by judicial fines and, since the Reformation, by ecclesiastical tribute which had formerly been diverted to Rome. Even when every source was squeezed dry it never amounted to more than £300,000 a year and, despite the famous Elizabethan parsimony, was becoming barely adequate for peacetime needs, let alone a continuing war situation. Elizabeth was close-fisted because she had to be, but there were economies she could not make. In an intensely status-conscious age, when a man's or an institution's potency was largely measured by his or its outward show, the Queen was obliged to maintain a suitably magnificent establishment or run the risk of being under-valued, and in an age of personal monarchy the Crown inevitably represented the fountain-head of all patronage. Ambitious men looking for jobs, impecunious peers hoping for hand-outs (the Queen wasn't the only one with appearances to keep up), businessmen on the make, social climbers impatient for honours, everyone with an axe to grind, a career to advance or a favour to seek gravitated towards the Court, and they could not all be disappointed. Everyone naturally expected to pay for a word in the right ear, and palace functionaries living on subsistence wages grew fat on the never-ending queues of petitioners who haunted the corridors and anterooms of power.

Of course it was a bad and a ramshackle system, wide open to every kind of abuse and cause of much of the corruption which spread like a cancer through the body politic. But although the Queen complained bitterly and often that she was surrounded by beggars and although the problem of making ends meet grew steadily more acute, she was as much a prisoner of the system as any of her subjects. As much as any member of the House of Commons she recoiled from the idea of increased taxation, and this was not just because taxation was unpopular. The more the Crown had to depend on Parliament for money, the more insistently that body would demand a say in matters which the Queen regarded as being none of their business and the harder it would be to maintain discipline. Elizabeth had in the past fought and won several pitched battles with the Commons in defence of her prerogative, but that was before the financial situation had become so threatening.

In 1589 the Commons came up with two private members' bills designed to redress various long-standing grievances against the malpractices of the royal purveyors and officials of the Court of Exchequer, but the Queen rejected them both. If the purveyors, officers of her own household, and the officers of her own court of her own revenues had been acting unlawfully, then 'her Majesty was of herself both able and willing to see due reformation' and would do so without assistance from anybody. Least of all, she indicated crossly, did she require assistance from those busy young gentlemen in the Commons who appeared to suffer from an uncontrollable itch to meddle in her private affairs.

The Commons of 1589 was a somewhat less obstreperous assemblage than some of its predecessors, but it was not to be put off with a mere royal scolding. A committee was set up and recommended that in 'humble and dutiful wise' this House should 'exhibit unto her Majesty the causes and reasons' which moved them to proceed with the two disputed bills. Such a course, it was felt, would best stand with the liberties and honour of the Commons, and the Speaker was instructed to make 'most humble petition and suit . . . that her Majesty would vouchsafe her most gracious favour' in the matter. Elizabeth agreed to receive a small deputation and, so the Speaker presently reported to the House, received it with 'most comfortable and gracious speeches . . . of her Highness's great and inestimable loving care towards her loving subjects; yea, more than of her own self, or than any of them have of themselves'.

All this, of course, was part of the recognised ritual of communication between Queen and Parliament played out in public, while the serious business of negotiation went on behind the scenes. The result of this particular bout was made known on 17 March, when the Speaker announced her Majesty's pleasure that four members of the Commons should be appointed to confer with a committee of Privy Councillors and Household officials over the drawing up of a new set of regulations to govern the purveyors in the discharge of their thankless task of provisioning the Court. A similar procedure seems to have been adopted with regard to the Court of Exchequer, with four MPs being invited to join a royal commission of enquiry in a consultative capacity. It was a typical Elizabethan compromise, which safeguarded the Queen's prerogative while, at the same time, allowing Parliament some outlet for its reforming zeal and giving the Commons at least an illusion of participation. Compromise in matters of this kind was, in fact, becoming increasingly necessary if the Tudor constitution was to have any chance of survival in a society rapidly outgrowing its paternalistic confines.

But in spite of the trouble it sometimes gave her, Elizabeth never really doubted her ability to manage the House of Commons. Infinitely more dangerous, in her opinion, were those who sought to use the Commons as an instrument in their campaign to undermine the authority of the Crown in the name of religious reform. When the Elizabethan Religious Settlement, as embodied in the Act of Uniformity of 1559, was first reached, there had been an influential body of opinion, both inside and outside Parliament, which would have liked to see a more radical, that is a more Protestant, church in England, more closely modelled on John Calvin's Genevan empire. On the other hand, the Queen, to whom all forms of Calvinism were anathema, would have preferred a settlement nearer the idiosyncratic form of Anglo-Catholicism evolved by her father and in which she herself had been brought up. In 1559 it had been necessary to make some concessions to radical sensibilities, but the Act of Uniformity marked the absolute limit to which Elizabeth was prepared to go and as presently became clear, this was one of the issues over which she was emphatically not prepared to compromise.

Despite their sovereign lady's disappointing lack of godly zeal, the radical or Puritan party never gave up hope of securing further reform and purging the Church of England of the last remaining vestiges of Romish idolatry, of such symbols and practices as the wearing of surplices, the use of the ring in marriage and the sign of the cross at baptism, the churching of women and kneeling at communion. Although never more than a minority, they were nevertheless a formidable minority, utterly committed to the righteousness of their cause and able to count on powerful support in high places – Francis Walsingham, Francis Knollys, the Earl of Leicester and Lord Burghley were all known to sympathise with some at least of their aims.

During the seventies and early eighties Puritan strength and organisation grew steadily within the Church itself, leading to the formation of the so-called Classical movement with groups of progressive clergy meeting together in private in *classes* and synods for prayer, for self-examination under the stimulus of brotherly censure, for exposition of the Scriptures and the discussion of problems of common interest. This may sound harmless enough, and the objectives of many of those attending such gatherings were unexceptionable in themselves: the remedying of certain all too obvious abuses in the administration of the Anglican

Church, the attainment of a higher standard of morals and education in the ministry, and a striving after greater 'purity' in religion generally. But the leaders of the movement, men like John Field and Thomas Cartwright, were planning a revolution. Adepts at the revolutionary arts of propaganda, of exploiting legitimate grievances and of infiltration, they were, in short, attempting to set up a 'shadow' church, 'the embryo of the Presbyterian Discipline lying as yet in the wombe of Episcopacy', intended to penetrate the established order from within and, in due course, quietly to take it over.

Under the 'Presbyterian Discipline' each individual church would be governed by a consistory of ministers and lay elders, whose duties included the supervision of the rank and file by means of domiciliary visits. Then came the *classis*, meeting every six weeks or so and composed of the ministers and elders from twelve neighbouring parishes. Above the *classis* was the provincial synod, representing twelve *classes* and meeting twice a year and finally, at the apex of the pyramid the national synod. Experience of non-conformist sects abroad, notably the Huguenots in France, had proved this to be an extremely effective method of organising a subversive minority, capable of imposing strict control over its own members and of exerting pressure out of all proportion to its actual strength.

The greatest threat to the episcopal church and, by implication, to the State itself, lay in the fact that English Puritanism – unlike English Catholicism of the same period – was essentially a grass-roots movement and its leaders were able to appear as sincere, dedicated and highminded patriots. Indeed they *were* burningly sincere, dedicated and high-minded patriots – that was just what made them so dangerous; that and their skilful exploitation of those external circumstances working in their favour. Many moderate Anglicans, uneasily aware of corruption and 'worldliness' within the Church, were eager to see some measure of reform. Many loyal and muddle-headed Englishmen saw the left-wing preacher thundering from his pulpit as a diligent watch-dog barking against the Popish wolf and therefore worthy of encouragement.

The Queen, with her infallible instinct for such matters, saw deeper. Elizabeth detested doctrinaire zealots of any complexion, but while she could often sympathise with the predicament of her Catholic subjects, torn as they were between allegiance to their sovereign and their faith, she had no sympathy whatever with Puritanism. She realised, even if no one else did, that the logical end of the system advocated by the radical party would be a theocracy, leading to intolerable innovation and unspeakable tyranny. It would inevitably mean the end of royal supremacy as established by her father and would result in the subjection of the monarchy to a parcel of insolent, Bible punching upstarts, all claiming a direct line to the Almighty and licensed to pry into the private affairs of their betters. Elizabeth's autocratic Tudor soul revolted at the very idea; nor had she forgotten Calvin's teaching that subjects had a positive duty to overthrow and spit upon an ungodly prince. Jerusalem, or Geneva, she indicated flatly would be built in England over her dead body and throughout her reign she fought tenaciously to keep the stealthy encroachment of Puritanism at bay.

It was frequently an uphill struggle – many people, including members of her own Privy Council, wondering audibly why the Queen should be so hard on loyal followers of God's Word at a time when the papist beast was ravening at her door. Surely such doughty opponents of the common enemy might be forgiven a little harmless non-conformity? Unimpressed, Elizabeth demanded the suppression of all unauthorised prayer meetings and nagged the bishops to be on their guard, but it was not until 1583 that she acquired a really trustworthy lieutenant. John Whitgift, the new Archbishop of Canterbury, was a man after the Queen's own heart – a tough disciplinarian who finally shared her views on left-wing clergy and set about the business of rooting them out with more enthusiasm than tact.

The fury roused by the Archbishop's activities offered disconcerting proof of the strength and efficient organisation of the radical movement. *Classes* met excitedly behind locked doors to discuss tactics and the Privy Council was deluged with petitions and complaints. The Archbishop himself became the target of a concerted and bitter attack – tyrant, pope and knave were only some of the epithets flung at him – and even Lord Burghley felt bound to reproach him for proceedings which savoured of 'the Romish Inquisition'. Whitgift, a dour, obstinate individual, as convinced of the righteousness of his cause as any Puritan, had a scornfully dismissive way with criticism which alienated moderate as well as extreme opinion, and England was not to have a more generally hated ecclesiastic until the primacy of the unhappy Laud. Only a generation separated them – William Laud was a boy of ten when John Whitgift was enthroned at Canterbury – but Whitgift was the more fortunate, both in his generation and his patron. The Queen made it clear that she backed her Archbishop's hard-line policy absolutely and, to ram the point home, she admitted him to the Privy Council. He was, significantly, the first and only Elizabethan cleric to be so honoured.

But while Whitgift continued to pursue the Puritans through the Church courts, the real battle was fought out in the House of Commons, where the radical element had always been strongly represented. The Parliament of 1584 met in an atmosphere of rabid anti-Catholicism. Recent events such as the assassination of William of Orange, the discovery of the Throckmorton Plot and the continuing infiltration of the dreaded Jesuit missionaries had all helped to raise Protestant temperatures to sizzling point, and the stage could surely not have been better set for a left-wing assault. As a preliminary step, the Puritans did what they could to ensure the return of 'godly' members to the Nether House, and the conference or *classis* of Dedham in Essex urged that 'some of best credit and most forward for the Gospel' in every county should go up to London to further 'the cause of the Church'. This idea was evidently taken up, for it was noticed that groups of earnest furtherers of the Gospel 'were all day at the door of Parliament and some part of the night in the chambers of Parliament-men, effectually soliciting their business with them'. But no business, however effectually solicited, was going to get very far in the face of the Queen's implacable opposition to any Parliamentary interference in the government of the Church, and her implacable hostility towards the Puritan faction.

At the end of February 1585 she told a select gathering of councillors and bishops about private information received from abroad 'that the Papists were of hope to prevail again in England, for that her Protestants themselves misliked her. "And indeed, so they do", quoth she, "for I have heard that some of them of late have said that I was of no religion – neither hot nor cold, but such a one as one day would give God the vomit."' Papists and Puritans were united in one opinion at least, Elizabeth declared, 'for neither of them would have me to be Queen of England'; but, she added bitterly, there was an Italian proverb which said: 'From mine enemy let me defend myself; from a pretensed friend, good Lord deliver me.'

A few days after this outburst the Speaker was summoned abruptly to Greenwich and ordered to inform the Commons that there was to be no more meddling with Church affairs, 'neither in reformation of religion or of discipline', no tampering with the Prayer Book and no more disrespectful attacks on the bishops. The Queen, let no one forget it, was, next under God of course, Supreme Governor of the Church with full power and authority to reform any disorder in the same. She hoped no one doubted that as she had the power, so she had the goodwill 'to examine and redress whatsoever may be found amiss'. But 'resolutely she will receive no motion of innovation, nor alter or change any law whereby the religion or church of England standeth established at this day'. She had maintained the Church of England for twenty-seven years. She meant in like state, by God's grace, to continue it and leave it behind her.

This was plain speaking beyond any possibility of mistake and the Commons, who had been happily occupied in drawing up a shopping-list of reforms designed both to make a Church safe for Puritans and clip the wings of proud prelates like Dr Whitgift, 'found themselves so greatly moved and so deeply wounded as they could not devise which way to cure themselves again'. It seemed that either they must come into direct collision with their gracious sovereign – a course still unthinkable to many – or else 'suffer the liberties of their House to be infringed'. Again there was much discussion of tactics carried on 'in private sort', in the houses of left-wing sympathisers, in the upper rooms of taverns and quiet corners of the Palace of Westminster itself.

Several bright ideas emerged from these conclaves. Those in favour of confrontation pressed for the dismissal of the Speaker, 'for that he durst enterprise to go to the Queen without the privity of the House'; while others wanted one of their number to stand up and publicly 'refuse' her Majesty's commandment. More prudent spirits 'wished rather that some way might be wrought underhand that should as forcibly restore the liberty of the House as any violent action openly used'. In the end, old habits of deference to the sovereign and, indeed, of affection and respect, overcame the stirrings of revolution and it was agreed to make a gesture rather than a stand. A bill was therefore introduced for 'the better execution' of a statute dating from the thirteenth year of the reign which regulated admission to the ministry. As this concerned religion (and contained a controversial clause providing for the trial of a would-be pastor's suitability by a panel of twelve laymen) it was certainly defying the royal prohibition; but it could also have been argued that the Commons were only seeking to strengthen an existing law. In the event, the Queen, having successfully frustrated the main attack, wisely turned a blind eye, and the bill was quietly killed off in the Lords.

Another battle had been won, but Elizabeth was undoubtedly worried and upset by the Puritan agitation and in her speech at the end of the session she returned to the subject of religion, 'the ground on which all other matters ought to take root'. 'I am supposed to have many studies', she told the assembled Lords and Commons, 'but most philosophical. I must yield this to be true: that I suppose few, that be no professors, have read more.' Yet in her library God's book was not the most seldom read and anyone who doubted the sincerity of her faith did her too much wrong. 'For, if I were not persuaded that mine were the true way of God's will, God forbid I should live to prescribe it to you.' She saw many overbold with God Almighty, making too many subtle scannings of His blessed will, as lawyers did with human testaments. The presumption was so great that she could not suffer it. She would neither encourage Romanists ('what adversaries they be to mine estate is sufficiently known') nor tolerate new-fangledness, but do her best to guide both by God's holy true rule.

So far, in spite of everything, the Puritans had achieved little or nothing – except perhaps to draw attention to themselves – but they had no intention of abandoning the struggle. In the year and a half which elapsed before the next parliamentary session, the party machine was hard at work completing a major survey intended to provide supporting evidence for their complaints about the deplorable state of the clergy. This, it was hoped, would shock moderate public opinion and win support for the cause from conscientious laymen everywhere, but especially from those influential 'gentlemen of worship' in the shires and counties who had livings in their gift. The survey gleefully identified parish priests who were 'suspected of whoredome' and others 'scarce able to read', one who was an idle ruffian, another 'taken in adultery' and yet another who was 'a common gamester and pot-companion'.

These judgements were not notable for their Christian charity, but there's no doubt that standards generally were pretty low. Many parishes, especially the smaller rural ones, were too poor to attract able men and, in any case, there were not enough able men to go round. The shortage of educated, preaching clergy did not worry the Queen unduly. There was nothing like a little learning for giving a parson ideas above his station, and she was well aware that the most eloquent and persuasive preachers were most liable to be ardent Puritans. To her way of thinking, it was quite enough for the parish priest to be an honest man, capable of administering the sacraments as laid down in the Prayer Book and of reading homilies to the people. On the other hand, scandals in the ministry were obviously undesirable. They damaged the Church, making it vulnerable to attack from both left and right, and the bishops were therefore sharply admonished by their Supreme Governor to look well to their charges or face dismissal.

The hard-pressed Dr Whitgift and his bishops did their best. Articles passed by Convocation in 1585 laid down stricter rules about the qualifications to be required from candidates for ordination, and a genuine effort was being made to crack down on the more glaring instances of laxity and corruption. But the root-and-branch radicals – like root-and-branch radicals of every age – were not interested in moderate reform, except, of course, for propaganda purposes. What they wanted was a clean sweep – the abolition of 'the titles and names of Antichrist – as Lord's Grace, Lord Bishop, Dean, Archdeacon'. 'Let cathedral churches be utterly destroyed' urged one trigger-happy member of the brotherhood, for they were 'very dens of thieves, where the time and place of God's service, preaching and prayer is most filthily abused: in piping with organs; in singing, ringing and trolling of the Psalms . . . with squeaking of chanting choristers.' If these sinks of iniquity, together with all the lazy, loitering lubbards, dumb dogs, destroying drones and unskilful, sacrificing priests who frequented them, were done away with, then their revenues could be used for the maintenance of a learned ministry.

When Parliament met again in November 1586 the godly brethren, stimulated by the prospect of wholesale iconoclasm, girded their loins and once more descended on the capital. The first weeks of the session were, however, monopolised by the momentous business of winding up the earthly affairs of Mary Queen of Scots, and the reformers were obliged to wait until nearly the end of February 1587 before launching a fresh assault. Then, despite a warning that the Commons were especially commanded by her Majesty to take heed 'that none care be given or time afforded the wearisome solicitation of those that commonly be called Puritans, wherewithal the late Parliaments have been exceedingly importuned', Anthony Cope, one of the Puritan members, rose to move the reading of a 'Bill and a Book'.

The Speaker, guessing something of what was coming, tried vainly to intervene, but the organised left wing was ready to talk down any opposition. Several members spoke in favour of Cope's motion, among them Job Throckmorton – a red-hot radical and not to be confused with the Throckmorton of the Catholic plot. In a brilliant piece of special pleading he argued that the surest way for the safety, long life and prosperity of the Queen's majesty – chief cause of all their consultations – was 'to begin at the house of God and to prefer the reformation of Jerusalem before all the fleeting felicities of this mortal life', and went on to protest against the use of 'puritanism' as an opprobrious epithet. 'To bewail the distresses of God's children, it is puritanism. To reprove a man for swearing, it is puritanism. To banish an adulterer out of the house, it is puritanism. To make humble suit to her Majesty and the High Court of Parliament for a learned ministry, it is puritanism . . . I fear me we shall come shortly to this, that to do God and her Majesty good service shall be counted puritanism.'

Throckmorton and his friends carried the day, but godly zeal and brevity seldom go together and the Commons rose very late, agreeing to read Mr Cope's bill in the morning. They should have known better. Elizabeth, still suffering from the violent emotional reaction caused by the Queen of Scots' execution and in a mood to be exasperated by this latest manifestation of Puritan arrogance, acted overnight, ordering the Bill and the Book to be sent to her at Greenwich. Neither was calculated to reassure. The bill, after a long preamble, contained two clauses, one authorising the use of the Book which was, of course, a version of the Genevan Prayer Book incorporating a Presbyterian form of discipline. The second would, in effect, have abolished the Anglican Church, declaring all existing laws, customs, statutes, ordinances and constitutions concerning it to be 'utterly void and of none effect'!

While the Commons waited for the inevitable thunderclaps of royal wrath they continued defiantly to debate the state of the Church, and Peter Wentworth, another leading radical, delivered himself of a resounding series of demands for freedom of Parliamentary speech and action – demands which, if conceded, would have speedily hamstrung the monarchy and put an end to the ancient system of government by the sovereign in council. In the words of Professor Neale, greatest modern authority on the Elizabethan era, 'through the plottings of the godly brotherhood and their organised group of Parliamentary agents, Queen Elizabeth was menaced with revolution in Church and State'.

Queen Elizabeth, as might be expected, reacted vigorously. She knew all about the organised lobbying of members of Parliament and the semi-secret conferences being held by the Puritan members and their supporters. Extra-mural activities of this kind were not protected by privilege; they were, in fact, not far removed from conspiracy, and Wentworth, Cope and three others were arrested and committed to the Tower. At the same time, the government launched a counter-attack spear-headed by Sir Christopher Hatton. The Queen, he announced, had suppressed the Bill and the Book and there was to be no more argument about it but, in her 'concern for their contentment', she was prepared to tell the Commons why. Hatton then went on to spell out just what the consequences of extremist action would be. Did the House, he enquired, really want to alter the whole form and order of the familiar church service? Did it really want to do away with the Book of Common Prayer, which a whole generation of Englishmen had been brought up to think 'both good and godly'? In the Calvinist version, with its overwhelming emphasis on the sermon and extempore prayer, 'all or the most part is left to the minister's spirit' and the unlettered would be deprived of the comfort of well-known and loved incantations.

Turning from the spiritual to the material, Hatton wanted to know how the new order was to be financed. Every parish, he reminded his audience, even the poorest, would have to support at least one pastor and two deacons, 'besides I know not how many elders'. Leaving aside the question of where all these wise and godly men were to be found, they would certainly have to be paid for. The bishops and the cathedral churches might be despoiled, but that would not be enough. Sooner rather than later the surrender of the abbey lands and other church possessions filched at the Reformation, and on which so many family fortunes had been founded, would be demanded by the presbyteries. And what of the Queen? Her royal supremacy would be 'wholly abrogated by this Bill and Book' and without first fruits, tenths and clerical subsidies her revenues would be seriously depleted. The Crown was still bound to defend the realm, so how was the deficiency to be made up if not out of taxpayers' pockets? Worse than this, the Queen would be made subject to censure and even excommunication by the pastors, doctors and elders.

Hatton was followed by Sir Walter Mildmay, himself known to have Puritan sympathies, and Thomas Egerton, the Solicitor General, who between them completed the work of demolition, of isolating and exposing the extremist minority as 'men of small judgement and experience'. Remorselessly they listed the Acts of Parliament, including those aimed at the Catholic recusants, which would disappear, and pointed to the legal confusion which would result from the dismantling of the Church courts. What, for example, would happen to wills and testaments, to contracts of marriage and questions of bastardy and inheritance?

The House of Commons might tend towards radicalism in its religious opinions and thus be liable to become carried away by Puritan eloquence, but the knights and burgesses, the lawyers and landowners and businessmen who made up its solid, conservative, self-interested bulk were nobody's fools. Elizabeth had reckoned that if they could once be shocked into realising how their loyalty, their patriotism and their genuine concern for the Protestant faith were being exploited by the irresponsible few, they would draw back – and she was quite right. There was some grumbling in the ranks, some talk of petitioning the Queen to release the imprisoned members, some threats of a sit-down strike, but at the same time it was clear that the crisis was over, that the militant left wing had been defeated by a shrewdly calculated mixture of coercion and reasoned argument. The five members remained in gaol until the end of the session, and it was a sobered assembly which finally dispersed on 23 March.

The Puritan or Presbyterian movement had not been destroyed – surreptitious mini-Genevas continued to flourish in the Midlands, East Anglia and the London area – but after 1587 it lost its power base in Parliament, something it was not to regain in the Queen's lifetime. The movement suffered other set-backs in the last years of the eighties. The death of John Field, its brilliant organising secretary, in March 1588 was a serious loss and, as no other leader of comparable ability came forward to take his place, the cohesion and unity of purpose which had made the left wing so formidable earlier in the decade began to break down. Disappointment and frustration, too, betrayed some members of the fraternity into a grave error of judgement.

Puritans as well as Catholics had always made use of the secret printing press in their propaganda campaigns and in the autumn of 1588 the first of the Martin Marprelate tracts appeared on the streets. These remarkable productions – there were seven of them altogether – caused a sensation. Written in a vein of broad, sarcastic humour they lampooned the unfortunate bishops, both individually and collectively. They were irreverent, witty and clever and good for a cheap laugh – everybody was reading them and sniggering over them – but in the long run they were a mistake. Serious minded people were alienated by their levity and they went a long way towards disenchanting the more moderate Puritans, especially those in high places. 'As they shoot at bishops now', remarked the Earl of Hertford, 'so they will do at the nobility also, if they be suffered'; and Lord Burghley noted that 'care is to be taken to suppress all the turbulent Precisians who do violently seek to change the external government of the Church'.

The authorities were doing their utmost to suppress Martin Marprelate and in the summer of 1589 an accident to the cart transporting the secret press from Warrington to Manchester led to its capture. Several arrests were made and, although Martin's identity was never established, a lot of useful information had come into the government's hands during the course of its enquiries. As a result, by 1590 the Presbyterian underground was in disarray and its leaders in custody.

1590 was also a satisfactory year from the Queen's point of view in that it marked a welcome lull in foreign hostilities. Henry IV's victory over the Catholic League at Ivry in March had won him a temporary respite and no English troops were required to fight in France. The two sovereigns, however, kept in close touch. Elizabeth wrote regularly to her 'dearest brother' – in spite of what he was costing her, the King of France was a friend worth having – and the French ambassador received some distinguishing marks of royal attention. In August he was invited to Oatlands for a few days hunting and the Queen herself killed a deer for him, and in November a new envoy, the Vicomte de Turenne, was guest of honour at the Accession Day tilt.

In typically English fashion the custom of observing 17 November, the anniversary of the Queen's accession, as a public holiday seems to have originated out of a chance incident, possibly at Oxford in 1570. It may well have started even earlier. No one really seems to know for certain. What is certain is that by the fifteen-eighties Queen's Day had become a major national festival, and after 1588 the celebrations spread over to 19 November which happened to be St Elizabeth's Day. Up and down the country the occasion was marked by bonfires and feasting, by pageants and shows and pealing bells and, of course, sermons. It made a pleasant and harmless substitute for all the feast and saints' days which had disappeared from the calendar with the Roman Church – a day when the good Protestant people of England could joyfully triumph for purely Protestant reasons. 'The sacred seventeenth day' had, in fact, been gradually built up into a day of official rejoicing and thanksgiving, an annual opportunity for reminding the lieges of the manifold blessings they enjoyed under the beneficent rule of their gracious Queen: the pious and virtuous maiden who had delivered them from the tyranny and cruelty of the Bishop of Rome; the wise and merciful princess who had brought them peace at home, freedom and true religion.

The noblest Queen
That ever was seen
In England doth reign this day.
Now let us pray.
And keep holy-day
The seventeenth day November;
For joy of her Grace,
In every place,
Let us great praise render.

In the more unsophisticated provinces, the emphasis was on the Queen in her role of God's handmaiden, the scriptural heroine, the English Judith and Deborah and, although this could scarcely be admitted, a surrogate Virgin Mary. At Court, where the festivities centred around the Accession Day tournament, the cult took on a heavily romantic, neo-classical, neo-mediaeval bias with Elizabeth cast as Astraea, virgin goddess of justice, as Cynthia 'the Ladie of the Sea', as Diana, Belphoebe and Gloriana, the Faerie Queene – a semi-divine object of courtly love before whom the knights, drawn mainly from the ranks of the Gentlemen Pensioners and the younger nobility, came to render homage and devotion.

The tournament normally took place in the tiltyard at Whitehall, roughly the area occupied today by Horse Guards Parade, and the knights made their entrances in a variety of elaborate and expensive disguises. Some arrived riding in chariots drawn by strange beasts, by men, or apparently self-propelled, and from which they would vault in full armour on their chargers. Others, less confident of their horsemanship, entered already mounted. There were Black Knights, Wandering Knights, a Blind Knight from the Americas whose sight miraculously returned in the Queen's presence, Melancholy Knights, Unknown Knights, even Clownish Knights, all attended by retinues of servants, squires and lance-bearers suitably got up as wild men, or Indian princes, or sailors or shepherds according to the chosen theme. Each carried a shield on which his *impresa*, or device, was depicted and the more loaded with symbolism and allusion the more successful it was considered.

Often the allusion was topical. In 1590 the Earl of Essex appeared 'all in sable sad' and escorted by a funeral cortege. This was a reference to his recent disgrace with the Queen, for the previous April Essex had married Frances, daughter of Francis Walsingham and widow of Sir Philip Sidney. Apart from her well-known dislike of seeing any member of her court get married, Elizabeth had been particularly annoyed on this occasion because the wedding had taken place without her knowledge and because she considered the alliance an unworthy one – Essex was, after all, rather a special case. However, since the Earl was wise enough not to parade his bride, being pleased 'for her Majesty's better satisfaction' that she should live very retired in her mother's house, and since young Lady Essex showed no sign of wishing to put herself forward, the storm had blown over quite quickly. Essex was now noticed to be 'in good favour' again, and on 19 November he and the Earl of Cumberland and Lord Burgh 'did challenge all comers, six courses apiece, which was very honourably performed'.

Although jousting or tilting – two armoured knights charging one another at full gallop on either side of a parallel barrier with the object of shattering the opponent's lance – was no longer quite the rugged and realistic combat exercise it had once been, it still required enough athleticism and speed of reaction to make it primarily a young man's sport, and the 1590 tilt was marked by the retirement of the Queen's Champion. Sir Henry Lee had stage-managed the Accession Day tilts for the past ten years and had been largely responsible for making them into an entertainment worthy of Gloriana and her Court, but now at fifty-seven he felt the time had come to make way for a successor. The retiring Champion made his entry

> *. . . in rich embroidery*
> *And costly caparisons charged with crowns*
> *O'ershadowed with a withered running vine*

and when the tilting was over presented a charming tableau before the Queen: 'a Pavilion, made of white Taffeta, being in proportion like unto the sacred Temple of the Virgins Vestal' and seeming to consist upon pillars of porphyry, 'arched like unto a Church'. Inside this confection of the scene-painter's art were many lamps burning and an altar covered with cloth of gold on which had been laid out a selection of expensive gifts, 'which after by three Virgins were presented unto her Majesty'. The offering was accompanied by sweet music and the lutenist Robert Hales sang Dowland's setting of 'His golden locks time hath to silver turn'd'.

> *His helmet now shall make a hive for bees,*
> *And, lovers' sonnets turn'd to holy psalms,*
> *A man at arms must now serve on his knees,*
> *And feed on prayers, which are age his alms.*
> *But though from court to cottage he depart,*
> *His saint is sure of his unspotted heart.*
> *And when he saddest sits in homely cell,*
> *He'll teach his swains this carol for a song.*
> Blest be the hearts that wish my sovereign well,
> Curst be the souls that think her any wrong.
> *Goddess, allow this aged man his right,*
> *To be your bedesman now, that was your knight.*

The new Champion was George Clifford, Earl of Cumberland, but Henry Lee continued to help with staging the tournament – his knowledge and long experience of such matters were too valuable to waste – and he made positively his last appearance at James I's Accession Day tilt in March 1604. Nor can it be said that the old man turned entirely to a diet of prayers, for during the nineties he became the protector of the beautiful but notorious Anne Vavasour, who lived with him as his mistress at his country house in Oxfordshire.

Queen's Day was observed until the end of the reign and 'fair England's knights' continued to don their archaic panoply and play their obsolete game of chivalry

> *In honour of their mistress' holiday*
> *A gracious sport, fitting that golden time.*

At Court, where the occasion had taken on the character of a royal command performance and become an important event in the social calendar, there was naturally a strong element of axe-grinding as knight vied with knight to put on the most impressive show and offer the most exquisite compliment to majesty. In the country at large, everyone, equally naturally, welcomed the excuse to have a party and a break in the grinding routine of daily life. But celebration of 'the sacred seventeenth day' as the birthday of England's happiness, which had risen out of a spontaneous wave of indignant patriotism in the late sixties and early seventies, could not have flourished on into the more sober nineties if it had not continued to provide a necessary outlet for genuine emotion. Nor, despite the obvious self-interest and the deliberate official encouragement, could the cult of the Queen have existed in a rough, tough, individualistic society if it had not been rooted in genuine 'affectionate love'.

The glorification and idealisation of an ageing, over-dressed woman into a peculiar amalgam of biblical saint and classical goddess may seem excessive, even perhaps a trifle ridiculous, but to the Elizabethans, nurtured as they were on the Bible and the classics, it was entirely logical. The Queen's actual physical appearance had nothing to do with the matter, for by the fifteen-eighties Elizabeth had become an almost mystical symbol. She *was* Protestant England, a legitimate focus for swelling national pride. Besides this, in an age of upheaval and insecurity, when all sorts of unsettling new ideas were working their way to the surface, the Queen represented continuity, an instinctive confidence that as long as she reigned the Protestant God would continue to look after his own.

In her days every man shall eat in safety
Under his own vine what he plants, and sing
The merry songs of peace to all his neighbours.

When she had gone, what then?

39

Fair Stood the Wind for France

Seated between the Old World and the New,
A land there is no other land may touch,
Where reigns a Queen in peace and honour true;
Stories or fables to describe no such.
Never did Atlas such a burden bear,
As she, in holding up the world opprest;
Supplying with her virtue everywhere
Weakness of friends, errors of servants best.

Although the new decade had opened relatively quietly on the European front, Henry IV's early successes and Queen Elizabeth's intervention on his behalf were having the inevitable effect of driving the French Catholic party still further into the Spanish camp. In January 1590 the Catholic League – a powerful right-wing confederation of nobles, government officials, cities and, indeed, whole provinces – made a fresh appeal to the King of Spain and, as a result, a new agreement was reached between the champions of orthodoxy. Philip assumed the title of Protector of the Crown of France and was promised possession of certain towns, plus the exclusive and unrestricted use of all ports and harbours under the League with increased financial and military aid in its struggle to dislodge the heretic king. Spanish troops now began to move in from the Netherlands and that summer an army under the command of the great Duke of Parma himself marched down through Picardy, forcing Henry to abandon his siege of Paris. In the early autumn, three thousand Spaniards landed on the coast of Brittany and proceeded to occupy the town of Hennebon, which overlooks the modern naval base of Lorient. Rumours exaggerated the size of this invasion and for a while there were serious fears that Parma in the north and Don Juan d'Aguila in Brittany would join hands and between them seize the whole of the Channel coast from Brest to Calais. So, when the Vicomte de Turenne arrived in London in November, he found a ready audience for his master's urgent requests for help.

Elizabeth placed very little reliance on Henry's solemn undertakings to repay the money she was lending him, nor did she really expect that he would keep his promise to double the size of any army she sent to Brittany. In fact, she didn't trust him further than she could see him and it was this distrust which, paradoxically, made her continued involvement unavoidable. The King of France had half his kingdom still to conquer and, for all his fair words, the defence of the Channel ports looked like remaining pretty low on his list of priorities for some time to come; but to the English the security of those ports was vital, especially now that Spain had begun to rebuild her naval strength. Clearly another expedition would have to be mounted, and on 11 January 1591 Sir John Norris received his commission as General of the Queen's Army in Brittany.

In spite of the apparent urgency of the situation there were the usual delays and difficulties in extracting a nucleus of experienced troops from the Netherlands, the usual anguished complaints about the wretched quality of the new levies – Norris lamenting that one of the West Country's contingents was made up of 'the worst men and the worst furnished' he had ever seen, and 'so poor and weak that they will scarce endure the passage by sea'. What with one thing and another it was nearly the end of April before the expedition finally got away, and the beginning of May by the time it landed at Paimpol in northern Brittany.

The campaign turned out to be an indecisive affair. Towards the end of May, Norris, in conjunction with the local royalist leader, the Prince de Dombes, succeeded in capturing the town of Guingamp, but the rest of the summer was frittered away in skirmishing and generally manoeuvring for position – neither of the opposing armies being strong enough to force matters to a conclusion. In spite of constant rumours that reinforcements were on their way from Spain, none came after April, and although the Leaguer Duc de Mercoeur had claimed to be able to offer Philip a choice of the useful seaports of Brest, Morlaix and St Malo, the native Bretons had other ideas. At St Malo the townsfolk took the precaution of occupying the castle, while at Brest and Morlaix they were in a position to exercise a controlling influence over their military governors – the governor of Brest was, in any case, a staunch king's man. England and Spain both retained a toehold in Brittany and Norris's presence was at least helping to keep the Spaniards tied down in the southern part of the province, but otherwise remarkably little had been accomplished.

The Queen was not pleased. Needless to say, Henry had failed to support Norris as promised and, even more aggravating, the Prince de Dombes had been trying to lure the English inland to join him in a campaign in 'the high parts of Brittany' – nothing to do with securing the coast. Elizabeth wrote angrily threatening to withdraw her troops altogether unless the French kept their side of the bargain, but by this time she was committed to yet another cross-Channel adventure.

All through the spring of 1593 the King of France had continued to press his urgent need for reinforcements. He wanted money for German mercenaries to match Parma in Picardy, and he wanted military aid to help him meet the growing threat to Normandy. There was already a small English force in Dieppe under Roger Williams, but Honfleur and Fécamp had recently fallen into the hands of the League and now even Boulogne was in danger. Henry's immediate objective, so he said, was the capture of Rouen and this woke a sympathetic response in London. Rouen, lying as it did on the Seine midway between Paris and the sea, would not only be a valuable strategic base from which to reduce the other northern cities (Lord Burghley considered it even more valuable than Paris), but was also a great commercial centre which would provide a welcome outlet for English continental trade, now almost at a standstill. When, as a further inducement, Henry offered to allow the Queen's agents to collect the royal revenues from Rouen and Le Havre until his debts had been cleared, Elizabeth undertook to raise and equip four thousand men, paid for two months and commanded by no less a personality than the Earl of Essex.

The Queen had consented to this appointment very much against her better judgement, but the pressures on her were hard to withstand. In many ways Essex was the obvious choice. His popularity would help to hold the army together and his prestige would attract the better class of volunteer – an important consideration, as no more veterans could be drawn from the Netherlands. Lord Burghley, who had his own reasons for wanting the favourite temporarily out of the way, supported the idea and Essex himself was wild to go. Ever since the Portugal voyage he'd been growing increasingly bored with the tameness of his courtier's life and impatient for martial glory. Then again, the prospect of charging to the relief of a hard-pressed warrior king, fighting for his throne against all the odds, was exactly calculated to appeal to his ardently romantic nature – all the more so since the warrior king in question was taking every opportunity to curry favour with him. Essex had been deeply disappointed at missing the campaign in Brittany. Now he pestered the Queen to send him to France. On three occasions, so he told the King, he had knelt before her for as much as two hours at a time. Elizabeth surrendered, but her misgivings remained. Essex was still only twenty-three with no experience of high command. It seemed only too probable that he would do something silly, and she warned Henry that he would need the bridle rather than the spur.

Having got what he wanted, the new Lord General was in high spirits and quite untroubled by self-doubt. 'I am commanded into France for the establishing of the brave King in quiet possession of Normandy' he wrote to a friend, and was soon happily immersed in the delightful business of raising a troop of horse from among his own cronies and dependents. On 24 June letters went out to the counties ordering a levy of 3,400 men which, with the six hundred already in Dieppe, would make up the promised four thousand. The Lords Lieutenant had special instructions to pick only the best type of recruit, as many as possible from the train bands or militia, and the officers, too, were carefully chosen to include many of the new, younger men like John Wingfield and Thomas Baskerville who were making soldiering their profession.

The army which sailed for France at the end of July was probably the finest and best equipped of all the Elizabethan expeditionary forces, though one observer remarked that he had never known so gallant a troop go out of England with so many young and untrained commanders. In fact, the misfortunes which were to overtake the gallant troop cannot be blamed entirely on the youth of its captains and the inexperience of its general. When the English disembarked they found that Henry, so far from being ready and waiting to begin the siege of Rouen, was not even in Normandy. Instead he was still engaged a good hundred miles to the east at Noyon and the German mercenaries, paid for by the Queen, had not yet arrived. After spending a fortnight hanging about waiting for news, Essex left the army camped round Dieppe and, with only a small cavalry escort, set out on a hazardous cross-country journey through Leaguer-held territory to meet Henry near Compiègne. He entered the city to the sound of trumpets, resplendent in orange-tawny velvet and gold lace, and if the shabby King and his grim, battle-hardened companions found the spectacle a trifle comic, they were careful not to show it.

On the contrary, Henry set himself out to charm Queen Elizabeth's youthful Lieutenant. Apart from his renowned fighting qualities, the King of France was famous for his affability and his easy-going friendly ways. Everyone who came into contact with him felt the attraction of his warm, out-going personality and the impressionable Essex quickly succumbed. He spent three delightful days as the King's guest and it was agreed that the bulk of the royalist forces, under the veteran Marshal Biron, should start for Rouen at once, Henry promising to follow just as soon as the Germans put in an appearance.

Meanwhile, Essex had to get back to base and the return trip turned out to be quite an adventurous one. He and his party had to make a wide detour and do some hard riding to evade a strong Leaguer force out looking for them, and when they reached Pont de l'Arche, a town held for the King, it was thought advisable to send for the rest of the army. Thus reinforced, Essex could not resist the temptation to try and entice the governor of Rouen to come out and fight. Unhappily, in the resultant skirmish his younger brother, Walter, was killed and Essex himself, who had gone down with a nasty attack of fever, had to be carried back to camp in a litter.

His discomfiture was presently increased by a scolding from the Queen. Having had no news of her problem child for nearly three weeks Elizabeth was already querulous with anxiety, and when she heard what he'd been up to, she exploded. The Lieutenant and General of her forces had no business to go gallivanting round France without her knowledge or permission. He had risked his own life by his irresponsible behaviour and endangered the army, first by leaving it without proper leadership and then exposing it uselessly. This was bad enough and confirmed all her forebodings about the unsuitability of the appointment. But what infuriated the Queen more than anything else was the delay in getting to grips with the purpose of the expedition, caused by the King's failure to keep his solemn promise 'to join with us to the beginning of Rouen'. She was not appeased by explanations or excuses; nor was her temper improved when Marshal Biron, arriving in the vicinity of the city on 12 September, decided that the neighbouring towns of Gournay and Caudebec must be taken first.

The English assisted at the assault on Gournay, Essex joining the ranks and trailing a pike like any common soldier. No doubt he enjoyed himself, but he got another angry telling-off from London. He was again hazarding his life in a childish desire for vainglory, denigrating his high office and, by implication, the sovereign who had bestowed it on him.

Elizabeth had, by this time, more than half convinced herself that Essex and the King of France were ganging up on her. She suspected Henry of openly mocking her, of accepting her help while, at the same time, cynically disregarding her wishes and her instinctive reaction was to order the immediate withdrawal of all her troops, leaving the French to stew in their own juice. Only the knowledge that if she abandoned him now, Henry, a king without a crown making wars without money, would almost certainly go under, leaving Spain to fill the vacuum, prevented her from taking this satisfying form of revenge. Reluctantly she agreed that, provided the siege of Rouen was really about to begin at last, the army in Normandy might stay for another month or forty days beyond its original two months' contract – but on the clear understanding that Henry would be responsible for paying its wages. Essex she was determined to recall. He'd made it only too plain that he couldn't be trusted to conduct himself with the restraint and decorum required of a senior commander, and Elizabeth was sufficiently fond of him genuinely not to want to see him lose his life in some stupid piece of bravado.

Essex, for his part, was equally determined not to be dragged away just as things were getting interesting. He went over to England early in October and got a cold reception. 'I see your Majesty is constant to ruin me', he wrote sadly. In the end he spent a week with the Queen at Oatlands and managed to talk her into a more reasonable frame of mind. Back at Dieppe in the middle of the month he was writing in typical Essex vein: 'I will humbly beseech your Majesty that no cause but a great action of your own may draw me out of your sight, for the two windows of your privy chamber shall be the poles of my sphere where, as long as your Maj. will please to have me, I am fixed and immovable. When your Maj. thinks that heaven too good for me, I will not fall like a star, but be consumed like a vapour by the same sun that drew me up to such a height. While your Maj. gives me leave to say I love you, my fortune is as my affection, unmatchable. If ever you deny me that liberty, you may end my life, but never shake my constancy, for were the sweetness of your nature turned into the greatest bitterness that could be, it is not in your power, great Queen as you are, to make me love you less. Therefore, for the honour of your sex, show yourself constant in kindness . . .'

By the same post the newly returned Lord General sent the Council a report of the state of the army, which he had found 'in great disorder'. The soldiers in the camp at Arques were now officially in the pay of the King of France and, since this meant no pay, they were reacting in the traditional manner by foraging over the surrounding countryside, looting and burning as they went. According to Essex, 'the King's ministers do not give them that which they promised me, because they say our men spoil the King's subjects and live well upon the country' but, as the King himself freely admitted to Queen Elizabeth's ambassador, he had not five hundred crowns in his treasury. 'The state of France is most miserable and lamentable', reported Sir Henry Unton. The necessities of the poor King, it seemed, were such that he even wanted bread to eat. 'If I were not an eyewitness hereof, I could not believe it', declared the ambassador impressively.

Unless and until the King could take Rouen there would be no money to meet his obligations to the English or anyone else, but it was not just the fact that their pay was in arrears – a common enough condition of sixteenth century armies – which had demoralised the Queen's soldiers. When it came to the actual fighting, as they had already proved in the Netherlands, even the raw levies could hold their own in any company. What they could not stand was boredom. The gentlemen volunteers simply went home and there was a steady trickle of desertion from the ranks, but mostly they got drunk and went on the rampage, or went sick. Sickness – always the largest single cause of wastage – was taking an increasing toll from men stagnating in the insanitary compounds of Dieppe, so that by the end of October, when the siege did at long last look like beginning in earnest, fewer than fifteen hundred effectives remained out of the original four thousand.

Elizabeth still sharply resented the 'public affront' she considered she had received from the King of France. 'Be not displeased', she wrote to him in November, 'if I tell you roundly, that if you thus treat your friends, who . . . are serving you at a most important time, they will fail you hereafter at your greatest need.' However, now that Henry and his Germans had finally put in an appearance, the Queen, grumbling steadily that some people seemed to forget she had a realm of her own to provide for and had neither 'the eastern nor the western Indies' at her disposal, did what she could to ensure their success. A small detachment of pioneers and a thousand veterans from the Netherlands were sent to Normandy and the English army, much to its relief, was taken back into the pay of the blessed Queen. But in spite of these last ditch efforts the siege made little progress, dragging inconclusively through the winter and early spring until the Duke of Parma, making another of his lightning forays from the north, revictualled and reinforced the Rouen garrison and once again forced the King to withdraw.

Essex had gone home by this time. He had handed over his greatly reduced command to Roger Williams early in January and sailed for England, disenchanted, at least temporarily, with a military career. Nor was he the only person to be disillusioned about the French war. In its initial stages the Normandy campaign, wakening as it did romantic echoes of past glories, had made a particular appeal to the Queen's subjects. In March 1592 Lord Strange's company of actors capitalised on the public mood with a production of *Henry VI*, the work of a new writer, a civil young fellow by the name of William Shakespeare, who was just beginning to make his way in the profession. Enthusiasm, though, was already waning, and as time went on the authorities found it more and more difficult to raise suitable recruits for service overseas.

Between the years 1591 and 1595 Elizabeth somehow contrived to maintain a military presence strung out along the European coastline from Brittany in the south to Zeeland in the north. Apart from the heavy financial burden this entailed, the drain on the manpower of a small nation was not inconsiderable – bearing in mind that the mortality rate from dysentery, typhus, malaria and other forms of disease (not to mention all those who died of quite minor wounds for lack of the most basic medical care) was seldom far short of fifty per cent. Of the twenty thousand men who went to France between 1589 and 1595 no more than half returned.

The government, unhappily aware of the shortcomings of a system which had begun to lose its usefulness before the end of the Hundred Years' War, made various well-intentioned efforts to check the worst abuses and improve the lot of the private soldier. But jobbery, vested interest, public indifference, chronic shortage of cash and, perhaps most important, a total absence of corporate spirit among the men of war, were too strong for good intentions and combined to ensure that England's armed forces should continue to be scratch collections of untrained or, at best, half-trained civilians, ill-equipped, badly paid, shockingly fed, sometimes half-naked, and always mercilessly exploited by corrupt captains and profiteering contractors. In the circumstances it is hardly surprising that military service grew increasingly unpopular and the subject of 'great murmuring' by the families and friends of those liable to be called up. Draft dodging was a national pastime and as a result the levies came more and more to consist of the scourings of the slums and gaols who deserted at the first opportunity.

The Queen hated the whole business, the expense, the bare-faced cheating and the waste, but she dared not disengage as long as France remained precariously balanced on the edge of a pro-Spanish takeover, or while reports continued to come in of another great Armada building in the Spanish ports. If even half the rumours were true, it was clear that Philip's navy could no longer be written off as a spent force. Indeed, England had been given an unmistakable hint of her enemy's reviving strength back in August 1591, when

At Flores in the Azores Sir Richard Grenville lay,
And a pinnace, like a fluttered bird, came flying from far away:
'Spanish ships of war at sea! We have sighted fifty-three!'

Grenville in the *Revenge*, with Lord Thomas Howard in the *Defiance* and another half-dozen or so of the Queen's ships, had been cruising off the Azores all summer in the hope once more of catching the treasure fleet on its homeward voyage, and at the end of August they were at Flores taking on provisions and fresh water and cleaning out their filthy ballast. A look-out was being kept to the westward for the American flota but no one, it seems, had been anticipating trouble from the east. So it was fortunate that the Earl of Cumberland should also have been spending the summer in Spanish waters on a semi-private marauding expedition. It was he who had spotted the Spanish fleet putting out from Ferrol and despatched Captain William Middleton in the pinnace *Moonshine* 'both to discover their forces the more as also to give advice to my Lord Thomas of their approach'.

Even with Middleton's warning, the English at Flores were caught at a considerable disadvantage. An epidemic, probably typhus, had been raging in the squadron. There were ninety sick on the *Revenge*, nearly half her crew. The *Bonaventure*, commanded by Robert Cross, had 'not so many in health as could handle her mainsail' and the rest were in little better case. Many of the ships' companies were on shore, either lying sick and helpless or out on foraging expeditions; nor were the ships themselves, after four months at sea, in very fit condition. Some had not yet finished rummaging and were consequently 'very light for want of ballast'. Thomas Howard, a cousin of the Lord Admiral Howard of Effingham, may have been no coward but he was no fool either, and it was patently obvious that he was in no position to give battle against such odds. The only sensible course was to get as many of the crews as possible back on board and run for it while there was still time.

Just how much time there actually was is not very clear – certainly no more than twenty-four hours and probably less. But Howard in the flagship, together with the *Bonaventure*, the *Lion*, the *Foresight*, the *Crane* and a small miscellaneous flotilla of victuallers and pinnaces, were able to get windward of the approaching Spaniards and make a reasonably dignified exit. Not so the *Revenge*. She was the last ship to weigh anchor and had left it too late to go with the others. Just what had delayed her is something else which is not very clear. According to Walter Raleigh, Grenville waited 'to recover the men that were upon the island, which otherwise had been lost'.

. . . Sir Richard bore in hand all his sick men from the land
Very carefully and slow,
Men of Bideford in Devon,
And we laid them on the ballast down below.

A later and less sympathetic account says that Sir Richard 'being astern, and imagining this fleet to come from the Indies, and not to be the Armada of which they were informed, would by no means be persuaded by his master or company to cut his cable to follow his Admiral . . . nay, so headstrong, rash and unadvised he was that he offered violence to all that counselled him to the contrary'.

Whatever the truth of the matter, all the authorities agree that the *Revenge* could still have got clear by running before the wind to leeward. 'But Sir Richard utterly refused to turn from the enemy ('For I never turned my back upon Don or devil yet'), alleging that he would rather choose to die than to dishonour himself, his country, and her Majesty's ship.' It was now about five o'clock on the afternoon of 31 August. General Marcos de Aramburu, leading a squadron of galleons from Castile, was already close enough to exchange fire with the departing Howard and Don Alonso de Bazan, the Spanish Admiral, was coming up fast with the rest of the fleet. At this point the *Revenge* appears to have borne straight down on the enemy, Grenville 'persuading his company that he would pass through the two squadrons in despite of them, and enforce those of Seville to give him way'.

It was the act of a berserker – crazy, magnificent and suicidal. The *Revenge* was almost immediately grappled and boarded, first by the huge *San Felipe* and then by the *San Barnabe*, leader of the Biscayan contingent. Soon she lay surrounded, like a baited bull, 'having never less than two mighty galleons at her side and aboard her'. But, like a baited bull, she put up a epic resistance. The *San Felipe* 'having received the lower tier of the *Revenge* discharged with crossbar shot, shifted herself with all diligence from her sides, utterly misliking her entertainment', says Walter Raleigh. The rest made repeated attempts to board, hoping to force the stubborn Englishman by sheer weight of numbers, but still they were repulsed again and again, 'and at all times beaten back into their own ships or into the seas'. The battle continued intermittently all night:

And the sun went down, and the stars came out far
over the summer sea,

But never a moment ceased the fight of the one and
the fifty-three.
Ship after ship, the whole night long, their high-built
galleons came,
Ship after ship, the whole night long, with her battle-
thunder and flame.

Dawn broke and incredibly the *Revenge* was still there, and still fighting. She had accounted for three of the enemy, two so badly damaged that they presently sank and another with her prow destroyed down to the water, but she herself was in desperate case, with six foot of water in her hold, 'masts all beaten overboard, all her tackle cut asunder, her upper work altogether razed, and in effect . . . but the very foundations or bottom of a ship, nothing being left overhead either for flight or defence'. Powder was down to the last barrel, forty men had been killed and most of the rest hurt, so that the ship – what was left of her – was like a slaughter-house, filled with the blood and bodies of the dead and dying. Grenville had been shot in the head and body, but even in his present extremity this harsh-tempered, violent, quarrelsome man, pig-headed and brave to the edge of insanity, refused to discuss the possibility of surrender. There was for him an infinitely more satisfying way out and one, moreover, which would leave nothing of glory or victory to the Spaniards.

'Sink me the ship, Master Gunner – sink her, split
her in twain!
Fall into the hands of God, not into the hands of Spain!'

The master gunner, 'a most resolute man', was ready and eager for self-immolation, but a majority of the other survivors, feeling reasonably enough that they had earned a chance of life, overbore their leader. Honourable terms were agreed with Alonso de Bazan and Richard Grenville was carried reverentially aboard the Spanish flagship where, a few days later, he died, grumbling passionately, so it is said, about those traitors and dogs in his company who had crossed his will 'and would leave a shameful name for ever'.

Like the defeat of the Armada, the last fight of the *Revenge* is a vital part of the Elizabethan tradition, and with the passage of the centuries (and some assistance from Alfred Tennyson) has become absorbed into the national folk-memory – part of the recurring pattern of standing alone against the powers of darkness and of the peculiar English genius for creating triumph out of defeat.

The episode caused a considerable stir at the time, the Spanish navy naturally making the most of this rare achievement – its first and, as it turned out, only major prize of the war. An English prisoner in Lisbon Castle later recalled how he had seen one of King Philip's great galleons entering the river in her fighting sails, dressed overall with streamers and pennants, and letting fly all her ordnance 'for the taking of Sir Richard Grenville in the *Revenge*'. At the same time, awkward questions were being asked in Madrid as to why the whole of Howard's squadron had not been destroyed, considering the size of the force under Don Alonso de Bazan's command.

In England there was consternation. The *Revenge* was by no means the largest of the Queen's galleons, being rated at five hundred tons and one of the medium-sized, fast, heavily-armed warships built in the fifteen-seventies and eighties during the enlightened rule of Sir John Hawkins at the Navy Board. But she was a famous ship, chosen by Drake for the Armada campaign and specially associated with the glories of 1588. Her loss was therefore a special humiliation, and questions were asked in London about how she had come to be caught in such a compromising situation.

Fortunately for the islanders' self-esteem, God was once more about to demonstrate that he was an Englishman and a Protestant. No sooner had the returning American flota rendezvoused with de Bazan off the Azores than storms and hurricane force winds roared in from the west and north-west with catastrophic results. The Venetian ambassador in Madrid heard that thirty-one merchantmen and three men-of-war were missing, and other accounts put the losses in the two fleets at over seventy. Among the casualties was the battered remains of the *Revenge* which broke up on a cliff near the Island of Terceira. 'So it pleased them', wrote Walter Raleigh grimly, 'to honour the burial of that renowned ship, the *Revenge*, not suffering her to perish alone, for the great honour she achieved in her lifetime.'

The year's consignment of gold and silver from the mines of New Spain had not yet left Havana and so escaped the general holocaust, but even so Spanish shipping and commerce had suffered a major disaster and in the Azores it was being freely said that 'the taking of the *Revenge* was justly revenged upon them, and not by might or force of man, but by the power of God . . . and that he took part with Lutherans and heretics'. A more orthodox school of thought held that the shade of Sir Richard Grenville, being descended into Hell, had raised up all the devils to the revenge of his death.

The following summer, 1592, a privateering venture financed jointly by the Queen, Sir Walter Raleigh and a syndicate of London merchants hit the jackpot when they intercepted a huge Portuguese carrack homeward bound from the Far East. The *Madre de Dios*, at 1600 tons one of the largest ships afloat, was laden with gemstones and spices and rare drugs, with musk and ambergris, silks, calicoes and carpets, porcelain and elephants' teeth, coconuts, hides and ebony – the sort of prize every privateer dreamed of taking – and even after wholesale looting of the cargo on its way back to Plymouth, the principal shareholders netted a very satisfactory return.

But although the capture of the *Madre de Dios* naturally boosted morale, it was an isolated incident and one which helped to conceal a turning point in the war at sea; for the early fifteen-nineties marked the beginning of the end of those carefree days when tiny English squadrons could roam the Spanish shipping lanes at will. 'It is to be observed', wrote William Monson, 'that from the year the *Revenge* was taken . . . there was no summer but the King of Spain furnished a fleet for the guarding of his coasts and securing of his trade.' The King of Spain was, in fact, learning at last to defend himself and to adopt a regular convoy system for his treasure fleets. In spite of a chronic shortage of cash as acute as Elizabeth's own and made worse, as the Venetian ambassador remarked, by 'the delay and uncertainty in the arrival of the ships which ought to bring the silver from the Indies', Philip was persevering with an ambitious ship-building programme. In 1592 he had forty galleons under construction, as well as fast, ocean-going pinnaces to improve his naval communications. He was also taking steps to fortify the American ports of departure and to provide a secure base in the Azores – that vital area on which both East and West Indian routes converged. Privateering went on, of course, and continued to be a sizable thorn in the King's side, but the pickings were becoming progressively less easy – even the masters of the big merchantmen were no longer always playing the game according to the rules. They were beginning to fight their ships and, in most unsportsmanlike fashion, would sometimes prefer to destroy them than see their cargoes fall into English hands.

It wasn't only at sea that things were changing. Francis Walsingham had died in the spring of 1590 and now Hatton, too, was gone, together with lesser names like Walter Mildmay, Thomas Randolph, the Earl of Shrewsbury and Sir James Crofts. Of the old guard at Court and Council only Lord Hunsdon, Francis Knollys and Lord Burghley were left, so that when the Earl of Essex returned from France in January 1592 the field looked wide open for a promising young man seeking 'domestical greatness' – or almost wide open. Lord Burghley was now seventy-one and a martyr to gout or, more likely, arthritis; but he was still a regular attender at Council meetings and his pre-eminent position as pillar of the state remained unchallengeable.

Of the younger generation, Sir Walter Raleigh, once considered by Essex to be his most serious rival, was to fall disastrously out of favour with the Queen in the coming summer for getting Bess Throckmorton into trouble but, in any case, Elizabeth had never considered him suitable material for high office. Although the Earl had not yet realised it, a far greater threat to the sort of future he was planning for himself existed in the apparently insignificant person of Robert Cecil, Burghley's son by his second wife, the blue-stocking Mildred Cooke. Robert had been a sickly child with a deformed shoulder. He had grown into a slender, delicate-looking, under-sized young man (the Queen called him her Pigmy or, in more mellow mood, her Elf), but there was nothing under-sized about his intellectual capacities or his political ambitions and he enjoyed, of course, the inestimable advantage of being his father's son.

When Francis Walsingham died the Queen had not appointed another

Secretary of State, the office and its burdens being shouldered once again by old Burghley on the tacit understanding, so it seems, that his son should take over in due course. In May 1591 Elizabeth paid a formal state visit to Theobalds, the Burghleys' Hertfordshire mansion, staying for ten days at a cost to her hosts of over a thousand pounds. Broad hints were dropped by the family that everyone's workload would be eased if the son of the house were now to receive the Secretaryship; but although the Queen knighted young Robert during her visit and at the beginning of August (the week after Essex sailed for France) admitted him to the Privy Council, she did not, contrary to widespread expectations, make any official appointment. Robert Cecil was still in his twenties – he was about three years older than Robert Devereux – and still learning his trade; the Queen would wait and see how he shaped. But by the time Essex came home, little Cecil, 'his hands full of papers and head full of matter', had become a familiar sight in the corridors of Whitehall and it was an open secret that he was already dealing with most of the routine work of the secretariat.

The protagonists in The War of the Two Roberts, which was to dominate English political life during the second half of the nineties, had known one another since they were children when Essex, as a royal ward, had been placed in Lord Burghley's charge and spent several months in his guardian's household before going up to Cambridge. There is no record of any special relationship, friendly or otherwise, between the boys at that time – probably Essex felt no more than slightly contemptuous pity for a youth whose physical disabilities would surely condemn him to a life of clerking – and, since they had grown up, their paths had scarcely crossed, the Earl being fully occupied with his glamorous career as courtier, royal favourite and military man. Now, though, things were different. Essex would soon be twenty-five, war had disappointed him of glory for the second time and he was ready to turn his attention to politics where, sooner rather than later, he would be bound to come up against the Cecil family. Already he was inclined to blame Lord Burghley's influence for the Queen's irascibility during the Rouen campaign, and he'd been greatly put out at being passed over in the election for the Chancellorship of Oxford University – a prestigious office once held by his stepfather. Although the job went to a senior and well-qualified candidate, Essex characteristically took his rejection as a personal slight. Equally characteristically he suspected the machinations of enemies and wrote to Robert Cecil, whose support he had been canvassing: 'Sir R. I have been with the Queen and have had my answer. How it agrees with your letter you can judge, after you have spoken with the Queen. Whether you have mistaken the Queen, or used cunning with me, I know not. I will not condemn you, but leave you to think if it were your own case, whether you would not be jealous. Your friend, if I have cause. R. Essex.'

Essex continued to be conspicuous as a courtier but when, in February 1593, he too was sworn a member of the Privy Council, an enthusiastic friend reported that 'his lordship is become a new man – clean-forsaking all his youthful tricks, carrying himself with honourable gravity and singularly liked of both in Parliament and at Council-table, for his speeches and judgement'. Unquestionably the Earl possessed both brains and a talent for public life. When not blinded by paranoia he could put a point of view persuasively and had all the natural leader's flair for drawing men to his side. But in matters of statecraft and high politics he remained an amateur. To compete with such dedicated professionals as Lord Burghley and his son on anything approaching equal terms Essex needed professional allies, and before the end of 1592 he had found them.

The Elizabethan establishment was very much a family affair, almost all its leading figures being connected by blood or marriage or both, and Anthony and Francis Bacon were Lord Burghley's nephews – the sons of his wife's sister Ann who had married the lawyer Nicholas Bacon, Queen Elizabeth's first Lord Keeper. Both brothers possessed trained and brilliant minds. Both had been born into the highest political and intellectual circles. Both were ambitious, hard-working and astute. It might reasonably have been supposed that two such gifted and well-connected young gentlemen would experience no difficulty in making honourable and lucrative careers for themselves in the service of the state. But that was not how it had worked out. There was, it seemed, no place for the Bacons in a world dominated by Lord Burghley and the brothers had no hesitation in blaming their otherwise inexplicable lack of progress on the old man's jealousy and determination to reserve all the sweets of office for his son. Simplistic reasoning, and yet the Lord Treasurer's consistent refusal to advance his nephews' cause was surely rooted in some fundamental dislike and distrust. No doubt their homosexual proclivities had a good deal to do with it, but Burghley was a shrewd and experienced judge of human nature and perhaps he sensed something of the cold-hearted, conscienceless self-seeking which lay beneath the brilliance.

By the early fifteen-nineties Francis, now turned thirty and still no more than a back-bench M.P. practising law at Gray's Inn, had come to the conclusion that it was more than time to seek another patron. He turned to the Earl of Essex, that bright and rising star who, so he later affirmed, he had then held 'to be the fittest instrument to do good to the state' and, so he might have added, to Francis Bacon. The two became close friends and when, in February 1592, Anthony Bacon returned to England after an absence of twelve years spent mostly in the south of France, the younger brother lost no time in drawing the elder into his new orbit.

Anthony had never been strong and at thirty-three suffered from a painful and often crippling disease described as gout, but which was probably a form of arthritis, sometimes not recognised by sixteenth century medicine. Unlike the more robust Francis, he shrank from the rough and tumble of public life and sedulously avoided the Court – any suggestion that he should pay his duty to the Queen would at once bring on an acute flare-up of his bad leg. Paying his duty to the Earl of Essex was a very different matter. Anthony had been captivated at first sight by the 'rare perfections and virtues' of this handsome, courteous young nobleman and longed for an opportunity to show the Earl how much he honoured and esteemed his excellent gifts and how earnestly he desired to deserve his good opinion and love.

The opportunity to serve, in fact, lay ready to hand. During his residence in France Anthony had for some time been one of Francis Walsingham's most valued correspondents, passing on information from the agents who slipped to and fro across the Pyrenees and from merchants whose trading vessels plied between the ports of Spain and south-west France. He was also a personal friend and admirer of King Henry IV and had acquired numerous French contacts, both Protestant and Catholic. Since Walsingham's death the intelligence network so closely associated with his name had passed under the nominal control of Lord Burghley, but without Walsingham's organising genius and passionate commitment to the cause he served, the organisation no longer possessed its former cohesion and sense of purpose.

Here, then, was Anthony's chance. While brother Francis acted as the Earl's political counsellor, let Anthony take over responsibility for foreign affairs and build up his own intelligence service. His invalidism need be no bar to the work of collecting and collating agents' reports, and there could be no doubt as to the usefulness of the service he would be performing. Detailed, reliable information from abroad was always a precious commodity and vital to the successful conduct of affairs. If, with the Bacons' help, Essex could begin to assume the reputation for omniscience which had done so much for Francis Walsingham, it must infallibly raise his prestige with the Queen and give him the right to be regarded as a serious character. For the Bacons, of course, the scheme offered a not to be missed opportunity for attacking the Cecils on their own ground and opened up agreeable prospects of being in a position to display their talents independently of Cecil patronage.

It was therefore unfortunate that Francis should have picked this moment of all others to offend the Queen by opposing the supply bill in the Parliament of 1593. He may, as he subsequently assured his uncle Burghley, have been honestly obeying the voice of his conscience when he maintained that the proposal to collect a treble subsidy in three years would be an intolerable burden on the Queen's subjects, and drew a pathetic picture of gentlemen forced to sell their plate and farmers their brass pots. On the other hand, he may have seen an opportunity to court popularity with his fellow back-benchers in a tussle between the Lords and Commons over the latter's right to initiate taxation which had invoked the sacred name of privilege. Or he may, quite simply, have been unable to resist the temptation to show off and embarrass his cousin Robert who, with old Sir Thomas Heneage, was now responsible for managing government business in the Commons.

But for a man in Francis Bacon's position, the temporary discomfiture of Robert Cecil was a heavy price to pay for royal displeasure. The Earl of Essex and his friends were all too apt to make the expensive mistake of forgetting that England was ruled not by the Cecil family but by Elizabeth Tudor, and the Queen, increasingly harassed with financial problems, would not soon forgive anyone who made difficulties about money. Especially not at a time when, as the Lord Keeper had warned the Commons, the King of Spain 'breathed nothing but bloody revenge' and, with his navy rebuilt largely after the English pattern, was looking more dangerous even than in 1588.

Elizabeth had not been afraid of Philip in 1588 and she was not afraid now. 'For mine own part', she told Parliament at the end of the 1593 session, 'I protest I never feared, and what fear was my heart never knew. For I knew that my cause was ever just; and it standeth upon a sure foundation.' But however just the cause, it must still be defended. This would continue to cost money and money could not, as certain members in their simplicity appeared to believe, be picked out of the air. The Queen was well aware of the anomalies and inequities of a system of assessment which, while consistently failing to tap the country's undoubted wealth (the last double subsidy had yielded no more than £280,000), tended all too often to press hardest on the little man. Nevertheless, pious concern about the burden of taxation must sometimes have been supremely irritating to a pacifically-minded lady struggling to meet the inescapable and ever mounting costs of a war she detested.

None of this irritation could be allowed to appear in public of course, and the Queen's end of session address concluded with 'as great thanks as ever prince gave to loving subjects' for the treble subsidy which, it had finally been agreed, should be collected over a period of four years. Elizabeth had never, in her conscience, been willing to draw from her people more than they would contentedly give and she repeated her customary soothing assurances that her care for their welfare would always take precedence over all other worldly cares whatsoever. She could only hope that she would be able to last out the next four years when another Parliament would have to be patiently cajoled into loosening the purse-strings.

40

A Maid in an Island

Happy hour, happy day,
That Eliza came this way!
Great in honour, great in place,
Greater yet in giving grace,
Great in wisdom, great in mind,
But in both above her kind,
Great in virtue, great in name,
Yet in power beyond her fame.

Elizabeth was now approaching her sixtieth birthday but her health remained excellent. If anything it had improved – the nerve storms and sudden, violent stomach upsets of earlier decades seems to have disappeared. She worked long hours at her papers, often starting before dawn, and in times of crisis would be shut up in Council until late at night – as she grew older she slept less and less. But she still found time for recreation and the outdoor exercise she loved. Although music and dancing remained her favourite indoor pastimes, she was addicted to bear baiting and enjoyed the theatre. Plays were performed regularly at Court during the season and the Queen was always a good friend to actors, more than once intervening personally to protect their precarious livelihood from disapproving city fathers.

She was still passionately interested in clothes, and when the Bishop of London was tactless enough to preach before her on the vanity of decking the body too finely, her Majesty remarked tartly that if the bishop held more discourse on such matters, 'she would fit him for heaven, but he should walk thither without a staff, and leave his mantle behind him'. Perhaps, observed John Harington, who recorded the incident in his *Brief Notes and Remembrances*, the bishop had never sought her Highness's wardrobe, or he would have chosen another text!

With the possible exception of John Whitgift, Elizabeth had never held a very high opinion of bishops, and she would certainly not have tolerated even a hint of episcopal criticism of her taste in dress. In any case, clothes were an important part of her job, part of her showmanship expected of all sovereigns and, for Elizabeth, part of the business of emphasising her semi-magical *persona* of Virgin-Goddess-Queen. With this in mind, she wore a lot of white and silver, especially in her later years.

Another important part of the job which she kept going almost to the end was the annual summer progress. These famous journeyings not only provided a welcome break from routine, giving the Queen a chance to see something of her kingdom and take the temperature of opinion in the provinces, they were also invaluable as public relations exercises, an opportunity to display the reverse side of the royal image – the gracious, lovable mother-figure. 'In her progress', wrote Edmund Bohun, 'she was the most easy to be approached; private persons and magistrates, men and women, country people and children, came joyfully and without any fear, to wait upon her, and to see her. Her ears were then open to the complaints of the afflicted, and of those that had been in any way injured . . . She took with her own hand and read with the greatest goodness the petitions of the meanest rustics. And she would frequently assure them that she would take a particular care of their affairs; and she would ever be as good as her word . . . She was never seen angry with the most unseasonable, or uncourtly approach: she was never offended with the most impudent or importunate petitioner . . . Nor was there anything in the whole course of her reign that more won the hearts of the people, than this her wonderful facility and condescension, and the strange sweetness and pleasantness with which she entertained all that came to her.'

Elizabeth, in fact, never travelled further north than Norwich or father west than Bristol, but given the uncertainty of the times and the logistical problems involved in transporting, accommodating and feeding the Court, this is not such a bad record. Apart from Woodstock, which was only a hunting lodge and in poor repair, all the royal residences were clustered around London, so the Queen naturally expected to be put up at the great houses along her route.

Much has been written about the financial burden this enforced hospitality imposed on her hosts, but for those concerned the prestige conferred by the royal presence more than compensated for any inconvenience or expense. When, in August 1591, the Queen arrived to spend a week as the guest of Lord and Lady Montague at Cowdray, the mistress of the house was so overcome that she shed tears on the royal bosom, exclaiming 'Oh, happy time! Oh, joyful day!' All the same, the information that the houseparty's Sunday breakfast alone accounted for three oxen and a hundred and forty geese does give some indication of the strain which a progress could put on the resources of the favoured neighbourhood.

After leaving Cowdray, the Queen went on to visit Chichester, Portsmouth and Southampton, staying at Petworth and Tichfield. The return journey took in Basing, Odiham and Elvetham, where the Earl of Hertford had solved the accommodation problem by employing three hundred workmen to enlarge his house and erect a temporary encampment in the park. The centrepiece was a large rustic pavilion with a withdrawing room for the Queen at one end and overlooking a specially constructed artificial lake. The outsides of the walls were decorated with green boughs and clusters of ripe hazel nuts, while the inside had been hung with arras, the roof lined with wreaths of ivy leaves and the floor strewn with rushes and sweet herbs. It sounds delightful, but the practical Lord Hertford had also remembered to provide comfortable quarters for the royal footmen and their friends, the Queen's guard and the servants of her house, as well as 'a great common buttery', two extra kitchens, a scullery, a boiling-house for the great boiler and special lodgings for the cook.

Elizabeth was lavishly entertained with all the usual pageants, masques, fireworks, music and flattering verses:

Eliza is the fairest queen
That ever trod upon this green;
Eliza's eyes are blessed stars,
Inducing peace, subduing wars;
Eliza's hand is crystal bright,
Her words are balm, her looks are light;
Eliza's breast is that fair hill
Where virtue dwells, and sacred skill!
Oh, blessed be each day and hour,
Where sweet Eliza builds her bower!

The Queen was used to taking this sort of thing in her stride but there was a pleasant touch of originality in the performance of ten of the Earl's servants, all Somersetshire men, in their shirt-sleeves playing with a handball, 'at bord and cord, as they termed it' five against five on an improvised court under her window. This amused her Majesty so much that 'she graciously deigned to behold their pastime more than an hour and a half'.

In spite of persistent bad weather, the visit was considered to have been a rousing success. At her departure, her Majesty, 'notwithstanding the great rain', stayed her coach to give great thanks to a consort of dripping musicians who were playing her off the premises, at the same time assuring a gratified Earl of Hertford that the beginning, process and end of his entertainment had been so honourable that she would not forget it.

The following year, 1592, Elizabeth got as far as Sudeley in Gloucestershire, returning by way of Oxford for a formal visit to the University and a heavy programme of sermons, dinners, speeches, Latin orations and disputations. By the end of September she was at Rycote, where she could relax in the company of Henry Norris and his black-haired wife Margery, nicknamed Crow, whose four soldier sons were all to give their lives in the royal service.

Elizabeth had known the Norrises since the far-off days of her precarious girlhood and, like most ageing people, she clung to the friends of her own generation who could share her memories, her prejudices, her way of looking at the world. But, in the nature of things, such friends were growing steadily fewer in number. The future was pushing impatiently at the door and the Queen would have to come to terms with it.

In the circumstances, then, it was ironical that the stage should have been set for so exact a recreation of the past, with Robert Cecil ready to fill his father's old office of Secretary and the Earl of Essex, as it appeared, taking the place once occupied by his step-father – the place of royal plaything and companion, chief ornament and organiser of Court ceremonial, military figure-head when such was needed, and general counter-balance to the Cecil interest.

Although certainly aware of the antagonism existing between the younger men, the Queen seems largely to have discounted it. Burghley and Leicester, after all, had never liked or trusted one another but, under her watchful eye, they had learned to work more or less in harness, even grudgingly to respect one another's qualities. In any case, she had to make use of the material available and the fact that the gulf separating Robert Cecil and Robert Devereux proved in the end to be unbridgeable was her misfortune rather than her fault.

The fault, it must be said, rested largely with the Earl of Essex. The Cecil family had not survived for half a century in the political jungle by making unnecessary enemies and Robert Cecil was in very many, if not quite all, ways his father's son. Robert Devereux, though, owed little or nothing to his step-father. Leicester had been the Queen's creation, his career and his greatness founded entirely on her favour, while Essex's ancestors had been noble before ever the Tudors emerged from their Welsh mountains. Leicester's dependence on the Queen had been constantly emphasised by his widespread unpopularity, while Essex was the people's darling. Leicester, like his mistress, had grown up in a hard school; he had learned, if reluctantly, to accept the drawbacks of his position and the wisdom of putting his passions in his pocket. Essex, on the other hand, was constitutionally incapable of discretion. 'He can conceal nothing', observed one of his secretaries; 'he carries his love and his hatred on his forehead'.

The Earl's impetuous candour, his artless habit of saying exactly what he thought on any given occasion regardless of consequences, his single-minded, childlike pursuit of whatever happened to be his current objective were, of course, all part of his charm, though scarcely the most desirable characteristics in a would-be serious man of affairs. Had they been due only to the natural insensitivity of youth and inexperience, snags of this kind could most likely have been overcome. But, unhappily, they were rooted in a fundamental instability which grew steadily more apparent and finally wrecked the Queen's hopes of ever moulding Robert Devereux into a viable substitute for that other Robert, now six years in his grave. The peculiar relationship which had existed between Elizabeth and the Earl of Leicester had often been stormy, but it had rested on a sure foundation of genuine mutual regard – it could not otherwise have lasted as it did for more than forty years. By contrast, her relationship with Essex was becoming increasingly to be poisoned by an unhealthy mixture of mutual fear and resentment.

The uncomfortable truth was that Elizabeth and Essex could not do without each other. In an unforgiving world, ever watchful for the first sign of weakness, it was essential that Gloriana should be able to display her continued command of the homage of the rising generation, and especially of its most brilliant star. She could not afford to allow any whispers to get about that her powers were failing, that she could no longer control her young men. Considerations such as these, not the foolish infatuation of an elderly woman, explain her nervous irritability when Essex absented himself from Court without leave and her sometimes surprising tolerance of his importunities and bad manners. Essex, too, had to show the world that he, above all others, enjoyed first place in the Queen's affections, that he, above all others, could count on her generosity towards himself and his friends; for, however much he and some of his cronies might be beginning to regret it, the Queen remained the *fons et origo* of power and patronage. No man, however deserving, would get office or preferment without her word.

It was an issue of patronage which led to the first major trial of strength between Elizabeth and Essex. The Earl was naturally beset by scroungers but, to maintain his position, a public man had to be able to reward his servants, either directly out of his own resources, or indirectly by using his influence on their behalf, and Essex was chronically short of private resources. So, when he saw an opportunity to further the career of Francis Bacon, whose devoted behind-the-scenes labours were doing so much to establish him as a political force, he seized on it with the impulsive good-nature which was another of his many charms.

Had Essex stopped to think, even he might have realised how remote were the chances of getting Bacon considered for the forthcoming vacancy of Attorney General. Not merely was the Queen still so annoyed over his tactless behaviour in Parliament that she was refusing to speak to him, but there was already a well-fancied candidate for the post. Edward Coke, the present Solicitor General, was a notoriously rough-tongued, bad-tempered man but, as Speaker of the Commons, he had proved himself a reliable supporter of the Crown; he was nine years older than Bacon and had had far more experience in the courts. (Although the law was Bacon's profession, he seems to have spent remarkably little time actually practising it.) Not surprisingly, the Queen's senior advisers favoured Coke but Essex continued to pester her with his friend's claims throughout the autumn and winter of 1593, apparently unconscious of the fact that he was laying himself open to a humiliating rebuff. When Robert Cecil tried to point out that Bacon would have been better advised to apply for the Solicitorship, a thing that 'might be of easier digestion to the Queen', he refused to see the tacitly offered face-saver. 'Digest me no digestions', he exploded, 'for the Attorneyship is that I must have for Francis; and in that will I spend all my power, might, authority and amity, and with tooth and nail defend and procure the same for him against whomsoever.'

As for Elizabeth, she simply adopted a variation on the stone-walling tactics of which she was such a past mistress. Sometimes she would listen amiably enough to the Earl's vehement advocacy, while repeating her own objections: Bacon's recent offence had been great, he was too young, he lacked experience and Essex himself lacked the necessary judgement to advise her. At other times she would be too busy or too 'wayward' to be approached. Meanwhile the Attorneyship remained vacant. Only when Essex had at last run out of steam was Edward Coke's appointment quietly put through.

Her reaction to an equally vigorous campaign to get Bacon the despised Solicitorship was 'very reserved', though Essex, who certainly rated A for effort, would not let the matter rest until the Queen, 'in passion', bade him go to bed if he could talk of nothing else. 'Wherefore in passion', wrote Essex, 'I went away, saying while I was with her I could not but solicit for the cause and the man I so much affected, and therefore I would retire myself till I might be more graciously heard . . . Tomorrow I will go hence of purpose, and on Thursday I will write an expostulating letter to her. That night or upon Friday morning I will be here again, and follow on the same course, stirring a discontentment in her.'

This persistent bullying refusal to take no for an answer would have been enough to stir a discontentment in anyone, but all the same, Bacon was probably unlucky not to get the Solicitorship. Burghley and Robert Cecil were both ready to support his candidate and the job would have given him his longed-for chance to prove himself. But Elizabeth, while acknowledging that he had 'a great wit, and an excellent gift of speech, and much other good learning', would not give way. Her decision was no doubt influenced by an intuitive wariness of any man who had once let her down in public, and also very likely by disapproval of Bacon's lifestyle (she would have known all about his money troubles, his mounting debts and the pretty young men who frequented his chambers at Gray's Inn), but the overriding reason for his rejection was almost certainly the closeness of his connexion with Essex. The Queen was by now fully aware that the task of containing the Earl himself within reasonable bounds was going to become increasingly difficult – if once she let him start packing her service with his nominees it might well become impossible. Wise in the ways of men, she harboured no illusions about the true nature of Essex's feelings towards her, or about the sort of threat he could come to represent in the hands of abler, more subtle and more unscrupulous operators than himself.

Elizabeth continued to lavish caresses on her 'wild horse' – not for nothing had she taken *video et taceo* as one of her favourite mottos. At the Twelfth Night revels of 1594, when a play was performed and the dancing went on till one o'clock in the morning, the Queen presided on a high throne, richly adorned, looking, says one observer, 'as beautiful as ever I saw her; and next to her chair the Earl, with whom she often devised in sweet and favourable manner'. The Earl could still apparently get almost anything for himself – in July he got a useful present of four thousand pounds cash together with a sibylline warning to 'look to thyself, good Essex, and be wise to help thyself without giving thy enemies advantage, and my hand shall be readier to help thee than any other' – but it was beginning to be noticeable that he could get nothing for his friends.

Although Essex had been obliged to admit defeat in the matter of Francis Bacon, his own reputation and prestige were growing and he was now an internationally accepted part of the political scene. English envoys abroad, Thomas Bodley at The Hague, Thomas Edmondes in Paris and Robert Bowes in Edinburgh, sent him regular reports, and the King of Scots, who had reason to take a special interest in rising men of power south of the Border, wrote flatteringly friendly letters.

More embarrassing than flattering the dedication of *A Conference About the Next Succession to the Crown of England* to the Most Noble the Earl of Essex, 'for that no man', wrote the author, 'is in more high and eminent place and dignity at this day in our realm than yourself . . . and consequently no man like to have a greater part or sway in deciding of this great affair than your Honour'.

The *Conference*, a detailed survey of all existing heirs to the throne, both likely and unlikely, was printed in Antwerp in 1594 under the name of R. Doleman, a pseudonym only thinly concealing the identity of the Jesuit priest Robert Parsons, himself a synonym for Satan in English Protestant circles. Apart from this unfortunate circumstance, the succession, whose unsettled condition had overshadowed English politics for so long, remained a strictly taboo topic. The intrepid Peter Wentworth had attempted to raise it at the last session of Parliament and had gone to prison for his pains, and even the privileged Essex showed unmistakable signs of alarm when a copy of this latest production of Father Parsons' controversial pen reached the Queen. Elizabeth, however, chose to take the matter lightly. She had, after all, no cause to suspect Essex of trafficking with the pro-Spanish Catholic exiles (an imprudence he never was tempted to commit), and as a mark of confidence in this regard 'many letters sent to herself from foreign countries were delivered only to my Lord of Essex and he to answer them'.

By this time Essex was, in fact, acting as an unofficial unpaid Foreign Secretary, employing four secretaries to deal with his voluminous correspondence. The organisation set up and supervised by Anthony Bacon was ensuring that a wide range of confidential information reached Essex House as well as, if not before, it reached the Cecils and, just as the Bacons had calculated, was giving their patron valuable additional status. Sooner or later, though, the rival networks were bound to come into collision and then someone would get hurt. The clash came in 1594 and the victim was the unhappy Dr Ruy Lopez.

Ruy or Rodrigo Lopez, a Portuguese Jew converted to Protestant Christianity, had been settled in London since 1559 and by the mid-eighties was established as a successful and fashionable physician who numbered Francis Walsingham, the Earl of Leicester, the Earl of Essex and even the Queen herself among his patients. The origins of his career as a secret agent are obscure, but circumstances point to the arrival in England of Dom Antonio and his Portuguese retinue – several of whom Walsingham strongly and quite correctly suspected of being Spanish spies. The Portuguese doctor would have been an obvious choice of instrument to penetrate the activities of his compatriots and in April 1587 one Antonio de Vega was writing to inform Bernardino de Mendoza, King Philip's ambassador and spymaster in Paris, that he had gained over Dr Ruy Lopez 'with good promises' and converted him to his Majesty's service.

De Vega hinted that Dr Lopez would be prepared to dispose of Dom Antonio, by poison if necessary. But Mendoza was sceptical, the doctor reluctant to proceed without a written authorisation and so the matter rested. By 1590, however, Lopez had become heavily involved in the murky and hazardous world of spy and counter-spy. Manuel de Andrada, code-named David and one of the most efficient and energetic of Philip's agents, reported to Mendoza that, if he received his Majesty's order, Lopez was ready to help negotiate an arrangement with Spain, and that this was the time. He (Lopez) was confident that the Queen would concede any terms that were demanded of her, as she was in great alarm. If Andrada were given a passport allowing him to go to and fro, and Lopez had undertaken to see to this, then he would come secretly to London where Secretary Walsingham would speak to him. Lopez hoped that everything might be speedily settled to the King's satisfaction, but in any case, provided the secret was kept, he promised to continue to pass on the decisions taken by the Queen's Council and 'everything that happens of interest to his Majesty'. 'In very truth', Andrada concluded impressively, 'no person can report so well as he can, in consequence of his great influence with the Queen and Council.'

There seems no reason to doubt that Lopez was acting under instructions – the putting out of 'peace feelers' being a recognised method of keeping one's adversary off-balance, while at the same time finding out more about his intentions and current strength. It was, of course, a method recognised by both sides. After speeding 'David' on his way to Madrid, Mendoza recommended that he should be sent backwards and forwards to England under cover of the negotiation, 'so that he may be able to report what is going on there'. But by the time Andrada returned from his mission in the summer of 1591, Walsingham was dead and Lord Burghley seems to have been unconvinced of his value as a double agent. After some strenuous de-briefing, he was released into the custody of Dr Lopez and after about eighteen months went abroad again to gather news 'in the interests of England', but he became very dissatisfied with Burghley's niggardly rate of pay and threatened to take his services elsewhere.

Meanwhile, Lopez continued to be employed by the Cecils to monitor the various rather nebulous intrigues being hatched among the Portuguese expatriates in England and the Spanish vice-regal court at Brussels. Exactly why and when he first incurred the ill-will of the Earl of Essex is not clear, although one account says that he betrayed certain discreditable details about his noble patient's physique – a breach of professional etiquette which was promptly reported back. A more likely explanation is that Essex had got wind of the doctor's connexion with Andrada's trip to Spain, possibly from Antonio Perez, a renegade Spaniard now living in London under the Earl's protection, and therefore began to regard him with suspicion. Messages passing between members of the Portuguese community and incoming letters containing mysterious references to the price of pearls and the proposed purchase of 'a little musk and amber' were intercepted by Essex House, and in January 1594 Lopez was arrested.

Taken before Lord Burghley, Sir Robert Cecil and the Earl of Essex the doctor vehemently protested his innocence and a search of his house in Holborn revealed nothing incriminating, as Robert Cecil hastened to report to the Queen. The result, according to Anthony Standen, a prominent member of the Essex House fraternity, was that when the Earl came to Court a day or so later, the Queen turned on him, calling him 'a rash and temerarious youth' for making unfounded accusations against a poor man whose innocence she knew well enough. Malice and nothing else lay behind the attack on Dr Lopez, and she was particularly displeased because her honour was involved in the matter. But if, as seems likely, Elizabeth was hoping by a display of authority to scotch the scandal at birth and save a useful servant and friend, she had miscalculated badly.

Uncontrollably furious at such a rebuke, delivered in the presence of Cecil and the Lord Admiral, Essex slammed out of her presence and shut himself up in his private cabinet, refusing to emerge until 'atonement' had been made. The Admiral had to go to and fro smoothing things over, while the Earl flung himself into renewed interrogation of the prisoners (two other Portuguese were also in custody) and a fresh examination of the documents, scarcely pausing for food or sleep until he was satisfied that he had a convincing case. On 28 January he scribbled a triumphant note to Anthony Bacon: 'I have discovered a most dangerous and desperate treason. The point of conspiracy was her Majesty's death. The executioner should have been Dr Lopez: the manner poison. This I have so followed, as I will make it appear as clear as noon day.'

Whether or not Dr Lopez had ever crossed the debatable land separating counter-espionage from treason has long been a matter of purely academic interest; but the only evidence that he was 'deeply touched' in a murder plot consisted of 'confessions' wrung from exhausted and terrified prisoners, ready to say anything they thought would please. The one fact appearing as clear as noon day out of the whole malodorous mess was that once the word poison had been mentioned in connexion with the Queen, the unhappy doctor's doom was sealed. Neither Elizabeth nor the Cecils were prepared to risk a confrontation with Essex over such an emotive issue. Lopez was tried and condemned on 28 February in an atmosphere of intense popular excitement and, although there is some evidence to suggest that the Queen made an eleventh hour attempt to rescue him (she did ensure that his widow was provided for), he was executed at Tyburn the following June amid the joyful execrations of a howling mob.

To the general public Dr Lopez was yet another in a long line of would-be assassins threatening the Queen's precious life and his unmasking, while it had provoked a wave of vicious anti-Semitism, was soon forgotten in the more pressing concerns of daily life. To the Queen herself, to Lord Burghley and Robert Cecil the case had worrying implications, for it had provided a disagreeable illustration of the sort of power Essex was now able to exert and of the extraordinary difficulties of dealing with a man whose volcanic temper so often seemed to put him outside the recognised conventions of well-bred behaviour.

At the Accession Day tilts of 1595 Essex presented an elaborate Device written for him by Francis Bacon, and in which he appeared in the guise of the knight Erophilus, torn between the rival attractions of Love and Self-love, or the goddess Philautia. He is tormented by the importunities of 'a melancholy dreaming Hermit', representing Contemplation, 'a mutinous brain-sick Soldier', who is Fame, and 'a busy tedious Secretary', Experience – all persuasive orators for Philautia urging him to adopt their own particular course of life. In the end, Erophilus, through the mouthpiece of his Squire, predictably renounced Philautia and all her enchantments -- wandering Hermit, storming Soldier and hollow Statesman -- and makes up his mind henceforward to dedicate himself to the service of Love, in other words the Queen. 'For her recreation, he will confer with his muse: for her defence and honour, he will sacrifice his life in her wars, hoping to be embalmed in the sweet odours of her remembrance; to her service will he consecrate all his watchful endeavours; and will ever bear in his heart the picture of her beauty, in his actions of her will, and in his fortune of her grace and favour.'

Elizabeth sat through this somewhat windy performance, which contained several pretty obvious digs at the Cecils and was clearly intended still further to establish the Earl as principal champion of Queen and country in the public mind, but she did not appear unduly impressed. According to one of those present, she went off to bed remarking that 'if she had thought there had been so much said of her, she would not have been there that night'.

But if the Queen took a sceptical view of the quality of Essex's devotion as laid before her in the rhetorical flourishes of Francis Bacon, she was soon going to need his soldierly services, for the international situation was changing and, after a period of stalemate, the war looked like hotting up again.

In the early summer of 1593 Henry IV had made his well-known decision that Paris was worth a mass and in July of that year was formally received into the Catholic Church – a development which, despite her indignantly reproachful reaction, cannot really have come as any very great surprise to the Queen of England. It had been obvious for some time that Henry had little or no chance of ever persuading the French people to unite behind him as long as he remained a Protestant; but his conversion was still a blow to the common cause of European Protestantism, and brought with it the added danger that he might now be tempted to make a separate peace with Spain and repudiate his debts to his English ally. On the credit side, of course, the collapse of the Holy League meant that the King would at last be able to draw the revenues of all those wealthy northern towns which had so stubbornly refused to recognise him, and Elizabeth would at least be relieved of the burden of subsidising him.

As it turned out, Henry did not become self-supporting for nearly two years. With a Catholic sovereign once more on the throne of France, Philip's insubstantial dreams of bringing her permanently under Spanish 'protection' faded, but he was still maintaining a presence in Brittany which, by the early spring of 1594, had begun to close in on the strategic deep-water port of Brest. This was a threat Elizabeth could not ignore. 'I think there never happened a more dangerous enterprise for the state of your Majesty's country', wrote Sir John Norris, 'than this of the Spaniard to possess Brittany, which under humble correction I dare presume to say will prove as prejudicial for England as if they had possessed Ireland.'

The Queen quite agreed and that summer a task force of eight warships and four thousand men, under the joint command of Norris and Martin Frobisher, sailed from Portsmouth for the Breton coast. But having raised the siege of Brest and destroyed the Spanish fortress at Crozon, the expedition was recalled, the last of the garrison troops from around Paimpol leaving for home before the end of February 1595. The eight companies of English soldiers which had remained in Dieppe after the abortive Normandy campaign had already been withdrawn and although Henry's northern frontiers continued to be menaced by the Spanish army in Belgium, England's long and wearisome involvement in the French wars was now effectively at an end: a relief to everyone but especially to those who had always regarded it as an irritating distraction, diverting valuable resources from the proper business of all right-minded Englishmen -- the business of 'offending our capital enemy, the King of Spain'.

Certainly the naval war had languished during the early nineties and Francis Drake, unemployed since the Portuguese debacle of 1589, was itching to get to sea again – a restless urge which may not have been unconnected with the fact that the busy Earl of Cumberland, with his annual freebooting excursions to Spanish waters, was beginning to acquire something of the reputation for derring-do on the high seas which ten years earlier had been Drake's alone. At any rate, the most famous freebooter of them all, supported by that other veteran sea-dog John Hawkins, was now badgering the Queen to let him loose once more in the Caribbean.

The Queen hesitated and understandably so. At a time when she still did not know which way the King of France was going to jump, and was being reliably informed that preparations for the launching of another Armada were nearing completion, she felt far from convinced of the wisdom of allowing experienced sailors and precious ships to go off into the blue on what might well proved to be a wild goose chase. But 'as all actions of this nature promise good hope until they come to be performed, so did this the more in the opinion of all men, in respect of the eminence of the two Generals and their great experience', and in January 1595, after weeks of haggling and discussion, Elizabeth was at last persuaded to agree in principle to invest in another joint-stock type of expedition to the Spanish Main. But it was June before the arrangements were finalised, and even then serious doubts remained about the advisability of the project. These doubts were strengthened in July, when the remnants of the Spanish forces in Brittany staged a daring commando-style raid on the coast of Cornwall, burning Mousehole, Newlyn and Penzance before vanishing as suddenly as they had come. The raid itself was a flea-bite, but the fact that any Spaniards had actually succeeded in landing caused a disproportionate amount of alarm – especially to the population of Mousehole which decamped in a body.

The Queen was now in two minds whether to cancel the West Indian expedition altogether, or else perhaps combine it with a foray to Portugal and yet another attempt to intercept the returning treasure fleet. Drake and Hawkins objected that they had taken on too many soldiers for a purely naval operation; besides, if the purpose of the voyage were to be altered at this late stage, the Queen, by the terms of her contract, would have to meet all the expenses. If they encountered a Spanish fleet, the two Generals would naturally give battle, but they were not going to waste time hanging round the Azores waiting for the flota – that had been tried unsuccessfully too often. Spanish treasure must be sought at its fountain-head and Drake at least still clung to his old dream of seizing control of the Panamanian Isthmus. In the end, the deciding factor seems to have been a report reaching England that a galleon from the last treasure fleet with a cargo of gold and silver ducats worth £600,000 had been damaged at sea and forced to take refuge at Puerto Rico. The lure of such a prize proved too much for everyone and the fleet – six royal ships, with about a dozen armed merchantmen and others making the total up to twenty-seven – finally sailed from Plymouth at the end of August.

Things began to go wrong almost at once. There was friction between Drake and Hawkins from the start, and they nearly came to an open breach over Drake's obstinate insistence on attempting a landing at Las Palmas. Little was achieved by this, apart from still more delay, while the fleet's presence in the Canaries told the enemy all he needed to know about its ultimate destination. Misfortune struck again at Guadeloupe, when a group of well-armed Spanish frigates captured the *Francis*, a small vessel which had become separated from the main body of the expedition. These frigates, ironically enough, were also on their way to Puerto Rico to convoy the coveted treasure and were able to give the alarm, so that when the English arrived off San Juan on 12 November the city was waiting for them.

Morale on the ships was already low and became lower still when John Hawkins, architect of the Elizabethan navy but now a tired old man of sixty-three who should have been at home by his own fireside, sickened and died as the fleet dropped anchor. The attack on San Juan went ahead as planned, but it failed. The good old days when Spain's colonial outposts had been a happy hunting ground for roving bands of marauders were gone for ever, and in the harsher, more professional climate of the fifteen-nineties harbours like San Juan were protected by forts and shore batteries. Drake didn't give up easily – not with the thought of all that gold in the citadel – but after three days he was obliged to admit defeat, telling his disappointed crews that he would soon bring them to 'twenty places far more wealthy and easier to be gotten'. Accordingly the fleet stood across for the Spanish Main and, after some rather desultory and not especially profitable raiding of coastal settlements, came to the port of Nombre de Dios towards the end of December.

At one time, Nombre de Dios, a notoriously fever-ridden spot, had been the depot for all the gold and silver brought by sea from Peru to Panama and thence on mule-back across the Isthmus for shipment to Spain, but the traffic had been re-routed more than ten years ago to Puerto Bello, a few miles up the coast, and the former Treasure House of the World lay silent and deserted. Drake landed the army, 2,500 men under the command of Thomas Baskerville, but their attempt to force a way through the fifty-odd miles over the mountains to Panama ended in another fiasco. Too much time had been wasted. The governor of Panama City had had too much warning and was fully prepared to defend the passes. The English had no proper guides, the weather was bad, the terrain notoriously rugged and they were running short of food. They floundered on as far as the halfway mark and then gave up, the hardships and losses suffered on the march making many of them swear that they would 'never venture to buy gold at such a price again'.

Baskerville's failure seems to have taken much of the heart out of Drake, and he 'who was wont to rule fortune, now finding his error, and the difference between the present strength of the Indies and what it was when he first knew it, grew melancholy upon this defeat'. Since no one would yet face the prospect of returning empty-handed, it was decided to make for the Bay of Honduras and perhaps attack the settlements on Lake Nicaragua which were popularly and hopefully believed to be roofed and paved with gold. But the fleet got no further than the island of Escudo de Veragua. Sickness was already raging through the ships and now Drake himself, who had always seemed to bear a charmed life, fell victim to an acute form of dysentery. He died delirious on board the *Defiance* during the small hours of 28 January and they buried him at sea off Puerto Bello, saluted by all the cannon in the fleet, 'the trumpets in doleful manner echoing out this lamentation for so great a loss'.

Leaving their beloved General 'slung atween the round shot in Nombre Dios Bay', the expedition sailed sorrowfully for home on 8 February, fighting their way past a Spanish fleet which came out from Cartagena to intercept them. Apart from causing a good deal of alarm in Spain that winter not one of their objectives had been achieved, but they had at least finally learned that the fabled Indies were no longer vulnerable to the sort of casual, scrambling plunder which had won Francis Drake his early fame.

When Spain heard that the terrible El Draque was dead the merchants of Seville, whose profit margins and nervous systems had suffered so severely and so long from the depredations of the great corsair, illuminated their houses and addressed heartfelt thanks to the Almighty. As for King Philip, it was the best piece of news to come his way since the Bartholomew's Day massacre.

In England, and especially in Plymouth and the West Country, there was mourning; but generally speaking the disappearance of so great a figure of the age seems to have made less of an impression than might have been expected. Drake had, of course, been out of the public eye for several years and in the spring of 1596 there were new and stirring doings afoot all along the south coast. Ever since the previous November the military men had been urging the Queen to agree to another major attack on the Spanish mainland. If, as was widely believed, another Armada would be ready to sail by the summer of 1596 this, they argued, was the time for England to abandon her defensive posture and repeat the triumphant beard-singeing exploits of ten years ago.

Elizabeth, as usual, hesitated. She was worried about the Irish situation, where the Earl of Tyrone's revolt looked as if it might be about to turn into something serious, and at home a succession of bad harvests was beginning to cause distress in some parts of the country – hardly the most propitious moment to call for an increased war effort. On the other hand, she could see the point of another pre-emptive strike. She always had seen the point of them, but always found it hard to rid herself of the suspicion that she was being pressurised into taking unacceptable risks with precious, irreplaceable resources – as well as denuding the island of its first and only effective line of defence – in order to satisfy the greed and ambitions of the commanders. However precise and detailed her instructions, she knew from bitter experience that once the fleets and armies had sailed, control, for all practical purposes, was lost and she would be in the hands of the men on the spot. War was the one department where Elizabeth's femininity became a definite and inescapable handicap – not even she could take the field in person – and this was undoubtedly one, if not perhaps the chief, reason why she disliked it so much.

But on this occasion everyone was pressing for action, even old Lord Burghley being cautiously in favour, and on 18 March a commission was signed and sealed naming the Earl of Essex and the Lord Admiral Howard of Effingham as 'lieutenant-generals and governors of her Highness's navy and army' and authorising them to levy five thousand men for service overseas. The expedition was to destroy warships and stores in Spanish ports, to capture and destroy Spanish coastal towns and to seize whatever booty and prizes they could; but there was to be no unnecessary slaughter and no killing of non-combatants. Thomas Howard and Walter Raleigh (just returned from a voyage to the Orinoco and partially restored to favour) were appointed Vice and Rear-Admirals respectively and they, together with Francis Vere and Conyers Clifford representing the army and George Carew as Master of the Ordnance, were to form a Council to advise the two commanders. No action was to be undertaken without their consent, and the Lord Admiral also received private instructions from the Queen to make sure that Essex did not expose himself needlessly to danger. In other words, Charles Howard was to have the unenviable task of keeping his volatile colleague under control. Elizabeth had not forgotten that the last time the Earl had been entrusted with an important command there had been occasions when she did not know what he was doing, what he meant to do, or even where he was.

Preparations for the expedition were going forward smoothly, or at least as smoothly as such preparations ever did go forward, when, at the end of March, came the alarming intelligence that a Spanish force from the Netherlands, commanded by its new general, Archduke Albert of Austria, was at the gates of Calais, and for a time it looked as if the great sea-voyage would be shortened to a hasty cross-Channel rescue operation. Essex hurried down to Dover, where the bombardment could be clearly heard, and waited in a fever of impatience for orders to embark. But if there ever had been a chance of saving Calais, it was lost in the diplomatic sparring between London and Paris. Elizabeth couldn't resist the temptation to capitalize on this sudden opportunity to regain possession of the last outpost of England's old continental empire, whose loss back in her sister's reign had always rankled. The King of France, on the other hand, openly preferred to see the town in Spanish rather than English hands; or, as he put it, he would as lief be bitten by a dog as scratched by a cat. The King, in short, had no difficulty in reading the Queen of England's mind when he rejected her kind offer of succours for Calais on condition that it was placed in her hands by way of 'security' thereafter.

The matter was settled in mid-April by the fall of the town and, although Calais was not a large enough port to be of much use to an ocean-going fleet, the thought of the enemy ensconced on his very doorstep was enough to give every Englishman the shivers. To the military, a swift counter-stroke now seemed more than ever essential and they were, therefore, driven to distraction by the Queen's apparent perversity during the next few weeks. Just as with Drake and Hawkins the previous summer, she was 'daily in change of humour' about the future of the great voyage and at times 'almost resolute to stay it'. Alternatively, she considered the possibility of sending out a smaller expedition under the command of 'an inferior officer', Thomas Howard perhaps, or else of dispensing with a landing force altogether and letting the fleet go on its own.

Essex who, with the Admiral and Francis Vere, was down at Plymouth working furiously among the accumulating chaos of stores, ships and soldiers, began rapidly to run out of his never very plentiful supply of patience. 'The Queen wrangles with our action for no cause but because it is in hand', he wrote bitterly. 'If this force were going to France, she would then fear as much the issue there as she doth in our intended journey. I know I shall never do her service but against her will.' In his letters to Robert Cecil he complained pathetically about the Queen's coldness and ingratitude, 'I receive no one word of comfort or favour by letter, message, or any means whatsoever.' He was working harder than any gentleman of his degree had ever done before to bring some sort of order out of the prevailing confusion, and to get the army trained and organised; yet he was so far from receiving any thanks from her Majesty that anyone would think he had, through 'fault or misfortune', lost her troops. On 12 May he pointed out that he was also being put to considerable personal expense. He had not touched a penny of the Queen's money, but was having to pay lendings to about five thousand soldiers. 'I maintain all the poor captains and their officers', he went on, 'I have a little world eating upon me in my house, am fain to relieve most of the captains and gentlemen and many of the soldiers that come from the Indies; and yet I complain not of charge, but of want of direction and certainty in your resolutions.'

Elizabeth was, of course, nagged by the new anxiety of the Spanish presence in Calais and disappointed and worried by the failure of the West Indian venture; but the principal factor influencing her 'want of direction and certainty' most likely had to do with the negotiations currently proceeding with the French. On 16 May, after several weeks of tough bargaining, a new offensive and defensive alliance was concluded and signed by King Henry's representatives at Greenwich, and eight days later the Queen's letters authorising the departure of the expedition reached Plymouth. To Essex she had written: 'I make this humble bill of requests to Him that all makes and does, that with his benign hand He will shadow you so, as all harm may light beside you, and all that may be best hap to your share; that your return may make you better, and me gladder. Let your companion, my most faithful Charles, be sure that his name is not left out in this petition. God bless you both, as I would be if I were there, which, whether I wish or not, He alone doth know.'

The fleet sailed from Cawsand Bay on 3 June. It made an impressive and beautiful sight, as even the Spaniards were presently to admit, this great Armada of seventeen royal galleons and about a dozen London men-of-war, reinforced by a strong Dutch contingent which, with transports, victuallers, flyboats, pinnaces and hangers-on, brought the total to around a hundred and fifty ships great and small.

The English were divided into four squadrons, the Lord Admiral leading the first in the *Ark Royal*, then Essex in the *Repulse*, Thomas Howard in the *Merhonour* and Walter Raleigh bringing up the rear in the *Warspite*, each squadron wearing distinguishing colours of crimson, orange tawny, blue and white. Among the soldiers were to be found the usual quota of gentlemen volunteers and 'green-headed youths, covered with feathers, and gold and silver lace', but the standard in general was high, the county levies being stiffened by two thousand veterans from the Netherlands commanded by that first-rate professional, Sir Francis Vere.

All in all, the expedition which set course for the North Cape of Spain in June 1596, a fair north-easterly wind filling its sails and taking with it the Queen's prayers for its good success 'with the least loss of English blood', was certainly the largest and grandest of any that had yet gone to war with King Philip. Whether or not the Protestant deity would listen to his handmaiden and 'speed the victory' remained to be seen.

41

Great Eliza's Glorious Name

Faire branche of Honor, flower of Chevalrie!
That fillest England with thy triumphs fame,
Joy have thou of thy noble victorie,
And endless happinesse of thine own name
That promiseth the same;
That through thy prowesse, and victorious armes,
Thy country may be freed from forraine armes;
And great Eliza's glorious name may ring
Through all the world, fill'd with thy wide Alarmes,
Which some brave muse may sing
To ages following . . .

After a long run of failures and disappointments, everything went right for the summer expedition of 1596. The weather co-operated, blowing the fleet swiftly southwards, and for once security seems to have been good – many people, both in Spain and on the fleet itself, apparently believing until almost the last moment that it must be making for Lisbon. So, when the English were sighted off the Bay of Cales, or Cadiz, early in the morning of 20 June, surprise was complete.

In the attack which followed, two of Philip's capital warships were captured and two (one of them the *San Felipe*, which had been the first to grapple with the *Revenge* at Flores five years before) were sunk with appalling loss of life among their crews, as recorded by the young John Donne:

So all were lost which in the ship were found:
They in the sea being burnt, they in the burnt ship
drowned.

After the holocaust in the outer harbour – 'if any man had a desire to see hell itself, it was there most lively figured', commented Walter Raleigh – no further resistance was offered and everyone stormed ashore, the commanders anxiously jostling one another for the greatest share of any available glory in true Elizabethan style. All the same, it was a pity that, in the general excitement, merchant shipping valued at twelve million ducats trapped in the inner harbour at Puerto Real should have been overlooked until too late, the Spaniards themselves having set fire to it.

A pleasurable and profitable fortnight passed in ransacking the city, 'the pearl of Andalusia', and then the question arose of what next? Essex wanted to hold Cadiz and use it as a base for further operations designed to cut King Philip off from 'his golden Indian streams'. As he later pointed out, 'Lisbon and Seville are the cisterns that first receive the wealth, and the Bay of Cales and the river of Tagus the ports whereby the King of Spain's fleets for the Indies ever go forth and to which they ever return: so as impeach him in these places and we impeach him in all.' This was true enough, and certainly the present large and well-found expedition could have remained on the Spanish coast at least for long enough to inflict some further and perhaps even decisive damage. But Essex was overruled by a majority of his fellow commanders. The plain truth, of course, was that the majority considered honour had been satisfied and were now in a hurry to get home with their swag. Even if the Council of War had voted to stay, it is more than doubtful whether they could have controlled the rest of the army which, bulging with the spoil of Cadiz, had frankly lost its enthusiasm for 'greater enterprises'. As William Monson, captain of the *Rainbow*, was to put it, 'some men's desires homeward were so great, that no reason could prevail with, or persuade them'.

The fleet therefore sailed for home, pausing only to make a landing at Faro on the Algarve coast of Portugal, 'a place of no resistance or wealth' according to Monson. It did, however, yield an interesting collection of books and manuscripts belonging to the local bishop, which were subsequently presented by Essex to his friend Thomas Bodley who was engaged in founding a new library at Oxford. Off the Rock of Lisbon the Generals took Council again and Essex, supported by Lord Thomas Howard and the Dutch admiral, offered 'with great earnestness' to stay behind with no more than a dozen ships for as long as their victuals lasted, in the hope of intercepting either the treasure fleet or the East Indian carracks. But again he was overruled by a majority headed by Walter Raleigh, who had no intention of letting their enterprising colleague out of their sight, and the expedition continued on its homeward way – incidentally missing the treasure fleet by no more than a couple of days.

When the first reports from Cadiz reached her, the Queen had been generous in her praise. 'You have made me famous, dreadful and renowned', she wrote, 'not more for your Victory than for your Courage . . . Let the Army know I care not so much for being Queen, as that I am sovereign of such subjects.' But this blaze of royal sunshine soon began to cloud over and by the time the expedition returned to its home ports in early August a distinctly chilly wind was blowing from Whitehall.

Elizabeth had not been best pleased to hear that the shipping at Puerto Real had been given time to destroy its valuable cargoes. Nor was she pleased that a fleet which had cost her fifty thousand pounds to equip and which could have kept the seas for several more weeks, had come stampeding home without even attempting to seize the Indian flotas. Annoyance turned to rage when the reason for this indecent haste became apparent and it was realised just how much of the booty from Cadiz had found its way into unauthorised hands. When the Lord Admiral actually had the gall to ask for more money to pay the wages of soldiers and mariners already weighted down with plunder which should have gone into the exchequer, the Queen exploded. She had always known how it would be, 'rather an action of honour and virtue against the enemy, and particular profit by spoil to the army, than any way profitable to ourself'. The government fought a protracted and determined battle to separate the army from its ill-gotten gains, but without any very noticeable success. Sir Anthony Ashley, the Secretary-at-War, who had sailed with the fleet especially to watch over the Crown's interests had feathered his nest with the others, and it was being whispered at Court 'that the Queen should not hereafter be troubled with beggars, all were become so rich at Cadiz'.

Both commanders-in-chief came in for a share of royal displeasure, her Majesty not hesitating to remind them of their large promises of 'great profit and gain' which would more than repay all expenses and without which, she declared, she would never have agreed to the voyage in the first place. But her particular wrath seems to have been reserved for the Earl of Essex. He had been prevented from publishing his own version of the Action at Cadiz and the Queen was heard to say 'that she had hitherto, to her great damage, been contented to follow the earl's humours; and now he had had his desire; but from henceforth she would please herself, and serve her own'.

Essex, who had returned home with a beard and looking older – he would, after all, be twenty-nine that autumn – accepted his 'crabbed fortune' gloomily. 'I see', he wrote to faithful Anthony Bacon, 'the fruits of these kinds of employments, and I assure you I am as much distasted with the glorious greatness of a favourite, as I was before with the supposed happiness of a courtier, and call to mind the words of the wisest man that ever lived, who, speaking of man's works, cryeth out, Vanity of vanities, all is vanity.'

But if the Queen saw Cadiz as a hollow victory which had not even paid for itself, there is no doubt that it had scored an immense *succès d'estime*. The taking of the city had been another humiliating slap in the face for the King of Spain, another brilliant demonstration of English audacity, and the island's international prestige was back where it had stood in Armada year. 'Great is the Queen of England!' they were exclaiming in Venice, 'Oh, what a woman, if she were only a Christian!', which last unfortunate misapprehension Dr Hawkyns, the royal agent, did his best to correct by circulating copies of the prayer specially composed by the Queen of England for her army's success.

At home, the victory, hollow or not, came as a much needed fillip to a war-weary nation and no matter what was being said at Court, the Londoners had no hesitation in ascribing all the glory to the Earl of Essex. A sermon preached at St Paul's by Dr William Barlow sounding his lordship's 'worthy fame, his justice, wisdom, valour and noble carriage in the action' was received with sustained applause by the congregation, and even in Spain Essex was being acclaimed as a great captain and praised for his courtesy, clemency and magnanimity.

None of this made him any more popular with the Queen. Even when his judgement was vindicated by news of the safe return of the treasure fleet barely forty-eight hours after the English had left Cape Roca, her temper did not improve to any marked degree; although the Earl's 'backward friends', who had been busy putting it about that the real credit for Cadiz belonged to Walter Raleigh and the Lord Admiral, fell suddenly silent. Among other things, Elizabeth was angry about the excessive number of knighthoods conferred by Essex during the expedition. She expected this privilege to be used sparingly by her commanders in the field, for otherwise it cheapened honour – something she had always been careful to avoid. What was more, an Essex knight would become an Essex man and, in the Queen's opinion, his lordship's military clientele was already too numerous for comfort.

The chief bone of contention, however, remained the financial deficit, and as the weeks went by and it grew increasingly obvious that only a small proportion of the spoil of Cadiz was ever going to be recovered, the Queen swore that Essex should pay for his carelessness and his prodigality with her money. Had he not made the soldiers dance *and* paid the piper? In short, she intended to confiscate his share of the ransoms paid by the wealthy Spanish prisoners.

When Lord Burghley, feeling perhaps that matters had gone far enough, was rash enough to intervene, Elizabeth turned on him with 'words of indignity', calling him coward and miscreant and accusing him of regarding the Earl of Essex more than herself. This very unfair attack (which, incidentally, is revealing of her intense nervous irritation at this time) wounded the old man deeply, and he wrote to Essex complaining that he was between Scylla and Charybdis. 'Her Majesty chargeth and condemneth me for favouring of you against her. Your lordship contrariwise misliketh me for pleasing of her Majesty to offend you.' Essex, to do him justice, replied gracefully, but Anthony Bacon could not resist crowing that: 'Our Earl, God be thanked! hath with the bright beams of his valour and virtue scattered the clouds and cleared the mists that malicious envy had stirred up against his matchless merit; which hath made the Old Fox to crouch and whine, and to insinuate himself by a very submissive letter to my lord of Essex.'

Although the ill-tempered aftermath of Cadiz continued to rumble on in the background, there is no question that, in the autumn of 1596, my lord of Essex was riding high. Hailed as the English Scipio, he had become a popular hero such as even Francis Drake had never been – a cult figure surrounded by an adoring entourage, his every public appearance drawing an eager, jostling crowd. Internationally his reputation now stood almost, if not quite, as high as the Queen's. The King of France addressed him as 'Cousin' and foreign diplomats were careful to pay as much respect to Essex House as to Lord Burghley himself. Amidst all this adulation only the founder member of the Essex party stood aside, taking a long cool look at the phenomenon he had helped to create.

Francis Bacon was worried. The significance of Sir Robert Cecil's long-delayed appointment as Secretary while Essex was safely out of the way playing soldiers had not escaped his notice, and ever since the expedition's return he had been watching the political barometer with close attention. At last, in the first week of October, he wrote a long, minutely considered letter to his patron. He would yield to none in true congratulation, but felt bound by duty and friendship to speak his mind – to offer both counsel and warning. Above all, Essex must keep the Queen's trust and favour: 'if this be not the beginning, of any other course I see no end'. But was he going the right way about it? What, after all, was the Queen to think of 'a man of a nature not to be ruled; that hath the advantage of my affection and knoweth it; of an estate not grounded to his greatness; of a popular reputation; of a military dependence: I demand', asked Bacon forthrightly, 'whether there can be a more dangerous image than this represented to any monarch living, much more to a lady, and of her Majesty's apprehension?'

Bacon clearly feared for the future if this unfortunate 'image' was allowed to become fixed in the Queen's mind, and he went on to urge his lordship first and foremost to try and remove the impression that he was 'not rulable'. He must be more attentive, appear more amenable to her Majesty's wishes, take more trouble to please her in small ways, and make his pretty speeches as if he really meant them. As for his 'military dependence', let him keep the substance of it if he must, but for heaven's sake stop flaunting it before a nervous Queen, who was known to love peace, to hate the expense and uncertainty of war and who might easily grow suspicious of a subject with too great a military following. Bacon who, like the queen, was a lover of peace would have much preferred to see Essex delegate martial matters to a subordinate and himself seek a civilian office like that of Lord Privy Seal which, as he wistfully pointed out, was a fine honour and a quiet place worth a thousand pounds a year with, moreover, 'a kind of superintendence over the Secretary'.

All this, of course, would have been excellent advice for a man seriously seeking to consolidate his power and influence in the state, but it was of little use to a maverick like Essex, whose restless self-destructive spirit would always reject the sensible, the politic course. In any case, it would by now have been difficult, if not impossible, for him to have relinquished his military role. After Cadiz he was irrevocably type-cast as England's leading man of war, and there was to be more work for him that autumn.

Even while Bacon was composing his carefully rounded periods, the King of Spain, roused from the lethargy of old age and mortal sickness by the disgrace of seeing one of his principal ports fall so effortlessly into enemy hands – he was said to wish to live only till he might satisfy his vengeance – was hustling his reluctant admirals into an immediate counter-attack, despite the lateness of the season. On 10 October the Venetian ambassador in Madrid reported that great preparations were going on in Lisbon under the command of Don Martin de Padilla, Adelantado or Governor of Castile. A fleet of ninety-odd miscellaneous craft had been assembled of which, according to the Venetian ambassador, a third would be fit to fight. 'There are 12,000 men on board', he went on, 'including seamen. Ships and munitions are very poor; there is a great lack of biscuit.' However, the extent of the preparations, the variety of the provisions and the anxiety of the Adelantado were leading people to believe that he meant to sail as soon as possible. His destination remained a closely guarded secret, 'but common conjecture points to Ireland or England'.

Intelligence reports reaching Anthony Bacon from his agent at Fuenterrabia and letters from a spy entrenched in the Escorial itself had already given warning that Spain was on the move, and towards the end of October the crews of some captured Portuguese caravels confirmed that the Armada had already sailed. The Queen at once turned to the Earl of Essex to organise a Council of War and the whole of the south of England was put on general alert. The militia was mobilised, warning beacons prepared, strategic points along the coast reinforced, and contingency plans for a scorched earth policy in case of an enemy landing were drawn up. After its summer service the navy was laid up in harbour for refitting, but five vessels were already in commission in the Channel and at the beginning of November others were issued for the hasty provisioning of another sixteen. The alarm lasted about a month but no more was heard of the Spanish fleet. Not until Christmas did reliable news come in that it had been scattered by a storm off Cape Finisterre and driven back onto its own coasts with heavy losses.

For the Queen 1596 had been an eventful and an upsetting year, and one which had seen the disappearance of still more familiar faces. In April John Puckering, Lord Keeper of the Great Seal, died of an apoplexy and Elizabeth had at once replaced him by Sir Thomas Egerton, a friend of Essex but an able and experienced lawyer whose talents she valued. The office of Lord Keeper was, in fact, the same as Lord Chancellor, but the latter title was only bestowed on those of noble or gentle blood and Egerton had risen from the ranks. After she had handed him his seals in a ceremony in the Privy Chamber, the Queen, wearing a gown of straw-coloured satin heavily trimmed with silver and standing on a Turkey carpet under the cloth of estate, remarked that she had begun with a Lord Keeper, Nicholas Bacon – 'and he was a wise man, I tell you' – and would end with a Lord Keeper. Lord Burghley, who was also present, exclaimed: 'God forbid, madam. I hope you shall bury four or five more.' 'No', said Elizabeth, 'this is the last' and burst into tears. Egerton murmured awkwardly that the first Lord Keeper had indeed been a wise man, but the Queen still wept, 'clapping her hand on her heart', and turned away, saying: 'None of the Lord Treasurer's men will come to fetch him so long as I am here. (Burghley now had to be carried in a chair.) Therefore I will be gone.' At the door, perhaps to cover her embarrassment at this uncharacteristic breakdown, she suddenly shouted: 'He will never be an honest man until he be sworn. Swear him! Swear him!'

Her first cousin, Henry Carey Lord Hunsdon, son of her maternal aunt Mary Boleyn, also died that spring and was followed in July by Essex's grandfather, that stout old Puritan Francis Knollys. But in spite of these unwelcome intimations of mortality, it was very rare for the Queen to give way to melancholy and foreign visitors were greatly struck by her elegance and vitality. The Duke of Württemberg, who saw her in 1592, had declared, with possibly rather more enthusiasm than accuracy, that to judge from her person and appearance she need not yield much to a girl of sixteen; while in 1595 another German had been deeply impressed by the splendour and richness of her Court and by the fact that her Majesty, dressed in a red robe interwoven with gold thread and sparkling with diamonds, had stood talking to him for more than a full hour by the clock – something which he considered astonishing for a Queen of such great age and eminence.

Of course no one could any longer pretend that the Queen was still in the prime of life, but her stamina and her resilience were surely astonishing as, at sixty-three, she continued to cope with a daily diet of problems which might have daunted any working monarch. Apart from the perennial anxieties about money and the fluctuating international situation, Elizabeth was now seriously worried by economic depression and 'dearth' at home. 1596 had been the third consecutive drenching summer when crops rotted in the ground and food prices rose to unprecedented heights. In the north wheat was up to eighteen shillings a bushel, rye to fifteen shillings and even at these famine prices hard to come by. Local authorities did their best to provide relief; some grain was imported from Germany and Denmark, and the Privy Council issued a stream of regulations intended to prevent hoarding and profiteering. But still the poor died of want and hungry children cried in the streets, 'not knowing where to have bread'. There were bread riots in Oxfordshire and some other places that autumn and a good deal of hot-headed talk by men with empty bellies, while the justices of the peace lived in dread of more widespread disturbances. After the boom years of the seventies and early eighties trade was in recession, and the law and order situation was not improved by the numbers of discharged soldiers now being thrown onto the labour market. Many of these unfortunates, unable or unwilling to return to a life of honest toil, took to roaming the countryside in gangs, terrorising isolated villages and farmsteads, or else gathered in the cities – a social nuisance and ready-made fodder for agitators and trouble-makers.

Then there was always the Earl of Essex. His lordship had come back from Cadiz in one of his hair-shirt moods, attending prayers regularly and prepared to devote himself entirely to business with, so he said, 'no ambition but her Majesty's gracious favour and the reputation of well serving her'. Unfortunately it was not a lasting mood. At the beginning of 1597 plans were already under discussion for yet another 'design against Spain' to be undertaken in the summer, and the Earls of Cumberland and Essex both put forward schemes for an attack on Ferrol, where yet another Armada was being laboriously collected. Essex's plan was, typically, the more grandiose. He wanted a large amphibious force of the kind which had gone to Cadiz – a fleet of ten or twelve Queen's ships, supported by twelve Londoners and twenty Dutchmen, with an army of five thousand and a free hand for himself. Elizabeth was lukewarm; there were rumours that Walter Raleigh and Lord Thomas Howard might be promoted to command and the upshot was a furious row between Queen and favourite. Essex took to his bed – a ploy he was to make use of more and more as time went on. Meanwhile Sir Robert Cecil was noted to be in great credit, the Queen spending most of the day in 'private and secret conference' with her new Secretary.

The changing state of the parties was naturally a matter of intense interest at Court, and that assiduous correspondent Rowland Whyte informed Sir Robert Sidney in a letter dated 19 February that the Earl of Essex had 'kept in' for a full fortnight, although the Queen often sent to see him and he, too, was going privately to see her almost every day. On 25 February Whyte had met my lord of Essex coming out of his chamber in his gown and nightcap and was able to report that there had been a reconciliation. 'Her Majesty', he wrote, 'as I heard, resolved to break him of his will, and to pull down his great heart, who found it a thing impossible, and says he holds it from the mother's side; but all is well again, and no doubt he will grow a mighty man in our State.'

Two days later there was more trouble, with Essex in the sulks again and announcing that he meant to visit his estates in Wales for his health's sake. 'Truly', commented Rowland Whyte, 'he leads here a very unquiet life.' Robert Cecil had apparently been to see him on a conciliatory mission which 'took not that success which was looked for' and now, again according to Whyte, Walter Raleigh was often very private with the Earl, having become 'a mediator for peace' between his lordship and the Secretary.

In the middle of these delicate negotiations came the death of Lord Cobham, Warden of the Cinque Ports. Essex was pushing Robert Sidney, younger brother of the dead hero Philip Sidney and currently Governor of Flushing, as his candidate for the vacant office, but the Queen rejected him out of hand. Sidney was too young, and, in any case, was already fully occupied with his present job. Besides, she added, it would be an insult to the Brooke family to bestow the Wardenship on a man of lesser rank and indicated that she had more or less decided to give it to the new Lord Cobham.

Essex, who as usual was making the affair an issue of confidence, retorted that if Robert Sidney's rank was not high enough, he would stand himself. At a Council meeting on 7 March he declared that he had cause to hate Lord Cobham for his villainous dealing (Henry Brooke had been one of the more outspoken critics of the Cadiz operation), and if the Queen were to grace so unworthy a man, then he, Essex, would have every reason to think himself little regarded by her.

Nevertheless, two days later, the Queen told him that she had definitely decided that Lord Cobham should have the Cinque Ports. In a furious temper the Earl at once got ready to set out on his Welsh journey, but he was recalled before he had left London and in a private interview Elizabeth offered to make him Master of the Ordnance. This was an important military post and just the kind of office which Francis Bacon had tried to warn him against, but Essex accepted without a second thought and, for the time being at least, was happy again.

Although the fleet was now being put into commission, a good deal of doubt remained as to what, if any, aggressive action would be attempted in 1597. Reports coming in from Spain of famine, desertion and sickness at Ferrol seemed to discount any immediate danger from that quarter, and one school of thought still held that the recovery of Calais ought to have first priority. This had been suggested to the King of France – a relieving force on the same conditions as before with the Earl of Essex in command – but the King is said to have replied, 'with a disdainful smile', that he was sure her Majesty would never allow his cousin of Essex to leave her skirts. To bait the lioness was to invite a punishing swipe of her claws and this insult, being faithfully repeated back, provoked four lines written in her Majesty's own hand which caused the King to change colour and almost to strike the messenger. Anthony Bacon was afraid that, if the story were true, 'some effects' would follow, and certainly Anglo-French relations took a distinctly chilly turn that summer.

Nothing had been decided when, on 18 April, at a dinner party at Essex House, Robert Cecil, Essex and Walter Raleigh agreed to settle their differences. The alliance was based on mutual self-interest. Cecil was angling in his quiet way for the Chancellorship of the Duchy of Lancaster. Raleigh wanted to get back his old job of Captain of the Guard, and in return offered to find victuals at ninepence a day for six thousand men for any forthcoming venture, while Essex, who was determined to have sole command this time, wanted all the support he could get. The new triumvirate made a formidable combination and by the end of the month Rowland Whyte was able to tell Robert Sidney that 'our preparation for sea for her Majesty's fleet goes well forward, so doth the victualling of six thousand foot, on expectation of some secret enterprise against the common enemy'.

Three weeks later came the usual hitch. 'Here', wrote Whyte, 'hath been much ado between the Queen and the Lords about the preparation for sea; some of them urging the necessity of setting it forward for her safety; but she opposing it, by no danger appearing towards her anywhere, and that she will not make wars, but arm for defence; understanding how much of her treasure was spent already in victual, both for ships and soldiers at land. She was extremely angry with them that made such haste in it, and at Lord Burghley for suffering it, seeing no greater occasion.' It seemed that no reason or persuasion could prevail and the Queen had given orders 'to stay all proceeding'. 'How her Majesty may be wrought to fulfil the most earnest desire of some to have it go forward', added Whyte, 'time must make it known.'

Time made it known within a few days, Elizabeth's struggles having been overcome, probably by sheer weight of numbers. The expedition was on again and Essex was 'to be chief of all'. With the Cecils behind him he had become well nigh irresistible; everything was still love and kindness between them and 'all furtherance given to his desires, especially in the matter now in hand'.

Walter Raleigh, too, was getting his reward. At the beginning of June Robert Cecil had brought him in to see the Queen, who received him graciously and reinstated him as Captain of the Guard. Elizabeth was pleased to have her old friend back. She took him out riding with her that evening and he was soon back on the old footing, coming and going boldly in the Privy Chamber 'as he was used to do'. All this took place in Essex's absence, but the Court knew it had his approval.

Having got his own way, the Earl, as always, was ready to call the whole world brother and, in any case, he was often away from Court these days. His steward, Gilly Meyrick, told Rowland Whyte complacently that his lordship was so full of the business now in hand that everyone must have patience till his return, when he would be able to do something for his friends.

Essex, in fact, looked all set for further glory and on 15 June his commission as 'lieutenant-general and admiral of our army and navy' was signed by the Queen. His instructions were to go first to Ferrol and destroy the Spanish fleet. 'For the doing whereof, you . . . will discreetly in God's name and with the least danger and loss of our people, expedite this special service for the ruin of the enemy, especially by the destruction of his ships; which being well executed, there is no cause for us to doubt of any peril to come for a long time, though his mind be never so malicious.' It was 1589 all over again, for only after accomplishing this 'special service' was the Lord General authorised to stand over to the Azores in pursuit of that eternal chimera, the treasure fleet, and also to explore the possibility of establishing a permanent base on the island of Terceira – that other long-cherished but by now impractical dream.

The expedition was a large one, much on the lines of the previous year's – seventeen of the Queen's ships and twenty-four troop carriers. Thomas Howard and Walter Raleigh were sailing as vice and rear admirals as before, and the fleet would again be reinforced by a strong Dutch squadron. Everyone was hoping for another Cadiz and Essex, setting out on his first independent naval command, wrote to the Queen that he would strive to be worthy of so high a grace and so blessed a happiness.

Unfortunately, the Islands Voyage, as it came to be known, got off to a disastrous start. Contrary winds in the Channel delayed the rendezvous at Plymouth for the best part of a month, while morale sagged and provisions were eaten up at an alarming rate. At last, on Sunday 10 July, they were able to get away, but almost immediately a great storm blew up from the south-west and raged for four horrible days. The fleet soon lost contact and ships and men suffered severely from the tremendous buffeting of wind and sea. It was too much for Walter Raleigh and too much for Essex, although he hung on as long as he dared, and by the nineteenth everyone except Lord Thomas Howard, who had triumphantly ridden out the gale and was now cruising off Corunna, had crawled exhaustedly back to port.

It was a bitter disappointment. There had been no actual losses but most of the ships were in need of repair – Essex's own flagship, the *Merhonour*, was leaking so badly that he had had to abandon her – and this would mean more delay with the campaigning season already well advanced. They would also need more provisions, which would mean more expense. The Earl wrote off anxiously to London – this was just the kind of setback calculated to annoy the Queen and perhaps make her decide to cancel the whole operation – but he was lucky enough to catch her in a relaxed mood. She was thankful that the fleet and its commanders were safe. She was willing for the voyage to continue, and would send the *Lion* to replace the crippled *Merhonour* with another three months' provisions, though, wrote Robert Cecil, 'she stuck at that at first'. Clearly the Cecil influence was still favourable and in another letter Sir Robert assured the absent Essex that 'the Queen is so disposed now to have us all love you, that she and I do every night talk like angels of you'.

It was while the two admirals were working like demons to refit and get to sea again that the famous episode of the Polish ambassador took place.

This had begun as a routine piece of diplomatic business, but as the Queen preserved pleasant memories of the King of Poland's father, who had visited her once long ago in her giddy courting days, and as his envoy was said to be a handsome, well-spoken fellow, she decided to honour him with a public reception in the Presence Chamber, with the lords and officers of the Court gathered round making an occasion of it.

The ambassador was duly brought in, attired in a long robe of black velvet 'well jewelled and buttoned', and kissed hands before retiring a few paces to make his oration; while the Queen, standing under the canopy of estate, waited to listen kindly to the usual complimentary Latin address. But it was not a complimentary address. On the contrary, the Polish ambassador was uttering threats. His master, he said, complained that, despite repeated protests, the Queen was allowing his ships and merchants to be spoiled in the pursuance of her quarrel with Spain, thus violating the laws of nature and of nations. By attempting to prohibit their freedom of trade, the Queen was assuming a superiority over other princes which he found intolerable and would no longer endure. He regarded Spain as his friend, and if her Majesty would not speedily reform these abuses, then he would do it for her.

For an ambassador supposedly come in peace to launch such an unheralded attack was, of course, a shocking breach of protocol and his audience heard him out in frozen silence. But if the King of Poland had expected to flummox the Queen of England, he was about to be disappointed. Her Majesty took up the challenge without hesitation, and there and then in fluent and flawless off-the-cuff Latin, proceeded to wipe the floor with his unhappy spokesman. 'Expectavi legationem, mihi vero querelam adduxisti . . .' If the King were really responsible for such language, then it must be attributed to youth and inexperience and also, no doubt, to the fact that he was a king not by right of blood but only by election. As for the ambassador, he might consider himself an educated man who had read many books, but clearly he had never come across the chapter which prescribed the proper forms to be used between kings and princes. If it were not for his privileged status, she added, she would have dealt with his impertinence 'in another style'. She then dismissed him contemptuously, promising to appoint some of her Council 'to see upon what ground this clamour of yours hath its foundation'.

Justly pleased with her performance, Elizabeth is said to have turned to the awed and admiring bystanders, exclaiming 'God's death, my lords! I have been enforced this day to scour up my old Latin that hath lain long rusting.' A little later she remarked wistfully that she wished the Earl of Essex might have been present to hear her and Robert Cecil, taking the hint, had a full account of the incident sent down to Plymouth. Essex – harassed by problems of sickness, desertion and shortage of victual, while persistent south-westerly gales continued to keep the fleet bottled up in harbour – nevertheless made haste to send congratulations on her Majesty's princely triumph over 'the braving Polack'. Surely she was made of the same stuff of which the ancients believed the heroes to be formed – 'that is, her mind of gold, her body of brass'.

The Earl may well have wished similar heroic attributes for himself during those frustrating weeks of struggle to salvage something from the wreckage of his great command. 'Such contrariety of winds and such extreme weather at this time of year, hath not been seen', he wrote dispiritedly to his secretary, Edward Reynolds. All the same, he intended, by God's grace, to live at sea until winter came in. 'We will fare hardly, but we will offer to dispute the cause with the Adelantado if he mean to look abroad this year.'

It was more than half way through August before a much depleted expedition finally set sail, Essex having at the last moment decided to discharge nearly all his infantry, keeping only the hard core of veterans who had come with Francis Vere from the Netherlands. This, of course, meant that there would now be no chance of landing at Ferrol and, although the Queen was still insisting on a naval assault, Robert Cecil no longer expected to see any results beyond 'the keeping up of the journey's reputation, by keeping the sea as long as the time of year doth serve for the Spaniards to come out, and to lie off at the Islands to interrupt the Indian fleet'.

In the event, Essex and Raleigh never went to Ferrol at all. Relying on reports that the Adelantado was too weak to come out anyway and using the weather as a convenient excuse (the fleet had again been separated by gales), they disobeyed instructions just as Drake had done before them and rendezvoused at the Azores on 14 September. Here they found that the treasure ships had not yet arrived, nor had the usual escort sailed to meet them. Hopes of making a killing rose sharply but Essex, either from over-excitement or over-anxiety or both, proceeded to behave like a neurotic sheepdog, constantly chasing after shadows and regrettably failing to inform his rear admiral of his movements.

It was during one of the Lord General's sudden darts over the horizon that Walter Raleigh performed the only noteworthy exploit of the entire campaign, landing at Fayal, one of the islands in the central group, and taking the town. When Essex returned he was furious at having been cheated of the 'honour' and a full-scale row developed with Essex, egged on by the more hysterical members of his entourage, threatening to court martial Raleigh for going ashore without orders, and Raleigh, who was not a man to stand for nonsense of this kind, threatening to take himself and his squadron home. In the end good old Thomas Howard managed to patch things up, persuading Essex to accept an apology and Raleigh to make one, but it was a fragile truce and feelings continued to run high between the Earl's followers and Raleigh's Westcountrymen.

Leaving the Dutch to guard the southern approaches, the English fleet now moved in a body to La Gratiosa in the north. The flota, which was expected at any moment, would arrive from the west and would have to be intercepted before it reached sanctuary in the heavily fortified roadstead at Terceira, but on 27 September the Earl of Essex, for reasons which remain mysterious, decided to make for St Michael's, the easternmost island, arriving at dawn on the twenty-ninth. Meanwhile, the flota, accompanied by eight galleons of the Indian Guard, had duly appeared on the western horizon and, before the English could retrieve their general's horrifying blunder, had sailed placidly into the Angra Road at Terceira and anchored under the protection of the most formidable shore batteries then known.

In 1585 Drake had missed the treasure fleet by a margin of twelve hours for reasons 'best known to God'. Essex had missed it by a margin of three hours, in circumstances which could only be explained by his own shortcomings as a commander. William Monson in the *Rainbow*, who had the mortifying experience of actually encountering the flota but being unable to impede its progress, considered that none of the captains could be blamed. 'All', he wrote later, 'is to be attributed to the want of experience in my lord and his flexible nature to be over-ruled.'

Since it would have been suicidal to attempt a direct assault on Terceira with the forces at its disposal, the expedition's only remaining hope – and that was a forlorn one – was to try and take one of the other islands, replenish their supplies and then hang on until the Spaniards were forced to put to sea. Accordingly the fleet sailed despondently back to St Michael's. Here it was agreed that while Raleigh created a diversion off Punta Delgada, Essex should take his soldiers round the headland and make a landing at Villa Franca where the coast was more sheltered. He would then march across country to take the town and fort of St Michael's from the rear. The first part of this plan was carried out but, having discovered Villa Franca to be a pleasant spot, well provided with the comforts of life, the army showed a marked reluctance to leave it. Essex listened to his officers' gloomy assessments of the probable hazards of the overland journey and the difficulties likely to be experienced in taking St Michael's from any angle and, with his usual weakness for cheap popularity, allowed himself to be persuaded. They would stay where they were and send for the fleet to join them, but not just yet – all those thirsty seamen would soon dispose of the wine and other goodies so thoughtfully left behind by the inhabitants of the town. It was an inexcusable decision whichever way you looked at it, made still worse by the deliberate failure to inform Walter Raleigh, left in suspense on the other side of the island with many of his ships beginning to run short of fresh water.

But while the fleet waited, at first puzzled and then angry, a prize offered itself which might very satisfactorily have wiped the army's eye. A huge East India carrack, homeward bound and fully laden, was sighted making trustfully for the road at St Michael's and, hardly daring to breathe, Raleigh ordered all flags to be struck, not a move to be made, until she had rounded the point. It could so easily have been the *Madre de Dios* all over again, if one of the Dutch captains had not lost his head and opened fire at almost the last moment. The carrack took fright and helped by a sudden shift of wind was able to run herself aground under the guns of the fort. The townspeople swarmed out to help unload her and by the time the English flyboats had managed to cover the three intervening miles of choppy water, her captain had set her alight.

This was the last straw as far as the sailors were concerned, for if Essex had kept his part of the bargain, the shore would have been in the hands of the army and some fortunes at least would have been made. The fleet had had enough and this final fiasco marked the end of a useless and inglorious voyage, remarkable for nothing but bad luck, bad judgement and bad feeling. In any case, it was now October, the weather was breaking up and everyone wanted to go home. The army was re-embarked and, after watering at Villa Franca, the expedition prepared to sail. Little attempt was made to keep formation and when a brief storm blew up, scattering the squadrons, they simply steered their own course for Plymouth, the more weatherly ships drawing ahead and leaving stragglers to fend for themselves. This rush for home was due primarily to the desire of individual captains to get their stories in first, since none of the disgruntled and disappointed crews was yet aware that they had company; that on 9 October, the very day they had left the Islands, the fleet in Ferrol so casually ignored by Essex and Raleigh had put to sea and was making for the Channel ahead of them.

The moment he realised that the English fleet was heading for the Azores, Philip of Spain had become possessed by the resolve to seize this apparently heaven-sent opportunity to sink his teeth into his arch-enemy while she lay virtually undefended. The King knew that he was dying. He knew that this would be his last opportunity to do God's work and, sweeping aside all objections, ignoring 'the unwillingness to sail which filled the minds of everyone . . . and of the absolute lack of all that was essential to the success of the enterprise', he literally drove the unhappy Adelantado of Castile to sea.

Don Martin's orders were to sail for Brittany and pick up the squadron of galleys which was still based on the little port of Blavet. He was then to cross to Cornwall, capture Falmouth and establish a base there, before returning to the Scillies to lie in wait for the English fleet. 'On winning a victory, as was expected, he was again to enter Falmouth and land the rest of his troops. From Falmouth he was to press forward and capture all he could.'

Whether Philip, carried away as most people seemed to believe by a passion for revenge, really expected this ingenious plan to result in the subjugation of England, or whether he was simply hoping to frighten Elizabeth into deserting her Dutch allies and agreeing to make peace on his terms, it is impossible to say. But, as the Venetian ambassador later remarked, no impartial observer had ever thought for a moment that, in a bad season, with a weak Armada, the King's 'violent resolution' could possibly result in anything except another humiliating failure. Nevertheless, late, creaky, ill-prepared, ill-equipped and reluctant though it was, the Armada got as far as Brittany and some of the ships were actually sighted off the Lizard.

An attack in such circumstances, with her own fleet straggling home in disorder after an unsuccessful voyage, was the sort of nightmare which had always haunted the Queen, and when Essex arrived in Plymouth on 26 October, he found that 'the Spaniards were upon the coast' and everyone in an acute state of alarm. The Earl, who was probably not sorry to have attention diverted from his own recent performance, prepared to rise magnificently to the occasion and assist at the destruction of a fleet which he should have finished off three months ago. 'If we do not bestir ourselves as never men did', he wrote excitedly, 'let us be counted not worthy to serve such a Queen.' As soon as he had set his sick men ashore and taken on fresh water, he would be out with as many ships as he could, even if they had to eat ropes' ends and drink rain water.

The Queen was not pleased with Essex, who had 'given the enemy leisure and courage to attempt us', but in this emergency she authorised him to assume command and take whatever action seemed necessary, with the proviso that he must not leave England unprotected upon any 'light advertisement'. However, if the Spaniards appeared to be making for Ireland, then he should follow them. It would not be necessary to eat ropes. 'For treasure, for victual, and what may be fit for us to send, you shall find that you serve a Prince neither void of care nor judgement what to do that is fit in cases of this consequence.'

As it turned out, no action was necessary. A brisk north-easterly was already scattering Don Martin's unenthusiastic fleet, and by the end of the month they were scuttling thankfully for home. It was the last Armada – just as the Islands Voyage was to be last big combined operation in Spanish waters. Although no one yet realised it, the stormy, unfruitful autumn of 1597 marked the end of an era.

42

A Very Great Princess

Love wing'd my Hopes and taught me how to fly
Far from base earth, but not to mount too high:
For true pleasure
Live in measure,
Which if men forsake,
Blinded they into folly run and grief for pleasure take.

'We may say, and that truly, that God fought for us . . . for certainly the enemy's designs were dangerous, and not to be diverted by our force; but by His will who would not suffer the Spaniards in any of their attempts to set footing in England.' This, at least, was the considered verdict of William Monson on the Armada of 1597 and one which was most probably shared by Queen Elizabeth. Having once more been obliged to watch her men of war deliberately disobeying their instructions with what might have been very serious consequences, it would hardly be surprising if she had come to regard the Almighty as her only reliable supporter.

Nor was it surprising that the Earl of Essex should have received a chilly welcome when he returned to Court at the end of October. The Queen had been listening to Walter Raleigh's friends and made no secret of her anger and disappointment with her commander-in-chief. It was the return from Cadiz all over again, but this time there was no compensating triumph. This time, too, Essex, himself deeply disappointed, overtired, irritable and on the defensive, was in no mood of resignation and quickly found a grievance of his own to exploit.

After church on Sunday, 23 October, in a grand ceremony in the Presence Chamber, the Queen had conferred the earldom of Nottingham on Charles Howard – an event made the more noticeable by the extreme rarity of Elizabethan peerages. Some people might have seen this one as a well-deserved, if belated, recognition of a distinguished servant of the Crown. Essex chose to see it as a deliberate insult, taking special umbrage over the wording of Howard's patent, which not only mentioned his great services against the Armada of 1588, but also in the action at Cadiz, the credit for which, in Essex's opinion, belonged to him alone. To make matters worse, the new earl, as Lord High Admiral and Lord Steward of the present Parliament, would now take precedence over him on public and state occasions – a humiliation Essex was not prepared to endure. He took himself off to his house at Wanstead on the pretext of having to attend to his own long-neglected affairs and proceeded to indulge in an attack of galloping self-pity. Being Essex, of course, he was over-reacting, but the timing of Charles Howard's elevation does lead to the suspicion that it had been intended, if not as a direct snub, at least as a strong hint that the Queen's favour was not to be considered as anyone's exclusive property.

The absence of my lord of Essex naturally became the chief topic of conversation at Court, Rowland Whyte speculating that the peace concluded between him and Robert Cecil would once more 'burst out to terms of unkindness'. The Queen, faced with this fresh evidence of irresponsibility in one who, like it or not, was still a popular hero and a leading public figure, grumbled that a prince was not to be contested withal by a subject, but she would not take up the challenge. She would not order Essex to return, his place and duty ought to be enough to command him, she said, and Lord Hunsdon was able to tell the sulking Achilles that he could find 'nothing but comfort and kindness towards your lordship, if you will but turn about and take it'.

In spite of strenuous efforts by his well-wishers to make him see the futility of his behaviour, Essex stayed obstinately at Wanstead for a full fortnight and, for the sake of appearances, Elizabeth was obliged to accept the excuse of his 'want of health'. When at last he condescended to come back to town, he persisted in his refusal to take his seat in Parliament or attend Council meetings, in case he should meet the Lord Admiral and be unable to control himself. He insisted that the Queen should be pleased to see the wrong done unto him and that the wording of the Earl of Nottingham's patent should be altered – a demand which the Earl of Nottingham understandably refused even to consider. An element of fantasy was introduced into the situation when Essex offered to settle the matter by personal combat, either with the Lord Admiral himself (a man twice his age, who had cried off the Islands Voyage because of indisposition of body'), or with one of his sons or kinsmen. Christmas approached and still the quarrel and its various ramifications were keeping the Court in a state of uproar. 'Here is such ado about it', reported Rowland Whyte, 'as it troubles this Place and all other proceedings.' 'All other proceedings' was the key phrase, for by December Essex's tantrums had begun to interfere with the progress of an important item of international business.

The Kings of France and Spain were now moving towards a settlement of their differences, and the King of France – mindful of his treaty obligations not to conclude a separate peace – had despatched a special envoy to London charged with the delicate task of discovering how Queen Elizabeth would react to the idea of taking part in joint negotiations with Spain. Elizabeth was naturally anxious that her Council should present a united front on such a vital issue and it would, of course, be acutely embarrassing if Essex, as a particular friend of Henry IV's, refused to meet his ambassador. André Hurault, Sieur de Maisse, was therefore kept waiting for his first audience while renewed behind-the-scenes moves were made to pacify the intransigent Earl.

De Maisse, an experienced and skilful diplomat, soon became maliciously aware of the English government's predicament, nor did it take him long to evaluate the probable response to his mission. The Queen, he thought, was inclined to peace and would welcome it, if some way could be found of including the Netherlands. Old Lord Burghley, too, was likely to be in favour, and where he led, his son and the rest of the Cecil faction would follow. Opposition could, however, be expected from the Essex party, for while de Maisse did not believe that the Earl would be so rash as to speak openly in favour of war, he undoubtedly had no desire for peace. Why should he, after all? 'He is courageous and ambitious', commented the ambassador, 'and a man of great designs, hoping to attain glory by arms, and to win renown more and more.' With the coming of peace, his shining public image would quickly fade and he would become no more than just another Council lord, forever playing second fiddle to Mr Secretary and falling ever deeper into debt.

André de Maisse was a conscientious man, keeping a faithful daily record of his observations of the English Court. The Queen, in particular, fascinated him and from the pages of his journal there emerges an unforgettable picture of Elizabeth as she was in the fortieth year of her reign.

The ambassador was finally summoned to the presence on 8 December and found the Queen *en déshabillé*. She told him that she had had a boil on her face which had made her feel wretched, and although she apologised profusely for receiving him in her nightgown, his first impression was of a somewhat outlandish old lady, wearing a great reddish coloured wig covered with gold and silver spangles, and perpetually fidgeting – twisting and untwisting her long hanging sleeves, or jerking open the front of her robe 'as if she was too hot'. Her face was long and thin and appeared very aged, and her teeth were discoloured and uneven. Many of them were missing, so that it was difficult to understand her when she spoke quickly. The whole effect was definitely weird, and yet the charismatic grace and dignity were still unmistakable.

Elizabeth was at her most affable, ordering a stool to be brought for de Maisse and telling him to remain covered. But, he wrote, 'all the time she spoke she would often rise from her chair and appear to be very impatient with what I was saying. She would complain that the fire was hurting her eyes, though there was a great screen before it and she six or seven feet away; yet did she give orders to have it extinguished, making them bring water to pour upon it. She told me that she was well pleased to stand up, and that she used to speak thus with the ambassadors who came to seek her and used sometimes to tire them, of which they would on occasion complain. I begged her not to overtire herself in any way, and I rose when she did; and then she sat down again, and so did I. At my departure she rose . . . and again began to say that she was grieved that all the gentlemen I had brought should see her in that condition, and she called to see them. They made their reverence before her, one after the other, and she embraced them all with great charm and smiling countenance.'

When de Maisse saw the Queen again a week later, she was looking better and was rather more conventionally dressed, in black taffeta bound with gold lace and lined with crimson over a petticoat of white damask. All the same, he noticed that 'when she raises her head she has a trick of putting both hands on her gown and opening it insomuch that all her belly can be seen'. During the course of conversation Elizabeth often referred to herself as 'foolish and old', saying she was sorry that de Maisse, who had known so many wise men and great princes, should come at length to see a poor woman and a foolish. The ambassador, who knew better than to be taken in by this kind of talk, remarked that the Queen liked to speak slightingly of her intelligence 'so that she may give occasion to commend her'. She was obviously pleased when he praised her judgement and prudence, but said modestly 'that it was but natural that she should have some knowledge of the affairs of the world, being called thereto so young'. 'When anyone speaks of her beauty', wrote de Maisse, 'she says that she was never beautiful, although she had that reputation thirty years ago. Nevertheless, she speaks of her beauty as often as she can.'

The Earl of Essex was still conspicuously absent from the gathering in the Privy Chamber and de Maisse was afraid that until he returned to Court 'they (the English) will do nothing in good earnest in the business which I have discussed'. But now, at last, there were signs of a breakthrough. Rowland Whyte, writing a few days before Christmas, was able to tell Robert Sidney that 'the gallant Earl doth now show himself in more public sort than he did', and shortly afterwards the word went round that Essex was to be given the office of Earl Marshal which would restore his precedence over the Lord Admiral. The Admiral was not pleased and went off in a huff to his house at Chelsea, but the deadlock seemed to have been broken and when de Maisse had his third audience with the Queen on Christmas Eve he found her in excellent spirits, wearing a very low cut gown of cloth of silver and listening to a pavane being played to her on the spinet.

Elizabeth had obviously warmed to the urbane and civilised Frenchman and was taking a good deal of trouble over him, chatting freely on a wide range of subjects from music to religion, reminiscing and entertaining him with a selection of anecdotes from her extensive repertoire. 'Whilst I was treating with her in the matter of my charge', de Maisse recorded, 'she would often make such digressions, either expressly to gain time . . .

or because it is her natural way. Then would she excuse herself, saying, "Master Ambassador, you will say of the tales I am telling you that they are mere gullery. See what it is to have to do with old women such as I am".' But the ambassador thought that apart from her face, which looked old, and her bad teeth, it would not be possible to see a woman of so fine and vigorous disposition, both in mind and body. She knew all the ancient histories, he wrote, and 'one can say nothing to her on which she will not make some apt comment'. In fact, despite her various little oddities, he had come to feel an enormous respect for the Queen. 'She is a very great princess who knows everything' was his considered judgement.

Elizabeth had promised that de Maisse should confer with her Council on the matter in hand, but it seemed that the Earl of Essex was still making difficulties and was now threatening to go back to the country again. De Maisse thought this was very foolish, for the Earl would only be giving his enemies a further opportunity to make mischief behind his back, and if he persisted in 'withdrawing' himself in this fashion the Queen might well begin to suspect that he was up to no good. The ambassador did not pretend to understand all the mysterious ins and outs of the quarrel, but he was becoming more than a little irritated by it and grumbled in his journal that 'the King's affairs remain at a standstill by reason of these trifles'.

A few days later he heard that there had been a reconciliation and all the Court was rejoicing, but another week went by before Essex was finally satisfied with the wording of his patent and had been ceremoniously installed as Earl Marshal. The way was now clear at last for a meeting of the full Council and, as de Maisse had anticipated, everyone appeared to be cautiously in favour of peace except Essex, who sat sulkily silent through most of the proceedings. The ambassador was told that the Queen had decided to send her own commissioners to France to take counsel with his Majesty as to what should be done and, since this was a game for three players, she understood that the Dutch would also be sending representatives. De Maisse pointed out that he had been kept waiting six weeks for this not very startling resolution and put in an urgent plea that the commissioners should be despatched as soon as possible with full powers to treat 'as much for war as for peace'.

When the meeting broke up, he went to take his leave of the Queen who apologised for having detained him so long and then drew him aside for a private word. There was no creature on earth who bore the King of France so much affection, or so greatly desired his welfare and prosperity as she did, but at the same time she must beg him to consider her position. She was only a woman, old and capable of nothing by herself. She had to deal with nobles of divers humours and a people who, although they made great demonstrations of love towards her, were notoriously fickle and inconstant, and as a result she was beset by fears and troubles on every side.

From even a short acquaintance with her Majesty, this affecting picture of a poor, helpless old lady must have struck de Maisse as a trifle unconvincing; and no doubt the Queen was equally sceptical of his earnest assurances concerning the King's undiminished goodwill and gratitude for past favours, and his intention, once his own affairs were straightened out, of repaying the like to his friends – an oblique reference to the matter of King Henry's formidable debt to the English treasury, which had come up more than once during the past six weeks. However, the two parted on the best of terms, Elizabeth saying that she was glad to have known de Maisse and would always think most highly of his merits. She turned to the Admiral, who happened to be standing near, and ordered him to make sure the ambassador was given a good ship for his passage home, adding with a laugh that he might be taken prisoner by the Spaniards, to which de Maisse replied gallantly that marching under the Queen's banner he had no need to fear them.

Before de Maisse left the country he paid the usual round of farewell courtesy visits and saw the Earl of Essex alone for the first time. Essex still seemed rather gloomy and out of sorts, referring to the 'great cloud' which had hung over him ever since his return from the Azores but which was now, he hoped, beginning to dissipate. He told the ambassador that he had been suggested as one of the commissioners to go to France but had excused himself, because he knew the peace party would blame him if the talks failed. He went on to remark that in England, as in France, there were contrary parties each with their own designs, adding that in England they suffered from delay and inconstancy 'which proceeded chiefly from the sex of the Queen'.

Essex was evidently of the opinion that he had received no more than bare justice in his recent contest with Elizabeth, but as usual failed to appreciate that the battle should never have been fought at all. The Queen had no taste for farce under duress and it seems reasonable to assume that this latest exhibition had destroyed any lingering remnants of her personal fondness for Robert Devereux. Once more, though, it appeared to be well on the surface. Essex was back in his accustomed place at Court and Robert Cecil had persuaded the Queen to show unusual generosity over the disposal of some cargoes of cochineal brought back from the Islands Voyage, as well as making his lordship an unconditional gift of seven thousand pounds. The arguments the Secretary had used with her Majesty were not revealed but there was no secret about his motives, for it was about to be Cecil's turn to go abroad. He had been nominated to lead the forthcoming delegation to France, leaving Essex to take his place at the Queen's right hand, and in typically Cecilian fashion was taking every precaution to secure his rear. Rowland Whyte heard that 'he was resolved not to stir one foot till the Earl of Essex did assure him that nothing should pass here that might be a prejudice or offensive unto him'.

As it turned out, Cecil needn't have worried. Francis Bacon, making one final attempt to offer sensible political advice, had urged Essex to start taking an interest in Irish affairs which, 'being mixed with matter of war', should be congenial to him – quite apart from the fact that anyone who could make a constructive contribution towards solving the Irish problem would certainly gain in credit and reputation. But although my lord of Essex was reported to be in very diligent attendance upon the Queen and 'in some sort takes upon him the despatching of all business in the absence of Mr. Secretary', he squandered what was to be his last opportunity to re-establish himself with her Majesty by nagging her to agree to receive his mother at Court.

The former Countess of Leicester, now married for the third time to Christopher Blount, one of her son's cronies, was a woman of considerable physical attractions, forceful personality and slightly doubtful reputation. The Queen had loathed her ever since the mid-sixties when she and the Earl of Leicester had first embarked on an ostentatious flirtation, and after her marriage with Leicester she became a non-person as far as Elizabeth was concerned. The prospect of being obliged to see her again was distasteful to say the least but Lady Leicester, as she was still known, would not let the matter drop and eventually, probably for the sake of peace, the Queen gave in. The two women met briefly in the Privy Chamber and embraced, but this was as far as Elizabeth was prepared to go. When she heard that Lettice wanted a repeat performance with more publicity, she refused with 'some wonted unkind words'. Mother and son had gained a technical victory, but neither achieved anything in the long run by 'importuning the Queen in these unpleasing matters'.

The spring of 1598 marked the lull which preceded the last great crisis of the reign. The Queen was reported to be very well and celebrated the Garter Feast of St George's Day in splendid style. Elizabeth had now become one of the great tourist attractions of the western world and whenever she was in London foreign visitors flocked to Greenwich or Whitehall or Hampton Court to see the Sunday church parade. Paul Hentzner, a German lawyer bear-leading a young nobleman on the Grand Tour, was at Greenwich that summer and, together with other selected outsiders, was admitted to the Presence Chamber to watch the Queen and her ladies pass by on their way to the chapel, escorted by the great officers of state and guarded by a contingent of gentlemen pensioners with their gilt battle axes.

Hentzner must have had a good view, for he described the Queen as looking 'very majestic, her face oblong, fair but wrinkled, her eyes small, yet black and pleasant, her nose a little hooked, her lips narrow and her teeth black'. (All the English were inclined to have bad teeth, a defect which, in Hentzner's opinion, was due to their inordinate fondness for sweetmeats.) Elizabeth was wearing a pair of very fine pearl earrings and a small crown on top of an obvious red wig. 'Her bosom was uncovered, as all the English ladies have it till they marry; and she had on a necklace of exceeding fine jewels. Her hands were small, her fingers long, and her stature neither tall nor low; her air was stately, her manner of speaking mild and obliging.' That particular Sunday she was dressed in white silk bordered with pearls the size of beans, and over it a mantle of black silk shot with silver threads, her train being carried by a marchioness. Hentzner was much impressed by all this magnificence and as the Queen passed, he says, 'she spoke very graciously, first to one, then to another, whether foreign ministers, or those who attended for different reasons, in English, French and Italian; for besides being well skilled in Greek, Latin and the languages I have mentioned, she is mistress of Spanish, Scotch and Dutch'. He remarked on the great respect with which she was treated. 'Whoever speaks to her, it is kneeling; now and then she raises some with her hand. While we were there . . . a Bohemian baron had letters to present to her, and she, after pulling off her glove, gave him her right hand to kiss, sparkling with rings and jewels, a mark of particular favour. Wherever she turned her face, as she was going along, everybody fell down on their knees.'

While the Queen was at prayer, the visitors were able to watch the ceremonial laying of the royal dinner table – the various officials responsible for spreading the cloth and carrying the bread and salt prostrating themselves and behaving with as much awe and reverence as if the Queen had been present. The meal itself, served on gilt plate, was brought in by the yeomen of the guard in their scarlet coats while the hall rang with the braying of trumpets and rattle of kettle drums. After each dish had been assayed, or tasted, for poison, the maids of honour appeared and, 'with particular solemnity', lifted the meat off the table and bore it away to the private apartments. 'The Queen dines and sups alone', wrote Hentzner, 'with very few attendants, and it is very seldom that anybody, foreigner or native, is admitted at that time, and then only at the intercession of somebody in power.' Paul Hentzner did not command that sort of influence and had to be content with the public part of the show; but just to have seen the great Queen of England go by on her way to church was something well worth storing up to tell one's grandchildren about.

The tourists who came to gaze and to admire the splendour of the English Court, who strained to catch a glimpse of the incredible woman around whom all this well-ordered, pompous ritual revolved, naturally knew nothing of the tensions building up behind the glittering and bejewelled facade as the Queen grew older and the power struggle rending the younger generation intensified. To the outward eye Gloriana at sixty-four still appeared to be fully in command, universally loved, feared and respected. It was an appearance which had at all cost to be maintained. Only the Queen herself knew the cost in terms of mental and physical strain, or how fragile the facade of power really was. She knew that the greedy, ruthless condottiere surrounding the Earl of Essex were becoming increasingly impatient of an old woman's rule and that the old order, the old system of checks and balances, the old game of playing one faction against the other which, in the last resort, had depended on the willingness of the factions to abide by its unwritten rules, was slowly but inexorably sliding out of control. The new men, who knew little and cared less of the past and its painfully accumulated conventions, were thinking of the future, of a time when they would no longer be encumbered by a living monument, her hands clamped firmly on the purse strings, her iron will damming the golden stream of patronage and preferment which might flow so freely from a more easy-going monarch.

The danger that such men would not be prepared to wait for nature to take its course – although in large part neutralised by their general incompetence and lack of cohesion – was by no means imaginary. In Scotland James Stuart, his naturally suspicious mind poisoned against the Cecils by his friend Essex, was also becoming increasingly dissatisfied with his admittedly anomalous position, and was busy intriguing abroad for support for his claim to be publicly recognised as the Queen's heir; while in the shadow world inhabited by spies, informers, political refugees and Catholic exiles, rumours proliferated that the King of Scots 'would attempt to gather the fruit before it is ripe'.

But troublesome though he might be, Elizabeth never doubted her ability to deal with young James. Of far more pressing concern in the summer of 1598 was the question of peace with Spain. Robert Cecil and his colleagues had returned home in April to report the failure of their mission to the King of France. Henry, with an empty treasury and a shattered country to rebuild, was set on peace without delay and, after safeguarding the rights of his Huguenot subjects by the Edict of Nantes, he signed a separate treaty with Spain at Vervins that May, but he stipulated that the English were to be granted a period of six months to decide whether or not they wanted to join in.

That both the Queen and Lord Burghley wanted peace is not in doubt. Its advantages were too obvious. The frightening drain on the exchequer would be checked, European trade would revive and the Irish rebels, cut off from any hope of Spanish aid, could be dealt with more or less at leisure. But it was not, of course, as simple as that. As the Earl of Essex passionately pointed out, the Queen and her advisers were proposing to negotiate with a nation which, for as long as most people could remember, had been dedicated to the destruction of Protestant England and all she stood for. It was impossible, he argued, to deal in good faith with a popish Prince who never treated with heretics but to deceive them, and who would simply seize the chance of a breathing space to re-group and re-arm while England allowed her military force to decay. Philip and his successors would think it no crime to break a treaty any time it suited them. Even if they did, they could easily obtain the Pope's absolution.

After all, were they not still bound to obey *Regnans in Excelsis*, the bull of excommunication which enjoined the Catholic powers to depose the bastard, heretical and usurping Queen of England by fair means or foul?

This was a familiar argument and had been used in pre-Armada days by councillors terrified that the Queen, in her reluctance to commit herself to all-out war, might be lured into dropping her guard by false hopes of peace. But the situation was very different now. Ten years after the Armada no one could seriously maintain that England was any longer in danger of invasion. She could not afford to go on fighting a holy war just for the sake of it and thus run the risk of incurring the disapproval of world opinion as an obstinate disturber of the peace. At one of the last Council meetings he attended Lord Burghley told Essex that he breathed nothing but war, slaughter and blood and, drawing out his prayer-book, the old man pointed solemnly to the words of the psalm: 'the bloodthirsty and deceitful men shall not live out half their days'.

This well-known incident proved prophetic enough, but Essex was not to be silenced by psalms and he proceeded to bring the debate out into the open by publishing – or allowing Anthony Bacon to publish – a letter in which he defended himself vigorously against those critics who accused him of war-mongering and of using his influence to prolong the conflict at a time when peace might be had, in order to further his own career and serve the selfish interest of his military followers. This letter, or Apology as it became known, was a naked appeal to the passions and prejudices of the mob over the government's head and it naturally infuriated both the Queen and the Cecils. But in the final analysis it was not the Earl of Essex who blocked the road to peace.

The Dutch people had suffered bitterly in their twenty year long struggle for freedom from the overlordship of Spain. By the mid-nineties, though, the United Provinces or States of Holland were at last beginning to emerge as an independent nation (Philip's ill-advised intervention in French affairs had helped to take the pressure off them at a crucial moment), and nothing and nobody was going to persuade them to accept even the most carefully hedged form of compromise, even the most nominal form of Spanish sovereignty – always supposing Spain was disposed to be so generous. Elizabeth had never cared for the Hollanders, regarding them as greedy, stubborn, ungrateful and Calvinist, but she could scarcely in honour abandon them now. Nor, for that matter, could she risk exposing them to a renewed onslaught from the south, perhaps wasting all the precious lives and treasure which had been poured in aid across the North Sea and saying goodbye to any hope of repayment of her numerous loans. So Francis Vere went back to strengthen the bonds uniting the two remaining members of the Triple Alliance, and the war in the Netherlands went on. But it had at least become a limited war and was, in its way, quite useful as a military training ground.

The other major problem which continued to preoccupy the Queen and her Council was, of course, Ireland, where the situation had been steadily deteriorating over the past two years and where the English presence was now effectively confined to the area of the Pale around Dublin. The appointment of a new Lord Deputy had become a matter of urgency but, not surprisingly, no one was eager to be banished to a country which had earned the reputation of a white man's grave, or to accept an office which in recent years had generally led to the financial ruin as well as the death of its incumbent.

The subject came up for discussion again early in July at a meeting which consisted of the Queen, the Earl of Essex, the Lord Admiral, Sir Robert Cecil and Thomas Windebank, Clerk of the Signet. The Queen's favoured candidate was William Knollys, Essex's uncle and one of his principal supporters on the Council. Essex proposed Sir George Carew, an able man but, more to the point, a prominent member of the Cecil faction and one who might with advantage to the Earl be taken out of circulation. The Queen rejected the suggestion out of hand. Essex persisted. The argument grew heated and then suddenly exploded into a violent scene. According to the brief, dispassionate account left by the historian William Camden, who probably had it from Robert Cecil, Essex turned his back on the Queen in a deliberate gesture of contempt. Elizabeth, thus provoked, lost her temper and boxed his ears, telling him to go and be hanged! The Earl made as if to draw his sword and, as the Lord Admiral hastily made to intervene, swore that he neither could not would take such an insult from anyone. He would not have endured it even from King Henry VIII himself! There was, one may imagine, a second's horrified silence before Essex flung away and slammed himself out of the room.

It had been an ugly and revealing episode which reflected no particular credit on either of the contestants, both of whom were now standing stiffly on their dignity. Essex, who had retreated to Wanstead, characteristically considered himself the injured party, as he made abundantly clear in a letter to the Queen reproaching her for 'the intolerable wrong you have done both me and yourself'. 'I am sorry to write thus much', he went on, 'for I cannot think your mind so dishonourable but that you punish yourself for it, how little soever you care for me. But I desire whatsoever falls out, that your Majesty should be without excuse, you knowing yourself to be the cause, and all the world wondering at the effect. I was never proud, till your Majesty sought to make me too base. And now since my destiny is no better, my despair shall be as my love was, without repentance . . . I must commend my faith to be judged by Him who judgeth all hearts, since on earth I find no right. Wishing your Majesty all comforts and joys in the world, and no greater punishment for your wrongs to me, than to know the faith of him you have lost, and the baseness of those you shall keep.'

This was a pretty amazing letter for any sixteenth century subject to address to the monarch and William Knollys, writing to his nephew about the middle of July, could only say that 'between her Majesty running into her princely power and your lordship's persisting in your settled resolution, I am so confounded as I know not how nor what to persuade. I will therefore leave it to God's work, to whom I heartily pray to settle your heart in a right course; your Sovereign, your country, and God's cause never having more need of you than now'. Sir William more than hinted that her Majesty would be prepared to accept an apology and ended with a plea that 'if in substance you may have a good peace, I beseech your lordship not to stand upon the form of treaty'.

But Essex refused to budge and a few days later his friend Lord Keeper Egerton took a hand. 'I will not presume to advise you', he wrote, 'but shoot my bolt as near the mark as I can and tell you what I think . . . You are not so far gone but you may well return. The return is safe, but the progress dangerous and desperate in this course you hold. If you have enemies, you do that for them which they could never do for themselves; whilst you leave your friends to open shame and contempt, forsake yourself, overthrow your fortunes, and ruinate your honour and reputation, giving that comfort to our foreign foes, as greater they cannot have . . . You forsake your country when it hath most need of your help and counsel: and lastly, you fail in your indissoluble duty, which you owe to your most gracious Sovereign.'

The best, indeed the only, way out of the present impasse Egerton concluded was 'not to contend and strive, but humbly to submit'. 'When it is evident that great good may ensue of it to your friends, your country and Sovereign, and extreme harm by the contrary, there can be no dishonour or hurt to yield, but in not doing it, is dishonour and impiety. The difficulty, my good Lord, is to conquer yourself, which is the height of all true valour and fortitude.'

This was plain speaking and Essex responded with some even plainer. He repudiated the charge that he was forsaking his country at a time of need. 'If my country had at this time any need of my public service, her Majesty, that governs the same, would not have driven me into a private kind of life.' The only indissoluble duty which he owed the Queen was that of allegiance 'which I never will, nor never can, fail in'. He had been content in the past to do her Majesty the service of a clerk, but could never serve her as a villein or slave.

As for Egerton's advice to yield and submit – 'I can neither yield myself to be guilty, or this imputation laid upon me to be just. I owe so much to the Author of all Truth, as I can never yield falsehood to be truth, nor truth falsehood . . . When the vilest of all indignities are done unto me, doth religion enforce me to sue? Doth God require it? Is it impiety not to do it? What, cannot Princes err? Cannot subjects receive wrong? Is an earthly power or authority infinite? Pardon me, pardon me, my good Lord, I can never subscribe to these principles . . . Let those who mean to make their profit of Princes show to have no sense of Princes' injuries; let them acknowledge an infinite absoluteness on earth, that do not believe in an absolute infiniteness in heaven.'

It would be easy to assume from the tone of this letter that, instead of being asked to say he was sorry for having been rude to the Queen, at the very least Essex's paternity was in question or that he'd been accused of some heinous form of treason. In fact, in the sixteenth century context, the sentiments expressed in it were not far short of treason. If any less favoured individual had stood up in public and said anything of the kind, he would quickly have found himself in serious trouble. But my lord of Essex, it appeared, remained a law unto himself and the Queen continued to ignore him.

As it happened, the Queen had other things on her mind just then, for Lord Burghley was failing at last and Elizabeth was sitting at her old friend's bedside feeding him his gruel. In his last letter to his son, the dying man wrote: 'I pray you diligently and effectually let her Majesty understand how her singular kindness doth overcome my power to acquit it, who though she will not be a mother (remembering all those years when he had tried so hard to get her married), yet she showeth herself by feeding me with her own princely hand, as a careful nurse, and if I may be weaned to feed myself, I shall be more ready to serve her on earth, if not, I hope to be in heaven a servitor for her and God's church.' And he added a postscript. 'Serve God by serving of the Queen, for all other service is indeed bondage to the devil.'

Burghley died on 4 August, having served the Queen for very nearly forty years, and for Elizabeth it was a break with the past more complete than any she had yet known. Her association with William Cecil went back to childhood days when, as a rising young government servant, he had been friendly with her much-loved governess Katherine Ashley. When she was sixteen the princess, who knew an honest man when she saw one, took the opportunity of attaching him to her interests by asking him to act as Surveyor of her landed property at a salary of twenty pounds a year. They kept in discreet touch during the dangerous years which followed and almost her first act as Queen had been to appoint him Principal Secretary of State. 'This judgement I have of you', she said on that occasion, 'that you will not be corrupted by any manner of gift and that you will be faithful to the state; and that without respect of my private will you will give me that counsel which you think best.' She had never had occasion to alter that judgement and their partnership remains something unique in history. Lord Burghley, wrote his friend William Camden, was 'a singular man for honesty, gravity, temperance, industry and justice. Hereunto was added a fluent and elegant speech . . . wisdom strengthened by experience and seasoned with exceeding moderation and most approved fidelity . . . In a word, the Queen was most happy in so great a Councillor and to his wholesome counsels the state of England for ever shall be beholden'.

When they brought her the news of his death, Elizabeth went away to mourn in private. But she made no attempt on this occasion to hide her grief. It was noticed that for months afterwards she could not speak Burghley's name without tears and would turn aside when other people brought it up. Her godson, John Harington, found this very understandable. When, after all, would the realm see such a man again, or such a mistress have such a servant. 'Well might one weep when the other died', he commented.

Meanwhile, the Earl of Essex, that so much less admirable servant of the state, was still absent from his appointed place and his friends, many of whom had built their own careers on his influence and patronage, were growing increasingly worried. As William Knollys pointed out, this was no time to be away from Court if the Earl wanted any say in the disposal of Lord Burghley's offices. 'Remember, I beseech you', he went on, 'that there is no contesting between sovereignty and obedience, and I fear the longer your lordship doth persist in this careless humour of her Majesty, the more her heart will be hardened, and I pray God your contending with her in this manner do not breed such a hatred in her, as will never be reclaimed.'

Shortly after this, Essex was summoned to attend a Council meeting at the Lord Keeper's house. He came, but declined to take any part in the proceedings unless the Queen agreed to see and listen to him first. She would not and he went away again. How long the stalemate might have continued is impossible to say, but before the end of August outside events supervened and made the domestic quarrels of the English Court seem more than usually irrelevant. On the fourteenth of the month the army in Ireland, some four thousand men under the command of Sir Henry Bagenal, had marched out of Armagh in a show of strength to relieve the garrison of a key fort on the Blackwater river, only to be outflanked and overwhelmed by the rebel forces under the Earl of Tyrone. Bagenal himself and half his army, including some of the best officers, were killed and the survivors driven back in disorder to Armagh.

The disaster at the Yellow Ford brought the running sore of Ireland to a festering head. The news also brought the Earl of Essex back to town. He was present at a Council meeting on the 22nd, but still the Queen would not see him, nor would she accept a written memorandum of advice on the Irish crisis, and it began at last to dawn on Essex that this time she was not playing games. Her Majesty had been heard to remark that the Earl had played long enough upon her and that now she meant to play awhile upon him, 'and so stand as much upon her greatness as he hath done upon stomach'. In other words, as she had already made clear in messages to Essex, he must apologise and 'submit' before he could hope to return even to limited favour.

Essex appeared prominently among the five hundred black-hooded mourners at Lord Burghley's funeral and was noticed to carry 'the heaviest countenance of the company', although at least one cynical observer was moved to speculate on how much of this gloom was due to grief for the departed and how much to 'his own disfavours'.

The Earl vanished to Wanstead again as soon as the funeral was over and conveniently went down with an ague. His fever may or may not have been genuine, but it did offer both sides an opportunity to retreat from their heavily entrenched positions without too much loss of face. Elizabeth, always concerned in cases of sickness, sent the invalid a kind message, followed by one of her own doctors, and let it be known that the gentlemen of the household might visit him without causing offence. By the second week of September he had recovered and was back at Court and apparently back in favour. By the beginning of October, Robert Cecil, writing to Thomas Edmondes in Paris, mentioned casually that any misunderstandings between her Majesty and his lordship 'was now clearly removed, and all very well settled again'.

This time, though, few people believed the reconciliation to be genuine. Francis Bacon, in a letter of congratulation to the Earl on his reinstatement, hoped that this would be the last of his 'eclipses' and that 'upon this experience may grow more perfect knowledge, and upon knowledge more true consent' between him and the Queen. But from his own knowledge of his patron, Bacon was probably more optimistic than convinced. What passed between Elizabeth and Essex in private is a matter of conjecture – all the same, it seems logical to suppose that this was the occasion of the Queen's warning to content himself with displeasing her and insolently despising her person, but to be very careful indeed of touching her sceptre. Of the numerous warnings Essex received during the course of his career it was this one, above all others, which he would have been wise to heed, but there is little indication that he did so. Within a matter of weeks he was back at his old tricks of trying to bully the Queen into giving him Lord Burghley's influential and potentially very profitable Mastership of the Court of Wards. The Queen took no notice. Burghley's Lord Treasurership went to Lord Buckhurst and, in the fullness of time, the Court of Wards was bestowed on the dead man's son.

There had been another notable death that summer when, on 10 September, Philip of Spain finally succumbed to the disease which was consuming him. It's hardly likely that Elizabeth shed tears for her old antagonist, but his going snapped another link and it is tempting to wonder if, when the news reached her, her thoughts went back to that long-ago summer when she had flirted discreetly with her sister's husband in the gardens of Hampton Court, while Queen Mary waited in desperate, deluded optimism to bear the half-Hapsburg son who would have altered the course of European history. Nearly half a century had gone by since Philip's brief sojourn in England as Mary Tudor's consort, but Elizabeth would certainly not have forgotten her first and only personal contact with the man to whom she was destined to be bound by ties of enmity as compelling in their way as those of love.

But the Queen had small leisure for dwelling on the past. Now, in what were to be the closing years of her life, she must turn to face new challenges to her authority and to the security of her realm – challenges as urgent and dangerous in their way as any she had met before and which were to drain the last of her strength.

43
The General of Our Gracious Empress

Now Scipio sails to Affrick far from home,
The Lord of Hosts and battles be his guide;
Now when green trees begin to bud and bloom,
On Irish seas Eliza's ships shall ride:
A warlike band of worthy knights, I hope,
Are arm'd for fight, a bloody brunt to bide,
With rebels shall both might and manhood cope,
Our country's right and quarrel to be tried:
Right makes Wrong blush, and Truth bids Falsehood fly,
The sword is drawn, Tyrone's dispatch draws nigh.

The Irish problem, now occupying the attention of Queen and Council to the exclusion of almost everything else, was not, of course, a new one. It had been a matter of intermittent concern throughout the Tudor century and its origins, which were geographical and ethnic quite as much if not more than political, went back even further.

The Plantagenet kings, with their numerous other outside interests, had been content to exercise their feudal overlordship of Ireland at second-hand and, apart from a few brief personal incursions, had left control of the island's affairs in the hands of the Anglo-Norman feudal barons, 'planted' there after the Conquest. These families, notably the Burkes, the Butlers of Ormonde and the Fitzgeralds of Desmond and Kildare, had intermarried extensively with the Irish tribal aristocracy and over the years had become almost totally absorbed into Irish tribal society. But so long as they were left undisturbed to pursue their private struggles for ascendancy among themselves and over the native clans or septs, they were willing enough to stay loyal to the Crown.

This mutually convenient state of affairs began to come to an end with the arrival of the new dynasty. The mighty Geraldines of Kildare had taken the Yorkist side in the English civil wars and Ireland therefore became a natural breeding-ground for Yorkist resistance, forcing the first Tudor monarch to intervene. Henry VII's attempt to impose a form of direct rule met with only partial success, and when the Yorkist challenge fizzled out, he let the experiment lapse, recalling his Lord Deputy and allowing the great Earl of Kildare to resume his position of uncrowned king.

The next encounter came in the 1530s when Henry VIII and Thomas Cromwell, conscious of the danger of papal interference in their revolutionary doings via the Irish back door, began to place new English officials in key offices and to establish a permanent presence in Dublin, to the acute irritation of the 'old' English. The Fitzgeralds revolted, but on their own they were no match for Tudor imperialism and their reign was finally brought to an end by a judicious mixture of treachery and gunpowder. In 1541 Henry adopted the title of King of Ireland and embarked on a determined campaign to anglicise and civilise the wild Irish, persuading some of the chieftains – notably the O'Neills of Ulster – to surrender their tribal independence in exchange for English-style peerages and an oath of allegiance. Again, this policy enjoyed a superficial short-term success, but the task of grafting an alien system of law, language and land tenure onto a primitive and uncomprehending pastoral society by 'circumspect and politic ways' was beyond the capabilities of the Tudor machine. The Earl of Surrey, who held the office of Lord Lieutenant in 1520, had given it as his poor opinion that Ireland would never be brought to good order and due subjection but only by conquest, and time was to prove him right. Nevertheless, conquest continued to be regarded as a last resort by successive Tudor governments.

Under Mary, and later under Elizabeth, efforts were made to speed up the civilising process by bringing in more English settlers who would, it was hoped, insert a solid and industrious wedge whose loyalty could be relied on in time of trouble. Richard Grenville and Walter Raleigh both invested heavily in these new 'plantations' and so, to a lesser extent, did Edmund Spenser the poet. But the immigrants led a precarious existence, constantly harassed by the wild Irish, much as the early American colonists were harassed by wild Indians, and few stood the course. Many of them, indeed, rented their holdings back to the dispossessed tribes, thus defeating the whole object of the exercise and laying the foundations of the notorious absentee landlord syndrome. By the end of the 1580s, despite the endeavours of successive Elizabethan Lord Deputies to bring the Queen's ungrateful Irish subjects the benefits of the rule of her law, the fact had to be faced that Ireland was as far, if not further, from becoming peacefully integrated into the English social system as it had been in the previous generation, and by this time, of course, the religious aspect was providing additional complications.

Henry VIII's Reformation had made no martyrs in Ireland for the sufficient reason that, St Patrick regardless, the indigenous population of the Island of Saints continued to set very much greater store by their own charms and spells and esoteric deities than on the Roman form of worship – in its way just as foreign to the Gaelic culture as the doctrines evolved by Martin Luther, John Calvin or the second Henry Tudor. But Ireland's long isolation from the mainstream of European life was coming to an end and, as the shock waves of the ideological revolution convulsing Western Christendom spread inexorably outwards, certain Irishmen began to grasp the fact that here was a weapon capable of being turned against the Anglo-Saxon intruder. The tide of religious fanaticism which was to cause such untold suffering in the unhappy island did not reach its flood until the next century, but already it offered a focal point of resistance, a force potentially powerful enough to unite the perpetually squabbling tribes and transform their localised resentments into a holy war to drive out the heretics.

The first manifestation of this new initiative showed itself in the Earl of Desmond's rebellion of 1579–80. The rising was savagely suppressed but thereafter there was a fairly constant traffic between Ireland, Spain and Rome, as the missionary priests of the Counter-Reformation worked to consolidate the Catholic revival, especially in the south and west. After the failure of the 1588 Armada Philip began seriously to reflect on the strategic advantages of establishing a bridgehead on Irish soil – the ill-fated expedition of 1596 had, in fact, been intended for an Irish destination – and Irish leaders, through their priestly emissaries, continued to press urgently for Spanish aid.

In the circumstances, therefore, it was ironical that the crisis situation facing Queen Elizabeth's government in 1598 should have originated in the north, in Ulster, the most backward and least Christianised of all the Irish provinces. It was ironical, too, that Ulster's paramount chief should have been by far the most sophisticated and able figure Ireland had yet produced, an astute and plausible politician as well as an efficient military commander. But Hugh O'Neill, Earl of Tyrone, had been brought up in England at the Sidneys' great house at Penshurst, absorbing all the enemy could teach him and storing it away for future use. A devious and patient man, he was content to bide his time and his defection, when it came, was well-thought-out and well-organised.

Although careful to present his cause as a crusade for the extirpation of heresy – the only banner under which he could hope for Spanish support and the equally essential support of his fellow chieftains – Tyrone's real motives were political. He was determined to preserve the old Celtic order in his own territories and with it, of course, his own local supremacy; but there is little doubt that he also dreamed of seeing the English driven out altogether and of setting himself up as High King of an independent and re-celticized Ireland. In 1598 that dream looked tantalisingly close to becoming a reality, for his brilliant victory at the Yellow Ford had lit a spark of revolt which ran like wildfire through the whole country. Everywhere the tribes were out, emerging from their impenetrable bogs and mountains to indulge themselves in an orgy of killing, burning and looting. The English settlers, among them Edmund Spenser, had to run for their lives to the doubtful sanctuary of the towns and even the Pale itself could no longer be regarded as safe. This was Tyrone's moment and an opportunity for mischief-making which Spain could hardly fail to exploit. Unless decisive action were taken quickly Ireland would be lost – a disaster in terms of England's national security and prestige which was not to be contemplated.

An army big enough and strong enough to reconquer the island and re-establish the authority of the Crown would somehow have to be raised and dispatched before the new King of Spain could provide the artillery which Tyrone lacked. This was not in dispute. The tricky problem now exercising Queen and Council was the identity of the new Lord Deputy and commander-in-chief. Elizabeth suggested Lord Mountjoy who, as Charles Blount, had first attracted her attention ten years earlier and as a result had been challenged to a duel by the brash young Earl of Essex. Mountjoy had subsequently become a prominent member of the Essex set – his brother had married Lady Leicester and he himself was well known to be the lover of the Earl's fascinating sister, Penelope Rich. All the same, Essex opposed his friend's appointment. He was inexperienced, too bookish and 'not considerable enough by his fortunes and alliances' to attract a following. Such an important job required 'some prime man of the nobility, strong in power, honour and wealth, in favour with military men, who had been before general of an army'. A description by which, as few people failed to notice, the Earl 'seemed to point the finger at himself'.

Did Essex really want the Irish command, or was he by some sinister but unspecified means manoeuvred into it by his enemies, as some of his biographers have hinted? In fact, he was, as he himself admitted, tied by the reputation he had worked so hard to build. If, as he claimed, he was indeed the greatest man in the kingdom, then he could hardly shirk the greatest task when it presented itself – 'his honour could not stand without undertaking it'. In any case, Elizabeth had made up her mind. 'Into Ireland I go', wrote the Earl at the beginning of January 1599, 'the Queen hath irrevocably decreed it.'

It seemed a strange decision, both then and later. Mountjoy's secretary, Fynes Moryson, remarked that his lordship's embracing of military courses and his popular estimation had made him so much suspected of his sovereign, 'as his greatness was now judged to depend as much on her majesty's fear of him, as her love of him. And in this respect he might seem to the queen most unfit for that service . . . The vulgar gave ominous acclamations to his enterprise; but wiser men rather wished than hoped happy effects either to his private or the public good.' Another contemporary observer was frankly puzzled. Robert Markham, writing from the Court to John Harington, who was to go with the army in Ireland, reported that 'in all outward semblance' the Queen had forgiven

Essex for his shocking behaviour of the previous summer and was now apparently content to place every confidence in the man 'who so lately sought other treatment at her hands'; but her real feelings were anyone's guess and 'what betydeth the Lord Deputy is known to Him only who knoweth all'. For his part, Markham expected trouble and went on to warn the Queen's merry godson (who had recently been in disgrace with his formidable godmother for writing naughty verses to amuse the maids of honour) to be very careful not to meddle in politics while he was away, 'nor give your jesting too freely among those you know not'. There would be spies in the camp and it was a time when sensible men kept their opinions to themselves.

The general atmosphere of foreboding was intensified that February when Dr John Hayward brought out his history of *The First Part of the Life and Reign of King Henry IV* and dedicated it to the Earl of Essex. Eighteen months earlier, when the Lord Chamberlain's Men were performing William Shakespeare's *Richard II* in which that monarch is deposed by his cousin Henry Bolingbroke, it had seemed to the more politically aware members of the audience that the playwright had been drawing from life in his description of the usurper's methods of courting popularity.

Off goes his bonnet to an oyster-wench;
A brace of draymen bid God speed him well,
And had the tribute of his supple knee,
With 'Thanks, my countrymen, my loving friends';
As were our England in reversion his,
And he our subjects' next degree in hope.

The historical parallel was far from exact and certainly it would be difficult to trace any noticeable resemblance between Elizabeth Tudor and the unfortunate Richard Plantagenet, but the fact that the romantic image of Essex as a second Bolingbroke should have gained even a passing currency demonstrates the strength of his hold on the public imagination. The Queen was well aware of the existence of the comparison and took furious exception to John Hayward's little book. Yet, at the same time, she was entrusting Essex with a large and well-equipped army which would be operating within the boundaries of her own realm. She was allowing him virtually untrammelled power in the exercise of his command and had also, though reluctantly, agreed to sign a licence enabling him to return to England at his own discretion.

So why did she do it? The suggestion that it was all part of a deep-laid plot, master-minded by Robert Cecil and intended to give Essex enough rope to hang himself, is surely about as paranoiac as the Earl himself. The Irish crisis posed a real and urgent threat, not something to play politics with, and raising the army had just about scraped the treasury bare. If Cecil was planning the destruction of his rival, he could hardly have picked a more expensive and chancy way of doing it. A more likely, if less dramatic, explanation is that the Queen, as much as the Earl, had found herself a prisoner of his reputation. In spite of all that had happened since, the glory of Cadiz still clung to Essex, giving him, both in the eyes of the general public and of the military caste, an inalienable right to lead any major expedition. Besides this, of course, his position as Earl Marshal did give him a proscriptive right to command the Queen's armies, a fact Elizabeth could scarcely ignore without courting further domestic uproar. Then, again, the choice of suitable alternatives was severely limited, Walter Raleigh having wisely refused to become involved. Service in Ireland was notoriously unpopular at all levels, but the soldiers would follow the magic name of Essex where they might not follow anybody else and one is driven to the conclusion that, at a time when speed was of the essence, Elizabeth simply took the line of least resistance and hoped for the best – though her misgivings must certainly have been as strong as Robert Markham's.

Essex's own mood see-sawed between over-confidence and gloom. 'I have beaten Knollys and Mountjoy in the Council', he wrote to John Harington, 'and by God I will beat Tyrone in the field; for nothing worthy her Majesty's honour hath yet been achieved.' But in a letter to Lord Willoughby he spoke of his 'private problems and nightly disputations', dwelling with customary obsessiveness on all the 'practising enemies' who would take advantage of his absence to drop their poison in the Queen's ear. The war itself would be hard and while failure was dangerous, too much success would only lead to further envy and suspicion.

By the time the new Lord Lieutenant left to take up his duties towards the end of March, his gloom had deepened. Elizabeth had vetoed his appointment of the young Earl of Southampton as General of the Horse, nor would she allow his stepfather, Sir Christopher Blount, to be made a member of the Council of Ireland and Essex was already convinced that everyone at home was against him. He complained constantly and fluently of lack of support and understanding, and whined that he was being sent to perform an exceptionally difficult task without the inward comfort or outward demonstration of her Majesty's favour. The Earl was not helping himself by this characteristic orgy of self-pity, but no one minimised the formidable nature of his task.

To the average Elizabethan, Ireland was a soggy, savage wilderness where no sensible person would willingly set foot. The Spaniards soon came to regard it as a land fit only for the Prince of Hell and the average civilised Englishman agreed with them. The English could see nothing romantic or even faintly admirable in the ancient Celtic tribal system. To them the habits and customs of the wild Irish were barbarous, unhygienic and generally just plain nasty. They were horrified by the backwardness, the filth, the inefficiency and laziness of a people whose favourite sports appeared to be cattle-raiding and killing one another, and were shocked by the tyranny of their chiefs. To the soldier, Ireland offered no possibility of profit or glory, but only an excellent chance of dying miserably of dysentery or marsh fever – if, that is, he escaped being knocked on the head by some axe- or club-wielding tribesman. Elizabethan soldiers were no strangers to hardship but Irish hardships held special terrors, perhaps because of the untamed and uncharted nature of their surroundings. On the continent, in France or the Netherlands, the landscape was at least tolerably familiar, with towns and highways and cultivated fields, the enemy recognisable as a fellow human being and not a half-naked, howling hairy savage. Usually soaked to the skin, cold, disorientated and fed up, the troops grumbled that they would rather go to the gallows than the Irish wars and deserted in droves at every opportunity.

To the army commander, campaigning in Ireland presented tactical and logistical problems of an acute kind. It was, of course, classic guerilla war territory, with all the initial advantages on the side of an enemy fighting on his own ground, especially an enemy apparently able to subsist on grass and to be virtually independent of clothing, shelter and other such basic amenities of life. Communications and supply became a nightmare in a country where such roads as existed were often impassable to wheeled traffic and rain fell with deadly persistence. Corruption, that universal bugbear of sixteenth century warfare, was rampant – with their pay, as always, in arrears, the soldiers sold their arms and even their clothes to Irish middlemen who sold them back to the rebels at a substantial profit – and an additional dreamlike quality was provided by the numbers of Irish who joined the English army, melting away or changing sides as the fancy took them.

Although Tyrone, more than any other Irish leader, had been able to unite and discipline his forces and arm them, at least in part, with pikes and other modern weapons, the English had, or should have had, the edge in superior organisation, technique and equipment. But soldiering in Ireland would always be a specialised affair, very different from continental war as understood by the professionals and demanding special talents and expertise which few professionals, had had the chance to develop. Certainly Essex, himself no more than an enthusiastic and occasionally lucky amateur, had never developed them and from the start he floundered hopelessly out of his depth.

It had been agreed in London that his first and most important operation must be to lead the army into Tyrone's Ulster power-base and there seek to destroy the rebellion at its source. But on arrival in Dublin, the Lord Lieutenant allowed the Council of Ireland to persuade him to postpone the march north until later in the season and deal first with the troubles in Leinster and Munster, where the rebels had recently been reinforced by Tyrone. Accordingly, early in May, he set off on a circular tour of the south, penetrating as far as Limerick. 'This people against whom we fight hath able bodies, good use of the arms they carry, boldness enough to attempt, and quickness in apprehending any advantage they see offered them', he reported to the Privy Council from Kilkenny, where he had been welcomed by the townsfolk with speeches and rush-strewn streets. 'The advantage we have is more horse, which will command all champaigns; in our order, which these savages have not; and in the extraordinary courage and spirit of our men of quality. But, to meet with these helps, the rebels fight in woods and bogs, where horse are utterly unserviceable; they use the advantage of lightness and swiftness in going off, when they find our order too strong for them to encounter; and, as for the last advantage, I protest to your lordships it doth as much trouble me as help me. For my remembering how unequal a wager it is to adventure the lives of noblemen and gentlemen against rogues and naked beggars, makes me take more care to contain our best men than to use their courages against the rebels.'

Essex returned to Dublin on 11 July, with nothing to show for his southern jaunt but the loss of a third of his army and the waste of two months' valuable time. He expected blame and wrote defensively to London, still harping on his old theme of the enemies waiting to stab him in the back and who would now, in the dark, give him wound upon wound. The Queen was not impressed by this sort of talk, she had heard it all too often before; nor was she impressed by her general's performance in the field and on 19 July she despatched the first of a series of stinging rebukes.

'If you compare the time that is run on', complained her Majesty, 'and the excessive charges that is spent, with the effect of anything wrought by this voyage . . . you needs must think that we, that have the eyes of foreign Princes upon our actions, and have the hearts of people to comfort and cherish, who groan under the burden of continual levies and impositions, which are occasioned by these late actions, can little please ourselves hitherto with anything that hath been effected . . . Whereunto we will add this one thing, that doth more displease us than any charge or expense that happens, which is, that it must be the Queen of England's fortune (who hath held down the greatest enemy she had), to make a base bush kern to be accounted so famous a rebel, as to be a person against whom so many thousands of foot and horse, besides the force of all the nobility of that kingdom must be thought too little to be employed.'

This, of course, was the heart of the matter and Essex's failure to go north and confront Tyrone was rousing Elizabeth to a fury of frustration. 'When we call to mind . . . the scandal it would be to our honour to leave that proud rebel unassailed . . . we must now plainly charge you, according to the duty you owe us, so to unite soundness of judgement to the zeal you have to do us service, and with all speed to pass thither in such order, as the axe may be put to the root of that tree.'

The Queen was angry that Essex, in direct disobedience to her orders, had made Southampton General of the Horse and she was going to be even angrier when she discovered how many knighthoods he had conferred, but she remained rigidly determined to hold him to the Ulster expedition. 'You know right well', she reminded him, 'when we yielded to this excessive charge it was laid upon no other foundation than that to which yourself did ever advise us as much as any, which was to assail the Northern Traitor, and to plant garrisons in his country, it being ever your firm opinion, amongst others of our Council, to conclude that all that was done in other kind in Ireland, was but waste and consumption'.

The Earl had been confident that he alone could deal with Tyrone and Elizabeth was not going to let him forget it, pointing out that he'd been given ample facilities to do the job as well as power and authority 'more ample than ever any had, or ever shall have'. So, concluded her Majesty, it was more than time that he stopped breaking the soldiers' hearts and wasting his strength on 'inferior rebels' and did something to justify the large promises made at his departure, 'to the intent that all these six months' charges prove not fruitless'. To ram the point home (and perhaps to insure against any rash impulse on his lordship's part), she revoked his licence to return. He was now on no account to leave his post until he had 'reduced things in the north', and even then not without prior permission.

To the unhappy Essex who, like others before him, was learning how very different Ireland looked from Dublin than it did from London, the Queen's reproaches were hammer blows on an already bruised ego. He had staked his whole future on his ability to succeed where others had failed only to find himself failing more dismally than the rest. In the present disease-ridden and demoralised state of the army he knew that any attempt to confront Tyrone must end in still further humiliation, but the Queen's attitude made it plain that she was in no mood to listen to excuses and all the time the Cecil influence at Court would be growing stronger. It was a desperate situation which seemed to call for a desperate solution and wild schemes were flitting through his head for taking two or three thousand men, landing in Wales, where he could count on a following, and then marching on London to remove his enemies from the Council by force of arms.

The Lord Lieutenant discussed this plan with his two most intimate cronies, Southampton and Christopher Blount, who, so they later deposed, did everything they could to dissuade him, suggesting that he should instead seek a private interview with the Queen, taking with him no more than 'a competent number' of hand-picked supporters for his personal protection. First, though, he must make at least a token appearance in Ulster.

Essex had already, by the middle of August, been in secret contact with Tyrone, who had sent messages via an intermediary that if the Queen's deputy would follow his lead, he would make him the greatest man that ever was in England. It was the first step on a slippery path but, when Essex led the remnants of his army north at the beginning of September, he probably had no real treasonable intent in mind – his only thought being somehow to find a way out of his present intolerable predicament.

The armies met at Ardee in Louth, where Tyrone paraded his forces just out of range in a nicely calculated display of strength. He then sent to suggest a parley, offering his 'submission' and, after some public huffing and puffing by Essex, the two leaders met at the ford of Bellaclynth. They talked alone together for half an hour and it seems more than likely that Essex poured out his grievances and received offers of support – upon conditions. Tyrone outlined his peace terms, which amounted to little short of Irish autonomy, and Essex promised to deliver them to the Queen. At a second meeting, held on the following day with commissioners from both sides present, a six week truce was agreed, renewable for periods of six weeks until May 1600. The rebels would remain in possession of all the territory they held on the date of this agreement and the English undertook to establish no more forts or garrisons.

The Irish leader then retired into 'the heart of his country' with every reason to feel satisfied with the summer's work. He had made the Queen of England's great army dance to his piping and the Queen's most famous general look uncommonly foolish at negligible cost to himself. He was confidently expecting Spanish reinforcements to arrive before the spring and had gained all the time he needed. Essex, on the other hand, had gained nothing – it would be difficult to disguise his arrangement with Tyrone as anything but abject surrender, and his unwitnessed conversation with a notorious traitor would obviously be capable of the worst possible interpretations.

When the Queen heard what was going on, she wrote: 'We that trust you with a kingdom are far from mistrusting you with a traitor, yet both for comeliness, example, and your own discharge, we marvel you would carry it no better.' Essex had not yet dared to tell her about the terms of the truce, so that her Majesty, as she tartly pointed out, could not tell 'but by divination' what to think of the issue of his proceedings. She was sure of only one thing, 'that you have prospered so ill for us by your warfare, as we cannot but be very jealous lest you should be as well overtaken by the treaty'. 'To trust this traitor upon oath', she went on, 'is to trust a devil upon his religion. To trust him upon pledges is a mere illusory . . . And, therefore, whatever order you take with him, yet unless he yield to have garrisons planted in his own country to master him . . . and to come over to us personally here, we shall doubt you do but piece up a hollow peace, and so the end prove worse than the beginning.'

Whether or not Essex actually received this letter, written on 17 September, seems doubtful, but in any case he had already made up his mind. He must see the Queen and make her understand how impossible it all was. He could not – would not – stay in Ireland another week. On the twenty-fourth he handed over or, more accurately, flung his responsibilities to Archbishop Loftus and the Earl of Ormonde and, taking the Earl of Southampton and a small group of kindred spirits, set off on a mad dash for home. After reaching England the little party rode hard down through the Midlands and by the early hours of Friday, 28 September, were clattering through the streets of Westminster. The Court was at Nonesuch, which meant crossing the river by the Lambeth ferry and more riding through the Surrey lanes, muddy from a wet autumn.

If Essex had a plan in his head, it was to take the Queen by surprise and this time to get his story in first, and to begin with it looked as if his crazy gamble might be going to succeed. 'Upon Michaelmas Eve, about ten o'clock in the morning, my Lord of Essex lighted at Court Gate in post, and made all haste up to the Presence, and so to the Privy Chamber, and stayed not till he came to the Queen's bedchamber, where he found the Queen newly up, the hair about her face; he kneeled unto her, kissed her hands, and had some private speech with her, which seemed to give him great contentment; for coming from her Majesty to go shift himself in his chamber, he was very pleasant, and thanked God, though he had suffered much trouble and storms abroad, he found a sweet calm at home. 'Tis much wondered at here, that he went so boldly to her Majesty's presence, she not being ready, and he so full of dirt and mire, that his very face was full of it.'

Thus Rowland Whyte's account of this famous confrontation between the gaunt, haggard old woman, the scanty white hair, usually so carefully concealed, hanging in wisps over her unpainted face, and the sweaty, mud-spattered man kneeling breathless at her feet. News of the Earl's approach had, in fact, preceded him by about fifteen minutes, but it had not reached the Queen and she therefore had no means of knowing whether or not he had brought his army with him, whether the palace might already be in his hands, her own handful of largely ornamental guards overwhelmed and she herself a prisoner. It was a nasty moment, not made any easier by the fact that she had been caught unawares, half-dressed and without her wig, but Elizabeth showed no signs of discomposure. Thinking on her feet, she smiled kindly on her unwelcome visitor, spoke to him soothingly and got rid of him as soon as she could by suggesting that he should wash and change before they talked again. Within an hour he was back and stayed with her until dinner-time. Still all seemed to be well and Essex went down to dinner flanked by his friends the Earls of Worcester and Rutland, and the Lords Mountjoy and Rich, while the ladies and gentlemen, avid with curiosity over this unexpected development, clustered round to hear his traveller's tales of Ireland. Only Mr Secretary, with Walter Raleigh, the Lords Grey and Cobham, the Earl of Shrewsbury, the Lord Admiral and Lord Thomas Howard remained aloof. Clearly some kind of showdown was imminent and all those whose careers and livelihoods depended on keeping in with the right people were sniffing the air like dogs. 'As God help me', wrote Rowland Whyte on that dramatic Friday, 'it is a very dangerous time here; for the heads of both factions being here, a man cannot tell how to govern himself towards them.'

In the afternoon Essex went to the Queen again, 'but found her much changed in that small time, for she began to call him to question for his return, and was not satisfied in the manner of his coming away, and leaving all things at so great hazard'. By this time, of course, Elizabeth had been able to take stock of the situation and to realise that this was not, after all, the armed coup she had feared. On the contrary, the great man had, in effect, run home to mother and was still apparently relying on her indulgence, or her dependence, to save him from the consequences of his gross mismanagement of her affairs and betrayal of her trust. But the days when Essex could sweet talk his way back into the Queen's good graces were long past. For nearly ten years she had put up with his tantrums, his bad manners, his arrogance and his broken promises, at the same time jealously watching his power and his prestige increase. Now that he had presented her with the long awaited opportunity to cut him down to size she meant to make full use of it. But she was still feeling her way in a highly volatile atmosphere, and when she finally dismissed him with a curt command to confer with her Council she can have had no idea that she would never see him again.

Only four members of the Council were actually present at Nonesuch and Essex spent an hour trying unsuccessfully to justify his actions to them. Meanwhile messengers were sent riding urgently to summon the rest and, late that evening, the Court heard that my Lord of Essex had been ordered to keep his chamber. Next day the full Council assembled and sat in conclave all morning before calling the Earl to appear before them. The clerks were sent out and behind closed doors Robert Cecil proceeded to read out the list of his crimes. He had contemptuously disobeyed the Queen's instructions by returning to England; many of his letters from Ireland had been presumptuous; his proceedings in Ireland had been contrary to what was agreed before he left; his coming away had been rash; he had been over-bold in going to her Majesty's presence in her bedchamber, and he had made too many idle knights. Significantly, there was no mention of his incautious dealings with Tyrone and outsiders heard that never man answered 'with more gravity or discretion to these matters laid to his charge'. After three hours' grilling he was released and returned to his quarters, while the Council deliberated for only fifteen minutes before going to make their report to the Queen. She listened without comment and told them she would think it over.

Some time during the weekend Essex received a visit from his old friend and mentor Francis Bacon, who said consolingly (and surprisingly for such a normally percipient individual) that he thought this present trouble was only a mist which would soon clear away. But he went on to urge his lordship not to try and pretend that the truce with Tyrone was anything but an inglorious shuffling up of 'a prosecution which was not very fortunate', not to let the Queen think she would be obliged to send him back to Ireland and, above all, to continue to seek access to her, 'seriously, sportingly, every way'. This might have been good advice in different circumstances but neither Francis Bacon nor anyone else, except perhaps Robert Cecil, had yet begun to grasp the real nature of the Queen's resentment against her former favourite, or the bitterness of her fury over the Irish debacle. By Monday morning she had made up her mind about the Earl's immediate future and Essex was informed that he was to be committed to the custody of the Lord Keeper at York House, there to remain during her Majesty's pleasure.

It was a decision clearly intended to make her displeasure manifest and, at the same time, to take the heat out of the situation. A period of house arrest, which no one expected to last more than a few weeks, in the charge of a man well known to be his friend was not likely to rouse even the most fervent Essex man to drastic action, but London was already filling up with a riff-raff of deserters from Ireland, 'all sorts of knights, captains, officers and soldiers', whose presence increased the risk of disturbance and also, incidentally, added fresh fuel to the Queen's simmering rage.

John Harington, who was among those who had followed their general home and was besides a recipient of an Irish knighthood, soon discovered this to be one of the occasions when her Majesty's demeanour 'left no doubtings whose daughter she was'. His first encounter with his godmother was not auspicious. 'What, did the fool bring you too?' she snorted. 'Go back to your business!' 'She chafed much', Harington was to recall some years later, 'walked fastly to and fro, looked with discomposure in her visage; and, I remember, she catched my girdle when I kneeled to her, and swore, "By God's Son I am no Queen; that *man* is above me. Who gave him command to come here so soon? I did send him on other business."' Elizabeth then insisted on seeing the diary which her godson had kept during the Irish campaign and swore again, 'by God's Son, we were all idle knaves, and the Lord Deputy worse, for wasting our time and her commands in such wise.' Harington did his best to explain about the peculiar difficulties and problems to be met with in Ireland, but found it impossible to make her listen, 'for her choler did outrun all reason'. However, after some four or five days, he received a summons to Whitehall and the Queen, in calmer mood, put him through a searching interrogation. 'Until I come to heaven', wrote Sir John, 'I shall never come before a statelier judge again, nor one that can temper majesty, wisdom, learning, choler, and favour, better than her Highness did at that time.' All the same, when he was bid 'Go home', he did not stay to be bidden twice.

'If all the Irish rebels had been at my heels, I should not have had better speed, for I did now flee from one whom I both loved and feared too.'

Meanwhile, the prisoner at York House had fallen sick, suffering from nervous collapse aggravated by dysentery, 'the Irish flux', which he had brought back with him from Dublin. 'He is grown very ill and weak by Grief', reported Rowland Whyte, 'and craves nothing more than that he may quickly know what her Majesty will do with him; he eats little, sleeps less, and only sustains life by continual drinking, which increases the Rheum.' There seems no reason to doubt that on this occasion Essex's mental and physical distress was genuine enough and, as the weeks went by with no hint of any softening in the Queen's attitude, sympathy for his plight increased. No official explanation of his mysterious disgrace had yet been given out and the Londoners, whose special favourite he was, were naturally growing restive, the more so since rumour had it that all the Lords of the Council had spoken in favour of his release. All the usual indicators as to the state of public opinion – ale-house talk, sermons and broadsheets – were pointing to storm and obviously it was high time the Queen took some action to justify herself.

At the end of the legal term it was customary for the Lord Keeper to deliver an exhortation to the people in the Court of Star Chamber – this being the Privy Council wearing its judicial hat – and, after some hesitation, Elizabeth made up her mind to use this opportunity to issue a statement listing the Earl's offences. Francis Bacon thought she was making a mistake and warned that such a one-sided proceeding would lead to complaints 'that my lord was wounded upon his back, and that justice had her balance taken from her, which ever consisted of an accusation and defence'. At the same time, Bacon came out strongly against any form of open trial, pointing out that Essex was an eloquent, well-spoken man who would also enjoy the advantage of overwhelming public sympathy; that, in short, the Queen was likely to come off worst in public examination of the matter, and he therefore advised her to find some way of wrapping it up privately.

To be told that she stood in danger of losing a popularity context with Essex confirmed the Queen's deepest fears and did nothing to improve her temper. Nevertheless, she stuck to her decision and, indeed, it is not easy to see what else she could have done at this juncture. To have climbed down and restored Essex to his former attendance 'with some addition of honour to take away discontent', as Bacon suggested, would not merely have been a stupendous sacrifice of pride but, more seriously, would undoubtedly have been taken by the Essex faction as a confession of weakness to be seized on and exploited. On the other hand, the time for a trial was not yet. Elizabeth knew as well as anyone that if and when that time arrived, the government must be in a position to present a cast-iron case.

Accordingly, on 29 November, all the privy councillors and judges assembled in the Star Chamber to make a public declaration 'for the satisfaction of the world' of the Earl of Essex's imprisonment, and 'for the reformation of divers abuses offered to her Majesty and her Council . . . by many dangerous libels cast abroad in Court, city and country, as also be table and alehouse talk abroad, both in city and country, to the great scandal of her Majesty and her Council.' There were many seditious people spread abroad to breed rebellion, declared Lord Keeper Egerton sternly, who had been uttering false and slanderous speeches against the Queen and her advisers concerning 'the marshalling of the affairs and state of Ireland'. Such people were no better than traitors, and he straightly charged all judges, justices and other officers to make stringent efforts to bring them to book.

Egerton then went on to deal with Irish affairs in detail. Far from being unreasonable or neglectful, the Queen, he said, had shown her special care for the government and good of her subjects in Ireland by sending her most famous commander against the rebels 'with so large a commission as never had any before . . . and that for the doing of this service, there was such an army, and such provision in every way, as the Earl himself could ask or thought fit'. But the plain facts were that my lord had acted 'clean contrary' to the plan of campaign he himself had helped to formulate. He had 'frivolously spent and consumed her Majesty's treasure, victuals and munition, and lost most part of his army'. He had confessed privately with the enemy and discussed a peace on such unfavourable terms 'as was not fit for any Prince to grant'. Lastly, he had deserted his post in disobedience to her Majesty's express commands given under her own hand. The Lord Treasurer, Lord Buckhurst, took up the story to spell out the ruinous cost of the Irish operation – three hundred thousand pounds between April and September; and the Lord Admiral added his voice, remarking scornfully that with such an army Essex might have gone all through Spain.

One of those present grumbled that the throng was so great and some of the lords spoke so softly that he could scarcely hear what was being said – Robert Cecil made a long and largely inaudible speech confirming that the Queen had written forbidding Essex to return to England – but on the whole the main object of the exercise seems to have been achieved. Although feeling continued to run high and scurrilous graffiti directed against Cecil appeared even on the palace walls, at least the more responsible sections of the community were now aware that the Queen had substantial grounds for her displeasure.

Despite persistent rumours that the Earl was to be committed to the Tower, nothing had been said about his future but, by the first week of December, it began to look as if the problem might be going to resolve itself in a particularly final manner. Essex was said to be critically ill and Elizabeth ordered eight leading physicians to examine the patient and advise her on his case. Their prognosis was not hopeful, for they found his liver 'stopped and perished', his guts and entrails exulcerated and could only suggest gentle glisters to keep him clean within. Looking rather pensive, the Queen sent one of her own doctors to York House with some of her special broth and a message that his lordship should comfort himself, adding that if she might with honour come to visit him, she would do so. This looked a hopeful sign but most people feared it had come too late, for Essex was now so weak that he had to be lifted on a sheet when his bed was made and scoured of all black matter, 'as if the strength of nature were quite gone'.

Since his condition had become so serious he had been moved, by royal command, into the Lord Keeper's own bed-chamber and his wife was allowed to go to him. Francis Essex cannot have known much happiness in her married life, but she appears always to have accepted her husband's neglect and his not infrequent infidelities in a proper spirit of Christian resignation, and to have stood staunchly by him in his disgrace. Although only just risen from her latest childbed, she had done her best to plead his cause, haunting the ante-rooms of power dressed in unrelieved black and, once leave had been granted, dutifully spent every day from six in the morning till seven at night – the permitted visiting hours – at his bedside. The fallen favourite was being publicly prayed for in the city churches and a few days before Christmas, when a rumour got around that he was dead, the bells tolled for him. But Essex was not dead. He was, in fact, a little better and a week or so later was able to sit up and to eat at a table.

As he recovered, the Queen's heart hardened again. She herself was in excellent health. The Court, which had moved out to Richmond, was crowded and gay for the Christmas holidays and her Majesty often to be seen relaxing in the Presence Chamber, playing cards with the Lord Treasurer and Mr Secretary or watching her ladies performing the new country dances – no doubt beating time to the music and calling out criticisms, as André de Maisse had reported was her habit. The year before she had danced with the Earl of Essex at the Twelfth Night festivities, but if she missed his company now she gave no sign of it.

44

THE MADCAPS ALL IN RIOT

Sweet England's pride is gone!
welladay! welladay!

Brave honour graced him still,
gallantly, gallantly;
He ne'er did deed of ill,
well it is known;
But Envy, that foul fiend,
whose malice ne'er did end,
Hath brought true virtue's friend
unto his thrall.

A new century had begun with England still at war with Spain – a war which had already lasted more than fifteen years – but the queen had not given up hope of securing the 'safe honourable peace' which every sensible Englishman was longing for and there had been much conferring with the Dutch ambassador during the winter. In Spain, too, where a new king faced the problems of an empty treasury and a nation war-weary to the point of exhaustion, a negotiated settlement would have been welcomed thankfully. In October 1599, Archduke Albert of Austria who, with his wife, old Philip's favourite child the Infanta Isabella, now ruled the Spanish Netherlands, had sent an envoy secretly to London and in the spring of 1600 representatives of both sides met at Boulogne. But the talks broke down over a point of procedure and, in any case, the English remained firm in their insistence on satisfactory guarantees for the Dutch and on trading concessions in Spanish America.

The war at sea had now largely passed back into private hands. Individual privateers continued to cruise the sea lanes in search of prizes and in 1598 the Earl of Cumberland, succeeding where Drake and Hawkins had failed, captured Puerto Rico but took no treasure worth mentioning. In the summer of 1599 there had been another invasion scare, when a young Genoese adventurer in the Spanish service brought off a brilliant dash up the Channel and through the Dover Straits to Sluys with a fleet of six galleys. But there were to be no more major naval confrontations and the war was steadily losing momentum both by sea and land. The Anglo-Dutch victory at Nieuport in 1600 virtually settled the issue in the Netherlands and thereafter the English presence could safely be reduced to little more than the garrisons in Flushing and the other cautionary towns.

This was just as well, for in Ireland the situation was rapidly going from bad to catastrophic. Elizabeth had been forced to ratify Essex's infamous truce (which, needless to say, was already being broken) and the winter of 1599 saw Tyrone lording it unchallenged over the tribes. Aware that only bad weather and Spanish incapacity had so far prevented active intervention from that quarter, the Queen reverted to her original plan of appointing Lord Mountjoy as her Lord Deputy. Mountjoy at first protested. He was not strong and feared, so he said, that the Irish climate would be the death of him. He was also worried about Essex. The previous summer he had taken it on himself to get in touch with King James to assure him that 'my lord of Essex was free from those ambitious conceits which some of his enemies had sought to possess the world withal', that his lordship fully supported James's claim to be recognised as heir apparent, and to propose some joint action should now be discussed with a view to persuading the Queen to reconsider her stubborn refusal to make the recognition official.

Mountjoy, it was said later, had been motivated principally by his affection for Essex 'who by loss of her Majesty was like to run a dangerous course unless he took a course to strengthen himself by that means' (in other words, sought protection from James), and by an honest conviction that only the formal declaration of a Protestant successor would serve to safeguard the country against the machinations of undesirable pretenders. Ever since the death of Mary Queen of Scots, the Spanish royal family had been making the most of their dash of Plantagenet blood – the Infanta Isabella being the most favoured replacement for Queen Elizabeth in extreme Catholic circles.

Lord Mountjoy may have been guilty of nothing worse than officiousness in the summer of 1599, but once his appointment as Lord Deputy was confirmed he began to be drawn into new schemes for using the army in Ireland as an instrument of coercion at home. Having sworn an oath to defend the Queen to the uttermost during her lifetime, and taken the precaution of extracting a similar solemn undertaking from the Earl of Southampton, the army's commander agreed to send another letter to James, suggesting that a contingent of four or five thousand of his men, acting in conjunction with the Scots, might be brought over to support 'the party that my lord of Essex would make head withal' in a show of force impressive enough to compel Elizabeth to name the King as her heir, restore Essex to favour and dismiss Robert Cecil.

Such a plan, if attempted, must have had disastrous consequences, but luckily for all concerned, by the time the messenger, who had been closely shadowed by Cecil's spies, returned from the north bringing a friendly but carefully non-committal answer from James, Mountjoy had left for Ireland.

Once in Dublin, removed from the influence of the Essex wild men and, perhaps even more important, from Penelope Rich, a strong-minded lady devoted to her brother, he was able to see things in a clearer light. When Southampton joined him towards the end of April, bearing a letter from Essex and eager for action, he was absorbed in the challenge of his new job and no longer interested in playing with fire. His friend was clearly out of immediate danger and Mountjoy who, left to himself, possessed a good deal of common sense, flatly refused to have anything to do with an enterprise intended merely to restore the Earl's fortunes and satisfy his private ambitions.

The secret had been well kept, but even so Robert Cecil and the Queen already knew something and no doubt guessed a lot more about the activities of the Essex party in Scotland and elsewhere. In spite of this, Essex had not been committed to the Tower. On the contrary, his position had improved a little. On 20 March, to the intense relief of the Lord Keeper, he had at least been allowed to return to Essex House, empty now and stripped of its paraphernalia of power. The busy staff of secretaries, the secret agents coming and going on their mysterious errands, the jostling queues of petitioners and place-seekers, the visiting dignitaries, the courtiers and captains and hangers-on who had once filled it with bustle and the illusion of greatness had vanished. Even Lady Essex, the Earl's mother and sisters and Lady Southampton were required to find alternative accommodation before he was installed with only a bare handful of servants and a government-appointed custodian to keep him company.

The problem of his future remained unsolved. The Queen had wanted to bring him to trial in the Star Chamber not, so she said, to destroy him, but to make him know himself and his duty towards her. Elizabeth was becoming increasingly worried by the bad publicity she had been getting over the Essex affair and was especially anxious to refute the charge that the Earl had been condemned unheard; but Robert Cecil, like Francis Bacon, strongly opposed any form of public proceeding at this stage and instead persuaded her Majesty to accept a letter of humble submission.

Walter Raleigh, evidently afraid that Cecil was going soft over Essex, wrote to warn him that 'if you take it for good counsel to relent towards this tyrant, you will repent when it shall be too late. His malice is fixed and will not evaporate by any your mild courses . . . The less you make him, the less he shall be able to harm you and yours; and if her Majesty's favour fail him, he will again decline into a common person . . . Lose not your advantage. If you do, I read your destiny.' This advice was almost certainly unnecessary. Cecil harboured no more illusions than Walter Raleigh about the fixity of Essex's malice, and could read his own destiny just as clearly if he lost his present advantage. But Mr Secretary, who had borne the brunt of the odium resulting from the Earl's disgrace, who commanded no popular following and depended entirely on the support of an ageing Queen, was understandably reluctant to pass the point of no return until he could feel a hundred per cent certain of his ground. The Star Chamber trial, which had been set for early February, was cancelled and another four months passed before a satisfactory compromise had been hammered out.

On 5 June 1600 Essex was summoned to appear before a special tribunal of Privy Councillors and judges sitting at York House under the chairmanship of the Lord Keeper to hear the charges against him, to give his answer and receive judgement. No witnesses could be called, no formal record kept and, as a further concession to the prisoner's special status, her Majesty had been graciously pleased to allow the proceedings to be held in a private place. However, since the tribunal's primary purpose was that of a public relations exercise, an invited audience of two hundred persons, carefully chosen for their standing and influence in the community, was present to see justice done.

The government's case opened with a reminder of the Queen's generosity. She had not only forgiven Essex ten thousand pounds worth of his debts to her before he left for Ireland, but had given him nearly as much again to buy horses and outfit himself for the campaign and was even now – despite the ingratitude with which her bounty had been repaid – unwilling to subject him to the rigours of an ordinary criminal trial. She had therefore directed that his misdeeds should receive 'before a great, honourable and selected council, a full and deliberate, and yet in respect a private, mild and gracious hearing'.

The Attorney General then rehearsed the Earl's various sins of commission and omission in Ireland: his appointment of Southampton as General of the Horse in defiance of the Queen's veto; his useless journey into Leinster and Munster which had ruined any chance of success in Ulster; his indiscriminate making of knights, again in disobedience to orders; his dishonourable and dangerous conference with the arch-rebel Tyrone; and his contemptuous leaving of his post contrary to her Majesty's absolute mandate. Edward Coke spoke in his usual hectoring style and could not resist the jibe that 'before my lord went into Ireland he vaunted and boasted that he would *fight* with none but Tyrone himself . . . But when he came thither, then no such matter, for he goes another way, it appeareth plainly he meant nothing less than to fight with Tyrone!'

The Solicitor General followed with a dissertation on the parlous state of Ireland since his lordship's return, which only went to show how little he had achieved, for Tyrone had now become more insolent than ever. Last, and perhaps most significant, Francis Bacon, as one of the Queen's learned counsel, rose to complete the case for the prosecution. After expressing the hope that all present would realise that any bond of duty he owed to the Earl had been temporarily laid aside, Bacon also described the unmitigated hash which his former patron had made of the Irish command. He went on to introduce two other matters – Essex's indiscreet letter to Thomas Egerton at the time of the ear-boxing row two years previously, and his patronage of Dr Hayward's tactless *History of Henry IV* – both of which had demonstrated undutifulness and disrespect.

When at last it came to Essex's turn, he spoke with becoming humility of the great sorrow and affliction which had fallen on him, and of the depth of his inner remorse. Since the Queen had been gracious enough to spare him the humiliation of a Star Chamber trial, he had resolved to give up all thought of attempting to justify his actions, he said. Instead, he would freely acknowledge, with grief and contrition, whatever faults of error, negligence or rashness it pleased her Majesty to impute to him. But the Attorney General had seemed to call his loyalty in question, and he would be doing God and his conscience a great wrong if he did not justify himself as an honest man. Speaking with passion and every appearance of sincerity, his lordship cried out that he would tear the heart out of his breast with his own hands if ever a disloyal idea had entered it.

Aware that the audience was showing ominous signs of responding to this display of eloquence, Lord Keeper Egerton hurriedly intervened to point out that no one had accused my lord of Essex of disloyalty, he was charged merely with contempt and disobedience and such affecting protestations were therefore irrelevant. His bubble pricked, Essex subsided, contenting himself with a pathetic plea that his former colleagues would make a just and honourable report of the disordered speeches which were the best an aching head and weakened body could utter. One by one the eighteen members of the tribunal then proceeded to give their opinion of the case, all agreeing that the Earl had been guilty of grave dereliction of duty, that he should be suspended from his various offices and remain under house arrest until such time as the Queen was pleased to release him.

Although many of the spectators shed tears to see 'him that was the mignon of Fortune now unworthy of the least honour', and Rowland Whyte heard that it had been 'a most pitiful and lamentable sight', the charade at York House had gone a long way towards destroying Essex's credibility as a public figure in the eyes of sensible men. Even more valuable from the government's point of view was the news coming in from Ireland, where Lord Mountjoy, ably assisted by Sir George Carew, was already beginning to make headway against the rebels; proving that with patience, persistence and determination – prosaic qualities notably lacking in the Earl of Essex – the Irish problem was not after all so insoluble as everyone had been led to believe.

It was widely expected that having made her point and taught Essex a lesson not even he could misunderstand, the Queen would soon relent, at least to the extent of restoring his freedom of movement, but what would happen after that was still anybody's guess. One thing, though, was certain. Unless he was eventually allowed to return to Court, his lordship's career was finished. Elizabeth might drop hints that once she was fully satisfied as to the sincerity of his repentance she would consider using his services again, but few people in a position to know anything of the inside story could bring themselves to believe that the Earl would ever again be trusted with a responsible office. Equally, it was hard to visualise him retiring unprotesting into private life.

If Elizabeth was worried about the situation, she rarely showed it. She seemed as active as ever, going briskly about her usual routine of work and pleasure, watching the bear baiting, a French tight-rope artist, taking long walks in Greenwich Park and dining with friends. All the same, Essex was obviously very much on her mind. Ten days after the tribunal had sat at York House, she was present at the social event of the season – the wedding at Blackfriars of Anne Russell, one of her favourite maids of honour, to Lord Herbert, the Earl of Worcester's heir. One of the entertainments provided at the marriage feast was a masque performed by eight ladies of the Court and when one of them, Mary Fitton, went to the Queen and wooed her to dance, her Majesty asked what character she represented. 'Affection', answered the girl. 'Affection', said Elizabeth sourly, 'affection is false', but she rose and joined the dancing.

During the previous summer some rather sinister rumours had been going about that the Queen was ailing, but this August Rowland Whyte told Robert Sidney that her Majesty was in very good health and went abroad every day to ride and hunt. Plans for a long progress were being discussed and when some of the older members of the household grumbled (progresses could be pretty uncomfortable affairs for those who no longer found it amusing to sleep in a tent), Elizabeth, who would be sixty-seven in September, snapped that the old could stay behind and the young and able go with her. In the end, though, she had second thoughts and went no further than Surrey, to Nonesuch, best-loved of her country houses, and Oatlands where the Court was given over to hunting and sports and the Queen said to be 'very merry and well'.

It was, perhaps, wiser to stay close to the centre. Essex, as anticipated, had now been relieved of his keeper and on 26 August was at last told he was free to go where he liked – except to Court. He announced that he meant to live quietly in the country, but his plea to be allowed the consolation of coming to kiss her Majesty's 'fair correcting hand' before retiring into solitude went unheeded. Outwardly the Earl was behaving with exemplary patience. There had been no tantrums, no outbursts of petulance, and his letters to the Queen positively crawled with penitence. But though Elizabeth sometimes sighed over them, she was not convinced and she was right – affection and contrition were both false.

Essex had not yet given up hope of Mountjoy and had already sent Sir Charles Danvers, another of his cronies, back to Ireland to remind the Lord Deputy of former promises and ask for his support in a bid to unseat

Robert Cecil. Danvers, went, not very optimistically, and found Mountjoy unsympathetic. Charles Blount, always hitherto overshadowed by the Devereux family, was enjoying his first experience of independent power (though this did not prevent him from complaining that he was not appreciated at home), and was discovering in himself an unexpected talent for command. He was, therefore, less and less inclined to put a promising career at risk by becoming involved in crack-brained schemes of rehabilitating my lord of Essex. He told Danvers that my lord must be content to 'recover again by ordinary means the Queen's ordinary favour'. When he came home he would naturally do what he could for him in the way of friendship, but in the mean time strongly advised him not to do anything rash.

Baulked, Essex turned again to Scotland and another messenger was sent north to warn James that unless he took steps to insist on his right to be named as the Queen's heir without further delay, he might find himself displaced by the Spanish princess, whose claim was favoured by one of the Queen's principal councillors – Cecil again. The Earl had 'infallible proof' that Cecil, in his anxiety for peace at any price, was plotting to hand England over to the Spaniards: he had been heard to say he could prove the Infanta's title to be better than that of any other competitor to the Crown; the Catholics, especially the Jesuits, were being treated with suspicious lenience; and the country was now almost entirely in the hands of Cecil supporters. Walter Raleigh was Captain of Jersey and commanded the whole of the West Country, Kent and the Cinque Ports were controlled by Lord Cobham and in Ireland, Munster, the province which of all others was 'fittest for the Spaniards' designs', had already been procured for Sir George Carew. As well as this, 'the treasure, the sinews of action, and the navy, the walls of this realm', were commanded by the Lord Treasurer and the Lord Admiral, two great officers of state well known to be 'principally loved by the principal Secretary'. The King of Scots, in short, had better realise that the Earl of Essex was his only friend and Essex urged him to send a reliable ambassador with whom his lordship could safely confer and decide on a joint plan of action. The cautious James was sufficiently alarmed by these scaremongering tactics to commit himself to a few lines of 'disguised' writing which Essex carried about with him in a little black bag hung round his neck, but by the time the reliable ambassador reached London, the Earl was no longer in a position to make use of their services.

Autumn was now approaching and still no one knew for certain whether the Queen meant to forgive Essex or not. His friends were still hopeful, finding it difficult to believe that any creature of flesh and blood could go on resisting the heartrending appeals of her humblest, faithfulest and more than most devoted vassal, the pining, languishing, despairing Essex. Other people took a more detached view, but everyone was watching to see what would happen at Michaelmas, when the Earl's 'farm' or monopoly of the duties on imported sweet wines fell due for renewal – or otherwise.

Many of Essex's past troubles, and a great deal of his present desperation, stemmed from his chronic financial problems which had always left him heavily dependent on the Queen's generosity. A man in his position, living precariously on an enormous overdraft of goodwill, quite simply could not afford to retire into private life and wait patiently until such time as it might please her Majesty to notice him again. If the farm of sweet wines, which represented a major source of his income, were to be withheld, the big shiny bubble of confidence on which his career and his ostentatious lifestyle had been balanced for so long would be seen to have burst, and his creditors would close in to strip him naked.

Elizbeth knew this as well as anyone. She told Francis Bacon that my lord of Essex had written her some very dutiful letters, and she had been moved by them; but what she had taken to be the abundance of his heart, she now found was merely a preparation for a suit for the renewing of his farm. Bacon, as the Queen no doubt also knew, had helped to draft some of these moving letters. Despite his appearance at York House, the canny Francis was still keeping a foot in the Essex camp and, according to his own testimony, begging her Majesty 'not utterly to extinguish my lord's desire to do her service'. Her Majesty remained unresponsive. Michaelmas came and went and nothing was said. Essex had returned to town, living very quietly and keeping his gates closed to visitors, but there was no summons to Court, no suggestion that he was considered to have served his sentence. On 18 October he made one last attempt to soften the Queen. 'My soul cries out unto your Majesty for grace', he wrote, 'for access, and for an end of this exile. If your Majesty grant this suit, you are most gracious, whatsoever else you deny or take away. If this cannot be obtained, I must doubt whether that the means to preserve life, and the granted liberty, have been favours or punishments; for till I may appear in your gracious presence, and kiss your Majesty's fair correcting hand, time itself is a perpetual night, and the whole world but a sepulchre unto your Majesty's humblest vassal.'

Still nothing, and then, at the end of the month, came the announcement that the farm of sweet wines would not be renewed and would for the present be kept in the Queen's own hands. On the face of it, this was fair enough. It was now more than a year since the Earl of Essex had taken any part in affairs of state, and the state had, after all, managed quite well without him. In some ways it had managed rather better. The business of government had not been disrupted by any explosions of umbrage and in Ireland the troops had at last got their tails up. They were actually fighting and winning battles, and 'beating the rebels from their bogs'. In the circumstances, there was really no reason why his lordship should continue to be rewarded out of public funds –

indeed, he might think himself lucky to have escaped the heavy fine and imprisonment in the Tower which, as the Lord Keeper had told him bluntly, would undoubtedly have followed a Star Chamber trial.

Essex, of course, being Essex could only see that he had been rejected, cast out and accursed; that he had humbled himself into the dust to no purpose, while the arch-enemy watched and gloated. Ahead lay nothing but ruin and disgrace, and as hope died, self-control frayed and finally snapped. Sir John Harington, who ventured to visit the Earl about this time, gave it as his opinion that 'ambition thwarted in its career doth speedily lead on to madness' – a conviction strengthened by the alarming manner in which Essex had shifted from sorrow and repentance to rage and rebellion, so suddenly 'as well proveth him devoid of good reason and right mind'. During their conversation, he began to talk so wildly that Sir John, who had once before nearly been wrecked on the Essex coast as he put it, hurriedly made his excuses and left. 'Thank heaven I am safe at home', he wrote, 'and if I go in such troubles again, I deserve the gallows for a meddling fool! His speeches of the Queen becometh no man who hath *mens sana in corpore sano*'. This may perhaps have been the occasion of the venomous remark always attributed to Essex that the Queen's mind had become as crooked as her carcase. Certainly he said something of the sort and, according to Harington, 'the man's soul seemeth tossed to and fro, like the waves of a troubled sea'.

Christmas approached and the Court settled down at Whitehall for the holiday season. Sir Robert Cecil invited the Queen to dinner, preparing to receive her 'with all fine and exquisite curiosity', and on Twelfth Night her Majesty feasted the Muscovy ambassador. The Orsini Duke of Bracciano, cousin of the new French Queen Marie de Medici, was also over on a private visit and being 'very graciously' entertained by Elizabeth, who danced measures and galliards before him 'to show that she is not so old as some would have her'. Everything seemed very much as usual. The musicians played, the children of the Chapel Royal sang as sweetly as ever, the trumpets sounded and the scarlet-coated yeomen of the guard performed their stately dinner-time ritual with the gold plate, while at the centre of the stage the Queen smiled and danced and made elegant small-talk with her distinguished guests, apparently unconcerned by the knowledge that less than a mile from the Palace a handful of angry, embittered men were plotting to overthrow her government.

Having abruptly abandoned his role of penitent and recluse, the Earl of Essex had now opened his doors to anyone who cared to enter, and a varied assortment of old friends and new were availing themselves of the opportunity to make common cause with the people's Robert. They ranged from wild young bucks like the Earl of Rutland and Southampton to militant young Catholics like Robert Catesby and Francis Thresham, from veterans of Essex campaigns like Christopher Blunt, Sir John Davies,

Sir Charles Danvers and the Governor of Plymouth Sir Ferdinando Gorges, to the Earl's secretary, Greek scholar Henry Cuffe, and included a rabble of impoverished lords and gentlemen who had all, for one reason or another, lost out in the harshly competitive Elizabethan rat-race. Pushing in behind the nobility and gentry came the bully boys and hoodlums, the discharged soldiers and unemployed captains, the petty criminals and professional trouble-seekers – 'swordsmen, bold confident fellows, men of broken fortunes, discontented persons, and such as saucily used their tongues in railing against all men' – every one of them ready for mischief and united, from earl to cutpurse, by their penury, their sense of grievance and their greed.

The general ambition of this promising assemblage was simple enough: to divert as much as possible of the life-giving stream of profit and perquisite flowing from the Crown into their own pockets, or to seize the Queen and become their own carvers, as the coarser element put it. But while they were strong on threats, when it came down to the actual ways and means of toppling a strong and widely popular regime, the would-be demagogues of Essex House became noticeably less self-confident. Detailed plans for taking over the Court, thus enabling Essex 'to present himself to the Queen' and enforce his demands – the dismissal of Robert Cecil, Raleigh, Cobham et al, their replacement by his own nominees and the calling of a Parliament to punish all enemies of the people – were discussed at a meeting chaired by the Earl of Southampton, but no firm decision was reached. The whole enterprise might yet have fizzled out in talk had not a small group of firebrands, impatient for some sort of action, brought matters to a head by bribing the reluctant company at the Globe Theatre to put on a special performance of Master Shakespeare's Tragedy of King Richard the Second.

For Essex's followers to demand to be entertained by the spectacle of a king being deposed and murdered – bearing in mind the comparison which had already been drawn between the Earl and Henry Bolingbroke – could only be construed as deliberate provocation, and the Queen and Robert Cecil, who had been keeping a close watch over the comings and goings at Essex House during the past three months, were left with no option but to take up the challenge. The same evening – it was Saturday, 7 February – the Privy Council met in emergency session to consider how best to deal with a potentially explosive situation.

The so-called Essex Rebellion is sometimes shrugged off as the grotesque bungling of a desperate man, half-crazed with disappointment, and hardly to be taken seriously. But it is always easy to be wise after the event and no one sitting round the Council table that Saturday evening felt in the least amused. Whitehall was virtually undefended and was, in any case, a rambling rabbit warren of a place almost impossible to secure. It would be highly vulnerable to a surprise attack, and there were some dangerous and determined characters among the mob now gathered a bare twenty minutes march away. If once they got into the precincts of the Palace, no one could say with certainty whether all the courtiers could be relied on to remain loyal; nor was it absolutely certain how the City would react. Essex, after all, was still Essex, the darling of the Londoners.

However, it was decided not to over-react and the Lords of the Council agreed to try and nip trouble in the bud by sending for Essex to appear before them forthwith. But their emissary, Secretary John Herbert, returned alone bringing word that the Earl had positively refused to come. He was not well, he said, and besides had been warned that the summons was a trap and Raleigh and Cobham were planning to murder him. This sounded ominous, as did Herbert's report of the scene at Essex House. So, first thing next morning, a warning was sent to the Lord Mayor to be ready for possible disturbances, while a final effort was made to bring Essex to his senses.

At ten o'clock an impressive deputation consisting of Lord Keeper Egerton, Lord Chief Justice Popham, the Earl of Worcester and Sir William Knollys arrived at the gates of Essex House demanding admission in the Queen's name. They found the courtyard 'full of men assembled together in very tumultuous sort' and Essex himself surrounded by his sidekicks, Southampton and Rutland, the Lords Sandys and Mounteagle, Christopher Blount, Charles Danvers and 'many other knights and gentlemen and other persons unknown'. Trying to make himself heard over the general hubbub, Egerton told the Earl that they had come from her Majesty to 'understand the cause of this their assembly, and to let them know that if they had any particular cause of grief against any persons whatsoever, it should be heard, and they should have justice'. Hereupon, according to Egerton's own account, 'the Earl of Essex, with a very loud voice, declared that his life was sought, and that he should have been murdered in his bed; that he had been perfidiously dealt with; that his hand had been counterfeited, and letters written in his name; and that therefore they were assembled there to defend their lives, with much other speech to like effect.'

Although Essex had pretty plainly passed beyond any appeal to reason, the Lord Keeper persisted bravely, repeatedly asking his lordship to let them understand his griefs in private, and commanding the jeering, jostling, cat-calling mob on their allegiance to lay down their weapons and depart. At last, Essex turned to go into the house and the deputation followed, pursued by insults and yells of 'Kill them! Kill them!' and 'Cast the Great Seal out of the window!' But once inside, instead of the private interview they had been hoping for, the Queen's representatives found themselves rudely locked up in a back chamber, the Earl telling them to be patient while he went into London 'to take order with the Mayor and Sheriffs for the City'.

The rest of the events of that Sunday – Essex's wild impromptu dash through the city streets, shouting hysterically that a plot was laid for his life and England was sold to the Spaniards, while the people came out to stare in open-mouthed amazement at the extraordinary sight of the hero of Cadiz running sweating and sobbing past their doors; his ignominious failure to win support or even credulity for his 'cause' and the final scrambling retreat to Essex House to find that his hostages had been released – all these are too familiar to need further repetition here. Nothing now remained for the Earl, stranded among the ruins of his lurid fantasy world, but to barricade his doors, burn his private papers and prepare to sell his life dearly. In the end, though, there wasn't even a heroic last stand. Soon after ten o'clock that night Essex and Southampton surrendered tamely enough to a force commanded by the Lord Admiral, and the Queen, who had sworn not to sleep until she knew they had been taken, was able to go to bed. The rebellion had lasted exactly twelve hours.

The rest of the Essex story is soon told. He and Southampton were arraigned together at Westminster Hall on 19 February before a jury of their peers, charged with conspiring with others to deprive and depose the Queen's majesty from her royal state and dignity, to procure her death and destruction and subvert the government of the realm; with having refused to disperse their disorderly company when called upon to do so by her Majesty's Privy Councillors, with imprisoning the said Councillors, and issuing into the City of London with a number of armed men with intent to persuade the citizens to join with them. Both the accused pleaded not guilty and defended themselves resolutely. Essex's 'boldness' was especially remarked on and, according to the letter-writer John Chamberlain, 'a man might easily perceive that as he had ever lived popularly, so his chief care was to leave a good opinion in the people's minds now at parting.' But the trial itself, like all treason trials of the period, was little more than a formal exercise, notable chiefly for the reappearance of the agile Francis Bacon among counsel for the prosecution and a dramatic confrontation between Essex and Robert Cecil.

Robert Cecil had put up with a good deal from Essex over the years, patiently enduring a long and spiteful campaign of smears and sneers and insults, but now he was determined to nail the nastiest slander of them all – that he had been deliberately plotting to sell England out to Spain. So, when his lordship repeated in open court that he had heard it reported how 'Mr. Secretary should say that the Infanta's title to the crown (after her Majesty) was as good as any other', Mr Secretary suddenly emerged from the hidden corner where he had been following the proceedings and, falling on his knees before the presiding judge, challenged Essex to name his sources for 'so false and foul an accusation'. Essex hedged and squirmed and passed the buck to the Earl of Southampton, but Cecil persisted and eventually it came out that the whole of the 'England is sold to the Spaniards' bogey was based on a casual remark made some two years earlier to Sir William Knollys. He and the Secretary had been walking in the garden at Court one morning discussing among other things the treatise by R. Doleman (alias Robert Parsons) on the *Next Succession to the Crown of England*, and Cecil had observed that it was a strange impudence on the part of Doleman to give an equal high right in the succession to the Infanta as any other. The Secretary of State had triumphantly vindicated his honour and made my lord of Essex look both foolish and malevolent.

Indeed, from Cecil's point of view, everything was turning out very satisfactorily. He felt reasonably certain that he had got to the bottom of the conspiracy – the evidence of Sir John Davies, Christopher Blount, Charles Danvers and Ferdinando Gorges gave a clear picture of the discussions at Drury House and the plot to seize the Queen, and two days after his trial Essex, influenced by his favourite chaplain, had been seized with a desire to purge himself of guilt by telling all. In a long written statement he poured out every detail of his own and his friends' activities over the past eighteen months; he named names from Lord Mountjoy downwards and confessed himself to be 'the greatest, the most vilest and most unthankfullest traitor that ever was born'. This was very helpful and not only confirmed much that the government already knew or guessed, but added quite a lot of interesting new information. Fortunately, though, the Earl's impetuous eruption of 8 February had made it possible to suppress the most damaging of these revelations and Cecil could congratulate himself on a very smooth operation, handled without causing embarrassment to such public figures as Mountjoy and the King of Scots.

As for the Queen, she had shown all her usual cool confident courage on the day of the insurrection, remarking that God who had placed her in that seat would maintain her in it, and showing an alarming readiness to go out on the streets in person 'to see what any rebel of them all durst do against her'. But after the crisis came reaction. John Harington, who seems to have had quite a talent for turning up at awkward moments, was at Court just as the madcaps were all in riot, and found her Majesty in a fractious mood – refusing to eat, not bothering to change her dress and making the household's life a misery.

'I must not say much, even by this trusty and sure messenger', wrote Harington to Sir Hugh Portman; 'but the many evil plots and designs have overcome all her Highness' sweet temper. She walks much in her privy chamber, and stamps with her feet at ill news, and thrusts her rusty sword at times into the arras in great rage.' The sight of Harington reminded Elizabeth of his Irish knighthood, still a sore point, and she sent him packing with a sharp message delivered by Lord Buckhurst: 'Go tell that witty fellow, my godson, to get home; it is no season now to fool it here.' Sir John knew better than to argue and hurriedly took to his boots and returned to the plough in bad weather.

The Queen typically concealed her unease under a royal display of bad temper, 'swearing at those that cause her griefs in such wise, to the no small discomfort of all about her'; but the anxieties of the early months of 1601 had undoubtedly taken their toll – visiting Robert Sidney at Penshurst she called for a stick and 'seemed much wearied in walking about the house'. It wasn't only Essex's final and fatal defiance – that had, after all, been expected in some form or other. Far more disturbing was the knowledge that a man like Mountjoy had actually contemplated leading his army against her and that even such an old friend as Peregrine Bertie, Lord Willoughby, now Governor of Berwick, had helped the Earl's messengers on their way into Scotland. It was a sign of the changing times that 'now the wit of the fox is everywhere on foot, so as hardly one faithful or virtuous man may be found'; but worse still, it was a sign that Gloriana's old magic was beginning to lose its potency.

It seems likely that it was reflections of this kind rather than personal grief for Essex which were responsible for Elizabeth's reportedly increasing tendency to mope by herself in a darkened room. Despite the various bogus romantic legends which grew up around the event, the Queen showed less reluctance than usual when it came to signing the Earl's death warrant, for though she might be saddened by the ignoble end of a once brilliant and beautiful young man, she never hesitated over its necessity. Essex had committed the two unforgivable sins – he would have touched her sceptre and he had tried to turn her own Londoners against her.

Elizabeth has often been blamed for her inept handling of Essex. At the time of his Irish fiasco, Francis Bacon thought she was making a mistake to criticise and discontent him as she did, and yet put so much military power into his hands. Robert Naunton, writing some thirty years later, commented on the 'violent indulgency of the Queen . . . towards this lord' as well as on 'a fault in the object of her grace, my lord himself, who drew in too fast, like a child sucking on an over-uberous nurse'. Naunton believed that 'had there been a more decent decorum observed in both, or either of those, without doubt the unity of their affections had been more permanent, and not so in and out as they were, like an instrument ill-tuned and lapsing into discord'.

Certainly, in the early and still unclouded years of their relationship, Elizabeth had over-indulged her pretty, red-headed boyfriend, allowing him to form an undesirably inflated idea of his own importance. It had also been a serious error of judgement to send him to Ireland as she did. But, at the same time, it is surely debatable whether any prodigies of tact or skill would have made any difference in the end in this classic case of hubris and nemesis. The conjunction of a young, essentially violent and unstable man, whose ambitions constantly outran his capabilities, and an ageing, autocratic woman, subject to the fears and stresses which afflict all ageing autocrats, can only have resulted in 'an instrument ill-tuned'. Essex's tragedy was that he could not be content with the position of domestical greatness which was his for the asking; Elizabeth's the bitter realisation that what she had to offer was not enough.

Essex paid the price of treason to the headsman on Ash Wednesday, 25 February 1601, acknowledging 'with thankfulness to God, that he was thus justly spewed out of the realm'. A few weeks later four of his fellow conspirators his stepfather Christopher Blount, his secretary Henry Cuffe, his friend Charles Danvers and his steward Gilly Meyrick followed him into eternity, but these were the only members of his party to suffer the death penalty. Even the Earl of Southampton had his sentence commuted to imprisonment in the Tower and lived to become an ornament of a Court where he was far more at home. Francis Bacon, too, would gather the harvest of his patient pragmatism in the next reign, but his crippled brother Anthony did not survive to share it. Faithful to his former patron to the end, he died that spring in debt and obscurity.

Essex was gone, and with him went the last flicker of the old, turbulent, baronial England, in which an over-mighty subject could challenge the central power of the state, even the throne itself, and hope to win. Essex was gone, though his memory lived on and the people mourned their dead hero in sentimental ballads which were heard even around the Court. 'Sweet England's pride is gone', they sang, but they and England and England's Queen were all very much better off without him.

One result of his disappearance from the political arena was a dramatic improvement in Anglo-Scottish relations. The ambassadors who were to have conferred with the Earl of Essex on the best means of enforcing James's demand for immediate recognition as heir apparent arrived in London in March, in nice time to congratulate the Queen on her lucky escape from the Essex conspiracy. Being sensible men, who could see how the land lay, they approached Robert Cecil instead and Cecil quickly seized the opportunity to reassure them of his impeccable devotion to their master, for it was time to start thinking seriously about the future.

The succession had been a major cause of anxiety and dissension in the past – Elizabeth's inflexible refusal to name her heir or even to allow the subject to be discussed had raised a series of storms in Parliament and elsewhere – but since the death of Mary Queen of Scots the problem had lost much of its immediacy. The exiled Catholic community and its allies might continue to discuss it with feverish intensity among themselves, but the majority of Englishmen had gradually grown accustomed to the idea that Mary's son James, who was after all doubly descended from Henry VII, the first Tudor king, would in due time come to occupy his great-grandfather's throne. Indeed, he had no serious competitor, with the possible exception of his first cousin Lady Arbella Stuart. Her claim was dynastically inferior but it could be argued in her favour that she had been born in the realm, while James was technically a foreigner.

There were those who might have been prepared to support her. Not everyone fancied the idea of a Scottish king, especially the son of that well-known Jezebel Mary Stuart, and Lady Arbella had from time to time been an object of interest to the Catholics as a possibly useful pawn in their endless convoluted intrigues to unseat Queen Elizabeth. But the Queen had never given her any sign of encouragement and, apart from a brief visit to Court as a child, Arbella had spent virtually all her life in the wilds of Derbyshire under the eye of her maternal grandmother, the formidable Dowager Countess of Shrewsbury, better known as Bess of Hardwick. In fact, it would probably be true to say that outside Court and political circles, few people were even aware of her existence and Robert Cecil meant to ensure that it stayed that way, for Robert Cecil was about to stake his political career on stage-managing a smooth transference of power when the time came.

Obviously the first thing was to win James's confidence and endeavour to undo the damage of years of Essex's mischief-making, and Cecil therefore embarked on a correspondence with the King which he took elaborate precautions to keep secret from everyone, including and especially the Queen lest, as he put it, her 'age and orbity, joined to the jealousy of her sex, might have moved her to think ill of that which helped to preserve her'. There can be no doubt but that Elizabeth had always regarded James as her rightful heir, witness her care to safeguard his position at the time of his mother's execution, and she no doubt guessed quite accurately what her Secretary was up to, but so long as the matter remained an official 'secret', she was content. She trusted Cecil, in the circumstances she had to trust him, and he did not betray her. Here, at least, was one faithful and virtuous man, for despite the bad press he has consistently received from historians dazzled by Essex's spurious glamour and despite the fact that he was not quite the man his father had been, Robert Cecil served the Queen loyally at a time when she would have been most vulnerable to deceit.

He soon had James eating out of his hand, and once that notoriously jumpy individual was convinced that he had at last acquired a competent and trustworthy friend at the English Court, his flirtations with the Catholic powers stopped abruptly. The fact that Cecil was able to negotiate an increase in his pension also helped. He also stopped pestering for recognition, assuring the Secretary that henceforward he would be content to wait for God's good time, rather than hazard the breaking of his neck 'by climbing of hedges and ditches for pulling of unripe fruit'. The fact that 'little Cecil' received cheering promises of favours to come, 'quhen it shall please God that the king shall succiede to his richt', did not alter the other fact that his tactful management of James protected Elizabeth's last years from unnecessary alarms and ensured a peaceful hand-over to the new branch of the family business.

45

A Taper of True Virgin Wax

An aged princess; many days shall see her,
And yet no day without a deed to crown it.
Would I had known no more! but she must die,
She must, the saints must have her, yet a virgin;
A most unspotted lily shall she pass
To the ground, and all the world shall mourn her.

By the summer of 1601 the Queen appeared to have recovered from the traumas of the Essex rebellion and was once more immersed in her usual round of activities. At the beginning of August Sir William Browne, deputy Governor of Flushing, came over to report on the situation in the Netherlands, where Ostend was currently being besieged by Archduke Albert. Elizabeth gave him an audience on Sunday morning after church, while walking in Sir William Clark's garden, and was at her most affable. 'I had no sooner kissed her sacred hands', wrote Browne, 'but that she presently made me stand up, and spoke somewhat loud, and said, Come hither, Browne; and pronounced that she held me for an old faithful servant of hers, and said, I must give content to Browne, or some such speeches. And then the train following her, she said, Stand, stand back, will you not let us speak but you will be hearers? And then walked a turn or two, protesting her most gracious opinion of myself . . . She called for a stool which was set under a tree, and I began to kneel, but she would not suffer me, in so much as that after two or three denials which I made to kneel, still she was pleased to say that she would not speak with me unless I stood up.'

These preliminaries disposed of, her Majesty 'discoursed of many things' and Browne found her to be remarkably well informed. She complained about lack of support from the Dutch, and when Browne attempted to defend them: 'Tush! Browne, saith she, I know more than thou dost. When I heard, said she, that they were at the first with their army as high as Nymegen, I knew then that no good would be done . . . I looked they should have come down nearer Ostend, or have taken some town in the part of Brabant or Flanders that might have startled the enemy. And that they promised me, or else I would not have let them have so many men.' She went on to talk of the French king and the support he had promised to the Dutch. Browne answered that 'the French king rather marvelled at their foolish boldness in venturing their army so far, than that he ever gave them any assurance to join with them'. But the Queen would not have it. 'Tush! Browne, said she, do not I know that Bucenval was written to, and written to again, to move the army to go that way and that then he would help them.' Browne answered slyly that if it were so, then her Majesty must think it was but a French promise. The conversation ranged over other topics, Browne could not remember 'all the discourses we had', but the end was that he 'received perfect joy by being so favoured of her Majesty, as that I shall think of it during life'.

Elizabeth gave unalloyed pleasure to another faithful subject that month, when she received the learned antiquarian and lawyer William Lambarde in the privy chamber at Greenwich. Lambarde, in his capacity of Keeper of the Records at the Tower of London, had compiled an inventory, or Pandecta, of the documents in his charge and had intended to present it to the Queen by the Countess of Warwick, but her Majesty would have none of that – if a subject of hers did her a service, then she would thankfully accept it from his own hands. She opened the book, read the epistle and title aloud, and at once began to ask intelligent questions about the meaning of certain technical terms, saying she would be a scholar in her age, and thought it no scorn to learn during her life. But when she reached the reign of Richard the Second, she was unfortunately reminded of recent events and exclaimed 'I am Richard. Know ye not that?' 'Such a wicked imagination', answered Lambarde, 'was determined and attempted by a most unkind gentleman – the most adorned creature that ever your Majesty made.' 'He that will forget God', observed her Majesty piously, 'will also forget his benefactors'.

Elizabeth went all through Lambarde's work, with obvious interest, and finally commended the gratified author 'not only for the pains therein taken, but also for that she had not received, since her first coming to the crown, any one thing that brought therewith so great a delectation to her, and so', he recorded, 'being called away to prayer, she put the book in her bosom, having forbidden me from the first to fall on my knee before her, concluding, "Farewell, good and honest Lambarde!"'

The Queen's summer progress that year took her to Reading and then on into Hampshire, where she stayed for nearly a fortnight at Basing as the guest of the Marquis of Winchester and entertained a grand embassy from France, headed by the Duc de Biron, which had been put up at The Vine, the stately home of Lord Sandys. The Vine was hastily embellished with extra plate, hangings and furniture borrowed from the Tower and Hampton Court. There was an exchange of visits, with hunting and feasting, and Elizabeth was able to boast 'that she had done more than any of her ancestors had ever done, or any other prince in Christendom was able to do – namely, in her Hampshire progress this year, entertained a royal ambassador royally in her subjects' houses'.

The party broke up on 19 September and Elizabeth started back towards Windsor, preoccupied by ominous news from Ireland. Early in the month a fleet of thirty-three ships, great and small, had set sail from Lisbon carrying nearly five thousand troops, a battery of siege guns and a quantity of spare arms and ammunition under the command of Don Juan of Aguila, the same who had once established the Spanish foothold in Brittany and master-minded the raid on Mousehole. This fleet was the long-heralded assistance for Tyrone and the Irish rebels, and on 23 September the Spaniards were disembarking at Kinsale to the west of Cork.

The Irish situation in general had eased considerably since Sir Henry Docwra had succeeded in establishing himself with a small independent force at Derby at the head of Lough Foyle in the heart of rebel territory; but this latest development put all the hard-won gains of the past eighteen months in jeopardy, for if de Aguila once joined forces with Tyrone the English would be hopelessly outnumbered. 'If we beat them', Mountjoy told Robert Cecil as soon as news of the landing reached him, 'let it not trouble you though you hear all Ireland doth revolt . . . if we do not, all providence bestowed on any other place is vain.' Clearly the next few weeks would see the turning point of the war in Ireland and perhaps the turning point of the whole long, bitter struggle. In London extra reinforcements were being hastily levied and a squadron of the fleet under Sir Richard Leveson was ordered to the coast of Munster, while the Queen wrote to her Lord Deputy in her own hand: 'Tell our army from us . . . that every hundred of them will beat a thousand, and every thousand theirs doubled. I am the bolder to pronounce it in His name, that hath ever protected my righteous cause, in which I bless them all. And putting you in the first place, I end, scribbling in haste, Your loving sovereign, E.R.'

Mountjoy had marched on Kinsale with the minimum of delay, for although it might be beyond his powers to dislodge the invaders by a direct assault, it was vitally important to prevent their breaking out of the bridgehead and making contact with the rebel army. Fortunately, with the threat of the English force at Derry in his rear preying on his mind and hampering his freedom of movement, Tyrone was slow in arriving. Mountjoy and George Carew were therefore able to get into position around Kinsale and, as autumn drew on, the campaign developed into a grim race to bombard the Spaniards out before the Irish came up.

Meanwhile, at Westminster, the Queen was meeting Parliament for the thirteenth and last time. As usual, the government was in urgent need of money. It was a year since the final instalment of the treble subsidy granted in 1597–98 had been collected and, but for the uproar caused by the Essex affair, the members would no doubt have been summoned sooner. Elizabeth was still selling land and even jewellery but, despite all her frugal housekeeping, the state was now sliding inexorably towards bankruptcy, a slide which the huge additional expense of the Irish war was doing nothing to halt.

The session began badly. Owing to some official blunder a number of MPs were shut out of the Lords and so missed the Lord Keeper's opening address, and there was another awkward moment, due to more bad management, when the Queen was jostled in the crowd of Commoners as she came out of the Upper House. 'She moved her hand to have more room; whereupon one of the gentlemen ushers said openly: "Back, masters, make room." And one answered stoutly behind: "If you will hang us, we can make no more room." Which the Queen seemed not to hear, though she heaved up her head, and looked that way towards him that spake.'

This was the first Parliament since old Lord Burghley's death and his skill and experience in handling government affairs were soon missed, as a first-class row blew up in the Commons over the so-called monopolies. These, like Essex's farm of sweet wines, were patents issued by the Crown granting to individuals the sole right to manufacture, import or export certain commodities ranging from starch to leather, from playing cards to glass and salt, and had long been a source of grievance. From the Crown's point of view, of course, they offered a temptingly easy and inexpensive way of rewarding deserving cases or placating importunate suitors; but they led naturally to all sorts of irritating abuses, to artificial shortages, inflated prices and the curtailment of freedom of choice and private enterprise. Probably, though, the greatest single cause of aggravation was that fact that corrupt or oppressive patent-holders could not be proceeded against in the courts. One member described the system as ending only in beggary and bondage to the subject, another attacked the monopolists as 'these bloodsuckers of the Commonwealth', yet another was to enquire sarcastically when bread would be added to the list and answered himself by declaring that if action were not taken now, bread would be there by the next Parliament.

The issue soon resolved itself into a matter of principle, for the monopolies were not a simple question of bad law which could be reformed by legislation. They were personal grants made by the Queen of her own authority and could only be revoked or withdrawn by her. They came, in short, within the royal prerogative which she guarded so jealously. The Commons knew they were on dangerous ground; nevertheless they proceeded to appoint a committee to discuss the subject. One faction urged the passing of a private member's bill entitled 'An Act for Explanation of the Common Law in certain cases of Letters Patent' – in other words what amounted to a direct attack on the prerogative; while another, more moderate, suggested petitioning the Queen to revoke all monopolies grievous to the subject and to permit the passage of an Act withdrawing such patents from the protection of the prerogative, so that their validity might be tested at Common Law.

No decision was reached but the agitation was growing and, as in the case of the Puritan campaigns of the past, had begun to show ominous signs of spreading beyond the confines of the Palace of Westminster. Propaganda sheets were being circulated and non-parliamentary supporters of the bill crowded in to lobby the members, declaring that they were Commonwealth men who desired the House 'to take compassion of their griefs, they being spoiled, imprisoned and robbed by monopolists'.

It was clear that the Commons had now fairly got their teeth into the monopolies and were not to be shaken loose by promises – they had been given promises before. Nor were they to be bullied. Cecil tried this and made matters worse. Worst of all from the government's point of view was the fact that the reading of the vital subsidy bill was being delayed. The holding up of supplies was a familiar weapon on the Commons' armoury, but in present circumstances it was an irresistible one. With the Spaniards on Irish soil, this was no time for a trial of strength, especially on such a doubtful moral issue. The Queen would have to yield, and on 24 November she yielded. On the following day the Speaker rose to inform the House that her Majesty, having learned to her surprise and distress that divers patents were proving grievous to her subjects, intended to take present order for the reformation of anything evil. Robert Cecil then spoke to confirm the royal message. He assured the House that a proclamation giving effect to the promised reformation would be issued without delay and went on to review those monopolies which were to be revoked at once. Every man, in future, would have salt as cheap as he could make or buy it and be able to eat his meat 'more savourly'. Those with weak stomachs would find vinegar set at liberty, and cold stomachs acqua vitae. Those who desired 'to go sprucely in their ruffs' would find starch cheaper, and so on through a long list. When Elizabeth gave way, she always did so handsomely. All the same, when the proclamation duly appeared two days later, it contained a clause re-affirming the power and validity of the prerogative royal and warned the lieges of the penalties which still awaited those who 'seditiously or contemptuously' presumed to call it in question. This was a face-saver, but it also made it plain that the Queen had not given way on principle. The proclamation was a device forced upon her by the necessity of the moment, and was intended to deflect Parliament from attempting to extend its legislative powers into forbidden territory. It was emphatically not a licence to do so.

But the Commons, rapturously welcoming so notable an instance of royal magnanimity, were in no mood for looking gift horses in the mouth. Some wept for joy and all were eager to show their loyal gratitude by giving the subsidy bill its first reading at once. Others wanted to do more, and on the afternoon of Monday, 30 September, a deputation of some hundred and fifty members headed by the Speaker filled the Council Chamber at Whitehall to offer their most humble and hearty thanks in person.

The Queen's reply has become known to history as her 'Golden Speech' and, famous though it is, it still deserves quoting as a classic example of the way in which Elizabeth fished for men's souls, using so sweet a bait that no one could escape her network. 'I do assure you', she told her audience on this occasion, 'there is no prince that loves his subjects better, or whose love can countervail our love. There is no jewel, be it of never so rich a price, which I set before this jewel: I mean your love. For I do esteem it more than any treasure or riches; for that we know how to prize, but love and thanks I count unvaluable. And, though God hath raised me high, yet this I count the glory of my crown, that I have reigned with your loves . . . Therefore, I have cause to wish nothing more than to content the subject; and that is a duty which I owe. Neither do I desire to live longer days than I may see your prosperity; and that is my only desire.'

The Queen went on to thank the Commons for the taxes they were voting her and then told the kneeling deputation to stand up, for she would yet trouble them with longer speech. She touched again on the subject of the monopolies, expressing pious gratitude to those of the Lower House who had brought the matter to her attention. 'For, had I not received a knowledge from you, I might have fallen into the lapse of an error, only for lack of true information . . . That my grants should be grievous to my people and oppressions privileged under colour of our patents, our kingly dignity shall not suffer it. Yea, when I heard it, I could give no rest unto my thoughts until I had reformed it.'

Elizabeth had ever been used to set the Last Judgement Day before her eyes, and she went on: 'I know the title of a King is a glorious title; but assure yourself that the shining glory of princely authority hath not so dazzled the eyes of our understanding, but that we well know and remember that we also are to yield an account of our actions before the great Judge. To be a King and wear a crown is a thing more glorious to them that see it, than it is pleasant to them that bear it. For myself, I was never so much enticed with the glorious name of a King or royal authority of a Queen, as delighted that God hath made me His instrument to maintain His truth and glory, and to defend this Kingdom from peril, dishonour, tyranny and oppression.

'There will never Queen sit in my seat with more zeal to my country, care for my subjects, and that will sooner with willingness venture her life for your good and safety, than myself. For it is my desire to live nor reign no longer than my life and reign shall be for your good. And though you have had and may have many princes more mighty and wise sitting in this seat, yet you never had nor shall have any that will be more careful and loving.'

And she ended: 'This, Mr. Speaker, I pray you deliver unto the House, to whom heartily recommend me. And so I commit you all to your best fortunes and further counsels. And I pray you, Mr. Comptroller, Mr.

Secretary, and you of my Council, that before these gentlemen go into their countries, you bring them all to kiss my hand.'

After this splendidly emotional occasion, the rest of the session passed relatively uneventfully, and an unprecedented quadruple subsidy was granted without too much grumbling. Between two and three o'clock in the afternoon of 19 December the Queen came down to the Lords to dissolve what she evidently believed would be her last Parliament, and after the ceremony of the royal assent she rose unexpectedly to make her valedictory address.

'Before your going down at the end of the Parliament', she said, 'I thought good to deliver unto you certain notes for your observation, that serve aptly for the present time, to be imparted afterward where you shall come abroad – to this end, that you by me, and other by you, may understand to what prince, and how affected to the good of this estate, you have declared yourselves so loving subjects.'

As far as home affairs were concerned, she believed 'yourselves can witness that I never entered into the examination of any cause without advisement, carrying ever a single eye to justice and truth; for, though I were content to hear matters argued and debated pro and contra, as all princes must that will understand what is right, yet I look ever as it were upon a plain table wherein is written neither partiality nor prejudice. My care was ever by proceeding justly and uprightly to conserve my people's love, which I account a gift of God.' When it came to the gloomy subject of finance: 'Beside your dutiful supplies for defence of the public . . . I have diminished my own revenue that I might add to your security, and been content to be a taper of true virgin wax, to waste myself and spend my life that I might give light and comfort to those that live under me.'

Elizabeth then referred briefly to Spanish aggression. 'The strange devices, practices and stratagems, never heard of nor written of before – that have been attempted, not only against my own person . . . but by invasion of the State itself, by those that did not only threaten to come, but came at the last in very deed, with their whole fleet – have been in number many, and by preparation dangerous; though it hath pleased God by many hard escapes and hazards . . . to make me an instrument of His holy will in delivering the State from danger and myself from dishonour. All that I challenge to myself is that I have been studious and industrious, in confidence of His grace and goodness, as a careful head to defend the body.'

Turning at last to 'foreign courses', the Queen took God to witness 'that I never gave just cause of war to any Prince . . . nor had any greater ambition than to maintain my own State in security and peace', and she went on to trace in some detail the origins of the war in the Netherlands and justify her own eventual intervention. At the same time, Elizabeth wanted her subjects to know 'that my care is neither to continue war nor conclude a peace, but for your good; and that you may perceive how free your Queen is from any cause of these attempts that have been made on her, unless to save her people or defend her state to be censured. This testimony', she declared, 'I would have you carry hence for the world to know: that your Sovereign is more careful of your conservation than of herself, and will daily crave of God that they that wish you best may never wish in vain.'

Elizabeth, great actress as she was, was taking her final curtain – the Bishop of Durham thought he had never heard her 'in better vein' – and rendering a solemn account of her stewardship to a body which had caused her a good deal of trouble over the years but which she had always dealt with honestly according to her lights. It was fitting that the long association between Queen and Parliament should have ended on this stately and graceful note, but it was perhaps just as well that it ended when it did.

The Queen, which her invincibly old-fashioned views on the sanctity of the prerogative royal, on the concept of the people guided and ruled for their own good by a wise, careful and loving sovereign, had never pretended to regard the noisy, self-opinionated assembly at Westminster as an auxiliary branch of government. Government was very definitely her business – undertaken with the advice and assistance of Councillors appointed by herself. The Commons were granted freedom of speech, within limits defined by established custom, and Elizabeth respected them as a representative sounding-board of public opinion, but she had never hesitated to scold them for wasting time in 'vain discourses and tedious orations', or for attempting to meddle with matters 'beyond the reach of a subject's brain to mention' – matters which had included such vital political issues as religion, her marriage and the succession. Nor did she ever hesitate to remind them of the undoubted fact that as she alone had the authority to summon Parliament, to continue it at her good pleasure and dissolve it when she thought good, so she also had the power 'to appoint unto them . . . what causes they were to treat of' and assent or dissent to anything decided by them. Parliament was the servant, albeit the valued servant, of the Crown but never its master, for it was unthinkable that the feet should direct the head.

This philosophy had led to some notable confrontations in the past, when an understandably nervous and sometimes dangerously fanatical House of Commons had fought to do their sovereign lady good against her will. But thanks in part to a deeply ingrained veneration for the mystique of kingship, in part to the shared perils of subversion from within and invasion from without which had drawn Queen and people together, and in part to Elizabeth's own peculiar brand of magic, confrontation had never developed into head-on collision. It was a state of affairs which could not have lasted. The delicately balanced special relationship with Parliament which the Queen had just, but only just, maintained to the end was doomed by the forces of history and not even a ruler of her genius could have maintained it for much longer.

The Commons was rapidly discovering its own strength and, more important, how to organise and direct that strength (some valuable lessons had been absorbed during the Puritan agitations of the eighties). Values were changing and an increasingly articulate and self-confident middle-class of lawyers and landed gentry was less inclined to accept the Tudor ideality of the paternalistic state, readier to question the God-given superiority of the sovereign. On a more practical level, it was realising the potency of that old, cold truth that he who pays the piper can, in the last resort, call the tune. The time was fast approaching, if indeed it had not already arrived, when the Crown could no longer 'live of its own', even in peacetime, when it would become dependent on the goodwill of Parliament for survival. The revolutionary concept of the sovereign Parliament was not yet openly acknowledged – if any member of the 1601 assembly had been told that within half a century it would have arrogated supreme power to itself and assisted at the judicial execution of the Lord's anointed, he would no doubt have been genuinely appalled – but the seeds of revolution had already lain some twenty years in the ground and would need only the warmth generated by righteous anger to germinate with frightening speed.

By the second week of January 1602 news came in from Ireland which did much to cheer the last full year of the Queen's life. Early in December the English naval squadron commanded by Sir Richard Leveson had distinguished itself by annihilating a Spanish fleet bringing reinforcements and supplies to de Aguila, and on the twenty-third Mountjoy's army won an overwhelming victory over Tyrone for the loss of one officer and a dozen men. Tyrone himself was wounded and it was the end of the by now thoroughly disenchanted Spaniards, who surrendered to the Lord Deputy in return for free passage home. It was the beginning of the end, too, for Tyrone and his dream of an independent Gaelic Ireland. It was also the beginning of the modern Irish problem, but this the Queen could hardly have been expected to foresee as she wrote her glowing thanks to Mountjoy, adding one of her scribbled postscripts to the official despatch: 'For yourself, we can but acknowledge your diligence, and dangerous adventure, and cherish and judge of you as your careful Sovereign.'

Relieved of her most immediate anxieties, Elizabeth was ready to authorise a small-scale naval expedition (the first for five years) in Spanish waters and by the end of March Richard Leveson and William Monson were at sea with a force of eight galleons and some smaller craft. It was Leveson who at long last actually encountered the fabled treasure fleet off the Azores, but with apparently only four warships with him at the time he could do little against sixteen heavily armed galleons of the Indian Guard. He did, however, succeed in cutting out one great carrack sheltering in the Lisbon river, and in London the Privy Council, with memories of bitter past experience, took every precaution to prevent her cargo from falling into the hands of the sharks at Plymouth. 'Here is order taken', wrote John Chamberlain, 'that no goldsmiths or jewellers shall go into the west countrie', and Fulk Greville was sent down with instructions to have the prize brought round to Portsmouth for unloading.

Leveson and William Monson between them kept the sea till autumn, but the war was coming to an end now on all fronts. Elizabeth Tudor may not have been a great war-leader, but then she had never wanted to be. Her aims had always been essentially defensive – to save her people and defend her state. Nor was the emerging society she ruled as yet sufficiently well-organised or disciplined to see and seize all its opportunities in a type of naval warfare which was still very largely in the experimental stage. But some vital lessons had been learned and, although it had taken a quarter of a century of suffering and death, the war's great objective, the restoration of a balance of power in Europe, had been achieved. The French monarchy had been helped back on to its feet and freed from the fear of a Spanish take-over. In the Netherlands, the Dutch of Holland and Zeeland – an increasingly prosperous oligarchy soon to challenge their English allies for maritime supremacy – were no longer threatened by renewed Spanish hegemony. The predominantly Catholic southern provinces of Flanders and Brabant remained under Spanish and, later, Austrian rule, but that would protect them from a predatory France and it would be another hundred years before England would again have to fight to secure her frontiers across the North Sea. In Ireland, too, the vulnerable back door was once more locked and bolted, at least for the foreseeable future. Considering the resources at her disposal, the Queen had no reason to feel ashamed of her record, even as a reluctant commander-in-chief.

At home the great dearth of the mid-nineties was over, trade was reviving and new markets and new horizons were being eagerly explored in both the Old World and the New; while the programme of social and economic legislation undertaken during the last decade of the reign had laid the foundations of a system of poor relief which endured for centuries. For very many people the quality of life was showing a steady improvement for, despite increased taxation, the heaviest financial burden of the war had fallen on the Queen rather than her subjects. By the end Elizabeth had been forced to realise practically all the wealth which had accrued to the Crown by her father's nationalisation of Church property at the time of the Reformation. The monarchy was thus seriously weakened – as her successors were to discover – but Elizabeth had preserved her personal authority and safeguarded her realm and had considered the price worth paying.

The religious controversies which had overshadowed so much of the political life of the country for so many years of the Tudor century had now, at last, reached a kind of stalemate. Thanks to the work of churchmen like John Whitgift, Richard Bancroft, Bishop of London and the great Anglican polemicist Richard Hooker, the Church of England was probably in a healthier state than at any time since the Settlement of 1559. The aggressive Puritanism of the eighties had faded, and although Puritanism was by no means dead, it was no longer openly attacking the Established Church. In any case, the radicals cherished strong hopes of King James, who had after all been reared in the presbyterianism of the Church of Scotland, and were content to await developments. The Catholic revival, too, which had caused such a crescendo of alarm and fury in the early eighties, could no longer be represented as a serious threat to national unity. The suffering and sacrifice of the small devoted band of missionary priests trained in the seminaries of Douai and Rheims, and at the English College in Rome, had ensured that the Faith would survive, but they had come too late and too few to reverse the Protestant tide. By the nineties the sudden surge of spiritual fervour among the native Catholics, which had reached its zenith about the time of the famous mission of the Jesuit Fathers Campion and Parsons, was largely spent. A small percentage of the population still clung, and would continue to cling, to its convictions in the face of every discouragement from social ostracism to the death penalty. But constant pressure, a constant sense of insecurity and the wounding imputation of disloyalty to Queen and country were doing their work, and although the Catholics too had hopes of James (at least they would be relieved of the embarrassment of trying to reconcile obedience to the Pope with allegiance to an excommunicated sovereign), not even the most optimistic was expecting more than perhaps a measure of toleration for their diminishing numbers.

For Elizabeth the fact that an actively anti-Jesuit, anti-Spanish faction had now begun to emerge from the ranks of the English Catholics could be taken as a satisfying vindication of her policy of refusal to countenance religious persecution on anything resembling the Continental model. She would not, and could not of course, ever have granted her Catholic subjects freedom of worship, but she who had always refused to make windows into men's souls had never demanded more than outward compliance with her laws, and could never be persuaded that Englishmen who happened to be Catholics must also necessarily be traitors. It was a position which had needed courage to maintain in the menacing atmosphere of the early 1580s, but the Queen had never wavered from it. As always, once she had made up her mind on a matter of principle, she was immovable. The exact nature of her own religious principles has often been debated, but she herself summed it up neatly enough when she remarked to André de Maisse in 1597 that there was only one Jesus Christ and one faith, and all the rest was a dispute about trifles or, she might have added, about power.

There can have been few people living in that second year of the new century who knew more about the exercise of power than the old Queen of England. 'She only is a King! She only knows how to rule!' her former sparring partner the King of France had exclaimed in unfeigned admiration after the Essex revolt, and the King's astute Minister of Finance, the Duc de Sully, who came on a private mission to London in the summer of 1601, was deeply impressed by her Majesty's grasp of affairs and of political realities. 'She drew me aside', he was to recall to his Memoirs, 'that she might speak to me with the greatest freedom on the present state of affairs in Europe; and this she did with such strength and clearness, beginning from the Treaty of Vervins, that I was convinced this great Queen was truly worthy of that high reputation she had acquired.'

Elizabeth referred to the necessity of containing the power of the House of Hapsburg within just bounds and went on to outline her views on the way in which the other European powers ought to combine, 'so that none of them might be capable of giving umbrage to the rest'. 'These were not the only reflections made by the queen of England', wrote Sully; 'she said many other things, which appeared to me so just and sensible, that I was filled with astonishment and admiration. It is not unusual to behold princes form great designs; their sphere of action so forcibly inclines them to this . . . but to be able to distinguish and form only such as are reasonable; wisely to regulate the conduct of them; to foresee and guard against all obstacles in such a manner, that when they happen, nothing more will be necessary than to apply the remedies prepared long before – this is what few princes are capable of.' And at the end of their conversation, Sully's verdict was little different from that reached by his compatriot de Maisse four years earlier. 'I cannot bestow praises upon the Queen of England that would be equal to the merit which I discovered in her in this short time, both as to the qualities of the heart and the understanding.'

Not merely was Elizabeth's intellect unimpaired by advancing age, physically she was still in astonishingly good shape. She danced with the Duc de Nevers, who visited her in April 1602, and in September another foreign nobleman reported catching a glimpse of her walking in her garden as briskly as an eighteen-year-old. There was no long progress that year but the Queen paid a round of visits in the London area, finishing up at Oatlands, and Robert Cecil noted that she had not been in better health for years, riding ten miles in a day and hunting without apparent ill-effects. In September the Earl of Worcester wrote to the Earl of Shrewsbury: 'We are frolic here at Court; much dancing in the Privy Chamber of country dances before the Queen's Majesty who is exceedingly pleased therewith.' Later in the month, when Elizabeth had entered her seventieth year, another courtier remarked in a letter to the Countess of Shrewsbury: 'The best news I can yet write you ladyship is of the Queen's health and disposition of body, which I assure you is excellent good. And I have not seen her every way better disposed these many years.'

Like her father, Elizabeth had been fortunate in inheriting the splendid constitution of their Yorkist forebears, but unlike him had never abused it. She had always been fastidious in matters of personal hygiene; had always taken plenty of fresh air and exercise, and was noticeably abstemious over food and drink. She had also, wisely, avoided the ministrations of the royal physicians whenever possible. Probably, though, the real reason for her continued well-being was the fact that she had been lucky enough to spend her life doing work she enjoyed and was supremely good at.

It was true that during her last months she suffered from occasional fits of melancholy. In June she told the French ambassador that 'she was a-weary of life' and went on with a sigh to speak of Essex; while someone told one of King James's friends that 'our Queen is troubled with a rheum in her arm which vexeth her very much . . . She sleepeth not so much by day as she used, neither taketh rest by night.' And he added, for good measure, that her delight was to sit in the dark and sometimes with shedding tears, to bewail Essex. Well, naturally, the great days were over, and Elizabeth knew it. Without an Essex to attract the young men the Court was no longer such a brilliant social centre, and despite the Queen's refusal even now to permit any public mention of her successor, some of the younger element had already begun to turn their eyes northward – Sir John Harington found some less mindful of what they were soon to lose, than of what they might perchance hereafter get.

All the same, it was quite a gay autumn. Queen's Day, the forty-fourth anniversary of her accession, passed with 'the ordinary solemnity'. There were many young runners at the tilting and the Court fool, who appeared on a pony no bigger than a bull mastiff, 'had good audience of her Majesty and made her very merry'. At the beginning of December she was present at a house-warming party at Robert Cecil's and seemed to enjoy herself. Lord Hunsdon gave a grand dinner later in the month, and on the twenty-second the Lord Admiral entertained his sovereign at Arundel House. Christmas was spent at Whitehall and, thanks to the efforts of the new Comptroller Sir Edward Wotton, it was more cheerful than anyone had expected. Indeed, John Chamberlain reported that 'the Court hath flourished more than ordinary' with dancing, bear-baiting and plays.

But not even Elizabeth was immortal – though to James of Scotland it must sometimes have seemed as if she might be – and John Harington, who had come to town for the Christmas season, was shocked at the change he saw in her. 'Our dear Queen, my royal godmother and this state's most natural mother', he wrote to his wife down in Somerset, 'doth now bear show of human infirmity, too fast for that evil which we shall get by her death, and too slow for that good which she shall get by her releasement from pains and misery.'

Harington found the Queen 'in most pitiable state'. Unfortunately, the sight of her godson always brought a vivid reminder of Essex and the Irish disaster and she at once brought the subject up, 'dropped a tear and smote her bosom'. Sir John tried to divert her by reading her some of his witty verses. 'Whereat she smiled once, and was pleased to say: "When thou dost feel creeping time at thy gate, these fooleries will please thee less; I am past my relish for such matters."' She was eating hardly anything now and for the first time there were signs that her memory was beginning to fail. 'But who', wrote Harington sadly, 'shall say that "your Highness hath forgotten"?'

But he must have seen her on a bad day, for she rallied again and in January she was said to be 'very well'. She was still in harness, still dealing with mopping-up operations in Ireland and negotiating the conditions for Tyrone's surrender. There was talk of sending another fleet to blockade the Spanish ports that summer, and plans were being discussed for raising an auxiliary fleet of private ships to guard commerce in the Channel from Spanish privateers and the Dunkirk pirates.

On 21 January the Court moved down to Richmond. The weather had turned very cold, but Elizabeth insisted on wearing 'summer-like garments' and on 6 February she received Giovanni Scaramelli – the first Venetian ambassador appointed to her Court since her accession – resplendently dressed in white and silver, her hair 'of a light colour never made by nature' and apparently in good spirits. She addressed Scaramelli in his own language, and said at the end of the audience: 'I do not know if I have spoken Italian well; still I think so, for I learnt it when a child and believe I have not forgotten it.'

Then, towards the end of February, she lost her cousin and closest woman friend, the Countess of Nottingham, granddaughter of her aunt Mary Boleyn. Elizabeth's mood of wretchedness returned and this time she did not throw it off. Early in March, Lady Nottingham's brother, Robert Carey, came down to Richmond and found the Queen in one of her withdrawing chambers, sitting huddled on a pile of cushions. 'I kissed her hand', he recorded in his Memoirs, 'and told her it was my chiefest happiness to see her in safety, and in health, which I wished might long continue. She took me by the hand, and wrung it hard, and said, "No, Robin, I am not well", and then discoursed with me of her indisposition, and that her heart had been sad and heavy for ten or twelve days; and in her discourse, she fetched not so few as forty or fifty great sighs. I was grieved at the first to see her in this plight; for in all my lifetime before, I never knew her fetch a sigh, but when the Queen of Scots was beheaded.'

Carey did what he could 'to persuade her from this melancholy humour', but found it was too deeply rooted in her heart and hardly to be removed. This was on a Saturday evening. Next day the Queen was not well enough to go to church and heard the service lying on cushions in her privy chamber. 'From that day forwards', says Carey, 'she grew worse and worse. She remained upon her cushions four days and nights at the least. All about her could not persuade her, either to take any sustenance, or go to bed.'

The French ambassador told his master on 19 March that 'Queen Elizabeth had been very much indisposed for the last fourteen days, having scarcely slept at all during that period, and eaten much less than usual, being seized with such a restlessness that, though she had no decided fever, she felt a great heat in her stomach, and a continual thirst, which obliged her every moment to take something to abate it, and to prevent the phlegm, with which she was sometimes oppressed, from choking her.'

The immediate physical cause of the Queen's last illness seems to have been a streptococcal throat infection, possibly connected with dental sepsis, but evidently pneumonia soon set in. Still no one could persuade her to go to bed until, at last, the Lord Admiral, who had left the Court in mourning for his wife, was fetched back and, partly by persuasion, partly by force, he succeeded in getting her off her cushions and into bed. There, temporarily, she felt a little better. There temporarily, she felt a little better and was able to swallow some broth, but 'there was no hope of recovery, because she refused all remedies'.

Elizabeth had said repeatedly that she had no desire to live longer than would be for her subjects' good, and now it seemed as if she felt her task was done. She had outlived her century, outlived nearly all her friends, outlived her usefulness to her beloved country and she was very tired. Recently the coronation ring, outward and visible token of her symbolic marriage with the people of England which for nearly forty-five years had never left her finger, had grown into the flesh and had to be cut away. It was an omen. 'The Queen grew worse and worse', said Robert Carey significantly, 'because she would be so.' She lay speechless and semi-conscious, her eyes open, one finger in her mouth, the power flowing out of her, the great golden dangerous world in which she had played so valiant a part fading into darkness.

But there was still one last important duty to be performed, and about six o'clock in the evening of Wednesday, 23 March she made signs asking for the Archbishop of Canterbury and her chaplains to be summoned. Robert Carey was among the company in the bedchamber and sat upon his knees, full of tears to see that heavy sight. 'Her Majesty', he remembered, 'lay upon her back, with one hand in the bed, and the other without. The Bishop kneeled down by her, and examined her first of her faith; and she so punctually answered all his several questions, by lifting up her eyes, and holding up her hand, as it was a comfort to all the beholders. Then the good man told her plainly what she was, and what she was come to; and though she had been long a great Queen here upon earth, yet shortly she was to yield an account of her stewardship to the King of Kings. After this he began to pray, and all that were by did answer him.'

Old John Whitgift prayed till his knees were weary and then blessed the dying woman and made to rise and leave her. But she would not let him go, making a sign with her hand which Lady Scrope interpreted as a desire that he would pray still. After another 'long half hour' he tried again to leave, and again 'she made a sign to have him continue in prayer. He did so for half-an-hour more, with earnest cries to God for her soul's health, which he uttered with that fervency of spirit, as the Queen, to all our sight, much rejoiced thereat, and gave testimony to us of all her Christian and comfortable end. By this time it grew late, and every one departed, all but her women that attended her.'

'This that I heard with my ears, and did see with my eyes', says Robert Carey, 'I thought it my duty to set down and affirm it for a truth, upon the faith of a Christian, because I know there have been many false lies reported of the end and death of that good lady.'

Elizabeth slipped away between two and three o'clock on the morning of 24 March, 'mildly like a lamb, easily like a ripe apple from the tree', and Carey, who had been standing by with a horse ready saddled, set out in pouring rain on the first stage of his wild ride north to tell the King of Scotland that the long wait was over – that the last English sovereign of the English nation was at peace.

46

Epilogue: Queen Elizabeth of Famous Memory

No oblivion shall ever bury the glory of her name. For her happy and renowned memory still liveth and shall for ever live in the minds of men.

The belief that one of Queen Elizabeth's last conscious acts had been to indicate her wish to be succeeded by the King of Scots was current within a few days of her death. Robert Carey repeats the story, but does not say he witnessed the occasion, and the French ambassador reported that, while he already knew the Council intended to proclaim James at once, Elizabeth herself had named no successor. It seems more likely that she who had always dreaded the prospect of being 'buried alive' had remained silent to the end, and that all the convenient tales of death-bed recognition were no more than precautionary propaganda circulated by a prudent government.

In fact, they proved unnecessary. King James's proclamation was duly read on the morning of 24 March at the gates of Whitehall and in Cheapside and the people listened quietly, with great expectation but 'no great shouting'. 'I think the sorrow for her Majesty's departure was so deep in many hearts', wrote the diarist John Manningham, 'they could not so suddenly show any great joy.' Watch was kept at every gate and street 'to prevent garboils', but there was no tumult, no contradiction, no hint of disorder in the city. During the winter Arbella Stuart had made a desperate last-minute attempt to draw attention to herself, but the poor woman was no match for Robert Cecil and the transference of power had been accomplished without a hitch. There was no mention of Lady Arbella, not a whisper of the Spanish claim. Bonfires were lit and church bells rung to celebrate the new reign and 'every man went about his business as readily, as peaceably, as securely as though there had been no change, nor any news ever heard of competitors'. For those who could remember the hag-ridden days of the seventies and early eighties, this peaceful transition provided a final vindication of Elizabeth's policy over the succession; for those who still mourned the Earl of Essex it was a vindication of the trust she had reposed in Robert Cecil, but for very many of her contemporaries England would never be the same again.

The Queen was carried to her tomb in Westminster Abbey on 28 April, at which time, John Stow recorded in his Annals, 'the City of Westminster was surcharged with multitudes of all sorts of people, in the streets, houses, windows, leads, and gutters, who came to see the obsequy. And when they beheld her statue or effigy, lying on the coffin, set forth in royal robes, having a crown upon the head thereof, and a ball and sceptre in either hand, there was such a general sighing, groaning and weeping, as the like hath not been seen or known in the memory of man – neither doth any history mention any people, time or state, to make like lamentation for the death of their sovereign.'

What sort of woman was she, this great Queen, and how can her achievement best be summed up? Among her surviving friends, John Harington, who both loved and feared her, blessed her memory for all her goodness to himself and his family. 'I never did find greater show of understanding and learning than she was blessed with', he wrote after her death. Robert Cecil, who had served her declining years, remembered her as 'more than a man and, in troth, sometimes less than a woman'; but although he was to prosper under the new regime, he would always remember her too as 'our blessed Queen'. 'I wish I waited now in her Presence Chamber, with ease at my foot, and rest in my bed', he was to write to Harington. Lord Burghley, who of all the Elizabethans is surely best qualified to give an opinion, said of her that she 'was the wisest woman that ever was, for she understood the interests and dispositions of all the princes in her time, and was so perfect in the knowledge of her own realm, that no councillor she had could tell her anything she did not know before'.

That the Queen's greatest strength lay in her matchless skill in promoting and exploiting her unique relationship with the people of England can scarcely be disputed. Their love affair had begun in the first months of the reign and to the end of her life she never forgot its importance – never made the mistake of taking it for granted. Once, 'in merry sort', she asked her godson's wife how she kept her husband's good will and love, and when Mary Harington replied that she always sought to persuade him of her own affection, 'and in so doing did command his', the Queen exclaimed: 'Go to, go to, mistress, you are wisely bent I find; after such sort do I keep the good will of all my husbands, my good people; for if they did not rest assured of some special love toward them, they would not readily yield me such good obedience.' Three years after her death, in a letter to his cousin Markham, Harington himself recalled that: 'Her speech did win all affections, and her subjects did try to show all love to her commands; for she would say, "her state did require her to command what she knew her people would willingly do from their own love to her." Herewith did she show her wisdom fully: for who did choose to lose her confidence; or who would withhold a show of love and obedience, when their Sovereign said it was their own choice, and not her compulsion?'

Like her father and her Yorkist grandfather before her, Elizabeth knew all about the truth of the somewhat cynical maxim that 'the common people oftentimes more esteem and take for greater kindness a little courtesy, than a great benefit'. Of course she traded on her charm – stories of the Queen's 'condescension' to the 'meaner sort' of her subjects are legion – and of course much of it was done for effect. Of course there was self-interest on both sides. But that there was also sincerity is not in question – a love affair does not stand the test of over forty years nourished on self-interest alone. Beneath all the bad poetry, the heavily allegorical pageants, the painstaking Latin orations and the romantic extravaganzas of the Gloriana cult, there lay a solid sub-stratum of mutual need, affection and respect.

The Queen, observed Bishop Mandell Creighton, one of the more percipient of her nineteenth century biographers, 'represented England as no other ruler ever did. For the greater part of her long reign the fortunes of England absolutely depended upon her life, and not only the fortunes of England, but those of Europe as well . . . In asking England to rally round her, Elizabeth knew that she could not demand any great sacrifices on her behalf. By cultivating personal loyalty, by demanding it in exaggerated form, she was not merely feeding her personal vanity; she was creating a habit which was necessary for the maintenance of her government.' And he goes on: 'Elizabeth's imperishable claim to greatness lies in her instinctive sympathy with her people.'

The contemporary historian and schoolmaster, William Camden, would have agreed with the Victorian Bishop in this assessment of the Queen. 'Though beset by divers nations, her mortal enemies', he wrote, 'she held the most stout and warlike nation of the English four and forty years and upwards, not only in awe and duty, but even in peace also. Insomuch as, in all England, for so many years, never any mortal man heard the trumpet sound the charge to battle.'

As far as her own people were concerned, this was undoubtedly the Queen's greatest achievement – that she had so satisfactorily defied the might of Spain and of Antichrist, while at the same time keeping the war out of English territory. And given the passions of the times, it was a very great achievement indeed. 'She found herself a sane woman in a universe of violent maniacs', wrote Lytton Strachey in his *Elizabeth and Essex*, 'between contending forces of terrific intensity – the rival nationalisms of France and Spain, the rival religions of Rome and Calvin; for years it had seemed inevitable that she should be crushed by one or other of them, and she had survived because she had been able to meet the extremes around her with her own extremes of cunning and prevarication. It so happened that the subtlety of her intellect was exactly adapted to the complexities of her environment. The balance of power between France and Spain, the balance of factions in France and Scotland, the swaying fortunes of the Netherlands, gave scope for a tortuosity of diplomacy which has never been completely unravelled to this day . . . Religious persons at the time were distressed by her conduct, and imperialist historians have wrung their hands over her since. Why could she not suppress her hesitations and chicaneries and take a noble risk? Why did she not step forth, boldly and frankly, as the leader of Protestant Europe, accept the sovereignty of Holland, and fight the good fight to destroy Catholicism and transfer the Spanish Empire to the rule of England? The answer is that she cared for none of these things. She understood her true nature and her true mission better than her critics.'

In the field of foreign policy Elizabeth has frequently been accused of tergiversation, indecision, faint-heartedness and plain dishonesty, but behind the baffling pallisade which she deliberately erected to conceal her real intentions it is now possible to see that her underlying purpose was paradoxically not only extremely simple but unwavering in its aim – to keep her people, her kingdom and her throne peaceful, prosperous and secure. In order to achieve that aim and stay dryshod in the quicksand of European politics, the Queen was prepared to shift her ground as often as seemed necessary, for the more confusion and uncertainty she could create in the minds of others, the more freedom of action she retained for herself.

The diplomatic poker game as played by Elizabeth Tudor demanded strong nerves and unremitting concentration. The fact that it also demanded subtlety, subterfuge and a high degree of histrionic ability only added to its zest. There can be no doubt that Elizabeth enjoyed the game for its own sake – certainly her skill as a player has never been equalled. Its justification is that it paid off. Throughout the bloody wars which tore sixteenth century Europe apart no foot of English countryside was laid waste – except, of course, the unlucky village of Mousehole. No English farmstead was burned down, no English town looted or put to the sword, no Englishman, woman or child slaughtered by an invading army. This was Elizabeth's objective, and if her methods of gaining it have laid her open to charges of selfishness and deceit she would have thought it cheap at the price.

The fact that the war was building the foundations of English sea-power and thus of so much of her future greatness scarcely concerned the Queen. She knew all about the importance of sea-power as it affected the struggle with Spain, but she was no visionary and if she cherished no dreams of empire, neither, it should be remembered, did the majority of those doughty entrepreneurs sailing uncharted oceans in vessels in which nowadays one would hesitate to cross the English Channel. They, like the Queen, were preoccupied with the purely practical considerations of trade and profit.

Elizabeth was, above all, an immensely shrewd and successful practical politician, completely at home in the arcane mysteries of her craft, but she was no political theorist. Partly through pressure of circumstances and partly from natural inclination, she was content to live from day to day, dealing with problems as they arose. It is arguable that if she had been readier to move with the times, to look ahead and to recognise the necessity of admitting Parliament at least to junior partnership, the history of the seventeenth century might have taken a different course. But that was not Elizabeth's way and, in any case, she would have regarded any such action as a gross betrayal of everything she stood for. For nearly forty-five years it had been her sacred trust to maintain intact the power, authority and prestige of the Crown, and she had done just that.

To what extent she realised that the system she had so stoutly upheld was crumbling beneath her feet; that the system of government which had been accepted as the natural order of things since Saxon times was doomed, must be a matter for speculation. But that was not Elizabeth's concern. She had held the breach. By sheer force of will she had kept the future at bay and was handing on her inheritance undiminished. The future would be for her successors, for the sickly baby in Scotland and the four-year-old son of Robert and Elizabeth Cromwell of Huntingdon.

Sources and Bibliography

Part One: The Young Elizabeth

Manuscript Sources

State Papers, Domestic. In the Public Record Office.

Printed Sources (Contemporary)

Acts of the Privy Council, ed. J.R. Dasent, vols. 1–6, 1890.
Ascham, Roger, *The Whole Works of Roger Ascham*, ed. with a Life of the Author by Rev. Dr Giles, 1865.
Bedingfield, Henry, *Papers*, ed. C.R. Manning, Norfolk and Norwich Archaeological Society, 1855.
Burghley, William Cecil, Lord, *State Papers*, ed. Samuel Haynes, 1740.
Calendar of State Papers, Domestic, ed. Robert Lemon.
Calendar of State Papers, Spanish, ed. Gayangos, Hume and Tyler.
Calender of State Papers, Spanish, Elizabeth, ed. Hume.
Calendar of State Papers, Venetian, ed. Rawdon Brown.
Cavendish, George, *The Life and Death of Cardinal Wolsey*, ed. Richard S. Sylvester in *Two Early Tudor Lives*, New Haven, Conn., 1962.
The Chronicle and Political Papers of King Edward VI, ed. W.K. Jordan, 1966.
Chronicle of King Henry VIII of England, trans. and ed. Martin A.S. Hume, 1889.
A Chronicle of London, ed. N.H. Nicolas, 1827.
Chronicle of Queen Jane and Two Years of Queen Mary, ed. J.G. Nichols, Camden Society, 1850.
Chronicle of Greyfriars, ed. J.G. Nichols, Camden Society, 1852.
Clifford, Henry, *Life of Jane Dormer*, ed. Joseph Stevenson, 1887.
Elizabeth I, *The Letters of Queen Elizabeth*, ed. G.B. Harrison, 1935.
Erasmus, Desiderius, *The Epistles of Erasmus*, trans. and ed. Francis Morgan Nichols, 1901.
Foxe, John, *Acts and Monuments*, ed. S.R. Cattley and G. Townsend, 1839.
Giustinian, Sebastian, *Four Years at the Court of Henry VIII (1515–1519), A Selection of the Despatches of Sebastian Giustinian*, trans. and ed. Rawdon Brown, 1854.

Gonzales, Tomás, *Documents from Simancas Relating to the Reign of Queen Elizabeth (1558–1568)*, trans. and ed. Spencer Hall, 1865.

Green, Mrs Everett, *Letters of Royal and Illustrious Ladies*, 1846.

Gregory, William, *William Gregory's Chronicle. The Historical Collections of a London Citizen*, ed. J. Gairdner, Camden Society, 1876.

Hall, Edward, *Chronicle*, ed. Sir Henry Ellis, 1809.

Harington, Sir John, *Nugae Antique*, ed. Thomas Park, 1804.

Hayward, John, *Annals of the First Four Years of the Reign of Queen Elizabeth*, ed. John Bruce, Camden Society, 1840.

——, *The Life of Edward VI*, in White Kennett et al., Complete History of England (1706), vol. ii.

Hearne, Thomas, *Sylloge Epistolarum*, in Titus Livius, *Viva Henrici Quinti*, ed. Hearne, 1716.

Heywood, Thomas, *England's Elizabeth*, Harleian Miscellany, 1813.

Holinshed, Rafael, *Chronicles*, 1807–8.

Household Expenses of the Princess Elizabeth, at Hatfield, 1551–2, ed. P.C.S. Smythe, Camden Miscellany 2, 1853.

Leti, Gregorio, *Historia o vero vita di Elizabetta regina d'Inghilterra*, French, translation, 2 pts, Amsterdam, 1692.

Letters and Papers, Foreign and Domestic, of the Reign of Henry VIII, ed. Brewer, Gairdner and Brodie, 1862.

Machyn, Henry, *Diary*, ed. J.G. Nichols, Camden Society, 1848.

Madden, F., *The Privy Purse Expenses of the Princess Mary*, 1831.

Mumby, F.A., *The Girlhood of Queen Elizabeth*, 1909.

Naunton, Robert, *Fragmenta Regalia*, ed. Edward Arber, 1895.

Nichols, J., *Progresses and Public Processions of Queen Elizabeth*, 1823.

Proceedings and Ordinances of the Privy Council, ed. N.H. Nicolas, 1835.

Raumer, F.L.G. von, *History of the 16th and 17th Centuries*, 1835.

Roper, William, *The Life of Sir Thomas More*, ed. Davis P. Harding in *Two Early Tudor Lives*, New Haven, Conn., 1962.

Rymer, Thomas, *Foedera*, vol. X, 1704.

State Papers, Henry VIII, vol. I, 1830.

Stow, John, *Annals*, ed. E. Howes, 1631.

Strype, John, *Ecclesiastical Memorials*, 1822.

——, *Life of John Aylmer*, 1821.

Tytler, P.F., *England under the Reigns of Edward VI and Mary*, 1839.

Vergil, Polydore, *The Anglica Historia of Polydore Vergil (1485–1537)*, ed. Denys Hay, Camden Society, 1950.

——, *English History Comprising the Reigns of Henry VI, Edward IV and Richard III*, ed. Ellis, Camden Society, 1844.

Wriothesley, Charles, *A Chronicle of England during the Reign of the Tudors*, ed. William D. Hamilton, Camden Society, 2 vols, 1875.

Later Works

Bindoff, S.T., *Tudor England*, Harmondsworth, 1950.
Chamberlin, Frederick, *The Private Character of Queen Elizabeth*, 1921.
Chambers, R.W., *Sir Thomas More*, 1935.
Chapman, Hester, *The Last Tudor King*, 1958.
Chrimes, S.B., *Lancastrians, Yorkists and Henry VII*, 1964.
Chrimes, S.B., *Henry VII*, 1972.
Evans, HT., *Wales and the Wars of the Roses*, 1915.
Fraser, Antonia, *The Six Wives of Henry VIII*, 1992.
Friedmann, Paul, *Anne Boleyn, a Chapter of English History, 1527–1536*, 1884.
Gairdner, James, 'Mary and Anne Boleyn', *English Historical Review*, vol. 8 (1893).
Griffiths, Ralph A. and Thomas, Roger S., *The Making of the Tudor Dynasty*, 1985.
Harbison, E.H., *Rival Ambassadors at the Court of Queen Mary*, Princeton, N.J., 1940.
Howard, G., *Lady Jane Grey and Her Times*, 1822.
Howe, Bea, *A Galaxy of Governesses*, 1954.
Ives, E.W., *Anne Boleyn*, Oxford, 1986.
Jenkins, Elizabeth, *Elizabeth the Great*, 1958.
Johnson, Paul, *Elizabeth I*, 1974.
Jones, Sir Thomas Artemus, 'Owen Tudor's Marriage', *Bulletin of the Board of Celtic Studies*, vol. XI (1943).
Jordan, W.K., *Edward VI: The Young King*, 1968.
Jordan, W.K., *Edward VI: The Threshold of Power*, 1970.
Loades, D.M., *Two Tudor Conspiracies*, 1905.
Mackie, J.D., *The Earlier Tudors*, 1952.
MacNalty, Sir A.S., *Elizabeth Tudor – The Lonely Queen*, 1954.
——, *Henry VIII – A Difficult Patient*, 1952.
Mattingly, Garrett, *Catherine of Aragon*, 1942.
Muir, Kenneth, *Life and Letters of Sir Thomas Wyatt*, Liverpool, 1963.
Neale, J.E., 'The Accession of Elizabeth I', in *Essays in Elizabethan History*, 1958.
——, *Queen Elizabeth I*, 1934.
Paget, Hugh, 'The Youth of Anne Boleyn', *Bulletin of the Institute of Historical Research*, 55, 1981.
Parsons, W.I.E., *Some Notes on the Boleyn Family*, Norfolk and Norwich Archaeological Society, 1935.
Prescott, H.F.M., *Mary Tudor*, revised ed., 1952.
Read, Conyers, *Mr Secretary Cecil and Queen Elizabeth*, 1955.
Routh, E.M.G., *A Memoir of Lady Margaret Beaufort*, 1924.
Rowse, A.L., *Bosworth Field and the Wars of the Roses*, 1966.

Ryan, Laurence V., *Roger Ascham*, Stanford, Calif., 1963.
Scarisbrick, J.J., *Henry VIII*, 1997.
Storey, R.E., *The Reign of Henry VII*, 1968.
Strickland, Agnes, *Life of Queen Elizabeth I*, Everyman ed., 1906.
——, *Lives of the Queens of England*, 8 vols, 1875.
Temperley, Gladys, *Henry VII*, 1914.
Wiesener, Louis, *The Youth of Queen Elizabeth I*, trans. C.M. Yonge, 2 vols, 1879.
Williams, David, 'The Family of Henry VII', *History Today*, vol. iv (1954).
Williams, Neville, *Elizabeth: Queen of England*, 1967.

Part Two: Danger to Elizabeth

Notes on Sources

As this book is written by a non-specialist for other non-specialists it would have been pretentious to include the full apparatus of notes and bibliography. Any specialists who should happen to read it will, of course, immediately recognise the material used but for those general readers who may be interested, the following is an indication of the sources I have drawn upon most heavily.

General Surveys

The dust of this ancient battle has only recently begun to settle and consequently it is only within the present century that dispassionate general surveys have begun to appear. Generally acknowledged as the foremost of these is *England and the Catholic Church under Queen Elizabeth* by A.O. Meyer, translated by J.R. McKee, first published in 1916 and re-issued with an introduction by John Bossy in 1967. Two modern accounts from the Catholic point of view are *The English Catholics in the Reign of Elizabeth* by J.H. Pollen (1920) which takes the story up to 1580, and *The Reformation in England*, Vol. 3 by Philip Hughes (1954). *Papists and Puritans* by Patrick McGrath (1967) deals, as the title suggests, with both types of Elizabethan non-conformity.

For the Reformation movement in general, *The English Reformation to 1558* by T.M. Parker, Oxford, 1950, covers the early stages clearly and concisely. Two wider modern surveys are *The Reformation* by Owen Chadwick, Vol. 3 of The Pelican History of the Church, revised edition published in 1968, and *The English Reformation* by A.G. Dickens, revised edition issued in The Fontana Library in 1967. An older but still objective account is *The English Church in the reigns of Elizabeth and James I* by Walter H. Frere (1904). Two other still older histories from the Protestant and Catholic viewpoints respectively are *The Annals of the Reformation* by John Strype in four volumes, Oxford, 1824, and Charles Dodd's *The Church History of England from 1500 to the year 1688*, edited by Mark A. Tierney in five volumes (1839–43). Both are valuable for the printed documents they contain.

For the political background which is an inseparable part of the story of the Elizabethan Catholics *Before the Armada, the Growth of English Foreign Policy 1485–1588* by R.B. Wernham (1966) is a general survey, while *The Shaping of the Elizabethan Regime* by Wallace MacCaffrey (1969) deals with a specific period in detail. See also *Elizabeth I and the Unity of England* by Joel Hurstfield (1960). William Camden's *History of the most renowned and virtuous Princess Elizabeth, late Queen of England* (1630) is the nearest thing we have to a contemporary political history of the reign and is invaluable as a source. Indispensable for anyone writing about Elizabethan politics are Conyers Read's two great studies of Elizabethan statesmen: *Mr Secretary Walsingham and the Policy of Queen Elizabeth* (1925) and *Mr Secretary Cecil and Queen Elizabeth* (1955) followed by *Lord Burghley and Queen Elizabeth* (1960). For proceedings in Parliament I have leaned heavily and gratefully on Professor J.E. Neale's classic *Elizabeth I and her Parliaments* (1953 and 1957).

Prologue

The Queen of Scots' own recollections of her flight into England are preserved in *Memorials of Mary Stuart* by Claude Nau, ed. J. Stevenson, Edinburgh, 1883. See also *The Life of Mary Queen of Scots* by Agnes Strickland, Vol. 2 (1873) and, of course, the biography *Mary Queen of Scots* by Antonia Fraser (1969). The letters of Richard Lowther and Francis Knollys are to be found in the *Calendar of State Papers Relating to Scotland and Mary Queen of Scots*, Vol. 2. The Spanish Ambassador's comments are in the *C.S.P. Spanish, Elizabeth*, Vol. 2. William Camden's *History* describes the English government's reactions and many of the documents are printed in *The Fall of Mary Stuart* by F.A. Mumby (1921).

Chapter 14

The descriptions of Elizabeth as princess are in the *Calendar of State Papers*, Venetian, Vol. 6, Pt. 2, and the reports of the Italian agent in London, Il Schifanoya, which are an invaluable source for the first year of the reign, appear in *C.S.P. Venetian*, Vol. 7. For foreign affairs with special reference to France see *C.S.P., Foreign, Elizabeth*, Vol. I and *A Full View of the Public Transactions in the Reign of Queen Elizabeth*, ed. Patrick Forbes (1740); for Rome *Anglo-Roman Relations 1558–1565* C.G. Bayne, Oxford, 1913; for Spain *C.S.P. Spanish, Elizabeth*, Vol. I and *Documents from Simancas Relating to the Reign of Queen Elizabeth* T. Gonzalez, ed. Spencer Hall (1865). For the Parliament of 1559 see *Elizabeth I and her*

Parliaments, Vol. I, J.E. Neale and for the point of view of the reformers in particular, Strype's *Annals* Vol. I, Pt. 2 and the *Zurich Letters*, Vol. 7, ed. H. Robinson, Parker Society, Cambridge, 1846.

Chapter 15
For the Protestant view on the fate of the Marian Bishops see Strype, Vol. I, Pts. I and 2. For a contemporary Catholic account see *The Rise and Growth of the Anglican Schism* by Nicholas Sander with a Continuation by Edward Rishton, trans. and ed. by David Lewis (1877). Two relatively modern studies of the religious settlement are, from the Anglican viewpoint, *The Elizabethan Clergy, and the Settlement of Religion, 1558–64* by Henry Gee, Oxford, 1898 and, from the Catholic side, *The Elizabethan Religious Settlement, a study of contemporary documents* by H.N. Birt (1907). Another contemporary Catholic appraisal – the Report prepared by Nicholas Sander for Cardinal Moroni – is printed in *Miscellanea* Vol. I, Catholic Record Society (1905). For an account of the Catholic emigrés and of the propaganda war see *The English Catholic Refugees on the Continent* by Peter Guilday, New York, 1914, and *Elizabethan Recusant Prose, 1559–1582*, A.C. Southern (1950). For the provisions of the Acts of Supremacy and Uniformity see *The Tudor Constitution: Documents and Commentary* by G.R. Elton, Cambridge, 1960 and also McGrath, *Papists and Puritans*. The Oath of Supremacy is printed in Gee. Catholic reaction to the new order in England can be found in *C.S.P., Rome*, Vol. I and the activities of King Philip's ambassador in *C.S.P., Spanish, Eliz.*, Vol. I. For the survey of Justices of the Peace, see *Letters from the Bishops to the Privy Council, 1564*, ed. Mary Bateson, Miscellany, Camden Society Vol. 53, N.S. (1895).

Chapter 16
There is only one relatively modern biography of William Allen, *An Elizabethan Cardinal* by Martin Haile (1914), written from the Catholic viewpoint. For the founding of the Seminary at Douai see *First and Second Diaries of the English College, Douai*, edited and with a valuable Historical Introduction by T.F. Knox (1878), also *Letters and Memorials of William Allen*, ed. T.F. Knox (1882).

For Mary Stuart's first widowhood, see Nicholas Throckmorton's dispatches in the *C.S.P. Foreign, Elizabeth*, Vols. 3 and 4; for the English intervention in Scotland in 1559–60 the *C.S.P. Scottish* Vol. I and Read's *Mr Secretary Cecil*. Maitland's account of his interview with Elizabeth is printed in *A Letter from Mary Queen of Scots to the Duke of Guise, Jan. 1562* by J.H. Pollen, Scot. Hist. Soc. xliii (1904). Other documents relating to this period are also printed in *Elizabeth and Mary Stuart: The Beginning of the Feud* by F.A. Mumby, Boston, 1914.

Chapter 17
The dispatches of Geurau de Spes are printed in the *C.S.P. Spanish, Eliz.* Vol. 2. See also *Mr Secretary Cecil* for the crisis of 1569. Many of the documents relating to the Rising in the North are printed in *Memorials of the Rebellion of 1569*, ed. Cuthbert Sharp (1840). A modern, Catholic study of the Ridolfi affair is *The Dangerous Queen* by Francis Edwards (1964). See also *The Marvellous Chance* by Francis Edwards (1968). Documents – letters, depositions and confessions are printed in *Collection of State Papers . . . left by William Cecil, Lord Burghley* ed. Samuel Haynes and William Murdin, Vol. 2 (1740–59) and in *Illustrations of British History* by E. Lodge (1838).

The Bull *Regnans in Excelsis* is printed in Camden and also in J.H. Pollen's *The English Catholics in the Reign of Elizabeth*. Bishop Jewel's counter-blast – 'A view of a seditious bull' -- can be found in *The Works of John Jewel*, 4th portion, Parker Society (1850).

For the Parliaments of 1571 and 1572 and the resulting legislation see Neale, *Elizabeth I and her Parliaments*, Vol. I and McGrath, *Papists and Puritans.*

Chapter 18
See Strype for the general reaction of St Bartholomew and Murdin for the plan to send Mary back to Scotland. *The Catholic Laity in Elizabethan England, 1558–1603* by W.R. Trimble, Harvard University Press, 1964 contains a useful survey of the conditions under which the English Catholics lived. There is a wealth of more detailed information in the *Acts of the Privy Council*, ed. J.R. Dasent (1890–1907), in the *State Papers, Domestic, Elizabeth* preserved at the Public Record Office and in the Cecil Papers at Hatfield House (see the Historical Manuscripts Commission Reports). More material still, which is outside the scope of this book, has been printed in the various *Miscellanea* of the Catholic Record Society, in *Recusant History* and in the Journals and Proceedings of a number of county Archaeological Societies.

For the continuing success of William Allen's foundation at Douai see the *First and Second Diaries of the English College.*

Sources for the story of Cuthbert Mayne are *A Briefe Historie of the Glorious Martyrdom of XII Reverend Priests* by William Allen ed. J.H. Pollen (1908), *The Troubles of Our Catholic Forefathers* by John Morris (1872) and the *Acts of the Privy Council.* See also *Sir Richard Grenville of the Revenge* by A.L. Rowse (1937). For other and later martyrs see *Memoirs of the Missionary Priests* by Richard Challoner ed. J.H. Pollen (1923), *Lives of the English Martyrs* by Bede Camm (1905) and *Unpublished Documents Relating to the English Martyrs, 1584–1603*, ed. J.H. Pollen, Catholic Record Society, Vol. 5 (1908).

Chapter 19
For foreign affairs in the 1570s see *C.S.P. Foreign*, Vols. 8, 9 and 11, also *C.S.P. Spanish, Elizabeth*, Vol. 2, Read's *Mr Secretary Walsingham* and R.B. Wernham's *Before the Armada.*

The troubles afflicting the Seminary at Douai in the late 1570s are chronicled in the *First and Second Diaries of the English College*. For the founding of the English College at Rome and its early teething troubles see above – also Robert Parsons' account of Domestical Difficulties in *Miscellanea* Vol. 2, Catholic Record Society (1906), the *Letters and Memorials of Father Robert Parsons*, ed. L. Hicks, Catholic Record Society No. 39 (1942) and, for the daily life at the College, *The English Romayne Life* by Anthony Munday, printed in the Harleian Miscellany, VII (1746).

Chapter 20
For the Jesuits see Records of the *English Province of the Society of Jesus*, ed. Henry Foley (1877–1884). The standard biography of Edmund Campion is still *Edmund Campion* by Richard Simpson (1867) which prints a number of letters and documents, but see also Edmund Campion by Evelyn Waugh (1935). There is, oddly enough, no biography of the able, complex and controversial Robert Parsons. His own fragmentary Memoirs are printed in *Miscellanea* 2 and 4, Catholic Record Society (1906 and 1907) and there is a valuable Introduction by Leo Hicks to the *Letters and Memorials*. Campion's *Bragge* is printed in Simpson and also in Pollen's *The English Catholics in the Reign of Elizabeth.*

Chapter 21
See above for the adventures of Campion and Parsons. See Neale, *Elizabeth I and her Parliaments*, Vol. I for the Parliament of 1581.

Chapter 22
See Simpson for the trial of Edmund Campion. Lord Burghley's Execution of Justice is printed in *Somers Tracts*, in the Harleian Miscellany and in Holinshed's *Chronicle*. William Allen's True Sincere and Modest Defence of the English Catholics is printed in The Catholic Library No. 2 (1914). See also *The Execution of Justice* by William Cecil and *A True, Sincere and Modest Defence of English Catholics* by William Allen, ed. Robert M. Kingdon, New York, 1964. For the Lennox-Guise-Throckmorton affair see Read's *Mr Secretary Walsingham*, the *C.S.P. Scottish*, Vol. 6, *C.S.P., Spanish, Elizabeth*, Vol. 3. *The Letters and Memorials of William Allen* and the *Letters and Memorials of Father Robert Parsons*. The official account of the Throckmorton Plot is printed in the Harleian Miscellany, Vol. 3. For the Bond of Association and the Parliament of 1584–5 see Neale's *Elizabeth I and her Parliaments*, Vol. 2. For the Parry Plot see Read's *Mr Secretary Walsingham*, Holinshed's Chronicle and William Camden's *History*; also *An*

Elizabethan Problem by L. Hicks (1964) and *The Strange Case of Dr William Parry – the Career of Agent-Provocateur* by L. Hicks, *Studies*, Dublin, 1948.

Chapter 23

See Neale's *Elizabeth I and her Parliaments*, Vol. 2 for the Parliaments of 1585 and 1586. For the 'second wave' of the Jesuit invasion see *Letters and Memorials of Robert Parsons*, also *John Gerard – The Autobiography of an Elizabethan*, trans. and ed. Philip Caraman, Longmans Green, 1951, and *William Weston – The Autobiography of an Elizabethan*, trans. and ed. Philip Caraman, Longmans Green, 1955. For the laity at this period, see Trimble's *The Catholic Laity in Elizabethan England* and for Robert Southwell, J.H. Pollen's *English Martyrs*. There is a full account of the Babington affair in *Mary Queen of Scots and the Babington Plot* by J.H. Pollen, Scot. Hist. Soc. 3rd series, iii (1922). See also Read's *Mr Secretary Walsingham* and *The Letter-Books of Sir Amias Paulet* by John Morris (1874).

Epilogue – 24

The Defeat of the Spanish Armada by Garrett Mattingly (1959) is an outstanding account. William Allen's *Admonition to the Nobility and People of England and Ireland* which, although he may not have written it himself, was issued in his name, was reprinted in 1842. For Catholic plans for the succession see *Letters and Memorials of William Allen* and *Letters and Memorials of Robert Parsons*.

Part Three: Marriage with My Kingdom

Notes on Sources

References to the various marriage projects discussed for the child Elizabeth are to be found scattered through the later volumes of the compendious *Letters and Papers, Foreign and Domestic, of the Reign of Henry VIII* (1862–1910); also in the despatches of Eustace Chapuys printed in the *Calendar of State Papers*, Spanish (1862–1954), vols V and VI.

The fullest source for the Seymour episode is *A Collection of State Papers, 1542–70*, from *Letters and Memorials Left by William Cecil, Lord Burghley, at Hatfield*, ed. Samuel Haynes (1740). Further references can be found in P.F. Tyler, *England under the Reign of Edward VI and Mary* (1839), and *The Literary Remains of King Edward VI*, ed. J.G. Nichols (Roxburghe Club, 1857), while many of the original documents are in the *State Papers*, Domestic, Edward VI, vol. VI, at the Public Record Office. For the remainder of Edward's reign, see the *Calendar of State Papers*, Spanish, vols

IX, X and XI, and the *Calendar of State Papers*, Foreign, Edward VI and Mary (1861).

For Mary's reign, the best and most detailed account is given by Simon Renard in the *Calendar of State Papers*, Spanish, vols XI, XII and XIII, but see also the *Calendar of State Papers*, Venetian, vol. vi. Other contemporary sources include *The Chronicle of Queen Jane and Two Years of Queen Mary*, ed. J.G. Nichols (Camden Society, 1850); *Chronicle of the Greyfriars*, ed. J.G. Nichols (Camden Society, 1852); *The Diary of Henry Machyn*, ed. J.G. Nichols (Camden Society, 1848); Charles Wriothesley, *A Chronicle of England during the Reigns of the Tudors*, ed. William D. Hamilton (Camden Society, 1875); and John Foxe, *Acts and Monuments*, ed. S.R. Cattley and G. Townsend (1839), which contains a highly coloured description of Elizabeth's troubles in 1554. Many of the documents relating to this period are printed in F.A. Mumby, *The Girlhood of Queen Elizabeth* (1909); and two other extremely useful modern works are H.F.M. Prescott, *Mary Tudor* (1952), and E.H. Harbison, *Rival Ambassadors at the Court of Queen Mary* (Princeton, 1940).

The marriage projects, likely and unlikely, of Elizabeth as Queen run through all the histories of the first twenty-five years of her reign, but again the most detailed contemporary source is provided by the despatches of King Philip's ambassadors in the *Calendar of State Papers*, Spanish, Elizabeth, vols I, II, and III. There was no Venetian representative in England after 1559, but the *Calendar of State Papers*, Venetian, vol. VII, contains quite a few references to the Queen's courtships relayed by the Venetian agents in Paris. *The Calendar of State Papers*, Foreign, Elizabeth, in numerous volumes, contains many of the letters and reports of her own ambassadors overseas; while, for the reports of the Emperor's special envoys during the interminable negotiations over the Austrian marriage, see *Queen Elizabeth and Some Foreigners*, ed. Victor von Klarwill, trans. T.H. Nash (1928).

The best general account of the Amy Robsart affair is George Adlard, *Amye Robsart and the Earl of Leycester* (1870); and two modern books on the subject of Elizabeth and Robert Dudley are Milton Waldman, *Elizabeth and Leicester* (1944), and Elizabeth Jenkins, *Elizabeth and Leicester* (1961). A recent biography of Leicester is *Sweet Robin* by Derek Wilson, Hamish Hamilton (1981).

Most of the documents relative to Queen Mary of Scots during the 1560s are printed in F.A. Mumby, *Elizabeth and Mary Stuart* (Boston, Mass., 1914), and the same author's *The Fall of Mary Stuart* (1921), but see also the *Calendar of State Papers Relating to Scotland and Mary, Queen of Scots, 1547–1603.*

For Elizabeth's encounters with Parliament, J.E. Neale's classic work *Queen Elizabeth and Her Parliament*, 2 vols (1953–7), is an invaluable guide and so, for the general political background, is Conyers Read's two-volume biography of William Cecil, *Mr Secretary Cecil and Queen Elizabeth* (1955) and *Lord Burghley and Queen Elizabeth* (1960).

For foreign policy and the French marriage projects, see Conyers Read's *Mr Secretary Walsingham*, vols I and II (1925, reprinted 1967). Many of the documents relating to the Anjou courtship are printed in *The Compleat Ambassador*, ed. Dudley Digges (1655); and, for Alençon, see *State Papers Relating to Affairs 1571–96, from Papers Left by Lord Burghley at Hatfield*, ed. W. Murdin (1759). There is also a detailed general account in M.A.S. Hume, *The Courtships of Queen Elizabeth* (1898; revised ed., 1904).

Other miscellaneous sources of contemporary material include William Camden's *Annals of the Reign of Queen Elizabeth* (best English edition, 1688); the *Hardwicke State Papers, 1501–1726*, 2 vols (1778); *Illustrations of British History*, ed. E. Lodge, 3 vols (1838); and T. Wright, *Queen Elizabeth and Her Times*, 2 vols (1838).

Of the innumerable modern biographies of Elizabeth, J.E. Neale's *Queen Elizabeth I*, first published in 1934 and reprinted many times, remains the best. Elizabeth Jenkins, *Elizabeth the Great* (1958), and Neville Williams, *Elizabeth I, Queen of England* (1967) are both good on the personal side, and Paul Johnson's *Elizabeth I. A Study in Power and Intellect* (1974), is first-rate on Elizabeth as a political animal.

Part Four: Elizabeth Regina

Notes on Sources

These notes, like those appended to the individual chapters, are intended only as a guide for the general reader to the more easily accessible source material and are very far from being an exhaustive catalogue. Anyone wishing to dig more deeply into the vast mass of material which does exist should refer in the first instance to the *Bibliography of British History: Tudor Period, 1485–1603*, ed. Conyers Read, 2nd edn (London, 1959).

E.P. Cheyney's two-volume *History of England* (New York, 1914–26) remains the standard modern survey of the post-Armada period and is good on political institutions, if somewhat marred by a strong anti-Elizabeth bias.

Other helpful modern works include: A.L. Rowse, *The Expansion of Elizabethan England* (London, 1955); the second volume of J.E. Neale's definitive *Queen Elizabeth and Her Parliaments* (London, 1957); two classics by the great naval historian J.S. Corbett, *Drake and the Tudor Navy*, 2 vols (London, 1898–9) and *The Successors of Drake* (London, 1900); M.A.S. Hume, *Treason and Plot* (London, 1901); Patrick McGrath, *Papists and*

Puritans under Elizabeth I (London, 1967); and Roy Strong, *The Cult of Elizabeth* (London, 1977).

Biographies of Elizabeth continue to proliferate, but J.E. Neale's *Queen Elizabeth I*, first published in 1934 and reprinted many times since, is still the best to my mind. Of the older lives, Mandell Creighton's *Queen Elizabeth* (London, 1896) is the most perceptive; and, for an excellent recent one, Paul Johnson's *Elizabeth I: A Study in Power and Intellect* (London, 1974).

Other biographies covering this period are generally rather thin on the ground. For Robert Cecil there is *The Second Cecil: the Rise to Power, 1563–1604, of Sir Robert Cecil*, P.M. Handover (London, 1959) and *Robert Cecil, First Earl of Salisbury: Servant of Two Sovereigns*, Alan Haynes (London, 1989). For Essex we have two volumes of W.B. Devereux's *Lives and Letters of the Devereux, Earls of Essex* (London, 1853) which are chiefly useful for the documents they print. Lytton Strachey's classic *Elizabeth and Essex* (London, 1928) is perhaps better regarded as literature than as history. More recent are G.B. Harrison's *The Life and Death of Robert Devereux, Earl of Essex* (London, 1937) and Robert Lacey's *Robert, Earl of Essex: An Elizabeth Icarus* (London, 1971). Most recent of all, *Polarisation of Elizabethan Politics: Political Career of Robert Devereux, 2nd Earl of Essex, 1585–97*, Paul E.J. Hammer (Cambridge, 1999). Daphne du Maurier's *Golden Lads* (London, 1975) is a fascinating study of the Bacon brothers, especially of the little-known Anthony. For Francis there is also James Spedding's *The Letters and Life of Francis Bacon*, 2 vols (London, 1890), which prints a lot of useful material relating to his relationship with Essex.

Of contemporary printed sources the following are basic. *Annals of Queen Elizabeth* by William Camden, master at Westminster School and a friend of Lord Burghley; originally written in Latin, the best English translation is by H. Norton (London, 1688). Thomas Birch, *Memoirs of the Reign of Queen Elizabeth*, 2 vols (London, 1754), drawn chiefly from the Bacon manuscripts in Lambeth Palace Library. *The Sidney Papers*, ed. Arthur Collins, 2 vols (London, 1746), which contain the letters written to Robert Sidney during his governorship of Flushing by his agent at Court, Rowland Whyte, and are particularly valuable regarding the downfall of Essex. *The Letters of John Chamberlain*, ed. N.E. McClure, 2 vols (Philadelphia, Pa., 1939), gives most of the gossip for the final years of the reign, and John Harington's *Nugae Antiquae*, ed. Thomas Park, 2 vols (London, 1804), prints the letters, miscellaneous papers and jottings of the Queen's merry godson.

Other source collections include: Robert Naunton's *Fragmenta Regalia: or Observations on the Late Queen Elizabeth, Her Times and Her Favourites*, reprinted by Edward Arber (London, 1895); John Nichols, *The Progresses and Public Processions of Queen Elizabeth*, 3 vols (London, 1823); Thomas Wright, *Queen Elizabeth and Her Times* (London, 1838); and E. Lodge, *Illustrations of British History*, 3 vols (London, 1838).

The Calendar of State Papers, Spanish, Elizabeth vol. IV (London, 1899), and *The Calendar of State Papers*, Venetian, vols. VIII and IX (London, 1894, 1898), all contain relevant material, with especial reference to the Armadas of the 1590s. Although there was no official Venetian ambassador accredited to London until the very end of Elizabeth's reign, the Venetians always took a close and informed interest in the Anglo-Spanish conflict.

Prologue

The best modern account of the Armada is Garrett Mattingley, *The Defeat of the Spanish Armada*, Cape, 1959, but see also Michael Lewis; *The Spanish Armada*, Batsford, 1960 and A.M. Hadfield, *Time to Finish the Game*, J.M. Dent, 1964. Most of the documents are printed in J.K. Laughton, *The Defeat of the Spanish Armada*, 2 vols., Navy Record Society, 1894.

For a description of the visit to Tilbury, see J. Nichols, *The Progressions of Queen Elizabeth*, vol. II.

Chapter 37

The fullest description of the procession to St Paul's is to be found in Nichols's *Progresses and Processions of Queen Elizabeth*, vol. II. Another account appears in Emmanuel van Meteren's narrative of the defeat of the Spanish Armada printed in Richard Hakluyt, *Principal Navigations*, Everyman's Library, vol. VI; and there is also a reference in Camden's Annals.

Harington's *Nugae Antiquae* is the best single source for personal descriptions of Elizabeth in later life, but there are also, of course, numerous other references scattered through the memoirs and correspondence of the period; for example, John Clapham's *Observations Concerning the Life and Reign of Queen Elizabeth*, ed. E.P. and Conyers Read (Philadelphia, Pa., 1951), and letters in Lodge's *Illustrations of British History*, vol. II.

For the Earl of Leicester's death, see *Calendar of State Papers, Spanish, Elizabeth* (C.S.P. Span. Elizabeth), vol. IV, pp. 420–1 and 431. For the rise of Essex, see Naunton's *Fragmenta Regalia* and Devereux, *Lives and Letters of the Devereux, Earls of Essex*, vol. I.

The aftermath of the attempted Spanish invasion of 1588 and European reaction to its failure can be followed in *C.S.P. Span. Elizabeth*, vol. IV and *Calendar of State Papers, Venetian* (*C.S.P. Ven.*), vol. VIII. The Venetian despatches are especially valuable, being usually well informed and unbiased.

For a detailed, modern and scholarly account of the great Portugal expedition of 1589, R.B. Wernham's two articles. 'Queen Elizabeth and the Portugal Expedition', *English Historical Review*, vol. LXVI (Jan. and April 1951), are of the greatest value. See also Corbett's *Drake and the Tudor Navy*; Cheyney's *History of England*, vol. I; William Monson's *Naval*

Tracts, ed. M. Oppenheim, vol. I (Navy Records Society, 1902); and *Acts of the Privy Council*, ed. J.R. Dasent, vol. XVII. Other sources include: Devereux, *Earls of Essex*; Lodge, *Illustrations of British History*; *C.S.P. Ven.*, vol. VIII; Birch, *Memoirs of the Reign of Queen Elizabeth*, vol. I; and Anthony Wingfield's narrative in Hakluyt, *Principal Navigations*, vol. VI.

Chapter 38

The aftermath of the Portugal voyage can be followed in Anthony Wingfield's narrative; in Monson's *Naval Tracts*, vol. I; in the despatches of the Venetian ambassador in Madrid, *C.S.P. Ven.*, vol. VIII; and in *Acts of the Privy Council*, vol. XVIII.

For a general account of the activities of the privateers, see Rowse, *Expansion of Elizabethan England*; also, of course, references in Hakluyt's *Principal Navigations*, and in Monson's *Naval Tracts*, vol. I, which contains an account of Frobisher's and Hawkins's 1590 expedition.

For Anglo-French affairs in 1589, see Cheyney, *History of England*, vol. I, and Conyers Read, *Lord Burghley and Queen Elizabeth* (London, 1960). *Acts of the Privy Council*, vol. XVIII, contains a lot of detail regarding the organisation of the 1589 expeditionary force; and Lady Georgina Bertie's *Five Generations of a Loyal House* (London, 1845) contains Lord Willoughby's journal of the campaign itself. Lord Burghley's letter to the Earl of Shrewsbury is printed in Lodge, *Illustrations of British History*, vol. II.

For the Parliament of 1589 and all other parliamentary proceedings, see Neale's invaluable *Queen Elizabeth and Her Parliaments* – in this case, vol. II.

There is a considerable literature on the growth of the Puritan and Presbyterian movements in England, but McGrath's *Papists and Puritans under Elizabeth I* provides a lucid general introduction to a highly complicated subject and contains notes and a full bibliography.

Roy Strong's *The Cult of Elizabeth* contains an illuminating account of both the Accession Day celebrations and the Accession Day tilts, but see also J.E. Neale's *Essays in Elizabethan History* (London, 1958), and E.C. Wilson's scholarly survey, *England's Eliza* (Cambridge, Mass., 1939). George Peele describes the 1590 tilt in his *Polyhymnia: Works*, ed. A.H. Bullen (London, 1888), vol. II.

Chapter 39

For a general survey of the European situation in the early 1590s, see Cheyney, *History of England*, vol. I; and, for an account of the Brittany campaign in particular, Thomas Churchyard, *Service of Sir John Norris in Brittany in 1591* (London, 1602).

The main sources for the operations in Normandy in 1591–2 are: Birch, *Memoirs of the Reign of Queen Elizabeth*, vol. I; *The Correspondence of Sir Henry Unton* (Roxburghe Club, 1847); 'Journal of the Siege of Rouen,' in *Camden Society Miscellany*, vol. I (1847); and *English Historical Review*, vol. XVII. Essex's letters are to be found in Devereux, *Earls of Essex*, vol. I; and see also *Letters of Queen Elizabeth*, ed. G.B. Harrison (London, 1935). For a valuable modern account of the campaign, see the article by R.B. Werham, 'Queen Elizabeth and the Siege of Rouen', in *Transactions of the Royal Historical Society*, 4th series, vol. XV.

The classic description of the last fight of the *Revenge* was written by Sir Walter Raleigh shortly after the event, and is printed in *Somers Tracts*, vol. I (1809), in Edward Arber's *English Reprints* (1871), and in Hakluyt's *Principal Navigations* (1903 ed.), vol. VII. But see also Monson's *Naval Tracts*, vol. I, and A.L. Rowse, *Sir Richard Grenville of the 'Revenge'* (London, 1937).

For the *Madre de Dios* affairs: Monson's *Naval Tracts*, vol. I; Rowse, *Expansion of Elizabethan England*; and letters printed in Wright's *Queen Elizabeth and Her Times*, vol. II.

For the genesis of the Essex–Cecil feud, see Read, *Burghley and Queen Elizabeth*, and also Essex's correspondence in Devereux, *Earls of Essex*, vol. I. Much of Anthony Bacon's correspondence is printed in Birch, *Memoirs of the Reign of Queen Elizabeth*. See also Spedding, *Letters and Life of Francis Bacon*, vol. I, and Daphne du Maurier's penetrating study, *Golden Lads*.

For the Parliament of 1593, see Neale, *Elizabeth and Her Parliaments*, vol. II.

Chapter 40

For the Queen's journeyings of 1591 and 1592, see Nichols, *Progresses of Queen Elizabeth*, vol. III.

The story of the struggle to get the Attorneyship for Francis can be found in Spedding, *Letters and Life of Francis Bacon*, vol. I, and in Birch, *Memoirs of the Reign of Queen Elizabeth*, vol. I; but see also Devereux, *Earls of Essex*, vol. I, and Harrison, *Robert Devereux*.

The main sources for the Lopez affair are Birch, *Memoirs of the Reign of Queen Elizabeth*, vol. I, and Hume, *Treason and Plot*; but see also *C.S.P. Span. Elizabeth*, vol. IV, and Arthur Dimock, 'The Conspiracy of Dr Lopez', in *English Historical Review*, July 1894.

The 'Device' presented by Essex at the Accession Day tilts of 1595 is printed in Spedding, *Letters and Life of Francis Bacon*, and also described by Rowland Whyte in *Sidney papers*, vol. I.

For a general account of the political situation in France following the King's conversion, see Cheyney, *History of England*, vol. I. For a more detailed view of Anglo-French diplomatic relations from 1592 onwards, see Thomas Birch, *An Historical View of the Negotiations between the Courts of England, France and Brussels . . . Extracted from the State Papers of Sir Thomas Edmondes*, and G.G. Butler, *The Edmondes Papers* (Roxburghe Club, 1973). The last expedition to Brittany in 1594–5 is described in Monson, *Naval Tracts*, vol. I.

The Drake–Hawkins voyage of 1595 is also covered in Monson, *Naval Tracts*, vol. I, and a contemporary account by one of the participants is Thomas Maynarde's *Sir Francis Drake His Voyage, 1595*, ed. W.D. Colley, *Hakluyt Society*, vol. IV (1849). See also, of course, Corbett's classic *Drake and the Tudor Navy*.

For the fall of Calais, the negotiations leading to the Treaty of Greenwich, and the preparatory stages of the great expedition of 1596, see: Cheyney, *History of England*, vol. II; Read, *Burghley and Queen Elizabeth*; Birch, *Memoirs of the Reign of Queen Elizabeth*, vols. I and II; Sidney Papers, vol. I; Devereux, *Earls of Essex*, vol. I; Harrison, *Robert Devereux*; and Monson, *Naval Tracts*, vol. I.

Chapter 41

For an authoritative modern account of the Cadiz voyage, see Corbett, *Successors of Drake*. Other sources include Monson, *Naval Tracts*, vols. I and II; Hakluyt's *Principal Navigations*; Sir Walter Raleigh's *Relation of the Cadiz Action*, printed in *Works*, 8 vols (Oxford, 1829), vol. VIII; and Sir William Slingsby, *The Voyage to Calais*, Navy Record Society, vol. XX (1902). See also L.W. Henry, 'The Earl of Essex as Strategist and Military Organiser (1596–97)', in *English Historical Review*, vol. LXVIII (1953).

For the aftermath of Cadiz, see: *Acts of the Privy Council*, vol. XXVI; Birch, *Memoirs of the Reign of Queen Elizabeth*, vol. II; and Devereux, *Earls of Essex*, vol. I.

Francis Bacon's famous letter of advice to his patron is printed in Birch, *Memoirs of the Reign of Queen Elizabeth*, vol. Ii, in Devereux, *Earls of Essex*, vol. I, and in Spedding, *Letters and Life of Francis Bacon*, vol. II.

For the Armada of 1596, see: Birch, *Memoirs of the Reign of Queen Elizabeth*, vol. II; Monson, *Naval Tracts*, vol. II; Corbett, *Successors of Drake*; Hume, *Treason and Plot*; and, of course, *C.S.P. Ven.*, vol. IX, and *C.S.P. Span. Elizabeth*, vol. IV.

The episode of swearing in the Lord Keeper in 1596 is described in Read, *Burghley and Queen Elizabeth*, and in Joel Hurstfield, *Elizabeth I and the Unity of England* (London, 1960).

For foreign impressions of the Queen in the early 1590s, see W.B. Rye, *England as Seen by Foreigners* (London, 1865), and Victor von Klarwill, *Queen Elizabeth and Some Foreigners*, trans. T.N. Nash (London, 1928).

For the great dearth of 1594–7, see: William Camden's and John Stow's respective *Annals: Acts of the Privy Council*, vol. XXVI; and also the general account in Cheyney, *History of England*, vol. II.

The manoeuvrings at Court during 1596–7 are described in the splendidly gossipy letters of Rowland Whyte, Robert Sidney's agent, and printed in *Sidney papers*, vol. II. See also Birch, *Memoirs of the Reign of Queen Elizabeth*, vol. II; Devereux, *Earls of Essex*, vol. I; and Harrison, *Robert Devereux*.

For the Islands Voyage and the 1597 Armada, the main sources are: Corbett, *Successors of Drake*; Monson, *Naval Tracts*, vol. II; Hakluyt, *Principal Navigations*; Devereux, *Earls of Essex*, vol. I; Hume, *Treason and Plot*; and *C.S.P. Ven.* and *Span., Elizabeth.*

Chapter 42

The row which resulted from Charles Howard's promotion is described by Rowland Whyte in his letters to Robert Sidney (*Sidney Papers*, vol. II), but see also: Birch, *Memoirs of the Reign of Queen Elizabeth*, vol. II; Devereux, *Earls of Essex*, vol. i; and Harrison, *Robert Devereux.*

For André de Maisse's mission and his impressions of the Queen and the Court, see his *Journal*, trans. and with an introduction by G.B. Harrison and R.A. Jones (London, 1931).

For Cecil's precautions before leaving for France and also the 'reconciliation' with Lady Leicester, see *Sidney Papers*, vol. II.

Paul Hentzner's account of his visit to England is printed in Nichols, *Progresses of Queen Elizabeth*, vol. III, and also in Rye, *England as Seen by Foreigners*.

For a general account of the intrigues being carried on by King James with the European powers during the 1590s, see Hume, *Treason and Plot.*

Essex's Apology concerning his reasons for wishing to continue the war with Spain is printed in Devereux, *Earls of Essex*, vol. I, and the prayer-book incident is described by Camden in his *Annals.*

The great face-slapping row is also related by Camden, and the correspondence which followed is printed in Birch, Devereux and Harrison.

For Burghley's last letter, see Wright, *Queen Elizabeth and Her Times*, vol. II; and, for the Queen's reaction to his death, see William Knollys's letter to Essex printed in Birch, *Memoirs of the Reign of Queen Elizabeth*, vol. II, p. 390, and also Harington, *Nugae Antiquae*, vol. I, pp. 173 and 244.

For Essex's return to Court after the Yellow Ford disaster, see Birch, Harrison and Devereux. His appearance at Lord Burghley's funeral is described in Letters of John Chamberlain, vol. I; and Bacon's letter is printed in Spedding, Letters and Life of Francis Bacon, vol. II.

Chapter 43

The history of Elizabethan Ireland is, like all Irish history, exceedingly complicated and there is in consequence a voluminous literature on the subject. For a catalogue of contemporary sources and later works up to 1959, see the section on Ireland in *Bibliography of British History: Tudor Period, 1485–1603*, ed. Read. The standard general survey, however, remains Richard Bagwell, *Ireland under the Tudors*, 3 vols (London, 1885). See also the illuminating chapters on Ireland in: Rowse, *Expansion of Elizabethan England*; R. Dudley Edwards, 'Ireland, Elizabeth I and the Counter-Reformation', in *Elizabethan Government and Society* (London, 1961); and Cyril Falls, *Elizabeth's Irish Wars* (London, 1950).

The build-up to Essex's appointment as Lord-Lieutenant may be followed in Camden's *Annals*, in Birch's *Memoirs of the Reign of Queen Elizabeth*, vol. II, in Harrison's *Robert Devereux* and, of course, in the relevant volumes of the *Calendar of State Papers, Ireland* (*C.S.P., Ireland*). Robert Markham's and Essex's letters to John Harington can be found in Harington's *Nugae Antiquae*, vol. I, which also contains Harington's Irish journal.

Most of the correspondence between Essex and the Queen during his absence is printed in Devereux, *Earls of Essex*, vol. II, in Harrison's *Robert Devereux and Letters of Queen Elizabeth*, but see also *C.S.P. Ireland*.

For Essex's confabulations with Tyrone and his plans for a coup d'état in 1599, see the depositions printed as Additional Evidences in Spedding, *Letters and Life of Francis Bacon*, vol. II.

Rowland Whyte's letters to Robert Sidney, printed in *Sidney Papers*, vol. II, are a primary source for Essex's dramatic arrival at Nonesuch and for the events of the autumn, but see also Harington, *Nugae Antiquae*, vol. I, and Spedding, *Letters and Life of Francis Bacon*, vol. II.

Chapter 44

There are brief discussions of the peace negotiations with Spain in Rowse, *Expansion of Elizabethan England*, and Cheyney, *History of England*, vol. II, pp. 449–60; but also see *Calendar of State Papers, Domestic* (*C.S.P. Domestic*), 1598–1601, and *Sidney Papers*, vol. II.

For the continuing war on sea and land, see: Rowse, *Expansion of Elizabethan England*; Corbett, *Successors of Drake*; and Clements R. Markham, *The Fighting Veres* (London, 1888).

For the appointment of Lord Mountjoy as Lord Deputy of Ireland, see *Sidney Papers*, vol. II, and Birch, *Memoirs of the Reign of Queen Elizabeth*, vol. II. His correspondence with King James is revealed in Charles Danvers's confession, printed in Spedding, *Letters and Life of Francis Bacon*, and the appendix of *Correspondence of King James of Scotland with Sir Robert Cecil*, ed. John Bruce (Camden Society, 1861).

For Essex's return to Essex House, see: *Sidney Papers*, vol. II; *Letters of John Chamberlain*, vol. I; and Devereux, *Earls of Essex*, vol. II. Walter Raleigh's letter to Cecil is printed in E. Edwards, *Life of Sir Walter Raleigh*, 2 vols (London, 1868), vol. II. Accounts of the proceedings at York House in June 1600 can be found in: *Sidney Papers*, vol. II; Birch, *Memoirs of the Reign of Queen Elizabeth*, vol. II; Spedding, *Letters and Life of Francis Bacon*, vol. II; and Devereux, *Earls of Essex*. See also Harrison, *Robert Devereux*.

See *Letters of John Chamberlain* and *Sidney Papers* for Elizabeth in the summer of 1600, and Devereux, *Earls of Essex*, for most of Essex's letters.

The plottings of the autumn and winter 1600–1 can be followed in the confessions printed in Spedding, *Letters and Life of Francis Bacon*, vol. II, and appendix to *Correspondence of King James and Robert Cecil*. See Devereux, *Earls of Essex*, for Essex's last letters to the Queen, and Harington, *Nugae Antiquae*, vol. I, for his attitude towards her.

For the rebellion itself, see: Camden's *Annals*; Devereux, *Earls of Essex*, vol. II; Birch, *Memoirs of the Reign of Queen Elizabeth*, vol. II; *Acts of the Privy Council*; and *C.S.P. Domestic*. There is an account of Essex's trial in D. Jardine, *Criminal Trials*, vol. I (1832), but see also: Spedding, *Letters and Life of Francis Bacon*, vol. II; Devereux, *Earls of Essex*; and Harrison, *Robert Devereux*. For the Queen's reaction, see Harington, *Nugae Antiquae*; and Robert Naunton's comments appear in his *Fragmenta Regalia*.

Cecil's correspondence with James is printed in the Camden Society's *Correspondence of King James and Robert Cecil*.

Chapter 45

The Queen's encounter with Sir William Browne is described by himself in *Sidney Papers*, vol. II, and an account of her interview with William Lambarde appears in Nichols's *Progresses of Queen Elizabeth*, vol. III.

For a general account of the Spanish landing at Kinsale, see the relevant chapters in Rowse, *Expansion of Elizabethan England*, and Corbett, *Successors of Drake*. For more detail: *C.S.P. Ireland*; Fynes Morison, *Itinerary* (Glasgow, 1907–8); and Falls, *Elizabeth's Irish Wars*. Some of Elizabeth's letters to Mountjoy are printed in *Letters of Queen Elizabeth*.

There is a lucid discussion of the monopolies in Cheyney, *History of England*, vol. II; but, for a detailed account of proceedings in the Parliament of 1601 and the definitive text of the Golden Speech, see Neale, *Queen Elizabeth and Her Parliaments*, vol. II.

For the end of the war in Ireland, see second paragraph above, and, for Leveson's and Monson's exploit at sea, Corbett's *Successors of Drake* and Monson's *Naval Tracts*, vol. II. For the closing stages of the war in general, see Corbett, *Successors of Drake*; Rowse, *Expansion of Elizabethan England*; and Markham, *Fighting Veres*.

There is a useful and detailed summary of the religious situation at the end of the reign in McGrath, *Papists and Puritans*.

For the Queen's journeyings in the summer of 1601, see Nichols, *Progresses of Queen Elizabeth*, vol. III; and, for Sully's impressions, *Memoirs of the Duc de Sully*, trans. Charlotte Lennox, vol. II (London, 1756).

Glimpses of the Queen in the last year of her life can be found in: *Letters of John Chamberlain*; Lodge, *Illustrations of British History*, vol. II; *Sidney Papers*, vol. II; Nichols, *Progresses of Queen Elizabeth*, vol. III; and Harington, *Nugae Antiquae*. See *C.S.P. Ven.*, 1592–1603, for her interview with Scaramelli.

The best and most reliable account of her last illness and death is printed in *Memoirs of the Life of Robert Carey*, ed. Sir Walter Scott (Edinburgh, 1808). The French ambassador's letters are printed in Birch, *Memoirs of the Reign of Queen Elizabeth*, vol. II; and see also *Letters of John Chamberlain*, and *The Diary of John Manningham*, ed. John Bruce (Camden Society, 1868).

Notes and Abbreviations

A.P.C.	*Acts of the Privy Council*, ed. J.R. Dasent
Ascham, *Works*	*The Whole Works of Roger Ascham*, ed. Rev. Dr Giles
Bedingfield, *Papers*	Henry Bedingfield, *Papers*, ed. C.R. Manning
Chron. Greyfriars	*Chronicle of the Greyfriars*, ed. J.G. Nichols
Chron. Henry VIII	*Chronicle of King Henry VIII of England*, trans. and ed. Martin A.S. Hume
Chron. Queen Jane	*Chronicle of Queen Jane and Two Years of Queen Mary*, ed. J.G. Nichols
C.S.P. Dom.	*Calendar of State Papers, Domestic*, ed. Robert Lemon
C.S.P. Foreign	*Calendar of State Papers*, Foreign
C.S.P. Span.	*Calendar of State Papers*, Spanish, ed. Gayangos, Hume and Tyler
C.S.P. Span. Eliz.	*Calendar of State Papers*, Spanish, Elizabeth, ed. Hume
C.S.P. Ven.	*Calendar of State Papers*, Venetian, ed. Rawdon Brown
Edward VI	*The Literary Remains of King Edward VI*, ed. J.G. Nichols
Foxe	John Foxe, *Acts and Monuments*, ed. Cattley and Townsend
Hall	Edward Hall, *Chronicle*, ed. Sir Henry Ellis
Haynes	Lord Burghley, *State Papers*, ed. Samuel Haynes
Hayward, *Annals*	John Hayward, *Annals of the First Four Years of the Reign of Queen Elizabeth*, ed. John Bruce
Hayward, *Life of Edward VI*	John Hayward, *The Life of Edward VI*
Hearne, *Sylloge*	Thomas Hearne, *Sylloge Epistolarum*
Holinshed	Rafael Holinshed, *Chronicles*
L. & P.	*Letters and Papers, Foreign and Domestic, of the Reign of Henry VIII*, ed. Brewer, Gairdner and Brodie
Machyn, *Diary*	Henry Machyn, *Diary*, ed. J.G. Nichols
MacNalty, *Elizabeth Tudor*	Sir A.S. MacNalty, *Elizabeth Tudor – The Lonely Queen*
MacNalty, *Henry VIII*	Sir A.S. MacNalty, *Henry VIII – A Difficult Patient*
Scotland	*Calendar of State Papers Relating to Scotland and Mary, Queen of Scots, 1547–1603*
S.P. Dom.	*State Papers*, Domestic
S.P. *Henry VIII*	*State Papers*, Henry VIII, vol. I
Strickland, *Lives*	Agnes Strickland, *Lives of the Queen of England*
Strype, *Aylmer*	John Strype, *Life of John Aylmer*
Strype, *Memorials*	John Strype, *Ecclesiastical Memorials*
Tytler	P.F. Tytler, *England under the Reigns of Edward VI and Mary*

Vergil	Polydore Vergil, *English History Comprising the Reigns of Henry VI, Edward IV and Richard III*, ed. Ellis
Wriothesley	Charles Wriothesley, *A Chronicle of England during the Reigns of the Tudors*, ed. William D. Hamilton

Part One: The Young Elizabeth

Prologue: Part One

1 Hall
2 Chron. Henry VIII
3 Wriothesley

Chapter 1. A Gentleman of Wales

1 D. Williams, 'The Family of Henry VII', *History Today*, vol. IV (1954).
2 Sir Thomas Artemus Jones, 'Owen Tudor's Marriage', *Bulletin of the Board of Celtic Studies*, vol. XI (1943).
3 *Proceedings and Ordinances of the Privy Council*, ed. N.H. Nicolas, vol. V (1835).
4 *Chronicle of London*, ed. N.H. Nicolas (1827).
5 T. Rymer, *Foedera*, vol. X (1704).
6 *William Gregory's Chronicle*, ed. J. Gairdner (1876).
7 Vergil, ed. Ellis.
8 John Stow, *Annals* ed. E. Howes (1631).
9 Vergil.
10 Vergil.
11 Vergil.
12 Hall.

Chapter 2. The King's Great Matter

1 *Epistles of Erasmus*, ed. F.M. Nichols (1901).
2 Sebastian Giustinian, *Four Years at the Court of Henry VIII*, trans. and ed. R. Brown (1854), vol. I.
3 R.W. Chambers, *Thomas More* (1935).
4 *Four Years at the Court of Henry VIII*, vol. 2.
5 *L. & P.*, vol. 2, pt I (1113).
6 Hall.
7 W. Roper, *Life of Sir Thomas More*, ed. D.P. Harding (1935).
8 G. Mattingly, *Catherine of Aragon* (1942).
9 G. Cavendish, *Life and Death of Cardinal Wolsey*, ed. R.S. Sylvester (1959).
10 *C.S.P. Ven.*, vol. IV (1824).
11 Cavendish, *Life and Death of Cardinal Wolsey.*
12 Hall.
13 *C.S.P. Span.*, vol. IV, pt I.

Chapter 3. 'An Incredible Fierce Desire to Eat Apples'

1 H.F.M. Prescott, *Mary Tudor* (1952). See also P. Friedmann, *Anne Boleyn* (1884).
2 *S.P. Henry VIII*, vol. I (1830).
3 *C.S.P. Span.*, vol. IV, pt 2.
4 State Papers.
5 *Chron. Henry VIII.*
6 *C.S.P. Span*, vol. IV, pt 2.
7 *C.S.P. Span.*
8 State Papers.
9 Ibid.
10 *C.S.P. Span.*, vol. IV, pt 2.
11 Wriothesley.
12 *C.S.P. Span.*, vol. IV, pt 2.
13 Hall.
14 *C.S.P. Span.*, vol. IV, pt 2.
15 *L. & P.*, vol. VI.
16 Ibid., vol. VI.
17 Ibid., vol. VI.
18 *C.S.P. Span.*, vol. IV, pt 2.
19 *State Papers.*
20 *C.S.P. Span.*, vol. IV, pt 2.
21 Wriothesley.
22 *L. & P.*, vol. VII (509).

23 *C.S.P. Span.*, vol. V, pt 1.
24 State Papers. See also *L. & P.*, vol. IX (568).
25 *C.S.P. Span.*, vol. V, pt 1.

Chapter 4. 'Anne Sans Tête'

1 Wriothesley.
2 *L. & P.*, vol. X.
3 Ibid., vol. X.
4 Hall.
5 Wriothesley.
6 *L. & P.*, vol. X.
7 Ibid., vol. X.
8 Ibid., vol. X.
9 Ibid., vol. X.
10 Ibid., vol. X.
11 Ibid., vol. X.
12 *C.S.P. Span.*, vol. V, pt 2.
13 *L. & P.*, vol. X.
14 *Chron. Henry VIII.*
15 *C.S.P. Span.*, vol. V, pt 2.
16 Wriothesley.
17 Hearne, *Sylloge.*
18 Ibid.
19 Ibid.
20 Wriothesley.
21 *C.S.P. Span.*, vol. V, pt 2.
22 *L. & P.*, vol. XI.
23 Ibid., vol. XI.

Chapter 5. 'The King's Daughter'

1 *C.S.P. Span.*, vol. V, pt 2.
2 Hearne, *Sylloge.*
3 *L. & P.*, vol. XI.
4 Wriothesley.
5 *L. & P.*, vol. XIi, pt 2.
6 Ibid., vol. XI.
7 Hearne, *Sylloge.*
8 *L. & P.*, vol. XIV, pt 2.
9 Ibid., vol. XV.
10 Ibid., vol. XVI.
11 T. Heywood, *England's Elizabeth*, Harleian Miscellany (1813).
12 Ibid.
13 *Letters of Queen Elizabeth*, ed. G.B. Harrison (1935).
14 J.J. Scarisbrick, *Henry VIII* (1968) p. 485 and n. See also MacNalty, *Henry VIII.*
15 F.A. Mumby, *Girlhood of Queen Elizabeth* (1909).

Chapter 6. Elizabeth's Admiral

1 Tytler.
2 *A.P.C.*, vol. 2.
3 *L. & P.*, vol. XVI.
4 Hearne, *Sylloge.*
5 Ibid.
6 Strickland, *Lives*, vol. 5.
7 Strickland, *Lives.*
8 Mrs Everett Green, *Letters of Royal and Illustrious Ladies* (1846).
9 Strype, *Memorials.*
10 Haynes.
11 Ibid.
12 H. Clifford, *Life of Jane Dormer*, ed. J. Stevenson (1887).
13 Haynes.
14 Ibid.
15 *S.P. Dom.*, Edward VI, vol. 6.
16 Haynes.
17 Ibid.
18 Ascham, *Works*, vol. I.
19 Ascham, *Works.*
20 Hayward, *Life of Edward VI.*
21 Haynes.
22 F.L.G. von Raumer, *History of the 16th and 17th Centuries* (1835), vol. 2.
23 Ascham, *Works.*
24 Ascham, *Works.*
25 Haynes.
26 Tytler.

Chapter 7. 'The Peril that Might Ensue'

1 Haynes.
2 Ibid.
3 Tytler, vol. I.
4 Hearne, *Sylloge.*
5 Ibid.
6 Tytler, vol. I.
7 Haynes.

8 *S.P. Dom.*, Edward VI, vol. 6.
9 Tytler, vol. I.
10 Haynes.
11 Tytler, vol. I.
12 Haynes.
13 Ibid.
14 Tytler, vol. I.
15 Haynes.
16 *S.P. Dom.*, Edward VI, vol. 6.
17 Haynes.
18 Ibid.
19 *S.P. Dom.*, Edward VI, vol. 6.
20 *A.P.C.*, vol. 2.
21 Haynes.
22 Tytler, vol. I.
23 Haynes.
24 Ibid.
25 Ibid.
26 Ibid.
27 Ibid.
28 Ibid.
29 Ibid.
30 Ibid.
31 Agnes Strickland, *Life of Queen Elizabeth* (1906).

Chapter 8. Sweet Sister Temperance

1 *A.P.C.*, vol. 2.
2 Ibid., vol. 2.
3 Ibid., vol. 2.
4 Ibid., vol. 2.
5 Ibid., vol. 2.
6 Ibid., vol. 2.
7 Ibid., vol. 2.
8 Ibid., vol. 2.
9 Strype, *Memorials*, vol. 2, pt I.
10 Ibid., vol. 2, pt I.
11 Clifford, *Life of Jane Dormer*, ed. Stevenson.
12 Strickland, *Life of Queen Elizabeth I.*
13 Haynes.
14 Tytler, vol. I.
15 Strype, Memorials, vol. 2, pt 2.
16 Holinshed, vol. 3, p. 1014.
17 Ascham, *Works*, vol. I, pt I.
18 Ascham, *Works.*
19 Strype, *Aylmer.*
20 *C.S.P. Span.*, vol. IX, p. 489.
21 Hearne, *Sylloge.*
22 *A.P.C.*, vol. 3.
23 *C.S.P. Span.*, vol. X.
24 Ibid., vol. X.
25 R. Naunton, *Fragmenta Regalia*, ed. E. Arber (1895).
26 Strickland, *Life of Queen Elizabeth I.*
27 Strype, *Aylmer.*
28 Tytler, vol. I.
29 *Household Expenses of the Princess Elizabeth*, ed. P.C.S. Smythe (1953).
30 Machyn, *Diary.*

Chapter 9. The Queen's Sister

1 Hearne, *Sylloge.*
2 *C.S.P. Span.*, vol XI.
3 *Chron. Greyfriars.*
4 G. Howard, *Lady Jane Grey and Her Times* (1822).
5 Machyn, *Diary.*
6 Wriothesley, vol. 2.
7 *Chron. Queen Jane.*
8 Ibid.
9 Wriothesley.
10 Prescott, *Mary Tudor.*
11 *A.P.C.*, vol. 4.
12 *C.S.P. Span.*, vol. XI.
13 Mumby, *Girlhood of Queen Elizabeth.*
14 *C.S.P. Span.*, vol. XI.
15 Ibid., vol. XI.
16 Ibid., vol. XI.
17 Ibid., vol. XI.
18 Ibid., vol. XI.
19 Wriothesley and Machyn.
20 *C.S.P. Span.*, vol. XI.
21 Ibid., vol. XI.
22 Clifford, *Life of Jane Dormer*, ed. Stevenson.
23 Mumby, *Girlhood of Queen Elizabeth.*
24 *C.S.P. Span.*, vol. XI.
25 Ibid., vol. XI.
26 Ibid., vol. XI.

Chapter 10. 'We Are All Englishmen'

1 *C.S.P., Span.*, vol. XI.
2 Tytler, vol. 2.
3 Mumby, *Girlhood of Queen Elizabeth.*
4 *Chron. Queen Jane.*
5 Ibid.
6 Ibid.
7 Hearne, *Sylloge.*
8 Strype, *Memorials*, vol. 3, pt I.
9 *Chron. Queen Jane.*
10 Ibid.
11 Tytler, vol. 2.
12 MacNalty, *Elizabeth Tudor.*
13 *C.S.P., Span.*, vol. XIi.
14 Machyn, *Diary.*
15 *C.S.P. Span.*, vol. XII.
16 Holinshed, vol. 4.
17 Tytler, vol. 2.
18 Foxe, vol. VIII.
19 Foxe.
20 *S.P. Dom.*, Edward VI and Mary.
21 *C.S.P. Span.*, vol. XII.
22 Foxe.
23 Foxe; Holinshed; *Chron. Queen Jane.*

Chapter 11. Elizabeth, Prisoner

1 *C.S.P. Span.*, vol. XII.
2 Ibid., vol. XII.
3 Foxe, vol. VIII.
4 Sir John Harington, *Nugae Antiquae*, ed. T. Park (1804).
5 *C.S.P. Span.*, vol. XII.
6 Foxe.
7 Ibid.
8 Strype, *Memorials*, vol. 3, pt 2.
9 *C.S.P. Span.*, vol. XII.
10 Foxe.
11 Mumby, *Girlhood of Queen Elizabeth.*
12 Foxe.
13 Bedingfield, *Papers.*
14 Foxe.
15 Bedingfield, *Papers.*
16 Ibid.
17 Ibid.
18 Ibid.
19 Foxe; Holinshed, vol. 4.
20 Strickland, *Life of Queen Elizabeth I.*
21 Bedingfield, *Papers.*
22 Ibid.
23 *C.S.P. Span.*, vol. XIII.
24 Bedingfield, *Papers.*
25 Prescott, *Mary Tudor.*
26 Foxe.
27 Ibid.

Chapter 12. 'A Second Person'

1 *C.S.P. Ven.*, vol. VI, pt I.
2 Machyn, *Diary*; *C.S.P. Ven.*, vol. VI, pt I.
3 Tytler, vol. 2.
4 *C.S.P. Ven.*, vol. VI, pt 2.
5 Ibid., vol. VI, pt I.
6 Machyn, *Diary*; *C.S.P. Ven.*, vol. VI, pt i.
7 L. Wiesener, *Youth of Queen Elizabeth* (1879).
8 *C.S.P. Ven.*, vol. VI, pt I.
9 Ascham, *Works.*
10 Machyn, *Diary.*
11 Wiesener, *Youth of Queen Elizabeth.*
12 See D.M. Loades, *Two Tudor Conspiracies* (1965).
13 *C.S.P. Ven.*, vol. VI, pt 2.
14 Ibid., vol. VI, pt I.
15 Wiesener, *Youth of Queen Elizabeth.*
16 *C.S.P. Ven.*, vol. VI, pt I.
17 Ibid., vol. VI, pt I.
18 Ibid., vol. VI, pt I.
19 Strype, *Memorials*, vol. 3, pt I.
20 Ibid., vol. 3, pt I.
21 *C.S.P. Ven.*, vol. VI, pt I.
22 Machyn, *Diary*; *C.S.P. Ven.*, vol. VI, pt 2.
23 *C.S.P. Ven.*, vol. VI, pt 2.
24 Wiesener, *Youth of Queen Elizabeth.* Also E.H. Harbison, *Rival Ambassadors at the Court of Queen Mary* (1940).
25 *C.S.P. Ven.*, vol. VI, pt 2.
26 Ibid., vol. VI, pt 2.
27 Wiesener, *Youth of Queen Elizabeth.* Also Harbison, *Rival Ambassadors.*
28 *A.P.C.*, vol. VI.

Chapter 13. England's Elizabeth

1 *C.S.P. Ven.*, vol. VI, pt 2.
2 Strype, *Memorials*, vol. 3, pt 2.
3 Wiesener, *Youth of Queen Elizabeth*, vol. 2.
4 *C.S.P. Ven.*, vol. VI, pt 3.
5 Ibid., vol. VI, pt 3.
6 Strype, *Memorials*, vol. 3, pt 2. See also Prescott, *Mary Tudor.*
7 *C.S.P. Ven.*, vol. VI, pt 2.
8 Ibid., vol. VI, pt 2.
9 Ibid., vol. VI, pt 3.
10 Machyn, *Diary*. See also Wiesener, *Youth of Queen Elizabeth*, vol. 2, pp. 246–55.
11 *C.S.P. Span.*, vol. XIII.
12 Harleian MS., quoted in Strickland, *Life of Queen Elizabeth I.*
13 *C.S.P. Span.*, vol. XIII.
14 Ibid., vol. XIII.
15 Prescott, *Mary Tudor.*
16 Hayward, *Annals.*
17 *C.S.P. Span.*, vol. XIII.
18 Gonzales, *Documents from Simancas Relating to the Reign of Elizabeth.*
19 Naunton, *Fragmenta Regalia.*
20 Machyn, *Diary.*
21 Holinshed, vol. 4.
22 Quoted in C. Read, *Mr Secretary Cecil and Queen Elizabeth* (1955).
23 Holinshed.
24 Machyn, *Diary.*
25 Hayward, *Annals.*
26 Quoted in Read, *Mr Secretary Cecil.*
27 *C.S.P. Span.* Eliz., vol. I.
28 Hayward, *Annals.*
29 *C.S.P. Ven.*, vol. VII.
30 Holinshed, vol. 4.

Part Three: Marriage with my Kingdom

Prologue

1 *C.S.P. Foreign*, Mary, 537.
2 Ibid. 542.
3 Ibid. 537.
4 Thomas Coryat, *Coryat's Crudities* (Glasgow, 1905), vol. 1.

Chapter 25. The King's Last Daughter

1 *C.S.P. Span.*, vol. IV, pt 2, 789.
2 Hall.
3 *L. & P.*, vol. VI, 807.
4 Ibid. vol. VI, 1425.
5 Ibid. vol. VII, 366.
6 *Statutes of the Realm*, vol. III, quoted in G.R. Elton, *The Tudor Constitution* (1960), p. 355.
7 *L. & P.*, vol. V, 1485–6. See also Hall and *C.S.P. Ven.*, vol. IV, 822–4.
8 *L. & P.*, vol. VII, 1298.
9 Ibid. vol. VIi, 1060.
10 Ibid. vol. VII, 1483.
11 Ibid. vol. VIII, 174.
12 *Statutes of the Realm*, vol. III, quoted in Elton, *Tudor Constitution*, p. 6.
13 *L. & P.*, vol. VIII, 174.
14 *C.S.P. Span.*, vol. V, pt 1, 112.
15 *L. & P.*, vol. VIII, 174.
16 Ibid. 339–43, 548, 555, 557.
17 Ibid. 189.
18 *C.S.P. Span.*, vol. V, pt 1, 139, p. 420.
19 *L. & P.*, vol. VIII, 793.
20 Ibid. 846, 909.
21 Ibid. 910, see also 340.
22 Ibid. 554.
23 Ibid. 909, 1044, 1052.
24 *C.S.P. Span.*, vol. V, pt 1, 213, p. 554.
25 Ibid. 238, and *L. & P.*, vol. IX.
26 *C.S.P. Span.*, vol. V, pt 1, 246.
27 *L. & P.*, vol. X, 308.
28 Wriothesley, vol. 1.
29 *L. & P.*, vol. XII, pt 1, 815.
30 Ibid. vol. XIII, pt 1, 274, 338.
31 Ibid. vol. XIII, pt 1, 241, 255, 273, 329, 338; pt 2, 484.
32 Ibid. vol. XIII, pt 2, 622, p. 241.
33 Ibid. vol. XVI, 885.
34 Ibid. 1090.
35 Ibid. 1090.
36 *C.S.P. Span.*, vol. VI, pt 2, 20.
37 *L. & P.*, vol. XVII, 371.

38 Ibid. vol. XVIII, pt 1, 364.
39 *State Papers and Letters of Sir Ralph Sadler*, ed. A. Clifford, 3 vols (1809), vol. I, p. 129.
40 *L. & P.*, vol. XVIII, pt 1, 509.
41 Ibid. vol. XIX, pt 2, 470.
42 Ibid. vol. XX, pt 1, 90, 91.
43 Ibid. pt 2, 639 (3), 764, 856, 891, 1038.

Chapter 26. The Noblest Man Unmarried in This Land

1 *L. & P.*, vol. XXI, 634.
2 *C.S.P. Span.*, vol. IX, 7 Mar 1547.
3 *S.P. Dom.*, Edward VI, vol. vi.
4 Edward VI.
5 Haynes.
6 Ibid.
7 S.P. Dom, Edward VI, vol. VI.
8 Haynes.
9 Ibid.
10 Ibid.
11 ibid.
12 Tytler, vol. I.
13 S.P. Dom., Edward VI, vol. VI.
14 Tytler, vol. I.
15 Haynes.
16 Ibid.
17 Ibid.
18 S.P. Dom., Edward VI, vol. VI.
19 Haynes.
20 Ibid.
21 Ibid.
22 *Acts of the Privy Council of England*, vol. II.
23 *C.S.P. Span.*, vol. IX, 19 Mar 1549.
24 Haynes.
25 *C.S.P. Span.*, vol. IX, 19 Dec 1549.
26 Ibid. vol. X, 4 Nov 1550, p. 186.
27 Ibid. 1 Mar 1551, p. 230.
28 Ibid. June 1551, p. 299.
29 *C.S.P. Foreign*, Edward VI, 30 Aug 1551, p. 164.
30 *C.S.P. San.*, vol. X, 6 July 1551, p. 325; 14 Sept 1551, p. 369; 16 Nov 1551, p. 394.
31 *C.S.P. Foreign*, Edward VI, 11 Mar 1553, p. 255.
32 Ibid. 15 Feb 1553, p. 245.
33 *C.S.P. Span.*, vol. XI, 30 May 1553, p. 46.
34 Edward VI.
35 *C.S.P. Span.*, vol. XI, 11 July 1553, p. 81.

Chapter 27. Le Plus Beau Gentilhomme D'Angleterre

1 *Edward VI.*
2 *Greyfriars Chron.*; *C.S.P. Span.*, vol. XI, 6 Aug 1553, p. 152.
3 Ibid. 22 July 1553, p. 114.
4 Ibid. 14 Aug 1553.
5 Ibid. 15 Aug 1553.
6 Ibid. 8 Sept 1553.
7 H.F.M. Prescott, *Mary Tudor*, p. 212; E.H. Harbison, *Rival Ambassadors at the Court of Queen Mary*, p. 79.
8 *C.S.P. Span.*, vol. XI, 14 Sept 1553, p. 236.
9 Ibid. 20 Sept 1553, p. 247.
10 Ibid. 12 Oct 1553.
11 Ibid. 12 Oct 1553, p. 291.
12 Ibid. late in Aug 1553, p. 195.
13 Ibid. 12 Oct 1553, p. 292.
14 Ibid. 19 Oct 1553, p. 307.
15 Ibid. 31 Oct 1553, p. 328.
16 Ibid. 4 Nov 1553, pp. 334–5.
17 Ibid. 28 Nov 1553.
18 Ibid. 24 Dec 1553.
19 Ibid. 4 Nov 1553, p. 333.
20 Ibid. 6 Nov 1553, pp. 342–3.
21 Ibid. 20 Nov 1553, p. 372.
22 Ibid. 17 Nov 1553, p. 364.
23 De Noailles to the King of France, 14 Dec 1553, in F.A. Mumby, *The Girlhood of Queen Elizabeth*, p. 97.
24 Ibid.
25 Harbison, *Rival Ambassadors*, pp. 121–2.
26 Ibid. pp. 126–7.

27 *C.S.P. Span.*, vol. XII, 24 Feb 1554, p. 125.
28 Ibid. 8 Mar 1554, pp. 139–40.
29 Ibid. 14 Mar 1554.
30 Ibid. 22 Mar 1554, pp. 166–7.
31 Ibid. 27 Mar 1554.
32 Ibid. 22 Apr 1554.
33 Ibid. 3 Apr 1554, p. 201.
34 Ibid. 1 May 1554.

Chapter 28. No Alliance More Advantageous Than That With the Duke of Savoy

1 *Chron. Queen Jane*, app. X, John Elder's letter.
2 *C.S.P. Span.*, vol. XII, 8 Mar 1554.
3 *Chron. Queen Jane.*
4 *C.S.P. Span.*, vol. XIII, July 1554, p. 11.
5 Ibid. 17 Aug 1554.
6 Ibid. 24 Aug 1554.
7 Ibid. 17 Aug and 18 Sept 1554.
8 Ibid. 14 Nov 1554, p. 90.
9 Ibid. 14 Nov 1554, p. 92.
10 Ibid. p. 104 n.
11 Ibid. Mar/Apr 1555, p. 151.
12 Ibid. Mar/Apr 1555, p. 152.
13 *C.S.P. Ven.*, vol. VI, pt I, 8 Apr 1555.
14 Foxe, vol. VIII.
15 *C.S.P. Span.*, vol. XIII, 24 June 1555.
16 *C.S.P. Ven.*, vol. VI, pt 2, 13 May 1557, p. 1059.
17 Ibid. pt I, 21 Apr 1556.
18 Ibid. pt I, 28 Apr 1556, p. 423.
19 Ibid. pt I, 19 July 1556, p. 532.
20 Ibid. pt 2, 13 May 1557, p. 1060.
21 Ibid. pt I, 9 June 1556.
22 Ibid. pt I, p. 571 n.
23 *C.S.P. Span.*, vol. XIII, 20 Mar 1556.
24 *C.S.P. Ven.*, vol. VI, pt I, 10 Oct 1556.
25 Ibid. pt 2, 27 Dec 1556, p. 887.
26 Ibid. pt 2, 26 Apr 1557.
27 Ibid. pt 3, 29 Oct 1558, p. 1538.
28 *C.S.P. Span.*, vol. XIII, Mar(?) (?) 1558, p. 372.
29 Mumby, *Girlhood*, pp. 236–8.
30 *C.S.P. Ven.*, vol. XIII, 1 May 1558, pp. 379–80.
31 *C.S.P. Ven.*, vol. VI, pt 3, 29 Oct 1558, p. 1538.
32 *Documents from Simancas relating to the Reign of Elizabeth*, 1558–68, trans. T. Gonzalez (1865).
33 Machyn.

Chapter 29. I Am Already Wedded to an Husband

1 Printed by J.E. Neale in *English Historical Review* (July 1950), p. 305.
2 *C.S.P. Ven.*, vol. VI, pt 3, 10 Dec 1558.
3 *C.S.P. Span.*, Elizabeth, vol. I, 21 Nov 1558.
4 Ibid. 14 Dec 1558.
5 Ibid. 14 Dec 1558.
6 Ibid. 14 Dec 1558, p. 9.
7 Ibid. 10 Jan 1559.
8 Ibid. 10 Jan 1559.
9 Ibid. 31 Jan 1559.
10 William Camden, *Annals of the Reign of Queen Elizabeth.*
11 Ibid.
12 J.E. Neale, *Queen Elizabeth and Her Parliaments*, vol. I.
13 Ibid.
14 *C.S.P. Span.*, Elizabeth, vol. I, 20 Feb 1559.
15 Ibid. 11 Apr 1559, p. 51.
16 *Queen Elizabeth and Some Foreigners*, ed. Victor von Klarwill, pp. 28–9.
17 Ibid. Report of Count von Helfenstein, pp. 31–45.
18 Ibid. pp. 46–7.
19 See Neale, *Queen Elizabeth and Her Parliaments*, vol. 1.
20 *C.S.P. Span.*, Elizabeth, vol. I, 11 Apr 1559, p. 49.
21 Ibid. 12 Apr 1559, p. 54.
22 Ibid. 12 Apr 1559, p. 53.
23 Ibid. 18 Apr 1559, p. 57.
24 Ibid. 18 Apr 1559, p. 57.
25 Ibid. 29 Apr 1559, p. 63.
26 Ibid. 10 May 1559, p. 67.
27 *C.S.P. Ven.*, vol. vii, 10 May 1559.

Chapter 30. The Emperor So Desires Me For a Daughter

1 *C.S.P. Span.*, Elizabeth, vol. I, 30 May 1559.
2 *Queen Elizabeth and Some Foreigners.*
3 *C.S.P. Span.*, Elizabeth, vol. I.
4 *Queen Elizabeth and Some Foreigners.*
5 Ibid.
6 *C.S.P. Span.*, Elizabeth, vol. I, 1 July 1559.
7 Forbes, *A Full View of the Reign of Queen Elizabeth*, 2 vols (1740); see also F.A. Mumby, *Elizabeth and Mary Stuart.*
8 *C.S.P. Span.*, Elizabeth, vol. I, 1 July 1559, p. 82.
9 Ibid. 7 Sept 1559.
10 Ibid. 7 Sept 1559.
11 Ibid. 2 Oct 1559.
12 Ibid. 2 Oct 1559.
13 Mumby, *Elizabeth and Mary Stuart*, pp. 77–9.
14 Haynes; see also Mumby, *Elizabeth and Mary Stuart*, p. 67.
15 *Queen Elizabeth and Some Foreigners.*
16 Ibid.
17 *C.S.P. Span.*, Elizabeth, vol. I, 13 Nov 1559.
18 Ibid.
19 Ibid.
20 *Queen Elizabeth and Some Foreigners.*

Chapter 31. Lord Robert Would Be Better in Paradise

1 *C.S.P. Span.*, Elizabeth, vol. I, 19 Feb 1560.
2 Ibid. 28 Mar 1560.
3 Ibid. 11 Sept 1560.
4 George Adlard, *Amye Robsart and the Earl of Leycester*, p. 35.
5 Ibid. p. 36.
6 Ibid. p. 32.
7 Ibid. pp. 36–7.
8 Ibid. pp. 38–9.
9 Haynes.
10 Adlard, *Amye Robsart*, p. 40.
11 Aird, 'The Death of Amy Robsart', *English Historical Review*, Jan 1956.
12 *C.S.P. Span.*, Elizabeth, vol. I, III, 10 Oct 1560.
13 *C.S.P. Foreign*, Elizabeth, vol. III, 10 Oct 1560.
14 Printed in E.S. Beesley, *Queen Elizabeth* (1892).
15 *C.S.P. Span.*, Elizabeth, vol. I, 15 Oct 1560.
16 *Hardwicke State Papers*, 1501–1726, vol. I, p. 167.
17 Mumby, *Elizabeth and Mary Stuart*, p. 153.
18 *C.S.P. Foreign*, Elizabeth, vol. III, 30 Dec 1560.
19 *C.S.P. Span.*, Elizabeth, vol. I, 22 Jan 1561.
20 Ibid. 23 Feb 1561.
21 Ibid. 23 Feb 1561, pp. 181–2.
22 Ibid. 25 Mar 1561, pp. 187–8.
23 Ibid. 25 Mar 1561, p. 188.
24 Ibid. 12 Apr 1561, p. 194.
25 Ibid. 5 May 1561, pp. 200–2.

Chapter 32. Without a Certain Heir, Living and Known

1 *C.S.P. Span.*, Elizabeth, vol. I, 30 June 1561.
2 See Mumby, *Elizabeth and Mary Stuart*, ch. V, for documents.
3 See Hester Chapman, *Two Tudor Portraits* (1960).
4 *C.S.P. Span.*, Elizabeth, vol. I, 27 Nov 1561.
5 Ibid. 31 June 1562, pp. 225–6.
6 Ibid. 20 June 1562, p. 248.
7 Ibid. 25 Oct 1562, p. 262.
8 Ibid. 25 Oct 1562, nos 189 and 190, pp. 262–3.
9 Ibid. 25 Oct 1562, nos 189 and 190, p. 263.
10 Ibid. 30 Nov 1562.
11 Neale, *Queen Elizabeth I and Her Parliaments*, vol. I, p. 94.
12 Ibid. pp. 105–6.
13 Ibid. pp. 109–10.

14 Ibid. pp. 107–9.
15 *C.S.P. Span.*, Elizabeth, vol. I, 7 Feb 1963, p. 296.
16 Neale, *Queen Elizabeth I and Her Parliaments*, vol. 1, p. 127.
17 *A Letter from Mary Queen of Scots to the Duke of Guise*, January, 1562 (Scottish Historical Society, 1904).
18 *C.S.P. Span.*, Elizabeth, vol. I, 28 Mar 1563, p. 313.
19 Scotland, vol. II, pp. 56–8. See also Mumby, *Elizabeth and Mary Stuart*, p. 307.
20 James Melville, *Memoirs of His Own Life* (1549–93), ed. T. Thomson (Bannatyne Club, 1827).
21 Ibid.
22 Conyers Read, *Mr Secretary Cecil and Queen Elizabeth*, p. 318.
23 Mumby, *Elizabeth and Mary Stuart*, p. 378.
24 Ibid. p. 382.

Chapter 33. Talk Is All of the Archduke

1 *Queen Elizabeth and Some Foreigners*, pp. 173–6.
2 Ibid. pp. 180 ff.
3 Ibid. p. 201.
4 T. Wright, *Queen Elizabeth and Her Times*, vol. I, pp. 183–5.
5 *C.S.P. Span.*, Elizabeth, vol. I, 5 May 1565, p. 429.
6 Ibid. 16 June 1565, p. 437; 25 June 1565, p. 439.
7 *Scotland*, vol. II, 30 Mar 1565.
8 Sir Robert Naunton, *Fragmenta Regalia* (1824).
9 *C.S.P. Span.*, Elizabeth, vol. I, 9 June 1565, pp. 435–6.
10 Haynes, p. 444.
11 *C.S.P. Span.*, Elizabeth, vol. I, 23 July 1565, p. 454; 3 Sept 1565, p. 472.
12 *C.S.P. Ven.*, vol. VII, 19 Feb 1566, p. 374.
13 *C.S.P. Span.*, Elizabeth, vol. I, 4 Feb 1566, p. 523; 28 Jan 1566, p. 514; 20 Aug 1565; *C.S.P. Ven.*, vol. VII, 1 June 1566, p. 381.
14 *Queen Elizabeth and Some Foreigners*, pp. 240 ff; *C.S.P. Span.*, Elizabeth, vol. I, 23 July 1565, pp. 452–3.
15 *Queen Elizabeth and Some Foreigners*, pp. 248–9.
16 *C.S.P. Span.*, Elizabeth, vol. I, 6 Aug 1565, p. 461.
17 *Queen Elizabeth and Some Foreigners*, pp. 218 and 229.
18 Ibid. pp. 239–42.
19 Ibid. p. 228.
20 *C.S.P. Span.*, Elizabeth, vol. I, 13 Aug 1565, pp. 465–6.
21 Wright, *Queen Elizabeth and Her Times*, vol. 1, pp. 206–7.
22 *C.S.P. Span.*, Elizabeth, vol. I, 11 Apr 1566, p. 540.
23 Neale, *Queen Elizabeth and Her Parliaments*, vol. I, p. 136.
24 Ibid., vol. I, p. 140.
25 *C.S.P. Span.*, Elizabeth, vol. I, 19 Oct 1566, p. 589.
26 Ibid. 26 Oct 1566.
27 Neale, *Queen Elizabeth and Her Parliaments*, vol. I, p. 142.
28 *C.S.P. Span.*, Elizabeth, vol. I, 4 Nov 1566, pp. 591–2.
29 Ibid. p. 593.
30 Neale, *Queen Elizabeth and Her Parliaments*, vol. I, pp. 146–50.
31 Ibid. pp. 163–4.
32 *Illustrations of British History*, ed. E. Lodge, vol. I, pp. 366–7.
33 Ibid. pp. 368–73; *Queen Elizabeth and Some Foreigners*, pp. 269, 275 and 295.
34 Ibid.; *C.S.P. Ven.*, vol. VII, 22 Jan 1568, p. 410.

Chapter 34. To Marry With France

1 *C.S.P. Span.*, Elizabeth, vol. II, 8 Jan 1569.
2 Ibid. vol. I, 24 Mar 1565, pp. 409–10.
3 François de Salignac de la Mothe Fénélon, *Correspondence*, ii vols

(1827–9), vol. III, pp. 414–20; see also Read, *Mr Secretary Walsingham*, vol. I, p. 101.

4 *C.S.P. Span.*, Elizabeth, vol. II, 22 Jan 1571.

5 Ibid. p. 295 n.

6 *The Compleat Ambassador*, ed. Dudley Digges, p. 97.

7 *C.S.P. Dom.*, Elizabeth, Addenda, vol. VII, pp. 328–32.

8 *C.S.P. Span.*, Elizabeth, vol. II, 10 May 1571, p. 309.

9 *C.S.P. Ven.*, vol. VII, 7 June 1571, p. 468.

10 Ibid. 28 Sept 1571, p. 476.

11 *C.S.P. Foreign*, Elizabeth, vol. IX, 8 Oct 1571, pp. 544–5.

12 Ibid. vol. X, Jan 1572.

13 John Strype, *The Life of Sir Thomas Smith* (Oxford, 1820), p. 11.

14 *C.S.P. Foreign*, Elizabeth, vol. X, and Strype, Smith, p. 112.

15 Ibid. pp. 112–13.

16 *Compleat Ambassador*, p. 218.

17 Ibid. pp. 219–21. See also Read, *Walsingham*, vol. I, pp. 206–7.

18 Fénélon, *Correspondence*, vol. V, p. 121.

19 Ibid. vol. V, pp. 120–33, and *Compleat Ambassador*, p. 246. See also Read, *Lord Burghley and Queen Elizabeth*, pp. 89–90.

20 *Compleat Ambassador*, p. 259. See also Read, *Walsingham*, vol. I, p. 235.

Chapter 35. A Frog He Would A-Wooing Go

1 Read, *Walsingham*, vol. II, pp. 3–4. See also Read, *Lord Burghley and Queen Elizabeth*, pp. 200–2.

2 *C.S.P. Span.*, Elizabeth, vol. II, 26 Feb 1579.

3 *Lettres de Catherine de Médicis*, 10 vols (1880–1909), vol. 7, 29 Mar 1579. See Read, *Walsingham*, vol. II, pp. 14–18.

4 *Illustrations of British History*, vol. II, p. 212.

5 Read, *Walsingham*, vol. II, pp. 14–18.

6 Printed in Read, *Lord Burghley and Queen Elizabeth*, pp. 210–11.

7 *C.S.P. Span.*, Elizabeth, vol. II, 3 May 1579, p. 669.

8 Ibid. 14 May 1579.

9 Ibid. 14 May 1579, p. 675.

10 Camden, *Annals.*

11 Wright, *Queen Elizabeth and Her Times*, vol. II, pp. 103 5.

12 *C.S.P. Span.*, Elizabeth, vol. II, 24 June 1579.

13 M.A.S. Hume, *The Courtships of Queen Elizabeth*, p. 212.

14 *C.S.P. Span.*, Elizabeth, vol. II, 25 Aug 1579, p. 693.

15 Ibid.

16 J.A. Froude, *History of England from the Fall of Wolsey to the Death of Elizabeth*, 12 vols (1856–70), vol. XI, p. 175.

17 Philip Sidney, *Works*, 4 vols (1922–6), vol. III, pp. 51–60.

18 *State Papers . . . Left by Lord Burghley at Hatfield*, ed. W. Murdin, pp. 322–36.

19 Ibid. pp. 336–7.

20 Ibid. p. 337.

21 ibid.

22 *C.S.P. Span.*, Elizabeth, vol. II, 11 Nov 1579.

23 Ibid. 28 Nov 1579.

24 Ibid. 28 Nov 1579, p. 705.

25 *Calendar of Salisbury Manuscripts*, vol. II, pp. 275–6.

26 Read, *Walsingham*, vol. II, pp. 75–6.

27 Hume, *Courtships*, pp. 235–6.

28 *C.S.P. Span.*, Elizabeth, vol. III, 11 Nov 1581, pp. 211–12.

29 Ibid. 22 Nov 1581, p. 226.

30 Camden, *Annals.*

INDEX